THE ECONOMIC SYSTEM IN THE UK

THIRD EDITION

EDITED BY
DEREK MORRIS

OXFORD UNIVERSITY PRESS
1985

Oxford University Press, Walton Street, Oxford OX2 6DP

LONDON NEW YORK TORONTO
DELHI BOMBAY CALCUTTA MADRAS KARACHI
KUALA LUMPUR SINGAPORE HONG KONG TOKYO
NAIROBI DAR ES SALAAM CAPE TOWN
MELBOURNE AUCKLAND
AND ASSOCIATED COMPANIES IN
BEIRUT BERLIN IBADEN MEXICO CITY NICOSIA

Oxford is a trade mark of Oxford University Press

Published in the United States by Oxford University Press, New York

First published 1977
Reprinted 1977, 1978
Second edition 1979
Reprinted 1981
Third Edition 1985

British Library Cataloguing in Publication Data

The Economic system in the UK—3rd ed.
1. Great Britain—Economic conditions—1945–
I. Morris, Derek J.
330.941'0858   HC256.6
ISBN 0–19–877224–6
ISBN 0–19–877235–1 Pbk

Library of Congress Cataloging in Publication Data

The Economic system in the UK.
Bibliography: p.
Includes index.
1. Great Britain—Economic conditions—1945– —Addresses, essays, lectures. 2. Industry and state—Great Britain—Addresses, essays, lectures. 3. Economics—Addresses, essays, lectures.
I. Morris, Derek
II. Title: Economic system in the U.K.
HC256.6.E24 1984 338.941 84–22618
ISBN 0–19–877224–6
ISBN 0–19–877235–1 (pbk.)

Typeset by Cotswold Typesetting Ltd, Gloucester
Printed in Great Britain by Butler & Tanner, Frome

For
George Richardson and Ray Kidwell
and in memory of
Norman Leyland and Neville Ward Perkins

Preface to the Third Edition

This book is mainly, though not exclusively, intended for non-specialist and certain specialist students in economics (see p. 5). It attempts to explain the general principles underlying both the working of the UK economy and Government economic policy whilst meeting two other objectives. These are, first, that it should be intelligible to the introductory reader who is prepared to study it carefully, whether he or she is a student or a member of the general public, and, second, that at the same time, the book should examine at least some of the complexities which are frequently excluded in introductory texts but which cannot be avoided if day-to-day developments in the economy are to be properly understood. (See section 1.2 of Chapter 1 for further discussion of these objectives.)

These aims reflect the origins of the first edition of the book, namely the Oxford University Business Summer School, which has now been held every July for the last 30 years. It is of four weeks' duration and has developed into an intensive course in economics for middle-level managers from the public and private sectors, primarily those who are regarded by their companies or departments as likely to reach board level or its equivalent and who are therefore likely to require a good understanding of how the economy works and how it impinges on companies' behaviour, objectives and performance.

Teaching on this course revealed the lack of a book which, while presuming no previous knowledge of economics, could none the less provide enough depth for its readers to comprehend many of the often intricate and complex economic issues of the day. Initially internal pamphlets were prepared to meet the gap but were subsequently found useful for a wider audience. Eventually the range of topics was expanded, the amount of detail increased, further introductory material included and the complete collection published as *The Economic System in the UK* in 1977. It was hoped that this would provide a series of useful articles on specific issues but also a coherent introduction to the working of the UK as a whole.

Since then the book has been used by a wide variety of readers including university and polytechnic students, people on numerous professional courses, at colleges of further education and a number taking A level economics as well, together with those in industry and government who had constituted the original audience.

It is now five years since the second edition appeared in 1979. That period has seen some of the most traumatic changes in the UK economy since the war. Mass unemployment has re-emerged as a persistent feature, inflation has both risen to very high levels and then fallen to levels significantly lower than was thought possible. North Sea oil production has risen from virtually zero to its expected maximum rate with powerful consequences for the structure and competitiveness of the economy. Growth over the period as a whole has none the less remained very low indeed. Equally important there has been a substantial change in the conduct of economic policy, the origins, execution, and impact of which are of the greatest significance. At the same time there has been a growing awareness of both the historical context of the UK's economic problems and the international pressures to which the UK is increasingly exposed. All these factors and a number of less major ones are reflected in the third edition of *The Economic System in the UK*, which has been very substantially extended and re-written. There are ten entirely new chapters, four re-written by new authors, and four completely re-written by existing authors. All but three of the remaining eleven have been revised and updated during 1983/4, and though some gaps still inevitably exist it is hoped that the third edition offers a moderately comprehensive introduction to the workings of the UK economy.

For such a task the authorship has, not surprisingly, expanded. While almost all the authors are currently or were in the past academic economists, the twenty authors include amongst them some from industry, others from financial institutions and some with experience of Whitehall in addition to those in academic posts in Oxford and elsewhere. This is an important element in the attempt to ensure that the book remains valuable to those whose day-to-day responsibilities present them with problems of economic analysis in the UK. In order of the chapters, Hywel Jones is the Director of the Henley Centre for Forecasting; Kenneth Mayhew is Fellow in Economics, Pembroke College, Oxford; David Mayes was recently Senior Lecturer at Exeter University and Editor of the National Institute Economic Review (NIER) and is now Chief Statistician at the National Economic Development Office; Peter Sinclair is Fellow in Economics, Brasenose College, Oxford; Andrew Graham, formerly economic adviser at Downing Street and a member of the Wilson Committee on the Financial System in the UK, is Fellow in Economics at Balliol College, Oxford; Roger Bootle, previously lecturer in economics at St. Anne's College, Oxford is now Chief Economist at Capel-Cure Myers in the City of London; Derek Robinson, former Chairman of the (now renamed) Social Science Research Council is a Fellow in Economics at Magdalen College, Oxford. Christopher Allsopp is Fellow in Economics at New College, Oxford, Economic Director of Oxford Economic Forecasting and a former adviser to the Bank of England and the Organisation for Economic Co-operation and Development (OECD); Michael Surrey, a former editor of NIER, is Professor of Economics at Leeds University; Donald Hay is Fellow in Economics at Jesus College, Oxford; Andrea Boltho, formerly with the OECD is a Fellow in Economics at Magdalen College, Oxford; Jeremy Hardie, now a Director of John Swire and Sons Ltd, is former Deputy Chairman of the Monopolies and Mergers Commission; Brian Tew is External Professor at Loughborough University of Technology; Correlli Barnett is Keeper of the Archives and Fellow of Churchill College, Cambridge; Peter Landymore is an Economic Adviser at the National Economic Development Office (NEDO); Geoffrey Hobbs is in the Group Planning Department of ICI plc; Michael Brech is Head of the Finance for Industry Section of NEDO; John Whiteman is Senior

Economist at Unilever plc; David Stout is Chief Economist with the same company and a former Economic Director of NEDO. The editor is Fellow in Economics at Oriel College, Oxford, Chairman of Oxford Economic Forecasting and until recently the Economic Director of the National Economic Development Office. With all their teaching, research, and other responsibilities, the editor much appreciates the willingness of the contributors to find time under such circumstances to prepare chapters for the third edition. It should be stressed that all contribute in a personal capacity and in no case can the views expressed be attributable to the organization for which a contributor works.

All the contributors have written in areas of their own expertise. This naturally leads to differences of viewpoint and emphasis. The editorial function has been exercised, not to remove any such differences, but to generate as far as possible a framework within which different schools of thought can be described, compared, and evaluated. Unnecessary duplication has been avoided where possible, but different chapters have occasionally required re-presentation and development of earlier points to preserve the sense or flow of argument.

Some of the chapters, for example chapters 12 and 13 on demand management, contain some more advanced material. But there is a progression in the book, in terms of both level and content, which it is hoped will make such chapters accessible to all. Part II for example provides the groundwork for the early policy chapters, which in turn examine the elements drawn together in chapters 12 and 13. Several contributors have offered comments and criticism on other chapters, and the editor is indebted to them for this. Similarly, a number of other colleagues have provided detailed comments and criticisms on early drafts, and suggestions for the final one. This has proved extremely helpful. The assistance of various students in reading and commenting on several chapters has likewise proved invaluable. All remaining errors of fact, argument, or judgement are of course our responsibility alone.

An inordinately large number of people are involved in producing a book with twenty authors. The editor would particularly like to thank Tim Bezley who provided invaluable editorial assistance in the later stages of preparation; Liz Moore who as copy-editor was faced with a plethora of problems of consistency of style and whose efforts went well beyond the call of duty; and to Andrew Schuller who, as the person responsible for getting the book actually published, must have had many a disturbed night but never showed it. In addition all the contributors would like to express their thanks to the array of typists who together produced two and sometimes three drafts of approaching half a million words. Finally, as with earlier editions, virtually every contributor already had other heavy full-time commitments. As a result most of the writing of the book has had to come out of already greatly squeezed leisure time. We would all once again like to thank very much those in our personal lives who have borne the brunt of this pressure.

Oriel College   Derek Morris
1 October 1984

Contents

PART I

PART II—ECONOMIC BEHAVIOUR

PART III—MACROECONOMIC POLICY

PART IV—THE INTERNATIONAL CONTEXT OF
THE UK

PART V—LONG-TERM ECONOMIC GROWTH IN THE UK

PART VI—INDUSTRIAL POLICY ISSUES

PART VII—CONCLUSIONS

PART I

I

Introduction

D. J. MORRIS

1.1. Background to the Book

1.1.1. The Performance of the UK Economy

The impact of the economy on all aspects of life has never been more evident. Governments, politicians, and civil servants are more preoccupied with economic performance both domestically and internationally than ever before; company sales, costs, and profits are often heavily determined by the general level of activity in the economy. At both managerial and shop-floor level the number of jobs available as well as the incomes received are often seen as more dependent on the state of the national economy and nationwide policies on employment than on the decisions of the particular company concerned. Most important of all, individual living standards are seen as determined by factors which lie far beyond the ability of the individual to influence, and this is true whether the individual is an employer or employee, a housewife, pensioner, student, or child.

This impact would probably have been less noticed or emphasized if it had in general been viewed as a beneficial one. In fact, the performance of the UK economy has been almost universally regarded as poor. Three distinct, though not necessarily unrelated, aspects of this performance can be identified. First, in the late 1960s and through the 1970s the underlying rates of both unemployment and inflation started to rise significantly. Living standards on average grew more slowly from the mid 1970s and in 1974–5 actually fell, albeit temporarily, for the first time since the war. There was continued worry about the UK's level of competitiveness *vis-à-vis* other countries, the balance of payments went into record deficit in the second half of the 1970s, and the value of the pound internationally fell very heavily. By the early 1980s some aspects of this picture had improved; the rate of inflation had fallen very substantially and the balance of payments, mainly as a result of North Sea oil, moved into record surplus in 1981–2. But other aspects had not; economic growth remained slow, with another period of negative growth being experienced in 1980 and 1981. The value of sterling rose to a very high level, once again generating serious concern about the UK's competitiveness. Most damaging of all, unemployment rose to over 3 million, or almost 1 in 8 of the work-force, over 1 million of whom had been unemployed for at least a year. This represented a social and economic cost not experienced in the UK for half a century.

Second, and looking over a somewhat longer period, the UK economy has been subject to almost continuous cyclical fluctuations in the general level of activity. These, together with the changes in economic policy associated with them, have created great difficulties for those in the public (government) and private sectors who are attempting to plan for and achieve sustained long-term economic growth and development.

Third, and probably most serious of all, is the poor performance of the UK economy over at least thirty years (and, it now appears, much longer) when compared to nearly all other developed countries in the world. The level of output per man (labour productivity) is relatively low and has for almost all of this period increased at a slower rate than in other countries. Living standards have consequently grown at a slower rate than elsewhere. The average level of competitiveness of British goods abroad has been inadequate and has only been temporarily sustained through successive depreciations of sterling.

The general result is that while both the causes of, and solutions to, this poor performance are a central topic of discussion and dispute in industrial, academic, and government circles, there is little disagreement with the judgement that the economy has failed to behave as it should. Consumer prices are thought too high, wages too low, production costs too high and profits too low, taxation is frequently regarded as excessive not only by those paying the highest levels, and the provision of goods and services by private companies, nationalized industries, and government agencies is often regarded as inadquate in terms of quantity and quality, or both.

1.1.2. Purpose of the Book

Two very important repercussions of this situation may be noted. First, there is an increasing need for all those involved in any way in the economic processes of production, distribution, and sales, or in the management of the economy as a whole, to have a good grasp of the fundamentals and some of the complexities involved in the operation of the economy. This includes managers, civil servants, union representatives, and politicians. Many of them feel, in a way which they did not several years ago, that they need the economic training necessary to understand what is happening in the economy, to assess its likely behaviour in the future and to recognize the limitations which inter-dependence of unions, management, and government places on all three. Their difficulty is the limited time available for this purpose, and it was with this in mind that the Oxford University Business Summer School (despite its somewhat inappropriate title) developed into an intensive one-month course in economics. Earlier editions of this book originally stemmed from some of the written material used on the course. While much has been added since then the book none the less retains some of the characteristics of a crash course and, as one objective, the provision of an introduction to economics for those who will have little or no opportunity to pursue an extended course in the subject.

A second repercussion of the pervasive impact of the economy has been a rapidly growing interest in the subject of economics on the part of students.

This arises partly because the tendency for economic considerations to dominate issues is increasing, a tendency that will place ever greater demands on the economic literacy of the future managers, civil servants, and trade unionists which many of today's students will become. In addition, however, it arises from a general and very sensible desire to comprehend the economic issues that constrain and determine so many human activities in all walks of life. An understanding of the very powerful, but often unanalysed, forces at work in society may increasingly be regarded as a central factor in the process of education, and economic forces represent some of the most powerful ones. This book is therefore very much directed at students, and the latest edition has been prepared partly as a result of the use made of earlier editions for teaching purposes. But it is very far from being a conventional introductory textbook and it is therefore necessary to be explicit about the two particular types of student for whom it is intended.

First, there is an increasing number of students at universities, polytechnics, business schools, and many other institutions who, though not specializing in economics, nevertheless wish to study it to some extent, so that they will be better informed about their economic environment and better equipped to judge the performance of economists and politicians in the attempts they make to manage the economy. There are all too many cases, however, where the course for such non-specialists has been little more than the introductory work of those doing specialist courses in economics. This is unfortunate as the demands of the two groups are quite different. There are many aspects of economic analysis (often abstract, rigorous, and complex) which are appropriate for a three-year course because there is sufficient time available to reach a relatively high level of sophistication. The introduction to a specialist course therefore rightly emphasizes the tools of analysis, starting with the simplest, most basic ones, and building up gradually. Initially, therefore, it makes sense to abstract from the economic environment and its complexities until the modes of analysis have been grasped. If the non-specialist is provided with only the first part of such a programme he can easily end up with a few pieces of simple deductive theory, little evidence on how to apply them (or even on whether they are applicable at all as they stand), little understanding of the economy, and the misguided belief that economic theory and the real world have little connection.

In fact, the needs of the non-specialist are much closer to those of management, civil servants, etc., namely an introduction to economics which reduces technical analysis to the minimum necessary to understand the systematic forces at work in the economy; which avoids the elaborations required to understand detailed problems that the student will never face, and which are not central to general economic activity; but which nevertheless brings out the complexity of the central issues, permits assessment of the controversies existing in the area of economic policy, and assists the formation of his own judgement on the vast literature of economics poured out each week in newspapers, journals, and all manner of government publications.

Second, many of the later chapters in Parts III to VI look at difficult, controversial, and often not easily understood areas of economics. Some will stretch non-specialists, but should be quite intelligible to them given that they have read the more introductory chapters in Part II. In addition, however, specialists, for whom Part II would be unnecessary, may well find the later chapters useful material as an introduction to the applied side of their course. These chapters summarize particular areas, identify the main issues and problems, and give some preliminary guidance on their analysis, thus providing a perspective prior to more detailed examination.

There are also, of course, many students not studying economics at all who none the less feel that some understanding of it is essential nowadays. It is hoped that this book will prove useful for them in pursuing this objective.

One other point needs stressing. The content and analysis are almost entirely economic. A number of issues of great interest and conern which have important economic aspects, for example social welfare and housing and environmental policies, are not covered. Many of the economic principles involved are examined, however, so that the text can provide introductory material for those whose course centres on such issues.

To repeat, this is not a textbook of economics in the normal sense. Its aim is to help those without either the time or the inclination to pursue a full economics course to absorb quickly the general principles of economics and economic policy, so that they have a sound basis for critical assessment of the economy, day by day. Neither economic theory, history, nor economic institutions is examined except in so far as it is necessary to this end. The book is elementary in the sense that no previous economics is presumed. It is not elementary, however, in the sense of being highly simplified or very extended in its step-by-step build-up of a picture of the economy. Often a paragraph must suffice where a standard textbook would spend many pages, and from the non-economist it therefore requires careful attention and considerable thought.

Such an approach, dictated by the origin and aim of the book, has evident dangers which must not be conveniently overlooked. Many qualifications and implications can only be hinted at, and much of the argument behind particular conclusions can only be summarized briefly. The most serious problem, however, is that there are still many uncertainties and many controversies (not always in the same areas!) in economics, the reasons for which are discussed below, which complicate the explanation of the corresponding economic phenomena. Every effort has been made, however, to see that the pressures of space have not prevented a statement and some examination of these problems, as they are important elements in the understanding of the current economic situation.

1.2. Historical Development in Economics

1.2.1. Pre-Keynesian Economics

It is conventional to define economics as the study of the allocation of scarce resources— in other words the study of who produces which non-freely available goods and services and who receives them. In practice, and in general terms, this means the analysis of the factors, including price, that determine (i) the amount of a product or service which its suppliers wish to supply; (ii) the amount prospective purchasers 'demand', i.e. can and wish to pay for; (iii) the price which then equates the supply and demand; and (iv) the amount of the good or service then exchanged. This approach has been applied to all sorts of 'products' and 'services', including not only tangible goods and intangible services bought and sold, e.g. cars, bread, haircuts, insurance, but also different financial assets like company shares, money itself, and also labour services. Each was presumed to have a 'price' determined by supply and demand, though in some cases this 'price' was different from the conventional notion associated with that word. In addition, this approach was applied at various levels; the individual producer, the total market[1] for a product, the economy as a whole.

In each case the same basic market mechanism was presumed to operate unless there was direct interference with it. the essence of this mechanism was, first, that a *market-clearing price* existed in each case, and second, that the market if left to itself would *find* that market-clearing price. If at a going price demand (in the sense given above) exceeded supply then competition amongst potential purchasers to buy would drive the price upward. This would induce suppliers attracted by the higher price to supply more and purchasers discouraged by the higher prices to purchase less. The excess of demand over supply would tend to disappear. This process would continue until the price was reached at which no excess demand existed. This price therefore 'cleared' the market in the sense that supply and demand were now equal, with no supplier left with unwanted stock and no purchaser willing to buy at the prevailing price left unsatisfied.

It was not, of course, suggested that suppliers and customers generally haggle between and amongst themselves to determine the market-clearing price. In most cases it was recognized that suppliers would in the short-term set the prices which any customer had to pay to obtain the product concerned. Rather it was suggested that if manufacturers, wholesalers, and retailers found *over a longer period* that they were unable to meet the demand for a product, then price rises would, if permitted, generally occur. Price reductions would tend to occur if, over a period, suppliers were left holding unsold stock. Given this it appeared reasonable to adopt the market mechanism described above as a simple picture of the longer-term tendency inherent in most if not all unrestricted markets.

This essentially very simple and very plausible view of the basic economic force at work in the world has in fact been one of the most controversial ideas propounded this century. Failure to recognize its inappropriateness on the one hand, and persistent refusal to recognize its basic truth on the other, have both been given by different people as reasons for economic and social loss on a vast scale, not least in the UK. Much of the current controversy in economics (which is discussed later) can be traced to disagreement over the extent to which this picture facilitates or distorts analysis of economic problems. In order to explain this it is useful to focus on one particular market to which the analysis has been applied, especially in the early decades of this century, namely the 'market' for labour. The 'price' of labour on which, amongst other things, the

---

[1] By 'market' we simply mean all the suppliers and all the potential customers for a product. No physical market in a particular location is implied.

supply and demand for labour was supposed to depend was the *real* (as opposed to *money*) wage of that labour. As the distinction between a real and a monetary variable is used repeatedly it will be useful to emphasize the difference straight away.

A wage of £40 per week is a monetary variable because it is the wage in terms of *money*. Nothing is said about the wage level in terms of what it could buy. The latter is known as the *real* wage. For example, if a wage level doubles from £20 per week to £40 per week, and at the same time the price of everything available in the shops doubles, it should be clear that in real terms the wage is unchanged. The recipient can still only buy the same volume of real goods as before. His money wage has, however, doubled. In the same way, suppose an individual has an amount of money—£100—in the bank. This money balance is a monetary variable. If all prices double, and his money balance stays at £100, his *real* balance is halved—his money balance will only buy half as much as before. The distinction is important partly because people may react in different ways to changes in real and monetary variables, and partly because their impact on people's well-being will be different.[2]

The supply of labour was argued to be dependent on *real* wages because over the long term a man deciding whether and how much to work is not concerned with the number of pounds he earns *per se*, but with what he can buy with his wage. (This tendency to think in real terms is very much more obvious since the experience of much higher rates of inflation.) Similarly, the demand by companies for labour was thought to be dependent on real wage levels because a higher money wage would be no disincentive to employ labour if the price of the goods produced by that labour had gone up proportionately. The implication of the market mechanism in this case was that over the long term all who wished for employment could obtain it, provided that there was no interference with the ability of the individual firms and employees to bargain with each other over the latter's real wages.[3] In the short term there might be unemployment as a result of shifts in demand from one firm to another, or from one country to another, but in either case if those without jobs could freely compete for jobs, offering to work for lower wages if a pool of unemployed existed, but able to obtain higher wages if there was a shortage of labour, then it was argued that any such unemployed person could eventually obtain a new job. In general the only unemployment existing at any point of time would be essentially temporary, except for voluntary unemployment comprising those

---

[2] Real variables can only be given as index numbers which are related to the value of the real variable in a 'base' year. Thus the real wage might be said to be 113 in 1974 with 1970 = 100. The 1974 figure is calculated as

$$\frac{W1974}{P1974} \bigg/ \frac{W1970}{P1970} \times 100$$

where W indicates the average wage level in the year specified, and P indicates the average price level in the year specified. With real variables given by corresponding monetary ones divided by the price level it is clear that real wages only rise if money wages rise faster than prices and vice versa.

[3] Although bargains will be struck in terms of money wages, any suggested money wage implies a particular real wage given the price level (or expected changes in it over the period the wage will be paid).

who did not wish to work at prevailing wage levels. Long-term involuntary unemployment was not possible on this view, *unless* it was caused by some interference with the free workings of the market, keeping the real wage level above that at which firms would wish to employ all those who wished to work.

1.2.2. The Keynesian Revolution

In the 1930s a new approach was developed, primarily by John Maynard Keynes, which later completely altered most people's way of thinking about economic problems and which at heart challenged the picture of the market mechanism described.

Keynes's work stemmed from observation of long-term involuntary mass unemployment in the interwar years, despite falls in wages, and his belief that *even if there was no interference in the process of wage setting*, there would not necessarily be a tendency towards full employment. Keynes therefore regarded the then existing economic theory as fundamentally wrong, and so set out to provide a new explanation of how the economic system functioned.

This new approach focused on the *aggregate* demand for goods and services. If this fell in the *short term* for any reason, firms would find themselves over-producing. Stocks of finished goods would accumulate, overtime working would be reduced, and some people would lose their jobs. Keynes accepted that eventually they might take on new jobs at lower wages, but *initially* they would look for new work at a wage roughly comparable to their previous wage. During this period their lack of income would greatly reduce their power to buy goods, and firms would find themselves facing *further* reductions in demand as a result. By the time the unemployed had come round to working for the lower wage at which they could all have been employed, the further reductions in demand could easily mean that this wage was itself too high. There might well therefore still be some unemployment, further falls in demand for goods, and yet more unemployment. The *long-term* position under which everyone accepted a wage low enough to ensure full employment might, therefore, be delayed for a very long time indeed as unemployment caused lower demand, causing further unemployment. In fact the economy could, as a result of the short-run recession, run into long-run stagnation. Firms would be unwilling to employ more people because there was no increase in demand for their products, but no increase in demand would occur because there was not the necessary increase in employment and wage payments to permit people in aggregate to spend more. Those unemployed would still want to buy goods and services, but they would not be able to back this up with ready money. Without wages their 'demand' would be ineffective and without increased *effective* demand, firms would not employ more people or pay them wages.

Much more will be said about the Keynesian model in later chapters. Several points are of immediate interest, however. First, Keynes saw that when demand fell the initial impact was on the *volume of output* and, therefore, on employment, rather than on *prices*. Although prices and wages might start to fall as firms and employees began to recognize that the fall in demand was not just a temporary fluctuation, the short-term fall in output and employment, and the consequent further falls in both, would *amplify* the initial fall of demand into a major recession of long duration. This was in sharp contrast to the previous view that changes in *prices* (wages) would tend to *reduce* the existing excess demand or supply. Keynes's approach, therefore, heavily emphasized the response of output and employment rather than of prices and wages.

Second, the earlier idea of a supply of labour which, if it exceeded demand for its services, would compete for jobs and reduce wages, largely disappears. There is, of course, a supply of labour, and potentially it might compete for jobs if there is unemployment, but the tendency to search first for another job at the existing wage entails a period of zero or low wage for those unemployed, reduced expenditure, and further falls in employment which undermine the effect of eventually accepting a lower wage. Only the demand for labour is then important, indeed crucial, because only rises in demand can halt the process.

To solve the problem, aggregate demand had to be increased. If the public did not have the income to increase its expenditure, and firms did not have sufficient expectation of future increases in demand to increase expenditure on new factories, machinery, etc., then, Keynes argued, the government would have to intervene to achieve the expenditure increase. Instead of the previous emphasis, therefore, on non-intervention by government in economic behaviour to avoid interference with the automatic equilibrating of supply and demand by the market (i.e. price) mechanism, Keynes laid emphasis on the need for active intervention by government to avoid long periods of high unemployment. After the war the acceptance of Keynes's views led to continuous use of government monetary and fiscal policy (both discussed at length later on) to attain and maintain levels of virtually full employment. This intervention into the economic life of the nation, so familiar since the war, stems directly, though not solely, from the Keynesian view that, left to itself, the economy might well stagnate with high unemployment.

1.2.3. Macro- and Microeconomics

It may have been noticed that the difference in the pre-Keynesian[4] and Keynesian views does not lie solely in their disagreement about how people respond to situations in which supply and demand are unequal. The Keynesian view crucially focused on a circularity of economic effects. In order to emphasize this let us consider an individual firm employing labour and selling its products. In general, a negligible proportion of its output will be bought by its own employees. If the firm increased production by employing more people, it would simply move into a situation of over-production, for virtually none of the extra wages it paid out would be used to purchase the firm's increased production. For the economy as a whole, however, the amount supplied and the amount demanded were seen to be related in a circular fashion. An increase in *aggregate* production would increase *aggregate* income which in turn would lead to increased *aggregate* demand for products. While it is therefore generally useful to presume that the factors determining how much *one supplier* (or even a group of suppliers, e.g. an industry) wishes to supply and the factors

---

[4] Usually termed 'neo-classical'.

determining how much purchasers wish to buy are separate, it is definitely not legitimate to imagine that these are separate at the level of the *national economy*. In consequence, the methods of analysing the two levels are very different.

Analysis which concerns itself with only a part of the economy, e.g. one consumer, one firm, one industry, such that the circular effects described can be ignored, is termed microeconomic analysis. That which examines the behaviour of the whole economy is termed macroeconomics, and it must explicitly recognize the circularity.

This distinction, which is of considerable importance in economics, will be observed in several chapters later on, with microeconomic analysis of individual sectors of the economy subsequently put together into a macro-economic analysis of the whole. But it is nevertheless appropriate to stress certain features of macroeconomic analysis at this point.

Clearly, it must involve the analysis of aggregates (in fact much of microeconomics does as well), because it examines the aggregate impact of countless millions of decisions and the general trends that result. Four important observations must be made on this, each of them fairly obvious when stated, but often not fully appreciated. First, suggested macroeconomic relationships cannot be shown to be invalid by individual observations at the microeconomic level. If hypotheses concerning the behaviour of aggregate variables are to be tested adequately, the tests must involve the *aggregate* variables concerned. No damage is done to the hypothesis that high-wage earners spend more by meeting a man who saves nearly all his £300 per week. Second, and stemming from this, it is frequently very misleading to judge any such hypothesis only by reflection on one's own behaviour or experience. Different individuals may act differently, and different types of institutions may operate in totally different ways. At best such introspection is a fertile source of hypotheses; it is no basis for testing them. Third, much economic analysis must operate at a fairly high degree of abstraction. Most of the myriad influences on any decision are of little concern. It is only the major systematic influences which are important and these may not always be the most obvious.

Fourth, an important feature of the Keynesian approach was the fact that government could intervene at the macroeconomic level, changing taxation, public expenditure, the availability of credit, etc., to ensure full employment, but without intervening at the micreconomic level. No selective interference in specific firms or industries was required, unless they exhibited specific problems. Total employment would be influenced without detailed control of any of the thousands of firms which provided it. This emerges more clearly later but one implication should be singled out. The fact that particular cases will arise where a macroeconomic policy is counterproductive cannot be taken by itself as evidence that the policy is unsuccessful *per se*, perverse as this may seem to the particular individual concerned. Only widespread examples based on a wide survey can give some indication of the success or otherwise of a macroeconomic policy.

The macro/micro distinction is by no means a rigid one, as will be seen. In addition, it is increasingly argued that this classification fails to recognize the giant companies now in existence which, though being individual firms, are so large that they can frequently influence the performance of the whole economy. These firms generally operate in several different countries, and this multinational aspect creates new opportunities and new problems for both the firm itself at the microeconomic level, and for the countries they operate in at the macroeconomic level: the framework of economic analysis may therefore need to develop in order to cope with this phenomenon.

1.2.4. Post-Keynesian Developments

Three important distinctions have been introduced above: supply and demand; micro- and macroeconomics; the short term and the long term. This would suggest that both supply and demand factors could be analysed at both the micro- and macroeconomic levels over both the short term and the long term. However, while each category can easily be identified at the micro-economic level, the interrelation of supply and demand frequently makes for complications at the macroeconomic level. Some approaches emphasize the demand aspect, some the supply side, while others focus specifically on the interrelationship between them. In particular, short-term macroeconomic analysis has been primarily one of demand factors. This emphasis arises mainly from the fact that demand conditions appear much more flexible than supply ones in the short term. The goods and services which an economy can supply will primarily depend on the labour force available, the capital equipment in existence, the quality of each, the efficiency with which they operate, and the technology they embody. None of these can change very much in the short term. Furthermore, evidence appears to suggest that the total amount the UK economy can supply increases at a fairly stable rate of perhaps 3 per cent or so each year, though a number of the contributory factors may themselves depend on the particular demand conditions that have existed, suggesting that a significant change in demand might radically change this situation.

Aggregate demand, on the other hand, is much less stable. It has grown at up to 6 per cent in some years, and fallen in others. As a result, demand tends to determine what proportion of the existing labour force and capital stock available is actually employed over the short term, and short-term macro-economic policy has therefore heavily concentrated on influencing demand.

Over the longer term, economic forces and government policy have in the past both tended to bring the growth of demand into line with the growth of the capacity of the economy to supply. With regard to the long term, therefore, the focus of attention has shifted to the supply side—in particular the supply of factors listed above such as capital, labour, their quality, etc. which together determine or influence the economy's overall supply capacity. Demand factors cannot, for the reason given, be ignored in this. For example, the growth of the capital stock will depend partly on the demand industrialists expect for their products; and another supply factor, labour efficiency, as measured by average output per man (labour productivity) appears to be dependent on changes in the level of demand. None the less, the long-term focus has been on the determinants of the *supply of inputs* as opposed to the short-term focus on the determinants of *demand for output*.

Keynes himself had much to say on these longer-term issues, and many economists have used a Keynesian framework to analyse supply and demand relationships over the longer term. It is nevertheless true that in the hands of some commentators the term 'Keynesian' has not unnaturally become more specifically associated with the short-term management of aggregate demand that became so all-pervasive in the 1950s, 1960s, and 1970s. This short-term Keynesian macroeconomic analysis and policy has recently come under considerable attack for a number of reasons. At a superficial level this could be explained by the fact that unemployment has recently climbed to historically very high levels again, but at a deeper level lie several more fundamental explanations.

First, Keynes was concerned to solve the immediate and pressing problem in the 1930s of unemployment. Since then new problems have arisen besides this one, in particular inflation. The Keynesian model was little concerned with the problem of persistently rising prices, primarily because the 1930s were years of relatively little movement in the average level of prices. In the 1950s, and even more in the 1960s and 1970s, the existence of gradual and then accelerating inflation has changed this. The Keynesian model, like pre-Keynesian ones, accepted that if demand rose above the capacity of the economy to supply, i.e. if full employment of either labour and/or capital was reached, then because the volume of output could no longer rise, shortages would occur and prices would start to rise. Keynes himself argued that even at somewhat below full employment of labour there would be a tendency to inflation, a prediction which experience after the Second World War appears to have confirmed. But the appearance of very rapid inflation despite considerable unemployment is apparently a different phenomenon which requires different analysis and new solutions. This had led to suggestions that the Keynesian framework is inappropriate for the task of developing anti-inflationary policies, and indeed many Keynesians favour direct control to prevent excessive rises in prices and incomes.

More seriously, the late 1950s and 1960s have seen the development of economic theory which implies serious faults in the Keynesian analysis, and as a result an inevitable lack of success in the application of policies based on it. Much of this theory stems initially from work by Professor Milton Friedman, and in several central areas of concern—fiscal policy, monetary policy, inflation—this school has done much to expose problems of Keynesian analysis. Lying behind much of it is the pre-Keynesian view that over the long term it is the response of price to excess demand or supply that dominates, and that many of our difficulties, not least that of inflation, are due to the preoccupation there has been with short-term output-manipulating policies to the exclusion of the long-term price repercussions they generate. In later chapters, therefore, we shall be concerned to present a picture of the economy in terms of which both approaches (and others where relevant) can be understood and compared. In terms of *explaining* the behaviour of the economy a synthesis of the two is emerging, but considerable differences of emphasis exist which can generate very different approaches as far as *policy prescription* is concerned.

Inflation, however, is not the only new problem to have arisen in the UK since the war. Another is the slow rate of economic growth and advance in real living standards. While this has been rapid in comparison with the inter-war period, it has been significantly slower than in nearly all the other industrialized countries of the world. Here again many have thought the Keynesian framework inappropriate. The problem seems inherently long term and to a considerable extent one which arises from the unwillingness or inability of firms to expand their supply potential because inputs to the productive process are inadequate, unreliable, inefficient, or too expensive. Intervention on the supply side is therefore likely to be required and quite possibly on a more microeconomic basis if particular industries or even particular firms can be identified as sources of poor performance. This raises the need for new analysis and reappraisal of the desirability and efficiency of government economic policy.

Furthermore, it may be that poor economic growth generates further poor economic growth. A number of ways in which this might occur are discussed later. If this is so then the problems facing the economy might be very deep-seated and the measures needed to get out of such a vicious circle might well be both quantitatively and qualitatively different from those thought appropriate if the economy was in a more healthy position. Here again the basic Keynesian analysis could be inadequate for the purpose of creating useful economic policies.

Finally, in recent years increasing attention has been paid to the relative rate of increase of demand of different sectors of the economy over the *medium term* of four or five years. This has focused on whether consumer expenditure and government expenditure are growing too fast, thus pre-empting resources that are not then available to produce the capital goods and exports necessary for future growth and a healthy balance of payments. This inevitably raises political as well as economic problems, but the longer-term background to demand analysis has raised new issues the implications of which are far from clear at the present time.

Economics is therefore at an interesting and crucial stage in its development. The relative stability of the post-war period has been severely shaken, inflation and growth problems have arisen which appear difficult to analyse or influence, and the post-war economic orthodoxy has been challenged at both theoretical and policy levels. New approaches to managing the economy have emerged, inflation has fallen but mass unemployment has again emerged.

1.3. Conflict and Methodology in Economics

1.3.1. Disagreement in Economics

It is perhaps not surprising in the circumstances that economics should itself be under attack. Certainly politicians, industrialists, the media, and the public generally have all in differing degrees been critical, in part because economists have appeared unable to provide answers to the many problems besetting the UK economy already referred to. Like most blanket criticism there is some truth and some inaccuracy in this view. For example, a valid criticism is that despite many microeconomic investigations by economists and others, including various government agencies (the Monopolies Commission, the National Board for Prices and Incomes, etc.), relatively little work has been done at that level to compare different firms, especially in different countries, in order to identify some of the factors lying behind the UK's poor economic performance. To some extent this may be because companies are reluctant to allow outside investigation and comparison of their operations, but economists also have been less ready to examine at the microeconomic level such factors as the comparative efficiency of management and work-force in terms of their education, skills and training, union organization, industrial relations and management techniques, company financing, research, innovation and development, etc., despite their obvious economic impact.

Criticism is less obviously valid with regard to the difficulties experienced in controlling the economy in order to avoid excessive instability. It is undoubtedly true that lack of complete understanding of the economic forces at work exacerbates the inherent problems. In particular, policies have been less successful than they would otherwise have been because the *speed* with which certain economic phenomena operate is difficult to judge. Yet against this it must be said that initially very little previous evidence existed to indicate, for example, how quickly demand might respond to government policy, nor can it be ignored that the existence of new situations in the economy—active government intervention, near-full employment, more rapid growth and inflation in the 1950s and 1960s; the reversal of all four in the 1980s, with two severe energy price shocks in between—might well render previous evidence irrelevant. In fact, considerable progress has been made even in the last ten years in developing a picture of the economy in terms of which many earlier difficulties can be understood, and avoided in future. The shocks to which the economic system has been subject have, however, increased, tending to obscure the advances that have been made.

There is relatively little validity in the view that the post-1973 period, which resulted in virtually none of the country's economic objectives being achieved, represented a major failure of economic analysis. Not only was the crisis of 1973–6 initially caused by factors largely out of control of the UK, but economic analysis was in fact rather successful in predicting the likely course of the crisis and in indicating the severity of the different policy options needed to deal with it. In the earlier 1980s few foresaw just how severe recession would be, particularly in its effect on unemployment, and the associated fall in inflation has been slightly greater than most predicted, but the interrelated set of economic forces underlying the behaviour of the economy, though complex, are probably now reasonably well understood, despite the turbulence of recent years. Such successes and failures in economics could each be illustrated many times over.

Lying behind all this is a rather more complex criticism—that economists disagree amongst themselves. This has already been implied in the description of the Keynesian approach and some of the reactions to it. It is disturbing, and confusing, when, in receiving professional economic advice, one is aware that a different opinion would be given by another economist, and so it is important to ask why this should happen. There are two factors, each of which generates controversy wherever it occurs in the field of human study, but which only come together in the social sciences. First, there is the impossibility of doing laboratory tests. Many scientific controversies can be settled by testing in specially designed laboratory conditions with all distorting influences removed. Wherever this is not possible, for example in many areas of medical science, astronomy, and archaeology, controversy is always present. The same is true of economics. In a situation in which a vast range of forces is at work, but where no possibility exists for temporarily removing some or holding them constant, the question of how to test, and indeed what constitutes a good test, becomes extremely complex and controversial, as is discussed below.

Second, economics cannot be divorced from politics, and whenever the latter appears, for example in history, sociology, some literature, and in the study of politics itself, controversy is widespread. If the development of an economy over time were completely determined independent of any action by any person in society, then even though economic conditions affected people greatly, the study of it would be as non-political as meteorology. Man would not be able to influence the economic environment. Given that this is not so, and that people's actions can and do partly determine others' well-being through their influence on economic conditions, economics is inevitably partly political. In the areas economists study, the assumptions they use, the constraints they recognize, and the policies they suggest, they cannot completely remove their own social and political standpoint. It is not surprising, therefore, that some important economic controversies closely parallel some political ones.

It is the presence of both these factors that makes most social sciences both particularly interesting and particularly difficult. In practice there is far less disagreement in economics than casual commentary suggests but, faced with these two potentially serious causes of controversy, economists have had to examine their approach and methods of analysis very closely, developing certain ground rules and reasonable means of testing the hypotheses they construct.

1.3.2. Positive and Normative Economics

An important distinction frequently made in economic analysis, therefore, is one between *positive* and *normative* economics. In essence, the difference between them is very straightforward. Normative economics includes statements about what *ought or ought not* to occur in economic affairs, e.g. the view that inflation ought to be reduced. Positive economics includes hypotheses and statements about what *does or does not* occur in economic affairs, e.g. inflation will be reduced if, other things being equal, productivity growth improves. The latter, it is argued, can be assessed by reference to empirical data, whereas the former is based on the personal value-judgements of the speaker. Thus argument over whether higher unemployment would reduce inflation is potentially capable of being settled by analysis of the facts. Argument over whether it is more important to reduce inflation or to reduce unemployment is *per se* not capable of being so resolved, as the argument hinges on the value the two sides place on the different hardships the two phenomena occasion. The fact that differences of view based on different value-judgements may be unresolvable creates difficulties if economic judgements depend on them.

It may be thought, and is often argued, that given this distinction, provided economists stick to positive economics, no value-judgements will be involved and no 'political' controversy can creep in. Indeed, economists have examined in considerable detail how far they can go in making recommendations divorced from value-judgements. As will be seen, the answer in both theory and practice is that they cannot go all that far. This is not always sufficiently emphasized, but is particularly important in the present context where much of what follows is devoted to understanding government economic policy, with its explicit blend of economics and politics. These issues are therefore considered in more detail later in the book.

1.3.3. *Testing Economic Hypotheses*

Even within the framework of positive economics there still is the second cause of disagreement in economics—the difficulty of testing hypotheses. Economic analysis essentially consists of constructing *models* and testing them. A model comprises three elements: a set of simplifying *assumptions*; a set of *deductions* from them; and a resulting *prediction* which then represents a hypothesis which can be tested empirically. The purpose of the assumptions is to simplify the process of investigation, e.g. many considerations will operate in the determination of the expenditure by consumers in Britain this year, but in analysing consumer expenditure we assume away or abstract from those which are thought to be of relatively minor importance, and concentrate on a few key factors which appear important at the aggregate level.

It may be immediately obvious what follows from these assumptions, e.g. if we assume all influences other than incomes to be unimportant in determining expenditure, then it follows immediately that we are predicting that expenditure will be determined by income. In other cases it will not be obvious, and a series of logical deductions will have to be made, e.g. if we assume that a firm (i) tries always to maximize its profits, and (ii) is a monopolist, we can deduce (given several other assumptions in addition) with the use of a model what would happen to its price if profits tax was increased. Here the prediction to be made is much less obvious, but can be deduced dependent on the assumptions made.

Given the assumptions and the deductions we end up with predictions which we can then go on to test. If the prediction is not borne out it could be because of faulty deductions, but in general will be because the simplifying assumptions have removed from consideration one or more factors that are significant influences on the matter under examination. In general, attempts will be made to reformulate the model if its predictions are not borne out by empirical observation.

Clearly, the testing of models or hypotheses is an important part of this whole process. In fact, a very large amount of testing now goes on in economics, and the literature abounds with the results of this testing. For many introductory readers this generates what might be termed the 'magic wand' effect. A piece of perhaps very simple theory is explained, data relevant to it are (sometimes) presented, and then some results are presented which claim to validate the theoretical analysis. It is clear what has been done and why, but it is not clear *how* it has been done, rather as if a magic wand had been waved to achieve the result.

Many quite difficult issues are involved in testing hypotheses in economics, and it is necessary to say a little about this, not because the reader is likely to do any testing himself, but because it is important that as much as possible of the mystery surrounding the principles involved can be removed so that he will have a better idea of the proper weight to be attached to the results of tests which he encounters.

It is best to take a very simple example. Suppose it is hypothesized that the level of firms' aggregate investment expenditure on new factories, plant, and machinery depends on the profits that firms in aggregate earn. If this is so one would expect some correlation between aggregate investment expenditure and firms' aggregate profits. The first and most major difficulty is in find out whether this supposed correlation exists.

In principle nothing would seem simpler, provided the information on aggregate investment and aggregate profits is available. A graph could be plotted, as shown in Figure 1.1, with investment expenditure measured

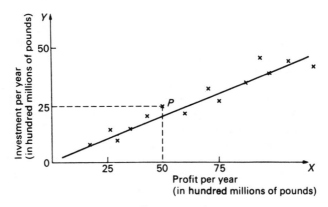

FIG. 1.1

vertically along the axis OY and profits measured horizontally along the axis OX. Each piece of information, which includes one level of profit (for example, £5,000 million per year) and the corresponding level of investment (for example, £2,500 million per year) could be represented on the diagram by a point (in this case the point labelled P). This is found by moving to the right from O a distance corresponding to £5,000 million per year and then upwards a distance corresponding to £2,500 million per year. The same could then be done for each piece of information, giving a scatter of points in the figure. If these lie roughly in a line, as shown, then it does appear that as profits get higher so investment does; otherwise not.

Now let us consider the problems. These can be split into two groups, the first of which concerns the difficulty of correctly specifying the relationship to be tested. Six separate though related points are involved.

(i) Which measure of investment and profits do we use? In the former, for example, we may or may not include the replacement investment that occurs when existing machinery becomes obsolete. We may or may not include, along with the investment of manufacturing industries, investment in agriculture, mining, and retail trades, etc. Perhaps factories should be treated separately from machinery, and similarly for transport equipment, etc. In the profit figures we may use pre-tax profits, post-tax profits, profits before payment of company interest payments on loans, or profits after payment of this, etc.

(ii) Next it has to be checked whether we are dealing with *stocks* or *flows* or a mixture. A stock variable is one like employment, or job vacancies, for example, which has a particular value at a particular point in time. The total amount of money in an economy and the total amount of capital—plant and machinery, etc.—are two other very important ones. All have the characteristic that we can at least in theory specify the level or amount at the point of time chosen, e.g. at the end of each month, the middle of each year, etc. A flow, on the other hand, is a variable the value of which cannot be specified unless a *period of time* is defined. An individual's spending can be so much per day or per week, etc., but a figure for spending has no meaning unless the period is stated or implied. A wage of £600 means nothing unless we know if it is per week, per month, or per year.

In our example both investment expenditure and profits are flows. If we have a stock and a flow—for example, if we want to correlate investment expenditure and the total stock of capital—then there is the problem of deciding which *period* for the flow variable to put with which *date* for the stock variable.

(iii) Next it has to be decided whether to use a *cross-sectional* or a *time-series* approach. In the first we look across firms, industries, or countries for a particular period, i.e. each piece of information in the diagram includes the investment done and profits made, for example, in a particular country during 1975. The correlation, if it exists, suggests that countries with higher profits carried out higher investment, at least in 1975. This cross-sectional result could be checked by repeating the analysis of 1974, 1973, etc. Problems begin to arise of course if the cross-sectional correlation works for some years, but not for others.

In the time-series approach we take one particular firm, industry, or country and look at it over a number of months or years. In this case each unit of information is the investment and profits of, e.g., the chosen country for each of a number of years past. If the correlation exists it suggests that when profits rise investment rises, and vice versa, at least for the country examined. Difficulties arise here if the correlation appears to exist for some periods, but not others, or if, as can happen, the correlation exists over a long period but not over shorter ones contained in the longer one, or vice versa. Such difficulties are further compounded if the evidence from cross-sectional and time-series studies do not agree.

(iv) In both cross-sectional and time-series studies there is a problem in deciding what *time-lags* are involved. In either approach, does one hypothesize that investment in 1975 depends on profits in 1975, or on profits in 1974, 1973, etc., or partly on each of them? If the latter, how far back should one go, and what importance should be attached to each year relative to the other? The argument over whether the fall in investment in 1970–1 was the fault of the Conservative Government in power at the time, or the previous Labour Government, is a good example of the difficulty.

(v) Worse still, what if the main influence on investment is *expected* profits? No solid evidence is available on the latter, and researchers may be forced to use data from questionnaires about business expectations or to attempt to identify the current factors that determine expectations about the future.

(vi) To say that investment depends on profits says nothing about the form of the relationship. Investment might be proportional to profits, might comprise one part independent of profits and another part dependent on them, could rise progressively faster the higher profits become, and so on. A particular form has to be specified for any actual test (though several different ones may be tried).

The next set of problems are statistical. There will almost certainly be a whole range of other influences on investment expenditure, and the probability is therefore that the data points will look as shown in Figure 1.2, rather than as

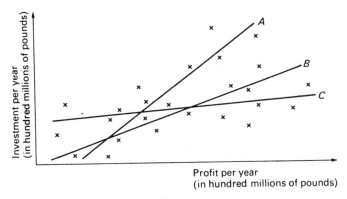

Profit per year
(in hundred millions of pounds)

FIG. 1.2

in Figure 1.1. Ignoring the lines *A*, *B*, and *C* for the moment, the points do indicate in a very vague and rough way a correlation between investment and profits, but how do we decide if the correlation is a good enough one on which to base analysis and policy? This leads to a further set of problems in trying to decide whether the data justify the hypothesis that the two are related in the way specified.

Two main problems arise. First, it does not help much just to look at Figure 1.2. Any of a number of lines (*A*, *B*, and *C* are but three examples) could be the line that best fits the points shown. *Econometric* analysis provides ways of finding out which line is the 'best fit'. This generally means finding the line such that if one calculates how far each point is vertically off the line, squares this amount, and adds up the total for all the points, the figure is less than it would be for any other possible line. A main argument for squaring the deviations between the points and the line is that large deviations count very heavily indeed against a line.

The second problem is to decide whether the line found is 'good enough'. Suppose line *B* in Figure 1.2 were found to be the best fit. Our belief in the hypothesized correlation will be much weaker than if the situation represented in Figure 1.1 had been the result of the empirical work (even if the line shown there was identical to line *B*), because the points are much more widely dispersed in Figure 1.2. A measure is therefore established (called a squared correlation coefficient) which measures how well the best-fit line fits the data points. If all the points lie exactly on the line it will have a value of 1. If at the other extreme the points are completely random it will have a value of 0. The line in Figure 1.1 would therefore have a correlation coefficient much nearer to 1 than line *B* in Figure 1.2.

In rough terms we can say that if the squared correlation coefficient is 0·7 then 70 per cent of the observed variation in investment is associated with variations in profits. When is such a coefficient high enough? The answer is that it all depends. At one extreme so little is known about some economic phenomena and they are so unpredictable that a value of 0·5 or 0·6 is quite useful. At the other extreme it may be disastrous if a major economic variable cannot be predicted to 98 per cent accuracy. In addition, the variable may be sufficiently stable that just using last year's figures will regularly give at least 95 per cent accuracy. Clearly here explanatory hypotheses require much higher correlation coefficients than in the first case.

The above points are largely technical. There is, however, another type of difficulty involved in testing hypotheses, that of inference. This is more philosophical in nature and more fundamental. To start with, it is often the case that one can find a correlation for the past which does not continue into the future, thus undermining the use of the correlation as a basis for accurate prediction of future behaviour. This may be because of other influences, because the relationship identified was partly or completely coincidental, or because people's behaviour has changed, probably as a result of new circumstances. For example, if working people tend to save a higher proportion of their income when unemployment becomes very high, because of the fear of further unemployment it induces, then this will invalidate any stable relationship which explains savings if that relationship was identified previously at a time when unemployment was never high enough to have this effect. Such an effect could, of course, have been hypothesized before, but would have been impossible to test.

A more serious version of this occurs if phenomena which hitherto appeared to have little economic effect and could be ignored by economic analysis start to have an effect. An increased awareness of income inequalities, or a changed political climate in which previous income differentials are no longer passively accepted, may both have powerful effects on inflation, productivity, and growth, but require extensive research, new modes of thinking, and new tools of analysis before these effects can be properly integrated into the mainstream of economics. In an extreme case the whole of our previous observations may become suspect. In the meantime existing analysis is inadequate. It could even be that people change their behaviour because they come to recognize that policy will radically alter the progress of the economy, thus invalidating the relationships on which economic analysis and the policy itself were initially based.

The most fundamental problem, however, is that even if a correlation is good and does continue to hold over time, it says nothing about the *direction of causality*. Suppose that it is found cross-sectionally that countries with high rates of economic growth generally have high levels of investment expenditure, and vice versa. Do we conclude (a) that higher investment causes faster growth by expanding an economy's capacity to produce faster, (b) that faster growth leads to higher investment expenditure by creating more profitable opportunities to invest, (c) that both faster growth *and* higher investment are caused by some third factor, for example a high level of managerial efficiency? The simple correlation throws no light on this, yet the implications for policy are very different in the three cases.

Several of these difficulties have indicated the possible significance of other variables besides the two mentioned. In fact it is an ever-present problem that any one economic variable tends to depend on quite a number of others. Econometric techniques have been developed to deal with this. (Conceptually the approach is as before, though it is difficult to portray diagramatically because the value of one variable is now explained by two or more others.) In such cases, fortunately, we can in principle not only find out econometrically how much of the variability of the former is 'explained' by variations in all the others, but also how important each separate variable is.

This, however, raises a new problem in deducing a causal relation from a statistical one. Suppose investment, profits, and total expenditure on all goods and services in the UK all rise and fall together. It may be that rises in total expenditure raise profits and also raise investment *directly*, the latter effect being because of shortages of the industrial capacity required to produce the goods demanded. Alternatively, it may be *only when profits rise* in response to the rise in total expenditure that investment rises. Again it is hard to tell simply from the data which hypothesis is correct, and again the policy implications of the two interpretations can be quite different.

Many other difficulties exist. It may be that the relationship examined is not linear, i.e. the best-fit line on the diagram is not a straight line at all, but a flattening or rising curve. There may be two or three separate causal links between two variables, one suggesting they rise and fall together, another suggesting the reverse. Frequently, an economic variable may depend on inherently unmeasurable factors. In some cases, for example the effect of imposing or removing credit controls, this is dealt with by introducing a so-called 'dummy' variable, the value of which changes (0, 1, etc.) according to whether controls are operating or not. In other cases a 'proxy' variable, one that is likely to change in line with the unmeasurable variable but which is itself measurable, has to be identified. Worse still, a great number of variables may all be interrelated in a large number of relationships, making analysis of any part of the system inadequate, but making analysis of the whole system highly complex.

In this case it may be necessary to identify each separate relationship, formulate it as an equation, put all the equations together simultaneously, and mathematically deduce the overall relationship between two or more variables. This can then be tested, but it is often very difficult to know which *individual* relationship hypothesized is incorrect if the *overall* prediction is not borne out.

Some cases are so complex that the above method is inappropriate. At this stage the model frequently has to be programmed into a computer and a battery of further techniques used to identify the predictions that arise from combining a large number of separate hypothesized relationships. Enough has been said though to illustrate the potential problems.

In many important cases the complexities are sufficiently great that it has been questioned whether testing of the type described is appropriate at all. The game of chess has been used here as a useful analogy. In chess all the relationships of the pieces to each other are known completely, as is the overall objective. In both ways the situation is much simpler than that which exists in the economy yet one would have great difficulty in empirically testing the hypothesis that a particular move was more likely to achieve checkmate than another. Rather, it is argued, one would seek the views of an expert chess player. Similarly, for the solution of economic problems it may, in some cases at least, be impossible to do reliable testing and be more important to obtain the judgement of those who have had success in making economic judgements previously. One important role of the study of economic history is to help provide the perspective, insight, and experience which such judgement requires. In practice some combination of prediction based on correlation and judgement based on experience is likely to be better than emphasis on either one alone.

1.4. Outline of the Book

Against this brief background it is possible to describe the structure and content of the book. The rest of it is split into six parts. Part II summarizes in fairly condensed form the basic economic forces at work in the economy. In six chapters it covers macro- and microeconomic behaviour and domestic and international aspects, mainly within a 'positive' framework. As in the other parts, each chapter draws on concepts and arguments presented earlier in the book, but is otherwise as self-contained as possible.

Chapter 2 includes a simple introduction to consumer theory at the microeconomic level and includes some elementary tools of analysis used widely in economics. The analysis is then placed in a macroeconomic context. While the framework is essentially Keynesian in that it focuses on volume rather than price adjustment mechanisms, post-Keynesian developments which introduce longer-term considerations ignored by Keynes are also discussed.

Chapter 3 examines the behaviour of firms in some detail, reflecting the origins of the book in the teaching of managers. Nothing emphasized more strongly the gap between the theory of the firm taught to most economics students and the behaviour of actual companies than the attempt to teach the former to businessmen at the Oxford University Business Summer School. This is due partly to differences of purpose and partly to the different levels of abstraction involved, but it also derived from the largely static equilibrium-based analysis used in economics as compared to the dynamic disequilibrium situation which most real-world firms face. None the less there are significant links between the two approaches, each of which has much to gain from the other, and Chapter 3 attempts to present a picture of firms' behaviour which can act as a basis for linking the two. The first part focuses on company decisions and accounts. Industrial economic analysis and the basis of the theory of the firm are developed as abstractions from this and focus on those particular economic forces likely to be most important in the long-term economic development of firms.

Chapter 4 introduces the economic behaviour of employees into the picture. Many key elements of economic performance to do with inflation, unemployment, and competitiveness revolve around the 'labour market'—the extent to which people want work, the availability of jobs, levels and forms of pay, and the influence of trade unions in the determination of these. How they interact, particularly as unemployment has risen heavily, is one of the central issues in current economic analysis. Chapter 5 then places the behaviour of consumers, firms, and employees in a macroeconomic context; introduces the monetary sector of the economy into the picture; briefly introduces international trade and government economic behaviour; and looks at several of the approaches developed to explain the behaviour of the economy as a whole. Both longer-term supply-side aspects and shorter-term, demand-oriented ones are covered. This core chapter introduces a large number of the ideas upon which subsequent chapters build and draws out some of the basic links between them. Chapter 6 then develops the international aspect in view of its vital importance to the UK economy as well as to other economies. International accounts and trade, the balance of payments, and the exchange rate are all discussed briefly so that some appreciation of these rather complex matters can be gained.

Given the framework of Chapters 2 to 6, Part II concludes in Chapter 7 with a more detailed examination of the two interrelated problems that have been of most immediate consequence in the UK in the last twenty years, inflation and unemployment. Chapter 7 reviews the course of both, the factors underlying them, and the links between them.

Having described in Part II the working of the UK economy and some of the problems it generates, Part III looks at the range of economic policies that have been applied to overcome them. Chapter 8 commences by looking in general terms at the issues involved in identifying objectives and selecting economic instruments to pursue them in an overtly political framework, and discusses the frequently ignored complexities of policy formation in an industrially developed democracy such as the UK. This is followed by three chapters dealing in turn with public finance, monetary policy, and incomes policy. Chapters 12 and 13 then focus on the interrelationships between fiscal and monetary policy and on this basis consider the central issue of demand management, both in theory and in practice, in earlier periods of higher growth and employment and more recently. Though somewhat more advanced in content, in terms of current macroeconomic policy issues these two chapters are the central ones in the book, and should be accessible to all who have read the earlier chapters. Part III concludes with a chapter describing how the UK economy is modelled in order to be able to make realistic forecasts and to simulate suggested changes in policy or in performance in order to find out and measure the likely consequences.

Parts IV and V put the recent behaviour of the UK economy in, respectively, an international and a longer-term context. The UK, both in terms of trade and in financial flows, is very exposed to what is happening in the rest of the world. So integrated have the economic links between countries become that it is very difficult to understand clearly the pressures on the UK without taking the international dimension into account. The first three chapters of Part IV look at the major influences in trade terms. Chapter 15 examines global trade developments generally, the factors underlying them, and, in particular, the impact of newly industrializing countries on the Western developed nations. Chapter 16 reviews the economic performance of Europe into which the UK, in economic terms, has been increasingly absorbed; Chapter 17 is on the economic performance of Japan which, apart from oil, has probably been the single most important influence on the trade performance of most European countries including the UK. This chapter also examines reasons for the phenomenal economic success of Japan to see if there are clues to improved performance in the UK. Chapter 18, on the international monetary system, examines financial aspects of the global economy, looking especially at the impact of exchange and interest rates, financial flows between countries, and the provision of reserves from which to be able to settle international payments. Chapter 19 then focuses specifically on the linkages between countries, the ways in which each has been constrained by the behaviour of others, and the record of attempts to prevent major economies simultaneously limiting each other in their individual attempts to improve performance. Taken together these chapters portray in some detail the often severe limitations imposed upon economic policy in the UK as a result of its international context.

Part V introduces a quite different and more speculative type of perspective but one which has received increasing attention recently and one which again suggests rather severe constraints on the behaviour of the UK economy. This is the historical perspective. Chapter 20 introduces the section with an analysis of economic growth in the UK since the war. This is a convenient and familiar period over which to look at UK growth, and one which makes it possible to illustrate most of the factors that have been suggested as reasons for the UK's slow rate of growth relative to other countries. The significant slow down in productivity growth after 1973 is described and reference also made to the recent signs of some reversion to faster producitivity growth in the 1980s.

In recent years, however, it has become increasingly clear that economic growth in the UK may have been relatively poor over a much longer period. Chapter 21 looks at some of the evidence for this and some of the suggested reasons. As the educational and training levels of the work-force in the UK appear prominently in this, Chapter 22 focuses on the topic specifically. Finally in this part, Chapter 23 looks at the pattern of growth over the very long term, exploring the at first sight rather curious, and until recently very ill-researched, notion that there may be 'waves' or cycles of activity over as long as fifty years which may go some way to explain the problems of the 1970s and 1980s in comparison to the rapidly expansionary phase of the 1950s and 1960s. As in Part IV so here, these chapters taken together cover in some detail the long-term constraints on the performance of the UK economy and on the opportunities for people to alter it for the better.

Serious as the constraints of the UK's international position and historically poor performance may be, they do not mean that the long-term path of the UK economy cannot be improved. Over many years there have been many attempts to raise economic performance, and these may loosely be referred to under the collective heading of industrial policy. This therefore is the subject matter of Part VI. Chapter 24 is an overtly more theoretical chapter which sets out the ground rules in terms of which economists have traditionally tried to assess such issues as the 'correct' price for a nationalized industry to charge or the advantages of 'competitively' determined prices. It therefore describes the type of analysis that underlies much of the thinking about nationalized industries and competition policy.

Policies towards these two issues are of particular significance in their own right and are covered in Chapters 25 and 26. Chapter 27 discusses one industry of sufficient importance to warrant individual attention, namely the development and impact of North Sea Oil. Finally, in this part, Chapter 28 reviews the main elements of the numerous other ways in which governments have sought to influence industrial performance.

Part VII comprises one chapter which tries to draw together certain of the main threads from earlier chapters. On this basis it gives a brief overview of the position of the UK economy in 1984 and, in terms of a number of key aspects— unemployment, macroeconomic policy, growth, etc.—looks at trends as they seem most likely to develop in the future.

Selected bibliographies are to be found at the end of each chapter where appropriate. In most cases these have been split into a Section A of main references on the subject discussed, and a Section B of a broader nature indicating possible sources on various aspects touched upon in the chapter.

PART II

ECONOMIC BEHAVIOUR

2

Consumer Behaviour

H. G. JONES

2.1 Introduction

Any modern developed economy typically includes millions of individuals who spend their different incomes on literally thousands of different goods and services. In the United Kingdom the *Family Expenditure Survey*[1] provides a wealth of detailed information on the pattern of expenditure of UK households at a particular point in time. Although, like all useful statistical compilations, it represents a necessary compromise between detail and clarity, it does reveal the bewildering *complexity* and *diversity* of household expenditure. The factors influencing the behaviour of households, both individually and considered together, in determining the pattern of expenditure, constitute the subject-matter of this chapter. Although it is convenient if, as in the *Family Expenditure Survey*, attention is concentrated on natural groups of individual consumers—the 'household' or the 'income unit'—almost all of the discussion and analysis does apply to the individual as much as to the household.

It is appropriate that our survey of the workings of the economy should begin with a discussion of the economic behaviour of households, for they constitute one of the principal groups of actors on the economic stage. In an economy such as the United Kingdom's, a typical household sells, or attempts to sell, its labour services to employers and receives, as proceeds of the sale, labour income. Moreover, the household may own financial assets (such as savings certificates, shares, etc.) and non-financial assets (such as property) from which it also derives income. The household's income may also include payments from the government in the form of social security payments, old age pensions, etc. With its income the household purchases goods and services, pays taxes, and, perhaps, saves. Although much of this book is concerned with macroeconomic policies and problems, it is important to remember that beneath many important macroeconomic aggregates—e.g. the level of unemployment or the flow of aggregate consumption expenditure—lie the individual households whose independent decisions and responses have generated, or contributed to, the macroeconomic phenomenon in question.

In this chapter we concentrate on the economic behaviour of the household as a *buyer* of commodities rather than as a seller of labour, although the

[1] Dept. of Employment, Government Statistical Office.

framework of thought, centred upon household *choice*, can easily be applied to these other economic activities. Our emphasis is on the simple analysis of general tendencies. We cannot, and probably should not, hope to *describe* adequately the economic behaviour of all households in their role as buyers. Even the *Family Expenditure Survey*, for all its wealth of detail, cannot mirror reality, and our objective will be to represent and summarize adequately the major characteristics of household economic behaviour.

One final introductory point should be made. For at least two centuries successive generations of economists have attempted to analyse the economic behaviour of the household. Countless textbooks and monographs have been written on even small parts of the subject. It should be clear that a brief chapter cannot hope to encapsulate all the rich variety of results, hypotheses, and conclusions that have been arrived at in that period. This chapter, in keeping with the overall purpose of the book, aims to provide only the basic framework of thought and the main points required for an understanding of later parts of the book. Consequently, we rely heavily on assertion, and many important topics have to be ignored or merely alluded to.

2.2. Household Demand for Goods and Services

2.2.1. The Law of Demand

Consider an individual household (or, indeed, an individual consumer). In any time period (e.g. week, month, or year) its pattern of expenditure will, in general, depend upon the *household's preferences or tastes*, the *prices* of goods and services, and the household's *income*. The basic problem for the household is to *choose* a collection of products or 'shopping list' which is feasible in the sense that it can be paid for given the household's income and the prices of goods and services. The chosen set of products should, moreover, be considered by the household as preferable to (or at least as good as) any other feasible set. Thus the preferences and choices of all households are, in general, constrained by available income and the prices of goods and services. Now, some discussion is required to elucidate and elaborate the precise meaning of the foregoing remarks. In the present section we assume that the concept of household income-per-period is unambiguous and, in particular, that household income is constant or fixed. Thus we discuss here the influences upon the demand for goods and services of preferences and prices *given a fixed income*. The variety of ways of conceiving of household income are discussed in the next section.

We have already stated that the object of choice for a particular household in any period is a list of the quantities of each product and each service that the household purchases. It is convenient, at this point, to draw a distinction between *durable* and *non-durable* goods. Some goods (non-durables) are, by their very nature, purchased so as to be immediately consumed, e.g. food and drink. But one can easily think of other goods (durables) whose purchase is, in general, based on the assumption that the goods can be expected to provide services over a relatively long period of time, e.g. a washing machine or a car. (It is, of course, possible to purchase a bottle of good wine as an investment rather than for consumption, and such an example illustrates the fact that the distinction between durable and non-durable goods does not really stem from an intrinsic property of the goods but from the motivation for purchase, and planned use.) We draw the distinction because the factors influencing the demand for durables are quite likely to be rather different from the factors determining the demand for non-durables. We return to these considerations in the next section.

In analysing the economic behaviour of the household as a purchaser, the economist often assumes that every individual consumer and every individual household has a complete set of preferences which do not change and which determine his choice of goods in any buying situation. Thus it is as though each household simply observes a whole series of possible shopping lists and simply chooses the one that is 'best' on the basis of the household's given preferences.[2]

The treatment of household preferences as *data*—in the sense that they are simply assumed to be given and unchanging—removes from the analysis a large variety of influences which may affect preferences. They may simply change with the passage of time—because, for example, of a desire for change *per se* or because the average age of a household is changing such that children's toys and perambulators no longer appear so desirable. Household preferences will be influenced by the current state of knowledge concerning the available goods and services, and are likely to change as more information becomes available as a result of experience or deliberate search. In particular, it is worth noticing that many consumers, in the absence of more 'objective' information (such as *Which* magazine reports) as to the quality of goods, habitually use the *price* of a good as a rough index of its quality. Advertising expenditures of all kinds are likely to alter household preferences—both between different brands of similar products and, possibly, between different products. Preferences may be moulded by all manner of psychological and sociological influences. Thus, for example, the pattern of household expenditure may be influenced by a desire to 'keep up with the Joneses' or by a desire to be different from other families in the neighbourhood. Changing views of the future may markedly alter current preferences.

It seems clear, therefore, that in attempting to analyse the economic behaviour of the household, the assumption of a given set of preferences is very powerful and must be handled with care. Its usefulness lies in the fact that in terms of broad classes of goods and services the influences discussed above do not, taking the population as a whole, usually change quickly or vary much in intensity. As a consequence, people's preferences between the major goods and services that are available tend to remain fairly stable. In addition, such changes as do occur may have little or no effect on the *total* level of consumer spending. Thus the assumption of given preferences may not, in fact, constitute a particularly serious distortion of reality—and it certainly provides a simple framework for much useful analysis.

Accepting the foregoing difficulties, imagine a household with a fixed set of preferences that is considering how much to buy of a certain commodity (which is considered desirable by the household) given its income and *given that the prices of all other goods and services are known and fixed*. Introspection and observation

---

[2] These preferences are usually assumed to satisfy a series of axioms or assumptions from which behavioural predictions can be derived.

reveal[3] one of the best known of all economic propositions—sometimes known as the Law of Demand. The quantity of any commodity—say, beer—that a household plans to buy will, in general, be inversely related to the price of that commodity.[4] Thus the demand for beer can be said to be a 'function' of (i.e. depend upon) the price of beer and this idea can be succinctly summarized by writing $D_B = f(p_B)$ where D_B represents the demand for beer, p_B represents the price of beer, and the expression $f(p_B)$ represents the functional relationship, namely that the former depends on the latter.

The so-called Law of Demand is illustrated in Figure 2.1. The curve DD

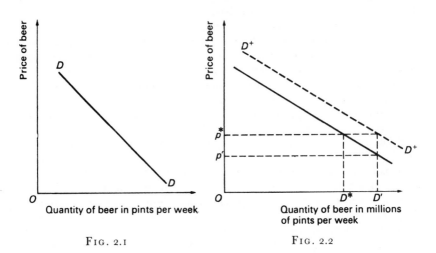

Fig. 2.1   Fig. 2.2

indicates the quantities of beer that a particular household will, given its preferences and income, plan to buy at different prices. This 'demand curve'[5] or 'demand function' is drawn as downward sloping, reflecting our statement of the Law of Demand. Different households will, depending upon their relative liking for beer, have different demand curves but, given the Law of Demand, all the curves will be downward sloping.

If, for each possible price of beer, the quantities that *all* households would buy at that price are added together horizontally we *obtain the market demand curve* illustrated in Figure 2.2. The market demand curve, which shows the total demand for beer at each price, is again downward sloping and is, in fact, conceptually very similar to the individual demand curve—apart from the change in the scale of the horizontal axis from 'pints per week' to 'millions of

[3] This proposition, together with possible exceptions, can be rigorously derived on the basis of a small set of assumptions concerning household preferences. Section 2.4 of this chapter constitutes a brief illustration of the method. For more detail see Green [3], Chaps. 2–4.

[4] The principal source of possible exceptions to the 'Law' is discussed in section 2.2.4 and elaborated in section 2.4.

[5] Economists refer to demand 'curves' even though the diagram illustrates a straight line! A line is, of course, a limiting case of the class of all curves.

pints per week'. At the price $p*$ households as a whole plan to buy a quantity $OF*$ of beer whereas at the lower price p', households would like to buy the larger quantity OD'.

Market demand curves for particular commodities can be estimated by statistical means and used as practical tools for government and business. In this book, however, we are more concerned with the *concept* of the market demand for any commodity being, in general, inversely related to the price of that commodity.

It is important to distinguish between movements *along* any given market demand curve and *shifts* in the whole demand curve. An increase in the desired quantity of beer from $OD*$ to OD' may come about as a result of a fall in the price of beer as discussed above. The same change could, however, arise as a result of changes in the preferences of households such that, at every price, they are prepared to buy more beer. The market demand curve consequently shifts to the right—as illustrated by the dotted curve D^+D^+ in Figure 2.2.

In considering the effect of a change in price on the demand for a product, it is important to recognize that there may be delays or 'time-lags' in the response of consumers. Thus, for example, quite a considerable time might elapse following an increase in the price of petrol before the demand for it fell.

2.2.2. *The Price Elasticity of Demand*

The fall in the price of beer from $p*$ to p' illustrated in Figure 2.2 generated an increase in the quantity demanded from $OD*$ to OD'. The demand for some goods will be more responsive to changes in price than others. A simple measure of the relative responsiveness of demand to changes in price is called the 'price elasticity of demand' and is defined as follows:

$$E_p = \frac{\text{percentage change in quantity demanded}}{\text{percentage change in price}}$$

where E_p signifies the price elasticity of demand for a commodity. Thus if a 1 per cent fall in *price* generates a 1 per cent increase in *quantity demanded* then the *price* elasticity of demand is said to be 1.[6] If, on the other hand, a 1 per cent fall in price generates a 2 per cent increase in quantity demanded then the price elasticity of demand is 2 and demand is described as *relatively elastic* (i.e. the elasticity is above 1). If, finally, a 1 per cent decrease in price generates a $\frac{1}{2}$ per cent increase in demand then the elasticity of demand is $\frac{1}{2}$ and demand is described as *relatively inelastic* (less than 1). The definitions can, of course, be symmetrically stated for an increase in price. Two extreme cases can be defined. If demand is totally unresponsive to a change in price (in which case the demand curve is a vertical straight line) then the elasticity of demand is zero and demand is said to be perfectly inelastic. If, at the other extreme, demand is *so* responsive to price that the slightest fall in price would induce households to attempt to buy infinite quantities of the good (in which case the demand curve

---

[6] Since a *fall* in price generates an *increase* in demand (i.e. price and demand move in opposite directions) the elasticity of demand is inherently negative. In practice, the sign is ignored so that this elasticity is said to be 1 rather than -1.

would be a horizontal straight line) then E_p would be infinite and demand 'perfectly elastic'.

It is easy to think of the demand for necessities as being rather inelastic while the demand for luxuries might be expected to be rather elastic—but the ambiguity in the definition of the terms 'luxury' and 'necessity' means that it is rather difficult to make statements of this kind, and possibly quite misleading.

It is important to note that the elasticity of demand[7] for a commodity might well change through time so that the measured elasticity might be very different depending upon the time period over which the change in demand was measured. Consider, for example, the effect of a large increase in the price of electricity. Some considerable time might elapse before any significant change in the quantity of electricity used occurred, for households would already be committed to the use of electricity because of previous purchases of electrical equipment. Thus in the short run the demand for electricity might appear highly inelastic. As time elapsed, however, a higher proportion of households might avoid electrical equipment in favour of, for example, gas central heating, with the result that the long-run elasticity of demand for electricity might be considerably higher. This distinction is of considerable importance in some later chapters.

The elasticity of demand for a commodity may be very important for policy purposes. Consider a commodity whose elasticity is 1. We know, therefore, that a 1 per cent increase in price will generate a 1 per cent fall in demand and it should be clear that, in this case, there will be *no change in total expenditure* on the commodity—the loss of sales being just balanced by the increased price. If, on the other hand, the demand for some commodity is relatively elastic—say, 2— then a 1 per cent increase in price will generate a 2 per cent fall in demand, and total expenditure on that commodity will consequently *fall*. Finally, it should now be clear that if demand is relatively inelastic as 1 per cent increase in price will generate a less than proportionate fall in demand, and total expenditure on that commodity will increase.

Thus decisions concerning prices, whether they be made by private companies or nationalized enterprises, will be much influenced by the elasticity of demand of the product concerned.

2.2.3. Complements and Substitutes

Thus far we have discussed the demand for an individual commodity on the assumption that prices of other goods and services are constant, and we have concluded that the demand for any commodity is usually inversely related to its own price. If we relax this assumption, it is immediately clear that the demand for any commodity will no longer depend simply on its own price but also on the prices of other goods. The demand for beer will depend in part on the prices of whisky and cider, etc., and the demand for cars will, in part, depend upon the price of petrol. Any economy is very interdependent in the sense that changes in any one part of the system may affect all other parts of the system. Thus, in

---

[7] Although there are other types of elasticity of demand beside the price elasticity of demand, the latter is so frequently used that it is often simply called 'the elasticity of demand'.

principle, the demand for any commodity will not only depend upon its own price but also on its price relative to the prices of *all* other commodities. In practice, of course, we would expect the prices of only some other commodities to be particularly quantitatively significant. In the above examples, whisky can be seen to be a partial *substitute* for beer in the sense of being an alternative alcoholic drink, and there can be little doubt that a halving of the price of whisky in the United Kingdom would reduce the demand for beer. On the other hand, petrol and cars are *complementary* and a large increase in the price of petrol might be expected to reduce the demand for cars.[8] Thus, it is clear that our demand function should, at a minimum, include some other prices—i.e. $D_B = f(p_B, \bar{p})$ where D_B the price of beer and $\bar{p}$ represents a list of the prices of other goods which are relevant to the demand for beer.

Before proceeding to the next section, it is worth noticing that the demand for any commodity might be influenced not only by its own price and the prices of other goods but also by its *expected price* and the expected prices of other goods. If households believe that the price of a washing machine is going to rise then they may bring forward in time the planned purchase of the commodity so as to avoid the effects of the price increase. Furthermore one might generally expect the effect of expected future prices to be much more significant for the demand for durable goods—for the exact timing of the purchase is probably more open to choice. We return to this subject in section 2.3.

2.2.4. *Analysing the Effect of a Change in Price*

Most of the preceding discussion of the Law of Demand is both intuitive and familiar. 'Everybody' knows that, other things being equal, a decrease in the price of a good or service is likely to lead to an overall increase in purchases of the good or service—and vice versa. It is, however, worth thinking a little more about the matter. A decrease in the relative price of, say, bread does imply that households with 'normal' preferences will be inclined to purchase more bread and less of other commodities. The decrease in price makes the good relatively more attractive (assuming that it is desirable in the first place) and the tendency to 'substitute' towards the good in preference to other available goods is a natural consequence of most forms of household preference. It is, however, worth noting that a decrease in the price of a good effectively *increases the real income* of a household—in the sense that the same income is sufficient to buy more of *all* goods. Consider a situation in which a particular good (say bread, potatoes, or rice for a low-income family) constitutes a very important part of the total household budget. A fall in the price of the good implies a substantial improvement in the real income of the household and, in particular, it can now buy (at least) the same volume of the good as previously *and* increase its spending on other goods.

A little reflection will confirm that this 'income effect' of the change in price could lead to an increase *or* a *decrease* in the demand for the good. It is easy to think of particular commodities that might be considered 'inferior' by a

---

[8] The concept of a substitute or a complement is more complicated that it appears here. See Green [3], Chap. 5 for further detail.

household—in the sense that at higher levels of real income the household would consume less of the commodity in question. Thus, for example, a low-income household might consume a large amount of rice but would prefer to consume more meat. A *decrease* in the price of rice would 'normally' lead to an increase in the consumption of rice—but it is clear that the effect of such a decrease in the *real income* of the household *could* lead to a *decrease* in the consumption of rice and an increase in the consumption of meat. The Law of Demand *does* apply in most cases—but the principal exceptions to the 'Law' stem from the possibility that the 'income effect' of a change in price may outweigh the natural tendency to consume more of a cheaper good. This point is elaborated in section 2.4.

2.3. Household Income

2.3.1. The Concept of Income

In section 2.2 we concentrated on the effects of prices upon the demand for commodities, on the assumption of a fixed and unambiguous idea of household income. In the present section we elaborate on the idea of income as a fundamental constraint preventing the unfettered expression of household preferences *given* the prices of commodities.

Consider, once again, an individual household facing fixed and known prices for all commodities. Given its income, its problem is to allocate that income amongst the available goods so as to purchase the consumption bundle or shopping list that it likes best. But what precisely is meant by 'household income'? In any period a typical household will receive a measurable income from a variety of sources and depending upon a variety of factors. Firstly, this 'measured income' will typically include a large component of labour income in the form of wages or salaries and this labour income will in turn depend upon wage rates, salary scales, the amount of overtime or short-time workings, etc. Moreover, the typical household's labour income will be paid net of various taxes, social security contributions, and pension contributions that are deductable at source. Thus it is clear that the measured disposable labour income depends upon a large variety of factors many of which are effectively outside the household's control. On the other hand, it is clear that *some* of the factors determining income, and, in particular, the amount of overtime worked and the wage demands made by labour representatives, *are* partially under the control of the household. Thus the response of households to either decreases in their incomes (as a result, say, of income tax increases) or to increases in the prices of goods may be to work more overtime, or demand that their unions apply for wage increases, thus attempting to maintain the previous income level.

Secondly, the measured income of a typical household in any period may include sums accruing from the ownership of various forms of wealth. Thus interest may be paid on building society or bank savings, dividends may be paid as a result of the ownership of shares, or rents paid as a result of the ownership of property. Furthermore, the typical household may receive a variety of payments from the state in the form of pensions, unemployment pay, or various forms of subsidy. Finally, the measured income of a typical household may, in any period, include a variety of transitory components of the 'windfall' variety—e.g. unexpected gifts, gambling winnings, or tax repayments.

Now, the measured income of a household clearly forms part of the constraint on its expenditure in any period of time but, equally clearly, that is not the whole story. Many items in any household's shopping list, and in particular durable goods such as cars and washing machines, simply could not be financed out of the measured income of any individual period. Such purchases are typically financed by various forms of borrowing—consumer credit, hire purchase, bank overdrafts, bank loans, or, in the case of house purchase, mortgage loans. Whether an individual household can, in any period, contract for such items will depend, *inter alia*, on availability of finance, the cost of finance in terms of the rate of interest charged on the loan, and, in general terms, the ability of the household to make the appropriate repayments. It is clear that we are moving away from the idea that current measured income is invariably the decisive constraint upon household expenditure. What may be more germane, particularly in terms of determining the demand for durable goods, is some concept of long-term, 'normal' or 'permanent' income[9] based upon the household's past income experience and its reasonable *expectations* of future income. For example, if a household has every reason to believe that its measured income will steadily increase through time (consider a young couple in which the income earner is on a rising salary scale in a secure job), then one might expect that the pattern of borrowing and expenditure will vary in a systematic way through the lifetime of the household, with expenditure exceeding measured income in the early years. The amount by which expenditure could be allowed to exceed income would stem from the household's own prudence and the lender's desire to minimize the possibility of default—but ultimately the *expectation of measured income* over time would constitute the decisive constraint. These expectations will, of course, be determined by a very large variety of factors—the ability of the income earner, the probability of continuous employment, the probability of promotion, the expectation of wage increases, etc. It follows that, although the Law of Demand may be expected to hold in general, the demand for particular commodities may be much more sensitive to such factors as incomes, prevailing consumer credit regulations, rates of interest, the general availability of credit, etc. than to their prices.

2.3.2. A Household's Total Consumption Demand

Our discussion has indicated that a household's income and the relative price of a good are two major determinants of its demand for the good. When we come to examine the household's *total* demand for all goods, then real income, i.e. effective purchasing power, becomes the main determinant, with relative

[9] These ideas were principally derived in the context of the theory of the aggregate consumption function (see section 2.5) in macroeconomics. For a flavour, consult Friedman [12].

prices determining the *composition* of consumption rather than the total. A change in the relative price of one good may change the household's total demand, but this effect arises because the price change results in a new real income—the household's money income can buy more of all goods if the price of one good falls. Current and expected income are therefore the main determinants of a household's *total* demand for goods.

As a matter of common observation, however, not all income is consumed. The remainder represents saving, and we need to examine what might determine a household's desire to save before we can fully specify the relationship between income and consumption.

The going level of interest rates that can be earned on savings will usually be one determinant of the proportion of income that a household is prepared to save. But the relationship between aggregate saving and interest rates is difficult to generalize about because two different factors are involved. First, the higher the interest rate available the more incentive there is to save, tending to increase saving out of a given income. Second, if the purpose of saving is to provide a given benefit, e.g. a fixed income in retirement, then a higher rate of interest will provide this income from a *smaller* capital sum, and the incentive to save is thus reduced.

A second, and probably much more important, determinant of the proportion of a household's income which is saved is the level of income itself. Low-income households which have greater difficulty in meeting their basic needs—for housing, food, clothing, and so on—will probably be unable to save more than a very small fraction of income, if that, while relatively well-off households, facing a choice at the margin whether to buy (relative) luxury goods and services, can ordinarily be expected to save a significant proportion of income.

Another factor influencing saving is the variability of income over time. Since an important motive for saving is as a precaution against the uncertainty of the future, it is likely that people with fluctuating incomes—for example, farmers—are more likely to save a relatively high proportion of their incomes than people with secure and steady incomes, for example many white-collar workers.

In fact, this conclusion follows directly from our previous discussion of the income constraint. If measured income is classified partly as 'permanent' income, i.e. that part regarded as secure and likely to persist, and partly as transitory, i.e. insecure, variable, or largely random (either positive or negative), and consumption is regarded as a function of permanent income, then two households with the same average measured income, one of which is stable, the other less so, will have different saving propensities. The household with the more fluctuating income will have the lower 'permanent' income and hence will consume less and save more of the measured or actual current income.

Finally, the amount of wealth owned by a household is also likely to affect saving behaviour. Generally speaking, a household which has a substantial amount of assets which could, if necessary, be realized in order to meet unforeseen contingencies will have less need to save out of current income.

All these factors, by influencing decisions to save, will influence a household's final decisions on how much to spend.

2.4. Theoretical Demand Analysis

2.4.1. Indifference Curves

Most of the discussion of the previous sections has been heuristic and intuitive. In the present section we re-examine the behaviour of consumers in a slightly more theoretical manner which can be utilized to analyse a whole range of choice situations.[10] For simplicity, we consider the case of a household (or individual consumer) that must choose how to allocate its fixed income between two goods, bread and ale, that are on sale at fixed and known prices. Although we conduct the analysis in terms of only two goods, all of the ideas outlined below will, in fact, apply however many goods can be purchased.

Our primary requirement for any theoretical analysis of the choice behaviour of a household is some means of representing its preferences. The *object of choice* for the household is a 'bundle' of certain quantities of bread and certain quantities of ale. Consider any two bundles of bread and ale—say, x and x'.[11] An elemental requirement for household choice is that it knows either that it prefers x to x' or that it prefers x' to x or that it is indifferent between the two bundles. We also assume that 'goods are good' in the sense that (a) if a bundle x includes more of *both* bread and ale than a bundle x', then x must be preferred to x', and (b) if a bundle x includes *at least as much of either* bread or ale and *more* of the other good than another bundle x' then x must be preferred to x'.

Given these preliminaries, we can introduce the idea of an *indifference curve* and an *indifference map* as a means of simply representing household preference, as is shown in Figure 2.3. The vertical axis of the diagram is measured in terms of quantities of bread and the horizontal axis is measured in terms of quantities of ale. Each point in the figure therefore represents a bundle of bread and ale— e.g. the point x represents a bundle of 3 loaves of bread and 4 pints of ale. The curve *II*, which is called an 'indifference curve', is a line joining all bundles of bread and ale that are considered equivalent or 'indifferent' by the household under consideration. Thus, for example, the curve shows us that the household is indifferent between the bundles x, x', and x''. Given our assumptions, the indifference curve must slope downwards to the right. Consider the bundle x on the indifference curve *II*. All bundles to the north-east of x (in the area marked P for preferred) must be preferred to x, for they contain more ale *and* bread. Moreover, all bundles lying on the vertical line above x and the horizontal line to the right of x must be preferred to x, for they contain the same amount of ale and more bread or the same amount of bread and more ale. Similarly, all bundles to the south-west of x (in the area marked W for 'worse') must be considered inferior to x, for they contain less bread *and* ale. Finally, all bundles

---

[10] The ideas in this section underlie much of the technical analysis of economic decisions and are essential for those formally studing economics; but if the earlier exposition of this chapter is clear then subsequent chapters will be perfectly intelligible even if this section is omitted.

[11] Thus, for example, the 'bundle' x might contain three leaves of bread and four pints of beer, while x' might contain two loaves and five pints.

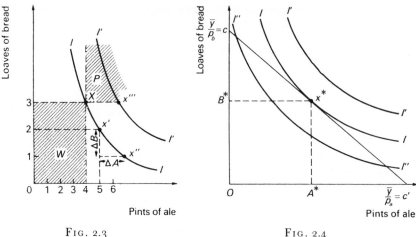

FIG. 2.3   FIG. 2.4

lying on the vertical line below x and the horizontal line to the left of x must be considered inferior, for they either contain the same amount of ale and less bread or the same amount of bread and less ale. Thus all bundles that are indifferent to x *must* lie to the north-west or the south-east of x—and the indifference curves are therefore downward sloping.

The slope of an indifference curve has an important economic meaning. Consider a small move along an indifference curve—from x' to x'' in Figure 2.3. Such a move involves a reduction, ΔB, in the quantity of bread (the symbol Δ simply means 'a change in') and an increase, ΔA, in the quantity of ale which, given the household's particular preferences, *just compensates* the household for the loss of bread, such that bundle x'' is indifferent to bundle x'. Now, by analogy to the conventional idea of the slope of a hill (the distance 'up' divided by the distance along), the slope of the indifference curve between x' and x'' is approximately $\Delta B/\Delta A$—i.e. the ratio of the loss of bread to the quantity of ale that just compensates for the loss. This slope is called the household's *marginal rate of substitution* of ale for bread (MRS_b^a).[12]

The curve II is simply a typical curve of a household's *indifference map* which consists of a large set of indifference curves which fill up the whole diagram.

[12] Another way of looking at the slope of the indifference curve is as follows. Assume for the sake of argument that a person can measure the 'utility' that he derives from consuming a particular good. We define *marginal utility* as the additional utility or satisfaction that a person obtains from having one more unit of a good. In general, we presume that this will decline the more units one has (the third bar of chocolate gives less additional utility than the second, the second less than the first). If the marginal utilities of two goods, for an individual, given he has a certain amount of each, are six and three respectively, then the individual could exchange one unit of the former for two of the latter and be no better or worse off. This would be a shift along the indifference curve with a marginal rate of substitution of $2/1$, i.e. 2. This of course was found from the ratio of the marginal utilities hence

$$\frac{MU_1}{MU_2} = MRS_1^2.$$

Thus $I'I'$ is another typical indifference curve, but it is crucial that the reader should note that *every* bundle on this curve is preferred to every point on the lower indifference curve II—the consumer is indifferent between all points on II, and indifferent between all points on $I'I'$, but point x''' on the latter is preferred to point x' on the former, since x''' contains more bread *and* ale. Therefore any point on $I'I'$ is preferred to any point on II. Thus a move to a higher indifference curve (i.e. in a north-easterly direction) implies improvement for the household. The complete indifference map is a relatively simple theoretical way of summarizing the preferences of a household. The objective of any household will be to attain a bundle of bread and ale on the *highest possible* indifference curve. The word 'possible' in the previous sentence leads us automatically to examine the constraint of the household's income.

2.4.2. *The Budget Line*

Considering Figure 2.4, if a household has a fixed income $£\bar{y}$, and spends all of it on bread at a price of p_B it will obtain a quantity $£\bar{y}/p_B$ of bread, and we assume that this quantity equals OC for the household under consideration. Similarly, if the household spends all of the fixed income, $£\bar{y}$, on ale at a price p_a it will obtain a quantity, $£\bar{y}/p_a$, of ale, and this quantity equals OC' in Figure 2.4. The line joining the point C to the C' is known as the *budget* line. It represents all the different *combinations* of bread and ale that the household can obtain by spending its fixed income on mixtures of bread and ale at the prices p_b and p_a. As more ale is bought, so less bread can be bought. The slope of the budget line will equal the distance OC divided by the distance OC'—i.e.

$$\frac{£\bar{y}}{p_b} \div \frac{£\bar{y}}{p_a} = \frac{p_a}{p_b}.$$

Thus the slope of the budget line equals the ratio of the prices of the commodities.

2.4.3. *The Analysis of Decisions*

We are now in a position to analyse the household's allocation of income between bread and ale. It is clear that, given the fixed income of the household, it can only buy bundles in the triangle OCC' of Figure 2.4 or bundles actually on the budget line. But we have already stated that the household's objective is to attain the highest indifference curve, so, on our assumptions, the household will buy the bundle x^* (consisting of OB^* of bread and OA^* of ale) at the point where the budget line is tangential to the indifference curve II. All higher indifference curves, like $I'I'$, are outside the triangle OCC' and all lower ones, like $I''I''$, represent less preferred positions. At the point x^* the slope of the indifference curve, the household's marginal rate of substitution of ale for bread, is equal to the slope of the budget line, the ratio of the prices of ale and bread.

The indifference curve apparatus can be used to analyse the effects of the change in price of one of the commodities with the household's income remaining constant. Assume that the price of ale falls. If the household spent all of its fixed income, $£\bar{y}$, on ale then it could, after the price fall, buy more ale.

The budget line will consequently move as shown in Figure 2.5. The original budget line is *CC'*. After the fall in the price of ale the new budget line is *CD*. Originally, the household purchased the bundle of bread and ale represented by the point *x* on the indifference curve *II*. After the price fall the household purchases the new bundle, *x'*, including more ale and more bread, and is, given its own preference, better off—for the new bundle is on the higher indifference curve *I'I'*. Thus Figure 2.5 provides an indifference curve representation of our heuristic law of demand—the fall in the price of ale has increased the household's demand for ale. This is known as the price effect. The demand for bread has also increased even though the absolute price of bread has remained unchanged, because the price of another good—ale—has changed.

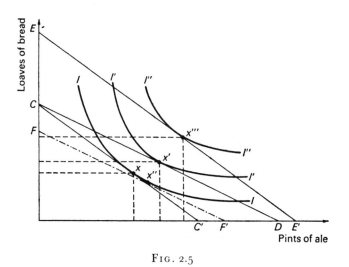

FIG. 2.5

2.4.4. Income and Substitution Effects

The same apparatus can be used to show the effect of a change in the other major determinant of consumer expenditure by a household, namely income. Imagine that, starting with budget line *CC'*, there is an increase in the income of the household, but no change in the relative prices of the two products. Instead of *OC* being the maximum amount of bread that could be bought it is now *OE*, and instead of *OC'* being the maximum amount of ale that could be bought it is now *OE'*. The budget line moves outwards from the origin (point *O*), indicating that more can now be bought. The slope of the new budget line *EE'* will be the same as that of *CC'*. This follows from the fact that the relative prices of the two products have not changed, but can be seen diagrammatically from the fact that if income increased *z* per cent then *both* the maximum amount of bread and the maximum amount of ale able to be bought must have increased by *z* per cent.

The new consumption bundle will be *x'''*, comprising more bread and ale.

The change in the demand for a product as a result of a change in income is sometimes known simply as the 'income effect'.[12]

It should be noticed that the income effect may, for certain products over certain income ranges, be negative. A traditional textbook example often cited is margarine, which many consumers consider inferior to butter. Thus an increase in income could lead consumers to switch to butter, reducing the demand for margarine.[14] This is shown diagrammatically in Figure 2.6. The distance *xy* represents the *fall* in demand for margarine resulting from the rise in income.

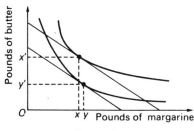

F IG . 2.6

Having examined the income effect, the change in the household's demand for bread and ale following a fall in the price of ale can be analysed a little more thoroughly. We saw in Figure 2.5 that, following the fall in the price of ale, the household was 'better off' in the sense of attaining a higher indifference curve. Assume now that the household is made such that it is no better or worse off than prior to the price change, i.e. income is reduced so that the household can only just attain the original indifference curve *II*. The dotted line *FF'* in Figure 2.5 represents such a reduction in income in that it is parallel to the new budget line *CD*. Its slope represents the new price ratio following the fall in the price of ale. It is now possible to decompose the whole move from the bundle *x* to the bundle *x'* (as a result of the fall in p_a), i.e. the price effect, into two separate components or 'effects'. In Figure 2.5 the move from *x* to *x''* is called the *substitution effect* of the price fall—for it represents the tendency for the household to substitute towards the relatively cheaper good (ale) *even though* its income has been reduced so that it remains on the same indifference curve. Given our assumptions on the shape of the household's indifference curves, the substitution effect invariably implies that more will be demanded of the good whose price has fallen. The move from *x''* to *x'* in Figure 2.5 is the *income effect* of the price change, for it represents that part of the change in the demand for commodities that stems from the fact that the fall in the price of ale has

[13] The income effect can be measured by the *income* elasticity of demand, i.e. percentage change in the quantity of a good demanded, divided by the percentage change in income.

[14] The current emphasis on the possible health advantages of margarine has, in fact, meant that this product is frequently no longer regarded as inferior, especially by high-income groups concerned with the possibility of heart disease.

increased the real income or effective purchasing power of the household.
Although this may seem rather complicated, the intuition is fairly simple. If the
price of ale falls, the household will normally buy more ale for *two* reasons.
Firstly, ale is relatively cheaper *vis-à-vis* bread and there is an automatic
tendency to buy more of the relatively cheaper good—i.e. the substitution
effect. Secondly, the fall in the price of ale means that the household's fixed
income, $\pounds \bar{y}$, has increased in the sense that it will now buy more goods—this is
the income effect.

In general, as shown in Figure 2.5, both the income and substitution effects
tend to increase the demand for a product whose price has fallen. In the case of
an 'inferior good' the income effect will be negative and tend to offset the
substitution effect. If it is sufficiently strong to completely offset it, then we
would have a case in which a fall in price actually led to a reduction in demand.
This should not be confused with the case where, because price is taken as a
guide to quality, consumers buy less of a product when its price falls in the belief
that it is a lower-quality (i.e. different) product.

We have introduced the ideas of income and substitution effects in the
context of changes in the prices of goods. It is important to note that the ideas
are, in fact, remarkably general.

We can, for example, analyse the effect of interest rates on consumption with
the same theoretical apparatus. To simplify, let us ignore future income and see
how much of a household's current income it consumes in the current time
period and how much in a future time period. The situation is portrayed in
Figure 2.7. Current consumption, C_t, is plotted on the vertical axis and future

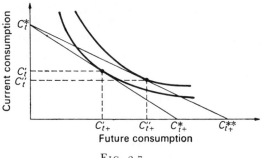

FIG. 2.7

consumption, C_{t+}, on the horizontal one. If all the income were spent today C_t*
could be purchased. If all of it were spent tomorrow C_t*_+ could be purchased.
This will be higher than C_t* because interest could be earned on the income in the
intervening period. The budget line is the line $C_t* - C_{t+}^*$. Given the indifference
curves shown, which indicate the household's preferences as between current
and future consumption, C_t' will be spent today and C_{t+}' tomorrow. If the
interest rate were to rise, then maximum future consumption could be higher
and the budget constraint would shift to $C_t* - C_{t+}^{**}$. Now current consumption
would be C_t'' and future consumption C_{t+}''.

Any income saved for the future will earn a higher interest rate, so overall income will have increased. There is, therefore, an overall income effect tending to increase both current and future consumption. There is also a substitution effect as the household substitutes relatively cheaper future consumption for relatively expensive current consumption. This tends to increase future consumption and to reduce current consumption. Adding the two effects together, future consumption will increase for both reasons, but current consumption may rise or fall, dependent on whether the income or substitution effect is stronger (in the diagram we have current consumption falling—a stronger substitution effect). Thus the response of current consumption to interest rates can be interpreted in terms of the substitution and income effects.

Secondly, consider the reaction of a worker to a decrease in income tax rates. Such a decrease *increases* the net wage earned per hour and, by implication, increases the 'price' (i.e. the amount of income foregone) of leisure. Conventional demand analysis would imply that the worker would consequently consume less leisure and do more work—for leisure is now 'more expensive'. If, however, the income effect is very strong, then it is quite possible that the worker will, in fact, increase the amount of leisure taken and work less, being still able to preserve his consumptions standards, i.e. the tendency to substitute more work is offset by the increase in leisure as a result of the higher real income obtainable. The concepts of income and substitution effects are very widely applicable in economics.

2.5. Aggregate Spending and Saving

2.5.1. Total Consumer Expenditure

In examining the *pattern* of consumer expenditure by a particular household, the emphasis of economic analysis is clearly based on the significance of relative prices. If, on the other hand, we are interested in the *total* expenditure of households on all goods then the focus is on real disposable *income*. In his *General Theory of Employment, Interest and Money*, Lord Keynes [14] introduced and elaborated the idea that total consumer expenditure in any economy would typically depend primarily on the level of income. This concept of a 'consumption function' has become central to much macroeconomic discussion and is used throughout this book. The basic ideas are quite simple and can be appreciated by examining the relationship between total expenditure and income for a particular household.

2.5.2. The Cross-Sectional Consumption Function

A household's *total* demand for goods and services can be illustrated in simplified form by plotting *a consumption function*, i.e. the relationship between household expenditure and its main determinants. We simplify here by assuming that only income is important, and ignore the other influences, e.g.

interest rates, that were previously discussed.[15] Following the previous chapter, there are two different ways of examining consumer behaviour graphically. First, a *cross-sectional* consumption function may be plotted as in Figure 2.8. This shows permanent income on the horizontal axis and consumption on the vertical axis. Thus consumption function CC indicates that, at a certain time, a household with permanent income Y_1 has consumption of C_1.

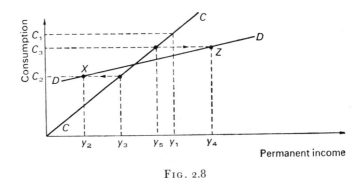

F IG . 2.8

As we move across the economy from the lowest to the highest permanent-income households (i.e. rightwards) so consumption increases. In practice there are serious difficulties in plotting this consumption function because we cannot directly measure households' permanent income, but only their *actual* income. Plotting consumption against actual income tends to give a much flatter consumption function, e.g. like DD in Figure 2.8. To see why, consider households with a very low actual income, e.g. Y_2. Although some households on this actual income will be receiving higher income than their (*very* low) permanent incomes, the majority will be temporarily on incomes significantly lower than their permanent incomes which might be at a point like Y_3. It is this income level which determines their consumption spending shown by C_2, and plotting this against actual income gives the point X.

Similarly, households with very higher actual incomes (Y_4) will tend to contain a large proportion who temporarily are receiving more than their permanent income (Y_5) with the result that consumption is at C_3 and the point plotted empirically will be Z. Thus the consumption function *appears* as the flatter line DD when we plot consumption against actual income cross-sectionally.[16]

2.5.3. The Time-Series Consumption Function

We can also plot a household's expenditure over time. A *time-series* consumption function is shown in Figure 2.9. This looks very similar to the consumption

---

[15] The rationale for this is that it allows us to further analyse consumer behaviour while not precluding a discussion of the other influences when examining real-world situations.

[16] It may be noted that the line DD is consistent with the argument above that low-income groups will tend to save a smaller proportion of their incomes than high-income groups.

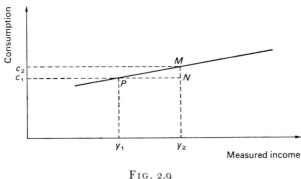

F IG. 2.9

function in Figure 2.8, but it is significantly different because we are now plotting the consumption behaviour of *one household* through time and against measured income, e.g. in 1971 the household's income was Y_1, consumption C_1. In 1972 they were Y_2 and C_2 respectively, and so on. If all a household's future income were known with certainty and were all included as permanent income, then the household could adjust its consumption immediately to that level and maintain a constant level of consumption throughout a lifetime of changing (generally rising) income. This would give a very flat time-series consumption function. In practice, of course, income over only a relatively short period of time, e.g. three or four years, can be reasonably relied upon as secure, and so households are continually revising (usually upwards) their notion of their permanent income, and changing their consumption over time. The time-series consumption function therefore slopes upwards, as shown in Figure 2.9.

2.5.4. *The Marginal Propensity to Consume*

The slope of the consumption function is of particular importance, and is known as the *marginal propensity to consume*. Suppose income rises from Y_1 to Y_2. Consumption rises from C_1 to C_2. Out of the additional or 'marginal' income of $Y_2 - Y_1$ the household has a propensity to consume $C_2 - C_1$ extra. The marginal propensity to consume is simply the additional consumption as a proportion of the additional income, i.e. $C_2 - C_1/(Y_2 - Y_1)$. But $C_2 - C_1$ equals the distance MN, and $Y_2 - Y_1$ equals the distance NP, so that the marginal propensity to consume equals MN/NP, which is the slope of consumption function.[17] The importance of this measure will be seen later.

2.6. Consumer Expenditure in the UK

2.6.1. *Recent Trends in Consumer Expenditure*

The National Accounts of the UK indicate that total consumer spending amounted to some £165 billion in 1982 compared with a level of £9·4 billion in 1950. It is obviously not the case that the actual volume of goods purchased has increased by 1,700 per cent. A very substantial part of the increase is associated

[17] By analogy with the gradient of a hill—the distance 'up' divided by the distance 'along'.

with the increase in prices over the period. Thus, in order to assess the real trend in consumer spending it is necessary to 'deflate' the numbers by an appropriate price index. The Retail Price Index (RPI), published by the Department of Employment, is probably the best-known price index in the UK—and it shows that prices have increased by more than 800 per cent since 1950. The RPI is calculated on the basis of regular surveys of the prices actually ruling in the shops. The index is then 'weighted' in terms of the relative importance of the goods concerned in the 'average' household budget. Thus, for example, an increase in the price of bread would have a relatively substantial effect on the index—whereas a doubling of the price of fur coats would hardly affect the index at all. Appendix 1 lists some of the weights used in the current RPI.

Figure 2.10 illustrates the long-run trend in the volume of consumer spending since 1953. It is noteworthy that until 1974 there was not a single year

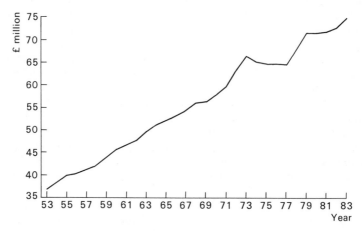

FIG. 2.10. Real Consumers' Expenditure 1952–1983 (£ million, constant prices).

in which the total volume of consumer spending actually *fell* compared with the previous year. Despite the decline in 1974–6 the upward trend was resumed and even the very severe recession of 1980–1 did little more than slow down the growth of consumer spending. A central feature of UK economic life does seem to be that the British consumer continues to increase the volume of spending through thick and thin—in contrast to many other countries (but note the discussion of personal saving in Section 2.6.3).

2.6.2. Changes in the Pattern of Consumer Expenditure

The *pattern* of consumer spending in the UK has, however, changed quite substantially. Table 2.1 illustrates the principal trends in the main categories of consumer spending. The decline in the proportion of total spending attributable to food consumption is quite marked as is the increase in the importance of durables and automobiles. These broad trends are, however, common to most high-income countries.

TABLE 2.1. *Consumers' Expenditure: Component Categories**
(per cent)

	1952	1962	1972	1982
Food	25·5	23·5	18·9	16·9
Alcoholic drinks and tobacco	12·3	11·3	11·0	10·2
Housing	15·1	14·1	14·1	14·3
Fuel and light	4·9	5·0	4·5	4·2
Clothing	7·0	7·6	7·8	9·0
Durable household goods	2·8	3·8	4·7	6·1
Cars and motor cycles	0·6	2·1	4·4	3·2
Other goods and services	33·3	33·2	34·6	36·1

* Consumer spending at constant (1975) prices as a percentage of total UK consumer spending.
Source: CSO, *Economic Trends*, Annual Supplement 1983.

2.6.3. *Household Savings Trends*

Figure 2.11 illustrates the behaviour of the UK personal savings ratio between 1953 and 1983. Although the Central Statistical Office has made major revisions in its estimates of the savings ratio over the past few years, it is clear from the figure that there was a marked *increase* in the proportion of income saved during the 1970s—and, moreover, a marked decrease in 1982 and 1983. Thus, the savings ratio did not exceed 10 per cent (on an annual basis) in the twenty years from 1953 to 1972—and did not *fall below* 10 per cent from 1973 to 1983. While the discussion in section 2.3.2 suggests that the proportion of household income saved might gradually increase over time, many observers were initially puzzled by the marked increase in the savings ratio in the face of

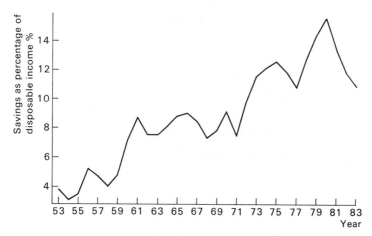

FIG. 2.11. Personal Savings Ratio (Percentage of Disposable Income) 1953–1983.

rising inflation—for 'common sense' would suggest that households would consume more (particularly durables) and save less if inflation increases. Reflection on the discussion of household income and expectations in section 2.3 gives some possible clues to this phenomenon. If households are saving for a *target* (e.g. the deposit on a new house, a new car, or retirement) then an *unexpected* increase in inflation will mean that they must save more than they had planned if they are to achieve their target. Equally, a faster rate of inflation may cause the real value of households' financial assets to fall. If households attempt to rebuild their holdings back to their previous real level this will also cause the savings ratio to rise. Similarly, if inflation *fell* more rapidly than was expected, then the savings ratio might be expected to fall—and it is interesting to note that the very rapid fall in inflation in 1982–3 was accompanied by a fall in the personal savings ratio to the lowest level since the early 1970s. We return to this issue in subsequent chapters.

2.7. Conclusion

In this chapter we have outlined some of the principal factors influencing the demand for commodities. We have seen the importance of preferences, relative prices, and incomes in the demand for a commodity, and the central importance of income in the determination of a household's total demand for commodities. We have introduced the concepts of elasticity, the consumption function, and various different ideas of income. We have also referred to the role of wealth, interest rates, and expectations. Each of these factors will be seen to be important in the analysis of the working of the economic system.

Appendix 1

TABLE 2.2. *Weights in the UK Retail Price Index, 1983*
(per cent)

Food	20·3
Alcoholic drink	7·8
Tobacco	3·9
Housing	13·7
Fuel and light	6·9
Durable household goods	6·4
Clothing and footwear	7·4
Transport and vehicles	15·9
Miscellaneous goods	7·5
Services	6.3
Meals outside the home	3·9
Total	100·0

Source: *Monthly Digest of Statistics* (Jan. 1984).

Bibliography

SECTION A

[1] BAUMOL, W. J. *Economic Theory and Operation Analysis* (Prentice-Hall International, 1972).
Chap. 9 of this book is an intermediate exposition of the theory of demand. Chap. 10 is an extremely useful elementary discussion of the empirical determination of demand relationships.
[2] BROOMAN, F. S. *Macroeconomics* (George Allen and Unwin, 1970).
Chap. 5 of this basic macroeconomics text provides a useful exposition of the basic ideas associated with the aggregate consumption function.
[3] GREEN, H. A. J. *Consumer Theory* (Penguin, 1971).
This book provides an excellent exposition and survey of all the principal ideas associated with the macroeconomic theory of consumer behaviour. Although more advanced than some of the texts listed, it can be followed by anyone who is prepared to read patiently.
[4] JOHNSON, M. B. *Household Behaviour: Consumption Income and Wealth* (Penguin, 1971).
A useful survey of the principal ideas of aggregate consumption behaviour.
[5] LIPSEY, R. G. *An Introduction to Positive Economics* (Weidenfeld and Nicholson, 1975).
Chaps. 5–7, 10, and 14–16 of this well-known textbook provide an elementary account of the theory of demand. Chap. 37 is an exposition of the consumption function.
[6] SAMUELSON, P. A. *Economics* (McGraw-Hill, 1973).
Chaps. 4, 20–2 of this justly famous introductory textbook provide a simple exposition of basic ideas of demand theory. Chap. 11 is a simple introduction to the idea of the consumption function.
[7] SCITOVSKY, T. *Welfare and Competition* (George Allen and Unwin, 1971). Chaps. 3 and 4 constitute a neat and clear exposition of the theory of consumer choice. Chap. 5 provides a useful discussion of the worker's choice between work and leisure.

SECTION B

[8] DEATON, A. and MUELLBAUER, J. *Economics and Consumer Behaviour* (Cambridge University Press, 1980).
[9] DUESENBERRY, J. S. *Income, Saving and the Theory of Consumer Behaviour* (Oxford University Press, 1967).
[10] EVANS, M. K. *Macroeconomic Activity: theory, Forecasting and Control* (Harper and Row, 1969), Chaps. 2 and 3.
[11] FARRELL, M. J. 'The New Theories of the Consumption Function', *Economic Journal* (Dec. 1959).
[12] FRIEDMAN, M. *A Theory of the Consumption Function* (N.B.E.R. Princeton University Press, 1957).
[13] GHEZ, G. R. and BECKER, G. S. *The allocation of Time and Goods over the Life-cycle* (Columbia University Press, 1975).
[14] KEYNES, J. M. *The General Theory of Employment, Interest and Money* (Macmillan, 1936), Chaps. 9 and 10.
[15] LANCASTER, K. *Consumer Demand: A New Approach* (Columbia University Press, 1971).
[16] MAYER, T. *Permanent Income, Wealth and Consumption* (University of California Press, 1972).

[17] PYATT, G. *Priority Patterns and the Demand for Household Durable Goods* (Cambridge University Press, 1964).

[18] WORKING, E. J. 'What do Statistical Demand Curves Show?' *Quarterly Journal of Economics* (1927).

3

The Behaviour of Firms

D. J. MORRIS

3.1. Central Elements in Firms' Behaviour

3.1.1. A Basic Framework

There are currently over 260,000 business enterprises of one form or another in the United Kingdom concerned with the production, transport, and trading of goods and services. (Of these over 10,000 are overseas-owned, including some very large ones.) They range from very small one-man private companies to giant firms whose annual turnover runs into many billions of pounds. They differ in their legal constitution and regulation, their financing, organization and decision procedures, their types of ownership, the number of production stages they cover, the competition they face, and many other characteristics. As a consequence, many differences may be seen in the impact on them of both the prevailing economic conditions and government economic policy.

Despite this, there are a number of similarities in their economic behaviour, which are considerably more important than the differences. All need to obtain finance, all need some inputs of labour and materials, and all have to determine a selling price for their products or services. It is with these sorts of common activities that we will be concerned in examining the behaviour of the private sector.

The purpose is, first, to provide a framework in terms of which the activities and performance of any particular business enterprise can be understood and interpreted, and, second, to provide a further step in the analysis of the economic system in the UK as a whole.

Figure 3.1 summarizes the framework, giving an outline of the 'typical' company. With only unimportant exceptions almost all businesses engage in the activities it depicts. It highlights the firm's internal operations and the external influences on them. The diagram is a circular one, each of the anti-clockwise arrows indicating a relationship to be mentioned. We start with the boxes marked 'demand conditions' and 'supply conditions'.

3.1.2. Demand Conditions

The previous chapter explained the derivation of the market demand curve for a product, showing the total demand for a product at each possible price, given

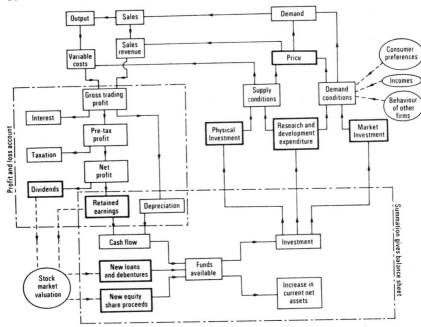

FIG. 3.1. (The author is indebted to Donald Hay of Jesus College, Oxford, for the idea behind this presentation.)

the prices of other goods, consumers' preferences, and incomes (see p. 32). If any of these latter three change, the demand curve will shift its position.

If a firm were a monopolist (sole supplier) in the production of a good, then the market demand curve would also be the demand curve facing the firm, and would tell us the demand which the firm would receive for each possible price. In general, however, there will be other firms producing either identical or similar products, and the demand curve facing the firm will depend on these other firms. In particular, it will depend on (a) the number of such firms and their size, (b) the degree of similarity of the products they produce, and (c) the type of competitive behaviour they exhibit, e.g. the prices they set, their sales policy, etc. The possibility that new firms might start to compete by introducing similar products may also be important. Figure 3.1 shows these, i.e. consumer preferences, incomes, and the behaviour of other firms as external influences (dotted lines) on the demand conditions facing the firm. The other determinants we examine below.

3.1.3. Supply Conditions

To meet demand, finished goods must be produced from the firm's input of materials. It will need factors of production to do this, premises, employees, capital equipment.[1] Some of these inputs, particularly premises and equipment, are fixed in the short term; it may take several years for a firm to expand them. *Fixed costs* are the overhead costs associated with such inputs; they are independent of the firm's current rate of production. Other costs associated with factors of production which are flexible in supply at short notice are termed *variable costs*, and these are affected by the current production rate. At a given time, therefore, a firm will be incurring some fixed costs which it cannot avoid, e.g. rental on land, depreciation[2] on capital equipment; and some variable costs, the level of which depends on its decision on how much output currently to produce, e.g. raw materials, wages.

Paradoxically, part of a company's profits, as measured in its financial accounts, should be regarded as a cost, like wages for example. Just as wages are what the company has to pay to obtain the services of its labour force, without which the company could not continue, so there is some (perhaps ill-defined) minimal level of profits which has to be received over a period by the owners, if the company is to retain their services as providers of finance for business operations entailing financial risks, again without which the company could not continue. Hence, one 'cost' to the firm is this required level of profit, usually termed 'normal profit'. It may be a fixed or variable cost, dependent on whether it varies with the level of output in the short term or not. These cost factors represent the supply conditions of the firm.

3.1.4. Pricing

Given these demand and supply conditions, a firm must decide upon its selling prices. How this is done is examined in detail later, but, as Figure 3.1 indicates (given the firm's demand curve), the price set will determine the actual demand for the product and hence the sales made by the firm. Assuming for the moment no change in the level of finished product inventory (unsold stock) held by the firm, output must adjust to this level of sales. As described above, the employment of some factors of production can be adjusted to this level of output, but not others. Once this adjustment has occurred, both fixed and variable costs are determined for the firm. The difference between the revenue from the sales made (i.e. price × quantity sold) and the variable costs incurred corresponds approximately to the firm's gross trading profit (or loss).

3.1.5. The Profit and Loss Account

Out of these gross trading profits various fixed costs will have to be met. First, interest charges on funds borrowed (and trade debts) will have to be paid. A

---

[1] 'Capital' can refer either to physical capital—factories, machinery, etc.—or to financial capital—the funds available for projects. The term will be qualified if the context does not indicate which is meant.

[2] i.e. the proportion of previous capital expenditure attributable to the current time period. In fact, the wear and tear of a machine in a particular year is partly due to the passage of time (and hence is an unavoidable fixed cost) and partly due to usage (and hence is an avoidable variable cost). In general, however, firms make a series of annual fixed notional depreciation allowances independent of production levels, the final total of which equals the initial capital cost of the equipment. If two or more products use the same equipment, serious problems arise in deciding how much of the depreciation cost is attributable to each product.

firm may borrow either by negotiating a specific loan, usually from a bank of one sort or another, or by issuing debentures (i.e. certificates entitling the holder to a specified amount of interest) to individuals or financial institutions.[3] With either type of borrowing the interest payable is a first charge on the firm's gross trading profits.

Second, the firm will deduct a sum for depreciation. This operation is an accounting one, and does not involve any flow of funds from the firm. In order to calculate the 'true' accounting profit of the company, i.e. the excess of revenue over *all* costs, this deduction has to be made from gross trading profits to allow for the cost of the machinery used in the current year, even though it was purchased in previous years. In other words, although the expenditure on a piece of capital equipment may occur at a single point of time, and out of the company's retained profits, the cost of this to the company is represented in its accounts as a series of annual deductions from gross trading profit prior to the calculation of 'profit before taxation'. The total of these depreciation charges for any piece of equipment may sum to the original cost, known as the 'historic' cost, of the equipment to the company, or to the company's estimate of how much it will cost to replace the equipment when it wears out or becomes obsolete, dependent on the depreciation method used.[4] (But for tax purposes a standard method must be used.)

Only that part of gross trading profit left after deduction of interest and allowance for depreciation is liable to tax, payment of which leaves the company's net profit. This belongs to the owners of the firm who may remove all or some of it from the firm for their own purposes as dividends, or they may leave it in the firm for future use. In the case of firms owned by the shareholders, but run by salaried managers, the latter usually decide what dividend the shareholders may receive, and what proportion of net profit will be retained by the firm. It is always legally possible for the shareholders to appoint new managers, however, if they are unsatisfied with the dividends received, and they are always free to sell their shares.

A statement known as the *profit and loss account* is usually published annually by firms as part of their published accounts (and in most cases is legally required), showing the amount and breakdown of gross trading profit into interest, depreciation, taxation, dividends, and retained earnings. These items are, therefore, boxed together in Figure 3.1 under the heading 'profit and loss account'. Table 3.1 shows the aggregate profit and loss account for all industrial companies in the UK, and the equivalent figures for manufacturing and non-manufacturing companies respectively.

3.1.6. The Balance Sheet

The funds available to the firm for expenditure on new capital equipment, research, etc., indeed on anything not already covered under expenditure on variable costs, comes from three main sources:

(a) The gross trading profit, minus the funds that have flowed out of the firm

[3] These may generally, like shares, be bought and sold in the stock market.
[4] Practice also differs on the methods used to allocate the total cost across the expected life of the equipment.

TABLE 3.1. *Aggregate Profit and Loss Account of all Industrial Companies, Manufacturing Companies, and Non-manufacturing Companies in the UK in 1979* (£ million)

	All	Manufacturing	Non-manufacturing
Gross trading profit	36,363	17,007	19,356
Other income*	2,888	1,542	1,346
Total income	39,251	18,549	20,702
less Interest†	−7,675	−3,504	−4,171
less Depreciation	−7,978	−4,397	−3,581
Pre-tax profit	23,598	10,648	12,950
less Taxation‡	−9,270	−3,651	−5,619
Net profit	14,328	6,997	7,331
less Dividends§	−5,241	−2,609	−2,632
Retained earnings¶	9,087	4,388	4,699

Includes:

* Income from listed and unlisted investments; other revenue income; prior-year adjustments (other than tax).

† Interest on bank and short-term loans; hire of plant and machinery; interest on long-term loans.

‡ All current UK and overseas taxation; deferred taxation.

§ Minority shareholders' interest.

¶ Net of deferred taxation.

Source: *Company Finance Monitor*, MA3 (HMSO).

in the form of interest, tax, and dividends. This, however, as Figure 3.1 shows, is equal to the depreciation charge set aside at the beginning, plus the retained earnings left after the various cash outflows. The sum of retained earnings and depreciation is usually known by the rather misleading term 'cash flow'. The fact that depreciation is a source of cash should not lead one to conclude that an increased depreciation charge would necessarily increase the cash flow. An *increased* depreciation charge would *reduce* profit before taxation by a similar amount, and if the tax bill and dividends paid were the same as before, retained earnings would be lower by exactly the amount that depreciation had increased. If, however, the reduced profit before taxation led to a lower tax bill and lower dividends, both of which are very likely, then cash flow would be higher than before. But it is only by causing a change in one or both of taxation and dividends that a change in the depreciation charge can alter the firm's cash flow, even though it is often referred to as a source of cash.

(b) New funds may be raised by issuing new debentures, and raising new loans.

(c) Alternatively, or in addition, the firm may issue new equity shares to new or existing shareholders. The extent to which these can be carried out will partly depend on the valuation the stock market places on the company, which in turn will be heavily influenced by the dividends paid and/or expected, and the prospects for future growth of the company as a result of its retained earnings.

These funds may be spent on various types of long-term investment projects. If not, they may be used to pay off current liabilities (i.e. debts the company must stand ready to pay off at short notice), or used to build up stocks and work-in-progress, increase holdings of short-term financial assets (e.g. government securities), or left in current or deposit accounts with a bank. These would occur either because the firm regarded the current level of these assets as too low in the light of possible demands upon them, or because cash flow exceeded the sums required to finance current investment plans. Stocks, financial assets, cash, and short-term debts owed to the company are termed 'current assets' as either they are cash, or can be turned into cash very quickly. *Net* current assets, equal to current assets minus current liabilities, will therefore rise by the amount of funds available which are not used for long-term investment.

Clearly, what flows into the 'funds available' box must equal what flows out in any time period,[5] i.e.

$$
\left.\begin{array}{l}
\text{Retained Earnings} + \text{Depreciation} \\
+ \text{Net New Loans and Debentures} \\
+ \text{New Equity Issue}
\end{array}\right\} = \left\{\begin{array}{l}
\text{Investment} \\
+ \text{Increase in Net Current} \\
\text{Assets}
\end{array}\right.
$$

Therefore, the sum of the amounts on the left-hand side for all previous time periods equals the sum of those on the right for all previous time periods. The sum of all previous retained earnings is termed the 'reserves' of the firm, but it should be stressed that they do not constitute any reserve of funds in the normal sense, all of it having flowed already into investment, or increases in net current assets. The sum of all equity issues is usually split up into two parts, (i) the funds that would have been raised if all shares had been bought by investors at their nominal face value (known as par value), and (ii) the difference between this and the amount actually received. The latter would be higher or lower, depending on the demand for the shares in the stock market when they were issued. In general this share 'premium' is positive.

Summing over all previous periods, and subtracting total depreciation from both sides, we get:

$$
\left.\begin{array}{l}
\text{Shares at Par Value} \\
+ \text{Share Premium} \\
+ \text{Reserves} \\
+ \text{Debentures} \\
+ \text{Loans (long-term)}
\end{array}\right\} = \left\{\begin{array}{l}
\text{Total Capital Expenditure} \\
- \text{Total Depreciation} \\
+ \text{Net Current Assets}
\end{array}\right.
$$

It should be noted that only *long-term* loans are included on the left. Short-term ones which might have to be paid soon are current liabilities and are subtracted

---

[5] Bearing in mind that money retained, e.g. in a current account, counts as an increase in current assets.

from the right-hand side in calculating current net assets. Total capital expenditure minus total depreciation to date is the current value of the firm's fixed assets according to its books—and is known as the 'written-down' value of its fixed assets, or simply net fixed assets.

This table is a simplified presentation of the firm's *balance sheet* which is also usually published once a year.[6] The total of either column is generally known as the *capital employed*, and it is a measure of the capital available to the firm over the medium term. It can be calculated either from the sources of funds (left-hand) or from the uses (right-hand). The ratio of net profit to capital employed is often taken as a major indicator of a firm's economic performance.[7] Table 3.2 gives the aggregate balance sheet for all industrial companies in the UK, and the equivalent figures for manufacturing and non-manufacturing respectively.

3.1.7. The Medium and the Long Term

It was stated earlier that in the short term the demand and supply (or cost) conditions facing a firm are more or less fixed. Over a somewhat longer period—the *medium term*—the demand curve facing the firm may to some extent be controlled by the firm through market investment, i.e. advertising, promotional schemes, etc.[8] In the long term, as defined above, the cost conditions will be changed by the capital investment which the firm carries out. A third use of the funds available is research and development. This may be directed towards the production process, thus again changing the cost conditions of the firm over the long term, or may be in the form of product development which will change the demand conditions over the long term by changing the products available.

These three uses of funds shown in Figure 3.1 will, of course, have to be co-ordinated—process research to improve production performance and reduce costs; capital investment which embodies the new process; capital investment for the production of new products, and marketing and advertising to establish or improve the demand for the product. By means of these expenditure decisions the cost and demand conditions which constrain the firm in the short run can to some extent be manipulated over the medium and long term, provided the funds can be made available. This to a great extent depends on the

---

[6] The items are boxed together in Fig. 3.1 under the heading 'summation gives balance sheet'. An older alternative form arises if current liabilities are added to both sides. The right-hand side is then the company's *total assets* (capital and current). The left-hand side is its *total liabilities* (debentures, loans, and current liabilities owed to people other than the owners of the company; shares at par value, share premium, and reserves 'owed' by the company as a legal entity to its owners).

[7] Very serious problems arise in company accounts under inflationary conditions, e.g. the depreciation allowances may sum to far less than the cost of replacing a machine when it is scrapped; assets and liabilities fixed in monetary terms will have declining real values; a large part of accounted profit may be used up simply in maintaining constant stock levels at higher prices, etc. See P. Kirkman, *Inflation Accounting* (Association of Business Programmes, 1975). Also Report of the Sandilands Committee of Enquiry into Inflation Accounting.

[8] In practice, much market investment expenditure is regarded as a recurrent cost and, therefore, deducted from sales revenue along with other variable costs in calculating gross trading profit. In this case the expenditure is financed directly out of sales revenue, without becoming part of 'trading profit' and 'cash available'.

TABLE 3.2. *Aggregate Balance Sheet of all Industrial Companies, Manufacturing Companies, and Non-manufacturing Companies in the UK in 1979* (£ million)

	All	Manufacturing	Non-manufacturing
Shares at par value and share premium*	82,073	45,099	36,974
Reserves	22,961	13,785	9,176
Debentures	6,322	3,487	2,835
Long-term loans	11,083	4,833	6,250
Deferred taxation†	8,137	3,951	4,186
Total net assets	130,576	71,155	59,421
Net fixed assets	89,586	43,570	46,016
Stocks	62,910	37,872	25,038
Debtors and prepayments	58,453	32,935	25,518
Cash	13,270	7,117	6,153
Other assets‡	14,403	5,182	9,221
Total current assets	149,036	83,106	65,930
Short-term loans	31,519	15,760	15,759
Creditors and accruals	67,667	35,301	32,366
Dividends, interest, and tax due§	8,860	4,460	4,400
Total current liabilities	108,046	55,521	52,525
Net current assets	40,990	27,585	13,405
Total net assets	130,576	71,155	59,421

* Not shown separately for aggregate figures.

† Taxes due but not yet paid are, until that time, a further source of funds. Various schemes which defer some tax indefinitely mean that this item can be very large.

‡ Includes: government grants receivable; investments; tax instruments.

§ Any such items due for payment within the year are regarded as a current liability. The tax element will affect a part of the source of funds from deferred taxation, but this will be only a small part of the total sources of funds.

Source: *Company Finance Monitor*, MA3 (HMSO).

firm's profits, not only because they are a major source of funds, but also because they are a main determinant of whether new funds will be made available in the form of loans, debenture stock, and equity shares. Hence there is a circularity. The firm can only actively influence its cost and demand conditions in the long term if it can generate adequate funds from the current cost and demand situation or, if this is poor, attract support from creditors convinced of its future improvement.

3.1.8. The Firm's Decisions and the Firm's Accounts

Eight of the boxes in Figure 3.1 are in heavier surround. These, out of the many decisions taken in firms, indicate the seven[9] main ones with which we shall be concerned. Three are financial, namely:

(i) The division of net profit between dividends and retained earnings.
(ii) The funds to be raised through new borrowing.
(iii) The funds to be raised through new equity issue.

The results of these decisions will appear directly in the firm's financial statements.

The other four decisions are also vital in determining the firm's performance and profitability. The expenditure decisions (market investment, research and development, and physical investment) are major elements in determining the cost and demand conditions, which, together with the pricing decision, determine profitability. Although, therefore, the main statements of a firm's position are given in its balance sheet and profit and loss account, economists have generally been more concerned with the pricing and investment decisions, because these are the main determinants of the firm's performance as a user of scarce resources. The financial statements primarily describe this performance, rather than analyse the behaviour that has led to it.

3.1.9. the Firm's Objectives

One thing is missing from Figure 3.1. Each type of decision is taken on the basis of certain criteria, and these will be chosen in the light of the firm's objectives. There is much controversy over what these are, and we will here simply note four main ones:

(i) Profit. Maintaining or increasing the level of profits is a central objective. Firstly, in smaller firms the profits earned may represent the main or only source of income for the directors, while in firms with shareholders, profits are necessary to pay the dividends which ultimately justify the holding of the shares.[10]

Secondly, profits are essential if funds are to be available for the various types of investment described. Thirdly, the rate of return on capital employed (i.e. ratio of net profit to capital employed) is often regarded as an indicator of how successful a firm has been. Both the firm's pricing and various investment decisions will be designed at least to maintain current profit levels, and more generally, over the longer term, to increase them as much as possible, subject to any constraining effects that result from pursuit of other objectives.

(ii) Size. Most business decision-takers are partly concerned to increase the size of their firm, be this measured in terms of assets, sales, or turnover. Partly, large size may help to maintain profits through its effect in allowing greater specialization; in allowing lower average costs per unit of output to be obtained

---

[9] Two boxes refer to what is essentially one decision—the division of net profit *between* dividends and retained earnings.

[10] Alternatively, it may be argued that the managers attempt to increase the value of their shareholders' equity as much as possible, but this will depend principally on profits and the firm's financial decisions.

from larger plant; and through economizing in such things as purchasing, advertising, training, etc. It may also lead to an element of market domination by the firm, with consequent gains in its competitive position. Thirdly, managers in large firms generally control more resources, have larger staffs and higher salaries, all of which contribute to their satisfaction. Finally, a certain amount of prestige attaches to the managers of large firms, which again is a reason for them attempting to increase the size of their firms.

(iii) Growth. Consequent upon this desire for size, managers may well want their companies to grow as fast as possible. This requires that firms tie their different decisions together effectively, e.g. lower prices and more advertising may ensure faster growth of demand for their products, but both these things reduce the margin of profit and perhaps the supply of funds for future investment. Thus the pricing, finance, and expenditure decisions have to be properly co-ordinated if the funds available are going to grow as fast as the demand for the firm's products.

(iv) Security. Pursuit of any objective clearly requires that the firm be financially viable, which implies maintaining sufficient net current assets and adequate cash flow to be secure against bad trading conditions. In addition, the directors of publicly quoted companies will be concerned to ensure dividend payments and stock market valuation adequate to satisfy shareholders, and to thus secure themselves against the possibility of replacement or take-over.

Many other influences will be present, but these four, specified in broad terms, are reasonably comprehensive, well attested to by firms' executives and well supported by various empirical studies of firms' behaviour.

Having looked at the flow of funds, the financial statements of firms, and the objectives of firms, we now go on to look at the decisions which are central—pricing, investment, and finance.

3.2. Pricing

3.2.1. Introduction

Firms use a very large number of procedures for setting prices, dependent on their objectives, their products, their organizational characteristics, and the competitive pressures they face. Here we identify only the major methods of pricing, but this will be enough for us later to identify both the response of firms to their external situation—the behaviour of the economy and government economic policy—and their role in the allocation of resources in an economy with a large private sector. We follow the framework of Figure 3.1 by examining first the dependence of price on cost and demand conditions, and then the impact of income, consumer preferences, and other firms on price behaviour.

3.2.2. Average Cost Pricing

By far the most prevalent form of price behaviour is to calculate the variable costs incurred per unit of production in a specified period, and to add percentages to this figure to arrive at a price. The first percentage is to allow for the fixed costs attributable to the production being priced—and the second is to provide a margin of profit. As the amount sold partly depends on price, this procedure only makes sense if (as quite often happens) average variable costs per unit do not vary much with the level of production (at least for a 'normal' range of output levels) and so can be calculated independently of the demand that results from the price set. If demand turned out to be particularly high or low, however, then actual average costs might differ from the 'standard' ones on which the price was based, and the price set would probably be reconsidered.

The main problem is to identify the factors which determine the size of the two percentages added. The first will depend on the ratio of the firm's fixed costs to its variable costs, but will only be a rough approximation to this ratio because it changes somewhat every time output—and, therefore, variable cost—changes. More important is the second percentage, for in choosing this the firm, given the first addition to cost, determines its overall gross 'mark-up' on average variable cost. The main factors influencing the size of this gross mark-up are examined in the next five sections.

3.2.3. Profit Maximizing in the Short Term

One possible objective, given the cost and demand conditions, will be to set price exclusively to maximize current profits. Given the level of average costs, a high gross mark-up will give a high profit per unit sold, but will result in a high price and a lower number of units sold, while a low mark-up will give high demand, but a low profit per unit sold. In general, therefore, there will be an intermediate price which maximizes profit. This profit-maximizing price will depend on the price elasticity of demand (described in Chapter 2). If this is low, then a high gross mark-up will be required to maximize profit because demand is reduced very little by the high profit per unit. If this elasticity is high, a lower mark-up will be required because a relatively very large increase in demand can be obtained in return for the lower profit per unit. In fact, it can be shown that the gross mark-up on average variable cost, expressed as a percentage *of the price*, must equal $1/E$, where E is the price elasticity of demand,[11] if short-run profits are to be maximized, and this shows clearly that the higher the elasticity of demand the lower the profit-maximizing mark-up. Much market research is designed to discover the sensitivity of demand to price (and by implication the elasticity of demand) in order to determine a profit-maximizing price.

Frequently, no actual calculation of the elasticity of demand will be made, however, because changes in demand will be indicated by decreased stocks of finished goods, higher utilization of capacity, and lengthening order books, and executives will be able, on the basis of past experience, to judge approximately the magnitude of the mark-up required to establish or re-establish more or less maximum profits, if they are required. Potentially very costly market research is therefore avoided.[12] Figure 3.2 explains the price set.

The vertical axis measures various cost and revenue characteristics of the

---

[11] Assuming average variable costs are constant, no matter what the output level. See Appendix 1 for a proof of this.

[12] Charging 'what the market will bear' is generally an intuitive attempt to find the price which gives the best trade-off between profit margin and demand.

firm, each as a function of the level of output in the short term. As fixed costs are a given fixed sum, the average fixed cost per unit of output will be lower the higher the level of output, and this is shown by the average fixed cost curve which falls continuously as output increases. The average variable cost curve shows average variable cost falling at first, as a result of economies of bulk buying, better use of labour, savings on fuel, maintenance, etc., becoming constant over a range, and then eventually rising as overtime becomes more prevalent, machine utilization becomes excessive, etc. Adding the two curves together vertically gives the total cost of production per unit of output, termed the average total cost curve. There will, of course, be a different average total cost curve for each possible size of plant.

Constant returns to scale are said to exist if an *X* per cent increase in all factors of production increases output by *X* per cent. If the cost of all factors of production are unchanging, constant returns to scale imply that the average total cost curve for larger-scale operations will have the same minimum level. *Economies of scale* imply a larger than *X* per cent increase in output, with lower minimum average total cost therefore (again assuming the price of all factors of production fixed) for larger scale. The opposite case is known as *diseconomies of scale*.

Superimposed on these curves, we put the demand curve for the product, from Chapter 2. This is labelled the average revenue curve, because average revenue equals total revenue/output which equals (price × output)/output which equals price. Hence the average revenue curve relating average revenue to output sold is the same as the demand curve which relates price to output sold.

To discover the price which maximizes current profits, we introduce the *marginal cost* and *marginal revenue* curves shown in Figure 3.2. Marginal cost is defined as the change in total cost which occurs when output is increased by one unit, and marginal revenue as the change in total revenue. The curves show marginal cost and marginal revenue for different output levels.[13] The concept of marginal cost is of central importance in many resource allocation issues, as will be seen. Here it is crucial because a firm only maximizes current profits if it produces a level of output at which marginal cost equals marginal revenue (Q^* in Figure 3.2). If output is at a lower level than this, generally meaning marginal revenue is above marginal cost (see Figure 3.2), then production of one more unit of output will add more to revenue than to cost, and therefore increase total profit. If output is at a higher level, generally meaning marginal cost is above marginal revenue, then the last unit of output produced has added more to cost than revenue, thus reducing profits, and production should be cut back to increase profits. Only at an output level where marginal cost equals marginal revenue (Q^*) can profits not be increased by reducing or increasing output. To generate demand at this level requires a price of P^*, as shown by the demand (average revenue) curve. The profit-maximizing gross mark-up as a percentage of price is $1/E$ (see p. 82), because this is the margin which logically

---

[13] Note that the marginal cost curve coincides with the average variable cost curve when the latter is horizontal. With variable cost per unit constant (and fixed costs fixed) the addition to total cost from one extra unit (marginal cost) equals the additional variable cost per unit.

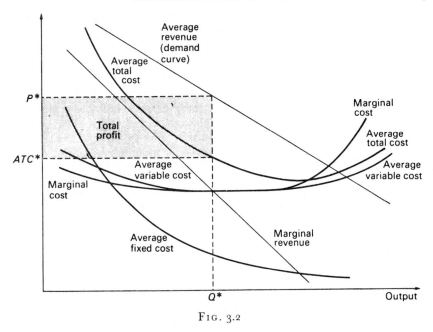

FIG. 3.2

ensures that marginal cost equals marginal revenue. Average total cost is ATC^* and total profit equals the profit per unit $(P^* - ATC^*)$ multiplied by the number of units sold (Q^*).

This analysis allows us to examine the implications of the other main influences on demand (see Figure 3.1). Income, preferences, and other firms all affect the profit-maximizing price by influencing the elasticity of demand.

3.2.4. Impact of Income

As the last chapter indicated, increases in income will generally increase the level of demand facing a firm.[14] This may or may not lower the price elasticity of demand, dependent on the specific form of the relationship between price, income, and demand. Thus the mark-up of a profit maximizer might rise, but not necessarily. His price would rise if the increase in output raised average variable costs, for example through paying more for raw materials now in short supply, or higher wages to retain the labour force. Net profit would then rise disproportionately fast because the fixed cost element to be deducted from the higher gross profit would not have changed.

3.2.5. Impact of Consumer Preference

The price elasticity of demand may be expected to be partly determined by the tastes or preferences of consumers. An individual is less likely to reduce

---

[14] Even if a product is 'inferior' for some consumers, the firm's demand will only fall if this is true for a sufficiently large number of consumers.

consumption in response to a price rise if he regards the product as a necessity (resulting in a low price elasticity of demand) than if he regards it as inessential. This would suggest a high profit-maximizing mark-up on necessities, but this may not be observed in practice either because of the impact of other influences on the price elasticity of demand (see below) or because high-income consumers regard as essential products which low-income consumers have to regard as luxuries.

3.2.6. The Existence of Close Substitutes

With regard to the impact of other firms, three central aspects can be identified. First, the degree of similarity (in the consumer's view) between the firm's product and that of one or more other firms, i.e. the extent to which these are close substitutes for each other. If one or more firms do produce a close substitute, then purchasers will be very ready to switch to a competitor if the first firm raises its price. This means that the elasticity of demand is high and the profit-maximizing price low.

At one extreme, if one or more other independent firms produce a product which consumers regard as identical, then, in the absence of transport costs, the elasticity of demand would tend to become infinite and the gross mark-up zero. In interpreting this theoretical extreme, two points must be stressed. (a) No contribution will be made towards covering fixed costs, implying losses. If this situation continued, the firm would eventually leave the industry. In the long term, however, *all* costs are variable and long-run considerations would lead the firm to base price on long-run average *total* costs, thus avoiding these losses. (b) Normal profit is part of cost. A zero gross mark-up does not, therefore, imply zero profit as conventionally defined in company accounts, but only that no profit in excess of the amount required by the firm to continue operating will be made.[15]

At the other extreme is the case of monopoly. No other firm produces a substitute, the elasticity of demand will tend to be lower and profits higher. While conceptually this is very clear, in practice it is more difficult to determine the extent of monopoly power. Even sole suppliers of a product may find they face competition from different products which none the less provide some of the services of the monopolized product. The definition of a market within which a firm may or may not monopolize production is therefore often very difficult and ultimately depends on the degree of substitutability considered high enough to warrant products being regarded as in the 'same' market. Even a monopolist may face some constraints if he faces a monopoly *buyer* (known as a monopsonist), for example if he supplies components to a sole user of them. This situation is known as *bilateral monopoly*.

[15] 'Perfect competition' is said to prevail if the product is homogeneous and divisible, if there are many quite independent buyers and sellers, if there are no transport costs, barriers to entry by new firms, rigidities in the movement of factors of production, or limitations on people's information about the market. These rigorous conditions ensure a horizontal demand curve. Few examples, if any, actually exist, but the model provides a useful bench mark for comparison and over the long term may give valid predictions of economic behaviour.

3.2.7. The Number of Close Substitutes

Second, irrespective of the number of firms producing close substitutes, if the profit margin or demand for the product is inadequate, then the firm will either have to improve its efficiency and therefore lower its average costs, switch to other products, advertise more, or begin to go out of business. In this way the prices other firms set exert a competitive pressure on the firm.

If, however, there are very few firms—an industrial structure known as oligopoly—an additional and quite direct pressure may be exerted on the price policy of any one of them. A price change by one firm will tend to have a marked effect on the demand facing the others.[16] Retaliation of some sort is therefore likely, making it difficult or impossible for the first firm to know the full effect of its new price policy. More specifically, if a firm thinks that a price rise will result in a large loss of demand because it expects none of its competitors to follow, and if it thinks that a reduction in price will gain it little extra demand because the competitors will be forced to follow, then any change of price may lead to lower profits, resulting in considerable price rigidities over a period, despite changes in cost and/or demand conditions.[17]

This will generally only be a temporary phenomenon, however, because

(a) firms may collude or develop a price 'leader';
(b) frequently one firm will eventually take the chance of a price rise, and others may then in fact take the opportunity to follow;[18]
(c) boom conditions may easily make one or more firms prepared to raise prices in the expectation that other firms, faced with rising costs, are anxious to do the same, and in the knowledge that demand is running at a relatively high level anyway.

Oligopolistic firms will ideally need to estimate all the different possible results of each possible new price, and develop some criterion for selecting the 'best' strategy—an approach known as game theory. In practice the number of alternatives and uncertainty about both the economic environment and other firms' reactions may lead to adoption of simple, well-tried, and well-known rules of thumb.

3.2.8. Barriers to New Entry

The third factor is the possibility that *new* firms will compete by commencing production of a close substitute. In some cases strong forces will operate to prevent this, e.g. if a firm has established a dominant market position through brand advertising; if particular scarce skills, technical know-how, etc. are necessary in the product line; if the processes used are patented; if a very large initial outlay is required to commence production; if competitive production

---

[16] Giving a high *cross*-elasticity of demand, defined as the ratio of proportionate change in the quantity of one firm's demand to the proportionate change in the price set by *another* firm.

[17] This gives rise to a *kinked* demand curve, so called because of the shape of the demand curve that portrays it. It should be noted that many other types of expectations may exist, giving different implications for price policy.

[18] It is frequently profit maximizing for a second firm to follow, *given* that the first raises prices, and knowledge of this may itself lead to the first firm raising prices.

can only be carried out on the very large scale necessary to generate very low average costs. To the extent that such barriers do *not* exist, the threat of new competition can usually only be thwarted by a deliberate policy of keeping profits sufficiently low, so that there will be no inducement for new firms to come into the market, or inducement sufficiently low to substantially reduce the rate of new entry.

Thus even a relatively simple analysis of firms' pricing behaviour must take account of the impact of income, preferences, the existence and number of close substitutes, and the threat of new competition. But this still ignores at least five further elements which complicate the situation. These are the existence of objectives other than profit maximization; the interdependence of pricing and other decisions in determining the firm's overall performance; the use of advertising as an additional determinant of demand; the fact that all the elements mentioned may be expected to vary over time; and the possibility of a firm foresaking a purely independent approach to its price policy. These we now consider.

3.2.9. Target Return Pricing

Firms frequently select a margin in order to obtain a previously specified target level of profits, or to allow a required return to be obtained from a specific capital project. This can arise for two reasons:

(1) Objectives such as the maximization of the firm's growth rate require, as we have seen, a particular level of profits in relation to capital employed. Too high a level makes more funds available, but tends to reduce the growth of demand; too low a level leads to an inadequate supply of funds. By experience managers will come to know the sort of profit levels required to ensure that the firm's development is not hindered by inadequate supply of funds or inadequate demand for goods. Their price decisions may then be seen as attempts to generate approximately this target level of profits, or target return on capital employed.

(2) Even if profit maximization is their only objective, firms generally will not know if they are achieving it. A useful way of proceeding, therefore, is to try new products as they are developed, retaining only those which give reasonable profits, and rejecting the others. Firms may, therefore, apply a given profit margin to all products, continuing production over the long term with only those products which can be successful with this target margin. This provides another reason why firms often take price decisions systematically on the basis of required target profits.

3.2.10 The Product Package

For many consumer products, firms attempt to provide an overall 'package'—a particular product of particular specification aimed at a particular type of consumer in a specified income bracket with advertising, packaging, and presentation designed specifically for him, and at a price that attracts him. This attraction is based partly on the price relative to his income, partly on what he deduces from the price about the supposed quality of the product, and partly on the implications for status and social position of being the type of person who pays that sort of price for such a product. The emphasis put on this approach by marketing executives, plus the many instances where demand has been higher despite higher prices, both indicate the extent to which it is the *combination* of price and other features which determines the demand for the product. In this situation, firms faced with inadequate margins may attempt to reduce costs, even at the expense of some change in product specification, rather than change the price and the associated attraction of the product. Again it is the interrelation of price decisions with others—this time product specification and marketing—which leads to a different approach than that implied by simple short-run profit maximizing.

3.2.11. *Life Cycle Pricing*

The relative importance of the different factors influencing price policy may well alter over the life of a product, and this can lead to the forward planning of price variation over the life of the product to take account of the change. There are a number of forms of this, but a typical one involves a high initial price when the product is launched, as a result of the high average costs of small-scale production and the high mark-up obtainable in the absence of close substitutes. If the product is successful, price is reduced significantly (in real terms) as large-scale production reduces average costs, mark-ups are reduced to deter at least some potential entrants, and as the introduction of new close substitutes begins to raise the price elasticity of demand. The main pressure may well be to expand production as rapidly as possible to obtain the potential economies of scale first, and achieve a dominant market position. Finally, the market stabilizes, often dominated by a small number of firms, with a fairly stable price and margin, and strong competitive pressures not to vary them independently of competitors' reactions.

3.2.12. *Restrictions on Price Competition*

In situations of acute price competition, particularly those where high fixed costs mean that even a relatively small reduction of demand results in losses, firms frequently wish to resort to some form of agreement to regulate prices. There is a whole spectrum of possible types of regulation, running from explicit co-ordination of prices, discounts, quantities, etc. at one extreme, to the most vague and purely implicit understanding, based only on experience of past price behaviour. In general, however, we may distinguish three main types:

(i) Collusion, where firms secretly, or occasionally openly, agree on a price for their product which they will all maintain, thus preventing competitive price-cutting which might be harmful to them in the long run.

(ii) Price leadership. In some cases, particularly where a dominant firm exists, there may be a specific agreement or a tacit understanding that all firms will set a price equal to (or related in some determined manner to) the price set by the price leader. His price changes are a signal for the others to follow suit.

(iii) Information agreements, in which firms simply supply information on their price changes and related aspects, e.g. quality specifications, either prior to the actual change or after it. There is therefore no actual agreement on price levels, but the information supplied can serve as a vehicle for obtaining greater uniformity of prices, if this is desired.

In conclusion, there are a large number of factors to be taken into consideration when pricing behaviour is examined. To draw out the implications of such behaviour for efficiency and resource allocation is very difficult, but none the less essential if industrial performance is to be properly understood.

3.3. Financial Decisions

3.3.1. The Cost of Finance

The firm's financial decisions are important because they help to determine the amount of funds available, and the cost to the firm of obtaining those funds. Section 3.1 identified four main sources, namely depreciation provision, retaining earnings, short-, medium-, and long-term borrowing, and equity issue. We therefore look at what determines the cost and availability of each.

It might be thought that there is no cost to the firm of depreciation provision and retained earnings, because no interest has to be paid to obtain them. This is incorrect. There is what is known as an *opportunity cost* to the owners of the firm. This is the cost involved in foregoing the returns available if resources were to be used in the best alternative way. By utilizing the funds, the firm deprives the owners (shareholders) of the opportunity of receiving the funds in the form of dividends.[19] If they were fully paid out the owners could invest the funds elsewhere and earn a return. Foregoing this return is a cost to them, and it will only be in the owners' interest for the firm to retain the funds if it can use them more profitably.

The situation is complicated by the tax position. Corporation Tax is levied on taxable company profits. Two items are generally deducted from gross profits to arrive at taxable profits: the depreciation allowance allowed by the Inland Revenue (which will generally depend on existing law on investment incentives and bears no relation to a 'normal' wear and tear provision) and interest charges on the company's financial obligations (bank overdraft, trade debt, loans, and debentures). The company then splits the post-tax profits between dividends and retained-earnings. If dividends are liable to *further* tax—the shareholders' income tax for example—the tax system is said to have a pro-retention bias, which will reduce the cost of internal funds relative to new equity financing. This is because if funds are retained, all of them can be used to earn a return for the shareholder, but if paid out, only that part left after payment of the additional taxation is available to earn more in the same (or another) company. The tax system can be designed to have a neutral, pro-, or anti-retentions bias.

Borrowing over whatever period in general involves a fixed interest cost over the life of the loan, though many loans, e.g. overdraft facilities, mortgages, involve an interest rate that can be altered at the discretion of the lender. Again, taxation reduces the effective cost of these capital funds because interest

---

[19] Using depreciation provision to pay dividends may, however, change the tax position and hence the funds available, besides being subject to various constraints.

charges are a tax-deductible cost, i.e. if the loan had not been incurred, profits would have been higher because of the absence of interest charges. However, taxation would also have been higher as a result of the higher profits, and the firm's net profit position would have been improved by only the post-tax amount. It is this amount foregone because of the interest charges which is the *effective cost* therefore. If the interest rate is 12 per cent and the company tax rate is 40 per cent, the effective cost is

$$(1 - 0.4) \times 0.12 = 0.072 = 7.2 \text{ per cent.}$$

The cost of new equity funds is more complicated to determine in practice. It depends on the yield that potential shareholders require to be prepared to buy shares, and thereby provide funds. The yield comes partly through dividends, and partly through appreciation in share prices. The latter will depend heavily on the firm's continuing ability to earn higher profits in the future, and this will require retained earnings. Therefore while too high a level of retained earnings can cause people to sell shares because the current dividend is inadequate, too low a level can also cause them to sell shares because there is too little prospect of future earnings increase. In both cases share prices fall, and the firm's decision on how to split net profits between dividends and retained earnings must partly be an attempt to find the intermediate level of retained earnings that keeps the share price as high as possible.[20] Maximization of the firm's share valuation may be an objective in itself, but in addition it will reduce the cost of equity finance. If in a given economic situation with a known stream of dividends share prices fall, it means that current or prospective shareholders will pay less for a claim on the future stream of dividends, implying that they require a higher return on their outlay than previously. New equity funds will only be forthcoming if this higher return can be earned, and so the cost of new equity finance will be higher. To the extent that managers are more concerned that their firm grows fast, they will tend to retain more earnings for growth than if they were only concerned to increase the value of the firm's equity.

3.3.2. Gearing

A firm is legally required to pay loan interest, which is therefore a first charge on its trading profit, but only subsequently pays dividends if it can and so chooses. Except in bankruptcy, therefore, the return to the *lender*, unlike the return to a *shareholder*, is known and certain. The higher variability of dividend payments means that the average return required by debenture holders is often less than that required by shareholders.[21] Given this, and the greater tax

[20] Some economists have shown that under certain assumptions the share valuation will be dependent on earnings, but independent of the proportion retained. The assumptions are, however, very restrictive, e.g. a perfect market for financial capital, no tax effects, etc.

[21] Two things may offset this: (a) the prospect of capital gains for the shareholder; (b) inflation will cut the real value of interest received, but may not cut the real value of dividends or capital gains received if these keep pace with inflation. A 'reverse yield gap' can then appear between interest rates and equity yields, and this is not uncommon. Equity finance is none the less quite expensive for the company in this situation because it is one which will only continue as long as equities really *are* a 'hedge' against inflation, i.e. as long as the company can maintain earnings in line with inflation.

advantage with loans, the effective cost of borrowing is frequently less than the effective cost of new equity finance, and often less than that of internal cash flow. Considerable cost savings arise therefore from increasing the proportion of a firm's total finance which is provided by loans (i.e. debt finance). On this basis the overall (weighted) average cost of capital funds will be lower, the higher the proportion of debt finance. There will, however, be a limit to the extent of this effect. If debt finance becomes a high proportion of total finance, interest charges will be high relative to dividends. If trading profits fall, dividends can always be cancelled, but interest must be paid, and so the existence of a high proportion of interest charges increases the probability that a fall in gross trading profits will bankrupt the firm. In addition, the percentage reduction in dividends consequent upon a fall in gross trading profits will be greater the higher the ratio of debt to equity finance, unless firms act to stabilize their dividend payments over time. Both equity holders and lenders will therefore be at a greater risk. The former will sell shares, reducing the price and increasing the cost of equity finance. The latter will ask for higher interest to offset the risk (or sell debenture, depressing the price and giving the same effect), and the cost of all types of finance will therefore rise. After a point, therefore, more debt finance can only be raised if the firm will accept a higher cost of capital.

The ratio of debt finance to total finance is known as the gearing ratio, and it follows from the above that there will be an optimal gearing ratio which minimizes the cost of capital (though in practice there may be quite a range of gearing ratios that give approximately minimum cost of capital).[22]

3.3.3. The Availability of Finance

We may summarize by saying that firms either attempt to retain that proportion of earnings which maximizes share value, or the maximum proportion consistent with maintaining acceptable share values and equity yields. They raise funds externally if required, but the declining profitability of the uses to which more and more funds may be put will eventually lead to a reduction in share valuation again, putting a limit on the total external finance that can be raised. The proportion of the external finance borrowed will be increased until it no longer makes a significant difference to the firm's cost of

[22] Two factors may interfere with this: (i) If the borrowing firm assesses the possibility of its not being able to maintain interest payments as more serious than does the lender of the funds, then the firm may deliberately choose to keep its gearing ratio below the level which minimizes the weighted cost of capital. (ii) An investor holding shares in a highly geared company may find it more profitable to borrow funds himself and invest them, together with his own funds, in a low-geared company. This allows him to increase his overall return while facing the same proportionate interest charges as before. (The difference being that it is the investor who pays them out of his dividends, rather than the company paying them before giving the investor his dividend.) This type of behaviour is not widespread, but the consequent switch from geared to ungeared company shares depresses the price of the former relative to the latter, and hence raises the former's weighted cost of capital. This could then, to some extent, offset the lower cost of finance that moderate gearing normally brings. See F. Modigliani and M. Miller, 'The Cost of Capital, Corporation Finance and the Theory of Investment', *American Economic Review* (1958) for the original (and difficult) statement of this view.

capital, unless halted by consideration of the borrower's risk. A typical firm might finance approximately two-thirds of its investment by retaining half its earnings, a sixth by new debt finance, and a sixth by new equity finance, giving an average value of rather less than 20 per cent for the gearing ratio.

Given these decisions, both the amount of funds available and the average cost of them are given. There will be little further scope to increase the amount (except by drastically increasing the cost) or to decrease the cost (except by cutting back on the amount raised). The cost and availability of funds for investment will then largely depend on the net profits earned, the level of interest rates on borrowing, and the yield required by shareholders. The last in turn depends partly on the interest that can be earned by lending rather than holding shares, partly on the level of profits being made, and, more importantly, on the likelihood or otherwise that the firm will continue to make profits in the future to finance further dividends, investment, and growth. The two central determinants, therefore, of a firm's ability to finance its investment expenditure are the current and expected level of net profits, and the level of interest rates.

3.4. Investment Expenditure

3.4.1. Investment Objectives and Investment Planning

It was stated earlier that, in general terms, companies are primarily concerned with the profitability, size or rate of growth, and security of their operations. At any one time, however, it may be very difficult, particularly in a large company, for its managers to identify those business opportunities the pursuit of which will most aid these objectives. This arises partly because of uncertainties as to the future course of economic events, and the impact of different possible strategies on the company's objectives; partly because of the complexity of the repercussions which occur as a result of the decisions taken at board level concerning major company developments, and finally because of the interdependence of the objectives specified.

Much effort is often spent, therefore, in establishing formal or informal means of making major business decisions amenable to careful and rational analysis and decision-taking. Three mechanisms in particular are important:

(i) Company planning. Long-range planning will frequently be carried out as a means of establishing a coherent picture of how the company may attain its objectives, within which the rationale for, and consistency of, individual decisions can be evaluated. This first requires identifying a consistent set of objectives, which itself is far from easy. On the financial side, a company can generally increase its finance over time: (a) by increasing its return on capital employed. This directly increases the funds available internally and generally makes it easier to raise new loans and new equity finance externally; (b) by reducing its net current assets or by raising new loans in the absence of an improvement in profitability. Both these latter two tend to increase the financial risks facing the firms, however, with the possible consequence that shareholders will sell their shares, depressing the share price on the stock market. Thus the growth of supply of funds tends to be directly related to profitability and inversely related to security.

Growth of demand for a firm's product will depend partly on the state of the market and the nature of the product. If these are conducive to commercial success then higher growth and higher profitability will generally result. Given the particular rate of growth and profitability determined by the market, a firm will generally only be able to obtain *faster* growth if it is prepared to sacrifice some of its profitability (and vice versa), e.g. growth of demand can generally be increased by lowering prices to encourage new customers; by increased advertising and promotional expenditure for the same reason; by developing new markets geographically; and by developing new products as a means of expanding its operations faster than might be possible within the confines of the existing product range. Each of these will frequently reduce profitability, however, unless the new markets are notably more profitable than existing ones; and so faster growth of demand will be attainable only at the expense of lower profitability.

Even in this very simple example, therefore, there are several relationships between different objectives which will limit the ability of the company to identify a plan that will ensure that the growth of demand for company products is matched by growth in its supply of funds. This can be illustrated, as in Figure 3.3 (based on an approach by Marris [38]).

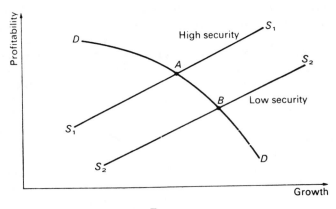

F IG . 3.3

The line DD indicates the inverse relation between profitability and growth of demand. S_1S_1 shows the direct relation between profitability and growth of supply of funds, for a given level of security. If a lower level of security can be risked then the line shifts rightwards, e.g. to S_2S_2, indicating a faster growth of supply of funds at any given level of profitability. The construction of a plan that ensures consistency between finance and production growth can be thought of as attempts, within this stylized approach, to identify points like A and B, and to select one which gives adequate security (i.e. an SS curve not too far to the right), and the preferred balance of profitability and growth. The selecting of objectives, construction of corporate plans, and identification of the corresponding financial plans are therefore three major functions of the senior levels within many companies' managements.

(ii) *Decentralization*. Once the overall plan is clear, the next step involves working out its implications for different parts of the company, and indicating the sort of decisions that it entails. The degree of diversification, the average profit margins, and the major capital projects required can be estimated and analysed. In addition, those lower down the company responsible for this aspect of operations will need to be constantly looking for and investigating the business opportunities likely to improve the company's performance as measured by its objectives. In particular, this requires the search for investment opportunities within one or more of various categories of expenditure, each of which can be interpreted as a type of investment likely to further the objectives stated. In a comprehensive classification this would include; (a) replacement of obsolete or unworkable equipment; (b) reduction of unit costs through modification and improvement of production processes; (c) expansion of plant to meet expected demand increases; (d) plant and machinery for the production of new models or new products; (e) the production of a previously purchased inputs (sourcing); (f) provision of distribution facilities; (g) offices, canteen, and recreational facilities; (h) equipment necessary for research and development prior to full commercial production.[23]

These reasons for investment, derived from the high-level objectives, may themselves be broken down further and converted into more specific form. Particular cost levels, capacity utilization levels, market shares, etc. will be watched, extrapolated in various ways, and used to indicate exactly when investment in different categories becomes potentially desirable. Thus not only are the general requirements of the overall plan filtered downwards, but opportunities to pursue company objectives are monitored and information on them filtered upwards, both to allow revision of plans in the light of changes in the economic environment, and for the purpose of final selection of projects considered necessary or desirable in the light of the company's current situation and future plans.

3.4.2. Investment Criteria

The third mechanism is to utilize specific investment criteria. As a result of the company's overall plans it will have a fairly good indication of the return on capital (and cash flow) required, the funds available, and the minimum cost of obtaining those funds (see previous section). As specific investment projects are formulated, they will in general be evaluated, not only in relation to the overall strategy, but also in the light of specific profit or cash flow criteria, to ensure that the targets envisaged are being met, that the return is greater than the cost of obtaining the funds to be used, and that there are not other projects which might offer a higher return if the funds were to be directed to them instead.

---

[23] In principle, almost all of these might be carried through by acquisition of another company's existing assets, as well as by the construction of new plant etc.

The three most widespread types of criteria are:

(i) Payback. From the estimated cost of the project, forecast running costs and revenue it is calculated how many years must elapse before the project has paid for itself, i.e. before the total accumulated revenue, net of running costs, exceeds the initial capital cost.[24] Only if the figure is below the maximum acceptable or 'cut-off' number of years is the project itself acceptable.

(ii) Accounting rate of return. The average annual profit (net or gross of tax) is calculated and expressed as a percentage of the initial capital cost. This must then exceed the chosen minimum satisfactory cut-off level.

Both of these suffer from some fairly obvious deficiencies. The former takes no account of revenue earned after the payback period, while the latter does not allow for the fact that revenue earned today is worth more than the same nominal amount of revenue in the future. This is because the revenue received earlier can be used to earn interest or a return of some form during the intervening period. For these reasons there is increasing and already widespread use of more sophisticated criteria which allow for these elements.

(iii) Discounted cash flow (DCF). Suppose a firm spends £100 now on a project which will result in £110 accruing to the firm in one year, and nothing more. The rate of return of 10 per cent is found by expressing the net gain $(110 - 100 = 10)$ as a fraction of the initial sum, i.e.

$$r = \frac{110 - 100}{100} = \frac{1}{10} \text{ (i.e. 10 per cent)}$$

where r is the rate of return.

This equation may be rewritten[25] as

$$100 = \frac{110}{1 + r} \tag{1}$$

and the rate of return is the value of r which satisfies this equation. If the £110 were reinvested, to obtain £121 in two years' time, then for the second year

$$r = \frac{121 - 110}{110} = \frac{1}{10}$$

again, and this may similarly be rewritten

$$110 = \frac{121}{1 + r}.$$

Putting $121/(1 + r)$ instead of 110, therefore, in equation (1) gives

$$100 = \frac{121}{(1 + r)^2}. \tag{2}$$

---

[24] In practice, many complications arise in the use of this, and the other criteria. Here only the general nature of the criteria is outlined.

[25] Multiplying both sides by 100, adding 100 to each side, and dividing both sides by $(1 + r)$.

Thus £100 invested now to generate £121 in two years' time would represent a return of 10 per cent per annum, and this would be found by solving equation (2). More generally, if the initial investment outlay is C, and the sum expected back is A, after t years, the rate of return, r, is found by solving the equation

$$C = \frac{A}{(1+r)^t}$$

and equations (1) and (2) are just specific examples of this. Typically, firms receive varying cash inflows over a period of years. If we call these A_1 in year 1, A_2 in year 2, etc. up to A_n in year n, the last year of the project, then the formula becomes

$$C = \frac{A_1}{1+r} + \frac{A_2}{(1+r)^2} + \frac{A_3}{(1+r)^3} + \cdots + \frac{A_n}{(1+r)^n}. \tag{3}$$

This is the basis of the discounted cash flow methods. The company can estimate the future net cash flows expected from an investment project (the As), estimate the initial capital cost (C), and then find the value of r that solves the equation. The variable r is called the internal rate of return of the project (IRR), and can be compared with either the cost of obtaining the funds, the internal rate of return on alternative uses of the funds, or a cut-off rate which may itself reflect these.

The advantage of this approach is that it takes into account *all* the cash flows associated with the project, but discounts them (i.e. reduces them in value in the calculation) by a larger amount the further they are in the future. Each term in the formula represents not the actual cash inflow for the year concerned, but the value of it to someone *now* who could earn the internal rate of return on it if he had it now, i.e. the *present value* of the future cash flow.[26]

3.4.3. *The Optimal Capital Stock*

Simplifying somewhat, we can envisage a company identifying the internal rate of return on a whole range of capital projects (existing and potential) and ranking them from left to right in descending order of their IRR. This is shown in Figure 3.4 by the line AA. The position of this line will reflect all the relevant cost and revenue factors influencing the desired capital stock, e.g. a higher level of wage cost could shift the line, with those projects involving little employment moving nearer the vertical axis relative to those involving high employment levels. The company also selects a cut-off point (10 per cent in Figure 3.4) as described above. The optimal situation for the company will be to have in operation all those projects for which the internal rate of return supersedes the cut-off rate, i.e. projects up to point K^*. This will maximize profits if the cut-off

---

[26] An alternative method—the Net Present Value method—utilizes the same formula, but substitutes the cut-off rate for r, and solves the right-hand side (the As and r being then known) to obtain the present value of the future stream of cash flows. The present cost of obtaining them, namely C, is then subtracted to find the net present value. The project is then acceptable if this figure is positive. The two methods have different advantages and disadvantages, and in certain situations can give conflicting answers. See Baumol [5], Chap. 19.

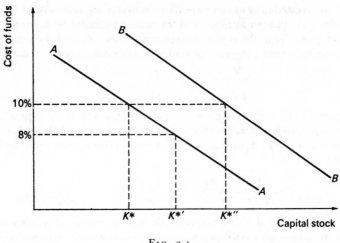

FIG. 3.4

rate reflects the cost of raising funds, and will maximize management utility generally if the cut-off rate is that rate consistent with the company's plans derived from its growth, profit, and security objectives. (Note that in this situation the cut-off rate will partly be chosen in the light of the capital stock desired.) If the actual capital stock existing is equal to K^*, then no further investment in plant and machinery would be necessary.

3.4.4. The Determinants of Investment Expenditure

If now the cost of raising funds were to fall, such that the company's cut-off rate fell to 8 per cent, the optimal capital stock would rise to $K^{*'}$, and further capital to the value of $K^{*'} - K^*$ would be desired. The rate of investment, i.e. the capital expenditure per year, per month, etc., is a flow variable and depends not only on the fall in the cost of borrowing (which determines how much new capital stock is required) but also on how rapidly the expenditure can be carried out. This in turn is a function of a number of factors—the extent to which the funds are immediately available, the degree of spare capacity in the capital goods industry, the time involved in planning expansion, placing orders, and carrying out construction, being the main ones. However, the *total* investment to be carried out will largely depend on the change in borrowing costs. As has been seen, the general level of interest rates will be a major factor in determining the cost to a company of obtaining funds and so interest rate changes may be expected to bear an inverse relationship to investment expenditure (having allowed for other determinants, to be discussed).

This is but one factor, however. If a company expects an increase in demand for its products, this will usually lead to an increase in the future expected cash flow associated with its capital projects. The value of A_1, A_2, etc. in the DCF formula will be higher even though C, the initial capital cost, is the same. In solving equation (3), therefore, r will be higher for each project. In Figure 3.4

the line AA, known as the marginal-efficiency-of-capital schedule, will be higher, e.g. at BB, indicating the higher internal rate of return than before that can be obtained for each unit of capital. Such a change in expected demand will, as before, raise the desired capital stock, in this case to $K^{*\prime\prime}$, and tend to bring about investment expenditure at a rate determined as described above. Thus indications that demand is going to rise to a level where the desired capital stock is above the currently existing one, e.g. rising levels of income, are likely to bring about increased investment expenditure. This relationship, known as the 'accelerator', appears to be a particularly powerful one in the determination of investment expenditure. It should be noted that both influences on investment will tend to work in reverse as well, with falling income levels and rising interest rates tending to inhibit investment.

We have so far assumed a single cut-off rate, dependent on the cost of obtaining funds, but the section on finance decisions indicated that the different sources of funds will have different costs. Typically, a company will generate some internal finance from depreciation and retained earnings (see p. 70), which have an opportunity cost, and raise some external finance from further bank borrowing, further issue of fixed-interest debenture stock, and issue of new equity shares. The cut-off rate might then be the cost of obtaining the most expensive funds that the company typically uses; or it might be some weighted average of the costs of the different sources of funds; or the company could construct different cut-off rates dependent on the type of finance that was to be raised for the investment expenditure being contemplated. In nearly all cases an increase in the amount of funds internally generated will tend to increase the amount of investment carried out. This is because in all cases the marginal projects that, prior to the increase in cash flow, were just not worth carrying out, will now become attractive, i.e. the internal rate of return was actually not high enough to make it profitable to raise funds externally for the projects, but will be comfortably above the relatively low cost of internal funds, if they can be generated in greater quantity. This can be shown diagrammatically as in Figure 3.5.

The MCF curve shows the marginal cost of funds as the company moves from the cheapest to the most expensive sources. The line II indicates for the particular situation the amount of new investment which would be profitable at different levels of the cost of funds. The increase in cash flow pushes the curve outwards to the right, also pushing the intersection with the II curve to the right. Thus internal cash flow is another important determinant of investment. This, it will be remembered, is comprised of depreciation allowance and retained earnings, both of which are individually important. The depreciation charge will reflect (abstracting from various investment incentive allowances) the size of the existing capital stock, which, by determining the likely replacement requirements, will have a bearing on the investment carried out. Retained earnings will primarily depend on the net profit earned, particularly if firms attempts to stabilize their dividend payments over time, and these earnings will also be significant as a guide to the prospective profitability of future investment. Thus the capital stock, profitability, and cash flow all help to explain the overall level of fixed investment, in addition to changes in interest

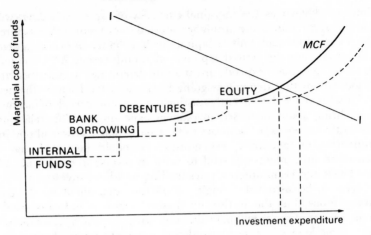

FIG. 3.5

rates and market demand levels. Finally, and implied by the above, movements in stock market prices, by changing the effective cost of raising new equity finance, may also play an important role in determining how much equity-financed investment will occur. Furthermore, if a fall in share prices scares some creditors, it can raise the cost of new debentures and even bank borrowing as well.

Four other factors must also be stressed. Firstly, investment expenditure must be planned long in advance, and also earn profits well into the future. *Expectation* of demand levels, interest rates, etc. are therefore vital, and expectations are much more volatile and rapidly changing in the light of economic events, than the events themselves. This adds a strong element of unpredictability to investment expenditure, making it more difficult to manipulate by government policy, and more dependent on the general level of confidence about future profitability. Secondly, different types of investment will be more responsive to different determinants. Replacement investment will depend more on the capital stock, expansion more on expected demand, stock investment more on the (opportunity) cost of holding the stocks, etc.[27] Thirdly, different determinants may have more influence at different stages of the trade-cycle, e.g. demand factors in a slump where funds are available but there is inadequate demand; cost and availability of funds if these are short during an upswing in the economy or if they are inadequate in a period of recession coupled with cost inflation. Finally, very long lags may exist between changes in demand, interest rates, etc. and consequent changes in investment expenditure. Only if it is forecast that all spare capacity will be eliminated, stock levels run down, and that excess demand will not be purely temporary, will investment plans be made, funds ear-marked, etc. All this takes

---

[27] Housing investment will depend to a great extent on interest rates, because of the significance of mortgage interest relative to incomes in determining how many houses the public can afford.

considerable time prior to a decision to invest, which itself will precede by months, or even years, the full utilization of the plant concerned.

3.4.5. *Research and Development*

Investment in research and development can in theory be dealt with by the DCF approach, but in practice it is usually almost impossible to make any reliable estimate of the expected future cash flows. It cannot be known whether research and development will lead to a saleable product or usable process, nor what they might be, or entail. Firms therefore frequently have to adopt a more rule-or-thumb approach, e.g. a constant research and development budget per year, or one which represents a specified proportion of total sales revenue, but adjusted in the light of particularly favourable or unfavourable circumstances. For specific research and development projects a higher cost of capital figure is frequently utilized to allow for the greater risk of failure with an unknown venture. In addition, firms have to ensure that such high-risk projects are generally not financed by borrowing on a large scale, but by the safer method of provision of new equity finance or retained earnings. Otherwise failure of the project will not be able to be accommodated by a reduction or cancellation of dividends, and the requirement to pay interest may result in bankruptcy. In practice, people would be very unwilling to lend at fixed rates of interest for a high-risk project, thus making this form of finance either very expensive or unavailable for such project.

Research and development investment, if successful, results in the firm possessing valuable information rather than a productive process itself. Unlike most valuable assets, however, no ordinary market could develop for it, because no one would pay very much for plans, designs, formulae, etc. unless they had a good idea as to their content and use. But if these are known then there is no point in paying for them. This situation is addressed by the patent system under which a firm, by registering a patent on its findings, can ensure either that someone else must pay the firm to use the information, even though anyone can see the information, or that it can develop its research commercially, safe in the knowledge that it will have a monopoly on the design, etc. for a certain period (though others may attempt to develop very similar processes which do not flout the patent act).

Patents restrict the diffusion of new products and processes through an industry, but there are also other obstacles to this. The need for new finance for the physical investment which embodies new advances may hamper their application; it may be more profitable to use a new design rather than an older one if one has a choice of either, but often more profitable to continue with the older design if the firm already has equipment embodying it rather than to scrap it and replace it with the newer design. For the DCF calculation the net cash flows appropriate to the capital outlay on the new equipment (minus any scrap value of the old) should *not* be the cash flows that will result from the operation of the new plant, but only the *additional* ones on top of those accruing to the existing equipment as a result of the lower costs. For all these reasons, research and development expenditure may be not only relatively insensitive to all the factors described above, except availability of funds, but also slow in its impact on the existing cost conditions.

3.4.6. Market Investment

This may be in the form of advertising, but often involves promotional campaigns, bonus payments (or discounts) dependent on sales, stock displayed, etc. It has partly an informative function, but also a persuasive one. It is debatable whether total demand is influenced greatly by the persuasive aspect, but market shares are strongly influenced by it. It will tend to proliferate where the gross profit impact of $£X$ of advertising is greater than $£X$; where oligopolistic structure makes price-cutting an unprofitable means of competition; and where the image of the product is an important element in the overall package being offered. In some cases an industrial equilibrium can be reached where an imbalance of market investment between firms is roughly matched, in profit terms, by an imbalance on price. In others the effectiveness of advertising ensures that all firms engage in similar amounts of advertising, which may then simply counter each other. The impact of this on the efficiency with which resources are being used is an element in public policy to be examined later.

3.5. Conclusion

This chapter has looked at the main decisions which firms take and the major considerations involved in taking those decisions. It has indicated that companies potentially have some control over their profitability, growth, and security, but that their pricing, finance, and investment decisions which promote these ends are all to a greater or lesser extent constrained—by consumers, the actions of other companies, and by a range of economic factors largely beyond their control, including market demand, interest rates, input costs, equity values, availability of loanable funds, to name only the more important. The chapter provides a basis for understanding and predicting the impact on companies of such factors. But in addition it provides an explanation of the main determinants of company pricing and expenditure decisions which together are two vital elements in the explanation of the general price level, inflation, and employment. This chapter is therefore one more component in the general picture of how the economy works.

Appendix 1

Marginal revenue (MR) is the first derivative of total revenue (TR) (i.e. the rate of change of total revenue with respect to changes in output). If P is price, Q is output,

$$\text{then } MR = \frac{d(TR)}{dQ} = \frac{d(PQ)}{dQ} = \frac{QdP}{dQ} + P = P\left(\frac{QdP}{PdQ} + 1\right).$$

$$\text{the price elasticity of demand equals} -\frac{dQ}{Q}\bigg/\frac{dP}{P} = -\frac{PdQ}{QdP}.$$

$$\text{Therefore } MR = P\left(-\frac{1}{E} + 1\right) = P\left(1 - \frac{1}{E}\right)$$

$$\text{and } \frac{P - MR}{P} = 1 - \frac{MR}{P} = 1 - \left(1 - \frac{1}{E}\right) = \frac{1}{E}.$$

profit maximization requires $MR = MC$ (marginal cost) and therefore requires $\frac{P - MC}{P} = \frac{1}{E}$. If average variable cost (AVC) is constant, $MC = AVC$ and profit maximization requires that the profit margin as a fraction of the price $\frac{P - AVC}{P} = \frac{1}{E}$.

Bibliography

SECTION A

A number of good introductory textbooks exist which cover the basic theory of Supply and Demand, Perfect Competition, Monopoly, Oligopoly, and Monopolistic Competition. The best-known British one is:
[1] LIPSEY, R. *Introduction to Positive Economics*, 6th edn. (Weidenfeld and Nicolson, 1983).
A good American alternative is:
[2] SAMUELSON, P. *Economics*, 11th edn. (McGraw-Hill, 1980).
More concise is:
[3] KOUTSOYIANNIS, A. *Modern Microeconomics*, 2nd edn. (Macmillan, 1979).
Those who prefer a more mathematical approach should read:
[4] COHEN, K. and CYERT, P. *Theory of the Firm*, 2nd edn. (Prentice-Hall, 1975), esp. Chaps. 1–2.
or
[5] BAUMOL, W. *Economic Theory and Operations Analysis*, 2nd edn. (Prentice-Hall, 1965).

These are very largely theoretical. More empirically orientated work on Industrial Economics covering firms' objectives, costs and pricing, market structure, etc. includes:
[6] NEEDHAM, D. *Economic Analysis & Industrial Structure* (Holt, Rinehart, and Winston, 1969).
[7] DEVINE, P *et al. Introduction to Industrial Economics* (George Allen and Unwin, 1974).
[8] PICKERING, J. *Industrial Structure and Market Conduct* (Martin Robertson, 1974).
[9] KOUTSOYIANNIS, A. *Non-Price Decisions: The Firm in a Modern Context* (Macmillan, 1982).
[10] COWLING, K. *Monopoly Capitalism* (Macmillan, 1982).

Major texts on industrial economics are, in the UK,
[11] MORRIS, D. and HAY, D. *Industrial Economics: Theory and Evidence* (Oxford University Press, 1979).
and in the US,
[12] SCHERER, F. *Industrial Market Structure and Economic Performance*, 2nd edn. (Rand McNally, 1982).
For a text which is more oriented to business decisions see:
[13] LIVESEY, F. *Economics* (Polytech, 1972).
A different picture of industrial behaviour is provided in:
[14] GALBRAITH, K. *The New Industrial State* (Hamilton, 1967).

For an introduction to Company Accounts and Accounting see one of:
[15] BULL, R. *Accounting in Business* (Butterworth, 1972).
[16] HENDRIKSEN, E. *Accounting Theory* (Irwin, 1970).
[17] TRICKER, R. *The Accountant in Management* (Batsford, 1967).

Introductory texts on Managerial Theories of the Firm and Managerial Economics include:
[18] WILDSMITH, J. *Managerial Theories of the Firm* (Martin Robertson, 1973).
[19] SAVAGE, C. and SMALL, J. *Introduction to Managerial Economics* (Hutchinson, 1967).
[20] HAGUE, D. *Managerial Economics* (Longmans, 1969).
[21] CURWEN, P. *Managerial Economics* (Macmillan, 1974).
[22] PAISH, F. *Business Finance*, 4th edn. (Pitman, 1968).
[23] MIDGLEY, K. and BURNS, R. *Business Finance and the Capital Market* (Macmillan, 1969).

SECTION B

More advanced reading under various headings is as follows:

Collected Articles
[24] NEEDHAM, D. (ed.). *Readings in the Economics of Industrial Organisation* (Holt, Rinehart, and Winston, 1971).
[25] ARCHIBALD, G. (ed.). *Readings in the Theory of the Firm* (Penguin, 1971).
[26] YAMEY, B. (ed.). *The Economics of Industrial Structure* (Penguin, 1973).
[27] ROWLEY, C. (ed.). *Readings in Industrial Economics* (Macmillan, 1972), 2 vols.
[28] COWLING, K. (ed.). *Market Structure and Corporate Behaviour* (Gray-Mills, 1972).

Pricing and Markets
[29] HAWKINS, C. *Theory of the Firm* (Macmillan, 1973).
[30] UTTON, M. *Industrial Concentration* (Penguin, 1970).
[31] SILBERSTON, A. 'Price Behaviour of Firms', *Economic Journal*, LXXX (1970).
[32] COWLING, K. *et al. Mergers and Economic Performance* (Oxford University Press, 1980).
[33] BAUMOL, W. J., PANZAR, J. C., and WILLIG, R. D. *Contestable Markets and the Theory of Industry Structure* (Harcourt, Brace, and Jovanovich, 1982).

Cost Structure
[34] SILBERSTON, A. 'Economics of Scale in Theory and Practice', *Economic Journal*, LXXXII (Special Issue, 1972).
[35] PRATTEN, C. *Economics of Scale in Manufacturing Industries*, Department of Applied Economics Occasional Paper, No. 28 (Cambridge University Press, 1971).
[36] HALDI, J. and WHITCOMB, D. 'Economics of Scale in Industrial Plants', *Journal of Political Economy* (Aug. 1967).
[37] LEIBENSTEIN, H. *General X-Efficiency Theory and Economic Development* (Oxford University Press, 1978).

Development of Firms
[38] MARRIS, R. *The Economic Theory of Managerial Capitalism* (Macmillan, 1966).
[39] PENROSE, E. *Theory of the Growth of the Firm* (Blackwell, 1959).
[40] McKINTOSH, A. *The Development of Firms* (Cambridge University Press, 1963).
[41] CYERT, R. and MARCH, J. *Behavioural Theory of the Firm* (Prentice-Hall, 1963).
[42] HESS, J. D. *The Economics of Organization* (North-Holland, 1983).

Investment and Finance

[43] BIERMAN, H. and SMIDT, S. *The Capital Budgeting Decision* (Collier-Macmillan, 1966).

[44] HAWKINS, C. and PEARCE, I. *Capital Investment Appraisal* (Macmillan, 1971).

[45] ROBICHEK, A. A. and MYERS, S. L. *Optimal Financing Decisions* (Prentice-Hall), 1965).

[46] BARNA, T. *Investment and Growth Policies in British Industrial Firms*, NIESR Occasional Paper, No. 20 (Cambridge University Press, 1962).

[47] BAUMOL, W. *The Stock Exchange and Economic Efficiency* (Fordham University Press, 1965).

[48] MERRETT, A. and SYKES, A. *The Finance and Analysis of Capital Projects* (Longmans, 1963).

[49] —— —— *Capital Budgeting and Company Finance*, 2nd edn. (Longmans, 1973).

[50] KIRKMAN, P. *Inflation Accounting* (Assoc. Business Programmes, 1975).

Advertising

[51] SCHMALENSEE, R. *The Economics of Advertising* (North-Holland, 1972).

[52] BACKMAN, J. *Advertising and Competition* (University of London Press, 1968).

[53] COWLING, K. *et al. Advertising and Economic Behaviour* (Macmillan, 1975).

Research and Development

[54] FREEMAN, C. *The Economics of Industrial Innovation* (Penguin, 1974).

[55] MANSFIELD, E. *The Economics of Technical Change* (Longmans, 1969).

[56] SALTER, W. *Productivity and Technical Change* (Cambridge University Press, 1960).

[57] ROSENBERG, N (ed.). *Economics of Technical Change* (Penguin, 1971).

[58] NELSON, R. R. and WINTER, S. G. *An Evolutionary Theory of Economic Change* (Belknap Press, 1982).

[59] STONEMAN, P. *The Economic Analysis of Technological Change* (Oxford University Press, 1983).

Oligopoly Theory

[60] DIXIT, A. K. 'Recent Developments in Oligopoly Theory', *American Economic Review* (May 1982).

[61] FRIEDMAN, J. W. *Oligopoly Theory* (Cambridge University Press, 1983).

Unquoted Companies

[62] HAY, D. and MORRIS, D. *Unquoted Companies* (Macmillan, 1984).

4

Employee Behaviour

K. MAYHEW

4.1. Introduction

In 1982 the total working population in the UK was 25·997 million. Of these, 23·165 million were in work, leaving 2·832 million recorded as unemployed. Figure 4.1 illustrates the path of the total working population and the employed labour force between 1970 and 1982. The trend most notable from this figure is a general increase in the level of unemployment, attributable to changes in the working population as well as to changes in the employed labour force. We shall see below that the size of the total working population is influenced by a number of factors; by such decisions as when people choose to leave full-time education or whether married women enter the labour force. The age structure of the population is also important in determining how total working population is related to population as a whole. Explaining what determines the level of employment is a major objective of this book.

It is unwise to think only in terms of aggregates. We must look also at the composition of the labour force. In 1982, 16·439 million were employed full time, 4·556 million part time, and 2·170 million were self-employed. It is important to understand how and why the figures for such disaggregated categories move when interpreting the overall movement in the level of employment. For example, if a change in aggregate employment could be explained mainly by a change in self-employment then we would wish, in our explanation, to look predominantly at factors influencing the self-employed. In 1982, 13·181 million of the UK labour force was male and 9·984 million were female, often doing very different types of work. In fact in the 1970s the number of women in work increased by 803,000 while the number of men in work fell by 875,000. This is also of interest in explaining aggregate behaviour.

The nature of jobs varies greatly. Table 4.1 gives the sectoral breakdown for June 1983 and Table 4.2 the occupational breakdown for 1980. If we look at movements in the disaggregated components of the work-force we are again assisted in our understanding of the aggregate. For example, we might wish to look at how employment has changed in the traditional manufacturing industries as compared with new 'high-technology' industries. Also of interest is the division of workers between the private and the public sectors. In 1982, of the total employed labour force, 29·6 per cent was employed in the latter.

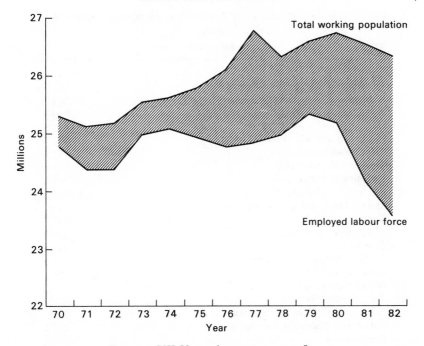

FIG. 4.1. UK Unemployment, 1970–1982.
Source: *Annual Abstract of Statistics.*

Aggregate employment is therefore very diverse in nature. The same is also true of employee behaviour generally, be this in terms of hours worked, earnings bargained for and received, levels and type of output generated. The purpose of this chapter is to draw out some of the *main* factors that influence employee behaviour across the board, as far as that is possible. It looks first at the factors influencing the demand faced by employees for their labour, then those affecting the supply of labour offered by employees. Unions are examined separately as having a particularly important role in the matter.

4.2. The Employer

4.2.1. Marginal Productivity Theory and the Demand for Labour

In examining the number of workers an employer would like to employ it is convenient to start with the traditional idea that he is concerned over the long term to maximize the profits he can make. For many this will be a reasonable approximation to what they are trying to do. For others, examined in more detail in the previous chapter (e.g. those trying to maximize their growth rate), the implications for their employment decisions may not be dramatically different in kind.

Suppose that an employer can take on as many people as he wishes at a going wage rate, but that each new employee adds less and less additional output. A

TABLE 4.1. *Sectoral Breakdown of Employees in Employment in the UK, June 1983*
(thousands)

All	20,651·0
Agriculture, forestry, and fishing	344·8
Mining and quarrying	324·8
Food, drink, and tobacco	604·9
Coal and petroleum products	25·5
Chemicals and allied industries	387·8
Metal manufacture	294·6
Mechanical engineering	722·2
Instrument engineering	128·9
Electrical engineering	642·3
Shipbuilding and marine engineering	140·5
Vehicles	550·7
Metal goods not elsewhere specified	430·0
Textiles	299·4
Leather, leather goods, and fur	28·6
Clothing and footwear	260·1
Bricks, pottery, glass, cement, etc	206·5
Timber, furniture, etc.	202·2
Paper, printing, and publishing	493·1
Other manufacturing industries	237·3
Construction	1,024·4
Gas, electricity, and water	330·9
Transport and communication	1,363·4
Distributive trades	2,655·8
Insurance, banking, finance, and business services	1,299·9
Professional and scientific services	3,660·3
Miscellaneous services	2,496·3
Public administration	1,495·7

Source: *Employment Gazette* (Oct. 1983).

profit-maximizing employer will continue to hire employees up to the point where the return from the last additional or 'marginal' employee is just equal to the cost of that employee. All the workers he is then employing add at least as much to revenue as they do to cost, but an extra employee would add more to cost than to revenue. Returns on labour are therefore maximized because the employer is employing all those with a positive net return and employing none with a negative net return. We can present this simple framework diagrammatically. First we construct a demand curve for labour which indicates the maximum the employer will pay for any given quantity of labour. In the simplest textbook case this can be constructed as in Figure 4.2. Figure 4.2(a) describes the *total physical product* (*TPP*), i.e. total real output of labour, as employment of labour increases, holding all other inputs constant. It shows that as extra units of labour are added, *TPP* rises, first at an increasing rate and then at a diminishing rate. Ultimately, however, extra input of labour actually

TABLE 4.2. *Occupational Breakdown of Employees in Employment in the UK, 1980*
(thousands)

Managers and administrators	2,129
Education professions	984
Health professions, etc.	986
Other professions	562
Literary, artistic, and sports occupations	447
Engineers, scientists, etc.	576
Technicians, draughtsmen	601
Clerical occupations	4,056
Sales occupations	1,417
Supervisors, foremen n.e.c.*	104
Engineering craftsmen	2,143
Other transferable craftsmen	907
Non-transferable craftsmen	675
Skilled operatives	622
Other operatives	4,712
Security occupations	386
Personal service occupations	2,932
Other occupations	789
Non-manual occupations	11,755
Manual occupations	13,271
All occupations†	25,026

* Because of classification problems this group covers engineering foremen and transport inspectors and supervisors only.
† Excluding HM Forces.

Source: University of Warwick, Institute for Employment Research, *Review of the Economy and Employment* (Summer 1983).

causes total product to fall. In Figure 4.2(b) we derive, from the *TPP* curve, *marginal* and *average* physical product curves. The former, known as the *marginal physical product* (*MPP*), shows the *addition* to total physical product from each additional employee and diagrammatically is measured by the steepness of the slope of the *TPP* curve. The *average physical product* (*APP*) is simply the *TPP* at any point divided by the number of employees necessary to produce it. This is shown graphically for *OA* employees as the distance *AB* (*TPP*) divided by *OA*, the number of employees. (*APP* is therefore measured by the slope of the line *OB*.)

That part of the *MPP* curve which is negative is irrelevant to the demand for labour because over this range each additional employee is *reducing* total output. Nor need we concentrate on the range where *APP* is rising; if real output per man is not only high enough to cover costs per man but *rises* with each additional man, then clearly profits will normally be rising with each additional man, and no profit-maximizing firm would halt recruitment in this

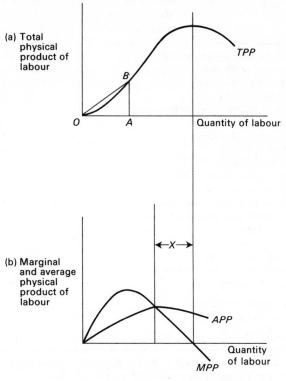

(a) Total
physical
product of
labour

TPP

B

O   *A*   Quantity of labour

(b) Marginal
and average
physical
product of
labour

←*X*→

APP

Quantity
of labour

MPP

FIG. 4.2

range. The remaining portion of the *MPP* curve, shown in Figure 4.2(b) by the
range *X*, is multiplied by the *marginal revenue (MR)* obtained from the extra
output, i.e. the addition to total revenue which each extra or marginal unit of
output generates (see p. 64), to yield *marginal revenue product*
($MRP = MPP \times MR$), the addition to company revenue generated by employing the extra person. Graphing this against employment gives a first
approximation to the labour demand curve because it shows the extra revenue
that each new employee can add to the company.

To see why it is only a first step, it is helpful to consider the special case of a
firm in a perfectly competitive product market, as described on p. 66. Here the
firm faces a constant price (P) so that $MR = P$, and the *MRP* curve is often
described as the *value of marginal product (VMP)* curve which is found from
$P = MPP$. In addition to the output price, the quantity and price of other
inputs or factors of production are held constant. We take first the quantity of
other factors. Some of them will be close substitutes for labour, and their
marginal product will therefore be reduced as more labour is used. Others will
have their marginal product increased by the hiring of additional labour. Let
us presume that, on balance, other factors are of this latter type.

Figure 4.3 plots the *VMP* line and, also on the vertical axis, the cost of labour, i.e. the wage rate. It can be seen that if the wage rate falls from W_0 to W_1 then there will be a movement along the *VMP* curve leading to an expansion in employment from N_0 to N_1. Given our assumptions in the previous paragraph, the fall in the price of labour and resulting increase in its use means that the marginal productivity of the other factors of production increases (i.e. an extra item of capital will be more productive than before because it has more labour with which to work). Therefore there will be a shift to the right of the marginal productivity curves of other factors therefore which, at a given cost for these factors, leads to a rise in *their* use. This will, by the same process in reverse, increase labour utilization, which is represented in Figure 4.3 by a shift to the right of the *VMP* schedule to VMP_2. At the lower wage W_1, this now implies that N_2 labour is employed, and the overall relationship between the wage rate and the demand for labour is given by the line *AA*.

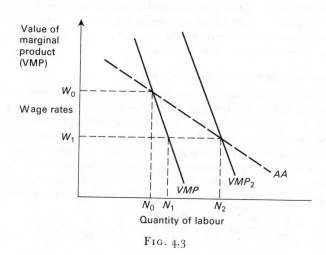

FIG. 4.3

If the marginal product of other factors is increased as more labour is used, then the demand for labour is *more* elastic than would appear from a single *VMP* schedule. The latter would suggest that a change in the wage rate from W_0 to W_1 would change employment from N_0 to N_1, whereas it actually changes from N_0 to N_2, if we take the shift of *VMP* to VMP_2 into account. The elasticity referred to here is defined as the proportionate change in the quantity of labour demanded divided by the proportionate change in the wage rate. Greater elasticity thus implies a larger quantity response for a given change in the wage rate. We might think of the change from N_0 to N_1 implied by the fall from W_0 to W_1 as giving us the short-run elasticity, while the eventual move to N_2 gives us a long-run elasticity. The time taken for these effects to occur will of course depend on the nature of the productive process.

If we now take the case of a firm *not* operating in perfect competition then price and marginal revenue do not remain equal and constant as output is increased, i.e. as more labour is employed (see Chapter 3, section 3.2). We therefore have separate *MRP* and *VMP* schedules. It is now the *MRP* schedule which is crucial in explaining employment decisions. This will affect the *AA* curve in Figure 4.3. Specifically, it would become less elastic. This is because any increase in output with a downward sloping demand curve results in a lower marginal revenue. We must also consider the case where a firm is large enough to influence the price of factors it purchases by its own actions. In such a case, if the firm buys more of such factors this constitutes an increase in demand for these factors and thus a rise in their price. This would also reduce the elasticity of the *AA* schedule.

There is no real sense, therefore, in which we can regard *VMP* or *MRP* curves as indicating labour demand. In the simple example given here we can say little more than that the demand curve for labour slopes downwards. For this reason the approach taken here has only weak predictive power. One notable way in which the behaviour suggested by this model does not agree with reality is that employers appear to react to wage changes less than it suggests. This led a number of economists to investigate the possibility that labour was a partially *fixed* (or quasi-fixed) factor of production.

4.2.2. Labour as a Quasi-fixed Factor of Production

There are various costs associated with labour other than direct pay.[1] These include search, hiring, and training costs. The employer's maximizing decision now becomes very different from the period-to-period equalization of marginal returns and costs. Labour is hired up to the point where the discounted present value of the marginal worker is zero (or discounted returns are equal to the discounted costs of hiring a worker). The notion of discounting was introduced in Chapter 3, section 3.4.2, in the analysis of investment criteria. Taking a discount rate, r, we can express our new criterion for hiring workers as

$$\sum_{i=0}^{N} \frac{Ri}{(1+r)^i} = \sum_{i=0}^{N} \frac{Wi}{(1+r)^i} + S_0 + H_0 + \sum_{i=0}^{N} \frac{Ti}{(1+r)^i}$$

where $\sum_{i=0}^{N}$ is to be read as 'the sum of . . . from period 0 (now) until period N', the expected length of employment with the firm. S, H, and T are search, hiring, and training costs respectively and R and W are the returns and wage costs. The left-hand side of the equation is simply the discounted value of the returns to the worker. The right-hand side has search and hiring costs which are incurred only once, i.e. at the time when the worker is hired (in period 0). Also on the right-hand side are the present discounted values of wage and training costs.

In the early years of his stay, it is likely that the costs of a worker will exceed his value to the firm. The employer, therefore, will try to recover these costs in later years by paying less than the value of his later output, so that for the marginal worker his present value to the firm overall would be zero. This provides a very different model from the traditional one. Instead of equating

[1] Still the best article describing labour as a quasi-fixed factor is Oi [28].

costs and benefits from period to period, they are equated over the worker's whole stay. As an example of the predictive implications of this, assume there is a recession which drives down the value of marginal product. In the traditional case, the employer has to dismiss the workers since he is not meeting his variable costs. In the quasi-fixed factor case, the value of marginal product may remain above the wage even allowing for the recession. If so, the employer is covering his variable cost and some of his initial fixed costs. Although his original employment decision is rendered incorrect, he will not necessarily sack the worker. If he does so he may have to make a redundancy payment and, once the recession is over, he will have to meet the fixed costs of searching for hiring, and training new workers. The employer will consider whether this is a more expensive course of action than retaining the original employee unproductively as long as the recession lasts. It is this which accounts for the well-known phenomenon of labour hoarding which has been a characteristic of most British slumps. It also explains why unemployment rates for unskilled workers rise more rapidly than unemployment rates generally. It is because the fixed costs of employing an unskilled worker are low and therefore the unskilled are much nearer to being variable factors of production than are their more skilled colleagues. The development of the theory of labour as a quasi-fixed factor leads us some distance from the competitive markets of traditional theory, and we shall explore this in the following section.

4.2.3. Internal Labour Markets

An internal labour market (ILM)[2] is one which to some degree is insulated from external market forces—employers can make independent decisions about wages and conditions of employment. Features of the ILM are clear administrative rules and procedures about things such as promotion and seniority payments. It might also have 'limited ports of entry'—these imply that only a few types of job are filled by external recruitment; the others are filled by promoting or regrading the existing work-force. Whilst large parts of the public sector in Britain possess such limited ports of entry (the administrative civil service, for example), they appear to be less common in the private sector.[3] Fortunately, their presence is not critical for our argument. Internalization of the labour market can be said to be present where *one or both parties to the employment contract has an incentive to reduce labour turnover.* We can see the significance of this by relating it to the theory developed in the previous section.

Training can be of two types. It can lead to the acquisition of a specific skill or of a general skill. The former is one which can be used only in the firm where it is learnt; the latter is fully usable in other firms. These are obviously extreme cases and most skills are somewhere in between. As an illustrative exercise, however, we shall employ the two extremes. If the skill involved is specific, then the employer can safely pay for it. In doing so he may well incur losses early in a

---

[2] An early exposition of internal labour market theory is Doeringer and Piore [3].
[3] See, for example, MacKay *et al.* [24].

worker's stay, but can recoup them subsequently. To give an example, suppose that a worker arrives with a value of marginal product (VMP) of 20 per period which after specific training has risen to 30; at some point the employer can pay (say) 25 and thus make good his early losses. There is no danger that the employee will leave as a consequence because he is still being paid more than he could get elsewhere, where his VMP would still be 20. Conversely, if the skill were general, pure theory would tell us that the employer would have no incentive to pay for its acquisition. To use the same example, if the employer tried to recover his training costs by paying 25 then the worker would have an incentive to leave since he would be able to obtain 30 elsewhere.

Where specific skills are involved, the employer has no need to take institutional action to reduce labour turnover. But the worker will in some ways feel trapped in the firm. His *human capital* is specific to the firm and will be left behind if he decides to leave. (See section 4.3.2 for elaboration of this concept.) He may well try, therefore, to obtain rewards for doing what he has to do anyway. In other words, he will ask his union to press for the sort of security and promotion provisions which are a feature of the internal labour market. The union will have latitude for pressing for such things because there will be no unique equilibrium wage or level of employment. This is because there is a *bilateral monopoly*. The employer is a monopsonist because he is the only person who demands these skills; the workers are monopoly suppliers since, in the short run at least, they are the only people who possess these skills (see Appendix 1).

In the case of general skills, the *employer* will have an incentive to construct an internal labour market to control labour turnover. Although in theory he should not pay for the acquisition of such skills, in fact he will do so for two reasons. First, because of imperfect capital markets, workers will be unable to borrow the sort of money needed to finance the training themselves, and if the employer needs such skills, he will have to pay for them himself. Second, in reality the employer may have little idea whether a particular skill is general or not, but he will presume that there is some element of generality. The employer, therefore, runs into the sort of danger we described above when he tries to recoup his costs. As a means of reducing the risks involved, he will attempt to design an internal labour market to discourage turnover. Overall, therefore, with either type of skill, either employees or employers, and generally both, will have some desire to control labour turnover by internalization of the labour market.

The discussion thus far has concerned internalization by plant or firm. This is often known as vertical internalization. There is another type of internal labour market, the horizontal one. In this case workers may be mobile between different employers, but always remain within the same occupation. As between the employers as a group and the employees in the occupation as a group, similar arguments apply. It may also be that the rewards of the ILM are a way of stimulating workers to greater effort.

The introduction of internal labour markets implies that plants or firms are to some degree 'protected' from market forces and that there may be no such thing as a unique equilibrium wage. The extent of this phenomenon depends on the strength of the supply response to differences of pay between plants or occupations. This issue will be considered later.

4.3. The Worker

4.3.1. Traditional Theories of Participation Rates and Hours of Work

The traditional analysis starts with a trade-off between leisure and income (or other goods). In Figure 4.4(a), each indifference curve represents a constant level of utility for an individual which is attainable through the various combinations of leisure and income shown along the curve. The slope of the budget line is given by the hourly wage rate and thus it depicts the rate at which the individual can trade off leisure for income. The individual maximizes his utility where an indifference curve is just tangent to the budget line; this represents the highest attainable utility, and implies that he will work for $(24 - x)$ hours and have x hours of leisure.

At first sight this seems to be a reasonable—albeit simple-minded— approach to the hours decision, but it would seem to have nothing to say about the decision whether or not to participate in the labour market at all. However, a simple amendment to the budget line alters this. Each individual has a certain

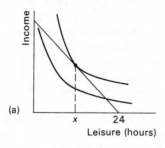

(a)

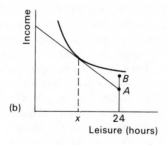

(b)

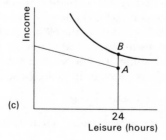

(c)

FIG. 4.4

amount of income even if he does not work. For the average prime-age male this would be social security benefit, any unearned income, and his wife's earnings. The sum total of these is likely to be small relative to potential earnings, and is represented by the vertical section of the budget line in Figure 4.4(b). The distance AB represents social security benefits which would be lost if the individual started work. Given normal tastes between income and leisure (i.e. leisure is not an inferior good, see Chapter 2, section 2.4.4), it is almost inevitable that the indifference curve will be tangent to the budget line well to the left of this vertical segment. In other words, marginal changes in wage rates and in tastes will affect hours worked but will not affect the basic decision to participate in the labour market. This corresponds well with reality since the participation rates of prime-age males are stable and well over 90 per cent. But consider married women and the young and old of both sexes. For all of these groups the vertical segment of the budget line is likely to be high. Married women, if not working, can rely upon the incomes of their spouses which have traditionally been higher than female earnings. Young people can rely on state grants for education and on the support of their parents. Older people (i.e. those between 55 and retiring age) may be able to rely on pensions and incomes from their personal savings. Given this high vertical segment of the budget line it is quite probable that an indifference curve may be tangent at point B as shown in Figure 4.4(c). In other words, for these groups marginal changes in tastes or in wage rates might alter the decision whether to participate or not. And again, this would accord with experience. Participation rates are lower than for prime-age males and subject to more variability over time.

This simple approach has some merit. Certainly more sophisticated theoretical and empirical work has found it difficult to add to the understanding of labour supply. The main historical phenomena to be explained are a secular rise in the participation rates of married women and a fall in those of the young and old of both sexes. Can econometric analysis reveal anything about these developments beyond what is common sense?[4] Econometricians started by employing a version of the hours-leisure model as the basis of their thinking. They included as independent variables a person's own wage rate and the spouse's wage rate. Increases in the former can have both income and substitution effects (see p. 42). The income effect increases the demand for leisure, leisure being a normal good; the substitution effect reduces the demand for leisure since it has now become relatively more expensive in terms of opportunity cost. An increase in the spouse's wage has a simple income effect increasing the demand for leisure. A basic problem econometricians face is accounting for changes in 'tastes' over time. Unless they can do this adequately, their measure of the elasticity of demand for work and leisure with respect to own wage and spouse's wage are unreliable. Unfortunately they find it difficult to do so if they have to rely upon crude 'proxy' variables[5] to measure changes in complex social phenomena and to

[4] Recent surveys of empirical work on labour supply are Greenhalgh and Mayhew [17] for the UK and Heckman *et al.* [18] for the US.

[5] i.e. an observable measure that is thought to be correlated with the unobservable variable presumed to be important.

model complicated interactions. A vast amount of empirical work has made some progress.[6] But much is still unexplained, though it seems reasonable to conclude that in the case of married women, changing attitudes to women in society have to be considered an important factor. In the case of the declining participation rates of the young and old, rising wealth has played a part.

Actual hours worked have fallen since the war.[7] Standard hours of work have declined even more, but their falls have been concentrated at particular times. For many workers, they fell from 48 to 44 in a few years after the Second World War. A 42-hour week became common between 1960 and 1962, and there was a push towards a 40-hour week in the late 1960s. We are currently seeing moves towards an even shorter working week. Each time before, overtime hours increased partially to make good the fall, so that the decline in actual hours was not as great. The cause of this decline on the supply side is presumably linked to the rise in income and therefore to increased demand for leisure; but too often econometric work does not consider the demand side where there may also have been forces making for a reduction in hours. A similar comment can be made on studies of participation. In summary, the traditional work on participation rates and hours is based upon the simple but attractive hours-leisure choice model which gives some insights. However, it has proved hard to move beyond the simple and general to more sophisticated and detailed explanations.

4.3.2. Supply of Labour to Occupations

The traditional approach to this topic employs human capital analysis.[8] Human capital theory analyses a particular employee in a manner analogous to a capital item such as plant or machinery. The value of the employee is altered through education and training just as the value of plant would be altered by computerization, for example. We can, therefore, talk of investing in people as well as investing in ordinary capital goods. According to human capital theory, people invest in their human capital up to a point where the marginal costs involved equal the marginal gain. As a result the greater the length, intensity, and expense of training required to enter an occupation, the higher will be its earnings. In addition, the supply of labour to a particular occupation can be altered by changing its relative pay.

A number of criticisms have been made of this approach which involve questioning its assumptions. Most commonly questioned is the implied view that individuals make such pecuniary decisions about their education, particularly at relatively young ages. Clearly the sorts of choices people make when deciding, for example, which university to apply to or which course to take are influenced by considerations other than pecuniary or even economic ones. However, like all economic analysis, human capital theory deals with decisions at the margin, and at the margin it seems reasonable to presume that pecuniary considerations will be important. Certainly, decisions by broad numbers of people on how many years of post-school education to pursue may

---

[6] For an excellent and comprehensive evaluation, see Killingsworth [21].

[7] For a detailed discussion, see Leslie [23].

[8] The classic exposition of human capital theory is Becker [9]. A shorter and simpler version is Schultz [34].

well, over time, be influenced by perception of what this will do to later earning capacity.

A less common but more telling difficulty concerns a sort of fallacy of composition which is best illustrated by an example. Imagine a typist travelling home on the London underground in the early 1970s. Reading her newspaper, she notices that jobs for software computer operators are paying far more than she is currently earning. Glancing above the heads of the passengers opposite she sees advertisements for private schools offering computer courses. Investigating, she finds that these courses are short and relatively inexpensive and she makes a classic human capital decision, leaving her job as a typist, scraping together a few hundred pounds, and a month later emerging as a software operator. Her only problem is that thousands of other typists were travelling home on the underground at the same time and made the same sensible decision. Unfortunately their mass action would drive down the earnings of computer software operators, thus invalidating their own initial calculations. Perhaps the best course of action for this typist would have been to do nothing. This is not to deny that human-capital-type calculations are sensible ones to make, but to stress that they are a much more complicated affair than might at first be apparent.

Criticisms of human capital theory can also be made at the empirical level. First, how is it translated into testable form? Its prediction is that earnings are related to human capital, but how is human capital to be represented in a testable equation? The original human capital theorists used years of schooling as a proxy. This is clearly inadequate, since it implies that all those, for example, leaving school at the minimum age have identical human capital endowments, or that all those emerging with a BA from a given university have exactly the same endowment. More recent work has used the level of qualifications obtained, including, in estimating equations, dummy variables for as many qualifications for which data are available.[9] Although this represents an improvement on the earlier approach, it is still inadequate, for again it implies that anyone with a certain university degree has just as much human capital as another person with that degree—which is clearly fallacious. Even if the final estimating equation is thought to be a reasonable representation of the theory, the problem is that it is also consistent with a multitude of other possible hypotheses. For example, it could be that earnings are influenced by family background. Equally, educational attainment may be a function of family background. Since both earnings and education depend upon the same variable, they will be correlated, though this correlation implies no causal connection.

In addition, the econometric results are not fully convincing. Only a small part of the pattern of occupational attainment or of earnings is explained by human-capital-type variables. Even the early human capital work included, in addition to education, age and/or experience as a determining variable. Subsequent work included other supply-side variables, such as family background, physical characteristics, such as health or strength,

[9] For examples of such recent work, see Layard [22].

and mental characteristics, such as drive, dynamism, determination, and ability.[10] Though regression equations containing these additional variables explain a greater porportion of the observed patterns of earnings, many problems remain. In particular, because many of the explanatory variables are themselves correlated, it is impossible to be certain as to the precise importance of any one of them; in addition it is hard to know the mechanism through which a variable has an impact on earnings or occupational attainment.

But for our purposes there are two critical points. The first is that occupational attainment is not simply a function of purposeful decision as implied by the human capital theorists. It depends also on social and environmental characteristics which are impossible or slow to change.[11] Second, all the variables so far considered are supply-side variables; such work almost totally ignores the influence of the demand side. The more extreme proponents of the demand-side view became known as 'segmented labour market' theorists.[12]

Segmented labour market theory is an umbrella term covering a variety of theories and observations. Relying in part on Thurow [37], a reasonably comprehensive approach is as follows. It has three stages. The first is that the labour market is divided into two or more segments between which lifetime mobility is virtually zero. In the simplest case, the better (or primary) segment is characterized by internal labour markets. In the primary segment employers are concerned to recruit workers who are reliable and trainable. They arrive in their jobs without any directly usable skills, but the employer is willing to go to the expense of providing them with these skills, and accordingly wishes to keep them for as long as possible in order to reap the return from his investment. Hence, we can see internal labour markets developing where the employer sets up the institutions and procedures which will be designed to encourage such long stays with his firm. By contrast, the nature of the jobs performed in the secondary labour market is such that employers merely require bodies. It does not matter who they are or that they have no particular skills. The employer therefore invests little in their training and is indifferent to turnover. The first stage of the theory, therefore, is an exposition of internal labour markets. Segmentation occurs in the extreme version of the theory because of limited ports of entry. If an individual misses the good jobs early in his career, he can never catch up.

The second stage involves describing a process by which people are assigned to one or other of the segments at the beginning of their working lives. Education by itself does not increase the labour market productivity of individuals. Instead it signals that they have the sort of characteristics which make them reliable and trainable and good material for the internal labour market. In other words, it provides people with a credential. Potential entrants

[10] See Lydall's chapter in Atkinson [8].

[11] Some researchers went so far as to suggest the possibility that a large proportion of the relevant characteristics were determined either genetically or by very early environment, Taubman [36] for example. Goldberger [16] has shown that, with present knowledge, it is impossible to isolate the relative importance of these forces.

[12] For an excellent survey, see Cain [6].

form a queue according to their educational qualifications and, perhaps, according to other variables, such as race or sex. Employers in the primary sector hire from the head of the queue whilst those in the secondary sector hire from the tail. People, therefore, are assigned to one or another segment according to their position in the queue.

The third stage of the theory concerns how earnings are determined. There are two possibilities. The one which departs least from traditional theory, and which was extensively developed by Thurow, still relies on wages being related to marginal productivity; but instead of being a function of the individual's skills and capacities, marginal productivity is now purely a function of the nature of the job. For example, beyond the minimum qualifications needed to enter a particular job, it is argued that additional qualifications and skills will not enable a worker to be vastly more productive. In other words, the range of performance is circumscribed by the nature of the job itself. Overall, educational qualifications would still be correlated with subsequent earnings but through a very different mechanism than in the simple human capital theory approach. A second and more radical approach to the determination of pay is that the relative earnings of different jobs are determined not by marginal productivity principles at all but by social conventions.

The empirical evidence does not support such extreme views (see Mayhew and Rosewell [27]), but there are still some important conclusions to be drawn from all this. In so far as occupational choice depends upon educational or training decisions, it will be only loosely related to relative wages of occupations and movements in those relative wages. In so far as the internal labour market is important, we have a situation where, to some extent at least, demand for particular occupations creates its own supply. The easy division between demand and supply has been lost.

4.3.3. Supply Responsiveness to Relative Wage Signals

The success with which internal labour markets can survive and be insulated from the external market depends on supply responsiveness to relative wages. This is the case both for movements within an occupation between plants and for movements between occupations themselves. In an uncertain world, supply response can take place only when information about the various options has been obtained. Therefore, we need to turn to *search theory*, which is concerned with decisions that people make about how much information to obtain before making a choice. According to Stigler's [35] exposition, there will never be enough search to acquire sufficient information to eliminate all wage dispersion in a local labour market. Stigler takes an almost ideal world in which once an individual has discovered the relative merits of the firms which he has searched, he can be certain that the ranking of those firms remains constant for as long as he desires.

In Figure 4.5, the *MC* curve portrays the marginal cost of search whilst the *MG* curve portrays the marginal gain. In neo-classical style, the worker stops searching where the marginal cost equals the marginal gain. If there are positive marginal costs of search there will be insufficient search to eliminate all earnings dispersion, since there are still marginal gains unrealized. If one then

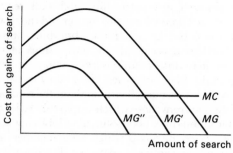

FIG. 4.5

relaxes the assumption that the rankings of firms remain constant for all time, the worker will evaluate his likely gains over a much shorter future period and thus the *MG* curve will move inwards to *MG'*. This implies that in the face of more uncertainty of this type there will be still *less* search and therefore less supply response. On top of this, the existence of internal labour markets implies that there is a range of earnings for any given grade of labour within a firm. Empirical work suggests that these ranges overlap each other (Mayhew [25]). Thus although an individual may be able to choose a firm on the basis of its starting rate, he will not be certain whether this will remain the best firm for him in the future since he will not know how well he will progress in that firm, nor will he know how he could have progressed in other firms, with lower starting rates, that he might have chosen. Because of this there will be a further leftward shift of the *MG* curve (to *MG"*) and even less search.

The implications of all this are that supply responses are weak in terms both of movements of a given type of labour between plants and of movements between occupations. This is a generalized case of bilateral monopoly and implies that there is no unique equilibrium set of relative wages nor equilibrium employment levels. It is against this background that the union has scope for its activities. All of this carries important implications for theories of inflation at the macroeconomic level. It suggests that such theories should be put firmly in a bargaining context; and, whatever determining variables are thought to be significant, that a variety of wage outcomes are consistent with any given value of these variables.

4.4. The Union

4.4.1. *The Range of Discretion*

If the labour market produces unique equilibrium wages, then the only scope the union has for affecting the wage or employment outcome is to influence either the supply or demand curves of labour. The union can restrict supply through a number of tactics. For those unions representing skilled workers, they can control entry through apprenticeships and skill regulations. Unions representing the less skilled do not have this option and they have to control the supply of workers through the threat of force, obtaining manning agreements, and threatening blacklegs if an employer shows signs of using non-union labour. It is less common to think of unions influencing the demand-for-labour curve, but they might do this in two ways. First, they might establish worker control of a company and thus make decisions about the company's demand for labour which are different from those which would otherwise have been made. Second, public sector unions may take political or lobbying action to influence the demand for the services or goods which their members supply.

All these possibilities are relatively restricted. But once the concept of the unique equilibrium wage is abandoned and it is established that there is a range of discretion, then the bargaining scope for the union is immensely greater. In particular, it has scope to exercise aims other than those which are just purely economic ones of maximizing the wage bill of its membership or some other crude economically measured variable—e.g. conditions at work, security, etc.

4.4.2. Why People Join Unions

For some, political motives may be uppermost—they join the union in the same spirit as they might join a political party. Such people are probably rare. The economic motive is likely to be predominant. The prime motivation might sometimes be defensive and sometimes aggressive. They may feel a need to protect themselves against a strong monopsonistic employer. They may wish to shelter from market forces which frighten them. Or there may be an opportunity to exploit a position of worker power to push aggressively for higher wages. Whilst an important focus will be on pay, there will also be concern for non-pay matters such as security, or safety, or training. But however strong these motives and desires, an individual might still feel that it is in his interests *not* to join the union. As long as all others in the plant are members, he is likely to get all the benefits of membership without paying any of the costs. In other words he might decide to be a 'free-rider'. The problem for the unions is that others might start to behave in a similar manner. If too many free-riders are allowed, reduced membership might directly harm the union's bargaining power. Certainly its financial position is harmed. To attempt to minimize this problem, the union might try to obtain a closed shop. Even if it does not go this far, it is likely that other tactics will be used in order to keep up membership.

Some writers suggest that the benefits of being a union member are in fact an illusion. They argue that those who first form the union obtain a gain, but that the advantage that the union obtains remains constant thereafter. People will try to join in order to obtain this gain. But there will be competition between aspirant members driving up the price of entry, either directly, through increasing union dues, or in some other way. The cost of entry will increase until the marginal costs equal the marginal gains. Thus all those who are not founder members of the union will get only the benefits they have paid for. They will obtain no net gain.

This thesis seems most plausible in the context of the sort of union which is able to maintain high pay by controlling entry into an occupation, and which strictly controls the number of entrants. Individuals wishing to enter the union can be seen as (say) taxi drivers trying to buy one of the limited number of licenses to operate in a particular city, forcing up the price of licenses until at the margin there is no net advantage. The case is an extreme one, but even here it is not clear that only founders benefit from union membership. It is only at the margin that there is no net gain. There may be intra-marginal gains for many new entrants. The general argument becomes even weaker if we relax some of the assumptions made thus far. Not everyone is able or willing to join a union. If the union gains are in part the result of economies of scale, then they may increase as the union increases in size. A piece of evidence often cited by the adherents of this approach is that in both the US and the UK membership dues over time have fallen as a percentage of average pay. They conclude that this was necessary because gains have been falling. Although there is probably some grain of truth in this, it seems safe to conclude that for the average trade unionist the advantages he gains from his membership are greater than the costs.

4.4.3. Union Aims

As with any other collective organization, it can be very misleading to talk of *the* aims or objectives of the union. It is composed of many different administrative units and more informal coalitions. The aspirations, perceptions, and priorities of these groups may diverge. The interests of one group may conflict with those of another. Those who read about post-war industrial relations will be struck, for instance, by the move in many sectors from national to plant bargaining, with a concomitant shift of power from the national leadership to the lay officers (or shop stewards) at the plant. Within any one of these groups or coalitions there are likely to be similar conflicts between individuals. These comments are important in understanding the Ross/Dunlop debate which, although it started well over thirty years ago, is still a live issue. The debate is often interpreted as one where Dunlop emphasized the primacy of the economic aims of unions (particularly their desire to increase pay as much as possible) and where Ross argued that the political aims of union leaders were paramount, particularly their desire to maintain the integrity and unity of their organization. In one sense that is a fair description of conflicting views on what might motivate union leadership. But the two approaches are not necessarily in such stark conflict. They could be interpreted as concentrating on two entirely different elements of policy formulation. Ross was concerned with how policy is decided, with the conflicts and strains this might impose on unity, and with how the issue is resolved. Dunlop, by contrast, did not concern himself with such details of decision making, contending that whatever the process of internal policy formulation might be, the final objectives of the unions are essentially economic in character.

Subsequent economic work has tended to accept Dunlop's approach, presuming that policy formulation—however revealing for the purposes of political or industrial relations studies—can be ignored when analysing the economic impact of the union.

It has usually suggested that unions maximize some relatively simply measurable economic variable; Dunlop himself argued that the union generally tried to fix wages so as to maximize membership. Others have suggested different objectives. To give just a couple of examples, De Menil [10] suggested that it was the difference between total wage income under unionization and wage income under competitive conditions; Farber [13], the expected utility of the median-aged union member. More recently, further sophistication has been introduced into this sort of approach, Oswald [29], for instance, introducing uncertainty into the model, and also contrasting a monopoly model of union behaviour with what he calls a co-operative union model. The former envisages trade unions as maximizing against a given labour demand curve. The latter sees them as choosing a wage and employment combination out of the range that is feasible for the company, which amounts to the union maximizing its utility subject to a minimum profit constraint.

Thus there is a lively debate amongst economists concerning both how the aims of unions are best captured for analytical purposes, and the market context into which to place trade unions. Much that is useful emerges from this approach, but a failure to consider more explicitly the *process* of internal policy formulation may lead economists to miss some interesting phenomena. For example, some industries experienced a squeezing of skill differentials in the early 1970s. There are a whole complex of possible reasons, but one likely contributory factor was a changing balance of power in some unions between the skilled and unskilled. What this illustrates is the possibility that the range of discretion gives unions the ability to concentrate on aims other than those which maximize earnings or some other such variable. In particular, it indicates the possibility that on occasions political aims may predominate and especially the need to preserve internal unity.

4.4.4. Union Strategies

At the outset of negotiations, the union generally makes an initial demand, the employer an initial offer. As negotiations proceed, the union moderates its demand and the employer increases his offer, both sides employing threats and bluffs against the other. If, at the end of the day, there is still a large gap between the parties, then there may be arbitration, conciliation, or mediation provisions, written into the bargaining procedure, which are brought into play. In other cases, the parties may decide to appoint a mediator or an arbitrator on a one-off basis. In the last resort the union will attempt to achieve its aims through force. This may involve a go-slow, work-to-rule and, as an ultimate sanction, a strike. Economists have not had great success in explaining either the pattern of strikes through time or the pattern at any point in time across industries, regions, or occupations. An important reason for this failure is that the branch of economic theory most frequently used as the basis for the analysis of strikes—bargaining theory—is in fact of limited use for the purpose. This is because it generally relies on a very narrow economic concept of rational behaviour, on the assumption of perfect knowledge, and so predicts a unique equilibrium wage outcome. In such circumstances neither side would perceive advantage in a strike. Recently researchers have seen as their way out of this difficulty the construction of models of strike activity which rely upon imperfect information or even irrationality. In other words, they have started to analyse strikes as mistakes.[13] There are two possible types of mistake. The first is an inadequacy in bargaining machinery—in the procedures and rules which help to make an industrial relations system work. The second concerns strategies and actions based on wrong information or where the two sides have received different information flows. That both have some credibility is undeniable. For example, one possible explanation of the rising trend of stoppages in all British industries, except coal-mining, between the mid-1950s and the early 1970s, might well be that as plant bargaining developed in importance, the procedures and rules of the game failed to develop at an equal pace, thus leading to frequent breakdowns of negotiations. As an example of the second type of error, it is arguable that the information flows received by the two bargaining parties are at the maximum divergence just before the turning point of the cycle. As the economy moves towards the boom, the unions will be making demands based upon the good times of the recent past. The employer, by contrast, will realize from his order books that bad times are around the corner. He will tell this to the unions, but they are used to this sort of bluff and may well refuse to be convinced. The two sides will, therefore, be acting on different information flows, and the likelihood of a breakdown of negotiations is high. It may be this which explains the positive correlation of strike activity with the business cycle.

4.4.5. *The Impact of the Union on the Distribution of Income*

Much econometric work has been done recently to try to measure the union/non-union pay differential.[14] Because many workers who are not members of unions are effectively beneficiaries of union agreements, for example a few employees in an otherwise unionized factory, some investigators have estimated a slightly different differential—between those covered by collective agreements and those not. Whichever is measured, there are similar methodological difficulties. Their basis is the problem of evaluating what would have happened in the absence of a union. The ideal would be to have two groups who are identical in all respects—in their skills and qualifications and in the industry and the area of the country in which they work—except that one group is unionized and one is not. Unfortunately such direct observations are not generally available, and therefore econometricians have had to estimate what the non-union wage might have been. This involves estimating an earnings equation, sometimes across industries, sometimes across occupations, and sometimes across individuals, which incorporates a range of variables that help to determine earnings. Whilst the precise formulation of such equations varies from author to author, none of them are fully satisfactory, either in terms

[13] As an example of this type of literature, see Addison and Siebert [2]. Mayhew [26] gives a brief survey of economic work on strike activity.

[14] Parsley [30] gives a review of both the American and British evidence.

of the basic theory or in terms of the amount of the dispersion of earnings 'explained'. Since the union/non-union differential is effectively calculated as a residual, this calculation must be unreliable when the fundamental earnings equation on which it is based is itself subject to doubt. Estimates of the differential have varied very widely, but it seems reasonable to presume that some positive differential does exist. However, a number of mainly American writers have questioned whether this reflects a true gain for union members. One line of attack is to argue, as described on p. 102, that it is only those who are fortunate enough to be in a job when it is first unionized who benefit.

We have seen, however, some objections to this. Duncan and Stafford [11] have a different way of trying to show that there is a reduced net gain from unionization. They argue that the working conditions in a unionized firm are worse than elsewhere. In particular, they mention regimentation and the use of formal rules and procedures. These represent a disutility to workers and at the extreme would cancel out all of the beneficial wage effects. Whether or not they do is an empirical question; and Duncan and Stafford conclude that in fact they are only partially offsetting.

This line of argument is not totally convincing. Even if one accepted the correlation between unionization and the sort of unfavourable working conditions that Duncan and Stafford mention, this is not to argue that there is a *causal* connection. Even if there is one, it might not run from unionization to working conditions, as would be needed for the Duncan and Stafford argument to hold; it might well run in the opposite direction. But there is a more obvious problem with their argument, which is that there are also many favourable non-wage conditions associated with unionization. The union may negotiate greater job security or health and safety at work or many other such benefits for the worker.

In summary, despite the recent American attempts to show that there are offsetting non-wage disadvantages to being a member of a union, it seems reasonable to conclude that in net terms the worker gains an advantage from union membership. However, to state that the union creates a differential between its own members and non-unionized workers is not necessarily to imply that the overall dispersion of earnings is widened. This depends not only on the differential between the two groups but on dispersion within each group. Freeman [14] has provided some evidence from the US to show that *within* the union group, the effect of unionization is to narrow dispersion. *A priori*, therefore, it is impossible to make any generalization about the consequences of unionization for the overall dispersion of earnings.

Given that the union does achieve some advantage for its members, at whose expense is this gain won? It may be at nobody's, if there are matching productivity increases. Generally, economists have argued that the net union impact on productivity is negative. Recently some writers, for example Freeman and Medoff [15], have questioned this. But even they find it hard to argue that the union-induced productivity increases are sufficient to cover the higher pay they get for their members. The union gain, therefore, is likely to be at the expense of either non-union labour or of capital. Unfortunately there has been no adequate work measuring the relative importance of each. But there is a substantial body of evidence measuring the relative shares of capital and labour—profits and wages—in total income.

In both Britain and America the share of profits has declined secularly since about the early 1960s.[15] Until then the share of labour showed no systematic time trend, at least when compared with the last 20 years, netting out effects of the change in the share of the rentier and the self-employed and excluding agriculture and government. Several theories try to explain changes in factor shares, but three of them can be used to provide a sensible picture. These are marginal productivity theory, mark-up pricing theory, and a 'trade union power' theory. If we take the ratio $WL/\Pi K$, where W is the unit wage cost, L is the quantity of labour, Π is in the price per unit of capital, and K is the quantity of capital, then if this ratio remains constant, so do factor shares. If it increases, labour's share increases. The ratio can be expressed as a product of two separate ratios: in other words, $W/\Pi \cdot L/K$. The first term in this is the relative price of the factors of production, labour and capital; the second is the relative quantities of labour and capital.

Marginal productivity theory gives us the concept of the *elasticity of substitution* between factors of production which is defined as a percentage change in relative factor quantities employed consequent upon any percentage change in their relative prices. By definition, if labour's share was constant through a long part of this century then either neither of the two ratios above could have changed, or the elasticity of substitution was equal to one, thus implying that as price ratios changed quantity ratios changed equi-proportionally in the opposite direction.

If the elasticity of substitution was equal to one in the early part of the century, then it is clear that it became less than one thereafter. This is because labour has become more of a fixed factor of production. Given that the elasticity of substitution is less than one, then if W/Π has increased, L/K will have fallen but by proportionately less. Thus their product will have increased, as will labour's share.

It seems plausible to argue that W/Π has indeed increased. A major theory of wage inflation is based on the concept of a target increase in the net real wage (see Henry *et al.* [19]). This implies that unions not only have a reactive role, reacting to preserve living standards when threatened by expectations of rising prices or increased income taxation, but that they also have an initiatory role. Even if expected price and tax changes were zero the union would be pushing for money wage increases to meet an aspiration target for increases in the real wage. Econometric evidence indicates that, at least until recently, the unions' push for this target was subject to an unemployment constraint that was certainly not binding.[16] In other words, a version of 'trade union power' theory explains, at least in part, the rise in W. The power of trade unions was their ability to push hard despite rising unemployment. They could do this because,

[15] A good survey of earlier developments in this area for the United States is Reder [32]. A similar survey for Britain is Phelps Brown [31].

[16] There has recently been some debate as to exactly how binding the demand or unemployment constraint was. The debate continues, but it is plausible to argue that in the private sector at least the constraint had some significant effect.

until the mid-1970s, British governments were quite explicitly committed t
maintaining full employment, and thus a worker could be confident that even
high wage demands led to redundancy in his own firm, there would be plenty c
alternative jobs around.

Mark-up pricing theory helps us to understand why employers have bee
unable to pass increased wages on to prices to their full extent. It predicts tha
employers will mark up prices by as big a percentage as possible over cost;
subject to the constraint of competition. Although domestically industria
concentration has increased, this has been more than offset by the increase
openness of the British economy, not least as a consequence of internationa
agreements. We thus have an explanation for the rise in W/Π and a plausib
hypothesis as to why L/K will have fallen by proportionately less and thus wh
labour's share has increased. The role of the union in this has been to push up V
but it has also had a part in creating the type of labour market and the climat
of opinion which has made labour more a fixed factor, thus reducing th
elasticity of substitution. If this is correct then at least some of the gains to unio
members have been at the expense of capital.

This raises the question of whether in the long term there has been a net *cost* t
union members because of poorer growth resulting from inadequate profits t
finance investment. But this controversial area brings in many other aspects c
the behaviour of the economy, and cannot be tackled on the basis of the mor
microeconomic perspective of this chapter.

4.5. Summary

This chapter started with a very simple model explaining the demand whic
workers face for their labour. The rest of it has illustrated both the need, bu
also the difficulty, of going beyond this to understand the considerations whic
are likely to affect both the demand and supply of labour in practic
Employers will consider a range of costs and prospective returns in determinin
their demand for labour; decisions by employees on whether and to what exten
to seek employment depend on a whole variety of factors; both employers an
employees are involved in, and respond to, influences within the firm whicl
may weaken substantially the impact of the labour market outside the firm
There will often be a substantial amount of indeterminacy in the interaction c
the supply and demand for labour, and this plays a crucial part i
understanding the role of unions in the labour market. In short, while it i
convenient to refer to the supply and demand for labour and their interactio
as a 'labour market', it is clear that it may operate in ways quite different fron
markets for goods and services.

It also emerges that there is still much to be learnt about these matters. This i
important because, as will become clearer later in the book, the behaviour an
interaction of employers and employees is a crucial element in determinin
many important aspects of economic performance, including output, employ
ment, productivity, and inflation. Much of the differences of view that exist o
determination of these economic variables reflect the lack of complet
understanding of the labour market.

Appendix 1

In Figure 4.6, the union (U) as a monopoly supplier, can control demand (D) and thus operates on the marginal revenue curve (MR). It equates marginal revenue with the marginal cost of supplying labour (S). The union would aim, therefore, for a level of employment L_U and a wage of W_U, though it could settle as low as $W\mathrm{min}.U$

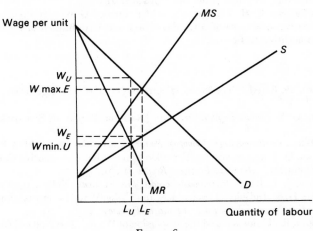

FIG. 4.6

The employer (E), as a monopoly buyer, can control supply and thus operates on the curve marginal to the supply curve (MS). He equates the marginal cost with the marginal revenue of labour (D). The employer, therefore, would aim for employment at L_E, and would offer W_E, though he could afford to offer $W\mathrm{max}.E$. There is, therefore, indeterminacy with respect both to the wage rate and to the level of employment; and thus there is scope for bargaining.

Bibliography

SECTION A

[1] KING, J. E. (ed.). *Readings in Labour Economics* (Oxford University Press, 1980).
A selection of readings covering the issues raised in this chapter, and many more besides. Excellent introductions to each section by the editor.
[2] ADDISON, J. T. and SIEBERT, W. J. *The Market for Labor: An Analytical Treatment* (Goodyear, 1979).
A very comprehensive textbook. Rather difficult but worth the effort.
[3] DOERINGER, P. and PIORE, M. *Internal Labor Markets and Manpower Analysis* (Heath, 1971).
An influential book on an important theme of this chapter—internal labour markets.

[4] BAIN, G. (ed.). *Industrial Relations in Britain* (Blackwell, 1983).
Contains a section on labour economics. It also has a rich array of detail on the role and purpose of unions, and on the collective bargaining structure.
[5] ATKINSON, A. B. *The Economics of Inequality*, 2nd edn. (Oxford University Press, 1983).
A clearly written text on a wide range of distributional issues.
[6] CAIN, G. 'The Challenge of Segmented Labor Market Theories to Orthodox Theory,*Journal of Economic Literature* (1976), 1215–57.
A survey article covering many of the 'alternative' developments. Much has happened in this sphere since its publication, but still worth reading.
[7] PHELPS BROWN, E. H. *The Inequality of Pay* (Oxford University Press, 1977).
A comprehensive treatment of wage dispersion and pay differentials. Covers many countries in addition to Britain.

SECTION B

[8] ATKINSON, A. B. (ed.). *The Personal Distribution of Income* (George Allen and Unwin, 1976).
[9] BECKER, G. S. *Human Capital*, 2nd edn. (National Bureau of Economic Research, 1975).
[10] DE MENIL, G. *Bargaining: Monopoly Power Versus Union Power* (MIT Press, 1971).
[11] DUNCAN, G. J. and STAFFORD, F. P. 'Do Union Members Receive Compensating Wage Differentials?', *American Economic Review* (1980), 335–71.
[12] DUNLOP, J. T. *Wage Determination Under Trade Unions* (Kelley, 1950).
[13] FARBER, H. S. 'Individual Preferences and Union Wage Determination: The Case of United Mine Workers', *Journal of Political Economy* (1978), 923–42.
[14] FREEMAN, R. 'Unionism and the Dispersion of Wages', *Industrial and Labor Relations Review* (1980), 3–23.
[15] FREEMAN, R. B. and MEDOFF, J. 'The Two Faces of Unionism', *Public Interest* (Fall, 1979).
[16] GOLDBERGER, A. S. 'Heritability', *Economica* (1979), 327–47.
[17] GREENHALGH, C. A. and MAYHEW, K. 'Labour Supply in Great Britain: Theory and Evidence', in Hornstein *et al.* [20].
[18] HECKMAN, J. J. *et al.* 'Empirical Evidence on Static Labour Supply Models: A Survey of Recent Developments', in Hornstein *et al.* [20].
[19] HENRY, S. G. B., SAWYER, M. C., and SMITH, P. 'Models of Inflation in the United Kingdom', *National Institute Economic Review* (Aug. 1976), 60–71.
[20] HORNSTEIN, Z., GRICE, J., and WEBB, A. (eds.). *The Economics of the Labour Market* (HMSO, 1981).
[21] KILLINGSWORTH, M. R. *Labor Supply* (Cambridge University Press, 1983).
[22] LAYARD, R. (ed.). *Journal of Political Economy*, Supplement (Oct. 1979).
[23] LESLIE, D. 'Hours and Overtime in British and U.S. Manufacturing', *British Journal of Industrial Relations* (1976), 194–201.
[24] MACKAY, D. I., BODDY, D., BRACK, J., DIACK, J. A., and JONES, N. *Labour Markets Under Different Employment Conditions* (George Allen and Unwin, 1971).
[25] MAYHEW, K. 'Earnings Dispersion in Local Labour Markets', *Oxford Bulletin of Economics and Statistics* (May 1977).
[26] —— —— 'Economists and Strikes', *Oxford Bulletin of Economics and Statistics* (1979), 1–19.
[27] MAYHEW, K. and ROSEWELL, B. C. 'Labour Market Segmentation in Britain', *Oxford Bulletin of Economics and Statistics* (1979), 81–115.
[28] OI, W. 'Labor as a Quasi-fixed Factor of Production', *Journal of Political Economy* (1962), 538–55.

[29] Oswald, A. J. 'Uncertainty and the Trade Union', *Economics Letters* (1982), 105–11.

[30] Parsley, C. J. 'Labor Unions and Wages: a Survey', *Journal of Economic Literature* (1980), 1–31.

[31] Phelps Brown, E. H. *Pay and Profits* (Manchester University Press, 1968).

[32] Reder, M. W. 'Alternative Theories of Labor's Share', in Abramovitz, M. (eds.), *The Allocation of Economic Resources* (Stanford University Press, 1959).

[33] Ross, A. M. *Trade Union Wage Policy* (University of California Press, 1948).

[34] Schultz, J. W. 'Investment in Human Capital', *American Economic Review* (1961), 1–17.

[35] Stigler, G. 'Information in the Labor Market', *Journal of Political Economy* (1962), 94–105.

[36] Taubman, P. J. *Income and Distribution and Redistribution* (Addison-Wesley, 1978).

[37] Thurow, L. *Generating Inequality* (Basic Books, 1975).

5

The Domestic Economy[1]

D. G. MAYES

5.1. An Outline of the Economy

5.1.1. The Overall Structure of the Economy

The previous three chapters have analysed the behaviour of three of the main economic groups in the private sector of the economy, namely people as consumers, people as employees, and companies. The purpose of the current chapter is to fit these parts, along with others, into a framework within which we can consider the UK economy as a whole. Economic activity takes the form of production by economic *agents* and *transactions* among them. These agents are households (which may be just single individuals); firms, from the self-employed person to the multi-million pound multinational company, whether in private or public industry, spanning the whole range of industrial, commercial, and financial activity; and government, both local and central. The transactions between them take the form of exchanges or transfers of goods, services, and financial claims. Financial claims are such things as saving certificates and stocks and shares, and notes, coins, and bank or building society deposits which the holder is entitled to use for transactions. In the typical transaction one person *exchanges* money in order to purchase goods or services from another. But exchanges can be of the form of a swap, one set of goods for another set of goods, or one claim for another, e.g. buying government stock with a cheque. Other transactions involve only a *transfer* from one agent to another without a reciprocal action to balance it. In their simplest form these would be gifts, but other transactions where any element of exchange is at best indirect, such as the payment of taxes or the receipt of social security benefits are also described as transfers.

In order to provide a clear explanation of economic behaviour in an economy out of the multitude of transactions which are taking place it is necessary to group them into categories of activity which between them cover the range of actions which economic agents can take. The three groups of agents we have distinguished: households, firms, and the government undertake a sequence of actions which are set out in a stylized diagrammatic form in Figure 5.1.

The primary activity in the economy is usually thought of as the *production of* goods and services. This is undertaken by people working for firms or for

[1] The helpful comments of John Black on chapters 5, 12 and 13 are gratefully acknowledged.

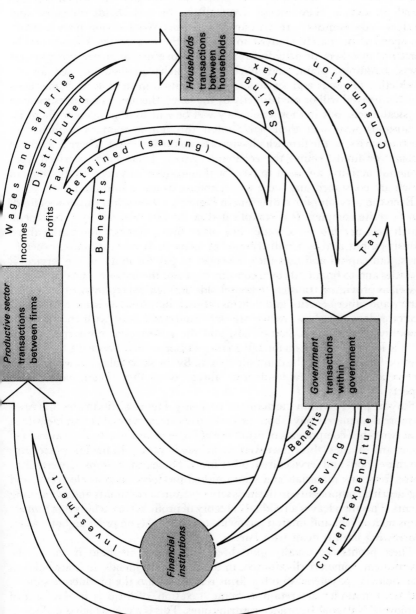

FIG. 5.1. The Flow of Funds in the Domestic Economy.

government and its enterprises, or indeed for themselves, through 'self employment'. For this employment people are paid an *income* which they can spend or save as they choose. Expenditure by households on goods and services—consumption—returns straight to firms. What income households do not spend immediately is saved to spend in the future. These funds can be borrowed by others, principally firms and the government, to invest in physical assets, buildings, plant, and machinery, which can then be used for the production of goods and services for consumption in the future. Some funds which are saved will be used directly by the savers themselves for investment in physical assets, but in most cases they will be lent by the savers to financial institutions who will then lend, often through a complex sequence of intermediaries, to the firm which wishes to do the investing. There is a flow of income, or funds, round the economic system. These funds, derived from economic activity, are used to pay for the products of that activity, some of which are consumed and some which endure as assets into the future.

Even the very simplified diagram in Figure 5.1 shows that this flow of funds can be quite complex. It is complicated in the first instance by government which acts not just as a trader like other firms, through the nationalized industries, but also as a redistributor of incomes. It taxes incomes, expenditures, and capital and uses these revenues to pay for much of the services it provides and to finance its own consumption and the incomes of its employees as well as providing transfers to households through unemployment, supplementary and other benefits, and to firms through industrial assistance. What the diagram does not show, as we are only concerned here with the domestic economy, is that firms, households, and the government use some of their income for expenditure on foreign goods—imports—and hence the further use of some funds is lost to the domestic system. By the same token, however, firms receive an inflow of new funds from abroad when they obtain payment for exports.

Staying purely within the domestic economy, Figure 5.1 indicates that firms do more than merely pay labour and sell goods and services. We can identify at least two other components of firms' use of funds in addition to the payment of wages and salaries (three if we were to include imports). In the first place firms purchase goods and services from other firms. These transactions between firms range from raw materials and semi-finished products, such as electronic and engineering components, to business services from accountants and advertising agents. This then leaves a residual category of profit, if we exclude more minor items such as rent and interest payments to households on previous borrowing. (Borrowing itself is dealt with later.)

These profits are usually split three ways: some are paid in tax to the government, some are distributed, in the form of dividends, to households as shareholders (payments to other firms remain within the productive sector) and the remainder are retained. Some 'taxation' of firms is in the form of employers' National Insurance contributions. This is a cost which is deducted, in accounting terms, before calculation of profits. It is not shown separately to avoid confusing the diagram. (In the same way, employees' National Insurance contributions and personal income tax are paid by firms directly to the government through the Pay As You Earn system and are never actually received by households. However, some income taxation is not deducted 'at source' in this manner and it is therefore all shown as if it were paid by households to the government.)

The incomes paid out by firms (and by the government in its role as producer) for use of labour (wages and salaries) or for the use of capital (interest, dividends, and rent) flow on round the circle shown in Figure 5.1, with all spending decisions, either on consumption or on investment goods, eventually reaching the productive sector again. The amount of funds and the way in which they flow round the system depend upon the decisions of economic agents: firms in their production and employment decisions, households through their choice of job and the determination of the rate of pay, government through taxation and expenditure, and households again through their tastes and consumption patterns. Changes in these decisions will affect the pattern of flows. There could, for example, be a stimulus from outside the economy in the form of an increase in the demand for British goods. Provided firms could increase production they would receive an increased inflow of funds which would flow back down the chain of production in the productive sector. It would result in an increased outflow of wages and salaries to pay for the labour to make the goods. These increased wages and salaries would then be saved or spent on consumption. Consumption provides a further increase in demand for goods and services and hence inflow for the productive sector, thereby starting another cycle through the system. These decisions and the responses to stimuli form the heart of macroeconomic enquiry.

In grouping and adding together transactions, the responses of individual economic agents to various stimuli quickly become blurred. For example, consumers' expenditure on food is little affected by interest rates as such expenditure tends to be made directly from current income. Expenditure on motor cars on the other hand is substantially affected by interest rates and hire-purchase terms, as virtually nobody earns enough to buy a car by a simple cash transaction out of his pocket. Previous income which has been saved has to be used, and in many cases agreements to borrow sums of money to be repaid in instalments over the future, with interest, have to be entered into.

If all consumers' expenditure is aggregated it will appear that changes in interest rates have little effect on activity, whereas if one disaggregated further it would be seen that some parts of the economy were substantially affected, with an interest rate fall leading to an increased demand for various consumer durables which in turn will stimulate their output and hence incomes and employment. Since, to follow the motor car example a little further, car production is concentrated in a relatively small number of areas, it is important for regional employment and social policy to be able to trace through the effects of such an initial stimulus.

The highly aggregative perspective also gives inadequate recognition of the crucial role of financial intermediaries in the economic system in enabling transactions to take place at all. For although we are discussing a system of economic activity which is 'real'—the goods produced do exist, even if for only a short time in the case of certain consumption goods such as bread or milk—

the transactions occurring in the system for the most part involve the exchange or transfer of financial claims all of which stem from the activity of some financial intermediary, be it a bank or a building society or a stockbroker. In the simplest case, where notes and coins change hands, the intermediary only acted as the provider of the cash in the first place. However, for more than half of all households the normal way of undertaking transactions entails first that all (or in some cases only a proportion of) income is paid directly into a bank, crediting the householder's account at that bank. The householder then either draws out cash from the bank to spend, or writes cheques on his account whereby the bank transfers money from the householder's account to the seller's account, which is typically held in a different bank, by means of book-keeping adjustments in both banks. These financial transactions are highly developed in the UK economy and involve many different financial intermediaries. This movement or 'flow' of funds in the economy is extremely important in enabling economic activity to take place, and forms an integral part of the working of the economic system. Indeed it might almost be viewed as the oil which enables the wheels of economic activity in turn.

A key facet of this activity lies in the ability of financial intermediaries to allow 'idle' funds which are not needed by the holder to be used by another economic agent who wishes to undertake economic activity but has no such funds. Most households do not spend their incomes immediately they receive them, even if they spend them all by the time they receive their next income payment. If during that period they keep that income as cash in their pocket then no one else can use it. If, however, they lend it, typically by leaving it in a bank or putting it in a building society, that money can be re-lent to somebody else who can then use it to undertake transactions. The lender in the meantime normally receives an interest payment from the borrower for the privilege of using funds to which he would not otherwise have a title. Money lent to banks in the form of deposits on current account does not usually earn a rate of interest, but this is normally thought to be offset by the services that the bank provides to the lender 'free'—security, chequeing facilities, ease of access, etc.

Since the bank does not have to match the individual lender with the individual borrower it can lend money for long periods of time even if each individual deposit is only made for a short period of time. Although lending by households to financial institutions may partly go to other households to finance additional consumption through overdrafts and instalment credit, or to finance house purchase through mortgages, lending to firms also occurs and helps to finance investment. It is important not to confuse two senses of the word 'investment'. In the economic sense, investment is the expenditure on new physical assets which will endure into the next time period, while investment in the financial sense is the purchase of a claim, for example a share in a firm or a building society. Therefore, in the economic sense this financial investment is viewed as *saving*—the use of income not spent on consumption.

Some elements of these more disaggregated issues are examined in some detail later on. For the moment the explanation of activity in this chapter remains highly aggregative, and deliberately so, in order to concentrate attention on the overall view, thus inevitably losing some of the richness of individual behaviour. But it is only through such an aggregate perspective that one can hope to understand the main forces affecting the economic system as a whole.

5.1.2. *The National Accounts*

Total economic activity in the UK is measured by a system of National Accounts. While economic activity in total can be thought of as the sum of goods and services produced in the economy during a particular time period, it is clear from Figure 5.1 that this total activity can be measured from two other points of view, income and expenditure. The value of production can readily be equated to what is spent in purchasing it. These inflows of funds to the firm are then by definition either paid out to households in the form of wages and salaries or kept as income for the firm in the form of profits. We are clearly interested not just in total activity, but in the components of each of these three accounts in their own right in order to study the behaviour of all groups of economic agents and their contribution to determining economic activity.

However, for the income, product, and expenditure aggregates to be equal in total, intermediate transactions between firms must not be double-counted. For example, the value of a final product sold to a household, such as a television, incorporates the value of all its components, although these may have been the product of a different firm. To avoid double-counting the economic value of a firm's product or activity is the total value of its output *less* the value of inputs it purchased from other firms.

Thus there is a clear distinction between the total *value of transactions* in the economy on the one hand, and the *value of economic activity* on the other. A retailer in selling an article is himself only contributing one part of all the inputs of economic activity that have gone to make up the final product. He is not the sole producer. There has in most cases been a chain of production starting with the provider of the raw materials and progressing through a series of stages of manufacture from rough castings to components to the finished article, and then on through the wholesaler and the retailer and only then to the consumer himself, each firm adding something to the product, even if it is just its transportation from the point of production to the point of sale. (The same amount of activity could or course take place within a single firm if it happened to control all the stages of production without any transactions occurring until final sale.) Thus the total value of all transactions will be many times the final value of the economic activity as represented by the product. In a similar sense the sale of an existing asset from one owner to another is a transaction, but it does not alter the value of the assets of the country. In such cases, the economic activity which takes place relates only to the value of the services that the seller or his intermediary, say an auctioneer, provides in undertaking the sale. Thus the sum of productive activity in any time period is the value of the goods and services produced during that period where the goods and services are valued only once. In principle this would be by valuing them only when they are finally completed, i.e. when they are purchased as consumption or investment goods or services.

In this way production and expenditure could be measured identically.

However, the firm may not keep any record of whether an individual sale is to final rather than intermediate demand. Hence the total is found by summing the value added to the product by *each* producer, i.e. the value of output less the value of inputs purchased from other producers, a sum which each producer can compute fairly readily. The sum of value-added over *all* stages of production is thus equal to the value of final product and is not altered by changes in the number of different firms involved in the production process if the final value is the same.

The value-added of the firm is what is not paid to other producers and hence comprises wages and salaries, which is the only remaining cost of production, and profits. As is shown in Figure 5.1, wages and salaries and profits form total final incomes and hence in turn the value of activity measured as the sum of incomes is equal to the value measured as the sum of production and as the sum of final expenditure.

Having established the equivalence of production, expenditure, and income measures for valuing economic activity, we can now set out the form of the published National Accounts, which provide the data which form the basis of analysis and explanation of economic activity in the United Kingdom.

In talking about economic activity the emphasis in terms of the words used is on production, with the aggregate of productive activity within the economy being labelled *Gross Domestic Product* (GDP). This is the sum of finished goods and services produced within the economy. However, the emphasis in the published National Accounts, which are summarized in Table 5.1, is on incomes and expenditures, where the incomes are the incomes earned in the production of the goods and services which constitute GDP and the expenditures are those made on the same goods and services, as explained in the previous section.

The build-up of GDP from the point of view of expenditure is given on the left-hand side of Table 5.1 and that from incomes on the right-hand side. The table follows the nomenclature and format of the accounts as set out in their source, *National Income and Expenditure*, usually referred to as the Blue Book. This entails that the expressions used are sometimes slightly different from those in common use in order to make them more accurate descriptions of the activity involved. The accounts shown come from the first two tables in the Blue Book (Tables 1.1 and 1.2). Expenditure is here shown on two bases as in the Blue Book. These are referred to as expenditure at 'market prices' and at 'factor cost'. Income is shown here on only one base, namely 'after providing for stock appreciation'; it is however also available in the Blue Book 'before providing for stock appreciation'.

What distinguishes these different bases? We first look at the expenditure tables. Under normal circumstances expenditures are valued at the prices at which transactions take place—at *market prices*—but these prices do not indicate what the producers actually receive for themselves because many goods and services are taxed, principally by VAT and excise duties, and some others are subsidized. But taxes and subsidies are not part of production; they merely redistribute the incomes generated. It is therefore the practice of the National Accounts, in trying to estimate the value of productive activity, to value both

TABLE 5.1. *Income and Expenditure Accounts for the UK, 1982*
(£ million)

Expenditure	at market prices	at factor cost	Income	after providing for stock appreciation
Consumers' expenditure	167,128	136,538	Income from employment	155,133
General government final consumption	60,082	55,624	Income from self-employment(c)	19,738
Gross domestic fixed-capital formation	42,172	37,776	Gross trading profits of companies (c), (d)	30,279
Value of physical increase in stocks and work in progress	−1,162		Gross trading surplus of public corporations (c)	8,662
Total domestic expenditure	268,220	229,938	Gross trading surplus of general government enterprises (c)	18
Exports of goods and services	73,128	69,780	Rent (c)	16,166
Total Final Expenditure (TFE)	341,348	299,718	Imputed charge for consumption of non-trading capital	2,507
less Imports of goods and services	−67,165(a)	−67,165		
Gross Domestic Product (GDP)	274,183(b)	232,553	**Gross Domestic Product** (income based)	232,503
Net property income from abroad	1,577	1,577	Residual error	50
Gross National Product (GNP) (at market prices)	275,760		**Gross Domestic Product** (expenditure based)	232,553
less Adjustment to factor cost		−41,630		
Gross National Product (GNP) (at factor cost)		234,130		
less Capital consumption		−33,057		
National Income (i.e. net national product)		201,073		

Notes:
(a) Excluding taxes on expenditure levied on imports.
(b) Including taxes on expenditure levied on imports.
(c) Before providing for depreciations.
(d) Including financial institutions.

Source: *National Income and Expenditure, 1983.*

incomes and expenditures without allowing taxes and subsidies to affect the figures. Expenditures are therefore measured after tax payments on them have been deducted and subsidies added on, to reflect the actual production cost, and are then said to be at *factor cost*, the second column in the Table 5.1. It is only recently that the individual items of expenditure have been shown at factor cost in summary form. In older editions of the Blue Book only the first column is shown, with a single lump-sum 'adjustment to factor cost' subtracted near the bottom of the column. Indeed it is still the case that initial estimates of expenditure are published only in terms of market prices and thus any analysis of the economy which relies on recent quarterly data, as, for example, do all the main forecasting models, will be in terms of market prices, with only the single adjustment.

The distinction between market prices and factor cost is not necessary in the income-based table of the Blue Book as incomes are generated only from the actual production occurring and the figures will already be on the basis of factor cost. Also, in keeping with the principle that taxes and subsidies are only redistributions, incomes are valued before deduction of income tax, corporation tax, and other taxes on incomes and without including transfer incomes derived from the government in the form of unemployment benefit, supplementary benefit, old-age pensions, and other such grants.

The specific items of expenditure on final goods and services set out in the left-hand side of Table 5.1 are derived from the expenditure flows accruing to firms in Figure 5.1. Ignoring intermediate flows, we can see that total expenditure by people within the economy is composed of consumers' expenditure (C), which represents well over half the total of all expenditure; government consumption spending (G), for example on current expenditure on the health services, education, the police force, etc. (denoted as 'general government final consumption'); the investment component of government spending in Figure 5.1 is, in the accounts, added into the next item in Table 5.1, namely fixed investment (denoted as 'gross domestic fixed capital formation') in plant, machinery, equipment, and buildings, including housing in both the public and private sectors (I_F).

The next item is stockbuilding (I_S) (denoted as the 'value of the physical increase in stocks and work in progress'). At first sight it appears strange to include stockbuilding because, by definition, these are products which have *not* been sold and on which therefore there has been no expenditure. But they have been produced and those who made them have received an income. Stocks are therefore regarded in effect as having been 'bought by the company from itself as an 'investment', or means of generating funds in the future. This enables the three forms of accounts—product, income, and expenditure—to remain consistent. When the stocks are sold, they count as expenditure under one of the other heads, but, being a reduction in stocks, count as an offsetting negative amount under the stockbuilding heading. No double-counting is involved therefore, nor is there any problem from price inflation raising the value of stocks between their acquisition and their sale, as the change is measured in volume not value terms.

The sum of these components gives total expenditure by people *within* the economy. However, *Total Final Expenditure* (TFE) also includes what is spent by foreign countries on UK goods and services, namely exports (X). This new total still differs from GDP because TFE includes expenditure on goods and services produced abroad, imports (M). GDP, which only measures activity in the UK, does not. Thus

$$GDP = C + G + I_F + I_S + X - M \qquad (1)$$

where all are valued at factor cost. If the components of expenditure are valued at market prices then we have to subtract a factor cost adjustment (FCA) to bring the right-hand side into line with GDP at factor cost. Both formulations are to found later in the book. For simplicity, in this chapter we assume that the expenditure components are already valued at factor cost, and no adjustment is therefore necessary. Table 5.1 goes on to set out two further economic aggregates which are wide used, *Gross National Product* (GNP) and *National Income*.

The conceptual difference between GDP and GNP is quite simple: the former is the product of the country and the latter the product of the residents of the country. These differ because some individuals and companies are resident in the UK but receive income, in the form of rents, interest payments, profits, and dividends, from abroad. Similarly some such incomes will be earned in the UK but paid to people and companies abroad. For the UK the former is normally larger and so GNP is GDP *plus* the balance of these two income flows. This latter flow is referred to as net 'property' income because it is composed of incomes derived from owning real or financial property. Payments for goods and services from other countries have already been included under exports and imports.

The final item in the expenditure-based table is normally referred to (bearing in mind the equivalence of expenditure and income) as national income. This is only ever considered on a factor cost basis, and measures the value of production of the economy *net* of the assets of the country which have been used up during the year, i.e. net of capital consumption as measured by depreciation. This means that the investment figure in this total is measured net and not gross of depreciation and hence represents the change in the value of the stock of capital assets over the year.

The right-hand side of Table 5.1 considers GDP from the point of view of the sum of incomes. In general terms it covers the income-generating flows emanating from the productive sector in Figure 5.1, i.e., different forms of wages and salaries, rents, and various elements of profits (surpluses) gross of, and therefore including, interest payments. (The other two outflows in Figure 5.1—intermediate goods and services and imported inputs—are, as in the expenditure-based calculation, excluded.) The first four items in the income table are self-explanatory. In the fifth item, 'general government enterprises' are simply those parts of government which operate as trading concerns but are not specifically set up as public corporations.

Before consider the other items, the heading of the column of figures 'after providing for stock appreciation' needs explaining. If an item has been made in one period but sold in the next, having been added to stocks in the interim, its actual sale price may be higher than the price it would have fetched had it been sold immediately in the first period. This difference is known as 'stock appreciation' and unless it is deducted from incomes, the sum of accumulated incomes will, in a world of price inflation, exceed the sum of accumulated production. (Stockbuilding in the expenditure table also excludes stock appreciation so that both methods of calculating GDP are consistent.)

The two other items in the main income table are rent and one with the complex title 'imputed charge for consumption of non-trading capital', which is the benefit which non-profit making institutions and the government derive from physical capital which they use in the course of activities that do not involve commercial trading. This follows from the concept that if a capital asset has positive value then it must generate a flow of services as time passes. Thus housing generates a valuable service in each year, which in some cases can be valued easily because the services are sold—i.e. tenants pay rent to landlords. Owner-occupiers on the other hand derive similar benefits from their houses but do not make actual payments. 'Rent' therefore includes an element of *imputed* income for owner-occupiers and the 'imputed charge for consumption of non-trading capital' covers the other cases where no charge is actually made. Of course, to make the accounts balance, consumers' expenditure also includes imputed payments by non-profit making institutions for the capital benefits they receive, and imputed payments by owner-occupiers for the use of their housing. The government's imputed payments for the benefits from its capital are included in G. These adjustments appear rather tortuous, but there would be a clear distortion in the National Accounts if the benefits of, for example, housing were included when paid for by tenants but not when received by owner-occupiers.

The total of all these items is once again Gross Domestic Product. It is already at factor cost and no deduction has been made for depreciation of capital.

Since incomes are summed independently of expenditures, excluding the imputed items we have just discussed, the two sums will only be identical if they are exact, or by chance. Since considerable estimation is involved in the calculation of the various component items—it would be totally infeasible to record every transaction—one would not expect the two accounts to have the same totals except by chance. The requirement for usefulness of the components is that the size of the discrepancy must not be so large that it calls the quality of the components into question. The discrepancy shown for 1982 the 'residual error', is less than 1 per cent of GDP and is usually less than 2 per cent. The error is entered in the income account for convenience and the expenditure-based measure used in the further calculation of GNP and national income. However, for other purposes economists use whichever of the three measures of GDP seems most appropriate for the issue in question, or indeed some weighted average of the three.

An increase in GDP from one year to the next can reflect either an increase in prices or an increase in the volume of activity, or both. To distinguish these changes in GDP are usually measured in *real* terms, i.e. having allowed for the effect of inflation, and GDP in a given year is often expressed as the value it *would* have if prices had not changed since a previous base date. Currently real GDP is expressed *at 1980 prices*. Though the specific calculations are very detailed, the principle is straightforward; nominal GDP in a given year (i.e. GDP at the then current level of prices) is divided by, or *deflated* by, a price index, often known as a *deflator*, the value of which reflects the inflation which has occurred since the chosen base date. (See p. 48 for discussion of the Retail Price Index.) The price index used for GDP is known as the *GDP deflator* and represents the price of a weighted basket of all the main goods and services which go to make up GDP.

Real GDP per head of the population is frequently used as the best measure of living standards in an economy. There are dangers in this. Many important factors affecting living standards, for example work done in the home, voluntary work, etc., do not enter the National Accounts. Some important public services, for example health and education, can only be entered in the accounts as the value of the resources they use, but may be more or less valuable. The degree of equality or inequality in the *distribution* of income will be important, as indeed will the distribution of expenditure as between consumer goods, welfare services, defence expenditure, etc. In the accounts, each is entered either at the market value at which it is exchanged, or, where no market-determined value exists, for example in public health provision, defence, etc., at the value of the inputs used. But provided these factors do not change rapidly then, over significant periods of time, real GDP per head is probably the best systematic measure. Similarly it can be used for international comparisons of living standards provided that the factors mentioned above are not too dissimilar.

5.1.3. Further Consideration of Output

The economic activities covered in the two Blue Book tables are classified in two specific ways, namely according to the type of expenditure and the form of income generated. But for many purposes it is useful to have a *sectoral* breakdown of output.

Because production is heterogeneous, output is recorded in terms of index numbers, thus permitting the aggregation of gallons of liquid, feet of film, tons of steel, thousands of televisions, the monetary measurement of other items, and so on. The individual categories are combined by a series of weights, shown for aggregate industries in table 5.2, from which it is immediately clear that in 1980 the share of manufacturing in output was only 26·6 per cent (lower still in 1982). Indeed industrial production, a more detailed breakdown of which is given on the right-hand side of the table, is only 40 per cent of total output, smaller in size than the total of the service sectors.

The use of activity in a fixed particular year, such as 1980 in the published indices, as the basis for the weights for five successive years can give a somewhat misleading picture in aggregate if in the meantime there are major changes in economic structure in the UK. The exploitation of North Sea oil is the most dramatic example. Oil and gas production had a share of 0·027 per cent in industrial output in 1975 and 12·3 per cent in 1981 (in constant prices). However, the move out of manufacturing is also of substantial importance.

TABLE 5.2. Index Numbers of Output at Constant Factor Cost, 1982
(1980 = 100)

All output	Weight per 1,000 in 1980	Output in 1982 where 1980 = 100	Production industries	Weight per 1,000	1982
Agriculture, forestry, and fishing	22	112·5	Energy and water supply		
Production			Coal and coke	41	93·2
Energy and water supply	95	110·1	Extraction of mineral oil and natural gas	123	125·7
Manufacturing	266	92·4	Mineral oil processing	15	92·8
Total production	361	97·1	Other energy and water supply	85	98·6
Construction	63	91·4	Total energy and water supply	264	110·1
Total production and construction	424	96·2	Manufacturing		
Distribution, hotels and catering, repairs	128	99·3	Metals	25	103·7
Transport and Communication			Other minerals and mineral products	41	95·0
Transport	46	96·8	Chemicals and man-made fibres	56	99·9
Communication	26	104·9	Metal goods not elsewhere specified	45	93·5
Total transport and communication	72	99·6	Food, drink, and tobacco	99	98·9
Banking, finance, insurance, business services, and leasing	116	110	Mechanical engineering	106	90·6
Ownership of dwellings	62	103	Electrical and instrument engineering	95	96·0
Public administration, national defence, and compulsory social security	69	98	Motor vehicles and parts	42	81·6
			Textiles	24	87·3
			Clothing, footwear, and leather	28	88·4
Education and health services	87	101	Paper, printing, and publishing	68	90·7
Other services	61	94	Other manufacturing industries	58	88·0
Adjustment for financial services	-41	110	Total manufacturing	736	92·4
Gross Domestic Product	1,000	99·0	Total production	1,000	97·1
			Total production and construction		96·2

Because of the complexity of the productive process a detailed analysis of inter-industry linkages takes place only every four to six years and takes many years to process. While it is relatively easy for industries to identify what commodities they have each bought and sold it is much more difficult to estimate the specific links between them, i.e. what inputs of commodities are used in the production of other commodities and what purchases are made by one industry from another industry. As a result we have a very inaccurate view of the consequences for the whole range of industries of changes in the pattern of final demand. The summary description of the interrelationships, periodically prepared, is based on a matrix, with all industries listed along both axes. The intersection of any row and column gives the flow of goods and services from the industry in that column to the industry in that row. It is then possible to calculate what inputs are required *per unit of output* of each industry by dividing through each column of inputs by the output of the same industry. This creates what is known as the *input–output matrix* and from this basis we can calculate for any postulated output of one industry the inputs required from all other industries, provided the structure described by the input–output matrix does not change. This is a very strong assumption and patterns tend to change quite substantially as time passes. The most recent input–output tables are for 1979 (*Business Monitor*, PA1004), published in 1983, and hence may be out of date for industries where there has been substantial technical change.

5.2. Money in the Economy

5.2.1. The Functions of Money

All the flows of income we have considered thus far have been measured in 'money' terms, but we have not actually discussed the role of money as such in the economic system. Money is the term used for certain types of financial assets (see below). These endure from one period to the next. Therefore, when money is used as a means of payment in transactions, it is not used up in the transaction. Thus the same *stock* of money can be passed from agent to agent in the course of the *flow* of transactions. (See p. 19 for further discussion of this distinction.) the more rapidly money changes hands the greater the value of transactions that can occur in a particular time period from a given stock of money.

Money has three main functions: it acts as a *unit of account*, in terms of which the value of assets and transactions can be measured; it is a *means of payment* for goods and services, wages paid, etc.; and it is a *financial asset*, acting as a 'store of value'. Given these functions, there are two main motives for economic agents to hold money: (i) for transactions, (ii) as an asset or 'speculation'. The asset-holding motive is viewed as speculative because agents have a choice of a range of financial and real assets in which they can hold their wealth, of which money is only one. The choice of assets is affected by three main factors: (i) the expected rate of return, (ii) risk, (iii) liquidity. *The rate of return* on an asset is the difference between its value at the end of a period and its value at the beginning, usually expressed as a percentage per year. Thus a pound note has the same nominal value as time goes by and hence a zero rate of return.

However, once money is lent from one agent to another it is usual for the lender to receive a rate of interest. If the financial claim received in return for the money has a fixed face value, like a deposit with the Post Office, the rate of return and the rate of interest are one and the same thing. Physical assets—houses, pictures, etc.—on the other hand do not attract a rate of interest but they do have a rate of return (which may be negative) because their price changes. Other financial assets, like government bonds, have both a flexible price and a rate of interest and hence the return is a combination of the two (as is explained in more detail below).

Clearly any asset which does not have both a known future value and a known rate of interest over the future is the subject of *risk*. In general, higher expected rates of return have to be offered to induce people to hold riskier assets. However, assets like money which are 'riskless' in nominal terms have an element of risk in real terms. Because the rate of price inflation is variable and not know with certainty the purchasing power of money in the future is unknown. Hence rates of return and rates of interest are often compared in real terms, i.e. net of the expected rate of price inflation. A riskless asset in real terms is one whose value is linked to the rate of price inflation.

The concept of *liquidity* is also related to the rate of return. The liquidity of an asset reflects the ease with which it can be turned into final means of payment without loss, with the implication that cash, being a means of payment, is perfectly liquid. There are both monetary costs and time delays in turning other assets into cash so that for example insurance policies are very illiquid assets while cheque accounts are highly liquid. Overall, there will be a range of financial and real assets, each with a return, degree of risk (nominal and real), and liquidity.

We have used the word 'money' as if it had a clear and simple definition; however, many different definitions of what constitutes money are used in practice. Taking its 'means of payment' function as a criterion, it is evident that the sum total of notes and coin in circulation is part of the money supply. So too is the total of current accounts with commercial banks, since these, which change hands when a bank honours cheques drawn on such accounts, are fully accepted means of payment. But should deposit accounts with the commercial banks, or share accounts in building societies, also be included? Such accounts differ from 'pure' money in bearing interest and sometimes in being subject to restrictions (in the form of the requirement to give notice of withdrawal) which mean they are not completely liquid. On the other hand, these accounts can in practice be drawn upon, at least up to a point, quite freely and can thus effectively serve as a means of payment in Britain, therefore, a number of different measures have generally been used, some narrow, including only totally liquid assets, others more broad and including still highly but less than totally liquid assets. (See p. 305 *et seq* for a full definition of them all.)

The ambiguity of a range of definitions may seem rather out of place given the relative simplicity of the definitions of the income flows we outlined earlier, but it reflects the inevitable difficulties which revolve around the role of money in the economy. On the other hand money is used for more than one purpose, while on the other many other financial assets are close substitutes for it.

Narrow definitions exclude some assets used for transactions, but if the definition is broadened to account for the full stock of what is used for transactions, then the value of assets included which are held for non-transactions purposes rises as well. In short, there is no clear division between money and non-money.

5.2.2. The Role of Banks

Much of the difficulty comes from the special role of banks as opposed to other financial intermediaries, such as building societies, in the creation of money. If money is defined purely in terms of notes and coin then it is physically held by some economic agent or other. As soon as bank accounts are brought into the definition the problem becomes more complicated. To take the simplest case, if a person pays cash into his bank the bank has both a new asset—the notes and coin paid in—and a new liability—it owes the customer that amount of money and has to stand ready to pay it on demand. The customer no longer has the cash asset but he does have the equivalent amount in his bank account, which is just another form in which he can hold his asset. This bank deposit is his asset, but the bank's liability. In the transaction no new money came into the hands of the public. The gain in terms of the bank deposit was exactly balanced by the loss from the public's hands of the cash.

A similar case is if one person pays a cheque to another. In this case the recipient of the cheque pays it into his bank, which sends it to the bank of the man who wrote (or 'drew') the cheque. In honouring the cheque this bank will transfer the equivalent amount from its *own* account at the Bank of England to that of the recipient's bank there. At the same time the account of the drawer of the cheque is reduced at his bank and that of the recipient rises at his. The increased liability of this latter bank to its customer is exactly matched by the increased asset it holds, namely its increased account at the Bank of England (known as Bankers' Deposits). Total liabilities of the banking system have not changed, however, and nor has the money supply. (In practice there will be many transactions occurring between the banks in both directions. These go through a central clearing house and only the net credit or debit between banks need be settled through the banks' own deposits at the Bank of England.)

If, however, a customer obtains a bank *loan* the situation is different. This *creates* deposits at the bank, and represents an increase in the money supply. This can be most easily seen if we imagine the customer drawing a cheque on the loan facility. The deposit moves to the bank of the recipient of the cheque; for him it represents an asset, and for his bank a liability. It is part of the money supply. But no reduction in deposits has occurred at the first bank. The customer stands liable to pay back the loan, but the recipient of the cheque now has a bank deposit (which can go from bank to bank in payment for transactions) which did not exist before the loan was given. In this way banks can create deposits and hence increase the money supply.

The mere creation of a loan or overdraft *facility* does nothing directly to change the bank's assets or liabilities. But when the customer writes a cheque on the overdraft, the bank gains one asset and loses another. It loses some of its Bankers' Deposits, as described above, in honouring the transaction. It gains an asset in that the customer now has a debt or liability to the bank. More than this, though, it is an interest-earning asset, and this is the way in which banks earn their profits. Nearly all a bank's assets are in the form of loans of one form or another on which it earns interest.

If this were the only consideration banks would lend in order to earn the highest return possible on all their assets, subject to considerations of default by the borrower. But they must also retain the confidence of their customers, who may wish to withdraw their deposits at any time in the form of cash. In general, therefore, the banks will hold some of their assets in cash; some in very liquid assets, so that although a return is earned on them they can very readily be turned into cash; and some in less liquid assets with a higher return, and so on. In this way they will attempt to make prudent provision for possible withdrawals, but not forego any profit opportunity consistent with this.

Listed below is a simplified version of a bank's asset structure:

(1) *Notes and coin in the tills.*

(2) *Bankers' Deposits.* Commercial banks' deposits at the Bank of England.

(3) *Money at call.* Money lent to Discount Houses and returnable on demand. Discount Houses primarily act as financial intermediaries, borrowing funds from lenders and lending them on to those wishing to borrow.

(4) *Money at short notice.* Similar, except repayment may be over a longer period, e.g. up to fourteen days.

(5) *Treasury Bills.* Government debt or IOUs issued regularly by the Treasury through the Bank of England, interest-earning and repayable by the Bank of England, as the government's bank, three months from the date of issue.

(6) *Government bonds.* Like Treasury Bills, these are obligations of the government but have longer lives, and the 'maturity' date at which they are redeemed may be many years in the future.

(7) *Loans.* With fixed or variable interest charges, often for a fixed period to finance a particular investment project or major purchase by a customer.

(8) *Advances.* Overdrafts to customers, repayable on demand in theory but often very illiquid since they cannot be traded and could not be repaid by the customer if the attempt was made to call them in quickly; these generally earn the highest rate of interest of any of the bank's assets.

Since banks can grant overdraft facilities and thereby create accounts on which customers can write cheques it is within the banks' power to create money. On the face of things, there need be no limit to this power. But in practice, prudence requires that each bank should keep a minimum reserve of cash in order to meet the demand for withdrawals. If this minimum reserve were, say, 10 per cent of total deposits, then the bank would be limited to a maximum volume of deposits equal to ten times the amount of cash actually held.

In practice the banks keep a prudently large ratio of cash *and liquid assets* to deposits. This minimizes the interest foregone through holding cash while ensuring that sufficient cash can always be found to meet any demand for withdrawals. Given the importance that the major banks have in the economic system these ratios are, not surprisingly, regulated by the Bank of England so that there is no reasonable chance of a bank coming anywhere near failing to meet its obligations. The suspicion of likely failure will clearly lead to a banking collapse as a bank cannot call in its loans as fast as depositors can ask for their money back. There therefore has to be absolute confidence in the system and this is provided through the role of the Bank of England. Provided that banks follow the prudential rules, the Bank of England will lend to them to enable them to meet all obligations.

Normally this is done indirectly via the Discount Houses. Traditionally, if banks were short of funds and called in their lending to the Discount Houses, thus leaving the latter short of funds, they would always replenish their funds by borrowing from the Bank of England. This was known as the 'lender of last resort' function of the Bank of England, but it could choose whether to relieve the shortage at going market rates or at the higher, penal Bank Rate. This subsequently became the *Minimum Lending Rate* (MLR) which was set in the light of market rates themselves. Subsequently the Bank of England modified the practice still further, becoming very specific over the assets that it would regard as collateral for its lending (see Chapter 10 on monetary policy).

Returning to the required ratios of certain assets to deposits, the so-called *reserve assets* are currently defined as: Bankers' Deposits at the Bank of England; all government debt with less than a year to maturity; funds lodged at call or short notice with the Discount Houses and the stock exchange; short-term local authority bills; and (subject to an upper limit of 2 per cent of total assets) very safe commercial bills. The required reserve asset ratio is $12\frac{1}{2}$ per cent. Thus deposits can be up to eight times $(100/12\frac{1}{2}$ per cent $= 8)$ as large as this asset base. This is a crucial element in the government's control of the money supply, to which we now turn.

5.2.3. The Control of the Money Supply and the Role of Government

The government, by its sheer size, has a major effect on the stock of money through the course of its own transactions. It may also wish to affect the money suppply as part of general economic policy. This section only considers how that is done. An introduction as to why it might want to is given in the following sections, and the issues are developed in detail in chapter 10.

The government buys goods and services from firms, pays its employees, collects taxes, and distributes benefits, all of which will involve transactions through the banking system. Furthermore as time goes by various previous borrowings, Treasury Bills, National Savings Certificates, government stock, etc. fall due for repayment. When the government makes such payments it puts new bank deposits in the hands of the public. All other things being equal, this increases the money supply. When the government receives payments from the public, it reduces the money supply. Normally government expenditure exceeds revenue, and the resulting deficit will, in the absence of any offsetting action, lead automatically to an equivalent increase in the money supply.

In fact there are two other types of government action which affect this. First the government can and generally does borrow to offset some or all (or even more than the total) of its deficit. This can happen indefinitely because other sectors of the economy regularly wish to save, i.e. run a surplus every year and want to lend that surplus in order to earn interest on it. The government can borrow in a number of ways: from banks, from the non-bank private sector, and from abroad (or of course it can print the money it requires for excess of expenditure over receipts, but this is in practice very limited). If it borrows from banks or prints money then there is no reduction in commercial bank deposits, and the money supply will still be higher than before, as explained above. Alternatively, the government can borrow from the private sector by selling government securities, National Savings Certificates, etc. The securities will have a variety of 'lives', from Treasury Bills, which are repayable after three months, to bonds, which can have any maturity date from a few years to over twenty years hence. (The longest-dated bond at present is Treasury $2\frac{1}{2}$ per cent index-linked 2020; some undated stock, which may never be repaid, has also been sold in the past.) In each case the sale results in bank deposits being transferred to the government, offsetting the the increase in the money supply which would otherwise have occurred.

The government can also control the money supply through the operations of the Bank of England, which can buy or sell government debt in order to change the level of bank deposits, a process which is known as 'open market operations'. Suppose that the government sells £1 million of bonds to a large company. The latter pays by a cheque drawn on its commercial bank, transferring deposits to the government. When cleared, this results in a transfer from Bankers' Deposits to Public Deposits (the government's account at the Bank of England). The commercial banks' total assets and liabilities have fallen by the same amount, as have reserve assets. The $12\frac{1}{2}$ per cent ratio is no longer maintained. The commercial banks must now reduce their non-reserve assets. If we assume there is no way that the banks can collectively augment their reserves this will in fact lead to a multiple contraction of non-reserve assets. With a $12\frac{1}{2}$ per cent ratio, a reduction of £1 of reserve assets necessitates a reduction of £8 of bank deposits overall. A single commercial bank could replenish its reserve assets but only at the expense of those of another bank. In principle therefore the Bank of England can bring about changes in the money supply, independent of its borrowing *requirement* as determined by its expenditure and receipts. The Bank of England can also call for further deposits from the banks, thus in effect increasing the reserve ratio, and it can try to influence the banks by what is known as 'moral suasion' persuading them to restrict lending.

However, the government's control of the money supply is not absolute, partly because the government's borrowing requirement and money supply targets may conflict, but mainly because of limitations in the Bank of England's control. For the government to borrow it must offer a competitive rate of interest since it must attract funds from other sources. It may therefore still be possible for banks to charge sufficiently high rates of interest to borrowers that they are prepared to pay higher rates to borrow reserve assets themselves, thereby frustrating Bank of England attempts to restrict their lending. Restraining the banking sector may merely push borrowing on to other financial intermediaries which are not constrained in the same way as banks. Also, there are always relatively illiquid assets in the banks' portfolio of assets which, albeit at a loss, can be converted into liquid assets in the reserve asset base. If the loss is outweighed by the return from being able to continue lending on overdrafts then this reduces to some extent the control which the Bank of England can exercise.

5.2.4. *Money and the Economic System*

The money stock can be related to the transactions which take place in the economy by a simple definition:

$$MV = PT$$

where M is the stock of money, V is the number of times that stock is used over the time period in making transactions, referred to as the *velocity of circulation*, P is the price level, and T is the number of transactions that took place. This is merely a definition because each side of the equation is simply a different way of measuring the nominal value of all the transactions that have occurred in a particular period. It does not tell us how the other three components would change if one component were to alter. Since T is not really measurable it is often replaced by Y, real income (GDP at factor cost and constant prices). P is then the GDP deflator, and V becomes the *income* velocity of circulation—the number of times that the money stock is used in the transactions that generate real income, Y. Definitional changes make an assessment of the value of V, from the formula $V = PY/M$, difficult, but it appears to have fluctuated in the range 2–3 over the last ten years. If it were possible to suggest that V was relatively unaffected by changes in M, a given percentage change in M would require the same percentage change in nominal GDP, i.e. $P.Y$. It would not of course explain causation nor how that change was split up between price inflation and real income growth.

In practice there is some variability in V. In part it may occur because money is held for both speculative and transactional reasons. If money were purely an oil for the wheels of the transactions system a more stable value of V could be expected. But speculative or idle balances are, as we noted earlier, sensitive to the rate of return on other assets, principally rates of interest in the money market. These interest rates are very much market determined. If firms or the government wish to borrow more, say, for investment, interest rates will tend to rise, but if the supply of funds increases, say, from overseas, interest rates will tend to fall.

The response of idle balances to these interest rate movements will tend to be largely speculative. For example, if interest rates are thought likely to fall, the holding of government bonds will become attractive. To illustrate this, consider a government loan with a nominal rate of interest, say 'Treasury $2\frac{1}{2}$ per cent', and no given redemption date. This means that each nominal £100 unit yields fixed interest of £2·50 per annum. However, at the time of writing the market rate of interest for undated bonds is 10 per cent. The market price of this bond, with a face value of £100, is therefore £25, as $2\frac{1}{2}$ per cent of £100 equals 10 per cent of £25. If the market rate of interest were to rise to $12\frac{1}{2}$ per cent then the price of the £100 bond would fall to £20 because only at this price does a return of £2.50 represent $12\frac{1}{2}$ per cent. By retaining his holding the investor would make an interest gain over the year of £2.50, but this would be more than offset by the capital loss of £5 as the market value of the asset fell. He would thus prefer to hold cash rather than the bond. Expectations of a rise in interest rates will thus tend to increase idle (or speculative) money balances and, conversely, expectations of a fall will tend to diminish them. Most government bonds are dated, which complicates the issue. Since there is a certain date of redemption the price of the bond incorporates two elements, the differential between its nominal rate of interest and the market rate, and the rate of return on an annual basis which will be achieved between now and redemption, when the bond will be repaid by the government at its face value of £100.

To some extent a rise in interest rates may lead people to expect still further increases. But more generally they will base expectations on interest rates in relation to the level thought appropriate or 'normal' for the current state of the economy. Given that people do have some such notion of a 'normal' rate of interest over a particular (often rather short) period, then it is clear that, in general, rates of interest higher than the normal rate will lead to expectations of a fall in interest rates, and lower rates than normal to expectations of a rise.[2]

The precise shape of this inverse relationship needs further analysis. As set out above, the argument implies an 'all-or-nothing' decision by each investor— all cash if interest rates are expected to rise, and all bonds if they are expected to fall. A smooth inverse relationship for the economy as a whole will result only if (a) different investors' notions of the 'normal' rate of interest (and hence expectations about future movements of the actual rate) differ, or (b) each investor recognizes the uncertainty of the future, and thus hedges his bets by holding both cash and bonds (though in differing proportions according to his expectations). These two possibilities are not, of course, mutually exclusive. Finally, there may be some lower limit to the rate of interest at which expectations of a rise (and thus of capital losses) are virtually unanimous, and the desire to hold bonds is negligible; and an upper limit at which unanimity of expectations of a fall (and thus of capital gains) reduce idle balances to zero.

So far the analysis has focused on decisions as between holding money or holding bonds. However, bonds are only a part of the portfolio of assets that economic agents hold, which includes houses and other physical assets as well as a whole range of financial assets. Changes in the relative rates of return on these assets will cause people to alter the composition of their portfolio. In equilibrium, a portfolio of assets will be held such that each asset is held up to the point at which its expected rate of return at the margin (allowing for the disadvantages of illiquidity, as well as for the expected capital gain and financial yield) is equal for all assets. If this were not so, one could gain overall by switching from an asset with a lower return at the margin, obtaining instead the higher return at the margin of another asset. An increase in the supply of

---

[2] In one respect this is too simplified, in that it leaves inflation out of account. If prices generally are rising then any given nominal return on a bond—interest plus expected appreciation—will represent a lower return in real terms. It is the real return expected from holding a bond, as opposed to not holding it, that will normally influence decisions in the manner described.

money will then disturb this equilibrium by causing holdings of money to be too high and depressing its 'return' at the margin below those of other assets. There will be a tendency to move towards a new equilibrium as people switch their excess money holdings into other assets. The key question is how far along the spectrum of assets this adjustment will go. At one extreme it may be that the bulk of the adjustment will take place at the 'short' end—here will be a switch into short-term bonds which will raise their price, but beyond this the adjustment will begin to weaken. Any further effects on the economy will be the consequence of any fall in longer-term interest rates—mainly on the incentive to invest, but this latter effect may still be rather small. At the other extreme the adjustment could proceed much further along the spectrum, ultimately increasing expenditure on consumer and investment goods. This might emerge as an increase in real activity or in inflation or some combination of the two.

It might be thought that such questions could easily be settled by statistical analysis designed to discover whether there is or is not a strong correlation between changes in money and changes in demand for different assets. A number of such studies have in fact been carried out, but there are formidable complications. In particular the use of the term 'money supply' for the money stock is confusing as the supply of money can respond to the demand, especially if the authorities, as has commonly been the case, try to avoid excessive fluctuations in interest rates. We consider the implications of this later. The next step is to examine the determinants of income and expenditure and to explain the interrelation of the elements in the structure we have outlined in section 5.1.

5.3. The Determinants of Aggregate Economic Activity

In the previous sections we have set out a categorization of the main forms of economic activity. This enables us to consider the determinants of that activity and their interrelation. In practice this involves three interrelated steps: the formation of theories about behaviour, the estimation of the parameters of such behaviour in practice using the data which have been collected, and the testing of the validity of those theories in the light of the estimates. They are interrelated because the testing of the theories may result in their rejection and our having to revise our ideas. Human behaviour is sufficiently variable that the data available on economic activity do not enable us to put forward any single model which most economists would accept as providing the best explanation in quantitative terms of the components of aggregate activity. There are for example several econometric models of the economy of which those estimated by the Treasury, the National Institute of Economic and Social Research, and the London Business School are among the best known.

Although these models differ in detail in important ways there is general acceptance among economists of the major determinants of behaviour. The disagreements about their relative importance and the actual values of the parameters, however, have important consequences for views about the way in which the economy as a whole behaves, and in particular with regard to the way it responds to such stimuli as changes in government policy and discovery of major natural resources, for example. Some models, such as those of the University of Liverpool, the Cambridge Economic Policy Group, and the City University Business School, have quite substantially different properties.

The degree of agreement about the determinants of behaviour, however, is sufficiently great that we can, in this section, set them out for the main activities explained in section 5.1, with only limited qualification for the range of opinion. In the following section we then examine briefly the implication of these differences of view for the conduct of economic policy. Until that point, however, we will not concern ourselves with anything but major differences of view about the detailed nature of behaviour.

5.3.1. *The Supply Side*

The system of income and expenditure accounts, which provide the main source of information on economic activity, focuses attention on the demand for goods and services rather than on supply. Indeed, in our brief exposition of the components of aggregate activity, equation (1)

$$(GDP = C + G + I_F + I_S + X - M),$$

we looked at it explicitly from the point of view of expenditures. For most of the rest of this section we will continue with that bias, because in the shorter term it is expenditure that determines output and employment. But it should be borne in mind throughout that there are factors affecting the *supply* of goods and services as well as the demand for them. (Indeed, analysis in terms of demand and supply factors can be applied to money, labour, and assets as well as goods and services.) These supply factors are also very important and in the longer term are a main determinant of the expenditures that people are prepared to make (see chapter 20).

In the case of goods and services, 'supply' is mainly determined by the decisions of firms, which in their broadest sense also include individuals trading on their own behalf. When looking at these decisions it is important to be explicit about what is being supplied, for it is rarely just a physical product. Normally it includes a number of other characteristics and associated services, such as quality, time to delivery, reliability, after-sales service, ease of operation, and several others in quite a long list of items, whose importance may be difficult to quantify. In trying to sell its 'output' the firm has to consider both price and these non-price factors, which are not usually independent.

The price the firm is willing to set or prepared to accept for its output will be primarily affected by its cost structure and of course its attitude to profits. These costs stem from the three main inputs to the productive process, labour, capital, and other purchased inputs. Subject to trying to meet the non-price characteristics of the product which are demanded it is clearly in the interests of the firm to try to keep its costs (per unit of output) as low as possible. In each case costs are a combination of the price of the inputs and the quantity of them required for each unit of output—again not independent items because capital, labour, and produced inputs such as energy are substitutes to various extents.

The quantitative relation between inputs and output—productivity of factors—is crucial in the determination of supply. The productivity of labour depends primarily upon its quality, in terms of skills and training, the capital and materials with which it has to work, and the efficiency with which it is employed. By the same token the productivity of capital depends upon its quality, usually thought of in terms of the technology it embodies, the skills of the people using it, and the way in which it is used in the production process. Thus the productivity of capital falls for any given item if it is idle, poorly maintained, or misused. The importance of the quality of produced inputs is often neglected. A highly skilled labour force with the most up-to-date equipment may nevertheless have low productivity if it is working with poor materials. Changes in supply can thus occur because of changes in the quality of inputs, changes in the efficiency with which the inputs are used, and changes in the relative proportions of inputs, as well as any change in the whole scale of production. All of these may lead to changes in firms' cost structures.

Thus while the firm is a supplier of products it is itself simultaneously a demander of capital, labour, and purchased inputs. In the case of both capital and labour, although the firm wishes to use capital and labour in the productive process, the nature of the transaction is more complex. Capital items, such as buildings, machinery, vehicles, etc., normally last more than one time period, so changes in any one period, investment, are a combination of new additions to the stock of capital (gross investment) and reductions in the existing stock, because it has worn out or been scrapped, i.e. through depreciation or capital consumption. Investment thus represents an attempt to move towards the desired capital stock for production under the required cost conditions.

The firm as a demander of labour (discussed in more detail in Chapter 4) wishes to purchase a number of man-hours, but because of rigidities over the number of hours of employment for a given individual per week, the demand is to a great extent for a number of employees with particular skills. Here prices, rather than being set competitively by firms, are negotiated primarily by trade unions and employees. The supply of labour, while constrained by demographic considerations—the number of people of working age in the country—is also affected by the proportion who wish to work—the participation rate—which varies by age and as between men and women.

The supply of labour is thus affected by the relative returns to being employed compared with being without a job. However, as mentioned earlier, labour is not homogeneous and can be classified by its skills. Since skills have to be acquired over time, there can be surpluses in one part of the labour market and shortages elsewhere at the same time. Such divisions of the labour market can also be geographic as the labour supplied must be in the same place as the labour demands for it to be employed. Hence, there are wide differences in unemployment rates among the regions of the country.

While the quality of the capital stock can be increased purely by investment in more up-to-date machinery it can also be increased as the result of research and development, as can the quality and type of products. Expenditure on such research and development, if successful, will tend to result in innovations in products or processes which may increase the technical efficiency of production (i.e. increase output relative to inputs used) or increase the quality of the product, or indeed introduce new products altogether. Factors influencing the supply of these inputs are considered in more detail in Parts V and VI of this book.

5.3.2. The Demand-Side Framework

One of the problems of looking at the economy from the point of view of the National Accounts is that it is like trying to understand what is going on in a video film which has been frozen at a particular frame. Attempts to carry out static single-period analysis of the economy are always going to be difficult because economic behaviour is inherently dynamic. The economy adjusts to stimuli over time, indeed, there are many economists who believe that the UK economy and even the world economy has its own harmonic path, causing it to follow a series of regular or irregular cycles round a trend in activity. Others who do not share this explicit belief are nevertheless happy to conduct their analysis of the economy using large-scale econometric models which themselves have dynamic cyclical properties.

It is important not to confuse the fact that the National Accounts, by definition, balance in any given time period with any notion of 'equilibrium'. Even if an economy is exhibiting signs of drastic change within a year such as 1980, with unemployment rising rapidly and price inflation high and rising, nevertheless the sum of incomes will equal the sum of expenditures. Equilibrium only exists when supply and demand are equated in each market at the prevailing price level (or in the dynamic equivalent of this static description). Such circumstances never prevail for the economy as a whole as human behaviour is too variable and subject to too many and varied shocks for the process of adjustment ever to be completed. (There are, however, some senses in which the economy can be in dynamic equilibrium in that the adjustment itself is optimal at any particular time, which we shall discuss in the next section.)

The explanation of the components of economic activity in the pages which follow is rarely in terms of immediate adjustment within the same time period. While the overall activity may show a cyclical path, the components of it do not necessarily follow the same path—some may lead it and others lag it. Between them they contribute to the overall picture and through an intricate web of interrelated causation explain the path of activity. This pattern can be affected in two ways, first by changes in the value of the determinants of behaviour and second by changes in that behaviour. For example, if foreign incomes rise demand for exports is likely to rise as well, leading to a stimulus which can feed right through the UK economy. As an illustration of the second case, severe financial pressure on companies may mean that they change their attitude towards employment. For example they may consider instituting redundancy proceedings, which under normal fluctuations they would not consider, as opposed to not replacing people when they leave.

In what follows we seek to set out the main features of these interrelations looking at the main components of economic activity which have been set out above, starting with the categories of expenditure as ordered in equation (1).

5.3.3. Household Expenditure

The decision over how much of a householder's income to consume is a complex one, far more so than the simple accounting definition that what is not consumed is saved would seem to imply. As is clear from Chapter 2, the householder as consumer can hold physical and financial assets as well as consuming during the current time period. The physical assets, principally houses and consumer durables, give the consumer a stream of benefits over the lifetime of the asset. The purchase of thse items is essentially a discrete activity. A consumer buying a dishwasher which lasts for ten years may pay for the item in full in the first year of its life. Taking all consumers together this lumpiness should be ironed out, because for every one consumer buying a dishwasher this year there will tend to be nine others who bought their dishwashers in each of the preceding nine years and do not yet need to replace them. However, there are two drawbacks to this assumption. The first is that the population is not sufficiently homogeneous in terms of its age and household structure nor in its wealth distribution that the pattern of consumption can be assumed to be constant over a period of ten years. Secondly, the products themselves are not a constant set. Most obviously, dishwashers produced today have facilities different from those purchased ten years ago—they are quieter, use less electricity, are more efficient, fit more items into the same space (and are widely thought to be less durable). More importantly there are products on the market which did not exist ten years ago: video recorders, personal computers, food processors, electric sandwich makers, coffee makers, etc.—not a short list, nor a trivial portion of expenditure.

As new products are introduced they are often initially relatively expensive, but as they enter the market in volume their relative price falls and consumption increases rapidly. However, as a larger and larger proportion of the population acquires the product the rate of purchase falls until it reaches a level largely reflecting the demand for replacement. But product innovations are not made at a constant rate, nor are they of equal impact. As a result consumption patterns vary quite substantially over time; while expenditure on motor cars and motor cycles was 3·9 per cent of the total in 1971, it was 2·9 per cent in 1981, while that on radio, electrical, and other durable goods rose from 1·8 per cent to 3·4 per cent over the same period (consumers' expenditure as a whole is about two-thirds of total GDP and the most important single component of expenditure.)

The consumption decision is related to the rest of the economy in three respects: first from its determinants, second from the simultaneous decisions that are implied for the other uses of income, and third for the consequential effects. Taking the first of these, the main determinant is real personal disposable income in the current and recent periods, as this is the main factor determining the purchasing power available. But the holding of existing assets, both real and financial, interest rates and credit terms and expectations of the future, particularly with regard to price inflation, will also be important (see Chapter 2.) Although it may have only a small effect on the total of consumers' expenditure it is also important to know what the *nature* of the change in real personal income is. For example, changes in income of the form of social security, pensions, or similar current grants tend to be reflected almost entirely in changes in consumption, while changes in higher rates of taxation will tend to have a much greater effect on savings.

It must also be borne in mind that households make *investment* decisions as well. In our simple flow of funds picture (Figure 5.1) investment in capital assets was treated as if it could be undertaken only by firms and the government. However, the construction of private sector dwellings and their purchase by owner-occupiers mean that households can also acquire capital assets. The proportion of personal incomes going into investment in housing has been falling over the last decade as a whole, particularly in the second half. Partly this is due to long-term trends, in particular a relatively stable total population (although there is an increasing number of households within that total) and a stock of dwellings that has risen sufficiently faster than the number of households so that there are now substantially more dwellings than households. Future expenditure on housebuilding is thus unlikely ever to return to the high levels of the 1950s and 1960s (in real terms).

Finally it must be recalled that the part of consumers' expenditure formed by 'rent' on owner-occupied dwellings is imputed. Since it makes no material difference to the nature of a particular house whether it is lived in by the owner or by someone else who pays rent it also seems unreasonable to suggest that GDP should be higher, the higher the proportion of households who rent their homes. Hence personal disposable income and consumers' expenditure are increased by an equal amount for rent received imputed to the 'owner' and rent paid imputed to the occupier. The imputation was equal to 6 per cent of consumers' expenditure in 1981 (having risen from 4 per cent since 1971), reflecting the rise in owner occupation and the increase in the relative price of housing.

Turning to the simultaneous effects on other uses of income, consumption decisions clearly constrain what is saved. But saving is not purely a residual item. A range of factors will influence how much people wish to save. The level and expected movement of interest rates will have an effect; but of great importance, particularly in obtaining the rise of the proportion of income saved in the 1970s, is the role of changes in the price level. The position here is complex, because not only do these changes affect real personal disposable income through the deflation of nominal incomes but they also affect behaviour through their effect on the value of existing wealth, particularly financial wealth, and through their effect on expectations of the future. The key point is that it is not so much changes in the price level which seem to matter as *changes in the rate of price inflation*. Under increasing rates of inflation some incomes and prices will lag behind as the system seeks to adjust; hence it becomes necessary to make provision for these discrepancies in the form of increased saving. It is the uncertainty involved which will tend to lead to increased 'precautionary' saving rather than a high or low level of inflation.

Moreover, if inflation accelerates then more has to be saved than previously planned if a saver is to amass the amount necessary for an intended purchase in the future. Many will also need to save more to try to restore the original value of financial assets where real value has been eroded by inflation. To the extent that inflation has raised nominal interest rates, this erosion of value will have been all the greater.

Another important influence has been observed from changes in the level of unemployment. Although savings may be different under different rates of employment, as an economy moves towards higher unemployment it is suggested that the fear of unemployment will itself lead people to save a higher proportion of their incomes. It is yet to be revealed whether this is symmetric, so that consumption *rises* in the expectation of *re-employment*. At the same time there is anecdotal evidence of a surge in spending in the short run because of the lump sums received from redundancy payments.

Changes as between consumption and saving will reflect a balance of all the determinants of both types of behaviour. But flexibility in consumers' behaviour is somewhat less than it might otherwise appear because of the existence of contractual saving, particularly for occupational saving schemes (see [32]). Over half of gross personal sector savings goes into contractual savings schemes. Between 1971 and 1981 the percentage of personal disposable income going into savings rose from $7\frac{1}{2}$ per cent to $13\frac{1}{2}$ per cent. Thus the contractual savings ratio in 1981 was the same as the *total* savings ratio in 1971. By their very nature contractual savings contributions are relatively long-term commitments, and rapid decline in the savings ratio in this area is unlikely. Thus although a substantial proportion of the rise in the savings ratio over the last decade may be due to increases in the factors described above, it is unlikely that the ratio can fall right back to the levels of the early 1970s, even if all the causes of upward movement were reversed.

Feeding on from the consumption decision is the consequence for the productive sector. The important question is whether it is domestic producers who meet the demand or foreign producers via imports. This will depend on the whole range of supply factors previously discussed—design, quality, reliability, delivery, marketing, etc.—as well as on costs of production as reflected in the price. The exchange rate will then play an important part in determining the competitiveness of domestic versus foreign production, at least in the short run. We will see how these interrelationships between different parts of the economy fit together in more detail in section 5.4 and in Chapter 14.

5.3.4. *Fixed Investment and Stockbuilding*

Both fixed investment and stockbuilding are categories of *accumulation* because they involve the creation of items which are carried forward from one accounting period to the next, but they are distinguished in equation (1) because their determinants are rather different, as is their contribution to overall activity in the economy.

As was explained in the previous chapter, the productive process involves the transformation of raw materials (and other purchased inputs) into finished products through the use of 'capital' and labour. The existing capital stock, consisting of dwellings, other buildings, plant, machinery, and vehicles, is decreased in any time period as it is scrapped, damaged, or destroyed, and increased by investment and purchases of new items. The capital stock, next to personal wealth, is one of the most difficult items to measure in the National Accounts for several practical reasons.

In the first place it is difficult to find out what capital firms have and then, even if one could find out, it is difficult to provide a valuation of this capital. Clearly the historical cost would be inappropriate as the National Accounts are in current prices. Simple revaluation by an appropriate price index does not solve the problem as an old item is not worth the same as a new one. As there is no real second-hand market for much of the stock no useful second-hand prices are known. Therefore only rules of thumb can be used and 'capital consumption', the amount of the capital stock presumed used up in our time period, shown in Table 5.1, is estimated by a series of conventions which take into account the known values of past investment, the likely life of the asset, and the appropriate price index of revaluation.

Thus while it may be possible to know what is being added to the capital stock of the country it is much more difficult to form an accurate view of what capital there is for future expansion of the economy. It is therefore not possible to say with any accuracy the amount that production could increase with the existing capital facilities if the willingness or demand to do so were to exist. In any case capital is not homogeneous and the additional output obtainable from unused or under-utilized capital may be very different from that of existing capital still being fully used. Indeed, since expansion will not come across the board it is important to identify in what industries it will come and what is the nature of the capital stock and investment there. Only then can we form a view of the potential for expansion.

While it may be possible to determine what the desired level of the capital stock would be for any level of expected output given the nature of the transformation process (see pp. 77-9) economists have had considerable difficulty in explaining how firms move towards these desired levels by a process of investment as time passes. Since output is related to the capital stock, changes in capital as reflected in investment tend to be related to *changes* in output, thus generating a much more cyclically fluctuating response of investment than that observed for activity in the economy as a whole. Indeed, other sectors, such as consumption and government current expenditure, have tended to stabilize activity. Investment therefore tends to be related to output with a complicated lag, modified by current limitations, such as company cash flow. Perhaps rather surprisingly given that investment projects are often appraised in terms of a rate of return, little influence has been identified from interest rates (whether nominal or real), and the response to a wide range of government incentive schemes, while easy to predict in theory, has been difficult to determine in practice [35]. The shape of the lagged effect from output, with little influence from the present or recent past, building up fairly quickly and then dying away slowly thereafter, reflects the fact there are several causes of delay which prevent investment decisions having immediate effect. Even before this there is a delay while firms make up their minds what to do. The distribution of the lagged effect estimated for UK manufacturing industry of the period 1957-75 is shown in Figure 5.2.

Investment in stocks has a more complex interrelation with the behaviour of

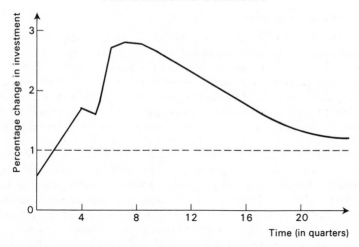

FIG. 5.2. Response of Investment to a Single Increase of Output by 1 per cent in Quarter Zero.

Source: Bean [29].

the economy. Firms at all levels of the production chain need to hold stocks of inputs and finished output, both because purchases may need to be 'lumpy' in order to obtain quantity discounts and because demand may be uneven. Productive processes will similarly entail that there is inevitably some work-in-progress which may have a considerable value. In a static world stocks would fluctuate round some particular stock–output ratio (stock–sales ratio in the case of the distributive trades) but in a changing world suppliers need to change stocks in advance of sales changes.

However, in practice sales forecasts are often wrong. If a supplier fails to foresee a downturn then his stocks will rise, whereas with correct foresight output would have fallen before sales, thus allowing stocks to fall. The consequence of this perverse movement in stocks due to poor forecasting is that stocks fluctuate more than proportionately to output. In fact in many cases stockbuilding changes form the largest component of changes in activity as a whole.

It is important to emphasize that it is *changes* in the level of stocks which reflect changes in activity in the economy, not the level of stocks. If stock levels remain unchanged throughout a year then there will have been no productive activity over and above that which went into the goods and services actually sold.

In an inflationary world an item which is stockpiled will tend to increase in value between the time it is produced and the time it is sold. This is reflected in the item called stock appreciation in Table 5.1. In order to try to value products identically when they are finished and when they are actually sold the change in the value of a given level of stocks during the year (or quarter) is deducted from GDP, as it does not represent any activity. Stockbuilding is purely the value of the physical increase in stocks and work-in-progress.

5.3.5. Government Expenditure

Government expenditure cannot be subjected to the same degree of economic explanation because its form and distribution are largely a matter for political decision. It is an artibrary matter whether particular activities such as steel-making or coal production lie in the public or private sectors, but items which fall in the public sector may be subject to many non-economic criteria which do not lend themselves to any formal explanation of behaviour. In what follows, therefore, we shall treat government expenditure as being the result of policy decision. However, it is not legitimate to assume that this means that government expenditure is in some sense separable from the rest of activity. Clearly, of course, the government as a producer of goods and services contributes to overall activity like any other productive enterprise, purchasing inputs from other producers both at home and abroad and paying its employees. However, some government transfer payments are directly related to economic activity. As unemployment changes so do benefit payments, thus generating an automatic counter-cyclical influence on overall activity. Furthermore, in a world of constrained resources a government can bid away resources from other sectors. If a government tries to spend more on UK goods, for example, and production cannot respond to this increase in demand it may result in a fall in private sector consumption of the goods or in a fall in exports. In financial markets, government attempts to borrow more may bid funds away from the private sector and hence some private sector expenditure may not take place, offsetting the increase in public expenditure. This phenomenon, known as 'crowding-out' is discussed in more detail in the next section (and in Chapter 10).

5.3.6. Exports and Imports

International trade is dealt with extensively in the next chapter so we consider its role here only within the context of the domestic economy. Exports and imports reflect respectively an injection and a leakage in the domestic system. The payment for exports brings in funds from abroad and the activity generated in their production contributes to the general cycle of activity, generating incomes and purchases of inputs and intermediate goods. Imports on the other hand represent a loss of the ability to pass on activity round the cycle. Payments made abroad for goods and services tend to contribute largely to economic activity in those foreign countries and only incidentally, in most cases, are UK exports inputs to goods which this country then imports.

The importance in the interrelation of traded goods with the rest of the economy is that it is the domestic purchaser who chooses whether to buy a domestic or a foreign product, so that domestic expenditure determinants and imports are highly related. Exports on the other hand are largely determined by foreign demand conditions and hence introduce an important different influence on domestic activity.

5.3.7. Sectoral Balances

The expenditures discussed in the previous section are not necessarily made by sectors which have adequate funds to meet them. To work out the net flows between sectors we have to total each sector's incomes, and its expenditures, in a specific period. The *sectoral balance* (deficit or surplus) in that period is the difference between the two. Since by definition the sum of incomes is equal to the sum of expenditures, the net deficits/surpluses summed across *all* sectors must also be zero. The deficit sectors therefore have to borrow from those in surplus.

We can conveniently divide economic agents into the public sector and the private sector, but there are two components of the private sector, the personal and the corporate sectors, which have very different patterns of behaviour. By and large the personal sector spends less than it earns and lends to the corporate and public sectors, which spend more than they earn. Thus the personal sector acquires a stock of financial claims on the corporate and public sectors.

The picture is in practice more complicated because of the role of the financial sector, banks, unit trusts, insurance companies, etc. The financial sector takes deposits from the personal sector and then re-lends to the corporate sector and government. The proportion of claims in the form of stocks and shares held directly by the personal sector is relatively small, the large financial institutions dominating the stock market.

If we include the foreign sector in the picture the sum across all four sectors, personal, corporate, public, and foreign, must be zero by definition. In this case the surplus of the foreign sector is basically imports less exports. Imports provide the foreign sector's income and exports its expenditure. (In practice it is the full current account balance which is the surplus/deficit, i.e. after allowing for net profits, interest, dividends, and transfers from abroad, as well as net trade in goods and services.)

That the sum of all the sector balances—surpluses and deficits—equals zero holds by definition. As such it tells us nothing new about behaviour. But, as will be seen, it is none the less an important definition. All deficits have to be financed from surpluses, and if this should prove difficult for any reason then that will constrain expenditure plans and/or cause additional income to be sought. Analysis of the determinants of behaviour of the different sections that ignored this constraint could lead to inaccurate or indeed inconsistent and therefore non-feasible forecasts of future behaviour. In addition the cost of sectoral deficits and the accumulated borrowings feature in the determination of incomes, through interest and dividends, for both paying and receiving sectors. It is to the generation of incomes that we now turn.

5.3.8. Prices and Incomes

For each individual productive enterprise, its contribution to GDP is its 'value-added', the value of its output less the value of the produced inputs it has purchased from other suppliers. The remainder of the firm's costs will lie in its labour bill and anything then left will be gross profits. Although a firm's motivation may relate to its profits, treating profits last in the components of the firm's activity has considerable validity. The individual firm has little control over the prices of its purchased inputs, including the price of labour, except where the firm is large. In the second place many firms are very much 'price-takers' in the sense that they are selling a product where larger competitors are tending to set the pace. Discussions of the determination of wage levels and price levels therefore tend to be couched in terms of macroeconomic relations. In the next section we shall identify the main theories that have been advanced to explain them. Here we shall for the moment merely concern outselves only with the basic interrelations of the domestic economic system.

Wages in the UK tend to be subject to an annual sequence of bargaining beginning in the autumn and ending when the negotiators take their summer holidays. The exact nature of their determination is a matter of great controversy among economists and several theories seem to be consistent with the past, yet forecasts of the future based on them have not performed well. There are, however, several factors which are common to all of them. In the first place, there is no reason why any particular level of nominal wages and prices should prevail. If the Bank of England were to announce that henceforward there was to be a new pound which was equal to two old pounds this need have no effect on real activity, even though anything denominated in pounds would have its price halved. The process of exchange would be unchanged because no change in relative prices is involved, just a redrawing of the units of measurement. The determination of wages is thus usually discussed in relation to *real wages* and to *rates of change of nominal wages*.

It is not surprising that wages and prices are intimately related. If wage bargainers seek an objective in terms of real wages then changes in prices will lead to changes in wages. In the same way, because wage costs are frequently the largest element in total costs wage changes will tend to be reflected in price changes in an effort to protect profits.

While the terms 'wages' and 'earnings' are often used interchangeably it is important to sort out their various components. The term 'earnings' refers to both wages and salaries, i.e. all income from employment. This includes not just basic pay at whatever are the prevailing wage *rates* but all overtime and other incidental payments. In Figure 5.3 the Average Earnings Index (AEI), the thick line, is contrasted with the Retail Price Index (RPI), the thin line. The general path of the two series is similar with the exception of the period 1977–9 where in the first part of the period inflation in earnings continued to fall even when the price inflation fall was arrested, while in 1978 earnings inflation rose while the decline in price inflation bottomed out. The lags and leads between prices and wages are clearly complex, and while wages led the way to decreasing inflation in 1974–5 after the first oil crisis, prices led in the second oil crisis in 1980.

Neither earnings nor wages reflect either what the employee receives nor what the employer pays in labour costs. Take-home pay, which is what actually affects the employee's ability to spend, is reduced by income taxes, National Insurance contributions, and pension contributions. The dashed lined in the top half of Figure 5.3 takes the first two of thse into account. The Tax and Price Index (TPI) tries to provide the appropriate deflator for real post-tax income. Thus when increases in the TPI are larger than increases in the RPI this entails that taxation has increased relative to the prevailing level of activity. When

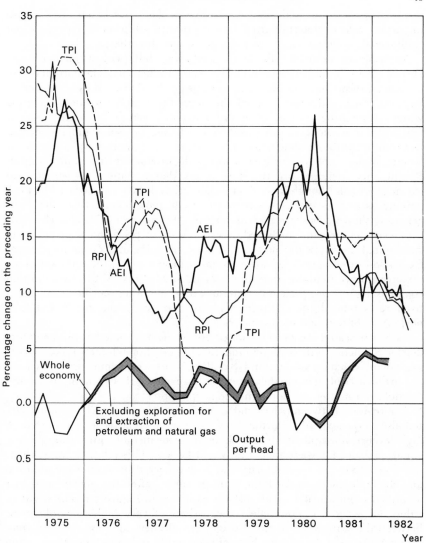

FIG. 5.3. Earnings, Prices, and Output per Head, 1975–1982. (RPI—Retail Price Index; TPI—Trade and Price Index; AEI—Average Earnings Index; 'output per head' is the index of real GDP per person employed.)

Source: *Employment Gazette.*

TPI growth is less than AEI growth, *real* post-tax incomes rise and when it is higher they fall, ignoring the difference in base values.

The employer on the other hand also has to contribute to National Insurance revenues on behalf of each employee and to make the 'non-contributory' part of payments to pension funds for each employee. The government thus has an important role in determining labour costs in addition to its role as an employer through which it can influence wages directly.

An employer can try to offset an increased wage bill (per head) in two ways. He can reduce employment or he can increase productivity. The bottom line in Figure 5.3 shows how productivity (output per head) varied over the period 1975–82. Such differences record the degree to which earnings can grow without generating price increases or having an adverse effect on the share of real profits in income, because productivity change shows how much more can be produced with the same amount of labour or, put another way, how much labour input can be reduced while still producing the same output. Productivity increases are therefore a key determinant of *sustainable* real earnings growth, though large fluctuations around them can occur. The most striking gains in real wages occurred in 1978, though since then they have generally shown a positive increase except after tax in 1981 and early 1982.

Government income is affected in several ways by price and wage inflation. As nominal wages rise during the year the share going in taxation increases as fixed allowances against tax form a smaller proportion of the total and some taxpayers move to higher rates of tax. Value-added tax (VAT) by definition compensates fully for price inflation but excise and other specific duties are at fixed rates related to quantities sold (or produced) and hence fall as a porportion of the total cost as prices rise.

As North Sea oil has been exploited government income has become more dependent on prices in a different manner. Oil taxation is largely related to the price of oil which is expressed in US dollars. Thus tax revenues are related not just to the price of oil but to the rate of foreign exchange between the pound and the dollar, a matter developed in the next chapter.

The relation between prices and wages is not just affected by productivity but also by the general performance of the economy relative to its resources. A high level of unemployment was thought to mean that, other things being equal, pressure for wage increases would be less. This relation is not clear, however. Up to 1967 a regularity had been observed between wage inflation and unemployment, named the Phillips curve (after the person who first identified it empirically), with a shape as shown in Figure 5.4. The negative values for wage inflation reflect the periods of very high unemployment between the wars when nominal wages actually fell, although less fast than prices. Since 1967 the relation has not been stable and in so far as there is any particular relation it seems to be rather more between *changes* in unemployment and *changes* in wages. Thus it is perhaps not so much the fact of being unemployed as the fear of becoming unemployed which dampens wage rises. This central issue is explored fully in Chapter 7.

The above sections have referred to all the components of macroeconomic behaviour as set out in Figure 5.1 and to the individual items in the income and expenditure accounts in Table 5.1. However, the determination of incomes is incomplete in that our discussion of earnings has been in terms of earnings per head. Total incomes require knowledge of both average earnings and the number of earners. We therefore need to consider employment also, which in

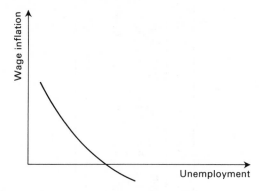

FIG. 5.4. The Phillips Curve.

itself, and more particularly in its consequences for unemployment, is a macro-economic variable of major importance for economic policy.

5.3.9. Employment and Unemployment

Employment in principle is derived as a result of the combination of the output decision and the labour requirements of that output, though given the difficulty in legal and cost terms of reducing employment in practice, this picture is too simple (see Chapter 4). In addition the labour requirement per unit of output will itself be variable to some extent. None the less, the most feasible means of identifying likely employment trends is to infer the employment implications of likely output trends, coupled with estimates of the growth of productivity. It should be noted that *unemployment* depends not just on employment but also on the number of people who wish to work, a wish which in turn is affected by employment opportunities and by the level of benefit available to the unemployed. As is shown in Table 5.3, while the population as a whole has changed hardly at all over the last decade, the population of working age (school-leaving to retirement) has increased. Thus even with constant employment and a constant participation rate, as defined by the third row in the table, unemployment would have risen after 1973–4. As it is, while the population of working age has not yet stopped rising, the labour force reached a maximum in 1978 and fell by nearly 1 million by 1982, compared with a fall in employment of $2\frac{1}{4}$ million since 1979.

5.3.10. The Behaviour of the Economy as a Whole

Up to this point we have looked at the determinants of behaviour one by one and have filled out the whole of the income and expenditure accounting system as well as the sectoral balances and portfolios of assets. To complete the picture we should consider how a shock to the system feeds right round the circular flow of income. Here we shall do this only in a simple mechanical sense as the next section is devoted to a discussion of different theories of the operation of the economy.

TABLE 5.3. *Employment and Unemployment*

	1971	1972	1973	1974	1975	1976	1977	1978	1979	1980	1981	1982
Total population (millions)	55·6	55·8	55·9	55·9	55·9	55·9	55·9	55·8	55·9	55·9	55·8	56·0
Population of working age as % of total	62·7	62·5	62·5	62·5	62·6	62·8	63·2	63·4	63·7	64·0	64·0	64·0
Fully employed as % of population of working age	70·0	69·9	71·5	71·7	71·2	70·5	70·4	70·5	70·3	68·3	65·2	63·5
Unemployed as % of labour force	2·9	3·2	2·3	2·1	3·4	5·1	5·5	5·5	5·1	6·4	9·6	10·6

Source: *Annual Abstract of Statistics* (mid-year estimates).

Let us take first of all a shock to the system which is in the form of increased optimism about the future which leads to an increase in fixed investment which we can denote ΔI_F (the Δ sign is to be read as 'the change in'). We could however have taken as an example any shock to the system which came from a determinant 'outside' it—an increase in the demand for exports, a change in tax rates—anything which did not involve a change in economic agents' responses to the same stimuli, i.e. it is a change in the stimuli, not a change in the reactions to them which is being considered.

Taking equation (1) we can see that the accounting definition requires that if we started with a set of values

$$GDP = C + G + I_F + I_S + X - M \tag{1}$$

we now have

$$GDP^* = C + G + (I_F + \Delta I_F) + I_S + X - M \tag{2}$$

where $\Delta I_F = GDP^* - GDP$. However, the increase in output required to produce the extra investment goods will have fed right through the productive process and will have generated extra incomes to pay people for producing the extra goods. Some of this extra income will be spent by households on consumption. Let us denote this increase in consumption as ΔC; we then have

$$GDP^{**} = (C + \Delta C) + G + (I_F + \Delta I_F) + I_S + X - M \tag{3}$$

where $GDP^{**} - GDP^* = \Delta C$.

This extra consumption in turn will entail higher sales and production by firms, which will generate yet further increases *some* of which will be spent on consumption goods and so on. The final amount by which GDP increases as a result of the initial increase in investment will therefore be some multiple of the original increase.

If we take a very simplified economy we can see this concept of a 'multiplier' rather more clearly. Let us suppose there is no government or foreign sector. Then, neglecting stockbuilding, equation (1) becomes

$$Y = C + I_F \tag{4}$$

where Y is used to denote this simplified form of total activity. Let us also suppose that consumers choose to spend a fixed proportion, b, of any increase in their income on consumption, then for any change in income, ΔY, the consequent change in consumption is

$$\Delta C = b \Delta Y. \tag{5}$$

(This also assumes all incomes are received by households.) We can now rewrite equations (2) and (3) more simply as

$$Y^* = C + I_F + \Delta I_F. \tag{6}$$

ΔC is then equal to $b(Y^* - Y) = b\Delta I_F$, and

$$Y^{**} = C + \Delta C + I_F + \Delta I_F \tag{7}$$

i.e. $\Delta C = Y^{**} - Y^*$.

The next step in the sequence is that a proportion b of the further increase in income $(Y^{**} - Y^*)$ will be spent on consumption:

$$b(Y^{**} - Y^*) = b[\Delta C] = b[b\Delta I_F] = b^2 \Delta I_F. \tag{8}$$

Thus each time round the cycle, income increases by a proportion b of the increase the previous time round. The total increase, Y^T, will therefore be the sum of this sequence:

$$\Delta Y^T = \Delta I_F + b\Delta I_F + b^2 \Delta I_F + b^3 \Delta I_F + \cdots + b^N \Delta I_F + \cdots \tag{9}$$

Fortunately it is easy to calculate ΔY^T. If we multiply both sides of equation (9) by b:

$$b\Delta Y^T = b\Delta I_F + b^2 \Delta I_F + b^3 \Delta I_F + b^4 \Delta I_F + \cdots + b^{N+1} \Delta I_F + \cdots \tag{10}$$

and subtract equation (10) from equation (9):

$$\Delta Y^T - b\Delta Y^T = \Delta I_F, \tag{11}$$

all other terms cancelling out, the term at the end of the series being infinitely small if $0 < b < 1$, which it must be to permit both saving and consumption. Rearranging equation (11):

$$(1 - b)\Delta Y^T = \Delta I_F \tag{12}$$

and dividing by $(1 - b)$ we see that

$$\Delta Y^T = \frac{1}{(1 - b)} \cdot \Delta I_F. \tag{13}$$

The term $1/(1 - b)$ is the 'multiplier', the multiple of the initial shock by which income finally changes.

This multiplier has a specific meaning. b in equation (5) is defined as the 'marginal propensity to consume', the proportion of any change in income which is spent on consumption. $(1 - b)$ is clearly the marginal propensity to save (MPS), as all income is spent on consumption or saved and the multiplier is thus $1/\text{MPS}$. For example if $\text{MPS} = \frac{1}{4}$ any change in investment would change income by four times that amount.

The multiplier process described above occurs because increased expenditure, arising as a result of increased income, itself constitutes income for the recipients of the payments made. In theory the process could go on indefinitely, but in practice it tails away, because at each stage not all of the increase in income goes forward as a further round of expenditure. In the simple model above there is a leakage at each stage into saving. In reality there are other leakages, i.e. diversion of income away from a further round of spending in the country, the two main forms of which are payments of income tax and expenditure on imports.

If these are introduced we can construct a simple model as follows:

$$Y = C + I + G + X - M. \tag{14}$$

This is the national income identity with government expenditure, exports, and imports reintroduced.

$$C = b(Y - T). \tag{15}$$

This is a consumption function showing consumption as dependent on post-tax income, where T is taxation on incomes.

$$M = d(Y - T). \tag{16}$$

This is an import function, showing that imports, like consumption, are dependent on the level of post-tax income.

Finally we assume for simplicity that taxation on income is proportional to that income:

$$T = tY \tag{17}$$

where t is the tax rate on income. Substituting equations (15), (16), and (17) into equation (14) gives

$$Y = b(Y - tY) + I + G + X - d(Y - tY). \tag{18}$$

Rearranging this with all the terms containing Y on one side:

$$Y - bY + btY + dY - dtY = I + G + X \tag{19}$$

and therefore

$$Y = \{1/(1 - b + bt + d - dt)\} \times (I + G + X). \tag{20}$$

Therefore any increase in I, G, or X will have an effect on Y which is $1/(1 - b + bt + d - dt)$ larger. We again have a multiplier but, not surprisingly, it is a more complicated expression. There is, however, a simple way of regarding this or indeed any multiplier so derived. Imagine someone receiving an increase in income of ΔY. An amount, $t\Delta Y$, goes in tax, leaving $\Delta Y(1 - t)$. A proportion of this is saved, i.e. not spent on consumer goods, $(1 - b)$, and a porportion is spent but on imported goods, d. The total amount of post-tax income not going on into a new round of domestic expenditure is therefore $\Delta Y(1 - b + d)$. Overall therefore the leakage is

$$t\Delta Y + \Delta Y(1 - t)(1 - b + d) = \Delta Y(1 - b + bt + d - dt).$$

We can see therefore that the multiplier is the reciprocal of the proportion of an increase in income which leaks away. This is generally true, whatever the actual leakages involved.

In practice multipliers can be calculated for the economy from detailed models which have been estimated on past behaviour, as is explained in the next section. However, they take into account the much greater complexity of the flow of income and behaviour in the money and asset markets in response to the initial shock. Clearly more is lost to the system in practice as any income spent on imports flows to foreign countries. Also, attempts to spend more entail increased borrowing which may increase interest rates and hence lower borrowing and activity elsewhere. It may also increase the money supply. The increased activity may put pressure on costs and have some impact on price inflation, leading to reduced consumption in order to maintain the real value of households' financial assets. All these factors tend to reduce the multiplier and hence although the marginal propensity to save in the UK at present may be less than 10 per cent, the multiplier is not greater than 10; in fact it is much nearer unity and, as is discussed in the next section, it has been suggested that it is less than unity, or even zero, because of all the offsetting influences.

The multiplier will tend to vary according to the nature of the initial shock. An increase in public expenditure on construction work will have a high proportion of feedback, initially through the flow of income because there is very little import content in construction work. Changes in the tax and benefit system which benefit high-income earners, say a reduction in the top rate of income tax, will have a different impact from an increase in Family Income Supplement, as both the marginal propensity to save and the import content of consumption of the two groups will be different.

An important feature to note about this form of multiplier analysis is that equations (1) to (13) were timeless. The calculation merely states what the eventual outcome will be—it does not say how long it will take to get there. The flows through the circle of income take place at varying rates in the order we described, but assessments of the level of activity in any particular accounting period will merely observe a section of the process. Multipliers calculated from models do in practice have such a time path and, most importantly, do not necessarily converge steadily towards the value $1/(1-b)$ in increasingly small steps. In addition a rise in income resulting from a boost to investment may itself lead to more investment in anticipation of increased expenditure. This further complicates the pattern of response in practice, and can in principle generate significant fluctuations in income, expenditure, and output. Certainly the UK economy shows cycles in behaviour, and models which try to represent that behaviour also generate cycles. Hence the effects on total income of an initial increase in expenditure may oscillate as time passes, although if subsequently undisturbed may tend to converge to some value eventually.

Such oscillation can be demonstrated more fully if we add only one equation to our economy, at present encapsulated by equations (4) and (5), *and* if we also add in the time path. The new equation reflects that investment is also determined within the system, as suggested above. If output changes, investment will also need to change to increase the capital stock. The important feature of this relation is that output is related to capital and hence investment is related to the *change* in output, not its level. So let us suggest simply that

$$I_{Ft} = c(Y_{t-1} - Y_{t-2}) \qquad (21)$$

where t denotes the time period. This suggests that investment adjusts to the change in output with a lag. (There will also need to be investment even when output does not change in order to replace capital consumed during the year, but for simplicity this is left out.)

If we take round values for b and c, say $\frac{1}{2}$ and 0.4, and a shock of 10 units maintained at that level, then the pattern of development would be as in Table 5.4. In period $t=1$ investment is assumed to increase by 10 for reasons which are unrelated to equation (21)—the government decides to invest more for example. This shock feeds through to income via the multiplier, which is 2 as $b=\frac{1}{2}$, and hence in $t=1$ the increase in income, ΔY_t, is 20. As the marginal propensity to consume is one-half, consumption increases by half the change in income, i.e. $\Delta C_t = 10$.

TABLE 5.4. *The Interaction of the Multiplier and the Accelerator*

t (1)	ΔC_t (2)	ΔC_t^T (3)	I_{Ft} (4)	ΔY_t (5)	ΔY_t^T (6)	I_{Ft}^* (7)
0	0	0	0	0	0	0
1	10	10	0	20	20	10
2	8	18	8	16	36	10
3	−1·6	16·4	6·4	−3·2	32·8	10
4	−7·7	8·7	−1·3	−15·4	17·4	10
5	−4·9	3·8	−6·2	−9·8	7·6	10
6	−2·3	6·1	−3·9	4·6	12·2	10
7	5·7	11·8	1·8	11·4	23·6	10
8	2·8	14·6	4·6	5·6	29·2	10
9	−2·4	12·2	2·2	−4·8	24·4	10
10	−4·2	8·0	−2·0	−8·4	16·0	10
11	−1·4	6·6	−3·4	−2·8	13·2	10
12	2·3	8·9	−1·1	4·6	17·8	10
13	0·0	20·1	0·1	−10·0	30·2	10
14	−5·1	15·1	−10·0	−15·1	15·1	10
15	−7·5	7·6	−15·1	−12·6	2·5	10
16	−6·3	1·3	−12·6	−3·8	−1·3	10

In period 2, investment $I_{Ft} = 0.4(20) = 8$. There is thus a further injection of 8 units into the system which through the multiplier increases income (column 5 in Table 5.4) by a further 16 units to a total of 36 (column 6). Half of this increase is again consumption because of the marginal propensity to consume of one-half. By period 3 the initial impetus is lost. The investment from the lagged change in income falls to $0.4(16) = 6.4$, so that total income is *lower* in period 3 than in period 2 (by $8 - 6.4$ (the fall in investment) multiplied by 2 (the multiplier), which equals 3·2. The lagged effect of this leads to disinvestment in period 4.

In a world with only the multiplier the final outcome would have been a rise in income of 20 units. When the investment relation is added this is still the final outcome, but there are oscillations round it. As is clear from Table 5.4, there are peaks in the response in periods 2 and 8 and troughs in periods 4 and 10, and the fluctuations continue indefinitely, steadily narrowing in on the 20-unit increase. The investment relation is known as the 'accelerator' and the outcome of its interaction with the multiplier will show explosive, steadily covergent, decreasing or increasing oscillating progress according to the values of b and c.

Again this is only a simplification and in the next sections we shall examine how the different relations in the economy contribute to the complex reaction to any shock to behaviour. In practice, although fixed investment does show wider variations than economic activity as a whole, a much larger contribution to the cycle is made by stockbuilding. Stocks tend to accumulate when there is a downturn in demand, until producers realize and cut back output. Since they can sell from this excess stock to meet demand, output is cut back further than

TABLE 5.5. *Contribution of Stockbuilding to Changes in GDP*

	Value of physical increase in stocks (£bn 1980) (1)	Increase in GDP (£bn 1980) (2)	Contribution of stock change to GDP change ((1)/(2) as %)
1976	1·1	6·9	15·9
1977	2·6	2·7	96·3
1978	2·1	5·6	37·5
1979	2·5	3·4	73·5
1980	− 3·2	− 5·4	59·3
1981	− 2·7	− 2·0	135·0
1982	− 1·0	4·3	− 23·3
1983	0·4*	6·2*	6·5

* Estimated.

Source: *Economic Trends.*

demand. Similarly, if demand rises it will initially be met by running down stocks. If we take the period from 1976 to 1983 (Table 5.5), stockbuilding changes in the same direction as GDP in all years except 1982, and contributed more than half of the change on four out of the eight occasions. The effect is most striking in the downturn. GDP fell by £7·4 billion between 1979 and 1981, while stockbuilding fell by £6·9 billion in the cycle. Other parts of the economy, however, such as the tax and benefits system, tend to reduce economic fluctuations, and the final outcome is the product of the interaction of all the components of income, output, and expenditure and requires quite a detailed model to represent it adequately.

5.4. Interactions of Macroeconomic Behaviour

5.4.1. *Some Different Views of How Transactions Interact*

The previous section has looked at a number of individual aspects of the economy. But a macroeconomic perspective looks at the economy as a whole, and we now go on to look at the interrelations that make up aggregate behaviour.

Consideration of the economy often concentrates on the behaviour of three 'markets', one for goods and services, hereinafter 'goods' for short, one for labour, and one for money. Sometimes this is extended to include a fourth market, that for 'bonds', which are thought of as being a representative financial asset which earns a rate of interest. Each of these markets exists because there are suppliers of the 'commodity' in question—goods, money, labour, etc.—and demanders of it; trade takes place at a price, which is a wage in the case of labour and a rate of interest in the case of money.

In such a simple world it is possible to trace through the interactions of the main influences on the economy and to set out the conditions necessary for the optimal operation of the economic system. Much of the controversy between macroeconomists can be explained in terms of how these four 'markets' operate and how they interact through the interrelated demands and supplies of economic agents. In particular the controversy focuses on how the markets react to discrepancies between supply and demand. At one extreme there is the view that markets 'clear', i.e. if the demand for goods exceeds the supply and prices are flexible, then supply will be brought into equality with demand by an increase in prices. In this case prices always adjust to keep supply and demand in equilibrium, while at the other extreme there is the view that prices do not necessarily adjust and hence the main markets in the economy are usually out of equilibrium.

In the 'neo-classical' approach there is a series of aggregated markets which are assumed to 'clear' simultaneously and more or less instantaneously. To quote a recent exponent, 'an excess supply of any particular product or asset will generate price changes for the asset which in turn will repercuss onto other assets and their prices' [30].[3] In this form of approach therefore it is prices that adjust and not quantities if the system is knocked out of equilibrium. Provided a solution to the system of the three markets is feasible then it will be possible to achieve some state of equilibrium. In a dynamic world this equilibrium state would involve the expansion of economic activity at its 'natural' rate, determined by the growth of inputs and technology, the maintenance of either no price inflation or at least inflation at a constant rate, and a 'natural' rate of unemployment. These 'natural' rates are such as to permit the system to move forward in price equilibrium, with all markets clearing. They entail also that the money stock shall expand at a rate consistent with the maintenance of this equilibrium. They are not maximal rates. Activity could expand faster but increased price inflation would result.

The Keynesian system on the other hand, although dealing with similarly aggregated markets, specifies a short period of equilibrium in which prices do not necessarily respond and quantities have to adjust. Thus if there is excess demand, rationing takes place in the sense that some of the demand goes unsatisfied. If there is then deficient demand, with wages not responding, unemployment results. The traditional Keynesian 'cure' for unemployment is to increase demand, i.e. to try to expand some of the demand categories in equation (1) by government policy. In the simplest case clearly this could be done by increasing government expenditure, either current or investment. Otherwise tax changes and incentives could be used to affect the categories of private sector expenditure.

This expansion must have consequences for the flow of funds and for the money supply and it is at this point that there is a further divergence of opinion, between those of a Keynesian persuasion and those of a more monetarist view.

[3] It is not suggested that this is an accurate description of day-to-day behaviour; rather, that over time the behaviour of the economy, at least for some important purposes, can best be understood and explained on this basis. In this sense an economic theory is rather like a map; it is simplified presentation of reality, the best form of which depends on the purpose (e.g. road map, ordinance survey, large- or small-scale, etc.).

(It is important to note the distinction between Keynes and 'Keynesians'; in particular that many of the simplifications and rationalizations introduced by Keynesians do not accord with Keynes's own statements.) At one extreme it may be argued that while increased government expenditure, carried out to increase demand, will require increased government borrowing and/or the putting of more bank deposits in the hands of the public, thereby increasing the money supply, neither of these consequences will have any severe offsetting effect. This is based on the view, first, that expenditures in the economy will not fall significantly if government borrowing pushes up interest rates; second, that financing increased government expenditure by allowing the money supply to increase could offset any undesirable rise in interest rates; third, that prices both of goods and labour are based on costs—of production and of living respectively—so that inflation will not, under conditions of spare capacity, increase as a consequence of the monetary expansion; and fourth, that the effects on the exchange rate do not interfere. Alternatively it may be believed that all these effects could occur, threatening to offset the demand expansion, but that other policy actions can be taken to offset them. An important feature therefore behind the Keynesian system is that a stimulus by the government feeds through to the rest of the economy and is not stifled by offsetting factors. Thus a stimulus to public investment will lead to increased incomes being paid out and increased demand for supplying firms, the suppliers will need to increase output and expand capacity, the income earners will in turn spend their incomes increasing demand elsewhere in the economy, and so on in a multiplicative process where the final result may be substantially higher than the initial stimulus. This cycle of expansion is damped by losses from the system, particularly by saving and by imports. If domestic production responds only slowly to an increase in demand then consumers will tend to purchase foreign goods and the benefits of the expansion will accrue abroad. But the overall effect is still viewed as positive and not necessarily offset as a result of the methods employed to finance the expansion. There are two corollaries from this; the first is that to have the greatest effect on activity the nature of the expenditure increase needs to be as closely related to domestic output as possible—e.g. through construction or certain service sectors—and the second is that stimuli will tend to be more effective when there is considerable slack capacity than when there is not.

Before contrasting this with the monetarist approach, it is worth noting an interesting perspective on this approach which has been brought out through detailed reappraisal of Keynes's work. The reappraisal, primarily due to Clower [31] and Leijonhufvud [37], accepted the basic proposition that prices do not change quickly to clear markets. It brings out that if only the unemployed had jobs and a commensurate income to spend they would generate the demand in the economy which would justify their employment. But the absence of such income constrains their purchasing power, which in turn leads to a continuation of unemployment. The mechanism would, of course, be indirect and does not imply that the individual, if re-employed, would purchase his own output; merely that the demand generated across the board would be sufficient to justify the employment across the board. In this scheme of affairs the problem is to move from the deficient position and make the *potential* demand effective.

One of the difficulties with this Keynesian system is the treatment of views about the future. Although Keynes himself had quite highly developed views about the role of expectations of the future in governing current actions, post-war Keynesians made little use of this. This feature of the dynamic structure of behaviour was, however, extensively developed in the monetarist critique of the Keynesian approach (see p. 162).

A Keynesian views of the world is of particular interest given persistent mass unemployment. But for much of the post-war period, demand did not appear deficient and frequently seemed to be running ahead of supply. Under these circumstances in the Keynesian world there is an 'inflationary gap'; supply cannot expand fast enough given the capacity currently available. Various indicators can be used of such a lack of capacity: the level of unemployment, the ratio of unemployment to vacancies, or the level of GDP relative to the trend rate of growth drawn through the highest points of each upswing in GDP, as illustrated in Figure 5.5. The indicators all rest on the assumption, supported

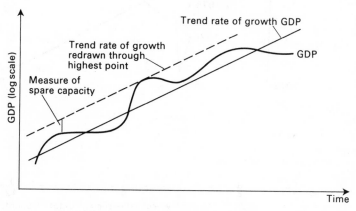

FIG. 5.5. The Pressure of Demand.

by experience, that there are limits to the rate of growth of productivity, i.e. output per head. If therefore there is little unemployment, further demand can only be met by the limited productivity gains and not by increasing labour input. If quantities cannot increase sufficiently then in the Keynesian system prices will adjust upwards. What the Keynesian system does not suggest is how this process of price inflation will end or at what price level it will stabilize. Up until 1967 the Phillips curve was thought to offer a statement of the long-run trade-off between unemployment and wage inflation (and hence price inflation, given the substantial contribution that wages make to total costs). Since then average rates of both price inflation and unemployment have risen from 3 per cent and 2 per cent respectively in 1956–64 to 16 per cent and 4½ per cent in 1974–80 (where price inflation is measured by the percentage change over four quarters earlier of the consumers' expenditure deflator, and unemployment is measured as a percentage of the UK labour force seasonally adjusted, excluding school-leavers). Since then inflation has fallen back to the 4–6 per cent range, but unemployment has risen to around 12 per cent. The path of inflation and unemployment shown in Figure 5.6, therefore, exhibits not a path of adjustment round a stable relation, but two sequences of price acceleration and decceleration while unemployment rose, thus giving a hooped path. This does not of course imply that the future will necessarily be a continuing series of hoops at ever higher levels of unemployment.

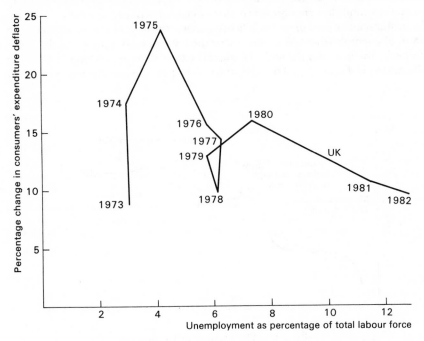

FIG. 5.6. Inflation and Unemployment in the UK, 1973–1982.

We now turn to the monetarist approach. This incorporates a number of features that can be outlined in terms already introduced above. These are, first, that markets clear and that in the long term unemployment will adjust to its 'natural' level; second, that price inflation is not indeterminate but can be explained by monetary phenomena; and third, that the financial repercussions of expansionary government policy will eventually cause full crowding-out of the initial increase in output. These elements are interrelated. In the monetarist approach, the existence of *changes in the rate of price inflation* indicate (ignoring the presence of lagged effects) that the level of unemployment is not at its 'natural level'. This comes about because the supply of labour, and indeed the demand for it, is thought to depend upon real wages. At the natural rate of unemployment, supply and demand are equal at a given *real* wage. Real wages tell us nothing about nominal wages and prices, merely that they move together without any particular tendency for one to run ahead of the other and (hence) alter the rate of inflation. Such destabilization can come from the supply of money. At the natural rate of unemployment, and hence output, the demand for money will depend upon prices and output. If the money supply rises faster than is necessary to meet this demand then people will hold more money than they require in equilibrium. They will respond to this by increasing expenditure, thus increasing demand rather more than supply. This will be met by a faster rate of price inflation than was previously experienced.

Initially, with prices rising faster than earnings, employers can increase profits and will be encouraged to take on more people. But this position cannot be maintained indefinitely given that real wages are falling. Either wage inflation increases to catch up with price inflation, the advantage to employers disappears and employment falls back to its 'natural' rate, or employers try to maintain their advantage by still faster price rises.

This adjustment process therefore *accelerates* the rate of inflation, it does not merely raise prices. This gives a view of the world in which, in equilibrium, unemployment and output would be at their natural rate and the money supply would increase at a rate commensurate with the natural rate of increase of output (as generated by the effect of innovation and the incorporation of technological change on productivity) and whatever rate of price inflation seemed desirable. This might not necessarily be zero; adjustments occur across different markets as prices change and there appears to be some asymmetry in this, suggesting that change is facilitated more readily by price rises in expanding areas than falls in declining ones. This might entail that a small positive rate of price inflation was preferred to a zero rate. But any attempt to move to a lower level of unemployment by expanding output would be unsuccessful. Either there would be crowding-out as interest rates (and with them the exchange rate) rose; or, if temporarily successful, there would be *ever-increasing* inflation until unemployment rose back to its natural rate. All this is examined in more detail in Chapter 7.

5.4.2. *Implications for Policy*

There are many aims of economic policy which relate not just to the avoidance of unnecessary unemployment, the elimination of high rates of price inflation, and the obtaining of as high a standard of living as possible, but to other specific objectives such as equality of income distribution, minimum standards of housing and education, and a long list of others. Here we shall merely consider how policy might be used to achieve the simple major aims in the framework of the domestic economy which has been set out and see how the policy prescription is altered according to one's view of the nature of the interrelations within the economy and the transmission of stimuli.

In the simplified Keynesian system the policy prescription is straight-forward. In order to move the economy towards a level where it is operating at its maximum sustainable rate of increase, demand needs to be expanded by governmental action, because rigidity of nominal wages and many prices will make the self-adjustment of the economy a slow process. Similarly the government should act to prevent too rapid growth and too low unemployment because this will generate an inflationary gap. There are minimum levels for unemployment because employees are not interchangeable. Skills may be required in one area while those unemployed may have different attributes, where 'areas' can be either geographic or refer to particular sorts of crafts. This individual mismatch will itself entail that there are costs as the system tries to adjust. Because the price level is not primarily determined by real activity a government might well be advised to maintain a prices and incomes policy to influence wages and prices directly. If all transactions were indexed for the rate of price inflation it is by no means clear that inflation would have much harmful effect by itself, except in the administrative costs of running such a system—involving frequent relabelling and rebasing. It is because the prices of different items move at different rates, and thus to the disadvantage of those selling or owning assets whose prices can move less quickly, that a world of rapid inflation is disliked. Furthermore, it is such variability and unpredictability which make a major contribution to the costs of society as a whole because planning and organization become difficult. It becomes necessary to maintain a higher level of liquidity in order to cover contingencies which in itself will tend to reduce the rate of growth by reducing consumption and investment.

The government has available to it a wide range of fiscal and monetary instruments with which to try to achieve its objectives. However, it is clear that it is not possible to calculate the policy required exactly and hence achieve the government's aims. In the first place there is, as we have noted, a trade-off between outcomes, particularly between economic growth and price inflation, and the trade-off is much more complex when the foreign sector is introduced (see next chapter.) It is not possible to assign a particular policy instrument to each objective and maximize them independently. For example, if a government wishes to give the consumer more choice about how to use his income and yet raise the same total sum in taxation it can institute a switch from income taxation to expenditure taxation as the government did in 1979, reducing the basic rate of income tax from 33 to 30 per cent and increasing VAT from the twin rates of 8 and $12\frac{1}{2}$ per cent to a uniform 15 per cent. This may have no effect on real personal disposable income because while disposable incomes are raised by the tax cut, prices are raised by the VAT increase. This move is thus contrary in the short term to the aim of reducing the rate of price inflation. Indeed it may be substantially so in the longer term, although the tax change is a once-and-for-all increase in itself, it may have a knock-on effect as it feeds through on to subsequent wage increases—wage bargainers not being able to accept that further nominal wage increases are not required as real personal disposable incomes are not changed by the tax package as a whole.

It is a matter of choice for the government as to which particular fiscal changes to use. Income and expenditure tax changes have a fairly quick impact on real incomes and hence consumption patterns, especially if concentrated on low-income groups or essential goods like food, electricity, gas, or housing.

However, government expenditure increases have a much more immediate effect on employment and domestic output. Indeed it is by no means clear that the final multiplier effects of different uses of the same-sized initial fiscal expansion in monetary terms will be the same once the variations in the time path have been taken into account, nor will the final effect on the balance of government revenues necessarily be the same. A sophisticated policy in these terms may actually seek to exploit the different time paths of effects to try to offset the cycles which seem to affect economic activity as a whole. Thus a policy which has an impact effect in the short run but none at all in the long run may nevertheless be worthwhile because of the timing of its positive and negative phases. However, there is a premium on accuracy in such sophisticated policy and it has frequently been argued (Dow [34] being the seminal case) that UK policy-making has actually made the fluctuations in the economy worse by getting the timing wrong.

In a simplified monetarist system, the policy implications are also clear, but quite different. Output and employment in the long term are determined by the 'natural' rate; any attempt to stabilize the economy at a higher level will generate accelerating inflation and eventually be unsuccessful. Even if unemployment is above the natural rate, this does not indicate a role for fiscal expansion by government. It is not necessary because the movement of price and wage expectations downwards will gradually permit the economy to move back to its natural rate of unemployment. Indeed fiscal expansion may be counterproductive both in slowing the downward revision of expectations and in eventually generating a level of unemployment lower than the natural rate. This would then set inflationary pressures off again.

Though the government cannot therefore control the long-term path of output and employment in the monetarist system (other than by measures which change the natural rate, which for the moment we leave aside) it nevertheless determines the rate of inflation. Using the monetary identity

$$MV = PY$$

which we discussed earlier, with V, the velocity of circulation, presumed constant and Y, real GDP, tending to its natural level, the rate of increase in prices depends entirely on the rate of growth of the money supply, which is assumed to be under the control of the monetary authorities. It may of course be that in an immediate sense, a rising level of prices is the result of rising costs, but the latter are viewed as able to occur in the long term only to the extent that increases in the money supply permit this. The main government objective therefore is to set clear monetary targets and adhere to them. A low target, if achieved, will generate low inflation, and the clear determination to adhere to the targets will influence people's expectations so that the latter adjust quickly.

In this view of the world, the trade-offs inherent in the Keynesian view disappear. In the long term there is no trade-off between inflation and unemployment. Fiscal policy becomes secondary to monetary policy. Too high a level of government spending relative to tax revenue either has to be financed by increases in the money supply, which is inflationary, or, in order to avoid this, has to be financed by borrowing. But this drives up interest rates and 'crowds out' expenditure on investment and consumer durables, thereby offsetting any temporary expansion generated by higher government spending and/or lower taxation.

Clearly there is no role for 'fine-tuning' here. Partly the argument against fine-tuning is just that it is too difficult to get right, either because of the unpredictability of the timing and the size of its effects, or because of the way in which it can be nullified by the normal 'random' shocks to the economy. A more comprehensive objection to this form of fine-tuning comes from those who argue that it merely destabilizes activity and has no long-run benefit because agents in the economy can work out its effects and take offsetting action. In the extreme case this is based on a combination of a strict monetarist view of the economy and the *Theory of Rational Expectations*. Most suggestions about how expectations of future values of economic variables such as prices are formed involve the use of past behaviour and any indicators of the future that are available. Schemes of expectations formation which involve people getting the answer wrong in a consistent manner are usually rejected but rational expectations make a stronger assumption than this, namely, that the distribution of people's expectations is the same as the distribution of actual values of the variable for the future. People are thus correct on average in their expectations, because they would change their expectations formation process if this were not so, and therefore they behave as if they knew how the economy worked.

The consequences of this for economic policy depend upon the 'model' of behaviour by which the economy is supposed to work. If it is the basic monetarist scheme, then people can see through the effects of an attempt to expand the economy. They anticipate the price effect straight away and therefore try to make up the real value of their financial assets to take account of the expected price rise, thus cutting back on consumption and offsetting the governmental attempt to expand. There are in practice, however, several restraints on the rate of adjustment, not least through the lags in the operation of the labour market (see [39]). While firms can raise their prices reasonably quickly wage contracts tend to be negotiated annually, hence frustrating rapid adjustment of wages.

This process of rational expectation includes expectation of the way the government will react. Indeed with rational expectations the only way that stimuli to the economy can have any real effect is if they are not expected. Thus the random shocks, such as oil crises and natural disasters, can have effects since they have not been allowed for, but otherwise the appropriate role for a government is to have a clearly stated policy about how it proposes to facilitate the economy to develop at its natural rate so that people can form expectations readily and to enable rapid adjustment.

It does not, however, follow that simple rules or fixed values for policy variables are appropriate; the inherent cyclical nature of the economy can generate a fluctuating result from a constant input, and the use of constant policy rules may amplify fluctuations by offsetting the effect of 'automatic stabilizers' already built into the system. For example, welfare benefits systems automatically act to help to even out the fluctuations in income caused by fluctuations in output and employment; trying to hold the budget deficit to a pre-assigned value can, under these circumstances, amplify the fluctuations that would otherwise have occurred.

Although we have characterized the transmission of effects in the economy in a deliberately simplified way it is clearly crucial for the appropriate policy choice as to how the interactions do take place in a dynamic framework. The position is greatly complicated by the addition of the foreign sector and the need to strive for balance between economies as well as within the domestic one. Subsequent chapters develop these issues and refine the views set out here.

5.5. The Domestic Economy since 1960

5.5.1. Structural Change 1960–1982

Table 5.1 sets out a picture of the domestic economy as described by the National Accounts. We could now examine the National Accounts for earlier years, but since they are expressed in the prices of each individual year comparison would be very difficult as the result of price inflation. Table 5.6 therefore shows 1961 and 1982 in the prices of a single year, 1980, to eliminate the effects of price inflation. Over that 21-year period economic activity in the UK increased by a half, but this increase was unevenly distributed over the categories of expenditure. International trade became strikingly more important, growing 1–1½ times. (The discrepancy between the movement in exports and that in imports occurs because two single years are chosen for the comparison; it happens that the first has a trade deficit and the second a substantial surplus.) The importance of investment appears to have fallen, growing by 10 percentage points less than activity as a whole. There also appears to have been a more-than-proportionate increase in indirect taxation (adjustment to factor cost). Lastly net property income from abroad has grown very little over two decades. In part this reflects the results of the exploitation of North Sea oil which involved considerable foreign investment which then earned an income for the foreign investors.

The structure of activity can be seen to have changes far more striking if we examine output rather than expenditure, as in Table 5.7. Although output overall still of course increases by about a half, several categories of activity have actually fallen; construction, motor vehicles and parts, clothing, footwear and leather, other transport, equipment, textiles, metals, metal goods not elsewhere specified (n.e.s.), and coal and coke, very markedly in the case of the last three categories. The biggest rise, quite naturally, is extraction of mineral oil and natural gas, reflecting the exploitation of North Sea resources. In general, outside the public sector, manufacturing output has increased at less than half the pace of overall activity and the other categories have risen compensatingly faster. However, there are some clear exceptions in manu-facturing to the general sluggishness: chemicals, electrical and instrument engineering (which includes electronics), and drink and tobacco. The major non-manufacturing gainers are communications, banking, finance, insurance business services and leasing and agriculture. While the former two are

TABLE 5.6. *UK Expenditure 1961 and 1982 at 1980 Market Prices*

	1961* (£m)	1982	1982/1961 (%)
Consumers' expenditure	89,628	138,865	55
General government final consumption	32,133	49,011	53
Gross domestic fixed capital formation	26,284	37,614	43
Value of physical increase in stocks and work in progress	1,357	− 1,031	—
Total domestic expenditure	149,579	224,459	50
Exports of goods and services	25,676	62,789	145
Total Final Expenditure	174,770	287,248	64
less Imports of goods and services	− 26,742	− 57,997	117
Gross Domestic Product (at market prices)	147,972	229,251	55
Adjustment to factor cost	− 19,503	− 30,927	59
Gross Domestic Product (at factor cost)	128,545	198,324	54
Net property income from abroad	1,233	1,362	10
Gross National Product (at factor cost)	129,963	199,686	54
less Capital consumption	− 12,333	− 29,114	136
National Income	117,321	170,572	45

Source: *National Income and Expenditure.*

* The 1961 figures in 1980 prices do not add up in the Blue Book as a result of changing the price base.

explicable in terms of modern technology, the rise in agriculture can largely be attributed to the consequences of UK membership of the EC and consequently higher agricultural prices.

While comparing single years can always be somewhat misleading because of wide short-run fluctuations, it is very clear from Table 5.7 that there have been major changes over the last few years; a fall of 20 per cent compared with 1979 for textiles and metals goods and of over 30 per cent for metals and man-made fibres. (In 1980 all values are 100·0 as the base year.) The relative decline in manufacturing over 1961–84 in fact comprises a relative increase over 1961–73, (manufacturing increased by 48 per cent while GDP as a whole increased by 41 per cent) and a rapid absolute decline (15 per cent) between 1979 and 1982.

5.5.2. *The Business Cycle and Policy since the 1960s*

It is thus very important to consider the development of activity over time. The

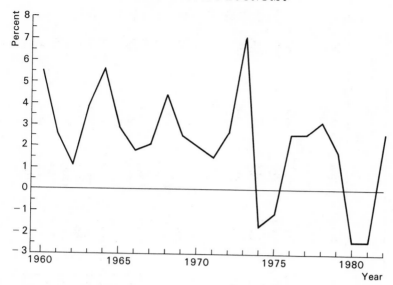

F IG. 5.7. Growth of UK Gross Domestic Product, 1960–1982 (per cent). Average measure in 1975 prices at factor cost.

Source: *Economic Trends*.

path of total activity is shown in Figure 5.7. Up to 1974 output rose every year but by varying amounts. There is a clear business cycle with peaks in 1960, 1964, 1968, and 1973 and a duration of 4–5 years. The next cycle with a peak in 1978 fits into this framework but with a dramatic trough in 1974–5 following the first oil crisis, while the most recent cycle has probably not yet reached its peak. In many ways 1973 seems to represent a watershed. It was the year of fastest growth and thereafter the economy never got back to the sustained rate of growth it had had in the 1960s.

(i) 1960–1973

Up to 1973 the cyclical pattern in the economy was not merely marked but thought to be largely explicable. Partly it arose from the interaction of the multiplier and accelerator as described on pp. 152–3. But also, as the economy expanded much of the increased income went into imports, worsening the balance of payments. Pressure on resources tended to drive up wages and prices and at some stage the government moved into slow up the rate of change of activity by a contractionary budget and thereby reverse the payments deficit and slow the rate of inflation. Then as the rate of growth turned down the government would seek to stimulate the economy again by some combination of tax concessions and public expenditure increases. It was thus trying to manage demand in the economy to meet the objectives of a high rate of growth, stable prices, and low unemployment, etc. with the avoidance of persistent balance of payments difficulties. (This process is described in detail in Chapter

TABLE 5.7. *UK Output 1961–1982*
(index numbers at constant factor cost, 1980 = 100)

	Weight*	1961	1973	1979	1982	1982/1961 (%)
Agriculture, forestry, and fishing	22	62·2	87·4	89·8	112·5	81
Production						
Energy and water supply:						
Coal and coke	15	204·9	114·0	97·6	93·2	−55
Extraction of mineral oil and natural gas	44	0·1	2·2	98·4	125·7	1,300
Mineral oil processing	5	67·8	126·9	113·7	92·8	37
Other energy and water supply	31	47·6	87·1	102·2	98·6	107
Total	95	44·8	55·8	100·3	110·1	146
Manufacturing (revised definition)						
Metals	9	..	155·1	132·2	100·8	−33†
Other minerals and mineral products	15	74·9	128·6	112·2	94·4	26
Chemicals	24	45·1	96·4	110·5	101·0	124
Man-made fibres	1	45·4	175·6	137·0	68·0	50
Metal goods n.e.s.	16	..	139·4	120·6	78·0	−41†
Mechanical engineering	38	83·6	115·2	108·4	89·7	7
Electrical and instrument engineering	34	48·6	95·6	100·9	96·1	98
Motor vehicles and parts	15	87·2	139·4	118·7	81·6	−6
Other transport equipment	14	115·2	100·5	92·4	99·0	−14
Food	24	79·2	99·0	100·5	102·4	29
Drink and tobacco	12	54·9	89·8	101·9	91·6	67
Textiles	9	110·3	149·2	120·9	87·0	−21
Clothing, footwear, and leather	10	95·6	111·2	115·2	87·8	−8
Paper, printing, and publishing	24	79·4	109·6	108·0	90·6	14
All other manufacturing (including timber, furniture, rubber, and plastics)	21	66·0	120·4	116·0	87·8	33
Total	266	77·3	114·1	109·5	92·4	20

Total production	361	67·9	99·4	107·1	97·1	26
Construction	63	93·9	122·4	105·6	91·4	−3
Total production and construction	424	71·6	102·5	106·9	96·2	34
Distribution, hotels and catering, repairs	128	78·5	107·0	109·0	99·3	26
Transport and communication						
Transport	46	69·8	100·8	103·9	96·6	38
Communication	26	43·4	81·8	97·4	104·9	142
Total	72	60·8	93·6	101·5	99·6	64
Banking, finance, insurance, business services, and leasing	116	47·0	81·0	97·0	110·0	134
Ownership of dwellings	62	66·0	87·0	99·0	103·0	56
Public administration, national defence, and compulsory social security	69	84·0	99·0	99·0	98·0	17
Education and health services	87	56·0	82·0	99·0	101·0	80
Other services‡	61	66·0	82·0	95·0	94·0	42
Adjustment for financial services	−41	..	80·0	95·0	110·0	150§
Gross Domestic Product	1,000	68·0	96·4	103·3	99·0	46

* The weights are proportional to the distribution of net output in 1980 and are used to combine the indices from 1978 onwards.
† 1982/1968.
‡ Comprising classes 92, 94, 96–99 and oo of the Standard Industrial Classification, revised 1980.
§ 1982/1963.

Source: *National Income and Expenditure.*

13 on demand management in practice.) Apart from the last year the UK operated a fixed exchange rate system throughout the period which was changed only in November 1967 by a devaluation from \$2.80/£ to \$2.40/£. Thus, since the relative price of traded goods could not otherwise be affected, balance of trade deficits were generally corrected by reducing the demand for imports through general deflation of the economy. After 1972 this constraint no longer applied in the same way.

In looking at economic performance and policy in this period, it is important to note that over the period 1960–73 governments changed four times. In 1960 the Conservatives were in power with Harold Macmillan as Prime Minister. He was replaced for a year by Sir Alec Douglas-Hume when he resigned through ill-health in October 1963. In the main during that period economic policy took the form of changes to indirect taxes and hire-purchase controls. Also, in 1961 the UK had applied (for the first time) to join the Common Market and negotiations lasted for over a year until vetoed by France in early 1963. This period in early 1963 is also remembered for an extremely severe cold spell which in econometric terms is found to disturb many estimated macroeconomic relationships. One of the other major facets of economic policy over the cycle was the attempt to control wage inflation more directly by an incomes policy, with a zero norm in 1961–2, subsequently raised progressively. Macmillan also tried to increase growth and the rate of structural reorganization in the economy, setting up in 1962 the tripartite National Economic Development Council of government ministers and the leaders of the TUC and CBI.

In October 1964 the Labour Party won the general election by a narrow majority and Harold Wilson became Prime Minister. The recovery in the economy began to peter out despite a high level of activity in policy-making with the creation of a Department of Economic Affairs under George Brown and the publication of a National Plan looking ahead to the end of the decade. The balance of payments had already moved into deficit and budgets in November 1964 and April 1965 sought an improvement. Monetary policy was also used quite extensively and a series of incomes policies with special provision for benefits from productivity agreements implemented. An import surcharge of 15 per cent (later reduced to 10 per cent) was introduced in 1964 to aid the task of improving the balance of payments and a £50 personal travel allowance limit was imposed in 1966. While the Budgets of 1966 and 1967 were largely neutral, those of 1968 and 1969 were again deflationary and the slight recovery in activity following the devaluation in 1967 was not sustained. The 1966 Budget introduced the innovation of the Selective Employment Tax (SET) which, with the Regional Employment Premium (1967), sought to encourage labour to move from services to manufacturing areas and to increase jobs in areas of highest unemployment.

Around the end of the 1960s the economic picture in the UK changed quite markedly. Up to 1969 the annual rate of price inflation had not exceeded 5 per cent since the Korean war. It has not, except for a brief period in 1983, fallen below it since. Similarly unemployment had not normally risen above $2\frac{1}{2}$ per cent of the labour force (employed plus unemployed) until 1969 and has not fallen below it since. However, while price inflation has had wild fluctuations since, rising to nearly 25 per cent in 1975 and falling to 8 per cent in 1978 before rising to 18 per cent again in 1980 and dropping to around 5 per cent by 1983, unemployment has shown a much more steadily rising profile, with falls only in 1972–3 and 1978–9.

In 1970 the Conservatives were returned to power and several important changes in policy took place. 1971 saw the introduction of Competition and Credit Control by the Bank of England, which sought to give a system of more flexible controls over the banking system and to encourage more competition between banks. The major upshot, however, was a rapid expansion in the money supply. Hire-purchase restrictions were abolished. The Budgets from 1970–4 were all expansionary, particularly that of 1972.

The UK finally succeeded in joining the EC at the beginning of 1973. VAT was introduced that year, partly to bring the UK into line with the EC, and purchase tax and SET abolished. Bank Rate was replaced by Minimum Lending Rate (MLR) which was more closely related to Treasury Bill yields in the autumn of 1972.

As the economy began to grow more rapidly so did price inflation. The so-called '$n-1$' incomes policy of the previous years—trying to make each wage settlement smaller than the previous one—was replaced by a freeze and then a low ceiling. In 1973 a much greater innovation was introduced in the form of threshold payments, which were that for every 1 per cent increase in prices above 7 per cent wages were also to rise. While it was hoped that these clauses would on the whole not have to be invoked the timing could not have been more unfortunate. In December 1973 the price of crude oil was doubled by OPEC, before any oil was obtained from the North Sea (June 1975). A massive balance of payments deficit ensued, but the exchange rate fell only slowly, picking up speed in the second half of 1975 until it reached an all-time low at the end of 1976. At the same time as the oil crisis the UK faced a serious strike by coal miners. This crippled electricity production which was dependent on coal and the industry had to operate a three-day week to conserve fuel. The surge in prices caused by the rise in oil prices and the feedthrough from the previous monetary and fiscal expansions all came through together. The domestic economy was constrained by the three-day week and the miners' strike, and the overall inflationary consequences were very severe. The stimulus of the previous year was counteracted extremely rapidly, and in retrospect the events of 1973–4 marked a substantial break in the development of the post-war economy.

(ii) 1974–1983

The government chose to call a general election largely on their handling of the miners' strike and lost (a second general election in October returned Harold Wilson to power with an overall majority). Initially the government tried to avoid contractionary measures and further control of incomes, but a strong incomes policy, the 'Social Contract', arranged with the co-operation of the trade unions, helped to bring wage rates down in advance of prices in three successive years until 1978, when no agreement could be reached. In 1977 an attempt was made to achieve a bargain of a tax cut in return for wage restraint. Although the government deficit widened sharply in 1974–6 increasing attention began to be paid to the Public Sector Borrowing Requirement (PSBR) as an aim of policy, aided by discussion with the International Monetary Fund (IMF) to finance massive loans to offset the effects of the oil shock. In particular restraint was agreed on public expenditure. Increasing use was made of monetary policy, and monetary targets were introduced in 1977.

There was thus a considerable change in the flavour of economic policy even before the 1979 election when Mrs Thatcher and the Conservatives again came to power. The 1979 Budget, which was delayed until after the election, involved a switch from direct to indirect taxation. This in itself added over 3 per cent to the price level, which, combined with the already rising wage rates after the collapse of the Social Contract, led to a new burst of price inflation. Interest rates were raised substantially in the autumn and a Medium-Term Financial Strategy (MTFS) was developed which involved a series of declining targets for the PSBR as a ratio of GDP and for the money supply. This was mainly to be achieved by the restraint of public expenditure rather than increases in taxation. Nevertheless domestic demand turned down in advance of the second oil crisis which followed further OPEC price rises. Since the UK was a substantial oil producer by then the rise in the price of oil further stimulated the exchange rate, which had been rising slowly from its low point in 1976–7. This was despite a large outflow of capital for foreign investment following the abolition of exchange controls in late 1979. As activity fell and unemployment rose, the government introduced a range of measures to sustain employment, particularly for young people who were especially badly affected. However, this was all within the terms of the MTFS which meant that the government fiscal stance did not respond counter-cyclically to the previous extent—income tax allowances and thresholds were not raised in line with inflation in the 1981 Budget. But by 1982, as inflation fell sharply, there was some slackening in the stance and the economy began to recover slowly. The 1972–82 recession was characterized by an unusually heavy fall in employment relative to output. Also, the fall in output was itself heavily concentrated in manufacturing industry which was hit on the one hand by the general fall in demand and on the other by the unfavourable movement in an exchange rate dominated by oil and the government's restrictive monetary policy. The effect on price inflation was very powerful, lowering it, in 1983, to below 5 per cent for the first time since the 1960s. While there was no general incomes policy, salaries were heavily restricted in the public sector in sharp contrast to a comparability exercise conducted in 1979 which led to substantial public sector pay rises.

This rapid fall in employment entailed a very rapid rise in labour productivity which helped to regain some of the lost competitiveness of previous years. The pressures on the economy, and on firms in particular, seemed to be so great that difficult decisions which would lead to increased efficiency and that had previously been postponed, not least through worries about trade union reaction, were accelerated. As the economy moved into 1983, growth accelerated, helped by a fall in the savings ratio as inflation fell, and by a small fiscal stimulus. But the growth of activity in 1982–3, though strong, was not sufficient to increase employment and stem the rise in unemployment effectively.

Also, one of the major features of the recovery was the rise in consumption of durable goods (especially motor cars) after hire-purchase controls were abolished again in late 1982. However, as on previous occasions much of the benefits of this consumer boom were lost to UK manufacturers as a disproportionate share of the demand went to imports. Thus while major changes may have been wrought on British industry by the severity of the recession it is not clear that many of the fundamental problems restraining UK growth were solved as a result.

5.6. Conclusions

In this chapter we have set out a brief overview of the various parts of the domestic economy and the way in which they interact. The transactions between economic agents can be summarized in a simple framework of a circular flow of incomes, where the process of production of goods and services by firms entails the payment of wages and salaries to employees. These wages and salaries form the income of households which is in turn spent on goods and services or saved. Firms also earn incomes in the form of profits which they can distribute or use for investment in assets. The government as the other main agent in the economy also features in the flow of incomes both as an employer and as a redistributor of incomes, away from some in the form of taxation and to others in benefits and grants. This descriptive scheme sets out the main forms of economic activity in the economy, but it does not quantify them nor does it provide an explanation of why they take place. Quantification takes place through a system of National Accounts whereby total activity in the economy can be measured as the sum of incomes, or as the sum of expenditures, or as the sum of output. However, these accounts do not cover the measurement of the wealth of the nation and the way it is held in the form of physical assets— buildings, plant, machinery, etc.—or financial assets—money, stocks and shares, bank deposits, for example. They cover *additions* to wealth and *changes* in the net holdings of funds by the various sectors of the economy.

The subject of macroeconomics and the main purpose of the chapter is much more than a pure description of activity and an accounting system, it is the explanation of the determinants of the behaviour described. It therefore concentrates on the actions of the groups of economic agents. For example, firms have to decide upon how much to produce and what inputs of materials, labour, and capital to use in production. Households decide on the basis of their incomes, their wealth, their expectations of the future, and relative prices what they will spend on the various sorts of goods and services.

It is, however, important to look at the operations of the economy as a whole so that we can see the consequences of the sum of individual decisions for issues such as unemployment, price inflation, and economic growth. As part of this general view the chapter explains the role of money in the economy. The determination of government policy and the way it can affect the working of the economy are also best introduced at this aggregate level and the chapter traces through the ways in which fiscal and monetary policy operates.

While there is considerable consensus among economists over the determinants of the main components of economic activity, there are sharply contrasting views held about the way in which the economy as a whole operates and the consequences this has for the effectiveness of the economy and the way shocks are transmitted through the system. The chapter therefore discusses the main elements of the two most well-known schools of thought, the Keynesian and monetarist views of the economic system, outlining their major points of difference. Thus there are expositions of the arguments about the way in which markets operate, the role of portfolio behaviour, the financing mechanism, and expectations. It is then possible to trace out the consequences of these differences in terms of the way in which a shock is fed through the economic system, with the operation of the multiplier modified by the operation of other relations such as the accelerator and the degree to which any of the authorities' attempts to stimulate demand merely 'crowd out' activity elsewhere in product, financial, and labour markets.

In order to see how the system has operated in practice there is a brief exposition of the behaviour of the UK economy over the period from 1960 to the present day. This highlights the way in which economic policy has evolved from the era of stop–go, through the attempts at economic planning and intervention, the change from fixed to floating exchange rates and the first oil crisis, to the recent recession and the operation of the Medium-Term Financial Strategy.

This chapter thus provides the core from which many of the subsequent chapters develop. Thus although the treatment of ideas here is purely introductory in order to provide a clear overall view of the working of the domestic economic system, those ideas are taken up later in detail. In the first place the international dimension is developed in the next chapter with the discussion of the balance of payments and the rate of exchange. This is followed in Chapter 7 by the consideration of the most prominent policy problem, inflation and unemployment. Chapters 8 and 9 discuss the public sector in more detail, the former looking at the objectives and instruments of policy and the latter at the public sector itself, examining expenditure, taxation, and the PSBR. The next four chapters then look at how macroeconomic policy can be used and how it has been used in practice in the UK over the last few years. This set of chapters begins with one on monetary policy followed by one on pay and is concluded by two which deal with demand management as a whole. The first of this pair deals with theory and measurement and the second with the way in which the policies have evolved in practice. In order to look at these various issues in quantitative terms it is necessary to specify and estimate economic models of the whole economy with which one can examine the nature of the interrelations in behaviour, look at the effects of different policies, and forecast what the consequences of actions are likely to be in the future. Chapter 14 therefore deals with this whole subject of modelling the economy.

Bibliography

SELECTIVE READING

The next few chapters of this book probably provide the most suitable follow up to this chapter, but there are many other avenues of suitable further reading.

The same two basic texts by Lipsey and Samuelson cited in the Bibliography to Chapter 3 ([1] and [2]) provide a good introduction to macroeconomics as well. However, there are some more specific texts on the subject, for example:

[1] JACKSON, D. *Introduction to Economics: Theory and Data* (Macmillan, 1982) follows a very empirical approach to the subject while

[2] DERNBERG, T. *Macroeconomics*, 6th edn. (McGraw-Hill, 1982) is a very widely used mainstream text book on the theory. A less formal exposition can be found in:

[3] ROWAN, D. C. *Output, Inflation and Growth*, 3rd edn. (Macmillan, 1983).

Two further recent books provide differing approaches to the subject:

[4] GODLEY, W. and CRIPPS, F. *Macroeconomics* (Oxford University Press, 1983).

[5] GREENWAY, D. and SHAW, G. K. *Macroeconomics: Theory and Policy in the UK* (Martin Robertson, 1983).

but one older text relating to the US economy still provides one of the best empirical approaches to the subject:

[6] EVANS, M. K. *Macroeconomic Activity* (Harper and Row, 1969).

There are three main areas of further reading on specific topics which are worth highlighting: (a) the main controversies over the theories of macroeconomic behaviour, (b) rational expectations and the new classical economics, (c) empirically based discussions of the UK's economic problems and performance.

(a) Macroeconomic Controversies

There are three well-known discussions of competing theories:

[7] CHRYSTAL, K. A. *Controversies in Macroeconomics*, 2nd edn. (Philip Allan, 1983).

[8] CUTHBERTSON, K. *Macroeconomic Policy* (Macmillan, 1979).

[9] STEIN, J. L. *Monetarist, Keynesian and New Classical Economics* (Basil Blackwell, 1983).

(b) Rational Expectations

[10] SHAW, G. K. *Rational Expectations* (Wheatsheaf, 1984).

[11] BEGG, D. K. H. *The Rational Expectations Revolution in Macroeconomics* (Philip Allan, 1982).

[12] MINFORD, A. P. L. and PEEL, D. A. *Rational Expectations and the New Macroeconomics* (Martin Robertson, 1983).

(c) The UK's Economic Problems and Performance

[13] PREST, A. R. and COPPOCK, D. J. (eds.). *The UK Economy—A Manual of Applied Economics*, 8th edn. (Weidenfeld and Nicolson, 1984).

[14] WORSWICK, G. D. N. and ADY, P. (eds.). *The British Economy in the 1950s* (Oxford University Press, 1962).

[15] DOW, J. C. R. *The Management of the British Economy 1984–60* (Cambridge University Press, 1964).

[16] BECKERMAN, W. (ed.). *The Labour Government's Economic Record 1964–70* (Duckworth, 1972).

[17] CAVES, R. (ed.). *Britain's Economic Prospects* (Brookings Institution, 1968).

[18] BLACKABY, F. T. (ed.). *British Economic Policy 1960–74* (Cambridge University Press, 1978).

[19] CAIRNCROSS, A. *Britain's Economic Prospects Reconsidered* (George Allen and Unwin, 1971).

[20] BACON, R. and ELTIS, W. *Britain's Economic Problem: Too Few Producers* (Macmillan, 1978).

[21] CAVES, R. E. and KRAUSE, L. B. (eds.). *Britain's Economic Performance* (Brookings Institution, 1980).

[22] MAUNDER, P. (ed.). *The British Economy in the 1970s* (Heinemann, 1980).

[23] POSNER, M. (ed.). *Demand Management* (Heinemann, 1978).

[24] VINES, D., Maciejowski, J. M. and MEADE, J. E. *Demand Management* (George Allen and Unwin), 1983).

Regular surveys of the British economy are contained in:

[25] *National Institute Economic Review* (quarterly).

[26] *Bank of England Quarterly Bulletin.*

[27] OECD, *Economic Survey* (annual).

[28] OECD, *Economic Outlook* (half-yearly).

REFERENCES IN THE TEXT

[29] BEAN, C. 'An econometric Model of Manufacturing Investment in the UK', Government Economic Service Working Paper, No. 29 (HM Treasury, 1979).

[30] BEENSTOCK, M. *A Neoclassical Analysis of Macroeconomic Policy* (Cambridge University Press, 1980).

[31] CLOWER, R. 'The Keynesian Counter-revolution: A Theoretical Reappraisal', in Hahn, F. H. and Brechling, F. P. R. (eds.), *The Theory of Interest Rates* (Macmillan, 1965).

[32] CUTHBERTSON, K. 'The Measurement and Behaviour of the UK Saving Ratio in the 1970s', *National Institute Economic Review*, 99 (Feb. 1982).

[33] DEATON, A. 'Involuntary Saving Through Unanticipated Inflation', *American Economic Review*, **67**/5 (Dec. 1977), 899–910.

[34] Dow [15].

[35] HAY, D. A. and MORRIS, D. J. *Industrial Economics: Theory and Evidence* (Oxford University Press, 1979).

[36] LAURY, J. S. E., LEWIS, G. R., and ORMEROD, P. A. 'Properties of Macroeconomic Models of the UK Economy: A Comparative Study', *National Institute Economic Review*, 83 (Feb. 1978).

[37] LEIJONHUFVUD, A. *On Keynesian Economics and the Economics of Keynes* (Oxford University Press, 1968).

[38] MAYES, D. G. *Applications of Econometrics* (Prentice-Hall, 1981).

[39] —— —— 'The Controversy over Rational Expectations', *National Institute Economic Review*, 96 (May 1981).

[40] —— —— 'Analysis and Forecasting at the National Institute' (Cambridge University Press, forthcoming).

[41] SAVAGE, D. 'The Channels of Monetary Influence: A Survey of the Empirical Evidence', *National Institute Economic Review*, 83 (Feb. 1978).

6

The Balance of Payments and the
Exchange Rate

P. J. N. SINCLAIR

6.1. The Balance of Payments

6.1.1. Introduction

The previous chapter began to fit together the various sectors of the economy. Inevitably, its description of the foreign trade sector was purely introductory. In this chapter we expand upon this area, examining the different types of international transactions that occur, the way these are treated in the balance of payments accounts, the short- and long-term determinants of each type of transaction, and the problems that can arise with a country's international economic transactions. We look also at the key role played by the exchange rate.

6.1.2. International Economic Transactions and Exchange Rates

In principle, international economic transactions resemble domestic transactions. Companies, governments, and households buy and sell, borrow and lend. Transactions are international when the parties to them do not all reside in the same country. Since most countries have their own currency for use in domestic transactions, international transactions will typically involve at least one party in the use of foreign currency. The relative price of one currency in terms of another is called the *exchange rate*. If the exchange rate between sterling and the US dollar is 1·60, for example, £1 is worth US $1·60, and $1 is worth 62½p. At one extreme, exchange rates may be fixed. This means that the monetary authorities in either or both of the countries concerned intervene in the currency markets to keep the exchange rate at, or very close to, a specified number. At the other extreme, exchange rates may be floating freely. In this case the countries' Central Banks stand aside and allow market forces to determine exchange rates. Between these extremes, there are several other possibilities: a 'managed' or 'dirty' float, where Central Bank intervention is periodic, but not continuous; upper and lower limits, which may be quite widely separated, between which the exchange rate may float; and there may be a fixed exchange rate for certain transactions, and other rates, perhaps freely floating rates, for others. Let us now consider an example of an international economic transaction under fixed exchange rates.

A UK exporter receives dollars as the proceeds of his sale of goods in the United States. He is likely to want to exchange these dollars for sterling, through a bank. The bank will probably surrender the dollars to the Bank of England, and the bank's balance with the Bank of England will rise correspondingly. The Bank of England will place the dollars in the official reserves of gold and foreign currencies held in its *Exchange Equalization Account*. To prevent any increase in bank deposits—simple or multiple—the Bank of England will then sell Treasury Bills equal in value to the increase in reserves, thus removing from the banks sterling deposits equal to those which the exporter originally gained.

A number of factors complicate this. First, there will be importers anxious to obtain foreign currency to carry out purchases. This process then operates in reverse, with importers demanding foreign currency from the banks as opposed to exporters supplying it. Only the excess of exports over imports will be reflected in the reserves. Second, international transactions need not be conducted in dollars. Japanese yen, German marks, or any currency—even sterling—may be used. If sterling is employed, the adjustments described will occur abroad, but not in Britain. Third, the Central Bank need not undertake offsetting open market operations in bills or bonds whenever there is a rise or fall in reserves. If it does not, it effectively permits the domestic money supply to go up (down) whenever reserves rise (fall).

Fourth, international transactions are not restricted to exports and imports. They also include transactions in assets. A UK firm which builds a factory in Spain, for instance, will need pesetas. These pesetas must be bought, in the foreign exchange market, from exporters who have earned pesetas, or from someone lending pesetas to UK residents or to the British Government, or from the reserves of the Bank of England. More generally, any outflow of foreign currency must be financed by an inflow of foreign currency, or out of reserves. This is true irrespective of whether the inflow is the result of export earnings, foreign investment in the UK, or international loans to the UK.

Finally, the Bank of England may choose not to buy (or sell) foreign currency. If, instead, it decides to keep its reserves constant, it will be the exchange rate—not the reserves—which bears the strain of any imbalance in the market. For example, if there is an excess supply of dollars, and an excess demand for sterling, the price of the dollar will fall in terms of sterling, to 'clear' the market; sterling will appreciate against the dollar (e.g. from £1 = $1·50 to £1 = $1·60). This will happen under a system of freely floating exchange rates. Alternatively, the Bank of England may choose some compromise between meeting any excess supply or demand for foreign exchange at existing exchange rates, and freely floating exchange rates. This would be an example of managed floating.

6.1.3. The Balance of Payments Accounts

A country's balance of payments accounts record all economic transactions that its residents undertake with foreigners in a given period (normally a year). These transactions are broken down in two ways. We distinguish between *credit* items and *debit* items, and between *current* transactions in commodities and services and *capital* transactions in assets; this is set out in Table 6.1.

The top left cell covers income earned from abroad. This income is earned from the sale overseas of a country's goods and services ('invisibles'), and 'property' income received from abroad in the form of interest payments, dividends, royalties, and repatriated profits by any domestic resident (household or firm). The cell on the top right is the mirror image of this from the rest of the world's point of view. It includes everything the residents of other countries earn or receive as income from the home country's residents. The difference between the two cells gives the *current account balance*. This is in surplus if the value of all entries in the top left cell exceeds that of those in the top right. In contrast, a current account deficit implies that income from abroad is less than expenditure abroad.

TABLE 6.1

	Credit items ($+$)	Debit items ($-$)

Current account	Exports of goods
	Exports of services
	Property income received
	  from abroad
		Imports of goods
		Imports of services
		Property income paid
		  abroad

Capital account	Investment from abroad Borrowing from abroad Fall in reserves	Investment abroad Lending abroad Rise in reserves

The bottom left cell covers, first, all capital transactions which are credits in the sense that they represent an inflow of funds from abroad. These may be for the direct construction of new plant and machinery in the UK; the purchase of existing assets (real or financial) from UK residents; borrowing by individuals or firms at home; 'official' borrowing by the government (both short term and long term); and other short-term inflows, for example for speculative purposes.

Second, this cell contains any *fall* in reserves which comprise the gold and foreign currency reserves held by the country's government or Central Banks. It may seem strange that this should appear on the credit side. This in fact is not only necessary from an accounting viewpoint: there is good reason for it. A fall in reserves will occur if total debits exceed total credits: that is, if the right-hand column exceeds the left-hand one. The difference between these two will equal the fall in reserves. Adding this to the left-hand side will, therefore, result in total credits equalling total debits. The fall in reserves is an *alternative* to an inflow of funds, and hence appears in the column identifying funds flowing in. The real significance of all entries in the cell is that they all represent decreases in the community's net wealth. This is clearly so in the case of a loss of foreign currency from the reserves, but is no less true if physical assets are bought up by foreigners or if loans are accepted from them. The bottom right cell is the opposite. It comprises all capital debits, including rises in reserves;[1] and every item in it can be thought of as a rise in the community's net wealth.

If the bottom right cell is subtracted from the bottom left, one derives the capital account surplus (a deficit if this produces a negative number).

The overall picture could be disaggregated by country, and much can be learnt by examining the extent to which trade and capital movements *vis-à-vis* particular countries or trading blocs vary relative to those with other countries. The more fundamental disaggregation, however, is by the nature of transaction. Britain's current account balance can be split into (i) its visible part comprising net exports of foodstuffs, raw materials, machinery, textiles, fuel, transport equipment, chemicals, consumer goods (durable and non-durable), and other goods, (ii) net invisible exports comprising net earnings on tourism, insurance, banking, shipping, aviation, other services, net property income from abroad, transfers from abroad, and payments for government services. The main components of a capital account balance follow the distinctions already drawn: net capital inflows for government or private direct investment, net 'portfolio' investment in the form of purchases of existing real assets, bonds, equities, etc., official (government) net borrowing from overseas, net inflows of short-term capital (holdings of sterling purchased with foreign currency which may rapidly be sold again), and falls in the reserves (see above).

6.1.4. Measures of Imbalance

Before investigating the UK's balance of payments in more detail, we must briefly examine the (in fact rather complex) question of what is meant by a 'balance of payments deficit'. If all transactions have been recorded correctly, the overall balance of payments must balance exactly. An excess of expenditure over income implies more foreign currency abroad than is received from abroad. The extra foreign currency must either come from borrowing or from the reserves, or both. Each of these generates a surplus on the capital account which offsets the deficit generated by the excess expenditure.

This overall balance arises from the principles of accounting used. To see how successfully a country is performing in its foreign trade and payments, it is necessary to look at one or more subtotals or balances between different subtotals within the overall accounts. For example, the movement of the reserves will be important because of the constraints imposed on a country if these are inadequate to finance temporary excesses of expenditure over income. The total value of exports will give some idea of how well a country is competing in export marekts, particularly if we examine exports in real terms. In general, however, such figures provide limited information. A rise in the reserves may represent only a high level of loans; increased exports may be more than offset by increased imports. There are, therefore, a number of more useful figures each of which represents the balance between certain inflows and outflows. These are:

(i) The visible trade balance: the surplus (or deficit if it is negative) of the value of visible exports over visible imports.

---

[1] In fact a rise in reserves is shown as a *minus* amount on the credit side.

(ii) The current account balance: the surplus or deficit of all visible and invisible trade items, including net property income from abroad.

(iii) The Balance for Official Financing (BOF), formally,

$$BOF \equiv net\ official\ short\text{-}term\ borrowing + \text{net loss of reserves}$$

where 'net official short-term borrowing' is confined to transactions with overseas monetary authorities (other Central Banks and, until recently, the International Monetary Fund) and foreign currency lending by the government. This formulation recognizes that short-term capital movements may frequently be beyond government control as well. For example, expectations of a revaluation of another currency may cause heavy short-term capital outflows.

Table 6.2 contains estimates of the UK's balance of payments for the period 1974–83. It is illuminating to compare 1974 with 1977 and 1980. In 1974, the visible and current balances were in record deficit. These deficits exceeded $6\frac{1}{2}$ per cent and $4\frac{1}{2}$ per cent of national income, a figure unparalleled in peacetime. But BOF in 1974 was in deficit by much less than the current account, and in fact reserves rose in that year. In 1977 there was an enormous surplus on BOF, thanks to a large inflow on the capital account; but the current account was in slight surplus, and visible trade in substantial deficit. By 1983 the UK had begun to run a visible trade surplus for only the fourth time this century, primarily as a result of North Sea oil exports (and replacement of oil imports). There was a rather larger surplus on current account, and a surplus, too, on BOF. (Note that the minus sign indicates a *rise* in reserves.) All three definitions of surplus or deficit gave the same sign in 1980.

A further noteworthy feature of Table 6.2 is the fact that BOF was far from zero in each of the ten years shown. This was despite the fact that sterling was floating throughout the period. It demonstrates that the Bank of England was intervening in the foreign exchange markets, sometimes to keep the exchange rate up (as in 1973–6) and sometimes, as in 1977 in particular, to keep it down. In section 6.3 we shall examine and attempt to explain the large swings in the exchange rate for sterling that have occurred since it began to float in 1972. This inevitably involves the balance of payments record for the period as well.

The next part of this chapter will analyse the factors that lie behind such surpluses and deficits—the major influences at work on imports, exports, and the capital account.

6.1.5. The Determination of Imports

It is easiest to begin with imports. The determinants of these can be seen and distinguished by referring to the factors that generally determine the demand for any product—tastes, income, and the price of the product relative to the price of other products. The last of these will depend partly on the relative cost of production of the goods, which in turn will depend on the cost of the factors of production required and the technology which combines them. In the absence of restrictions most international trade can be explained in terms of these four aspects: cost of factors of production, technology, tastes, and incomes.

TABLE 6.2. *UK balance of payments, 1974–1983*

(£ million)

	Current transactions								Balancing item	Investment and other capital flows					Official financing	
	Visible balance	Balance of services	Interest, profits, and dividends		Transfers		Current balance			Private investment (net)	Investment in UK public sector (net)	Investment in banking sector (net)	Miscellaneous	Total	Reserves	Other
			Balance	*of which general government*	Balance	*of which balance of general govt. with EC*										
1974	−5,351	+1,075	+1,415	−352	−417	−54	−3,278	+30		+876	−231	+1,440	−483	+1,602	−105	+1,751
1975	−3,333	+1,515	+773	−514	−468	+16	−1,513	−106		+160	−297	+276	15	+154	+655	+810
1976	−3,929	+2,503	+1,365	−648	−775	−221	−836	+183		−357	+30	−1,613	−1,035	−2,975	+853	+2,775
1977	−2,284	+3,338	+116	−721	−1,116	−452	+54	+3,141		+633	+1,135	+1,887	+511	+4,166	−9,588	+2,227
1978	−1,542	+3,816	+661	−594	−1,777	−925	+1,158	+1,979		−2,630	−546	−644	−443	−4,263	+2,329	−1,203
1979	−3,449	+4,071	+990	−540	−2,265	−1,076	−653	+217		−3,110	+748	+4,917	−409	+2,146	−1,059	−651
1980	+1,233	+4,267	−186	−606	−2,079	−825	+3,235	−155		−3,495	+1,443	+2,429	−2,265	−1,888	−291	−901
1981	+3,008	+4,249	+1,257	−668	−1,967	−530	+6,547	+156		−7,447	+119	+997	−1,217	−7,548	+2,419	−1,574
1982	+2,119	+3,853	+1,515	−800	−2,109	−721	+5,378	−3,712		−7,624	−48	+5,446	−724	−2,950	+1,421	−137
1983	−954						+2,016									

Source: *National Institute Economic Review*, 107 (Feb. 1984).

(a) *Cost of factors of production.* A country will tend to import products which require a relatively high input of those factors of production with which it is relatively poorly endowed. For example, the UK imports lamb and butter from New Zealand despite transport costs, because these products require much land relative to labour, and because New Zealand has an abundance of land relative to its labour force, when compared to the UK. The abundance of land will tend to make it relatively cheap, and this would give rise to relatively low costs for such products. Similarly, a country with little capital per man compared to other countries may tend to import products which are capital-intensive in production, again because the relative abundance of capital abroad may make such products relatively cheaper.

(b) *Technology.* Another reason may be technology: Britain imports, for example, certain components for television sets from Japan, some pharmaceutical products from Switzerland, and several types of aeroplane and computers from the United States. In each case, the exporting country generally has a relative technical lead in their manufacture; indeed, because of the heavy cost of small-scale production, patents, and other obstacles to the international transmission of knowledge, these commodities may not even be produced in Britain at all. Also, the potential lead that a country might have in the production of a particular commodity might remain unfulfilled: managerial inefficiency, the inadequate exploitation of available technology, or market imperfections could in fact be large enough for the product concerned to be imported, not exported.

Such factors will cause differences in product prices, but the crucial question is whether they generate different *relative* prices.

An opportunity for profitable commodity arbitrage exists whenever product price ratios differe between countries—or, at least, differ by enough to outweigh the costs of 'trading'. Arbitrage means buying cheap and selling dear in pursuit of a safe profit. Suppose that one ton of copper costs five times as much as one ton of coffee in London, while in New York their respective prices are $1,600 and $800. Suppose that a trader can buy and sell in limitless amounts at these prices, and that trade impediments (transport costs and government trade restrictions) are negligible. The trader can take one ton of copper from New York to London and barter it for five tons of coffee, which he can sell in New York for $4,000. This will bring him a clear profit of $2,400. If, instead, the trader took copper from London to New York and coffee in the reverse direction, he would make a substantial loss. If international trading is to be profitable, it will imply that the pattern of commodity trade between countries follows the *Principle of Comparative Advantage*: goods are taken from sources where they are (or would otherwise be) relatively cheap to destinations where they are (or would otherwise be) relatively dear. What is important is the difference in the *ratios* of the commodity prices; the result that the trader will make profits by shipping copper from New York to London and coffee back was obtained without actually stipulating that sterling prices for either good in London. The conclusion about the direction of trade would not change, either, if the New York prices doubled or halved or decupled while retaining the same ratio.

If traders cannot collude, and trading impediments are negligible, commodity arbitrage will 'unite' the two markets for coffee and copper; the new common price ratio will settle somewhere between 5:1 and 2:1. At this stage, the arbitrage profits will have disappeared, and the gains from trade will accrue as rises in real national income in either the US or the UK, or (most probably) in both. The Principle of Comparative Advantage can now be seen to have a normative implication: if planners are to decide which commodities Britain should export and import, they should ensure that the trading pattern corresponds with, and does not run counter to, the direction of trade one would predict if there were free competition in all markets. For further analysis see Chapter 20, where this issue is considered in a multilateral trading context.

The relative price of exports to imports is known as the *terms of trade*—the ratio of a price index of exports to a price index of imports. This therefore represents the import-purchasing power of a given volume of a country's exports. A rise in the terms of trade is known as an 'improvement', and implies that fewer exports have to be sold to obtain the foreign currency necessary to purchase a given volume of imports. Less work is required, therefore, to obtain the imports, and this represents a rise in the standard of living. Notice, however, that an improvement in the terms of trade can worsen the balance of payments if the relatively high price of exports leads to a big reduction in demand for them (see below).

Between mid-1971 and mid-1974 Britain's terms of trade fell, or deteriorated, by some 25 per cent, implying that she had to increase the volume of her exports by one-third if she was to 'pay for' the same volume of imports. The cause of this deterioration, with its grave implications for the standard of living in Britain, lay chiefly in the fourfold increase in the price of imported oil (1973–4) and the sharp rise in the price of food and raw materials that occurred between 1972 and 1974. In the eight years after 1974, Britain's terms of trade improved by nearly 20 per cent, so that most of the deterioration in the previous three years was regained by 1982.

Demand factors can also influence relative prices of products, and this leads us to the other two main influences on trade—tastes and income.

(c) *Tastes*. The third possible cause lies on the demand side. The size of British imports of tea, port, sherry, and champagne is partly explained by the lack of domestic production (for climatic reasons), but partly also because of a traditionally high level of consumption in comparison with many other European countries, reflecting different tastes. If domestic consumers were forbidden to buy these imported products, the price of them in Britain would be much higher: the price rise would be essential, to choke off the demand in excess of that which the UK could produce. In some cases, the product might cease to be available at any price, no matter how high.

In each example, the foreign country is a cheaper source of supply than Britain. By and large, the lower the level of foreign costs and prices, the greater the probability that a particular commodity will be imported, and—if it is already imported—the greater the volume of imports. But the effect of a change in the foreign supply price on the *value* of imports is ambiguous. In Britain's case, the demand for imported manufactures is reasonably sensitive to price: if their price goes up, all else being equal, customers may turn to domestic suppliers or buy less, the total volume of these imports falls and the total value of imports may therefore fall, despite the higher price level. This is not true, however, of imported foodstuffs, metal, and fuel. The demand for these commodities is very insensitive (inelastic) to price, at least in the short run, and it is very hard, or impossible, for domestic suppliers either to begin or to increase production quickly. So an increase in these prices leads to an almost equi-proportionate rise in the total value of the imports. The period 1972–4 provides a recent and dramatic example of this with respect to raw materials.

(d) *Income.* In addition to these price and cost influences on imports, there is the powerful effect of changes in *aggregate* demand at home. In a boom, with incomes rising, the demand for most commodities rises. In the early stages some domestic producers can increase their own sales and output roughly in pace, so imports as a whole rise little faster than demand itself. In some sectors, however, the boom may start to eat into stocks of materials, and attempts by producers to re-stock lead to sharp rises in imports. As the boom progresses, more and more bottlenecks appear: steel, bricks, machine tools, consumer durables all run short, as the limits of current domestic production are reached. Further rises in demand then begin to spill over almost entirely into imports. After the boom breaks, and demand starts to ebb away, the ratio of imports to national income stops rising and often starts to drop back.

Can the government affect the level of imports? The strong influence that aggregate demand can have suggests that it can do so by demand management policy (monetary and fiscal policy). Reflation will expand imports; deflation will cut them, or at least check their rate of rise. Yet these policies work slowly, taking perhaps as long as eighteen months to have maximum effect. As well as monetary and fiscal policy (which alters the *level* of expenditure), there are instruments to *redirect* expenditure away from imports towards domestically produced goods. Examples are tariffs and import quotas (which restrict the volume of imports) and devaluing the currency, which will in all probability reduce the value of imports measured in foreign currency. More formally, a devaluation will generally reduce the outflow of foreign exchange on imports if the price elasticity of demand for imports is above zero. For this implies at least some reduction in demand as a result of the higher sterling price of imports in the UK consequent upon devaluation.

6.1.6. The Determination of Exports

The determinants of a country's exports should now be clear— they are, by definition, the rest of the world's imports. Certain commodities are exported because endowments of resources, technology, or tastes confer a comparative cost-advantage on the home country's industries. Provided that foreign demand is sufficiently responsive to price, the total value of a particular category of exports will be enhanced if there is a fall in the export price (in particular, a fall relative to the prices and costs of overseas producers), or anything, therefore, which at existing exchange rates leads to lower UK prices, e.g. a fall in domestic demand, or even an expansion in the supply of domestic products. But if foreign demand responds little to price, any of these will tend to cut the total value of exports—the price will drop by a higher proportion than the resulting rise in the volume of foreign sales.

The response of foreign currency earnings on exports to a devaluation of the exchange rate depends not only on the elasticity of demand for exports but also on the extent to which exporters alter their foreign currency export prices. Suppose there is a devaluation of X per cent. At one extreme, with the home currency price constant, the export price in foreign currency would drop by the full amount of devaluation, X per cent. In this case, the value of total exports in foreign exchange will rise if, and only if, there is a more than offsetting rise in the volume of exports—if and only if foreign demand is more than unit-elastic. At the other extreme, for example, if a country is a very small competitor in international markets, the foreign exchange price of its exports will be outside its control and quite unaffected by the devaluation. The home currency price will rise however, and the foreign exchange value of total exports will rise only if this induces increased supply of exports (i.e. if, and only if, the domestic elasticity of supply of exports exceeds zero). In Britain's case, there is evidence (Artus [9], Cairncross and Eichengreen [17], Junz and Rhomberg [42], and an earlier study of devaluation, National Institute [45]) that foreign demand is reasonably price-elastic. Junz's study suggests that if Britain's producers raise their export prices by 1 per cent relative to those of other manufacturing nations, the volume of their exports will drop (relative to the figure it would have reached) by perhaps 2 per cent about one or two years later (suggesting an elasticity of demand of approximately 2) and possibly even more after that. This suggests that a 1 per cent rise in export prices, all else being equal, will eventually clip about 1 per cent off the total value of sales. It also implies that devaluation is likely to have a favourable effect on the current account, at least if sufficient time is allowed to elapse.

It is important to note, however, that under certain conditions the initial effects of devaluation on the current account could be perverse. Suppose that British exporters always quote their prices in sterling, and importers into Britain quote in foreign currency. Balance of trade statistics measure the difference between the value of exports leaving Britain and the value of imports arriving. Since deliveries lag behind orders placed—in some cases by as much as two years or more—the volume of both exports and imports in the months after devaluation will be only minimally affected by it. In the meantime, given our assumption that international traders quote prices in the currency of the 'source' country, the trade balance will actually deteriorate and may take several months to register an overall improvement. This is the 'J curve' effect, named after the shape of the time path the trade figures take in a diagram with time on the horizontal azis and trade balance on the vertical. The J curve depends crucially, of course, on our price-quotation assumption. If instead one is to assume that traders quote prices in the currency of the 'destination' country (British exports to Holland set in prices denominated in Dutch florins, Dutch exports to Britain in sterling)—no less plausible—devaluation gives the British trade balance an artificial, temporary boost: the florin value of British imports drops while there is, temporarily, no change in the florin value of

British exports. Another reason why the J curve might not appear is that devaluations are often predicted with some degree of accuracy, at least as to date. Traders expecting a sterling devaluation will advance imports into Britain and delay exports from Britain, so that exports in subsequent periods are temporarily swollen and imports temporarily cut.

There are other potential difficulties with devaluation. In a severe world slump, it may be hard for a country to win additional export orders if it devalues. Other countries may place an effective ceiling on its exports, either informally or in the form of a specific quota. Then there is the chance that devaluation may provoke retaliation by other countries. In the longer run, increased export earnings brought about by devaluation may be undermined as a consequence of other effects. A payments surplus may lead to financial inflows which increase domestic money supply, and thereby increase domestic spending on exportable and importable goods. A payments improvement will tend to increase national income, with similar effects. Increases in the domestic prices of traded goods, coupled with increased demand for labour in the traded industries, will stimulate rises in domestic money usage rates. This in turn will raise domestic exporters' costs, squeeze their profit margins, and cancel at least some and perhaps all of the initial improvement in competitiveness. We return to these issues in section 6.2.4.

Overall, the exchange rate can be a powerful weapon if (i) foreign demand is elastic, so that devaluation raises the total foreign exchange value of exports, (ii) domestic production of exportables can be stepped up, and (iii) if devaluation does not trigger off a burst of domestic inflation which negates the competitiveness advantage established. Incomes policy to contain domestic wage costs—provided it works—has analogous consequences.

Besides price, or domestic supply the other major factor influencing a country's exports is the size of demand in other countries: just as a boom at home tends to raise imports, so a boom abroad usually stimulates exports. As well as this, mention should be made of non-price influences on exports (delivery dates, advertising, the quality of distribution and after-sales servicing, and impressions of the product's reliability) which are widely thought to have had an adverse effect on Britain's export performance in recent years.

The government can influence exports in a variety of ways, which will be examined in greater detail later. Export subsidies increase the volume of exports, and raise the value as well provided that foreign demand is elastic; if it is inelastic, export receipts go down with an export subsidy and would increase with an export tax.

Domestic deflation of aggregate demand, through restrictive monetary or fiscal policy, should have effects similar to an export subsidy—encouraging a switch by producers from selling at home to selling overseas. In practice, however, Britain's exports tend to rise faster than average in booms and slower than average in slumps. This could be explained by the multiplier effect of exports on demand, or by some synchronization of rising demand, both home and abroad. In fact there has been a mild positive association since the war between the pressure of demand in Britain and that in other developed countries, and overall the direct effects of demand management policy on exports remain uncertain.

Even in 1980, when real national income fell heavily and with unexpected severity, the volume of exports registered negligible change, despite the presumably depressive effects of the rising relative unit labour costs and falling relative profitability of exports apparent in Table 6.5.

6.1.7. Invisibles

Both exports and imports were seen also to contain 'invisible' elements—trade in services like tourism, insurance, shipping, and banking. In general, however, invisible exports and imports respond to the same influences as their visible counterparts. Countries will tend to have a surplus on these items if they have a comparative advantage in the generation of the services they cover, as a result of relative efficiency and abundance of the more important factors of production. The UK has generally been in such a position, for many years turning a visible trade deficit into a current account surplus. Rising world income will again generally improve the position.

International transfer payments are also included in the current account of the balance of payments. An example would be funds remitted overseas by a foreigner working temporarily in the UK. As Table 6.3 shows, transfers have been persistently negative in recent years. Usually at least one-third of the deficit on transfers is attributable to overseas payments by the UK government. These include net payments to the European Communities. For the most part these represent Britain's net contribution to the EEC Common Agricultural Policy (CAP). The costs of this policy account for some 70 per cent of the total EEC budget. Under CAP, there is free trade in agricultural commodities inside the EEC but the prices are set independently of world prices, which are typically more variable and somewhat lower (often far lower) than inside the EEC. The CAP prices for grain and dairy products are pitched so high that large surpluses are frequent. After storage, such surpluses are dumped overseas at a fraction of their production cost, or, occasionally, destroyed. The costs of CAP are borne partly by levies on surviving imports of food from outside the EEC, and partly by contributions from national value-added tax revenues. CAP does not therefore favour a country with modest agricultural output and dependence on imports, such as the UK. Hence the substantial British official payments under CAP, which would indeed have been far heavier in recent years but for the generosity of the West German Government.

The final item in the current account—net property income from overseas—needs further explanation. In the case of the UK this has been a large positive item for several decades—often over 1 per cent of national income. Traditionally, the income accruing to British owners of foreign assets (chiefly, interest on loans to foreign and Commonwealth governments and companies, dividends from overseas companies, and profit repatriation by overseas subsidiaries of UK-based firms) has greatly exceeded the corresponding outflows to overseas owners of assets in the UK. Yet such has been the scale of net overseas borrowing (chiefly by the public sector) in recent years—accompanied by a sharp rise in interest rates—that net property income from overseas has fallen to much lower values. The greater the accumulated borrowing, the higher the total cost of servicing the debt. The rise in interest rates has been important since little of the borrowing has been long term, at rates of interest fixed for long periods. On the other hand, perhaps the chief reason for the rise in nominal interest rates on loans—a worldwide phenomenon since the war, but especially pronounced in Britain—has been the increasing realization and expectation of inflation.

Unless nominal interest rates rise in line with expectations of inflation, borrowers are keen to borrow, expecting to repay debts later when the real value has fallen; lenders become reluctant to lend in this form, and eventually the excess demand will force interest rates up. If inflation persists, Britain will find that the real value of her debts falls, and that the interest paid on them contains, in real terms, a concealed repayment of capital. Since Britain's overseas assets are less dominated by financial as opposed to real assets than her liabilities, there are some grounds for thinking that there might be a reversal of the downward trend of net property income from abroad in the 1980s and 1990s. Indeed, the data for 1981 and 1982 in Table 6.2 already point in this direction.

6.1.8. The Determinants of the Capital Account

Turning attention to the capital account of the balance of payments, we find that its determinants are much more complex. The crucial influence on international *direct* investment—the construction of industrial plant by one country's residents in another country—is the expectation of relative returns on capital at home and overseas. The higher the rate of profit expected on investment in Britain, the greater the direct capital imports; conversely, a rise in expected returns overseas will induce direct capital exports. Differences in expected returns from a similar direct investment in two countries might be explained by different unit labour costs (differences in either wage rates or productivity per man), by geography (leading to transport cost savings or natural resource cost savings in one area rather than another), or different government policies towards taxation or protection by subsidy, tariffs against imports, or preferential taxation. Other factors at work on international direct investment may include the desire to reduce risk or enhance prestige by dispersing production in several countries.

International *portfolio* investment occurs when one country's residents acquire existing assets (irrespective of location) from another's residents. Example of portfolio capital exports from Britain are purchases by Britons from Frenchmen of shares in a Germany company, American Government bonds, a Paris office block, or an English farm. Although it seems at first sight paradoxical that the purchase of an English farm by a UK resident could be a capital export, it must be remembered that, given he purchases it from a Frenchman, he will in general need francs to do it. *Ceteris paribus*, this represents a drain on the UK's reserve holdings of foreign currency, and in this vital respect is exactly like the purchase of a Paris office block from a Frenchman.

The motives that underlie such investment may or may not be pecuniary. Some holders of wealth will wish to maximize the expected stream of returns

TABLE 6.3. *UK Balance of Payments Current Account, 1972–1983*
(£ million, seasonally adjusted)

| | Visible trade | | | Invisibles | | | Balances | | | Current balance |
	Exports (f.o.b.)	Imports (f.o.b.)	Balance	Credits	Debits	Total	Services	IPD	Transfers	
1972	9,437	10,185	−748	6,300	5,329	+971	+701	+538	−268	+223
1973	11,937	14,523	−2,586	8,506	6,899	+1 607	+786	+1,257	−436	−979
1974	16,394	21,745	−5,351	10,503	8,430	+2,073	+1,075	+1,415	−417	−3,278
1975	19,330	22,663	−3,333	11,457	9,637	+1,820	+1,515	+773	−468	−1,513
1976	25,191	29,120	−3,929	15,039	11,946	+3,093	+2,503	+1,365	−775	−836
1977	31,728	34,012	−2,284	16,847	14,509	+2,338	+3,338	+116	−1,116	+54
1978	35,063	36,605	−1,542	19,130	16,430	+2,700	+3,816	+661	−1,777	+1,158
1979	40,687	44,136	−3,449	23,804	21,008	+2,795	+4,071	+990	−2,265	−653
1980	47,415	46,182	+1,233	25,943	23,941	+2,002	+4,267	−186	−2,079	+3,235
1981	50,977	47,969	+3,008	29,760	26,221	+3,539	+4,249	+1,257	−1,967	+6,547
1982	55,546	53,427	+2,119	31,734	28,475	+3,259	+3,853	+1,515	−2,109	+5,378
1978 2	8,790	8,949	−159	4,669	3,975	+694	+845	+237	−388	+535
3	8,854	9,411	−557	4,947	4,197	+750	+1,027	+185	−462	+193
4	9,137	9,401	−264	5,051	4,250	+801	+1,030	+167	−396	+537

1979 1	8,313	9,746	−1,433	5,538	4,643	+895	+1,013	+388	−506	−538
2	10,759	11,238	−479	5,667	5,135	+532	+954	81	−503	+53
3	10,497	11,220	−723	6,240	5,417	+823	+1,056	+377	−610	+100
4	11,118	11,932	−814	6,359	5,813	+546	+1,048	+144	−646	−268
1980 1	11,997	12,394	−397	6,587	6,049	+538	+1,101	−101	−462	+141
2	11,914	12,166	−252	6,572	6,261	+311	+1,067	−162	−594	+59
3	11,692	10,931	+761	6,245	5,822	+423	+1,015	−13	−579	+1,184
4	11,812	10,691	+1,121	6,539	5,809	+730	+1,084	+90	−444	+1,851
1981 1	11,854	10,224	+1,630	6,943	6,073	+870	+1,129	+245	−504	+2,500
2	12,229	11,103	+1,126	7,084	6,137	+947	+1,080	+394	−527	+2,073
3	13,142	13,279	−137	7,594	6,928	+666	+1,014	+289	−637	+529
4	13,752	13,363	+389	8,139	7,083	+1,056	+1,026	+329	−299	+1,445
1	13,470	13,243	+227	7,590	6,959	+631	+1,062	+58	−489	+858
2	13,788	13,678	+110	7,941	7,109	+832	+1,037	+416	−621	+942
3	13,702	13,135	+567	7,887	7,203	+684	+817	+423	−556	+1,251
4	14,586	13,371	+1,215	8,316	7,204	+1,112	+937	+618	−443	+2,327
1983 1	14,773	14,936	−163	8,290	7,346	+944	+1,120	+356	−532	+781
2	14,677	15,346	−669	8,300	7,802	+498	+1,212	−37	−677	−171
3	14,903	15,198	−295	8,552	7,654	+898	+1,081	+172	−355	+603

Source: *Economic Trends*, 363 (Jan. 1984).

from it. Others may temper concern for yield with anxiety about risk and try to diversify their portfolio and avoid holding particularly risky assets unless there is a high average expectation of return. Yet others may hold assets abroad (holiday cottages for instance) for their 'psychic' yield. British companies may acquire foreign firms to add to profits, or facilitate expansion.

There is one important feature that direct and portfolio investment have in common: they are, by and large, non-recurrent. Suppose that expectations in Britain of profits in the Swiss chemical industry rise. British individuals will now be more likely to buy shares in these firms, and British chemical companies to consider setting up a new Swiss subsidiary. The timing of any investment that takes place is hard to predict; particularly in the latter case it may take some time, while in the former the shares may rise so much that they no longer appear worth buying. But once any Swiss assets have been acquired—financed, for example, by borrowing or the sale of assets elsewhere—further flows in that particular direction are unlikely to take place (unless, of course, expectations change once more).

Short-term capital movements (SCM) in many ways resemble portfolio investment, and the two are hard to distinguish in practice. The essential characteristic of SCM is the high degree of liquidity of the assets bought and sold. Suppose a company transfers a bank deposit from sterling into US dollars, or sells British Government bonds nearing maturity and buys similar obligations of the US Government. Either constitutes SCM from Britain to the United States. The bank deposits and bonds are liquid: they have a certain or near-certain value, expressed in a particular currency and can rapidly be converted back. Why should such SCM occur?

There are two major influences on SCM: relative interest rates and expected exchange rates. The first is clear. If a firm can borrow at one rate, and lend at a higher one, it can exploit the discrepancy in the market and make profits at low risk. If it can lend at one rate in one financial centre and lend at a higher one in another, we may expect it to switch any funds it has in the former to the latter, if it is adequately informed about the opportunities confronting it. Interest rate differentials between countries may, therefore, induce SCM. Furthermore, in special conditions (if borrowers and lenders can contract at practically the same rate of interest in any one financial centre, if the costs of negotiating loans and transferring funds are negligible, and if there is general confidence that prevailing exchange rates will not change over time) SCM will tend to equalize interest rates internationally. Even a slight discrepancy in interest rates between financial centres will trigger off SCM from the centre with lower rates to the markets where they are higher. This will tend to depress the latter and raise the former, leading back to equalization of the rates of interest.

But these conditions rarely if ever, apply. In particular, exchange rates between currencies can and do change. Even when currencies are pegged to each other—as under the Bretton Woods system for currencies which operated from after the Second World War until August 1971 (see later)—there is always a finite chance that the 'peg' may change; and the limits of permitted fluctuation of the exchange rate (perhaps 1 per cent or so either side of the 'central' rate) still expose a company moving funds to some danger of exchange loss; for example, if it borrows now for three months in sterling, and immediately lends (at a slighly higher rate) for three months in French francs, it will be faced with losses if there turns out to have been an appreciable fall in the sterling value of the franc when the three months are up. The francs it receives back are worth appreciably less in sterling than the amount it has to pay to settle its original debt.

6.1.9. The Forward Market

In fact, the company can insure itself against this risk by selling francs on the three months' forward market. This involves the following: the company enters a contract (with a bank or another firm) to deliver x million French francs at a stipulated future—in this case, three months later—in return for a promise of a guaranteed sum in sterling, which it will receive at that time. This contract eliminates the risk from exchange rate changes.

If a firm notices that it can buy 12 francs per pound *now* (the 'spot' rate) and can pre-sell them three months forward at 11·88 francs per pound, then sterling is said to be at a 1 per cent discount forward against the franc. In other words,

$$\frac{0 \cdot 12}{12} \text{ or 1 per cent fewer francs}$$

are required to buy back the pounds, than the pounds can currently buy, and if the interest rate that can be earned on sterling and on francs is the same, buying the francs now and pre-selling them would result in a 1 per cent profit over the three-month period. If, however, three month interest rates in London on sterling were 3 per cent higher than those in Paris on francs, then it would be more profitable to stay in sterling rather than buy the francs and pre-sell them. There is what is known as a 'covered interest differential' of 2 per cent in favour of London, since the relevant London interest interest rate exceeds the relevant Paris one by more than the discount. If three-month interest rates in London fell by $2\frac{1}{2}$ per cent, the covered interest differential would favour Paris ($\frac{1}{2}$ per cent) and the company would be likely to move its funds into francs and pre-sell them—another example of arbitrage.

SCM respond, therefore, to covered interest differentials—interest differentials minus the relevant forward discount; and there is some tendency for the movements to close the gap that occasions them. In the above example sizeable SCM from London to Paris tend to raise the spot (and weaken the forward) franc relative to the pound, and to lower interest rates in Paris while raising them in London. All four effects tend to remove the covered interest differential in favour of Paris. Formally the differential is:

$$\frac{\text{spot value of pound in francs} - \text{forward value of pound in francs}}{\text{spot value of pound in francs}}$$

$$- (\text{London interest rate} - \text{Paris interest rate}).$$

The spot sale of sterling and forward repurchase of them both decrease the value of the first term, while the rise in London interest rates and fall in Paris ones both raise the value of the second term. Overall, therefore, the covered interest differential diminishes. Various sorts of friction (commissions, taxes, transactions costs) usually stop the covered interest differential from vanishing completely, although it is often very small. Economic analysis of the balance of payments and exchange rates often starts from the assumption that covered interest differentials are negligible. This is known as the *Covered Interest Parity Condition*.

We have already examined the sort of factors which influence interest rates. Rising demand will tend to raise them, recession reduce them; government measures to ease credit and expand the level of bank deposits may exert a sharp—but perhaps temporary—downward pressure; increased borrowing, whether by firms or government, will tend to raise them. Expectations about future short-term rates of interest will play an important part in determining the present levels of long-term rates of interest (see Chapter 10), and any expected inflation will tend to be reflected in current nominal rates of interest.

What, however, governs forward exchange rates? A major influence here is speculation. If the relevant officials in a large number of companies and banks involved in international transactions suddenly come to expect that sterling will fall in value (spot) against the German mark over the next few months, it is fairly certain to fall in value in *forward* trading against the mark *now*. If it were not to, there would be too many willing sellers of forward sterling and buyers of forward marks, all backing their view that the marks they are buying forward will be worth more in three months than they are at present. The three months' forward discount of the pound against the mark that emerges is an approximate measure of the market's average expectation now of what the spot rate will be in three months' time. But the measure is only approximate; there are other types of transaction, besides speculation, which impinge on the forward foreign exchange markets. Traders also have recourse to them. An importer who must pay a bill denominated in a foreign currency at a stipulated future date, and expects to receive domestic currency for the goods, may well wish to insure himself against the risk of devaluation of the home currency in the intervening period, by buying the foreign currency forward. Similarly, exporters with future receipts in a foreign currency, and costs to meet denominated in home currency, may hedge (against the possibility of revaluation, this time) by selling the foreign currency forward, thus guaranteeing the home currency value of that foreign currency against a possible fall in the value of the foreign currency. The set of forward exchange rates—generally for delivery one, three, six, and twelve months forward—is, therefore, determined by the market forces of speculation, traders' hedging against exchange risk, and SCM 'arbitrage) on covered interest differentials. These forces may, of course, be tempered by regulation or intervention on the part of governments.

This completes the analysis of the components of a country's balance of payments and the major influences at work on them. To summarize, factors making for a weak external position include: a domestic boom (raising imports); a recession abroad (restricting exports); a high ratio of domestic costs to foreign prices (this amounts to an overvalued exchange rate, and usually implies a weak current account, and a danger of a net outflow of direct and portfolio investment); lower interest rates at home than abroad, and/or expectations of future depreciation of the currency (stimulating adverse SCM).

6.2. Balance of Payments Adjustment

6.2.1. Automatic Equilibrium Mechanisms

To explain the parts as we have done above is not necessarily to explain the whole. Broadly, there are two schools of thought about the balance of payments. The more optimistic one maintains that balance of payments deficits—or disequilibria—are usually transient phenomena, and that *automatic forces* are brought into play to reverse surpluses or deficits. According to this view, *government intervention* to influence components of the external accounts is rarely justified, and often pointless or even harmful. The other more pessimistic one considers that there may be violent swings in a country's balance of payments position, with a serious danger that market forces may even be destabilizing. This school emphasizes the need for swift, intelligent government intervention in times of trouble; it often favours controls on international capital flows, and even on commodity trade as well.

It is not hard to construct models of the economy which demonstrate that each school *can* be right, given certain assumptions. For instance, suppose that there are two countries, X and Y. The exchange rate between their currencies is fixed. The capital account always balances so that the current account surplus (deficit) always accompanies some gain (loss) in reserves. Suppose that there is a positive association between each country's reserves and its money stock, and between its money stock and its price level. The current account of each deteriorates if its price level rises relative to that in the other. Suppose also that X is in surplus on its current account. X must gain reserves from Y. The money supply and, therefore, prices in X will tend to rise relative to prices in Y. So X's current account surplus must fall. It will continue falling until it disappears, because the mechanism will keep operating while country X is in surplus. This is known as the *price-specie flow mechanism*. It was used to explain the working of the Gold Standard (see later) and to dissuade governments from trying to increase their reserves of gold. In fact, the mechanism does not predict that current account deficits or surpluses must disappear in all circumstances. If real income in X grows faster than in Y, the demand for money, and therefore for reserves, should rise faster in X than in Y as well. In a two-country world with a fixed exchange rate, this would imply a persistent tendency to surplus in country X. Only this would enable X to gain a growing share of the world's reserves. The price-specie flow mechanism predicts no tendency to surplus or deficits under fixed exchange rates, when all countries' demands for reserves grow at a common rate.

Similar results may follow in other circumstances. Imagine now that the two countries' currencies are free to float against each other. X is again in surplus. This means that households and firms in Y must pay more to X's residents for their imports than they are earning from exports to X, and so there is a higher demand for X's currency than the supply of it; X's currency can be expected to rise in value against Y's (which is in excess supply) pushing up the price of X's exports to Y. The effect of this will probably be to cut X's surplus. X's companies will see their profit margins on sales to country Y whittled down, or the purchases of their customers in country Y cut back in response to price rises. Again, the process may continue until X's surplus vanishes. All that is needed to guarantee this result is the assumption that the excess demand for a country's currency invariably goes down if its value rises in terms of other countries' currencies. This model constitutes the basis of the argument in favour of floating exchange rates. (It, and the price-specie flow model, are closely related to the monetarist view of macroeconomics outlined in the previous chapter, and to the monetary approach to exchange rates which is investigated in section 6.3.)

6.2.2. The Need for Intervention

By contrast, the pessimists can establish their point of view (again, given the right assumptions) in a Keynesian macroeconomic framework. Suppose that prices of goods, labour, and assets are rather inflexible, and that changes in them can be ignored. (This assumption—whether realistic or not—is far cruder than Keynes's own model of the economy.) Income, or output, can change, however, via the multiplier process in response to changes in any component of aggregate demand, of which exports to other countries is one. Output in aggregate cannot exceed the limits set by productive potential, but may fall short of them. Once more, there are two countries, X and Y. There is now no reason to expect the current accounts of either to balance—at least in the short run—for these depend on the level of incomes (and hence imports) in the two countries. The two countries' income levels are, of course, interdependent, since a boom in one country will raise exports (and hence income) in the other, but there is no guarantee that the deficit in one country as a result of a rise in income will, via the surplus in the other country, generate an increase of income in the second country sufficient to move both countries back to balance of payments equilibrium.

A current account deficit implies net sales of assets to foreigners, which must include the possibility of a drain on reserves. If the government considers this dangerous for the future it may be driven to deflate home demand (using fiscal or monetary weapons), unless it can persuade the other country to reflate or accept a new exchange rate. Yet the pessimists often argue that changing the exchange rate (devaluing, if an improvement in the current account is needed) is an unreliable remedy. If domestic demand for imports and foreign demand for exports are both sufficiently inelastic (price-insensitive), the effect on the current account may well be perverse. If it is not perverse, they suggest, there still remains the possibility that the improvement in exports will give rise to such a big multiplier increase in domestic demand—and hence imports—that the final position could be little better, or even worse, than the first. Equally serious, and perhaps rather more likely, is the possibility that the higher cost of imports will raise prices generally, generating a demand for wage increases which, if granted, further worsens the country's competitive position internationally. They also fear the possibility of destabilizing capital movements (further flights from a currency if its value has recently fallen). For these reasons they often oppose the case for floating exchange rates, challenging the assumption given in section 6.2.1 that the world's excess demand for sterling always rises if its price comes down. Above all, Keynesian pessimists insist that the price system is insufficiently flexible and complete for all markets to clear continuously.

6.2.3. The Causes of a Deficit

It is clear that both schools' arguments are based on theoretical possibilities. There can be no general theoretical grounds for preferring one view to another. In practice, the questions of whether the government should take action to correct balance of payments disequilibria, and if so, how, can only be answered when one knows the source of the disequilibrium, the strength of the key relationships, and the time-lags involved.

A balance of payments deficit on current account can be treated as an excess domestic demand in a particular set of markets, namely the markets for current tradable commodities (current, because the goods are purchased now; tradables, because they comprise goods which can be imported or exported, unlike, for instance, haircuts, for which international transport costs are prohibitive).

The usual explanation given for the UK's traditional tendency towards excess demand for current tradable goods is that higher- or faster-rising production costs in the UK have undermined our ability to compete either in foreign markets with our exports, or in the domestic market against imports.

This description is not wholly unreasonable, but it conflates a number of possible effects that may be at work. More formally, we can give at least four different answers to the question, Why should excess demand for current tradable goods exist? These are:

(i) Too high a real wage for labour, given its productivity level. This may well imply unemployment (excess supply of labour).

(ii) Too high a price of *non*-traded goods (restaurant meals, bricks, haircuts, and so on) in terms of traded goods. Non-traded goods will be in excess supply.

(iii) An excess supply of money in the portfolios of UK residents (companies and firms).

(iv) An excess supply of future goods. A borrower has an excess demand for present goods, matched by a net offer (excess supply) of future goods in exchange.[2] If reserves are constant, net borrowing by UK residents from foreign residents necessarily entails a current account deficit.

We consider these separately. A rise in real wages relative to productivity implies a rise in the real cost to a firm of each employee relative to the real output of each employee. There will, therefore, be an incentive to reduce production and employment. Firms will, with a given level of productivity,

---

[2] The hypothesis that excess demand (i.e. a shortage) in one market must be matched by an excess supply (i.e. a glut) in at least one other market, is known as Walras's Law.

only increase production if they can obtain higher prices relative to their wage costs or a fall in wages relative to their prices. In either case this amounts to saying that they require a fall in *real* wages if they are to increase production and employment. In the meantime, with the level of wages too high relative to prices, aggregate spending in money terms will exceed domestic production, and the gap in an open economy may, to some considerable extent, be plugged by imports. The optimistic view is that unemployment will reduce the real wage, thus raising domestic production and employment. Against this is Keynes's pessimistic view, amply attested by evidence, that falls in money wage rates are no longer likely in contemporary conditions; and rises in prices may well not reduce real wages if people obtain wage rises to compensate for the price rises.

Similar results occur if output per man falls or rises less rapidly than real wages. Any inefficiency, managerial or otherwise, which leads to inadequate productivity will, therefore, result in an increased probability of an excess of demand over supply of current tradable products, and hence an increased probability of a tendency towards a current account deficit.

In the second case (non-traded goods) the explanation of the current account deficit is that the price of non-traded goods (haircuts, bricks, etc.) is too high relative to the price of goods that are imported and exported. The relatively low price of the latter means that demand for traded goods rises, but domestic production falls, giving a gap between demand and domestic supply which is filled by imports. Anything which generates a low price for tradables relative to the price of non-tradables will have this effect, but UK experiences suggest the major reason. More rapid increases in UK production costs may well increase the price of non-traded goods which face no international competition more than the price of traded goods, where international competition acts to restrain price rises. The consequent deterioration of profits in export industries gives an incentive for producers to concentrate more on non-traded goods, diminishing the domestic supply of just those products for which demand is increasing as a result of their relatively declining price.

What is needed here to remove the disequilibrium is a rise in the relative price of internationally traded goods. This would tend to switch domestic production into these goods and switch domestic expenditure away from them. The optimistic view suggests that the excess supply of non-traded goods will itself tend to bring down their price, and that the excess demand for traded goods will itself tend to put up their price, thus generating the required changes in relative prices, and 'correcting' the market discrepancy. Even if this is true, however, the mechanism will almost certainly operate very slowly. It is hard to see how the price of non-traded goods can fall quickly or easily, especially if money wages are inflexible downwards. If the change in relative prices comes purely through a rise in the price of traded goods, then a general tendency to inflation may be set in motion.

If there is an excess supply of money in Britain, the portfolios (asset holdings) of a number of firms and households will be out of balance. In an economy without external transactions, this imbalance—which must induce those holding what they consider to be too much money to attempt to run-down their balances—will set in motion rises in the demand for, and prices of, alternatives to money. Houses, shares, bonds, consumer durables, and capital equipment are examples of such alternatives. Either directly (monetarist) or indirectly (Keynesian), there is likely to be upwards pressure on the price of all goods, and labour too. The inflation may continue—accompanied, perhaps, by some expansion in real output—until an increasing demand for money to finance the increasing value of transactions is brought up to meet the supply. But in an open economy (like Britain) much of the pressure from the excess money can be let off in other ways: through increased imports and capital exports. The optimistic view of this will be that it cannot go on for too long: *unless*, that is, the British Government prevents the loss in reserves from leading to a fall in the domestic money supply, or governments abroad stop their swelling reserves having any upwards effect on their own domestic money supplies, or the demand for money is growing more slowly in Britain than in the rest of the world (when, as we saw in section 6.2.1, the deficit would tend to persist).

The pessimistic view is that few countries permit losses in reserves to lead to rapid or large falls in their domestic money supply, and even fewer allow rises in reserves to be reflected in rapid or large rises in it. In fact the Exchange Equilization Account of the Bank of England has operated in Britain since April 1932 to insulate domestic monetary conditions as much as possible from at least the effects of SCM on reserves. In recent years Germany and Switzerland have tried to repel inward SCM by penalizing foreign-owned deposits, and both have held their internal money supply down in periods when reserves were rising. On the other hand, there is growing evidence that countries governments or Central Banks are unable to prevent balance of payments surpluses (deficits) from having some positive (negative) effect on their domestic money supplies. Decaluwé and Steinherr [26], for instance, find that West Germany has only succeeded in 'sterilizing' about one-half of its balance of payments surplus. In Britain, substantial capital inflows in 1977, which reached their peak in October, eventually forced the authorities into allowing sterling to float upwards. The Exchange Equilization Account device of selling bonds on the open market to 'mop up' the extra holdings of sterling failed to work completely: interest rates rose with bond sales, which merely attracted further capital inflows.

Turning to the fourth possibility, it may be that UK residents have decided to save less and spend more. In other words, they prefer more consumption of current goods, and less of goods in the future. This creates an extra demand for current goods, including tradables. More of these are imported, less may be exported, and the current account goes into deficit. As we saw, this must imply a net sale of assets (including reserves) to foreigners. The excess spending on imports today has thereby reduced the ability of the community to spend on imports tomorrow, and there may well be an excess supply of goods for delivery (at various dates) in the future.

The optimistic view is that when tomorrow comes the then lower demand for traded goods will result in a compensating current account surplus. On the pessimistic side, however, people may be spending more today, not because of a decision to switch from future to present consumption, but because of excessively optimistic expectations of how well off they are going to be (their long-run or 'permanent' income). In this case they may strive to keep up their expenditure later on, and regret their earlier spending, both aspects implying that it would be in the community's interest to curb the high current spending. In practice, it would be very difficult to decide whether the optimistic or pessimistic interpretation was correct.

6.2.4. Correcting Instruments

It therefore seems arguable that the automatic market mechanism in each case works too slowly, so that government intervention may be required. This may simply be the arrangement of official loans to offset the outflow of reserves until the relevant market mechanism removes the deficit. But if this is inadequate and the government has to intervene more directly, the appropriate action differs from case to case.

It is easiest to start by considering the case where the price of non-traded goods relative to that of traded goods is too high. Devaluation is the most attractive remedy here, precisely because it corrects the imbalance between higher-priced profitable non-traded goods, and lower-priced unprofitable traded goods. The devaluation raises the sterling price of tradables, making them less attractive to import but more profitable to produce for export. Meanwhile domestic demand will switch towards non-traded goods, so the current account will improve. Devaluation is therefore a good example of an *expenditure-switching* instrument because its role is to switch expenditure from one type of good to another.

The effectiveness of devaluation in these circumstances arises from the fact that it directly redresses the particular type of disequilibrium. It is unlikely to have any *permanent* effects on the long-run equilibrium value of 'real' variables in the economy. (Real variables include all quantities, and relative prices of goods, such as the price ratio of traded to non-traded goods.) The likelihood of a negligible permanent effect can be understood by noting that devaluation is a change in the relative price of two countries' monies. It is the exchange rate counterpart to expanding the domestic money supply. Consequently, if devaluation is accompanied or followed by increases in the money supply, it cannot be expected to exert any long-run effect. Its major potential advantage is as a *short-run instrument* in certain well-defined circumstances. An excess supply of non-traded goods and an excess demand for traded goods, as described above, is a good example of this. Devaluation will speed up the return to equilibrium, which will be particularly useful if the domestic nominal price of non-traded goods is inflexible downwards.

If excess supply of money is the problem, the government could take steps to cut the size or rate of growth of the money supply. Devaluation could still help, if it is not accompanied by a rise in the domestic money supply, because it will tend to raise the domestic price of all goods traded internationally. This will increase the demand for money, and thereby lower the excess supply. The monetary restriction might appear more suitable because it avoids these inflationary tendencies, and because devaluation will disturb the relative price of traded and non-traded goods—unnecessarily in this situation. Against this, monetary restriction is likely to increase unemployment for a period, whereas devaluation will tend to generate *more* employment as firms in export and import-substitute industries begin to expand production, and the multiplier repercussions of this are felt.

The next case—inadequate saving—may call for deflation of aggregate demand, for example by increasing taxes. This means that the government ensures the abstention from consumption that is necessary to give current account balance. Any subsequent increase in personal saving can be offset in its effect on consumption by lowering taxes. The process is slow, however. The only component of aggregate demand to react quickly to fiscal cuts or tighter credit is consumers' expenditure on durables. There is a sizeable effect within three or four months, which is particularly marked if hire-purchase regulations have been tightened or eased. The long-run effect, however, is negligible, because the main effect is only to delay such purchases. Other consumption expenditures exhibit inertia, responding only slowly to changes in real disposable income. Investment expenditures do appear to be affected by both interest rates and the level of national income; but here there is little response for up to a year, and a complicated and obscure sequence of adjustments in the five or six quarters after this.

These are both examples of *expenditure-reducing* instruments. They operate through their effect on the level of total expenditure rather than through switching expenditure from one class of goods to another.

There are several possible ways, in theory, out of the last difficulty—the excessive level of real wages relative to labour productivity.

Incomes policy might restrain money wages, and then real wages; devaluation would cut the foreign exchange value of money wages, thereby cutting import demand; longer-term policies might be designed to improve industrial productivity, lower unit costs, and improve profitability in export industries at existing world prices. But experience in recent years makes one unconvinced that any of them is likely to be very effective. Incomes policies in Britain thus far appear to have had at best a minor, temporary, and diminishing impact on money wage rises. Devaluations, particularly by small countries, seem to lead rather quickly to compensating wage demands (a matter of hours in the case of Israel in November 1974). Much of the evidence in Britain suggests that cyclical rises in output, employment, and productivity are quickly followed by higher (and possibly accelerating) rises in money wage rates: if price rises lower real wages they do so only at the cost of more rapid inflation.

One remaining possible solution to the problem is to restrict imports by quotas or tariffs. Quotas set specific upper limits to import volumes. Tariffs can discourage imports by raising the internal domestic price of the importables concerned: this tends to cut home demand for them, and to stimulate domestic production to meet part of the demand at the same time. The main difference between quotas and tariffs is that the government will receive some revenue with a tariff, while under quotas the fortunate importers gain by being able to charge the higher price (unless the government auctions import licences). Another difference is that if there is only one domestic producer of the importable good, he will still be forced to compete with imports—albeit on easier terms—with a tariff, while a quota will confer monopoly power upon him. Another consequence of import restriction—given there are initially spare resources—will be to raise domestic output in the economy as a whole, unless foreign retaliation is substantial enough to damage export sales seriously. Its major disadvantage—besides its illegality under the General Agreement on Tariffs and Trade, and its dangers of inducing retaliation—is that it misallocates resources. Consumers are unable to purchase those combinations of goods that they would freely have chosen in the absence of import restrictions; production is switched (wastefully) away from industries in which the country enjoys a comparative cost advantage, towards those in which it does not. Any advantage accruing from import restriction can, in principle, always be achieved at less cost by other means. In general, no economic transaction (of which international commodity trade is an example) is entered into, unless the parties to it each expect to derive benefit from it. Any restriction on these transactions will normally be detrimental to those whom it affects—and it can be proved that, under certain conditions, everyone in the world could be made better off without them. It can also be shown that devaluation is usually a superior instrument to import restriction, since it is much likelier to have a large and favourable effect on the domestic supply of exports. This point is established by Scott and Little [50], although it has been disputed in the British context in a somewhat idiosyncratic model presented in the *Economic Policy Review* [37].

An economy suffering from substantial involuntary unemployment might benefit by applying quotas on its imports, or it might lose. But even if it does benefit, the quota is an indirect, partial way of securing a reduction in unemployment. A distortion is in general best-corrected directly, not indirectly. This line of argument suggests a hierarchy of instruments for removing the unemployment.

(a) First best: an economy-wide employment subsidy. This goes straight to the heart of the problem and corrects the distortion directly.

(b) Second best: either an economy-wide production subsidy or an employment subsidy confined to a particular sector. Neither of these are as good as the first best. The economy-wide production subsidy increases the demand for *other* factors, as well as energy, land, and capital. This is a distortion if it is only labour which is in excess supply. An employment subsidy confined to certain sectors has the drawback of altering the composition of production. Capital, for example, is diverted wastefully to sectors favoured by the subsidy from those which are not.

(c) Third best: a sector-confined production subsidy. This combines the disadvantages of the two second-best instruments.

(d) Fourth best: a measure such as devaluation, which operates as a sector-confined production-subsidy-plus-consumption-tax. (The sector to which the production subsidy and consumption tax are confined in this case comprises traded goods industries.) This is worse still since it also creates a consumption distortion.

(e) Fifth best: measures such as an import tariff, which act as a subsector-confined consumption-tax-plus-production-subsidy. This is inferior to the fourth-best solution as it is still more restricted in application. (The subsector in the case of an import tariff comprises 'importables'.)

(f) Sixth best: measures such as an import *quota*, which act as a subsector-confined consumption-tax-plus-production-subsidy, *together* with a windfall transfer to surviving importers and a possible grant of monopoly power to a domestic producer of import substitutes.

In the absence of additional distortions and ignoring distributional effects as between different groups in society, this ranking order of measures is unambiguously correct.

This analysis has demonstrated various possible disequilibria in other markets which can be associated with a current account deficit on the balance of payments: too much money; too many non-traded goods; a surplus of promises to deliver commodities in the future; too much unemployment. None calls for exactly the same remedy; no remedy is free from potential drawbacks; there are grounds for hoping that these disequilibria will indeed eventually disappear of their own accord, but there must be serious doubts that such automatic tendencies—if they exist—are rapid enough.

A balance of payments deficit is usually the external symptom of some internal inflationary pressure. A deficit under fixed exchange rates would register itself as depreciation under floating rates. It is to the study of adjustment under floating rates that we now turn.

6.3. Adjustment under Floating Exchange Rates

6.3.1. The Monetary Approach to Exchange Rates

Probably the best place to begin the study of floating exchange rates is with the view of the idealized economy portrayed by the 'optimists' of section 6.2. All prices are perfectly flexible. All markets clear continuously. Under these circumstances, movements in a country's exchange rate will be the external symptom of relative inflation. Any tendency for prices to rise more swiftly in country X than in country Y will be registered by a depreciation of X's currency in terms of Y's. To the question of what can cause prices to rise faster in one country than in another, proponents of the monetary approach to exchange rates have a simple answer. Since an exchange rate is the price of one country's money in terms of another's, the explanation of exchange rate changes must be monetary too.

Consider the market for money, and assume that this now clears continuously. Note the contrast with the monetary approach to the balance of payments under fixed exchange rates, which stresses that a surplus or deficit on the balance of payments reflects an excess supply or demand for money.) Call the real demand for money in country X Z_x and let M_x and P_x denote respectively the nominal money supply and the appropriate index of prices in country X. Similarly, Z_y, M_y, and P_y represent these variables for country Y.

Continuous money market clearance implies

$$P_x \mathcal{Z}_x = M_x$$

$$P_y \mathcal{Z}_y = M_y.$$

Furthermore, in proportional rates of change, equation (1) becomes

$$\hat{P}_x = \hat{M}_x - \hat{\mathcal{Z}}_x$$

$$\hat{P}_y = \hat{M}_y - \hat{\mathcal{Z}}_y.$$

In equation (2), the hat ($\hat{\ }$) over a variable represents the proportionate rate of change over time. Equation (2) tells us that the rate of inflation ($\hat{P}$) equals the amount by which the rate of growth of the money supply ($\hat{M}$) exceeds the growth of the real demand for money ($\hat{\mathcal{Z}}$).

The easiest way to bring the exchange rate into the story is to invoke the *Commodity Arbitrage Condition* (CAC). The CAC states that merchants leave no unexploited opportunity for international arbitrage in commodities. In the case of a commodity j that can be traded freely and costlessly across national boundaries, the CAC predicts that

$$P_{jx} = P_{jy} E_{xy}$$

where P_{jx} and P_{jy} are the local-currency prices of j in X and Y, and E_{xy} is the price of Y's currency in terms of X's. A rise in E_{xy} means that Y's currency is depreciating against X's, and X's appreciating against Y's. In proportional rates of change, the CAC gives us

$$\hat{P}_{jx} = \hat{P}_{jy} + \hat{E}_{xy}.$$

Now if all goods are freely tradable, and the two countries' residents employ a common index for prices, we can infer that the rate of depreciation of X's currency in terms of Y's exactly matches its relative inflation rate:

$$\hat{P}_x = \hat{P}_y + \hat{E}_{xy}.$$

Indeed, equation (5) can be extended to a world with trade barriers, such as tariffs and transport costs: all that matters is that any trade barriers remain unchanged.

There are three ways of reading equation (5). One is to take the right-hand side variables as exogenous. This gives us the so-called Scandinavian model of inflation: a country catches inflation from the rest of the world (if exchange rates are given) or as a result of exchange rate depreciation. A second interpretation is to freeze $\hat{P}_x$ and $\hat{P}_y$ and treat equation (5) as determining $\hat{E}_{xy}$. This is the *Purchasing Power Parity Theory* of exchange rates: if prices rise faster in one country than in another, the latter's exchange rate will be bid up against the former in order to preserve parity of purchasing power of money.

The third way of reading equation (5) is to take all three variables as *jointly* determined by the equation. This is much more appealing and realistic than placing clamps on some of the variables and pretending that they are not all interdependent. But if we take this challenging and superior approach, we need more equations. Otherwise, the variables are left dangling, unexplained. Where are these extra equations to come from?

The monetary approach to exchange rates provides a simple answer: from the money market equation (2). We can combine equations (2) and (5) to eliminate the inflation terms and solve for the exchange rate trend:

$$\hat{E}_{xy} = (\hat{M}_x - \hat{Z}_x) - (\hat{M}_y - \hat{Z}_y). \tag{6}$$

Now equation (6) says that X's depreciation against Y's currency equals the excess money supply growth in X, less than in Y. Alternatively, the slower the relative growth in the money supply $(\hat{M}_x - \hat{M}_y)$, and the faster the relative growth in the real demand for money $(\hat{Z}_x - \hat{Z}_y)$, the more X's currency will tend to appreciate against Y's. Factors that could raise the real demand for money, Z, include:

(a) a rise in wealth;

(b) a rise in real income, either now or expected in the future;

(c) a fall in nominal interest rates on alternative assets, perhaps due to lower expectations of inflation;

(d) increased uncertainty about the cost or availability of funds for emergency borrowing;

(e) fiscal and institutional phenomena, such as a switch from direct to indirect taxation.

The monetary approach to exchange rates has much to commend it. It is simple, logically consistent, and highly plausible, at least as a long-run relationship. But—at least in the embryonic form given in equation (6)—it is subject to several qualifications. Eight qualifications stand out:

(1) Z is not directly observable, and has to be proxied, for example by real income.

(2) There may be complex socio-political pressures underlying M_x and M_y, which may be related back to other economic variables.

(3) There is strong empirical evidence (for example Frenkel [34]) against the CAC and Purchasing Power Parity Theory, at least as short-run relationships, during the 1970s.

(4) The appropriate price indices are very hard to identify and almost certain to differ between countries. This becomes especially problematical when relative prices change.

(5) Some markets do *not* clear continuously.

(6) In the crude form presented above, but not in more sophisticated versions, no role is given to expectations.

(7) The analysis should not be restricted to the demand for and supply of money, but extended to market-clearance conditions for a wider set of assets, including bonds.

(8) When Z is proxied by variables such as real income, equation (6) is not well attested by the data. Evidence of tests (for example Hacche and Townend [38]) lends at best very lukewarm empirical support.

6.3.2. A Simple Keynesian Approach

A different view of exchange rate determination, which emphasizes the role of unit labour cost trends in different countries, can be obtained from examining the identity for the wage share (α) in output, Q:

$$WL/PQ \equiv \alpha.$$

Here, W, L, and P denote respectively the money wage rate, the level of employment, and the price level. Expressing this in proportionate rates of change, and rearranging, we have

$$\hat{P} \equiv \hat{W} - \hat{\alpha} - (\hat{Q} - \hat{L}). \tag{7}$$

Equation (7) states that inflation must equal the increase in money wage rates, minus the increase in the wage share of output, minus the growth of labour productivity $(\hat{Q} - \hat{L})$. The growth in unit labour costs equals $\hat{W} - (\hat{Q} - \hat{L})$. Expressing equation (7) with subscripts x and y to denote countries X and Y, and combining it with equation (5), we may derive

$$\hat{E}_{xy} = (\hat{W}_x - \hat{W}_y) - (\hat{\alpha}_x - \hat{\alpha}_y) - \{(\hat{Q}_x - \hat{L}_x) - (\hat{Q}_y - \hat{L}_y)\}. \tag{8}$$

According to equation (8), the rate of depreciation of X's currency against Y's will equal X's relative money wage increase, corrected for relative productivity growth and for the relative change in labour's share in output. Equation (8) may be called a Keynesian approach to exchange rate determination. This is so because it was Keynes who first stressed that money wage rates may respond only weakly to economic influences. Their movement could be spontaneous, and at least temporarily independent of economic variables. Some historic instances can be adduced to support equation (8). In June 1968, the French Prime Minister Pompidou conceded generous money wage increases to stop a general strike. Little over a year later, the French Government felt it necessary to devalue the franc to restore international competitiveness. The giddy downward spiral of sterling in 1975–6 followed a sharp increase, to over 25 per cent, in the level of British pay settlement increases in 1974. But there are also counter-instances: the British wage explosion of 1979 actually accompanied a pronounced appreciation of sterling. International differences among OECD countries in unit labour costs, expressed in a common currency, have in fact become much wider and more turbulent during the 1970s, when exchange rates have been floating, than in the previous two decades when exchange rates were fixed. Furthermore, even when the evidence does seem to support equation (8), as in the UK in 1974–6, it can be argued that the 1974 jump in money wage increases was *not* spontaneous. It followed hard upon a sharply increased rate of growth of the money supply (between 16 per cent and 28 per cent per annum from mid-1971 to end-1973, depending on definition). Furthermore there is growing empirical support (see, for example, Sargan [48]) for the view that money wage increases are dependent on an approximately one-to-one basis with actual, or expected, inflation. These considerations suggest that equation (8) can at best only *describe* the process of exchange rate changes (and the evidence suggests that it even fails to do this satisfactorily). It cannot fully *explain* it.

6.3.3. Exchange Rate Overshooting in Theory and Practice

The simple monetary approach assumes that the labour market, and other markets, function smoothly and perfectly. The Keynesian approach gives money wage rates an independent 'life of their own'. The truth appears to lie somewhere in the middle. Money wage rates do respond to economic influences, but sometimes very sluggishly, and especially so in a downward direction.

If certain markets display a sluggish response of prices to disequilibria, floating exchange rates may over-react to stimuli. This phenomenon is known as 'overshooting'. Consider the following example. Suppose that the appropriate index for prices in an open economy, X, is a geometric average of two (national-currency) prices: the price of traded goods, P_{TX}, and the price of non-traded goods, P_{NX}, both expressed in X's currency. Suppose that P_{NX} is temporarily frozen, presumably reflecting frozen money wage rates, but that P_{TX} obeys the CAC, as in equations (3) and (4), by virtue of international trade. Suppose that the real demand for money in X, Z_x, is frozen, and that the money supply, M_x, suddenly rises by 10 per cent.

If the money market in X is to clear the fact that Z_x cannot change means that the price index, P, must go up by 10 per cent. But since the non-traded goods price is frozen, the only flexible element in the price index, P_{TX}, must go up by more to compensate. In fact P_{TX} must increase by about 20 per cent to bring P up to 10 per cent, and choke off the excess supply of money. If the price of traded goods abroad is exogenously given, the only way this can happen, given the CAC, is for X's exchange rate to depreciate by about 20 per cent. This result bears repetition. A sudden increase in X's money supply causes a much larger than equi-proportionate depreciation. Later on, however, the exchange rate will swing back towards its long-run equilibrium value (which will imply an eventual depreciation of about 10 per cent only, assuming that there are no subsequent changes in monetary conditions at home or abroad). This happens because sooner or later the prices of non-traded goods (and money wage rates) in X will go up in line with the jump in the money supply.

This explanation of 'overshooting' is very simple. The phenomenon was first analysed in detail by Dornbusch [29]. A more sophisticated story than the one we have just considered was developed in detail by Buiter and Miller [14] among others, and summarized by Sinclair [52]. It runs as follows. Suppose, following our earlier idea in section 6.3.1, that the demand for real money in X, Z_x, is negatively related to the nominal rate of interest in X, R_x. Suppose too that the covered interest parity condition keeps $R_x - R_y$ equal to the forward discount on X's currency against Y's, and that this in turn equals the market's mean expectation of the rate of depreciation of X's currency against Y's. Finally, suppose that exchange rate expectations are formed by agents who believe (and are not systematically wrong in this belief) that the economy will work as described by the monetary approach outlined in section 6.3.1.

Consider, in this model, the effect of news, suddenly made public, that X's monetary authority plans to keep the future growth of the money supply, M_x below levels previously anticipated. This means that participants in foreign exchange markets will be predicting slower depreciation (or faster appreciation) for X's currency. This in turn will cut the forward discount on X's currency (or raise the premium) and, given foreign interest rates, bring domestic nominal interest rates down.

The fall in R_x now causes a return of confidence in X's money for X's residents. Z_x rises now. But if the current value of M_x is given, the price index in country X must fall in order to preserve equilibrium in X's money market. This requires an immediate appreciation of X's exchange rate. This will be amplified, in the short run, if certain domestic prices in X are temporarily frozen, but will still occur even if they are not. One may conclude that revised expectations of tighter (looser) monetary policy in the *future* will cause the spot exchange rate to jump (or drop) *now*.

6.4. Sterling and the Balance of Payments since 1972

Armed with these ideas, we can now turn to the record of sterling and the United Kingdom's balance of payments since floating began in June 1972. Table 6.3 earlier in this chapter presented current account balance of payments statistics. The current balance was in deficit in five of the eleven years between 1972 and 1983 (1973, 1974, 1975, 1976, and 1979). Of these, the 1974 deficit was by far the largest. It represented over 3 per cent of national income in that year. What explained this was, above all, the fourfold rise in oil prices that occurred between 1973 and 1974. At this time, Britain had to meet all her oil needs from imports.

Oil also accounts for the strongly positive trend in the current balance which can be seen in the years that follow 1974. This time, it is not so much oil price changes as the cumulative effect of replacing oil imports by North Sea oil that explains much of the trend. Even the visible trade balance, which had been positive for only three previous years in the century, had swung into surplus by 1980. But there were non-oil phenomena at work, too. The years 1973-4 and 1979 represent business cycle peaks, when imports are often heavily swollen as a result of high domestic demand. 1975, 1980, and 1981, on the other hand, were years of recession, when imports grew only slowly in nominal value and fell steeply in real terms. The aggregate statistics for the current account conceal important structural changes, such as the rapid increases in certain categories of imports of manufactures (particularly vehicles) witnessed in the 1970s, and pronounced growth in exports of services. Other noteworthy developments included a massive inflow of short-term capital in 1977, most of it transferring from the United States. This explains most of the unprecedented fourfold jump in Britain's official reserves during 1977 (see Table 6.4) when the current account was barely in surplus. Since 1979, when foreign exchange controls on exports of capital by British residents were relaxed, the capital account of the balance of payments has been dominated by sizeable outflow of long-term capital.

Such are the major swings in the balance of payments that have occurred

TABLE 9.1. *Public Expenditure in 1982 and Selected Earlier Years*

		Ratio to GNP					£ million	
		1961	1971	1976	1981	1982	1981	1982
1	Military defence	7·05	5·51	5·50	6·04	6·31	12,639	14,497
2	Civil defence	0·03	0·01	0·02	0·01	0·01	27	38
3	External relations	0·52	0·78	0·91	0·91	0·96	1,908	2,198
4	Roads and public lighting	1·12	1·68	1·40	1·17	1·25	2,583	3,039
5	Transport and communication	2·16	1·11	0·96	0·96	0·88	2,029	2,054
6	Employment services	0·13	0·35	0·61	1·11	1·00	2,357	2,338
7	Other industry and trade	2·72	4·12	2·46	1·69	1·58	3,449	3,543
8	Research not included elsewhere	0·47	0·46	0·42	0·44	0·44	910	995
10	Housing	2·27	2·62	4·52	2·72	2·42	5,603	5,484
11	Water, sewerage, refuse disposal	0·78	0·95	0·58	0·58	0·55	1,278	1,327
12	Public health services	0·10	0·13	0·17	0·16	0·16	332	368
13	Land drainage, coastal protection	0·08	0·07	0·10	0·12	0·13	247	307
14	Parks	0·20	0·26	0·38	0·39	0·39	843	905
15	Libraries, museums, arts	0·14	0·22	0·29	0·29	0·27	624	659
16	Other local government	0·39	0·58	0·75	0·57	0·57	1,110	1,221
17	Police	0·64	0·88	1·02	1·24	1·29	2,551	2,934
18	Prisons	0·09	0·15	0·21	0·26	0·24	545	554
19	Parliament and law courts	0·13	0·20	0·31	0·40	0·42	852	983
20	Fire service	0·15	0·19	0·22	0·24	0·23	561	606
21	Education	4·14	5·79	6·45	6·47	6·30	13,259	14,292
22	School meals, milk, welfare foods	0·38	0·32	0·40	0·24	0·22	515	531
23	National health service	3·80	4·49	5·38	6·31	6·15	13,087	14,014
24	Social security benefits	6·65	8·61	9·95	12·95	13·69	27,498	31,914
25	Personal social services	0·27	0·62	1·04	1·18	1·18	2,548	2,806
26	Finance and tax collection	0·57	0·65	0·68	0·71	0·69	1,521	1,630
27	Other	0·47	0·31	0·38	0·19	0·30	279	498
28	Debt interest	5·13	4·17	4·78	6·18	6·07	13,218	14,265
29	Non-trading capital consumption	0·62	0·70	0·80	0·90	0·89	2,018	2,205
30	Total expenditure by public authorities	42·78	46·93	51·75	55·27	55·44	116,060	128,044

Source: Adapted from *National Income and Expenditure* (1982 and 1983).

from 1961 to 1976. Some of this is explained by demographic changes and the higher political emphasis placed on these categories of spending over this period, but also by rates of pay boosted in line with, and occasionally above, earnings elsewhere in the economy, where productivity was growing by 3 per cent per year, even though conventional measures of labour productivity changed little in health and education. This 'relative price effect' also explains the rising trend of expenditure on prisons, Parliament and law courts, the fire service, and finance and tax collection. The modest jump in debt interest from 5·1 per cent to 6·1 per cent of GNP between 1961 and 1982 occurred despite a downward trend in the ratio of National Debt to GNP. It reflected the sharp increase in expected inflation which was built into the interest payments offered on newly issued government debt. Main items to have fallen as a percentage of GNP since 1976 are industry and trade, agriculture etc., and housing, the last of these by 2 percentage points back to its level in the 1960s.

9.2. Public Goods

Public goods are goods which can be consumed collectively. One person's enjoyment of a public good in no way prevents someone else's. What is more, no one can be prevented from enjoying public goods if he wishes to: exclusion is impossible. They are contrasted with a private good (apples, for instance) from which generally only one person can derive satisfaction; and from other goods or amenities from which exclusion is possible, although they may share other characteristics of public goods. Because exclusion is impossible, direct charges for consumption are impossible.

One example of public goods is collective defence. Any benefits X feels it confers on him are in no sense at the expense of someone else's deriving them either. This is not to suggest that everyone must benefit from expenditure on defence. X may be a pacifist: he may consider that some types of defence spending are more likely to jeopardize his security than increase it; he may feel that it threatens something dear to him. The point simply is that, good or bad, defence can only be 'consumed' collectively.

Other types of public good are not hard to find: the task, assumed by public authorities, of containing, and eliminating, contagious diseases; TV and radio waves—the fact the X's set receives them does not stop Y's doing so as well; good architecture, at least on the outside of buildings, displaying a public face. The judiciary and the police are also public goods. One of the most important of all public goods, with profound economic effects, is knowledge—knowledge at least, which is unappropriable. The saving in the costs of gathering information afforded by the Yellow Pages of Telephone Directories is a simple example.

A decentralized market system will probably not, by itself, provide public goods in the required amount. This is because the extent to which X contribute toward the provision of public goods will only to an insignificant extent affec how much X can himself consume. What matters for X's consumption is what i provided by everyone together; and that in turn depends on what the million of others provide. In these circumstances it will pay people to understate thei demand for public goods and this may make it hard for public authorities t decide how much to provide. If a city council sends a questionnaire to al inhabitants, asking them to put a monetary value on the benefit they would ge from a doubling of the local police force, but pointing out that each household will be called on to pay some proportion of the value it states, plenty c households will reply, 'nothing'—not because the extra policemen ar valueless to them but because the increase in their numbers, and the benefi each household derives, will be seen to depend primarily on the answers of others. All your really get from being honest is a bigger tax demand.

The only realistic solution to this problem involves communal action, organizing our collective affairs together. But what is the most *efficient* way of doing this? Pareto defined one state of affairs, X, as superior to another, Y, if no member of society is better off in Y than in X and at least one is better off in X. Derivation of the specific rules by which to determine the optimal provision of a public good is rather complex and more appropriately tackled in chapter 24 on resource allocation: but it must be stressed that since everyone can consume a public good, society's demand for a public good is found by adding the individual's demand curves for it *vertically*, i.e. the benefit from any given amount of a public good is the summation of the benefit each individual would receive from it. (This is in sharp contrast to a private good where total demand at each possible price is found by summing individuals' demand curves *horizontally*.)

While the Pareto criterion is in principle straightforward, in practice there are many difficulties. Many alternatives X and Y involve some being better off and some worse off—and there then has to be some mechanism for compensating the losers. Even ignoring this, the application of the Pareto principle requires estimates to be made of the benefits people receive from public goods and this is frequently difficult or impossible.

Public goods are, of course, costly to provide in aggregate, and, clearly, some limit must be placed upon them. In practice, the decision on how much should be provided lies with government; and their guesses of the sum of individual benefits, however intuitive or inaccurate, are often influenced by pressure groups and periodic elections. What must be noticed, however, is that public goods have to be paid for by some system of levies or taxes on the citizens themselves.

9.3. Subsidies

9.3.1. The Economic Efficiency Argument and its Applications

The second category of public expenditure we identified was the losses or subsidies on various undertakings, which governments assume.

A common justification for an economic undertaking to run at a loss is as follows. Everyone should be free to buy another unit of any private good at the same price; and this 'same price' should equal the extra costs, to society as a whole, involved in making another unit of the good available. These two precepts are necessarily true only in an ideal world, and very probably need modification in the presence of distortions elsewhere in the economy. The implication is that everyone should be free to buy at a price equal to marginal cost. (See chapter 24 for elaboration of this concept.)

Marginal cost need not equal average cost. Marginal cost means the addition to total cost involved in providing the last or the next unit, when the size of the unit is very small. The average cost is the total cost divided by the number of units provided. Only when average cost does not alter with output will the two be equal. This could occur in some cases—labour-intensive operations, for instance, like services or baking bread, where the technical advantages or disadvantages to be had from altering the scale of provision are minimal. But in other cases there can be a wide gap between marginal cost and average cost. Two obvious instances are bridges and museums, two goods usually provided publicly. One extra journey across a bridge or visit to a museum costs those providing the service hardly anything at all. Until the facilities become congested, it costs other users nothing either; but when the point of congestion is reached the *external* marginal cost—in the form of extra delay imposed on *other* users—becomes appreciable, even though the 'internal' marginal cost stays negligible. The average cost, however, may be considerable. The correct price to charge people who cross the bridge or visit the museum is (in ideal conditions) the *marginal cost to society*. Unless the facility is congested, this is nothing. So the bridge toll and museum entry charge should be set at zero except when they are congested. Any positive charge will produce economic loss—society is, as a whole, the poorer (in terms of time and fuel wasted) for having the toll. But there is one obvious and awkward implication of not having tolls or charges. The fixed costs of providing the facilities are not met. Taxation is an obvious possible source.

Several nationalized industries are in a similar position to the bridge or museum owners. Transport and telecommunication are the obvious cases. The marginal cost of allowing another passenger on a train or a bus is very low, so long as the facilities are uncongested. Similarly with a telephone call. But these organizations have heavy costs to bear in total—a large wage bill to pay and a large debt on which to pay interest. These can be met, in part, by charging the higher social marginal costs which occur when the facilities are congested— peak-time railway travellers and telephone callers impose external costs (delays, inconvenience, and so on) on other would-be users. Alternatively *long-run* marginal cost can be used, where this refers to the additional cost of producing an extra amount of output or service presuming *all* inputs, including capital, to be variable. But this can still result in losses if long-run marginal cost is below average cost. (These points will be developed in Chapter 25.) Another method of raising revenue to meet losses otherwise resulting from optimal pricing rules is to levy fixed contributions to meet the fixed costs, although this often merges at national level into taxation. Just as a club levies subscriptions on members to defray costs, and charges marginal costs only for the use of facilities whenever they are used, telephone subscribers are charged quarterly rentals, and owners of vehicles and television sets charged for annual licences, which are independent of the use of the service made. All such charges are fixed, and so do not affect the marginal price which everyone who pays them faces. But there may well still be an overall loss. General taxation is then needed to meet it.

9.3.2. Subsidies to Agriculture

Subsidies are given sometimes to specific industries. The best British example is perhaps agriculture. This has been subsidized since 1928 through exemption from rates, since 1930 through cheap loans, and since 1932, starting with wheat, through price regulation and price support. A major purpose of these subsidies has been to conserve a domestic agricultural industry in the face of competition from frequently low-priced imports; it has been felt to confer strategic and aesthetic social benefits; hence the marginal social cost of domestic output is less than the marginal commercial cost faced by farmers. So the price farmers receive for many of their products has been stabilized at levels often much higher than import prices. The traditional device for doing this was 'deficiency payments', a system now dismantled in conformity with EEC regulations. The deficiency payment scheme kept prices to consumers at the world level (plus the obvious mark-ups for distribution), and shielded farmers from the losses this would involve by paying them, when necessary, a deficiency payment above this. By contrast, the EEC's Common Agricultural Policy keeps the domestic price to farmers and buyers within prescribed limits, and taxes or subsidizes imports of food to keep their price in line with the domestic price. This has nearly always meant taxing food imports with tariffs, a policy seen earlier to be suspect. The figure of £1,524 million for 1981 in Table 9.1 greatly understates, therefore, the true level of subsidies paid to British agriculture.

9.3.3. Subsidies to Aviation

Another British instance of an industry subsidized heavily is aviation. The subsidy is often indirect, as the government is a major purchaser of military aeroplanes, and the price paid is calculated to cover all costs and give a 'fair' rate of profit. The government also defrays all the costs of abortive projects; and it has been known to require the state airlines to buy British, if necessary even subsidizing them as the price for this. The justification of the subsidy must be that the strategic importance of a domestic aircraft industry, and 'spill-over' benefits to other industries from research and development, keep marginal social costs below the marginal commercial costs confronting the manufacturer. The need to keep unemployment down or the exchange rate up have also been offered as reasons, but they are uncompelling, since economically more efficient means are at hand to reach these objectives.

9.3.4. Other Subsidies to Private Industry

Other subsidies paid to private industries have usually had a more specific purpose, and a more complicated method of operation. Since the 1930s, and more especially the 1960s, increasingly lavish subsidies on investment have been available for manufacturing firms operating in various regions of Britain where unemployment was seen to be below the national average. The Department of Scientific and Industrial Research was set up in 1916 to encourage and subsidize research in industry; and in recent years quite generous tax treatment has been given for research and development expenditure. Investment in manufacturing, irrespective of location, has been encourage at various times by tax allowances (from 1959 to 1966 and from 1970), cash grants (between January 1066 to 1970), and (at least until 1984) increasingly generous depreciation allowances against tax. The purpose of the research and investment incentives has been to guide industry towards a socially correct' set of choices between consumption now and investment for consumption later. This can be done by offering the incentive of greater expected profit, or by increasing the cash flow for such projects if capital markets are imperfect and do not therefore provide the funds.

The common thread between all these subsidies or losses has been that attempts to justify them depend on *economic efficiency*. Pricing at average cost for bridges, museums, telephones, and railways was seen to lead to waste; in ideal conditions, they, and all other goods, should be priced at marginal cost. In these four cases—to which one might add many others—pricing at or near marginal cost is likely to lead to losses. The agriculture and aviation cases were slightly different. Here the crucial factor was the *external* benefits (greater security and so on) alleged to accrue from domestic production. Subsidies were one method—perhaps the most efficient method—of ensuring that these benefits were reaped to the correct extent. Then we saw specific subsidies or allowances (for regional development or investment, for instance) being given. In this case, the justification must be that the market place *malfunctions*. Unemployment in a particular region ought to lower wages there, relative to other areas, and so induce a double switch: workers to the work in the other areas, and work to the workers in the area concerned, but this does not happen sufficiently. If society invests too little and consumes too much, the shortage of capital should be signalled in the form of a high enough reward to investors and savers to correct the misallocation. But, for various reasons, this does not happen either, or happens too slowly. Hence the subsidy. Research may combine the external benefits and market malfunctioning arguments—not all the gains from successful research go to the researcher, and some may accrue free, at once or after the patent expires, to others; also there may be an 'intertemporal' fault in the market which places too low a value on any form of investment, of which research is one. Unfortunately, some subsidies given cannot easily be justified under any of these criteria; and the calculation of 'correct' prices, 'external' benefits, and 'marginal' costs is so beset with mathematical, political, or philosophical problems that all we can attempt are the crudest and most tentative of guesses. But before moving on to the third object of taxation—redistribution—we should look at the last type of justifiable subsidy.

9.4. Merit Goods

Merit goods are goods which buyers may for some reason undervalue. Education is an often-quoted example. The point is that if there were no state subsidy or state provision of education, then parents would decide on the level of education their children received. In many cases the parents could be feckless and disregard their children's interests. The children themselves might indeed be no better judges of their interests at the time either. So education is subsidized and, also, attendance made compulsory. In many societies, it is available free. The argument does not necessarily imply that the state should itself control all the schools, merely that education should be cheap, in relation to costs, *or* compulsory. The fact that it is generally *both* is partly explained by the income-distribution argument we consider next. Health is similar to education; both the merit good and income-distribution arguments are relevant. We may bitterly regret not having visited our doctor for an early diagnosis; cheap, or free, or, alternatively, compulsory access to him may guide us to make 'better' decisions. And again, parents may pay inadequate attention to their children's health. But the provision of a free medical service may also be a way of making the distribution of income less unequal, and of compensating those unlucky enough to be prone to illness. Also, in contagious disease we have a case of a pure public 'bad'; so anything to halt or cure it is a public good. These two merit goods—education and health—are dominant items of public expenditure, frequently consuming, together, one-seventh or so of society's total economic resources.

9.5. Income Redistribution

9.5.1. Factors Influencing the Distribution of Income

How the market place parcels out income to the citizens in a society is a complex matter. National income may be decomposed into earned income (wages and salaries) and unearned income (rent, profits, and interest). Virtually everyone receives unearned income, in cash or kind. Consumer durables, houses, inherited stocks and shares, accumulated savings, and pension rights all confer a yield of service or income. These assets constitute wealth (a stock), and unearned income, both psychic and pecuniary, is the yield (a flow) of wealth. About two-fifths of the population are also workers: usually some 90 per ccent of the male population aged between 20 and 65, and about 50 per cent of the female population in this age range, receive earned income in return for work. Nearly the entire population—all but the youngest and oldest—are workers in a wider sense: at the least they perform jobs, as it happens unpriced in the market place, for themselves or their household, in the house or the garden. The fruits of labour, and, more particularly, the income from wealth, are unevenly spread over the population; but there can hardly be any family with no income at all from both sources, even before the substantial adjustments by the government are carried out. The inequality in wealth and income arises from differences in ability, inheritance, accumulated savings, market power, and luck.

9.5.2. The Welfare Arguments

No area in economics elicits greater controversy than the question of what constitutes an optimum distribution of income. Any answer is necessarily normative, not positive; and this difficulty is further compounded by the fact that individuals will differ in their answers, and even disagree about whether or how they can formulate general principles for debating the topic.

Marx and Proudhon challenged the moral basis of property rights and the unearned income that accrues from them in capitalist or pre-capitalist societies. Marx also believed that labour income (earned income) should be spread evenly. Complete equality was a moral precept, for which no independent justification was offered or thought to be necessary. The utilitarian approach to the question suggests that the distribution of income is best when redistribution has equalized the marginal utility of money for everyone. This implies complete equality of incomes if, and only if, everyone has the same relationship between money and utility—the same utility function.[1] It produces strange results when, for example, poor health prevents someone enjoying money as much as others. It is also open to other objections: can one individual's marginal utility of money be measured, or compared with that of some else? A recent attempt to answer the problem has relied on the concept of a hypothetical social contract which would be drawn up between everyone if they were unaware of what their actual position in the hierarchy of incomes would actually be. They would be so alarmed, the argument runs, of falling into the poorest set that they would assent to a distribution of incomes which maximized the absolute income of the poorest set. This would result in complete equality provided that the volume of work done, and goods produced, did not fall as the marginal rate of tax on incomes was raised to 100 per cent— or if individuals were deprived of any freedom to choose their hours and intensity of work. But if these liberties are protected, and the disincentive effects of high marginal rates of income tax are perceptible, the hypothetical contract to maximize the absolute income of the poorest set will impose less than total equality of incomes [34], [14], [33].

It has sometimes been held that the income a person receives is a true reflection of the value placed by society on the (marginal product of) his wealth and work; and that this constitutes a case against any redistribution of incomes. The first proposition is falsified in practice by the imperfections in factor and other markets; the second is no less a value-judgement than any of the pleas for complete or limited equality discussed earlier.

9.5.3. Methods and Scale of Redistribution

Redistribution has its origins in the 1563 Poor Law, and has been transformed and extended beyond recognition in this century. Since the war the scale of assistance has steadily risen in real terms, although there is much evidence that the take-up rate of this assistance is still quite low.

The beneficiaries of redistribution may receive income in cash or kind. The redistribution in kind takes the form primarily of merit goods freely available to all in equal amounts. Although these goods can be enjoyed (if they will) by the better off (at least, in the case of 'blanket' provision), the provision of merit goods is still redistributive since the costs are not spread equally over the population, but bear much more heavily on the higher-income groups. Education and health are the obvious examples. But there are other types of redistribution in kind as well: cheap butter (1973–4) and beef (1974) for old age pensioners.

Cash benefits include unemployment and sickness benefit; old age pensions; supplementary benefit; since 1971 Family Income Supplement (for those on low earned income); child allowance; maternity benefits and assistance for widowhood or disablement; rent rebates for local authority and private tenants on low income (introduced by the Housing Finance Act, 1972); and

---

[1] With the further assumption that the marginal utility of money diminishes the more money one has.

abatements in prescription charges for medicines bought by families in need or old age pensioners (an exception to their general reintroduction in 1968). Attempts to suppress politically sensitive symptoms of inflation led to 'blanket' subsidies on mortgage interest rates (1973, 1974) and some items of food (milk, 1973–6; bread, cheese, and butter, 1974–6).

Redistribution has gainers; it also, obviously, has losers. So it must generally involve taxes. How redistributive taxation in fact is depends on its degree of 'progessivity'. A tax is progressive if the *proportion* of income paid in tax is higher for higher-income groups, regressive if it is lower for them. Assessing the effect of the tax system on the distribution of income is difficult, since incomes are spread over a continuous scale, and it is possible for a tax to cut the ratio of the highest 25 per cent to the lowest 25 per cent, let us say, but raise it between the highest and lowest 10 per cent. In general, income taxes are strongly progressive, since an increasingly large chunk of income is lopped off in tax for every in crease in the scale above about £18,000 per annum. Taxes on consumption may be regressive or progressive, depending on whether expenditure on the goods concerned is a higher or a lower proportion of low-income budgets than high-income budgets. The net effect of taxation in Britain in much of the nineteenth century has been thought to be slightly regressive. The picture is different now, although some commodities with a low income-elasticity of demand do bear a heavy rate of tax (see section 7.2 of this chapter). Tables 9.2 and 9.3 give some impression of the effect of income tax on the distribution of income.

9.6. The National Debt

Lastly, we come to our fourth need for taxes: to pay interest on the National Debt. The National Debt is the sum total of the *government's* interest-bearing obligations. The case for continuing to pay interest on government borrowing from the public is both moral and prudential: it will have to pay prohibitive interest on future borrowings if it has reneged in the past. In large measure, these debts are explained by the excess of government spending over the tax receipts in the two world wars. The First World War more than decupled the central government's interest-bearing debt from £650 million to over £7,000 million, and the Second World War nearly trebled it by adding another £14,000 million or so. The thirty-eight years after 1945 saw it rise by another £105,000 million. Table 9.4 gives the most recent estimate available, and shows how the debt is broken down by the type of obligation and the nature of its holder. Fortunately for the tax payer most of these debts are in the form of long-term fixed-interest bonds; he has been shielded from much of the unparalleled rise in nominal interest rates that has occurred since the last war. To the luckless holder, of course, this has meant a sharp fall in the nominal value of his bonds, and a remorselessly negative real return apart from brief periods. Inflation (the growing expectations of which were the main cause of the rising interest rates) has helped to whittle away the real value of interest payments, too. But for fresh debt, newly issued to cover the current budget deficit, or to redeem old bonds falling due, the expectation of inflation has an

TABLE 9.2. *Distribution of Income, Before Tax in 1978–1979*

Range of incomes		Number of tax units	Income before tax	Taxes on income	Income after tax
		Thousands		——— £ million———	
Income before tax					
Not under	Under				
£	£				
	1,000	1,411	987	3	984
1,000	1,500	3,670	4,844	43	4,801
1,500	2,000	2,974	5,234	215	5,019
2,000	2,500	2,701	6,075	475	5,600
2,500	3,000	2,263	6,223	712	5,511
3,000	3,500	1,975	6,415	879	5,536
3,500	4,000	1,815	6,801	998	5,803
4,000	4,500	1,698	7,208	1,124	6,084
4,500	5,000	1,652	7,833	1,277	6,556
5,000	6,000	2,855	15,599	2,644	12,955
6,000	7,000	2,173	14,037	2,508	11,529
7,000	8,000	1,460	10,885	2,053	8,832
8,000	10,000	1,394	12,385	2,575	9,810
10,000	12,000	458	5,004	1,175	3,829
12,000	15,000	310	4,091	1,073	3,018
15,000	20,000	160	2,745	855	1,890
20,000	30,000	76	1,822	737	1,085
30,000 and over		31	1,422	839	583
Total		29,076	119,610	20,185	99,425
Income not included in the classification by ranges		..	13,667	..	..
Total income of households		..	133,277	..	..

Source: *National Income and Expenditure* (1982).

odd effect: if the new debt is not indexed,[2] the interest payments will reflect fears of inflation and effectively force the government into a fast rate of amortization of the debt in real terms. At the time of writing, for example, the government must offer £9·50 per year interest to borrow £100 for a long period (say, thirty years)—and if inflation occurs at a rate of 10 per cent per year, nearly half the real value of the loan will have been already paid off after seven years. If the annual rate of inflation comes down to single figures, however, the burden of debt-servicing on future tax payers becomes more onerous. These points constitute some of the justification for indexing government borrowing. Indexed government bonds have been issued since 1981. Their yield is approximately 3·0 per cent. If this real rate of interest measures the true, real cost of debt-servicing once the optical illusions and distortions arising from

[2] A bond is fully indexed against inflation if both the interest payments (coupon) and redemption value are guaranteed in real terms.

TABLE 9.3. *Distribution of Income after Tax in 1978–1979*

Range of incomes		Number of tax units	Income before tax	Taxes on income	Income after tax
		Thousands		—£ million—	
Income after tax					
Not under	Under				
£	£				
	1,000	1,446	1,023	9	1,014
1,000	1,500	3,895	5,257	123	5,134
1,500	2,000	3,685	6,988	543	6,445
2,000	2,500	3,320	8,405	943	7,462
2,500	3,000	2,691	8,491	1,100	7,391
3,000	3,500	2,340	8,931	1,329	7,602
3,500	4,000	2,090	9,310	1,476	7,834
4,000	4,500	1,961	9,945	1,614	8,331
4,500	5,000	1,714	9,774	1,638	8,136
5,000	6,000	2,593	17,172	3,048	14,124
6,000	7,000	1,602	12,757	2,459	10,298
7,000	8,000	791	7,513	1,636	5,877
8,000	10,000	595	7,044	1,739	5,305
10,000	12,000	199	3,110	943	2,167
12,000	15,000	94	1,891	679	1,212
15,000	20,000	47	1,342	568	774
20,000	30,000	11	515	253	262
30,000 and over		2	142	85	57
Total		29,076	119,610	20,185	99,425
Income not included in the classification by ranges		..	13,667	..	..
Total income of households		..	133,277	..	..

Source: *National Income and Expenditure* (1982).

expected inflation are removed, the real debt-servicing cost (row 28 in Table 9.1) would have been about £3,500 million in 1981, rather than £13,088 million. Since the government's financial deficits fail to take this into account, and have recently fluctuated around £10,000 million, it may be argued that the real government deficit has been negligible in the early 1980s. Indeed, Professor Miller of Warwick University estimates that the government was running a budget surplus in 1981 and 1982.

The National Debt has grown simply because of budget deficits. These are likely in wartime, as military expenditure soars. Inflation may produce deficits too—'fiscal boost' as it is known—because tax payments on average lag behind government spending. There is also, as was seen in Chapter 5, an argument for being prepared to deliberately 'unbalance' the budget when the pressure of aggregate demand is too low or too high and if the alternative weapon, monetary policy, works too slowly. This argument is originally due to Keynes but is also supported by Milton Friedman. The idea is that 'fiscal stabilizers'

TABLE 9.4. *Estimated Distribution of the Sterling National Debt, 31 March 1983*
(£ millions Nominal values(a) *Market values in italics (b)*)

	Total debt	Percentage of market holdings	Treasury Bills	Stocks					
				Total		Up to 5 years to maturity	Over 5 years and up to 15 years	Over 15 years and undated	marketable debt
Market holdings									
Other public sector									
Public corporations	791		8	59	*59*	29	30	—	724
Local authorities	74		—	71	*69*	18	18	35	3
Total	865	0·8	8	130	*128*	47	48	35	727
Monetary sector (c)									
Discount market	341		60	280		240	20	20	1
Other	6,268		318	5,875		4,462	1,343	70	75
Total	6,609	5·9	378	6,155	*6,291*	4,702	1,363	90	76
Other financial institutions									
Insurance companies	27,401		..	27,401	*27,494*	2,699	11,228	13,474	—
Building societies	9,206		11	9,023	*8,883*	6,618	2,383	22	172
Local authority pension funds	2,946		..	2,946	*2,950*	23	891	2,032	—
Other public sector pension funds	5,256		..	5,256	*5,233*	99	1,240	3,917	—
Private sector pension funds	10,181		..	10,180	*10,161*	347	2,902	6,931	1
Investment trusts	205		..	205	*205*	56	93	56	—
Unit trusts	344		..	344	*347*	33	148	163	—
Other	40		..	40	*42*	—	34	6	—
Total	55,579	49·9	11	55,395	*55,315*	9,875	18,919	26,601	173

Central monetary institutions	2,191		404	471	*463*	366	105	—	1,714
Other	2,927		72	2,469	*2,452*	1,443	917	109	—
	4,773		60	4,700	*4,798*	466	3,368	866	1
Total	9,891	8·9	536	7,640	*7,713*	2,275	4,390	975	1,715
Other holders									
Public Trustee and various non-corporate bodies	520		99	420	*413*	60	237	123	1
Individuals and private trusts (d)	28,642		··	12,593	*12,681*	3,263	6,460	2,870	16,049
Industrial and commercial companies	··		268(e)						
Other (residual)	3,353		—	1,110	*5,124*	3,893	1,378	71	1,975
	5,991			4,232					1,759
Total	38,506	34·5	367	18,355	*18,218*	7,216	8,075	3,064	19,784
Total market holdings	111,450	100·0	1,300	87,675	*87,665*	24,115	32,795	30,765	22,475
Official holdings	14,100		684	8,739	*8,653*	3,520	3,695	1,524	4,677
Total sterling debt	**125,550**		**1,984**	**96,414**	*96,318*	**27,635**	**34,490**	**32,289(f)**	**27,152**
of which Nationalized industries' stocks guaranteed by the Government	224		224		*140*		224		—

·· not available, assumed negligible.
— nil or less than £1 million.

(a) With some exceptions.
(b) Some of these estimates are based on reported market values at end-December 1982 and cash transactions in the first quarter of 1983; certain others rely on broad nominal/market value ratios.
(c) Excludes the Bank of England, Banking Department (which is included among official holders). Holdings of stocks are at book value or cost.
(d) Direct holdings only.
(e) The residual after holders of Treasury Bills have been identified; the total may thus include unidentified holdings, and differences in valuation, in other sectors.
(f) Of which, undated £3·259 million.

Source: *Bank of England Quarterly Bulletin* (Dec. 1983).

should be 'built in'; when demand is high, tax receipts should exceed government spending; when low, fall short. We must, however, distinguish the effects of a change in the budget deficit from the budget deficit level itself. Keynes's theory is that a rise in the deficit or fall in the surplus will be expansionary (if this is the result of an increase in government spending or of a fall in tax rates), raising output if there are spare resources, and raising prices in any case, but especially if there are none. This is because government spending must rise, or consumption spending must rise somewhat if tax rates fall; and the multiplier chimes in, steadily if slowly, to amplify the effect. For monetarists, two things are important: the level of the deficit, and whether the gap is covered in part or in whole by raising the money supply. Demand and prices will go up if the existence of a deficit leads the government to raise the money supply. If the deficit is financed by sales of bonds to the domestic non-bank public, on the other hand, the money supply need not change. If the community as a whole treats the newly issued bonds as part of its net wealth, interest rates may rise as a result of a rise in the *demand for money* (which occurs indirectly due to increased private sector spending, and directly due to the increase in wealth). But if, as Barro [13] argues, the community regards bonds as equivalent to deferred taxation, net wealth, and also interest rates, should remain unaffected (see also [15], [19], and [20]). We shall return briefly to this macroeconomic aspect of public finance after analysing the British system of taxation.

9.7. Sources of Government Revenue

The sources of government revenue can be broken down in several ways. Some is precepted by local authorities, through rates; most accrues to central government; some comes from the gross trading surpluses of public corporations. A second distinction is between current receipts and capital receipts; a third between direct taxation (levied on income and capital) and indirect taxation (from taxes on expenditure).

9.7.1. Taxes on Income and Capital

For many years the biggest single revenue-raiser has been income tax. It was expected to yield some £30,800 million in the financial year 1982–3. All income—wages, salaries, commissions, bonuses, dividends, interest, and rent—is subject to tax. There is a personal allowance for a single person, which untaxed: this is £2,005 per year in 1984–5. Married couples receive a combined allowance of £3,155, although since 1971 they have been able to opt, up to a certain limit, for separate tax assessment. There are further allowances for dependent relatives, for the blind, for a housekeeper, for certain necessary working and other expenses, for covenants, and—a very substantial item—for all interest on loans or mortgages (up to £30,000) secured on the family house. When these allowances have been subtracted, all income above this is taxed at a standard rate of 30 per cent. (These are the rates in force for the year 1984–5.) Any excess of income (after allowances) above £15,400 is taxed more heavily: the rate goes up in 5 per cent steps, from 40 per cent on income between

£15,400 and £18,200 until a level of 55 per cent is reached on any income (less allowances) between £30,600 and £38,100 per annum. Above that, there is a top rate of 60 per cent. Investment income derived from the ownership of assets (receipts of dividends, interest, and rent) was subject to an additional levy of 15 per cent on any excess over £7,100 (more than those over 65), but this additional levy was abolished in 1984. Rather higher rates of tax are levied on high incomes in New Zealand and some Scandinavian countries; British tax rates in this range are similar to those prevailing in North America or the rest of Western Europe.

At present levels, income tax receipts amount to some 11 per cent of GNP. This compares with 7 per cent in 1929 and 10½ per cent in 1960. From 1960 until 1979, the burden of income tax increased most on sections of income between £3,200 and £7,700 per annum, and above £21,000 (in 1984 values). This was explained chiefly by the fact that the thresholds at which the tax rates started to operate often failed to keep pace with inflation, and consequently came down sharply in real terms. In 1979, the standard rate was cut by one-eleventh, and high rates by much more. To make good the lost revenue, the standard rate of Value-Added Tax was almost doubled. These changes made the distribution of after-tax real incomes considerably less equal.

Nearly all sources of government revenue have the drawback that they distort choices. Income tax is no exception. It distorts the individual's choices between leisure and commodities. It is (in general) a necessary condition for economic efficiency that the rate at which an individual is prepared to exchange his leisure for commodities at the margin should equal the marginal rate at which firms can transform his leisure into commodities. If these marginal rates were unequal, the individual and the owners of a firm could both become better off—to no one else's detriment—by bargaining some other exchange of labour for goods. Suppose, for example, a man will only give up one hour of leisure for £2, but that a firm can produce a commodity valued at £3 by employing him for that hour. It would be to everyone's benefit if the firm employed him for any sum between £2 and £3. The firm would make a profit and the man would gain more than the £2 necessary to compensate him for the loss of his leisure. A 50 per cent income tax would prevent this occurring because £1·50 is not sufficient to induce the man to work. A good illustration of the distortion this brings is the way it persuades individuals to forsake comparative advantage, to some extent, by 'doing it yourself'. Furthermore, as the marginal rate of income tax is increased, the leisure of the individual concerned comes to acquire more and more the character of a public bad (the opposite of a public good). This is so because all other citizens have to forgo the advantages they would derive from his work, through his tax payments. Against this, increases in tax rates can often lead people to work longer hours, especially if they treat the leisure they retain as complementary with the commodities they buy. The damaging disincentive effects of income tax might be avoided if it were possible to tax ability to earn rather than actual earnings. For example, an IQ tax might be a way of achieving this. Obvious drawbacks to this would include its inequity (to the extent that IQ fails to measure earning capacity), the opportunities for fraud, and the distorting disincentive effects on investment in 'human capital'. It might also be possible to lessen the disadvantages of marginal taxation on income by heavy taxes on goods complementary with leisure (golf balls and alcohol, for instance).

In fact the case for taxes on income is based on two points: they are often a relatively costless way of obtaining some of the vast financial resources the state needs to support its transfers and expenditure; and they are a very convenient way of achieving whatever redistribution it is aiming for. Yet it might be noted that some research on the latter has come up with recommendations for far lower marginal rates of tax—especially on top incomes—than present British levels [28]. A further point on marginal tax rates: the effect of the recent trend to selective welfare benefits (e.g. income-related rent and rate rebates, social security payments, and Family Income Supplement) has been to increase substantially the effective marginal rate of tax on those who take them up. In some cases this can reach 100 per cent. So the effective marginal rate is often at its maximum on both very low and very high incomes. Finally, the payment of transfers is likely to weaken the incentive to work: see [16] and [24].

The other major direct tax is Corporation Tax: tax on the profits of companies. In recent years it has come to yield about £5,000 million per annum. The figure fluctuates: profits themselves are a volatile element in the national income, rising in booms and falling in slumps; companies could, until 1984, set against Corporation Tax the depreciation of their investment virtually when they liked; and the timing and rates of charge do change. Since 1973 Corporation Tax has been based on an 'imputations' system. Profits, net of permissible depreciation and other allowances (e.g. interest on borrowing), are taxed (from 1974 to 1984) at 52 per cent but are scheduled to fall to 35 per cent by 1985–7, with lower rates for small companies. The company can then split the residue as it chooses between dividends for its shareholders and retained earnings. Dividends are then deemed to have paid income tax at the standard rate; the shareholder pays more tax only if his income from all sources exceeds about £18,000. If his income is very low he gets a refund. From November 1974 until April 1984 companies were able to subtract much of the cost of stock appreciation from their trading profits before Corporation Tax was levied. The excess of the annual increase in the book value of stocks over 15 per cent of gross trading profits was the deduction allowed after 1976. This provision was technically an indefinite deferral of tax, not an outright and unqualified exemption. Its removal in 1984 reflects success in reducing inflation to 5 per cent or so. But in years of rapid inflation, stock relief (when combined with tax deductibility of depreciation and interest charges) made the yield of Corporation Tax on retained earnings very modest. Kay and King [1] estimated that Corporation Tax payments made by Britain's leading industrial companies averaged less than $3\frac{1}{2}$ per cent of profits in 1977. This figure has certainly risen.

The large falls in Corporation Tax rates announced in 1984 for 1984–7 have been accompanied by the progressive elimination of first-year investment allowances. This is expected to offset the loss of revenue from lower rates of tax. The aim behind these changes is to simplify the system of taxes on companies.

The system previously in operation (from 1965 to 1973) had favoured profit retention in the company (see Chapter 3); this was achieved by double taxation net of Corporation Tax (then at lower rates, which oscillated between 40 and 45 per cent). There is controversy about the wisdom of the 1973 changes [26, 38].

On levels of tax, comparisons are hard, since systems differ; but British rates of Corporation Tax—at least until the 1974 reform which deferred tax due on profits attributable to stock appreciation—were on average somewhat above equivalent rates abroad. On the question of incidence—who finally pay Corporation Tax—there is little firm evidence to suggest that it is passed on fully or quickly to the customer in the form of higher prices, and some evidence to suggest that it is not. In certain circumstances, it may be passed backwards on to employees in the form of lower wages than otherwise. But probably the major burden is borne by the owners of companies.

The direct taxes on capital were estimated to yield £1,885 million in 1982–3: £600 million from Capital Gains Tax (introduced in 1961, extended in 1965, and much modified since); £10 million from estate duties (introduced in their modern form in 1894 and greatly extended later); £810 million from Stamp Duty (an ancient tax on the transfer of assets, currently levied at a rate of 1 per cent); and £465 million from Capital Transfer Tax, which has now started to replace estate duties.

A Petroleum Revenue Tax has been established to tax revenue from the sale of North Sea oil. Its current rate is set at 70 per cent (in 1983). Together with Supplementary Petroleum Duty, which it is intended to phase out, Petroleum Revenue Tax was expected to yield some £4,300 million in 1982–3. The unanticipated drop in oil prices will have reduced this figure somewhat.

9.7.2. Taxes on Expenditure

Central government's taxes on expenditure were estimated to yield £34,500 million in 1982–83. Of this, nearly £15,000 million can from Value-Added Tax (VAT). Brought in in 1973 to replace other types of indirect tax (purchase tax on 'luxuries' and SET on the employment of labour in service industries), VAT is charged at various rates on businesses' value-added—the excess of gross sales over their payments to other businesses. This amounts to paying the VAT rate on sales value and recovering the tax paid by suppliers on their sales value. Some activities are zero-rated, paying no tax on their sales, but recovering the tax paid on purchases from other firms; food and housing are important examples. Others are exempt: the tax paid on purchases is not recovered, but tax is not charged on their sales. About one-third of the value of total output of goods and services is liable to VAT at a rate (since July 1979) of 15 per cent.

France and Germany introduced VAT in January 1968; the telling case for bringing it in here was perhaps the need to conform with Common Market practice. Collection costs—borne in large part by the businesses themselves—appear to be higher for VAT than for the taxes it replaced. One important feature is that it is rebated on exports and applied to imports. The effects of the switchover to VAT on the distribution of income are thought to have been negligible—the rates of tax on the chief items of expenditure in low-income budgets remained the same (often zero)—and there was little overall impact on the cost of living. One can assume that VAT, like all expenditure taxes, is generally passed on fully to the customer. Two further arguments were made for VAT: the previous tax base for expenditure was held to be too narrow (and hence inefficient for demand management policy) and too uneven (in an ideal world, the relative prices of two goods facing consumers should deviate as little as possible from their relative marginal costs of production). Both these defects could, however, have been remedied by evening up the old taxes.

Central government's other expected receipts from taxes on expenditure come chiefly (in 1982–3) from motoring (£5,100 million from petrol and oil, £1,854 million from Motor Vehicle Duty—Road Fund—and £600 million from a special tax on top of VAT on the sale of new cars); from smoking (£3,525 million) and alcoholic drink (£3,275 million); and from gambling (£350 million). Virtually all countries have substantial taxes on these activities. The goods concerned are usually treated as 'demerit' goods, or at least, relatively inessential; and they all have low price-elasticity of demand—implying that they are lucrative sources of tax revenue to the Exchequer and that heavy taxation on them may have less serious consequences for consumers' welfare than it would on more price-elastic goods (see [18]). As most of these duties are specific (a tax on a unit of quantity) they tend to drop in real terms during inflation: the fact that they were held roughly constant in money terms between December 1968 and March 1974, for instance, meant that they fell by over 35 per cent in real terms in that period. Since inflation may raise the state's spending faster than its tax receipts, this can produce the 'fiscal boost' mentioned earlier. There is therefore a strong case for keeping indirect taxation in line with the general price index. One property that these taxes have is widely felt to be opprobrious. They tend to be regressive: consumption of petrol, drink, and tobacco usually accounts for a higher share of low-income budgets than high-income ones. Expenditure on, for example, tobacco, appears to be virtually independent of income levels.

9.7.3. Other Sources of Central and Local Government Revenue

Other central government receipts include the proceeds of tariffs on imports ('Protective Duties' brough in over £1,300 million in 1982–3). As was seen in Chapter 6, duties on imports must in one sense be inefficient, at least at the world level, for they contravene the rule that the price ratios for goods that one buyer faces should be as close as possible to the price ratios facing others. But import duties have usually proved cheap to collect; and it has to be remembered that virtually all other taxes create some distortion. Besides tariffs, £754 million was estimated to have come from television licences, £512 million from a special gas levy, £321 million from interest and dividends received by the government on assets it owns, £5,000 million from various other sources, and about £35,000 million from contributions from employers and employees to National Insurance, including over £3,400 million from a National Insurance Surcharge. (This last was abolished in 1984.)

The National Insurance Fund is designed to be self-balancing. Contributions are levied upon employer and employee in roughly equal measure to defray the costs of providing pensions, and sickness, disability, unemployment, and other benefits. The levy upon employees emounts to 9 per cent of earnings in 1983–4 for the great majority of workers.

Turning our attention to the local authorities, we find that on average just over half of their income takes the form of grants from central government. Much of the rest is raised locally through rates on residential, commercial, and industrial property. In 1982–3 rates generated some £10,500 million net of the rate rebates. The other major local source of revenue is rents on municipally owned property, which, together with interest and dividends, brought in some £6,000 million that year. Rates are levied on the imputed rentable value of property; for a number of reasons, they are unpopular. Inflation and recent increases in the real volume of local authority spending have increased them sharply in money terms; they are more conspicuous than taxes on income or expenditure; it is often felt unfair that they are not related to income or to any measure of ability to pay. Yet there is something to commend rates. The structure of national taxation creates a large bias in the relative desirability of saving through house buying and saving through other means (for instance, by buying shares). Dividends from shares, and interest from loans, are liable to Corporation and/or income tax. But the imputed rent on an owner-occupant's dwelling is untaxed in Britain (although it is liable to tax in the Netherlands, for example). Interest on mortgages or loans to buy houses can be set against the borrower's income for tax purposes, at least for the first house, where as interest on borrowing to buy shares is not tax-deductible. There is usually no tax on any capital gains made on the sale of a house, but capital gains on shares are taxed. Rates go some way to redress these biases. Furthermore, if rates were replaced by additions to income or expenditure taxes, there could be a serious added disincentive to work, since the effective marginal rate of tax would have to go up sharply.

9.7.4. Microeconomic Criteria for Taxes

There are two microeconomic criteria on which to assess a tax: economic efficiency, and equity. Taxes inevitably affect the allocation of resources, usually, but not necessarily, for the worse. They influence consumers' choices between goods, and between goods and leisure; they alter wealth holders' allocation of assets in their portfolios; and they bear on production and factor-hiring decisions by firms. There are also the costs of collection, never wholly borne by the state, which represent a deadweight loss. Taxes can improve economic efficiency if they are applied on the output of industries experiencing increasing costs of production (where marginal cost exceeds average cost) or on firms imposing external costs on other firms or citizens (pollution, for example). The damage they bring will be low if they are levied on the consumption of goods for which demand is inelastic, or on factors of production of which the supply is inelastic. The second criterion—equity—is hard to apply for many reasons. Individuals' views about the 'ideal' distribution of incomes are difficult to assess. The correct balance between efficiency and equity—in so far as they conflict—can only be a matter of subjective judgement.

9.8. Note on the Macroeconomic Effects of Budgetary Changes

Besides those already mentioned, there is a further use to which changes in government spending and taxation can be put. Both can be altered, for *macroeconomic* purposes, to affect the future path of national income. Spending may be cut, or taxes increased, when aggregate demand is felt to be rising too fast, for example. Taxes may be cut to stimulate labour supply, risk-bearing, and investment. Public sector capital spending may be increased to expand, as well as redirect, the economy's productive capacity in future years. In addition the budget deficit (the amount by which the government's spending exceeds it revenue) may have powerful and pervasive macroeconomic effects, as was seen in section 9.6. Yet the exact size of the deficit is hard to define [15]. The broadest definition of the public sector embraces central government, local government, and the nationalized industries; for some purposes, this is the appropriate definition, but for others, one may wish to confine attention, perhaps, to central government alone. Another difficulty is the distinction between the current and capital accounts of public authorities. Borrowing to finance capital investment is quite different from borrowing to finance current spending.

The sale of assets is at present treated as negative expenditure by the public sector. But if the deficit and borrowing requirements are kept down for a while by the sale of public sector assets (such as shares in nationalized industries, or council houses), this is only borrowing under another name. Lastly, there are the statistical distortions, already noted, to which inflation gives rise. These problems are looked at in some detail in Chapters 12 and 13 on demand management.

Bibliography

SECTION A

An outstanding textbook has been written on taxation in the UK:
[1] KAY, J. A. and KING, M. A. *The British Tax System*, 3rd edn. (Oxford University Press, 1983).

The theory of taxation and public expenditure is discussed in:
[2] ATKINSON, A. B. and STIGLITZ, J. E. *Lectures on Public Economics* (McGraw-Hill, 1980).
[3] BLINDER, A. S. and SOLOW, R. M. *et al. The Economics of Public Finance* (Brookings Institution, 1974).
[4] BROWN, C. V. and JACKSON, P. M. *Public Sector Economics*, 2nd edn. (Martin Robertson, 1982).
[2] is excellent, but advanced and technical. [3] and [4] are more accessible to the non-specialist.

Empirical evidence on taxation is surveyed critically and very readably in the contributions to:
[5] AARON, H. J. and PECHMAN, J. (eds.) *How Taxes Affect Economic Behavior* (Brookings Institution, 1981).

The United Kingdom's systems of taxes, transfers, and subsidies have been the subject of a recent report:

[6] MEADE, J. E. *et al.* *The Structure and Reform of Direct Taxation* (Institute for Fiscal Studies, 1978).

On income distribution and redistribution, the following are strongly recommended:
[7] ATKINSON, A. B. *The Economics of Inequality* (Oxford University Press, 2nd edn., 1983).
[8] SEN, A. K. *On Economic Inequality* (Oxford University Press, 1973).

On the history and possible macroeconomic effects of the growth of public expenditure, see:
[9] BACON, R. W. and ELTIS, W. A. *Britain's Economic Problem: Too Few Producers*, 2nd edn. (Macmillan, 1978).
[10] PEACOCK, A. T. and WISEMAN, J. *The Growth of Public Expenditure in the UK*, 2nd edn. (Unwin, 1967).

SECTION B

Other works of general interest on aspects of public finance include:

[11] AARON, H. J. (ed.). *The Value Added Tax: Lessons from Europe* (Brookings Institution, 1981).
[12] ATKINSON, A. B. (ed.). *Wealth, Income and Inequality* (Penguin, 1973).
[13] BARRO, R. J. 'Are Government Bonds Net Wealth?', *Journal of Political Economy* (1974).
[14] BARRY, B. M. *The Liberal Theory of Justice* (Oxford University Press, 1973).
[15] BUITER, W. H. 'Measurement of the Public Sector Deficit and its Implications for Policy Evaluation and Design', *IMF Staff Papers* (1983).
[16] DANZIGER, S., HAVEMAN, R. and PLOTNICK, A. 'How Income Transfers Affect Work, Savings and the Income Distribution', *Journal of Economic Literature* (1981).
[17] DIAMOND, P. A. and MIRRLEES, J. A. 'Optimum Taxation and Public Production', *American Economic Review* (Mar./June 1971).
[18] DIXIT, A. K. 'On the Optimum Structure of Commodity Taxes', *American Economic Review* (1970).
[19] FELDSTEIN, M. S. 'Government Deficits and Aggregate Demand', *Journal of Monetary Economics* (1982).
[20] FRIEDMAN, B. 'Crowding Out or Crowding In: The Economic Consequences of Government Deficits', *Brookings Papers on Economic Activity* (1978).
[21] FUCHS, V. R. (ed.). *Economic Aspects of Health* (National Bureau of Economic Research, 1982).
[22] GORDON, R. 'The Shifting of Corporation Tax', *American Economic Review* (1967).
[23] GRILICHES, Z. 'Estimating the Returns to Schooling: Some Econometric Problems', *Econometrica* (1977).
[24] HANOCK, G. and HONIG, M. 'The Labour Supply Curve Under Income Maintenance Programs', *Journal of Public Economics* (1978).
[25] HICKS, Lady U. K. *Public Finance*, 3rd edn. (Oxford University Press, 1968).
[26] KAY, J. A. 'The Taxation of Corporate Income and Capital Gains', *Oxford Economic Papers* (1974).
[27] LITTLE, I. M. D. and FLEMMING, J. S. *Why we Need a Wealth Tax* (Methuen, 1974).
[28] MIRRLEES, J. E. 'An Exploration in the Theory of Optimum Income Taxation', *Review of Economic Studies* (1971).
[29] MOODY, T. and SMITH, K. G. D. 'An Evaluation of Subsidies to British Manufacturing Industry', *Oxford Economic Papers* (1975).

[30] NORDHAUS, W. D. 'The Political Business Cycle', *Review of Economic Studies* (1975).

[31] PHELPS, E. S. (ed.). *Economic Justice* (Penguin, 1973), especially Chaps. 16 (Atkinson), 18 (Phelps), and 19 (Arrow).

[32] PIGOU, A. C. *A Study in Public Finance*, 3rd edn. (Macmillan, 1947).

[33] *Quarterly Journal of Economics*, 'Symposium on Rawls' (Nov. 1974).

[34] RAWLS, J. *A Theory of Justice* (Oxford University Press, 1972).

[35] SAMUELSON, P. A. 'Diagrammatic Exposition of a Theory of Public Expenditure', *Review of Economics and Statistics* (1955).

[36] SEBOLD, F. D. 'The Short-run Shifting of Coporation Tax: A Simultaneous Equations Approach', *Review of Economics and Statistics* (1979).

[37] WEBB, M. G. *The Economics of Nationalized Industries* (Nelson, 1973).

[38] WHALLEY, J. 'A General Equilibrium Assessment on the 1973 UK Tax Reform', *Economica* (1975).

I I

Government and Pay

D. ROBINSON

.1. Pay Bargaining

examining the impact of government on pay levels it is necessary to be clear
out the many factors which determine wages. But, as has been discussed in
~apter 4, economic theory leaves us with areas of indeterminacy on the
estion of what determines wage levels and wage increases. Neither the
andard textbook models based on individual behaviour, nor the adaptations
nich include trade unions, manage to capture sufficient behavioural features
the real world to explain the processes and course of wage determination
tisfactorily. The micro models are insufficiently comprehensive and the
acro models, while sometimes displaying intellectual and mathematical
gance, do not provide very good forecasts of wage movements. Part of the
use of these deficiencies lies in the use of open-ended or indeterminate factors,
ch as 'net advantages' or 'the natural rate of unemployment' (see Chapters 4
d 7), to explain pay levels, or changes in them. As far as real life is concerned,
ages and salaries are determined, not only by economic forces but also by
cial and political forces, and in particular by people's views about fairness. Of
l economic questions and issues there is none in which the importance of
ople's beliefs about what is or is not fair is as great, as pervasive, or as
fluential as the question of wages and relative wages.

There are still a number of people whose terms and conditions of
1ployment—their rate of pay, hours of work, job content, fringe benefits, and
on—are determined by individual bargaining and agreement between
emselves and an employer. However, some of these apparently 'free-market'
age and salary levels are, in practice, very much influenced by views as to
hat is the trade union or 'going' rate. For the majority of blue-collar
1ployees terms and conditions of employment are determined by collective
argaining. There are about 3 million workers covered by Wages Councils (or
e Agricultural Wages Board) where basic or minimum terms and conditions
employment are fixed by Orders with statutory effect. These are intended to
otect workers in low-paying industries, but there are sizeable pockets of low-
id workers in uncovered industries [18]. It is important to have a clear
cture of the factors which are of most significance in determining pay within
is collective-bargaining framework before going on to examine the impact of
vernment on the process.

11.2. Factors in Pay Determination

11.2.1. The Level of Bargaining

Even where wages or salaries are determined by collective bargaining there ca be considerable differences between industries and groups in the methods bargaining and the ways in which pay is actually determined. In man industries there is bargaining at various levels, while in others, a sing industry-wide agreement may determine the actual rate of pay.

At one end of the spectrum an industry-wide agreement, probably made by Joint Industrial Council (JIC) or some other joint body composed representatives of trade unions and employers, will establish a negotiated ra of pay which is in effect standard throughout the firms covered by th agreement. In some other cases the industry agreement (which is often referre to as the national agreement) lays down only a minimum rate of pay whic individual firms can improve upon if they so wish. In many parts of the publ sector, particularly where white-collar workers are concerned, an effective ra of pay or incremental salary scale will be determined by collective bargainin; arbitration, or some other form of wage determination. While these publ sector agreements are also frequently referred to as national agreements, the differ in one important respect from the JIC or similar agreements in th private sector, namely that there is basically only one employer on th employer's side of the bargaining table and it is administratively easier t ensure that the standard rates of pay will be adhered to. There has howeve been a growth of supplementary payments to manual workers in public secto industries as various types of productivity bonuses have been introduced. The: are generally determined on a decentralized basis, thereby reducing th importance of the industry agreement as the sole determinant of pay.

In the private manufacturing sector there has been a significant transform ation. In the Sixties, multi-employer agreements dominated. By 1978 tw thirds of manual and three-quarters of non-manual employees were covered t a formal bargaining structure of single-employer agreements. These migh cover a single plant or a number of plants in the same company. Mult employer, national, or JIC agreements still exist. They are particularl important in industries, such as clothing and printing, which have many sma employers, and for small companies elsewhere, but the balance has shifted [3 There are a number of implications of this change. The reduced importance industry agreements led to the abolition in 1982 of the Department Employment's Index of Wage Rates and Minimum Entitlements, thereb effectively ending the discussion, or, at least, an informed discussion based o analysis, of wage drift—the difference between the movement of these wag rates on the one hand and of average earnings, which include a whole range additional payments, on the other. Private sector pay disputes are much mor likely to be confined to companies rather than affect a whole industry. Ther may be greater variation in pay settlements if companies respond more to th particular factors affecting them and less to industry-based pressures comparability. This may not mean the end of comparability as a criterion i pay bargaining, but rather a shift in the selection of comparators. As industry

de pay bargaining becomes less important, it becomes more difficult for any
vernment which is concerned to influence the outcome of collective
rgaining to collect and assimilate useful information and then design the
propriate policies. This may be made even more difficult by the fact that
any blue-collar workers receive some part of their pay from piecework or
her types of payments-by-results systems. There is an extremely wide range of
centives and bonuses in addition to a bewildering assortment of methods of
ating pay to output or performance.
Trade unions in a Western society are fundamentally and necessarily
rgaining organizations. It is their purpose to bargain in order to defend and
prove the conditions of their members and if, at certain levels or at certain
nes, they cannot bargain about pay, they will bargain about something else.
iis is particularly important when changes are made in the bargaining
stem. For example, if plant, industry, or company-level bargaining is
troduced to replace fragmented shop-floor bargaining, the shop stewards will
ve lost an important role and it is unlikely that they will be content to give up
rgaining altogether.
The level at which bargaining takes place can influence the type of
rgaining and the way in which it is carried out. Even in theory it is difficult to
oduce an explanation that leads to the same level of pay emerging from a
igle industry negotiation as would emerge from a series of fragmented or
int-level bargains. A single national bargain which settles the effective rate of
y will channel all the *pay* pressure into the one negotiation (although of
urse there may be bargaining at lower levels about such things as grading and
grading, which can be equivalent to a pay rise, manning ratios, the effort
rgain, and so on). This is one reason why pay negotiations in the public
tor may more frequently lead to national or industry-wide strikes or work-
-rule activities.
With a piecework payment system there may be almost constant bargaining.
anges in methods of working, or in materials or product design, etc., all
ovide opportunities for a revision of the piecework prices. It is never clear
m the outside, nor sometimes from the inside, whether pieceworkers'
rnings have increased because they are producing more output at constant
cework rates, or because the rates have been increased, or because of some
mbination of these, complicated by new work for which new rates have had
be set. The actual weekly gross pay may also vary considerably from week to
ek as a result of changes in the amount of overtime worked (or paid, whether
s actually worked or not) and the incidence of shift working, which usually
racts an additional premium.
The combined effect of these factors is that an employee's pay-packet may be
mposed of a number of different items which have been determined at
ferent levels of bargaining by different groups of people and representatives
response to different pressures or arguments, and which may, or may not, be
egrated through a coherent relation of pay to effort, to labour shortages, or
concepts of equity and fairness. There may be considerable scope for the
justment and manipulation of many pay-packets from week to week and a
ethora of allowances and bonuses which, with the opportunities for regrading

into a higher pay category, all provide different employers with some variety of opportunity to adjust pay. These factors should be borne in mind when considering incomes policies.

11.2.2. Pay Claims: Defensive

Pay determination by collective bargaining can be separated into two part. There is the pay claim and the pay settlement. Unfortunately, there does n appear to be any explanation, simple or complicated, that will satisfactori account for the level of claims that are forthcoming. On some occasion economic arguments may dominate a trade union's behaviour, on other mo political considerations, perhaps the perceived obligation on trade unic leaders not to fall behind other unions, or the tactics of a group within the unic which is seeking to obtain control (the nearest analogy might be the behaviou of directors in relation to dividends when a take-over threat is made ar resisted), or the fact that some officials are seeking re-election, or a ne leadership is seeking to establish its own mark on the union, or a membershi drive, and so on. Similar possibilities arise if it is a workgroup rather than union which is submitting the pay claim. On some occasions the processes b which a claim is formulated may influence its size. If a union conferen determines the specific size of the claim it may represent aspiration more than realistic assessment of what is obtainable (assuming this can be made), or may be an attempt to embarrass those who will actually have to negotiate. does appear that claims formulated by those who will subsequently have negotiate for them are generally lower than those formulated by people who c not have the responsibility for attaining them.

It is useful to separate claims into defensive claims, which seek to mainta some previously established position or relationship, and offensive claim which seek to improve on past positions or relationships. There are two aspec to a defensive claim:

(i) Normally a change in price levels provides a minimum floor to a wa claim on the grounds that living standards should be at least maintained. unions become more sophisticated in their bargaining, increases in direct tax may provide grounds for a defensive claim. Although the Retail Price Ind (RPI) is generally taken as an indication of price movements there may I some particular items that are more sensitive than others so that an increase i say, rents may have a greater effect on stimulating claims that an equivale increase in the overall RPI which was spread more evenly over other item

(ii) The maintenance or restoration of pay relationships which may ha changed as a result of a pay settlement by some other group generates stror defensive claims even if the cause of an increase in pay of the comparitor w supply and demand. Frequently, past relationships and history are regarded powerful arguments in support of fairness. While there may not always certainty as to which other groups a particular union will use for the comparisons, there are a number of broadly recognized orbits of compariso Here a distinction should be made between *internal* comparisons, or relativitie which are made with other groups in the same industry, company, or plant, b which have their pay determined in a separate bargaining unit, and extern relativities which are made with groups outside. Differentials are used to refer to pay relationships within the same bargaining unit.

11.2.3. Pay Claims: Offensive

Offensive wage claims arise from a group's attempts to *improve* its relative position or living standard. These can be based on such things as changes in productivity, altered job content, changed skill requirements, or profitability. Just as defensive claims are based on a perception of fairness, so too can fairness influence or determine an offensive claim. If job content is changed it is seen as fair that the workers affected should receive more pay, and this perception of fairness is independent of the prevailing state of supply and demand for that type of labour. The particular criterion adopted to justify an offensive claim may change with circumstances.

Because perceptions of fairness—which, to a greater or lesser degree, may be held jointly by the two sides of the bargaining table—extend beyond the coverage of the bargaining unit, it is frequently not possible for one set of negotiations to ensure that some desired relationship with the pay of another bargaining unit is actually achieved or maintained. The other group may negate or reverse the desired result.[1] A successful offensive claim by one group therefore often leads to defensive claims based on past pay relationships by others. This can make it extremely difficult to change pay relationships in an accepted or agreed way, since different interpretations of fairness are introduced by different groups. It is because pay claims are often based on pay movements elsewhere, which may themselves have been strongly influenced by economic factors, and because of the interaction between offensive and defensive claims, or between claims based on fairness and those caused by economic factors, that a system of 'free' collective bargaining often leads to repercussive actions which can add force to a wage–wage spiral. It is crucial to bear in mind that claims will be generated as a result of the views and perceptions of those who believe they are affected by changes elsewhere. It is less important whether 'outsiders' consider the pay relationships fair than that the 'insiders', those concerned, do so.

11.2.4. Real Wage Targets

The view that trade unions have certain real wage levels as their bargaining objectives has led to some new developments in the analysis of wage movements and inflation. Put simply, the view is that unions press for certain real wage levels so that they respond to changes in prices and also to changes in taxation and similar imposts which affect their real disposable income. The target may include improvements in real wages, perhaps reflecting productivity changes or some 'expected' trend rate of past improvement, and individual bargaining groups may incorporate comparisons with other groups as well. The difficulty with this approach is that it usually starts from the assumption that the real wage sought in any period is the actual real wage of the previous period plus

[1] See [37] and Pay Board, *Anomalies*, Advisory Report 1 (Cmnd. 5439, Sept. 1973) for a more detailed discussion.

adjustments for the desired or target increase in real net income and an
allowance for expected price changes. It may be objected that the previous
period's real wage was less than desired or was unacceptable as a long-term
position but tolerated for a time in the belief that it would be corrected at the
next settlement. The 'improvement' factor then becomes uncertain or a non-
constant. In any event there is no firm reason to suppose that the target
improvement in real net earnings is a constant. Further, despite the
assumptions which some economists make about 'rational' behaviour, there is
no convincing evidence that British trade unions normally pay great attention
in their wage bargaining to the rate of inflation *expected* to occur over the period
for which pay is being determined. Much more importance is given to
compensation for past price increases, and the recent movement in the Retail
Price Index is often taken as the starting point in the preparation of a wage
claim and in the subsequent bargaining. However, there is some statistical
evidence which is not inconsistent with the view that over the post-war period
the determinants of wage change have altered, with market forces becoming
weaker and bargaining power a more important influence [1]. It may be, of
course, that bargaining power is itself a function of market forces. We just do
not know what determines relative power in collective bargaining and, perhaps
equally important, militancy, or the propensity to use power (Robinson in
[15]).

11.2.5. Pay Settlements

If pay claims are determined by a range of complicated factors, which make
them difficult to analyse, pay *settlements* are either determined by a simple set of
factors or by even more complicated ones. A simple explanation would use
market forces, supply and demand, as the sole determinants of pay levels and
pay increases. The discussion of the Phillips curve in Chapter 7 suggests that at
the aggregate or macro level such an explanation is not satisfactory, and is little
better if earnings rather than wage rates are focused upon. At the micro
(industry and firm) level the evidence, although patchy and incomplete in
coverage, is even less convincing.[2] Various institutional factors, bargaining
practices, payment systems, militancy, union and workgroup attitudes, as well
as a range of factors on the employers' side, need to be brought in if some even
roughly realistic explanation is to be forthcoming.

  In practice there need be little systematic relationship between claim and
settlement. Many people believe that settlements are about half-way between
the claims and the employer's offer, but even in arbitration cases where this is
supposed to hold most firmly, there is little evidence to justify th
interpretation. Since the Second World War, employers have not generally
sought to obtain pay cuts. The lowest offer in arbitration might therefore be
seen as zero. If arbitrators merely split the difference, unions seeking to
maximize increases in rates of pay ought to ask for as large an amount as they
like, knowing they will get half of it. But unions do not in fact do this. On

----

[2] See K. G. J. C. Knowles and D. Robinson, 'Wage Movements in Coventry', *B.O.U.I.E.S.*, 3
(Feb. 1969).

ason is that their own views of what is fair and reasonable impose constraints.
lso, they have views as to the number of people, primarily their members, who
ould be employed to receive that rate of pay. This is influenced by their view
 the employer's ability to pay certain levels, and so in some way depends on
rofitability. In the public sector this might be influenced by views of
overnment policy on nationalized industries' deficits or pricing policy. This
robably leads to an area of acceptable settlements rather than a precise figure,
ut if a defensive claim is pursued based on a specific relationship, then the
nion and its members may be committed to a precise amount.

The more that a pay-packet is composed of a number of items, each of which
 decided by different people in response to different factors or for different
urposes, the more difficult it may be to say that anyone actually determined
e level of pay, although, of course, the various decision-taking levels may
ave paid some regard to what happened elsewhere. In other cases, while there
ay have been the performance or ritual of bargaining, the increase in pay has
een employer-led in response to his views of the need to recruit or retain labour
 a tight market.

It does not follow, of course, that a union's views of fairness necessarily lead to
e appropriate settlement, nor that those making defensive claims will receive
xactly what the comparison group received. Much depends on how similar the
ttlements are expected to be, and while there is some consistency in some pay
lationships, this is not necessarily the same as rigidity, and there is often more
ariation than either an extreme 'labour market' or 'coercive comparison' view
ould suggest. The observed results will vary according to the particular
easurement of pay that is used.

There is, as a result, little agreement about the factors that actually do cause
ay movements. Nor is there agreement about what should cause pay
ovements. Both collective bargaining and arbitration in this country are
arked by absence of agreement about the criteria that should determined
ay.[3] While this leads to an agnostic view of pay determination it is clear that
any groups and unions believe that fairness and comparability in some sense
ould influence pay. Conflicts between normative views and actuality lead to
ressures to change the existing situation, and because normative views
emselves change one ought not to expect any permanent solution.

.2.6. Changes in Earnings 1961–1982

igures 11.1 and 11.2 illustrate the annual percentage changes in average
eekly and hourly earnings from 1961. Because of alterations in the source of
e statistics provided by the Department of Employment it is not possible to
ow a continuous series over the full period. Figure 11.1 refers to full-time

[3] The main exception was the adoption of Pay Research in the Civil Service as a method of
etermining princples and the Pay Research Unit which discovers the facts. For an account of this
stem see Pay Board Advisory Report 1, op. cit., and *Civil Service Science Group*, Advisory Report 3
mnd. 5602, Apr. 1974). The Police, following the Edmund-Davies Report which led to new pay
vels, receive percentage increases equal to the percentage rise in average earnings. The Fire
rvice has an agreement by which a qualified fireman receives the upper quartile of male manual
rnings as shown in the *New Earnings Survey*.

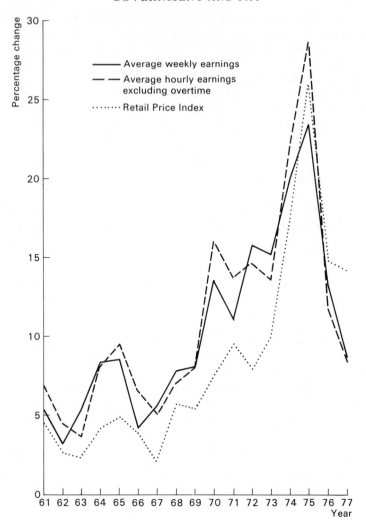

F IG. 11.1. Annual Percentage Change in Average Weekly and Hourly Earnings of Fu
time Manual Workers, and Retail Price Index, 1961–1977 (October to October).

manual workers. Hourly earnings are estimated by subtracting the standar
hours from the number of hours actually worked and assuming that the
overtime hours were paid at time-and-a-half. This method may lead to som
errors but was the only way of obtaining estimates of hourly earnings before tl
New Earnings Survey was introduced. Figure 11.2 shows the annual rate
change of weekly and hourly earnings for all employees, manual and no
manual. Overtime premia are excluded from the calculations of average hour
earnings. Two marked features are the very large increase in pay after tl

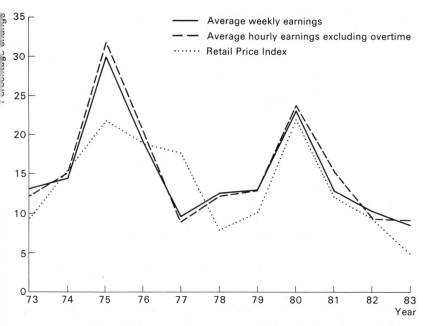

FIG. 11.2. Annual Percentage Change in Average Weekly and Hourly Earnings, All Services and Industries, and Retail Price Index, 1973–1983 (April to April).

ending of the statutory incomes policy in 1974, and the reduction in real pay during the Social Contract, particularly in 1977 (see Table 11.1 later in the chapter).

There have been many attempts to explain the movements in pay by the construction of econometric models (see Chapter 14) but none has provided both satisfactory explanations of past movements and reliable forecasts of future ones. It is of particular note that the general level of earnings increases is not significantly lower in the early 1980s, with over 3 million unemployed, than it was in the early 1970s, with around 1 million unemployed. To the extent therefore that the level of unemployment, as an indicator of excess supply in the labour market', was used in part to explain the path of earnings, this has been demoted in importance. Those approaches which see a strong role for demand in determining earnings increases have therefore tended to switch more to output itself, which can rise and permit increased earnings even if unemployment is not affected, or to *changes* in unemployment as having an impact while they last, but with no further impact (apart from time-lags) once unemployment stabilizes at any given level. Either approach suggests that any sizeable and sustained growth of output could lead to an appreciable acceleration of earnings inflation despite the existence of widespread and generalized unemployment.

This has two important implications. First, the elements of bargaining and

pay determination which we have been considering are crucial components i‹
understanding the issue of pay levels and inflation. No ordinary market woul‹
have an inherent tendency to rising prices largely irrespective of the levels o‹
excess supply. Second, attempts to reconcile low unemployment and lo‹
inflation will have to encompass significant structural change of some kind—i‹
bargaining, work patterns, etc.—or the introduction of policy measures tha‹
can in some way control earnings inflation despite fast growth, risin‹
employment, and falling unemployment.

11.3. The Government's Role in Pay Settlements

11.3.1. The Basis of Government Involvement

In theory it might be possible for a government to take the view that wha‹
happens to pay is the result of either market forces or institutional an‹
bargaining processes and that it is no part of its duty or obligation to becom‹
involved. In practice this choice is not open to it for two main reasons. First, it ‹
itself directly a large employer, and is widely regarded as responsible, directl‹
or indirectly, for the pay of public sector employees who make up some 30 pe‹
cent of the total work-force. Second, government is expected to accep‹
responsibility for the general management of the economy, inflation, incom‹
distribution, full employment, and so on. Government cannot therefore choos‹
to opt out of concern for pay developments. However, it can choose how it wil‹
accept its responsibilities, and the types of policies it will introduce to seek t‹
attain some form of combination of different objectives.

Government's choice has been from three main types of policies, although, c‹
course, it has not confined itself to only one of them at any given time. There ha‹
been a tendency to switch the main emphasis from one to another, sometimes‹
perhaps, with insufficient regard for the necessity to ensure that all polic‹
approaches are, so far as is possible, co-ordinated and consistent. Often we ar‹
impressed by the difficulties and failures of the type of approach most recentl‹
adopted with perhaps an underestimation of the difficulties that will be face‹
by an alternative policy.

11.3.2. General Economic Policies

These may be demand management policies or just monetary policy. It i‹
hoped that pay levels will change as a result of changes in the general level o‹
economic activity. The intention is that pay (and price) decisions will b‹
influenced by the changed economic environment as decision takers respond t‹
the prevailing economic forces. In addition to these 'pure' economic forces‹
expectations may be changed as a result of easing or tightening economi‹
pressures, and these expectations may feed through on the workers' and trad‹
union side to influence their wage demands, and on the employers' side b‹
affecting their demand for labour and thus their willingness to increase pay i‹
order to recruit or retain a satisfactory labour force. If there was a singl‹
determinant, or single set of determinants, of expectations that was related in ‹
constant way to the economic circumstances or to some economic variables‹

then we could by-pass expectations and relate pay developments directly to the variables. It is because there is not, or we have not been able to discover it, that we introduce the concept of expectations. This does not mean, however, that we know how these expectations are determined, or how they will react to changing economic circumstances.

Some place rather less weight on economic forces and wish to introduce other factors of an institutional, political, and social nature. The view, therefore, of whether demand management works, or can work, in an effective way on pay development, depends on two judgements. First, that the pressure of economic forces is the sole important criterion. Even if economic forces were interpreted very narrowly as solely the pressure of demand, the evidence would seem to be against this position. Moreover, even if economic forces are the sole or major determinant, it is still unclear as to what exactly will happen; for example, there could be fewer jobs at higher wages or more jobs at lower wages. Second, it has to be decided, if the pure economic view is rejected, whether the other factors are constant over time or whether they can and do vary. What we can say with some certainty is that the old economic relationships between demand and wage inflation do not seem to hold in the same form and that this is probably due to changes in attitudes on the part of workers and trade unions.

It is as though unions have questioned the belief that they are necessarily weaker, or all of them are weaker, when unemployment rises. The UK has experienced rising unemployment at times when prices are rising quickly and defensive pay claims are being pushed. Also, a contracting or depressed economy affects firms too. While some may become more determined to concede only small wage increases and many will shed labour, perhaps heavily, it may be that some of them conclude that they cannot afford to have a strike, and so they opt to pay what they do not appear to be able to afford in the long run because they cannot afford not to do so in the short run. There is also the question of the effect of demand management policies on the public sector. On occasions governments have tried to use the public sector to set the pace for pay settlements for the rest of the economy. On other occasions the need of the private sector to give relatively large pay rises has generated comparability pay claims.

Demand management policies as they were exercised in the 1960s and much of the 1970s increasingly did not seem able satisfactorily to contain the inflationary pressures within the UK economy, whether the initiating pressures were domestic or international in origin. As we have suggested, this is in part because the reactions and responses of people who are able to influence the rate of inflation and pay developments are uncertain and changing. It is also due to the fact that governments have tended to believe that there are certain limits beyond which they should not use demand management policies. The containment of inflation is only one of government's objectives. Amongst other things it has also sought to maintain a high level of employment, encourage economic growth, affect the distribution of income, pursue a regional policy, and maintain free collective bargaining. Whether demand management 'works' partly depends on the effect on unemployment, income distribution, etc. of successful control of inflation. If governments believe that much higher levels of unemployment are policitically tolerable the constraints on the extent to which the economy can be squeezed are eased and contractionary policies may then have greater effect in moderating pay increases.

If workers hold the view that increased prices, whatever the cause (e.g. higher unit costs, higher import prices, or higher indirect taxation), provide sufficient grounds for increases in money wages, then demand management measures which lead to increased prices might well themselves generate additional pay demand. Contractionary measures require that there be reductions in living standards somewhere in the economy and the crucial question is whether people will accept this. While workers and unions react more quickly and directly to measures which increase the cost of living they are increasingly adopting a more sophisticated approach, so that the effect of direct taxation, National Insurance contributions, and social security provisions are taken into account in the formulation of their pay claims. This is incorporated in the real wage target approach. While it would be too extreme to say that these responses will negate any disinflationary consequences of contraction there is sufficient validity in them to give concern about the ability of demand management measures alone to moderate inflation indefinitely. Certainly their contribution to the control of inflation, particularly if operated in association with other policies, may frequently be very unclear depending specifically on how they influence unit costs and prices.

In some ways as a response to this broad view the Labour Government in the late 1970s introduced cuts in direct taxation as part of a package designed to influence wage bargaining. This is an interesting inversion of an argument which sought to establish that increases in direct taxation led to pressure for higher increases. If the latter is correct, it would appear reasonable to conclude that reductions in direct taxes will lead to smaller wage increases. But this may not be so. If settlements would have been x per cent but direct increases lead to them being $(x+y)$ per cent, it may be that reducing direct taxes will still lead to pressure for x per cent even though the government's intention is that the settlement should be for $(x-z)$ per cent, where z is the effect of the reduction of direct taxation. It really depends on what determines the pressure for, and success in obtaining, the x per cent increase.

Here the structure of bargaining and the distribution of power or decision-taking processes within the trade unions may well be crucial. National trade union leaders, briefed by research departments, are well able to appreciate that an increase in direct taxation leaves their members, or many of them, worse off, and so they demand the extra y per cent to defend real living standards as well as pressing for the x per cent as part of an offensive pay claim. However, if taxes are reduced they may well be under pressures from within their own union to go for the x per cent. Even though the leadership may be persuaded that the tax cut is as good as a z per cent wage increase, rank-and-file members, or the activists and shop stewards, may not agree to forgo the opportunity to obtain the full x per cent. Moreover, from the union's viewpoint, a tax reduction worth z per cent can never be as good as a pay increase of z per cent. For it is less easily demonstrated that the tax cut was obtained by trade union action. After all, it came from the government which will, understandably, seek to obtain political credit for the action. Trade unions need to persuade people to join and remain in membership. They have to be able to demonstrate the advantages of union membership.

Governments may therefore obtain some advantageous response in wage bargaining to tax reductions, but these cannot be relied on to occur automatically. The extent of the response, and its reliability, depend upon whether the structure of bargaining and the union organization are such that trade union leaders are able to provide the necessary degree of commitment on the part of their members. Alternatively, the government may go over the heads of the union leadership, and by appealing directly to union members, perhaps as part of the electorate, persuade them to modify their bargaining behaviour.

The Thatcher Government, committed to a monetarist approach, placed the brunt of its counter-inflation action on control of the money supply. In part this is based on the belief that it will influence pay developments by establishing a total amount of aggregate monetary demand which will act rather like a form of wage fund. If there is only a certain amount of aggregate money demand in an economy there would appear to be a simple relationship between the average level of money wages and the level of employment which can be funded from that aggregate. If wages rise by more than the percentage increase in the money supply, employment, according to this approach, must fall. Following the discussion of expectations in Chapters 5 and 7, the announcement of the government's plans to control the growth of money supply within certain targets might be expected to affect expectations of future price movements and therefore exert moderating pressures on wage claims and settlements. Acceptance of the expectations-augmented Phillips curve leads to the abandonment of demand management as way of increasing employment, or of controlling the economy. Monetary policy determines the rate of inflation, although in some versions it is possible for trade unions to add to inflationary pressures, but only at the expense of higher unemployment. The usual conclusion of the monetarist school is that employment settles round the natural rate (or the NAIRU) and inflation depends upon changes in the supply of money.

Even if it were possible to define and control the money supply there are difficulties about this view of monetary policy and its effects on the labour market. The public sector might not operate in the same way as the private sector is assumed to do in the theory, and the public sector may initiate pay settlements which feed through to the rest of the economy. The Thatcher Government has recognized this by introducing cash limits for government spending with external financing limits (EFLs) for public corporations to create in effect an administratively determined monetarist environment. Higher pay settlements inevitably reduce the number of jobs if overall cash finance is limited. There is no evidence available to show that expected inflation plays much, if any, role in British pay determination. Real wages of some groups can, and do, fall on occasions, and there is no reason to believe that the expectations-augmented curve for any expected rate of inflation remains located in the same place through time.

The sharp reduction in the rate of increase of money wages during the period of the Thatcher Government appears to have far more to do with the very large and sustained increase in unemployment, possibly reinforced by the associated structural measures, than to the implementation of a strict monetary policy, exerting effective control over the money supply. Elements of policy have contributed indirectly, through pushing up the level of unemployment, most notably interest rates, the exchange rate, and the fiscal stance; but apart from the exchange rate (to some extent) there does not appear to have been any strong *direct* route of impact via expectations.

11.3.3 Structural Changes

The second main type of measures open to government can be regarded as structural. This approach rests on a belief that there are distortions, blockages, or impediments in the way in which the economy operates, such that if they can be reduced or removed it might be possible to improve the workings of the economy. For example, a particular skill or occupation may be in short supply. We might expect employers to bid up wages for that sort of labour which in turn might have the effect of reducing demand for it and of increasing its supply as more people are attracted by the relatively higher wages. However, if, in the process, other occupations press for higher wages to maintain some past pay relationship, then general inflation occurs; relative wages do not change quickly, and the time period of adjustment, if left to the market, is lengthy. Government-introduced or -sponsored training schemes might therefore be established in order to speed up the adjustment process and perhaps moderate the inflationary effects.

A more comprehensive approach is an active manpower policy. The original Swedish advocacy of an active manpower policy was related to the Swedish solidaristic wage policy. The manpower side was seen as an essential link in an overall approach which included trade union wage strategy, concern for the lower paid, economic development, macroeconomic policy, and other narrower question of labour supply.

There has long been concern about the adequacy of industrial training in Britain [12]. Fewer British school-leavers go on to apprenticeships or other further skill training than our major competitors. *The New Training Initiative*[4] led to a guarantee from September 1983 of a full year's training to all unemployed 16-year-old school-leavers in the year they leave school, with provisions, but no guarantee, for 17-year-old leavers. In a full year this will cost over £1 billion.

However, in November 1981 the government announced its intention to reduce the number of Industrial Training Boards (ITBs) from twenty-three ITBs covering about 55 per cent of the work-force to just seven. From 1982–3 reliance was, in the main, to be placed on the voluntary provision of training and retraining, with the costs borne by industry instead of statutory requirements to support an ITB by levy. While there were criticisms of the uneven quality or, in some cases, appropriateness of the training provided

---

[4] Cmnd. 8455, HMSO, Dec. 1981.

under some ITBs, and while in the worsening economic conditions industry was anxious to free itself of the training levy and associated costs, it is difficult to reconcile the move to voluntarism with the need for increased and improved training for adults as well as school-leavers. 'The role of manpower policy must be to ensure that new skill requirements are met, economically important developments are not delayed through shortages of key skills, and individuals have opportunities to adapt to the changing needs of the economy.'[5] There is no more reason to believe that employers will voluntarily provide the necessary training and retraining in the future than they did in the past. 'Since the last war there has been a persistent shortage in industry of skilled manpower and industry's own arrangements failed to cure it.'[6] If it is believed that the future need for retraining and adaptation in response to technological change and fiercer competition will be even greater than in the past the reversion to an essentially voluntary system of training may be particularly inopportune.

The changes in employment patterns, particularly the move from manufacturing to the services sector, combined with technological change, add an extra dimension to manpower policy. It is not merely in order to ease inflationary bottlenecks arising from shortages of certain types of labour, but in order to ensure provision of employment opportunities at all, that training programmes are essential. Structural changes which improve the speed with which the labour market adapts to changing conditions ought to be a feature of a growth economy.

Anti-monopoly legislation or provisions against restrictive trade practices can be seen as structural measures designed to reduce the rate of increase of prices. Other measures to help regional development, encourage investment, and provide redundancy pay to help workers adjust to job change are part of the same approach (see Chapters 24 and 28).

In recent years the structural approach has also tried to tackle the *processes* of industrial relations and collective bargaining by proposals for industrial relations reform (Robinson in [15]). Running through the various proposals has been the view that changes in the way in which industrial relations are carried out, and some shifts in the balance of power, either between unions and management, or between union leaders and their members, would make some contribution to easing inflationary pressures. This was spelled out very clearly by Roy Jenkins, then Chancellor of the Exchequer, in the 1969 Budget statement. He said that the then existing climate of industrial relations was a serious obstacle to the attainment of economic objectives and that there was a need to facilitate the smooth working of the process of collective bargaining to prevent the occurrence of unnecessary and damaging disputes which were totally incompatible with the nation's economic objectives. It was for this reason that the government had decided to implement without delay some of the more important provisions incorporated in the White Paper *In Place of Strife*. In the even the government was unable to get its legislation through the

---

[5] MSC, *Manpower Review* (1982).
[6] Lord Donovan in *Hotel and Catering Industry Training Board v. Automobile Proprietary Ltd.* (1969), W.L.R. 697, p. 702.

Commons. What is important, however, is that both the then Labour Government and the succeeding Conservative administrations believed that reform of industrial relations was either necessary of desirable, not only to reduce the incidence of industrial disputes, but also to ease the inflationary pressures from wage settlements.

Both the Labour Government's White Paper and the subsequent Conservative legislation appeared to support the view that some disputes and wage pressures were the result of trade union leadership insisting on larger pay rises than the rank and file would themselves press for. There seemed to be a belief that trade union leadership was more militant than the membership and that members might be led or coerced into action to support excessive demands. Legislation which changed the structure of decision-taking and the processes by which decisions were taken and strike action initiated therefore appeared attractive. The issue of whether the balance of power in collective bargaining should be shifted, assuming that legislation is able to do this, focuses on two issues: first, whether the workers' side is considered to have too much power *vis-à-vis* the employers, and second, whether trade union officials accurately reflect the views of their members.

The answer to the first question will be based primarily on judgements about what one things *ought* to happen. These judgements will necessarily involve various views about the distribution of income, the causes and effects of trade unions, industrial democracy, and the general distribution of power and decision-making authority in industry and society generally. On the second question there is frequently a tendency for people to allow their view of the content of the decision to influence their judgement of why or how the decision was made. This is perhaps nowhere more prevalent than in the question of whether trade union officials lead and manipulate the views of their members or whether they reflect them, sometimes in a moderating way.

Other recent structural changes in the UK include limitations on picketing and industrial action, increased financial liabilities on both employers and trade unions in cases of unfair dismissal for non-union membership where a 'closed shop' agreement operates, and the making of unlawful any union-labour only contracts, as provided in the Employment Acts of 1980 and 1982.

The Thatcher Government has abolished Schedule 11 of the Employment Protection Act 1971 which enabled wage levels set by collective bargaining to be obtained by workers not themselves covered by similar bargaining arrangements. It has in addition rescinded the Fair Wages Resolution which required public contractors to observe terms and conditions as good as those determined by collective bargaining. These can be seen as attempts to reduce the institutional constraints which prevent market forces from operating on individual wage settlements, thereby 'freeing' those decisions to make them respond more closely to the prevailing economic conditions in the industry or locality. The same philosophy led to the renunciation of the system of Pay Research for the Civil Service in 1981 and the refusal of the government to go to arbitration at the request of the Civil Service unions, notwithstanding an agreement to do so.

Changes may be made which affect individuals rather than trade unions.

Many monetarists emphasize the importance of the level of unemployment benefits in influencing wage levels. It is argued that the replacement ratio—the ratio of net income when out of work to net income when in work—provides a floor below which wages cannot fall, and therefore builds inflation or institutional rigidity into the pay system leading to higher wages than would be the case were the replacement ratio lower [27]. There is however little evidence to suggest that high replacement ratios are responsible for much current unemployment; the 3 million plus who are unemployed in 1983–4 are not the result of voluntary unemployment decisions. Nevertheless, the Thatcher Government has adopted measures to increase the incentive of the unemployed to find work (Robinson in [15]).

11.3.4. Prices and Incomes Policies

The third main group of measures is prices and incomes policies. The essence of all these policies is that those responsible for taking wage and price decisions are expected to take decisions which are different from those which they would take in the same economic circumstances but without the existence of the prices and incomes policy. Thus, instead of seeking to reduce the pressure of demand to obtain lower wage increases, or shift the balance of power by restricting the use of the strike weapon or some other form of sanction, a prices and incomes policy seeks to reduce the rate of increase of money wages (or prices) by inducing people to take decisions that they know are different from what they *could* and *would* have taken. In practice, of course, it may not be possible to know precisely what they would have done.

Thus an incomes policy can be seen as saying to wage bargainers, 'You could get a settlement of ten per cent but we want you to settle for eight.' Or it might say, 'If you settle for the ten per cent you would have got anyway, we want you to do so on certain additional conditions which will increase efficiency and so reduce costs and prices.' While there may well be a whole series of other features of a prices and incomes policy, this one is essential, and if it is thought that it is not possible to obtain decisions that are different from those imposed by economic or market forces, there is no point in pursuing an incomes policy. It is therefore a necessary condition for the successful operation of a prices and income policy that there is enough flexibility in price and wage determination to allow changes in the decisions actually taken. There is a wide range of possible methods of inducing changed behaviour in pay determination, ranging from exhortation and moral pressures on the one extreme to strict legal control on the other. At various times since 1945 British governments have tried the whole range of options.

A chronology of the main provisions of incomes policies is given in Table 11.1. Governments have sometimes introduced pay standstills with legal backing (the Labour Government in July 1966 and the Conservative Government in November 1972). Both of these were followed by periods of statutory control of pay increases of differing complexity and severity, with organizations created to apply the rules. In the case of the Labour Government's policy there was already an organization, the National Board for

TABLE 11.1. *Incomes Policy: A Chronology of Main Events*

April 1962	Following standstill from November 1961, voluntary norm of $2-2\frac{1}{2}$ per cent. Exceptions for productivity, labour allocation, and comparability. *Incomes Policy: the Next Step*, Cmnd. 1626.
November 1962	Establishment of National Incomes Commission to advise on wage settlements or claims.
February 1965	NPBI to be established. Government expects voluntary co-operation from unions and employers but will consider statutory authority if experience shows this to be necessary. *Machinery of Prices and Incomes Policy*, Cmnd. 2577.
April 1965	The National Plan assumed a growth rate of 4 per cent p.a. providing a 'norm' for money incomes of $3-3\frac{1}{2}$ per cent p.a. Pay increases above the norm should be confined to four cases: (1) where employees make a direct contribution to increasing productivity; (2) to obtain desirable distribution of manpower; (3) pay too low to maintain a reasonable standard of living; (4) pay seriously out of line with that of similar work. *Prices and Incomes Policy*, Cmnd. 2639.
July 1966	Statutory freeze on pay for six months. *Prices and Incomes Standstill*, Cmnd. 3073.
November 1966	Severe restraint to continue to end June 1967. Zero norm with exceptions, only in exceptional circumstances, for productivity, low pay, and, very exceptionally, manpower distribution and comparability. Restriction Orders could be placed on increases in excess of policy provisions under Part IV of Prices and Incomes Act 1966 which was activated in October 1966. *Prices and Incomes Standstill: Period of Severe Restraint*, Cmnd. 3150.
July 1967	Zero norm, no one can be entitled to a minimum increase. Four exception clauses of April 1965 (Cmnd. 2639) return. *Prices and Incomes Policy After June 30, 1967*, Cmnd. 3235. Sections 4 and 6 of Prices and Incomes Act 1967 operative. Government able to impose standstill on individual settlements pending investigation.
April 1968	Zero norm but increases up to $3\frac{1}{2}$ per cent p.a. permitted under the four exception clauses with exemptions from ceiling for genuine productivity bargains. Power to delay settlements when referred to NBPI to be extended to twelve months. *Productivity, Prices and Income Policy in 1968 and 1969*, Cmnd. 3590.
January 1970	Settlements should be within $2\frac{1}{2}-4\frac{1}{2}$ per cent. Exceptional increases permitted for productivity, reorganization of pay structures, lowpaid workers, equal pay, labour allocations, and public sector pay. *Productivity, Prices and Incomes Policy After 1969*, Cmnd. 4237.
1971-2	Rather more informal policy of $n-1$, whereby settlements should be 1 per cent lower than previous ones. Public sector to set example.
November 1972	*Stage I*. Statutory pay standstill. *A Programme for Controlling Inflation: the First Stage*, Cmnd. 5125.
April 1973	*Stage II*. Pay Board established. Statutory policy norm £1 plus 4 per cent. Twelve-month rule between settlements. Exceptions for

TABLE 11.1—*continued*

	prior settlements. *The Programme for Controlling Inflation: The Second Stage*, Cmnd. 5205.
November 1973	*Stage III*. Statutory norm of 7 per cent or £2·25, whichever higher, plus threshold arrangements. Additional 1 per cent for flexibility, up to 3½ per cent for productivity, staged movements towards equal pay, unsocial hours, extra holidays up to 3 weeks plus 1 January. Threshold increases of 40p a week for each 1 per cent increase in the RPI above 7 per cent of October 1973 level. *The Price and Pay Code for Stage 3: A Consultative Document*, Cmnd. 5444, and *Stage Pay Code*, S.I. No. 1785.
1974–5	Government sought voluntary restraint by trade unions. Settlements to compensate for price rise since last settlement. Compulsory element in Pay Code provision regarding allowable pay rise for price increases. Moves to equal-pay and low-pay exceptions.
1975–6	Social Contract continued with maximum increase of £6. No increases for those earning £8,500 or more p.a. Exceptions for moves to equal pay. Voluntary, with Price Code provisions. *The Attack on Inflation*, Cmnd. 6151.
1976–7	Social Contract, voluntary, with Price Code provisions. Norm of 5 per cent with minimum of £2·50 and maximum of £4.
1977–8	No agreement with TUC on guidelines other than twelve-month rule. As government agrees with TUC on desirability of return to free collective bargaining it was not thought appropriate to stipulate a specific figure for individual negotiators. If national target of 10 per cent increase in earnings to be achieved the general level of settlements must be well within single figures. Price Code provisions continue. *The Attack on Inflation after 31st July 1977*, Cmnd. 6882.
1978–9	No agreement with TUC. Government sought limit of 5 per cent with extra for productivity agreements. Higher increases for lower paid. Public sector disputes led to establishment of the Clegg Comparability Commission (see Kessler in [15]).
1979	No formal comprehensive incomes policy. Cash limits for public sector.

Prices and Incomes, in existence but its powers were considerably increased after the standstill. The Conservative Government created the Pay Board and Prices Commission to apply its rules from April 1973. Attempts to obtain an incomes policy as a result of voluntary agreement took place in December 1964 with the Declaration of Intent, agreed by government, unions, and employers, and in 1974 with the Social Contract, agreed by government and the TUC. It is not intended to provide here any detailed history of these various approaches, but only to draw some general conclusions about the use of various forms of incomes policy.

Exhortation alone may not be sufficient to obtain moderation in pay settlements. A crucial factor is whether those whose actions are subject to the exhortation believe that it is in their interest to change their behaviour. This requires that there be some view as to which set of people is responsible for making pay settlements. As we have seen, sometimes this may be trade union officials, sometimes shop stewards, sometimes arbitrators and third parties, and sometimes employers. It is reasonable to believe that they are much more likely to change their behaviour if they believe that their own interests will be furthered by their so doing, although, of course, it is possible that they might do so in order that some other interest, that of another group or of society as a whole, might be furthered.

For it to have much chance of success exhortation needs to be in somewhat specific terms. Even if we assume that 'men of goodwill' will respond, they need to know what they are supposed to do. Some indication of the extent of restraint or modification to their behaviour is necessary. In the early post-war years government's approach was based on macroeconomic considerations: the aggregate rate of increase in money incomes should be kept in line with the aggregate or average rate of increase of productivity. This can be done in two ways. The first is to tie all pay increases to the increase in national productivity. This means that some sectors face rising costs as pay rises faster than productivity does in those sectors, giving price rises, and some face falling costs, giving offsetting price reductions. But this divorce of pay increases from the productivity of the industry or firm concerned creates great pressures on the policy, particularly from the sectors with fast-rising productivity.

In some cases it may be that, with existing payment systems, pay in a firm will automatically rise with productivity, for example if there is a piecework system which links them together. If employees believe they are 'entitled' to a pay settlement based on the national increase in productivity, they may well conclude that there is no need for them to participate in measures to increase productivity in their employment, so that the actual increase in productivity could be less than expected.

If, as an alternative, the approach is to link pay and productivity in each plant, firm, or industry, so that a group of workers receives an increase related to the change in their productivity, there will be different reactive pressures emanating from defensive pay claims based on comparability. Tight links between pay and productivity on this basis would require significant changes in attitudes towards fairness and comparability. There are also many workers for whom it is extremely difficult to measure productivity because of the problems of quantifying their output, for example policemen or teachers. In many situations, even though it may be possible to indicate that there has been a rise in productivity it is unclear why this has happened—whether it was the result of a direct contribution by the work-force or whether because of increased or improved capital equipment or technological progress. Also, the decrease in the importance of industry-level bargaining means that it would be much more difficult to apply a productivity–pay norm on an industry basis.

An important conclusion, which is relevant whether the approach is based on exhortation or legislative intervention, is that while the macroeconomic relationship between pay movements and productivity increases may be the central theme in the package of government economic objectives, the

mplementation of pay policies to attain this objective must recognize the
microeconomic realities of the processes of pay determination and the existence
f extremely powerful, albeit variable and varying, concepts of fairness.

A modification of exhortation is the creation of some degree of consensus
between government and those responsible or mainly responsible for pay
determination. Government may seek to obtain tripartite agreement to a set of
rules which should govern pay movements, or bipartite agreement with either
the trade unions or, less frequently perhaps, the employers. The success of this
approach will depend on the extent to which those responsible for making the
agreement in good faith are actually able to ensure that their good intentions
are translated into modified behaviour. For obvious institutional and
representational reasons the consensus or agreement is likely to be made with
the national leadership or unions and/or employers. In practice, this leadership
may not be able to exert dominant influence over the actual pay decisions. This
may depend on the structure of bargaining as well as on the extent of the
opportunity for national leadership to influence the behaviour of members
Brown in [15]). Thus, if the Donovan Commission's interpretation that trade
unions, particularly in their relationships with shop stewards, workgroups, and
members, are too weak rather than too strong is correct, then government
should not expect trade unions to be able suddenly to obtain greater strength in
the sense of being able to commit their members to pay restraint. They may not
have the *de facto* power to do so.

The use of voluntary agreements, or preference for them over statutory
methods, rests on a belief that voluntary commitment to moral obligations,
perhaps in a bargained situation where government has altered its economic
and social policies to allow the unions and/or employers to obtain some of their
objectives, is a more effective way of influencing behaviour than the use of
coercion through legislation.

The 1975 Social Contract reflects this approach. The TUC and Labour
Government arrived at a consensus on the broad social and economic policies
to be implemented by government and in return the TUC agreed to support a
voluntary pay policy. This involved the TUC in accepting some responsibility
for ensuring that member unions accepted the obligations imposed upon them.
It also meant that the unions within the TUC had to agree on the content of the
policy, a flat-rate increase rather than, say, a percentage increase, with the
consequential effects on differentials. Both of these points subjected the TUC to
considerable internal pressures and stresses. The great virtue of this approach is
that the unions themselves will seek to ensure the observance of the policy. A
weakness is that if they believe that the government has not delivered the
economic policies or circumstances that they expected they will withdraw their
support, and, of course, there are circumstances in which government believes
that it is unable to guarantee the creation of specific economic situations—a
particular level of employment, for example—because of factors outside its own
control. A consequence of tripartite or bipartite approaches to incomes policy is
that there will be much more 'bargaining' about the government's economic
policies and this will focus attention on the effects of these policies on such
things as real disposable income, income distribution, employment levels, etc.

If the government believes that voluntary enforcement or compliance is unlikely to prove sufficient, it may introduce legislation limiting the increases which are permitted. Legislative intervention has not hitherto taken the form of insisting that certain increases be given for incomes policy purposes. The rules have been allowable maxima. The adoption of legislative controls requires two main decisions to be taken. First, who is to apply the rules? Second, what should be the content of the rules? The questions have been put in this order because it is generally the case that the method of administration imposes constraints on the type of rules that can be introduced.

The 1965 Labour Government's incomes policy was implemented by the appropriate government departments, with the National Board for Prices and Incomes (NBPI) asked to provide advisory reports when departments wished them to do so. The 1974 Pay Board created by the Conservative Government was different in that it had statutory authority to implement the rules which Parliament had laid down in a pay code. (The advisory reports of the Pay Board had no legally binding effects and were much more like the previous NBPI reports.) A very rough analogy is that the NBPI was in a similar position to the Monopolies Commission while the Pay Board was more like the Restrictive Trade Practices Court, except that it had no power to judge on wider 'interests', for example those of consumers or purchasers, etc., which would have given an element of discretion (see Chapter 26).

The choice of the rules reflects both the social and economic objectives sought. If the decisions of the agency are, in the absence of specific intervention by a minister or Parliament, to be legally enforceable, it follows, given our system of parliamentary democracy and accountability, that the agency will not be empowered to make decisions which are discretionary, based on its own value-judgements. Thus terms such as 'in the national interest' or 'desirable restructuring of a payment system' are unlikely to be introduced as grounds on which the agency can permit exceptionally large pay increases. The provisions of the Pay Code for the Pay Board were therefore much more prescribed (in the sense that they were expressed in objective or quasi-objective and measurable terms) than were the exception clauses of the documents which provided guidance for the NBPI. What this means is that government can provide for differentiated, but not discretionary, treatment in the code. If an exception clause cannot be stated in objective terms it is extremely difficult for it to be included in a statutory policy that is implemented by an independent agency whose decisions are legally enforceable. If discretionary clauses are introduced it is unlikely that an independent agency can implement them, as opposed to the offering of advice to a minister, and therefore the implementation and enforcement will ultimately have to lie with ministers. In so far as this requires decisions on individual settlements, the implementation of the policy is much more likely to become a political process rather than an administrative one

Perhaps the most striking difference in the approach of the Pay Board and that of the NBPI was that the former in its advisory reports[7] placed great

---

[7] See especially [37], which proposed setting up a special Relativities Board to consider claim for special treatment within a statutory incomes policy. This reflected the belief that no matter how well the permitted exception clauses were written there would be occasions when special treatment might be necessary, but determined on grounds which could not satisfactorily be set out in quantifiable and objective terms; some element of judgement would be necessary.

emphasis on the importance of relative pay and concepts of fairness and the effect these had on influencing the acceptability of a policy, while the NBPI discounted these factors and emphasized productivity. Stage III of the Conservative policy in 1973 introduced a form of index-linking through the threshold provisions. In part this was to offer guarantees against inflation and might also have influenced the size of the pay limit, which it was thought would be acceptable. The vital question is whether a threshold provision or some other form of indexation makes inflation worse by ensuring an increase in labour costs when prices rise, or helps by reducing the size of the general norm. A major problem arises if government believes that it has to obtain a reduction in living standards, perhaps because of a significant change in the terms of trade. Any policy here can face difficulties, but indexation may make these far worse.

Policies have not simply been measures to hold down money wages and prices. They have contained varying provisions designed to make some changes in the distribution of income or to change relative pay. In all cases they sought to inject some elements of value-judgement into pay relationships. This is crucial. If trade unions and workers are to be induced to settle for less than they could have obtained in money terms they will need to be persuaded that they will receive other benefits which are considered worthwhile by them. Income redistribution is often one such benefit which is offered, or, perhaps more accurately, the possibility of achieving some degree of redistribution is offered if those responsible for decision-taking wish, or are able, to take advantage of it.

When government seeks to influence the development of wages at the macro level through incomes policy it has to do so by influencing developments at the micro level, i.e. it must seek to influence the actual changes in pay at whatever level these are determined, and these vary considerably from industry to industry and job to job. Moreover, it is reasonable to expect that changes will be made in the levels at which decisions are taken as a response to the creation of the incomes policy itself. In a modern economy such as the United Kingdom's where trade unions represent an important part of the work-force, it is important that a government embarking on incomes policy should try to obtain the agreement and consent of the unions to its measures, and if this is not possible, then at least their acquiescence and the avoidance of overt and direct rejection.

Unless it is thought that an incomes policy can be imposed on unions, employers, and workgroups irrespective of its prevailing economic and social policies, government has to recognize that there might well be a trade-off between incomes policy and demand management or other measures. Government might well not be able to choose the combination of items it wishes from the full range of possible measures which are, prima facie, open to it. If, at the same time, it is accepted that various themes of policy should be mutually supportive then the possibility may easily arise that an acceptable and effective combination of measures is not politically available.

There is a tendency to condemn incomes policies on the grounds that they have always failed, or always lead to a subsequent explosion which results in the overall position being no better or even worse. Several points should be borne in mind when considering these criticisms. The policy is frequently judged against one or both of two criteria: (a) the statement of policy objectives made by its advocates when it was introduced, and (b) the extrapolation of some past trends to provide a yardstick against which the actual economic out-turn can be measured. One of the difficulties of using the declared objectives of those introducing incomes policy as the criteria for evaluation is that an important part of the declaration of objectives is to influence behaviour. Sometimes this may lead to the policy being couched in terms that overstate the extent of change that is really expected. The difficulty is that if the actual results are too far removed from the expectations generated by the public advocacy, credibility is lost in the next phase of the policy.

If the extrapolation of past trends is used as a yardstick the appropriate test is to compare what happened with what *would* have happened in the absence of incomes policy. This of course requires some forecast of what would have happened in the absence of the policy, and this is notoriously difficult to make. While there are econometric techniques for producing these forecasts they depend heavily upon assuming fairly constant relationships between various economic variables, for example wages, unemployment, and productivity, and if, as has been suggested earlier, these relationships have been changing, the usefulness of the forecasts is accordingly reduced. Moreover, the forecasts or the econometric equations from which they are derived tend to regard economic policies as consisting of only two types, 'incomes policy on', or 'incomes policy off'. If the 'off' periods consist of various and changing combinations of *other* policy measures it cannot be assumed that there is a constant relationship between pay awards and unemployment in the absence of income policies.

There have been numerous attempts to quantify the effects of incomes policies (Henry in [7]). Overall the results are consistent with the view that incomes policies generally have their desired effects while the policy operates but that wages and real wages tend to increase faster when the policies are ended. While this may not seem a particularly favourable outcome in view of the very considerable strains and conflicts that may be generated by incomes policies, it should be remembered that on occasions obtaining a postponement of pay increases might be an important part of a government's economic strategy (see Mayhew in [15]). Moreover it may be that the repercussions which seem to follow incomes policies occur because the policies did not last long enough to obtain the desired effects in changing collective bargaining behaviour.

There are finally two other points relevant to evaluation of incomes policies. People paradoxically seem to adopt much more stringent tests for incomes policies than they do for other policy measures. Thus demand management measures which have not been successful in containing inflation while maintaining full employment are not condemned merely on that ground, yet incomes policy may be. All evaluation of policies, in the real world of government decision-taking, should be between the policy adopted and the other policies which were considered as realistic reasonable alternatives. It is of little value to make comparisons with perfect systems; perfect systems of running an economy are not given to man.

The other point is that a distinction needs to be drawn between the content of the policy and its application. If it is concluded that an incomes policy failed it must be decided whether this was because the policy provisions were inappropriate and perhaps excessively generous in an anti-inflation sense, or whether it was because people did not observe the policy provisions. Because they have frequently contained exception clauses allowing increases in excess of the norm, it is very difficult accurately to quantify what should have happened to aggregate pay during an incomes policy. In one case where it was possible the Pay Board concluded that on the whole the 1973–4 policy was well observed [37], [38]. Also, changes in the occupational and industrial composition of the work-force can lead to movements in aggregate pay, and it is difficult to know whether these changes are accurate reflections of underlying economic developments or are devices to avoid the constraints of incomes policy.

Income policies are sometimes criticized on the grounds that they lead to excessive bureaucratic intervention in pay and related matters, thereby creating distortions which have harmful economic effects. According to the content of the policy they may lead to a greater squeezing of differentials than would have occurred. Labour turnover may increase as individuals, by changing their employer, obtain the higher pay they may be denied by incomes policy. Phoney productivity deals may be arranged in order to benefit from an exception clause and payment-by-result schemes may be deliberately abused in order to increase earnings beyond the limits of the norm. Most incomes policies in the UK have been in periods of tight labour markets so that employers and unions may collude to beat the policy in the pursuit of their separate sectional interests.

Each of these criticisms may have some justification. However, it does not follow that the 'distortions' are movements away from some theoretically perfect or desirable position. The real world is full of distortions; political choice requires us to select which package of distortions and benefits we prefer. The narrowing of differentials has often been a deliberate objective of incomes policies which have sought to improve the relative position of the low paid, and this cannot, of course, be done without squeezing some differentials. If some provisions of some policies have been abused as a result of collusion between employers and unions this is a criticism of the content and implementation of particular policies rather than of incomes policies as a whole.

Many trade unions object to incomes policies as unwarranted interference with free collective bargaining. The defence of free collective bargaining, which means the absence of state intervention not only in the processes, but mainly in the results, of bargaining, is not only the pursuit of some sectional interest by unions; it is frequently seen by those who defend it as a necessary condition of a democratic society. Certainly totalitarian governments, of the Left or the Right, seek to destroy or suborn trade unions to their own ends. Many trade unionists therefore believe that their continued existence and freedom to participate in collective bargaining as it has developed are fundamental to democratic society. This is why a temporary enforced freeze may actually be easier to obtain than a full-scale statutory incomes policy. The former is regarded as a passing phase but the latter could lead to permanent restrictions on the results of collective bargaining. The principle of free collective bargaining is not in fact, in the UK, absolute. Unions accept that there are legal limitations on their freedom to negotiate certain terms and conditions, for example they cannot now negotiate different rates of pay for men and women performing the same tasks in the same establishment. There are other restrictions associated with equal opportunity and race relations legislation. However, these are not in themselves seen as attacking the basic rights of union to bargain freely, probably because the results they seek to avoid are themselves accepted, or not openly challenged, by unions.

Unions may agree to voluntary restraint on pay, as in the Social Contract. This is not seen as presenting the same threat of government intervention in collective bargaining since it occurs with the agreement of the unions, but many of them are deeply suspicious that voluntary participation might encourage statutory restraint. Trade union leaders are also exposed to challenges from below if members and activists do not accept the need for voluntary pay restraint, not as a general requirement, but as something to apply to themselves. There is a major problem in reconciling the view that there ought to be general restraint to reduce inflation and the widely held view of each group that it is a special case deserving some special treatment within the general restraint.

11.3.5. Partial Incomes Policies

The Thatcher Government, while publicly eschewing incomes policy, has in practice introduced partial incomes policies for parts of the public sector. The main vehicle has been the use of cash limits which were reintroduced in 1976–7 by the Treasury as the main means of control over public expenditure, replacing the volume control method which had emerged. However, since 1979–80 they are being used for purposes for which they were never originally intended. By including an allowance for further pay rises in forward expenditure provisions the government is devolving its responsibilities as an employer so that it does not appear to set a 'going rate'. But cash limits provide an unclear and variable limit [17]. The government limits the amount of public funds to be made available to an organization in the next financial year. To do this some provision is made for inflation and future pay settlements in order to arrive at an appropriate 'volume' figure in terms of next year's costs. The allowance for pay increases which is included does not necessarily limit pay settlements to that percentage increase as it may be possible to make some 'savings' on the pay bill by not filling vacancies immediately. If this is not possible the only way in which pay settlements can exceed the increase in the pay component of the cash limit is by reducing the number employed. Thus, cash limits are being used to influence pay settlements. Different limits can be set for different parts of the public sector, thereby allowing some degree of flexibility rather than having a single 'norm' for all sectors. The police and fire services are special cases in that they have agreed systems of pay determination which link them to movements in the Average Earnings Index and the upper quartile of adult male manual workers respectively.

Governments will always be tempted to adopt partial policies for the public sector. Indeed, in one sense they cannot avoid doing so for they must have some policy for public sector pay. A government which gives high priority to control of public expenditure and the PSBR will find it difficult to maintain those pay systems for the public sector which, in effect, require it to abdicate control over large areas of public expenditure. This is one reason why both comparability and unilateral access to arbitration have been withdrawn from the Civil Service. The former because pay levels were determined by levels paid outside the Civil Service and the latter because arbitrators might make awards contrary to the government's views (Kessler, and Hunter, in [15]).

11.3.6. Tax-Based Incomes Policies

In an attempt to avoid some of the perceived difficulties of traditional incomes policies there have been proposals for tax-based income policies (TIPs) (Bosanquet in [15], and [23]). Essentially the proposals suggest that a tax be levied on increases in pay which exceed some norm. Wootton proposed as a short-term measure that the tax be levied on individual pay earners who received increases in excess of a norm [34]. But this would penalize those on incremental scales, those benefiting from genuine payment by result schemes, those working genuine productive overtime, and those who accepted promotion or moved to a better-paying job. As the proposal was envisaged as a temporary measure, these difficulties might have been tolerable but they would be unacceptable for any sustained period. Other proposals would impose the tax on employers. Thus, if average hourly earnings, or some other measure of pay, rose by more than the permitted rate, employers would pay a tax related to the amount of the excess pay increase. If the tax is actually charged irrespective of the profitability of the enterprise, it works rather like a fine, although a fine-based incomes policy sounds much more punitive and less neutral than a TIP (Bosanquet in [15]). If the charge is levied on profits it may be inapplicable to many companies and the public sector. It is claimed that this approach would allow collective bargaining to continue unhindered by any central bureaucracy or statutory intervention. Market forces are allowed to operate; if companies cannot afford to pay the tax they can be expected to resist pay settlements in excess of the norm. Efficient and profitable enterprises would be able to pay higher wages to attract labour. The main counter-inflationary impact of a TIP lies in the encouragement it gives to employers to resist pay settlements in excess of the norm. Each percentage excess increase attracts an additional cost according to the rate of tax.

The main exponents of TIPs are American and for them there is nothing startlingly new in proposals to use the tax system as a form of incomes policy. The American Internal Revenue Service has experience of implementing pay policy of the traditional sort. The British Inland Revenue has no such experience and it would be a major administrative innovation to use it for this purpose. It would be even more innovative for them to collect details of hours worked if the basis of the control was hourly earnings.

There are four main problems about TIPs. First, it is difficult to see how it could be applied to the public sector. Even the nationalized industries would be difficult. Those which make losses would be in no different position than they are now. Their ability to pay wages and incur other costs in excess of their receipts depends upon government policy regarding financial support and pricing. Imposing an additional tax would not alter this basic position.

Second, it is far from clear that such a tax would exert a great restraining influence on pay settlements. In some sectors the higher tax would be passed on in the form of higher prices. It does not follow that those who incurred the first payment of the tax would turn out to be those who bore the ultimate incidence, or that those who insisted on higher pay settlements would be the ones who would suffer loss of jobs as a result of reduction in product demand. Unlike virtue, policy-goal breaking does not always bring its own reward in the form of punishment. Moreover the *impact* on pay would vary across enterprises and industries according to their ability to pass on the tax in higher prices. To the extent that this led to considerably greater variations in pay increases between groups of workers and to the disruption of established pay relationships and linkages it would undoubtedly lead to industrial unrest. It might be thought that there should be greater flexibility in relative pay and that the forces of coercive comparison and fairness are undesirable and economically harmful in that they lead to misallocation of resources. It does not follow, however, that it will be easy, or even possible, to change this, and certainly not without great difficulties. Changes which may be imposed during adverse economic circumstances may not endure an improvement in the economy.

Third, it would be administratively difficult to obtain a satisfactory pay basis for calculating the norm. If average earnings per worker were used it would encourage part-time employment and 'ghost' workers. If hourly earnings are used it would encourage phoney overtime or even payment for overtime not worked. Moreover, even genuine overtime would penalize the firm since the premium element would count against the norm.

It may be desirable to discourage the widespread use of overtime in order to create more employment opportunities, although it does not follow that employers will hire more labour even if they are penalized for, or prevented from, working regular overtime. The non-wage costs of additional employees, such as the employer's National Insurance contributions, and the apparent reluctance of employers to expand their labour force in present conditions, may inhibit job expansion. The inclusion of other premia payment in the earnings which are compared with the norm would inhibit the extension of shiftworking and the more efficient use of capital equipment.

Fourth, neither of the bargaining parties may give much weight to a tax which is imposed only after some time-lag. The perceived short-run bargaining needs may well dominate. It might be proposed that the tax be assessed and levied more frequently than on an annual basis. This would cause considerable unfairness to some enterprises which have seasonal fluctuations in the occupational composition of their work-force. In some jobs earnings vary seasonally.

Finally, it is not feasible for there to be exception clauses with a TIP. The very nature of these proposals is their simple single element. It is just not possible to base a policy that is expected to be anything other than short-term on a single criterion of the percentage increase in earnings regardless of the cause of that increase. Neither is it desirable to do so. Increases in earning in hemselves are not inflationary; it depends on what is happening to productivity. If extra productivity growth is not rewarded by higher pay, xcept perhaps indirectly by adjustment of the general norm, there will be little ncentive to increase productivity. Firms which increased both productivity nd pay would be taxed for their efficiency.

1.4. Conclusions

Government cannot ignore pay developments, nor can it choose to opt out and eave pay developments to be determined by market forces or whatever else letermines them. To do so would mean that the rest of economic policy was in ffect dependent on what happened to pay, and this would involve too great an bdication over too many crucial areas of policy. The real choice facing government is in the selection of methods or combination of methods. But hoose it must. Because pay levels and pay changes are influenced by social and nstitutional factors, particularly people's views of fairness, any measures which ffect one group will have repercussions on others. The implementation of policies determined by consideration of macroeconomic factors must pay egard to the actualities of pay determination at micro level. If people's perception of fairness and equity coincided with economic factors and with uch changes as may be necessary on economic grounds, for example to obtain a necessary allocation or reallocation of labour, it might be much easier to nfluence pay development. But they do not, or at least do not seem to do so ufficiently well to permit significant changes to be introduced quickly and easily.

The monetarist approach of the Thatcher Government seems to have had a ignificant effect on curbing wage increases. However, this has been associated with extremely high levels of unemployment. It may be that political attitudes have changed so that these high levels are now tolerable, but they represent a remendous waste of resources and foregone economic activity. The structural measures which have been introduced to shift the balance of power and to try to educe militancy may also appear to be important contributory measures, but t is far from clear whether they will have any effect, or in fact be operable, if the economy improves. Certainly there is insufficient evidence to suggest that they have led to any shift in underlying attitudes; apparent changes may represent trategic withdrawals in the face of adverse current conditions rather than any ong-lasting change in attitudes and behaviour.

Incomes policies make certain issues surrounding relative pay levels explicit and so focus attention upon these very sensitive areas. If they are successful they emphasize that many people are receiving smaller increases in *money* wages than hey might otherwise have done, although the increases may be larger in real erms in the longer run. This inevitably creates problems inside trade unions as the leadership is pressed to obtain larger money increases in the shorter run. At a time when the national leadership of trade unions is less able to commit its membership to any policy as a result of the decentralization of decision-taking and the effective devolution of power inside unions, the stresses thus generated makes the implementation of a policy more difficult. A paradox is that at the same time as it is more difficult for national leadership to commit their membership in this way to the effective observance of restraint, the development of tripartite or bipartite discussions or agreements on general economic policy measures requires that the national leadership should take part in realistic discussions with government about *quid pro quos*.

None the less, it is difficult to foresee government abandoning for long the option of incomes policy. Even governments which are politically or philosophically opposed to the concept will generally be compelled by the force of economic events to use some elements from this range of policy measures. At the end of the day it is probably the lack of an effective alternative for reconciling high employment and low inflation which will lead governments to turn to incomes policies; these policies may have disadvantages, but when the drawbacks of other policies are experienced the possible advantages of incomes policies will seem relatively more attractive. Each policy will also be a response to the perceived lessons of the last one(s).

At the same time the problems of government as an employer with responsibility for the public sector will compel it to take a more positive role than merely reacting to general economic circumstances which can be handled by demand management or monetary policies alone. This will lead to forms of partial policies. They may be restrictive, as with cash limits as currently applied, or they may try to remove public sector pay from the arena of industrial conflict by establishing forms of comparability, as with the Clegg Commission (Kessler in [15]). The public sector will occupy an important place in government's pay problems.

Proposals for adaptations of traditional incomes policies, such as TIPs, will be put forward in an attempt to avoid the perceived problems of previous policies. Unless a government advocates them as long-term features of economic control they will not have much chance. Governments have turned to incomes policies as short-term solutions to immediate pressing problems. TIPs are not appropriate for this.

Because incomes policies have been regarded as short-term measures imposed by the overwhelming necessities of current adverse economic circumstances there has been relatively little attempt to work out longer-run policies. If expectations and attitudes really do lie at the heart of the problem then measures which are seen as only short-run ones will not be sufficient to secure the necessary changes. Incomes policy would have a much better chance of success if it were designed to obtain these longer-term changes even at the expense of some of its more immediate effects, but it is doubtful whether this is politically feasible at the present time.

Bibliography

SECTION A

[1] ARTIS, M., GREEN, C. J., LESLIE, D., and SMITH, G. W. (eds.). *Demand Management, Supply Constraints and Inflation* (Manchester University Press, 1982).
Essays on aspects of demand management, labour supply, and wage developments. Some good summaries of recent research work.

] Brittan, S. and Lilley, P. *The Delusion of Incomes Policy* (Temple Smith, London,
)77).
rong attack on incomes policies written from a monetarist standpoint.
] Brown, W. (ed.). *The Changing Contours of British Industrial Relations* (Basil Blackwell,
xford, 1981).
ery good survey of the changing level of bargaining in British manufacturing industry.
nalysis of incidence of different types of industrial action by size of plant, manual, and
n-manual employees separately.
] Chater, R. E. J., Dean, A., and Elliott, R. E. F. (eds.). *Incomes Policy* (Clarendon
ess, Oxford, 1981).
ollection of essays discussing different aspects of incomes policies and the case for and
gainst.
] Clegg, H. A. *How to Run an Incomes Policy and Why We Made Such a Mess of the Last One*
Heinemann, London, 1971).
] —— —— *The Changing System of Industrial Relations in Great Britain*, revised edn. (Basil
Iackwell, Oxford, 1982).
standard text on industrial relations with good chapters on the development of
comes policies. The various types of bargaining institutions and methods of payments
re described in their historical setting.
] Fallick, J. L. and Elliott, R. F. (eds.). *Incomes Policies, Inflation and Relative Pay*
George Allen and Unwin, London, 1981).
ome good essays on incomes policies. Contains useful summaries of events and
mpirical results.
] Fels, A. *The British Prices and Incomes Board* (Cambridge University Press, 1972).
he most comprehensive survey of the role, operation, and methods of inquiry of the
IBPI yet published.
] Jackson, D., Turner, H. A., and Wilkinson, F. *Do Trade Unions Cause Inflation?*
Cambridge University Press, 1972).
iscusses British experience of inflation in comparison with other countries' experi-
nces. The second part argues that government tax policy influences pay claims by
ffecting take-home pay.
o] Jones, A. *The New Inflation: The Politics of Prices and Incomes* (André Deutsch and
enguin, London, 1973).
he former chairman of the NBPI discusses the need for an incomes policy. He
nphasizes the importance of productivity and the way in which pressures for wage
creases spread. The role of incomes policy in the overall framework of economic policy
well discussed.
1] National Board for Prices and Incomes. Various Reports, but especially Nos. 23,
5, and 123 on Productivity Bargaining, 65 on Payment by Results, and 83 on Job
valuation.
2] Prais, S. J. *Productivity and Industrial Structure* (Cambridge University Press, 1981).
xcellent detailed study of productivity in various British industries with chapters on
1e relationship between size of plant and labour relations. Argues that British
dustrial relations is an important cause of poor performance. Also compares industrial
aining in UK and competitors.
3] Robinson, D. *Wage Drift, Fringe Benefits and Manpower Distribution* (OECD, Paris,
968).
n introductory discussion of various methods of payment bringing out the wide range
f possible components of pay.
4] —— —— *Incomes Policy*, Ditchley Paper, No. 38 (Ditchley Park, 1971).
hort discussion of benefits and disadvantages of incomes policy. Compares other

methods of influencing inflation open to governments; based on an Anglo-America conference.

[15] ROBINSON, D. and MAYHEW, K. (eds.). *Pay Policies for the Future* (Oxford Universit Press, 1983).
Essays on the range of policies open to governments to influence pay. Mixture of applied economics and industrial relations.

[16] ULMAN, L. and FLANAGAN, R. J. *Wage Restraint: A Study of Incomes Policy in Wester Europe* (University of California Press, Berkeley, 1971).
A comparison of incomes policies in a number of countries which combines statistica analysis with an understanding of collective bargaining processes.

SECTION B

[17] BEVAN, R. G. 'Cash Limits', *Fiscal Studies*, 1/4 (Nov. 1980).
[18] CRAIG, C., RUBERY, J., TARLING, R., and WILKINSON, F. *Labour Market Structur, Industrial Organisation and Low Pay* (Cambridge University Press, 1982).
[19] DANIEL, W. W. and MCINTOSH, N. *The Right to Manage* (MacDonald, PEP, Londo1 1972).
[20] FAY, S. *Measure for Measure: Reforming the Trade Unions* (Chatto and Windu. Charles Knight, London, 1970).
[21] FLANDERS, A. *The Fawley Productivity Agreements* (Faber and Faber, London, 1964)
[22] HYMAN, R. and BROUGH, I. *Social Values and Industrial Relations* (Blackwell, Oxforc 1975).
[23] JACKMAN, R. and LAYARD, R. 'An Inflation Tax', *Fiscal Studies*, 3/1 (Mar. 1982)
[24] MACKAY, D. I., BODDY, D., BLACK, J., and JONES, N. *Labour Markets Under Differe1 Employment Conditions* (George Allen and Unwin, London, 1971).
[25] MCCARTHY, W. E. J. and ELLIS, N. D. *Management by Agreement* (Hutchinson, 1973)
[26] MEADE, J. E. *Stagflation, Vol. 1: Wage-Fixing* (George Allen and Unwin, Londo1 1982).
[27] PARKER, H. *The Moral Hazard of Social Benefits*, IEA Research Monographs, No. 3 (1982).
[28] ROBINSON, D. (ed.). *Local Labour Markets and Wage Structures* (Gower Press, Londor 1970).
[29] —— —— 'Labour Market Policies', in BECKERMAN, W. (ed.), *The Labou Government's Economic Record 1964–1970* (Duckworth, 1972).
[30] —— —— *Solidaristic Wage Policy in Sweden* (OECD, Paris, 1974).
[31] TAYLOR, R. *The Fifth Estate: Britain's Unions in the Modern World*, revised edn. (Pa: Books, London, 1980).
[32] Trades Union Congress. Annual Reports with verbatim reports of debates o incomes policy, industrial relations, and government economic policies.
[33] WEEKES, B., MELLISH, M., DICKENS, L., and LLOYD, J. *Industrial Relations and th Limits of the Law* (Blackwell, Oxford, 1975).
[34] WOOTTON, B. *Incomes Policy: An Inquest and a Proposal* (Davis Poynter, Londor 1974).
[35] WREN-LEWIS, S. 'A Model of Private Sector Earnings Behaviour', Governmen Economic Service Working Paper, No. 57 (Treasury Working Paper, No. 23) (HN Treasury, London, 1982).

Government Publications

[36] Department of Employment. *Prices and Earnings in 1951–69: An Econometric Assessmer* (HMSO, May 1971).

37] Pay Board. *Relativities*, Advisory Report 2 (Cmnd. 5535, HMSO, Jan. 1974).
38] —— —— 'Experiences of Operating a Statutory Incomes Policy' (Mimeo, July
974).
39] —— —— Quarterly Reports.

12
Demand Management Policy: Theory and Measurement

C. J. ALLSOPP and D. G. MAYES

12.1. Introduction

An outstanding feature of the period since the Second World War is the extent to which governments actively intervened to manage the economy. This is, perhaps, most apparent in the field of *demand management* policy—the purposeful management of the overall level of demand in the economy to achieve macroeconomic aims such as full employment, growth, or the avoidance of inflation. Nowhere did the commitment to demand management policy (or stabilization policy, as the Americans would call it) go further than in the United Kingdom: until, that is, the marked change in the direction of economic policy in the late 1970s.

A prime reason for the adoption of demand management as the cornerstone of economic policy was the development of the 'New Economics' and the scheme of economic theory associated with J. M. Keynes and others. These techniques, which had been found useful in wartime,[1] appeared to offer the means of achieving full employment and prosperity after the war: the new tools were eagerly grasped in the prevailing political climate which demanded a widening of government responsibilities to include the commitment to full employment and growth.

The techniques and practice of demand management are discussed in this chapter and in many other chapters of the book. Here, it is useful to start with a wider perspective. The idea of managing demand involved a *diagnosis* and a *prescription*. The diagnosis involved the claim that deficiencies or excesses of aggregate demand could arise which would have the deleterious effects of prolonged unemployment or inflationary pressure. The economy, if left uncontrolled, would exhibit unwelcome fluctuations in demand. The prescription was that deficient or excess demand should be eliminated (or, at least, mitigated) by *offsetting* monetary or fiscal policies carried out by the authorities.

Even to set out the reasons for managing demand in this way brings out some of the issues which form the main threads of this chapter and the next. The first is whether (or perhaps, more interestingly, when and under what circumstances) the diagnosis of deficient demand (potential or actual) as the problem

---

[1] One of Keynes' most influential writings [23] was *How to Pay for the War*, which was concerned with the problem of how to *reduce* private demand to make room for the war effort.

ing behind unemployment is correct. Certainly, this issue is contentious. The 'Treasury View' in the interwar period was that the reasons for unemployment y elsewhere—in structural change and in wages that were too high. Similarly, the post-war period, the most important element in the monetarist position is t the emphasis on money, but the denial of the demand manager's premise at in the absence of such management, larger fluctuations in demand would cur and would cause undersirable changes in activity.

A second set of issues concerns the instruments of policy and their efficacy in fecting demand. Generally, demand management policy is taken to be ncerned with monetary and, particularly, fiscal policy. There are, however, her instruments that affect expenditure and demand: for example, an change rate fall stimulates exports and slows import penetration; incentives a microeconomic kind may raise private investment. Evidently, demand anagement policy need not be concerned only with the balance of the budget. evertheless, much reliance has been placed on fiscal policy, especially in the K, and that is where the emphasis of this chapter lies. In looking at fiscal licy, however, it is well to bear in mind that there are different views about its fects. Many monetarist and 'new classical' economists, for example, deny that cal policy has any influence on demand and activity at all.[2] Thus, in arguing ainst fiscal stabilization policy, some economists adopt a two-pronged proach. Not only is fiscal stabilization not needed; it is not efficacious either.

A third issue is whether policy makers have, in practice, used the instruments policy to good effect. Some of the reasons why they might have been badly ed include poor forecasting performance and over-ambitious or otherwise appropriate targets. For example, attempts to 'fine tune' demand and tivity may have been overdone.

Any overall assessment is, however, difficult. Demand management seldom kes place in a 'vacuum' where the only economic problem is to find the 'right' vel of demand. In the first place, the appropriate or target level of demand d activity is subject to competing considerations, as, for example, between e claims of high employment and of counter-inflation policy. Second, the onomy will normally exhibit other economic problems which are not due to excessive or deficient level of demand but which nevertheless affect what is asible. A prime example, important through much of the post-war period in e UK, would be poor international competitiveness, showing itself as current balance of payments problems and acting as a constraint on fiscal and onetary policy. Another would be inadequate industrial profitability, ading to 'supply-side' difficulties of one kind or another.

These issues are developed in this chapter and the next. There is, though, other, largely historical, theme that cuts across them—the changing nphasis that was laid on demand management as time went by (a change hich became dramatic in the 1970s) and changing views about what demand anagement policy could and could not do. Broadly, in the early period, soon ter the war, there was recognition of the fragility of success: even with mand management, high employment and growth were seen as conditional

---

[2] See, for example, the discussion of the working of the Liverpool model in Chap. 14.

on the avoidance of significant problems elsewhere, such as balance payments difficulties or inflationary pressure in labour markets. It was, so speak, a question of getting policy right on a number of fronts simultaneousl Later—especially in the late 1950s–early 1960s period—there was a phas world-wide it seemed, of over-optimism about the perfectability of macr economic economic policy, and over-ambition about stabilization. Th optimism never went so far in the UK as in some other countries, part because, in the 1960s, policy makers were painfully aware of other constraint Their ambition was, however, evident in the attempts during the 1960s 'break out' of the 'strait-jacket'—by planning, by devaluation, by incom policies.

Around the mid-1960s the dominant paradigm for the analysis of econom policy had become that of objectives, instruments, and the 'trade-offs' betwee them.[3,4] These 'trade-off' ideas now seem out of line with the longer history economic policy-making. The most famous trade-off was that betwee inflation and unemployment—the Phillips curve [37]. With the developmer of the expectations-augmented Phillips curve and other versions of th 'accelerationist thesis',[5] the control of inflation came again to be regarded as necessary condition for success on other fronts including, especially, fu employment.[6] This change—whether justified or not—was of the highe importance: for if inflationary pressure unchecked led not to inflation, but accelerating inflation, then there was no alternative but to control it.

There remained scope for much dispute about how inflation should k controlled. The 1970s are marked by swings between the view that deman management policy itself should be turned against inflation and the alternativ that inflation should be tackled more directly, by incomes policies and th like—releasing the instruments of fiscal and monetary policy for their 'prope role of maintaining employment and growth. With the apparent failure of th various attempts at incomes policy to provide a permanent solution to th policy dilemma it was perhaps inevitable that demand management woul come to be directed more and more towards the objective of controllin inflation.

The 1970s seem to mark a progressive retreat from demand managemer with a move, apparently completed by the beginning of the 1980s, monetarist principles of economic policy. From a broader perspectiv however, this interpretation is oversimplified. It is more true to say that th policy instruments were *diverted* from their traditional role of maintainin demand and output to the control of nominal variables (such as money) in th cause of slowing inflation. Counter-inflation policy came to be formulated wit reference to intermediate targets (principally £M3, but also, if less formall

---

[3] For a famous example see Caves [10]. See also Chap. 5.

[4] For a discussion of this and the problems that arose see Chap. 8 in which the assignment policy instruments to objectives is discussed.

[5] i.e. that unemployment lower than a 'natural' rate would give not just higher inflation b *accelerating* inflation (see Friedman [15]). See also Chap. 7.

[6] See, for example, McCracken *et al.* [27]. For a discussion of the importance of this change ideas in the wider context of the European economy see Allsopp [1].

others such as public borrowing and the exchange rate) and the instruments of demand management policy—short-term interest rates, and, on the fiscal side, tax rates and public expenditure programmes—were extensively used to try and achieve the government's financial targets. Far from marking the end of 'fine-tuning', the late 1970s–early 1980s period can be seen as a phase of *policy activism* in pursuit not of stable and high employment, nor even of a particular inflation objective, but of intermediate financial targets.

The fact that both monetary and fiscal instruments continued to be used even under the Medium-Term Financial Strategy (MTFS)[7] should not, however, conceal the intellectual gulf that continued to divide the (broadly Keynesian) demand managers from those taking a more 'monetarist' or classical' line on policy. One fundamental difference (going right back to the early debates between Keynesians and classicials) was over the strength of any tendency for the economy to general full employment. On classical assumptions, demand management policy, if it worked at all, would only affect prices. The other major difference was over fiscal policy. Under the MTFS the role of fiscal policy was, in effect, to help in controlling the money supply. This contrasted with the traditional 'demand management' view which emphasized direct effects from fiscal policy onto economic activity or prices.

These themes are taken up in following sections. The chapter starts in section 2.2 with a sketch of an analytical framework within which demand management policy can be discussed. In order to provide some background to more recent concerns (for example the MTFS), demand management policy is looked at not just in terms of flows—such as the budget deficit—but also in terms of the *stocks* of assets/liabilities, such as public sector debt. This is followed, in section 12.3, by a discussion of how policy changes, and the effects of those changes on the economy, can be quantified. In the 1970s the measurement of the thrust of policy (especially fiscal policy) became highly controversial. In particular there are major issues as to whether the size of budget deficits, taken as an indicator of fiscal stance, should be adjusted for inflation and/or for the business cycle. All this is then used in the discussion of the practice of policy, which takes place in the next chapter.

2.2. The Framework of Demand Management Policy

Even in an economy which did not suffer from high unemployment or price inflation it would still be necessary for the government to avoid creating destabilizing shocks emanating from the public sector, and to provide a financial framework conducive to stable prices and orderly exchanges. But active demand management policies would only be needed in the presence of some kind of *market failure*: some departure from the perfectly functioning system of the theorists.[8]

The diagnosis of the unemployment and under-utilization of capacity of the

---

[7] Introduced in the spring 1980 Budget; see Chap. 13, p. 423–5.
[8] Thus, while opponents of demand management policies come under many labels, they are usually, first and foremost, 'market optimists'.

interwar years as due to deficiency of demand is associated with the name o᷈
Keynes.[9] In the standard Keynesian economic model, when the economy is a᷈
less than full capacity, *output* is determined by demand: and the management o᷈
economic activity and hence employment is effected by managing demand. I᷈
turn, aggregate demand and its components are taken as being influenced b᷈
the instruments of fiscal and monetary policy. The scope for policy action ca᷈
then be seen either as the desirability of eliminating or mitigating the *busines*
cycle or as the need to counteract some longer-term tendency to stagnation o᷈
cumulative decline.

12.2.1. Forecasting: The Income/Expenditure Approach

The almost universal starting point is the accounting identity linking th
expenditure components (the components of demand) with Gross Domesti
Product (see Chapter 5, p. 121).

$$GDP = C + I_F + I_S + G + (X - M) - FCA$$

where

C = consumers expenditure,
I_F = fixed capital formation,
I_S = stockbuilding,
G = government expenditure,
$(X - M)$ = exports minus imports,
FCA = factor cost adjustment.[10]

This accounting identity applies equally to quantities measured in currei
price (or nominal) terms or to quantities measured in *real* terms—i.e. at th
constant prices of some base year. In considering changes over time, howeve᷈
the distinction matters (where confusion could arise we use the term NGDP ᷈
refer to nominal GDP below). The income/expenditure approach focuses o᷈
real quantities. On the (Keynesian) assumption that spending determin᷈
output, GDP can be predicted on the basis of forecasts of the expenditu᷈
component such as consumption, investment, government spending, etc. The᷈
components themselves are related to the economic variables that affect the᷈
for example, consumption might be related (with lagged response) to person᷈
disposable income, interest rates, and inflation; exports to world trade and t᷈
exchange rate; and investment to past changes in output, profitability, a᷈
interest rates.

Of course, forecasting is not confined to projections for real GDP. Oth᷈
relationships are used to generate forecasts for employment and (introduci᷈
demographic and other factors affecting the labour supply) for unemploymer᷈
Moreover, it is obviously important to assess the future course of *prices* (a᷈
hence the rate of inflation) using, perhaps, information on the trend ᷈
international commodity prices, recent data on wage settlements and econom᷈
relationships such as one or other version of the 'Phillips curve' (relati᷈

---

[9] Though others such as Kalecki, or, in Sweden, Myrdal, have equal claim to priority.
[10] GDP is normally measured at factor cost, whereas the expenditure components are at mar᷈
prices. Factor cost adjustment reconciles the two, and is equal to indirect taxes net of subsidi᷈

flation to unemployment). Particularly when looking at financial interac-
ons and effects, interest focuses not on real GDP and the real expenditure
ows but on nominal or current price spending and on nominal GDP. In
actice, a full forecast may include projections for literally hundreds of
onomic variables, which are either of interest in themselves (e.g. GDP,
employment, inflation and the balance of payments) or are needed because
ey enter into the economic relationships of the *model*.
There are different views about the underlying economic relationships or
odel of the economy. In practice, forecasts are now usually made using one or
her of the large empirical models of the UK—such as that of the Treasury.[11]
ssuming that some procedure for generating forecasts exists, the likely
utcome over a run of quarters or years can be assessed against the
overnment's objectives, and, if necessary, remedial action set in train. At that
age interest focuses on the effect of the instruments of policy on the course of
e economy.

.2.2. *The Instruments of Policy*

principle a wide variety of economic parameters is under the government's
ntrol and could be used to influence demand and output. For example,
centive policies could influence private investment. Although this would
ormally be looked at as a 'supply-side' measure, incomes would be generated,
d there could be substantial direct and indirect effects on demand. Even
ore obviously, direct intervention would have both demand and supply
fects. Generally, however, demand management policy is thought of in terms
fiscal and monetary policy at the macroeconomic level.
It is not as easy as is sometimes supposed to distinguish the instruments of
olicy from their effects, or from intermediate objectives—indeed, any
assification depends on the model that it is assumed to hold. Broadly,
owever, the instruments of *fiscal policy* are the public expenditure decisions of
overnment, and the tax schedules in operation. The overall balance of the
udget, the deficit or surplus, is best thought of as an intermediate variable, or
ometimes) as an *intermediate target*. For much of the 1950s and 1960s, and to
me extent still today, demand management was thought of very largely as a
uestion of the government varying its budget deficit from year to year,
xpanding if it it wished to increase GDP and employment, reducing it if the
onomy appeared to be (or likely to be) overheating. These variations might
e achieved by changes in government expenditure or taxation or both. Views
out the instruments of *monetary policy* vary, but they are usually taken to include
e short-term interest rate, and funding policy, i.e. on how the budget deficit is
anced. The growth of the money supply itself, often taken as an *exogenous*
strument in textbook models, is (like the fiscal deficit) an intermediate
riable, often put forward as an intermediate target.

[11] For a discussion of the different properties of some of the major private forecasting models—
d some of the implications for policy—see, for example, Allsopp and Joshi [2]; Laury *et al.* [24];
ech [6]. Also Surrey's discussion in Chap. 14 of this volume.

12.2.3. Multipliers, Ready-Reckoners, and Policy Simulations

As noted, there is great dispute over most important economic relationshi and so over the model of the economy. Putting that problem on one si (assuming, for example, that a particular model is agreed to be useful), t effects of an instrument change on important economic variables—such GDP or inflation—can be computed. A simple example would be t 'multiplier' to be attached to a change in government expenditure to indica by how much greater the final effect on total expenditure would be (s pp. 149–52). Slightly more complex constructions, such as the balanced budg multiplier, which considers a simultaneous (balancing) change in tax a expenditure instruments, can also be carried out. The practical analogues such exercises are tabulations, derived from econometric models, of the effe through time of specified policy changes—such as a £1 million increase public spending, or a reduction of 1 per cent in the rate of VAT. Often su simulations are assembled in convenient form as a kind of 'ready reckoner' show the approximate effects of particular policy changes.

Larger changes, or more complex policy packages, can be investigated usin full-scale simulations of the effects as compared with some base run of t model. It needs stressing that such simulations are only as good as the model c which they are performed, and as controversy over how the economic syste functions has grown, so has scepticism about the usefulness of this kind approach. Nevertheless, they remain an important input into the polic making process, although they are assessed in the knowledge that the model (models) may in important respects be incomplete.

12.2.4. The Budget Deficit and Sectoral Flows

The basic national income accounting identity demands that, for a clos economic system, expenditure equals income and production. For an op economy with foreign trade, however, aggregate expenditure can exce income by the extent of the balance of payments deficit. Clearly, if the econon has, for example, a balance of payments deficit, then some one or other of t *domestic* sectors—households, companies, or government—is spending mo than it is receiving and therefore has a deficit.

More formally, the sectoral balances of the economy are connected, matter of accounting, by the identity

$$B = B_H + B_C + B_G$$

where

B = balance of payments on current account
(surplus measured as positive),
B_H = surplus of households,$\left.\right\}$ private sector
B_C = surplus of companies,
B_G = surplus of government.

In practice the sectoral balances for the domestic sectors (here, househol companies and government) are derived by looking at total incomes a expenditures for the sector concerned. Thus for households, their gross incon will include not only income from production (wages, salaries, rents a dividends)—which is the part of national income that accrues to households—but also transfers from other sectors, particularly transfer payments from the government. Taxes paid to the government can be subtracted to give net or disposable income, or treated as part of expenditure. Expenditure includes not only consumption (C) but also investment by households (principally housebuilding). For companies, their sectoral balance is, approximately, their net retained earnings after taxes, minus their expenditure on fixed investment and stocks.

Particular interest attaches to the position of the government. The budget surplus (B_g) is the balance between the total flow of receipts by government (principally taxes on households, companies, and on expenditure) and the flow of government expenditure which includes transfer payments to other sectors (e.g. social security, interest on the national debt) as well as government spending on goods and services (G).[12] This budget surplus (deficit if negative) has financial implications. If there is a surplus, the government is acquiring financial assets (usually by retiring its own debt). A budget deficit has to be *financed*, in effect by borrowing from the private sector or from overseas (so National Debt will normally rise). The *way* in which a deficit is financed will have *monetary implications* (see below).

The accounting identity implies that the government's position must be matched, or 'mirrored', in other sectors. Ignoring the external sector for the moment, this means that a *budget deficit* must be matched by a *private sector surplus*. And the government's borrowing to finance the deficit has its counterpart in the accumulation of financial assets by the private sector—i.e. by households or companies.

Looking at actual or forecast budget deficits together with the other sectoral balances may be useful from a number of points of view. The first point is historical. Clearly if the instruments of fiscal and monetary policy are directed purposefully to managing demand in the way described in section 12.2.2, then this implies a *tolerant* attitude to resulting changes in the government's financial position—in particular, it requires a tolerant attitude to any *deficits* that might result. Though the positive aspects of demand management are usually stressed, the negative aspect of tolerating budget deficits is equally important. Such toleration also contrasts strongly with the 'Treasury View' of the interwar period and with the revival of such views in the later 1970s.

Second, the sectoral balances are the usual link into the financial sectors of policy models. In the 1960s and early 1970s they were commonly used as a kind of consistency check on forecasts or simulations. If, for example, an implausibly large company sector deficit was in prospect, then judgemental adjustments to the forecast might be made to take account of the expected financial pressure.[13]

[12] There is always a question about the exact definition of the budget deficit/surplus. Should it refer to the whole of the public sector, including nationalized industries, or be restricted to general or central government? The budget deficit is related to, but is not identical with, the Public Sector Borrowing Requirement (PSBR) which, for example, includes borrowing by the government for on-lending to the private sector, and excludes asset sales.

[13] The classic case in the UK was after the first oil shock in 1973–4, when forecasts suggested that more or less the whole £3 billion impact of oil would fall on the company sector deficit. This subsequently happened, with predictable consequences for de-stocking, labour-shedding, etc.

More formally, the sectoral balances can feed into all sorts of relationships of the model, modifying its behaviour.

Third, from a theoretical or conceptual point of view, a focus on the sectoral deficits may give useful insights. The *private sector surplus*, i.e. the combined company sector plus personal sector net accumulation of financial assets, is its net *balance of saving over investment*; $(S-I)$ in the usual symbolism. In the simple model of the textbooks, S must equal I. Here, it is seen that private savings can exceed private investment if, and only if, the government runs a deficit or there is a balance of payments surplus (thus ensuring $S = I$ when all sectors are added together). Either a payments surplus or a government deficit can be seen as supplying financial assets to the private sector as a counterpart to an excess of savings over investment on their part.

This leads to an alternative, more financially oriented, view of stabilization policy. Recessionary forces can be seen as developing either due to a reduction in investment or due to an increased desire to save (i.e. a desire to accumulate financial assets). Either way, S tends to rise above I. If that is impossible, as it would be for the private sector if there were no government and no foreign trade, then stocks would rise as households reduce spending in order to build up their desired savings, and company spending on investment and wages would fall as companies try to restore *their* position. Downward adjustments via the 'multiplier' process are set in train—i.e. a recession develops. The tendency can be checked, however, if the government goes into deficit (dis-saves, de-cumulates financial assets) to *allow* the private sector to go into surplus and to satisfy the excess desire to save. For Keynes, it was the tendency for the private sector, from time to time, to want to stop spending and to accumulate financial assets instead that lay behind the problem of slumps and unemployment. It could be checked by deficit spending.

12.2.5. Discretionary and Automatic Fiscal Stabilization

Clearly the sectoral balances, including the balance of the budget, are very far from being independent of the state of the economy. The budget deficit/surplus will be affected as an economy goes into a recession by a reduction in tax receipts, and by rises in some spending flows, such as unemployment and social security benefits. Similarly, the current balance will be affected as the demand for imports falls in recession. (There may even be some stimulus to exports as products are directed abroad.) These developments tend to generate budget deficits and balance of payments surpluses, allowing the private sector to accumulate the surplus it wants. They therefore act as *automatic stabilizers* of the economy.[14] So too does any tendency for private savings to fall in recession.

Automatic stabilization from the public sector has clearly been very important in the post-war period—reflecting the increased role of government and the rising share of public spending. Stabilization policy can go further, however, via *discretionary policy* (tax or expenditure changes) of a counter-cyclical kind. In the UK, much interest has focused on the question of whether

[14] The balance of payments effects described are those that would occur with *fixed* exchange rates. With the move to floating, this 'stabilizer' would not operate to anything like the same extent.

discretionary policy was, as practised in the 1950s and 1960s, stabilizing or destabilizing.

2.2.6. Stabilization and Monetary Policy

Clearly, if monetary policy affects the components of demand, then it could be used to stabilize the economy along with, or instead of, fiscal policy. In the 1950s and 1960s, monetary policy tended to be looked at in terms of interest rates. In terms of that paradigm, counter-cyclical variations in interest rates, if they could be engineered, and if they had sufficiently pwerful effects, could make a useful contribution to stabilization policy.

Looking at the need for stabilization, as in section 12.2.4, in terms of the desire by the private sector to accumulate or de-cumulate financial assets, interest rates could be seen as affecting both the supply of financial assets—via effects on the *decision to invest*—and the demand for financial assets via the *desire to save*. A fall in interest rates, stimulating investment and lowering savings, would, in principle, choke off any tendency to recession.

Indeed one of the neo-classical objections to the Keynesian framework was that interest rates would work in exactly this way *automatically*, and so stabilize the economy.[15] The market was assumed to equalize the demand and supply of funds at full employment. Keynesian monetary policy could be seen as justified if that mechanism failed, in which case market forces could be overriden by discretionary policy—i.e. by a Keynesian policy of monetary stabilization.[16] Monetary policy was not used very actively in this way in the UK—though it was in some other countries. Part of the reason was that it was thought, at the time, to have rather weak effects (see Chapters 10 and 13).

2.2.7. Financing the Budget Deficit: Monetary and Fiscal Policy

In simple models the budget deficit may be *financed* either by bonds or by changes in the amount of money held by the public. Strictly, the relevant monetary aggregate is Central Bank or *high-powered* money, and if the question is discussed at all, it is assumed that other, broader monetary aggregates—such as £M3—are related to it by some simple ratio. Thus, letting bonds be N, high-powered money H, and with Δ standing for the change in either,

$$- B_G = \Delta N + \Delta H.$$

The minus sign reflects that a deficit will be a negative value of B_G, but will require increases (positive changes) in N and H. Thus fiscal policy, as represented by the deficit, may, depending upon the *financing rule*, have monetary implications.

There are two polar cases corresponding to a deficit that is entirely monetized $(- B_G = \Delta H)$ or entirely bond-financed $(- B_G = \Delta N)$. In the bond-

[15] The main objection of the classicals was to the hypothesis that the unstable swings in demand would occur in the first place. If they tended to occur, however, fluctuations in interest rates would offset the tendency.

[16] Some writers in the neo-classical tradition have been careful to *assume* an enlightened and active monetary authority which keeps the economy at full employment.

financed case the money supply is fixed, whilst the fiscal stimulus occurs. In th
kind of example, a *neutral monetary policy* is implicitly defined as one in which th
supply of money does not change; and a *pure fiscal impact* is a *bond-financed defici*
In that framework (which, as will be seen, is not always helpful) there is
question about the effects of bond-financed deficits on interest rates, via th
mechanisms of *crowding-out*. Broadly, there are two reasons why, given th
money supply, interest rates would rise. The first is that, if the fiscal impuls
increases activity (and/or prices), then the demand for money rises fc
transactions reasons, tending to raise interest rates. Evidently this would ten
to choke off some of the expansionary impulse. The second is that the amount c
National Debt (bonds) in private portfolios would be *rising*, whilst the amoun
of money was fixed, which in likely circumstances would require higher intere
rates on government debt to persuade the public to hold the higher proportio
of bonds. (This latter effect is often termed *portfolio* crowding-out.) Monetaris
often argued that crowding-out would be complete, and that fiscal expansio
would simply lead to higher interest rates (with no change in activity) and
displacement of private sector activity by public sector activity.[17]

The reason this framework is not ideal is that monetary and fiscal effects ge
thoroughly mixed up. In effect, there is a combination of an expansionary fisca
policy and a tighter monetary policy: it is not surprising that some or all of th
fiscal expansion is offset and that overall the results are ambiguous.[18] It is bette
to define a pure fiscal policy change as involving a *balance of money and bon
finance*. One way—appropriate to the economic perceptions of the 1950s an
early 1960s—would be to choose (as the neutral case) a mix of money an
bonds that left interest rates unchanged. Another, which has conceptua
advantages, is to define fiscal policy in terms of changes in the total stock c
public sector debt (taken now to include high-powered money), with th
proportions of bonds and high-powered money unchanged.[19] Monetary polic
would then be defined in terms of *compositional* changes in the government
outstanding liabilities—including high-powered money. Thus a change i
monetary policy would come about through market operations of one kind o
another *taking the deficit as given*. In this framework, pure fiscal policy has n
crowding-out effects, at least of the type so far described,[20] though of cours
there remain interesting questions about the effects of monetary policy an
their relative importance compared with fiscal policy.[21]

[17] See, for example, Friedman's [16] evidence to the Treasury and Civil Service Committe
[18] Beyond this, the normal framework for the 'crowding-out' debate—the *IS-LM* framework c
the textbooks—mixes up flow effects (the fiscal deficit) with stock effects (the stock of mone
compared with the flow of production or the stock of bonds).
[19] In the more complex case the proportions of all public sector liabilities should be unchange
e.g. the proportion of bills to bonds, or bills to (high-powered) money.
[20] Alternative crowding-out effects still operate in the new classical framework, exemplified b
the Liverpool model (see Chapter 14, p. 467).
[21] There are also questions about the effects of a rise in public sector debt and high-powere
money (with composition unchanged) on interest rates, on activity, on prices, and on the capit
stock. In the long run there may be crowding-out of another kind if a rise in public debt displac
the private capital stock.

The separation of monetary and fiscal policy in this way[22]—so that monetary policy involves no change in the deficit, and fiscal policy is concerned with a change in the deficit financed in some *neutral* way—becomes even more important if another step towards realism is taken. In practice, most money is *inside money*—that is, it is not only an asset for whoever in the private sector holds it but a liability inside the private sector as well—of the *commercial banking system*. Money *is*, for most purposes, a deposit in a bank. Most of this inside money comes into being as a counterpart of the lending of the banks—the credit extended appearing as someone else's deposit (see Chapter 10). Inside money—which is what usually matters for monetary policy—may have very little direct connection with the high-powered money which results from monetization of a budget deficit.[23]

In what follows, fiscal policy is considered as involving some (approximately) neutral financing rule. Issues such as crowding-out still arise, but in the context of a relaxation of fiscal policy with a tightening of monetary policy—i.e. when the two types of policy are pulling in different directions. Clearly there *may* be circumstances when a tighter monetary policy might offset, or more than offset, a fiscal relaxation.

2.2.8. A Stock-Oriented Reformulation: National Debt

The sectoral balance approach looks at the *flows* of financial assets between sectors of the economy, i.e. at the pattern of the net acquisition of financial assets (NAFA) for the various sectors. Corresponding to these flows there are, of course, *stocks* of financial assets held by the various sectors, all of which represent someone else's liabilities.

If the assets of the whole of the private sector are considered, both real and financial, its *net* assets (i.e. net of any liabilities, and after cancelling out the network of claims and debts within the sector) may be seen as comprising three types of asset or wealth (W):

(i) Its capital stock (W_K).
(ii) Assets from abroad (W_F).
(iii) The liabilities of government—i.e. the public sector debt (W_G).

The first component, the value of the physical capital stock, which comprises buildings, plant and machinery, stocks of working capital, etc., obviously does not net out for the economy as a whole. It can be looked at either as a collection of physical objects, or often more conveniently, as the financial assets which

---

[22] Which is, for example, the framework adopted by Dow [12].
[23] Notes and coin are, in fact, available to the private sector on demand. In normal times, they enter the system in return for bills (especially Treasury Bills) given up by the banks. Thus as far as monetary *control* is concerned, notes and coin have little relevance. The outstanding government liabilities that do matter are bonds, bills, and Bankers' Balances at the Bank of England. The latter, though expremely important, are quantitatively small. If a shortage develops, banks bid against each other for funds, raising the short-term interest rate. The balances are replenishable by *discounting* bills at the Bank of England: the rate at which this is done used to be Bank Rate; subsequently the term changed to *Minimum Lending Rate*. Recently, the rate at which cash is supplied has been allowed to vary within an undisclosed band.

comprise *claims* on the capital stock, such as equities, corporate bonds, title deeds, etc. The physical stock is increased when net *investment* occurs.[24]

The second component represents the net claims of the economy on foreigners. This will rise if there is a balance of payments surplus on current account—implying a rise in financial assets held by the domestic economy.

The third component, public sector debt (W_G), comprises the liabilities of the government to its own citizens,[25] and should properly be taken as including high-powered or Central Bank money. It includes Treasury Bills held by the private sector, and government bonds of various maturities.[26]

Writing the total wealth of the private sector as W,

$$W = W_K + W_G + W_F.$$

A change in the financial wealth of the private sector (ΔW) is equal to private savings. Recalling that ΔW_K is private investment, ΔW_F is the balance of payments surplus, and ΔW_G is the budget deficit, we have

$$S = \Delta W = \Delta W_K + \Delta W_G + \Delta W_F$$

or

$$(S - I) = (-B_G) + (-B_F),$$

i.e. the surplus of the private sector is equal to the budget deficit plus the current account surplus of the balance of payments. This is just the sectoral balance identity in another form,[27] but this derivation from the stock, rather than flow, perspective has interesting consequences.

It was suggested above that the need for stablilization policy arose if there was an increase in the desire of the private sector to accumulate financial assets. Offsetting policy could be seen in terms of the public sector, via a budget deficit, supplying financial assets for the private sector to accumulate, i.e. *increasing public sector debt* to offset any excessive desire for 'wealth as such'.[28]

Though it makes little difference to the analysis of *disequilibrium* whether the problem of stabilization is looked at in terms of the *flows* (the budget deficit and the private sector surplus) or in terms of the *stocks* of financial assets, there is a question as to which is the better way of looking at longer-term tendencies. The conventional Keynesian analysis sees the budget deficit as *balancing* any difference between savings and investment flows in the private sector. This balance would then have implications for the *development* of *National Debt over time*, for example if savings tended to be larger than investment at full employment, then the National Debt would tend to rise. Alternatively attention could be focused on the private sector's demand for *wealth*, and on that component of financial wealth that would need to be supplied by the

---

[24] In practice the value of financial claims does not always accurately reflect the value of the physical stock of capital.

[25] The complication that the government may own foreign assets or have foreign liabilities ignored.

[26] For a discussion of the various concepts of national and public sector debt see Reid [39].

[27] This is a simplification. In practice ambiguities arise, e.g. about the treatment of capital gains/losses and about the effects of inflation.

[28] Cf. Keynes [22] Chap. 16: 'The problem [of unemployment] arises . . . because of a desire for *wealth as such*.' (Italics added.)

overnment—i.e. public sector debt. The determinants of the demand for
ublic debt could be complex,[29] but a natural and convenient *reference case*
ould be to consider the conditions under which public debt, as a proportion of
DP, remained constant.

.2.9. Public Debt and the Budget Deficit

uppose public debt (W_G) is a constant proportion (α) of nominal (i.e. current
rice) GDP, written as NGDP:

$$W_G = \alpha(\text{NGDP}).$$

he budget deficit $(-B_G) = \Delta W_G$. So,

$$-B_G = \Delta W_G = \alpha\Delta(\text{NGDP})$$

$$-B_G/\text{NGDP} = \alpha\{\Delta\text{NGDP}/\text{NGDP}\}.$$

he first term is the budget deficit expressed as a proportion of NGDP. The
ational Debt/NGDP ratio is α. The final term $\Delta\text{NGDP}/\text{NGDP}$ is the
roportionate rate of change of NGDP, i.e. it is the *rate of growth* of nominal
DP.

What the formula shows is that if NGDP is growing (either due to real
rowth, *or* due to inflation) then a budget deficit of a particular size is *required* if
e National Debt to NGDP ratio is to be unchanged. For example, if NGDP is
rowing at 12 per cent per annum (say, 2 per cent growth and 10 per cent
flation) and if the National Debt/NGDP ratio (α) is one half,[30] then a budget
eficit of 6 per cent of NGDP would be needed for the National Debt/NGDP
tio to be constant. With a larger (smaller) budget deficit, the ratio would be
sing (falling).[31] This formula is extremely important in interpreting the high
ublic sector deficits of the 1970s.

A slight extension of the formula is to break the growth of NGDP into a real
rowth component $\Delta\text{GDP}/\text{GDP}$, written as $\dot{y}$, and the rate of inflation $\Delta P/P$,
ritten as $\dot{p}$. Then

$$-B_G/\text{NGDP} = \alpha(\dot{y} + \dot{p})$$

d the (proportionate) deficit breaks into two bits. The first, $\alpha\dot{y}$, is necessary to
low for real growth. The second, $\alpha\dot{p}$, allows for *inflation*. This second
mponent is sometimes called the '*inflation tax*' and is the extent to which the
alue of National Debt outstanding—an asset for the people who hold it—is
roded by inflation. The formula then shows that to retain a constant National
ebt/NGDP ratio, the inflation tax must be *balanced* by a budget deficit.

Finally, the term $\alpha\dot{p}$ is a gain to the public sector which does not appear in the
nventional accounts. It can be argued that *really* the deficit of the public

[29] The demand for wealth could certainly be trended up or down. Moreover fluctuations in
ther the demand for (savings) or the supply of (investment) 'private' wealth could occur, and
ight need to be offset by counter-cyclical variations in National Debt.
[30] This figure is approximately that for the UK in the late 1970s.
[31] The National Debt/NGDP ratio would not normally explode or collapse. For example, if the
ficit were 12 per cent then the National Debt would converge on a new proportion of 100 per
nt of GDP.

sector is smaller than the nominal deficit by that amount. The *inflation-adjusted* or '*real*' deficit of the public sector allows for the erosion of public debt due to inflation. One of the simplest ways of adjusting the deficit for inflation is simply to net out the term αp as above.[32]

12.2.10. *Norms, Rules, and Discretion*

An important theme running through debates on demand management is whether to adopt certain rules or norms to follow, or whether discretion should be used at any point in time to adopt the policy stance that seems most appropriate at that time. One of the oldest of the suggested norms for fiscal policy is that the budget should be *balanced*. (This was the famous 'Treasury View' of the interwar period in the UK.) From the preceding, it can be seen that this amounts, equivalently, to the prescription of keeping National Debt constant in nominal terms, i.e. with no allowance for inflation. Any faster growth of nominal GDP would, *ceteris paribus*, result in a falling ratio of National Debt to nominal GDP. A suggestion, common enough in the interwar debates (and still often put forward) would treat the balanced budget rules as a *medium-term* target or norm. In the short term, counter-cyclical policy could allow budget deficits in recessionary periods, so long as they were offset by surpluses in the boom. This too can be seen as a rule for National Debt, but with room for rises and falls in it over the cycle.

It is easy to extend these rules—with marked implications for policy—to allow for budget positions, in the medium-term, which are not zero. One possibility is to look at the *structural budget* position, allowing for a difference between savings and investment flows at full employment.[33] Another is to extend the analysis to allow for growth and (possibly) inflation, as in the previous section. Further refinements to the fiscal norm could allow for trend movements (either up or down) in National Debt.

Any of these approaches stands in contrast to the conventional *demand management* view of the 1950s and 1960s in the UK when it was generally believed that *no* fiscal norm for the medium term was required. Rather, it was argued, short-term policy should be used to maintain full employment. The process of adjusting the economy year by year (on the basis of forecasts) was all that really mattered. It has already been noted that this involved a tolerant attitude to deficits, should they arise. It also involved the belief that such policies would not lead to any longer-term movements in National Debt of deleterious kind.

It was this latter view that came seriously under attack in the crowding-out debates of the later 1960s and early 1970s, where one of the main claims was that attempts at short-term stabilization would, via movements in National

---

[32] If a neutral fiscal policy is taken as one in which the National Debt/NGDP ratio is held constant, then there are strong arguments for this procedure. Alternatively, however, attention can be focused on the income of the public sector, allowing for real interest flows, capital gains and losses, etc. For inflation-adjusted figures see Taylor and Threadgold [40]: also, Miller [29], and Buiter [7].

[33] See, for example, the literature on the Dutch of German approaches [4], [11].

Debt, have deleterious longer-run consequences and should not therefore be an objective of policy.

Although a full analysis of these debates is beyond the scope of this chapter but see pp. 906–7 for a summary of the mechanism of crowding-out), it is important to bring out that much of the literature seems, from a practical point of view, beside the point. This can be illustrated simply. One type of argument was that deficits, if prolonged, would raise National Debt, which, because the latter represents assets of the private sector, would in turn have the direct effect of increasing spending and the demand for money. On the usual, but in this context unhelpful, assumption of a fixed supply of money, the rise in activity and the increased demand for money due to increases in wealth would raise *interest rates*. At some point the monetary tightening would come to dominate the fiscal stimulus. The latter would be crowded out by the former.

What this shows is two things. The first is that, against a fixed money supply, the amount that can be done by fiscal policy is limited, and indeed, attempts to push fiscal relaxation very far under these circumstances would produce undesirable consequences. This is not a conclusion that would surprise a policy maker, nor keep him awake at night. Some policies and policy mixes do not look sensible if pursued too far. The second is that *longer-term* effects should be taken into account. If they exist, this is undeniable. But if fiscal policy has longer-term effects, this is no argument that it should not be used actively in the short term so long as the longer-term feedbacks are understood, and so long as inappropriate financing policies are avoided.

It is true, of course, that some of the longer-term effects of short-term policy could be very awkward to forecast and to deal with, for example if short-term impact effects are later reversed. But in principle, they have little bearing on the debates between those who favour discretion and those who favour more or less fixed rules or norms. Ultimately, this issue must turn on:

(i) the degree of self-stabilization of the economy;
(ii) the skill of the authorities in forecasting economic developments and the effects of policy changes, and in executing policy;
(iii) the degree to which the authorities have other objectives and/or face constraints on their actions;
(iv) the feedback from the commitment to rules or norms (for monetary or fiscal policy) on to economic behaviour, especially via expectations.

The case for norms and rules becomes stronger the greater the degree of self-stabilization of the real economy, and the worse the authorities are at carrying out discretionary policy. A special importance may be assigned to rules or norms if the climate of expectations is favourably affected (i.e. condition (iv), feeding back to condition (i)).

12.3. Measuring Demand Management Policy and its Effects

In order to make any assessment of the impact of demand management policy over the last three decades it is is necessary to be able to measure the stance of policy and to quantify the effects of policy changes on the economy.

It is clear that measuring policy is not likely to be easy. The first difficulty—which is fundamental—is over what is meant by policy. There is usually an implicit reference standard, or 'norm' or 'neutral case', against which the setting of the policy instruments is measured. Sometimes the 'reference standard' is trivially obvious, as, for example, when a tax rate change is measured against the standard of no change in tax rates. But in practice 'no change' in an instrument will frequently *not* be a 'neutral' policy: for example, specific duties and tax thresholds would normally be expected to rise with inflation; government expenditure would be expected to rise in line with the growth of the economy. The implicit standards applied have changed substantially over time.[34]

Greater difficulties are apparent in trying to measure the overall 'stance' of fiscal or monetary policy using summary measures. In the first place, the measures themselves (for example the budget deficit or the money supply) may not correspond closely to the instruments of policy (cf. section 12.2.2). Second, the implicit standards of reference may vary considerably and are highly contentious. For example, fiscal stance might be assessed by looking at the budget deficit against an implicit norm of budget balance (cf. the discussion in section 12.2.10), or a more complex standard (such as the IMF's *cyclically neutral fiscal balance*)[35] might be used. The setting of monetary policy might be looked at in terms of the growth of the money supply as compared with zero growth, growth at the rate of inflation, growth at the rate of growth of nominal GDP, or growth against some explicit or implicit government target. These possibilities amount to focusing attention on, respectively, the nominal money supply, the 'real' money supply, the velocity of circulation, and the deviation from some target. Which, if any, is to be preferred depends upon the underlying model of the economy that is being applied and the purposes to which the measure is put.

Even if policy 'stance' and changes in policy can be adequately defined and measured, there is still the problem of quantifying the effects of policy or policy changes. In principle we are interested in *all* the effects of a particular policy (such as a tax change) on, for example, output, unemployment, the price level, and the balance of payments. In looking at the past, moreover, there were usually a great many policy actions going on, operating with lags, and the separate influences would be difficult to disentangle. A further problem is that some effects, such as those operating through expectations, are very hard to pin down. The enormous difficulties can, perhaps, be brought into focus by posing the question, 'What would have happened to the UK economy if the authorities had not used demand management policy over the last thirty years?'[36] There is no easy answer, but neither is it a question that should be avoided.

---

[34] For example, it used to be common practice to define all government expenditure changes as discretionary rather than viewing them against some normal growth of the economy [33].

[35] Described in IMF, *World Economic Outlook 1982*, App. A3. The concept is further discussed in following sections of this chapter.

[36] More realistically, since some policy instruments *have* to be set by the authorities, the counter-factual (reference) case is what would have happened if tax rates and monetary instruments had been set according to some longer-term set of rules, avoiding an *active* policy. The ambiguities creep in: what longer-term rules should be assumed?

In practice a number of ways of trying to measure the stance of demand management policy and its effects are in common use. We consider, in turn, the use of empirical models, the problems of measuring monetary stance, and summary measures of fiscal policy, such as the budget deficit. The concepts of the cyclically adjusted deficit and the inflation-adjusted deficit—both of increasing importance since the early 1970s as unemployment and inflation rose—are outlined.

12.3.1. The Use of Empirical Models

In principle it can be argued that what is needed is a fully articulated *empirical model* of the economy within which all the difficulties of defining neutral policy settings and quantifying the effects of policy can be sorted out. Though we are a long way from having such an ideal model, empirical macro-econometric models do exist, and, as noted, are used in producing forecasts and in designing policy responses. They can also be used in helping to analyse the past.

One way in which they are useful is in simulating the effects of particular changes in the policy instruments on the economy. Normally, this would be done by constructing some realistic or convenient *base run* as a standard of reference and then examining the difference that would be made by a specified change in policy. Such quantifications can be directly useful in assessing the effects of policy changes in the past (see Chapter 14).

One of the practical lessons from such simulations made on the 'mainstream' forecasting models[37] is that the effects of particular policy changes depend crucially on assumptions made about, for example, the setting of other policy instruments, or about important relationships in the model which the modellers may not be very sure about. Thus the effect of a tax cut on activity would depend on whether monetary targets are assumed to be adhered to and on whether the exchange rate was taken as fixed or allowed to move. It would also depend on assumptions made, for example, about the determinants of wages.[38] There is no unique effect of a policy change, but a whole range of possibilities depending upon the (sometimes rather arbitrary) assumptions made. Other results throw doubt on the use of summary indicators of stance—such as public borrowing. The models suggest that the effects of a given change in public borrowing depend greatly on how it is brought about, for example whether it is brought about by tax changes or expenditure changes and, within these categories, what type of tax or expenditure compenent is varied.[39] Or, looking at it the other way around, for (say) a *given* stimulus to the economy, the *effects on the deficit* depend on how the stimulus is applied. The implication is that (in these models) the public deficit is not always a good indicator of fiscal stance.

These results may suggest that the models should be used to produce more

[37] The Treasury, LBS, or NIESR models could all be described as 'mainstream' neo-Keynesian models.
[38] In using models for forecasting, the 'wage equation' (about which there is much empirical uncertainty) is often overridden, and wages are forecast 'judgementally'. For simulations, however, the assumed equation is of great importance. Sometimes more than one variant is used.
[39] For simulations using the Treasury model see Middleton *et al.* [28].

elaborate analyses of the effects of past policy, for example by comparing the actual course of the economy with the hypothetical path (computed via the model) that would result if the policy instruments had been set to develop according to some longer-term norm.[40] The difference would then show up the effect of policy (as against the norm or reference case assumed).

To insist on evaluating policy in terms of such models, however, has its own drawbacks. The practical difficulties of such exercises are very great. Beyond that, there are two more important difficulties: first, the results are only as good as the model on which the simulations are performed, and the models available are, inevitably, very imperfect. People will disagree, perhaps strongly, on what the underlying model should be, and the data will often not be good enough to discriminate between alternatives. The whole procedure loses much of its practical appeal if the model itself is in doubt. Indeed, the idea that there is one unchanging model is, at best, a convenient working hypothesis: there is every reason to suppose that economic behaviour changes over time.

Second, the expectations of economic agents and their perception of how the authorities will act are part of the economic system. Unless explicitly modelled, relationships fitted over the past will be quite misleading when the policy regime changes (for example from Keynesian policies to monetarist rules of the game). Aspects of behaviour that remained unchanged under a discretionary policy regime, and were incorporated into models as such, might well have been different under a regime of policy rules, thereby invalidating the results of a simulation of such rules on a model based on *actual* past behaviour. The solution to this problem (the Lucas critique [26]) is to go back to the microeconomic foundations of economic behaviour and expectation formulation. But in a macroeconomic policy context, this is a council of perfection. For these and other reasons there is still much to be said for older, cruder methods of assessment, such as relating summary measures of fiscal or monetary 'stance' to the cycle. Though in principle they too would only be appropriate on the basis of particular underlying models, in practice they may be somewhat less 'model-specific'— in part because they are less precise.

12.3.2. Monetary Stance

Particular difficulties are apparent in measuring monetary policy and assessing its impact. The basic reason for the difficulty is clear enough. There exists no articulated and *agreed* empirical model of the channels of monetary influence on the economy. Rather, different schools of thought have stressed different linkages, and hence different indicators of the setting of monetary policy (for example Keynesians tended to focus on interest rates, monetarists on the quantity of money). Moreover, some aspects of monetary policy, such as controls over the extension of credit, or 'moral suasion' (see Chapter 10), are inherently difficult to summarize in a quantitative way. Even if the indicators of policy could be agreed, there would remain much empirical uncertainty over the effects of (say) interest rates or money supply changes on the economy.

---

[40] For example, government expenditure growing with GDP, and with the overall proportionate tax-take constant.

The result of the difficulties is that studies of the importance of monetary policy have tended to evaluate it in a highly judgemental way. Overall assessments of monetary tightness/looseness—or stance—based on a number of different indicators are often informally examined as against movements in the economy,[41] without much overall quantification. This does not mean that monetary policy is unimportant; only that it is hard to measure.

Despite the difficulties described, it is useful to try to assess two different elements of monetary policy. The first is, in effect, the definition of a neutral policy. The second is the assessment of the actual setting of policy in relation to that reference case. In the 1950s and through much of the 1960s, a neutral policy tended to be evaluated by reference to interest rates (though it was not always clear what level was regarded as 'normal') and in terms of normal controls on the banking system and on hire-purchase. Monetary policy was, in effect, assessed as 'tight' if interest rates were above normal and controls stringent. Changes in stance could be similarly assessed. With the rise in inflation from the late 1960s onwards, an implicit reference case or 'norm' of unchanged nominal interest rates began to look far from *neutral*: fixing nominal interest rates as inflation rose would be a highly expansionary policy with falling *real* interest rates. One obvious response would be to change the implicit standard or 'norm' and use a *real* interest rate. Tightness/looseness could then be assessed by looking at whether *real* interest rates were 'high' or 'low' against the standard. This is, in fact, often done.

In practice, the 1970s saw a move toward assessing monetary policy in terms of the *quantity* of money, rather than real interest rates. If the quantity of money were fixed as inflation rose, then this would have almost the opposite effect from that of fixing nominal interest rates—policy would tighten. A fixed quantity of money is not a 'neutral' standard either. A good candidate for a *neutral* monetary policy would be a situation in which the quantity of money rose in line with nominal GDP—i.e. a situation in which the velocity of circulation of money remained unchanged. Monetary tightness/looseness could then be assessed in terms of monetary growth being slower/faster than the growth of nominal GDP—i.e. in terms of velocity tending to rise above normal, or fall below it.[42] (Note that normal velocity may be subject to a time trend or shifts from time to time, and that it would be affected by other variables, such as interest rates.)

There is certainly nothing necessarily *desirable* about a *neutral* stance with (say) money rising in line with nominal GDP. Definitionally, such a situation would be *accommodating*: if inflation rose it would be accommodated in the neutral case by increased money. On the contrary, it may be highly desirable to formulate policy so that it is *non-accommodating* against rises in inflation, and one way in which that could be done would be to formulate a *target* in terms of the (growth of) the nominal money supply. If nominal GDP and nominal money rose in line, then policy would be assessed as neutral according to the velocity

[41] As examples see Kareken [20] and OECD [34].

[42] Movements in velocity are commonly used as part of the overall evaluation of monetary policy, though there is frequently a difficulty in assessing whether a particular change indicates a change in 'tightness' or, alternatively, financial innovation.

criterion. On the other hand, if inflation accelerated, then (assuming the monetary targets were met) the velocity criterion would show a tightening—as it should. Conversely, a fall in inflation against a given target would automatically loosen policy.

The last example illustrates some of the complexities of assessing monetary policy in the 1970s and 1980s. In effect there are three concepts of monetary growth that are important: the actual growth; some concept of a neutral or accommodating stance; and a target. It is natural to think of monetary tightness in terms of the difference between the first two. A target too could be assessed as tight or loose (either *ex post* or against some projected path for inflation and growth) by reference to the neutral case. But the target itself, taken as an indication of the government's intentions, may (for example via expectations) itself affect monetary conditions and, in an extreme case, could itself be taken as an indicator of stance. For example, suppose, in an extreme 'monetarist' world that targets are instantly credible and that both the money supply *and* inflation quickly change when the announced target changes. It would then be found that there was no difference between target, neutral, and actual rates of growth of money. In such a perfect world they would all collapse into one; and the only indicator of monetary policy would be the money supply and its rate of growth. In particular no indicator of monetary tightness would be necessary, since with inflation reacting quickly to money, monetary policy would never be 'tight'. With more sluggish adjustments all three concepts, and the differences between them, are important in the overall assessment of 'stance'.

In practice it is common to go even further and, as well as looking at target monetary growth, actual monetary growth, and velocity,[43] to include both nominal and real interest rates as well as the exchange rate[44] as indicators of monetary stance. This is the procedure adopted in the next chapter in looking at the 1970–83 period. With so many indicators, any overall assessment remains essentially judgemental.

12.3.3. Summary Measures of Fiscal Policy

Fiscal stance too can be, and often is, evaluated in a judgemental way. Largely because the instruments of fiscal policy are more unambiguously defined, however, and because of a consensus (during the 1950s and 1960s) about the underlying income/expenditure model, fiscal effects are (or were taken to be) more easily summarized and measured than those of monetary policy.

One obvious measurement is to estimate the financial effects of *discretionary* tax and expenditure changes. In principle this is a fairly mechanical exercise for each tax or expenditure component identified (e.g. income tax, purchase tax, VAT, levels of pensions). The 'discretion' can be shown against some baseline of 'no policy change'. For taxes the reference case of 'no policy change' might include indexation of specific duties, income tax allowances, and perhaps even some tax bands with inflation.

On the expenditure side the concept of a discretionary change is harder to

---

[43] Or, equivalently, the real money supply in relation to the rate of growth of the economy.
[44] Again, in relation to some implicit norm: e.g. attention might be focused on the 'real' exchange rate.

in down. Unemployment benefit and other social security transfers are affected automatically by the cycle. Also, much of the public expenditure expansion of the post-war period reflected more or less inevitable increases in expenditure as pension schemes and the like matured, or coverage increased (see OECD [32]). In early studies (for example Musgrave and Musgrave [33]) all public expenditure was often treated as 'discretionary'; later writers have tended to define a 'norm' for public expenditure—such as growth in line with potential GDP—and to measure change relative to that standard [3].

The two sides of the accounts, revenue and expenditure, may be put together to give the effects of discretionary policy on the budget surplus or deficit.[45] Apart from the ambiguities about what is meant by discretionary policy,[46] the estimates seldom give much indication of the actual results for revenue and expenditure. In the first place automatic changes in tax or expenditure occur as well, due, for instance, to real growth, for example raising more people's real incomes into higher income tax brackets (fiscal drag), inflation (inflationary fiscal drag), and the cycle.[47] Second, the measures themselves have effects on the economy (for example a tax cut may stimulate output, raising the tax yield, and offsetting some or even all of the initial impact).

The budget position may be looked at directly to see the *ex post* result—which of course includes both the discretionary and automatic effects. Generally some measure of the public sector deficit/surplus is taken to be the best overall summary measure of fiscal positions. There are, however, several versions:

(i) *The actual deficit.* This shows the *ex post* position. It may nevertheless be interesting in showing the degree of *offset* to private sector saving provided by the public sector. In looking at some financial effects the actual deficit may be the most appropriate number.

(ii) *The cyclically adjusted deficit.* The motive behind this concept is to purge the raw figures of temporary fluctuations due to the automatic effects of the cycle. The resulting measure can be regarded as an indicator of the underlying or *structural budget* position; or variations in the adjusted deficit may be regarded as a better measure (than the unadjusted numbers) of *discretionary policy.*

(iii) The *weighted budget deficit.* In constructing this measure, different expenditure categories and tax flows are given different *demand weights.*[48] This concept can also be constructed on a cyclically adjusted basis.

(iv) The *inflation-adjusted deficit.* This takes into account the fact that the figures for the deficit are *distorted* by inflation. One simple procedure is to exclude the 'inflation tax' (see p. 379). The inflation-adjusted deficit may be a better indicator of fiscal stance.

[45] As is commonly done, for example, in official Budget Statements.
[46] In Budget Statements, policy on the expenditure side is often measured against some previous plan or commitment, which makes assessment particularly difficult.
[47] For estimates of some of these effects see Price [38]. Fiscal drag is the reason why most Chancellors in recent years have been able to cut taxes.
[48] For example, public expenditure might have a weight of unity, whereas taxes, paid out of income, some of which would otherwise be saved, have a lower weight. The import content of different components also varies—so they have differing effects on the domestic economy.

All these concepts (and combinations, such as the inflation-adjusted and cyclically adjusted deficit) have their uses, but tend to emphasize different things. The third approach—the weighted deficit—can be seen as justified on the basis of a short-term income/expenditure-type model where different impacts have different multiplier effects.[49] Use of this indicator can be seen as an approximation to the results that might be derived more directly from forecasting models (see section 12.3.1), and for recent years, model-derived estimates are usually to be preferred. The concept serves to remind us that, *in the short term* at least, the effect of a given budget change depends very much on the actual tax and expenditure changes that underlie it.

For other purposes—especially for analyses with a longer-term focus where the weighting of different components may seem inappropriate—the unweighted deficit may be preferred. There are controversial questions, however, over whether deficits should be *cyclically adjusted* and/or *inflation adjusted*. These adjustments are considered in turn.

12.3.4. Cyclical Adjustment

Cyclical adjustment may be justified in a much less model-specific way. At a very basic level it may be desirable to correct for the cycle and other temporary/reversible factors in looking at the budget deficit. This may then give an indication of the structural or underlying budgetary position; an indication which may be useful for a number of purposes. Changes in the underlying or structural position may be taken to indicate changes in fiscal stance, or the 'fiscal impulse',[50] in a given year.

In practice, cyclically adjusted deficits are usually calculated in a number of stages:

(i) The first—often controversial—is to construct a series for maximum feasible, or *potential*, GDP; or alternatively, and better, a series for trend GDP at some *average* utilization of labour and capital. Given this, a series of the *deviations* of actual from trend GDP can be computed.

(ii) The second is to estimate the effects of these deviations on the budget deficit.

(iii) The third, trivially, is to purge the actual budget deficit of cyclical effects by subtracting the estimates under (ii).

There is another way of looking at the procedure which is often illuminating. As discussed at the beginning of this section, measures of policy need to be evaluated, explicitly or implicitly, against some 'reference standard' or 'norm' which is taken as a neutral case. Suppose we set up, as a reference standard, a

---

[49] The measure could be a weighted budget deficit (as described) or the indicator could explicitly allow for multiplier effects. In the latter case the indicator could be larger than the weighted deficit by the overall 'multiplier'. This is now relatively small, not much greater than one, so the practical distinction is not very important. For an indicator which does show the multiplier effects see Hansen [17]. More recent OECD [36] indicators do not include multiplier effects.

[50] This is the term used by the IMF. The guideline concept of the 'cyclically neutral budget' was put forward in Germany by the semi-independent Council of Economic Experts, and later adopted by the IMF. See, for example, Dernberg [11]; also Bispham and Boltho [4], p. 294.

situation in which the economy is at trend levels of output and the budget deficit is zero.[51] Deficits of surpluses which arose simply because the economy was fluctuating about the trend would also be regarded as *neutral*. Comparing the actual deficit with the 'reference case' would then amount to focusing attention on the cyclically adjusted deficit.

The idea of a *cyclically neutral fiscal balance* is explicitly used by the IMF in its calculations of fiscal stance.[52] Basically, the procedure involves defining 'neutral' settings for government expenditure and receipts separately. From some base,[53] it is assumed that it would be 'neutral' for public expenditure to grow in line with *potential* GDP, and for tax receipts to grow with *actual* GDP. Alternatively, in the hypothetical neutral case, expenditure remains constant as a proportion of potential GDP, while taxes remain constant as a proportion of actual GDP. It can be seen that, when the economy deviates from its potential, the 'cyclically neutral' change in the deficit—i.e. the cyclical adjustment factor—simply allows for the overall tax-take to decline in proportion to the cyclical deviation.

Though there are advantages in being explicit about the concept of neutrality or normality being applied, the IMF's procedure can be seen as a particularly simple, indeed crude way, of computing the effects of deviation from potential on the deficit (i.e. stage (ii) above). A possible justification would be that the procedure sets up an especially simple 'reference case', and that no more need be read into it than that. On the other hand, it is desirable that the reference case be as realistic as possible; and it can be argued that better estimates of the effects of deviations from potential or average utilization do exist—for example from simulation studies using macroeconometric models. In fact in 1983 the IMF measures were made more realistic by recognizing that one component of government expenditure—unemployment benefit—also varies with the cycle and defining all movements in unemployment benefit as 'cyclically neutral'.[54]

In the 1970s the procedures of cyclical adjustment became highly controversial, mainly due to the large divergences from potential or average utilization that occurred, and the great increases in unemployment (especially in the early 1980s). It can be appreciated, for example, that if trend output were defined in relation to a figure for unemployment of (say) $2\frac{1}{2}$ per cent—the kind of figure that was often used in the 1960s—the computed cyclical adjustment in the early 1980s (with unemployment of the order of 12 per cent) would be very large.

The problem is not over cyclical adjustment *per se*, but over what baseline of trend output and employment should be used. The best way round the difficulty is to start from first principles and to be explicit about what is being assumed. The primary purpose of cyclical adjustment, it will be recalled, is to

---

[51] In practice, a budget position at trend output which was not zero could be used as a standard of reference. As far as the procedures for cyclical adjustment are concerned this would make little difference.

[52] See IMF, *World Economic Outlook 1982*, App. 3 and Tables 48, 49.

[53] Usually taken as the position in a particular year regarded as 'normal'.

[54] See IMF, *World Economic Outlook 1983*, App. A2, p. 110.

remove the effects of temporary/reversible fluctuations. Thus full or high potential is not the concept required: average unemployment or average capacity utilization would be a more natural and uncontentious baseline. Beyond that, there is an obvious difficulty where recent developments are out of line with past experience (as, for example, they were in 1982 and 1983 with very high levels of unemployment). Here there is really no alternative to making an explicit judgement about what *average* unemployment (or capacity utilization) is likely to be in the *future*—a judgement that involves an element too of a *target level*. Given such a judgement, cyclical adjustment can still be useful in assessing the underlying (or structural) budget position—in spite of the inevitable subjectivity.

The issues appear most clearly if the underlying 'neutral' or 'reference case' is made explicit. There is little dispute that recession and unemployment were a major cause of high deficits in the mid-1970s and early 1980s. The contentious question is whether at the same time *supply potential* fell, or (on another view), the natural rate of unemployment rose. If it did not, and the high unemployment that arose was regarded as a particularly severe but ultimately temporary deviation from normal, then a cyclically neutral stance would have been a substantial increase in the actual budget deficit. But if, for example, supply potential fell in 1974–5 (reflecting perhaps the OPEC shock) then a *neutral* policy would have been to raise taxes and to lower public expenditure in line with the change in supply. Against that concept of a 'neutral' response, an 'unchanged' fiscal policy with rising deficits due to unemployment would appear *expansionary*. The actual rises in budget deficits at that period should not be regarded as cyclically neutral. Similarly, if it were felt that high unemployment was, inevitably, going to continue for a long time, this should be reflected in the standard of reference, and the effects on the budget should not be regarded as cyclical.

12.3.5. Inflation Adjustment

Another serious difficulty in assessing the effects of fiscal policy and of budget deficits in the 1970s is the impact of inflation on the government's budget position. This led to measures of the budget deficit which are 'inflation adjusted' and which (as will be seen in Chapter 13) give a radically different picture from the raw or uncorrected figures.

There are two different issues which are so closely related that they tend to get mixed up. The first is that the government's (or the public sector's) income is *distorted* in times of inflation. A true measure of the deficit should allow for this distortion via some inflation adjustment. Strictly speaking this is a problem in *accounting*. Second, there is a problem of assessing fiscal policy and providing some (perhaps rough and ready) measure of its thrust—a measure of fiscal stance. One possibility is that *inflation-adjusted deficits* are also the best measure of fiscal stance, or at least substantially better than the uncorrected figures. It is this intuition that accounts for some of the confusion between the *measurement* of the public deficit and the *assessment* of stance—in that a single procedure is often used for both jobs. In principle, however, the computation of the 'real' position of the public sector and the assessment of fiscal stance are different issues.

Taking the accounting problem of inflation adjustment first, the basic reason why it is necessary is quite straightforward. The government (or the public sector) has outstanding liabilities denominated in money terms—namely, general government or public sector debt. As inflation proceeds, the real value of these liabilities declines so that, for this reason, the overall financial position of the government improves (the 'inflation tax').[55] This gain is not however computed as income or revenue in the conventional national income accounts—so the public sector's *real* position is mismeasured.[56]

Inflation adjustment consists of estimating this effect and adjusting the figures accordingly. The *inflation-adjusted deficit* is then the actual deficit *minus* the inflation adjustment. It is clear that the correction is substantial. If, for example, public sector debt were taken as 50 per cent of GDP, and inflation were 15 per cent (both realistic figures for much of the 1970s), the adjustment would be no less than $7\frac{1}{2}$ per cent of GDP.[57]

It is reasonable to suppose that if the budget deficit is badly mismeasured then it will be a poor measure of fiscal stance—quite apart from any other defects the deficit may have as a measure of the thrust of fiscal policy. Before the inflation-adjusted deficit can be accepted as preferable, however, further analysis is needed. One question is whether the size of the *actual deficit* itself is affected by inflation—as, for example, it is (via the automatic stabilizers) by recession and unemployment.

In fact there are good reasons to suppose, at least in the longer term, that the actual deficit *will* be affected by inflation, giving *prima facie* grounds for believing that some part at least of the high deficits observed in the 1970s is due to high inflation. Consider, by way of illustration, an economy in which National Debt is half GDP and in which inflation is proceeding at 15 per cent per annum. We have already seen that there is an 'inflation tax' benefitting the government, and 'paid' by the private sector, of $7\frac{1}{2}$ per cent of GDP. But if the inflation is well established and the economy has adapted to it, there is another aspect as well—the *rate of interest* paid on National Debt is likely to be high, reflecting inflation and the inflation tax. This high interest rate—and the associated flow of government expenditure—then compensates, wholly or in part, the private sector for the inflation tax.

In a simplified and 'perfect' world, the extra interest flow due to inflation, affecting nominal but not real interest rates,[58] would exactly compensate the

---

[55] If, for example, the debt at the beginning of the year were £1 billion and inflation were 15 per cent, then, in real terms, the debt would be worth £1/(1 + 0·15) billion at the end of the year. The gain would be (approximately) 15 per cent.

[56] Note that although the public sector gains from the 'inflation tax', the overall effect of inflation must take into account other effects, such as the tendency for nominal interest payments—part of government expenditure—to rise. In a fully adapted economy the government may neither gain nor lose from inflation (see following pages).

[57] The inflation adjustment is analogous to the gearing gain/loss which is taken into account in current cost-accounting methods for companies.

[58] The nominal interest rate (r) would then equal the rate of inflation $(\dot{p})$ plus the real interest rate (r^x) where the real interest rate was taken as given by the fundamentals of the economy, independent of inflation.

private holders of National Debt for the inflation tax,[59] so that there would be no change in the distribution of income between the public and private sectors. The *measured* budget deficit, and the counterpart surplus of the private sector, would, however, be affected—by the extent of the inflation tax. Specifically, the public sector would *appear* to be in deficit, corresponding to the enlarged interest payments due to inflation, and the private sector would *appear* to be in equivalent surplus. The measured deficit of the public sector and the measured surplus of the private sector would both be seriously distorted.

The counterpart to this distortion would be that the public sector would be increasing its liabilities to finance its deficit (for example by selling new gilt-edged stock) which would be accumulated by the private sector. In *real* terms, however, neither public nor private sectors would be altering their position. Another way of seeing the same point is to imagine that all government funding was done in terms of *indexed* securities, which paid only *real* interest. In this case the effects of inflation in boosting nominal interest payments, the deficit of the public sector, and the apparent surplus of the private sector would all disappear.

In this simplified case (with steady inflation) the inflation-adjusted budget deficit is clearly a much better measure of fiscal stance than the ordinary measured deficit. The latter would be simply misleading. In the complex real world, particularly if the government is using demand management policy in a counter-inflationary way, there is still a question as to what meaning should be given to the inflation-adjusted deficits. Much depends on what the fiscal stance is being measured against.

It is useful to go back to the idea of the 'neutral' case, or 'standard of reference', which lies behind any summary measury of fiscal stance. Specifically, there is a question as to what would be a neutral development of the budget deficit in times of inflation. Should no allowance for inflation be made—so that attention is focused on the unadjusted deficit—or should the neutral case be taken as one in which deficits rise to offset the 'inflation tax'? It is the latter case that provides the standard of reference for the inflation-adjusted deficit. But such a baseline could also be described as *accommodating* inflation.[60] Thus inflation-adjusted deficits measure fiscal stance relative to a situation of neutrality or accommodation.

The use of inflation-adjusted concepts of the deficit—or the PSBR—has led to some disquiet (see, for example, Minford [28]), in that focusing on them could be taken to imply an accommodating attitude to inflation. If inflation rose, the nominal deficit would simply rise with it, with no change in the 'real' deficit. In fact this kind of worry confuses two things: the measurement of fiscal stance, and policy prescription. In the situation described, fiscal policy could indeed be said to be accommodating inflation, and that is what the measure would show. There is no presumption, however, that such a policy would be

---

[59] It can be seen that the tax system is bound to mean that this neat result would not hold in practice.

[60] Cf. the discussion in section 12.3.2 of an accommodating monetary stance, and the use of velocity (or sometimes the real money supply) as a measure of monetary tightness. The analogy is close.

esirable, and many would agree that fiscal policy, measured as the inflation-djusted deficit, should be tightened if inflation were to rise. One special case of 'rule' that would do this would be to try to keep the *nominal deficit constant* as nflation rose, implying a tightening of fiscal policy. Thus the objection is not to he use of the inflation-adjusted deficit as a *measure*, but to its use as a *target*.

In the case of the economy which is fully adapted to inflation, a standard of eference in which deficits rise to affect the inflation tax appears entirely easonable: increased nominal interest payments balance the inflation tax and he problem appears to be largely one of distortion of the figures. But what bout the case where nominal interest flows do not fully adapt, where inflation *oes* hurt the private sector and benefit the public sector? (Often this will appear s capital losses to the private sector and gains to the public sector.) Again it is seful to go back to the 'reference case'. In the reference case losses to the rivate sector were offset by rises in the budget deficit—due, for example, to ower taxation or higher expenditures (other than interest). Even from the oint of view of the *behaviour* of the private sector this may not appear neutral if he response to the inflation tax is different than the response to other overnment taxes or expenditures. The question of whether one tax or xpenditure flow 'balances' another is a general problem—which led, for xample, to the concept of the weighted budget deficit discussed earlier. It may e that the inflation tax should be given a *low weight*—perhaps even zero. A zero veight given to the inflation tax would amount to ignoring inflation djustment when assessing fiscal stance and concentrating on the unadjusted igures as more relevant to economic developments.[61]

There is a final point to bring out. There is no reason why fiscal policy should ot be assessed against some other standard than 'accommodation' of inflation. 'or example, the government may have an explicit *target* for inflation. Looking t the actual deficit in relation to the deficit which would be appropriate at *arget* inflation may also be useful in assessing and describing fiscal stance—just s looking at the growth in the money supply against a target is one element in ssessing monetary policy. Moreover the target itself may be assessed as 'tight' r 'loose' in relation to the 'neutral' case, and give some idea of expected levelopments in the price level.

2.3.6. *Public Sector Debt as a Measure of Policy*

As noted earlier in sections 12.2.8 and 12.2.9, budget deficits and variations in he stock of public debt are related by identity so that 'norms' for public orrowing imply norms for the development of public debt and vice versa. ometimes it is useful or convenient to look at summary measures of fiscal tance in terms of the implications for public debt.

The nominal budget deficit is usually looked at against the implicit standard f zero. In 'stock' terms, the equivalent reference case is zero change in the

[61] Using the unadjusted figures amounts to ignoring the inflation tax *and* giving *full weight* to ominal interest flows. An alternative, sometimes used, would be to ignore the inflation tax *and* to et out nominal interest (entirely, or that part that is estimated as due to inflation). The 'adjusted' eficit would then be the actual deficit *minus* all or part of the interest on National Debt. In the fully dapated economy this would closely approximate the true inflation adjustment.

nominal amount of National Debt outstanding,[62] and toleration of government deficits different from zero implies toleration of rises or falls in National
Debt outstanding. The implicit standard of the cyclically adjusted deficit
accepts that cyclical movements in National Debt are (in effect) regarded as
neutral. (It would, of course, be possible to construct a cyclically adjusted series
for National or public sector debt.)

These examples bring out the essential *arbitrariness* of the implicit standard—
which is one of the advantages of looking at the stock data. National Debt has
been far from constant over the period since the war, nor has it shown a steady
trend. The common practice of looking at year-to-year *differences* in budget
deficits (cyclically adjusted or not) as measures of fiscal stance leaves the
question of the normal *level* of deficits to one side. Equivalently, that amounts to
ignoring the trend of National Debt and concentrating on variations about the
trend. (Thus there is an implicit assumption that the trend does not matter very
much, though variations, reflecting short-term fiscal impacts, do.)

The inflation-adjusted deficit (whether cyclically adjusted or not) has as its
'stock' counterpart the real National Debt—i.e. the value of public sector debt
deflated by the price level. The reference case of zero corresponds to no change
in the real National Debt, a standard which can be seen as accommodating
inflation in that rises in the price level are accommodated by rises in debt
outstanding. Again, it would be possible to allow for a trend in National Debt
as the implicit standard of neutrality—which would correspond to a standard
for the inflation-adjusted deficit which was different from zero. Using *differences*
between years in the inflation-adjusted deficit as a measure of fiscal impact
amounts, as before, to focusing on short-term variations and effectively
ignoring longer-term developments in the real public sector debt.

Finally, a particularly convenient reference standard is to look at the
conditions under which National Debt remains constant as a *proportion* of
nominal GDP. This amounts to adjusting for *real growth* as well as for inflation.
Recalling section 12.2.9, a norm for public sector debt as a proportion of
nominal GDP (say α in $W_G = \alpha(\text{NGDP})$, where W_G = public debt) implies, if it
holds over time:

$$-B_G/\text{NGDP} = \alpha(\dot{p} + \dot{y})$$

where $\dot{p}$ = the rate of inflation and $\dot{y}$ = the real rate of growth. That is, the
proportionate deficit of the public sector $(-B_G)/(\text{NGDP})$ is equal to the public
sector debt to NGDP ratio (α) multiplied by the rate of growth of nominal
GDP— the rate of inflation $(\dot{p})$ plus the rate of growth of real output, $(\dot{y})$.

Thus the establishment of a neutral or reference case as one in which the
public sector debt to nominal GDP ratio remained constant would amount to
setting the deficit as in the preceding equation. Within that, $\alpha\dot{p}$ is just the
inflation adjustment previously described. The other term, $\alpha\dot{y}$, reflects the fact
that 'neutrality' has been taken as National Debt moving proportionately to
GDP rather than as constant in real terms. Against such a standard there is an
extra adjustment—the growth adjustment $\alpha\dot{y}$. There is no reason why this
should not be computed, though it is seldom displayed.

---

[62] As noted earlier, there may be problems of reconciliation [39] and over the treatment of
capital gains/losses on existing holdings.

What this shows is that, in practice, looking at real National Debt, or at ational Debt as a proportion of nominal GDP, gives much the same formation as looking at inflation-adjusted figures.[63] Particularly in looking longer-term trends, the debt figures may be illuminating. It needs to be ressed, however, that there is certainly no presumption that α *should* be nstant, or that a focus on longer-term wealth effects is superior to looking at e 'flow effects' summarized by public deficits. (Which focus is better depends 1 the model of economic behaviour that, in principle, underlies any attempt at easurement: unfortunately that model is not known, let alone agreed.) ather, the message from the debt figures often appears to be almost the pposite: the variations in public sector debt over time that have occurred[64] row considerable doubt on the implicit standards which are often applied, plicitly or more often implicitly, in evaluating public sector deficits.

.3.7. *Further Complications*

scal policy has been looked at—as is traditional—in terms of the position of e public sector. Earlier, in looking at the need for stabilization policy, it was ggested that such policy could be seen as offsetting fluctuations (for example desired savings or the demand for financial wealth) emanating from the *ivate* sector, and in discussing economic behaviour it is generally the private ctor that is the focus of interest.

In a closed economy the surpluses or deficits of the public and private sectors irror each other and it does not matter whether fiscal policy is looked at terms of the public deficit or the private surplus. In an economy with foreign ade, however, the correspondence is not exact, and the private surplus differs om the public deficit by the extent of the balance of payments surplus on rrent account. Particularly when shocks—such as an oil crisis—emanate om abroad, it may be better to look at fiscal effects in terms of the private ctor's position rather than in terms of the public sector.

A more general difficulty sometimes arises. If there are known impacts on the ivate sector—such as the effects of a rise in the oil price—then it may appear at the public sector should, in some way, *offset* the known effects. In principle is gives rise to an even more complex standard of reference for evaluating cal (and monetary) policy—the standard of an offsetting policy.[65] Unfortu- itely there is seldom agreement over what an offsetting policy would be.

Finally we note that, in spite of the increased attention given to summary easures of stance in the 1970s and early 1980s, there is another way in which cal and monetary policy might be assessed—by its results. Thus in the short rm the question can be posed as to whether policy action had broadly the fects anticipated, and whether mistakes (such as forecasting errors) were tickly corrected. On this view, the best way to proceed is to chronicle the blicy actions that were taken, the mistakes that were made, and the results. his was, in effect, the way in which demand management policy was often

---

[63] The 'growth adjustment' is normally fairly small, and does not vary much over time.

[64] e.g. National Debt declined from some $2\frac{3}{4}$ times nominal GDP after the war to about half of minal GDP in the 1970s (see Chap. 13).

[65] The standard could even be an 'optimal' policy if such a policy can be established—e.g. by timal control techniques using one of the macroeconometric models.

assessed in the 1950s and 1960s.[66] With the breakdown of consensus in th
1970s, and the much greater problems of inflation and unemployment, interes
in the longer-term effects of fiscal and monetary policy generally increased
and, in part reflecting that, so did the use of relatively crude summary measure
of fiscal and monetary stance. Finally, from the late 1970s onwards, summar
measures of fiscal position (such as the Public Sector Borrowing Requirement)[67]
came, in effect, to be treated as targets for policy. Developments in them had
moreover, marked effects on expectations in domestic and internationa
financial markets.

In the next chapter, whose two sections look at the record of deman
management policy in the 1950s and 1960s, and in the period 1970–83, severa
different approaches are used. In many ways the most important is the record o
events which tries to detail what the authorities were trying to do, and th
extent to which they succeeded. Space permits only the merest sketch of th
history: nevertheless it is difficult to resist the conclusion that, over much of th
period, the demand management instruments produced the short-term result
that were expected and intended. The longer term is a different matter. Th
chief problems in the 1970s were inflation and the extent to which this shoul
be seen as *due* to demand management policy, and/or should be fought b
demand management policy. In the 1970s and early 1980s the question o
whether fiscal policy was tight or loose becomes crucial for any overa
assessment, and different indicators give very different pictures. Whils
unadjusted budget deficits suggest a loose policy, inflation- and cyclicall
adjusted figures indicate a generally tight policy, which became very tight i
the early 1980s.

Bibliography

[1] ALLSOPP, C. J. 'Inflation', in Boltho, A. (ed.) [5].
[2] ALLSOPP, C. J. and JOSHI, V. 'Alternative Strategies for the UK', *National Institut
Economic Review*, 91 (Feb. 1980), 96–103.
[3] ARTIS, M. 'Fiscal Policy for Stabilization', in Beckerman, W. (ed.), *The Labou
Government's Economic Record: 1964–70* (Duckworth, 1972).
[4] BISPHAM, J. and BOLTHO, A. 'Demand Mangagement', in Boltho, A. (ed.) [5], [1
[5] BOLTHO, A. (ed.). *The European Economy: Growth and Crisis* (Oxford University Pres
1982).
[6] BRECH, M. 'Comparative Structures and Properties of 5 Macroeconomic Models
the UK', National Economic Development Office Economic Working Paper, No. 1
(1983).
[7] BUITER, W. H. 'Measurement of the Public Sector Deficit and its Implications f
Policy Evaluation and Design', *IMF Staff Papers*, 30/2 (June, 1983).
[8] CAIRNCROSS, A. *Britain's Economic Prospects Reconsidered* (George Allen and Unwi
1970).
[9] CAIRNCROSS, F. (ed.). *Changing Perspectives on Economic Policy* (Oxford Universi
Press, 1981).
[10] CAVES, R. E. (ed.). *Britain's Economic Prospects* (George Allen and Unwin, 1968

[66] The classic example is Dow [12].
[67] Related to but not identical with the Public Sector Financial Deficit.

1] DERNBERG, T. 'Fiscal Analysis in the Federal Republic of Germany: The Cyclically utral Budget', *IMF Staff Papers* (Nov. 1975).

2] DOW, J. C. R. *The Management of the British Economy, 1945–60* (Cambridge University ess, 1964).

3] FELLNER, W. *et al. The Problem of Rising Prices* (OECD, Paris, 1964).

4] FFORDE, J. 'Setting Monetary Objectives', *Bank of England Quarterly Bulletin* (June, 83), 200–8.

5] FRIEDMAN, M. 'The Role of Monetary Policy', *American Economic Review* **58**/1 968), 1–17.

6] —— —— Memorandum in House of Commons [19].

7] HANSEN, N. *Fiscal Policy in Seven Countries, 1955–65* (OECD, 1969).

8] House of Commons. *Third Report from the Treasury and Civil service Committee: Monetary licy* HC (1980–1), 163, I, II, III.

9] —— —— *Memoranda on Monetary Policy* HC (1979–80) 720 and HC (1979–80) 720-.

0] KAREKEN, J. H. 'Monetary Policy', in Caves [10].

1] KENNEDY, M. C. 'The Economy as a Whole', in Prest, A. R. and Coppock, D. J. ds.). *The UK Economy: A Manual of Applied Economics*, 7th edn. (Weidenfeld and icholson, 1978).

2] KEYNES, J. M. *The General Theory of Employment, Interest and Money* (Macmillan, 36).

3] —— —— *How to Pay for the War* (Macmillan, 1940).

4] LAURY, J. S. E., LEWIS, G. R., and ORMEROD, P. A. 'Properties of Macroeconomic odels of the UK Economy: A Comparative Study', *National Institute Economic Review*, ; (Feb. 1978).

5] LITTLE, I. D. M. Review of Dow [11], *Economic Journal* (Dec. 1966).

6] LUCAS, R. E. 'Econometric Policy Evaluation: A Critique', *Journal of Monetary onomics*, Supplement 1 (1976).

7] McCRACKEN *et al. Towards Full Employment and Price Stability* (OECD, 1977).

8] MIDDLETON, P. E., MOWL, C. J., ODLING-SMEE, J. C., and RILEY, C. J. 'Monetary argets and the Public Sector Borrowing Targets' (City University, London, 1979).

9] MILLER, M. 'Inflation-Adjusting the Public Sector Financial Deficit: easurements and Implications for Policy', in Kay, J. (ed.), *The 1982 Budget* (London, 82).

0] MILLER, M. H. and BABBS, S. 'The True Cost of Debt Service and the Public Sector nancial Deficit', Mimeo (Apr. 1983).

1] MINFORD, A. P. L. Memoranda in House of Commons [18], [19].

2] MINFORD, A. P. L. and PEEL, D. *Rational Expectations and the New Macroeconomics* Martin Robertson, 1983).

3] MUSGRAVE, R. A. and MUSGRAVE, P. B. 'Fiscal Policy', in Caves [10].

4] OECD. *The Role of Monetary Policy in Demand Management* (Paris, 1975).

5] —— *Public Expenditure Trends* (Paris, June, 1978).

6] —— *Budget Indicators, Economic Outlook* Occasional Studies (July, 1978).

7] PHILLIPS, A. W. 'The Relationship Between Unemployment and the Rate of hange of Money Wages in the United Kingdom, 1861–1957', *Economica*, NS, **25**/100 958), 283–99.

8] PRICE, R. W. R. Chap. 4 in Blackaby, F. (ed.), *British Economic Policy, 1960–74* Heinemann, 1978).

9] REID, D. J. 'Public Sector Debt', *Economic Trends* (May, 1977), 100–9.

0] TAYLOR, C. T. and THREADGOLD, A. R. *Real National Savings and its Sectoral omposition*, Bank of England Discussion Paper, No. 6 (Oct. 1979).

1] HM Treasury. *Background to the Government's Economic Policy* in House of Commons 8].

13

Demand Management in Practice

C. J. ALLSOPP and D. G. MAYES

13.1. Introduction

The previous chapter looked at some of the main theoretical aspects of demand management, and in particular at the problems of measuring and assessing the impact of monetary and fiscal policy. This chapter now goes on to look at how demand management has worked in practice in the UK since the war. It does not attempt to give a year-by-year chronological account of all that happened such an approach would require a book in itself. Rather, it attempts to look at the main factors in the development and changing nature of demand management in this period, linking them to the more theoretical consideration developed in Chapter 12.

This chapter none the less remains predominantly chronological in that the next section looks at the 1950s and 1960s, and the following three sections at the period 1970–83. This division is more or less dictated by the changes that occurred between the two periods—changes in the behaviour of the economy the shocks to which it was subject, and in the thinking behind demand management. It also has the analytical advantage that such questions a whether demand management was, in practice, stabilizing or not can be discussed in their proper context, of the 1950s and 1960s in this case. The early period then forms a background to the much greater problems of assessing policy in the 1970s. The influence of expectations is discussed both in the context of the earlier period and, in a more technical sense, in the period 1970–83.

13.2. Demand Management in the 1950s and 1960s

Few economists or politicians looking forward immediately after the ending of the Second World War would have expected economic policy to be easy. The immediate problem was to return the economy from a wartime footing to normal peacetime development, involving the reabsorption of nearly a quarter of the labour force, the restructuring of trade patterns, and the progressive dismantling of controls and other restrictions on economic activity.

In the event, the period of reconstruction was completed remarkably smoothly under the post-war Labour governments of 1945–51—at least

mpared with the dislocation and inflation following the First World War.
is phase involved a great deal of purposeful intervention in the economy of
e detailed kind possible (indeed inevitable) whilst wartime controls continued.
also involved a major devaluation of the pound relative to the dollar of 30 per
nt in 1949, which was judged necessary if direct controls on exports and
ports and on sterling were to be reduced.[1] Clearly, these policies had major
ects both on *supply* and on aggregate demand—as well as on their sectoral
mposition.

At this time, the role of demand management policy was, as it had been in
rtime, essentially subsidiary. It was needed to ensure that, in aggregate,
mands on the system were neither excessive nor deficient.[2] To this end,
ccessive Labour Chancellors pursued fairly active budgetary policies.
onetary policy was not used actively. The wartime policy of 'cheap money'
s continued, with Bank Rate remaining at 2 per cent.

The era of demand management really starts, however, in the early 1950s
er the further shock of the Korean war, which led to a sharp increase in
flation (most obviously commodity price inflation, but followed by rapid
ge increases) and military expenditure at the expense of the civilian
onomy. By about 1952 or 1953, however, the structures of production and
mand had largely returned to a peacetime footing, and direct controls were
ing rapidly dismantled. The claim that an active policy of managing
mand would lead to the 'maintenance of a high and stable level of
ployment'[3] was about to be tested.

2.1. The Record

e experience of the 1950s and 1960s suggests both successes and failures.
ble 13.1 shows the development of some of the major economic variables
er the period. On the positive side, *unemployment* was kept very low during the
50s, and rose only a little during the 1960s. Indeed, average levels of
employment were far *lower* than the architects of demand management
licy had dared to hope for.[4] On the other hand, as the table shows
amatically, the story was one of successive cycles of 4–5 years' duration.
though, compared with the interwar years, and with earlier periods, the
cle was shortened and much attenuated, it was certainly not eliminated.
emand management appeared unable to 'fine tune' the economy. What came
be known as the 'stop–go' cycle remained. Table 13.1 also shows that balance
payments swings (often exacerbated by sterling crises) accompanied the
ings in activity. Likewise, the record on inflation was patchy. The 1950s

[1] The devaluation was also required in that existing policies did not appear to be able to
minate the deficit with the US. Generally, however, the desire to reduce controls progressively
ms to have been the most important factor, particularly in explaining the size of the devaluation,
dely thought, even at the time, to be excessive.

[2] This was a period in which many goods were directly rationed. Even with rationing in force,
wever, it is necessary to control aggregate demand if inflation is not to be generated in non-
tioned markets and to avoid generally stimulating the black market.

[3] *White Paper on Employment Policy* (1944).

[4] The original Beveridge Report had envisaged 'full employment' with unemployment at about
er cent of the labour force. This was later reduced to 3 per cent.

TABLE 13.1. *The UK Record 1950–1972*

	Growth* (% per annum)	Inflation† (% per annum)	Unemployment‡ (%)	Balance of payments§ (% GDP at market prices)
1950	3·1	2·9	1·6	2·4
1951	3·0	9·0	1·3	−2·5
1952	−0·4	9·4	2·2	1·0
1953	4·0	3·1	1·8	0·9
1954	4·0	1·7	1·5	0·7
1955	3·9	4·6	1·2	−0·8
1956	1·3	5·0	1·3	1·0
1957	1·6	3·6	1·6	1·1
1958	−0·3	3·2	2·2	1·6
1959	4·0	0·6	2·3	0·7
1960	5·5	1·1	1·7	−0·9
1961	2·6	3·3	1·6	0·2
1962	1·1	4·2	2·1	0·5
1963	3·9	2·0	2·6	0·4
1964	5·6	3·2	1·7	−1·1
1965	2·9	4·8	1·5	−0·1
1966	1·8	3·9	1·6	0·3
1967	2·1	2·4	2·5	−0·7
1968	4·4	4·8	2·5	−0·6
1969	2·5	5·4	2·5	1·1
1970	2·0	6·3	2·6	1·6
1971	1·5	9·4	3·4	2·0
1972	2·7	7·3	3·8	0·4

* At factor cost, average estimate.
† Retail Price Index, 'all items'.
‡ Unemployed as percentage of employed and unemployed.
§ Current balance as percentage of GDP at market prices.

Sources: *Economic Trends; British Labour Statistics; Annual Abstract of Statistics.*

started with very high inflation during the Korean war boom. This w
successfully contained and price rises declined rapidly [1]. But even in t
1950s, 'creeping inflation' at about 3–4 per cent per annum remained, whi
was much higher than in most previous periods of peacetime expansion. In t
1960s, inflation started to rise—a rise which accelerated in the early 1970
  The tendency for inflation to accelerate is one indication of longer-ter
deterioration in overall performance. A related difficulty was worseni
international competitiveness, which first (under the fixed exchange ra
system of Bretton Woods) exacerbated balance of payments difficulties a
then, in 1967, necessitated a 15 per cent devaluation of the pound. Finally,
the early 1960s, it was apparent that economic growth in Britain (though hi

the UK's own past standards) was pitiful in comparison to growth in other
estern European economies and Japan (see Chapters 16 and 17).

2.2 The Practice of Policy

roughout the 1950s and 1960s demand management policy was used
remely actively, with interventions of a monetary or fiscal kind often
curring several times in a year.[5] In the main, reliance was placed on fiscal
licy with changes in the Bank Rate (to which other short-term interest rates
re tied) being primarily used not for demand management purposes, but to
courage short-term inflows to finance the balance of payments. Generally,
licy makers at the time tended to play down the direct effects of interest rates
demand and activity, emphasizing instead the general state of liquidity and
dit in the economy. On this view—endorsed by the extremely influential
dcliffe Report in 1959[6]—demand could nevertheless be influenced (es-
cially as to timing) by monetary measures such as changes in hire-purchase
gulations, 'moral suasion' on the banks, calls for, or release of, special
posits, etc. Within fiscal policy, the emphasis was (for most of the period) on
cretionary changes in tax rather than expenditure. It was felt that public
enditure was not usually an appropriate instrument for short-term
bilization policy, although public expenditure changes were, nevertheless,
important source of variation in the economy.

This degree of activism, together with the tendency established early on for
licy to be framed as 'package deals' of monetary and fiscal measures, poses
ere problems for any overall assessment, or even description, of policy. The
50s and 1960s were the era of attempted 'fine-tuning' and the authorities
re reacting almost as if they were, to use the metaphor of the times, steering a
ip' buffeted by various shocks (the Korean war boom, Suez) to avoid various
stacles (balance of payments crises, inflationary pressure, excessive unem-
oyment). It is almost impossible, even with hindsight, to assess what would
ve happened if demand management policy had not been used, or had been
d less actively.

The problems of the 'stop–go' cycle and of the Labour Governments'
empts after 1964 to break out of it have been much analysed.[7] One of the first
ncerns to surface was whether demand management policy in the 1950s was
bilizing or whether, on the contrary, it had served to exacerbate the stop–go
cle. Dow [15], for example, concluded that it had been destabilizing. The
asons put forward as to why it might have been destablilizing were various,
nging from simple error (for example on forecasts), to over-ambition causing

For example, Bank Rate, which (apart from a brief rise, then fall, during 1939) had been
nstant at 2 per cent from 1932 to 1951, was changed twenty-four times by the Conservative
ministrations of 1951–64, and no less frequently by the subsequent Labour Governments. Hire-
rchase regulations were altered in all but a few years throughout the 1950s and 1960s. Other
netary measures, such as requests to the banks to limit advances and (after 1960) calls for special
posits, were frequent [23]. Fiscal changes were not confined to the annual Budget, but were
plemented by additional action in 'mini budgets' or, in the 1960s, by use of the 'regulator'.
⁶ Committee on the Workings of the Monetary System: Report (Cmnd. 827 HMSO, 1959).
⁷ For a full account of the period up to 1960, see Dow [15]. The period from 1951–67 is reviewed
for example, Musgrave and Musgrave [31]. For a general account of UK policy, see Surrey [39].

swings between external and internal objectives, to the cynical view that tⱨ swings in policy reflected the electoral cycle.[8] The important point to briⱨ out, however, is that complaints about the stop–go cycle were *not* directe against the idea of demand management, or even against fine-tuning. Tⱨ general thrust was to try to improve the practice of demand management ⱨ widening the range of the instruments, by better forecasting procedures, and ⱨ proper attention to lags, etc.

Though the main concern in the 1950s was to improve the conduct of polic 　by the late 1950s—and certainly by the early 1960s—an altogether moⱨ serious set of worries came to the fore. This was that the practice of demaⱨ management would turn out to be *incompatible*, in the longer term, with othⱨ objectives, such as stable prices or, under fixed exchange rates, with balance ◖ payments equilibrium. As noted in Chapter 12, this worry had never real been absent. The early demand managers always thought that success would ⱨ conditional on success in other areas, such as the balance of payments anⱨ especially, inflation. They were well aware of the 'orthodox' view, quiesceⱨ but never absent, that Keynesian-type policies would break down wit inflation.[9]

The concern with inflation led to experiments with incomes policies (real from Selwyn Lloyd's pay pause in 1961 onwards). But in the UK, tⱨ developing incompatibility tended to be perceived much more starkly as problem with the balance of payments and the defence of sterling. The stop–ⱨ cycle came to be described in these terms—as swings in policy betweⱨ incompatible objectives [31] and, with the developing trade-off ideas of tⱨ time, many suggested, from the early 1960s onwards, that compatibiliⱨ between external and internal balance could only be restored by devaluatioⱨ The prescription of devaluation was seen as freeing the demand managemeⱨ instruments for their proper purpose of pursuing high employment aⱨ growth.[10]

In the event, devaluation was delayed. The Labour Government attempte to square the circle by a combination of planning for growth (the Nationⱥ Plan) and incomes policy to affect competitiveness. Demand managemeⱨ policy became even more closely geared to external considerations (both befoⱨ

---

[8] e.g. the tax cut in 1955, which with hindsight appears particularly inappropriate, was follow within a month by a general election. After the election, policy was sharply reversed. Policy wⱨ expansionary before the 1959 general election (justifiably so, given the recession in 1958, but ⱨ stimulus, especially from public expenditure, was greatly overdone). Policy was agⱥ expansionary prior to the 1964 general election.

[9] The concern with the possible incompatibility of demand management and price stability clearly evident in an international report (Fellner *et al.* [16]) presented to the OEEC (later OECⱨ in 1961. The majority felt that wage-bargaining mechanisms would have to be brought into ⱨ compass of economic policy. The minority (Fellner and Lutz) favoured less ambitious targets a (slightly) higher levels of unemployment. See also Allsopp [1].

[10] It is notable that, in the 1960s, the 'incompatibility' was seen as between internal and exterⱨ balance rather than as the more fundamental problem of a conflict between inflation (accelerating inflation) and prolonged high activity. To an extent, price and cost pressures wⱨ treated as 'exogenous'. Many recognized, however, that devaluation would need to accompanied by measures to control inflation, such as incomes policy.

the devaluation of 1967, and afterwards when trying to make it work) and the National Plan was effectively jettisoned to protect the pound.

The experience of the 1960s raises a lot of questions, some of which are pursued by this chapter. Demand management policy continued to be used, but in an increasingly constrained environment. If anyone had ever believed that demand management policy would solve all economic problems at once, they were disappointed. In a way, there was a return to some of the perceptions of the reconstruction period. Demand management took its place as one amongst many instruments of policy: a necessary but far from sufficient condition for success. But in spite of the constraints on policy, unemployment in the 1960s, though a little higher than in the 1950s, was still very low by the standards of the interwar period or of the 1970s.[11] And the growth of output was no worse than in the 1950s either. Inflation, on the other hand, did accelerate—raising again, but now in much more acute form, the question of the compatibility of employment and price objectives. And there was another question too which was beginning to be posed: *was* it demand management that accounted for (relatively) high growth and high employment since the war? The difficulty of breaking out into even more rapid expansion could be taken as indicating that there were more fundamental forces at work. Perhaps growth and high employment had little to do with demand management, reflecting instead the natural buoyancy of the economy, and permissive monetary and fiscal policies served just to accommodate inflation.

3.2.3. Measuring Policy and its Effects in the 1950s and 1960s

It has been seen that policy actions of both monetary and fiscal kinds were taken very frequently in the 1950s and 1960s. As noted in Chapter 12 (pp. 384–6), the way in which *monetary policy* is assessed has changed greatly over the last decades. In the 1950s and 1960s the main indicator of policy—taken also to be the main instrument—was the level of interest rates, particularly short-term interest rates which were effectively tied to Bank Rate. Interest rate measures (expecially when used in the restrictive direction) were, however, generally accompanied by controls over the banking system, changes in hire-purchase regulations, and often fiscal measures as well. In practice the main objective of monetary policy tended to be the defence of sterling.

A result of the difficulties of measurement (see Chapter 12, pp. 384–6) is that studies of the effects of monetary policy on the cycle in the 1950s and 1960s usually refer vaguely to monetary tightening or loosening without much overall quantification. Figure 13.1 indicates movements in Bank Rate and their relationship with the cycle. The features that stand out are, first, the general rise in short-term nominal interest rates over the two decades—a movement which is paralleled by long rates (the rate on $2\frac{1}{2}$ per cent Consols rose from around 4 per cent in the first half of the 1950s to about 7 per cent in 1967 and 9 per cent in the early 1970s). The second is that most of the dramatic rises reflected sterling crises—in 1957, in 1961, in 1964, in 1966, and again in 1967

[11] The rise of unemployment in the late 1960s—to about 2–$2\frac{1}{2}$ per cent—was nevertheless an important source of concern at the time. See Cairncross [12], especially Chap. 1 (Matthews) and 'discussion'.

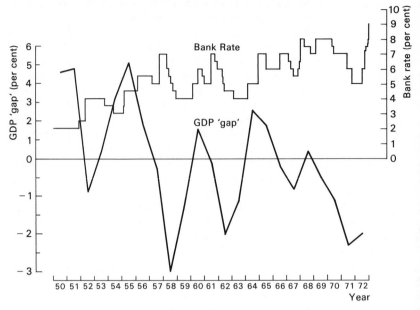

FIG. 13.1. Bank Rate and the Economic Cycle.

before devaluation. The continuing monetary tightness in the late 1960 (paralleled by fiscal restraint) reflected the desire of the authorities to make devaluation work.

The active role played by monetary policy and the tendency for fiscal and monetary actions to be framed as 'package deals' is a complicating factor surprisingly often ignored, in looking at the overall successes and failures c demand management policy over this period.

Turning to *fiscal policy*, Table 13.2 shows the sector balances over the period including the balance of the public sector. Although this is generally in defici (on average by some 2–3 per cent of GDP), most of this can be accounted for b borrowing by the nationalized industries; the position of genera government[12]—often regarded as a better indicator of fiscal policy—is neare to balance. A feature of the table is the substantial rise over the period i accumulation by the personal sector (from negative figures in the early 1950s which is approximately mirrored in the position of the company sector whos surplus declines. The variation in the public sector's position is not very marke from the mid-1950s onwards until the very large swing to surplus in 1969 an 1970. The counterpart to the fiscal tightening is seen in the company secto which moved sharply to deficit.

[12] The public sector includes general government and public corporations. General governme comprises central government and local authorities. The average deficit for public corporatio over the whole period 1950–72 was 1·85 per cent of GDP.

TABLE 13.2. *Sector Balances, 1950–1972*
(% of GDP at market prices)

	Public sector	Personal sector	Company sector*	Overseas sector
1950	2·7	− 2·9	3·8	− 3·7
1951	− 1·7	− 4·0	3·2	2·5
1952	− 3·5	− 0·5	4·9	− 0·8
1953	− 4·2	− 0·9	5·8	− 0·8
1954	− 2·4	− 2·1	5·2	− 0·7
1955	− 2·1	− 1·5	2·8	0·8
1956	− 2·6	—	3·6	− 1·0
1957	− 2·4	− 0·1	3·6	− 1·1
1958	− 2·0	− 0·6	4·1	− 1·6
1959	− 2·3	− 0·3	3·3	− 0·7
1960	− 2·8	1·1	0·8	0·9
1961	− 2·7	2·2	0·7	− 0·2
1962	− 1·8	1·7	0·6	− 0·5
1963	− 2·7	1·6	1·5	− 0·4
1964	− 2·8	1·8	—	1·1
1965	− 2·2	2·7	− 0·6	—
1966	− 2·2	3·0	− 0·4	− 0·3
1967	− 3·6	2·2	0·8	0·7
1968	− 2·2	1·1	0·5	0·6
1969	1·0	1·5	− 1·4	− 1·1
1970	1·3	2·8	− 2·5	− 1·6
1971	− 0·5	0·8	1·7	− 2·0
1972	− 2·4	2·2	0·6	− 0·4

* Includes financial and industrial companies as well as the residual error which has
een (somewhat arbitrarily) assigned to companies.

ource: *Economic Trends*, Annual Supplement (1983).

Table 13.3 shows the general government balance together with estimates of
the automatic effects of the cycle, and the cyclically adjusted deficit. Though
the adjustment procedure is crude, the variations in unemployment and in the
eviations of actual GDP from potential GDP (the GDP 'gap') in the 1950s and
960s, also shown in Figure 13.1, were relatively small, and the overall picture
ould probably not be much affected by making more sophisticated estimates
f the effects of the cycle. The outstanding features are that the deficit, whether
yclically adjusted or not, does not—except at the very beginning of the period
nd in 1960–70—vary greatly, and that what variation there is does not
orrelate in an offsetting way with the cycle. The interpretation of these
pparently paradoxical results is further examined in the following pages.

There is another indicator of the overall thrust of fiscal policy that (as
iscussed in Chapter 12, pp. 377–80 and 393–5) can also be examined—the

TABLE 13.3. *Measures of Budget Deficit*
(% of GDP at market prices)

	GDP 'gap'*	General government financial balance	Cyclically neutral balance	Cyclically adjusted balance
1950	2·3	4·0	0·8	3·2
1951	2·4	0·2	0·8	− 0·6
1952	− 0·9	− 1·8	− 0·3	− 1·5
1953	0·2	− 2·6	0·1	− 2·7
1954	1·6	− 1·0	0·5	− 1·5
1955	2·6	0·2	0·8	− 0·6
1956	0·9	− 0·7	0·3	− 1·0
1957	− 0·2	0·1	− 0·0	0·1
1958	− 3·0	0·5	− 0·9	1·4
1959	− 1·3	0·1	− 0·4	0·4
1960	0·8	− 1·0	0·3	− 1·3
1961	− 0·1	− 0·7	0·0	− 0·7
1962	− 2·0	0·0	− 0·6	0·6
1963	− 1·1	− 1·4	− 0·3	− 1·1
1964	1·3	− 1·1	0·4	− 1·5
1965	0·9	− 0·5	0·3	− 0·8
1966	− 0·2	− 0·0	0·7	− 0·7
1967	− 0·8	− 1·0	− 0·3	− 0·7
1968	0·2	− 0·5	0·1	− 0·5
1969	− 0·5	2·1	− 0·2	2·3
1970	− 1·1	3·0	− 0·5	3·5
1971	− 2·3	1·4	− 0·9	2·3
1972	− 2·0	− 1·3	− 0·7	− 0·6

* Proportionate deviation of actual from potential GDP, adjusted so that average gap, 1950–72, is zero.

Sources: GDP 'gap' figures from OECD (1972); general goverment financial balance from *Economic Trends*, Annual Supplement (1983); cyclical adjustment factors: authors' estimates.

variation in the stock of public sector debt. Figure 13.2 shows variations in *National Debt*,[13] in nominal money value and as a proportion of GDP, over a long period since 1855. Looking at the nominal amount outstanding it can be seen that the rise over the 1950s and 1960s was relatively modest, confirming that the budget (of central government) was not greatly in deficit. Indeed, the difference between the experience in the 1950s and 1960s, and the experience of

[13] The correspondence between the 'flow' deficit of general government and the stock concept of National Debt is not exact. In the first place, coverage differs—National Debt figures exclude local authority borrowings. Beyond this there are other problems of valuation and reconciliation (see Reid [35]). National Debt figures are, however, a reasonable proxy for the 'stock' effects of government borrowing and are available over a long period.

he interwar period—when the 'Treasury View' was that the budget should be balanced—is not very great. The dramatic change occurred in the 1970s as inflation accelerated and deficits rose.

The lower half of Figure 13.2, the ratio of National Debt to GDP, apparently tells a completely different story. The major rises in the real amount of debt outstanding in the two world wars is readily apparent, with National Debt peaking at about $2\frac{3}{4}$ *times* GDP after the Second World War. After that, there was a very rapid reduction during the 1950s and 1960s to reach a figure of about half of GDP by the mid-1970s. In a mechanical sense, the proportionate reduction was due to both real growth and to inflation. From this point of view, fiscal policy in the 1950s and 1960s seems, perhaps, surprisingly conservative.

As explained in Chapter 12 (pp. 379–80), focusing attention on the ratio of National Debt to GDP is similar to looking at deficit figures which are adjusted for *inflation* and *growth*. In the early 1950s, actual deficits would have had to be very high to maintain the National Debt/GDP ratio constant against real growth of $2\frac{1}{2}$–3 per cent per annum. (Indeed, if the National Debt/GDP ratio were 2, and growth were 3 per cent per annum, public deficits of some 6 per cent of GDP would have been necessary to maintain the National Debt/GDP ratio constant without making any allowances for inflation: for that to be covered' as well, even at the creeping rates of the 1950s and 1960s, further deficits of perhaps 8 per cent would have been required in the early part of the period.) Thus the debt figures indicate that through the 1950s and 1960s, the budget was in large *inflation- and growth adjusted* surplus.

There is, of course, nothing in the least sacrosanct or desirable about a constant National Debt/GDP ratio. The huge nominal deficits that would have been implied by such a policy after the war were never needed, and would probably never have been tolerated. Indeed, it can be argued that National Debt was excessive after the war, and that it was right that it should be paid off. From a demand management point of view, high levels of debt (which equal high levels of financial wealth held by the private sector) perhaps directly stimulated spending, necessitating a relatively restrictive fiscal policy to avoid excess demand. Certainly the very low level of personal savings—and the negative accumulation of financial assets (see Table 13.2)—in the early 1950s would be consistent with that view. Nevertheless the fact that, in the UK, the pursuit of very active demand management policies was consistent with such massive reductions in the proportionate amount of National Debt is interesting, suggesting as it does that public policy was not quite as expansionary as sometimes assumed. This is the more true as the period also saw a large amount of public sector capital formation, which—by analogy with the private sector—might appropriately be financed by borrowing.

13.2.4. Was Policy Stabilizing?

The question of whether policy was or was not stabilizing over the 1950s and 1960s is not just of historical interest. The perception that policy had been destabilizing and that 'fine-tuning' had failed was one of the factors that led to marked change in the direction of policy in the 1970s.

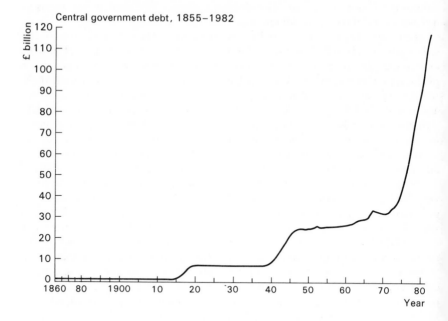

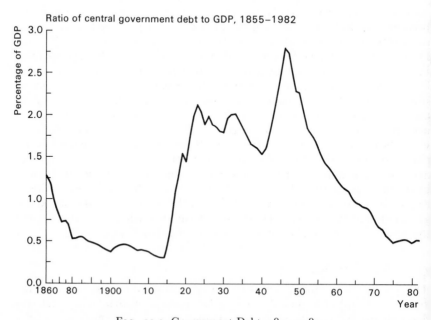

FIG. 13.2. Government Debt, 1855–1982.

Dow [15] suggested, in a famous passage[14] that policy had contributed to the fluctuations in the 1950s—a judgement that was challenged, at the time, by Little [26]. Subsequent studies have continued the debate. Matthews (in [8]) argued that too little attention had been given to endogenous cyclical tendencies which would tend to exonerate the policy makers. The Brookings Study [31] suggested policy was destablizing—a conclusion which was also challenged.[15] Most important of all was a study by Hansen [20] for the OECD, which looked at the experience of seven countries. The general conclusion was that fiscal policy had been highly effective in moderating fluctuations in economic activity—*except in the UK*. In the UK, according to his (admittedly crude) measures, policy had exacerbated the cycle. This conclusion too has been challenged by Boltho [6] who finds that if nationalized industries are excluded, then policy was 'stabilizing'—a conclusion that is strengthened if the trends used by Hansen are replaced by a more satisfactory series for potential output. Nevertheless, by comparison with other countries, the performance of UK policy (especially in the period 1955–65) undoubtedly remains very poor.[16]

The experience of the 1950s and 1960s can also be looked at in terms of the adjusted and unadjusted budget deficits shown in Table 13.3. The unadjusted figures, whilst they show considerable variation (confirming the tolerant attitude of the authorities referred to above) do not correlate in a counter-cyclical way with the cycle. The idea that demand management policy would work by offsetting swings in the private sector's desire to accumulate financial assets is not borne out over this period in the UK. The adjusted figures, a better measure of discretionary policy, are if anything negatively correlated with the gap between potential and actual GDP. On the face of it the destabilizing, or at least non-stabilizing, character of UK policy is confirmed.

But there are several major objections to taking this conclusion at face value. The first, stressed by many commentators, is that the authorities may not have intended to stabilize output in the way assumed. One reason could have been considerations of electoral gain.[17] Another could have been perfectly sensible reactions to shocks, such as the Suez crisis. And generally, as seen earlier, there may have been a developing conflict of objectives (between internal and external balance) which led in the event to actions which, normally judged, appear destabilizing. An example, clear from Tables 13.2 and 13.3, is the *intended* deflation in 1968–9 to try to make devaluation work: the causal story runs from the external requirement, to the budget tightening, to the cycle, rather than the budget deficit being determined in the light of the cycle. (It would only take a few such actions to produce a negative correlation between the budget deficit and the GDP gap.)

There is, indeed, evidence from Budget Statements and official forecasts that

[14] He wrote '. . . budgetary and monetary policy failed to be stabilising, and must on the contrary be regarded as having been positively destabilising' ([15], p. 384).

[15] See Matthews, Solow, Worswick, and Caves in Cairncross [12].

[16] It is notable that, according to Boltho, while all the other six countries investigated show a sharp fall in their success in 1966–77 (compared with 1955–65), the UK's performance improves.

[17] See the remarks of Lord Roberthall in Cairncross [12].

policy makers, over the period, got the result that they (albeit perhaps mistakenly) wanted. Table 13.4, derived from Kennedy [24], whilst subject to obvious qualifications[18] certainly suggests a degree of success. The major errors appear to have been in 1959, when output was under-forecast, and in 1962, when the direction of change was wrongly assessed.

The second point is that the failure to get rid of short-term fluctuations— whether they were intended or not—leaves open the question of the medium- or longer-term effects of demand management policy. None of the studies referred to can throw much light on what would have happened in the absence of demand management. Would growth have been much as experienced; or would major cumulative movements have occurred—perhaps leading to

TABLE 13.4. *Short-Term Targets and Forecasting Errors, UK, 1955–1972*

	Target use of potential output* (%)	Forecast and target change in GDP from year earlier† (%)	Actual change in GDP from year earlier‡ (%)	Error (forecast less actual) (%)
1955 (year)	99	2·9	3·7	− 0·8
1956 ,,	98	1·1	1·3	− 0·2
1957 ,,	87	1·3	1·6	− 0·3
1958 ,,	95	− 0·4	− 0·3	− 0·1
1959 (4th qr.)	94	2·8	6·9	− 4·1
1960 ,,	98	3·1	3·8	− 0·7
1961 ,,	94	1·8	2·1	− 0·3
1962 ,,	98	3·9	0·9	3·0
1963 ,,	97	4·6	6·3	− 1·7
1964 ,,	101	5·4	4·2	1·2
1965 ,,	100	2·7	2·7	0·0
1966 ,,	98	2·0	1·2	0·8
1967 ,,	97	3·1	2·0	1·1
1968 (2nd half)	97	3·6	5·0	− 1·4
1969 ,,	96	1·9	2·5	− 0·6
1970 ,,	97	3·6	1·8	1·8
1971 ,,	94	1·1	2·1	− 1·0
1972 ,,	98	5·5	2·8	2·7

* Potential output is GDP corresponding to 1·0 per cent unemployment: 1955–64 from M. C. Kennedy, 'Employment Policy—What Went Wrong?' in J. Robinson (ed.) *After Keynes* (Blackwell, 1974); 1965–72 are derived from the trend of potential output in University of Cambridge, Department of Applied Economics, *Economic Policy Review No I* (Feb. 1975).

† From Kennedy, op. cit., and from *Financial Statement and Budget Reports* (HMSO)
‡ Average estimate of GDP from *Economic Trends* (1977).

Source: Kennedy [24].

[18] e.g. forecasts need not be targets.

rolonged depression? Beside this much larger question the debates of the 960s over the efficiency or otherwise of fine-tuning seem relatively nimportant.[19]

3.2.5. Long-Term Effects of Demand Management: Expectations

`he experience of the UK with demand management in the 1950 and 1960s ppears somewhat paradoxical. Policy was very active, but on the face of it, not tabilizing. Budget deficits, though tolerated, were not very large, and in fact llowed a massive reduction in National Debt as a proportion of GDP. But pparently, full employment growth was achieved, even if growth was not as igh as other countries, and some cycle was left. The question obviously arises s to whether demand management had anything to do with the relative uccess achieved.

The conventional wisdom was, of course, that it did. Indeed, in the early 960s the claims made for demand management went further: it was argued hat, if only the strait-jacket of the balance of payments could be removed (by ncomes policies or by devaluation) and demand kept growing at a rapid rate, hen growth itself could be raised—from $2\frac{1}{2}$–3 per cent up to, say, 4 per cent.[20] `he attempts of both Maudling and of the post-1964 Labour Government to aise growth were predicated on this kind of optimism. In the event they did not ucceed—though it can be argued too that the underlying premiss was never eally tested since the constraints of the balance of payments and of inflationary ressure were never broken (see Beckerman [2] and Stewart [38]).

Against the demand management view it was argued that growth, at least in he longer term, depended on supply-side factors and was little influenced by lemand management. This view itself had Keynesian and classical variants.)n the Keynesian view, there was still a role for demand management policy in noderating the cycle: demand management may have helped to limit some of he larger swings in the UK, but, as seen, the evidence is not conclusive. On the tronger classical—later monetarist—view, fiscal policy was simply not needed, nd was ineffective, or at worst destabilizing. And permissive monetary policies erved, it was argued, simply to raise inflation.

In the nature of the case, it is very hard to prove or disprove the supply-side typothesis—that growth and other real economic developments would have urned out very much as they did turn out, even in the absence of demand nanagement. What can be said is that the situation was very much worse both efore and after the era of active policies—in the UK, and more generally in the vorld economy. That, however, is hardly conclusive.

Similarly, it would not be easy to refute the demand-side hypothesis. The atter does, however, need reinforcement to explain why, apparently, the roblems faced by the demand managers turned out to be much smaller than hey expected. It was thought that the authorities would need to carry out ather large counter-cyclical actions, and perhaps intervene in a more secular

---

[19] This is also the view of Dow [15]. See Cairncross [13], 'Record of Discussion'.
[20] This 'demand-side' thesis associated with (for example) Beckerman [3] and Kaldor [21] is escribed in Chap. 19.

way to raise the propensity to spend. By and large neither appear to have been necessary. The problem for the demand managers is to explain why, over the period, swings in demand and in financial behaviour seem to have been moderate, and why investment expenditure particularly, but also consumption, were so buoyant.

The most plausible missing link is expectations—or more loosely confidence. Passing over the immediate post-war years, the confidence developed that:

(i) the authorities were committed to high employment and growth;
(ii) they had the means at their disposal to achieve their aims.

Once these came to be taken for granted, the whole climate of expectations changed. Apart from cyclical difficulties—which were not eliminated—growth at something like productive potential came to be anticipated. This in turn reinforced investment, stabilized employment, and generated the confidence amongst consumers not to indulge in wide swings of optimism or pessimism which would be reflected in their savings behaviour.[21] Paradoxically, if the expectation of success really takes hold, the demand management instruments become signalling devices, signalling the intention of the authorities. Particularly in the 1950s, they appear to have worked in just that way. If the signal is strong, then the actual instruments of policy need to be only lightly applied: confidence does the rest.

Thus whilst confidence lasts, relatively stable financial behaviour would be expected. As seen, the sectoral balances do not show much movement—less in fact than in most countries. The movements that did occur—like the rise in personal accumulation in the 1960s—are matched by changes in the company sector, rather than offset by policy action. High investment (and, perhaps, an effect from high levels of National Debt on consumption) allow the balance of the economy to be struck, with, in effect, a government *surplus* allowing National Debt to be proportionately reduced, year after year. Again, whilst the consensus lasts, swings in behaviour, which would need offsetting action, do not occur.

On this view, however, the edifice was fragile. It *could* have been threatened by international developments, but, on the contrary, domestic confidence was reinforced by the buoyant international economy. It *was* threatened by developing worries over the balance of payments and inflation, and policy did become more difficult. Arguably, however, the overriding belief in the efficacy of policy and the objective of full employment persisted right up to the end of the 1960s. Devaluation, strains in the international financial system, and above all, inflation at home and abroad then faced policy makers with a set of difficulties to which they had no convincing answer. Their first response was in effect a reduction in the commitment to full employment. But equally important was a change in the climate of opinion: it was no longer taken for granted that the authorities had the means to deliver high employment, even if they wanted to.

---

[21] Alternatively it might be said that, with confidence in the future, they consumed on the basis of 'permanent income' (see Chap. 2, p. 37).

3.3. The Changing Role of Demand Management Policy: 1970–1983

The 1970s appear to mark a retreat from demand management policy towards older principles of 'sound finance' combined with more *laissez-faire* attitudes to the real economy. The move appears gradual at first—with hesitations and U-turns—but seems effectively complete with the Thatcher Government of 1979–83, which embraced explicitly monetarist principles of economic management.

The reality is more complex. The 1970s were a period during which there were major external shocks, notably the two oil crises, which, on the face of it, would have justified countervailing or offsetting policy action. In part because of these shocks, the 1970s were also a period of high and volatile inflation which, since exchange rates were allowed to float,[22] appeared now directly as a problem for domestic economic management.[23] Thus, first and foremost, the period is one in which the authorities can be seen as searching for methods of dealing with inflation—by demand management policy, or by other 'non-conventional' policies, such as incomes policy. Eventually, with the 1979–83 Government, the instruments of demand management policy were turned almost completely away from their traditional role of maintaining activity and employment, towards the counter-inflation objective.

At the same time—in part reflecting the weight given to the counter-inflation objective—there was a shift in emphasis towards reliance on monetary policy. Initially, at least, this owed rather little to the paradigms of academic monetarist theory, reflecting instead a pragmatic response to inflation and the move to floating exchange rates. Monetary targets when introduced (1976) were combined with a continuing emphasis on fiscal policy and on incomes policy: an eclecticism which was fully in the tradition of the 'package deal' approach of much of the 1950s and 1960s. Monetarism proper would have seen no role for fiscal policy in managing demand. Even when fiscal policy was dethroned with the more explicitly monetarist stance of the 1979 Thatcher Administration, it re-emerged (by one of those twists of analysis which are not uncommon in economics) as a principal tool for controlling the *money supply*. In the British version of monetarism, the Public Sector Borrowing Requirement (PSBR)—closely related to the budget deficit[24]—came to be seen as bearing on inflation (and/or activity) *via* money. Thus tight fiscal policies were an element, along with tight money, in a counter-inflation strategy [17]: a set of ideas formalized in the 1980 Budget with the Medium-Term Financial Strategy (MTFS). Thus, fiscal policy might be seen in a new light but it still had a crucial role to play in macroeconomic policy.

[22] The Bretton Woods system broke down in 1971, when the dollar was made inconvertible, and the world currencies floated. The system was patched up with the Smithsonian Agreement of December 1971, but the new set of fixed parities lasted only for a brief period. The pound was formally floated in 1972 (see Chap. 6).

[23] Arguably, of course, it always was: only if inflation could be treated as effectively exogenous could devaluation, or floating, be expected to transform the prospects for the UK.

[24] It differs mainly by including some borrowing done by the public sector for on-lending to the private sector; and by the 'accruals adjustment'. The latter arises in that the budget deficit (on a National Income Accounts basis) looks at taxes when they are incurred as liabilities; the PSBR looks at cash payments.

13.3.1. The Record: 1970–1983

An indication of the way in which the pattern of economic development changed from the beginning of the 1970s is provided in Table 13.5. While price inflation never reached 6 per cent before the 1970s, it never fell below it until the very end of the period in 1983. While unemployment never exceeded 2·6 per cent in the 1950s and 1960s, it never fell below this figure in the 1970s. After the first oil crisis at the end of 1973, it rose sharply, to about 4·5 per cent, only to rise again after 1979 to reach more than 13 per cent of the labour force in 1983. Growth throughout the period 1970–82 was even lower than in the previous decades ($1\frac{1}{2}$ per cent per annum), though the table suggests that it would be more illuminating to describe the experience in terms of two downward shifts in output following the two oil crises, with a period of roughly average growth (for the UK) of $2\frac{1}{2}$–3 per cent between them.

The table brings out too the peaks of price inflation that followed the two oil crises—and the decline that occurred in each case over the ensuing three years. The inflationary peak was somewhat worse after the first oil shock than the second. Another obvious difference was in the balance of payments: during the first crisis, there was a swing to deficit of 3–4 per cent of GDP, largely due to oil. The major swing to *surplus* after the second oil shock reflected the build-up of North Sea oil production (which was negligible in 1976) to self-sufficiency in

TABLE 13.5. *The UK Record 1970–1983*

	Growth* (% change)	Inflation† (% change)	Unemployment‡ (%)		Balance of payments§ (% GDP at market prices)
1970	2·0	6·3	2·6		1·6
1971	1·5	9·4	3·5		2·0
1972	2·7	7·3	3·8		0·3
1973	7·1	9·1	2·7		− 1·3
1974	− 1·7	16·0	2·7		− 3·9
1975	− 1·1	24·2	4·1		− 1·4
1976	2·6	16·5	5·7	*On*	− 0·7
1977	2·6	15·9	6·2	*new*	0·0
1978	3·2	8·3	6·1	*basis*	0·7
1979	1·8	13·4	5·7	5·3	− 0·3
1980	− 2·4	18·0	7·4	6·8	1·4
1981	− 2·4	11·9	11·4	10·5	2·6
1982	2·7	8·6		12·2	2·0
1983	3·0	4·6		13·0	0·7

* GDP average estimate using 1975 prices at factor cost.

† Retail Price Index, 'all items'.

‡ Unemployed as percentage of employed and unemployed; basis of measurement changed in 1982.

§ Current balance as percentage of GDP at market prices.

980, and to substantial *net exports* in 1981 and 1983. Obviously, one of the features to be explained is why the inflationary and recessionary experiences after the two oil 'crises' appear similar, in spite of the UK's move from dependence on oil imports to self-sufficiency by 1980.[25]

3.3.2. *The Conduct of Policy: The Heath Government 1970–1974*

The Heath Government, elected in 1970, started with a continuation of the squeeze initiated by the previous administration. The policy of tight demand management following the 1967 devaluation was bearing fruit in terms of the balance of payments, which had moved to surplus in 1969. On the other hand, inflationary pressure of a 'cost push' kind appeared strong, and something of a wage explosion followed the ending of the Labour Government's incomes policy.[26] In part as a result of the pressure of high wage increases against tight demand management policies, a major 'shake-out' of labour occurred and unemployment rose rapidly to reach the politically sensitive '1 million' in the winter of 1970–1. The squeeze is readily apparent from Table 13.6. The company sector deficit, normally a surplus in the 1960s, rose to $2\frac{1}{2}$ per cent of GDP in 1970, a swing to deficit which is comparable to the swings after the two oil crises of the 1970s.

TABLE 13.6. *Sector Balances, 1970–1982*
(% of GDP at market prices)

	Public sector	Personal sector	Company sector	Overseas sector
1970	1·3	2·8	−2·5	−1·6
1971	−0·5	0·8	1·7	−2·0
1972	−2·4	2·2	0·6	−0·4
1973	−3·7	4·0	−1·6	1·4
1974	−5·7	5·1	−3·4	4·0
1975	−7·2	5·5	0·3	1·4
1976	−6·7	4·8	1·2	0·7
1977	−4·1	3·8	0·3	0·0
1978	−4·8	5·6	−0·1	−0·6
1979	−4·3	6·7	−2·9	0·4
1980	−4·4	8·2	−2·6	−1·3
1981	−3·0	6·6	−1·1	−2·4
1982	−2·7	3·8	0·9	−2·0

Source: *Economic Trends Annual Supplement* 1983.

[25] Although the proportionate rise of oil prices was very different in the two oil crises approximately fourfold in 1973–4 and about double in 1979–80), the overall impact of the two oil crises in relation to the size of the world economy was similar: about $2–2\frac{1}{2}$ per cent of OECD countries' GDP in each case.

[26] This episode can be seen as the result of pent-up frustrations accumulated during the period of incomes policy or, perhaps, as part of an international phenomenon of militancy and cost push leading to wage explosions in many industrial countries at the end of the 1960s. On the latter view, the incomes policy postponed—to 1970—a wage explosion which would have occurred anyway. See for example, Nordhaus [32], Perry [33], and Soskice [37].

Along with a policy of tolerating somewhat higher levels of unemployment, the approach of the Heath Government, both to industrial policy and to pay bargaining, marked a move towards non-interventionist policies and a reliance on 'market forces'. More actively, there were commitments to join the EEC, to introduce a more 'flexible' framework for the operation of monetary policy, and to reform the laws relating to trade unions. The machinery of incomes policy was immediately wound up; intervention in industry was reduced and an Industrial Relations Act was introduced. Most importantly, direct controls over the banking system and credit flows were first reduced, and then swept away with the major monetary reforms of Competition and Credit Control in 1971 (see Chapter 10).

The policies of deflation and disengagement failed to lead to any perceptible reduction in the rate of pay increases. The sharp rise in unemployment together with increasing industrial unrest—reflecting both the proposed labour legislation and attempts to hold down public sector pay[27]—led to a so-called 'U-turn' or political *volte face*. The emphasis of policy changed back towards the maintenance of activity by demand management policy together with reliance on incomes policy to deal with inflation. A policy of letting bankrupt companies, however important, close was abandoned when Rolls-Royce and Upper Clyde Shipbuilders failed. At the same time a much more conciliatory attitude was adopted towards the unions. This change in emphasis, which by itself need not have led to any dramatic reversals of demand management policy, was, however, compounded by major errors of policy (in the expansionary direction) as well as serious shocks from the international economy.[28] (These somewhat extraneous factors are inevitably tangled up with perceptions of the U-turn, and give a partly spurious impression that the attitudinal shift was more dramatic in its effects than was really the case.)

The initial reflationary moves of the Heath Government appeared to have little effect, and much of the subsequent boom seems to have reflected the problem of underestimating the lags before policy takes effect. This in turn led to a greatly excessive stimulus, especially from public expenditure, in 1972–3. Another factor was the vast expansion in money and credit which followed the reform of the monetary system in 1971. Combined with the move to floating exchange rates internationally,[29] which encouraged the authorities in lowering interest rates to discourage undue appreciation of sterling relative to the dollar, monetary laxity fuelled both expansion and inflation—especially the house price boom of 1971–2. Finally, domestic errors were greatly reinforced by the inflationary boom in the world economy, which occurred at much the same time and for similar reasons—a factor which was not fully foreseen.

Two other features need to be brought out. The first is that it was publicly announced that any balance of payments difficulties resulting from expansion

---

[27] Which collapsed with the bitter miners' strike of the winter of 1971–2.

[28] See Chap. 19. The 'shocks' included the breakdown of Bretton Woods and the move to floating in 1971, the commodity price boom of 1972–3, and the oil crisis of 1973.

[29] The period from the summer of 1971 to the Smithsonian Agreement of December 1971 was known as the period of 'dirty floating'.

ould be dealt with, not by 'stop–go', but by allowing the pound to float
ownwards if necessary. The second is that any inflationary consequences of
xpansion itself, or of floating, were to be countered by incomes policies.
nitially, these were 'voluntary', with the public sector trying to set an example
y making the next wage rise 1 per cent smaller than the previous one.[30] In the
autumn of 1972, however, there was a compulsory freeze, followed in 1973 by
ecified limits (£1 per week plus 4 per cent). But the boom that followed the U-
urn was very rapid, with growth reaching about 7 per cent in 1973. As a result,
iflation, which had declined in the early stages of the incomes policy,
ccelerated again to over 9 per cent even before the oil crisis. In addition, the
973–4 wage round saw more generous limits, combined with *indexation* for
iflation over a basic threshold of 7 per cent. This policy was introduced in
973, before the oil crisis and at a time when the pressure from commodity price
ises was expected to fall off, or even reverse. Had these forecasts been correct,
he thresholds could have helped to bring down pay rises. In the event, with the
1assive (fourfold) rise in oil prices in December 1973,[31] they were a recipe for
isaster, effectively guaranteeing that the oil impact would feed through
apidly to wages.

Many lessons have been drawn from the experience of this period, 1970–3. In
1ct, as even the brief sketch in this section should make clear, lessons are
ifficult to discern. There were simply too many things going on at the same
ime—allowing almost any school of thought to see confirmation of its favourite
eliefs. Taking the U-turn first, this can be read as a sensible pragmatic
esponse to the failure of demand management to cure inflation, or as
idicating that much greater persistence and toleration of unemployment was
ecessary.[32] Whatever the merits of the U-turn, it gets mixed up with quite a
ifferent problem: a major failure in the *practice* of demand management policy
:ading, by 1973, to greatly excessive monetary demand in relation to supply.
.xcessive demand expansion can be explained by fiscal policies, monetary
olicy, or by developments in the international economy. And the rapid rise in
iflation, even before the oil crisis, can likewise be ascribed to domestic
1onetary and fiscal policies, or to commodity price inflation 'imported' from
broad (see Chapter 19).

3.3.3. Labour Governments: 1974–1979

`he Labour Government, elected after Mr Heath had gone to the country after
he 1974 miners' strike, was faced with the immediate aftermath of the oil crisis,
s well as the legacies of excessive expansion and other policy errors. The initial
esponse, and the subsequent policy moves when the government was re-elected
1 the autumn of 1974 with a working majority, were muddled and sometimes
ppeared inconsistent. There was no shortage of Budgets, with four in the first

---

[30] The so-called '$n-1$' policy.

[31] The oil crisis started in the autumn of 1973 with quantitative restrictions and a moderate price
ise. The main price rise occurred on 23 December 1973.

[32] Another aspect of the U-turn, arguably even more important than the swing round in demand
nanagement policy, was the change from a policy of curbing union power to a more permissive set
f attitudes.

year, involving first a mild contraction, and then some relaxation. But certain features of policy attitudes up to 1976 and then subsequently can and need to be brought out.

The first is that the Labour Administration publicly favoured a strategy of *offsetting* the international oil shock, both by maintaining domestic demand and by promoting international action to lessen the risk of world recession. Domestically, the situation was harder to assess, and policy attitudes more complex. Broadly, the position adopted in the immediate aftermath of the oil crisis was that some deflationary action was necessary to reduce *excess* demand (which included accepting some of the impact of oil itself) but that once excess demand was eliminated, any tendency to further recession and unemployment should be offset in a conventional Keynesian manner. Partly because of the unfavourable experiences during the recession of 1970–1, it was not felt that further rises in unemployment would be conducive to inflation control—they might even be counter-productive.[33]

In practice, policy was far from fully offsetting—and given the international response, that would probably have been impossible anyway. A notable feature is the swing to deficit in the company sector in 1974 to about 14 per cent of GDP. This was followed by government action to alleviate it but also by a strong move by companies to reduce stocks and to shed labour—the immediate causes of the deep recession in 1975 (see Table 13.6). Also apparent from the table is the sharp rise in the accumulation of financial assets by the personal sector to about 5 per cent of GDP in 1974–5 (compared with about $1\frac{1}{2}$ to 2 per cent on average in the 1960s). But although policy was not strongly offsetting in a *discretionary* way, the very high public sector deficits that resulted from the oil impact and the automatic effects of recession were tolerated in 1974–5 and subsequently, though less willingly, through to 1979. Thus in the 1970s, deficit finance does finally seem to play the role envisaged for it by the early Keynesians. (But see the discussion of inflation adjusted figures in the following pages.)

The Labour Administration's policy on inflation appeared initially perverse in that the damaging threshold agreements were not swept away but were allowed to raise wage rises in line with price inflation through much of 1974.[34] Generally, the approach was to rely on voluntary incomes policy to deal with the inflationary push from oil and commodity price rises: the initial Social Contract was, however, ineffective and wage inflation rose to over 30 per cent in 1975. The apparent loss of control was followed by a much stronger incomes policy, which had the feature of fixed rises for most workers and hence implied a progressive narrowing of differentials. This policy, combined with somewhat tighter demand management and a reduced political commitment to a rapid return to full employment, was apparently extremely successful: wage inflation tumbled down to reach about 8 per cent in 1977.[35] Price rises fell rapidly too,

[33] A position explicitly adopted by the Cambridge Economic Policy Group (CEPG).

[34] Many commentators have seen the continuation of thresholds as a major policy error accounting for Britain's exceptionally rapid rate of inflation in 1975. See, for example, Surrey [39]

[35] Average earnings, 3rd quarter 1977 on a year earlier. Wage rates came down even faster, to about 5 per cent over the same period.

elped by favourable movements in international primary commodity prices as
the rapid world upswing of 1976 petered out into 1977.

The third strand to bring out is the sharply changing policy towards the
exchange rate. Initially sterling seemed to gain strength from the oil crisis[36]
and the pound was 'surprisingly' high in 1974 and through much of 1975.
Government policy, however, was to seek a competitive pound as an aid to the
longer-term health of industry. The exchange rate was seen at this time—at
last in part—as an *instrument* of demand management policy: a low exchange
rate, favouring exports and discouraging imports, would directly stimulate the
economy in a way which did not require budgetary action. Indeed, a successful
strategy of export-led expansion, it was argued, would curtail the need for
deficit finance. The unfavourable aspects of a fall in the exchange rate—
especially in setting off inflation—were (as with the previous administration)
to be dealt with by incomes restraint.

This strategy, of managing the economy via the exchange rate with the back-
up of incomes policy, is interesting in that it marked a shift in the way in which
demand management policy was looked at. The policy shift owed a great deal
to the ideas of Kaldor and the Cambridge Economic Policy Group.[37] It
reflected, on the negative side, the disillusion which developed during the later
960s both with 'fine-tuning' and with conventional consumption-led
strategies of demand expansion. More particularly, it was felt that 'export-led
expansion' would have favourable effects on the structure of the economy and
that it would be sustainable.

There was a period in 1976 when the broad lines of this strategy seemed to be
succeeding. Wages and prices were coming under control, and there appeared
to be 'a new mood of realism' in wage bargaining. The world economy was
expanding again and British industry was highly competitive in terms of unit
costs of production. The balance of payments deficit had fallen sharply (0·7 per
cent of GDP in 1976) and North Sea oil was expected to build up in significant
quantities very soon. Despite this, and for reasons which still remain obscure,
there were a series of sterling crises through 1976, and a major run on the pound
in the last quarter. The proximate cause of the latter appeared to be an
article[38] in the *Sunday Times* (in October) suggesting that the visiting IMF
delegation would have a target for the dollar/pound parity of $1·50,
significantly lower than the current rate. It is likely that both the administration and some members of the IMF did have in mind an unofficial target for
sterling which would have maintained competitiveness, though not necessarily
as low as $1·50. In any case, market reaction was sudden and severe,
necessitating, it was argued, a conventional deflationary package with higher
interest rates and cuts in public expenditure. An IMF loan for balance of
payments and exchange rate support was negotiated with the signing of the
famous IMF Letter of Intent in December. This letter spelt out targets for
Domestic Credit Expansion (DCE) (see Chapter 10) and public sector

[36] Probably reflecting the build up of sterling balances by some of the OPEC oil producers and
uncertainty about the US response.
[37] See Kaldor [22]. Also Cambridge Economic Policy Group Reviews (various issues).
[38] By Malcolm Crawford.

borrowing. A monetary target of a somewhat informal kind (for M3) had already been introduced in July 1976: whilst the commitment to the IMF continued, domestic targets were, in effect, subordinate to the IMF's preferred measure of DCE. From 1977 onwards, announced targets for £M3 were an important part of government economic policy.

The IMF measures themselves were mainly important as an earnest of the government's intentions, marking as they did the abandonment of a 'low' exchange rate policy. The conversion was not initially complete, however. There was a spectacular turn-round in international sentiment in 1977 with strong capital inflows.[39] Upward pressure on the exchange rate was strongly and successfully resisted through much of 1977, via a policy of intervention and rapid reduction in interest rates. This policy was, however, abandoned in October—the exchange rate was 'uncapped'—as it was thought that monetary expansion arising from intervention was excessive. From that period on, the determination of the exchange rate was, in effect, left to market forces whilst attention was concentrated on domestic indicators of the thrust of policy—such as £M3 and the Public Sector Borrowing Requirement (PSBR).

Though this looks like the start of the so-called 'monetarist' policies pursued by the subsequent Conservative Administration, there is a very important difference, which is not just of degree. Though financial targets or indicators were well established from 1977 onwards, these were seen as a guidepost to markets of the general thrust of monetary and fiscal policy.[40] But the main weight of counter-inflation policy fell on *incomes restraint*.

Demand management policy clearly needed to be *consistent* with the general thrust of counter-inflation policy, and beyond that, a public commitment to monetary and other financial targets could be actively helpful in stabilizing financial markets and generally in increasing the credibility of the overall strategy.[41] The political attractions of such a 'package deal', especially for the monetary authorities, are apparent.

The 1977 and 1978 budgets were framed within the terms of this strategy, although incomes policy started to disintegrate and wage increases picked up. Some of the contradictions and pressures, particularly over the squeezing of skill differentials in successive phases of the incomes policy, came to a head in the 'winter of discontent' of 1978–9. In terms of its public credibility at least, the strategy lay in ruins.

The assessment of this period is taken up in following pages. Here it may be noted that, overall, performance was not too bad, though no significant progress was made in reducing the underlying rate of unemployment, which appeared to step up after the first oil crisis. Against the government's objectives, this was failure. The inflationary potential of the UK's wage-bargaining system was amply demonstrated by the extraordinarily unfavourable responses after the OPEC shock. But incomes policy was apparently very successful—for a time. But most importantly, there was the perception that two ways out of the

---

[39] North Sea oil started to affect the current account substantially in 1977, which moved into surplus.

[40] For an account of the objectives of monetary policy see Richardson [36], and Fforde [17].

[41] A view put forward in the international context, in the 'McCracken Report' [27].

JK's 'box' of macroeconomic difficulties had been tried and failed. A strategy f a low exchange rate and export-led expansion was jettisoned after 1976. inally, the lynch-pin of the whole strategy—incomes restraint—appeared to ail decisively in the 'winter of discontent'.

3.3.4. The Thatcher Government: 1979-1983

he Conservative Government, elected in May 1979, was committed to a set of olicies which were similar to those of the incoming 1970 Government—i.e. ismantling of incomes policies, reliance on market forces, and trade union eform—but with the additional commitment that, this time, there would be o U-turn. These policies were underpinned by an intellectual and ideological osition which was both stronger and less pragmatic than most post-war overnments had shown. Glossing over differences within the party, it espoused nonetarist doctrines of economic management together with a belief in supply- ide incentives and a commitment to a smaller role for the public sector.[42]

The positive feature of monetarism is that inflation should be controlled by ontrolling the money supply. In discussing demand management policy the *egative* feature is equally important: *fiscal policy* is regarded as ineffective or rrelevant as far as macroeconomic management is concerned and there is reater concentration upon taxes, public expenditure, and the budgetary osition for their *microeconomic* resource allocation effects, which may include ffects on the interest rate at full employment.[43] Thus, the fiscal management of he economy, as practised in the 1950s, 1960s, and 1970s is regarded by nonetarists as an illusion:to the extent that it did appear to have had effects, it vas because *monetary magnitudes* had been affected as well. And, in anything but he short term, the effects of monetary policy were on *prices*; the economy was elf-stabilizing—left to itself it would tend to produce the *natural rate of output* at he natural rate of unemployment.

These ideological strands are important in understanding economic policy t that time. But there is another element as well—the disillusion of non- nonetarist demand managers with incomes policies and with other attempts to reak the constraints operating on UK economic policy. It seems that many on-monetarists had come, however reluctantly, to the conclusion that the nstruments of demand management policy would have to be turned against nflation: that recession, possibly deep and prolonged, might have to be olerated in the interests of price stability. Tight demand management policies vould, of course, include strict control of the monetary aggregates.

At the risk of over-simplifying, it is possible to argue that there was a oalition in favour of tight policies against inflation composed of new nonetarists and pragmatic Keynesians. Within that coalition the monetarists vere mainly distinguished by their *optimism* that inflation could be controlled at elatively small cost by monetary restraint. By contrast, the pragmatic Keynesians still essentially demand managers, saw restraint as coming through oth monetary and fiscal policies and they were in the main pessimistic about

---

[42] Initially, at least, its monetarism can be thought of in terms of the Friedman school. Later, trong elements of the new classical theory (with rational expectations) became important.

[43] See, for example, [18] Friedman's evidence to the Treasury and Civil Service Committee.

the probable costs. The tension between these different views[44] has continued as a feature of the whole period since 1979.

There is a further aspect of the intellectual—or attitudinal map—that needs to be recalled and emphasized. We have seen that one way of looking at the difference between the new monetarists and the pragmatic Keynesians is that the monetarists believed that *only* money mattered, whereas the Keynesians believed that both monetary and fiscal policy mattered. The important gulf was in attitudes to fiscal policy. There is, however, another position which complicates this picture. Many British 'monetarists' started to argue that fiscal policy did matter, but *via* its effects on money. Public borrowing in particular needed to be controlled, not *per se*, but as an aid to monetary control. Though this left some British monetarists agreeing with the Keynesians that fiscal policy was important—and with both groups seeing reasons, ultimately of an anti-inflation nature, to favour tight policies—the convergence was only part way. Many important differences in the role assigned to fiscal policy remained, with one group concerned with monetary consequences, the other with demand consequences.

In practice, the new government was faced with the breakdown of the previous incomes policy, an acceleration in wages and, shortly afterwards, the effects of the second oil crisis—the major rises in oil prices in 1979 and 1980. Incomes policy was abolished, but not the comparability study and associated awards set in train by the previous government.[45] The June Budget was restrictive—but in conventional terms only mildly so. Minimum Lending Rate (MLR) was raised to 14 per cent.

The two features that stand out in the early months of that administration are first, the switch from direct to indirect taxation which directly contributed some $3\frac{1}{2}$ per cent to the price level and thus sharply increased the expected rate of inflation, and second, its handling of the oil price rises. The switch in taxes was widely regarded as dangerous as to timing and likely to lead to increased wage inflation.[46] In the event the wage reaction was large and rapid. The acceleration in inflation was a major reason for the rise in MLR to the crisis level of 17 per cent at the end of November. The full extent of oil price rises was not apparent in the summer of 1979: government policy, however, was to allow them to come through, which again had a major impact on the price level— perhaps another $2\frac{1}{2}$ to $3\frac{1}{2}$ per cent. Moreover, as far as the non-oil corporate sector was concerned, there was no offset comparable to the reduction in income tax which balanced the rise in VAT, so that the oil impact operated like a tax increase; from a conventional point of view it was directly demand reducing and price raising. This occurred in spite of the UK's near self-sufficiency in oil at that time (see section 13.2, and Chapter 27).

Initially the government was over-optimistic in hoping that holding the money supply ($\pounds M3$) in the range 7–11 per cent would control inflation without a major recession and that such control would turn out to be straightforward. Even looked at from a broadly monetarist perspective, the

---

[44] Reflected, for example, within the Conservative policy in the split between 'drys' and 'wets'.
[45] The so-called 'Clegg awards' applied mainly to the public sector.
[46] The broadly monetarist LBS forecasting unit was strongly against this move at that time.

government's difficulties were exacerbated by the rise in VAT and by the oil price rises and their 5–7 per cent addition to the general price level. The rise in inflation was one reason why interest rates had to rise sharply, which in turn was part of the reason for the strong upward pressure on the exchange rate, squeezing exposed sectors of industry [10]. In addition, the fiscal stance was, if account is taken of oil, allowed to tighten substantially, further exacerbating the difficulties of companies. The recession was widely predicted by the conventional (broadly Keynesian) forecasting models, but the true extent of the deflationary forces did not become apparent until around April–May of 1980 when the stockbuilding cycle really took hold and industrial production started to decline rapidly. The trough of the recession occurred in mid-1981, though manufacturing production continued to decline—reaching its low point in late 1982. By that time it had declined by nearly 20 per cent from its level in mid-1979.

13.3.5. The Medium-Term Financial Strategy

The strategy of the Conservative Government was spelt out much more formally in the Medium-Term Financial Strategy (MTFS), announced with the spring 1980 Budget. The basic idea was to set out a financial framework of (declining) monetary targets with a *consistent* path for public borrowing. The relevant indicator of public borrowing was taken to be the Public Sector Borrowing Requirement (PSBR) rather than the Public Sector Financial Deficit (PSFD). Although the projections for the PSBR as a proportion of GDP were often described (e.g. in the financial Press) as *targets*, this terminology was carefully avoided in official statements. The primary target remained the declining path for monetary growth—with public borrowing in a supportive role.

The key element in the MTFS was that fiscal policy should support or be consistent with monetary policy. The intention was to achieve a 'substantial reduction over the medium term in the PSBR as a proportion of GDP', though it was recognized that the relationship of the PSBR to GDP and to the growth of £M3 could, in the short run, be sensitive to such factors as the state of the cycle, the rate of inflation, and the structure of taxation and expenditure. Table 13.7 shows the projections set out in the 1980 *Financial Statement and Budget Report*, together with the out-turns. In the event, the projections shown in the table were not achieved. Taking the monetary targets first, there was a massive overshoot in the first year of the MTFS (1980–1). The 6–10 per cent target range was, however, retained for the next year but rebased to incorporate the previous overshoot. In spite of this, a further overshoot occurred, and in 1982–3 the concentration on a single monetary target was, in effect, abandoned. A new range of 8–12 per cent was adopted which was to apply to £M1 and PSL2, as well as £M3 (see Chapter 10). Over the three-year period from the start of the MTFS to March 1983, the *maximum* growth of £M3 envisaged was 37 per cent. Its actual growth was close to 50 per cent.

It is perhaps paradoxical that the projections for public borrowing were more nearly achieved—except in 1980–1. In that first year of the MTFS there was a large overshoot of £5 billion (target £8·5 billion, out-turn to £13·6

TABLE 13.7. *The 1980 Financial Statement Projections*

	Projected PSBR/GDP (%)	Actual PSBR/GDP (%)	Target £M3 (% change)	Actual £M3 (% change)
1978–9	$5\frac{1}{2}$	3·5		11·8
1979–80	$4\frac{3}{4}$	5·1	7–11	11·0
1980–1	$3\frac{3}{4}$	5·8	7–11	19·6
1981–2	3	3·4	6–10	13·0
1982–3	$2\frac{1}{4}$	3·1	5–9	11·2
1983–4	$1\frac{1}{2}$	3·2	4–8	9·0

billion) much of which was due to the unanticipated severity of the recession.[47] Though some allowance was made for this in projecting a PSBR of $4\frac{3}{4}$ per cent of GDP for 1981–2 in the 1981 Budget Statement (cf. the original projection of 3·0 per cent) the 1981 Budget was, in conventional terms, substantially *deflationary* in order to reduce the PSBR. These deflationary moves came when the economy was already in deep recession—and in conventional demand managers' terms, were strongly *pro-cyclical*. This policy—of raising taxes and cutting expenditure to meet financial targets in the midst of recession—appeared finally to mark the end of 'Keynesian' attitudes to fiscal policy.

Though the MTFS and policy based on it marked a major departure from conventional attitudes towards the management of demand, it certainly did not mean the end of fine-tuning or the abandonment of fiscal policy. On the contrary, the *instruments* of demand management policy were used actively. Short-term interest rates and funding policy were used to try and control money, and so so too were the instruments of fiscal policy (taxes and expenditure programmes) which were frequently varied in order to try to meet objectives for public borrowing and money. Thus it is probably best to see this period as marking the *diversion* of the instruments of demand management policy away from their traditional role of maintaining growth and full employment towards the achievement of *financial targets*, themselves part of a strategy against inflation. From a longer-term perspective, such diversion appears neither new, nor surprising. In the 1950s and 1960s, as we have seen, these self-same instruments were often used to meet balance of payments or anti-inflation objectives. The new element was not that they should be used in this way, but the Medium-Term Financial Strategy itself.

The rationale behind the MTFS was in certain respects obscure and ambiguous (see [41] and [25]). The emphasis on the PSBR and fiscal policy distinguished it from the straightforward monetarism of, for example, Friedman [18]. One strand, influential in the City, was the idea that broad money (£M3) and public borrowing were closely connected via the credit

---

[47] The Clegg awards (which were backdated) also boosted public expenditure.

counterparts of £M3, and the appearance within them of the PSBR.[48] It could be argued that the identity provided a framework within which fiscal and monetary policy could be looked at consistently [17], with a lower PSBR helping, *ceteris paribus*, in the achievement of lower monetary growth. But the identity itself, being an identity, carries no implications for any causal connection whatsoever. More specifically, changes in the PSBR could have effects on other items in the identity, depending on the state of the economy, in addition to changes in £M3 deriving from other causes, especially bank lending to the private sector. Perhaps more influential in the Treasury[49] was the idea that, in the longer term, there was some *portfolio* relationship between National Debt and money [11]. Since National Debt depended on the *cumulation* of public borrowing, this would mean that public borrowing needed to be controlled if money was to be controlled.

There remain some obscurities about what is meant by the 'portfolio relationship' and about the underlying causal mechanisms which are supposed to connect public borrowing, National Debt, and the money supply. For some purposes these do not matter—as when attention is focused only on equilibrium results, or on consistency.[50] But they do matter greatly—even to the extent of giving *diametrically* opposite predictions—when fiscal policy (public borrowing) is varied *relative* to a fixed money target. This is discussed further in section 13.4.3.

13.4. Measuring Policy in the 1970s

The general problems of measuring and assessing policy have been described in Chapter 12 and further discussed in the context of the 1950s and 1960s in the second section of this chapter. In the 1970s several additional problems arose which make the assessment of policy stance particularly problematic. The most important were:

(i) uncertainty about productive potential or trend output which makes the underlying fiscal position hard to assess;[51]

(ii) inflation and its impact on interest rates, on the demand for money, and on budget balances;

(iii) oil and its effects.

We consider the measurement of fiscal policy first before looking at monetary policy and the balance between monetary and fiscal policy.

---

[48] See Chap. 10. The counterpart identity relates the change in £M3 to its credit counterparts, is given on p. 311, and may be summarized as:

£M3 = PSBR − gilt sales to the non-bank private sector
+ bank lending to the non-bank private sector
+ change in non-deposit liabilities and external influences.

[49] Judging from its published statements, such as [41].
[50] The position adopted by the 'new classical' school. See, for example, Minford and Peel [30].
[51] In principle this poses problems for assessing monetary policy as well.

13.4.1. Summary measures of Fiscal Policy: 1970–1983

Arising out of the approaches followed in the 1960s, the traditional measure of overall fiscal stance became some concept of the 'full employment' or cyclically adjusted budget deficit. Some of the possible variants have been described in Chapter 12 (see pp. 388–90). In the 1970s all these measures became problematical (and therefore contentious) because assessment of trend or full-employment output itself became subject to much dispute. In particular, there is a serious question as to whether the *trend* and/or the *level* of potential output changed after 1973 (e.g. due to the oil impact) and similar questions about what happened in the early 1980s.

The reason that 'productive potential' or 'trend output' is so important is that cyclical adjustment procedures start by looking at the deviation of the economy from its trend and correcting the actual deficit for the automatic effects on the deficit of that divergence. Though both elements in the calculation are subject to uncertainty, it is the assessment of the actual position of the economy in relation to its potential or trend that has strong political connotations, especially when, as in the early 1980s, the economy is in deep recession with very high unemployment. Clearly, different assessments of the trend could lead to vastly different estimates of the underlying budgetary position.

It will be recalled that there are two, related, motives for cyclical adjustment: the first is to distinguish between the 'automatic' and 'discretionary' aspects of policy; the second is to remove the effects of temporary or reversible fluctuations on the budget position so as to be able to look at the underlying or structural situation. In either case it is necessary to construct an implicit 'norm' or reference case against which fluctuations can be measured.[52] It has been argued (see pp. 389–90) that the trend of output at average unemployment or average capacity utilization would be the most natural and uncontentious baseline. In the 1950s and 1960s, it was reasonably clear what that average was.[53] In the 1970s, and, especially, in the early 1980s, there has been a serious difficulty in that 'recent history' has been out of line with past experience, so that past averages might not be thought relevant to the 'future'. What, therefore, should be used as the baseline for the calculation of cyclical deviations?

The difficulties in establishing the baseline may be illustrated for the period 1974–9, between the two oil crises. At the time of the first oil crisis, there was no way of knowing what the trend would turn out to be: it was natural enough to project forward the trends established in the 1960s. Measured against such a trend, the cyclical adjustment factor would be persistent and growing in the 1970s: *ex post* the deviations do not look cyclical, nor were they reversed. Thus if

[52] In looking at the discretionary versus automatic effects of policy it is common practice to focus on *changes* in policy rather than on some absolute measure of 'stance'. If this is done, the *level* of trend or potential output often does not matter, since it is only necessary to establish a reference position of *no policy change*. The procedure is not really satisfactory, partly because the level often does matter (policy can be tight, even if not changing) and partly because the distinction between automatic and discretionary changes is hard to draw.

[53] The estimates shown in Table 13.3 of cyclical effects in the 1950s and 1960s are normalized to average out to zero over the period considered.

our concern is with cyclical adjustment and the underlying budgetary position it seems better, with hindsight, to allow for a shift downwards in trend output around 1973–4, and/or for a somewhat lower trend growth rate. If, however, the measure is being used to indicate what was happening to *discretionary* policy, building such a shift *into the baseline* may be misleading. When the shift occurred, measurement of policy stance could indicate that it was expansionary not because it 'really' was, but because it *failed to tighten* in line with the assumed fall in trend or potential. Thus whether such 'shifts' should be built into measures of cyclically adjusted budget balances depends upon the purposes for which they are designed as well as convenience. The important thing is that the underlying assumptions should be clear.

Table 13.8 shows two different measures of cyclically adjusted budget balances for the period 1970–82 which illustrate some of the issues. The first series, adapted from OECD sources, assumes that output was near 'trend' in 1973 and approached it again in 1978 and 1979 (cyclical adjustment factor just over half per cent of GDP). The other series, drawn from IMF sources, assumes a considerably lower level of trend output in the years 1973–6, reflecting, in the IMF's view, the 'supply shock' of oil. Both series measure cyclical effects in relation to some 'potential' trend rather than against some average level of utilization over the cycle—which is in effect impossible in the 1970s.[54] The

TABLE 13.8. *Cyclically Adjusted Measures of Fiscal Stance, 1970–1982*

	General government financial balance (% of GDP)	Cyclically neutral balance (% of GDP)		Cyclically adjusted balance (% of GDP)	
		I*	II†	I	II
1970	3·0	−0·5	—	3·5	—
1971	1·4	−0·7	—	2·1	—
1972	−1·3	−1·1	−1·1	−0·2	−0·2
1973	−2·7	0·1	0·6	−2·6	−3·3
1974	−3·8	−1·2	−0·3	−2·6	−3·5
1975	−4·6	−2·5	−1·8	−2·1	−2·8
1976	−4·9	−2·4	−1·7	−2·5	−3·2
1977	−3·2	−2·0	−1·8	−1·2	−1·4
1978	−4·2	−0·7	−1·1	−3·5	−3·1
1979	−3·2	−0·6	−0·9	−2·6	−2·3
1980	−3·3	−2·4	−2·1	−0·9	−1·2
1981	−2·6	−4·4	−3·5	+1·8	+0·9
1982	−1·7	−5·7	−3·8	+4·0	+2·1

* Based on OECD figures.   † Based on IMF figures.

Sources: Budget balance—*Economic Trends*; OECD adjustment—based on J. C. Chouraqui and R. W. R. Price, *Public Sector Deficits: Public and Policy Implications, Economic Outlook* Occasional Studies (June, 1983), Table 5; IMF adjustment—based on *World Economic Outlook*, 1981, 1982, and 1983.

[54] In fact, both the OECD and the IMF, in making use of the figures, stress year-to-year changes in the cyclically adjusted position as an indicator of fiscal policy—which means that the level of the trend line assumed does not matter.

effects of deviations from potential on the deficit are assessed differently: the OECD procedure uses estimates based on its INTERLINK world model;[55] the IMF figures use the concept of the cyclically neutral budget balance described in Chapter 12.

In spite of their defects the figures are suggestive. The OECD numbers indicate very little change in the 'underlying' fiscal position from 1973–6, with a tightening in 1977, and a relaxation in 1978. Equivalently, most of the rise in the deficit (especially in 1975) is measured as due to the automatic stabilizers. The IMF figures show a much more expansionary policy in these years which, as suggested above, is mainly due to its view that potential declined (relative to trend); or equivalently, that a policy of allowing the stabilizers to operate would not have been 'cyclically neutral'. Both sets of figures show a massive tightening of fiscal policy from 1979–82: by no less than $6\frac{1}{2}$ per cent of GDP according to the OECD and by about $4\frac{1}{2}$ per cent according to the IMF.[56]

Turning to the problems posed by inflation, it is clear that figures for public borrowing in the 1970s are distorted by high and variable rates of inflation in the ways outlined in Chapter 12. In practice, rather different figures for the inflation adjustment can result from different assumptions about the relevant rate of inflation (should it be the actual rate, some average rate, or some expected or anticipated rate?) and about relevant measures of liabilities outstanding. There are also questions about how capital gains and losses should be treated.[57] The figures in Table 13.9 use the methods developed by the Bank of England which amount, in effect, to computing the 'inflation adjustment' as the nominal value of net monetary debt outstanding multiplied by the rate of inflation during the year.[58]

The distortion due to inflation can be very large. Looking at the unadjusted figures, the decade since 1973 appears as a time when deficit finance was actively used to offset recessionary forces. Looking at the inflation-adjusted figures a very different picture results. The period at the end of the 1960s appears as one with very tight policy as budget surpluses were combined with accelerating inflation, and hence a substantial 'inflation tax'. The relaxation apparent in the nominal figures, of some $5\frac{1}{2}$ per cent of GDP from 1970–3, is still indicated in the inflation-adjusted data. The years of very high deficits in 1974 and 1975, however, appear in substantial inflation-adjusted *surplus*. The large relaxations appear to come in 1976 and again in 1978 with reductions in the inflation tax. The table also brings out the relatively small variation in the

[55] See OECD, *Economic Outlook* (July 1982), pp. 40–3.

[56] More recent procedures adopted by the IMF, which include treating all increases in unemployment benefits as 'cyclically neutral', increase the apparent tightening in the IMF method—so that the figures are close to those of the OECD. See IMF, *World Economic Outlook* (1983).

[57] For a discussion of some of these issues see Miller [28], and Buiter [9].

[58] For a discussion of the methods used see Taylor and Threadgold [40]. Very similar results would obtain from using the market value of debt [28], though varying treatments of the large losses in the mid-1970s (reflected in strongly negative *real* rates of interest) can lead to substantially different estimates of the 'inflation tax' in those years. In the period 1979–82, real interest rates were closer to their longer-term values, and most methods of adjustment give a broadly similar picture.

TABLE 13.9. *Inflation-Adjusted Measures of Fiscal Stance, 1967–1982*

	General government financial balance (% of GDP)	Inflation adjustment (% of GDP)	Inflation adjustment balance (% of GDP)	Cyclically and inflation adjusted balance (% of GDP)	General government debt (% of GDP)
1967	−1·0	1·0	0·0	−0·3	63·2
1968	−0·5	3·0	2·5	2·4	59·7
1969	2·1	3·0	5·1	5·3	56·9
1970	3·0	3·5	6·5	7·0	50·3
1971	1·4	3·7	5·1	5·8	45·0
1972	−1·3	3·3	2·0	3·1	42·2
1973	−2·7	3·7	1·0	0·9	38·6
1974	−3·8	7·2	3·4	4·6	35·5
1975	−4·6	7·3	2·7	5·2	32·0
1976	−4·9	4·1	−0·8	1·6	33·2
1977	−3·2	4·1	0·9	2·9	32·8
1978	−4·2	2·6	−1·6	−0·9	31·2
1979	−3·2	4·7	1·5	2·1	30·1
1980	−3·3	3·4	0·1	2·5	27·9
1981	−2·6	3·3	0·7	5·1	29·6
1982	−1·7	1·9	0·2	5·9	26·5

Note: All GDP figures are at market prices.

Source: *Economic Trends:* author's estimates.

inflation-adjusted balance in the years 1979–82: as the fourth column indicates, the assessment of fiscal policy as tight and tightening in the years 1979–83 depends crucially on the procedures of *cyclical* adjustment. The real issue (as far as fiscal policy is concerned) over that period is the justification or otherwise of the policy of offsetting the operation of the automatic stabilizers and, in effect, pursuing financial targets largely independently of the extent of recession.

The broad lines of this picture are confirmed by looking, not at the balance of the budget, but at the stock figures for general government debt (Table 13.9, last column). As has been pointed out (see pp. 393–5), looking at the stock of debt outstanding as a proportion of GDP is (apart from statistical difficulties of coverage and valuation) rather like looking at 'inflation and growth adjusted' balances. This indicator fell sharply from 63 per cent of GDP in 1967 to 26½ per cent in 1982, with particularly large declines in the ratio in the early 1970s when the inflation-adjusted surplus was high.

Finally, it is necessary to consider the complications introduced by the oil price rises of the 1970s—both in 1973–4, when the impact was entirely external, and in 1979–80 when, with self-sufficiency, it was internal as well. In order to take these impacts fully into account it is necessary to focus not on the public sector, but on the position of the *private* sector (see discussion in section 12.3.7 of

Chapter 12) and, for the second impact, to go beyond that and consider what an offsetting or neutral policy towards oil might have been.

In 1973, the external impact is readily apparent in the sectoral balances in Table 13.6, which shows the swing to surplus of the overseas sector (i.e. the swing to deficit of the current account of the balance of payments by some 3-4 per cent of GDP). An approximately corresponding swing is visible in the company sector position. Looking at the position in 1974, the surplus of the private sector was 1·7 per cent of GDP, smaller by 4 per cent of GDP than the Public Sector Financial Deficit.[59] Thus the fiscal tightening appears much stronger if attention is focused on the position of the private sector. An alternative way of looking at the issue, also outlined in Chapter 12, is to note than an offsetting policy would have been for the public sector to widen its deficit to counteract the external impact of oil, and then to measure what actually happened against such a standard or baseline of 'neutral' policy action.

During the second oil crisis in 1979-80 the UK was effectively self-sufficient in oil due to the build-up of North Sea production (see Chapter 27). This means that there was no comparable external impact on the UK to be taken into account in assessing fiscal policy. But as far as the *non-oil private sector* was concerned, the oil impact in the UK was very similar to that in other countries, and to the impact of 1973-4. The difference was that the price rise would have its main effect on the tax revenues of the UK Government. In principle this means that a 'neutral' policy towards oil could have been adopted, for example by lowering some other tax—such as Value-Added Tax—by an equivalent amount as the oil price rises came through.[60] There was a difficulty, however, in that much of the increased oil tax revenues would accrue to the government 3-4 years later since, in the short term, the oil companies operating in the North Sea could use various allowances. In the event, no offset to the oil impact was made (though it can always be claimed that without oil, taxes would have had to be raised). By the time the oil revenues did come through in large quantities to the Exchequer the recession itself had so swelled government spending—for example on unemployment benefit—that (given the MFTS) tax cuts were unlikely. The general point is that the oil price rises in 1979-80 had an impact on the private sector which was similar to that in other countries, with the effects on public revenue coming later. It is perhaps not surprising that the response of the private sector was no less strong.[61]

[59] Note that the figures in Tables 13.8 and 13.9 refer to the position of general government rather than the public sector. The latter includes the nationalized industries, which, in 1974 were in deficit by about 2 per cent of GDP.

[60] In principle, oil prices might have been left low in the UK: this would, however, have created difficulties and, arguably it was in any case optimal to match the world price rise. A rise in oil price (like an increase in duty) balanced by a fall in other indirect taxes would have had little impact on the current price level, or on demand, whilst maintaining the 'real' relative increase in the price of oil.

[61] In the rational and perfect world of the textbooks the private sector, though hit immediately by the price rises, would anticipate the future benefits via the tax system so that there would be no effect on spending. This did not appear to happen.

13.4.2. Monetary Stance: 1970–1982

Monetary stance, as has been seen, is even harder to summarize than fiscal stance. The notable feature of the 1970s was the increasing political importance given to monetary norms and targets, culminating in the MTFS. The main target variable was £M3—and in the period from about 1976 to 1983 this was taken as the main indicator of stance. There are, however, other indicators that can be used, separately or in combination. A selection is shown for reference in Table 13.10.

The rapid rise in £M3 after Competition and Credit Control (1972) is readily apparent, as is the rapid rise in 1980. In the former case, however, the ratio of £M3/GDP also rose substantially (equivalently, the velocity of circulation slowed)—an observation consistent with the view that monetary expansion was excessive. Monetarists would see this rise in the real money supply as a major reason for the subsequent surge in inflation. The difficulty is that the rapid inflation can also be explained by the world commodity price boom, oil price rises, and the like. Other narrower measures of money show nothing like so strong a movement.[62] The picture in 1980 is quite different: rapid growth of £M3 coincided with rapid growth in nominal GDP, and velocity was unaffected. The table also shows the course of interest rates, short and long, in nominal and real terms, bringing out the strongly negative real rates that obtained in the mid-1970s, and the relatively high real rates in 1981 and 1982. Also shown is the 'real' exchange rate—an indicator of competitiveness—showing the enormous rise from 1976 to 1980. This upward pressure on the exchange rate was frequently appealed to—especially in 1980—as an indicator of the general tightness of monetary stance in spite of the contrary indication from £M3.[63]

Though it is possible to make broad judgements about whether monetary stance was, in particular periods, 'tight' or 'loose', the effects of monetary variables on economic behaviour remain extremely hard to pin down. Some channels of interaction are well established—such as effects from interest rates and mortgage availability on housing. More pervasive effects from the monetary aggregates have proved hard to establish empirically. The effects of the exchange rate and competitiveness appear strong and (relatively speaking) reasonably predictable. In assessing policy over the period 1970–83, however, that is less helpful than it might seem since (at the time at least) there was considerable uncertainty as to what determined the exchange rate [9]. The spectacular rise from 1976 to 1980 has been ascribed to a number of factors, in particular a combination of North Sea oil and tight monetary and fiscal policies (see pp. 207–14) but quantification of the various effects is difficult. The likelihood of 'overshooting' in exchange rate movements (see Chapter 6, p. 205–6) also obscured just how tight (or otherwise) monetary policy was at the time.

---

[62] It is possible to account for this by the combination of excessive monetary growth and a switch out of M1—largely non-interest bearing—as nominal interest rates rose.
[63] See *Bank of England Quarterly Bulletin*, relevant issues.

TABLE 13.10. *Indicators of Monetary Stance*

| | £M3/GDP (%) | M1/GDP (%) | Mo/GDP (%) | Consumer prices increase 1 year ahead (%) | Interest rates | | | | Real exchange rate (1975(Q4)=100) | % change in £M3, year end (%) |
| | | | | | nominal | | real | | | |
					short(a) (%)	long(b) (%)	short(a) (%)	long(b) (%)		
1967	0·32	0·20		4·69	6·18	6·80	1·49	2·11	100·6	9·55
1968	0·33	0·20		5·64	7·45	7·55	1·81	1·91	91·6	7·76
1969	0·33	0·19		5·86	7·85	9·05	1·99	3·19	95·3	2·04
1970	0·32	0·19		8·43	7·25	9·22	−1·18	0·79	98·9	9·43
1971	0·32	0·19		6·54	5·68	8·87	−0·86	1·33	103·0	12·89
1972	0·35	0·19	0·07	8·65	5·92	8·91	−2·73	0·26	94·9	24·61
1973	0·38	0·18	0·07	17·16	10·00	10·56	−7·16	−6·60	86·0	27·17
1974	0·40	0·17	0·06	23·68	12·29	14·79	−11·39	−8·89	97·7	10·46
1975	0·35	0·15	0·06	15·72	10·38	14·39	−5·34	−1·33	100·1	6·73
1976	0·32	0·15	0·06	15·20	11·17	14·43	−4·03	−0·77	86·3	9·52
1977	0·29	0·14	0·05	8·80	8·88	12·73	0·08	3·93	92·9	10·20
1978	0·29	0·15	0·05	12·75	9·07	12·47	−3·68	−0·28	97·2	15·13
1979	0·28	0·15	0·05	16·23	13·71	12·99	−2·52	−3·24	117·0	12·71
1980	0·28	0·13	0·05	10·79	16·31	13·79	5·52	3·00	148·2	19·05
1981	0·30	0·13	0·05	8·07	13·25	14·74	5·18	6·67	131·2	13·26
1982	0·30	0·13	0·04	6·10	11·93	12·88	5·83	6·78	134·4	9·77
(1983 Q1)	0·30	0·13	0·04	6·16	10·01	11·35	3·85	5·19		

Notes:
(a) Bank Rate/Minimum Lending Rate.
(b) Gross redemption yield on 20-year government stock.
(c) Deflated by normalized unit labour costs.

Source: *Economic Trends; Financial Statistics.*

4.3. The Balance Between Monetary and Fiscal Policy

e have noted that one of the features of the period since 1970 was the swing of icial economic fashion, first towards monetarism, and then back (in part) wards fiscal policy in the form of targets for public borrowing. This was lected in an apparently increasing concern over the *consistency* of fiscal and netary policy, which became explicit with the Medium-Term Financial ategy.

In spite of the importance of the issues, however, the balance between netary and fiscal policy is extremely difficult to measure. Ideally, the stances monetary and fiscal policy need to be separately assessed before their relative sition can be judged. We have seen, however, how difficult it is to provide ambiguous measures. Nor is the claim that the relative strengths of monetary d fiscal actions can only be evaluated within a model of the economy useful in context of widespread disagreement over the model to be applied. Thus this tion, whilst looking at some of the indicators that might be used, is intended sound a note of caution: it is very difficult to measure the balance between netary and fiscal policy and accordingly hard to give empirical content to tements about 'consistency'—however desirable consistency might seem.

One approach to the problems is to look at the composition of the financial ets held by the private sector. (Cf. the discussion in section 12.2.7 of Chapter , where it is suggested that fiscal policy can be taken to be concerned with blic borrowing and public sector debt, whilst monetary policy is concerned th composition effects and/or interest changes.) To do this properly would volve examining the stocks of all financial assets held by the private sector king into account, for example, the major fall in stock market values in 73–4) and not just public sector assets/liabilities. This is not attempted here: vertheless Figure 13.3 shows the development of some financial stock/GDP ios over the period since 1967.

It is notable that narrow money (M1) shows relatively little variation over period apart from a downward trend (rise in velocity of circulation). The wnward trend is lower than that for public sector or general government bt up until about 1973; after that they are similar. There is more interest in mparing the development of £M3 with public sector debt.[64] The rise in M3 from 1971 to peak (as a proportion of GDP) in 1974 comes out clearly: the blic debt figures suggest a fiscal relaxation starting about two years later. If ything, the figure would lend mild support to the proposition that monetary icy was *relatively* loose from 1971–3 and that fiscal policy was relatively pansionary round about 1976–8 and that they were approximately in lance since. Any such categorization would, however, be subject to major veats about the interpretation to be given to summary indicators of monetary

---

[4] Note that in simple models, the money supply is often taken as being Central Bank money and omponent of public sector debt. Thus a comparison of the two would show the proportion that s 'monetized'. £M3, however, is predominantly *inside money*—a claim not on the government but the banking system. Base money is a relatively small proportion of £M3, and within base ney, Bankers' Balances held at the Bank of England (arguably the effective cash base of the em) are very small indeed. Thus any connection between public debt and money (if there is) would have to be indirect.

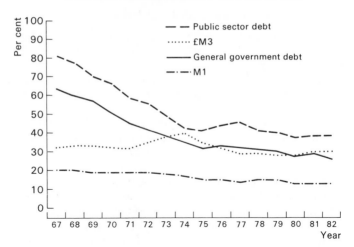

FIG. 13.3. Financial Asset Stocks (as a Proportion of GDP).

Sources: Miller and Babbs [29], Tables 8 and 9. *Financial Statistics.*

and fiscal stance outlined in previous sections. The main message of the figure appears to be *negative*: it is not easy to deduce that monetary and fiscal policy were inconsistent with each other—and in particular, in the period of monetary targets since 1976, it would be hard to argue that National Debt was 'excessive' in relation to £M3, or thereby posing problems for the control of money or for interest rates.

This rather negative conclusion is, perhaps, reinforced by Figure 13.4 which shows the increase in £M3 as a proportion of GDP, as well as the public sector balance, also as a proportion of GDP. The series move broadly together before 1969 and from about 1977 onwards. The intervening period is one of apparently major disturbance associated with Competition and Credit Control, with (world-wide) inflation, and with the first oil crisis. But there is certainly no evidence from the Figure to support the popular proposition that public borrowing 'caused money' to increase. On the contrary, looking only at the Figure, it would appear that the surge of money 'caused' the surge in public borrowing approximately two years later. But such casual correlations should not be regarded as significant: it is necessary to go behind the figures to what was actually happening. If that is done then it is just as plausible that the two series (taking the two series for the public sector balance together) have little *direct* connection. Both were affected by policy actions, but at different times; both were affected by inflation, by oil, and by world recession.

Finally, looking at the period from about 1978–82, it appears that fiscal and monetary policy were broadly 'consistent', at least in the sense that they appeared to be pulling in the same direction, and there were no large relative changes in the stock of money and public debt. This consistency, however, actually *conceals* the real policy issues which were about what would happen if monetary and fiscal policy were not consistent in the sense described.

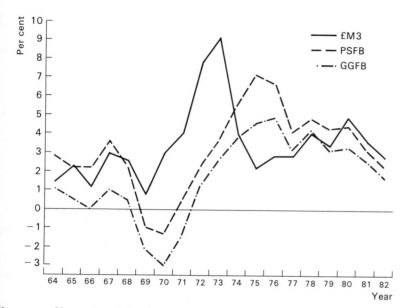

'IG. 13.4. Change in £M3, the Public Sector and General Government Financial Balances (as Proportions of GDP).

Sources: Table 13.3. *Financial Statistics. Economic Trends.*

particular, at the time, the main question was about the effects of a fiscal relaxation (PSBR increase) against a given monetary target. Where more than consistency' was at stake, views differed sharply.

One view was that a fiscal relaxation would have the traditional effects, raising nominal spending—even though there would be some effect due to crowding-out' via interest rate rises. (Conventional monetarists would see the crowding-out as complete, and fiscal policy as ineffective.) Against this there was (as we have noted in discussing the Medium-Term Financial Strategy) another view: that increases in public borrowing would expand public debt and, via a 'portfolio relationship', increase the demand for *money*. Thus the effect of a fiscal relaxation would be *either* to raise the money supply—which might raise price expectations and inflation—*or* to raise interest rates. In either case the effects were seen as entirely adverse. (Some appeared to argue that fiscal relaxations were, at one and the same time, inflationary via money *and* deflationary via interest rate rises.) Indeed, it was easy to go further and, by neglecting any *direct* effects of a fiscal relaxation on activity or prices, to see fiscal policy as perverse and argue that fiscal tightness would actually *promote* recovery.[65] Thus a concern with consistency hides some very important

[65] One mechanism could be via an effect of lower interest rates on the exchange rate, and hence the competitiveness of industry. Against any such effects, however (which are plausible enough) must be set the *direct* effects of fiscal tightening in lowering activity.

disagreements over the role of fiscal policy. For some, a more expansionary fiscal policy with 'unchanged' monetary stance (in fact a relative tightening) would have had some expansionary effect on the economy, albeit attentuated by some crowding-out; for others the effect would have been zero or even perverse. But the debate was at once different from, and more important than, whether there was or was not 'consistency' of monetary and fiscal policy.

There is little evidence for such perverse effects from fiscal policy in the 1970s—though adverse expectational effects in domestic and international financial markets presumably could cause them to occur. The 'portfolio approach' also has to face up to the evidence that public debt was low in the 1970s, by the UK's own historical standards, and that apparently vast variations have occurred in the ratio of National Debt to GDP and to money with no apparent effect on interest rates.[66] And more recent data are not favourable to the proposition that public borrowing causes money to expand, either. On the other hand, there is a great deal of evidence that fiscal policy has direct effects on spending of the conventional kind. The main difficulty in an adverse expectational climate is not that fiscal policy might have perverse effects, but that its conventional effects might lead to inflation rather than to increases in activity. This is a problem for demand management policy as a whole—i.e. taken to include both monetary and fiscal policy action.

13.5. Assessing the Period 1970–1983

Any evaluation of the role of demand management policy in the 1970s and early 1980s is bound to be difficult—both because of uncertainties over the underlying framework of analysis that should be applied, and because of the many difficulties of measurement outlined in the preceding section. At the time of writing it is, moreover, too soon for any full assessment of the MTFS. This section concentrates on two aspects which appear particularly important:

(i) The effects of demand management policy on activity and employment
(ii) Expectations and the credibility of policy.

13.5.1. Overall Effects on Activity and Employment

One of the questions raised by monetarist and new classical economists is whether demand management policy does, in fact, have any effect on the overall output of the economy. We have already seen that, in the 1950s and 1960s, the question is not quite as easy to answer positively as is sometimes assumed: partly because there was so much else going on and partly because there are reasons to suppose that a *successful* demand management policy would itself powerfully affect expectations and the behaviour of economic agents. In the 1970s the economy was subject to major shocks and, even more than in the 1950s and 1960s, demand management has to be seen as part of the overall economic management of the economy, along with policy towards the exchange rate, towards industry, and towards incomes restraint. Given the

---

[66] Figure 13.2 indicates that National Debt was some $2\frac{3}{4}$ *times* GDP after the Second World War and that interest rates were low.

buffeting the economy received it does not appear useful to try and assess whether demand management was in some overall sense *stabilizing*; nor would it be easy to argue that the practice of policy allowed a high and stable level of growth.

The shocks to which the economy was subject in the 1970s, and the conflicting and changing objectives, mean that the only real starting-point for an evaluation is to ask whether the instruments of policy had (at the time, or with the benefit of hindsight) reasonably predictable effects on the economy. Policy has already been discussed in qualitative terms in this Chapter, and for the most part demand management does seem to have had the kind of effects that were expected—at least as far as activity and unemployment were concerned. This assessment is subject to at least two important caveats: the first is that there are instances where errors were clearly made; the second is that, in the 1980s, whether the results are assessed as being consistent with expectation depends upon which model of the world is adopted (primarily monetarist or Keynesian).

It is however possible to go a bit further. Table 13.11 shows the forecasts published with each Budget Statement since 1969–70, together with estimates of the same year published with the next Budget statement, as well as the out-turn as estimated still later. Such published forecasts may of course not

TABLE 13.11. *Budget Forecasts and Out-turns, 1969–70*
to 1983–4
(percentage change)

	Forecast 1st half to 1st half year later	Estimate 1 year later	Out-turn
1969–70	2·9	3·1	2·0
1970–1	3·5	1·3	2·0
1971–2	3·1	3·9*	2·1
1972–3	5·9*	7·1*	8·9
1973–4	4·5	−4·5†	−2·3
1974–5	2·5†	2·5†	−0·7
1975–6	1·5	1·0	1·8
1976–7	4·0	1·0	3·0
1977–8	1·5	1·0	3·0
1978–9	3·0	1·0	2·2
1979–80	−1·0	−2·0	−0·7
1980–1	−1·5	−4·0	−3·8
1981–2	1·0	1·0	0·7
1982–3	2·0	1·4	2·4
1983–4	2·5		

* Estimates for individual years affected by local strikes.
† Estimates affected by miners' strike and three-day week.

Source: *Financial Statement and Budget Reports.*

represent all the information available to the Treasury at the time, but nevertheless give some indication of where the government thought the economy was going in the short term. Several things stand out from the table.

The first, at a rather mundane level, is the considerable variation (and, by implication, error) in estimates of the *recent past*. Sometimes the difference between the situation assessed at the time, and the picture that emerges later, is striking.[67] Moreover, in the early 1970s the statistics available to policy makers were much distorted by the hard-to-assess effects of the miners' strikes and the three-day week.

Otherwise, the picture that emerges is one of some consistency between forecasts and out-turns, but with important errors which are themselves illuminating.[68].

In the period 1970–3 the over-optimism about prospects for output in the first two years, followed by excessively rapid expansion later, comes out clearly. The data were much distorted by the miners' strike of 1971–2, but perhaps the most surprising thing is the degree to which that excessive upswing *was* anticipated with apparent complacency. The massive error in spring 1973 for prospects over the coming year 1973–4 is, of course, entirely understandable— since the oil shock was not anticipated at that time. The data for 1974–5 suggest that the impact of oil was underestimated, though yet again the statistical picture at the time, and subsequently, was clouded by the effects of strikes and the three-day week.

A notable feature is the extent to which the recession of the early 1980s was predicted—even officially, though some doubt was thrown at the time on the usefulness of such neo-Keynesian forecasts. The real error occurred in 1980 (after the steel strike), when it appeared that around April/May the economy 'fell over a cliff'. There was a sudden downward shift in output as industry came under intense pressure, and the stockbuilding cycle took hold.

Turning to other aspects of the story, one feature is that financial effects seem to have been important, though they remain very hard to quantify. Table 13.6 on sectoral balances indicates that each of the recessions—1970–1, 1974–5, and 1980–1—followed swings to deficit in the company sector[69] which were followed by stockbuilding reduction and 'shakeouts' of labour. The swings to deficit were for different reasons. The first was induced by fiscal policy (when Jenkins was Chancellor) which was tightened in order to make devaluation work. The second was largely the result of the external impact of oil. In the third, the exposed sectors of British industry were squeezed between high pay rises on the one hand and the strongly rising exchange rate on the other.

Cyclical adjustment, inflation adjustment, and the impact of oil have all been discussed in this chapter. Very broadly, the recession of 1974–5 can be

---

[67] Out-turn figures can vary from initial estimates for a host of reasons. Apart from more complete information, these include rebasing of the figures—e.g. from 1970-based figures to 1975 based figures.

[68] For an analysis of the forecasts and errors made by the National Institute over the whole period 1959–82 see *National Institute Economic Review* (Aug. 1983).

[69] Though the data are somewhat unreliable: the figures shown for the company sector deficit include the 'residual error' in computing the balances.

accounted for in conventional terms if allowance is made for oil and inflation. Indeed, full allowance in those years for the 'inflation tax' probably overstates the fiscal tightening and the impact on behaviour.[70] The fall of inflation under the Labour Government's incomes policy against continuing high nominal deficits can be seen as at least one factor behind the upswing in the late 1970s.[71] Certainly, taking inflation into account, it appears that fiscal stance became more accommodating at that time.

Looking at the various indicators of fiscal policy in the period 1979–83 from the conventional demand management point of view, an unprecedentedly severe fiscal squeeze is apparent, starting in 1979. Allowance for the effects of recession on public borrowing, or for inflation, suggests that the underlying (or structural) budget position was moved to surplus. Allowance for both together suggests a massive effective tightening of fiscal stance—perhaps by as much as 5 per cent of GDP. From this point of view there was never any difficulty in 'explaining' the 1980–1 recession. As noted earlier, however, there were aspects which were hard to account for. In particular, the rise in the real exchange rate (see Table 13.10) went much further than most people had expected, even allowing for high interest rates and North Sea oil. (See Chapter 6, pp. 205–6, for an analysis of 'overshooting' of the exchange rate.) Whatever the cause, it added to the recessionary forces as well as concentrating them on the exposed sectors of British industry.

In general terms too it appears that monetary policy had the kind of effects expected of it according to the conventional demand management view. The excessive expansion of credit and money in 1971 and 1972 has already been referred to. High nominal interest rates in late 1979 and 1980 were an additional factor bearing directly on industry in addition to affecting the exchange rate. The modest recovery that set in from about 1981 onwards[72] was driven by consumer spending, itself the result of reduced savings. A major reason for the reduction of savings was the rapid fall in inflation, but also the extension of credit—especially mortgage finance—reflecting generally easier financial conditions.

There is nothing in this to suggest that demand management policy had somehow stopped working in the 1970s. On the contrary, the overriding impression from forecasts and commentary at the time is that the instruments of policy, both fiscal and monetary, were actively used. Errors were made and some of them, such as the excessive stimulus to demand in 1972–3, were serious. But by and large they had the predicted effects. The difficulties lay elsewhere in the shocks to which the economy was subject, and in apparently incompatible objectives. Even more than in the 1960s, it became apparent that demand management was no panacea: whilst appropriate demand management

---

[70] The inflation tax, much of which worked like a tax on capital, is better seen as having effects which were spread out over several years.

[71] The upswing was also helped by a lag of wages behind prices which, as they decelerated, boosted disposable incomes.

[72] The recession appeared to reach a trough in mid-1981 if GDP figures are looked at. Manufacturing production reached its low point about one year later.

policies might be necessary for success, they were certainly not sufficient. Even in the 1980s when the *way* in which the instruments have been used has changed substantially, reflecting both different views of how the economy works and different priorities in objectives, still monetary and fiscal policy have played an important, and for the most part predictable, part in determining the behaviour of demand.

By far the most important problem was with inflation. Most of the twists and turns in policy can be seen as attempts to get to grips with high and volatile inflation. The instruments of demand management policy were turned against inflation in the early 1970s, but the experience appeared so unfavourable that the strategy was abandoned in favour of the 'alternative' of expansion plus incomes restraint. Incomes policy was the main counter-inflation strategy of the Labour Government in the second half of the 1970s, with demand management (and, after 1976, financial targets) playing a supportive role. Finally, still looking at the picture from from an eclectic demand management viewpoint, the instruments of policy were massively tightened against inflation in 1979–82, with predictable results on activity and unemployment. Inflation eventually responded, falling rapidly in 1980–3, but the 'trade-off' with unemployment was extremely unfavourable: unemployment rose to 3 million, a level which would have been politically unthinkable a decade earlier.

13.5.2. Expectations and the Credibility of Policy

As has been noted in a number of places in this chapter, extreme monetarist or neo-classical frameworks of analysis suggest no role for demand management policy in affecting activity or unemployment. Whilst details vary, the usual hypothesis is that fiscal policy has no effect—for example due to crowding-out via interest rates—and that monetary policy affects only prices. (In another version, closer to the spirit of the MTFS, fiscal policy may affect prices via money.)

These views have been most clearly expressed by proponents of the new classical macroeconomics. In such a world there is a 'natural level of output' which is determined by the general characteristics of the economic system. This natural rate is achieved when the economy is in equilibrium (all markets clear) and expectations are fulfilled. Output can, however, deviate from its natural rate if expectations are *incorrect*. The mechanism usually works from the supply side: if, for example, the rate of inflation is under-predicted, mistakes will be made and the real wage will fall. Firms, facing the lower real wage, expand output. These effects are likely to be temporary, however, and the economy reverts to its natural output as expectations (and contracts based on them) catch up with reality.

If prices and inflation are determined by the money supply, and if expectations of prices are *rational* (i.e. in this case dependent in turn on expected changes in the money supply),[73] then it is easy to see that only *unanticipated* changes in policy can have any effect. Anticipated changes in policy—i.e. in the

---

[73] Strictly speaking, it is better to say that the expectations are *consistent* with the assumed model. This leaves to one side the awkward question of whether it would be 'rational' to believe the model.

money supply—would not drive actual and expected prices apart, so there would be no effect on output.[74]

Such parables are obviously far removed from the practicalities of demand management policy. They have the virtue, however, of illustrating the importance of the 'model', of expectations, and of the interactions between them. In the 1950s and 1960s, the dominant view of the world was that prices, if not constant, were at least given; and that demand management policy would have its impact on real activity. It has already been suggested earlier that the *expectation* that policy worked in that way probably had powerful effects on economic behaviour. We have also seen, in looking at the 1970s, that *perceptions* of how economic policy worked and what it could do changed radically. Whether or not that change was justified, these perceptions fed through both into expectations and into actual economic behaviour—i.e. into the *model*. These in turn affect *how* policy works, and condition what is possible.

The most notable changes in the 1970s were, first, the developing recognition that inflation could be high and volatile, and second, that policy action could, in unfavourable circumstances, dissipate itself in inflation rather than growth. And with this recognition it became all too apparent that policy makers were highly constrained in what they could do. It became important that economic policy should be *credible*: if it was not credible, it was highly likely that reactions, especially in financial markets, would be adverse.

It is very difficult to quantify anything so vague as an expectational climate. But a number of examples of its importance can be tentatively put forward. The first, in the early 1970s, is the unexpectedly long lag before policy took effect—and the consequent overshoot. One explanation for this is that, even then, the expectation that the government could deliver more rapid growth had been shaken, leading to a 'wait and see' attitude. The second is the reaction of international financial markets in 1976, when it appears that perceptions of the authorities' exchange rate policy played a vital role. A third example, perhaps, is public scepticism about the Labour Government's incomes policy after the 'winter of discontent'.

The clearest example, however, is the Medium-Term Financial Strategy. This had the explicit objective of laying a credible financial framework for a disinflationary policy. One of the explanations put forward for the adverse responses of wages and inflation to the initial policies of the 1979 Conservative Government was that announced intentions for monetary targets were not sufficiently believed—they were not credible. Thus the climate of expectations was not changed, and the pressure of wage rises against tight policies led to recession. Adherence to the targets and projections of MTFS was seen as part of a strategy of radically altering the climate of expectations, and so lowering inflation.

It is more or less impossible to establish the part played by the MTFS in helping to lower inflation as compared with the more conventional effects of unemployment and the squeeze on industry. To the extent that it was helpful, it should have lowered unemployment compared with what it otherwise would

[74] For a discussion of these and other policy ineffectiveness results see Begg [4].

have been for any given progress against inflation. It is probable that it was an element in convincing economic agents that policy would continue to be non-accommodating—that there would be no U-turn. But whilst this represented a major change in attitudes and expectations, it is only on the monetarist model that non-accommodating policies solve the economic problem. For the monetarists and new classicists, output reverts to its 'natural' level and rate of growth, and macroeconomic policy affects only inflation. There is no case for an active demand management policy and no longer-term trade-off. But what if they are wrong?

The case for demand management policy, it will be recalled, rested on some sort of failure of the private sector of itself to generate high employment and stable growth. In the late 1970s, and early 1980s, the instruments of policy were, in effect, diverted to the control of inflation. Even if such policies were fully effective in stopping inflation, however, it would be only half a victory. Unless the optimism of the monetarists is justified, what is needed is a credible way of bringing the instruments of demand management policy back into use without rekindling inflation.

Bibliography

[1] ALLSOPP, C. J. 'Inflation', in [7].
[2] BECKERMAN, W. (ed.). *The Labour Government's Economic Record 1966–1970* (Duckworth, 1972).
[3] BECKERMAN, W. *et al. The British Economy in 1975* (Cambridge University Press, 1965).
[4] BEGG, D. *The Rational Expectations Revolution in Macroeconomics: Theories and Evidence* (Philip Allan, Oxford, 1982).
[5] BLACKABY, F. T. (ed.). *British Economic Policy, 1960–74* (Heinemann, 1978).
[6] BOLTHO, A. 'British Fiscal Policy 1955–1971: Stabilizing or Destabilizing?', *Oxford Bulletin of Economics and Statistics* (Nov. 1981).
[7] BOLTHO, A. (ed.). *The European Economy: Growth and Crisis* (Oxford University Press, 1982).
[8] BRONFENBRENNER, M. (ed.). *Is the Business Cycle Obsolete?* (Wiley Interscience, New York, 1969).
[9] BUITER, W. H. 'Measurement of the Public Sector Deficit and its Implications for Policy Evaluation and Design', *IMF Staff Papers*, **30**/2 (June 1983).
[10] BUITER, W. and MILLER, M. 'Thatcherism: The First Two Years', *Brookings Papers on Economic Activity* (1981).
[11] BURNS, T. and BUDD, A. 'The Role of the PSBR in Controlling the Money Supply' (London Business School, 1979).
[12] CAIRNCROSS, A. (ed.). *Britain's Economic Prospects Reconsidered* (George Allen and Unwin, 1970).
[13] CAIRNCROSS, F. (ed.). *Changing Perspectives on Economic Policy* (Oxford University Press, 1981).
[14] CAVES, R. E. (ed.). *Britain's Economic Prospects* (George Allen and Unwin, 1968).
[15] DOW, J. C. R. *The Management of the British Economy, 1945–60* (Cambridge University Press, 1964).
[16] FELLNER, W. *et al. The Problem of Rising Prices* (OECD, 1964).
[17] FFORDE, J. 'Setting Monetary Objectives', *Bank of England Quarterly Bulletin* (June, 1983), 200–8.

18] FRIEDMAN, M. Memorandum in House of Commons, *Memoranda on Monetary Policy*, IC (1979–80) (HMSO 1980).

19] HAACHE, G. and TOWNEND, J. 'Exchange Rate and Monetary Policy: Modelling terling's Effective Exchange Rate, 1972–80', in Eltis, W. and Sinclair, P. (eds.), *The Money Supply and the Exchange Rate* (Oxford University Press, 1981).

20] HANSEN, N. *Fiscal Policy in Seven Countries, 1955–1965* (OECD, 1969).

21] KALDOR, N. *Causes of the Slow Rate of Growth of the U.K.* (Cambridge University Press, 1966).

22] —— —— 'Conflicts in National Economic Objectives', *Economic Journal* 81 (Mar. 971).

23] KAREKEN, J. H. 'Monetary Policy', in [14].

24] KENNEDY, M. C. 'The Economy as a Whole', in [34].

25] LAWSON, N. 'Britain's Policy and Britain's Place in the International Financial Community', Speech given at the *Financial Times* Euromarkets Conference, London (21 an. 1980).

26] LITTLE, I. D. M. Review of Dow [15], *Economic Journal* (Dec. 1966).

27] McCRACKEN, P. W. *et al. Towards Full Employment and Price Stability* (OECD, 1977).

28] MILLER, M. 'Inflation Adjusting the Public Sector Financial Deficit: Measurements and Implication for Policy', in Kay, J. (ed.), *The 1983 Budget* (London, 1982).

29] MILLER, M. H. and BABBS, S. 'The True Cost of Debt Service and The Public ector Financial Deficit', Mimeo (Apr. 1983).

30] MINFORD, A. P. L. and PEEL, D. *Rational Expectations and the New Macroeconomics* Martin Robertson, 1983).

31] MUSGRAVE, R. A. and MUSGRAVE, P. B., 'Fiscal Policy', in [14].

32] NORDHAUS, W. D. 'The Worldwide Wage Explosion', *Brookings Papers on Economic ctivity*, 2 (1972).

33] PERRY, G. L. 'Determinants of Wage Inflation Around the World', *Brookings Papers n Economic Activity* (1975).

34] PREST, A. R. and COPPOCK, D. J. (eds.). *The UK Economy: A Manual of Applied conomics*, 7th edn. (Weidenfeld and Nicholson, 1978).

35] REID, D. J. 'Public Sector Debt', *Economic Trends* (May, 1977), 100–9.

36] RICHARDSON, G. Mais Lecture, City University (1978).

37] SOSKICE, D. 'Strike Waves and Wage Explosions 1968–70: An Economic nterpretation', in Crouch, C. and Pizzorno, A. (eds.), *The Resurgence of Class Conflict in Western Europe Since 1968* (London, 1978).

38] STEWART, M. *The Jeckyll and Hyde Years* (Dent, 1977).

39] SURREY, M. J. C. 'The United Kingdom', in [7].

40] TAYLOR, C. T. and THREADGOLD, A. R. *Real National Saving and its Sectoral 'omposition*, Bank of England Discussion Paper No. 6 (Oct. 1979).

41] HM Treasury. 'Background to the Government's Economic Policy' in *Third Report rom The Treasury's Civil Service Committee: Monetary Policy*, HC (1980–81), 163, III, HMSO 1981).

14

Modelling the Economy

M. J. C. SURREY

14.1. Introduction

In Chapter 5 a basic model of the economy was developed which served as a framework for much of the analysis of subsequent chapters. This basic model was highly schematic: it was intended to focus attention on the main elements in the determination of the level of economic activity, the level of employment, the state of the balance of payments, and so on, rather than to provide a realistic model of the way in which an economy such as that of the UK actually functions. The purpose of this chapter is to extend the basic model of Chapter 5 in the light of the analysis of the intervening chapters so as to arrive at a model which is sufficiently close to reality to serve as a tool with which to assess the economy. 'Assessment' here means understanding the primary causes of the past behaviour of the economy, being able to provide reasonably trustworthy forecasts of its future behaviour, and estimating the likely consequences of changes in policy or performance of the economy.

A number of models of the UK economy now exists. Each comprises a set of equations which summarize different main economic relationships in the economy. The basic forms of these equations are derived from theoretical considerations, but the precise formulation is determined in the light of historical data on the economy. These models are used both for forecasting and for simulating the effects of possible changes in the economy, and undergo modification and improvements as understanding of the economy increases.

In what follows, we first describe a basic structure which underlies several major, albeit different, models. We then go on to look at five major UK models, bringing out how and why they differ at the time of writing.

14.2. Developing a Theoretical Model

14.2.1. The Basic Flow Model

It is important to stress at the outset that the major econometric models of the economy to date have been essentially 'demand based'. This does not mean that the supply-side factors outlined in Chapter 5—the quality and size of the capital stock, available labour and its quality and skills, and the state of technological know-how and its degree of application—are ignored. Rather they are regarded as together determining the maximum output of the economy at any time, and as changing through time relatively slowly in comparison with such things as prices, interest rates, or expenditure. Most models predominantly concentrate, therefore, on demand as the determinant of the extent to which the capacity of the economy is in fact utilized, or the determinant, therefore, of such variables as output, employment, etc. Supply-side factors when required in such models are typically put in as a 'trend' increase in productivity, i.e. a constant percentage increase each year in the total output available from the inputs.

This is a major problem which step-by-step is being improved. For example, improvement in the skills of the labour force or in the efficiency of management may mean that a given demand-side boost will have a greater effect on output and less effect on inflation than otherwise, effects which can only be incorporated in demand-based models with difficulty. None the less such models can give useful forecasts and insights into the likely consequences of changes in the economy, especially over the shorter term, for example two to three years, during which time supply-side changes are rarely very significant.[1]

The most basic model comprises the expenditure identity for the economy,

$$Y = C + I + G + X - M - T_y,$$

together with the assumptions that consumption is a function of disposable income,

$$C = f(YD),$$

investment is a function of interest rates,

$$I = f(r),$$

and imports are a function of income,

$$M = f(Y),$$

together with the assumptions also that government expenditure and exports of goods and services are exogenously determined, that direct taxes, T_y (the difference between Y and Yd), are given, or are a simple function of the level of national income, and that the interest rate is either exogenously determined or is given by the equation of the supply of and demand for money. Figure 14.1 represents the simplest possible flow diagram.

This schematic model fails to correspond to all closely with reality in three distinct ways. First, it is incomplete, in the sense of omitting important macroeconomic variables and relationships—the most glaring omission is the price level and its determination. Second, it is excessively aggregated: for example, no distinction is drawn between different kinds of private investment, and there is no breakdown of income into wages and salaries, profits, and so on. Third, the relationships for the consumption function, the investment function, and the export and import functions (which take no account of changes in relative prices and exchange rates) are highly over-simplified.

---

[1] 1980–3 represents one period where productivity appeared to break away from its trend line, resulting in the need to correct forecasts based on the conventional approach. See Chap. 29.

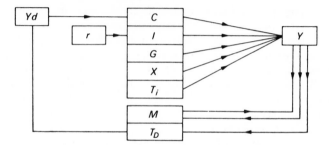

F1G. 14.1. Overall Expenditure Flow Chart.

What is the minimum degree of complication which is necessary to arrive at a 'realistic' macroeconomic model? The best way of answering this is to take each of the expenditure aggregates in turn.

14.2.2. Consumption

The first problem here is that the National Accounts' aggregate 'consumers' expenditure' lumps together both personal consumption proper (i.e. current expenditure by the personal sector on goods and services) and expenditure on durable goods. While consumption may depend only on disposable income, expenditure on durable goods is likely to be significantly affected by monetary factors, such as changes in the cost and availability of finance to persons, notably through hire-purchase and bank overdraft facilities. There is thus a strong case for treating the two components of consumers' expenditure separately.

The relevant concept of income is real personal disposable income (RPDI), which bears an extremely complex relationship to national income. There are several factors to be taken into account in passing from national income to RPDI:

(i) the distribution of national income between sectors;
(ii) transfers between sectors;
(iii) direct taxation;
(iv) changes in the price level.

(i) *The distribution of national income between sectors.* Income accruing directly to the personal sector comprises income from employment (wages and salaries together with income from self-employment), rent, and net receipts of interest. The wage and salary bill is the product of average earnings and the level of employment. Average earnings depend on both negotiated standard rates of pay and on a variety of other factors reflected as 'wage drift'—that is, the tendency for the gap between standard rates and actual earnings to vary independently of changes in standard rates (because of changes in the scarcity of labour, changes in the extent of pieceworking, and so on). Changes in standard rates of pay may be affected by the general pressure of demand for labour, but will tend to be affected by the rate of price inflation and the extent to which central negotiations attempt to compensate for past inflation or anticipate future inflation. Incomes policy, whether statutory or voluntary, explicit or implicit, can also have an important effect.

The volume of employment is generally dependent on the levels of real output and of labour productivity. There is a tendency for labour productivity to increase over time, but an increase in output in excess of the increase in labour productivity will raise employment, and a lower rate of increase of output will reduce employment. However, this relationship is likely to be characterized by a significant lag: the initial response to a rise in the volume of employment desired by employers may be to increase overtime working until new workers can be hired. The underlying rate of growth of productivity may itself change as well.

The remainder of income accruing directly to the personal sector is influenced by a variety of factors. Incomes from self-employment seem to move broadly in line with employment incomes, while incomes from rent and interest—though growing fairly steadily over time—are influenced by a host of factors, including monetary policy and legislation. However, little is known about the precise determinants of changes in incomes from these sources, and in forecasting, for example, projected movements are very much a matter of extrapolation and guesswork.

(ii) *Transfers between sectors*. The next step is to add in transfers of income from the company and public sectors to the personal sector. Transfers from the company sector—notably dividends—tend to depend, after a lag, on company profits (though companies' dividends policies generally mean that fluctuations in dividends are smaller than fluctuations in profits). Transfers from the public sector—pensions, social security benefits, and so on—are primarily determined by government decisions on rates of benefit, though a number of such payments (unemployment benefit and earnings-related benefits) will clearly reflect the pressure of demand and its effect on the levels of unemployment and earnings.[2]

(iii) *Direct taxation*. The main component of direct taxation of personal incomes is income tax. The amount of tax paid will depend primarily on the rates of tax and on the level of personal income, but because of the distinction between 'earned' and 'unearned' income the distribution of personal income between income from employment and other income will also be relevant.

(iv) *Changes in the price level*. Consumer prices (the index of prices which is relevant in arriving at the real value of personal disposable income) are generally considered to be set (before indirect taxes) on a cost-plus basis (see Chapter 3). A given profit margin is added to the average unit variable costs of production, which comprise labour costs and the unit costs of imported materials.[3] Unit labour costs, i.e. labour costs per unit of output, are the costs per man divided by output per man and therefore vary directly with earnings and inversely with labour productivity. The existence of lags in price-setting means that the assumption of an unchanging target profit margin does not

---

[2] Employers' contributions to National Insurance and private pension funds are treated in the National Accounts as imputed personal sector income which is automatically saved.

[3] The costs incurred in purchasing intermediate products and capital equipment will reflect these same two components elsewhere in the economy.

entail an unchanging profit share: if costs of production are increasing at an accelerating rate, actual profit margins will fall (if the lag in adjusting prices stays constant) even though the target profit margin remains unchanged. The contribution of indirect taxes to the Consumer Price Index depends primarily on the rates of the taxes, though it will also be affected by any shifts in the composition of consumers' expenditure between high- and low-taxed items.

The final stage is to relate consumers' expenditure to real personal disposable income. Even in its simplest form, this relationship must also take account, as we have already noted, of the influence of financial conditions on the availability of credit to finance expenditure on consumer durables. Another important aspect of the relationship is that it will almost certainly be characterized by a significant lag between changes in disposable income and changes in expenditure.

Figure 14.2 summarizes in diagrammatic form these relationships as they appear in the National Institute of Economic and Social Research forecasting model.

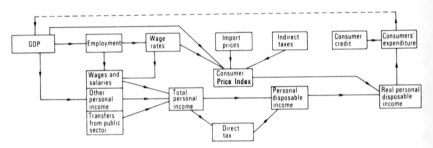

FIG. 14.2. Flow Chart of the Personal Sector.

14.2.3. Investment

The first need, in reaching a realistic model of the behaviour of private investment, is to recognize the importance of distinguishing several different kinds of investment. The most obvious distinction is between fixed investment and investment in stocks (or inventory investment). Within fixed investment, it is obviously necessary to treat investment in dwellings separately. The remainder of fixed investment can be classified by industry (notably manufacturing and non-manufacturing), or by type of asset (plant and machinery, new buildings and works, vehicles) or both. The main reason for distinguishing manufacturing investment from investment in other industries is that fluctuations in both output and investment in manufacturing industries tend to be more violent than in other industries. A distinction is usually drawn between investment in different types of assets because of the differing lifetimes of different capital assets. Thus investments in plant and machinery which have relatively short lives will tend to be influenced predominantly by expectation of future output levels, and much less by small changes in the cost of finance. Investments in new buildings and works, on the other hand, have a much longer life and a more certain rate of return (given long-run trends in production), so that the cost of finance can be expected to have a powerful influence while short-run fluctuations in output will have relatively little effect.

Private investment in dwellings is in fact powerfully influenced by financial factors. This reflects the factors governing both the demand for and the supply of new houses in the UK. Demand is highly sensitive to the liquidity position of the building societies, which in turn depends on the structure of interest rates among the various financial institutions competing for funds and on the relationship between interest rates and levels of personal income (since the building societies normally operate according to rules setting maximum allowable repayments—largely interest—in relation to income). On the supply side, most private housebuilding is speculative—that is, houses are not built to order—and thus builders are heavily dependent on the availability of credit during the period of building and before the sale of the completed house.

Investment in stocks is generally related to a simple—though lagged—way to changes in output. The presumption is that, other things being equal, stockholders will wish to maintain some fairly constant ratio of stocks— whether of raw materials, work-in-progress, or finished goods—to output. The desired level of stocks will thus vary directly with the level of output. Short-period changes in the level of stocks, or stockbuilding, will, however, be erratic both because of lags in the adjustment of actual stocks to the demand level and because of involuntary changes in the level of stocks caused by sharp changes in output or demand.

14.2.4. Other Items of Expenditure

Public expenditure—both current and capital—is generally treated as wholly exogenous. Decisions, whether by central government, local authorities, or public corporations, on such matters as defence spending, road construction, education, railways, etc., are not normally regarded as having passively or systematically to follow short-term fluctuations in the economy, but as capable of being determined separately.

Exports of goods and services are, at the most aggregate level, determined by world demand and the relative prices of UK and foreign goods. However, because of differing movements in demand and relative prices in different parts of the world and for different commodities, a case is often made for disaggregation of exports by destination or commodity, or both. Information about demand in different countries can often be obtained from forecasts made by international organizations such as the OECD. With the exception of the effects of changes in the levels of UK competitiveness (effects which are hard to ascertain except when there are very marked changes, such as those attributable to a devaluation), these determinants of the demand for exports are largely exogenous to the UK economy. It has, however, sometimes been argued that both the profitability of production for export relative to production for the home market and the pressure of domestic demand will influence the supply (as opposed to the demand) for exports.

Similarly, imports of goods and services will depend on both the volume of demand at home and on relative prices. Again, a distinction may be drawn between different commodities—as, for example, between basic raw materials, where demand is likely to be insensitive to cost but highly sensitive to changes in output, and finished consumer goods, where price relative to domestically produced substitutes will play a much larger role.

The net sum of all these aggregates gives Gross Domestic Product at market prices—that is, at prices which include indirect taxes. Since we are primarily interested in Gross Domestic Product (GDP) at factor cost in real terms (because the payment of the indirect tax element does not represent a demand for real resources), net indirect taxes must finally be deducted.[4] The effects of changes in indirect tax rates are reflected, as we saw earlier, in changes in (mainly) the Consumer Price Index, which alter the real purchasing power of given money incomes.

14.2.5. Wages and Prices

The rate of inflation is a policy problem in itself; it also has an important bearing on the determination of real variables, notably consumers' expenditure and exports and imports. Originally, most macroeconomic models based their account of the inflationary process on some form of the Phillips curve for the determination of money wages together with some kind of cost-plus pricing assumption. The first of these suggests that the rate of change of money wages will depend to some extent on the pressure of demand for labour (as reflected inversely in the level of unemployment); most modern versions also suggest that increases in money wages will compensate largely or fully for actual (or possibly expected) changes in the price level. The cost-plus pricing assumption implies that prices are normally set on the basis of a constant mark-up over variable unit costs. Unit costs comprise wage and salary costs per unit of output (so the growth of labour productivity is an influence) and the costs of imported inputs. The latter in turn will reflect both world prices and changes in the exchange rate.

Modelling wage formation has, however, proved very difficult, as will be clear from the issues described in Chapter 4. The equation in any model has frequently been 'overridden' (i.e. alternative figures substituted for those predicted by the equation) in the light of the most recent relevant information available, for example latest major wage settlements, robustness of recent wage bargaining, etc. Moreover different models, exploring alternative ways of explaining wage formation, have developed types of equations other than those based on the Phillips curve. These include versions which see the real wage in the long term as largely or completely independent of demand. Rather, it is exogenous, depending on a target which is largely independent of the economic

---

[4] This raises a technical point. Working at constant prices (in the case of the current UK National Accounts, 1980 prices), this means that net indirect taxes must be valued at 1980 'prices'—that is, at 1980 tax rates. This adjustment is known as the factor cost adjustment. Change in this adjustment thus reflect only changes in the pattern of real expenditure between high- and low-taxed items.

ituation, or is dependent on labour productivity, trade union power, the tax
tructure, and the terms of trade. Attempts have also been made to model the
upply of and demand for labour separately and then develop an equation
ased on putting the two together.

4.2.6. The Exchange Rate

'rior to 1972, the exchange rate was fixed, subject to only occasional negotiated
liscrete changes (as in 1949 and 1967). Since then, however, the rate has been
nore or less free to 'float'. This has posed a difficult problem for modellers of the
:conomy. Under a completely free float, and assuming (not unreasonably) that
oreign exchange markets are highly efficient, the level of the rate should be
letermined solely by the overall (current and capital) demand for and supply
if sterling. Accounting for movements in the exchange rate would then require
:omplete modelling of both the current and capital accounts of the balance of
)ayments. In practice, things have been even more complicated because of
acit or overt government intervention in the foreign exchange markets so as to
nfluence changes in the rate.

Modellers have typically, therefore, formulated hypotheses about how the
quilibrium exchange rate is determined; they have then added on rather *ad hoc*
actors intended to account for shorter-run deviations from this 'equilibrium'
evel. Typically, changes in the equilibrium rate are taken to be determined by
:hanges in UK and world inflation rates relative to each other. The underlying
ussumption is that in the long run the current account of the balance of
)ayments must be zero, and this means that exchange rate changes must be
uch as to preserve competitiveness. Short- (or even medium-) term deviations
rom the equilibrium level, however, will occur because of capital flows, for
:xample due to interest rate differentials or because of official intervention in
he foreign exchange markets.

4.2.7. The Monetary Sector

It is in their treatment of the monetary sector that models of the economy differ
nost (see section 14.3). Until about the mid-1970s, monetary channels of
nfluence were both weak and *ad hoc*. The authorities could control interest rates
lirectly (by varying Bank Rate or, later, Minimum Lending Rate), and could
nfluence the supply of credit by means of hire-purchase controls and directions
:o the Clearing Banks on lending policy. With growing concentration on
:ontrol of the money supply and with the associated recognition of the
interdependence of fiscal and monetary policy, however, a more formal
account of the monetary sector became necessary. Although there is little
common ground between the various models, the following framework of
analysis would probably be recognizable to them all.

The income–expenditure side of the model (at current prices) generates the
3ap between total general government expenditures and receipts—roughly,
the Public Sector Borrowing Requirement (PSBR). This can be financed in
three ways—by the issue of notes and coin, by borrowing from the banking

system, or by borrowing from the non-bank private sector (bond financing). (For the moment we ignore the overseas sector and possible movements in the exchange rate.) Since the volume of notes and coin held by the public is basically demand determined, the government's financing decision, given the PSBR, is essentially between selling more bonds (which will generally require higher interest rates) and borrowing from the banking system.

Turning to the balance sheet of the banks, in very simplified form, total lending, or assets, must equal total deposits, or liabilities. Lending in this simplified world is either to the public sector or to the private sector. Total deposits (sight and time), together with notes and coin, constitute sterling £M3, the 'broad' money supply, and control of £M3 therefore requires control of total bank deposits, which in turn means control of total bank lending.

The money supply can be reduced either by reducing lending to (borrowing by) the public sector or by reducing bank lending to the private sector. Given the size of the PSBR, the former means increasing sales of bonds (higher interest rates), the latter reduced lending by means of controls (or higher interest rates). If the government wishes to control the money supply without higher interest rates or restrictions on bank lending then, *ceteris paribus* and ignoring any subsequent effects, it can only do so by reducing the PSBR—that is, by adjusting fiscal policy.

It is this basic set of relationships which underlies the modelling of the monetary sector in a fixed exchange rate world. In this kind of model, the channels of monetary influence are—with the important exception of the exchange rate—through interest rate and credit availability effects on various kinds of expenditure. Thus interest rates may affect various kinds of fixed investment (notably in housing) while the availability of bank and other credit may have a significant effect on consumer spending (especially on durable goods) and on stockbuilding.

In a world of floating exchange rates, however, the picture is radically altered. Other things being equal, even quite a small rise in interest rates may have quite a powerful upward effect on the exchange rate (by attracting short-term international capital inflows). This in turn will have significant effects on both real output and prices. Real output will fall, as exports are discouraged and imports encouraged. There will, however, be a downward influence on the rate of price inflation via lower sterling import prices and a possible further induced reduction in wage settlements. In most conventional models, these monetary effects via the exchange rate are far more powerful than the monetary effects on domestic consumption and investment. The interaction of monetary conditions and the exchange rate has therefore become one of the most important elements in the modelling of the economy.

The above outline shows that a realistic model of the economy, while remaining broadly within the familiar framework of the national income expenditure identity, needs to account on the way for a wide variety of economic variables which the simple model ignores—the price level, average earnings, the distribution of income, the level and structure of interest rates, the availability of credit, and so on. The resulting larger model may be summarized by means of a further flow chart as in Figure 14.3.

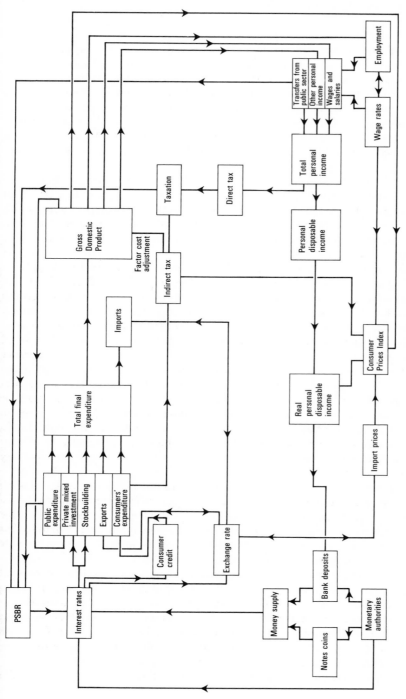

Fig. 14.3. Flow Chart of the Economy.

14.3. Modelling the Economy

14.3.1. Simulation

There are in existence several models of the UK economy constructed broadly along the lines set out in the preceding section. The most well known, and best documented, are those used in the preparation of short-term economic forecasts by HM Treasury, the National Institute of Economic and Social Research, and the London Business School. There are also two more recent—and less orthodox—models used in forecasting and policy analysis, those developed by the Cambridge Economic Policy Group and by Liverpool University. The characteristics and properties of these models are briefly described in section 14.4.

In principle, the analysis of such models should settle a number of fundamental questions. For example, Is the economy subject to a persistent business cycle? Are monetary factors important? Is the wage–price spiral stable or unstable? How powerful is the multiplier? and many more. These questions should be answerable using the techniques of simulation. The procedure is as follows: the model is 'solved'—i.e. the paths of the endogenous variables like GDP found—for chosen paths of all the exogenous variables. One exogenous variable is then changed and the model solved again. The differences between the two solutions then reflect the consequences of the change in the exogenous variable. Thus, for example, if the two exercises differ in having a uniformly different path of public expenditure, the resulting differences in the paths of GDP will show the resulting multiplier effect. Because of the lags in the system, the GDP differences will not be constant over time, even though the difference in public expenditure is. The multiplier value in the first period is known as the impact multiplier. The subsequent response of GDP will reflect any cyclical characteristics of the model—damped or explosive oscillations may be produced, or there may be a steady move towards or away from an equilibrium. If the model does tend towards an equilibrium, the multiplier in the new equilibrium is known as the dynamic multiplier. Similar exercises can be conducted to show the effects of changes in taxation, or in monetary variables or wages rates, and so on.

Unfortunately, little has so far been published on the results of such experiments with models of the UK. This is partly because the approach is a relatively new one but also because the models, being designed primarily for the production of forecasts, are often not well suited to this kind of analysis. For example, it may be found much more satisfactory to forecast private investment by means of investment intentions surveys than by means of a formal investment function. But a model which does not contain an investment function will throw little light on the behaviour of the economy under differing assumptions, for there will be no means of estimating effects on investment— one of the most crucial determinants of the dynamic behaviour of the economy. In addition, the models may be incomplete simply because of the absence of knowledge about the precise functioning of some parts of the economy— notably the financial sector and its influence on real variables.

Such evidence as is available suggests that there are marked differences between the behaviour of the economy under a fixed exchange rate regime and under a floating rate regime. Under fixed rates, the evidence tends to suggest that the UK economy was characterized by very highly damped oscillations, and that both impact and dynamic multipliers were fairly low—perhaps of the order of 1 and 2 respectively. More tentatively, there was little evidence of powerful monetary influences since the interest sensitivity of expenditures was generally found to be very low. Under floating exchange rates, these conclusions are quite substantially altered. Multipliers are markedly lower: an expansion of domestic demand leads to an exchange rate depreciation and then to both falling net exports and higher inflation. In some models there is evidence that these lead to a fall in demand sufficient fully to offset the initial stimulus: in other words the multiplier falls to zero, or there is 100 per cent 'crowding-out' of the expansion which would otherwise have occurred. A second aspect of models under floating exchange rates is that monetary policy becomes much more important in determining overall effects. For example an expansionary fiscal policy, accompanied by unchanged monetary growth, will cause a rise in interest rates (relative to foreign rates) which will put upward pressure on the exchange rate. This will be offset, to a greater or lesser extent, by the effect of higher imports on the current balance, putting downward pressure on the exchange rate. If the *net* effect is a higher exchange rate, then output and employment will tend to be depressed and inflation lowered. But if the same fiscal change is accompanied by an 'accommodating' increase in the money supply, then interest rates will be unaffected, the exchange rate will unambiguously fall, and higher output and employment, together with higher inflation, will follow.

14.3.2. Economic Forecasting

Most of the models of the kind described in general terms in section 14.3.1 have been constructed primarily for the purpose of making short-term economic forecasts. Such forecasts are generally for up to two years ahead, and are in terms of quarter-to-quarter (sometimes half-year to half-year) paths of the main variables, though these paths are intended to reflect the general 'shape' of future developments rather than precise quarterly movements.

The first step in making a forecast using such a model is to make projections of those variables which are regarded as 'exogenous'—that is, those which, because of the absence of simultaneous determination or 'feedback', will be unaffected by the outcome of the remainder of the forecast. Of the broad expenditure aggregates, this is usually thought to cover public expenditure and (largely) exports, while other elements will probably include import prices, tax rates (unless future changes have already been announced), public sector transfer payments to persons,[5] perhaps 'liquidity', and so on. The assumption that existing public expenditure programmes will be realized and that tax rates will remain unchanged reflects the assumption of 'unchanged policies' on which such forecasts are usually made. It depends on the acceptability of the

---

[5] Note that changes in inflation and unemployment rates can change these semi-automatically (see Chapter 12).

outcome of such a forecast whether clear recommendations for changes in policy can then be made.

The remainder of the model consists, broadly speaking, of a set of equations representing the economic relationships described in earlier chapters (which are presumed to operate together). Thus a rise in consumption will raise GDP, but this in turn will raise employment and average earnings and thus further increase consumption. If all the equations were linear the whole set could be solved algebraically, but this is extremely unlikely to be the case. Iterative methods are therefore used: a provisional likely path for GDP is selected and, through the various relationships of the model, this allows consequential paths for consumption, investment, and so on to be calculated. When these are added up, the resulting path for GDP will not normally agree with the initial assumption. A new revised path for GDP is therefore specified in the light of the consumption and investment 'forecasts' etc., and the solution of the model repeated. This process is repeated until consistency is achieved between the path of GDP and the total of the expenditure components given autonomously plus those dependent on GDP itself. Normally, of course, this is done with the aid of a computer.

Described thus baldly, the forecasting process seems comparatively mechanical. In practice, however, this is far from being the case. A wide variety of ambiguities and uncertainties must be taken account of. Some of these are now very briefly described: interested readers are referred to the Bibliography at the end of this chapter for more detail.

First, since economic data appear only some time, often considerable, after the event, the 'forecast' actually starts in the past. Partial information—on retail sales, industrial production, international trade, and so on—will be available for the recent past, but the picture of the economy over the last six months remains relatively incomplete.

Second, even the full National Accounts data are subject to revisions, often substantial, so that even the more distant past is not known with complete certainty.

Third, the formal econometric relationships which comprise the model can only be treated as rough guidelines to the behaviour of the economy in the future. In particular, such relationships will normally have 'fitted' the recent past with some inaccuracy, and the problem arises of what degree of 'inaccuracy' one should assume in the future.

Fourth, the forecast will be influenced by all kinds of unquantifiable factors for which a formal model cannot allow—the effect of the general level of confidence, to take only the most pervasive example.

Finally, although forecasts are generally made on the basis of the assumption of unchanged policies on the part of the government, it is frequently difficult to lend precision to the notion of what 'unchanged' means. No real problem arises with, for example, tax rates, but an 'unchanged' monetary policy cannot normally be uniquely defined,[6] still less the notion of, for example, 'continued severe restraint' on pay or prices.

[6] Does it, for example, mean that the money supply will continue to grow at the same rate as in the recent past, or that interest rates will be stabilized at their current levels?

Against these uncertainties, the forecaster can derive some help from various 'extraneous' or 'leading' indicators. Examples of the former are investment intentions surveys and surveys of business confidence. The latter, e.g. statistics of new orders, are variables that have been found generally to move up and down prior to a corresponding movement in GDP, and are thus of some help in predicting the latter.

It follows that a forecast made using any particular model will reflect not merely the character of the basic formal model, but, often more importantly, the judgement and intuition of the forecaster in employing the model.

14.3.3. The Use of Economic Forecasts

The main purpose of most macroeconomic forecasts is as an aid to the rational discussion of economic policy-making. As we have observed, the forecasts are generally based on the assumption of the continuation of existing policies; if the resulting forecast shows an unacceptable pattern of development of the economy, then some of the existing policies must be altered. Until the mid-1960s, this meant almost exclusively the use of fiscal policy and some aspects of monetary policy—notably the use of consumer credit regulations—to control the level of aggregate demand: in particular, to attempt to maintain constant pressure of demand in relation to capacity. This concentration on 'demand management' or 'fine-tuning' reflected the beliefs (explicit or implicit) firstly, that forecasting techniques and policy manipulations were adequate for the task of maintaining balance over a period of eighteen to twenty-four months ahead and, secondly, that the preservation of a stable pressure of demand at the right level would simultaneously prevent fluctuations in output and employment, prevent anything more than creeping inflation, preserve a stable balance of payments, and even raise the rate of economic growth.

The techniques of demand management were in principle simple: confronted with a situation in which, on existing policies, unemployment was projected to rise to an unacceptable level, a reflationary demand policy was called for. The forecasting process would be repeated with different, lower, sets of tax rates prevailing from the next Budget, and that policy package chosen which produced a stable level of unemployment. The changes would duly be made; a new forecast would be produced some months later which might again suggest some adjustment to the level of demand . . . and so the process continued. 'Brakes', 'accelerators', and 'tillers' became common terms in Chancellors' Budget Statements.

It gradually became clear, however, that short-term demand management of this kind was failing to produce the desired results. In the first place, it became increasingly apparent that simply controlling the level of demand was not sufficient to produce a tolerable rate of inflation, a satisfactory balance of payments, or an adequate rate of growth of production. The recognition of cost rather than demand factors in governing the rate of inflation reduced the relevance of demand management as a counter-inflationary policy. There was a realization that after allowing for cyclical fluctuations there was a persistent and growing fundamental disequilibrium in the balance of payments. And there was increasing dissatisfaction with the underlying rate of growth. The retreat from near-exclusive preoccupation with demand management wa reflected in the adoption at various times of prices and incomes policies devaluation (and later floating) of the exchange rate, and indicative economic planning. There was even mounting scepticism about the government's basic ability to manipulate demand so as to eliminate the vestiges of the business cycle in real output and employment. This inability seemed to stem from inadequate recognition of the lags involved both in implementing decisions and in the effects of their implementation on the economy at large. Changes in income tax rates, for example, cannot normally be put into effect for some months—to allow for PAYE codes to be changed; the consequential reduction in personal disposable income affects consumers' expenditure only with a lag and the effect of the subsequent rise in output on the level of private investment may extend well beyond the forecast period. Furthermore, caution on the part of government decision takers may have led them to delay acting in accordance with the forecasts until the projections were confirmed by the actual behaviour of the economy as reflected in, for example, the unemployment figures. But the delays already noted in connection with the collection of statistics (and the fact that unemployment, in particular, lags well behind changes in output) mean that such information was not available until far too long after action should have been taken. The total of all these lags, stretching from a change in the economy to the final impact of policy designed to redress the change, could be two, or even more, years. In the meantime, self-correcting forces might well have been in operation. In short, there is probably a broad consensus—with hindsight—that demand management measures were generally 'too much and too late'.

As the 1970s progressed it became clear that in a world of floating exchange rates, a number of 'rules of the game' were different. As we have already noted (p. 455), fiscal policy was at least weakened and monetary policy strengthened, and, in addition, the wage–price–exchange rate–import cost linkage made the rate of inflation much more volatile. For most model builders this has meant that both economic forecasting and policy analysis are now much more complex—though certainly no less vital—than they appeared to be ten to twenty years ago. Some, however, have concluded that the extreme weakening of fiscal policy when combined with a belief in the efficacy of market forces means that there is very little that governments can or should do to try to control the macroeconomy at all, other than setting a broad monetary framework characterized by a relatively low and stable growth of the various concepts of the money supply (see pp. 305–8) and a fiscal policy sufficiently tight to permit these monetary targets to be met at relatively low rates of interest.

14.3.4. Assessing Assessments

There is obviously no point in having economic forecasts unless they are reasonably accurate. But assessing how accurate forecasts have been is, perhaps surprisingly to many readers, so difficult as to verge on the impossible. There are three main problems. The first is that forecasts are of necessity made on the basis of assumptions about future economic policy which may—and

enerally do—turn out to be 'wrong'. The inverted commas are used because it
in fact the purpose of forecasts, in most cases, to alter policy. As described in
ction 14.3.2, 'unchanged policies' are often assumed in order to show what
olicy changes are likely to be needed if the (presumably unattractive)
evelopment of the economy is to be improved. Thus if a forecast is of a
cession on unchanged policies, say with GDP growth of 1 per cent per annum
ver the forecast period, and the government, on the basis of that forecast, takes
ction which raises the growth rate to 3 per cent, a simple comparison of the
orecast (1 per cent) with the out-turn (3 per cent) will suggest that the forecast
ad been extremely poor. But such a comparison is clearly logically invalid.
orecasters themselves try to overcome this by attempting subsequently to
correct' each forecast for the effects of policy changes after the forecast was
1ade, but this is a procedure of a complexity similar to that of making the
riginal forecast: a full-scale correction involves duplicating the original
orecast on the 'true' set of policy assumptions.

The second difficulty concerns the accuracy of the official statistics. These
atistics are (with a very few exceptions) only estimates of the quantities they
1easure, often based on incomplete or sample data. They are thus not only
1herently subject to margins of error, but also liable to revision as more
omplete information becomes available. Thus the picture the forecaster has of
1e recent behaviour of the economy—which will of course affect his forecast
1r the future—may later turn out to have been seriously misleading. To take
1st one example: the first official estimate of the change in real GDP between
1e fourth quarters of 1975 and 1976 (published in April 1977) was 2·1 per
ent; by August 1978 this had been revised to 4·1 per cent (that is, from below-
rend growth to significantly above-trend growth).

The third difficulty is a philosophical one: how accurate is 'accurate' in this
ontext? The general answer must be 'accurate enough to provide a reliable
asis for decision-making', but this is not easy to quantify. More forecasts are
erforce presented as tables of figures, frequently to two, three, or even more
ignificant figures. Yet few forecasters would seriously maintain that their
rocedures really allow them to say much more than that the balance of
ayments is expected to improve 'a little', 'significantly', or 'substantially', and
o on. This is, however, generally adequate for the informed discussion of
conomic policy options, but it makes still more nonsensical the precise
uantitative comparisons of forecasts and outcomes.

A useful contrast may be drawn with weather forecasting. Taking the above
hree points in reverse order, a weather forecaster will normally make
tatements like 'outbreaks of rain are likely tomorrow in many southern areas',
while an economic forecaster will tend to say things like 'GDP growth next year
s forecast to be 2·8 per cent' (though he really means 'output is likely to
ncrease at close to its trend rate'). Secondly, unlike the economic forecaster,
he weather forecaster is in no doubt about what happened 'yesterday'. And
nally, again unlike the economic forecaster, there is no human agency (at least
ntil the advent of successful rain-making techniques) to upset the forecast by
irect intervention, be this governments' changing policy, or the population
hanging its economic behaviour in response to forecast events.

14.4. Models of the UK Economy: A Review

There are now several fully developed econometric models of the UK used regularly for economic forecasting and for the analysis through simulation of different policy options. They include the models of HM Treasury, the National Institute of Economic and Social research (NIESR), the London Business School, the Cambridge Economic Policy Group (CEPG), and the University of Liverpool. Other models are being built, still others exist but are not so accessible to outsiders.

It might be thought that since there must, in the end, be one 'true' model of the economy then the fact that the existing models differ quite markedly from one another can only reflect 'mistakes' which ought to be eliminated. There is indeed growing interest in comparing the structures and properties of the models with a view to resolving some at least of the differences between them. But the fact remains that empirical econometric evidence is rarely conclusive in providing such resolution, and the models are likely to continue to display important differences attributable to different theoretical preconceptions as well as to different histories of development. The aim of this section is to provide only thumbnail sketches of the five models listed; more detailed analysis of the models is referred to in the Bibliography.

14.4.1. The Treasury Model

The foundation of the Treasury quarterly model is recognizably based on the kind of income/expenditure framework described earlier. The large scale of the model—well over 500 equations—gives a misleading impression of complexity since a large number of the equations and variables reflects only disaggregation and the need to provide detailed forecasts to other government departments.

Initially the model was in essence 'Keynesian' in the sense not only of being based on the real income/expenditure linkages but also in that the main channel for the influence of monetary policy was through interest rates. Thus real personal consumption depends primarily on real personal disposable income (though also on the levels of unemployment and of real wealth). Real private fixed investment (other than in housing) depends mainly on th expected level of output, but also on companies' cash flow and on interest rate. Investment in housing is more strongly influenced by interest rates as well a by the relative price of housing. Public sector current and capital expenditur is, in the model, treated as exogenous in real terms (that is, determined b autonomous government decisions about the real level of services to b provided). Finally, exports and imports are related to appropriate measures c demand and relative costs or prices—the volume of world trade and relativ wage costs in the case of exports, and of domestic real demand or output an relative prices in the case of imports.

The development of the monetary sector of the Treasury model seems to hav been, understandably, rather piecemeal. Until relatively recently, interest rat were predominantly determined by autonomous government decision (vi Bank Rate or, later, Minimum Lending Rate). Since the influence of monetar policy on the real side of the economy was predominantly through intere ates, there was thus no need for a 'monetary sector' at all. Only in 1979 was a fully developed monetary sector first included on an experimental basis, and the subsequent development of what is now quite a complex monetary sector reflects in part the need to model and forecast changes in the monetary aggregates themselves. With one major exception, noted below, there was no radical reassessment of the way in which monetary policy affects the economy. The supply of money was in essence implicit in the model, the most important element in the supply of money—bank lending to the private sector, which has an important influence on consumers' expenditure on durables—being effectively demand determined. Only in 1982 was an explicit demand for money function introduced, the main effect of which was to modify slightly the strength of the linkages between the money supply, interest rates, and income.

The exception concerns the modelling of the exchange rate (and, in consequence, the relative costs and relative prices terms in the export and import equations). In a world of floating exchange rates, but when the authorities can intervene in the market to influence the rate, exchange rate modelling is very difficult. In the Treasury model, monetary policy has an important influence on short-term changes in the exchange rate (and hence in both inflation and the volume of exports and imports) both through relative interest rates at home and abroad and (more obscurely) through relative money supplies at home and abroad. As seen below, monetary policy is also important in determining the long-run equilibrium value of the exchange rate.

Finally, the determination of the rate of inflation hinges on unit costs: wage and import costs and indirect taxes. Wage inflation was originally generated through an expectations-augmented Phillips curve with a *long-run* coefficient of unity on price inflation. There was thus a *short-run* trade-off between inflation and unemployment, which depended simply on the gap between labour demand (given by the level of output) and labour supply (taken as exogenous). The Phillips curve has now been replaced by an equation based on explicit modelling of demand and supply influences. The short run trade-off seen with the Phillips curve can now be seen through shifts in the demand for and supply of labour. But the Treasury model now also permits the existence of a *long-term* inflation/unemployment trade-off. Money wages also respond to changes in income tax rates as bargainers attempt to preserve after-tax real wages.

Examining the structure of an econometric model in this wort of way can of course give only a very loose qualitative impression of its overall characteristics. Various published simulation studies help to complete the picture by showing the net overall effects of the linkages involved. For example, a recent experiment shows the effects of a rise in exports caused by an exogenous rise in world trade. There is a rise in domestic output and employment initially. But the improvement in the current balance of payments drives up the exchange rate and so raises imports (as well as moderating the rise in exports). In the longer run, the net benefit to output is rather small. The inflation rate, however, improves: the upward influence of higher output and employment is more than offset by the effects of the higher exchange rate.

We may also look at the effect of a change in monetary policy. In this model money has both direct and indirect effects, the introduction of the former being a recent development. By direct effects of monetary policy we mean such things as the effect on bank lending or on expectations. In the Treasury model the most important direct effect is upon the exchange rate which is determined, in long-run equilibrium, by the domestic money supply relative to abroad. More recent versions of the model also permit the rate of growth of the money supply directly to influence the rate of convergence of the exchange rate to its long-run value. The indirect effects of monetary policy are through the more traditional Keynesian route, via interest rates. Due to the elasticities of money demand being low the impact of interest rate changes on money holdings are not significant. However, interest rate effects are important in exchange rate determination and in their real wealth effects, as we shall see later in the discussion of 'crowding-out'.

Overall, the model has changed significantly over time. For example, in the case of expansionary fiscal policy, conventional 'Keynesian' multiplier effects are largely offset by (a) the (weak) effect of higher interest rates on durables and investment expenditure, (b) the effect of higher demand on wages and hence on trade competitiveness, (c) the effect of higher nominal interest rates on real private net worth and hence on expenditure, and (d) a real balance effect whereby increased inflation reduces expenditure. The model, that is, displays substantial 'crowding-out'. In the case of monetary policy, the major effects come via the exchange rate and its influence on the rate of inflation, both directly and indirectly (as noted above).

In short, although traditionally a Keynesian model, the Treasury model has begun to incorporate more monetarist features such as real wealth effects in the 'crowding-out' mechanism and a direct effect of monetary policy on the exchange rate. At the same time, however, it has abandoned the Phillips curve in favour of an approach explicitly based on the supply and demand for labour. Within it however, a long-run inflation/unemployment trade-off, though severe, is permissible. As we shall see with most of the other major models, the interaction between the exchange rate and monetary policy has been developed.

14.4.2 The National Institute (NIESR) Model

Historically, the National Institute's interest in economic modelling and forecasting arose partly as the result of a perceived need for a public 'cross check' on Treasury exercises. At that time (1959–68), Treasury forecasts were not published and the Treasury forecasting model was not made publicly accessible until 1975. Perhaps not surprisingly, then, the Treasury and NIESR models are the most similar of the major models in existence. Like that of the Treasury, the NIESR model is income/expenditure based, with monetary policy operating domestically via interest rates, inflation explained through an expectations-augmented Phillips curve, and the exchange rate offering the most important linkage for the operation of monetary policy.

Differences between the NIESR and the Treasury models are thus primarily of detail and occasionally emphasis, rather than of basic philosophy or theory. In addition, the NIESR model is considerably smaller than that of the

Treasury, though this reflects mainly the degree of disaggregation employed rather than any difference in scope. Nevertheless, these apparently minor differences can have quite significant effects on the overall properties of the model as revealed by simulation studies—an awkward fact not always appreciated by those unfamiliar with econometric model-building.

There are few differences of major importance between the models on the income/expenditure side, save perhaps that the impact of interest rates on housing investment seems to be more strongly marked in the NIESR model. The monetary sector, though substantially less complex than that of the Treasury model, is more elegant and (to this writer) seems more theoretically appealing. It is firmly in the post-Keynesian monetary tradition in that one major domestic component of the money supply (monetary expansion by the government) is seen as the outcome of decisions by the government about the extent to which the budget deficit (PSBR) is to be financed by bond sales, while the other major component (bank lending to the private sector) is essentially demand-determined. The first element reflects the familiar proposition that the authorities can, given the size of the PSBR, control *either* the differential between long- and short-term interest rates *or* the degree of its own contribution to monetary expansion, but not both. The second element reflects the belief that (*ceteris paribus*) interest rates affect the *demand* for bank loans and thus the creation of money by the banking system. The 'missing link' is the short-term interest rate (the Treasury Bill rate), which is in effect determined partly by the US short-term rate (because of the effect of interest rate differentials on the exchange rate) and partly by direct government policy.

The operation of monetary policy is much more transparent in the NIESR model than in the Treasury model. Given US interest rates, there is a clear connection between short-term UK interest rate policy and exchange rate policy. Given short-term interest rate policy, there is an equally clear connection between long-term interest rate policy and the supply of money. Thus, for instance, given the PSBR, the pursuit of a money-supply target will affect only long-term interest rates and affect the real economy only to the (very limited) extent that these interest rates matter. The pursuit of monetary targets is, in itself, quite without point. It is this characteristic which most clearly places the NIESR model in the 'non-monetarist' camp despite the fact that its monetary sector is well developed.

There are significant differences between the NIESR and Treasury models so far as the determination of both the exchage rate and the rate of inflation are concerned. It is assumed that, in equilibrium, the exchange rate will tend to its purchasing power parity value (that is, will depend only on differential inflation rates) but that quite significant deviations from this equilibrium level will take place in the short to medium term. These deviations will reflect (a) changes in the UK/US short-term interest rate differential, and (b) the visible balance of payments (in real terms)—the latter apparently intended to indicate *expected* changes in the rate. Inflation is driven by a conventional expectations-augmented Phillips curve wage/price model but there is some inflation/unemployment trade-off even in the long run, as is generated by the Treasury model's explicit labour market modelling.

Perhaps the most revealing comparison between the Treasury and NIESR models in simulation mode is the extent to which, and channels through which, crowding-out takes place. As we noted earlier, crowding-out in the Treasury model is virtually complete in the medium term and in simulation occurs primarily through the effect of higher inflation on the earnings equation and the interaction between interest rates and the exchange rate. In the NIESR model this exchange rate effect is greater (because of the sharp deviations generated by interest rate effects). In addition, because of the absence of a real post-tax wage response, higher inflation coupled with the progressiveness of the income tax system actually reduce real personal disposable income and the volume of consumer spending, which generates some crowding-out (although only to a limited extent). The upshot is that crowding-out is, as in the Treasury model, virtually complete in the medium term, the principal influence, however, being interest rates and their effect on the exchange rate. If the NIESR model were to employ a target real post-tax wage equation, it seems that crowding-out would be reduced, though not substantially, due to the prominent role played by the exchange rate. The inflationary impact of increased public spending would, however, be increased.

14.4.3. The London Business School (LBS) Model

The LBS model began life at about the same time as the NIESR model (though the Institute has a rather longer history of formal forecasting). It has grown somewhat faster, and is now between the NIESR and Treasury models in size. Like the two other models, the real domestic side is based on the conventional income/expenditure framework, but the LBS model differs sharply in its account of the determination of the rate of inflation and the level of the exchange rate. It is on the treatment of these, therefore, that we focus.

Fundamental to the LBS analysis is the assumption that there exist stable demand for real balances functions for the UK on the one hand and for the rest of the world on the other. Combined with the assumption that purchasing power parity holds for small open economies like the UK, it follows that movements in the exchange rate depend primarily (given real incomes at home and abroad) on relative movements in UK and world money supplies. An increased rate of UK monetary growth (ceteris paribus) will, it is maintained, drive up the UK rate of inflation; the exchange rate will fall so as to preserve purchasing power parity. Money wages will follow (not cause) movements in domestic prices; real wages will grow in line with the growth of productivity.

This is, of course, a highly schematic summary of the early structure of the model. But it brings in to sharp relief the original and avowedly 'monetarist' nature of the LBS model. In practice, the model is much more complex: the exchange rate can depart in the short run from the purchasing power parity level, for example because of government intervention, and monetary policy operates through interest rates as well as directly on the rate of inflation. But the model none the less reflects a monetarist approach and provokes the same questions as that approach. In particular, is it causally legitimate to invert demand for real balances equations in order to derive a theory of the determination of the price level? And (a related question) can the rate growth of the money supply be treated as an exogenous, policy-determined variable?

At an empirical level the model provides rather an ambiguous view. The reason for this is that a number of key equations in the model are reduced-form rather than structural equations. First, the rate of growth of the UK money supply is made to depend on (*inter alia*) the rate of inflation, real GDP, the lagged ratio of the PSBR to GDP, and real interest rates. This seems to be an *ad hoc* mixture of supply and demand relationships consistent with a variety of underlying causal (structural) models and leaving obscure the role of policy choices over the financing of the PSBR. And, second, the fundamental exchange rate equation relates, on the left-hand side, the exchange rate multiplied by the ratio of UK to world money supplies to, on the right-hand side, the ratio of UK output to world industrial production (and other influences). Again, this leaves the underlying structure and causality rather obscure.

This use of under-specified reduced-form relationships makes the monetary side of the LBS model notably less sophisticated than that of the Treasury or of the NIESR. The assumption of a purely monetary theory of inflation and of the exchange rate, guarantees, however, that the LBS model will deliver recognizably 'monetarist' results in simulation studies.

More recently there have been some significant changes in the model. Earnings to some extent now depend on inflation; a cost-plus element is involved in price-setting; and interest rates have a weaker effect on expenditure but a stronger one on exchange rates. While these changes do not undermine the basic stance of the model, they do contribute to some extent to a convergence of the structures of the Treasury, NIESR, and LBS models.

Perhaps surprisingly, all three models that we have so far briefly examined deliver roughly the same *kind* of end result: a fiscal expansion will be broadly ineffective in real terms but will significantly worsen the rate of inflation and depreciate the exchange rate. Is this 'reduced form' agreement, despite remaining 'structural' differences between the models, encouraging or depressing? Encouraging, perhaps, to those who believe with Friedman that only predictive ability matters in economic policy-making. Depressing, though, to those who believe that econometric models have a role to play in judging between different theories of economic behaviour.

4.4.4. The Cambridge Economic Policy Group (CEPG) Model

The CEPG model was born in the early 1970s. Unlike the other models so far reviewed, it uses annual rather than quarterly data, largely reflecting the desire to produce medium-term rather than short-term (up to two years ahead) forecasts. It is sometimes described as an 'extreme Keynesian' model. This is in one sense accurate—very little attention is paid to monetary influences in the conventional sense—but in another highly misleading—the income/expenditure framework is quite unlike the familiar Keynesian treatment of consumption and investment.

Income/expenditure relationships are based, in the CEPG model, on the assumption that there are stable 'normal' ratios between stocks and flows in the economy—in particular between the stock of inventories and the flow of output, and between stocks of financial assets and flows of income. Thus, very schematically, if the total stock of private sector financial assets is a fixed proportion of current disposable private sector income, then the change in this stock—net acquisition of financial assets (NAFA)—will be the same fixed proportion of the change in disposable income. But NAFA itself is the excess of disposable income over private expenditure. Hence private expenditure is simply related to current and once-lagged disposable income.

In the early versions of the CEPG model, this account of the behaviour of the private sector (aggregating firms and households) led to the contention that the private sector's NAFA would tend to be small and stable. It followed that any fiscally induced change in the public sector's financial balance would lead to a parallel change in the overseas balance of payments—the original 'New Cambridge' proposition. Subsequent development of the model led to some complications, notably concerning the role of firms' inventories and the availability and cost of credit, and to some revision of the simple aggregation of firms and households. But the later account of the determination of private sector expenditure remains recognizably derived from the simple stock/flow analysis described above.

The monetary side of the model is quite simple. As usual, the PSBR is given essentially as the difference between (largely exogenous) public expenditure and (partly endogenous) tax receipts. More unusually, public sector borrowing from the banks is treated as exogenous, leaving public sector sales of bonds to the non-bank private sector as the residual element in the financing of the PSBR (cf. the NIESR treatment).

Inflation is essentially exogenous to the model. There is a predetermined post-tax real wage settlement which initially was not influenced by the pressure of demand in the labour market. However, more recently, unemployment as a proxy for demand pressure has appeared in the wage equation, though the impact is weak. Prices are given by a mark-up over unit costs, allowing for the trend increase in labour productivity. Thus, given the target real wage increase and trend productivity, the rate of inflation is governed by changes in tax rates (both direct and indirect) and changes in sterling import prices. Finally, the exchange rate is treated as a policy instrument even under a system of nationally free-floating exchange rates.

The properties of the CEPG model follow straightforwardly from its specification. An expansion of public spending will have no direct effect on inflation nor any significant crowding-out effects via the monetary sector. It will, however, lead to a marked worsening of the balance of payments. Cuts in tax rates will act similarly, but will (because of the target real net wage assumption) benefit the rate of inflation. In either case, but especially the former, the balance of payments effects will require some policy response—either a devaluation (which will exacerbate the inflation problem) or direct measures such as tariffs (which may not). From these properties follow familiar CEPG policy prescriptions, notably that reflation will need to be accompanied either by a combination of devaluation and an incomes policy or by direct

ontrols on imports if the consequences for the balance of payments and for
aflation are to be avoided.

4.4.5. The Liverpool Model

'he Liverpool model is a small annual model dating from the late 1970s. It
:ems still to be in a state of considerable flux. More than any of the other
1odels it is based on a clear set of theoretical propositions, with little or no
ttempt to test other possible hypotheses. This theoretical basis is essentially
1at of 'new classical' economics. Markets clear continuously, expectations are
ationally'[7] formed, and the rate of increase of the money supply determines
1e rate of increase of prices.

Central to the Liverpool model is the dependence of private expenditures on
·ealth rather than income and, consequently, it differs markedly from the
ther models discussed. The main changes in net worth arise through changes
a the value of the PSBR, the current account of the balance of payments, and
1vestment in new real assets. Inflation and interest rates emerge as important
a the model not only for the more traditional reasons, but also because of their
npact on the value of net worth. For example, interest rate changes alter the
apital values of existing government debt.

Changes in the long-run or 'natural' rate of unemployment can only be
rought about in the model by changes in the supply of labour schedule
10tably by increasing the incentive to work by cutting direct tax rates and/or
nemployment benefits) or by shifting the demand for labour schedule (for
xample if there were technological progress). Unions bargain implicitly in
:rms of a post-tax real wage and seek compensation in full for expected
aflation.

To get a sense of how the Liverpool model operates we may consider the
ffect of a fiscal stimulus financed by a combination of money creation and
ond sales. As the money supply rises this generates inflationary expectations
hich are reflected in higher wage settlements and higher nominal interest
ates. The effect of both inflation and higher nominal interest rates is to lead to
:valuation of real net wealth downwards and hence to a tendency for private
xpenditures to fall (a crowding-out effect). This fall in real net wealth is offset
） some extent by the rise in the PSBR, but not totally, because part of the fiscal
.imulus is bond-financed. If we turn to external effects, there is a depreciation
f the exchange rate which boosts net exports and thus contributes to overall
emand. However, inflation eventually erodes the gain in competitiveness,
:storing the initial value of the real exchange rate and of exports. In the long
un output is unchanged but inflation is higher.

The result of this fiscal stimulus can be compared with the effect of a purely
10netary stimulus which has a rapid effect on inflation through expectations.
'here are initial short-run effects on output but in the long run money is
1eutral', i.e. the whole of the monetary stimulus is translated into changes in
·rices. Thus neither fiscal nor monetary policy in the Liverpool model have any

---

[7] By expectations being 'rationally' formed in the Liverpool model we mean that agents in the
1odel are assumed to expect values of variables which are identical with the forecasts made by the
1odel.

long-run impact on output or employment. Random errors in expectations apart, therefore, the level of employment cannot be affected by changes in government policy—a standard 'new classical' proposition.

14.4.6. Assessing the Models

We remarked at the outset that it was for the reader to judge which model seemed the most convincing. But it may be worth drawing attention to some of the problems involved in making such an assessment.

Perhaps the most obvious criterion is, 'Which model forecasts best?' Unfortunately, this question is virtually impossible to answer. First, all forecasts make crucial assumptions about exogenous factors which will turn out to be false. Forecast failures on this account in no way reflect on the econometric model of the endogenous variables. These assumptions will include those concerning future government fiscal, monetary, and other policies, 'forecasts' of economic developments in other industrial countries, assumptions about oil and commodity prices, and implicit assumptions about institutional and political changes. To compare forecasts with out-turns without allowing for these non-model 'errors' will be a misleading guide to model performance. The only way round this is to 'reforecast' with hindsight, using correct (outcome) values for exogenous variables. Some modellers attempt to do this from time to time, but it is inevitably a resource-intensive and time-consuming task.

Second, forecasts made *using* an econometric model are not merely forecasts made *by* an econometric model. If an econometric relationship is correctly specified and estimated, its error term should be 'small' and random; for future periods the best expectation should be of zero errors in each period. But in practice econometric relationships will frequently display relatively large and systematic errors for recent periods. There will generally be little or no time to conduct a proper investigation into the reasons for this behaviour—it could be a change in behaviour, the sudden relevance of a new factor, or even poor official provisional data. The forecaster must judge as best he can how to project future values of the error term. If his judgement is good, he will produce an accurate forecast even though the econometric model was demonstrably poor.

A quite different criterion for judging between models might be, 'Which modellers have been most scientific and unprejudiced in their empirical work?' On the basis of published work it appears that the NIESR, the LBS, and the Treasury have undergone most change in the light of new evidence while the CEPG and Liverpool University have been the most committed to particular theoretical positions. Yet difficulties remain. The NIESR has been consistently accused of 'Keynesian bias', despite the work done on the monetary sector of its model; the LBS has continued to be regarded as 'monetarist' despite several moves away from this approach; and on the other hand, it may not be convincing to criticize (say) 'monetarist' groups for failing to explore alternative structural models if their avowed methodology leads them toward reduced-form (or even 'black-box') models.

None of this is very helpful to the reader who wants to know which model to ack. Perhaps the only safe—if disappointing—conclusion is that, despite the resources devoted to it, macroeconometric model-building is still in a relatively early stage of development. Whether progess is really possible is, of course, an even more vexed question.

4.4.7. Medium-Term Analysis

The CEPG and Liverpool models were primarily designed for forecasting for periods of several years ahead. The more 'orthodox' models, designed for quarterly forecasts up to two years ahead, were not. But during the 1970s, the econometric view grew that if a model is a satisfactory representation of the real world then it should be as valid for medium-term projections as for short-run forecasts. In practice this proved not to be the case. When 'stretched' to forecast up to five years ahead, the quarterly models tended to produce scenarios which were in one way or another seen as 'unrealistic'. These 'unrealistic' outcomes might include, for example, plainly absurd rates of accumulation or divesting of financial assets by one sector or another, or degrees of import penetration clearly inconsistent with anything like the present industrial structure.

The response of the builders of the quarterly models has typically been to 'impose' on their models a number of longer-run 'constraints' designed to produce 'acceptable' medium- and long-run properties. These might include unit elasticity of response of consumption to income (at a constant inflation rate), unit elasticities of response of exports and imports to world and domestic demand, unit income elasticity of demand for money (at constant interest rates), and so on.

This poses a severe dilemma for modellers. If an unconstrained model produces unrealistic medium-term scenarios, then its validity for short-run purposes must be called into question. If, on the other hand, a realtively large number of somewhat *ad hoc* constraints determines the medium-term characteristics of the model, econometric analysis tells us little more than the (relatively short-run) pattern of adjustment to the largely imposed medium-term solution. A sceptic could well argue that in the first case econometric analysis tells us incorrect things, and, in the second case, nothing of importance. Less tendentiously, the problem of medium-term forecasting has thrown up problems which many model builders have not yet satisfactorily resolved.

4.5. Summary and Conclusions

The difficulties in assessing the past and current behaviour of the economy and in predicting its future evolution have increased dramatically over the last fifteen years. Until then, major disturbances to world trade and prices were relatively rare and the economy's responses to such external shocks as there were—as well as to changes in economic policy—appeared to be both mild and stable. Within limits, it appeared possible for the authorities to aim successfully at a high level of employment with balance of payments equilibrium and a tolerable rate of inflation using only the management of effective demand through (mainly) fiscal policy.

Since the early 1970s, a number of developments have severely jolted that reassuring view. The breakdown of the Bretton Woods system of (broadly) fixed exchange rates had two important effects. First, it introduced a degree of instability into the international transmission of economic fluctuations, especially in prices. Second, it meant that monetary policy, through its impact on the exchange rate, assumed an importance which it had not previously had. Then the commodity price rises (particularly of oil) produced an inflationary shock of an unprecedented sort, bringing inflation to the forefront as an economic problem—but one for which, as yet, no fully satisfactory answer exists. Next, the experience of rapid inflation showed that inflation itself causes problems which neither modellers nor policy makers had anticipated—for example change in the values of financial assets and in people's savings behaviour. Policy responses, too, have changed. Partly because of the increased significance of monetary policy and partly because of the absence of any coherent alternative policy to deal with the problem of inflation, successive governments (both here and abroad) in the second half of the 1970s and the early 1980s pursued deflationary policies—usually presented as designed to 'control' public sector borrowing—which led to unprecedentedly high levels of unemployment and low rates of output growth.

Thus over the last decade fluctuations in both price inflation and real output have been greatly in excess of those experienced earlier. Understandably, modellers have not always correctly anticipated the behaviour of the economy in these 'new' circumstances. Yet one's impression—it can be little more—is that the sorry state of the UK economy in the early 1980s has been due, not to the failure of economic forecasters to predict events reasonably well, but to governments' failures to widen the range of policy instruments employed to cope with the emergence of grossly incompatible policy targets. Orthodox models can 'explain' quite adequately the general path of output and the wide fluctuations in inflation since the mid-1970s, given world developments, government policies, movements in the exchange rate, and the feeble influence of labour market pressure on wage settlements. But this has not been sufficient to remove controversy over the most appropriate policy responses that the behaviour of the economic system requires.

Bibliography

Regular assessments of the UK economy appear in:
[1] *National Institute Economic Review* (quarterly).
[2] London Business School, *Economic Outlook* (quarterly).
[3] Department of Applied Economics, Cambridge, *Economic Policy Review* (annual to 1982).
[4] HM Treasury, *Financial Statement and Budget Report* (annual).
[5] OECD, *Economic Survey* (annual).
[6] Bank of England, *Quarterly Review*.
[7] University of Liverpool, *Quarterly Economic Bulletin*.

Forecasts made by an independent group (ITEM), using the Treasury model, are summarized quarterly in the *Guardian*.

A simple (but early) account of forecasting using the NIESR model is:

8] SURREY, M. J. C. *The Analysis and Forecasting of the British Economy* (Cambridge/NIESR, 1971).

A recent introduction to economic modelling, together with brief surveys of the main models, is:

9] HOLDEN, K., PEEL, D. A., and THOMPSON, J. L. *Modelling the UK Economy* (Martin Robinson, 1982).

Comprehensive accounts of the Treasury, NIESR, LBS, and CEPG models are in Technical Manuals issued from time to time by the institutions involved. These are, however, almost entirely incomprehensible to the newcomer.

For a recent description and comparison of five major UK Models see:

10] BRECH, M. *Comparative Structures and Properties of Five Macroeconomic Models of the UK*. Economic Working Paper no. 10. (NEDO 1983).

Comparative simulation studies of the various models are multiplying rapidly. One useful example is:

11] LAURY, J., LEWIS, G., and ORMEROD, P. 'Properties of Macroeconomic Models of the UK Economy: A Comparative Study', *National Institute Economic Review* (Feb. 1978).

A useful survey of recent developments in model-building is:

12] ORMEROD, P. (ed.). *Economic Modelling* (Heinemann, 1979).

PART IV

THE INTERNATIONAL CONTEXT OF THE UK

15

International Trade and Development

D. A. HAY

15.1. The UK in the World Trading Economy

15.1.1. The UK as an Open Economy

The theme of this chapter and the following four in this part of the book is the United Kingdom as a trading economy placed in the context of a world economy that has undergone rapid and fundamental changes in the post-war period. Most have been developments over which the UK has had little or no control, though naturally the UK has played its part in the diplomacy that has attended institutional change such as the General Agreement on Tariffs and Trade (GATT), and latterly the commercial policy of the European Economic Community. However, the shifts in trade and competitiveness, instanced by the strength of German and Japanese exports in world markets, and the more recent growth if exports from the Newly Industrializing Countries, have been largely thrust upon the UK. This chapter seeks to document and explain these developments in the world economy. The main conclusion is that the UK economy has no option but to accept change and to adjust. The next two chapters look in more detail at the European and Japanese economies respectively, while Chapter 18 charts the development of the international monetary system. Finally in this part, Chapter 19 looks at the whole issue of international demand management as pursued in recent years.

Our starting point is the observation that the UK is an exceptionally 'open' economy. One simple indicator of the 'openness' of the economy is the ratio of exports and imports to Gross Domestic Product. This ratio is given at intervals since 1960 in Table 15.1. It is evident that a fifth of all production of goods and services has been destined for overseas markets in the period since 1960, and that this has been matched by imports to satisfy the requirements of UK industry and consumers. Furthermore the degree of dependence on foreign trade has increased over the period as the economy exports proportionately more of its product, and also imports more. These trends are considered in more detail in section 15.5 of this chapter, but it is important to note that the composition of trade, particularly of imports, has also changed over time. Thus the ratio of total manufacturing imports to output was only 12 per cent in 1963 but had risen to nearly 25 per cent by the end of the 1970s as imports penetrated the domestic market.

TABLE 15.1. *The Ratio of Imports and Exports to UK Gross Domestic Product,*
1960–1981
(percentages)

	Exports	Imports
1960	21·3	—
1964	19·7	21·3
1966	19·7	19·7
1969	22·7	22·0
1972	22·4	22·3
1975	26·6	28·1
1978	29·4	27·9
1981	27·3	24·4

Source: OECD, *Historical Statistics*;
OECD, *National Accounts.*

The openness of the UK economy to trade is also evident in comparisons with other leading industrial nations. Over most of the 1960s and 1970s both the export and import ratios were the highest observed. Only since 1980 have the West German ratios pulled ahead of those of the UK; major trading nations such as the United States and Japan have much lower ratios. Comparative figures for 1978 are given in Table 15.2.

TABLE 15.2. *The Ratio of Imports and Exports to GDP for Selected Industrial*
Countries, 1978
(percentages)

	UK	US	Japan	West Germany	France	Italy
Exports	29·4	8·3	11·2	25·4	21·3	26·8
Imports	27·9	9·7	9·5	22·8	20·3	24·2

Source: OECD, *Historical Statistics;* OECD, *National Accounts.*

The most obvious implication of 'openness' is that it is difficult to insulate the economy from what is happening to world trade. The UK economy is no exception in this respect. It is to developments in world trade in the last twenty years that we next turn. The description and explanation of these developments will occupy much of this chapter, but in the final section we return to the question of how the UK economy has responded, and what are the prospects for the future.

15.1.2. Recent Developments in World Trade

The 1960s were a period of unprecedented growth in world trade. From 1963–73 it grew at 8½ per cent per annum in volume terms, outstripping the growth rate of world output, which was about 6 per cent per annum. This was a period of progressive liberalization of world trade, which had beneficial consequences for economic progress generally. Table 15.3 shows how the broad sectors contributed to the total. The dominant role of manufacturing output and trade is evident. In terms of value, the proportion of trade accounted for by manufacturing increased from 52 per cent in 1963 to 61 per cent in 1973.

TABLE 15.3. *Growth Rates of World Production and World Exports, 1973–1981*
(average annual rate of change in volume, percentages)

	World output		Exports	
	1963–73	1973–81	1963–73	1973–81
Total	6	3	$8\frac{1}{2}$	$3\frac{1}{2}$
Agriculture	$2\frac{1}{2}$	2	4	$4\frac{1}{2}$
Minerals*	$5\frac{1}{2}$	1	7	$-2\frac{1}{2}$
Manufactures	7	$3\frac{1}{2}$	11	5

* Includes fuels and non-ferrous metals.

Source: GATT, *International Trade 1981–82* (Geneva, 1982), Table 1, p. 2 and Table 2, p. 3.

The regional composition of this trade is shown in Table 15.4. The growth of trade in manufactures enabled the major industrial countries to increase their share of world exports from 64 to 68 per cent over the decade 1963–73. They accounted for about four-fifths of all trade in manufactures, and this trade was predominantly between themselves. Developing countries, with their greater dependence on exports of primary products, experienced a slower growth in their export markets, and for this reason their share of world trade declined.

TABLE 15.4. *Regional Composition of World Trade, 1963–1981*
(percentages)

		1963	1973	1981
Industrial areas	exports	64	68	61
	imports	$64\frac{1}{2}$	$69\frac{1}{2}$	$63\frac{1}{2}$
Oil-exporting developing countries	exports	6	$7\frac{1}{2}$	14
	imports	3	$3\frac{1}{2}$	$7\frac{1}{2}$
Other developing countries	exports	$14\frac{1}{2}$	12	$13\frac{1}{2}$
	imports	18	$14\frac{1}{2}$	18
Eastern trading area	exports	12	10	$9\frac{1}{2}$
	imports	$11\frac{1}{2}$	10	9

Source: Reproduced from GATT, *International Trade 1981/82* (Geneva, 1982), Table 5, p. 7.

The 1970s' experience included some element of continuity with that of th 1960s, especially the continuing reduction in tariffs, offset to some extent by th growth of non-tariff barriers to trade. But Table 15.3 makes it clear tha average growth in both trade and output was sharply reduced in the perio 1973–81. Furthermore the growth of trade was somewhat unstable: in som years trade hardly grew at all, in other years it grew as much as in the best yeal of the 1960s. Agriculture was the only sector that managed to maintain th growth experience of 1963–73. At least part of the reason for this inferio growth performance is to be found in the two major shocks to the world tradin system in the 1970s: the transition from fixed to floating exchange rates, and th very large increases in the real price of oil. These shocks are discussed in sectio 15.4.

Table 15.4 also shows a marked drop in the share of industrialized countrie in world exports, from 68 per cent in 1973 to 61 per cent in 1981. This was th first time that their share had declined in the post-war period. The drop is evel more marked if trade *within* Europe is excluded: the share of industrialize countries in world exports then shows a drop of nearly 10 percentage point over the 1970s. North America became a less important market for Europeal exports, and US exports to other industrialized countries decreased from 62 t 54 per cent of their total exports. Exports from industrialized countries to oil exporting developing countries increased sharply, but not enough to offset th rise in the value of imports from those countries, brought about by the rise i the real price of petroleum over the period.

The decade 1965–75 also saw the emergence of a number of strong exportin countries in the Third World. In descending order of importance they were Hong Kong, Taiwan, South Korea, Mexico, Brazil, Yugoslavia, Singapore India, and Malaysia. These each had total manufactured exports of over $ billion in 1976, and accounted for 95 per cent of all the manufactured export from less developed countries. This group of countries has become known as th Newly Industrializing Countries (NICs). Their progress has been watche closely, as they are widely believed to have the potential to become new Japans Manufactured exports from the developing countries as a whole grew at a rat exceeding 16 per cent for the whole decade 1965–75. The NICs of Latil America and East Asia recorded growth rates of manufactured exports il excess of 20 per cent per annum in the same period. Furthermore all th projections are for rapid growth to continue despite the world recession of th 1970s, though the rate is likely to fall due to increased protectionism in th industrial economies. The destination of these exports reflects the pattern o world trade in manufactures as a whole: some two-thirds going to the industria economies, and the other third to other developing countries. Within the NICs Hong Kong, South Korea, and Taiwan are dominant, with some 63 per cent o all NIC manufactured exports in 1976.

In the next two sections we provide some explanations for the shiftin patterns of world trade just described. In the next section we explain some o the theories developed by international economists to account for the pattern o trade and specialization between trading nations. In section 15.3 we switcl attention to the institutional framework within which the post-war develop

1ent of trade has taken place, notably the general relaxation of previously
xisting barriers to trade.

5.2. Trade and Specialization

5.2.1. Comparative Advantage and International trade

`he modern theory of international trade is based on the concept of *comparative
dvantage*. This concept focuses on the rate at which an economy can increase its
utput of one good by giving up the production of another, assuming that all
esources in the economy are fully employed. The application of the concept to
nternational trade is best illustrated by an example.[1] Let us suppose that in
ngland only one extra ton of potatoes can be grown by giving up two tons of
heat, whereas in Ireland the situation is reversed, two extra tons of potatoes
eing possible if one ton of wheat is foregone. Then we would say that England
as a comparative advantage in growing wheat, and Ireland in growing
otatoes. It takes no great imagination to conclude that both parties can gain if
ngland puts resources into growing wheat, and Ireland into potatoes. Then
ngland can export wheat to Ireland, with potatoes being traded in the
pposite direction. Both countries can gain because they are using their
esources more productively, and aggregate output of wheat and potatoes is
ncreased. It is important to note that the argument is silent about the *absolute*
fficiency of production in the two countries. For example, climatic and soil
onditions could make English farmers more productive than their Irish
ounterparts in producing *both* potatoes and wheat. In that case English
armers will enjoy a higher standard of living than Irish farmers. But that is
rrelevant to the previous argument which relies solely on *comparative*, or
elative, efficiency in producing the two crops.

The theory is incomplete as a basic explanation of international trade
vithout some explanation of the determinants of comparative advantage. The
Ieckscher-Ohlin theory is one such explanation that is given considerable
ttention in the literature. The theory states that a country will specialize in
hose goods for which it has a particularly favourable resource endowment.
Thus a country with an abundance of labour will have a comparative
dvantage in the production of labour-intensive goods, will specialize in the
production of the same, and will also export them. The theory is usually
xpounded in terms of two factors of production, capital and labour. The goods
re ranked according to the ratio of capital to labour used in their production.
A labour-intensive economy is one where the overall ratio of supply of capital to
he supplies of labour is low relative to the other economies with which it trades.

Early attempts to demonstrate the validity of this simple model of trade gave
ome unexpected results, of which the most notable is the so-called *Leontief
aradox*. Examining the imports and exports of the US, Leontief estimated that
he imports were on the whole capital-intensive and the exports labour-
ntensive. This was exactly the reverse of what might have been expected, since
ssuredly the United States had a higher overall capital–labour ratio than any

---

[1] A fuller explanation of comparative advantage theories of trade is given in Appendix 1 of this
chapter.

of its major trading partners. This paradox stimulated a great deal of further development of the theory, and of empirical work seeking to unravel the mystery. An obvious possible explanation was that the United States might have a very high demand for capital-intensive products. However, studies have found a striking similarity between demand patterns in different economies, even where income per capita is very different. Hence this possibility was rejected as implausible. Much more weight has been given to studies that seek to extend the list of factors of production beyond just two, and to define these factors more accurately. Two particular examples are physical resources and 'human' capital. The importance of physical resources needs little stress. For example, an appropriate climate is a *sine qua non* for the production of tropical and sub-tropical commodities such as coffee, cocoa, and natural rubber.

The concept of 'human capital' reflects the fact that some workers are more highly trained than others (see Chapter 4, pp. 97–9). This may derive from formal education, or from training in specific skills including learning on the job. It is now accepted that physical resources and skilled labour provide much of the explanation for the Leontief paradox. Allowing for these, one finds that US manufacturing net exports are positively correlated with physical capital-intensity and the level of skills needed in production, and negatively correlated with requirements for most physical resources and for unskilled labour.

Another aspect of the Heckscher-Ohlin theory that has come under attack is the assumption of a common international technology available to all countries. It is apparent that most new technology is produced by the research and development of the advanced industrial economies of North America, Western Europe, and Japan. This will not be immediately available to other countries, unless transferred *within* a multinational corporation with production facilities outside those economies. The barriers to transference will be, at the very least, patent protection and industrial secrecy on the part of the originators of the new technology. Furthermore, less advanced economies may lack the technical skills to appreciate and apply the new technology. Technology transfer is not a costless operation, and therefore may involve substantial time-lags.

These observations have given rise to the 'technological gap' theories of trade. New technologies will first be applied in advanced countries and will give rise to exports early in the life of the technology. As the techniques become well known, production can be transferred to locations in less advanced economies which may have a comparative advantage. These economies will then start exporting to the advanced economies, which will in turn be moving on to even newer products and processes. This type of explanation of trade has been adduced to explain the emergence of manufactured exports from the Newly Industrializing Countries. Their exports include not only the traditional sectors—textiles, clothing, footwear—where they might be thought to have a comparative advantage in terms of abundant cheap labour. They also include some advanced products, such as electronic equipment for both domestic and industrial use, which require a considerable level of skill in manufacture. But these products are virtually all those with 'mature' technologies, which are well understood.

5.2.2. Trade in Differentiated Products

Perhaps the least attractive feature of the Heckscher-Ohlin theory is its failure to treat adequately the case of *differentiated products*. It is evident that a great deal of trade between advanced economies is in the form of 'intra-industry' trade, that is, an economy will both export and import *within* a broad classification of goods. The most obvious case is trade in cars, particularly within Western Europe. Britain exports some cars to the rest of Western Europe and simultaneously imports others. To define each type as a separate product, and then to explain that France must have a comparative advantage in making Renault cars, is only to avoid the question. We must add to the theory an analysis of differentiated product markets. One framework is to imagine a set of differentiated products, incorporating a range of underlying characteristics or qualities in different proportions. Thus size, comfort, fuel economy, and engine size might be appropriate in the case of motor cars. If consumer preferences are spread out over different combinations of characteristics, then clearly, differentiated products will be produced. However, there are also economies of long production runs in the manufacture of many differentiated products. Hence a limited number of differentiated products will be produced. The hypothesis is that a particular economy will produce a range of differentiated products which most closely corresponds to the tastes of its inhabitants, exporting to similar consumers in other countries and importing to satisfy those domestic consumers whose tastes do not conform to the national products.

The introduction of product differentiation has another consequence for understanding trade patterns. *Non-price* competition may be just as important as price competition in determining the trade successes of a particular economy. Attention to product specification and quality, the marketing of a product, and the provision of service can become the decisive features rather than price. There is evidence, for example, that despite the real appreciation of the yen and the mark in recent years, Japanese and German products have continued to enjoy growing penetration of world markets. They gain from superior design and marketing, despite rising prices.

Studies have suggested that as much as 60 per cent of all trade between the ten major OECD countries represents matching imports and exports within specific (three-digit) sectors of the Standard Industrial Trade Classification.[2] The next question is what characterizes the products which enter intra-industry trade, and what are the country characteristics that favour such trade between economies. One might expect intra-industry trade in differentiated products between economies which are at similar levels of development in terms of per capita incomes. These expectations have been broadly confirmed by statistical analyses, though there is much work still to be done in this area.

---

[2] But some of these 'sectors' actually comprise a wide variety of products, so the measure may be a statistical artefact. The only way to discover this is by inspecting trade flows at a still more disaggregated level, preferably at the level of individual products. Such studies suggest that disaggregation does indeed eliminate some trade previously identified as intra-industry. But possibly as much as half of all trade between the ten major OECD countries is properly so identified.

15.2.3. Trade Distortions: Tariffs, Subsidies, Non-tariff Barriers to Trade

Our discussion has proceeded thus far on the assumption that there are no obstacles to the free trade of goods between different countries. In practice, of course, there are numerous barriers to free trade. The geographical fact of distance introduces the barrier of transport costs that can reduce the profitability of trading over long distances, especially where the ratio of transport costs to unit values is high. However, this effect is somewhat mitigated by the structure of freight costs. A major element in transportation cost is the cost of trans-shipment—transferring, for example, the product from lorry or train to ship at a port. Once the merchandise is on the ship, then the marginal cost of transporting the good a further thousand miles may not be very great. But empirical studies have shown that distance between trading economies reduces trade.

The other major obstacles to trade are not natural barriers, but are created by deliberate actions by policy makers. The objective is always to protect domestic producers against overseas competition which would otherwise be able to undercut their prices.

The methods fall into three broad groups. The first is tariffs, that is, taxes on the entry of foreign products into the country, imposed at the point of entry, and usually set as a certain percentage of the value of the import. (This begs the question of how that value is defined, and regulations on that point are often complex to avoid evasion of duty by under-reporting of the value by the importer.) The second method is a direct subsidy to the operations of the domestic producers to enable them to meet the overseas competition, either in domestic or export markets. While such a subsidy does not overtly interfere with trade, the consequences are not totally dissimilar to those of tariffs, though there are some important differences. The subsidy itself is often concealed as a subsidy on the use of a factor of production—capital investment incentives, wage subsidies—rather than being a subsidy on the product itself. Alternatively it may take the form of subsidized financing of export business, such as export credits or special insurance for risky export deals. The third set of methods, non-tariff barriers to trade, has attracted a good deal of attention in recent years, and can take a multiplicity of forms. One form is just an addition to existing tariff barriers. The valuation of imported goods is arbitrarily inflated by the customs authorities in order to increase the import tariff that is paid. More common is the use of bureaucratic delays within an elaborate import-licensing system to increase the costs of a prospective importer, even though trade in the product is nominally 'free'. A similar manoeuvre is the introduction of complex regulations relating to product quality, including the requirement that products be subjected to rigorous evaluation in government-controlled laboratories. There is a very narrow line between what might be regarded as reasonable to protect domestic consumers, and what is certainly just a ploy to make importing more difficult and less profitable. Yet another method is the reserving of government procurement contracts to domestic firms only. Given the importance of such contracts in most Western economies, this effectively removes a substantial proportion of Gross Domestic Expenditure om the domain of free trade. Finally, non-tariff barriers may take the form of uantitative restrictions on imports. Quotas may be put on particular products r a group of products, and may specify the permitted level of imports from articular countries of origin.

A brief analysis of the effects of these government-erected barriers to trade is iven in Appendix 2 of this chapter. The essential points to grasp are that a uccessful barrier will increase domestic output in the protected sector, but at ie cost of consumers having to pay more for the good. Only a subsidy to omestic producers avoids the latter disagreeable consequence. But the overnment will have to find a means of paying the subsidy, probably from ixation, so the eventual burden will again rest on consumers. Governments ill favour tariffs as they produce revenue for the Exchequer. Quotas and other uantitative restrictions enable those importers lucky enough to obtain licenses) import to make high profits, at the expense of consumers. To sum up, any of ie barriers to trade provoke a misallocation of resources, and involves output)sses in a fully employed economy.

We therefore need to ask why protection of domestic industry is so videspread. One argument, with a long tradition, is that protection may be sed to encourage a nascent industry that needs time to establish itself. conomies of scale and the existence of a learning curve in production may rovide valid reasons. This 'infant industry' argument has been widely used to istify protectionist measures in the Third World. However, it cannot explain he protection afforded to long-established industries in many of the advanced conomies. The explanation must lie, first, with the capacity of industry lobbies) obtain protection from pliant governments despite the costs to the public-at-irge as consumers. The interest of the lobby is in preserving the employment nd profits afforded by protection. Second, protection of well-established ndustries is difficult to dismantle, given that competitors abroad in the same ndustry may well be protected also. There may be very great difficulties in iegotiating multilateral reduction of protection in a number of countries imultaneously, but few if any countries want to remove protection uni-aterally, in the hope that others will follow.

5.2.4. The Role of Multinational Companies

A further unrealistic aspect of the Heckscher-Ohlin theory of trade is the .ssumption that production and trade are carried on by firms that are ffectively perfect competitors. In practice a great deal of world trade riginates in large multinational corporations. One estimate is that 70 per cent f US exports in 1970 were accounted for by such enterprises. Under free trade his makes little difference to the international location of production so long as uch firms seek to minimize the global costs of their operations and are esponsive to the various determinants of comparative advantage. However, on he demand side, such corporations potentially could control markets in lifferent countries. A number of interesting questions arise. First, what are the leterminants of the decision by a multinational to invest in an economy to vhich it was previously exporting from another production location? Second, here are questions about the transfer of both product and process technology within multinationals. Third, many multinationals are vertically integrated, and trade flows can be generated by movements of intermediate products between production locations in different countries. It is important to know how such transfers are valued by the companies concerned, and whether such values represent international market values. The answer to all these questions is made more difficult by differences in corporate taxation between countries, by the existence of trade barriers, and by rules concerning the remittance of profits on foreign direct investment. Multinationals are frequently accused of manipulating their internal accounts by such practices as unrealistic pricing of transfers of goods or services *within* the corporation but between countries. Thus the company would wish to avoid making profits in an economy which taxed such profits highly or restricted their remittance abroad. This could be achieved by charging the subsidiary in that country inflated transfer prices for any services or intermediate goods it received from other parts of the corporation. This would result in an arbitrary inflation of the value of imports to that economy, and correspondingly lower capital remittances.

Empirical work on these questions has provided some partial answers. One conclusion is that the decision by a multinational to invest in an economy is often motivated by the desire to exploit the advantages of some 'intangible' asset such as a patent on a process or a differentiated product. In principle the former could be achieved by licensing the use of the patent to an independent firm within the country. But the costs of transferring the information may be high, and the multinational company will often prefer to invest for itself. The rationale for transferring production of a differentiated product will be the need to adapt the product and its marketing to local conditions. There is also some evidence of multinationals responding to cost differentials in process industries by relocating production of a labour-intensive part of the production process in an economy with cheap labour. This is the phenomenon of 'sourcing' that has been a feature of the microelectronic industry in the US: the labour-intensive production of components has been transferred to Far East economies. Furthermore, it is likely that multinationals reduce the time-lag in the spread of new technology from the advanced industrial countries. In particular they are able to provide a package of entrepreneurship, essential skills, and financial capital, any or all of which may be absent from a less developed economy.[3]

15.2.5. The Adjustment Problem

Our analysis has so far been unduly static. The world economy has been changing very rapidly and the pattern of comparative advantage is very far from static. The emergence of Japan as an industrial power in the past thirty years, and the increasing industrial potential of some Third World countries, are clear evidence of the importance of change. Furthermore there has been a

---

[3] This is not to prejudge the issue as to whether the outcomes are totally beneficial to the host country. A multinational may stifle local entrepreneurship by its capacity to compete on a large scale. It may also transfer technology which is more appropriate to developed-country conditions and bring with it all the skilled manpower required, thus lessening the employment impact on the local economy.

oncerted effort to reduce the restrictions that affect trade between countries, specially trade between the advanced industrial countries. So an economy may at any time find certain of its industrial sectors contracting rapidly in the face of competition from new producers overseas, while other sectors experience rapid growth. Naturally such change is not entirely painless, and governments and policy makers are frequently urged to intervene to arrest or modify the process. This is the 'adjustment problem'.

To get the flavour of this problem it is best to consider a specific case. We assume that a Third World country emerges as a strong competitor to domestic producers in the home market of an advanced economy. The price of the good falls and consumers switch to the imported good, benefiting from the lower price. The domestic industry contracts as revenues and profits fall. Workers are laid off. However, we can also identify effects in other sectors. The Third World economy is likely to spend the foreign exchange earnings on purchases of goods from the advanced economy which it is not in a position to produce itself. Thus output in other sectors will rise, and so will employment. Given suitable flexibility in labour markets the adjustment problem is resolved by workers switching jobs. Unfortunately that flexibility is not always available. If the labour is switching from a labour-intensive sector to a capital-intensive sector, the restoration of full employment may require a fall in wages. The situation may be made more difficult if the skills developed in the declining industry are irrelevant to the sector that is expanding, and so retraining is necessary. Furthermore, the two industries may have different regional location patterns so that workers have to transfer between regions.

Exactly the same kind of adjustment problem will arise where the authorities are considering the removal of protection from a protected sector. Without protection, the domestic sector will experience a decline of profits and employment. Consumers will benefit, and other sectors will expand.

The following paradox emerges. In most cases it is in the long-term interests of the economy to adjust. Our discussion of the gains from trade shows us that: it also shows that the *other* trading partner gains too. But these gains are the *net* outcome of considerable gross gains and losses accruing to different sectors of the community at different times. The essential point is that the losses are much more easily perceived than the gains. A particular industry, perhaps geographically concentrated, sees its markets slipping away, its factories closing, and its workers being made redundant as a direct consequence of import penetration. Adversity bring the trade association and the trade unions representing workers in the industry into a powerful alliance to lobby for government protection. Local political voices will be added in the case where the industry is geographically concentrated. Perceptions of the gains are much more diffuse. Consumers, who will benefit from cheap imports, are not a particularly powerful lobby. The output and employment gains are likely to be spread across several sectors, and not to be widely understood and appreciated. The consequence is that a government faces a powerful lobby for protection, with no other body to express a contrary view. If protection is conceded in terms of a tariff, the policy is costless to the government: indeed it will gain the tariff revenue. Non-tariff barriers are similarly costless, except for the sometimes substantial cost of administration. The alternative, a subsidy to the declining sector, is not likely to be granted: it is expensive to the government, and is likely to raise too many political questions.

Hence it will be a brave government that resists protectionist pressures, and insists on adjustment. Furthermore the costs of enabling adjustment to take place may themselves be substantial. Displaced workers will require unemployment benefit, and may require retraining facilities. Problems in particular regions may require expenditure on regional programmes.

15.3. International Trade Policy and Institutions

15.3.1. The General Agreement on Tariffs and Trade

During the 1930s international trade had been greatly restricted by the imposition of tariffs and other barriers to trade by governments anxious to protect their domestic markets from the consequences of the Depression. It was hoped by this means to secure domestic markets for domestic producers, and thus mitigate the impact of unemployment. The outcome was a spiral of retaliatory protectionist measures, and a sharp diminution in world trade. The General Agreement on Tariffs and Trade (GATT) was drafted in 1947 with the specific objectives of reducing barriers to trade, and of avoiding the tariff wars of the 1930s by creating a forum for multilateral discussions on international trade policy. GATT had eight signatories intially, with the US as a leading member in pressing for multilateral free trade.

The key principle of GATT is non-discrimination in trade. A GATT member accepts the most-favoured-nation (MFN) clause: it agrees not to give better treatment, in terms of access to the domestic market, to any single trading partner than it gives to all the contracting parties of GATT. The only exception to this clause is the creation of customs unions or free-trade areas, where tariffs between the members are reduced to zero.

The GATT negotiations made slow progress in the 1950s, though world trade grew rapidly. In 1962, the US made a major new initiative for tariff reductions that became known as the Kennedy Round. The American objective was to counter what it saw as the growing protectionism of the European Economic Community (EEC) and the European Free Trade Association (EFTA), where the promotion of free trade between members of these groupings was diverting attention from trade policy issues in relation to non-members. The negotiations at GATT dragged on until 1967, and what was finally agreed was very much less than the original aspirations of the US. Tariff reductions amounted on average to about 35 per cent of initial levels, and about one-third of all imports by the major industrial countries were affected. The main effect was on trade between the industrial countries. The tariff cuts were spread over five years to 1972. At the end of the process, the United States' tariffs on manufactured goods were in the range 10–20 per cent, as were those of the United Kingdom and Japan. EEC tariffs averaged 10 per cent, with a narrower spread.

The success of the Kennedy Round gave sufficient momentum for further negotiations between the US, the EEC, and Japan, who were the major participants in the Tokyo Round which was completed in 1979. The agreement will be implemented over a period of eight years, which began in 1980. The Kennedy Round had left only limited scope for further tariff reductions, though agreement was reached to halve existing tariff barriers on average, with larger reductions in those tariffs which had large initial values. Trade worth about $110 billion in 1976 will be affected. However, the impact is likely to be reduced by the 'exceptions lists' of products tabled by participants, effectively removing those products from consideration.

More significant than tariff reductions is the attempt made to get to grips with non-tariff barriers to trade. Agreement was reached on common rules for valuation of imports at customs, on limiting the preference shown to domestic suppliers in government contracts, and on simplification of rules for import licences. Codes governing government subsidies to industries were agreed. Progress was also made on reducing obstacles to trade arising from regulation on product safety or quality. Unfortunately, these agreements were reached in an atmosphere of increasing pressures for protection from within the participating economies. The experience of the latter half of the 1970s began to look like a repeat of the history of the 1930s, as governments came under pressure to protect domestic industry and employment from the effects of world recession. Symptoms of these pressures are apparent in the Tokyo Declaration, both in the 'exceptions list', and in the warning by the EEC that it was prepared to exercise its rights under GATT to apply safeguard measures against 'disruptive' imports. It remains to be seen whether the 1980s will continue the process of trade liberalization of the 1950s, 1960s, and 1970s, or whether there will be a general return to protectionist policies.

Two other features of GATT are worthy of note. The first is the implication of the agreements for trade between the advanced industrial economies and the countries of the Third World. This aspect will be dealt with later. The second is the fact that GATT has for the most part excluded agricultural products. In the 1950s, the US wished to protect its agricultural sector for domestic political reasons. The other signatories agreed to this, as a quid pro quo for tariff concessions by the US. Later the American stance was modified somewhat, but the EEC then developed a profoundly protectionist policy for its own agriculture in the Common Agricultural Policy. There is little prospect of any major liberalization of trade in agricultural products.

5.3.2. The European Economic Community

The rules of GATT made an exception from the most-favoured-nation clause in respect of regional groupings of economies. Two kinds of groupings are possible. The first, of which EFTA was the paradigm example, involves free trade between members, but each remains free to set its own external tariffs. The second, a customs union of which the EEC is the most important example, involves the members not only in free trade between members, but also in a common external tariff. In practice, too, the EEC has become involved in a wide range of other policies that might affect trade between members. Thus there have been moves to remove non-tariff barriers to trade that could arise from regulations relating to product quality and specification. Competition

policy has been extended to cover market behaviour involving one or mor
firms operating in different member countries, for example agreements abou
market sharing. Particular attention has been paid to subsidies and tax relief
offered by different member countries which could affect trade. Harmoniza
tion of indirect taxation is a long-term objective.

The EEC came into being on 1 January 1959, the basis being the Treaty c
Rome of 1957. The six initial members were Belgium, France, italy
Luxembourg, the Netherlands, and West Germany. Progress on removin,
tariff barriers between the members was rapid, and tariffs disappeared by 1966
Over the same period external tariffs were brought into line. Seven countrie
outside the EEC—Austria, Denmark, the UK, Norway, Portugal, Sweden
and Switzerland—formed EFTA in 1959, and by 1967 abolished all tariff
between them. These countries had stayed out of the EEC either because the
were not prepared to accept the *political* commitment to co-operation that wa
entailed, or because, like Britain, they saw their commercial interests in
maintaining strong trading links outside Europe which would have bee
damaged by accession to the EEC. However, since 1967 there has been
process of rapprochement between the members of the EEC and EFTA. Th
UK, Norway, and Denmark applied for membership of the EEC and wer
admitted in 1973. At the same time, free trade between the remaining EFT
countries and EEC members was established. Although EFTA member
retained control over their tariffs external to Europe, the progress that had bee
achieved under GATT meant that differences between those tariffs and th
external tariffs of the EEC were negligible for the majority of industria
products. Further extension of the EEC is taking place with the accession o
Greece, Spain, and Portugal.

The theory of customs unions is a complex area of economic analysis
Reduction of tariffs between two economies, while preserving commo
external trade barriers, has two effects. The first is that trade will be *created* b
each economy specializing in those products in which it has a comparativ
advantage and trading to reach higher levels of welfare. The conditions fo
gains are that the countries should have dissimilar economic structure
(reflecting different factor endowments). If the two economies are very similar
then the scope for gains will be limited. The second effect is that of trad
diversion. Assume that X, Y, and Z are three economies between which trade i
impeded by tariff barriers. For a particular good, X is a high-cost producer, Y
has lower costs, and Z has the lowest costs of all. The tariffs are such that X
imports from Z, despite the tariff, while Y produces for itself. X and Y now form
a customs union, maintaining the external tariff against Z. X now imports the
good in question from Y, as Y's costs are less than Z's costs plus the tariff. The
terms of trade of X, i.e. the ratio of its export to import prices, deteriorate as i
switches from a low-cost to a high-cost source of imports. This represents
welfare loss. The *price to domestic consumers* has fallen since supply from Y carrie
no tariff, but the total resources necessary to buy imports rises as a result of the
trade diversion. Assessing the gains and losses from trade creation and trad
diversion is therefore a complex matter empirically. However, studies that wer
made of the net benefits of Britain's entry to the EEC concluded that the gain

mounted to no more than 1 per cent of national income. In general the gains
re largest where the initial distortions created by tariffs are largest.

The smallness of the empirical estimates of gains from tariff reductions has
d some economists to emphasize other sources of gains. The first is related to
ie efficiency of firms. The suggestion is that oligopolistic industries within a
rotective tariff have no incentive to seek cost efficiency. The tariff enables
iem to agree (tacitly) on a high price, and then absorb the excess profits by
perating inefficiently and not striving to keep costs down. Cutting the tariff
xposes such a cosy arrangement to international competition. Domestic firms
ave to become cost efficient in order to survive. However, this scenario
epends on competitive behaviour by foreign suppliers. If they decide to join
ie domestic oligopoly, and take their share of the high profits, then
ompetitive gains will not accrue. The second source is dynamic economies.
'he idea is that specialization within the customs union will enable firms to
ealize economies of scale and thus make productivity gains. Alternatively the
rocess will involve capital investment in those sectors in which specialization
s occurring. The consequences will be embodiment of the most recent
echnologies in a substantial proportion of the capital stock of those sectors,
ith consequent beneficial impact on productivity. Unfortunately we have no
eal idea of how large these gains are likely to be. Proponents of the EEC often
oint to the rapid growth of the six EEC countries in the 1960s as evidence of
he dynamic gains of customs unions. However, it is just as plausible to
nterpret the period as one of exceptional growth rates throughout the OECD
rea, generated by Keynesian policies and investment optimism.

5.3.3. North–South Trade Policy

The GATT negotiations concentrated their efforts on trade liberalization
)etween the advanced industrial countries, collectively termed the North. The
leveloping countries of the South came to feel that GATT offered little that
vould help with their problems of economic development. In particular, the
nultilateral free-trade approach of GATT, with its most-favoured-nation
:lause, was difficult to reconcile with the policies of import-substituting
ndustrialization behind tariff walls that characterized many economies of the
'outh during the 1960s. So while twenty countries from the South participated
n the Kennedy Round negotiations of GATT, the South was not directly
nvolved in the Tokyo Round. Instead the South sought to promote its interests
hrough the United Nations Conferences on Trade and Development
UNCTAD), which had its first conference at Geneva in 1964 and has
ubsequently met at four-yearly intervals. Within UNCTAD the South has
)rganized itself into the Group of 77, to press the Southern countries' joint
nterests. More than 100 Southern countries are now associated with the group.

The interests of the South at UNCTAD have spread far beyond matters of
nternational trade alone. Its demands have been described as a call for a New
International Economic Order, the main features of which have been
)opularized in the report of the Brandt Commission. Our particular interest
ies in the area of trade. The South has consistently pressed for adoption of the
3eneralized System of Preferences (GSP), whereby developed economies grant

tariff reductions on designated imports from developed countries on a non reciprocal basis. The effects of this would be to *create* trade between developed and developing partners, and also to *divert* trade between the developed economy and its other Northern trading partners. Consideration of the latter effect led to the proposition that MFN tariff reductions *within* the North were inimical to the South, as the trade diversion effect of the GSP would be reduced. This proposition has been debated for the following reason. The GSP tariff reductions negotiated over the period 1964–71 contained a significant number of constraints. Thus agricultural and fishery products were excluded as were all textiles. Preferences were not extended to all countries on an equal basis, for example Taiwan was not included in the EEC scheme, and Hong Kong faced special restrictions in the Japanese scheme. Volume limits were set on a number of products of particular interest to developing countries exporters. The implication is that lower MFN tariffs, without conditions, might effectively give better access to Northern markets than the zero tariffs on the GSP 'with strings attached'. Against this it may be argued that MFN tariff reductions have not included a number of products of particular interest to Southern countries, and so the advantages of MFN are not so evident. Finally, GSP arrangements were given a ten-year time horizon which is arguably too short to establish a successful exporting industry in a Southern economy.

The GSP tariff reductions were implemented over the period 1971–6. Further agreements have also been implemented of which the Lomé Convention of 1975 between the EEC and forty-six developing nations in Africa, the Caribbean, and the Pacific is the most notable. However, it is arguable that little more can be done along these lines. First, it is noted that tariffs are now generally low, and hence GSP tariff reductions have little more than cosmetic value. But this ignores the 'cascading structure' of tariffs in the North, with higher rates on semi-manufactures than on raw materials, and even higher ones on final products. So the effective rate of protection certainly exceeds the nominal rates.[4] Furthermore the tariffs have remained high, particularly on those goods of interest to the developing countries. The second argument is that tariffs are no longer the real obstacle to trade. The real problem lies with non-tariff barriers. The rise of these barriers in the 1970s has been a particular concern of UNCTAD. In 1974 UNCTAD mooted the concept of a 'standstill' on the introduction of non-tariff barriers, and this was affirmed by both UNCTAD and the OECD countries. But the reality was somewhat different. All OECD countries have unilaterally introduced quantitative restrictions and other non-tariff barriers to trade under GATT Article 19, which refers to 'market disruption due to low-cost competition'. Negotiated trade restrictions have become common. One form of such restrictions with a long history is 'orderly marketing arrangements', of which the Multi-Fibre Agreement (MFA) of 1973 is the paradigm example. This covers the clothing and textile exports of Southern producers to the EEC which grew quickly in the early 1970s. The objective was to mitigate the EEC employment consequences of too rapid a growth in import penetration

---

[4] An explanation of the difference between 'nominal' and 'effective' rates of protection is given in Appendix 2 of this chapter.

However, the MFA has in fact become an instrument for blocking all growth in these imports. This is but one example of a number of such arrangements. It is not surprising therefore that the Tokyo Round under GATT made a major effort in respect of non-tariff barriers to trade, though once again the exceptions included many products of specific interest to the South.

It remains to be seen whether the international quest for freer trade, and for better access to Northern markets for Southern producers, which was such a feature of the 1960s, will be completely abandoned in the recessionary world of the 1980s. Certainly the rapid growth of non-tariff barriers in the latter half of the 1970s is not a favourable augury. They could easily cancel out all the gains from tariff reductions in the previous fifteen years. Furthermore they are much less 'objective' than declared tariff levels, and reductions are going to be much more difficult to negotiate in the future.

15.4. Problems of World Trade

Sections 15.2 and 15.3 have focused on long-run factors affecting the development of world trade since the 1950s. In this section we concentrate on three areas of particular concern to policy makers in the 1970s: the transition from fixed to floating exchange rates, the shocks arising from the sharp increases in the real price of oil, and the growing competition from the NICs.

15.4.1. Exchange Rates

The transition to floating exchange rates occurred in the period 1971–3, replacing the relatively fixed exchange rates of the Bretton Woods era (see Chapter 18 for a fuller description). In the very long run one would expect the changes in relative values of currencies to reflect differential rates of inflation in the different economies, such that *real* exchange rates remained unchanged. However, experience shows that very wide fluctuations have occurred in real exchange rates in the short term. Table 15.5 illustrates the point. This variability in real exchange rates is likely to have had adverse effects on the growth of trade in the 1970s and slowed down adjustment to new patterns of trade. Exporters and importers need to be reasonably secure in their estimates

TABLE 15.5. *Range of Fluctuations of Real Exchange Rates, 1970–1981* (quarterly values against 1970–9 mean values, percentages)

	UK	Japan	US	Germany	France	Italy
Maximum value	+39	+23	+20	+13	+7	+10
Minimum value	−15	−15	−12	−13	−12	−8
Range	54	38	32	26	19	18

Note: Real exchange rates are based on wholesale prices of manufactures.

Source: Commission of the European Communities, 'The Competitiveness of European Community Industry', III/387/82 (Mar. 1982).

of exchange rates in order to calculate the profitability of particular import and export contracts.

15.4.2. Oil Prices

A major shock to the world system was the doubling of the real price of oil by OPEC in 1973–4, and the repeat of the experience in 1979–80. During the decade the real price increased fivefold. The major effect was an alteration of the terms of trade between those countries which exported oil and those which exported manufactures. Given that substitution of non-oil energy sources could not be achieved immediately, trade balance required increased exports by the non-oil industrialized countries. Unfortunately, the process of adjustment was hindered by the failure of the oil exporters to spend their increased earnings from oil exports. The effect was a substantial deflation of world demand, only partly offset by the recycling of the oil revenues to financial markets of the industrialized countries.

Some indication of the size of this effect can be gauged from the share of fuels in the value of world exports. Having remained constant at about 10 per cent in the period 1963–73, the share rose sharply to 20 per cent in 1974 and to 24 per cent in 1980. This was despite a fall in the *volume* of fuel exports over the same period.

That the world training system had not completely adjusted to these shock by the end of the decade is suggested by a number of features of the current accounts of the balance of payments of the major trading groups, shown in Table 15.2. In particular the OPEC countries ran a substantial balance of payments surplus over the decade. The second oil price rise of 1979–80 restored the imbalance which the first price rise had brought, but which had been eroded in the interim. Thus in 1981 the traditional oil-exporting developing countries accounted for 14 per cent of world exports, but only $7\frac{1}{2}$ per cent of world imports. This trading surplus was reflected in very large deficits for other developing countries and rather smaller deficits for the industrialized countries.

15.4.3. The NICs

The rapid export growth of the NICs has been described in section 15.2, but the full impact of that growth is more apparent if the product composition is considered. As one might expect intuitively, textiles and clothing are important, comprising about 30 per cent of the total by value in 1976. More surprising is the fact that the share of engineering products was only slightly less, and that proportion has been increasing. Developing country exports in twelve different product groups increased by a multiple of at least nine over the period 1970–6: leather clothes, fur clothes, silk yarn and thread, telecommunications equipment, watches, motor vehicle parts, switchgear, piston engines accounting machines, electric power machinery, sound recorders, and domestic electrical equipment. It is noticeable that the last nine items in this list cannot be easily described as traditional products. Various attempts have been made to relate the export success of the NICs to the characteristics of the products in which they have specialized. The key determinant appears to be technology, the NICs having a revealed advantage in those products where the technology is well established and understood, and manufacturing processes are standardized. The product cycle theory dominates, with developing countries entering at the end of that cycle. Interestingly, other features, like capital-intensity and skill-intensity, do not appear to be a barrier to successful implantation of manufacturing industry in the NICs, though the large scale of operations does apparently put them at a comparative disadvantage *vis-à-vis* the industrial economies. One explanation for this pattern is that locations in the NICs have been increasingly sought by multinational companies, which can transfer the needed technology, capital, and key skills. For example, over 90 per cent of Singapore's exports in 1975 were accounted for by enterprises with a significant participation of foreign capital.

The aggregate impact of the NICs' manufactured exports on the industrial economies remains small. Despite their very rapid growth, less than one-tenth of the manufactured imports of the industrial countries originated in the NICs in 1980. However, the concentration on specific products was quite marked: the traditional industries—textiles, clothing, wood products, and leather— feature prominently. This can explain the recent growth of non-tariff barriers to trade in these products described at the end of section 15.3. Despite these protectionist reactions, competition from the NICs is likely to intensify as they diversify their industrial structure and seek new export markets. Furthermore there is a considerable number of other developing countries that are now seeking to emulate the success of the NICs. The adjustment problem posed for the advanced industrial countries will not be quickly or easily resolved.

15.5. The UK in the World Economy

The evolution of international trade policy described in section 15.3 has moved the UK from a relatively protected position in the immediate post-war period to being a very open economy indeed. There is free trade with the rest of Western Europe since the EEC, of which the UK is member, also has free trade with the former EFTA members. Successive rounds of tariff reductions under GATT, and the granting of tariff reductions to Third World producers under the Generalized System of Preferences, have greatly reduced the overall level of protection with respect to world trade in general. The result is that the UK has had to adjust, and in future will need to adjust further to competitive pressures in world markets.

In this context the recent behaviour of UK imports and exports is significant. In the 1960s and 1970s exports expanded by only $8\frac{1}{2}$ per cent for every 10 per cent increase in world trade. In consequence, the UK share of trade in manufactures declined as world trade grew. Exports do not appear to have been particularly sensitive to changes in relative costs, which reflect exchange rate movements and changes in unit labour costs. There was some response to the pressure of demand in the domestic market, but this was only slight. However, the most disturbing feature is a long-run trend decline in exports of about $2\frac{1}{2}$ per cent per annum. On the import side these results are matched.

The income elasticity of demand is 1·3 for semi-manufactures and 1·4 for finished manufactures. Price elasticities are low for semi-manufactures, but of the order of 0·9 for finished goods. The underlying growth of imports over time is $6\frac{1}{2}$ per cent per annum for semi-manufactures and 8 per cent per annum for finished manufactures. These apparently long-run adverse movements in both imports and exports are not easy to explain. One suggestion is that they reflect a period of adjustment in the specialization and trade of the UK in response to fundamental changes, like entry into the EEC, and to the NICs. A complementary explanation is non-price competition: the UK is not producing the 'right' products, reflecting comparative advantage in world markets.

We briefly consider this hypothesis in respect of UK trade with other advanced industrial countries and with the developing countries of the Third World. We begin with the EEC. It was always expected that UK industry would take some years to adjust to entry. The evidence is that imports rose sharply in the first four years after entry. Exports responded more slowly, but by the end of the decade were beginning to catch up. However, the UK's share of OECD trade in manufactures within Europe was only 11·8 per cent in 1980 compared to a share of 19·4 per cent in trade outside Europe. For comparison, the figures for France were 16·9 per cent and 18·1 per cent respectively. It is clear that the UK is not obtaining its anticipated share of European trade. One study of UK trade with the EEC in 1975 and 1976 failed to find any variables that could explain the pattern of specialization. None of the normal indicators of comparative advantage were significant in statistical analysis. Once again this could be taken as an indicator of a disequilibrium situation.

When UK trade with all the industrial countries, including Europe, is considered, a clearer picture emerges. Skill-intensity and human capital are positively correlated with success in trade (measured by the trade balance in a sector as a proportion of domestic consumption). There is a negative association with capital-intensity. However, the UK is *less* specialized than its OECD trading partners: they have gone much further in withdrawing from those sectors where they have comparative disadvantage and in building up sectors with a comparative advantage. A further finding about UK trade is that *within* sectors, the UK exports products with low unit values relative to Germany and France, and imports those with high unit values. If the unit value is interpreted as an indicator of the technological sophistication of the products, the conclusion is that the UK specializes in low-technology products which have low world-income elasticity of demand, and are particularly vulnerable to competition from the NICs.

UK trade with the developing countries displays a rather more pronounced pattern of specialization. UK comparative advantage is positively correlated with the skill-intensity or human capital-intensity of the product, and negatively with the capital-intensity. These are characteristics shared by all the industrialized economies. Moreover, the UK *does* concentrate on those sectors where it has a comparative advantage. Textiles, clothing, leather goods, man-made fibres, telephone equipment, motor cycles and cycles, rope, brushes and brooms, and games and sports equipment are sectors where developing countries have an unequivocal advantage in trade with the UK. But in the

:dium term, other UK sectors might expect import penetration—especially low unit-value engineering products, and perhaps in petrochemicals and astics, as OPEC countries build up their capacity in oil-related sectors. This description of the UK's position in the world trading economy may :m to invite a pessimistic conclusion. It appears that the UK is caught tween inability to compete with Germany, Japan, and other advanced dustrial economies in the production of sophisticated goods on the one hand, d an ever-increasing threat from the NICs in the production of standardized oducts on the other. However, this is misleading. Within a multilateral ading system an economy will be able to find some products in which it can de successfully, as the principle at work is *comparative* advantages, not *absolute* vantage. The question is which products those will be. The elementary :ory suggests that the supply of factors of production is an important terminant, and the empirical studies identify the key factors in the UK case skill-intensity. This is best interpreted as a surrogate for the degree of .earch and development effort put into a sector. Various studies have ncluded that while total resources devoted to research and development in e UK compare favourably with other industrial nations, those resources have en unduly concentrated in sectors where the returns have turn out to be :appointing, especially defence and aircraft. Other industrial countries have iced more emphasis on research and development into commercially viable oducts. The effect has been, as we explained above, that the unit values of K exports have tended to be low relative to those of the other industrial untries. The conclusion is not that we cannot export at all, but rather that K incomes in manufacturing reflect the lower value of the products. The only iy to escape this consequence is to give a greater priority to research and velopment investment in advanced technology sectors with prospects for :cess in world trade. The corollary is that the UK would at the same time thdraw from those sectors where the NICs have a comparative advantage d have already shown their capacity for import penetration. This presents e economy with the 'adjustment problem' which was discussed in general ms in section 15.2.5. A comprehensive quantitative study for the UK does t exist, but some illustrative figures can give us an order of magnitude. In the riod 1970–5, in the 24 industries most affected by developing country ports, 134,000 jobs were displaced due to imports from all sources, but :reased exports in the same sectors (but different goods) provided 42,000 new is. Of the net loss of 92,000 jobs, only 26,000 were due to developing country de. Displacement of labour due to productivity gains in these sectors was 2,000. But this is not a complete picture. As we saw in section 15.2.5, the veloping countries are likely to spend the foreign exchange earned from their :reased exports on purchases of more sophisticated goods. Thus over the riod 1970–7, the UK had a trade surplus with the NICs which was iintained by higher exports to the NICs offsetting increasing imports from em. The total employment loss was less than 2 per cent of the 1970 nufacturing employment, offset by an almost equivalent gain in jobs from :reased exports. This is in line with studies of adjustment in other European onomies. Trade has required workers to switch jobs rather than to lose them.

We conclude that unless there is a widespread return to protectionism, the UK has no option but to adjust to the pressures of world competition in trade. The 1970s were such a period of adjustment, and this probably explains the failure to discern any definite pattern of specialization in UK trade. The important question concerns the probable direction of specialization over the next two decades. The hope is that UK industry will respond to the challenge of world markets by moving 'up-market' to more sophisticated products in the high-technology sectors. Failure to do so will condemn the UK to a future in which real incomes can grow very little, and may even fall, as industry competes with low-cost producers in the NICs for a share of world markets in relatively standard and unsophisticated products.

Appendix 1: Explaining International Trade Patterns—Comparative Advantage Models

The explanation of the pattern of trade, and of the pattern of specialization of production between regions and countries, has been a preoccupation of economists since David Ricardo. The concept of *comparative advantage* has been central to the development of the theory and attempts to put the theory to the test. This concept is simultaneously deceptively simple and difficult to grasp. Let us suppose that we are considering the trade between only two countries (Britain and Portugal) in only two products (wine and cloth). Further suppose that five units of wine (measured in quantities, *not* values) require in Portugal the same resources as one unit of cloth. Thus the opportunity cost of cloth in terms of wine is five. In Britain the same ratio is unity: relative to cloth production, wine uses more resources than it does in Portugal (climatic factors could be the explanation). Then at least one and possibly both countries can gain by trade. Britain could make more cloth and less wine, gaining one unit of cloth for each unit of wine given up. Portugal can reduce cloth production and gain *five* units of wine for each unit of cloth given up. It can trade one unit of wine for one unit of cloth with Britain leaving Britain as well off as it was before. Portugal is better off by four units of wine. Portugal were willing to offer more than one unit of wine (though less than five) for each unit of cloth supplied by Britain, then Britain too would be better off.

It is important to note that the argument is based on *comparative*, or relative, cost advantages in the production of the products—Portugal in wine, Britain in cloth. *Absolute* advantages are not considered. For example, suppose that Portugal is more efficient than Britain in production of both goods, in the sense that fewer man-hours are required to produce both one unit of cloth and one unit of wine in Portugal than Britain. The previous argument carries through unaffected, as far as trade and specialization are concerned. However, the inhabitants of Portugal would be better off on average than those of Britain: they are more productive and hence can consume more. Further, the argument has been explained in terms of adjustments of production at the margin. However, if it is always the case that the ratio is five in Portugal and unity in Britain whatever the initial outputs of cloth and wine, then successive marginal adjustments will lead to Britain specializing completely in cloth and Portugal in wine. alternatively, the ratios change as the proportions of wine and cloth in total output are varied, then the process of specialization will cease when the ratios are equal in the two countries. The two cases are shown in the Figure 15.1.

In Figure 15.1(a) the production frontiers, which represent the maximum obtainable outputs given the technology and resources of the two countries, are straight lines exhibiting constant relative, or comparative, costs. Hence Britain will specialize at point

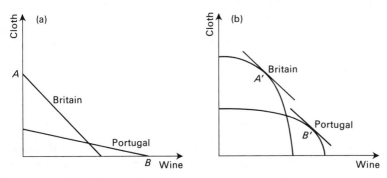

FIG. 15.1. Comparative Advantage Analysis.

all cloth) and Portugal at point B (all wine). This extreme pattern of specialization
l only be violated if one of the countries is smaller than the other and unable to supply
rld demand for the good in which it specializes. Then the larger country will have to
ke some of that good as well. In Figure 15.1(b) the production frontiers exhibit
reasing relative costs. Thus, in the British example, as more and more cloth is being
de so additional units of cloth require increasing sacrifice of units of wine. In this case
: two countries will specialize at points like A' and B', where comparative costs have
n equalized. The precise point will be determined by world demand (the sum of
nands in the two countries) at given relative price (cost) ratios. In general, as the
ce of wine relative to the price of cloth rises, so supply of wine rises, but world demand
it falls and the supply of cloth diminishes and demand for it rises. Equilibrium is
ained where supply equals demand in both markets simultaneously. The absolute
ces in each country will be denominated in local currency, and the values of the two
rencies will be determined in the market for foreign exchange, so that in the long run
: money values of trade in both directions are equal. This is not to deny that in the
rt run, the rate of exchange may be other than that which would equilibrate the
ney values of trade flows. Such a rate may be sustained by capital movements
ween the countries, or by the intervention of the monetary authorities supplying or
nanding foreign exchange, and thus running down or building up foreign exchange
erves. However, such phenomena cannot continue for ever. The authorities will run
: of reserves or not be willing to accumulate more. The international investors are
ely to vary the countries to which they make loans. Hence in the long run the pattern
rade is determined by the real factors which affect production in different countries,
d the discussion of these has been our primary concern in this chapter.
As a rule, countries are not observed to specialize in the production of a single traded
>d. (Traded goods are those which can enter international trade. Non-traded goods
: those which by their very nature, or because transport costs are prohibitive, are
ng to be consumed where they are produced. Haircuts are the paradigm example.)
nce we presume that production frontiers of different countries are more like those of
  than those of (a) in figure 15.1. We must now consider reasons as to why this should
so.
The traditional framework of analysis is the Heckscher-Ohlin model. The simplest
·sion of the model involves two traded goods produced by two factors of production,
d traded between two countries. Each good is produced by combining the factors of
·duction, say capital and labour, according to technological conditions described by
·duction functions which are the same in both countries: it is assumed that the

production functions for the two goods are such that at any ratio of factor prices one good will always have a more capital-intensive method of production than the other. The two countries are assumed to differ in their overall endowments of capital and labour, in that the *ratio* of capital to labour in one exceeds the same ratio in the other. Two conclusions about the production frontiers in the two countries can be deduced. The first is that they will be concave to the origin, as in Figure 15.1(b). The intuitive reason is that as resources are transferred from the production of the capital-intensive product (say cloth) to the production of the labour-intensive product (say wine), those resources are not as well suited to the production of wine. There is 'too much' capital and 'too little' labour. Hence the capital–labour ratio in wine-making must rise. But, by definition, wine is better suited to labour-intensive methods of production. Hence the more factors are released from cloth-making the *less* effective they are, at the margin, a making wine. Hence the production frontier exhibits diminishing marginal returns. The second conclusion is that the shape of the production frontier will be affected by the resource endowment. Thus a country with a high overall capital–labour ratio will find its resources better suited to the production of cloth, as shown by the production frontier for Britain in Figure 15.1(b). Conversely, a low overall capital–output ratio will provide the conditions for wine-making, as shown by the production frontier for Portugal in the same figure.

The final assumption of the Heckscher-Ohlin theory is that the markets for internationally traded goods may be treated as if they were perfectly competitive. Thus all firms entering world trade take the world prices of traded goods as given, and supply as much as will maximize their profits given their supply curves. A country will produce therefore, at the point where its production frontier has the same slope as the ratio of international prices, in order to maximize the value of its national income. These points are shown at A' for Britain and B' for Portugal in Figure 15.1(b). The significance of the shape of the production frontiers is now apparent. Britain will tend to specialize in cloth (a high ratio of cloth to wine in total output), and Portugal will tend to specialize in wine, at any given international price ratios for the two goods. To put it another way, the capital-intensive country, by endowment, will tend to specialize in the capital-intensive output.

To complete the analysis we must now consider trade between the two countries. First, we note that a country can trade along the international trade price line, and can thereby reach points *outside* its own production frontier. The potential for increased welfare is obvious. Second, we note that trade must 'balance': the supplies must equal the international demands for different goods at the international trade prices, or else these prices will adjust to clear the markets. Third, if different countries have roughly the same tastes (i.e. if at a given level of national income and at given price ratios the pattern of demand is not too dissimilar), we would expect a capital-intensive country specialize in capital-intensive products and to export them, importing in exchange the labour-intensive products for which its resource endowment makes it less suited produce. And conversely for a labour-intensive country, according to its resource endowment. But this no longer holds if demand patterns are very different internationally. Suppose that Britain not only specializes in cloth production but also (given the climate) has a high demand for cloth, then it is possible that Britain will also *import* cloth, and export wine to pay for it.

Appendix 2:

A full analysis of all the effects of trade distortions is beyond the scope of this appendix but a simple analysis will serve to illustrate some of them. Figure 15.2 enables a part

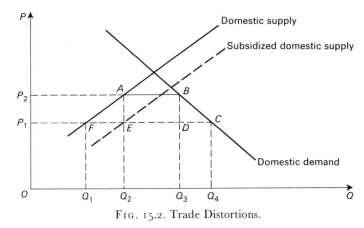

F IG . 15.2. Trade Distortions.

uilibrium analysis of the market in which the trade distortion occurs. What it cannot
ll us are the effects in related markets for both goods and factors of production—the
neral equilibrium effects. However, we will indicate what these might be.

Figure 15.2 shows the domestic market for a single homogeneous good. In the absence
trade distortions the good can be imported at a price P_1 and hence price competition
sures that this is the price in the domestic market. In these circumstances domestic
oducers will be willing to supply the market OQ_1 units of output, leaving the rest of the
arket, Q_1Q_4, to be supplied by imports. Suppose that a tariff is now imposed which
ises the import price to P_2. Domestic output increases to OQ_2. Imports now supply the
st of the domestic market, Q_2Q_3. Demand has fallen to OQ_3 because of the higher
ice. (A sufficiently high tariff could eliminate imports altogether, but with the
nsequence of a much higher price for consumers.) The 'costs' of protection can then be
timated approximately as follows. We assume that the area under the demand curve is
 indicator of the value to consumers of consuming the good in question (i.e. the sum of
ch unit demanded times the price it can command). As the quantity consumed goes
wn from OQ_4 to OQ_3, and the price rises from P_1 to P_2, the loss to consumers is the area
BCP_1. However, P_2AFP_1 of this will accrue to the domestic producers as increased
rplus, returns over and above what they need to cover their costs as shown by the
pply curve. Also, the area $ABDE$ will accrue to the government in tariff revenues.
ssuming no welfare implications in redistributing income from consumers to
oducers and the government, these two areas represent transfers which can be
nored. But that leaves the triangles AFE and BDC not accounted for. The first of these
presents a net production loss: domestic resources are being used expensively to
oduce goods that could be imported for the cost P_1 per unit. The second represents a
nsumer loss: consumers are being deprived of the satisfaction of consuming the
nount Q_3Q_4 which they would otherwise enjoy.

We may now compare this with the alternative policies available to the government.
n-tariff barriers that increase the costs for importers also raise the domestic price
vel, as in the tariff case. However, there is one important difference. The authorities no
nger collect the tariff revenue $ABDE$. Furthermore, if the barrier is by nature
reaucratic there will be additional waste of resources in setting up and maintaining
e bureaucratic system, not forgetting the scope for corruption in such a system. Prima

facie, there is a presumption that tariffs will be less costly. Quotas operate by allowing imports at the level $Q_2 Q_3$. This enables domestic producers to set the price P_2. In this case those importers who are fortunate enough to gain a part of the quota make profits per unit of $P_2 P_1$. Once again, it appears that the authorities would do better to impose a tariff. Finally, we may look at the operation of a subsidy. If the objective is to raise domestic output to OQ_2, this can be achieved by a subsidy which shifts the domestic supply curve down so that it passes through the point E. In this case there is no rise in the market price, and hence no loss to consumers. However, the authorities have to pay out $P_2 AEP_1$ in subsidy payments, and this will presumably have to be met from taxation. We also note that a subsidy is the only one of the policies described that not only protects domestic producers in the home market, but also enables them to compete more effectively in international markets. This would be the case in Figure 15.2 if the subsidy shifted the supply curve down so much that it lay below the point C.

The analysis so far has proceeded on the assumptions that markets are competitive, and that the supply of the good for imports is completely elastic at the world price P_1. The latter assumption is appropriate to an economy that is small in relation to the world economy. Dropping these two assumptions leads to the possibility that the introduction of trade distortions may lead to a decline in the foreign supply price. Various consequences follow. First, if the objective of the restriction on trade is to give incentives to domestic production, then a tariff will not be effective if foreign suppliers simply drop their price to compensate for the tariff. A quota will be more appropriate. Second, any reduction in the foreign supply price represents a real gain to the economy, as the terms of trade, the rate at which domestic output is traded for foreign goods, have improved. A sufficiently large improvement in terms of trade can affect the costs of a tariff, as noted previously. We note that a subsidy will not affect the terms of trade.

The general equilibrium consequences of protection are more complicated. The inadequacy of partial equilibrium analysis of one market is evident from the observation that expansion of output from OQ_1 to OQ_2 in a fully employed economy must represent the diminution of output in other sectors from which factors of production are drawn. The composition of national output will change, and this will have consequences for the returns to factors of production. Suppose, for example, that a labour-intensive sector is protected by the imposition of a tariff. An increase in output requires resources to be released from the capital-intensive sector. These resources are not in the 'ideal proportions' and the effect will be that both sectors will have a higher capital–labour ratio. Hence real wages will be higher, and the distribution of income will be different. The effect of protection on income distribution can explain some of the resistance to tariff reductions, and the powerful industry lobbies that frequently characterize protected sectors.

A rather different general equilibrium effect highlights the fact that nominal tariff rates on final products may be a very poor guide to the real 'effective' protection on the production of that product where there is a complex structure of tariffs. The basic insight is that protection is afforded to *value added* in production (the difference between the cost of the materials bought in and the value of final output). Thus if there is a 10 per cent tariff on a good where half of the final output value reflects imports available to domestic and foreign producers alike at given prices, then the effective production 20 per cent of value added. If three-quarters of the final output value reflect import then effective protection is 40 per cent of value added. Furthermore, the situation may be complicated if the inputs themselves are produced by firms that enjoy tariff protection in the domestic market. The nominal tariff, then, can give a very inadequate indication of the real protection enjoyed by domestic producers.

Bibliography

The UK in the World Trading Economy

[1] THIRLWALL, A. P. *Balance of Payments Theory and the UK Experience* (Macmillan, London and Basingstoke, 1980).
Chaps. 7–9 summarize much of the empirical literature relating to British trade performance.

[2] General Agreement on Tariffs and Trade (GATT). *International Trade 1981/82* (Geneva, 1982).
An annual publication providing commentary and statistics on broad developments in world trade.

Trade and Specialization

There are a number of excellent textbooks which give full treatments of trade theory, e.g.

[3] SODERSTEN, B. *International Economics*, 2nd edn. (Macmillan, London and Basingstoke, 1980).

[4] HELLER, R. H. *International Trade: Theory and Empirical Evidence*, 2nd edn. (Prentice-Hall, 1973).

The empirical literature seeking to test trade theory is vast—the following are a few of the more significant studies:

[5] HUFBAUER, G. C. 'The Impact of National Characteristics and Technology on the Commodity Composition of Trade in Manufactured Goods', in Vernon, R. (ed.), *The Technology Factor in International Trade* (NBER, New York, 1970).

[6] BALDWIN, R. E. 'Determinants of the Commodity Structure of US Trade', *American Economic Review*, **61** (1971), 126–146.

[7] HARKNESS, J. 'Factor Abundance and Comparative Advantage', *American Economic Review*, **68** (1978), 784–800.

Costs in transferring technology from advanced industrial countries to developing economies are central to the technology gap theories of trade. The following article is a study of those costs:

[8] TEECE, D, J. 'Technology Transfer by Multinational Firms: The Resource Cost of Transferring Technological Know-How', *Economic Journal*, **87** (1977), 242–61.

Intra-industry trade, or trade in differentiated products, is an important area of current research:

[9] GRUBEL, H. G. and LLOYD, P. J. *Intra-Industry Trade* (Macmillan, London and Basingstoke, 1975).

[10] CAVES, R. E. 'Intra-Industry Trade and Market Structure in the Industrial Countries', *Oxford Economic Papers*, **33** (1981), 203–23.

[11] HOCKING, R. D. 'Trade in Motor Cars Between the Major European Producers', *Economic Journal*, **90** (1980), 504–19.

A comprehensive analysis of tariffs and other barriers to trade is to be found in standard texts such as [3] and [4]. Effective protection is discussed in:

[12] CORDEN, W. M. *The Theory of Protection* (Oxford University Press, London, 1970).

A readable and accurate survey of the immense literature on the economics of multinational enterprises is given in:

[13] CAVES, R. E. *Multinational Enterprise and Economic Analysis* (Cambridge University Press, 1982).

The 'adjustment problem' and the various options for policy makers are described in the following:

[14] WOLF, M. *Adjustment Policies and Problems in Developed Countries*, World Bank Staff Working Paper No. 349 (Washington DC, 1979).

International Trade Policy and Institutions

A standard text such as [3] (Chaps. 17–20) provides more detail on the history of such institutions as GATT, UNCTAD, and the EEC. Other useful references are:

[15] BLACKHURST, R., MARIAN, N., and TUMLIR, J. *Trade Liberalisation, Protectionism and Interdependence* GATT Studies in International Trade, No. 5 (Geneva, 1977).

[16] ANJARIA, S. J., IQBAL, Z., KIRMANI, N., and PEREZ, L. L. *Developments in International Trade Policy* IMF Occasional Paper, No. 16 (Washington DC, Nov. 1982).

[17] DEARDORFF, A. V. and STERN, R. M. 'Economic Effects of the Tokyo Round', *Southern Economic Journal*, **49** (1983), 605–24.

[18] SWANN, D. *The Economics of the Common Market* (Penguin, 1970).

[19] Independent Commission on International Development Issues (the Brandt Commission). *North–South: A Programme for Survival* (Pan Books Ltd., London, 1980).

[20] BHAGWATI, J. N. (ed.). *The New International Economic Order: The North–South Debate* (MIT Press, Cambridge Mass., 1977).

[21] BALDWIN, R. E. and MURRAY, T. 'MFN Tariff Reductions and Developing Country Benefits under the GSP', *Economic Journal*, **87** (1977), 30–46.

[22] AHMAD, J. 'Tokyo Rounds of Trade Negotiations and the GSP', *Economic Journal*, **88** (1978), 285–95.

Problems of World Trade

For further discussion and references to the literature on the problems caused by floating exchange rates and the oil price 'shocks' see Chapters 6, 12, and 13. The adjustment problems arising from the exports of the NICs are described in [14], and in:

[23] Foreign and Commonwealth Office Working Group (Hayes Committee). *The Newly Industrialising Countries and the Adjustment Problem*, Government Economic Service Working Paper 18 (1979).

[24] EDWARDS, A. *The New Industrial Countries and Their Impact on Western Manufacturing* Special report No. 73 (Economist Intelligence Unit Ltd., London, 1979).

The UK in the World Economy

[1] and [23] are useful sources. Unfortunately there are no published recent studies of UK comparative advantage in international trade.

16

The European Economy

A. BOLTHO

6.1. Introduction

n the early 1950s Western Europe (excluding Ireland) accounted for some
5 per cent of Britain's foreign trade, and the six founding members of the EEC
or only 12½ per cent. By the early 1980s the former's share had more than
doubled to 52 per cent and the latter's had nearly trebled to 36 per cent. The
main counterpart to this rise was a steep decline (from over 40 per cent to less
han 20 per cent) in the importance of what used to be the Sterling Area. By
irtue of this very sharp redirection in trade flows, Britain's economy is now
probably more closely linked to that of Europe than it has ever been before. In
no year from the beginning of the nineteenth century did the share of trade with
he Continent (and a fortiori, therefore, with Western Europe) rise above 50 per
ent. And in no year (with the possible exception of the decade preeceding the
First World War) did the share of trade in total output rise to the record levels
of the early 1980s. Moreover, the progressively closer relationship of the United
Kingdom with the rest of Europe in the last thirty years has gone well beyond
oreign trade relations. The shares of invisible transactions, capital flows, and
migration to and from the Continent have also risen. Perhaps more
importantly, EEC membership has led to a process of harmonization with the
Community in a large number of areas, of which the switch to a decimal system
or currency, weights, and distances is probably the most glaring example.

In the time-span of a generation, therefore, the importance of Western
Europe in Britain's economic life has increased dramatically. In very many
areas, developments across the Channel now matter more than developments
across the North Atlantic, let alone in the Commonwealth. And the influence of
EEC policies and Western European trends is likely to increase. Integration
within the Community can be expected to continue (if, perhaps, at a slower
pace than in the 1970s); an elected European Parliament and possible future
moves towards monetary union may bring forth additional elements of supra-
nationality, and further impetus towards closer links would, of course, be
imparted if a tunnel were ever to be built under the Channel.

Any account of the UK economy which failed to cover the European
dimension would thus be very incomplete. This chapter provides a brief
discussion of some selected aspects of Western Europe's economic experience.

Section 16.2 puts forward a bird's eye view of post-war developments and section 16.3 of the economic policies followed by the major European countries. In both cases, the discussion is centred on the contrasts and parallels that can be drawn with Britain. Section 16.4 tackles more directly the interrelationship between the UK and the EEC, discussing, in particular, the first decade of 'Britain in Europe'.

16.2. Trends

The broad contours of Western Europe's post-war economic history are well known. Macroeconomic trends were extremely favourable during the quarter century to the early 1970s. Thereafter, largely because of accelerating inflation and two oil price shocks, performance worsened, particularly on the employment front, and by the early 1980s Europe found itself stuck in a phase of semi-stagnation. This section begins by discussing the growth experience and then moves on to consider the related issues of unemployment and inflation.

16.2.1. Growth Performance

Table 16.1 presents growth rates of output for selected Western European countries over a relatively long time-span. Two things stand out:

(i) The exceptional nature of the period 1953-73, relative to both earlier and recent trends.[1]
(ii) The exceptional position of the UK in the post-war period—while between 1870 and 1937 Britain's growth rate had been almost identical to that recorded by Continental Western Europe, it has been much lower since the Second World War.

Both these phenomena have brought forward a large number of explanations. Among those that have proved most popular in throwing light on the overall acceleration *vis-à-vis* earlier periods, pride of place has often been given to the availability in most countries of post-war Europe of abundant labour supplies and technologies—the former because of the presence of a large under-employed population on the land, the latter because of the possibility of importing advanced US production methods. Abundance meant that both labour and technology were relatively cheap, allowing enterprises to achieve high profits and hence high rates of investment. These, in turn, bolstered growth because of investment's crucial role in simultaneously raising supply, creating demand, and incorporating technological progress.

There is no doubt a good deal of truth in this explanation, which relies heavily on a Marx-Lewis dualistic theory of economic development.[2] It is unlikely, however, to be a sufficient explanation since the conditions of factor abundance it relies on were also present in earlier periods during which growth did not reach the levels of the 1950s and 1960s. Surplus labour was present in

[1] The growth rates recorded in the years 1946-53 were also exceptional, but for purely temporary reasons linked to the reconstruction effort.
[2] See Chap. 20 for a fuller explanation of this model.

TABLE 16.1. *Longer-Run GDP Trends in Europe*
(average annual percentage changes)

	1870–1913	1922–37	1953–73	1973–9	1975–82
United Kingdom	1·9	2·4	3·0	1·3	1·1
Western Europe, excluding the UK	2·0	2·5	5·1	2·6	2·3
France	1·6	1·8	5·3	3·1	2·6
Germany	2·8	3·2	5·5	2·4	2·4
Italy	1·5	2·3	5·3	2·6	2·7
Spain	0·8	1·7*	6·1†	2·7	1·6
Austria	2·4	0·8	5·7	3·0	2·7
Belgium	2·0	1·4	4·3	2·4	1·8
Netherlands	1·9	1·9	4·9	2·4	1·5
Sweden	2·8	3·5	3·9	1·8	0·9

* NNP, 1922–5.
† 1954–73.

Sources: Maddison [2]; P. Bairoch, 'Europe's Gross National Product: 1800–1975', *Journal of European Economic History* (Fall 1976); OECD, *National Accounts, 1951–1980*, Vol. I; OECD, *Economic Outlook* (July 1983).

the nineteenth and first half of the twentieth centuries (as shown by the levels of urban unemployment or by the high rates of internal and, particularly, international migration). And the US had already achieved a very substantial productivity lead over Europe well before 1950, which could have allowed massive imports of technology.[3]

This suggests that something else must have been at work in addition to cheap labour and new technology to explain the very pronounced gaps in European investment rates between the years 1953–73 and in both earlier and later periods. The theory of investment determination is far from settled, with competing hypotheses stressing the importance of financial factors, such as interest rates, or of 'real' factors, such as sales and capacity utilization levels. But whether a neo-classical or a Keynesian formulation is preferred, there is probably agreement on the proposition that entrepreneurial expectations play a crucial role, be these expectations of future profits, or of future demand, or of both. Hence, a more general explanation for the high rates of post-war investment and growth should throw light on why the whole climate of entrepreneurial expectations was more favourable in these years than it had been before (and after).

Two major sets of reasons can be advanced. First, the speed of the

[3] Thus, data presented in Maddison [2] show that overall man-hour productivity in Western Europe was close to 45 per cent of the US level in 1950—a figure not much lower than the 55 to 60 per cent levels for 1913 or 1929. This is confirmed by an earlier and more detailed investigation (Taussig [27]) which showed that US output per man was 1½ to 4 times greater than in Europe in selected industries in pre-First World War years.

reconstruction period probably created a momentum and generated favourable expectations—the growth rates recorded by the three major Continental countries in the later 1940s, at some 10 per cent per annum, were, after all, above anything that had ever been seen in Europe. In addition, the period probably saw a profound change in attitudes, encouraged by the social upheavals that followed the end of the war, which stimulated entrepreneurship after years of stagnation, enforced semi-autarchy, and war privation.[4]

Second, the same change in attitudes reflected, and was a reflection of, an even more important change in the policy stance of most of the European countries. In sharp contrast, for instance, to the experience following the First World War, policies in the late 1940s were at least broadly permissive and often openly expansionary, with governments much more committed than hitherto to growth and high employment. The climate of opinion surrounding the role and nature of state intervention in the economy had changed, partly because of the theoretical revolution pioneered by Keynes, partly because of the successful achievement of full employment during the war. And the introduction of more expansionary domestic policies was coupled at the international level by the adoption of new plans and institutions that buttressed high growth rates. Marshall aid ensured the relief of crucial bottlenecks, while the Bretton Woods Agreement promoted exchange rate stability and international trade liberalization.

In other words, the presence of a 'bigger and better' government ('bigger' because of the greater weight of public revenues and expenditures, 'better' because of the theoretical foundations which intervention had been given), and the creation of an international system of stable exchange rates and open trade, may well have been crucial factors bolstering entrepreneurial confidence in the reconstruction period and preserving it throughout the 1950s and 1960s. This confidence made for high rates of investment, which led to rapid improvements in productivity and competitiveness, particularly vis-à-vis the US, and maintained favourable balance of payments positions, thus further reinforcing optimistic expectations.[5] In a sense, private sector behaviour was based on 'rational expectations' of what governments would do in the event of a slowdown in growth, but the 'virtuous circle' that was initiated ultimately made such government intervention largely unnecessary.

This stress on the importance of economic policies can also throw light on the post-1973 deceleration. It is clear that so sudden and generalized a change in Europe's growth tempo could not have come from slowly moving supply factors. It is the loss of government credibility from the late 1960s onwards, as policies were seen to be unable to tackle rising inflation and unemployment, coupled with a much more restrictive policy stance after 1973, that more than anything else contributed to the entrepreneurial uncertainty that overtook Europe in the last decade.

Turning to Britain's experience, it is clear that the permissive factors of abundant labour and technology were less in evidence than across the Channel.

---

[4] A thesis put forward, for instance, by Olson [25].
[5] A mechanism similar to the one advanced in 'export-led' models of growth; see, for instance, Beckerman [19].

Britain had little urban unemployment at the outset of the period and could hardly rely on abundant labour in agriculture given that barely over 5 per cent of the work-force was employed in that sector in 1950, as against more than 30 per cent on the continent of Europe. Nor could immigration (an important source of manpower in several North-Western European countries) provide a sufficient supply of surplus labour—Ireland was too small, the Commonwealth a distant source which could, in any case, create social difficulties, while Southern Europe was never accepted, largely because British trade unions were strong enough to prevent the inflow of Mediterranean workers. Equally, the technology-import option was somewhat less open to Britain, at least throughout the 1950s, since UK productivity levels were at the time the highest in Europe and hence closer to those of North America.

On the side of the less tangible influences, a clear difference between Britain and the Continent emerges during the reconstruction period. Given that Britain's output level in 1945 was actually above that of 1938, there was no rapid growth spurt and no outburst of entrepreneurship helped by social upheavals. If anything, the massive transformation of that period (the creation of the Welfare State) may well have had the opposite effect on enterprise and risk-taking.

It was argued earlier, however, that greater government intervention in the economy and a stable international trading system were among the major forces propelling Europe into a self-sustaining growth process. The UK benefited from a stable world economy and was in the forefront of the countries which throughout the 1950s and 1960s used demand management instruments. These factors were, however, insufficient in Britain's case to generate acceleration because of a further characteristic of British policy-making that stands in sharp contrast to that of other European countries—the ultimate subordination of employment and income targets to the defence of the pound as a reserve currency and as a symbol of continuing pre-eminence on the world economic and political scene. Throughout the 1950s and until the belated 1967 devaluation, a binding balance of payments constraint thus dominated policy considerations. Whenever the trade balance deteriorated and a 'run on the pound' was feared, policies had to move into a restrictive direction which was then reverted as the danger receded—the outcome was the famous 'stop–go' cycle of short and probably destabilizing spurts and slowdowns in growth.

The long-term underlying reason for Britain's balance of payments problems was a lack of competitiveness—investment rates were insufficient relative to what was being achieved across the Channel (let alone in Japan), but each effort to raise them, by stimulating demand, endangered the trade balance, led to restrictive policies, and probably brought investment below what it would otherwise have been. By the time devaluation did come, it was probably too late. Successive sterling crises and stop–go policies had sapped entrepreneurial confidence, while relatively low income growth had generated rising frustrations. Three increasingly serious policy mistakes—excessive deflation in 1968–9 to accompany devaluation, an irresponsible reflation in 1972–3 at a time of a world-wide boom, and a prolonged period of unprecedented restriction in 1979–83—made matters worse. Despite the presence of North Sea oil, the UK's relative performance deteriorated yet further in the late 1970s and in the early 1980s.

16.2.2.Unemployment and Inflation

Europe's growth performance was paralleled by an equally favourable labour market performance (see Table 16.2). The virtual full employment most Western European countries recorded in the 1960s was an unprecedented achievement for industrial societies (and only matched by the equivalent successes of Eastern Europe and Japan at about the same time). Episodes of high employment had occurred at cyclical peaks in the urban sectors of the economy in earlier periods, but these had usually been shortlived. More importantly, they had hardly impinged on agricultural underemployment—a phenomenon which had virtually disappeared in most of Western Europe by the mid-1960s.

TABLE 16.2 *Longer-Run Unemployment Trends*
(per cent of the labour force)

	1923–37	1955–63	1964–73	1974–9	1980–2
United Kingdom	9·8	2·6	3·1	5·1	10·1
Western Europe, excluding the UK	··	2·5	2·1	4·5	7·3
France	··	1·5	2·2	5·0	7·2
Germany	7·5	1·7	0·8	3·2	4·5
Italy	4·4*	6·3	5·5	6·6	8·2
Spain	··	2·1	2·8	5·3	13·7
Austria	10·2†	2·8	1·7	1·8	2·6
Belgium	5·0	2·8	2·3	6·5	11·0
Netherlands	5·6	0·9	1·3	4·0	7·1
Sweden	4·2	2·1	2·1	1·9	2·5

* 1929–37 (excluding 1935–6).
† 1924–37.

Note: The data in the first two columns are not strictly comparable with the standardized figures shown for the years since 1964.

Sources: Maddison [2]; Boltho [1]; OECD, *Economic Outlook* (various issues).

This picture worsened markedly after the first oil shock when demand and supply forces combined in boosting unemployment from a 3 per cent rate in 1973 to 10 per cent a decade later. On the demand side, the main influence was the deceleration in growth, though the sharp income shift away from profit and towards wages in 1974–5 may also have played a role. On the supply side the working-age population bulged, while the labour force withdrawals that could have been expected in a period of low growth did not materialize as female participation rates went on rising.

Britain's employment performance in the 1950s and 1960s broadly matched that of Continental Western Europe and represented a dramatic improvement on earlier periods. In a sense, however, this favourable record worsened the country's competitiveness. Full employment was preserved despite unsatisfactory output developments because the growth of productivity lagged far behind that of most other countries in Western Europe. Indeed, the productivity differential between the two areas was, if anything, slightly more pronounced than the growth differential (British productivity rose by $2\frac{1}{2}$ per cent per annum between 1953 and 1973, that of the rest of Western Europe by $4\frac{1}{2}$ per cent).

Turning to inflation, Europe recorded a well-known acceleration both *vis-à-vis* earlier periods and within the post-war period itself (see Table 16.3). The virtual price stability of the years up to the First World War and throughout most of the interwar period gave way to inflation rates of some 2 per cent per annum in the 1950s, 4 per cent in the 1960s, and 10 per cent in the later 1970s. To some extent this deterioration can be interpreted as a lagged reaction to the favourable developments on the unemployment front. The gradual achievement of full employment must have been a powerful factor making for inflation even if the growth of wages accelerated in fits and spurts rather than along a smooth trend. A tightening labour market was accompanied, on the demand pull side, by increasingly ambitious economic policies that were attempting not

TABLE 16.3. *Longer-Run Inflation Trends*
(average annual percentage changes)

	1870–1913	1922–37	1952–61	1961–9	1969–73	1973–82
United Kingdom	− 0·2	− 1·2	2·4	3·8	8·0	14·7
Western Europe, excluding the UK	0·3	1·3	2·3	3·7	6·2	10.7
France	0·1	4·5	3·3	4·0	6·2	11·4
Germany	0·6	− 0·2*	1·3	2·5	5·3	4·9
Italy	0·6	− 0·2	2·0	4·1	6·5	16·9
Spain	. .	− 0·4†	5·2	6·7	8·4	16·9
Austria	0·1‡	2·4§	1·9	3·5	5·7	6·3
Belgium	—	5·3	1·2	3·2	5·1	8·1
Netherlands	1·1¶	− 1·9	2·1	4·7	6·8	6·9
Sweden	0·5	− 1·3	2·9	3·9	6·8	10·3

* 1924–37.
† 1920–35, Madrid only.
‡ 1874–1913.
§ 1923–37.
¶ 1900–13.

Sources: Maddison [2]; IMF, *International Financial Statistics* (1981 Yearbook).

only to fine tune activity but also to raise the provision of public services. Rapid growth may also have contributed to cost push forces by strengthening what have been called 'competing claims'[6]—the pressures stemming from rising aspirations amongst various interest groups in society as expectations of continuing income growth became generalized. Finally, inflation was given an added momentum by the supply shocks of 1973 and 1979.

Within this general picture, a distinction must be made between the broadly fixed exchange rate period of the 1950s and 1960s and the floating period of the 1970s. In the first two decades inflation rates were relatively similar across countries, even during the wage explosions of 1968–70. This similarity was largely imposed by economic policies that accepted the 'discipline' of the Bretton Woods system. The uniformity in inflation rates masked, however, the existence of underlying problems—in the German case, for instance, the difficulty of pursuing a monetary policy compatible with domestic aims, in the British case the existence of cost push pressures which translated themselves in low profitability, low investment, and low competitiveness.

When floating exchange rates were generalized, these pressures burst loose. Germany reacquired the freedom to choose its own rate of inflation; Britain, and also Italy, were able to expand more rapidly in the ultimately misguided hope that efforts to offset the deflationary effects of the first oil price rise, combined with currency depreciation, would sustain output. The hopes placed in the virtues of floating exchange rates turned out to be illusory and a slow deceleration of inflation had to be imposed in both countries by a combination of incomes policies and demand retrenchment. The second oil shock, as well as the breakdown of the incomes policies, undid much of what had been achieved between 1975 and 1978 and paved the way for a second attempt at bringing down the rate of price increases—an attempt which in Britain, at least, was eventually successful, if at a massive employment cost.

16.3. Policies

The preceding discussion has suggested that economic policies were an important contributory factor to Europe's performance in the post-war period. The present section tries to document this more fully by looking at the record of government action in three important areas: demand management, incomes policies, and longer-run growth policies.

16.3.1. Demand Management

Three major phases can be distinguished in the use of demand management in Western Europe over the period:

(i) An early phase during the 1950s in which conscious and continuous use of demand management policies was on the whole limited to a few countries.

(ii) A more interventionist phase in the 1960s which saw the spread of fine-tuning and policy activism throughout most of Western Europe.

[6] McCracken et al [23], p. 155.

(iii) A phase, from the early 1970s, in which active policies were still pursued (even if lip-service was increasingly being paid to doctrines of non-intervention), but in which the policy aims changed from output stabilization to inflation control.

The use of fiscal and monetary instruments for expenditure regulation spread only gradually through Europe after the war. Britain and Scandinavia were forerunners in this area and even in the 1950s attempted to iron out cyclical fluctuations. Elsewhere, however, growth and the reduction of structural unemployment were more important priorities than short-term stabilization. Monetary policy followed a low interest rate option, with the monetary aggregates made to accommodate rapid growth;[7] fiscal policy was usually expansionary though the momentum of growth limited the size of budget deficits or, as in Germany, led to sizeable surpluses.

This picture changed gradually during the 1960s as economic conditions altered. On the one hand full employment had now been achieved almost everywhere and the need was felt for instruments that could maintain it. On the other, inflation was creeping up while the 1958 return to currency convertibility was making the preservation of external equilibrium more difficult. Both these constraints required more frequent policy intervention. The use of monetary and fiscal instruments for fine-tuning purposes thus spread, with France and Italy joining the 'demand managers' in the early 1960s and Germany bringing up the rear in the second half of the decade.

The third phase embraces the 1970s and early 1980s—a period which, according to many, saw the rejection of the whole idea of demand management in favour of stable 'policy rules' for both fiscal instruments and, especially, monetary targets. Yet the practice of this period shows that intervention hardly diminished. What changed were neither the methods nor the frequency of policy action but, rather, the policy aims. From steady growth and continuous full employment, priority shifted increasingly to the control of inflation. The conversion was at first timid. In the early 1970s a restrictive stance was quickly superseded by a return to expansionary policies as unemployment figures edged up. After the 1973 oil price explosion the swing into restriction was more widespread and prolonged, but by 1978 a new and concerted attempt was made to reflate the world economy. After 1979, finally, restrictive policies were imposed and maintained in virtually all the European countries.

The claims, however, that such policies implied a withdrawal from day-to-day management of the economy were usually unwarranted. There was some evidence of this in Britain where new policies were pursued after 1979 with much greater dogmatic zeal than elsewhere. But neither France (under Barre) nor Germany went as far in rigidly pursuing a restrictive stance as did Britain. Even that paragon of financial orthodoxy, Switzerland, when threatened in 1978 by a revaluation that was only a fraction of that later suffered by the

---

[7] The broadly defined money supply rose by 13 per cent per annum over the decade in France, by 15 per cent in Italy, and by as much as $16\frac{1}{2}$ per cent in Germany, even though inflation was running at only $5\frac{1}{2}$, 3, and 2 per cent respectively.

pound, promptly dropped its monetary targets in favour of exchange rate stability.

Trying to assess whether demand management was a success in Europe is no easy task. Statistically, it is clear that output fluctuations were much less pronounced in the post-war period than earlier (a finding also corroborated by evidence for the United States [17]). Table 16.4 suggests that the more recent phase saw a remarkable degree of stability relative not only to the troubled

TABLE 16.4. *Variability of GDP Growth Rates*

	Standard deviation of annual percentage changes			Coefficient of variation of annual percentage changes		
	1870–1913	1922–37	1953–79	1870–1913	1922–37	1953–79
United Kingdom	2·2	3·4	1·8	1·2	1·4	0·7
Western Europe	1·5	3·5	1·6	0·8	1·4	0·4
France	3·7	4·5	1·5	2·3	2·5	0·3
Germany	2·2	8·7	2·9	0·8	2·7	0·6
Italy	3·3	4·0	2·4	2·2	1·7	0·5
Austria	2·3	5·4	2·5	1·0	6·7	0·5
Belgium	1·2	2·8	2·0	0·6	2·0	0·5
Netherlands	2·7*	2·9	2·4	1·1*	1·5	0·6
Sweden	2·4	4·1	1·9	0·9	1·2	0·6

* 1900–13.

Sources: Maddison [2]; OECD, *National Accounts, 1951–1980*, Vol. I.

interwar years but also to the much more peaceful period from 1870 to 1913. Not all of this stability was necessarily due to demand management. Thus, late nineteenth century fluctuations may have been somewhat more pronounced because agriculture was still a relatively large sector at the time and one that was more prone than the agriculture of today to sharp output changes on account of the weather. But the difference from earlier periods is too striking for this to be the whole explanation. Nor could purely fortuitous events, such as the desynchronization of the world economy in the 1950s and 1960s, provide a full answer—after all, the world of 1870–1913 seems to have been even more desynchronized according to the evidence of Table 16.4. Thus, it would appear that demand management policies had an effect, and possibly a powerful one, in stabilizing the Western European economies since the early 1950s.

This is confirmed by Table 16.5 which shows for selected countries estimates of the proportion of the underlying cycle which budgetary policy prevented from occurring in the years 1955–73. However tentative such calculations inevitably are, they support the idea that policy stabilized activity. The contribution seems to have been greatest in France, Spain, and Sweden, al

TABLE 16.5. *Effects of Fiscal Policy on GNP*
(stabilization of GNP growth around potential)

	Percentage stabilization achieved by general government, excluding public enterprises		
	1955–65	1966–71	1955–71
United Kingdom	18	20	18
Western Europe*	42	21	32
France†	53	39	50
Germany	52	8	27
Italy†	35	17	26
Spain†	..	31‡	40§
Belgium	32	..	..
Netherlands	..	11	23¶
Sweden	45	29	40

* Total of countries shown in this table.
† Measured on non-agricultural GNP.
‡ 1966–70.
§ 1963–70.
¶ 1962–71.

Source: Boltho [1].

ountries committed to a large degree of intervention in the economy. Italy and
e UK, on the other hand, performed less well, the former (probably) because
 the inadequacy of its policy instruments, the latter (possibly) because
op–go policies were overdone. Indeed, according to similar calculations
hich include the effects of nationalized industries' transactions, the British
udget may have actually destabilized the economy in the decade up to 1965.[8]
  An interesting finding that emerges from the table is that policy performance
eteriorated almost everywhere throughout the period. Partly this may have
een due to the increasing constraints stemming from inflation and the balance
 payments, partly from the greater ambitiousness of policy as time went by.
urtured by earlier achievements, governments became increasingly confident
at they could 'deliver' economic success, and in the process may have tried to
o too much' (Lindbeck [22], Chap. 12). A similar and possibly even more
egative conclusion might hold for the post-1973 period, though estimates such
 those shown in Table 16.5 would be less appropriate given that priorities had
vitched. A very simple, and inevitably imperfect, indicator of policy
erformance in these years could be a 'discomfort index' which tried to account
r successes or failures on the inflation and unemployment front. The figures
own in Table 16.6 give equal weights to the two indicators—a convenient but
rbitrary procedure, in so far as preferences between inflation and unemploy-
ent differed across countries and changed through time. As it stands, the
vidence suggests that the more restrictive countries of the Deutschmark
lock—Germany, Austria, and the Netherlands, as well as Switzerland (not

[8] Hansen [8]. See also Chap. 13.

TABLE 16.6. *The 'Discomfort Index'* *

	Absolute levels			Changes	
				1973 to 1979	1979 to 1982
	1973	1979	1982		
United Kingdom	12·3	19·0	21·1	6·7	2·1
Western Europe, excluding the UK	11·1	15·1	19·1	4·0	4·0
France	10·0	16·7	20·0	6·7	3·3
Germany	7·7	7·3	11·4	−0·4	4·1
Italy	17·0	22·2	25·4	5·2	3·2
Spain	13·9	24·1	30·3	10·2	6·2
Austria	8·8	5·8	8·8	−3·0	3·0
Belgium	9·7	12·9	21·7	3·2	8·8
Netherlands	10·3	8·3	15·5	−2·0	7·2
Sweden	9·2	9·4	11·7	0·2	2·3

* The 'discomfort index' is obtained by adding, with purely arbitrary *equal* weight the rate of consumer price inflation to the rate of unemployment.

Sources: IMF, *International Financial Statistics* (various issues); OECD, *Economic Outlo* (various issues).

shown in the table)—were the least unsuccessful. Though growth faltered an inflation accelerated almost everywhere, this group of countries fared a goo deal better than, for instance, Britain, Italy, or Spain, which had all tried, i the later 1970s, to preserve some of the earlier demand managemen achievements. But, for reasons explored in the next section, Sweden (an Norway), which had not abandoned the older aims, also performed relativel well.

16.3.2. Incomes Policies

This differential behaviour of countries during the last decade is largely function of the successes and failures of traditional demand managemen policies versus less traditional forms of incomes policies, in coping with wag and price pressures. When looking at the incomes policy experience of Wester Europe it is important, at the outset, to distinguish between the majc economies on the one hand and most of the smaller countries on the other

Among the larger economies, it is really only the UK which has seen frequent use of well-defined incomes policies. In France and Spain there hav so far been only two attempts at something similar—the prices and incom policy applied by the Mauroy Government in 1982–3 and the 'Monclo Agreements' of 1977–8—the former too recent, the latter too short lived t allow proper judgement as to their effects. Elsewhere, Italy saw a tacit (an successful) understanding on trade union wage moderation in the late 1970s, time at which the Communist Party was supporting a Centre–Left coalitio while in Germany, the 'Concerted Action' programme (followed by the 'soci partners' from 1967 to 1977) was only a (useful) exchange of views on likel

macroeconomic trends which may have influenced union behaviour but which
in no way laid down pay guidelines.

Inflation control was thus usually pursued by restraining demand.
Throughout the 1950s and 1960s such policies were broadly successful and
inflation was muted because of labour market flexibility. In the 1970s,
however, inflation control via tight policies became much more difficult. It
remained effective in Germany partly because of the presence of a large
immigrant labour force, partly because of the reformist nature of German
unionism. In France and Italy, on the other hand, restrictive measures were
much less successful, largely because labour markets had lost most of their
earlier flexibility and political constraints, unlike in post-1979 Britain, limited
the maximum feasible degree of tightness.

Among some of the smaller countries of Europe, however, the picture is very
different. Scandinavia, and also Austria and the Netherlands, have a long
history of incomes policies which, in some cases, have become almost
permanent features of their economies. There are two fundamental differences
between such permanent incomes policies and the variety of incomes policies
attempted in the UK. First, a high degree of unionization is accompanied by a
high degree of centralization, with virtually all unionized labour affiliated to a
strong national trade union federation. The same is true for employers.
Centralized wage formation thus becomes an almost inevitable outcome
which, by its very nature, is forced to take into account its consequences on the
country's macroeconomic situation. The general interest is perceived by both
participants whether the government is directly involved in the bargain or not.
It is true that wage drift at the plant level can partially undo the agreement
struck at the centre, but the room for manoeuvre of individual unions and firms
is institutionally much more limited than in the decentralized and staggered
bargaining system of Britain.

The second, less tangible but probably more important, difference relates to
these countries' much greater degree of consensus on what the primary socio-
economic aims should be. This contrasts sharply with the profound disagreements about economic priorities among the major parties, or the political and
even religious splits in the union movement, in Britain, France, or Italy.

The widespread application of centralized wage formation was not,
however, used mainly to control inflation which, in such small open economies
with (usually) pegged exchange rates, is virtually given by trends in the rest of
the world. Incomes policies were aimed at controlling the distribution of
income between wages and profits so as to maintain investment and growth. In
practice, it is unlikely that factor shares were, over the longer run, much
influenced by centralized wage formation. The evidence suggests that their
movement was close to that recorded in the larger economies and responded to
market forces. But incomes policies did achieve a much lower degree of open
strike conflict than in other European countries.

Moreover, in the troubled period which followed the two oil shocks, the
presence of a centralized bargaining machinery probably facilitated a
smoother adaptation to changed terms of trade and lower growth—the sharp
shift into wage income that followed the 1973 oil price increase was, for

instance, much less pronounced in the six countries here discussed. And if one took the very crude indicator shown in Table 16.6 (the 'discomfort index'), one would find that while in 1973 the six countries here considered ranked from third to eleventh place among sixteen Western European economies, by 1982 they were all clustered between the second and the eighth position—a further prima facie indication that centralized wage bargaining can improve, at least in relative terms, the economic performance of even small and very open economies.

16.3.3. Policies for Growth

In both the demand management and income policy areas, Britain probably tried to achieve 'too much'. Excessive reliance on fine-tuning and too detailed and frequent intervention in wage formation may, in the end, have had counter-productive results. There is another policy area, however, where, if anything, the opposite holds—that of what will be loosely called 'growth policies'. For the first fifteen to twenty years of the post-war period a major aim of British economic policy-making was the preservation of full employment, subject to the constraints of the balance of payments. Elsewhere on the Continent, however, this goal seemed less crucial. What was aimed at was the reconstruction and growth of the economy which, it was felt, would in turn bring about full employment. There were good reasons for this dichotomy in attitudes. Unemployment had been much higher in the interwar years in Britain than in France or Italy where growth, on the other hand, had been relatively low. And the presence of a large number of structurally unemployed at the outset of the post-war period, particularly in Germany and Italy, also made a short-run employment aim unfeasible.

As a consequence, the economic policy debate focused on longer-run issues. Initially, reconstruction provided a medium-term aim. With reconstruction completed and most of Europe launched onto a higher growth path, the exact nature of the targets changed, but they remained broadly structural. In France it was further modernization that was needed, it was felt, to withstand foreign competition; in Germany it was the restoration of foreign market shares lost during the war (and also the achievement of respectability via economic success); in Italy it was the industrialization of the South; in Spain, the strengthening of the regime via rises in living standards.

The instruments used to pursue these various aims differed across countries, depending largely on the degree of government intervention itself. At one extreme was Germany which (ostensibly) let the market run its course, and at the other, France with its plan and Spain with its corporatist structure, both of which seemed prone to constant and detailed interference in the economy. Yet in practice, the lines were more blurred. All these countries were conscious from the beginning that investment held the key to competitiveness and growth. 'Cheap money' was one of the policies pursued, with much less scepticism as to its effects on investment than there was in Britain, and this was supplemented by a variety of other direct and indirect encouragements.

In Germany the main instruments used were a tax policy which favoured profits relative to wages, providing not only liberal depreciation allowances but also substantial inducement to the reinvestment of buoyant profits, and a conservative expenditure policy which, via continuous budget surpluses, left funds available for the corporate sector. In France economic planning may have had some favourable effects on entrepreneurial expectations,[9] but of greater importance at a macroeconomic level were two aggressive devaluations of the currency (1957–8 and 1969) which strongly stimulated the profits and investment of the country's tradable sector. In addition, the government was conscious from the outset of structural weaknesses in certain industries that it felt were destined to grow rapidly in the world, and intervened actively to promote them via nationalization, state participation, specific subsidies, and public procurements. In Italy the absence of an efficient bureaucracy made such long-range intervention less viable. But during the 1960s in particular, the government was able to use the public corporations (whose weight in industry looms large) successfully to foster investment in the southern half of the country.

It is, of course, difficult to appreciate the overall effect of such policies. Individual examples of failure are forthcoming. The very capital-intensive nature of some of the investments made in southern Italy led to little employment creation and to few backward and forward linkage effects. The very ambitious French 'computer plan' was unable to create an independent and sufficiently competitive industry. German policies in favour of profits were eventually defeated by market forces which imposed a sharp redirection of income from capital to labour. But an overall, and admittedly impressionistic, judgement would none the less be that investment was positively helped by many of the public initiatives put into action.

Comparing the UK's policy experience with that of Western Europe, the impression that emerges is that, here too, Britain performed relatively poorly. Fine-tuning did not achieve a great degree of stability, incomes policies did not fulfil their aims, and growth policies were either absent (in the 1950s) or, when they came, belated (the attempt to institute indicative planning at a time of acute balance of payments difficulties) or misguided (the attempt to recreate 'dualism' by taxing service sector employment through SET). No doubt, policy mistakes were also made on the other side of the Channel, but in relative terms they were perhaps less frequent and/or serious.

16.4. The EEC

Begun in a modest way with the creation of the European Coal and Steel Community in the early 1950s, the European movement gathered momentum in the late 1950s when the Treaty of Rome was signed by the six original members of the Common Market, and was further reinforced by the accession of three new countries in 1973 (Britain, Denmark, and Ireland). By 1980, Greece had also entered the Community and it is not inconceivable that the Iberian peninsula will have joined by the mid-1980s. Over 80 per cent of Western Europe's GDP and population would then form part of a customs

[9] J.-J. Carré et al. [11], Chap. 14.

union and be subject to a significant integration process. This section looks first at the EEC's major achievement to date—the customs union—and then briefly considers the balance sheet of ten years of UK membership.

16.4.1. The Customs Union

Creation of the Common Market involved two major steps: abolition of intra-EEC trade barriers and establishment of a common external tariff. Both processes began in 1958 and were largely completed a decade later. Trade within the Community remains, however, distorted by numerous national regulations, hidden subsidies, and other non-tariff barriers. The Treaty of Rome stipulated that a Community competition policy should do away with such subtler obstacles to free trade, but the history of that policy has been chequered. While significant progress has been made in some areas via the imposition of standardized regulations, in others (for example the procurement policies of governments or the price policies of nationalized industries) progress has been slower. It has been even slower in what the founding fathers of the Community thought would be the customs union's natural complement—monetary union. The turmoil of the post-1973 period destroyed the ambitions in that field. It is true that the European Monetary System has brought some exchange rate stability to most of the EEC since 1979, but that stability has proved very fragile in the early 1980s and is, in any case, a far cry from what would be a full monetary union.

The bulk of the work done in trying to measure the impact of the EEC on member countries has concentrated on the two effects emphasized by customs union theory—trade creation and trade diversion (see Chapter 15, pp. 488–9). The first measures the welfare gains that follow from the abolition of tariffs on intra-customs-union trade if a country were now to choose imports from a cheap foreign source in preference to its hitherto protected and more expensive domestic industry; the second measures the losses which follow from the creation of an external common tariff if a country were now to purchase its imports from a relatively high-cost source within the union rather than from a cheaper, but tariff-ridden, source outside. It should be stressed that such effects assume that output levels are unchanged and that all countries remain at full employment throughout, i.e. abstract from virtually all the really interesting questions that creation of a customs union raises. A very rough summary of the many estimates made would suggest that trade creation exceeded trade diversion over the first decade of the EEC (by perhaps 10 per cent of EEC imports and 2 per cent of EEC Gross Domestic Product in 1970). If this is, in turn, translated into welfare terms, an estimate by Balassa suggests that the gains were much smaller—of the order of 0·15 per cent of GDP (Balassa [18]).

Even if such static effects were underestimated, it is clear that the main source of gains from the creation of the Community must lie elsewhere, i.e. in the dynamic advantages which it may have generated by raising the growth rates of member countries. This stimulus might have come from greater economies of scale as the size of the market expanded, from greater efficiency in production as protection was dismantled, and from the higher investment induced by both larger-scale production and intensified competition. There is nothing inevitable, however, about such favourable influences. Thus, the rapid integration of countries whose levels of development and labour productivity are not equal could generate favourable shocks in some but unfavourable ones in others. In the presence of nominal wage rigidity and with fixed exchange rates (or with exchange rate changes that are largely ineffectual), the more advanced countries could gain market shares in their less developed partners and thereby reduce the sizes of the latters' manufacturing sectors. Indeed, both France and Italy in the late 1950s clearly feared that Germany's dynamic industry would easily conquer their hitherto protected markets.

It is impossible to know whether such fears were proven right or wrong by the subsequent development of events. A superficial reading of the evidence suggests, however, that both France and Italy fared relatively well from the creation of the Common Market, as did the other EEC countries. Table 16.7, for instance, shows that growth accelerated in five out of the six countries during the first five years of the Common Market relative to the preceding five years (and remained high in the subsequent quinquennium), while investment ratios rose in all six member countries. It is true that 1958 was a mild recession year in Western Europe so that any through-time comparison which takes it as an end-point will be biased. None the less, it would appear unlikely that the EEC was associated with negative dynamic effects in its first decade of operation.

France and Italy appear to have been stimulated by the fear of greater

TABLE 16.7. *Growth and Investment after EEC Membership*

	GDP growth*			Investment ratios†		
	1953–8	1958–63	1963–8	1953–8	1958–63	1963–8
France	4·7	5·6	5·1	17·7	20·0	22·7
Germany	7·2	5·7	4·2	22·8	24·0	24·0
Italy	5·0	6·6	5·1	23·2	26·4	24·6
Belgium	2·7	4·6	4·3	19·6	21·5	23·8
Netherlands	4·0	4·9	5·6	20·7	21·5	24·6
Luxembourg	2·8	3·3	3·3	(27·9)	30·2	31·8
	1968–73	1973–8	1978–82	1968–73	1973–8	1978–82
United Kingdom	3·2	1·3	−0·3	20·4	19·1	17·9
Denmark	4·1	1·6	1·5	25·2	23·0	18·4
Ireland	4·8	4·4	2·0	25·3	25·5	27·6

* Average annual percentage changes.
† Gross fixed investment as percentage of GDP at constant prices.

Sources: OECD, *National Accounts, 1951–1980*, Vol. I; OECD, *Economic Outlook* (various issues).

German competition into a concerted investment and efficiency effort which transformed their industrial structures. Both countries, for instance, recorded sharp gains in world market shares for their manufactured exports (France's share went from $8\frac{1}{2}$ to 9 per cent, after having fallen in the preceding five years, Italy's rose from 4 to 6 per cent, following a 1 percentage point gain in the years 1953–8). And Belgium almost certainly benefited from its favourable geographical position at the heart of the EEC's most industrialized area, by attracting a large inflow of foreign (mainly US) direct investment.

16.4.2. Britain in Europe

The apparent galvanizing effect which the Common Market had on its six member countries in the 1960s was clearly an important argument in determining British membership in the 1970s. Strong hopes were placed in the beneficial effects which greater competition from, and closer links with, a dynamic area would have on British industry [28]. A decade later, many of these hopes seem to have evaporated in the wake of domestic de-industrialization and a vanishing trade surplus in manufactures. It remains an open question, however, whether the deterioration in Britain's industrial and foreign trade performance after 1973 was due (partly or entirely) to the EEC.

Some of the relevant evidence for trade in manufactures is shown in Figure 16.1. In the 1970s the shares of both British imports from the Six and the Six's imports from Britain rose, almost certainly reflecting trade creation. The interesting question is whether this benefited one area more than the other. The UK's disastrous bilateral trade performance since the early 1970s (not paralleled by an equivalent deterioration in trade with other countries) would prima facie suggest that Continental Europe was more successful at substituting its exports for uncompetitive British domestic production than vice versa. And this impressionistic judgement is confirmed by an econometric study (Fetherstone et al., [20]) showing that already by 1977 EEC membership had worsened Britain's manufacturing trade balance by perhaps £3 billion. It is true that a somewhat different estimate (Morgan [24] has arrived at a small gain (of the order of £300 million in 1977), but even if the methodology followed in that study were accepted, post-1977 developments would almost certainly nullify the findings.

The general, if very tentative, conclusion so far would thus be that the UK may well have lost, on the manufacturing side, from EEC membership. In other words, the hypothesis advanced earlier that a customs union may damage rather than benefit a relatively weaker member country could fit Britain's experience even if it did not apparently fit those of France and Italy. The reasons for these different responses lie probably in labour market and entrepreneurial reactions. France and Italy joined the Community at a time at which their trade unions were weak, surplus labour was still available, and business expectations had been buoyed up by the previous decade of unprecedentedly rapid growth. Britain, on the other hand, entered the Common Market after a quarter century of disappointing growth, with a much less confident managerial class, and with a strong and rigid trade union

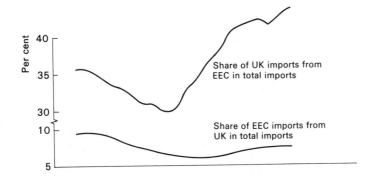

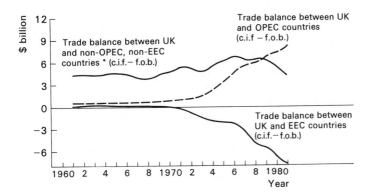

FIG. 16.1. *UK Trade in Manufactures†* *with the Six Original EEC Member Countries.*
(three-year moving averages).

* Including Denmark, Greece, and Ireland.
† SITC 5 to 8 less 68.
Source: OECD, *Statistics of Foreign Trade* (various issues).

movement. It is perhaps not surprising that the 'cold shower of competition' left the country weaker rather than stronger.

   The lack of success in manufacturing trade was compounded, as far as the balance of payments went, by a further budgetary problem. Despite special arrangements made at the time of entry and painful renegotiation of these arrangements in the early 1980s, Britain's net contribution to the Community's budget has been well in excess of that of all the other member countries with the exception of Germany. Indeed, the imbalance is even greater if further adjustments are made to the crude budgetary data so as to allow for the effects arising from the fact that agricultural trade is conducted at support prices that differ from world prices.[10] The main reason for Britain's imbalance stems from the workings of the Common Agricultural Policy. Since Britain still imports a large proportion of its food requirements from outside the EEC, it pays import levies on such purchases into the Community budget, and since its agricultural output is relatively small, it receives little price support expenditure from that budget.

The one area in which Britain may have benefited from EEC membership is that of direct investment inflows. US firms, which in the 1960s had invested heavily on the Continent so as to avoid the common external tariff, may have shifted their operations to Britain after 1973 in view, perhaps, of a common language and, more importantly, of relatively low labour costs. And Japanese firms, whose European investments were rapidly expanding in the 1970s may, for similar reasons, also have chosen the UK. The available evidence weakly supports this argument for US investment,[11] but the inflows in question are not sizeable and the estimates of long-term jobs created are hardly dramatic. Work by the Department of Industry [21] suggests, for instance, that all the direct investment decisions taken by foreign companies over the years 1979–82 yielded some 60,000 new jobs in manufacturing (or roughly 1 per cent of that sector's labour force). But not all of these decisions were, of course, taken because of Britain's EEC membership, while some of the jobs created may have been at the expense of employment in British-owned factories.

In the light of this very brief summary it could be argued that Britain's balance sheet is not strongly in favour of the EEC—the trade effects were probably negative, the budgetary position has been unfavourable almost uninterruptedly throughout the last decade and even if direct investment inflows were boosted by membership, this favourable impact pales into insignificance when compared to the large debit items. Yet withdrawal at present would not necessarily improve the economy's relative performance. Present and future budgetary payments would be avoided, but the abandonment of free trade with the Continent need not lead to symmetrical and favourable trade effects compensating those which were incurred during membership. The lack of a dynamic response to the 'cold shower of competition' does not, *per se*, ensure that a dynamic response will follow the imposition of protection. Historical experience abounds with examples of both successful and unsuccessful policies of import substitution. In some cases the knowledge that the domestic market would henceforth be protected generates favourable expectations and rekindles what Keynes called entrepreneurial 'animal spirits'. But in other cases that same knowledge can lead to a totally

[10] Two British studies suggest that such more comprehensive estimates would further boost the UK's net payments to the EEC; see Rollo and Warwick [26], and *Cambridge Economic Policy Review* (Apr. 1979).

[11] Inward US direct manufacturing investment was equal to 47 per cent of investment in the six original EEC countries in the years 1973–81, as against 43 per cent in the preceding decade. Japanese total direct investment, on the other hand, was at a peak in Britain, as a percentage of investment in the EEC, in the years 1970–4, but fell back thereafter.

ifferent reaction as both management and the work-force relax from their
arlier efforts and 'X-inefficiency' spreads in the economy. Britain's past
xperience of relatively low managerial adaptability and high labour market
igidity would prima facie suggest that the latter response could well
redominate.

6.5. Conclusions

The preceding brief treatment of trends and policies in Continental Western
Europe and in the UK has highlighted the latter's unsatisfactory performance.
Relative to earlier periods of its economic history, Britain was successful in the
thirty years from the Second World War. Growth was at least as rapid as before
nd full employment was maintained for a prolonged period of time. But seen
n relation to developments across the Channel, performance was clearly
mediocre. Indeed, given the sharp acceleration in world output and trade
rowth, the unprecedented stability of the international economy, and
Britain's favourable starting position, one could have expected a better
outcome.

Numerous reasons have been advanced to explain this relative lack of
uccess, such as an insufficiently elastic labour supply, too rigid a labour
market, or lingering international ambitions. Other reasons may stem from the
design and implementation of economic policies. Across the Channel, and until
he 1970s at least, implementation may have been helped in France, Italy, or
Spain by a higher degree of administrative centralization. Design, on the other
hand, may have benefited from the fact that, through the 1950s and 1960s,
conomic policies were seldom major political issues. No doubt, parties
promised continued or even growing prosperity, but the focus of most electoral
campaigns was usually political—liberalism versus Communism, the creation
of new institutions, electoral reform, decolonization, etc. In Britain, by
contrast, a major aspect of political campaigns was an economic platform
designed to put forward new and better blueprints for growth and employment. To some extent this was a function of the greater consensus of British
ociety on major political issues. Since neither of the two parties disagreed on
undamentals, they had to highlight their differences on economic themes. On
he Continent, instead, these were felt to be technical and best left to
bureaucrats and Central Banks.

Greater stress on economics need not, *per se*, have had unfavourable effects
had it not been accompanied in Britain by two further consequences—an
electoral cycle that led to an alternation of Conservative and Labour
administrations, and a stress on theoretical solutions. The first meant that
policies changed frequently, the second that these changes were doubly
destabilizing because of the dogmatic terms in which they were often put
forward—industries were nationalized and denationalized, fine-tuning was
pursued to the limit, monetarism was wholeheartedly embraced, each new
policy was put forward as *the* panacea which would solve Britain's economic
problem.

In most of Continental Western Europe, on the other hand, broad

Centre–Right or Centre–Left coalitions remained in power for long periods of time, while economic policies, when discussed, were usually tackled in highly pragmatic terms. As a consequence, there was much greater policy continuity and much less stress on theory. No Continental country engaged in as many varieties of incomes policies, none would have taken such major steps as the introduction of SET or of Competition and Credit Control on the basis of an inaugural university lecture or of recommendations coming from Chicago.

It is true, however, that as economic performance deteriorated in the 1970s, the Continental approach came closer to that of Britain. Government changes became more frequent and economic policy panaceas infiltrated electoral programmes as politicians increasingly resorted to the solutions propounded by the alchemists of the twentieth century. It is too soon to predict whether this will lead to a stop–go pattern of policies. The indications in the early 1980s, however, are that just as Britain moved closer to the Continent by joining the EEC, so the Continent was coming closer to Britain in adopting an electoral cycle heavily centred on economic issues that could well have similar unfavourable consequences on the economy as it has had in the United Kingdom.

Bibliography

SECTION A

A relatively recent work on Western Europe that looks at both cross-country trends and at country experience (and which has been heavily drawn upon in this chapter), is [1] A. Boltho (ed.), *The European Economy: Growth and Crisis* (Oxford, 1982). An equally recent book which sets Europe's performance in a broad historical perspective is [2] A. Maddison, *Phases of Capitalist Development* (Oxford, 1982). In the growth area, three interesting sources are: [3] N. Kaldor, *Causes of the Slow Rate of Economic Growth of the United Kingdom* (Cambridge, 1966); [4] C. P. Kindleberger, *Europe's Postwar Growth: The Role of Labor Supply* (Cambridge Mass., 1967); and [5] J. Cornwall, *Modern Capitalism* (London, 1977). On the inflation and incomes policy side, two major Brookings Institution studies are: [6] L. B. Krause and W. S. Salant (eds.), *Worldwide Inflation* (Washington, 1977) and [7] R. J. Flanagan, D. Soskice, and L. Ulman, *Unionism, Economic Stabilization and Incomes Policies* (Washington, 1983). Fiscal policy is treated in [8] B. Hansen, *Fiscal Policy in Seven Countries* (OECD, Paris, 1969) and monetary policy in several OECD country studies (for France, Germany, and Italy) as well as in two broader works: [9] *The Role of Monetary Policy in Demand Management* (Paris 1975) and [10] *Monetary Targets and Inflation Control* (Paris, 1979).

On individual countries, France is covered very exhaustively in [11] J.-J. Carré, P. Dubois, and E. Malinvaud, *French Economic Growth* (Oxford, 1976); Germany's 1950s and 1960s experience is analysed in [12] H. Giersch, *Growth, Cycles and Exchange Rates The Experience of West Germany* (Stockholm, 1970); while relatively recent English language surveys of Italy and Spain are [13] D. C. Templeman, *The Italian Economy* (New York, 1981) and [14] A. Wright, *The Spanish Economy, 1959–1976* (London, 1977). Finally, two works on EEC policies and trends are [15] P. Coffey (ed.), *Economic Policies of the Common Market* (London, 1979) and [16] A. M. El-Agraa (ed.), *The Economics of the European Community* (Oxford, 1980).

ECTION B

7] BAILEY, M. N. 'Stabilization Policy and Private Economic Behavior', *Brookings Papers on Economic Activity*, 1 (1978).
8] BALASSA, B. 'Trade Creation and Trade Diversion in the European Common Market: An Appraisal of the Evidence', in Balassa (ed.), *European Economic Integration* Amsterdam, 1975).
9] BECKERMAN, W. 'Projecting Europe's Growth', *Economic Journal* (Dec. 1962).
10] FETHERSTONE, M., MOORE, B., and RHODES, J. 'EEC Membership and UK Trade Manufactures', *Cambridge Journal of Economics* (Dec. 1979).
11] Invest in Britain Bureau, Department of Industry. *Inward Investment and the IBB, 1977–1982* (London, 1983).
12] LINDBECK, A. *Swedish Economic Policy* (London, 1975).
13] McCRACKEN, P. *et al.* *Towards Full Employment and Price Stability* (OECD, Paris, 1977).
14] MORGAN, A. D. 'The Balance of Payments and British Membership of the European Community', in Wallace, W. (ed.), *Britain in Europe* (London, 1980).
15] OLSON, M. *The Rise and Decline of Nations* (New Haven, 1982).
16] ROLLO, J. M. C. and WARWICK, K. S. *The CAP and Resource Flows Among EEC Member States*, Government Economic Service Working Paper, No. 29 (1979).
17] TAUSSIG, F. W. 'Labor Costs in the United States Compared With Costs Elsewhere', *Quarterly Journal of Economics* (Nov. 1924).
18] *White Paper on Britain and the European Communities* (Cmnd. 4289, HMSO, London, 1970).

17

The Japanese Economy

A. BOLTHO and C. J. M. HARDIE

1. Introduction

may appear somewhat incongruous that a chapter on Japan should appear
a book devoted to the British economy. Yet Japan's experience is important
the United Kingdom for at least three major reasons linked to that country's
st history, likely future impact on the world economy, and economic policies.
Historically, Britain and Japan have shared a number of common features—
se; both were first industrializers in their respective continents; both were per-
ps less advanced than the more ancient and/or powerful civilizations which
ighboured them in the middle of the eighteenth or nineteenth centuries, yet
th quickly overshadowed them. In the second half of the twentieth century,
wever, their economic histories have diverged dramatically. While in the
rly 1950s Britain accounted for nearly 8 per cent of the OECD area's GDP,
d Japan for barely 2½ per cent, thirty years later these shares had changed to
and 14½ per cent respectively. Japan's per capita income, from being some
per cent of Britain's level in 1950-1 had edged ahead by 1980-1. The
untry's achievement is perhaps even more apparent in a number of social
dicators. From what was a semi-developed economy in the 1940s, Japan has
w reached the second highest educational level in the world (after the United
ates) as well as the world's lowest infant mortality and highest life expectancy
tes (together with Scandinavia); it can also lay claim to a much lower
currence of crime than most countries and, probably, to one of the most equal
tterns of income distribution among market economies.

The extreme disparity in growth between Britain and Japan recorded over
e last thirty years is unlikely to be reversed in the foreseeable future. Most
asonable forecasts show Japan—with its natural sphere of economic influence
hich covers South-East Asia, Australia, and perhaps China and the US West
past—as the dominant economic entity of the next century. This might be of
ly intellectual curiosity if it were not that Japan and Britain interact with
ch other. Indeed, a number of Japan's past successes were probably acquired
Britain's expense. Thus, industrialization during the First World War was
eatly helped by the take-over of Asian markets which Britain was unable to
pply at the time, just as the penetration of European markets in the 1970s

began in the United Kingdom, seen as the EEC's 'weakest link'. Hence, awareness of Japan is important if only because the country is likely to continue to be a threat to much of British industry.

Finally, a study of why Japan was so successful may also suggest some lessons. This depends importantly on whether the 'Japanese model', if a model there is, is at all transplantable. Arguably, some of the reasons for Japan's successes may lay in cultural traits specific to that country. Yet there may also be other, and more institutional, elements which could be imitated. After all, Japan itself did for a long time borrow and adapt from the West.

This chapter's structure broadly follows the three main themes just outlined. Section 17.2 presents a bird's-eye view of the country's post-war development, looking in turn at the reconstruction phase, the years of 'super-growth', and the post-oil shock adjustment period. Section 17.3 briefly assesses Japan's external trade performance and the policies which made it possible, while section 17.4 takes a broader historical perspective by considering whether or not Japan is indeed 'unique'.

17.2. Post-War Growth

17.2.1. Reconstruction, 1945–1953

Japan's economy was probably affected by the war more than that of any other major belligerent country. Output in 1946 was down to its 1917–18 level, and output per capita (if such a comparison can be made) to the almost subsistence level of 1906. About one-quarter of the housing stock had been destroyed and the population had been swollen by some 6 million people who had returned from overseas possessions, while the almost total destruction of the merchant fleet implied that international trade had come to a virtual standstill.

Reconstruction was relatively rapid and by 1953 output had returned to its pre-war peak. But in contrast to the experience after 1953, Japan's growth in these years was not unique (Table 17.1). Other countries which had suffered from war destruction achieved similar results. Between 1946 and 1948 growth was driven by large budget deficits and a rapid expansion of the money supply. In 1949 the US occupation authorities, which until then had given the Japanese bureaucracy a free rein, intervened with a sharp squeeze which balanced the budget and stabilized the exchange rate. Growth faltered to barely 4 per cent, but the outbreak of the Korean war gave a new fillip to demand and in the three years to 1952 output rose by 45 per cent.

The early years of this period were a particularly troubled time. The dislocation of the economy and the inevitably permissive policies which were followed led to very rapid inflation. Prices were multiplied by a factor of 3 between 1945 and 1949 and black markets thrived. The current account of the balance of payments was propped up by US aid and military expenditure. Labour relations were tense, strikes were numerous, and factories were at times occupied and run by workers—indeed, a general strike nearly took place in early 1947. As well as social turmoil, the period also saw substantial institutional change. Three major reforms in particular were introduced by the

TABLE 17.1. *Selected Macroeconomic Indicators, 1945–1953*
(indices and average annual percentage changes)

	Output		Inflation	
	Level in 1946 (1938 = 100)	Change 1946–53	Change 1945–53	Level in 1953 (1945 = 100)
Japan	50·6	10·2	58	3,860
France	83·3	7·1	26	640
Germany	49·1	14·1	5	145
Italy	79·5	8·3	15	305
Soviet Union	83·4	10·2	··	··

urces: Ohkawa and Rosovsky [1]; Bank of Japan, *Hundred-Year Statistics of the Japanese onomy* (Tokyo, 1966); A. Maddison, *Economic Growth in Japan and the USSR* (London, 69); Maddison, *Phases of Capitalist Development* (Oxford, 1982).

cupation authorities—the dissolution of the more important pre-war dustrial groups, the re-creation of a trade union movement, and agricultural form. The first of these was quickly undone as Japan regained full sovereignty ter the 1952 Peace Treaty, the second was partly undone as a political shift to e Right and rapid economic growth transformed the aggressive nation-wide ions of the late 1940s into the much more compliant enterprise unions of the 50s, but agrarian reform remained. Thanks to it, one of the major reasons for e severe income inequalities of the pre-war period disappeared, as small vner-occupier farmers replaced the absentee landlords and landless peasants ho had hitherto accounted for close to 50 per cent of Japanese agriculture.

.2.2. 'Super-growth', 1953–1973

1952–4 the occupation had ended and the pre-war output peak had again en reached. Yet the Japan of the time was not confident in the future (in ntrast to the increasingly optimistic expectations that were spreading in 'estern Europe). The end of the Korean war had brought with it a slowdown activity and there were widespread fears that the economy would, at best, turn only to its longer-term 3 to 3½ per cent growth path. In particular, it was t that the forgoing of the use of war in the new Constitution had eliminated e single most important stimulus to economic growth, given that most of pan's expansion from the 1868 Meiji Restoration to the Korean war had rectly or indirectly been linked to imperialist conquest and military nflicts.[1]

Yet the next twenty years saw the most rapid expansion any country has ever itnessed, and this despite a minimum of defence expenditure and a colourless plomatic posture. Output and productivity growth were roughly double ose of the OECD area and some one-third faster than those of Eastern Europe

[1] S. Tsuru, *Essays on the Japanese Economy* (Tokyo, 1958), pp. 38–57 (the argument originally peared in an article published in 1953).

TABLE 17.2. *Output, Employment and Productivity, 1953–1973*
(average annual percentage changes)

	GDP	Employment	Productivity*
Japan	9·3	1·5	7·7
France	5·3	0·5	4·8
Germany	5·5	0·7	4·8
Italy	5·3	−0·2	5·5
United Kingdom	3·0	0·5	2·5
United States	3·4	1·7	1·7
Soviet Union†	7·6	2·0	5·5

* GDP per person employed.
† 1950–2 to 1967–9.

Sources: OECD, *National Accounts, 1951–1980;* OECD, *Manpower Statistics* and *Labour Force Statistics* (various issues); United Nations Economic Commission for Europe, *Economic Survey of Europe in 1971,* Pt. 1.

(Table 17.2). Cyclical fluctuations were quite sharp by the standards of other developed countries, but even in 'recession' years the growth of GDP never fell below 4½ per cent (or a rate *higher* than that of Britain in almost all years of the period).

The reasons for such an exceptional performance are many. On the input side, the rise in employment was somewhat faster than in the major Western European countries. More importantly, Japan witnessed an above-average growth in labour supply to the 'advanced' sector of the economy, thanks to the presence of numerous surplus workers in agriculture and in low-productivity handicraft and service activities. In other words, labour supply was 'abundant' or 'elastic' in the sense stressed by Marx, Lewis, or Kindleberger.[2] This allowed a growth of productivity in the industrial sector well above that of wages, and an almost uninterrupted rise in the share of profits in national income. Reinvestment of these profits, in turn, was a powerful factor making for high rates of investment and the rapid incorporation of foreign technology in the capital stock.

Per se, however, an abundant labour supply is merely a permissive factor (as is an abundant supply of technologies developed abroad). Its existence facilitates growth but does not generate it. Moreover, abundant labour had been present in pre-war Japan and had not led to growth rates of the order of to 10 per cent per annum. The reasons why, on this occasion, the permissive elements were exploited so much more successfully must be found in the economy's investment performance. The growth of investment was exceptional by both historical and other countries' standards. Relative to the interwar period, the share of gross fixed investment in GDP was already, in the 1950

[2] See Chap. 20 for an explanation of the contribution of elastic labour supplies to economic growth.

bove that of the years 1919–36. At constant (1975) prices it rose from just over 5 per cent in the early 1950s to a peak of 35 per cent in the early 1970s.[3] And his was accompanied by a similar rise in savings. At one point (1969–70), Gross National Savings (at current prices) were in Japan equivalent to 39 per cent of GDP, as against a British peak (at exactly the same time) barely above 0 per cent.

The importance of savings and, in particular, of personal savings, which in he early 1970s represented close to 20 per cent of household disposable income, as often been put forward as an explanation of Japan's high investment rate. Causation, however, runs in the opposite direction. Savings were not articularly high at the outset of this period and many of the 'structural' or exogenous' reasons that could have made for high personal savings at the time such as the presence of a large unincorporated sector, the influence of earlier nd more traditional patterns of living and consumption, or the absence f adequate social security provisions) became less important through me and could, therefore, have been expected to reduce the saving ratio. Yet it ose, largely as a consequence, rather than as a cause, of rapid growth. Growth oosted savings because, *inter alia*, it created an inevitable lag between income eceipts and consumption expenditure, because it facilitated wealth accumula-on, and because it boosted profits and thereby the bonus component of wage-ackets which, due partly to its lumpiness, is associated with above-average avings, etc. The dependence of savings on growth does not lessen their nportance for the Japanese economy. Without them an increasing investment ffort would have been associated with intolerable balance of payments and/or flation difficulties—but they were not the moving force behind the country's vestment performance.

Much more important was the behaviour of the public and corporate sectors. Government action in favour of investment, a constant factor in Japanese conomic policy-making over the last century, was significant in strengthening, r even generating, optimistic business expectations. When the favourable ffects of the reconstruction period and of the Korean war had evaporated, a eading role was taken by a succession of official blueprints and plans setting orth very ambitious targets either for specific industries (for example by the Ministry of International Trade and Industry (MITI) in the 1950s), or for the conomy as a whole (for example by the 'Income-Doubling Plan' of the early 960s). And these plans were accompanied by various forms of direct and ndirect encouragement (on which more in section 17.3), including the very mportant tacit insurance that a safety net would be provided by the authorities o any major company whose investment effort might threaten its short-run olvency.

Government intervention was accompanied by a highly dynamic corporate esponse. Firms invested, partly because they were helped by MITI; partly because, in a climate of rapid growth, expectations became increasingly uoyant, thus encouraging risk-taking and reinforcing both growth and xpectations; but partly also for more complex reasons linked to the country's

[3] Comparable figures for the UK, US, and Western Europe show rises from 19 to 20, 15 to 20, nd 20 to 24 per cent respectively.

company structure. Japanese industry is relatively oligopolistic, but Japanese oligopolies, unlike many of their Western counterparts, seems to have pursued aggressive, even apparently uncautious, strategies. For one thing, this was almost inevitable in markets which expanded by 10 to 15 per cent per annum—caution would have meant virtual disappearance. For another, Japanese firms were, throughout the 1950s and 1960s, facing a given stock of advanced foreign technology which could be imported on virtually identical terms. In such circumstances, not unlike the perfectly competitive firm of textbook models, they were virtually forced to innovate as rapidly as possible for fear of otherwise being made uncompetitive. Finally, it is arguable that the degree of competition between rival oligopolies was heightened by some social characteristics not always present in the West. As was said about the three major conglomerates: 'Each group feels itself obliged, *for reasons of prestige*, to obtain a share of every new industry as it appears and to hold its own in all fields with the rivals.'[4] In other words, established, but also newcomer firms, aimed not so much at short-run profit maximization but at achieving first rank in sales league tables in any particular sector.

A further peculiarity of Japan's growth in this period is that it was seldom interrupted by unemployment, inflation, or balance of payments constraints (Table 17.3). Unemployment was very low, by international standards, throughout these twenty years, and little affected by output fluctuations. This 'stickiness' reflected in part the institution of 'lifetime employment' (discussed in the next section). More importantly, it was a function of the labour absorption–disabsorption role played by small enterprises and agriculture, whose employment tended to follow a counter-cyclical pattern.

The inflation story is equally striking. The twenty years to 1973 witnessed the

TABLE 17.3. *Selected Macroeconomic Indicators, 1953–1973*

	Inflation*		Unemployment†	Current balance‡
	Consumer prices	Wholesale prices		
Japan	4·6	1·4	1·2	0·8
France	4·4	3·6	2·2	−0·1
Germany	2·6	1·5	0·8	1·0
Italy	3·7	2·4	5·5	0·7
United Kingdom	4·1	3·4	3·9	0·2
United States	2·6	2·0	4·4	1·9

* Average annual percentage changes.
† As percentage of the labour force, 1964–73.
‡ Annual averages, in US$ billion.

Sources: IMF, *International Financial Statistics*, Supplement on Price Statistics (1981) OECD, *Economic Outlook* (various issues); OECD, *Balance of Payments Statistics, 1950–196* and *1960–1977*.

[4] Allen [14], p. 192 (emphasis added).

west rate of wholesale price inflation in the OECD area, yet one of the highest
for consumer prices. This divergence mainly reflects the presence of what has
been called a 'dual' economy, i.e. the coexistence of large and highly productive
enterprises supplying modern industrial goods and of smaller and less efficient
firms providing the bulk of the food, services, and simpler manufactured
commodities which enter into the Consumer Price Index. Given similar wage
trends in the two sectors, but different productivity growth rates, inflation rates
diverge, an argument similar to that put forward by the 'Scandinavian' theory
of inflation,[5] even if some of the mechanisms differ.

An inflation rate of 4 to 5 per cent was unlikely to be a constraint on policy,
and virtual wholesale price stability could hardly imperil Japan's international
competitiveness. The external sector was none the less a constraint at the top of
the business cycle. From the early 1950s to the mid-1960s the current account
swung regularly into deficit as the economy overheated. Equally regularly, the
government restricted demand, but these policy-induced recessions were shortlived as imports quickly receded. In the intervening years of high growth Japan
laid the foundation for its eventual achievement of a structural current account
surplus.

7.2.3. Adjustment, 1973–1982

By 1973, and in sharp contrast to the situation twenty years earlier, Japan
exuded confidence—its growth rate was the highest in the world, its industry
was extremely competitive, and its prospects for future expansion seemed
almost limitless. As late as 1972, the Tanaka Plan for 'Rebuilding the Japanese
Archipelago' had been based on a 10 per cent annual growth assumption to
1985, and at about the same time a well-known futurologist [19] was
forecasting a GNP larger than that of the United States by the turn of the
twentieth century. The first oil shock shattered this picture by highlighting the
fragility of an economy more dependent on imported energy than virtually any
other in the OECD area. The growth tempo faltered. Output actually declined
in 1974, for the first time since the war, and its longer-run growth trend was
reduced to less than 4 per cent.

Yet while the break with the past was extremely sharp, Japan probably
weathered the difficult post-1973 period more successfully than any other
Western economy. This is the more surprising as at the outset of the crisis the
country's performance deteriorated very sharply (Table 17.4). Thus, consumer
price inflation ran at two-digit levels for three successive years and at its 1974
peak ($24\frac{1}{2}$ per cent) was virtually the highest in the OECD area. On the
external side, the 1974 current account deficit ($4\frac{1}{2}$ billion) was not as large as
that of Britain or of Italy ($8 billion), but the swing into deficit was more
pronounced. And though the 1974 decline in output was only marginal
(−1 per cent), the deceleration from the past was much sharper than
elsewhere. It was only on the unemployment front that the country's unique
position was preserved.

Despite the exceptional seriousness of the output, inflation, and balance of

---

[5] For a brief account of this theory, see Aukrust [15].

TABLE 17.4. *Performance of Major Economies after First Oil Shock* (differences between outcomes in 1974–5 and in 1969–73)

	GDP*	Consumer price inflation*	Unemployment†	Current balance‡
Japan	−7·4	10·6	0·4	−5·7
France	−3·9	6·5	0·9	−0·8
Germany	−4·8	1·2	1·8	5·6
Italy	−4·0	11·5	−0·2	−6·1
United Kingdom	−4·5	12·1	0·4	−6·4
United States	−4·1	5·1	2·0	11·0

* Differences in average annual percentage changes.
† Differences in percentages of the labour force.
‡ Differences in US$ billion, annual rates.

Sources: IMF, *International Financial Statistics* (1981 Yearbook); OECD, *Economic Outlook* (various issues).

payments experience of the mid-1970s, by the beginning of the 1980s Japan had overcome most of these difficulties (Table 17.5). Though growth had not returned to earlier rates, it had been well above that of other OECD countries. Inflation had decelerated to levels at times below those of the 1960s, the current account had, on several occasions, been in massive surplus, while measured unemployment had remained extremely low. More importantly, perhaps,

TABLE 17.5. *Performance of Major Economies, 1976–1982*

	GDP*†	Consumer price inflation†	Unemployment‡	Current balance§
Japan	4·6	5·1	2·1	3·3
France	2·2	11·3	6·0	−1·8
Germany	1·9	4·5	3·9	−1·1
Italy	2·2	16·5	7·5	−1·7
United Kingdom	0·6	12·6	7·8	3·5
United States	2·1	9·2	7·1	−3·9

* The two terminal years of this period are cyclically not strictly comparable (1976 was a year of rapid recovery, 1982 a year of semi-recession), but while this impairs growth comparisons with earlier periods, it does not impair inter-country comparisons.
† Average annual percentage changes.
‡ As percentage of the labour force.
§ Annual averages, in US$ billion.

Sources: IMF, *International Financial Statistics* (various issues); OECD, *Economic Outlook* (various issues).

international competitiveness seemed to have actually improved despite significant currency appreciation.

Two major reasons probably lie behind Japan's successful overcoming of a very serious situation: the response of economic policy and the presence of a very flexible labour market. Economic policies, which had contributed to the overheating of 1972–3, were forcefully used to tackle the inflation of 1973–4. A severe monetary squeeze, implemented as in the past via quantitative restrictions on lending (rather than via interest rate rises), had the desired effect—from a peak year-on-year rate of 26 per cent in October 1974, consumer price inflation had returned to a single-digit figure by August 1975.

Policies were also important in the subsequent revival in activity. Since private investment recovered only little, growth was stimulated by public expenditure. Fiscal policy remained relaxed until the early 1980s, with the budget deficit running at some 4 per cent of GDP in the years 1975–82—a figure *higher* than that for Britain. Nor were such relatively large deficits accompanied by the dangers economic theory often predicts—excessive monetary expansion and, therefore, inflation, or 'crowding-out'.[6] Budget deficits did not generate inflation since these deficits were financed by longer-term bond issues; and interest rates did not sky-rocket, partly because the Central Bank had legal control over financial institutions more or less to impose the absorption of rising public sector debt, and partly because household savings remained high and, given lower private investment levels, required some alternative assets for investment purposes.

A second and more important reason for Japan's successes in this period lies in the flexibility with which the labour market responded to the crisis. Prima facie, this may sound surprising. A number of well-publicized Japanese forms of labour relations suggests that flexibility is much more limited in Japan than in the West. Thus, the practice of 'permanent employment' (by which an employee, once hired, is assured of a job with the firm until retirement age) would seem to rule out dismissals even in the event of recession, while the custom of 'seniority wages' (by which earnings rise regularly with age) would seem to limit severely flexibility in the wage bill, even in the event of cash flow difficulties. In other words, neither the price nor the quantity of employment would seem to be at all flexible for a normal Japanese firm.

Yet in practice this picture is seriously misleading. First, permanent employment and seniority wages, in so far as they apply, cover only male workers in the public sector and in large-scale enterprises, or perhaps one-third of the labour force. Elsewhere in the economy, these practices are much less common. Nor are such phenomena unknown elsewhere. Wages rising with age are quite widespread in Western Europe as are longer-term forms of employment.[7] Second, even in Japan's large firms flexibility is assured by the presence of a 'temporary' labour force which does not benefit from the same rights (and which constitutes up to 10 per cent of the 'permanent' one), by the option of altering the length of the working week, and by the variability of one

[6] For a discussion of these in the British context, see Chap. 13.

[7] For some evidence on this, see Boltho [3], pp. 34–40.

important component of workers' earnings (bonus payments) which is linked
to firms' profitability.[8] Finally, flexibility has also been assured by the much
greater willingness of the labour force to adopt new technologies. Partly this is a
function of the bonus and enterprise union systems which create strong
common interests between workers and the firm; partly it is a function of
permanent employment, in those companies in which it exists, since the latter
rules out fears of 'technological unemployment'.

These various adjustment mechanisms received an added boost with the oil
crisis. The realization by company unions that their firms were facing a new
hostile environment facilitated wage moderation and, possibly, an even
speedier adoption of new technology. More importantly, the oil crisis and its
aftermath led to a significant shake-out of labour, particularly from large firms,
permanent employment practices notwithstanding. Table 17.6 illustrates how
the decline in employment in Japan's industrial sector was sharper, both
during the recession and in the medium term, than that of any other major
country except Germany (which had the option, denied to Japan, of reducing
the employment of immigrant workers).

TABLE 17.6. *Employment Adjustment in Major Economies after First Oil Shock*
(percentage changes at annual rates, seasonally adjusted)

	Recession period*		Medium-term trend 1973–9	
	Industrial production	Manufacturing employment	Industrial production	Manufacturing employment
Japan	− 0·1	− 2·8†	2·2	− 2·0†
France	—	− 1·6	1·9	− 1·2
Germany	− 0·2	− 3·9	1·6	− 2·1
Italy	− 0·7	− 0·3	2·7	0·3
United Kingdom	− 1·4	− 2·3	1·1	− 1·4
United States	0·2	− 1·6	2·7	0·7

* Periods have been chosen for each country so as to begin with the highest pre-
recession figure and end with the first quarter during which industrial production comes
closest to the pre-recession peak. The figures for employment have been lagged one
quarter. The exact periods for each country are as follows: Japan, 1974 qr.1–1978 qr.1;
France, 1974 qr.2–1976 qr.4; Germany, 1973 qr.4–1976 qr.4; Italy, 1974 qr.2–1976
qr.3; United Kingdom, 1973 qr.4–1977 qr.1; United States, 1973 qr.4–1976 qr.4.
† Regular employees with firms with 30 workers or more. Inclusion of smaller firms (5
to 29 employees) in which the employment declines were less pronounced, and of
temporary workers, for whom they were larger, reduces the recession period and
medium-term trend figures to 2 and 1 per cent respectively.

Sources: OECD, *Main Economic Indicators—Historical Statistics;* unpublished Japanese
Ministry of Labour data.

[8] Indeed, a recent econometric investigation [18] for eighteen OECD countries comes to the
conclusion that both real and nominal wage flexibility were highest in Japan (together with
Switzerland). For further evidence on the often greater variability of nominal wages and of labour
inputs in Japan relative to the US and Britain, see Gordon [17].

The reasons for such an unexpected outcome must be found in the nature of Japan's permanent employment system. This had never been enshrined in legal provisions—it had merely been a custom, originally developed in the 1920s, which had strengthened in the post-war period as expectations of 'permanent growth' spread in the economy. It was perfectly rational for firms expecting to face growth rates of 10 per cent per annum to develop institutions which ensured permanence of their own trained labour force. In other words, permanent employment was not an inherent characteristic of the economy, but mainly a function of rapid growth—when the growth momentum was broken, some adjustment was inevitable.

Yet this adjustment did not lead to open unemployment. The workers made redundant in large firms either withdrew from the labour force (prematurely retired and female employees), or found alternative employment, at times in other parts of the company's conglomerate, more usually in Japan's very important small-scale firms sector which acted as a 'shock absorber'.[9] Through the 1950s and 1960s this sector had shed labour and had seen some rise in its (well below average) wage levels; after 1973 it reacquired workers, but these workers had to accept relative falls in their earnings (Table 17.7). It was

TABLE 17.7. *Employment and Wage Changes by Size of Firm in Manufacturing* (deviations from overall average annual percentage change)

	Weight in 1979*	1955–73		1973–9	
		Employment	Wages†	Employment	Wages†
Size of firm‡					
1–9	19·9	− 0·8	0·9	2·2	..
10–29	19·0	− 1·4	1·2	2·0	− 1·4
30–99	19·4	0·1	0·4	0·4	− 0·7
100–299	15·3	1·2	− 0·4	− 0·7	− 0·1
300–999	13·1	1·4	− 1·0	− 2·0	0·4
over 1,000	13·3	0·6	− 1·2	− 3·1	0·5
Memorandum items:					
Actual change§	..	4·4	11·9	− 1·6	12·9¶

* In total manufacturing employment.
† Total cash earnings per employee.
‡ Number of employees.
§ Average annual percentage changes.
¶ Excluding firms with 1–9 employees.

Sources: *Japan Statistical Yearbook* (various issues); MITI, *Census of Manufactures* (various issues); MITI, *White Paper on Small and Medium Enterprises, 1981.*

[9] A MITI survey (quoted in [22]) on the 1974–6 labour response of major firms showed that well over 50 per cent of the corporation surveyed had transferred workers to other plants or to subsidiaries, but that none had had to resort to outright dismissals.

employment flexibility, in other words, which allowed Japan's large-scale firms to maintain their competitiveness in this period, and it was wage flexibility which prevented any substantial increase in unemployment.

17.3. External Performance and Policies

17.3.1. Foreign Trade

The text so far has hardly mentioned Japan's foreign trade. Yet this is probably the aspect of the country's economic experience which has most caught the outsider's attention. Japan's 'fame' is essentially a function of its phenomenal export successes (and reluctance to import). To the uninformed, Japan often appears as a highly protectionist country, whose principal activity is to produce for foreign markets and whose growth has been pulled up by exports to other countries. But while there clearly was, and may still be, some truth in the first of these three propositions, the other two do not really withstand analysis. Foreign trade dependence is not particularly high in Japan. The share of exports or imports in GDP was of the order of 14 per cent in the early 1980s, well below the 25 to 30 per cent ratios of countries such as Britain, France, Germany, or Italy. On a per capita basis, the value of British exports in 1979–80 was *double* that of Japan.

More interesting is the analytical question of whether Japanese growth was 'export-led'. A proper test of this hypothesis is beyond the scope of this brief chapter. But some evidence can be brought to bear on whether the expansion of exports was mainly related to growing demand for exports or to improved competitiveness. At a very aggregate level, Caves [16] has suggested a simple test based on familiar demand and supply curves. If the initial stimulus to growth comes from the foreign demand side, then prices and quantities should both shift in the same direction, while if growth is supply-led, then they should move in opposite directions. Over the twenty years to 1973, before inflation accelerated, Japan's export prices (in dollars) remained virtually stable, while the volume of Japanese exports was multiplied by 20.

A further indicator suggesting that demand changes abroad cannot have been of prime importance is provided by calculations showing that at the outset of the period both the commodity and the country compositions of Japan's exports were relatively 'unfavourable', i.e. concentrated in products and markets whose subsequent growth turned out to be below average.[10]

At a more disaggregated level, Figure 17.1 illustrates the development of output, imports, and exports for a number of commodities which cover a range of products in which Japan has, at one time or another, enjoyed a distinct comparative advantage, and which can often be taken as representative of wider sectors. The path shown by cotton yarn is that typical of the import-substitution pattern of a developing country, and was already discussed in such terms in Japan in the 1930s (see, for instance, Akamatsu [13]). Imports lead the way, followed by domestic production and, only after a lag, by exports. A

[10] NIESR, *Economic Review* (Aug. 1963); Economic Planning Agency, *Economic Survey of Japan, 1965–1966.*

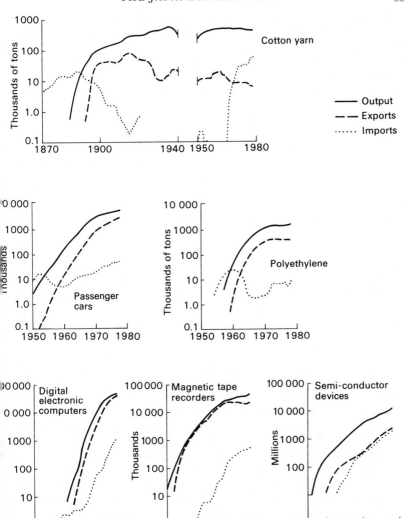

FIG. 17.1. Production, Exports, and Imports of Selected Commodities. (volumes; five-year moving averages; log-scales.)

Sources: Bank of Japan, *Economic Statistics Annual* and *Hundred-Year Statistics of the Japanese Economy* (Tokyo, 1966); Bureau of Statistics, Office of the Prime Minister, *Japan Statistical Yearbook* (various issues); Department of Finance, *Financial Annual of Japan* (various issues); HMSO, *Statistical Abstract for the Principal and Other Foreign Countries* (various issues); Ministry of Finance, *The Foreign Trade of Japan* and *Japan Exports and Imports* (various issues); MITI, *Industrial Statistics Monthly* (various issues) and *Kikai Tōkei Geppō* (Monthly Report on Machinery Statistics) (various issues); K. Ohkawa *et al., Estimates of Long-Term Economic Statistics of Japan*, Vol. II (Tokyo, 1979); Oriental Economist, *Foreign Trade of Japan* (Tokyo, 1935).

similar pattern, in a much shorter time-span, can be seen for cars and
representative modern chemical product. Imports are quickly replaced b
buoyant domestic output. Export drives follow only once significant sca
economies have been achieved and costs have been sufficiently reduced t
withstand foreign competition.[11] As a consequence, exports do not, for most c
the period, account for a major share of output. The same is no longer true fc
the latest products of Japan's technological revolution. Here imports ar
virtually non-existent, since by now Japan is a world leader in the particula
commodities chosen, and international competitiveness is achieved early in th
product cycle. Hence foreign demand plays a more important role as expor
soon become a major percentage of output. But for the bulk of Japan
successful exports, a supply-led theory would seem to be more appropriate
'Japan's rate of growth of exports has been high . . . because the rate of growt
of its economy and especially of its industry has been high . . . and not vic
versa' ([1], p. 173).

17.3.2. Policies

The fact that Japan's experience was not one of export-led growth, but one c
growth-led exports, does not mean that it was spontaneous. On the contrar
both the economy's overall expansion and the upstream movement of th
industrial structure, away from traditional, low income-elasticity of deman
commodities towards machinery and other high-technology products, wer
purposefully encouraged by the authorities. At a macroeconomic level, fisca
and monetary policies were almost continuously used to foster growth. Balanc
of payments difficulties or accelerating inflation did impose the need fc
restriction on specific occasions, but over the longer run the emphasis was in th
opposite direction. In a climate of optimistic expectations in which *ex-an*
investments exceeded *ex-ante* savings, the Central Bank made available (a
pegged interest rates) the funds that firms required. Fiscal policy, for its par
expanded supply in those areas of infrastructure most needed by the corpora
sector, while at the same time favouring capital formation more directly by
wide variety of tax concessions. The essential characteristic of these policies wa
their focus on investment and on longer-term growth rather than a concer
with the short term and fine-tuning, of the kind which dominated Britain
experience since the war. And concentration on the long term was greatl
helped by an unparalleled degree of political stability and continuity.

The same long-term approach is also evident in MITI's sectoral policie

---

[11] It has often been argued that Japan's (and for that matter Germany's) international success
were due to a head-start acquired thanks to the destruction of the war—Japanese industry w
rebuilt using the most modern equipment, while British industry, for instance, remained fetter
with obsolete technologies. Yet such an argument hardly stands up. It should be remembered th
Japan's manufacturing production rose fivefold in the 1950s (crude steel output, for instance, we
from 5 million tons in 1950 to 22 million tons in 1960, motor cycle production from 75,000 units i
1952 to 1·7 million units in 1962, etc.). Even if very advanced plants had been built at the outset
rather unlikely event given the small size of the existing and foreseeable market), the tempo
growth would have made these technologically obsolete within a short time-span. It was not
much war destruction as rapid growth which (continuously) renewed the Japanese capital stoc

most of which were concerned with the country's international competitiveness. MITI's achievement in contributing to the transformation of Japan's industrial structure stems from three major factors—its successful establishment of an environment favourable to investment and growth, its frequently correct selection of sectors to be encouraged, and its often imaginative choice of instruments and policies designed to achieve its aims.

At the most general level, MITI followed a 'dual' economic policy of protection vis-à-vis the rest of the world but of encouragement to competition within the economy [23]. At present, Japan has probably lower tariffs and fewer quotas than either the United States or the EEC (though informal barriers still exist for crucial sectors); until the late 1960s, however, it was a heavily protected country. Yet this protectionism was accompanied by a less interventionist strategy at home. MITI was ready to accept domestic competition—not, of course, the atomistic competition of the textbook, but the competition of large-scale oligopolies. It was this acceptance of fierce inter-group rivalry which allowed the mobility of resources and the rapid adoption of new technology which were essential if protectionism was to succeed.

MITI, in addition, also chose what it saw as being the 'winning sectors'. Initially, these were fairly obvious (coal, iron and steel, electricity, shipbuilding), but thereafter the choice was dictated by a forward-looking selection of areas in which world income elasticities of demand were thought to be high. Static comparative advantage criteria were blatantly ignored and Japan embarked on a purposeful programme of import substitution in capital- and technology-intensive industries. Throughout the 1950s the choice of sectors was in many ways mapped out by developments in more advanced countries. Even then, however, the 'Visions of the Future' went beyond the mere copying of successful foreign industries. To name but the best-known example—the first official plan for the encouragement of the electronics industry was launched in as early as 1957.

The instruments used by MITI to guide the economy into the desired direction were relatively straightforward in the 1950s (though in some instances, such as the allocation of a very lucrative sugar import quota to the shipbuilding industry as a disguised subsidy [24], the bureaucrats showed a high degree of ingenuity). Given the tight balance of payments situation, foreign exchange allocations were under official control, and 'Control of the foreign exchange budget meant control of the entire economy' ([2], p. 25). By licensing out the imports of raw material, machinery, and, especially, technology, MITI could effectively implement its priorities.[12]

As foreign trade and foreign exchange transactions were liberalized, direct controls gave way to what has been called 'administrative guidance'—a subtler system of persuasion rather than compulsion, a persuasion made more palatable, but also more pressing, by an array of both carrots and sticks. As an example, firms which complied with official wishes would be favoured with above-average quotas when MITI organized 'recession cartels' to weather periods of slowdown. Conversely, recalcitrant enterprises might not be given

[12] For an example, see Ozawa [21].

significant help for restructuring in the 'rationalization cartels' that were introduced in several industries after the first oil crises. A further indirect means of influence came via the dependence of companies on bank finance and of banks on Central Bank finance. Not only did this allow greater macroeconomic control, it also meant that the sectoral allocation of credit often responded to the signals provided by MITI.

This concentration on MITI's policies should not, however, make one lose sight of the other institutions that also shaped the country's post-war growth and, in particular, promoted its most dynamic element—investment:

Capital formation was encouraged in all possible ways—by the Bank of Japan's permissive . . . credit policies, by the Ministry of Finance's tax and other financial stimuli, by the M.I.T.I.'s investment guidance, insistence on protection, and selection of key sectors and infant industries. The ministries directed growth; the central bank financed it. . . . Japan is not, of course, the sole example of a government using the whole array of direct and indirect instruments in its hands to stimulate both over-all growth and a particular sectoral allocation of resources. . . . But among market economies Japan may well have been at the top of the scale for both the comprehensiveness and the efficiency of its governments' intervention ([3], p. 131).

Not much has changed since this summary judgement was written in 1974. Combined with the already mentioned flexibility of the labour market, this strengthens the expectation that Japanese economic performance will remain for some time still the most favourable in the industrialized world.

17.4. Is There a Japanese 'Model'?

In the 1950s and 1960s Japan's experience elicited relatively little comment in the West, where attention was focused on the more obvious successes of Germany, Italy, and, later, France. Japanese growth was comfortably attributed to a combination of low wages, catching up after the war, and a somewhat reprehensible ability to copy Western technology and products. As a matter of fact, these explanations were not good enough even at the time; if they were sufficient, they would have predicted explosive growth for countries such as India or Ethiopia, with even lower wages, even more to catch up, and an even wider technological gap to fill.

It was only when Japan continued, year after year, to show a growth rate of some 10 per cent per annum that something else seemed to be needed, beyond references to a highly productive capital stock and the benefits of protection. It was then that Westerners looking for explanations turned to history, culture, and national character. A new orthodoxy was developed (sometimes referred to as the theory of 'Japan exceptionalism'), which purported to show that Japan's experience was unique.

17.4.1. 'Japan exceptionalism'

The first element in the view that Japan's 'miracle' is inextricably linked with its cultural and social values is a reference to history. The Tokugawa regime, which effectively insulated Japan from trends in the rest of the world between

he middle of the seventeenth and the middle of the nineteenth centuries, also
ursued a policy of relentless indoctrination of the values of the Japanese brand
f Confucianism—frugality, consensus, and loyalty to the state and clan. It is
hese values, so it is argued, and the feudal nature of the society of that period,
hat can still be seen in today's industrial relations and industrial structure.

Equally important was the Meiji restoration—a response to intolerable
xternal pressures, partly military and colonialist, but above all economic. It
vas not possible for Japan to continue to exclude the West and its technology,
is had been done more or less successfully for hundreds of years. The changes
vhich had to take place would have three features. First, they had to be done
quickly. The gap between East and West was so huge, and the Western
ountries so dominant, that any delay meant facing, like China, the dangers of
dismemberment and quasi-colonial status. Second, the essential nature and
dentity of Japan had to be preserved. Tradition and the religious status of the
Emperor required this. Third, the state would play a very large role. This came
partly from the natural attitude in a theocracy that power, or at least
authenticity, arises from the centre. As much, it was the automatic response of a
emi-feudal society with no established tradition of the decentralized market
ystem which goes with widespread trading and production.

To some extent these three elements remain important to the present day.
The Japanese can make big changes in unison, fast. Their responses to post-war
reconstruction, to the oil shock of 1973, and to the problem of pollution, show
an easy acceptance of the idea that large (technical) problems can be solved
quickly, which has pretty much disappeared in the West except in parts of the
United States. Their hostility to imports, not only of manufactures, but also of
ervices, such as shipping and banking, is based at heart not on any calculation
of optimum tariff levels, or how to protect infant industries, but on an instinct
hat the outsider can be dangerous to Japanese interests and identity, and must
be kept out. Similarly, the role of the state, crucial in the early industrialization
period, continues today. The current British debate on where the demarcation
hould lie between the private and the public sector makes little sense to the
Japanese. The two were intertwined from the start of economic development,
and remain so.

The second important aspect which the theory of Japan exceptionalism puts
forward is the notion of collectivism, which stands in sharp contrast to the
Western ideas of individualism and which, it is often argued, goes back to a
combination of the feudal past, the rice-growing nature of Japanese
agriculture, and the values of consensus inherent in Confucianism.
Collectivism starts with the Japanese attitude to the family and the group—of
which the company is a particular example. Just as Japan is seen as a very
distinct entity which must be sharply distinguished from the rest of the world,
and demands extremes of loyalty, so the university class or the factory represent
a family which the ordinary Japanese naturally wants to play his part in
supporting.

As a consequence, consensus is the basis for action, not legality or authority.
Successful groups naturally depend on the agreement of their members, not the
application of a rule book or the superior power of the leader. This is why

Japanese firms are allegedly slow to come to decisions—it takes time to get all the members of a large group to feel comfortable with a conclusion—but very good at putting them into effect—there are no defeated factions to undermine the operation, and everybody knows enough about the decision and its rationale to understand how to make it work.

The hierarchy within the group depends above all on respect for seniors, which in turn reflects the more fundamental attitude to parents and teachers. A great deal of Japanese morals is to do with the formal repayment of debt to such patrons. A child owes everything to his mother and father: a pupil is eternally indebted to his teacher. It is easy to see how this attitude can be transferred to roles within a company. An employer naturally becomes a father or teacher figure. The company becomes the family. The manager and worker has a duty to repay what he owes to the company through diligence and loyalty. Loyalty includes a natural feeling of belonging to that group through thick and thin: hence the system of lifetime employment, which fits naturally with the idea of being a permanent member of the family. Seniority is the natural mechanism for promotion; that after all is how a father, and many teachers, get their status.

This notion of the firm (or of the conglomerate) as a family implies a corresponding duty for the employer. It is alleged, therefore, that if a large company sees demand in one part of its business declining—say, in textiles or shipbuilding—it cannot get rid of its workers, as would Courtaulds or Vickers. They must be found other work within the company. Certainly this appeared to be the case until the mid-1970s. Correspondingly, the labour force and its union do not resist job changes; work is guaranteed, but not work of a particular kind.

The third element of the theory is the popular notion of 'Japan Inc.', a notion which, again, draws heavily on both history and culture. The principal idea is that the Japanese are peculiarly competent at seeing what long-term products and markets Japan should concentrate on, and at co-ordinating public and private effort to hit those targets. The mechanism of co-ordination depends again, above all, on consensus. The politicians, industry, the Bank of Japan, and MITI (or whatever may be the relevant ministry) all work in the same direction. The politicians are more dependent on, and subservient to, the interests of business than in the West. The Civil Service understands better than the businessmen where the country's long-term interests lie, and is quite ruthless in withdrawing support (money, legislation, contracts) from sectors which are no longer progressive. Politics and the bureaucracy are much less concerned with the social services—which are rudimentary—and defence—which is limited by the Constitution to self-defence. Consensus is reinforced by relationships established at university: to be a member of a particular class at the University of Tokyo, in particular the Law Faculty, makes you part of a network of loyal acquaintances which covers all the main elements in the political/business/finance/bureaucratic system.

On this view of the matter, therefore, the Japanese have ended up with a uniquely effective machine for economic planning and co-ordination. It relies heavily on instinctive aptitudes for co-operation, shared objectives, natural loyalty, and the absence of that individualism which is at the heart of competition in the West. Modern technology requires heavy long-term investment, the ability to move the economy quickly in new directions, ruthless decisions to dispose of old industries, and social attitudes to change which allow far-sighted bureaucrats to achieve their purposes.

7.4.2. Scepticism and Doubt

If this account of how Japan works, and why it works well, is even half true, there is little for Westerners to do but admire an inimitable natural phenomenon, and reconcile themselves to prolonged inferiority. However, while there is no doubt some truth in it, particularly in the summary sketch of inter-personal relationships, it is also much exaggerated in many of its main features.

First, if indeed these various cultural and historical elements are so important, Japan ought to have shown an economic miracle in earlier periods of its modern history as well. Yet its growth rate between 1870 and 1940 was barely higher than that of Western Europe and actually below that of North America. Japan has not always been as it is now. Much of its post-1868 history is a story of dissenting peasants or military uprisings, intellectual ferment, poverty, and other upheavals very different from today's placid scene. This suggests that there is no timeless, changeless Japanese character which determines what the country is like or guarantees its economic success.

Second, many of the customs and institutions which loom so large in any account of Japan's economy (lifetime employment, seniority wages, company unions, extensive subcontracting, bonus payments, etc.) were often recent responses to economic developments, not permanent characteristics of Japanese society smoothly adapted in the move from feudalism to capitalism. In the early days of industrialization, the mobility of labour was extremely high and lifetime employment appeared for the first time only in the 1920s for a small élite of highly skilled workers. Similarly, early Japanese unions developed along craft or industrial lines and were often politicized, in contrast to their present-day successors. Nor were economic dualism or subcontracting the industrial equivalents of the timeless relationship between the feudal lord and his retainer, but a spontaneous market reaction to the rapid and unbalanced growth of the years 1915–29.

Third, as already mentioned, much of the previous account, even when true, is about the conspicuous large-scale sector of the economy where the giant companies operate, and where politicians and civil servants are involved. It ignores the much larger part of the economy—agriculture, small firms, subcontractors—to which little of the orthodoxy applies. In these sectors there is no lifetime employment, seniority system, government contracts, or vision of the 1990s.

Fourth, the apparatus of co-ordination and control, of which MITI and Japan Inc. are the symbols, are quite modern, and came as much from the military style of administration and politics which grew up in the 1930s and during the war. And the reality of fierce, at times ruthless, competition on the domestic market belies the impression of continuous and smooth co-operation and consensus. Even the effectiveness of MITI and of the government in general in masterminding the country's growth (to which this chapter broadly subscribes) is a controversial issue. A major survey of Japan's economy concluded on this topic that: 'While the government has certainly provided a favorable environment, the main impetus to growth has been private . . . Government intervention generally has tended (and intended) to accelerate trends already put in motion by private market forces.'[13]

Finally, it is odd how many of the allegedly virtuous features of Japanese society mirror features of Britain which this country has strenuously attempted to uproot. It is common belief in the United Kingdom that profitability is critical; that an 'old boy' network of promotion and pay is inefficient; that to have been to the same university is a poor basis for co-operation and agreement; that paternalism is inefficient and patronizing; that consensus thinking results in the lowest common denominator. These propositions may be true or false. But it will not do, in attributing causes to the success of Japan, to praise those features which, were they discovered in a company or a ministry in Britain, would be extirpated without hesitation.

17.5. Conclusions

The foregoing text has put forward a number of explanations for Japan's post-war successes. Some of these are of an economic nature—permissive supply conditions in terms of both labour and technology for much of the period, high rates of savings and investment, and a relatively flexible labour market. Others are more institutional—for instance protection and the role of government in fostering growth. Others, finally, stem from a complex social and historical background, such as the strong inter-group rivalry, which promotes fierce competition and 'excessive' investment, or the apparently greater degree of within-group consensus, which facilitates non-inflationary wage bargaining and united responses to external shocks.

Clearly, Japan's success story is not exceptional in the sense of being totally dependent on society and tradition. Yet the popular literature about Japan as 'number one' has often stressed such aspects. Partly this may be because the theory of 'exceptionalism' catches the eye and strengthens the West's incomprehension of the Japanese phenomenon. Party it may be because much of the literature on Japan comes from the United States, and the United States diverges more from Japan than any of the major Western European countries.

Many of Japan's apparently strange institutions, much of Japan's close government-business relationship, while absent across the Atlantic, can be found, if in different, and at times weaker, forms in Europe. Major reasons, no doubt, are that both Japan and Europe share a common feudal-agricultural past, as well as a long tradition of centralized government. From a European perspective, much of Japan's miracle is different in degree, not in kind, from what happened on the Continent in the post-war period.

In a sense, this conclusion is perhaps reassuring. There seems to be little that is unique or immutable about Japan. Its economic history over the last thirty

[13] H. Patrick and H. Rosovsky, 'Japan's Economic Performance: An Overview', in [5], p. 47

years may have raised fear or admiration, but in the past this was not always the case. As George Allen put it:

Today the typical Japanese is regarded as immensely hard-working, competent and reliable. But this was not the impression of Western residents in Japan in the early days of modernisation, and indeed much later. At a time when the furious rate at which English labourers worked excited the wonder of Continental Europeans, the qualities of the Japanese as producers were rated very low, and their national prospects were considered bleak. Contemporary Western observers commented on their indolence and their love of pleasure. In 1881 one of them wrote in the *Japan Herald* that 'a condition of moderate affluence' probably lay before the Japanese, but 'being content with little, they are not likely to achieve much'.[14]

Bibliography

SECTION A

The two best single sources on Japan's economy are perhaps [1] K. Ohkawa and H. Rosovsky, *Japanese Economic Growth* (Stanford, 1973) and [2] C. Johnson, *MITI and the Japanese Miracle* (Stanford, 1982). The first looks at the broad sweep of economic development from the beginning of the century to the early 1970s. The second is an in-depth examination of industrial policy-making which concentrates on the post-war period. A concise presentation of the post-war economy up to the first oil shock (from which a good deal of the material in sections 17.1 and 17.2 has been taken) can be found in [3] A. Boltho, *Japan—An Economic Survey* (Oxford, 1975), while for a Japanese view which takes the story to the later 1970s one can consult [4] T. Nakamura, *The Postwar Japanese Economy* (Tokyo, 1981). More detailed material appears in a collection of articles on all major aspects of the economy: [5] H. Patrick and H. Rosovsky (eds.), *Asia's New Giant* (Brookings Institution, Washington, 1976). The annual Economic Surveys of Japan by [6] the Economic Planning Agency and by [7] the OECD provide a running commentary.

For books less exclusively devoted to purely economic aspects, see, *inter alia*, [18] R. Benedict, *The Chrysanthemum and the Sword* (Boston 1946); [9] R. Dore, *British Factory—Japanese Factory* (London, 1973); [10] C. Nakane, *Japanese Society* (London, 1973); [11] M. Morishima, *Why has Japan 'Succeeded'?* (Cambridge, 1982); and an anthology of readings: [12] J. Livingstone, J. Moore, and F. Oldfather *The Japan Reader*, 2 vols. (London, 1976).

SECTION B

[13[AKAMATSU, K. 'A Theory of Unbalanced Growth in the World Economy', *Weltwirtschaftliches Archiv*, 2 (1961).
[14] ALLEN, G. C. *Japan's Economic Expansion* (London, 1965).
[15] AUKRUST, O. 'Inflation in the Open Economy', in Krause, L. B. and Salant, W. S. (eds.), *Worldwide Inflation* (Brookings Institution, Washington, 1977).
[16] CAVES, R. E. 'Export-Led Growth and the New Economic History', in Bhagwati, J. N. *et al.* (eds.), *Trade, Balance of Payments and Growth* (Amsterdam, 1971).
[17] GORDON, R. J. 'Why U.S. Wage and Employment Behaviour Differs from that in Britain and Japan', *Economic Journal* (Mar. 1982).
[18] GRUBB, D., JACKMAN, R., and LAYARD, R. 'Wage Rigidity and Unemployment in OECD Countries', *European Economic Review* (Mar./Apr. 1983).

[14] Nishiyama and Allen [20], p. 59.

[19] KAHN, H. *The Emerging Japanese Superstate* (London, 1971).

[20] NISHIYAMA, C. and ALLEN, G. C. *The Price of Prosperity*, Hobart Paper, No. 58 (London, 1974).

[21] OZAWA, T. 'Government Control over Technology Acquisition and Firms' Entry into New Sectors: The Experience of Japan's Synthetic Fibre Industry', *Cambridge Journal of Economics* (June 1980).

[22] SHIMADA, H. *The Japanese Employment System* (Japan Institute of Labour, Tokyo, 1980).

[23] SHINOHARA, M. 'Causes and Patterns in the Postwar Growth', *The Developing Economies* (Dec. 1970).

[24] TSURU, S. *The Mainsprings of Japanese Growth: A Turning Point?* (The Atlantic Institute, Paris, 1977).

18

The International Monetary System

J. H. B. TEW

8.1. Introduction

The international monetary arrangements described in this chapter are of the greatest importance both for the UK as a trading nation and for sterling as a currency in widespread international use. They have evolved very conderably in the course of the post-war period, and especially so on two occasions—the early 1960s, with the introduction of 'convertibility' of currencies as intended in the Bretton Woods Agreement of 1944, and again in the early 1970s, with the ending of the Bretton Woods regime by the transition from pegged to floating exchange rates.

8.2. The Bretton Woods Regime

8.2.1. Convertibility

The most important objective of the original Articles of Agreement of the International Monetary Fund (IMF), as signed at Bretton Woods in July 1944, was to restore after the war the 'convertibility' of currencies, such as had obtained under the Gold Standard of pre-1914 and post-1925. This earlier convertibility' had two distinct aspects:

(i) *Convertibility-in-the-market*, meaning that the holder of any one currency was free to sell it against another in any foreign exchange market, unhampered by exchange controls or other official regulations.

(ii) *Official convertibility*, meaning that the Central Banks of each country undertook official transactions in gold or in foreign exchange so as to keep the value of the home currency close to an official par value in terms of gold or in terms of some other currency (usually sterling) which was itself officially convertible into gold. (Thus the Bank of England assured the official convertibility of sterling by offering to buy gold at 77s.9d. a standard ounce and sell at 77s.10½d., while the Australian authorities assured the official convertibility of their currency by offering to buy or sell pounds sterling at approximately £E1 = £A1.)

The collapse of the Gold Standard in the early 1930s arose in the first instance from the discontinuance in 1931 of official convertibility by the UK and, several years later, by the US. The official convertibility of the dollar into gold (at a new price of $35 an ounce) was restored as from February 1934, but soon after the outbreak of war (and indeed earlier in the case of the Axis powers) convertibility-in-the-market was ended by the introduction, in virtually all industrial countries except the US and Canada, of an official monopoly of foreign exchange dealing, with fixed official prices.

So at the time of the Bretton Woods conference, the reform needed to re-establish the 'convertibility' required by the agreement was the dismantling of exchange controls and similar regulations which restricted free access to foreign exchange markets, at any rate for transactions on current account (the agreement specifically permitted the imposition of restrictions on capital transactions). The necessary reform was not, however, achieved by the Western European signatories of the agreement, or by Japan, until the early 1960s, so the 'Bretton Woods regime' did not come into operation until about a decade and a half after the Bretton Woods conference. In the intervening years most IMF members, outside North and Central America, appealed to Article XIV of the agreement, which permitted them, for an unspecified transitional period, to maintain, and to adapt to changing circumstances, any exchange controls and suchlike devices which they were enforcing at the time of signing the agreement. Then in February 1961, following some tentative moves in December 1958, ten countries which had hitherto availed themselves of Article XIV (Belgium, France, Germany, Eire, Italy, Luxembourg, the Netherlands, Peru, Sweden, and the UK) all agreed to emerge from the shelter of this Article, and assume the obligation under Article VIII to avoid restrictions on current payments. Japan followed suit in 1963. Thus convertibility-in-the-market was well re-established among the developed countries of the Western world (though less well among the developing countries) as from the early 1960s. It has remained in operation ever since, and has indeed been taken beyond the requirement of Article VIII by the progressive dismantling of official regulations on capital, as well as on current, transactions.

The other aspect of Bretton Woods convertibility, namely *official* convertibility, proved less durable, and came to an end in the early 1970s. Thus the Bretton Woods regime, as provided for in the original Articles of Agreement, lasted for little more than a decade. How was official convertibility operated during that decade? There was in effect a three-tier system of pegging exchange rates operated by virtually all the countries of the Western world:

(i) The US dollar was pegged to gold by the willingness of the US authorities to trade both ways in gold with other Central Banks at a fixed price of $35 an ounce. (This undertaking ended in 1971 with President Nixon's famous speech on 15 August—see Section 18.2.3.)

(ii) All the other major currencies, as well as most currencies of Latin America, were pegged to the US dollar by official transactions in dollars undertaken by the Central Bank responsible for the currency concerned. For example, in the early 1960s the Bank of England bought sterling for dollars in the market whenever its spot price would otherwise have fallen below $2.78 and sold whenever its price would otherwise have risen above $2.82. (When sterling was devalued in November 1967 these limits were lowered to $2.38 and $2.42 respectively.) Such pegging on the dollar was discontinued by the major industrial countries in the early 1970s: Canada floated her currency as from 1970, the UK as from June 1972, and most of Western Europe and Japan in the first quarter of 1973.

(iii) The countries of the Sterling Area (roughly the British Commonwealth except Canada) pegged to sterling in much the same way as sterling itself was pegged to the US dollar. These arrangements were abandoned soon after sterling was unpegged from the dollar in June 1972. Operating in much the same way as the Sterling Area, though much smaller, were the French-Franc Area, the Belgian-Franc Area, and the Dutch-Florin Area. Of these three, only the first has survived, and then only with a much-reduced membership.

18.2.2. The Dollar System

Let us now look more closely at the first two tiers, that is, at the dollar itself and the currencies pegged on the dollar. This 'dollar system', as we may call it, was *asymmetrical*, in the sense that the United States played a different role from the other countries operating the system and the US dollar a different role from the other currencies in the system:

First, the United States played a *passive* role, in that decisions about exchange rate parities with the dollar were taken individually by the other country concerned, in agreement with the executive board of the IMF. The United States did not have to be consulted, and so the official value of the US dollar in terms of other currencies was the outcome of decisions in which the US authorities did not directly participate. It might be objected that the US authorities could initiate a move to change the dollar price of gold, but (as the US Council of Economic Advisors [4] reported in January 1973) 'since most countries were pegging their rates to the dollar in the foreign exchange market, the United States could not be certain that a change in the price of gold would actually result in a change in the value of the dollar in terms of foreign currencies'; and in practice the US authorities never regarded a change in the dollar price of gold as a practicable device for changing the dollar's external value. The US role was also unique in that the official transactions in the foreign exchange market required to keep market rates close to their official parities were undertaken almost exclusively not by the US authorities but by the Central Banks of the other countries. For instance, official intervention in the dollar–sterling market was undertaken by the Bank of England, in the dollar–DM market by the Bundesbank, and so on. The US authorities sometimes undertook transactions with other countries' Central Banks (for example gold sales or currency swaps) to relieve them of the exchange risk on dollars acquired in *their* market transactions, but only very exceptionally did the US undertake official transactions with dealers in the market, so as to influence market rates.

Second, the role of the US currency, the dollar, was unique in that it was used by the other countries in the dollar system as, *de facto*, the standard of value in which they fixed the par value of their currencies and as the 'intervention currency' used by their Central Banks for exchanging against their own currency in their market transactions. Moreover the adoption of the dollar as the intervention currency by a Central Bank meant that it needed a stock-in-trade of dollars on which it would draw when it was supporting the home currency in the market and to which it would add when it was capping a rise of the home currency in the market: hence the widespread use of the US dollar as a reserve asset. It was not the *only* reserve asset held in official reserves, since Central Banks do not like to keep all their eggs in one basket, and in particular like to hold reserves of gold as well as of foreign exchange, as shown in Table 18.1. (Of course the US authorities, whose responsibility it was to maintain the official convertibility of the dollar into *gold*, held their reserves almost exclusively in gold, not in foreign exchange.)

The fact that official intervention in the foreign exchange market was undertaken not by the United States but by the other countries' Central Banks, using the US dollar as their intervention currency, meant that when the US dollar was weak in the market, the resulting market purchases of dollars by other countries' Central Banks increased the world total of official dollar reserves; and conversely when the dollar was strong. (In contrast, when the non-official[1] demand for dollars balanced the non-official supply, a weakness of one currency in relation to another would simply redistribute dollar reserves. Thus if sterling were weak in relation to the DM, the Bank of England would be selling dollars from UK official reserves while the Bundesbank would be buying dollars for German official reserves.)

We have now the key to an underlying paradox in the Bretton Woods system. On the one hand a steady growth of reserves, which the United States' trading partners had as their objective, required that they should be constantly buying dollars in the market, which would occur only if the dollar remained constantly weak; on the other hand, it is hardly a recommendation of a reserve currency that it should be constantly weak! Up to 1957 the dollar was not weak enough to provide for adequate reserve growth, but from 1958 to the mid-1960s it became decidedly weak, as it did again (and to a much greater degree) in the early 1970s (see Table 18.2). In consequence, countries got in the 1960s the reserve growth they wanted, and rather more than they wanted thereafter, but only by virtue of a progressive deterioration of the gold 'cover' for the US liabilities held by other countries' Central Banks, as is apparent from Table 18.1. Even before the end of the 1960s the regime was perceived not to be viable, in the long run, without major modification. Such a modification was indeed embarked upon in the late 1960s, when it was widely expected (quite contrary to what turned out to be the case) that the dollar's weakness was coming to an end. It was in 1968 decided, after protracted international negotiations, that the future growth of official reserves should henceforth be assured by the creation by the IMF of a new international reserve medium, Special Drawing Rights (SDRs); and in 1969 the IMF's Articles of Agreement

---

[1] 'Non-official' here means 'by transactors other than Central Banks'.

TABLE 18.1. *Total International Reserves, at End of Selected Years*
($ billion)

	1949	1958	1969	1972	1974	1980
Gold reserves*						
US	25	21	12	10	51	160
Other countries	8	17	27	29	139	420
Total ($bn)	33	38	39	39	190	580
Total as % of year's world imports	*55*	*38*	*15*	*10*	*24*	*30*
Non-metallic reserves						
US liabilities	3	10	16	62	77	157
Other	10	10	24	59	99	257
Total ($bn)	13	20	40	121	176	414
Total as % of year's world imports	*22*	*20*	*16*	*31*	*22*	*22*

* Gold is valued at its official price of $35 an ounce in 1947, 1958, and 1969 and of $38 in 1972; in 1974 and 1980, following the Martinique Agreement (see p. 560), it is valued at market price.

Sources: Triffin [15], p. 260; IMF, *Annual Report, 1976* and subsequent years; IMF, *International Financial Statistics Yearbook, 1979* and *1982*.

TABLE 18.2. *Reserve Transactions in US Dollars by US and Foreign Monetary Authorities*

(The sign + indicates 'tending to support the US dollar'; the sign − would indicate the unwinding of such support.)

	Annual averages ($ billion)
1950–7	+ 1
1958–64	+ 2½
1965–9	+ 0
1970–2	+ 17
1973–4	+ 7*
1975–6	+ 10½*
1977–8	+ 35½

* These amounts largely represent increases in OPEC's dollar holdings in the US, which in these years were being acquired as investments, rather than for the purpose of exchange rate management.

Source: Federal Reserve bank of New York, *Quarterly Review* (Summer 1980), p. 24.

were amended to permit the IMF to issue SDRs to its members.[2] Small issues were in fact made at the beginning of 1970, 1971, and 1972, but thereafter issues were discontinued until January 1979, since the continuing weakness of the dollar (disappointing earlier expectations) ensured an adequate (indeed, more than adequate[3]) growth in world reserves, without the issuance of more SDRs.

18.2.3. Problems of Financing

Official convertibility, as provided for under the Bretton Woods regime of the 1960s, implied that exchange rates were (by official market transactions) held close to official parities which were fixed through a procedure under Article IV of the Bretton Woods Agreement, but could be adjusted with the IMF's consent to deal with a 'fundamental disequilibrium'. Since exchange rates were fixed in this way, the immediate symptom of a *weak* currency was not that it suffered a marked fall in its market value but that it was getting official support in the market. Likewise, the immediate symptom of a *strong* currency was that it was coming on to the market through official transactions.

The financing of the official market transactions presented no very serious problem in the case of a currency which was only temporarily weak or temporarily strong, but difficulties arose, and became progressively more serious, when a currency was persistently weak (as were the US dollar and sterling) or persistently strong (as were the Swiss franc, the DM, and the yen). The nature of these difficulties will perhaps be immediately apparent from Table 18.3, but can be described in greater detail.

First, the authorities responsible for a persistently *strong* currency would find themselves persistently buying US dollars in the market with their own national currency, say the DM. This was embarrassing to them on two grounds: the currency they were buying (the dollar) was a weak one, and hence in any future adjustment of parities could prove to be a depreciating asset; and 'any country taking in foreign exchange in order to keep its exchange rate stable creates, in this process, additional high-powered money (Central Bank money). In the years of the immense dollar outflows from the US, i.e. from 1970 to 1973, this was largely responsible for the huge increases in the money stock of the industrial countries outside the United States'.[4]

Second, the authorities responsible for a persistently *weak* currency other

---

[2] SDRs are in effect a paper currency issued by the IMF and distributed to IMF members in proportion to their 'quotas' (which roughly reflect their relative importance in the world economy). An IMF member country which asserts its need to finance a balance of payments deficit is entitled to use its SDRs to obtain national currencies from other members, though prior to 1981 SDR balances had to be partially reconstituted following large and prolonged use.

[3] See Table 18.1 and section 18.3.5.

[4] From an address by Dr Emminger, then of the Bundesbank, to the European-Atlantic Group, London, 19 February 1976. If, in order to keep the DM–dollar exchange rate stable, the Bundesbank buys dollars in the market, it will pay for them by a cheque for (say) a million DM drawn on itself which the seller of the dollars will pay into his account at one of the German commercial banks. Thereby the commercial bank's deposit liabilities (counted as a component in the German money stock) will increase by a million DM, while on the assets side of its balance sheet its own deposit at the Bundesbank ('Central Bank money') will increase by a like amount.

TABLE 18.3. *Treatment of Disequilibria under the Bretton Woods Regime*

Policy options open to monetary authorities	Strong currency	Weak currency
	(Exchange rate would rise above parity in the absence of official sales in the market.)	(Exchange rate would fall below parity in the absence of official purchases in the market.)
1. Go on intervening in the foreign exchange market. (Intervention was done by the countries pegging on the dollar.)	(a) If the *dollar* was strong, its rise in the market was checked by the dollar sales of the weak-currency countries. (b) If any other currency was strong, its rise in the market was checked by dollar purchases by the country concerned.	(a) If the *dollar* was weak, it was supported in the market by the strong-currency countries. (b) If any other currency was weak, it was supported by the country concerned.
2. Adjustment via fiscal and/or monetary policy.	*Expansion*, e.g. tax cuts, lower interest rates.	*Deflation*, e.g. a tough budget, higher interest rates.
3. Adjustment via change of parity.	*Revaluation* (as with the DM in 1969).	*Devaluation* (as with the £ in 1967).
4. Exchange control or equivalent regulations.	Controls on capital inflows.	Controls on capital outflows.

than the dollar (say the pound sterling) faced the problem of the steady depletion of their reserves. The day of reckoning could be postponed by borrowing dollars from other Central Banks and by drawings on the IMF's General Account,[5] as the UK did from time to time (on an especially large scale as from 1964), but the time would eventually arrive when a further rescue operation could not be arranged on acceptable terms (as happened with the UK in November 1967, thereby forcing an adjustment of the sterling exchange rate).

Third, when the US dollar itself was weak, market support was given not by the US authorities but by the Central Banks of the strong-currency countries, whose unfavourable reactions have already been explained. The worry of the US authorities in these circumstances was the knowledge that the ultimate recourse of a foreign Central Bank embarrassed with an excessive stock of 'weak' dollars was to exercise its right of conversion into gold at the Federal Reserve Bank of New York; and that a persistently weak dollar meant that the US gold reserve became progressively smaller in relation to US liabilities to foreign Central Banks. (As Table 18.1 shows, such liabilities were at end-1958 covered twice over, but at end-1969 they were less than fully covered, and thereafter the coverage deteriorated still further.) Hence the US authorities came to fear a 'run' on the US gold reserve. The danger could be temporarily alleviated by official currency swaps and suchlike inter-Central Bank transactions, which in effect gave forward cover on part of the dollars held in foreign official reserves, but as time went by US anxiety steadily mounted, especially when the dollar weakened even further in the early 1970s, and ultimately provoked President Nixon, on 15 August 1971, to suspend the official convertibility of the dollar into gold.

18.2.4. Problems of Adjustment

The problems of financing could be avoided only by the adoption of measures of adjustment, that is, of measures which would tend to make the weak currency stronger and/or the strong currency weaker. Such measures (shown in tabular form in Table 18.3) were, however, far from being foolproof and painless, and were usually distinctly unattractive from a political standpoint.

The easiest corrective measure to take was the imposition of exchange control or equivalent restrictions on capital flows: on outflows in the case of countries with weak currencies and on inflows in the case of countries with strong currencies. Both kinds of restriction were imposed from time to time [8] but only the UK imposed them (on outflows, in this case) throughout the

[5] The IMF was set up by the Bretton Woods Agreement, and one of the responsibilities of it executive board, assisted by its permanent staff, is to give effect to the rules of behaviour as to exchange rates etc. accepted by the member countries on signing the Articles of Agreement. In addition, however, the IMF is a financial intermediary, affording financial assistance to member countries in balance of payments difficulties. In the original Articles (modified in the First Amendment by the creation of a Special Drawing Account) the financial activities of the IMF were all embraced in its General Account. This comprises a 'kitty' constituted by members subscriptions, augmented if needs be by borrowing, on which members in balance of payment difficulties may draw, to finance support for their currencies in the foreign exchange market, on terms and conditions laid down in the Articles and by decisions of the executive board.

uration of the Bretton Woods regime. In general, the developed countries laced little reliance on these devices, mainly because they could be evaded on scale which greatly limited their efficacy.

A much more efficacious measure for achieving adjustment would have been change in the setting of monetary and/or fiscal policy—a deflationary change 1 the case of a weak-currency country and an expansionary change in the case f a strong-currency country. However, governments had an understandable reference for setting the stance of their monetary and fiscal policies so as to chieve what they (or their electorates) considered to be optimal for the effect n the level of demand in the home economy rather than for the effect on the reign exchange market. Admittedly, weak-currency countries, such as the JK, were from time to time prepared to adopt a package of deflationary measures in support of the external value of their currency, but only *in extremis*. trong-currency countries, such as Germany, Switzerland, or Japan, were even ss willing to adopt expansionary measures, except when these were anyway eeded for other reasons, such as to counter a business recession or excessive nemployment.

Lastly, as shown in Table 18.3, there remained the option of seeking djustment by a change in exchange rates, but this remedy was adopted only elatedly and with the utmost reluctance, and for four reasons.

(i) The one-at-a-time procedure for adjusting parities under the Bretton Voods system was a deterrent to adjustment in that any one country was eluctant to take the initiative of repegging its curency, since it could never be ure how much the burden of adjustment might be shared by other countries hanging their pegs soon afterwards. (This procedural weakness was remedied n December 1971, when at the Smithsonian conference a multilateral enegotiation of parities was successfully achieved: see p. 561.) The extreme ase of this procedural weakness was the seeming inability of the United States o take an initiative at all, as explained earlier.

(ii) Even more important was the political obstacle to a change in rates, ttributed by Oort [11] to 'the political asymmetry between positive action nd non-action':

iovernments are rarely criticised for not changing the par value, and when they are, it is asy to silence such criticism by appealing to the national interest that forbids open ebate on such sensitive issues. A change of the par value, on the other hand, is a onscious, overt policy action that is unavoidably accompanied by all the trappings of a najor public decision: comments in the press, complaints from groups that are injured, vindfall profits and losses by 'speculators' and traders, book gains or losses for the entral bank or the Treasury, parliamentary debates, international repercussions, etc., tc. Behind all this commotion are the very real facts that a parity change does hurt ertain sectoral interests, particularly in the case of revaluation, and that a devaluation dds to cost-push inflation at home. Left to themselves, governments will continue to ake delayed, discontinuous action on parities.

(iii) The emergence of large and effectively integrated capital markets n conditions of currency convertibility created a huge and progressively ncreasing pool of liquid funds which may be switched between currencies for precautionary or speculative reasons.[6] Such switching is undertaken mainly by bankers and corporate treasurers in the hope of increasing the chance of capital gain or reducing that of capital loss: however, such operators have increasingly been prepared to take uncovered positions or make use of borrowed funds. Moreover, companies engaged in international trade may pursue the same aims not by a redeployment of liquid funds, but simply by a variation in the leads and lags in ordinary commercial payments. For example, a British importer can speculate against sterling by paying his foreign suppliers more promptly, a British exporter by giving his customers extended credit, and such practices are virtually immune to restraint by exchange control. How were these various kinds of transactions to be discouraged? In the course of the 1960s statesmen and officials came to believe that completely invariable pegged rates were the only effective device for preventing them. In a regime of pegged rates, as prescribed by the Bretton Woods Agreement, any change in parities leads to the expectation that further changes can occur in the future, and since there is never much doubt about the *direction* of a possible parity change, speculation is virtually risk-free. Hence the official dealers in the Central Banks of the major powers always feared the speculative consequences of any change in parities, or indeed of any official admission that such a change could ever be contemplated.

(iv) A more specifically *economic* reason for the unpopularity of exchange rate changes lies in the long time interval between administering the medicine and the recovery of the patient—a time interval which may include an initial period in which (due to the so-called *J*-curve phenomenon) the patient's condition deteriorates even further, before it begins to improve. The *J*-curve phenomenon takes its name from the disappointing behaviour of the UK trade balance following the devaluation of sterling by one-seventh (from \$2·80 to \$2·40) in November 1967: after the devaluation the course of the graph of the monthly trade balance was initially *downwards*, followed by a recovery which, however, did not come up to expectations until 1969 or even 1970. Why this long delay?

First, British manufacturers may have been initially slow in reducing the dollar price of their exports, and foreign manufacturers likewise slow in raising their sterling prices in the British market. This would mean that though exporting became more profitable and importing less profitable, so that *sellers* would have an incentive to export more and import less, they would be faced with no corresponding reaction on the part of *buyers*, who would have no price incentive to switch their purchases to British-made goods.

Second, even after export and import prices had been adjusted to reflect the devaluation of sterling, buyers did not quickly switch to British-made goods. The purchaser of almost any kind of manufactured article tends to be loyal to the brand, or the design, or the producing firm with which he is already familiar, and in consequence he is not readily induced (even by skilful marketing) to transfer his allegiance quickly to another source of supply following a change in relative prices. Let us suppose, by way of illustration, that the devaluation in 1967 by one-seventh led to a change in relative prices in a

[6] See [5], p. 25.

ther smaller proportion, say by 10 per cent. Then suppose that purchasers' itial response to the relative cheapening of British-made goods was for foreign rchasers to increase the quantity of British goods they bought by only 4 per nt, and for British purchasers to reduce by only 4 per cent the quantity of ported goods they bought: then UK exports would earn $6\frac{1}{2}$ per cent *less* in eign exchange[7] and this fall would probably be less than fully offset by the nultaneous 4 per cent fall in the UK's dollar expenditure on imports: hence e UK trade balance would initially deteriorate. Improvement in the balance uld occur only as purchasers, with the passage of time, became more sponsive to the price advantage of switching to a British source of supply, ovided, of course, that British sources of supply could also respond! For in actice there appear to have been supply bottlenecks which took some time to ar.

.3. The Collapse of Official Convertibility

3.1. The Chronology of Events

ie chronology of the main events in the early 1970s is set out in Table 18.4 lowing.

TABLE 18.4. *Chronology of Events in the Early 1970s*

1970	June	Canadian dollar unpegged from the US dollar.
1971	15 August	President Nixon's speech: suspension of convertibility of the US dollar into gold.
	18 December	Smithsonian Agreement. The Group of Ten agree on a revision of exchange rates and an increase from $35 to $38 in the official price of gold.
1972	March	The six original EEC members establish the 'snake' scheme for keeping their exchange rates in line.
	May	The new EEC members (UK, Eire, and Denmark) join the snake.
	June	Sterling unpegged from the dollar. UK, Eire, and Denmark defect from the snake.
	July	The IMF decides to set up the Committee of Twenty to report on the reform of the international monetary system.
	October	Denmark rejoins the snake.
1973	January	Swiss franc unpegged from the dollar.
	February	Lira and yen unpegged from the dollar and Italy defects from the snake. At a meeting in Paris on 12 February, the official price of gold raised from $38 to $42·2 and the dollar parities of the remaining pegged currencies revised upwards so as to keep their gold values unchanged.

[7] As the result of the devaluation, UK export prices (in dollars) fall in the ratio of 100 down to 90, ile the UK's export volume increases in the ratio of 100 up to 104. Hence UK export earnings (in llars) change in the ratio of 100×100 down to 90×104; that is, from 100 down to 93·6.

TABLE 18.4.—cont.

March		Two meetings in Paris, on the 9 and 16 March, of fourteen industrial countries (the nine EEC members plus the US, Canada, Japan, Switzerland, and Sweden) fail to agree on a further revision of dollar parities and opt for floating instead. The snake members thenceforth float jointly, the others individually, against the US dollar.
October		OPEC's first hike in oil prices.
1974	**June**	Publication of the Committee of Twenty's *Outline of Reform*.
16 December		French and US Presidents meet at Martinique and agree that Central Banks may value their official gold reserves at market price, instead of at $42·2 an ounce.

18.3.2. The Demise of Dollar Convertibility

Though, as we have seen, the Bretton Woods regime had many weaknesses, th proximate cause of its downfall was the reluctant shift of US official opinio▶ towards the conclusion that, despite all the problems associated with a▶ exchange rate adjustment, the persistent weakness of the dollar was incurabl unless such an adjustment could be forced on the United States' tradin▶ partners. Until the time of the devaluation of sterling in November 1967, th▶ United States had argued against all exchange rate changes, including an▶ change in sterling's parity, but in the event the international monetary syster survived sterling's depreciation, and thereafter the view gained ground in th▶ United States that what was needed to alleviate the plight of the dollar was general appreciation of other currencies, and especially of the DM and ye▶ above their then parities with the dollar. However, under the Bretton Woo◀ procedure it was the United States' partners that had to take the initiative, ◀ that all the United States could do was to exercise persuasion. But though son▶ other countries did take the required initiative, they acted so belatedly an▶ inadequately as to arouse in 1971, to quote one authority,

... increasing apprehension of a loss of United States competitive strength in wor▶ markets. As the weekly figures of dollar reserve gains abroad confirmed the generaliz◀ weakness of the dollar and the prospect that the United States deficit was rising w◀ above the abnormally high level of 1970, overt speculation began to appear in t▶ exchange markets in March, further swelling the torrent of dollars flowing to forei▶ markets. ... On Sunday, August 15, President Nixon announced a major new progra▶ of domestic and international economy measures ... With respect to internation▶ payments, the President introduced a 10 per cent temporary surcharge on dutiab▶ imports into the United States, and announced a temporary suspension of convertibili▶ of the dollar into gold and other assets [3].

The purpose of this drastic step was to force other countries to unpeg th◀ currencies from the dollar, and in this it was successful. Whether they were th◀ repegged at higher parities in relation to the dollar (as in fact happened December 1971) or whether they continued to float, was for the United Stat▶

this stage a matter of secondary importance which could be discussed in due
ie, after its partners had accepted the inevitability of a substantial
preciation of the dollar value of their currencies. In the US view, foreign
tesmen and officials could be made to give up the defence of their existing
gs only if the dollars they would thereby acquire were made inconvertible
o gold and so less desirable to hold. Hence the US decision to suspend
nvertibility for a 'temporary', but all the same indefinite, period. In any case
e US decision announced on 15 August 1971 would very soon have been
posed by the pressure of events, since the growing lack of confidence in the
llar would soon have produced a run on the US gold reserve on a scale such as
uld have quickly led to its exhaustion. So the suspension of dollar
nvertibility was inevitable in the absence of a major appreciation of other
rrencies, which in turn was not negotiable so long as the dollar remained
nvertible: this was the impasse from which President Nixon hoped to
ricate his country in his speech of 15 August, and he succeeded, though only
er four months of bitter negotiations in the forum of the Group of Ten.[8]
The deal was concluded in the Smithsonian building in Washington, on
December. In return for the ending of the 10 per cent surcharge imposed by
esident Nixon on 15 August, the other members of G-10 agreed to repeg on
e dollar at target rates ('central rates', as they were now to be called) which
ounted to a substantial depreciation of the dollar, though a smaller one than
e United States had wanted. In addition to these changes in target rates,
gging was henceforth to be less precise than under the Bretton Woods
angements, the previous limit of 1 per cent each side of parity being now
placed by one of $2\frac{1}{4}$ per cent each side of the central rate. Another ingredient
the Smithsonian package was an increase in the official price of gold from
5 to $38 an ounce. This change was without operational significance in that
e dollar was no longer officially convertible into gold, but for European
ntral Banks it had the advantage of maintaining the value of their reserve
ets, in terms of their local currency.
After the Smithsonian Agreement, the US dollar retained its role as
tervention currency and reserve medium, even though no longer convertible
to gold. Thus the post-Smithsonian regime may be described as a dollar
andard, under which the other currencies of the dollar system were officially
nvertible into the dollar, without the dollar being itself officially convertible
to any other reserve asset.
To an optimist it may well have seemed reasonable to hope at the end of 1971
at the world would peacefully settle down to an improved version of the
onetary regime of the 1960s—the improvement being that a technique had
w been found to repeg exchange rates by multilateral agreement, and
ereby to escape from the difficulty that the special role of the dollar deprived
e US authorities of the ability to devalue. However, as we shall see, things did
t in fact go so smoothly for the dollar standard; even in 1971 there were signs
at many statesmen and officials were wanting something different. Two

[8] The Group of Ten, alias G-10, comprises the US, Canada, Japan, the UK, France, Germany,
ly, Belgium, the Netherlands, and Sweden, with Switzerland as an associate member.

initiatives in this sense were particularly important: *first*, the EEC 'snake', and *second*, the 'Grand Design' worked out by Jeremy Morse and his fellow members of the Committee of Twenty (see section 18.3.4).

18.3.3. The Snake in the Tunnel

The Bretton Woods pegging arrangements, as they operated up to August 1971, required each country other than the United States to keep the market value of its currency within a 'tunnel', the ceiling of which was 1 per cent above its dollar parity and the floor 1 per cent below. The Smithsonian conference of December 1971 enlarged the tunnel to $2\frac{1}{4}$ per cent above and below the dollar parity (or central value, as it was now termed). Hence a European country's currency could fluctuate (from ceiling to floor, or vice versa) by $4\frac{1}{2}$ per cent in relation to the dollar. But if one European currency rose from floor to ceiling while another fell from ceiling to floor, their relative fluctuation would be 9 per cent. Such a large fluctuation as between two European currencies was repugnant to the EEC's aspiration to move by successive stages to eventual European monetary union, as mapped out in the Werner Report of October 1970. In this report, EEC Central Banks had been 'invited, from the beginning of the first stage [that is, as from January 1971] to restrict on an experimental basis the fluctuation of rates between Community currencies within narrower bands than those resulting from the application of the margins in force in relation to the dollar.'

In the light of the Werner Plan, the essentials of which were adopted by the Community's Council of Ministers in February 1971, the widening of the 'tunnel' accepted by G-10 at the Smithsonian conference was naturally seen as a step backwards, and as a challenge to EEC members to inaugurate specifically EEC arrangements for keeping fluctuations as between member countries' currencies within narrower limits. This was the purpose of the 'snake in the tunnel'. The dollar value of the member countries' currencies would be kept within the wide tunnel provided for in the Smithsonian Agreement, and supervised by the IMF; at the same time they would have their *relative* movements confined within a narrower EEC snake.

The essential characteristic of the snake scheme is that whenever the percentage by which the strongest currency's market value exceeds its par value *plus* that by which the weakest currency's market value falls short of its par value (all values being in terms of a common *numéraire*) together reach $2\frac{1}{2}$ per cent (half the amount permitted by the Smithsonian tunnel) then someone buys the weakest currency with the strongest. The 'someone' may be either the weak-currency country (debtor intervention) or the strong-currency country (creditor intervention) or both together. With creditor intervention, the intervening country buys the weak currency in the exchange market with its *own* currency, which it can make available as required; hence the only problem which arises is what to do with the weak currency which has been purchased. With debtor intervention, the intervening country has first to borrow from its partner the strong currency needed for purchasing its own weak currency in the market; hence the need for the so-called 'very short term' credit facility which was incorporated in the EEC scheme.

Whether the intervention is by the creditor or by the debtor country, a ttlement arrangement is needed by which periodically (monthly, in the EEC heme) the creditor countries can exchange their accumulation of weak rrency for a more acceptable reserve asset, and at the same time obtain ·payment of their 'very short term' credits, likewise in terms of an acceptable ·serve asset. The snake scheme provided that the monthly settlements should ǝ effected by the transfer by the debtors to the creditors of a mixed bag of ·serve assets selected on an agreed formula, which in practice usually ensured ₁at most of the settlement was in US dollars.[9]

The Community snake came into operation for the original six members in ₄arch 1972. The new members (the UK, Denmark, and Eire) joined the snake ₄ May 1972 but defected in June, when sterling was floated; Denmark rejoined ₄ October 1972, but the UK and Eire remained outside the scheme. Italy ft the snake in the February 1973 crisis (see section 18.3.5); France ft in January 1974, rejoined in July 1975, but left again in March 1976. On ₄e other hand, two non-EEC countries joined: Norway in May 1972 and ₄weden from March 1973 to August 1977. On the eve of the establishment of ₄e European Monetary System (EMS) in 1979 the snake membership ₄mprised Germany, Benelux, Denmark, and Norway. The EMS arrange- ₄ents retained the snake in a slightly modified form, with a membership ₄mprising all the then members of the EEC except for the UK, which has been ₄t of the snake continuously since June 1972.

.3.4. The Grand Design

here began in 1971 an ambitious initiative, or 'Grand Design', to replace the ₄etton Woods Agreement by a new charter which would explicitly displace ₄e US dollar in its twin roles of intervention currency and reserve currency. ₄ollar intervention would be replaced by multi-currency intervention, as in ₄e snake arrangements, and national currencies (in particular the dollar) ₄ould be replaced as reserve assets by SDRs issued by the IMF. The proposal r such a grand design was launched by Anthony Barber, then the British ₄hancellor of the Exchequer, at the IMF annual meeting in September 1971.

Initially Mr Barber's initiative was not very enthusiastically received, but in ₄ly 1972 the IMF governors decided to pursue the matter be setting up a ₄mmittee, the so-called Committee of Twenty (C-20), comprising ministers ₄om each of the twenty countries whose nationals were at that time members of ₄e IMF executive board. They also set up a similarly constituted committee at ₄puty level, of which the UK member, Jeremy Morse, was appointed ₄airman. His view, in June 1974, of what then happened was, in his own ₄ords [9]:

₄e set out in September 1972 . . . to build, as at Bretton Woods, a complete design for an ternational monetary system that would last for twenty-five years. This effort was ₄visaged to take about two years: in the first year, the establishment and resolution of

---

[9] Intervention under the procedure just described was mandatory when a currency rose or fell to ₄e limits permitted by the snake, but member countries had the option, frequently exercised, to ₄ervene before the limit was reached; in this case the intervention in practice took the form of a ₄arket transaction in US dollars.

the main issues; in the second year, the working out of detail and—about now—the translation of it all into legal form by way of amendments to the Articles of Agreement of the Fund. The first big wave to hit us was the double-headed exchange crisis of February/March 1973.

(This crisis, involving the transition from pegging to floating, is the subject of section 18.3.5.) 'Then', Morse said, 'the second and more unexpected wave, hit us—the towering rise in oil prices' (the subject of section 18.4.2.) Morse continued:

The C-20 meeting in January 1974, in Rome, changed tack. Recognizing that the return to par values and all that goes with it was likely to be delayed, they decided to switch to a more evolutionary process of reform, and to concentrate on those aspects that were most relevant to the present situation. So, since then, the Deputies have been collecting their work on the reformed system, principles and details, into a final version of the Outline which still leaves some issues open for later decision, and have also been preparing a package of immediate steps to deal with current problems.

So the Grand Design was duly published [7], though with many controversial issues still unresolved; then it was shelved indefinitely in favour of an alternative programme of comparatively modest 'evolutionary' reforms.

18.3.5. The Crisis of February/March 1973

Let us now consider the first of the 'big waves' which undermined the feasibility of the Grand Design—the exchange crisis in the first quarter of 1973. Though, as suggested earlier, an optimist might in December 1971 have supposed the new 'dollar standard' then inaugurated to be a viable regime, any such optimism proved to be unfounded: the regime collapsed in February/March 1973. What seems to have happened is that the knowledge that the dollar had been devalued, and could presumably be devalued again at any time by the Smithsonian procedure, led to a lack of confidence in the future stability of the Smithsonian central values. There was also the knowledge that these central values were the outcome of hard bargaining between the United States and it fellow members of G-10, in which the US had maintained that larger change would be needed to curb the dollar's weakness. It was known too that some influential Americans felt no commitment to central values of any kind and were perfectly ready for a transition to floating. As regards the other G-10 countries, it was known that those Central Banks which were the legal owners of their country's reserves[10] were liable to legal and political embarrassment if they made book losses on the local-currency value of their dollar holdings, and hence were increasingly reluctant to accumulate stocks of what might prove to be a depreciating asset. Even more important, it was known that the Central Banks of both Germany and Japan, in pegging at the Smithsonian central values, were accumulating reserves at a pace which they could clearly not tolerate much longer if they were to retain any control over the liquidity of their commercial banks.

The mounting dollar flood breached the dykes on 10 February 1973 when

[10] Most countries' official reserves are in fact owned by the Central Bank. The UK and the United States are the important exceptions.

e Japanese authorities suspended their market support for the dollar. The
isis was resolved, like that of 1971, by a multilateral negotiation on
2 February of new central values for the main currencies, though the lira and
e yen were left floating, along with the Canadian dollar (which had been
oating since June 1970), the UK and Irish pounds (since June 1972), and the
wiss franc (since January 1973). The revised pegs agreed on 12 February
chieved a general appreciation in relation to the dollar by repeating the
mithsonian gimmick of raising the official dollar price of gold, this time from
38 to $42·2 an ounce, while leaving unchanged the gold value of other
currencies.

Alas, the dollar flood still continued, and a further crisis broke in March
973. Its outcome was crucial to the evolution of the monetary system, since it
arked the discontinuance of pegging on the dollar by the major industrial
countries. This time the forum for resolving the crisis comprised the Group of
'en, including the associate member Switzerland, plus the three smaller EEC
countries: Denmark, Luxembourg, and Eire. Of these fourteen countries, the
EC countries in the snake (France, Germany, Benelux, and Denmark) agreed
to proceed with a joint float, in which they were joined by their snake partners,
weden and Norway. The UK, Italy, Canada, Japan, and Switzerland
continued to float individually, while Eire pegged on sterling. None of these
countries any longer pegged on the US dollar: thus for the fourteen countries
concerned this was the end of their experiment with the dollar standard. As
regards the other 100 or so members of the IMF, they followed a variety of
ractices. A few, mainly small countries, continued for a while with the old
terling Area practice of pegging on sterling. Many continued to peg on the
ollar. Several pegged on synthetic monetary units, comprising 'baskets' of a
umber of major currencies in fixed proportions.

8.4. The Floating Rate Regime

8.4.1. The Dollar Strengthens

'hough there had from the end of the 1960s been a growing body of influential
pinion, in the United States and to a lesser extent in the UK, which
aintained that floating was in principle better than pegging, and hence
elcomed the course of events in the first quarter of 1973, many statesmen and
fficials responsible for international monetary affairs in the G-10 countries
iewed with misgivings a system in which none of the major national currencies
as officially convertible either into gold or into dollars. If currencies were
ermitted to float freely, without any official market transactions, the day-to-
ay fluctuations in market rates would be too violent for bankers and traders to
arry on their normal business. If, on the other hand, currencies were managed
y official market intervention, countries might intervene at cross purposes;
oreover with floating rates the Bretton Woods rules of good behaviour,
esigned to prevent beggar-my-neighbour remedies for unemployment, would
o longer be applicable, since they presupposed pegged rates; hence one must

expect rounds of competitive exchange depreciation, such as had occurred in the 1930s.[11]

However, even in the course of 1973 floating was seen to be working better than had been expected. The event which began to build up confidence in the floating regime and led more and more statesmen and officials to regard it as viable for an indefinite period, and not just as a temporary expedient, was the realization that the dollar could rise, as well as fall, in the market. The US balance on current account improved dramatically in the second half of 1973. The medicine of exchange depreciation was at last working: the combined effect of the exchange rate adjustments at the Smithsonian conference and again in February 1973, together with the depreciation of the dollar under the floating regime, had by July 1973 reduced the dollar's value in terms of a weighted average of other major currencies by about 20 per cent as compared with mid-1970, and US prices of manufactures were getting distinctly more competitive. In addition there occurred in 1973 a rise in the prices of many primary products of which the United States is a net exporter, and this too helped the trade balance.

18.4.2. Oil Prices and the Dollar

Then later in 1973 came the OPEC decision to jack up the price of oil, which in two ways served to make the earlier build-up of dollar reserves now seem more of a blessing than a burden. In the first place it contributed to the rapid rise in commodity prices, which meant that the great increase in world non-metallic reserves as beween end-1969 and the spring of 1973, predominantly in the form of US liabilities, was soon overtaken by an even more rapid rise in the dollar value of world imports, as shown in Table 18.1.

In the second place, the oil-exporting countries (mainly members of OPEC did not increase their imports in line with the increase in the value of their exports. The oil exporters' balance of payments on current account was no less than $68 billion in 1974 and $32 billion in 1975 (see Table 18.5). These vast surpluses had to be settled in the first instance in dollars and sterling, predominantly the former, and were thereupon heavily invested in dollar denominated assets. Hence in most oil-importing countries there arose an enormous demand for dollars to pay for their oil. Oil-importing countries with

---

[11] A beggar-my-neighbour remedy for unemployment is one which, like a higher tariff on imports, is intended to divert demand from foreign to domestic sources of supply, and hence to induce greater employment at home at the expense of diminished employment in other countries. Such remedies were widely adopted in the Depression of the 1930s, but post-war were in abeyance until the onset of world depression in the 1980s. In the 1930s various beggar-my-neighbour devices were adopted in addition to tariffs: one such was the management of the exchange rate so as to give home-produced goods a competitive advantage over foreign goods, in circumstances when such exchange depreciation could not be defended as a necessary adjustment to deal with a weak currency.

The Bretton Woods Agreement was intended to guard against any reversion to the antisocial practices of the 1930s by prescribing fixed exchange rates, which could be devalued only with the approval of the IMF executive directors, who would withhold consent unless satisfied that the devaluation was needed to adjust a 'fundamental disequilibrium' in the balance of payments of the country intending to devalue.

TABLE 18.5. *Payments Balances on Current Account, 1973–1982*
($ billion)

	1973	1974	1975	1976	1977	1978	1979	1980	1981	1982
OECD members	−13	−23	5	−15	−22	12	−28	−70	−30	−31
Oil-exporting countries	6	68	32	40	25	4	60	109	59	4
Other developing countries	−6	−25	−32	−19	−13	−26	−41	−66	−81	−67

Source: *Bank of England Quarterly Bulletin* (1983).

large dollar reserves drew them down: those less well provided borrowed heavily, especially from private sector banks, as will be explained in section 18.4.5.

18.4.3. Policy Options

Whereas under Bretton Woods the symptom of weakness or strength of currencies had been official transactions undertaken in the foreign exchange market, the corresponding symptom under a floating rate regime is a rise or fall in market rates. Hence the policy decisions which now had to be taken, though they involved much the same range of options as under Bretton Woods (as may be seen by comparing Table 18.6 with Table 18.3), were now forced on the attention of officials and statesmen in a somewhat different form. Essentially, when they found their currency rising or falling in the market, they had to decide: 'Shall we just let it rise or fall [a policy which came to be called "benign neglect"] or shall we resist the change [a policy of "leaning against the wind"]?'[12] If they opted for the latter they still had to decide:

(i) on what occasions to lean against the wind, on what scale, and how persistently, in the face of persistent market pressure;
(ii) what instruments of policy to use, the main ones available being the same as under Bretton Woods, namely (a) official transactions in the foreign exchange market, and (b) fiscal and monetary policy, most especially interest rate policy.

The unfortunate statesmen and officials concerned quickly learned that the policy dilemmas which now faced them were much the same, and certainly no less acute, than those which had beset them under Bretton Woods. How in fact did they exercise their options?

There was in the United States a powerful school of academic thought, led by Professor Milton Friedman, which commended the virtues of benign neglect in an extreme form, with 'clean' floating (i.e. no official transactions at all in the foreign exchange market) and a monetary policy geared exclusively to the achievement of a prescribed steady rate of growth of the money stock. Friedman's extreme views were, however, countered by arguments which had a familiar ring to the statesmen and officials who had operated the Bretton Woods system in the 1960s.

First, Dr Oort's [11] political analysis (see p. 557) still remained valid. A rise in the exchange rate reduces the international competitiveness of home industries and hence antagonizes the workers and employers who are adversely affected; a fall in the exchange rate provokes a rise in the cost of living and may thereby lose the housewife's vote; hence the practising politician likes to let sleeping dogs lie, in the sense of holding the exchange rate *de facto* stable, even in the absence of any official commitment to peg it.

---

[12] There was in principle a third option, which was, however, in practice virtually never exercised: that of 'forcing the rate'; that is, of intervening to *accentuate* a change that was already occurring in the market.

TABLE 18.6. *Policy Options under the Floating Rate Regime, Post-1973*

Policy options open to monetary authorities	Strong currency	Weak currency
LEANING AGAINST THE WIND Intervention in the foreign exchange market.	(a) If the *dollar* is strong, its rise in the market may be checked by dollar sales by the weak-currency countries; sometimes also by DM purchases by the US. (b) If any other currency is strong, its rise in the market may be checked by dollar purchases by the country concerned.	(a) If the *dollar* is weak, it may be supported in the market by the strong-currency countries; sometimes also by DM sales by the US. (b) If any other currency is weak, it may be supported by the country concerned.
Adjustment via a change in fiscal and/or monetary policy.	Lower interest rates and possibly other expansionary measures.	Higher interest rates and possibly other deflationary measures.
Exchange control or equivalent regulations.	Controls on capital inflows.	Controls on capital outflows.
BENIGN NEGLECT	Currency allowed to appreciate in the market.	Currency allowed to depreciate in the market.

Second, international flows of short-term capital, induced by the same motives as under Bretton Woods, were even larger and more volatile post-1973 than in the 1960s. Friedman argued that under 'clean' floating, speculation would tend to be equilibrating, but central bankers often spoke instead of 'bandwagon effects' leading to 'overshooting', which could be avoided only by official 'smoothing transactions' in the foreign exchange market.

Third, overshooting might also arise due to the J-curve phenomenon (see p. 558). The initial impact of an exchange rate depreciation on external trade may be perverse in value terms, with the trade balance in value terms initially diminishing, before eventually increasing; likewise, *mutatis mutandis*, for an exchange rate appreciation.

Finally, the experience of the 1970s somewhat undermined the belief that a change in exchange rates could effect more than a temporary change in the relative prices of goods and services in different countries. As the Governor of the Bank of England put, in his Henry Thornton Lecture in June 1979:

Recent experience has indeed suggested that there are more serious limitations to the role flexible exchange rates can play in promoting adjustment than was earlier believed. . . . changes in costs arising from exchange rate movements appear nowadays to feed through into an economy more quickly and completely than used to be the case. . . . At the same time many economies have become significantly more open, more vulnerable to price and demand developments in their trading partners.

The result of these two developments appears to have been that adjustment in nominal exchange rates can no longer be relied upon to yield, for more than a relatively short period, as large an adjustment of real exchange rates as could once have been anticipated—in other words, exchange rate adjustment is, beyond the short-term, now likely to be less effective as a means of changing international competitiveness [12].

In the light of these considerations, it is not perhaps surprising that, since the transition from pegging to floating, no country has opted for 'benign neglect' in the extreme form commended by Milton Friedman. However, there have been wide differences of practice as between one country and another, and also as between one time and another in the same country, varying from something very close to 'benign neglect' on the one hand, to determined and prolonged 'leaning against the wind' on the other. And in the latter case there have also been differences of practice as between the relative degree of reliance placed on official market intervention, on the one hand, and on fiscal or monetary policy on the other.

As regards official *market intervention*, the Bank for International Settlement's Annual Report for 1977 gives a very useful snapshot of the policies of different countries as at mid-1977:

The Group of Ten countries, including Switzerland, can be divided into two main categories so far as their intervention policies are concerned, according to whether they limited themselves to intervention designed merely to smooth out day-to-day market conditions or whether, in addition, they operated in the markets in a way that brought about substantial changes in their net official reserves, including official, or officially inspired, borrowing. . . . the United States belongs in the first of the categories mentioned above, as did Canada until the November 1976 provincial elections in

uebec, while all the other Group of Ten countries, including Switzerland, belong in
e second. Germany, however, may be said to have a foot in both camps, belonging
th the United States so far as the Deutsche Mark/dollar rate is concerned but with its
low participants so far as interventions within the framework of the European joint
at are concerned [1].

his picture did not remain correct for very long, due to changes of tactics by
th the United States and the UK. In the case of the United States, the US
d German authorities at the end of 1977 jointly undertook much more
termined intervention to support the dollar against the DM. In a statement
21 December 1977, President Carter noted the emergence in the past year of
large deficit in the US trade and payments position. These deficits, he said,
ave contributed to some disorder in the exchange markets and rapid
ovements in exchange rates'. To counter such disorder, an agreement was
ncluded between the US Treasury and the Bundesbank on 4 January 1978,
der which the Bundesbank extended a credit line which the Treasury could
aw on to support the dollar in the market. This agreement was duly acted
on, and the same tactic of joint intervention on a substantial scale was
peated several times under the Carter Administration, as may be seen from
able 18.7. Then when the Reagan Administration came to power in 1981 it
verted to something closely akin to 'benign neglect' and ceased intervention
the foreign exchange market, except in March 1981 when the President was
ot, and again on rare subsequent occasions. The UK in 1977 made a U-turn
the opposite direction to the United States, as described in section 18.4.4.
If we now look at the attitude of the floating currency countries, as from
arch 1973, to the use of *monetary and fiscal policy* for purposes of leaning against
e wind (that is, for resisting or moderating changes in the value of their

TABLE 18.7. *US and German Official Support for the US dollar**
(DM billion)

Year	Period	DM billion
1977	Quarters 1 and 2	0·7
	Quarter 3	1·3
	Quarter 4	9·3
1978	Quarter 1	7·8
	Quarter 2	− 1·5
	1 July to mid-October	1·8
	mid-October to end-December	16·0
1979	January to April	− 9·9
	May to 13 June	− 4·1
	mid-June to 23 September	+ 18·6
	24 September to end-December	+ 2·8
1980	January to mid-April	− 13·9

* Market purchase of US dollars by the Bundesbank plus sales of DM
by the Federal Reserve Bank of New York.

Source: Deutsche Bundesbank, *Reports*, 1977, 1978, and 1979.

respective currencies in the foreign exchange market), we find that on the whole they preferred to reserve monetary and fiscal policy for use in influencing the state of the internal economy, in particular to keep the growth of the money stock on a predetermined path. Nevertheless there were a number of cases where the setting of monetary and/or fiscal policy was made more deflationary specifically to support a weakening currency, or more expansionary specifically to prevent the further appreciation of a strengthening currency. Examples of the former include, in the case of the United States, President Carter's package of measures in November 1978[13] and, in respect of the UK, the cases mentioned in section 18.4.4. Examples of the latter are the decisions taken by both Germany and Switzerland in 1978 to allow their monetary aggregates to exceed the target growth rates, rather than permit a further appreciation of their currencies in the market.

18.4.4. Benign Neglect in the US and UK

The countries where Milton Friedman's recipe of benign neglect was most influential were the US and the UK—partly, no doubt, thanks to the persuasiveness of monetarist literature but even more on account of the traumatic experience, in much of the 1960s, of having to live under the Bretton Woods system with an overvalued currency. The demise of Bretton Woods in the early 1970s seemed like an escape from an irksome strait-jacket: henceforth fiscal and monetary policy could be set by reference to the health of the internal economy, and a floating exchange rate would dispose of what had come to be considered a *self-inflicted* balance of payments problem. The central bankers concerned did not readily fall prey to such easy optimism, but crucial policy decisions are taken by ministers rather than by central bankers.

In the US case, benign neglect has been the received governmental doctrine throughout the floating rate regime except in the short period from President Carter's U-turn in 1978 until the end of his administration. In Britain's case benign neglect has held sway for only about half the time since sterling was floated in June 1972—namely in the first twelve months after June 1972 and again in the four years beginning October 1977—and even then the Friedmanite doctrine of clean floating was infringed on both occasions by recourse to modest official transactions in the foreign exchange market to iron out what were identified as temporary fluctuations.

The first period of UK benign neglect came to an end with the weakening of the pound as from mid-1973. The Bank of England then began to support sterling in the market, and continued to do so, on an increasing scale, until the autumn of 1976 (see Figure 18.1); moreover shortly afterwards, in July 1976 the Bank brought about 'a sharp upward shift in short-term rates in London with the 'objective of stabilizing the sterling exchange rate'.[14]

Sterling's weakness none the less continued and indeed reached crisis proportions in 1976, until Mr Healey's deflationary package towards the end of the year succeeded in restoring confidence.[15] Thereafter, thanks to the

---

[13] See [13], p. 208.
[14] See [2], pp. 249 and 316.
[15] *Midland Bank Review* (May 1977), p. 13.

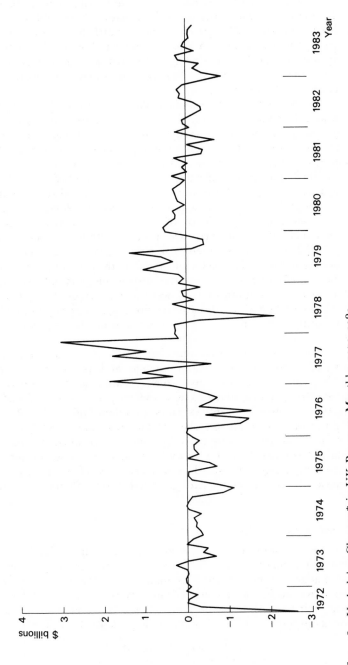

FIG. 18.1 Underlying Changes* in UK Reserves, Monthly, 1972–1983.
* That is, ignoring valuation changes, SDR issues, and the capital element of all public sector, IMF, and Central Bank debt transactions—which gives a series that is a good proxy for Bank of England intervention in the foreign exchange market.

remedial treatment and then a growing awareness of the implications of North Sea oil, the pound strengthened rapidly. The authorities continued to lean against the wind, but now in the opposite direction. They sold sterling on a massive scale, using the dollars thereby acquired partly to replenish the official reserve, partly to repay some of the dollars they had borrowed over the years 1973–6. In addition, the Bank of England allowed a rapid fall in money market interest rates, the Treasury Bill yield falling from 14 per cent in late 1976 to $4\frac{1}{2}$ per cent at end-October 1977.

Then in October 1977 the decision was taken to discontinue leaning against the wind, and the pound was allowed to rise in the market. Apart from April 1978, when the pound was temporarily weak and was strongly supported, the scale of the Bank's market transactions was appreciably reduced from October 1977 onwards, as Figure 18.1 shows. Moreover, short-term interest rates were steadily pushed upwards, especially after the advent of the Thatcher Administration, even though this must have greatly aggravated the appreciation of sterling: they reached a peak of 17 per cent in November 1979.

Why the U-turn in 1977? Clearly official concern had switched from the sterling exchange rate to the need to keep the growth of the money stock, as measured by £M3, within its targeted ceiling (see Chapter 10, p. 324). Official sales of sterling in the foreign exchange market in the earlier part of 1977 were seen to be contributing to the excessive growth of £M3; likewise the low interest rates in the autumn of 1977 were thought liable to aggravate the growth of bank lending which also was contributing to the growth of £M3. So a policy of leaning against the wind gave way to one much more akin to benign neglect.

A policy shift occurred in the opposite direction in 1981, with the progressive weakening of sterling in the foreign exchange market. Though in 1980 and 1981 £M3 was overshooting its target, it was becoming increasingly discredited as the guiding star for UK monetary policy: hence official policy came to favour a lowering of interest rates from their high peak in November 1979.[16] But in September and October 1981 the Bank dramatically intervened in the money market to *raise* rates by some 4 percentage points,[17] in a (successful) attempt to hold the sterling rate against selling pressure in the market. So benign neglect in the UK would seem to be a fair-weather doctrine, to be embraced when sterling is strong but liable to be abandoned when it is weak!

18.4.5. Shocks and Disequilibria

Except in the case of the US and UK experiments with 'benign neglect', the major industrial countries have (as we have seen) not infrequently sought to mitigate changes in their floating exchange rates, mainly by undertaking official transactions in the foreign exchange market, but sometimes also by modifying their fiscal and/or monetary policies. However, though they may have ironed out some of the market fluctuations, their efforts failed to prevent

---

[16] *Midland Bank Review* (Spring 1981), p. 13.
[17] *Midland Bank Review* (Summer 1982), p. 10.

very large changes in exchange rates as between the relevant currencies.[18] This was partly because the 1970s saw a rapid acceleration of inflation, at different rates in different countries, but even so *real* exchange rates were also highly volatile, as is shown for the period 1973–82 in Figure 18.2. In the case of the non-OPEC developing countries' currencies, most of which have continued to be pegged, devaluations against the major currency (or 'basket' of currencies) to which they have been pegged have been frequent, despite an enormous amount of official support.

Clearly, then, the international monetary system has been subject to substantial shocks:

(i) There have been enormous changes in the relative prices of manufactures,

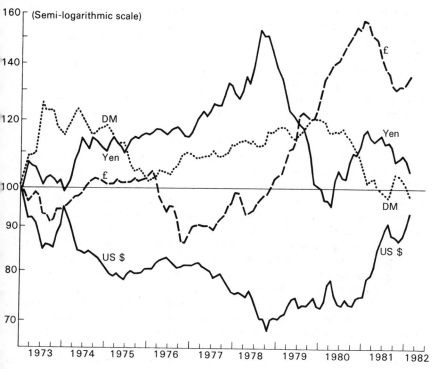

FIG. 18.2. Movements of Real Effective Exchange Rates in Terms of Relative Unit Labour Costs, Selected Industrial Countries; 1973–1982. (Monthly averages, indices: December 1972 = 100.)

Source: [1], 1982, p. 156.

[18] The 'relevant' currencies were not numerous, since some of the currencies which floated against the US dollar were bound together in the European snake. With the present snake membership, the relevant currencies are the DM (a proxy for all the snake), the US and Canadian dollars, the yen, the Swiss franc, and sterling. It should be said that the snake currencies are not bound together all that tightly, since the snake arrangements provide for a revision of parities, and a number of such revisions has in fact occurred, the last one in March 1983.

oil, and non-oil primary commodities in the last ten years. Over the eight year beginning with the first oil-price hike at the end of 1973, oil prices rose no less than tenfold, while those of manufactured goods little more than double and those of non-oil primary products by less than half (see [6], Table 9).

(ii) The impact of higher oil prices on the industrial countries' economies may be compared to a new excise duty, the revenue from which was largely saved instead of being spent on goods and services, and this deflationary impact was not fully offset by reflationary fiscal or monetary policies: indeed with the mounting fear of price inflation the policy stance of the industrial countries came to be markedly more *de*flationary. This is examined further in Chapter 19. In practice, growth in the industrial economies (taken as a whole) which had been running at an annual rate typically in the vicinity of $4\frac{1}{2}$ to 5 per cent before the first oil price rise, came to a virtual halt in 1974 and 1975. Then after a recovery in 1976, 1977 and 1978, it declined again to rates of 1 per cent per annum and less after the second oil price rise at the end of 1979 (see [6] Table 1).

(iii) A particular aspect of the industrial countries' reaction to the mounting fear of inflation has been their adoption of targets for the rate of growth of the money stock and/or monetary base, and their pursuit of such targets with relatively little regard (despite some important exceptions noted on page 572 for the effect of the consequential interest rate variations on international capital movements, and hence on exchange rates.

(iv) The main victims of these events have been the non-oil developing countries. Their oil bills increased greatly, until the collapse of oil prices in 1983. The business depression in the main markets for their export products depressed their export prices in relation not only to oil prices but also to the prices of the manufactures which they import. They themselves, unlike the industrial countries, sought—successfully up to 1980, though not in 1981, 1982 and 1983—to continue with their development programmes and to maintain the rate of output growth they achieved in the years before 1974. In consequence their balance of payments on current account deteriorated as that of the oil-exporting countries went into surplus (see Table 18.5).

(v) With the weakening of the oil market as from 1982, the difficulties faced by the non-oil developing countries spread to some of the oil producers, in particular those which had developed a voracious appetite for imports in connection with ambitious development programmes.

(vi) The financing of the developing countries' unfavourable current balance has been achieved mainly by their stepping up their borrowing from the big private sector banks. In consequence there has been, as shown in Table 18.8, an enormous increase in their outstanding debt, to no less than $626 billion at end-1982,[19] of which $210 billion was to banks (not including any of the $148 billion of export credit mostly guaranteed by the governments of the exporting countries). Some half of this debt (and considerably more than half of the debt to banks) was owed by some dozen developing countries (see Table 18.9).

---

[19] Excluding debts of an initial maturity of one year or less.

TABLE 18.8. *Total Disbursed Debt* of Developing Countries, End-Year 1971–1982*
($ billion)

	1971	1975	1976	1977	1978	1979	1980	1981	1982
Export credits	27	42	51	65	85	100	114	128	148
Bank loans (excluding export credits)	11	49	64	81	105	131	155	180	210
Multilateral organizations	10	22	26	33	40	47	56	65	76
Other	42	67	79	95	115	128	140	157	192
Total	90	180	220	274	345	406	465	530	626

* Excluding debts of an initial maturity of one year or less.

Source: [10], Table 1. the figures for 1981 are preliminary and for 1982 estimated.

TABLE 18.9. *Disbursed Debt* of Twelve Developing Countries, End-1981*
($ billion)

Brazil	66
Mexico	54
Spain	25
South Korea	21
Argentina	20
India	19
Indonesia	18
Algeria	17
Yugoslavia	17
Turkey	16
Venezuela	15
Egypt	14
Total	302

* Excluding debts of an initial maturity of one year or less.

Source: [10], Table 17.

(vii) The countries that borrowed heavily to sustain 'debt-led growth' through the 1970s suffered, in 1982 and 1983, a collapse in their credit standing; in consequence they now find themselves obliged to accept stringent austerity programmes in order to balance their international payments on the basis of the sharply reduced levels of capital inflow available to them. This represents a major setback to their economic development.

(viii) It also represents a setback for the lending banks, whose loans are having to be rescheduled as the only alternative to forcing their debtors into outright default.

The serious difficulties of the banks with their loans to the developing countries began in August 1982 with Mexico's inability to meet its obligations: in consequence the Mexican debt had to be rescheduled, and soon afterwards similar action was needed in the case of other Latin American borrowers, in particular Brazil and Argentina. Unfortunately for the banks, their difficulties with their Latin American customers occurred at a time when they had already run into problems with their Eastern European customers, especially with Poland; the total bank debt of Eastern Europe is large ($52 billion in September 1982)[20] and much of it needed to be rescheduled.

The rescheduling of international debts presents a problem of enormous complexity. A country like Mexico, and its residents, may be indebted to many hundreds of banks, as well as to governments and other lenders, and every debt is peculiar in its terms and conditions. Each of the lending banks, in its own immediate self-interest, would prefer to 'cut and run', rather than reschedule its outstanding debts, let alone continue with net lending. But banks *as a whole* cannot 'cut and run';if the debtor country is unable to repay its debts in total

[20] See [14], Table 5.

any one of the lending banks can obtain repayment only by getting other banks to take over the borrower's commitment, which however they will not want to do. Individual banks can of course refuse to undertake further net lending to their doubtful customers, and many were indeed beginning to act in this way in the latter part of 1982, but the consequences for the lending banks as a whole would in due course be disastrous, since the borrower would then be forced into default. Clearly, then, the best outcome for all the parties concerned is a rescheduling operation, tied in with an agreement by the borrowing country to pursue prudent economic policies and by the lending banks to continue net lending, albeit on a more modest scale than in the 1970s, to allow time for the borrower's prudent policies (usually involving measures of fiscal and monetary deflation) to take effect. But there are so many parties involved, and their respective interests so diverse and complicated, that in practice agreement is virtually impossible without the intervention of a public sector agency as a mediator. Even then, the mediating agency cannot expect to carry sufficient weight in the negotiations except by making a financial contribution in its own name. In practice the role of mediator has been assumed by the IMF, which took charge of the Mexican negotiations in 1982, holding out the promise of new IMF finance if all the other parties would co-operate on the lines put forward by the managing director; the Mexican case served as a precedent for subsequent rescheduling operations.

It is still too soon to say whether these reschedulings, actual or prospective, can stand the test of time, and in present circumstances it is still impossible to forecast whether outright defaults can be avoided or which countries' debts are ultimately at greatest risk. These questions depend on a number of factors that go far beyond the efforts being made, through the international monetary system, to contain the situation; they depend on the rate of world recovery, the policies adopted by the borrowing countries, the structure of their liabilities, the path of interest rates, and the price of oil. The issue is therefore returned to at the end of the next chapter (p. 617) where these factors can be accessed in the light of current trends in international macroeconomic policy.

But it is difficult to be very optimistic about the future outlook. Up to the present the lending banks have not had to face outright defaults, but they are none the less worried by the riskiness of a significant part of their outstanding international lending, as is shown by the large provisions they are now making against doubtful debts. As might be expected, they have become more cautious lenders, to domestic as well as to foreign borrowers. This may well constrain the part they are prepared to play in promoting world economic recovery. The prospect for the developing countries is especially bleak. Their ability to pay their way by exporting is conditional on the recovery of their depressed markets in the industrial countries. Their development programmes, hitherto financed to a considerable extent by bank loans, are now in jeopardy, except to the extent that finance from private sector banks can be replaced by public sector finance, coming mainly from the IMF and the World Bank. Steps are being taken to boost the lending of both these institutions, but it remains highly unlikely that the developing countries will be able to develop in the 1980s as they did in the 1970s.

Bibliography

SECTION A

[1] Bank for International Settlements, *Annual Report*, Nos. 47 and 52 (Basle, June 1977 and June 1982).
[2] BLACKABY, F. *et al. British Economic Policy 1960–74* (Cambridge University Press, 1978).
[3] COOMBS, C. A. 'Treasury and Federal Reserve Foreign Exchange Operations', in Federal Reserve Bank of New York, *Monthly Review* (Oct. 1971).
[4] *Economic Report of the President and the Annual Report of the Council of Economic Advisers* (US Government Printing Office, 1973).
[5] IMF. *The Role of Exchange Rates in the Adjustment of International Payments* (1970).
[6] ——. *World Economic Outlook*, Occasional Paper No. 9 (Apr. 1982).
[7] *International Monetary Reform: Documents of the Committee of Twenty* (IMF, 1974).
[8] MILLS, R. H. 'The Regulation of Short-Term Capital Movements in Major Industrial Countries', in Federal Reserve System, *Staff Economic Studies* (1972).
[9] MORSE, Sir J. Address on 7 June 1974, reproduced in IMF, *Finance and Development* (Sept. 1974).
[10] OECD. *External Debt of Developing Countries: 1982 Survey* (Paris, 1982).
[11] OORT, C. J. *Steps to International Monetary Order* (Per Jacobsson Foundation, Washington DC, 1974).
[12] RICHARDSON, G. (Governor of the Bank of England). Henry Thornton Lecture, June 1979, reproduced in *Bank of England Quarterly Bulletin* (Sept. 1979).
[13] TEW, B. *The Evolution of the International Monetary System 1945–81*, 2nd edn. (Hutchinson, 1982).
[14] Treasury and Civil Service Committee of the House of Commons. *Report on International Lending by Banks* (HMSO, Mar. 1983).
[15] TRIFFIN, R. 'The European Monetary System and the Dollar in the Framework of the World Monetary System', in Banca Nazionale del Lavoro, *Quarterly Review*, (Sept. 1982).

SECTION B

[16] COOPER, R. N., KENEN, P. B., DE MACEDO, J. B., and VAN YPERSELE, J. (eds.). *The International Monetary System under Flexible Exchange Rates* (Ballinger Publishing Co., Cambridge USA, 1982).
[17] HORSFIELD, J. K. *et al. The International Monetary Fund 1945–1965* (IMF, 1969).
[18] KILLICK, T. (ed.). *Adjustment and Financing in the Developing World* (IMF, 1982).
[19] LLEWELLYN, D. T. *International Financial Integration* (Macmillan, 1980).
[20] SOLOMON, R. *The International Monetary System* (Harper and Row, 1982).
[21] STRANGE, S. *International Monetary Relations*, Vol. 2 of *International Economic Relations of the Western World, 1959–71* (Oxford University Press, 1976).
[22] TRIFFIN, R. *Gold and the Dollar Crisis* (Yale University Press, 1961).
[23] DE VRIES, M. G. *The International Monetary Fund 1966–71: The System Under Stress* (IMF, 1977).
[24] DE VRIES, T. 'Jamaica, or the Non-Reform of the International Monetary System', *Foreign Affairs* (Apr. 1976).
[25] WILLIAMSON, J. *The Exchange Rate System* (Institute for International Economics, Washington, 1973).

19

International Macroeconomic Policy

C. J. ALLSOPP

19.1. Introduction

Economic policies are, by and large, formulated at the national level. It is important, however, to consider the ways in which they interact to bring about favourable or unfavourable results for the world economic system as a whole. Moreover, some problems, such as the oil impacts of the 1970s, are international in character and cannot be adequately from the viewpoint of any particular country.

The economic performance of the industrial countries deteriorated dramatically from around the late 1960s onwards. In the mid-1960s there was a climate of optimism that most economic problems, whether arising at the level of the individual economy, or at the level of the international system, could be dealt with by rational policy action. By the 1980s faith in the controllability of the international economy and in the power of governments to make much difference had mostly evaporated. Industrial countries had run into problems which were apparently intractable. The worsening international environment in turn reacted back onto individual economies and became a severe constraint on domestic policy action.

Malfunction on such a scale would have appeared unthinkable two decades earlier. This chapter brings together the main contributory factors, most of which have been explored individually in more detail in earlier chapters: the rise in inflation in the late 1960s and the breakdown of the Bretton Woods system of pegged exchange rates; the commodity price inflation of the early 1970s; the two oil crises of 1973–4 and 1979–80, and the international debt crisis of the early 1980s. The problems involved and the policy responses are analysed as a kind of case study of the considerations that are relevant and the additional difficulties that arise when economic policy is considered in an international context.

The emphasis is on *interactions* amongst the developed industrialized countries and on *short-term* policy. Longer-term considerations, such as the development of the international monetary system and resource availabilities, form the background to short-term policy, but are not themselves under discussion. Likewise, the situations of the developing countries, of OPEC, or of Communist countries are not analysed *per se*, but are looked at where relevant from the point of view of the industrialized OECD countries. In keeping with the objective of illustrating the problems involved, policy recommendations are avoided; and since the situation is still evolving, judgement on the most recent events cannot even be tempered by hindsight.

Though there is no supra-national authority with powers in any way comparable to those of national authorities, consultation and information exchange are continuous; countries have international obligations of both formal and informal kinds, and, on occasion, international pressure may have a decisive influence. Many contacts are formalized under one or other of the international institutions, such as the International Monetary Fund (IMF), or the Organization for Economic Co-operation and Development (OECD), but others may be more *ad hoc*, concerned with particular issues. Committees are set up at many different levels, ranging from purely technical working parties to ministerial meetings. Often the same set of problems will be discussed simultaneously in many different contexts; gradually a consensus may emerge, or there may be a formal agreement. The whole process is rather amorphous, often shrouded in diplomatic language, but is none the less an important element in policy formation.

Expected developments in the world economy are inputs into any national-forecasting exercise. National forecasts and, for that matter, policy targets may, however, be inconsistent with each other. It is one of the roles of international consultation to try to remove as far as possible these inconsistencies so as to arrive at a better overall consensus as to likely developments in the international economy. To this end, institutions such as the OECD and the IMF produce their own forecasts for individual countries as for world trade and payments. Of necessity, these forecasts have consistency thrust upon them.[1] Beyond this, international discussions are designed to influence policies, and to promote a co-operative approach to common problems. Sometimes international pressure is more than diplomatic, as when, for example, conditions (usually to deflate) are attached to the granting of an IMF loan.

The difficulties in achieving international consensus and a co-operative approach are of course immense. One aspect needs, however, to be stressed in an economics textbook. Meaningful co-operation requires consensus on the diagnosis and economic analysis of common problems. That consensus appeared to exist in the 1950s and 1960s. With increasing economic difficulties, however, serious disagreements and differences of view started to emerge. Even within the consensus framework of the late 1960s and early 1970s, views differed sharply on such questions as whether there was a 'trade-off' between inflation and unemployment; on whether fiscal or monetary policy should be emphasized; as to whether demand management policy, or, for example, exchange rate adjustment, should be used to correct international payments disequilibrium. Fundamental disagreement on how to run a rational world is an important stumbling-block, even if there are no other difficulties, such as national self-interest, in the way of achieving international co-operation. These

[1] As an example, balance of payments positions must be compatible with each other, whereas it is not uncommon for the aggregate of individual-country forecasts to violate the condition that one country's surplus is another country's deficit.

difficulties became far worse in the late 1970s and early 1980s as the whole basis of conventional macroeconomic policy came to be questioned, and to be replaced in some countries by 'monetarist' or supply-side economic ideologies.

19.2. The 1950s and 1960s

The outstanding characteristic of the 1950s and 1960s was the generally high rate of expansion of the industrialized countries. The growth of the non-socialist industrial world was about 5 per cent per annum—a rate unprecedented in any historical period of comparable length. This was a general expansion, with all industrial countries participating. Moreover, fluctuations associated with the business cycle were shorter and smaller, and in most countries took the form of fluctuations in the rate of growth rather than absolute declines in output as in the traditional definition of depression. World trade grew steadily at something like 8–9 per cent per annum.

This prolonged boom period raises two questions which we consider in turn. The first is, in effect, 'What went right?': what was it that accounts for the success achieved, and what was the general climate of international policy-making at the time? The second is, 'What went wrong?' Clearly, only a sketch of some of the considerations that are relevant can be attempted.

Despite many studies, the explanation of rapid and relatively stable growth in the 1950s and 1960s remains highly contentious (see Chapter 20). Eclectic views usually start by stressing various facilitating factors on the supply side. In most of the fast-growing countries, vast movements of labour occurred between sectors and between rural and urban occupations. International migration also played its part, especially in Europe.[2] This flexibility of labour supply is often regarded as a necessary condition for the growth that was achieved. Also on the supply side, the development of technology and, for many countries, the existence of a backlog of technical opportunities are regarded as important. Moreover, supplies of energy, raw materials, and food were plentiful and available at stable or declining prices.

In order to go further it seems essential to turn to the expenditure or demand side of the picture. Keynesian policies of demand management played a role both in maintaining expenditure, and in moderating the business cycle. The weight that should be given to the direct effects of stabilization policy is, however, uncertain. Many countries were slow to adopt demand management policies, and the extent of counter-cyclical intervention can also be questioned—was demand management policy, where practised, powerful enough to stabilize the economy? Others would point to automatic stabilizers, such as improved unemployment benefits, which help maintain expenditure during recessions, and the progressivity of the tax system, which increases taxation as incomes rise. The increasing role of government—of public expenditure generally—may have been an important stabilizing factor even if not used as a counter-cyclical tool, since a larger proportion of the economy may be independent of cyclical conditions.

Though there may be doubt about the direct effects of stabilization policies,

[2] See F. Bernabé, 'The Labour Market and Unemployment', in [8].

nevertheless the commitment to full employment and growth may have been vitally important. After the war, in Britain and in most other industrialized countries, the government took responsibility for the maintenance of employment and with Keynesian (or, especially during the reconstruction period, more directly interventionist) policies apparently had the means to achieve it. The success was phenomenal compared even with the hopes of the architects of such policies. Once it comes to be accepted that the government can and will maintain growth and employment, there is an important effect on the expectations of both investors and consumers. In recessionary periods, the best guess is that the economy will return to full employment within a few years. Such expectations are themselves powerfully stabilizing: consumption is maintained and investment plans become geared to the growth of productive potential. In such an environment, when governments are expected to succeed in their economic aims, stabilization policy may need to be only lightly applied. A corollary, however, is that problems of instability could get much worse if confidence in the ability of governments to achieve high employment and growth were severely shaken—as occurred in the 1970s.

There was another favourable factor: the tendency for the business cycle in different countries to be out of phase—when one group of countries was expanding fast, others tended to be moving towards recession. As a result world trade grew rather steadily. Until the 1970s, the most nearly coincident cycle was the recession of 1958, but at that time expensionary policy actions were taken in major countries early on, and recessionary forces were quickly reversed. Generally, the lack of synchronization meant both that individual economies were stabilized and that domestic demand management policies were easier to apply. The multiplier applying to individual countries was lower (because of the import leakage) than that which would apply to the system as a whole. Each bit was stabilized by all the rest. The buoyancy of world trade meant that the international transmission mechanisms worked much less strongly than in the interwar period. In turn this meant that individual countries had, or appeared to have, a considerable degree of national autonomy. Economic policy could be viewed in terms of *domestic* objectives and instruments, and the constraints imposed by the international economy (such as balance of payments problems) were, for most countries, relatively minor.[3]

Viewed from the present, several features of the rapid growth period appear fragile. Expectations could turn sour. International transmission effects, unless offset, were perhaps bound to increase over time, leading to problems of synchronization, external constraints, and a reduction of national autonomy. The supply side was getting less flexible both due to the using up of spare resources (such as underemployed labour in agriculture) and due to institutional changes, especially in the labour market. As some of these changes occurred it was perhaps inevitable that international payments adjustment problems would become more difficult, and fluctuations in the world economy harder to deal with.

The notable features of the late 1960s which suggest that instability in the

[3] An obvious exception to that generalization was the UK, which was subject to periodic balance of payments crises and an apparent inability to achieve both internal and external equilibrium.

world economy was increasing *before* the 1973 oil crisis were, first, the breakdown of the fixed exchange rate system set up after the war, and, second, the emergence of *inflation* as an international policy issue. A detailed description of the collapse of the Bretton Woods system has been given in Chapter 18. The final stages were entered when sterling was devalued in 1967. The existing set of exchange rates was called into question, and the dollar was in the front line of speculative attack. Persistent US balance of payments deficits—due largely to an outflow on capital account—had vastly swelled the quantity of externally held dollar balances. The first casualty was the price of gold, which had been stabilized at $35 to the ounce by the mechanism of the London Gold Pool. Fears about the position of the dollar led to massive buying of gold in March 1968. The system was, however, patched up. Gold continued to enter transactions between Central Banks at the official price, but was allowed to find its own level on the free market.

Uncertainty and speculation continued, however, and by the middle of 1971 convertibility of the dollar into gold was suspended, and all the world's major currencies were *de facto* floating. This period of floating ended with the Smithsonian Agreement of December 1971. At the time the realignment appeared to mark the end of a period of extreme uncertainty, but the newly established parities were themselves destined to be short lived. A little over a year later the dollar was again devalued, and floating currencies were again the rule.

These monetary uncertainties and exchange rate changes cannot, however, be seen in isolation from other developments. The most important problem to arise in the late 1960s was inflation, which accelerated both in North America and in Europe. In turn, differential inflation was one of the problems that put pressure on the fixed exchange rate system. (It was not the only one, however: the problem of longer-term improvements in the real competitiveness of Europe and Japan relative to the United States was at least equally important.)

Though the acceleration of inflation throughout the 1960s and 1970s is often presented as a continuous process, such a characterization is misleading. The rise in inflation in Europe and America in the late 1960s is hard to account for. Even in the United States, where the usual explanation runs in terms of excess monetary demand due to the Vietnam war and due to President Johnson's programmes 'for a great society', the trade-off was worsening and there appear to have been social and political forces of a cost push or 'competing claims' type as well. It was a time of protest and militancy. In Europe, conventional explanations in terms of demand pressure or monetary expansion fail. There was a series of wage explosisions in different countries (the most dramatic being that following *les événements* of May 1968 in France) and the rises coincided with shop-floor unrest. Thus in Europe the rise in inflation appeared to be due to wage push pressure, and the phenomenon raised the old fears that full employment and growth might be incompatible with a reasonable degree of price stability.[4]

[4] Wage explosions occurred in France in 1968, in Germany and Italy in 1969, and in the UK in 1970 (following the ending of the Labour Government's incomes policies). For a discussion of this important period see C. J. Allsopp, 'Inflation', in [8].

One possible explanation of increased inflationary pressure is that the unemployment and underemployment in Europe and America in the 1950s acted as a dampening factor, and that as the balance between supply potential and demand changed over the longer run, inflationary pressure was bound to increase. Another, which would be difficult to distinguish from the previous one, is that it was inevitable that expectations and aspirations would catch up with the actuality of rapid growth. The combination of expected real rises in living standards and the assumed ability of governments to guarantee full or near full employment would eventually mean that the inflationary problem, disguised for a time by unexpectedly good performance, would reappear.[5] In support, it could be argued that a number of the wage explosions had followed periods of slower growth and apparently frustrated expectations. And slower growing countries such as the United Kingdom had always appeared to have difficulties with cost push pressure.

The response to the rise in inflation and to the other problems of the late 1960s was that most countries deflated, which led to the approximately coincident 'mini recession' of 1970–1. Although the problem of inflation had become generalized, in the countries concerned it was the *domestic* wage–price spiral that was seen as the policy issue. This phase can be seen as an attempt in a number of countries simultaneously to make use of the traditional assumed trade-off between inflation and the pressure of demand to slow the rise in prices. From that period in the late 1960s onwards, the policy problem was increasingly dominated by inflation and by attempts to deal with it—by deflation, or (usually following a 'U-turn') by other techniques, such as incomes policy or a wage freeze.

The period of low pressure in demand in 1970 and 1971 set the stage for the world-wide coincident boom of 1972 and 1973. In part this was the result of normal cyclical developments from a starting-point in which many countries had a larger degree of slack than usual. But economic policies changed sharply to induce and to reinforce the expansion.

There were several elements in the reversal of policy positions. In the first place deflation, in a number of countries, appeared to be going too far. The US recession was larger and more prolonged than many had expected. The policy position was reversed; there were rapid increases in the money supply and the Federal budget position became more expansionary. It was not until the end of 1970 that the economy really started to grow again, and the turn-around in industrial production was even further delayed. In the United Kingdom, the period 1970–1 was marked by a severe rise in unemployment, which led to the famous 'U-turn'. The second element is that the slowdown appeared to have *disappointingly small effects on the course of price and wage inflation.* In Europe consumer prices continued to accelerate through to the middle of 1971. In the United States consumer price rises were somewhat lowered in 1971 and 1972. But even here there is a question as to whether the improvement reflected the lagged effect of lower demand pressures, or, alternatively, the beneficial effects of productivity gains at the beginning of the upswing, combined with the move

---

[5] See, for example, the discussion in McCracken *et al.* [6].

policies of prices and incomes control. It began to look as if the demand
anagement weapon for controlling price and wage rises was a very blunt
strument: if it worked at all, the costs in terms of unemployment and output
rgone appeared to be great—so great in some countries as to be beyond the
nit of political feasibility.

By 1971 nearly all major countries were in a strongly reflationary policy
sition. This coincided with strong pressure on the dollar. When conver-
ility of the dollar was suspended in the summer of 1971 an extra twist was
ven to expansionary policies. In the subsequent period of floating there was a
ndency for authorities to want to maintain their competitive position, and to
sist upward movements of their exchange rates. Monetary expansion, general
flation, and Central Bank intervention accompanied the float, leading to a
arp increase in the world money supply and a marked stimulus to demand. It
arguable that the fixed exchange rate system, up to this time, had tended to
ad to a deflationary bias in economic policy, as the onus of adjustment fell on
eak-currency countries who resisted devaluation by restrictive monetary and
cal policies. When countries floated, the tendencies were reversed: it was
rong-currency countries which were resisting revaluation by expansionary
licies. Confidence factors, however, due to the turmoil on exchange markets,
obably acted as a brake on expansion, until world monetary uncertainties
ere sharply reduced as a result of the Smithsonian realignment of December
71.

The boom that followed was very sharp. It was led by North America; Japan
d Italy joined in the general upswing rather later, but were soon expanding
ry fast indeed. By the first half of 1973 it appeared that the industrial
untries as a group were expanding at a rate of about 8 per cent per annum; a
te which was clearly unsustainable. The boom was marked by some unusual
atures. Inflation accelerated quickly, stimulated in the main by rapidly rising
mmodity prices. Supply constraints appeared early on, particularly in
imary processing sectors, so that capacity limitations became a brake on
pansion earlier than might have been expected. Many governments acted to
strain demand quite early in the boom. In the second half of 1973 the oil crisis
upted, with marked effects on industrialized economies which were already
wing down.

9.3. The Commodity Price Rise in 1972–3

9.3.1. History

he marked increase in the rate of inflation was an extremely worrying
henomenon given that the recessionary policies of the previous few years had
ad only a small effect, so that prices were already rising fast. At this time,
owever, the *increased* inflationary pressure arose, not from an intensification of
e domestic wage–price spiral, but from a world-wide rise in the prices of food
nd raw materials. The terms of trade started to move sharply in favour of
rimary procducers. To an individual country this raised a difficult policy
roblem in that the phenomenon was largely outside the scope of domestic

control. (Even for the United States, a large exporter of primary commoditi⬤
the inflationary stimulus had a quasi-exogenous character, arising as it d
from increased export demand.) For the world as a whole, however—or for t
industrialized countries as a group, which are about 80 per cent self-sufficie
in primary products—this inflationary stimulus could not be regarded
'exogenous'. It arose in part from sharply increased demands, reflecting t
speed and generality of the upswing in activity, and in part from supply-si⬤
difficulties.

In 1972 and 1973 primary commodity prices—both of food and of ra
materials—rose very sharply. *The Economist* index of world commodity sp
prices[6] fell during 1971 to 90 (taking 1970 as 100), rose to 109 in 1972, to 164
1973 as an average; was 193 in December 1973, and rose to over 200 in the fi⬤
part of 1974. The food component rose earlier (to 120 for the average of 197
and to an even greater extent. In October 1974 the index stood at no less th⬤
262. Spot food prices had risen $2\frac{3}{4}$ times compared with the situation in 197
Wheat and soya beans went up about fourfold.

These dramatic figures considerably overstate the effects of the commodi
price boom. As noted, transactions prices lag developments on the free marke
and, moreover, much food is domestically produced, with prices that tend to l
much more stable. Nevertheless, food prices in the United States rose l
$14\frac{1}{2}$ per cent in 1973 compared with 1972, and alone contributed about half tl
rise in the Consumer Price Index (CPI) of that year (6·2 per cent). In tl
United Kingdom the food price rise was smaller ($11\frac{1}{2}$ per cent), but the weig
of food in the CPI is greater. For the United Kingdom also, the food price ri⬤
contributed about half the total rise in the CPI of 9·2 per cent. It is probab⬤
that the rise in price of *imported* primary products (excluding oil) was abo⬤
30 per cent in 1973 on a *transaction* basis. It was about the same in 1974.
industrial materials are included as well, it is clear that the contribution
inflation of the rise in commodity prices was very great.

The reasons for the rise varied between commodities. In the case of foo
prices rose rapidly from the middle of 1972, reflecting global supply deficienci⬤
and sharp increases in demand. Crop failures in the Soviet Union, Australi⬤
and China, and many parts of South-East Asia, led to a 3 per cent fall in wor
grain production, exacerbated by a low stock position. The initiating cause
the rise in industrial raw materials was the sharp increase in world industri⬤
production—but here too the situation was worsened by supply-side di⬤
ficulties. In many products, the low prices of the 1960s had deterred investme⬤
in increased capacity. Problems were not confined to the primary industri⬤
themselves, but also appeared at the primary processing stage, whe
widespread capacity bottlenecks developed. In relation to the expansion
industrial production the spot price of industrial materials rose to a far great
extent than usual.

---

[6] The weighting of this index is based on imports into industrial countries rather than on wor
production. Fuel and oil prices are excluded. Spot prices are much more volatile than the avera
prices at which actual transactions take place. These are often based on longer-term contra⬤
between producers and consumers. Transaction prices may lag behind movements of the spot pri⬤
by as much as six or nine months.

An end to the boom was widely expected in the summer of 1973. But in October the Middle East war occurred, followed by the oil crisis. The general effect on expectations and speculation was such as to keep the commodity price boom going into the first half of 1974, when industrial materials did start coming down with characteristic sharpness. Food prices remained high, however, throughout 1974, as it became apparent that the crop year was not going to be as good as had been expected.

19.3.2. The Policy Problem

The additional stimulus to inflation came on top of inflation rates which were already regarded as highly unsatisfactory. In retreat from demand management policies as a cure for inflation, many countries were relying on prices and incomes controls to stem inflationary pressures during the upswing. (The most notable example was the introduction of the various phases of prices and incomes policy in the United States, starting with the price and wage freeze introduced during the second half of 1971.) In the first half of 1972 there were grounds for optimism that the rate of rise of consumer prices was moderating in North America, Europe, and Japan. But there was soon a dramatic acceleration, reflecting the effects of the commodity price boom. There was then a retreat from reliance on prices and incomes controls, which simply could not operate successfully in such unfavourable conditions. The price rises for food and raw materials were in such sensitive and important areas that incomes policies and the like could be of little help.

It is necessary to distinguish between different phenomena, all of which are often loosely described as inflation. A rise in the price of primary commodities has a direct effect on final goods prices—especially consumer prices. But the most important aspect is that the real incomes of those who pay the increased prices are reduced. There is a change in the distribution of income away from consumers in favour of those who gain from primary commodity production. If the deterioration in living standards were accepted by the consumers there would simply be a once-and-for-all increase in consumer prices. Inflation, as measured by consumer prices, would rise as commodity price rises worked their way through, but then stop. The process can be thought of as analogous to an increase in indirect taxation—which raises prices and lowers consumer real incomes. The really serious inflationary consequences of rising commodity prices are the effects that occur at the next stage. If the erosion of real income positions is *resisted*, there is an attendant increase in wage–price pressure, and the likelihood of spiralling inflation of a continuous kind. This is especially likely when increases occur in areas such as food prices which are important in the wage bargaining process. Higher money incomes may, in turn, further bid up commodity prices.

Seen in this way, there were two possible approaches to the policy problem. In the first place, it could be argued that the price rises were exceptional, brought about by excess world demand for commodities. Policy should be concentrated on lowering demand and increasing supply. The difficulty was that the problem arose in a global way, and any particular country could have only limited impact. The other possibility was that the change in terms of trade of primary producers was more permanent. In that case policy would have to concentrate on the problem of making sure that the changes in the distribution of real income were accepted without too great an acceleration in the wage–price spiral. Here again, however, there was room for disagreement. It could be argued that this case also called for deflationary policies. But it has to be remembered that deflation itself has an unfavourable effect on real income positions, and it is possible that this could further exacerbate cost–price pressures. In fact, the situation did lead to a move towards deflationary policies. In part this was seen as acting on commodity prices themselves. In part it was felt that domestic wage–price pressures would be minimized in this way—the trade-off again; but, most importantly, it became apparent that domestic demand pressures were building up in a number of important economies; and there is of course no disagreement that generalized excess demand is a cause of inflation, and should be avoided.

The analysis of the commodity price rise in terms of implied distribution of income changes brings out clearly the effects on aggregate expenditure. When income is transferred from one group to another, the impact depends on the relative spending propensities of the groups concerned. Thus if primary producers, who gained, spent on current goods and services exactly the same proportion as those who lost, there would be no aggregate effect. In fact, many primary producers—the less developed countries—are high spenders, so that on balance the effect may have been stimulating to expenditure. Though consumer real incomes were reduced, demand returned in the form of increased demand for exports. Lags are involved, of course, and as it turned out, less developed country demand for industrial-country exports grew very fast in 1973, and was maintained in 1974, when industrial countries were slowing down. Within a large primary-producing country such as the United States it is more difficult to be sure what the effect was. In fact, wage earner's real incomes were considerably eroded, and the farming sector, which gained is, traditionally, a high saver. It is probable that the income distribution changes were an important reason for the recessionary trends that developed in the United States.

It should be noted that the commodity price rise did *not* lead to any overall worsening of the balance of payments situation for the industrialized countries. This is in contrast to the oil price increase considered in the next section. The reason is quite straightforward. The impact was balanced by increased export demand from primary producers. There was no reason to suppose that less developed countries, in particular, would maintain balance of payments surpluses—there was no consequent tendency for world savings to increase. But relative balance of payments positions were affected. There was an improvement in the US balance, and a reduction of the Japanese surplus, thus contributing to an adjustment that the exchange rate changes of previous years had failed to achieve. For some countries, such as the United Kingdom, the adverse effects were in part responsible for further downward movement of the exchange rate, exacerbating inflationary problems. Germany and some other countries received some relief from the inflationary situation as their currencies rose in relation to the dollar.

4. The First Oil Crisis

October 1973 the Middle East war erupted. This was followed by the oil mbargo, with a restriction on supplies and a rise in price. Up until the end of 973 the major concern of policy makers was the threat of severe shortages of ergy, which would have an immediate effect on industrial supply potential d bring about widespread disruption. On 23 December the supply strictions were relaxed, but a massive price rise was announced, which ought the (landed) crude oil price to about $10\frac{1}{2}$, or about four times its ctober 1973 level. The oil crisis brought about massive political and economic oblems, which are still far from resolved. The following sections are intended illustrate the analytical problems involved. The analysis of the second oil isis, considered below, is very similar.

.4.1. The Embargo Period

the event the embargo was not very effective; crude oil shipments did not crease very much. Industrial production was not cut for lack of energy.[7] No vernment could know this at the time, however, and policy had to respond to e threat of shortage. Most countries introduced measures to cut energy mand—of varying severity; the effects of these were in some cases quite bstantial. The main effects, however, were indirect. Confidence and pectational factors became highly adverse, affecting particularly the demand r automobiles; and governmental policies became more cautious. In general, mand management policies moved considerably further towards restriction an might have been expected on the basis of the previous situation. In some untries, notably Japan, curbs on certain types of expenditure, especially vestment, were designed both to reduce aggregate demand and to economize energy.

Awareness of supply-side problems in general was considerably heightened, pecially with respect to primary commodities and the primary materials-roducing industries. Together with the heightened uncertainty this produced further rise in commodity prices, the rise appearing to have a strongly eculative element. The hoped-for decline in spot commodity prices failed to aterialize and was replaced with further substantial rises.[8] With the further l price rise of December 1973 it was clear that it was the problem of mmodity prices that would dominate economic policy discussions in the ort term; it was certain that the price rises would lead to a very substantial celeration of inflation, to rates in the 10–20 per cent per annum range, rates hich a few years previously would have been unthinkable.

.4.2. The Oil Price Rise

terms of its effects on domestic price levels, a rise in the price of oil has similar

---

[7] In the United Kingdom the 'oil shortage' was exacerbated by the miners' strike, which led to e introduction of the three-day working week in the early months of 1974.
[8] The threshold payment arrangements introduced in the United Kingdom in the autumn of 73 became a source of great problems owing to the rises in oil and other commodity prices. The verse effects of the UK terms of trade were bound to trigger the thresholds—contrary to the pectation of officials when they were introduced.

effects to other price rises affecting essential commodities. From this point
view, the massive oil price increase added to, rather than changed, t
problems faced by consuming countries. The unfamiliar aspect of the price r
was that there was no possibility that the increased oil revenues could be spe
in the short term. Thus producers—or some of them—were bound to run ve
large balance of payments surpluses, and consumer countries, as a grou
would have to run a correspondingly large deficit. For the same reason, the
price rise was deflationary, tending to lower aggregate spending in real tern

There are many ways in which the deflationary impact of the oil price r
can be conceptualized. In the first place, since there was a transfer of income
countries which could not spend all their increased revenue, there was
tendency for world savings to rise, with deflationary effects according
standard Keynesian analysis. An analogy which goes further is with an indir
tax increase (such as a rise in Value-Added Tax—or an increase in the exc
duty on oil). An indirect tax lowers, other things being equal, the real spendi
power of households and companies that pay the tax. The total effect, howev
depends on what is done with the proceeds of the tax. If it is spent by t
government, there is an 'injection' to balance the 'withdrawal' and t
deflationary impact is neutralized, or even reversed.[9] In the analysis of t
commodity price boom we have already come across this situation—t
increased revenue to producers was largely spent so that the deflationa
impact was offset. In the case of the oil impact, the increase in revenue (to
producers) could not be fully spent in the short run, so the impact w
deflationary. The increase in tax was external to the consuming countries,
that the balance of payments on current account was affected adversely.

The quantitative importance of the oil price rise can be gauged in terms
the approximate magnitude of some of the financial flows relative to t
aggregate Gross National Product of industrialized countries. The to
increased expenditure on imported oil by OECD countries was of the order
$65 billion in 1974—or about $1\frac{1}{2}$ per cent of their aggregate GNP. Thus,
average, the oil price impact was analogous to a rise in indirect taxation
about $1\frac{1}{2}$ per cent of GNP. However, the average includes the United Sta
and Canada. For other countries the impact was much larger—about $2\frac{1}{2}$ p
cent of GNP for Europe as a whole, and about 3 per cent for the Unit
Kingdom. These figures also indicate the direct mechanical effect on domes
price levels. There were additional effects on other countries—the non-c
producing less developed countries being adversely affected by abc
$10 billion.

But even in 1974 there was additional expenditure on imports by c
producing countries so that the net effect on current balance of payme
positions of OECD countries was smaller than $65 billion—perhaps $50
billion. This impact is a measure of the effect of the increased world savings

[9] If an 'income stream' is transferred from one group to another, the demand effect is neutra
the spending propensities of the two groups are the same. For then the depressive effect on the los
is exactly offset by increased expenditure by those who gain. In the case of a tax which is spent,
effect is usually stimulatory in the short run in that the government spends all the tax, whereas
private sector would have saved a proportion of the income forgone.

dustrialized countries—as far as they were concerned it represented that part the impact which was not 'recycled' in the form of increased export demand. In the event, however, the balance of payments position of industrialized untries only worsened by about $30 billion between 1973 and 1974—the ason being that there was a large increase in the surplus of OECD countries ith other non-oil-producing countries.[10] The surplus of OPEC countries creased by about $60 billion; the deficit of the non-oil-producing less veloped countries rose by about $25 billion.

The special feature of the oil impact was that, in effect, it was not possible for nsumers to pay fully for the increased oil bill at the time. Though the mmodity price rise and the oil price rise have similar effects on inflation, the mmodity price impact implied an immediate transfer of real resources to the neficiaries—in the form of increased exports—whereas the oil impact implies future or potential demand for exports rather than a current one. This is cause, initially, to the extent that oil producers increased their savings, there d to be a transfer of 'claims'—money, or other assets—from the consumers to e producers, rather than exports of real goods. To the extent that 'claims' are ansferred, rather than real goods and services, there is no necessity for the nsumer countries to lower their real expenditure flows—of consumption and vestment—in order to make 'room' for increased exports.

In fact, by 1975 the surplus of oil producers was much reduced, and the sorptive capacity of oil producers has been rising since. As this occurs, the oblem changes from one of debt management to the problem of an increased ansfer of *real* resources, with an attendant effect on potential real living andards in consumer countries. These problems are exactly those of the crease in the price of non-oil commodities. The assets accumulated by the oil oducers represent a deferred demand for real commodities, which eventually s to be met.

One aspect of the situation which may appear confusing needs to be brought it. In 1975 the current account deficit of OECD countries was eliminated. he major reason for this was the world recession. The lower activity had a bstantial effect in lowering the demand for imported oil, thus lowering the ficit directly. Even more importantly, low activity led to a cut-back in ports other than oil from developing countries, so that much of the 'oil ficit' was passed to them. It is estimated that in 1975 the deficit of the non-oil-oducing less developed countries worsened further to $37 billion. The surplus oil producers was still substantial at about $27 billion.[11] As was clear at the

---

[10] The increased surplus of industrialized countries with less developed countries was not, of urse, due, directly or exclusively, to the oil impact. The two major reasons were a favourable ild up of reserves by less developed countries in 1973, reflecting the commodity price rise, and the mp in activity in industrial countries.

[11] One of the difficulties is that different sources give different figures for surpluses and deficits er this period, due to differences in coverage, definition, etc. The figures quoted are from OECD, onomic Outlook (19 July 1979), Table 39. Earlier or later issues give somewhat different estimates. e IMF suggests that the industrial countries were in surplus in 1975 by $20 billion, and that the n-oil developing countries had a deficit of $46 billion (IMF, *World Economic Outlook*, 1983). The neral picture, especially of changes from year to year, is, however, similar in the two sources.

time, a revival of activity would lead automatically to a re-emergence of th
industrialized countries' deficit position—as did occur in 1976 and 1977.

19.4.3. International Payments Problems

If the increased balance of payments surplus of the oil-producing countries i
accepted as inevitable, it follows that other countries must suffer
deterioration in their aggregate current account position of similar magnitud
The danger, in such circumstances, is that countries may be unwilling to accep
the inevitable, and individually attempt to improve their position. This coul
involve competitive devaluations, competitive deflations, and trade restric
tions which would be very damaging to the world economy. Such beggar-my
neighbour policies would, moreover, be self-defeating in that the overa
balance of payments position would not be improved.

In order to avoid competitive reactions, it is necessary for countries to accep
a modification of traditional balance of payments targets, and aim, in effect, t
run deficits to the required extent. International debtors are needed to balanc
the saving of the oil-producing countries. In an ideal world some concept of
fair distribution of the burden would be worked out, and it would be clear
recognized that surplus positions were as damaging internationally as excessiv
deficit positions.

In 1974 and 1975, the first two years after the oil crisis, there was no serio
scramble for balance of payments positions. Nevertheless, there was
cumulative problem in that indebtedness to foreigners rises for as long as the
is a payments deficit. The increasing indebtedness has to be accepted, and is i
fact inevitable, for so long as the surpluses of the oil producers continue. It wa
very difficult indeed for some governments to countenance this.

Though 'willingness' to run balance of payments deficits is extremel
important if competitive reactions are to be avoided, it is not by itself sufficien
There is a supply side to the problem in that finance must be available to th
'willing' debtors. Indeed, attitudes to balance of payments deficits cannot b
regarded as independent of the supply of finance and the terms on which it
available.

In aggregate there can be no problem of financing the deficits. The o
producers have to accumulate assets and these must be the assets of the defic
countries. For the world as a whole there can be no problem of 'recycling'. I
this context the term itself is misleading. The financial counterpart to th
surplus of the producers and the deficit of the consumers is a transfer
ownership—of financial claims or real assets—from oil consumers to o
producers. Nevertheless, there may be considerable difficulties for individua
countries.

To simplify somewhat, the 'recycling' problem arises in that the surpl
countries may not want to build up assets from different countries in proportio
to the deficits they run. For example, if they want to accumulate assets entire
as dollars (claims on the United States), there may be a financing problem for
deficit country such as Italy. Though the balance of payments account, lik
other accounts, always balance—ex post, deficits are always financed—a defic
may not be financeable at existing rates of exchange, or with existing econom

policies. If a deficit country wishes to maintain its exchange rate (and other aspects of its economic policy) it has to make sure that there is a capital inflow to balance the current deficit, or make use of its reserves. The deficit country, in effect, must be able to borrow—or be in a position to run down a stock of internationally acceptable assets. There is no need for direct borrowing from oil producers. There may be a long chain of intermediaries; and in the process the composition of all sorts of asset portfolios may alter. The new claims on the deficit country or the assets released by it must be accepted somewhere in the system—but not necessarily by the oil producers. Thus it is the acceptability of claims on particular countries to the international financial community *in toto*, rather than to the oil producers, that is important.

The recycling problem was therefore simply the problem of making sure that those with balance of payments deficits could finance them with reasonable stability of the exchange rate, and on reasonable terms.

In 1974 and 1975 the major mechanism for ensuring that the demands for funds and the supplies of funds matched was the international capital market, i.e. the market in internationally mobile currencies and loans. The banking system accepted deposits from surplus countries (such as the low absorbers of OPEC) and on-lent them to countries with deficits. At this time the main issue appeared to be to prevent damaging reactions by *industrial* countries facing deficits: it was only later that it became apparent that the major recycling difficulties would concern the build-up of debt by the non-oil developing countries (see section 19.6.4).

The private market performed its function much more easily than had been generally expected. Nevertheless, there were some obvious difficulties in relying exclusively on private markets. One is that there is no guarantee that particular deficit countries can always obtain finance, so that they might be forced into actions judged to be internationally damaging. It is just those countries which most 'need' finance that are most likely to have difficulty in obtaining it on the free market. For this reason more formal official schemes to aid in the recycling process were proposed and introduced.

The basic principles of operation of various schemes were simple enough. The 'oil facility' of the International Monetary Fund, introduced in 1974 and considerably extended in 1975, was perhaps the simplest. Its basic mechanism was for the IMF to borrow directly from oil producers and other countries in a strong economic position, and to lend-on the funds to deficit countries with financing needs. The 'safety-net' scheme, run through the OECD (with the Bank for International Settlements as agent) was more complex, with two basic elements. In the first place, countries subscribe convertible currency to the fund directly, according to a set of quotas. As an alternative, however, countries could act as guarantors (up to an agreed amount) for international borrowing by the Support Fund. This scheme was not activated.

The problems with official intervention in the recycling process were political as well as technical. There were two particular areas of political disagreement which were important in the discussion of any official scheme. The first was the question of the appropriate policy response of a deficit country. On one side, there were those who felt that deflationary policies were the appropriate remedy for any deficit, so that any facility that allowed countries to be 'irresponsible' was therefore regarded as unacceptable. On the other side, many stressed that policy reactions to deficits and surpluses already tended to be asymmetrical—favouring overall restriction—and that the oil deficits would, in any case, tend to produce a strong deflationary bias. For this group, the object of a recycling scheme was not just to avoid particular financing difficulties, but to actively encourage more expansionary policies than would otherwise be the case. The other area of political divergence was the question as to how favourable any scheme would be to oil producers. One view was that they should have no special treatment, and, therefore, be as subject as others to declining financial asset values as a result of inflation. Against this, it was argued (especially by the French) that if oil supplies were to be maintained, some favourable 'home' for the oil monies would have to be provided— otherwise supply cut-backs would look increasingly attractive to producers.

Concern over the 'recycling' problem amongst the industrial countries was much reduced after 1975. The most important reason for the increased optimism was that industrialized countries, as a group, improved their balance of payments position substantially. As we have seen, however, only part of the improvement reflected increased demand for imports by oil producers. To a large extent, the problem was being disguised—or displaced—by the recession. The huge deficits being run by the non-oil-producing less developed countries obviously raised questions as to whether they could go on being financed—and also pointed to the possibility of downward adjustments of imports by the affected countries, which would become an additional deflationary factor in the world situation.[12] Another aspect was that, amongst the group of industrialized countries, there remained some very difficult balance of payments positions—especially among the smaller countries. Generally, however, policy makers in the industrial world accepted with relief the displacement of the debt problem to the non-oil developing countries (especially to some of the large Newly Industrializing Countries, such as Brazil or Mexico) and to Communist block countries (such as Poland). And for their part, the large borrowers appeared happy to accumulate international liabilities on which they were, until about 1980, paying negative *real* rates of interest. The more elaborate official schemes, either for recycling, or for surveillance, were for the most part quietly shelved.

19.4.4. Domestic Implications

Though the international problems raised by the oil price rise were reasonably clear and well understood, there was much less agreement on the implications for domestic economic policies.

It is useful as a first step to consider an artificial case, where the oil impact is completely neutralized. For this purpose it is convenient to simplify and to assume that all increases in revenues to oil producers are saved; there is no increased export demand. The inflationary and deflationary domestic effects

---

[12] By maintaining imports in spite of declining exports the less developed countries (as a group) operated as a powerful stabilizing force on the world economy in 1974.

ould be offset completely if oil were *de-taxed* to the extent of the price rise. In practice, this could be approximated by lowering existing taxes and duties. As ar as the domestic economy is concerned there would then be, in effect, no oil price rise, and no effects on aggregate demand *or inflation*. The implication, however, would be an increase in the public sector deficit to the extent of the oil impact, for government revenues would fall to the extent of the de-taxation, whilst government expenditure was maintained. We would have: oil impact quals change in current balance of payments deficit; equals change in public sector deficit.

The increase in the public sector deficit has to be financed. For simplicity, suppose it is financed by an increase in the money supply, or by an increase in the bond issue, or by some mixture of the two. If oil producers, or more generally foreigners, are prepared to hold, as assets, some mixture of money and government bonds or bills at existing exchange rates and interest rates then there need be no monetary impact either. The *domestically* held money supply and the domestically held bond supply could be unaltered.[13] The only thing that would have happened is that there would be an increase in externally held currency and/or debt instruments—and hence, of course, some increase in debt-servicing costs. In effect, we would have the oil, whereas they would have some pieces of paper representing a future claim on national resources and there would be no other effects.

This neutral case can be made less unrealistic. In the first place, it is not necessary to de-tax oil itself. If economy in the use of oil were desired, it would be better, for example, to lower other indirect taxes to the extent of the oil impact. The difference between the two cases is a standard exercise in budgetary analysis.

Secondly, it is unlikely that foreigners would so conveniently desire to hold public sector assets. If they wanted private sector assets instead, this would present a problem of intermediation, but no serious difficulties from a monetary point of view. In effect, the private sector would get the increased public sector debt and release the other assets for foreigners to hold. There would, however, normally be some changes in relative asset prices.

The most serious difficulty is one we have already come across. If the oil producers or, more accurately, international creditors in general, do not want to hold *any* of the debt instruments of the country concerned, there is a 'recycling' problem; the balance of payments deficit could only be financed if exchange rates or interest rates changed. It is notable that this is not an unfamiliar problem; it is simply an example of the general difficulty that international considerations limit domestic monetary freedom—though admittedly the problem appears in rather an extreme form.

If the impact is *not* offset by the public authorities, broadly along the lines of the simplified analysis above, then the *private* sector *must* run a deficit—i.e. its net asset position must deteriorate in line with the balance of payments deficit.

[13] This is a simplification. In practice, externally held assets of certain types can affect domestic credit creation, and hence the domestic money supply. The impacts depend, however, on the precise institutional and legal provisions surrounding banking ratios, and hence vary between countries.

It is this deterioration that leads to the deflationary effects, and which may also increase inflationary pressure. It is convenient to analyse the impacts separately for households and for companies. In an actual case, of course, both sectors would be affected simultaneously, so that the overall result would depend on some mixture of the two 'pure' cases considered.

Consider first the case where the household sector takes *all* the oil impact—by which it is meant that the deterioration in the financial position of the country (the adverse effect on the current balance) is entirely reflected in the household sector's financial position. This will be the case if there is no change in the government deficit, and no change in the net acquisition of financial assets by companies. In this situation the relation between the household sector's receipts and its expenditures must worsen to the extent of the oil impact. Consumers must be going more into debt or saving less than before. So much is a matter of accounting.

Though the worsening of the relation between household receipts and expenditures must happen—*ex post* it is a truism—the new situation may induce disequilibrating reactions. Of course, consumers might simply be willing to countenance the deterioration in their financial position, without altering real expenditures.[14] In this case there would be no effects on real aggregate demand. A more likely reaction, however, is that they will reduce expenditures in an attempt to restore their financial position—thus reducing real demand. For so long as the balance of payments deficit continues, however, they cannot be successful in lowering their expenditures in relation to their receipts. Their reduced expenditure simply works through, *in aggregate*, to produce a reduction in their income to the same extent. A cumulative process is likely to be set in train, which continues until households are willing to accept the deterioration in their financial position without further attempts to cut expenditure. This is nothing more than the familiar Keynesian multiplier effect. Equilibrium occurs when desired savings have fallen to the required extent, which, according to standard consumption function theory, only occurs at lower levels of demand and output.[15]

Another reaction is possible: faced with a deteriorating financial position, individuals may struggle harder to raise their income. The attempt to restore their real income position (again doomed to failure in aggregate) could lead to a sharp increase in inflationary pressure.

Now consider what happens if *companies* initially take all the oil impact.

[14] No change in real expenditures, since they are paying more for oil, would imply increased expenditure in money terms—hence with unchanged money incomes their savings must fall, or they must be going more into debt.

[15] The example is artificial in that most of the normal stabilizers are absent. (1) If the balance of payments deficit is unaltered, there is no 'import leakage'. (2) If the public sector deficit is unaltered, there is no automatic stabilizing effect due to unemployment benefit or tax decrease. (3) If the company sector deficit is unaltered, in effect company investment must decline *pari passu* with company income. The multiplier in this artificial example really would be the reciprocal of the marginal propensity to save out of personal disposable income—or about ten. If consumer investment—largely expenditure on housing—were also adversely affected, the full effects could be even larger. In the short run, of course, lags could be highly stabilizing. In practice, household savings tended to rise in 1974 and 1975—adding to instability.

(Suppose, for example, that consumers are protected, or somehow manage to avoid an deterioration in their financial position—so that household's net financial surplus or deficit position remains unchanged.) If the assumptions of no change in the foreign balance[16] and of no change in the public sector deficit are retained, then the 'pure' effect of the oil impact on the company sector can be analysed. In the standard Keynesian forecasting models employed at the time little attention was paid to the effect of financial variables on company expenditure. Here, however, it is suggested that financial effects may be very important, and more recent models include similar interactions.[17]

The deterioration in the current balance now implies, as an accounting identity, that the company sector must be spending more in relation to its receipts—it must be increasing its indebtedness—or lowering its surplus earnings. The extent of the deterioration is great; under the artificial assumptions adopted, it is equal to the oil impact itself. For the UK this would give a swing in 1974 relative to 1973 of nearly $6 billion, or slightly less than £3 billion.[18] If the oil impact is accepted as inevitable, and the other sectors of the economy do not 'allow' their financial positions to deteriorate, then this deterioration is inevitable, no matter what evasive action is taken.

The problem in this case is that though the corporate sector's position *must* deteriorate to this extent, company policy will be affected. In exactly the same way as for households, expenditures may be lowered—leading to lower investment and increasing unemployment. There may also be pressure from company accountants to raise prices—stimulating inflationary pressure. Equilibrium would occur, as before, when no further cuts in expenditure are induced, that is, when the deterioration in financial positions is accepted as inevitable.

The problem is cumulative, and the effects may be delayed. Adverse cash flow positions can be tolerated for a time; if prolonged, however, difficulties get worse, and reactions follow.

The domestic problem, for companies, is entirely analogous to the international balance of payments problem. There is a demand side—are companies willing to change their traditional operating criteria and taken on increased debt, or lower surpluses? If not, deflationary reactions will be set in train. Secondly, there is a *domestic* recycling problem. Those companies which are prepared to keep up expenditure, in spite of lower income, may look bad credit risks; they may not be able to raise the finance even though they desire to. Bankruptcy may follow, if they are not bailed out. The situation can be made easier if credit conditions ease; but the problem remains. They have to be willing to take on more debt (including, of course, floating new equity issues)—which they will only do if they feel that it is profitable on a long-term basis.

Surprisingly, perhaps, the possible effects on company liquidity were relatively neglected in early analyses of the oil crisis. It was felt by many that, if

[16] Other than the initial impact.

[17] Whilst the importance of financial linkages is now fully appreciated, the effects are still hard to estimate, and often appear to operate only after some threshold. The effects are often imposed judgementally.

[18] Or nearly 3 per cent of GDP in 1974.

consumers—through wage pressures—succeeded in protecting themselves, the deflationary impact would be lost. Experience through 1974 showed how wrong that view was. But there *can* be offsets, in certain circumstances, if the impact is taken by companies. Certain types of investment may be stimulated (energy exploration and saving). It is possible also that in some countries there is a typically *excess* demand for finance in the sense that firms are always willing to borrow more at existing interest rates if they can get credit—the system being kept in check by monetary availability factors. In circumstances of extreme willingness to accept higher liabilities—presumably due to profit expectations—there is no need for a deflationary response, unless monetary policy tightens further to contract the supply of credit.

But, in general, a relaxation of monetary policy may not easily counteract the flow impact on corporate financial positions. A relaxation may increase willingness to take on additional debt liabilities—either for cost or availability reasons—but need not. The liquidity difficulties do not arise from a tight monetary policy, but from a changed relationship between current receipts and current expenditures. The problems posed by such a situation can be considerably exacerbated by high interest rates and the difficulty of obtaining loans, but there may still be reactions of an expenditure-reducing kind even if monetary conditions are relatively easy.

We have considered three 'pure' cases corresponding to the oil impact being taken by government (public sector), by households, or by companies. Clearly, any actual case is a mixture of the pure cases. Some of the impact falls on households, some on firms, and the government takes some. In fact, however, it is likely that most of the impact will end up being taken by the government, *whether that is the intention or not*. The reason is that not much stabilization can be expected from either households or companies. The actions of the authorities make a great difference to the level of activity that results at the end of the disequilibrium process. At one extreme, if the authorities act to offset the impact there may be no downswing in activity. At the other extreme, if no action is taken, the offsetting increase in the public sector deficit position occurs automatically as a result of recession—due to increased transfer payments (especially unemployment benefits) and a decline in tax receipts.

An imposed swing in the current balance of payments position is like a change in the public sector deficit. When it happens, the economy is in disequilibrium. The impact may, in fact, be passed around from sector to sector before equilibrium is re-established. Suppose, for example, that the initial impact falls on consumers. Through a combination of reduced expenditure and successful wage demands the impact could be passed to companies. As we have seen, the response of companies could be to reduce expenditure (thus creating unemployment) and also, perhaps, to pass the impact back to consumers via price rises. The process of disequilibrium continues until the deterioration in financial positions is 'willingly' accepted by some sector or sectors. In practice, however, no great reduction in savings can be expected from consumers—in the 1974–5 recession savings rose. In the short term, dramatic increases in the deficit of the company sector are possible; but in the longer run these may not be sustainable. So the main stabilizing force is an induced rise in the public sector deficit as a result of the recession, which offsets the impact on the private sector. It is perhaps interesting that Keynes, writing at the start of the Depression in 1931, saw demand stabilizing due to government deficits—he did not appear to expect much stabilization from household savings [11], [12].

An interesting example of the sort of interactions that can occur is provided by price control in the United Kingdom in 1974. Consumers' real income positions were protected by threshold payments under Stage III. Companies were unable to pass on fully the effects of increased expenditure on inputs—back to consumers—because of price control, and also because of increased competition. Pressure developed, however, for a removal of price controls—and ultimately price control was relaxed. Paradoxically, however, the reduction in price control might not have been able to improve company financial positions. Obviously, if higher prices led to higher wages (because of threshholds) they would be self-defeating. But even if the price rises had 'stuck', it is arguable that they would not have improved the situation. By passing the impact back to consumers they would have set in train further reductions in consumer demand, adversely affecting company income, and so on. Only if the price rise led to a reduction in consumer savings would the financial balance of the company sector be improved.[19] But the reduction in price controls was not the only aid to companies in the second half of 1974. Part of the help to companies fell directly on the government deficit, and, in any case, it was found that the public sector deficit (combined capital and current account) had been rising very rapidly: so rapidly, indeed, that 'liquidity' difficulties looked like being temporary anyway.

19.5. Economic Policy Between the Two Oil Crises

19.5.1. The 1974–5 Recession

Industrialized countries, as a group, decelerated extremely sharply from the peak of 1973 into the worst recession since the Second World War. By the middle of 1975 recorded unemployment in OECD countries had risen to about 15 million, or about $5\frac{1}{2}$ per cent of the civilian labour force. Industrial output fell dramatically during the recession—by over 20 per cent in Japan, and by about 15 per cent in Germany and the United States. In the United Kingdom the fall was somewhat less—but still substantial. In the United States GNP fell by about $7\frac{1}{2}$ per cent from its peak in 1973 to a low point in the first half of 1975. For other industrialized countries taken as a group, GNP roughly stagnated over the same period. The volume of world trade, which had been buoyant since the war, was rapidly contracting in late 1974 and in the first half of 1975. The move to recession was accompanied by unprecedented rates of inflation and some very difficult balance of payments situations.

By the end of 1975 it was apparent that the three major countries which had led the way into recession—the United States, Japan, and Germany—had bottomed out during 1975. The United States recovery appeared well

[19] Of course, the reduction in price control was very important for some particular companies.

established. The extent of recovery in Japan, and especially in Germany, was more debatable. Many European countries however, were still experiencing the full effects of the world recession.

It is natural to ascribe the development of world recession to the commodity price boom and the oil crisis. But the direct effects of these events were probably less important than the indirect effects that came about owing to the policy response of governments. As noted, the demand-depressive effects could have been offset. In most cases they were not offset, and indeed demand management policies (especially monetary policy) moved towards restriction. Particularly in the three largest countries, the United States, Japan, and germany, restrictive policies were pursued as a conventional response to rapid rates of inflation.

There is no doubt that aggregate demand on a global basis was excessive in 1973. Some restriction was necessary, both to remove the supply constraints which were appearing and in order to stem the rise in commodity prices. Policy disagreements appeared, however, as to the extent of deflation and of unemployment that was desirable.

It was, of course, accepted as more or less inevitable that consumer prices would accelerate dramatically in 1974 as the increased oil and commodity prices were passed through. But the major fear was that after that stimulus tailed off, inflation would continue at high or even accelerating rate due to a domestic wage–price spiral. Some argued that the best way to minimize the ensuing wage–price spiral, and to make sure that inflation rates came down, was to deflate substantially and to rely on the traditional trade-off between inflation and unemployment. Others took the view that deflation beyond the point necessary to remove excess demand would have little effect on inflation, and might indeed intensify the struggle over income shares. Proponents of the latter view naturally tended also to favour the use of incomes policies or other 'non-conventional' anti-inflation policies. It is not surprising that the conventional policies of deflation and monetary control found least favour in those countries where past experience (and especially experience in 1970–1) suggested that the trade-off between inflation and unemployment was particularly unfavourable.

The large falls in domestic demand in the United States, Japan, and Germany largely account for the very uneven pattern of balance of payments surpluses and deficits that developed. The relative conjunctural positions meant that the overall deficit of the OECD area was concentrated on the smaller OECD countries. Though the United Kingdom found external finance easy to obtain, Italy and some of the smaller countries were more or less forced to take deflationary action as a result of financing problems. Nevertheless, the more extravagant fears of an immediate scramble for balance of payments positions turned out to be unfounded. In fact, by the first half of 1975 the deficit position of the OECD area had been almost eliminated. The most important reason for the turn-round was the world recession, which had the twin effects of sharply lowering oil imports and of lowering imports from the non-oil-producing less developed countries so that the 'deficit' was passed to them. As noted earlier, a recovery by industrialized countries was bound to lead to a re-emergence of the problems of a current balance of payments deficit for the OECD countries as a group.

The oil price rise did mean that deflationary impulses were more likely to be transmitted from one country to another. Those countries which did not deflate immediately (or deflated only moderately) were subject to a double impact. The recession in the large countries was bound to affect the development of their exports and worsen their balance of payments position; the oil crisis added to the problem in that the swing in the balance of payments was that much larger. This swing in turn tended to lead to a direct response through deflationary policy, and even in the absence of an explicit policy response tended to produce recessionary forces anyway, for the reasons explained earlier. Particularly where the impact fell on companies, the response tended to be delayed and it was easy to underestimate its magnitude.

Perhaps the most puzzling aspect of the 1973 world recession is that it was not more widely predicted—at least by official forecasters. Though in many countries the rise in unemployment was an intended response to the inflation problem, the recession took on a cumulative character which was not generally anticipated. Some remarks about the reasons for the underestimation of the deflationary forces can perhaps serve to draw together some of the points raised in previous sections.

A distinguishing feature of the 1973 boom and subsequent recession was that practically all countries were simultaneously affected. By the beginning of 1975 recessionary forces appeared to be operative in almost all countries. As noted in section 19.2 of this chapter, when countries move together, rather larger multiplier effects are to be expected. Moreover, the impact of the oil crisis and inflation on expectations and confidence was very substantial indeed. It is probable that many of the usual stabilizing elements were absent during the development of the recession, so that any adverse impacts would tend to have larger effects than usual.

Another element that should be given weight is the situation in 1973. It seems probably that many countries had already passed the turning-point and that a slowdown was already occurring. The deflationary moves and the effects of the oil crisis therefore came on top of a situation which was already recessionary. This illustrates that one of the most difficult elements in any forecasting exercise is the diagnosis of the current situation.

Forecasting procedures should capture the cumulative effects due to simultaneous movements. But forecasting is difficult when the situation passes outside the range of recent past experience. There was no precedent, for example, for the sharp contraction in world trade that occurred. But another element is that the lags appear to have been rather lengthy. For example, world trade was stabilized in 1974 to a remarkable extent by a maintenance of imports by less developed countries. It was only at the end of 1974 that world trade started to drop sharply. As noted, some of the financial effects in the deficit countries were delayed; such effects cumulate and appear to build up to some kind of a threshold. The result of the long lags was that it was easy to underestimate the effects still to come. Since in most countries inflation fears and balance of payments worries combined to produce deflationary or at least cautious policies, the recessionary forces developed considerable momentum.

In the course of the recession two further deflationary elements appeared. Households, which in more normal times would have been expected to stabilize the situation by lowering their savings, in fact sharply increased their savings with strongly deflationary results. The reasons for the rise in savings which occurred in many countries are debatable. Some of the rise may have been due to wealth effects following the extremely severe fall in real stock-market values all over the world. Some was probably precautionary—a response to rising unemployment and the general climate of uncertainty. The other element is that there was a very sharp adjustment of inventory levels by companies. Inventory accumulation appears to have continued well after the turn-round in final demand. In early 1975, however, there was a sharp reaction and an absolute reduction in the level of inventories for the OECD area as a whole.

In general, due to the long lags and the additional deflationary elements that appeared, it seems that disequilibrium in the world economy continued for much *longer* than usual, and so the recession developed much further. One major stabilizing element was that as the recession developed public sector deficits rose, in many countries, to unprecedented levels—far exceeding the oil impact. Much of the rise reflected the automatic stabilizer effects referred to earlier, but there were fiscal relaxations as well. The rise had to go beyond the oil impact or the balance of payments impact to offset the increased desire to save of consumers—and, in most countries, to allow for a build-up of financial assets to more normal levels by the company sector as well.

The situation at the beginning of 1976 well illustrated a major difficulty in forecasting economic developments. A number of the elements that contribute to the development of recession are self-reversing in character. Most obviously, inventory run-down comes to an end—as it did in the United States in mid-1975. High savings allow a reduction of consumer indebtedness and contribute to a revival of consumer spending. If companies are saving more than they are investing, they are building up their asset position, and as this happens this contributes to a revival of investment expenditure. These two elements mean that public sector deficits (the counterpart to increased saving by companies and households) may have *cumulative* effects on the level of activity. Most importantly, as activity recovers so do expectations—thus reinforcing the upswing in activity. These elements mean not only that it is hard to forecast turning-points, but also that it is very difficult to judge the strength of any upswing that develops. Much of course depends upon policy action. But there is a worry that if reflationary action is large enough then it may, almost inevitably, be too large, and tend to bring about a kind of political cycle as governments oscillate between the objectives of full employment and price stability.

19.5.2. Recovery and Slow Growth

The recovery in the second half of 1975 and in 1976 was characteristically sharp. World trade grew at about 12 per cent per annum, and there was a marked improvement in industrial production. Thus during 1976 it was still possible to argue that the recovery was on course, and that an over-strong response with a risk of renewed acceleration in inflation was as likely as too weak a response. Thus governments, many of whom were still primarily concerned with getting inflation down, tended to take a very cautious line. Fiscal policy became substantially more restrictive—with large reductions in government deficits—and monetary targets were adopted which were more cautious than in previous periods of upswing. In spite of these policies, world commodity prices were sharply raised by the turn-round. This volatility in commodity markets was another factor making for policy reactions which generally erred on the side of caution.

In fact the recovery never appeared soundly based. It depended on a reversal of the stockbuilding cycle, and a recovery of consumer durable demand from exceptionally depressed levels. As these natural, but temporary, factors faded, the recovery faltered, and growth in 1977 and 1978 was slow. World trade grew in those two years by only about $4\frac{1}{2}$ per cent per annum. The growth of GNP of the industrialized countries was about 3 to $3\frac{1}{2}$ per cent per annum, compared with the historical trend of about 5 per cent. These rates of expansion implied an increasing degree of slack and rising unemployment in most OECD countries.

With a continuation of slow growth and substantial disequilibrium in the world economy, it was natural that more fundamental worries should surface. Was the rapid growth of the 1950s and 1960s—which for all its faults began to look like a gold age—gone, never to return? Were rapid growth and stable prices incompatible, as many had always thought they would be? Did the end of the 1960s mark the beginning of a period of fundamental resource constraints, of the type publicized by the 'Club of Rome' and others? Were demand management policies—of both monetary and fiscal kinds—completely impotent or counter-productive in a period of volatile expectations? Was the problem structural, owing to inappropriate relative prices, labour market rigidities, and the like? Had there been a fundamental change in the propensity to invest, perhaps owing to declining profitability, itself resulting in part from the problem of 'competing claims' for a limited national output and inflationary pressure of the 'struggle over income shares' variety?

The awkward combination of problems faced—to varying degrees—by most industrialized countries should be no surprise. It was the natural result of an international system in disequilibrium. When one thing goes wrong, it is highly likely that all sorts of other problems will emerge as well. In practice it is extremely difficult to sort out cause from effect, the fundamental from the less fundamental.

A second observation comes out of the analysis presented in looking at the past, in section 18.2. There it was argued that the period of rapid and sustained expansion depended to an unknown extent on the expectation that full employment growth was the norm. Both the feasibility of government action and the objective of full employment and growth now came to be questioned. Such a change in expectations is likely, a priori, to markedly alter private sector responses. One of the distressing features of the recovery was that private investment expenditure did not recover nearly as much as usual. But if expectations were generally pessimistic, such a development is easy to account for.

But it is not only the private sector that came to be affected by pessimism about world growth prospects. The international transmission mechanisms appeared so strong that many countries had only limited domestic economic sovereignty. They were forced to base their own policy on expected developments elsewhere. Formally, this meant that a co-operative strategy might have been necessary. But at the international level there is of course no equivalent to the national authorities who, in the past, could, for better or worse, attempt to control the economy. International co-operative action is chancy and difficult. Any such strategy is extremely vulnerable to the risk that it might fail. And any strategy depends on there being agreement about what the problems are, and about what should be done about them.

19.5.3. Strategies

Soon after the oil crisis it was recognized that to get back to more acceptable developments in the world economy would take time. It was a medium-term problem. This recognition was reflected in the policy statements of governments and in the normative scenarios that were prepared—principally by the OECD (see, for example [7]). There was a substantial shift away from emphasis on short-term stabilization policy towards more medium-term objectives and planning. And by and large, such normative plans for the world economy (or at least the industrialized part of it) were endorsed by national governments. Why then, at least in 1977 and 1978, did such plans fail?

Before going into some of the difficulties, it is worth seeing what sort of developments for the world economy were being suggested. Table 19.1 shows some of the figures from an OECD scenario published in 1976. An obvious feature of the scenario is the high overall rate of expansion portrayed. The growth rate of $5\frac{1}{2}$ per cent per annum over a five-year period was slightly over the assumed growth of productive potential, so that if it occurred, it would have been expected to lead over the period to some reductions in unemployment. Several other features bring out its normative character. It was hoped to bring down inflation to about 5 per cent per annum by the end of the period. Within the scenario, high rates of growth of investment are shown. Finally, the figures for exports and imports would, at the exchange rates assumed, have led to some correction of the serious external payments imbalances at the beginning of the period.

Of course, that scenario was rapidly overtaken by events. The recovery year 1976 was the only time that the targets were even approximately met. And looking at the experience of individual countries in 1977 and 1978, the only one to approach its target was the United States. Germany's growth was about $2\frac{1}{2}$ per cent per annum. And in Japan, growth at 5 per cent owed a lot to buoyant exports. But such a plan or scenario remained relevant if it were thought of as being rolled forward for a year or so. A rate of growth of the world economy of $4\frac{1}{2}$ to $5\frac{1}{2}$ per cent per annum still appeared necessary in the medium term even to maintain the existing degree of slack in OECD countries. The target recovery track—the 'narrow path'—that was suggested in the

TABLE 19.1. *Growth Scenario to 1975–1980, Selected Figures*
(average annual percentage changes)

	Output	Investment	Exports	Imports	GNP/GDP deflator*
Total OECD	$5\frac{1}{2}$		$8\frac{1}{2}$	8	5
United States	$5\frac{3}{4}$	$11\frac{1}{4}$	8	9	$4\frac{1}{2}$
Canada	[	$8\frac{1}{4}$	9	$8\frac{1}{2}$	$5\frac{1}{2}$
Japan	7	$7\frac{1}{2}$	$10\frac{1}{2}$	$8\frac{1}{2}$	6
France	6	$7\frac{1}{2}$	$9\frac{1}{2}$	$11\frac{1}{2}$	6
Germany	5	$6\frac{1}{2}$	8	9	4
Italy	$4\frac{1}{2}$	$5\frac{1}{2}$	9	$7\frac{1}{4}$	7
UK	$3\frac{1}{2}$	$5\frac{1}{2}$	7	$4\frac{1}{2}$	6
Belgium	5	$7\frac{1}{4}$	9	10	$5\frac{1}{2}$
Netherlands	$4\frac{1}{2}$	3	$7\frac{1}{2}$	8	5
Sweden	$3\frac{1}{2}$	4	8	$6\frac{1}{2}$	$5\frac{1}{2}$
Switzerland	3	$\frac{3}{4}$	$4\frac{1}{2}$	$4\frac{1}{2}$	$3\frac{1}{2}$

* End-year (1980 compared with 1979), per cent per annum.

ource: OECD [7].

McCracken Report' [6] was an endorsement of the rate of growth put forward
n the scenario.

The popular term for the kind of objective adopted by OECD governments
n 1976 was the 'locomotive strategy'. This term referred to the view that the
strongest countries, with healthy external positions, who had made the greatest
inroads on inflation, should lead the way out of the recession, while the weaker
should lag somewhat in order to improve their balance of payments, and
because of the anti-inflation objective. Some of the obvious difficulties with
such indicative plans for the world economy are as follows:

(1) There may be disagreements over the targets that should be adopted.
(2) Even if the overall targets are accepted, it may appear to pay individual
    countries to go for lower growth in their own economies, in the hope that
    they will be pulled up by expansion elsewhere. But if generalized, such
    policies add up to slow world growth.
(3) Individual targets—even in the medium term—may be substantially
    out of line with the overall strategy.
(4) Domestic economic policy may be powerless to meet the targets, either
    because the instruments of policy do not work—or are misjudged—or
    because external considerations and other constraints may severely limit
    the scope for domestic action.

In general it would appear that any tendencies to overshoot or to fall short
should roughly balance. In practice they did not balance. Almost all the

uncertainties and constraining factors acted in a downward direction. Thus
was highly likely that slow growth would result.

The main reason for slow growth in 1977 and 1978 was the slow grow
performance of Germany and Japan. If two of the 'locomotives' undersho
substantially it is not surprising that the targets were not met. And the effect
undershoot had repercussions on international trade, and hence on the polici
of the weaker countries as well. Thus in 1978, as it became obvious that slo
growth was continuing, the locomotive strategy was in effect abandoned (mo
obviously in the run up to the Bonn summit of July 1978) and replaced with
looser idea of generalized expansionary policies, with weaker or 'convalescer
countries also expected to make some of the running. This new strategy becan
known as the 'convoy strategy'. The main result, however, was that German
did, at last, though with continuing reluctance, reflate fairly substantiall
Combined with other relaxations (in the UK for example) growth in the wor
economy did speed up, until it was brought sharply to an end by the even
surrounding the Iranian revolution and the second oil crisis.

19.6 The Second Oil Crisis: 1979–1980

19.6.1. The Magnitude of the Problem

Oil prices were relatively stable between 1974 and 1978, rising gently fro
around $11 per barrel to about $13.[20] This corresponded to a substantial fa
over the period in *real* terms of about 10–15 per cent. This period of stabili
came to an end in 1979: the price of crude oil rose to $19 per barrel in 1979,
over $31 per barrel in 1980, and to about $35 per barrel in 1981. Thus th
cumulative increase was about 2·7 *times*, or 170 per cent.[21] Allowing for gener
inflation, real oil prices approximately doubled.

The immediate event triggering these developments was the Irania
revolution in late 1978 and early 1979. Oil exports from Iran, previous
running at about 5 million barrels per day,[22] were suspended fro
27 December 1979 to 4 March 1979. When resumed, supplies were approx
mately 2 million barrels per day less than had been assumed in forwar
projections. Although much of the initial shortfall was made up by other OPE
producers, a deficiency remained, which was exacerbated by a cold winter i
the northern hemisphere, by low stocks, and by an increasing tendency towar
conservation of oil supplies by several producers inside and outside the OPE
group. In addition, structural changes in the world oil market had bee
occurring which markedly decreased its flexibility: in the circumstanc
security of supply became the dominant consideration for many buyers c
crude oil, and prices reacted strongly. It was the loss of flexibility, rather than
lasting supply shortfall, that largely explained the rapid oil price rises and th
disorderly conditions during 1979 and 1980.

---

[20] Weighted official/contract price of crude oil exports (f.o.b.). See OECD, *Economic Outlo*
(July 1983), Table 30.

[21] Ibid.

[22] Almost $\frac{1}{5}$ of the production of the oil-exporting countries.

The dangers in the situation as it developed in 1979 were obvious. In the
ort term, there was a need for direct measures of conservation to allow for the
building of stocks and to guard against the risk or severe shortages developing
the winter of 1979–80. Moreover, though in 1979 attention tended to focus
the immediate difficulties posed by shortages and rising prices, the real
gnificance of the events surrounding the Iranian revolution was longer term.
he projection forward of energy supplies and demands had always been a
azardous business: after the revolution many of the longer-term assumptions
pout OPEC behaviour and OPEC supply began to look totally unrealistic. In
onsumer countries too, delays in the development of alternatives to OPEC oil
nd in conservation measures suggested that the oil market was likely (*given*
asonable growth in the world economy) to be much tighter and much more
nstable than had been assumed. Thus pessimism about the longer-term
utlook was a major factor affecting price in the short term, especially as
peculation began to influence spot markets. It began to look as if there was a
ossibility that the growth of the world economy would be limited by the
vailability of a key industrial input.[23] (Later, as the world moved into
cession, and especially when the expected world recovery in 1982 failed to
aterialize, the oil market weakened greatly: in early 1983 OPEC output was
duced to less than half the level of 1979, and the 'official' price of crude was
duced to $29.[24] These developments were not, however, generally foreseen in
979 and 1980.)

Apart from worries over energy and oil supplies, OECD governments faced,
1 1979 and 1980, the macroeconomic consequences of the oil price rises for
iflation, for the balance of payments, and for growth. In principle, these were
milar to those that followed the first oil crisis: they came through, however,
onsiderably more slowly. For example, in mid-1979, oil prices had risen by
pproximately 60 per cent since December 1978: this meant that the increase
i the oil bill for industrialized countries as a proportion of GDP (a measure of
ie overall size of the oil impact) was then about half as large as in 1973–4.
rices went on rising, however, so that the full impact turned out to be about
ouble that—or, conveniently for the purposes of exposition—almost the same
ize' as in the earlier crisis of 1973–4. Thus the direct 'mechanical' impact of
ie second oil crisis was, like the first, about $2-2\frac{1}{2}$ per cent of most OECD
ountries' GDP, a figure which also indicates the direct impact on the final
rice level.[25]

9.6.2. *The Policy Response*

Ve have noted that, at the Bonn summit of 1978, some modest relationary
10ves to raise European growth rates and bring about a better balance in the

[23] The OECD suggested that there was an 'energy-warranted rate of growth' which might
ffectively constrain the growth of the world economy.
[24] The price for market crude was reduced by $5 on 14 March 1983.
[25] See, for example, IMF, *World Economic Outlook* (May 1980), OECD, *Economic Outlook* (27 July
980). Sympathetic rises in the prices of substitutes for imported oil (e.g. indigenous oil, gas, or
oal) meant that the overall impact would be larger.

world economy were agreed.[26] Growth did pick up, especially in Germany. This strategy was, however, never tested. Soon after, and purely coincidentally, the world economy ran into the inflationary and other difficulties of the second oil crisis. The accident of timing left the impression in some countries that the more relaxed policy stance was a major reason for the subsequent oil-induced price rises.

We have discussed in detail the problems posed by the first oil crisis, and the policy response. In large degree the problems posed by the second one—for inflation, and for real activity—were the same. The starting-point, however, differed in important ways. First, on the positive side, although there had been some reflation, the industrialized countries were in a much less fragile and over extended position than in 1973. (Though non-oil commodity prices started to rise from about the middle of 1978, raising fears of a renewal of inflation even before the Iranian revolution.) In most other respects, however, the situation was worse. Unemployment had stepped up from about 3 per cent before the first oil crisis to over 5 per cent afterwards.[27] Consumer price inflation was still running at the relatively high rate of about 8 per cent per annum; wage inflation was even worse. Above all, the many problems of adjustment set in train by the first oil crisis did not appear to have been solved except in a few countries.

The most important difference, however, was in the policy response adopted by OECD governments. After the first oil crisis there were, as we have seen, major disagreements about what best to do, centring on the vexed question of how to minimize the inflationary effects of the oil and commodity price rises. Some governments had tried to 'offset', though on balance the overall response was deflationary. With the second oil crisis, there appeared to be no disagreement at all: the response was immediately restrictive almost every where. No country appeared even to try to offset the inflationary/deflationary impact—not even the UK, which by 1980 was self-sufficient in oil, meaning that the oil impact was internal (see Chapters 13 and 27).

This important change in policy attitudes owed much to the experience of the period since 1973. In the first place there was a widespread feeling that those countries that had introduced restrictive fiscal and monetary policies after the first oil crisis had out-performed those which had not. In particular, there was admiration for German policy, where tight monetary policies (including monetary targets) appeared to have helped slow inflation much faster than elsewhere. One of the mechanisms was via exchange rate rises, which, in the German case, appeared to have helped inflation rather than worsening international competitiveness. Many countries appeared to feel that it was desirable to emulate that experience (however inconsistent such a policy

[26] The slowdown in Europe and Japan in 1977 is most apparent from data on industrial production. For the four major European countries it hardly changed during the year, before picking up in 1978. In Japan, too, industrial production was flat until it started to pick up in the second half of the year.

[27] Average for OECD countries: standardized definition. See OECD, *Economic Outlook* 'Historical Statistics, 1960–80'.

would be if widely adopted). Second, there is no doubt that those countries that had tried to offset the impact of oil whilst others deflated had, in a number of cases, got into trouble. (Italy, Denmark, and the UK had been forced into deflationary action. Sweden's attempts to bridge the recession had led to major difficulties, particularly with the balance of payments.) Third, there was the fact that in many countries, progress against inflation had been very slow and costly which—perhaps paradoxically—meant that the authorities were even less willing to risk a further upsurge. Finally—no doubt partly in response to the unfavourable developments of the 1970s—there had been a major change in the economic perceptions that underly policy action, away from the broadly Keynesian consensus of the 1960s towards more 'monetarist' modest of analysis. This was one factor (though by no means the only one) behind the widespread adoption of monetary targets in the late 1970s.

These factors operated to differing extents in the various countries—in many smaller OECD countries the dominant fear seems to have been of running into unsustainable external payments positions: the perception of economic policy remained broadly Keynesian, though they were locked into a world situation not of their making. These countries continued to preach the virtues of international co-operative action of a reflationary kind. By contrast, France under the 'Barre Plan'[28] more or less explicitly tried to emulate Germany. In the UK (after May 1979 when the Conservative Government was elected) monetarist ideas were extremely influential in determining the policy response (see Chapter 10). In the United States, which had been unexpectedly buoyant in the second half of 1978, fiscal and monetary policy were both tightened. The deflationary response was particularly marked in Germany, which was, in effect, caught off balance by the oil price rises, coming as they did just after a somewhat reluctant reflation.

Figure 19.1 shows some indicators of monetary and fiscal policy stance for the major OECD countries during the 1970s. It is notable that, after the first oil crisis, though nominal interest rates rose initially, real interest rates (i.e. after allowance for inflation) were strongly negative in the recession of 1974–5. They hovered round about zero between the two crises. The fiscal indicators show that the major swing to budget deficit in 1975 was not due just to the automatic effects of the recession on public expenditure and receipts, but also involved 'discretionary' fiscal relaxation.[29] The picture after 1979–80 is quite different. Nominal interest rates again rose sharply, but, as inflation moderated a little, did not come down. As a result real interest rates rose (to the order of 4 or 5 per cent in most OECD countries) and stayed there in 1981 and 1982. On the fiscal side, although budget deficits rose to reach over 4 per cent of GDP by 1982—a level comparable to that reached in 1975—the cyclically adjusted deficit *narrowed* throughout the period and was very small by 1981 and 1982. This indicates that discretionary fiscal policy, far from offsetting the impact of oil, was tightening over the period, and that more than the whole of the rise in

[28] So called after the Prime Minister Raymond Barre.
[29] See Chaps. 12 and 13 on UK demand management, for a discussion of the concepts involved.

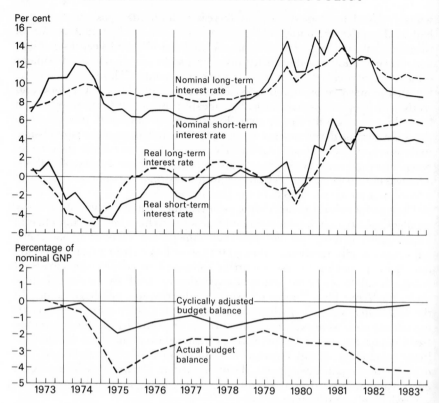

FIG. 19.1. Monetary and Fiscal Policy Indicators (Aggregates for Seven Major OECD Countries).

* OECD forecasts.

budget deficits in 1981 and 1982 could be accounted for by the effects of recession.[30]

19.6.3. The Delayed Recovery

It is useful to raise the question as to what, given the policies adopted, might be expected to happen to the OECD countries in reaction to the second oil shock. Any answer, however, depends upon the overall view of the economic system adopted (Keynesian or monetarist, for example) and it is clear that quantitative or qualitative 'forecasts' could differ a lot—and did in fact differ at the time. On a broadly Keynesian view, the impact was likely to be similar to

[30] It is also worth bearing in mind that fiscal stance in the United States—which has a large weight in the overall indicators—was rather different from elsewhere. Although policy was not offsetting, most estimates of discretionary policy in the US (or of the cyclically adjusted budget position) suggest that it was, over the period 1979–82, approximately neutral (though it varied from year to year). The fiscal tightening elsewhere (especially in Europe) thus tends to be understated by the aggregate indicators.

at after the first oil crisis. The *ex-ante* 'fiscal' impact of oil was contractionary
by about 2 per cent of OECD Gross Domestic Product. The much less extended
arting position meant, however, that a much slower, shallower recession
ight be anticipated—and at the time forecasts often referred to a 'saucer-
aped' recession. Restrictive fiscal and monetary policies, via the usual 'trade-
ff' involving unemployment, would be expected to curb inflation to an extent
rgely dependent on the severity of recession that was tolerated. On more
monetarist' lines of argument—and we have seen that monetarist modes of
inking had been gaining ground in a number of countries—the fiscal impact
f oil could be ignored. The chief problem would be the rise in inflation, which
if it occurred against 'non-accommodating' monetary targets, would, via real
alance effects (i.e. inflation reducing the real value of holdings of money) and
igh (real) interest rates, induce recession during the adjustment period. The
ore credible the commitment of the authorities to anti-inflationary monetary
olicy, the quicker would be the response of inflation, and the lower would be
he costs. There were also more eclectic views which, in effect, saw a non-
ccommodating monetary and fiscal framework as affecting inflation and
flationary expectations with, again, adverse effects on output and employ-
ent during the period of adjustment.

Thus, at the risk of over-simplification, it is possible to characterize the
revailing sentiment at the time as a guarded optimism that the initial
flationary effects would be less than after the first oil crisis, and that inflation
ould be rather more quickly contained; and that the recession would be less
ramatic, and less deep. Given that semi-optimistic consensus, it is not
urprising that there was relatively little pressure for offsetting policies. This
cquiescence can, however, best be seen as involving a coalition (amongst
fficials at least) between the broadly Keynesian 'demand managers', who felt
hat in the absence of other policies to deal with inflation, deflation and
ecession were inevitable (there was 'no alternative'), and those of—for want of
better word—'monetarist' persuasion, who thought that restrictive policies
ffered the best hope for inflation *and* for growth.

Table 19.2 shows what actually happened. The peak of inflation occurred in
he first half of 1980 at nearly 14 per cent,[31] which was only marginally better
han in 1974. The subsequent deceleration was very similar, but continued
onger, until by the first half of 1983 inflation had been brought down to about
$\frac{1}{2}$ per cent per annum, substantially better than in any period since the first oil
risis. The cost, however, was greater than generally anticipated. Initially,
;DP more or less stagnated in 1980 and there were signs of an upswing at the
eginning of 1981: it looked as if the optimistic predictions were coming true.
There was then, however, a sharp setback: the anticipated recovery in 1982
ailed to materialize and instead there was a further large contraction.
Recovery did set in with expansion in North America in 1983. The recovery
vas patchy, however, and most European countries remained depressed.
Jnemployment rose greatly, averaging about 9 per cent for the OECD area,

[31] For the total of OECD inflation was somewhat larger than indicated for the major seven
ountries in Table 19.2.

T A B L E 19.2. *Major Seven Countries, Indicators of Economic Performance*

	1973		1974		1975		1976		1977		1978		1979		1980		1981		1982		1983
	I	II	I	II	I	II	I	II	I	II	I	II	I	II	I	II	I	II	I	II	I
Consumer prices*	7·6	10·0	14·8	13·6	10·8	8·8	7·8	7·4	9·2	6·6	6·8	7·8	8·9	11·7	13·6	9·9	10·3	9·4	6·6	6·0	4·5
GDP growth†	8·7	2·3	−0·5	−0·8	−3·0	5·0	6·5	3·1	5·1	3·6	4·8	4·6	2·9	3·2	0·4	0	2·9	0·3	−1·1	0·6	2·0
Unemployment‡		3·4		3·7		5·5		5·5		5·4		5·1		5·0		5·6		6·5		7·9	8·5

* Percentage changes from previous periods, annual rates, not seasonally adjusted.
† Growth of real GDP, percentage changes from previous half-year, seasonally adjusted at annual rates.
‡ Standardized employment rates as a percentage of total labour force.

Source: OECD.

and $10\frac{1}{2}$ per cent in Europe by the first half of 1983.[32] It was estimated that about 33 million people were unemployed in the OECD countries, compared with about 19 million in 1979.

Two rather different accounts of the delay in recovery and the severity of recession gained currency. The first, which is consistent with the general line of analysis adopted in this chapter, was that tight (and tightening) monetary and fiscal policies meant that there was bound to be a reaction as severe or more severe than after the first oil crisis: the long lags reflected the more benign starting position, and the delay in recovery was due to the fact that policy—and especially fiscal policy—was further tightened as the recession developed. This was in contrast to the previous recession, where discretionary fiscal relaxations occurred early and stimulated recovery. On this view recovery, when it did come, reflected policy relaxations: in the United States because of large budget deficits, which had the conventional stimulating effects. In the UK, although fiscal policy tightened, the effects were outweighed by a consumer boom resulting from a removal of credit restraints, and easier finance.

The conventional demand management view of events contrasts with an alternative explanation, which was particularly influential in conditioning expectations in financial markets. This was that the second wave of recession resulted from the adverse effects of US budgetary policy. The relatively relaxed fiscal stance, it was argued, necessitated extremely high interest rates in order to control the money supply and to bring down inflation: high interest rates in turn had to be matched by other industrialized countries, so that high real interest rates became generalized throughout the world economy, exacerbating the debt crisis (see below) and recession. Recovery when it came in North America reflected the success of tight monetary policies in bringing down inflation (the real money supply rose in the US in 1982 by nearly 4 per cent after falling by $2\frac{1}{2}$ per cent in 1980, and by $3\frac{1}{2}$ per cent in 1981). On this view, far from being the engine of recovery, the US budget deficit (which rose to about 4 per cent of GDP in 1982) was the main *threat* to recovery, particularly as forward projections suggested further rises in the structural or underlying deficit.[33]

The alternative 'explanations' well illustrate the disparity of views which had developed by the early 1980s over the role of *fiscal* policy: even the direction of the effects seemed to be in doubt, threatening to paralyse policy-making. Against the conventional view that fiscal relaxation would aid recovery if it did not fuel inflation, an increasingly powerful body of opinion argued almost the exact opposite: that the effects of fiscal policy were *perverse* (presumably implying that a relaxation of fiscal policy would be price-*lowering*!). And although the idea of perverse effects from fiscal policy (going well beyond the full 'crowding-out' of the monetarists) appears extreme and ill-thought-out, there is no doubt that public borrowing in a number of countries started to have

---

[32] Unemployment was in excess of 12 per cent in the UK, Canada, Belgium, the Netherlands, and Spain. Japan, Sweden, Norway, and Switzerland succeeded in keeping unemployment low— less than 3 per cent.

[33] The central government fiscal balance for 1983 was forecast at 6·3 per cent of GDP by the IMF in *World Economic Outlook* (1983).

adverse *expectational* effects in financial markets. These effects could not be ignored by policy makers, however unjustified they might feel them to be.

To go into the question of the balance between monetary and fiscal policy in the US, or more generally into the economic effects to be expected from budget deficits and public borrowing, or into problems of explaining the high real rates of interest in the US and in the world economy in 1982 and 1983, would be beyond the scope of this chapter. Two points need, however, to be brought out. The first is that the *balance* of fiscal and monetary policy in a country such as the US could appear wrong even from the conventional demand management viewpoint. On that view, there is some trade-off between reliance on fiscal policy and on monetary policy, and it would be possible to argue that benefits would flow from a tighter fiscal policy matched by a more relaxed monetary policy. One of the benefits could be lower interest rates in the country itself, and perhaps in other countries as well. The second is that, in spite of the concern over US budget deficits at the time, it was not easy to account for the high US interest rates. The US deficit in 1982 was no larger than in 1975, and most of it was accounted for either by recession or by the effects of inflation (see, for example, Buiter [9]). Public sector debt was about one-quarter of GDP [10], which was vastly lower than after the war (when it was over 100 per cent of GDP) and well below average for industrial countries. To account for the upward pressure on interest rates it was necessary to appeal to anticipated future rises in the deficit, or, more crudely, to an adverse expectational climate.

The policy significance of the disputes over public borrowing was, however, clear. Nearly all countries were, in the early 1980s, sufficiently worried about large deficits to seek to contain them, and this led to some notable moves to tighten fiscal policy, especially in Germany and the UK (see Chapter 13). On one view of the interaction this was entirely beneficial: the IMF, for example, called repeatedly over this period for policy action to control and reduce budget deficits.[34] On the other hand, if the analysis of this chapter is accepted, such a prescription if actually followed was likely to be a recipe for disaster. If budget deficits were curtailed, then deficits elsewhere, in the private sector of industrial countries, in the Third World, or in Eastern Europe, would inevitably widen (or surpluses decline). Only if this policy were accompanied by such large favourable effects from lower interest rates and/or lower expectations of inflation as to outweigh the contractionary effects of the fiscal tightening (which is possible but unlikely) could the policy succeed.[35] in the absence of sufficiently large effects there would be an intensification of world recession and a further worsening of the international debt crisis.

---

[34] See IMF, *World Economic Outlook*, 1981, 1982, and 1983.

[35] If a budget deficit declines then, necessarily, some other surplus must decline or deficit increase. If, however, at the same time (or perhaps because of the reduced public sector deficit) interest rates decline, and/or credit availability increases, then the *desired* balance of the private sector would fall as investment picked up and savings declined. In principle, the effect on a desired balance could outweight the impact on actual balances. An example is provided by the UK in 1983, where cuts in public borrowing (as a proportion of GDP) were outweighed by a credit-financed consumer boom in the private sector.

19.6.4. The International Debt Crisis

The most spectacular manifestation of the economic difficulties set in train by the second oil crisis was the international debt crisis that developed from about 1981 onwards (see Chapter 18, pp. 574–80 for a description of the build-up of this problem). The difficulties of some large borrowers, such as Mexico, Brazil, and Argentina, were well publicized, as were the rescheduling and refinancing arrangements that were patched together. The problems were, however, remarkably widespread, and in early 1983 multilateral debt reschedulings had been arranged, or were under negotiation, for no less than twenty countries;[36] there were many more countries which, at least potentially, faced severe external problems. Clearly the difficulties of the non-oil developing countries were both a result of the adverse economic conditions following the second oil price rise, and a contributory factor.

One point needs to be brought out immediately: as the discussion of the recycling problem after the first oil crisis should indicate, there was always a severe risk of something like the debt crisis developing. Initial worries, which surfaced as suggested schemes for recycling, for an increased flow of official aid, and for surveillance, were put aside when it was found that the OPEC surpluses could be balanced by Third World (and Communist bloc) borrowing, with the private banking system acting as intermediary. It is worth recalling that in the years 1976–80 there was little but praise for the way in which private financial markets functioned and for the 'flexibility' of the banking system. Nor was there much public worry over the capacity of the borrowing countries to service their debts. All that changed with the debt crisis, and there was a widespread tendency to blame the irresponsibility of the banks and of the countries concerned. Irresponsibility there undoubtedly was, but much of it was due to 'benign neglect' (or even encouragement) by international financial institutions and by Central Banks. It is unhelpful to assign 'blame' when, basically, it was the international financial system that was at fault. It is more interesting to look at the factors that triggered the debt crisis, and (tentatively) to look at the question of whether debt really was, on a global scale (i.e. putting individual-country difficulties aside), excessive.

Table 19.3 shows some features of the non-oil developing countries and their indebtedness. The first aspect to bring out is their relatively rapid growth up until about 1980: at about 5 per cent per annum they were substantially out-performing the developed world. The rise in their balance of payments deficit to $46 billion after the first oil crisis and to $108 billion after the second stands out: in proportionate terms, however, the peak deficits were remarkably similar at 5·8 per cent and 6 per cent of GDP respectively. The total external indebtedness rose to over $600 billion in 1982 compared with $130 in 1973. Once again the rise needs to be brought into proportion: compared with GDP, indebtedness rose from 22 per cent in 1973, to $34\frac{1}{2}$ per cent in 1982.[37]

It is the *debt service ratios* that seem to show, most clearly, the developing problem. Total debt service rose from around 15–16 per cent of export earnings

---

[36] See IMF, *World Economic Outlook* (1983), p. 68.   [37] Ibid., p. 67.

TABLE 19.3. *Non-oil Developing Countries, Selected Indicators*

	1973	1974	1975	1976	1977	1978	1979	1980	1981	1982
Output (% p.a.)	6·1	5·4	3·3	6·0	5·2	5·4	4·6	4·3	2·4	0·9
Balance of payments (current account) ($bn)	-11	-37	-46	-33	-29	-41	-61	-89	-108	-87
External debt ($bn)	130	161	191	228	278	336	397	474	555	612
as % GDP	22	22	24	26	27	29	28	28	31	35
as % exports	115	105	122	126	126	130	119	113	125	143
Debt service ($bn)	18	22	25	28	35	50	65	76	95	107
as % exports	16	14	16	15	15	19	19	18	20	24
Interest	6	6	7	6	6	7	8	9	12	13
Amortization	10	8	9	9	9	12	11	8	9	11
Net borrowing from private banks*	10	19	23	21	15	26	36	53	53	25

* Rough estimate, broadly consistent with national balance of payments statistics of total net borrowing (short and long term) from private banks. See IMF, *World Economic Outlook* (1983), Table 25.

1973–5 to nearly 24 per cent in 1982. Apparently, one-quarter of these countries' export earnings were going simply to service their debts. Debt service ratios can, however, be very misleading, and it is necessary to consider what they show in more detail. There are two components, interest and amortization. The first of these shows a major rise, roughly doubling between the mid-1970s and 1982. Most of the rise was due to the rise in interest rates. The average interest rate on all outstanding debt (which includes large amounts at concessional rates) rose from about 6 per cent in 1976–9 to $9\frac{1}{4}$ per cent in 1980, and to $10\frac{3}{4}$ per cent in 1981, falling back a little in 1982.[38] It is also necessary to allow for *inflation*. In 1976–9, more than the whole of the interest rate paid would have been necessary to compensate the lenders for world inflation which was running at $7\frac{1}{2}$–8 per cent, i.e. the borrowers were paying *negative real interest rates*: the interest burden was negative. In the early 1980s, however, real interest rates, as seen earlier (Figure 19.1), were positive: even so, the continuing concessionary element meant that (on *average*) *the real interest burden was still not very high*.[39] As an indicator of the real burden of debt interest, debt service ratios, which concentrate on nominal flows, overstate the problems considerably.[40]

The amortization component can be even more misleading. What it indicates is the repayments due in a given year. If loans can be *refinanced* (or even increased in line with the growth of GDP) then the amortization component is not a burden at all. What it *does* indicate, which may *in adverse circumstances* be very important, is the extent of refinancing necessary in a given year. From this point of view, *nominal* interest rates are also important, indicating, along with amortization, the degree of recourse to international capital markets necessary and hence the degree of exposure to any difficulties that might arise.

We are now in a position to sketch the underlying elements behind the debt crisis. The indebtedness of the non-oil developing countries did increase (in proportion to GDP) during the 1970s, but it would be hard to argue, in aggregate, that the degree of indebtedness (or gearing) was excessive given their need for capital resources. In practice the burden was small given real interest rates which were low or negative. With the second oil crisis and its aftermath, however, the non-oil less developed countries were adversely affected in a number of ways simultaneously, which included:

(i) for most of them, an increased oil import bill;
(ii) sharply reduced export earnings, due to falls in the price of their major primary commodity exports, and due to the reduced volume of sales reflecting the recession in the industrial world;
(iii) a greatly increased nominal and real interest bill, especially for those which had most relied on private capital markets;
(iv) an increase in the value of their liabilities as the dollar rose relative to other currencies (since much of their debt was denominated in dollars).

[38] Ibid.
[39] Perhaps 2 or 3 per cent in 1981 and 1982.
[40] Consider, for example, a representative non-oil developing country in 1982 with a debt/GDP ratio of 35 per cent. At 3 per cent real interest, the real interest burden of external debt would be per cent of GDP, or about 4 per cent of export earnings.

Even these adverse factors might not have been sufficient to trigger a serio
crisis if the recession and high interest rates had been short lived. It was t
delay in recovery and the persistence of high real interest rates which rea
revealed the weaknesses of the system. Exposed countries had to have recour
more and more to the private banking system, which was less and less willing
provide finance. Net borrowing from private banks rose from about $26 billic
in 1978 to about $53 billion in 1980 and 1981. With the mounting crisis, th
was sharply reduced to about $25 billion in 1982 as countries institute
willingly or unwillingly, adjustment programmes, and as the banking syste
tried to reduce its exposure. The lack of availability of private funds meant th
the IMF, and the major Central Banks, were increasingly drawn in to promo
rescheduling schemes most of which involved rigorous adjustment programm
for the debtor countries, frequently beyond the limit of political feasibility

The situation was dangerous. Adjustment programmes instituted f
particular countries would, if successful, risk displacing the problems elsewhe
(for example, by intensifying world recession). For the system as a whole, t
debt problem did not appear out of control, and the main fear 'was fear itsel
But confidence could only be maintained if the adjustment of the most-expose
countries could be seen to be going ahead. Above all, what was needed w
confidence in world recovery, the expectation of which would transform t
prospects for commodity prices and export earnings for many of the debt
countries. The other need was for lower interest rates, which seemed to have g
stuck at a high level (and there was at least the possibility that uncertainty ov
the debt crisis itself was one factor behind high interest rates). In 1983, thou
more and more countries got into difficulties, underlying confidence d
improve, based mainly on recovery in the US, and the hope of it elsewhere.
remained obvious that any setback to the prospects for orderly world recover
could rapidly trigger a major crisis the consequences of which it was difficult
foresee.

A final general point needs to be made, about the perceptions of econom
policy makers at that time. It was clear that financial interactions in the wor
economy had become extremely adverse. The natural response was to call for
renewal of financial prudence and discipline at all levels. As far as the le
developed world was concerned, this meant adjustment programmes to low
balance of payments deficits, to reduce indebtedness, and to lower inflation. I
the developed world similar pressures were apparent (especially in tho
countries such as Belgium, Denmark, or Ireland which had borrowed heavi
abroad). Beyond this, there were insistent calls to lower public borrowing an
to control National Debt.[41] There was a severe danger that the general polic
prescription simply would not 'add up' for the world as a whole: if attempted,
would amount to countries, sectors, and individual economic agents all tryir
to run surpluses relative to each other, which is impossible. The result instea
would be a continuing recessionary bias, which, while it might be conducive
the control of inflation, risked renewed recession and slow growth and a
intensification of the financial problems that the policy was designed to cur

[41] i.e. internal debt of the public sector to its own citizens.

19.7. Concluding Remarks

Compared with the situation as it was perceived in the 1960s, economic policy makers now face a formidable array of constraints on the use of the instruments of macroeconomic policy. Individual countries have, in effect, only limited economic sovereignty, owing to the interaction of external influences and domestic difficulties. And even if external problems are put on one side, there is far less optimism about the feasibility of policy action to achieve the usual objectives of full employment and growth. Reflationary action may appear inconsistent with the goal of keeping inflation in check. Expectational factors in financial markets may make certain policies or combinations of policies impossible. And many of the problems—such as those of industrial structure and performance—do not, in any case, appear to be soluble in terms of macroeconomic policies alone.

It is important to stress that some of the factors that constrain the use of demand management policies for domestic objectives come about because of the interaction between national economies. In principle, these external constraints disappear from the world economy as a whole, or for the group of industrialized countries. Most obviously, at the level of the world economy, there can be no such thing as a balance of payments constraint. And exchange rates cannot all spiral down relative to each other. It would therefore be quite illegitimate to infer on the basis of the experience of individual countries that internationally co-ordinated action would be similarly constrained. The inference should be that the proper domain for certain types of policy action is now the world economy.

But many would go further and question whether even international action of a reflationary kind could work in the new circumstances. And the fact that there is doubt on this issue is extremely important—whether the doubt is well founded or not. By far the major issue is whether such action would be compatible with the control of inflation, nationally and internationally. There are many different reasons advanced in favour of the view that reflationary policy would be inappropriate. Very broadly, however, they fall into two groups. The first is simply the trade-off argument. Some argue that it may be necessary to have a prolonged period of low pressure of demand to bring down inflation. The second is more complex—but is basically an argument that the apparent under-utilization of resources is an illusion, and that supply potential for reflationary action is not there. A simple version would be to argue that the unemployment that exists is 'structural'. But there are more elaborate versions which argue that the present difficulties are not simply due to deficient demand or to a deterioration in the 'trade-off', but have their origin in, for example, inappropriate relative prices, low profitability, or a decline in investment opportunities. The appropriate remedies do not lie therefore within the sphere of macroeconomic policy.

It is not easy to evaluate these claims. The obvious alternative to the 'trade-off' is some form of incomes policy—and, as has been seen, much of economic policy since the mid-1960s is explicable in terms of swings of fashion between ways of attempting this control of inflation in circumstances where no method is costless, and no method can claim unambiguous success. The various structural arguments are even hard to evaluate. Low demand, however caused, is bound to create structural problems as capacity shrinks. And a concern about structural unemployment has been a feature of nearly all periods of depressed demand, from the interwar period onwards. But an important point is often missed. If supply-side policies to improve performance are adopted, it would normally be necessary to have an appropriate demand management policy as well. Demand management policies may be necessary rather than sufficient conditions for a solution to some of the problems now faced.

A final point needs to be brought out. The developments outlined in this chapter do not suggest that demand management policies ceased to work in the 1970s and early 1980s, nor do they suggest that they ceased to be used. On the contrary, most of the movements of the world economy appear explicable in terms of the shocks to which the system was subjected and the policy responses of governments. What did change was the environment in which policy had to operate. Economic policies became more constrained by the international economy. Even more importantly, they became far more constrained by the problem of inflation. The instruments of demand management policy, for the lack of an easy alternative, were diverted more and more away from their traditional role in maintaining employment and output, towards the control of inflation. As this occurred, more and more attention was given to nominal variables as intermediate targets—such as the money supply, public borrowing, or, in a few cases, the exchange rate. The process was accompanied by monetarist rhetoric—and expectations based on the monetarist model started to play an important (if not always benign) role, especially in financial markets.

The costs of attempting to control inflation in this way turned out to be very great, for the world economy, and for most individual nations. Indeed, the fears of the economic policy makers of the 1960s—that attempting to cure inflation by restrictive monetary and fiscal policies would be very expensive (if it was politically feasible at all)—were more than justified by events. But even if inflation is controlled in that way, that may not be the end of the policy problem. Only if the optimism of the monetarists—that once inflation is controlled, individual countries will revert to full employment growth—is justified, is the result satisfactory. Otherwise, what is required is some way of bringing the instruments of policy back into play without rekindling inflation.

Bibliography

Many of the works suggested at the end of other chapters are also relevant to the issue discussed in this chapter. The following list is intended only to give an indication of where some of the issues can be followed up. The best overall 'official' surveys of the international economic issues discussed in this chapter are:

[1] Bank for International Settlements (BIS). Annual Reports (June each year), various issues.

These reports contain topical descriptions and analysis of major economic developments. A particularly good source for comment on international financial difficulties ıch as the debt crisis. The 1972 report contains a useful summary of the history of the ɔllar and the lead-up to the Smithsonian Agreement of December 1971.

∙] Organization for Economic Co-operation and Development (OECD). *Economic utlook* (June and Dec. annually), various issues.
ɔrecasts for the world economy are presented biennially together with extensive ıscussion and analysis of major issues of current interest.

₃] International Monetary Fund (IMF). *World Economic Outlook* (published annually ınce 1980), various issues.
nalysis and comment on world economic issues. Covers developing countries as well as ∙ECD.

he issues are discussed in UK publications such as:

₄] *National Institute Economic Review* (quarterly), various issues.
₅] Cambridge Economic Policy Group (CEPG). *Economic Review*, various issues.

comprehensive survey of developments up to 1976 is:

₆] McCRACKEN, P. *et al.*, *Towards Full Employment and Price Stability* (OECD, Paris, ₃977).
ee also:

₇] OECD. *A Growth Scenario to 1980*, Special Supplement to *Economic Outlook*, 19 (July ₃976).

conomic policy in Europe since the war is comprehensively surveyed in:

₈] BOLTHO, A. (ed.). *The European Economy: Growth and Crisis*. (Oxford University Press, ₃982). See especially the chapters on Demand Management by Boltho and J. Bispham; nflation', by C. J. Allsopp; 'Inflation, A Monetarist Interpretation', by A. Budd and ∙. Dicks; and 'Growth', by Boltho—together with references there cited.

₉] BUITER, W. H. 'Measurement of the Public Sector Deficit and its Implications for olicy Evaluation and Design', *IMF Staff Papers*, **30**/2 June 1983).

₁0] PRICE, W. R. and CHOURAQUI, J.-C. *Public Sector Deficits, Problems and Policy nplications*, *Economic Outlook* Occasional Studies (OECD, June 1983).

ɔr Keynes's approach in the 1930s see:

₁1] KEYNES, J. M. 'An Economic Analysis of Unemployment'. Three lectures ɔntributed to the Harris Foundation series in Chicago, June 1931. Reprinted in *The ɔllected Writings of John Maynard Keynes*, Vol. XIII (Macmillan, 1973), pp. 343–67.
₁2] —— —— *The General Theory of Employment, Interest and Money* (Macmillan, 1936).

PART V

LONG-TERM ECONOMIC GROWTH
IN THE UK

20

Economic Growth

C. J. ALLSOPP

0.1. Introduction

During the 'long boom' of the 1950s and 1960s the developed countries enjoyed unprecedented rates of growth—as compared with either earlier trends or with the subsequent period of slowdown which set in from about 1973 onwards. During this period the policy objective of promoting high growth appeared to become more and more firmly established (especially in countries, such as the UK, which appeared to be performing relatively poorly). Nevertheless, in spite of the apparent success of high-growth policies and the general interest in the topic, understanding of the processes involved remained limited. With the more recent experience of world recessions and high inflation, the objective of growth has faded, but interest in the factors making for sustained and rapid expansion in the 1950s and 1960s has, if anything, been heightened.

This chapter surveys some of the approaches to the analysis of growth that have been suggested. It focuses first on the rapid growth period, when one of the main preoccupations was the problem of explaining why different developed countries grew at such different rates. This in turn relates to the slightly different question of how the industrialized countries as a group could grow so fast in that period. Finally, the period of slowdown since 1973 is considered. In a chapter on growth it is, of course, tempting to leave that period out, on the grounds that it was so disturbed that little can be said about longer-term trends. In spite of the difficulties, however, it does seem that the trend of growth slowed markedly in nearly all developed countries. Some of the possible explanations are examined.

In the United Kingdom there is a widespread feeling that growth performance has been inadequate for a very long time. Table 20.1 puts this claim in perspective. One of the most exceptional features is the very rapid expansion achieved by the United States before the First World War. There is nothing very remarkable about Britain's growth rate at that time or during the interwar years. In both periods the growth rate was about average for Europe. Such figures may, however, be misleading in that (a) they neglect the period of the First World War and its aftermath, when Britain did relatively badly, and (b) they take no account of variations in employment or hours worked. It can be argued (see Chapter 21) that if attention is focused on productivity—a better indicator of overall performance—then Britain's relatively poor record is long standing and that it has been falling behind compared with major competitor at least since the beginning of the twentieth century.

It is also clear from Table 20.1 (and from Table 20.2, which shows GDP pe employed person, or productivity) that Britain's post-war performance, up t 1973, was exceptionally good by its own historical standards. It is only in relative terms that there appeared to be a problem, with Britain effectively a the bottom of the 'growth league table'. Britain's relatively low growt persisted in the period of generalized slowdown after 1973. The tables als bring out the extent to which rapid growth in the 1950s and 1960s can be see as due to exceptional advances in Continental Europe and in Japan. When looking at explanations of differences in growth this should be borne in mind. I may be that the interesting question is not why Britain grew so slowly, but wh it was that some other countries were able to grow so fast. The shift of emphas to the positive factors favouring growth in this period may be particular important in looking at the reasons for the slowdown in the 1970s. Tables 20.

TABLE 20.1. *Growth of Total Output*
(average annual percentage changes)

	1870–1913	1922–37	1953–73	1973–9
United Kingdom	1·9	2·4	3·0	1·3
France	1·7	1·8	5·3	3·0
Germany	2·8	3·2	5·5	2·4
Italy	1·5	2·3	5·3	2·6
Austria	2·4	0·8	5·7	3·1
Belgium	2·0	1·4	4·3	2·3
Denmark	2·7	2·8	4·3	2·1
Ireland	—	1·5*	3·3	3·6
Finland	3·0	4·4	5·0	2·3
Netherlands	2·1	1·9	4·9	2·4
Norway	2·1	3·4	3·9	4·4
Spain	—	1·7†	6·1‡	2·0
Sweden	2·8	3·5	3·9	1·8
Switzerland	2·1	2·4§	4·6	−0·4
Europe	2·0	2·5	4·8	2·4
United States	4·1	2·1	3·4	2·7
Canada	3·8	2·3	5·0	3·2
Japan	2·5	3·9	9·6	4·1
OECD	2·7	2·4	4·5	2·7

* 1926–39.   † NNP 19822–35.   ‡ 1954–73.   § 1924–37.

Sources: Adapted from Table 1.1 in Boltho [11]: A. Maddison, *Phases of Capitalist Development* (Oxford, 1982); B. R. Mitchell, *European Historical Statistics, 1750–1970* (London, 1975); UNECE [61]; OECD, *National Accounts of OECD Countries 1950–1979*.

TABLE 20.2. *Productivity* Trends*
(average annual percentage changes)

	1953–79	1953–61	1961–73	1973–9
United Kingdom	2·2	2·0	2·9	1·2
France	4·3	5·0	4·6	2·8
Germany	4·4	5·2	4·5	3·2
Italy	4·6	5·5	5·6	1·5
Austria	4·8†	5·5‡	5·1	2·9
Belgium	3·3	2·8	4·1	2·3
Denmark	2·8§	3·2§	3·1	1·3
Finland	4·1	4·8	4·4	2·5
Ireland	3·5‡	3·4‡	4·3	2·2
Netherlands	3·4	3·1	4·2	2·3
Norway	2·8	3·1	2·9	2·2
Spain	5·0†	4·0†	6·0	4·2
Sweden	2·6§	3·0§	3·2	0·6
Switzerland	2·6§	3·1§	2·9	0·9
OECD Europe	3·8	4·1	4·3	2·3
United States	1·3	1·4	2·0	0·1
Canada	1·9	2·0	2·6	0·5
Japan	6·6	7·1	8·1	2·9
OECD	3·1	3·3	3·8	1·5

* GDP per employed person.
† 1954–79 and 1954–61.
‡ 1951–79 and 1951–61.
§ 1950–79 and 1950–61.

Sources: Adapted from Table 1.4 in Boltho [11]: OECD, *National Accounts of OECD Countries* and OECD, *Labour Force Statistics* (various issues); B. R. Mitchell, *European Historical Statistics, 1750–1970.*

nd 20.2 show that the deceleration was remarkably generalized, with only reland (which benefited from Common Market entry) and Norway (with a uge oil build-up) increasing their rates of growth in the 1973–9 period.

Before considering some of the approaches to the analysis of growth, it is as vell to look at some of the explanations, which, in their naive form at least, just ill not do. One problem is that many 'explanations' are not explanations of rowth at all, but of the level of output. Most commonly, this includes efficiency rguments, where the efficiency of someone, management or labour, is to blame or slow growth (and conversely gets the credit for fast growth). The point is imply that it is possible for an 'inefficient' economy to grow fast, or an efficient ne to grow slowly. In the first instance the effect of inefficiency should be on the vel of output rather than on growth. To be sure, while inefficiencies are being emoved, growth accelerates—in exactly the same way as when an economy noves from slump to boom—and it may be that inefficiencies can go on being

removed for a long time with marked effects in the medium term.[1] But t
establish an effect on long-run growth it is necessary to establish that the degre
of efficiency is changing over time. Of course, this does not imply tha
'efficiency' of various kinds can never affect growth in the long run. There ma
be reasons why the *level* of efficiency might influence, for example, the rate c
innovation and hence growth. The important point is that a connection mus
be established between the level of efficiency and some such factor—in man
arguments no attempt is made to do this.

Another set of 'explanations' which is suspect comprises those that associat
certain factors with growth and then assume that these factors cause growth
The problem is always that they might be a *result* of growth, or perhaps hav
nothing to do with it. It would be wrong to say, for example, that because Japa:
has a high growth rate and invests a lot, that investment causes growth. On th
other hand, it is clearly interesting that Japan has both high investment an
high growth, and we might want to make use of the hypothesis that there is
causal connection. The association, by itself, does not imply any causalit
whatsoever, though it may suggest that certain causal hypotheses ar
reasonable.

A related difficulty which goes even further is that it may be almos
impossible to find *any* factor that is truly exogenous to the growth proces
Simple economic models usually take the labour supply and technical progres
to be exogenous. In practice, however, labour supply can respond to growt
due to international migration and due to induced sectoral shifts (both thes
factors were important in Europe in the 1950s and 1960s). And the speed c
technical progress depends crucially on other aspects of the growth proces
such as the amount of investment which influences the rate at which it i
'embodied' in new equipment. What this means is that one should be wary c
attempts to find the ultimate causes of growth. A more modest objective is to tr
to examine some of the main contributory factors and to look at the interaction
and relationships that appear to be most important in shaping the process.

20.2. Supply-Side Approaches

20.2.1. Productive Potential

The development of demand management policies in the post-war perio
meant that there was no particular difficulty in altering the rate of growth c
the economy, from year to year, by altering demand.[2] As demand rise
however, constraints appear as the economy nears its supply potential—o
productive potential. This concept of productive potential is important fo
short-term policy—targets for demand must always be set in relation to som

---

[1] Indeed some of the best-known explanations of rapid growth do involve the progressi
removal of 'inefficiencies'—such as the reduction over time of the under-utilization of labour i
agriculture or other low-productivity sectors. There remains a question, however, as to wh
determines the rate at which it occurs, and why it happened in some countries and not others. S
section 20.6.

[2] In the 1970s, of course, the feasibility of using the instruments of demand management polic
came into question. Domestic policy action may be constrained by international repercussions c
by the priority given to other objectives—such as the control of inflation.

concept of productive potential—and it is with the *growth of productive potential* that we are usually concerned when economic growth is discussed. Actual growth rates of the economy obviously differ from the growth of productive potential—being higher when, for example, the economy moves from slump conditions to boom conditions, and lower in a situation when unemployment and excess capacity are building up. It is not too misleading to think of the growth of productive potential as that rate of growth which would maintain a constant level of unemployment.

There are many techniques in use for assessing productive potential. One of the simplest is to extrapolate growth between peaks of the business cycle. Though this may be adequate for many short-term applications it hardly contributes to an explanation of the growth of the economy. Much the same can be said of the techniques which rely on modifying observed levels of national output to take account of variations in unemployment, or capacity utilization indices, to give estimates of full employment or full capacity output. However, many measurements are based implicitly or explicitly on a theory of growth process.

The traditional approach to the problem of determining the productive potential of an economy (and by extension its growth) is to look at it in terms of the co-operating factors of production. In the last century these factors were often thought of as labour and land, a classification which reflected the importance of agriculture in the economy. Nowadays, the usual breakdown is in terms of labour and capital, and considerable weight is given to technical progress as an additional source of growth.

A simple approach is to assume that output depends on the inputs of the factors of production, according to some stable relationship which retains the same form over time. Such a relationship is often called a *production function*. Usually, the function is allowed to shift over time, so as to allow more output for a given input—the shifts representing the influence of increasing technical knowledge and of other factors which are not specifically included in the analysis. Normally, the relationship is assumed to be fairly flexible in that it allows capital and labour to be combined in different proportions to produce a given output.

The earliest results using this approach were obtained in the 1920s by Cobb and Douglas, and a particularly simple version of the production function, which is often used in empirical work, still bears their names. The Cobb-Douglas production function assumes that the elasticity of output with respect to either of the two inputs is constant. This means that if the labour input is increased by 1 per cent, output is assumed to increase by a fixed percentage, say a per cent, whilst if capital increased by 1 per cent, output increases by b per cent, these constants, a and b, being independent of actual output, or of the proportions in which capital and labour are combined.[3] This function has

---

[3] The mathematical formulation of the function is

$$Q = \text{constant } L^a K^b$$
$$\text{or } \log Q = \log C + a \log L + b \log K$$

where Q = output,
L = labour input,
K = capital input.

convenient properties, not least the implication that the growth of output can be though of as composed of a part dependent on labour and a part dependent on capital. Thus in symbols we can write

$$\dot{q} = a\dot{l} + b\dot{k}$$

where $\dot{q}$ stands for the rate of growth of output, and $\dot{l}$ and $\dot{k}$ for the rates of growth of labour and capital.[4]

In order to make the analysis more applicable to the real world, it is usual to introduce a residual term, which allows output to rise over time at a constant trend rate even if labour and capital do not rise. In that case, the above equation becomes

$$\dot{q} = r + a\dot{l} + b\dot{k}$$

and the rate of growth of ouput (or, strictly, productive potential) is now seen to be broken down into three components, one due to increase in labour, another due to increase in capital, and a third (r in the above equation) being simply a time trend, which, apart from genuine advances in technology, may represent anything else left out of the analysis.

This approach, using the Cobb-Douglas production function (or more complex formulations), can be used in order to try to establish an empirical relationship between the inputs into an economy and its output. Given the data, this is a statistical problem, and statistical measures of how well the hypothesis of a production function fits the data can be derived, as well as measures of the significance of individual coefficients. Such production functions can be fitted to data for one country, for a number of years (the time-series approach), or to data drawn from a number of different countries (the cross-section approach). Ideally, perhaps, both cross-section and time-series information should be used.

Although it is an attractive idea to fit production functions, there are a number of acute difficulties. When production functions were first fitted to time-series data, they seemed to give good results (a close fit) and the co-efficients came out sensibly at about $\frac{1}{3}$ for the capital coefficient (b) and $\frac{2}{3}$ for labour (a). However, difficulties soon appeared. It was found, for example, that the time trend 'explained' most of the growth. Since the time trend is really no explanation at all, this is a serious defect. Moreover, capital and labour usually grow together and their effects tend to get mixed up in time-series analysis.

Quite apart from these problems, there are a number of difficulties which make the interpretation of the results in terms of an aggregate production function very suspect. In the first place, is it right to expect a stable relationship between aggregate output change and the change in capital and labour inputs?

---

[4] The assumption made in many empirical studies that there are *constant returns to scale* can be seen to amount to the assumption that a and b add up to unity—for, then, a 1 per cent increase in capital and labour together would mean a 1 per cent increase in output. This assumption is not necessary, however, and the function can be used with either diminishing or increasing returns to scale. In the latter case a particular increase in the inputs would result in a more than proportionate rise in output.

Surely we might expect different results depending on which industries or firms were expanding? Second, there are grave theoretical and practical difficulties in using the concept of capital. The capital goods in use are a heterogeneous collection of physical objects. If they can be valued, they can be added up; but what values should be used? What about obsolescence and technical progress? When they were installed they represented a sum of money, but their cost even after allowance for depreciation may be a poor indicator of their value in production now. Finally, it may be wrong to interpret a fitted relationship between capital, labour, and output as being due to a production function. There are many other relationships which are likely to be important in the analysis of growth which could also lead to observed relationships between output, labour, and capital.

Though some of these problems can be dealt with, it is true that there is widespread dissatisfaction amongst economists with the aggregate production function. All sorts of sophisticated modifications have been tried, but, on the whole, the interpretation of the results still remains problematical. If enough assumptions about the world are made, the results can be interpreted in terms of these assumptions. But there is something unscientific about such a procedure.

Since so many of the difficulties, both practical and theoretical, arise because of the concept of capital, it is tempting, at least for short-term applications, to leave it out, and pick up its effect in the extrapolation of labour productivity (which will tend to rise the more capital labour has with which to work). In the United Kingdom productive potential is usually assessed simply in terms of the labour force, and of changes in productivity. The rate of growth of output can be written as the sum of the rates of growth of employment and the rate of growth of productivity (output per man). The rate of growth of labour supply can be projected on the basis of demographic data and assumptions about participation rates[5] and so on. It is common practice to add to this a trend rate of growth of productivity in order to project productive potential. During the 1950s and 1960s this usually resulted in an assessed growth of productive potential, for the British economy, of the order of 3 per cent per annum—i.e. something like the growth rate actually achieved.

Though such crude estimates are often good enough for short-term policy purposes, they are subject to serious limitations for medium-term work. A number of comments can be made. In the first place, there is an assumption that productivity growth is independent of output. If productivity is influenced by output growth, because of economies of scale for example, then the procedures should reflect this. Second, productivity is often projected simply as a trend. It would seem better to allow explicitly for the influence of capital accumulation on productivity growth, but it has, in fact, proved extremely difficult to establish empirically significant effects of capital accumulation on

---

[5] The participation rate is defined as the proportion of a given group that is economically active—i.e. that is at work or actively seeking work. The labour supply is usually projected by assuming that participation rates for particular age/sex groups of the population remain unchanged, or at least, are predictable.

productivity for the British economy. Third, it is questionable whether productivity projections for the aggregate of the economy are very useful. Better results might be achieved by disaggregating, at least down to broad sectors of the economy (agriculture, industry, services, etc.). Indeed, many would argue that a fairly fine industrial breakdown is necessary for productivity projections to be useful. For these reasons, amongst others, estimates of productive potential growth should be treated with care. In particular they do not imply that there is an immutable supply-determined growth rate which it is difficult to exceed.

The difficulties with the concept of productive potential were thrown into relief with the major slowdown in growth and productivity that occurred in most countries after 1973. Initially it was common practice to continue to project forward the trends of potential output established in the 1960s. As economies departed further and further away from that trend, however, it obviously came to have less and less significance, and various modifications were suggested. One possibility—which is further discussed in later sections of this chapter—is that the trend of potential output had slowed down. Another was that, around the time of the first oil crisis in 1973, there had been a once-and-for-all loss of potential output, which would mean that the potential line should be shifted down (though perhaps the trend would then continue parallel to the old line). Two particular arguments as to why that might have occurred are worth rehearsing. The first is that the oil shock may have led to the scrapping of capital equipment and other changes in structure which caused a loss of supply potential. The second, which is rather more complex, was the idea that the underlying rate of unemployment which would be compatable with the control of inflation—sometimes called the 'natural rate of unemployment'[6]—had risen, either due to structural changes in the labour market or, perhaps, due to increased inflationary pressure of a cost push of 'competing claims' kind. On these views the economy needed to shift down to a permanently higher level of unemployment. Finally, of course, productive potential could have been subject to both a shift down and a change in trend.

There is another difficulty which well illustrates the problems of analysing economic growth. One *hypothesis* about the slowdown in the 1970s is that productive potential fell—in which case the fall in supply potential becomes, in effect, the explanation of the change. But suppose growth slowed down for some other reason (such as the policies pursued) not connected with the supply side. Then in the medium term the capacity of the economy to produce would fall in line with the actual growth achieved (for it would not pay businessmen to keep capacity that was not utilized). Thus one would observe productive potential slowing down in this case too.[7] This means that, in practice, estimates of productive potential are never likely to diverge very far from the trend of

---

[6] See Chap. 7. The 'natural' rate of unemployment is that level which is consistent with neither an acceleration nor a deceleration in inflation. Sometimes the more neutral (if ugly) acronym NAIRU—the non-accelerating inflation rate of unemployment—is used.

[7] This problem is particularly acute if productivity—and hence unemployment—are also endogenous and respond to the slowdown.

growth actually achieved and, except in rare circumstances, it will be impossible to infer much about the causes of growth from such estimates.[8]

20.2.2. The Neo-Classical Approach

An approach which is of considerable importance in the literature on comparative growth rates makes use of a production function as described in the previous section, but with additional assumptions about the world which justify (if they are true) a particularly easy estimating procedure. The major additional assumption necessary is that capital and labour markets are *perfectly competitive*. Under perfect competition factor prices are determined by the *marginal products* of the factors, i.e. addition at the margin to output that results from employing one more unit of the factor (see Chapter 4).

The importance of the competitive assumption is that it allows estimation of the elasticities of output with respect to labour and to capital (the coefficients of the Cobb-Douglas production function, as in the previous section) simply by looking at the shares of national income which accrue to labour and to capital respectively—data which are nearly always available. There are obvious defects in the procedure, but let us see how it is justified under competition.

Marginal products are defined as follows. Given a production function, we can ask how much extra output an additional unit of labour would produce if all other inputs into the system were to remain fixed. The value of this extra output is the marginal product of labour, and under the competitive assumptions it is equal to the wage that labour receives. In a similar way the marginal product of capital is defined and set equal to the rent on capital.

Going back to the Cobb-Douglas production function of the previous section, the constant a, the labour coefficient, is defined as the *elasticity* of output with respect to the labour input:

$$a = \frac{\text{proportionate change in output}}{\text{proportionate change in labour input}}$$

given that capital is not varying. But this elasticity can be rewritten as

$$a = \frac{\text{change in output}}{\text{change in labour input}} \times \frac{\text{level of labour}}{\text{level of output}}$$

where all we have used is the definition of a proportionate change.

The first term in the last expression is, however, the marginal product of labour as defined above. If the competitive assumptions apply, then it is equal to the wage rate, and the whole expression is equal to the value of the total labour input divided by the value of output; that is, a is equal to *labour's share of national product*. By a precisely similar argument we can show that b, the capital elasticity, is equal to capital's share of national product—it is equal to total profits as a proportion of the national income.

[8] The exception would be if there were clear evidence for particular changes or 'shocks' to potential which preceded changes in growth. Even in the case of the oil crises of 1973–4 and 1979–80, however, estimates of the supply shock vary widely, and there is no conclusive evidence that supply changes caused the subsequent recessions or slow growth.

20.2.3. Growth Accounting

The assumptions of perfect competition under which the above 'factor shares' method is justified may seem so unrealistic that it may come as a surprise to find that the method is widely used in practice. In fact, a weaker justification i possible. It is rather natural to look for a measure of the growth of total input—a measure which includes both capital and labour. One such measure which has the virtue of simplicity is to define the growth of total factor input as the weighted sum of the growth rates of labour and capital input, the weights used being the shares accruing to labour and capital in the National Income Accounts. Such a measure can be regarded as a useful starting-point for the analysis of growth, even if it is not felt that the perfect competition assumptions apply. Total factor input is a concept widely used by economic historians.

As in the case of 'fitted' production functions, one of the main difficulties with the factor shares approach turned out to be that total factor input appeared to contribute very little to the explanation of growth. Most of growth appeared to be due to the 'residual factor', the unexplained rises in productivity. Moreover, differences in growth between countries appeared to be associated with differences in the residual, rather than differences in factor inputs. This led to attempts to refine the measurement of the inputs, and to cut down on the apparent importance of the residual.

Denison [17], in one of the best-known books on comparative growth rates uses an extension of the factor shares approach. In a cross-country analysis he estimates total factor input for each of nine countries. The inputs are 'corrected' to reflect increasing levels of education, changes in composition and utilization, and so on. Beyond this, differences in the residual between countries are in part explained by estimating the importance of structural shifts in the disposition of the labour force, and the influence of economies of scale. By appealing to a wide range of factors, Denison does succeed in cutting down the apparent importance of the residual very considerably.

It is not possible to do justice to such a major study in a short survey. We are concerned with the approach.[9] The difficulties are obvious. The assumptions may not apply. Even if they do the estimates may be rather inaccurate Moreover, the approach does not really explain growth—rather it imputes growth to various contributory factors. If it does this correctly it is a very useful starting-point, but at some stage it is necessary to consider the causal problem of how actually to affect growth in practice. It is implicitly assumed in the factor shares method that they way to affect growth is to have more of such factors as capital and labour, and that the causality runs from input to output. It is difficult to test this against the alternative hypothesis that, say, investment (and hence capital accumulation) is induced by output growth (probably through some mechanism involving expectations of future growth).

Finally, Denison's procedures do not involve fitting a production function to the data, so there is no *test* of the idea of a production function involved. It is

[9] Innumerable estimates are involved, many of which depend on special procedures and assumptions and cannot be understood simply in terms of the 'factor shares' method. See Denison [17]; Matthews [44].

assumed that the economy works in a particular way. If it does then the importance of various factors can be estimated in a mechanical way (apart from data difficulties). The only problem is how much of observed growth is left over at the end to be explained by 'residual factors'—i.e. is left unexplained.

Professor Denison is well aware of the difficulties. His view appears to be that this is a worthwhile exercise since one must start somewhere, and quantification of the effects is an exceedingly important, if hazardous, task. Certainly, his estimates are interesting even to those who may not agree with the underlying methodology.

Table 20.3 shows Denison's estimates for the contributions of total factor input and the 'residual' output per unit of input (productivity) to the growth of national income for the nine countries he studied. The period covered is 1950–62.

It can be seen that though the imputed contribution of the factor inputs is substantial, there is still much to be explained. More importantly, differences in growth between countries appear to be largely due to differences in the contribution of output per unit of input. Denison's estimates thus serve to emphasize the difficulty in explaining differences in growth rates by appeal to differing rates of growth of capital or labour inputs. As noted, however, Denison does not stop at this point, but proceeds to 'explain' the growth of output per unit of input by appeal to other influences, such as economies of scale and structural shifts in the disposition of the labour force. The latter factor, in particular, is estimated to be an important reason for differences between countries. The method used is discussed below.

20.3. Demand and Supply

The approaches to the growth problem described so far all concentrated on the development of supply potential—and explain the development of the economy in terms of the growth of labour and capital resources, and changes in the state of technology. Though there is clearly a need for some concept of the short-term supply potential of the economy (i.e. productive potential), it is not so self-evident that the explanation of growth in the longer term should run in terms of the supply of resources.

In the first place, a supply-oriented approach itself needs some supplementation. It may be reasonable enough to assume that the growth of the labour supply is an independent factor determined 'outside' the model by demographic factors; but the growth of the capital stock is itself influenced by the level of investment. In the pure supply-oriented approach it is not capital that is constraining, but the supply of investible resources—i.e. savings. In the short to medium run an increase in savings (a reduction in consumption) allows more to be invested, and speeds up capital accumulation.[10] Thus this view of the growth process often carries with it the policy prescription that the way to faster growth is to increase savings as a proportion of national income. Clearly,

[10] In the long run, on this theory, the capital–output ratio would rise—so that the growth of the capital stock would slow down again to its previous rate. Thus the growth rate would ultimately be independent of the proportion of savings. The *level* of output and output per head would, however, still be raised by the increased savings ratio. See, for example, Solow [59]; Jones [28].

TABLE 20.3. *Contributions to the Growth of National Income, 1950–1962*
(per cent per annum)

	Growth of national income	Labour	Capital	Contribution of: Total factor input	Output per unit of input
Germany	7·26	1·37	1·41	2·78	4·48
Italy	5·96	0·96	0·70	1·66	4·30
France	4·92	0·45	0·79	1·24	3·68
Netherlands	4·73	0·87	1·04	1·91	2·82
Denmark	3·51	0·59	0·96	1·55	1·96
Norway	3·45	0·15	0·89	1·04	2·41
United States	3·32	1·12	0·82	1·95	1·37
Belgium	3·20	0·76	0·41	1·17	2·03
United Kingdom	2·29	0·60	0·51	1·11	1·18

Source: Denison [17], Table 15.3.

there may be problems of a Keynesian kind in ensuring that increased savings, which reduce consumer expenditure, lead to, or are at least balanced by, increased investment expenditures.

In sharp contrast to those approaches which concentrate on the supply side, many explanations of growth emphasize the development over time of the various categories of expenditure (consumption, investment, etc.)—that is, the development of aggregate demand. It is natural to label such approaches 'demand-oriented'—or 'demand-side'. Clearly, the idea of a demand-side growth path develops out of the Keynesian model of income determination—by extension, the growth of the economy is seen as determined by the growth of aggregate demand. The growth of aggregate demand is, in turn, seen as dependent upon the behaviour of businessmen and households, as well as upon government policy and, of course, export demand. Variants of this general approach include some of the best-known hypotheses—such as that of export-led growth.

The terminology may suggest that demand-side growth paths are very easy to change—for example, by Keynesian policies. This would, however, be an incorrect inference. Any rate of growth, if established for some time, may be difficult to alter, and indeed may appear supply constrained. There are a number of reasons for this. In the first place, there may be a built-in tendency for things to continue unchanged if expectations are rigid. More importantly, it is natural to suppose that businessmen would, if a growth path were maintained for a reasonable length of time, adjust their capital stock to that growth path, so that the development of capital capacity would tend to be consistent with the growth that was achieved. Expansionary policies would tend to lead to supply problems and bottlenecks. As noted in section 20.2 the concept of productive potential would still appear to be applicable—defined, perhaps, in terms of capital capacity—but would, in fact, be of little use in explaining longer-term growth tendencies.

The obvious problem with the concept of a demand-side path is that there s no particular reason to suppose that such a path would be consistent with *full employment*, in that the rate of growth of demand for labour might not be equal to the rate of growth of supply of labour. It is this possible inconsistency which has attracted most attention from economists. It appears that the consequences of such a problem—either an increasing proportion of the labour force unemployed, or an increasing demand for labour in relation to its supply—are just not observed. Most developed countries appear, especially in the 1950s and 1960s, to have had growth at reasonably full employment, with no longer-run tendency for the amount of unemployment either to increase or decrease. Surely, therefore, there must be some interaction to ensure that demand for labour grows at the appropriate rate?

There are several possible answers to this. In the first place, it may be that the supply of labour is, in real economies, very variable, due to a potential for shifts between occupations, regions, and so on. The massive shifts in the disposition of the labour force in some fast-growing countries since the war would support this view. If such shifts occurred in response to growth, then growth itself can be explained as largely due to the development of demand. Even in the absence of such potential movements it may be that technology is such that shortages of labour are very easily overcome—so that labour supply is unimportant. Conversely, the labour force policies of firms (hoarding etc.) may be such as to disguise unemployment even if it exists—at least for a time.

The problem of how the demand side and the supply side interact is exceptionally important for practical policy, but there are many difficulties in the way of getting any answer. It is probable that different countries at different times are in different situations—in some, it may be that it is the supply of resources that is the crucial constraining factor. In others, it may be a demand-side problem, requiring a different policy approach. In general, it is likely that the two sides of the picture interact in a complex way.

20.4. Keynesian Problems in Growth Theory

20.4.1. Macroeconomic Consistency: The Warranted Rate of Growth

Though the idea of a 'demand-side' or 'expenditure-side' growth path is easy enough, there may be difficulties in achieving it. One problem has already been discussed. A demand-side growth path may not automatically give rise to full employment of the labour force. Another problem is that demand-side paths, if they exist, may have a tendency to be unstable—a divergence, once it starts, may tend to develop into a cumulative movement away from equilibrium.

The formal analysis usually starts from the simple Keynesian 'multiplier' model, with only two categories of expenditure—consumption and investment. Such models are usually considered statically—a simplification that is only valid in the short run (see Chapter 5). In particular, when considering growth, investment cannot be taken as 'autonomous'—given from outside the model. It is necessary to consider why businessmen invest, and also the results of a given level of investment.

Over time, the investment expenditures that are going on are, clearly adding to capital capacity. Aggregate demand, however, only expands to utilize the extra capital capacity that is produced if investment *rises*; it is a *rise in* investment which, through the multiplier, leads to a *rise* in aggregate demand. The problem is that there is no particular reason to suppose that the extra capacity produced in a given period will be fully utilized—no more and no less. There may be an inconsistency between the growth of capacity and the growth of demand, which if prolonged would, of course, tend to lead to a revision of investment expenditure—downwards if excess capacity is developing, upwards if a shortage of capacity appears.

Although, in general, there may be inconsistency between the development of capacity and the development of demand, the question arises as to whether it is possible to find a special case in which there is no inconsistency—in which capacity develops in line with demand. It turns out that there is: there is a particular rate of growth of the economy (often called the 'warranted' growth rate, (g)) which allows capacity and demand to grow in line with each other. For any other rate of growth the problem of inconsistency would arise (see Harrod [26], [27]).

There are many different ways in which the problem of inconsistency can be analysed. The approach adopted here is intended to focus as closely as possible on the likely behaviour reactions of businessmen and householders, so as to bring out practical problems. The point is that if inconsistency develops, then either households or businessmen are likely to be in 'disequilibrium' in the sense that they would not be satisfied with the way things were turning out and would, therefore, tend to change their expenditure plans.

Consider first the question of why businessmen invest. What determines aggregate investment expenditures? A simple hypothesis is that businessmen invest in order to expand capacity in line with expected changes in output or demand.[11] Formally, we may write:

$$I = v_r \, \Delta Ye$$

where I = investment,

ΔYe = expected change in output (Ye = expected output),

$v_r = (I/\Delta Ye)$ is a coefficient—the desired incremental capital–output ratio.

Since we are concerned with growth it is more convenient to consider proportions and proportionate changes, so it is useful to divide the above equation through by output Y, to get

$$\frac{I}{Y} = v_r \, \frac{\Delta Ye}{Y} \quad \text{or} \quad \frac{I}{Y} = v_r g_e,$$

and the hypothesis is that the investment–output ratio (I/Y) is directly related

[11] Neglecting, for simplicity, other reasons for investment such as capital deepening, or replacement.

o the expected rate of growth of demand $(\Delta Ye/Y = g_e)$ by some coefficient v_r which represents some desired, normal, or required incremental capital to output ratio.

In aggregate, this amounts to the hypothesis that the investment–output ratio for the economy depends upon the rate of growth expected by the business community. It is a simple idea. Suppose, for example, that the normal capital–output ratio were about 2. Then according to the formula, if expected growth were 3 per cent per annum then a (net) investment–output ratio of 6 per cent would be required. If, however, expected growth were 6 per cent per annum, then the investment–output ratio would have to be twice as large, at 12 per cent.

This is all very well and appears reasonably realistic. But under what circumstances will the investment that satisfies businessmen also lead to people being satisfied with the amount they are saving? Assume that investors invest as above. Then it follows that the *actual* savings rate is determined (for actual savings always equals actual investment—so much is a matter of accounting). So the condition that savers as well as investors should be satisfied with the situation is simply that *the growth expected by businessmen should lead them to want to invest the same amount as people want to save.* Formally, this means that

$$\frac{I}{Y} = v_r g_e = s_r.$$

The expected growth rate (g_e) must therefore be s_r/v_r if savers and investors are to be satisfied simultaneously.

So it is possible to solve the problem and satisfy the requirements (or desires) of both investors and savers—but only if the expected growth rate is appropriate. The particular growth rate that is appropriate, s_r/v_r, is what we have termed the warranted rate of growth (g_w) because it has the property that no inconsistencies arise. Investors are adding to capacity at the appropriate rate—and savers are saving what they want to save.[12] Since the warranted rate of growth depends upon two independently determined behavioural characteristics of the private sector—the desire to save, and the desired (incremental) capital–output ratio—it can be appreciated that the determination of a 'demand-side' growth path by expectations may not be quite so simple as at first appears. In fact, only if expected growth is equal to the 'warranted rate' (g_w) will the actual growth that comes about tend to correspond with expectation. If any other growth rate were expected, the result would tend to be inconsistent with the maintenance of that expectation over time, in that inconsistency and disequilibrium would result.

[12] This latter condition is simply the condition that the 'multiplier' relationship holds. In fact the warranted rate can also be written as

$$g_w = \frac{I}{m v_r}$$

where m is the multiplier. This follows since in the simple model the multiplier is the reciprocal of the *desired* saving ratio:

$$\left(m = \frac{I}{s_r} \right).$$

This problem was first analysed by Harrod [26], who pioneered growth theory and first used the formula for the warranted rate in 1939. Harrod defined the 'warranted' rate of growth (g_w) as that rate of growth 'which is consistent with people saving what they want to save, and having the capital goods they require for their purposes' ([26], p. 19). The warranted path can be thought of as that growth path that would keep the private sector happy, and continuing to do what it was doing in the past—i.e. continuing to grow at a steady rate. The warranted path thus depends on the concept of the desired savings ratio, and on the concept of the required capital–output ratio—that relationship between increments in output and increments in capacity which, if it obtained, would leave businessmen feeling 'in the upshot that they have done the right thing'. Put thus generally, it can be seen that the idea of the 'warranted' path has nothing to do with the constancy or otherwise of saving behaviour, or of the required capital–output ratio. It depends on the idea of there being two independent conditions for equilibrium (one for savers, one for investors) with no automatic mechanism for making sure that they will be simultaneously satisfied.[13]

20.4.2. Instability

The interpretation of the 'warranted' rate of growth is problematical. There are reasons for supposing that warranted paths, if they exist, would tend to be unstable—a chance divergence might set up forces taking the economy ever further away from the warranted path. The point is quite straightforward. If by chance, say, the economy were to grow at a different rate, the inconsistency problem would arise, and either savers or investors would be dissatisfied with the results—they would be out of equilibrium. But the likely reactions to the disequilibrium are such that they would tend to lead to further divergence from the warranted rate.

The easiest way to analyse this problem is to note that any *actual* growth rate can be written in a way which allows it to be compared with the warranted rate. Actual growth (g_a) can always be expressed as s/v, where s is the actual or observed savings ratio, and v is the actual, observed, incremental capital–output ratio. This is derived as follows:

$$g_a \equiv \frac{\Delta Y}{Y} \equiv \frac{\Delta Y}{I} \times \frac{I}{Y} \equiv \frac{\Delta Y}{I} \times \frac{S}{Y} \equiv \frac{s}{v}.$$

This is *always* true since all that has been used is the definition of v ($= I/\Delta Y$), the definition of s ($= S/Y$), and the accounting identity that, *ex post*, savings are always equal to investment $(S = I)$.

---

[13] Most growth models solve the problem posed by Harrod in rather unsatisfactory ways. The neo-classical school ignores the problem by dropping the idea of an independent investment function. The neo-Keynesian school usually allows savings to adjust to investment by changes in income distribution between wages and profits. Though this is a way out of the consistency problem, there remain problems as to the actual mechanism of adjustment in a dynamic setting. See, for example, [25], [28], [58].

Let us suppose that actual growth is above the warranted growth—perhaps by chance, or due to a wrong expectation. Then we have

$$g_a > g_w.$$

But from the definitions, this means that

$$\frac{s}{v} > \frac{s_r}{v_r}.$$

Such a divergence thus implies *either* that the actual savings rate (s) has turned out to be bigger than the desired savings rate (s_r) *or* that the actual incremental capital–output ratio (v) has turned out to be less than required (v_r). Thus *either* savers have saved more than they desired, *or* businessmen have invested less than they required. In either case there would be a tendency for expenditure plans to be revised upwards, further raising the growth of the economy and tending to lead to a cumulative upswing in the economy. In the case where actual growth turned out to be less than warranted, cumulative recessionary forces would tend to develop.

The tendency towards cumulative movements away from the warranted growth rate is suggestive of the phenomena of the business cycle. A fuller analysis would aim to develop a model of growth and cycles. The nature of the movements away from equilibrium is, however, very sensitive indeed to the precise assumptions made about the formation of expectations and the reactions of businessmen and households. But it is easy to see why there may be a problem. In the long run there are no 'autonomous' variables—everything is induced by everything else—and it is not surprising that 'instability' should be a problem.

20.4.3. A Policy Problem

In practice, instability may not be as severe as might be suggested by the preceding analysis. For an individual country, foreign trade may be powerfully stabilizing (so long as countries do not all move together).[14] Moreover, the problem of short-term instability over the trade-cycle may be regarded as a problem for short-term demand management policy. But what about the problem of a divergence between the warranted rate of growth and that rate of growth that would seem best for the economy in question? If the government has a target—for example, that the economy should grow at a rate which would lead to full employment over time—should policy action be designed, over the medium term, to bring the warranted rate of growth into line with the target? This is not a problem that has been faced in practice.

The argument that the warranted rate should be brought into line with a target rate of growth for the economy (such as the growth of 'productive potential') can be presented as follows. Suppose the authorities do succeed in managing the economy so that it grows in line with productive potential. Then it would seem natural to suppose that businessmen would come to expect such a

---

[14] Cf. Chap. 19 where it is suggested that the increased coincidence of policy problems and movements in demand and output have increased problems of instability on an international scale.

growth rate. It would clearly be desirable that their expectations should lead to the right rate of growth—this would minimize the need for policy action. But the condition that expectations should, by and large, be fulfilled is that growth should be at the warranted rate. If the warranted rate of growth were different from the growth of productive potential, then disequilibrating reactions would tend to occur and the task of maintaining growth in line with potential would be much more difficult.

This is a powerful argument. But there is a catch. If investment is in any case appropriate to the 'target' rate of growth, the policy amounts to controlling consumption to be appropriate to the investment that is going on. This is a highly likely response, and lends plausibility to the idea that favourable expectations can generate high investment and hence high growth—a feature of many explanations of rapid growth since the war. But what happens if investment is not high enough for the target growth? In the United Kingdom, for example, policy targets have usually involved the objective of raising growth. It turns out that the normal short-term response may be perverse from a medium-term point of view.

If it is desired to raise actual growth, then if 'warranted' growth is also to be raised, consumption needs to be lowered (desired savings need to be raised). What this amounts to is the policy prescription of lowering consumption to 'make room' for the extra investment required for higher target growth. The difficulty is very well known—there is no reason for investment to rise, and the policy might just swell unemployment. However, if the alternative of lowering taxes and stimulating consumption were pursued, the target growth might be achieved for a time—but only at the cost of instability. For such a policy *raises* actual growth but *reduces* the warranted growth—thus increasing disequilibrium. In practice, when investment does respond, there is then too much demand relative to supply, with the risk of an inflationary boom. This tendency for consumption-led booms to be unstable is beginning to be given the attention it deserves. Thus policy to raise growth needs simultaneously to lower consumption and to raise investment. The first is easy. The latter may be very difficult indeed, especially if expectations and confidence as to the longer term are adverse.[15]

20.5. Demand-Side Emphasis

20.5.1. Expectations

Some analyses and some policy prescriptions concentrate on the 'demand side' of the growth process. A practical example of such an approach—in fact an extreme one—is the 'expectations' approach. According to this view, businessmen's expectations are thought to be the most important factor affecting growth rates. If the business community expects that a particular growth rate is normal, then, so goes the argument, that is the growth rate that will tend to be achieved. There is clearly a great deal in this; it is known that expectations affect investment, and that investment will affect the growth of the

---

[15] For further discussion see Allsopp [2].

economy and its productive potential. Moreover, if the expectations held by businessmen are adverse, they may easily frustrate government targets. It may be hard to raise the growth rate without running into the problems of instability outlined in the previous section.

This view of growth can easily be abused. As it stands it does not really explain anything. It can be much improved, however, if something is said about what it is that affects expectations. One influence, which is extremely difficult to quantify, but which was probably very important, is governmental commitment to high employment and growth. If the authorities are seen to be committed to rapid expansion and full employment, and if they apparently have the means to achieve their objectives, the climate of expectations is favourable. Recessions are expected to be short lived, and the general expectation of continued expansion stimulates longer-term investment. After the war most governments took responsibility for economic management, and with the new instruments of demand management policy they had apparently the means to achieve their objectives. And as sustained expansion developed, the confidence engendered by success—at least in the rapidly growing countries—became more and more self-reinforcing. Paradoxically, the belief that the authorities could and would control the economy—whether well founded or not—may have made their task very much easier. Because of expectational effects, a successful demand management strategy may need to be only lightly applied. This is one of the reasons why it is so difficult to quantify the importance of government policy in the post-war period.

An obvious defect of the expectations approach is that, in its naïve form, it says nothing about supply-side influences at all—it just assumes their absence. It is necessary at least to specify what is happening on the supply side. It could be that there is unemployment, in which case the assumption that there are no supply limitations is reasonable. Often, however, the implicit assumption is not that there is unemployment, but that the combination of capital accumulation and technical progress is so powerful that almost any supply bottleneck can be overcome. If the labour is available, it will be used—if not, then technology will come to the rescue. This is an assertion about the nature and speed of technological advance which is in principle testable.

20.5.2. Export-Led Growth

One of the most fashionable demand-side exlanations of rapid growth in some countries is the 'export-led growth' hypothesis. To an individual country exports are a major 'exogenous' component of demand. If the economy is competitive and exports grow rapidly, strong multiplier effects can be expected. Indeed, if the authorities maintain domestic balance between savings and investment, the multiplier applying to an expansion of exports is $1/m$—where m is the marginal propensity to import. And as far as growth is concerned, exports 'rule the roost'. Since, as a matter of accounting, savings–investment balance domestically implies external balance—the current account of the balance of payments equal to zero—another way of conceptualizing the same result is to imagine that the authorities raise demand as fast as possible, consistent with equilibrium in the balance of payments. Thus uncompetitive countries are 'balance of payments constrained', and competitive countries which tend to generate surpluses are able to avoid that tendency by going for more rapid growth. The idea of export-led growth has often been advanced as an, at least partial, explanation of the rapid expansion phases in Germany, Japan, France, and Italy. And, of course, it is often suggested that the UK was uncompetitive and balance of payments constrained throughout much of the post-war period.

A related approach has been spelled out by Beckerman [6], writing in 1965—when, of course, exchange rates were still 'fixed'. There are many strands to his analysis, but a crude sketch would be as follows. Growth depends on expectations, but these in turn depend upon the balance of payments position of the country in question. The idea behind this link is that the business sector is well aware of the constraints that operate on a modern government, and if the balance of payments is in surplus, they will expect expansionary policies; whereas if it is in deficit, they will expect deflationary policies. Thus the climate of expectations is modified by the payments position.

To this expectations hypothesis are added certain other interactions. The first is between the rate of growth of the economy and the rate of growth of productivity in the economy. That such a relationship exists is well attested empirically, but of course it can be explained in many different ways. The effect of this relationship is that the balance of payments position affects not only the growth rate (because of expectations) but also the rate of growth of productivity in the economy. But a fast rate of growth of productivity will lead to a tendency for costs per unit of output to decline, and under a regime of fixed international exchange rates this will improve the country's competitive position in international markets.

Thus we get a feedback effect. A good balance of payments position stimulates fast growth which stimulates productivity, which lowers unit costs, which improves the competitive position, which improves the balance of payments position, and so on. Corresponding to this virtuous circle, there is a vicious one, where slow growth leads to a worsening payments position, and so to slower growth.

20.5.3. Indicative Planning

If exports are profitable and rapidly growing, and if expectations are favourable, there may be no need to stimulate investment. But if there is a policy objective of raising the rate of growth, there is an obvious question about how to start the process off. If the expectations of the business sector are inappropriate for fast growth, increased aggregate demand by itself might not be much of a help—there would be a danger of supply-side bottlenecks, inflationary pressure, and instability. It would obviously be desirable to lead the way with increased investment. But for this to be possible it is necessary that expectations should be revised upwards so that investment plans become consistent with the targeted rate of growth. No individual in the private sector can affect growth by himself—but in concert, if the business sector as a whole revised its expectation upwards, then the whole economy would grow faster. The idea behind indicative planning is that the publishing of a target rate of growth with a set of consistent plans for each sector of the economy can help to modify expectations and investment plans so that they are in fact consistent with the targeted growth. Clearly, if the business sector believes that the targets will be achieved, then they are more likely to behave accordingly, and the plan may have the desired results.

In practice, of course, indicative plans, whilst relying on expectational phenomena, do not concentrate exclusively on the demand side. It is an essential purpose of such plans to identify potential supply constraints, bottlenecks, etc.—and to break them. The government's role on the supply side may be very important. Much depends, of course, on the overall credibility of an indicative plan. They are vulnerable once they start to go wrong. The greater the governmental role, and the more it is seen to be committed to the plan targets, the more likely is the private sector to react in the desired way.

It is often claimed that indicative planning played a major role in stimulating French growth rates in the 1960s. In this country the closest approach to indicative planning was the National Plan of 1965. The plan and its failure have been the subject of many studies. In the event it was balance of payments problems that led to the abandonment of the plan. There is a question, however, of whether it would have been feasible even in the absence of payments problems. The plan suggested some shortage of labour if the targets were achieved. Would it have been possible to surmount this supply-side constraint? Would productivity have responded? We shall never know, but there is much international evidence which suggests that the labour supply position may be very important.

20.6. The Importance of Labour Supply

The previous section outlined certain approaches that concentrated on the development of the expenditure side (or demand side) of the economic growth problem. Such approaches are much more plausible if it can be shown that the labour supply is unlikely to be constraining. A number of studies have stressed the importance of shifts in the labour force from one sector of the economy to another in the post-war decades. The potentiality for such shifts makes approaches which concentrate on demand factors look much more reasonable.

There is no doubt that in the fast-growing countries of Western Europe and in Japan such shifts in the disposition of the labour force did in fact take place. Indeed, these shifts are the reason that, in a cross-country comparison, differences in growth appear to be almost entirely due to differences in the growth of productivity (output per man). With widely differing degrees of structural change, it is hardly surprising that there is no simple correlation between observed rates of growth of output and observed rates of growth of total employment. There are a number of different ways, however, in which the importance of these shifts might be assessed.

20.6.1. The 'Growth Accounting' Approach to Sectoral Shifts

As noted earlier, Denison [17] found changes in the disposition of the labour force to be important. He estimated the contribution of shifts in the labour force, both from agriculture to other sectors of the economy, and from self-employment into other activities. His method was to estimate the productivity of the labour force in the two sectors. Conceptually, imagine the transfer of a worker from agriculture to, say, industry and assess (i) how much extra output is produced by that worker in industry, and (ii) how much output is lost due to the worker leaving agriculture. If the productivity in the two sectors is different, there is certainly a gain due to the transfer—which would not already have been picked up in terms of total factor input (since no change in measured labour supply is involved). For the economy as a whole, the total effect can be found by multiplying the net effect per worker by the number of workers who transferred in a given time period.[16]

The problem with this method is to decide on the gains and losses in the two sectors, and any such estimates are rather arbitrary. Denison assumed that the proportionate gain in output in the non-farm sector was four-fifths of the proportionate gain in the non-farm labour force for the north-west European countries, and three-quarters for the United States and Italy. The figures for the loss in agriculture due to the transfer varied from country to country—from zero in Italy to one-third of average agricultural productivity in the UK and the US.

On the results of this method of calculation Denison ([17], p. 215) observed: 'The reduction in the over-allocation of resources to agriculture emerges as a principal source of growth in several countries and an important source in all but the United Kingdom. Differences in the gains from this source are responsible for much of the difference among countries in growth rates of national income per person employed.' The actual order of magnitude of the combined effect of movements from both agriculture and the self-employed can be gauged from the largest figure, for Italy, where on Denison's method the shifts accounted for 1·26 percentage points of their annual growth rate for the period 1950–62. The corresponding figure for the United Kingdom was 0·1 percentage points.

It is important to realize that Denison's estimates are concerned only with the effect of the shifts on productivity and growth as part of his general approach of imputing the growth that was achieved to various sources. It may well be that the true importance of the labour force transfer may have been much greater if such a transfer was a *necessary* condition for the achievement of other 'sources' of growth. For example, without the expansion of the labour force in the non-agricultural sectors, it might have been impossible to have so much capital accumulation. If so, the true importance of the labour transfer would be much understated by this method.

20.6.2. Labour as a Permissive Factor

An approach which gives a much more central role to intersectoral shifts in the labour force is that of Kindleberger [35]. He conceptualized the problem of the fast rates of growth achieved by some European countries in the post-war

---

[16] If the total employment changes between the two years used, the number who 'transferred' cannot be measured simply by the decline in agricultural employment.

period (he used the term 'super-growth') in terms of a model of the growth process which was designed to be of use when considering underdeveloped countries. The Lewis model [38] is a model of a *dual* economy which has an advanced modern sector coexisting with a backward non-monetized sector, which is usually thought of as agriculture. The backward sector is usually considered to be underemployed, so that labour can be taken out of it without adversely affecting the output of the sector. The importance of the backward sector in the Lewis model is that it provides the more modern sectors of the economy with a supply of labour over time—the labour force in agriculture can be run down without lowering the output of agriculture—and second, since there is an abundance of labour available for the industrial sector, real wages in industry are kept low. The mechanism of growth is that the profits that arise in industry are reinvested and increase the growth of industry. Labour is always available, and since the real wage is depressed due to the existence of the low-productivity sectors, profits in industry rise over time.[17] The rising profits generate an accelerating growth process. The rapid and accelerating growth process ends when so much labour has been taken out of the low-productivity sectors that they are no longer underemployed. At this point wages start to rise, cutting into profits and slowing the growth process.

Kindleberger suggested that some such mechanism as the Lewis process was behind the 'super-growth' experience of some Western European countries. As evidence of this he examined the labour supply situation in a number of countries in some detail. The thesis of the book is best put in Kindleberger's own words:

The major factor shaping the remarkable economic growth which most of Europe has experienced since 1950 has been the availability of a large supply of labour. The labour has come from a high rate of natural increase (the Netherlands), from transfers from agriculture to services and industry (Germany, France, Italy), from the immigration of unemployed and underemployed workers from the Mediterranean countries (France, Germany, and Switzerland). Those countries with no substantial increase in the labour supply—Britain, Belgium and the Scandinavian nations—on the whole have grown more slowly than the others ([35], p. 3).

Though it would not be right to think of the labour supply as merely a permissive factor for Kindleberger, his analysis of the supply side is not really an explanation of the fast rates of growth achieved in parts of Western Europe. Kindleberger, as others, tends to appeal to demand-side factors, such as the growth of exports, and policy action by governments as additional factors making for fast growth.

20.6.3. The Kaldor Approach

A rather similar thesis was in 1966 put forward independently by Kaldor [31], who also stressed the importance of shifts in the disposition of the labour force in explaining the very rapid rates of growth achieved by some countries. The focus of his analysis, however, was on the causes of the slow growth of the United Kingdom. His main claim was that Britain's poor performance could be

[17] In the formal model the stricter assumption of a constant real wage is made.

explained by the impossibility of such shifts, which meant that the United Kingdom, unlike most other countries, should be regarded as labour constrained.

The starting-point of his analysis was the (by now familiar) finding that in the 1950s and 1960s the rates of growth of output of developed countries seemed almost totally unrelated to the growth of employment.[18] Kaldor's innovation was to use a more disaggregated approach, and to focus on the manufacturing sector rather than on the total economy. For manufacturing, in contrast to the results for the economy as a whole, international cross-sectional studies suggested that there was a close relationship between the growth of output and that of labour input. The explanation of the contrast is, of course, simple enough. In those countries that were growing fast (such as Japan or Italy) intersectoral shifts in the labour force were occurring, so that rates of growth of employment in manufacturing substantially exceeded the rates of growth of the total labour force. There was, in effect, an internal source of labour.

The finding that for a subsector of the economy (manufacturing) there seemed to be a close relationship between labour input and output is hardly surprising. It is in fact just what would be expected, and is generally confirmed by time-series studies for individual countries.[19] It serves to illustrate, however, the dangers of aggregative analysis. Many had drawn the conclusion from cross-country results for the total economy that labour supply was unimportant. Kaldor's results served to re-establish the possibility of a labour-supply constrained growth process.

Kaldor argued that a rapid rate of growth of manufacturing was a necessary condition for rapid overall growth. (There are several reasons why it might be, including its role in foreign trade, or its importance as a kind of leading sector in the overall improvement of productivity.[20]) If manufacturing needs labour in order to grow, then the whole economy could be constrained if it were not forthcoming. This, he suggested, was the fundamental explanation of Britain's relatively poor performance. In contrast with the rapidly growing countries, Britain could gain very little from the rundown in agricultural employment.[21] Perhaps, even more importantly, levels of productivity and wages were rather equal between sectors in the UK, whereas in other countries relatively high manufacturing wages meant that that sector could attract labour as it needed.[22]

[18] In the earlier discussion of Denison's work, we have seen that, even if productivity is defined as output per unit of *total* factor input, differences between countries still appear (in large part) as differences in productivity growth, or in the 'residual'.

[19] The relationship may be between labour and output, or, in more complex formulations, between output and the inputs of labour and capital—i.e. a production function.

[20] For Kaldor, productivity improvements in much of the service sector were seen as *induced* by rising real wages, which in turn were influenced by productivity improvements in manufacturing.

[21] In 1968, 3 per cent of the labour force was left in agriculture in the UK compared with 4.8 per dent in the US, 10 per cent in Germany, $15\frac{1}{2}$ per cent in France, 20 per cent in Japan, and 22 per cent in Italy ([51], Table 8). The comparison is even more dramatic in 1950, when Germany had 25 per cent in agriculture, France 30 per cent, and Italy 45 per cent.

[22] Kaldor suggested that the UK was 'prematurely mature', by which he meant that there were few sectors which could lose labour, and that productivity and wage levels were equalized before high productivity had been achieved.

20.6.4. The Verdoorn Law

Whilst the important thing in explaining why a country might be labour constrained is a relationship between input and output (in effect, a production function), Kaldor also used the same relationship to explain why *productivity* growth was related to output growth in manufacturing. Such a relationship has come to be known as the 'Verdoorn Law'.[23]

Using data from twelve developed countries (for the period 1953–5 to 1963–4), the relationship he found between rates of growth of output and of employment for manufacturing was, approximately,[24]

$$\dot{e} = -1\cdot0 + 0\cdot5\dot{x}$$

(where $\dot{e}$ = the rate of growth of employment and $\dot{x}$ = the rate of growth of output) which would also imply a relationship between productivity and output (the Verdoorn Law) of

$$\dot{p} = 1\cdot0 + 0\cdot5x$$

where $\dot{p}$ = the rate of growth of output per person employed. Apart from suggesting that labour matters, the form of these relationships indicated that productivity in manufacturing may be *endogenous*, rising as growth rises. Kaldor himself, in accounting for the relationship, stressed the importance of economies of scale, both of the static kind and also of 'irreversible' and dynamic economies of scale due to the extension of the division of labour and markets, organizational economies, effects of learning by doing, and so on. Some of the effect could also be due to capital accumulation and technical advance embodied in new equipment.[25] It should be noted that a 'Verdoorn type' of relationship between growth and productivity is also a part of many other analyses of economic growth.

If a relationship of the Verdoorn type operates, then an economy which is forced to grow slowly due to labour shortage or inflexibilities is doubly constrained. Not only is growth directly limited, but, more importantly, the growth of output per man (and hence potential living standards) are also relatively slow. By contrast, a country with large reserves of labour experiences very rapid growth in productivity which is stimulated both by the reduction in

---

[23] After the Dutch economist P. J. Verdoorn, who first suggested it in 1949 (see [62]). Originally Verdoorn suggested that productivity rose with the square root of output—a factor very close to Kaldor's estimate for manufacturing. The term 'Verdoorn Law' is often now used more loosely to refer to the idea that productivity depends upon the growth achieved. The stricter version used by Kaldor has two elements: a relationship between productivity and growth and a relationship between growth and employment input—i.e. a production relationship showing strong economies of scale or growth.

[24] For simplicity of exposition the coefficients have been rounded. The actual equation was:

$$\dot{e} = 1\cdot03 + 0\cdot52\dot{x}; \quad (R^2 = 0\cdot84).$$

[25] The estimated Verdoorn coefficient (the elasticity of productivity with respect to output, $0\cdot5$ in the previous equation) tends to fall if allowance is made for the influence of investment or other measures of capital accumulation.

'over-manning' in low productivity sectors *and* by Verdoorn effects in manufacturing.[26]

Though 'immaturity' or dualism may explain why the growth of the total labour force appeared unimportant in the fast-growing countries, there is still a question as to whether the shifts in the disposition of the labour force were an 'exogenous' factor—which would explain rapid growth through some supply-side mechanism—or whether they were endogenous, induced by growth itself. Either hypothesis (combined with Verdoorn effects) could explain the observed pattern of productivity increases. On the hypothesis that the shifts were induced, some other explanation of growth in these countries is needed: Kaldor, like Kindleberger and others, cites 'demand-side' factors, such as policy and the growth of exports, as well as the 'stage of economic development'.[27] The supply-side and demand-side hypotheses have very different implications if growth slows down for reasons other than the drying up of labour resources. On the supply-side view, sectoral shifts continue and heavy unemployment results; on the other view, observed productivity growth would slow as sectors, previously operating as a source of labour, changed more slowly, or even started to go into reverse.[28]

20.7. Other Explanations

20.7.1. 'Technological Gap' and 'Catch-Up' Theories

As noted, the major differences between countries in growth performance appear statistically as differences in the rate of growth of productivity. We have already seen that the vast shifts in the disposition of the labour force between sectors in many of the rapidly growing countries can account for much of the difference in overall productivity performance. But even if attention is focused on a subsector such as manufacturing, differences in the rate of growth of productivity are striking.

One possible explanation of the divergences in productivity performance has already been referred to—the influence of economies of scale, of growth more generally, and of technology embodied in new equipment (owing perhaps to greater investment, or different types of investment induced by rapid growth). In this type of thesis the causality runs, in effect, from growth to productivity change. But there is, of course, a competing hypothesis—that the causality runs

[26] The analysis suggests that there should be a relationship between employment growth in manufacturing and the growth of productivity. This link was investigated directly by Cripps and Tarling [16], whose results were attacked by Rowthorn [55]. (See also Kaldor [34].) In practice even for the 1950s and 1960s, the relationship is not strong—which may not be very damaging given the likelihood of other influences on productivity growth.

[27] Kaldor argues that when a country is developing its own capital-goods producing sector one would expect a great reinforcement of the demand for industrial products which would be largely self-generating. He regards this as a characteristic of an intermediate stage of development, such as that achieved by Japan in the 1950s (see Kaldor [31] and [32]).

[28] In the 1970s some countries, such as Germany and Switzerland, were able to lower their dependence on immigrant workers, who were repatriated. Thus the employment and productivity consequences were external to the economy. The development of the 'black' economy in some other countries can also be seen as in part a response to low growth and low demand for labour.

ie other way, and that productivity performance—especially in
manufacturing—was the prime mover. On this view, a more rapid rate of
technical advance was the principal reason for the relatively good performance
of the rapidly growing countries.

Explanations based on technical advance run the risk of begging the
interesting question of why some countries were able to modernize more
quickly than others. But there is an important group of hypotheses which
attempt to provide some rationale. Many authors have noted that Japan and
many European countries were substantially behind the United States in levels
of output per head and in productivity at the start of the period. There was thus
an opportunity for these countries to catch up with the United States by
introducing best-practice technology. Productivity growth in the United
States, which was slow at about 2 per cent per annum, is often thought of as
representing genuine improvements in technology and organization. Other
countries could achieve much faster growth as they were catching up with the
leader. In Denison's work, the ultimate residual, after accounting for total
factor input, for sectoral shifts in the labour force, and for economies of scale, is
compared with the residual for the United States, and the difference is ascribed
to this phenomenon of technological catch-up.

One difficulty in sorting out the importance of this factor—and of other
factors—is that a number of the rapid growers had a technological backlog as
well as large reserve of under-utilized labour, and were in addition competitive
in international trade. Thus statistically it is more or less impossible at a simple
level to discriminate between the competing hypotheses.[29] Moreover, both
catch-up theories and theories based on elastic labour supplies would predict a
slowing down over time, as the gap was reduced, or as labour markets became
tighter. There is, however, one phenomenon which is hard to account for in
terms of the naïver gap explanations. At least until the early 1970s productivity
in manufacturing appeared to be accelerating in the rapidly growing countries.
The slowdown in growth and productivity in the 1970s is difficult to evaluate
because of the influence of the world recession—see section 20.9.) Another
difficulty is that such explanations—which regard convergence as natural—do
not explain why it was that many of the slow-growing countries, such as the
United Kingdom, did not participate and experienced slow growth.

0.7.2. Dynamic Efficiency

The previous sections have outlined some of the major strands of analysis that
have been applied to the problem of why growth rates differed so much in the
950s and 1960s. But some analysts stress quite different aspects, focusing not so
much on aggregative questions about the supply of resources or the
development of exports or government policy, but on more microeconomic
elements such as the degree of initiative or of innovation. It is particularly true
that in discussions of the United Kingdom's poor performance, it is common to
come across diagnoses which run in terms of poor innovative record, the

---

[29] For a discussion of the interrelationships between technology, capital, accumulation, and
labour supply see Cornwall [15].

inefficiency of British management, or the power of British trade unions. It i
even sometimes suggested that it is all to do with the 'British nationa
character'—whatever that is.

It is well to start by reiterating a caveat made at the beginning of thi
chapter. It is perfectly possible for inefficient economies to grow fast, and fo
efficient economies to grow slowly. In considering growth it is necessary to loo
for changes in efficiency over time or for those inefficiencies which migh
specifically affect growth performance. There is another problem. Objectiv
factors, such as the labour supply position, did obviously differ greatly betwee
countries. So, for example, did export competitiveness and exchange rat
policy. It would, in fact, seem unreasonable to try and explain the large
differences between the United Kingdom and its competitors in terms o
general sluggishness and inefficiency. There would still be a problem o
explaining what led to the inefficiency—and it might be slow growth. But ther
may be something in these views, and certainly from a policy point of view it i
desirable that inefficiencies, if they exist, should be identified and eliminated

One suggestion is that the low growth of productivity in the Unitec
Kingdom is due to inadequate expenditure on research and development. O
the surface, however, there is fairly strong negative evidence. The Unitec
Kingdom spends a lot relative to European competitors, and, in fact, it is th
two slowly growing countries, the United Kingdom and the United States
which seem to have concentrated most heavily in expenditure on research anc
development. However, it is possible to point to aspects of the Britisl
programme which appear unfavourable—such as the relative proportion spen
on basic research compared with developmental work, on defence comparec
with civil research and development, and so on (for a survey of this aspect se
[54]).

The most difficult assertions to test are those which suggest that the Unitec
Kingdom's growth rate is slow relative to competitors' due to the inefficiency o
British management or the structure of labour relations. How should on
measure the efficiency of a manager? Even more problematic is the question o
how one should measure the supposedly adverse effect of Britain's comple
industrial relations structure. One measurable aspect, the strike record
suggests that Britain was not particularly strike-prone compared with othe
countries (see, for example, [60]). Of course, the fact that influences ar
difficult to quantify does not mean that they are unimportant—only that we d
not know how important they are. It does mean, however, that assertions abou
relative efficiency and its effects on growth should be treated with som
scepticism.

20.8. The Rapid Growth Period in Restrospect

The rapid and sustained expansion of the 1950s and 1960s raises, as noted in th
introduction to this chapter, two related sets of questions. The first is why som
countries were able to grow so fast, whilst others (particularly the Unitec
Kingdom and, in terms of productivity and output per head, the United States
grew slowly. In short the issue is—to borrow the title of Denison's [17] book—

why growth rates differ'. The second is how the whole system was able to maintain such a fast rate of growth for more than twenty years.

The two questions interconnect. In particular, it may be that the explanation of exceptionally rapid growth in *some* countries (Japan and much of Western Europe) effectively accounts for the overall performance of the developed world. In favour of this view it can be pointed out that it is the fast growth in some countries that looks out of line with historical experience: trends in the US and the UK look much more ordinary. With the hindsight of the 1970s and early 1980s, however, that view seems to leave something out. The deceleration in the 1970s was remarkably generalized, with countries tending to maintain their relative ranking. It looks as if there were general factors behind the acceleration into the 1950s and 1960s and the slowdown since. And, looking forward, there is an interesting question as to whether the lower growth of the 1970s represents a reversion to 'normality'—in which case it can be expected to continue—or whether a return to the buoyant conditions of the 1950s and 1960s is possible.

Starting with the problem of explaining why growth rates differed, it should be clear that the difficulties do not arise because of a shortage of plausible explanations. Quite the contrary. But some degree of consensus can be detected. It does appear that nearly every study that has examined structural shifts in the disposition of the labour force has found that they were important—though the weight given to such shifts varies considerably with the methodology adopted. In the rapidly growing countries the shifts that were observed may have been necessary or permissive factors on the supply side. Without the potential for such shifts, fast growth would perhaps have been frustrated. The shifts can be interpreted, however, as originating on the side of supply, or of demand. On the supply-side view they provided a large, effective supply of labour which, by some mechanism, was then utilized. On the demand-side view, the shifts would themselves be explained largely as a result of rapid growth rather than as a cause.

Most studies also stress other favourable factors on the supply side, such as the ready availability of raw materials and energy at stable or declining prices, and the technological backlog that existed at the beginning of the post-war period.[30] Particularly for those countries that started with relatively low levels of productivity (especially compared with the United States) the potential for improvement was large, and 'catch-up' may have played some part in the rapid rates of growth of productivity achieved.

It is unlikely, however, that the permissive elements on the supply side could have been brought to play without the high levels of investment and rapid rates of growth of the capital stock that were such a feature of the fast-growth period. We have seen that one way of assessing the contribution of capital to growth is the 'factor shares' or 'growth accounting' method. But to the extent that improvements in organization, efficiency, and technology require, or are facilitated by, high investment, this method could understate the true importance of capital in the overall story.

[30] For a recent examination of the 'catch-up' hypothesis see Marris [42].

Although capital accumulation is often treated as if it were an exogenou factor operating from the 'supply side', this would obviously be a serious over simplification. Investment is affected by demand (and expectations of growth and is also a component of expenditure. In turn it has major effects on productivity and the supply side. The causal links run in many directions Moreover the significance of variations in investment behaviour no doub varies depending upon the circumstances of the economy. In some situation where supply constraints operate, it may indeed be best to see a rise in investment as raising productivity, and hence supply potential and growth. In others, the direct demand effects may be the more important. In yet others where growth was perhaps constrained for other reasons, a rise in investment say in manufacturing, could raise productivity in that sector, but via some mechanism such as induced changes in the sectoral disposition of the labour force, lower it elsewhere, and leave aggregate productivity unchanged.

Turning to the demand side of the picture it is again possible to detect some consensus. Most of the rapidly growing countries were competitive in international trade, and had rapidly growing exports. There is less agreemen about cause and effect: some would see the expansion in exports as coming about because of productivity and cost improvements in the domestic economy. Others subscribe to some model of export-led growth. Apart from exports, stress is sometimes laid on other expenditure components such as the buoyancy and growth of public expenditure programmes, and, of course investment.

The most difficult demand-side element to assess is the effect of policy— particularly demand management policy. One view, of course, is that policy activism had little to do with the longer-run trend of growth. Most writers however, have suggested that policy was important, particularly in initiating and maintaining a climate of optimism and favourable expectations tha growth would continue, justifying high and rising investment.[31] This aspect o policy, working indirectly through the expectations of private sector economi agents, is necessarily difficult to quantify (even the rapid growth of publi expenditure can itself be seen as in part engendered by the general climate o optimism and success). Nevertheless, as Boltho [11] has pointed out in analysing European experience, the most striking change between the pre-wa period and the post-war period was not in any of the factors on the supply side (they were permissive in the 1920s and 1930s too) but in the commitment to ful employment and growth and the policies followed by post-war governments There is thus a prima facie case that the policies pursued contributec importantly to the successes achieved.[32]

[31] See, for example, UNECE [61], Chap. 4; Maddison [39], Chaps. 2 and 4; Matthews [43] Cornwall [15]; Boltho [11].

[32] It is sometimes objected that government policy actions were too 'small' to explain the moderation of the business cycle and the acceleration of growth. However, such arguments miss th point about expectations. The commitment to high-growth policies, together with the belief tha policy instruments are available to achieve the objectives, powerfully alters private secto behaviour—especially the investment decision—so that the private sector does most of the work Paradoxically, demand management policies which are expected to succeed may need to be onl lightly applied. See section 20.5, Boltho [11], and for the United States, Baily [3].

In explaining rapid growth it is thus possible to tell an eclectic story of favourable elements on the demand side interacting with permissive factors on the supply side, which became powerfully reinforcing. The process received an initial boost from the reconstruction programmes after the war, but as time went on the expectation of continued growth probably became more and more important. High rates of growth were favourable to productivity improvements in manufacturing due to static and dynamic economies of scale (the Verdoorn Law) and due to high investment and the upgrading of technology. Rising real wages were in turn in part responsible for induced rises in productivity elsewhere—especially in services.[33] (Thus for the economy as a whole, the overall trend of productivity is endogenous.) In turn rapid rises in productivity in the fast-growing countries tended to increase export competitiveness, further reinforcing the demand-side elements. The favourable balance of payments position reacted back on to government policy: so too did growth itself, which led to buoyant tax revenues facilitating the expansion of public expenditure.

There is more controversy about the reasons for slow growth. This is especially true of the reasons advanced for the slow rate of growth of the United Kingdom. Kaldor and Kindleberger both stressed the labour supply situation acting as a constraint, overall or on manufacturing. Others have pointed to different supply-side factors such as a low level of investment, sluggish innovation,[34] restrictive practices, etc. But another group of explanations suggests that the problem did not lie on the supply side at all, but on the demand side. Of these, the most common are those that stress the balance of payments difficulties in the 1950s and 1960s, or, more generally, an uncompetitive exchange rate and the sluggish development of exports. The view that the UK was 'balance of payments constrained' was important in the run up to the devaluation of sterling—delayed until 1967. Proponents tended to assume that once the external constraint was removed, faster growth would follow—either automatically, or via more expansionary policies adopted by the authorities.

Experience from the mid-1960s onwards in the United Kingdom (and also in some other countries) may tend to favour the view that slow growth in Britain was no due to any fundamental supply-side factor such as a restricted labour supply. In the manufacturing sector, where, as noted, there did appear to be a good relationship between employment input and output, and hence the possibility of a labour constraint, productivity accelerated in the second half of the 1960s as a result of 'shake-outs' of labour and, also (according to some observers), as a result of an increase in investment (see, for example, Sargent [57]). This did not lead, however, to more rapid growth, but to the phenomenon which came to be known as 'de-industrialization' (see Blackaby [8]). The international cross-section evidence also suggests that the relationship between manufacturing output and labour input tended to break down in

---

[33] Kaldor, for example, argues that in many service sectors, such as distribution, productivity an adapt by changes in organization—such as the move to supermarkets—but that the changes are induced by rising costs. See Kaldor [31].

[34] See Gomulka [23] and [24].

other countries as well in the late 1960s and early 1970s. Productivity growth in manufacturing generally accelerated.[35] If the manufacturing sector can in fact grow fast, without a rapid growth of labour input, then this means that the idea that the UK was constrained by lack of labour is much less plausible.

But this period is not favourable to the 'balance of payments constraint' school either. Growth in the UK failed to accelerate in spite of improved competitiveness. One reason, of course, is that demand management policy was, in effect, diverted in the late 1960s to making devaluation work—so perhaps the hypothesis was not really tested. Much more fundamentally, however, devaluation (and later in the 1970s, the floating exchange rate) had the effect of diverting attention away from the external constraint *per se* to the more important difficulty of *domestic* wage–price pressure, which constrained the use of the demand management policy instruments and tended to frustrate any attempts at expansionary action.[36]

A focus on domestic inflationary pressure as the underlying reason for balance of payments difficulties and, later, for more direct constraints on policy in the United Kingdom raises again the question of the importance of Britain's relatively tight labour market in the story of slow growth. One extreme view is that inflationary pressure itself resulted from trying to grow faster than was warranted by the supply of labour. It seems likely, however, that other aspects of a more qualitative kind—such as Britain's poor industrial relations structure and the inflationary potential of the bargaining system—should be brought into the account. If the institutional structural were *relatively* adverse in the United Kingdom this would help to explain not only inflationary pressure as a constraint on policy, but also, more directly, poor productivity and slow innovation.

The issues can perhaps be brought into relief by looking not at the relative growth rates achieved, but at *levels* of productivity and output per capita. Nearly all countries started after the war well below the United States—productivity in Europe was perhaps half that in the US, and it was even lower in Japan. During the period of rapid growth most developed countries greatly narrowed the gap, and in some cases reversed it. The UK, on the other hand, did not, remaining about half as productive as the US. The self-reinforcing character of rapid growth must greatly have facilitated the transformation in the countries that experienced it. But slow growth in a relatively constrained economy seems inadequate as an explanation of the maintenance of relatively low productivity (quite apart from the apparent circularity). At a certain point the more direct question has to be posed: what accounts for low efficiency in Britain and how might the factors making for low productivity and poor competitiveness best be removed? And at that point the underlying differences between the 'demand-siders' and the 'supply-siders' emerge. Those who stress the demand side see the best chance of structural transformation as occurring in

---

[35] In several countries this seems to have been associated with advances in labour-saving investment. Some have argued that this exceptional period of productivity growth was bound to be short lived (Sargent [57]), or even that the figures indicate some kind of crisis of accumulation (Glyn [22], Mazier [46]).

[36] See Chap. 13 on demand management and Chap. 19 on international macroeconomic policy.

a situation of high and rising expenditure. The supply-siders would argue that the initiating impulse would have to come from the supply side, via improvements in work organization and technology.[37] But few would disagree that, in practice, rapid transformation necessarily involves a complex interaction of demand- and supply-side forces.

Returning to the problem of accounting for the generally high rate of growth of the developed countries, it is evident that the process described here had many of the characteristics of a (particularly prolonged) cyclical boom.[38] It can also be described in terms of a 'virtuous circle'.[39] Either description suggests a certain fragility in the process, which would be vulnerable either to developing constraints on the supply side, or to major shocks or policy difficulties arising on the demand side. Once the virtuous circle was broken it would be very difficult to sort out cause from effect, and a combination of unfavourable elements would be observed.[40] The resulting slower growth could, by putting into reverse some of the favourable factors outlined here, contribute to a slowdown in productivity growth in manufacturing and in other sectors of the economy.

As discussed in detail in other chapters,[41] Western developed countries appeared to be running into serious difficulties from about the mid-1960s onwards. The Bretton Woods system was breaking down, and inflationary pressure was building up both in the United States and in Europe. Furthermore, some of the supply-side elements which had facilitated rapid growth were beginning to diminish: the potential for major sectoral shifts in the labour force was drying up, immigration flows were starting to cause social and political pressures in much of Western Europe, and, above all, institutional and legal changes may have been making for less flexibility in labour markets (see Bernabé [7]). The scope for technological 'catch-up' in Europe and Japan had been much reduced by previous success, and there were beginning to be worries about the supply of some essential raw materials.

In spite of the developing problems, rapid growth, both of output and of productivity, continued more or less unchecked[42] until 1973, when the whole world went into recession during the first oil crisis. Investment continued at high levels in spite of mounting economic problems, and, if forecasts made at the time are any guide, general confidence that the 'Western' world would continue to grow at about $4\frac{1}{2}$ per cent per annum was maintained (see, for example, OECD [51]). The climate of optimism about prospects for medium-

---

[37] In an extreme version of this view, high demand, by 'feather-bedding' inefficiency, may be an adverse factor, slowing longer-run growth.

[38] See Matthews [45], 'Introduction'.

[39] This characterization is more normally applied to particularly fast-growing countries, with a corresponding vicious circle applying in the slow growers (Beckerman [6], Moore and Rhodes [48]). The same general ideas can, however, be applied to developed countries taken as a group.

[40] See also Allsopp [2].

[41] See especially Chap. 19.

[42] In the United States the growth of GDP per person employed slowed to about $1\frac{1}{2}$ per cent per annum in the period 1967–73. Productivity in US manufacturing continued to grow at about $3\frac{1}{2}$ per cent per annum during 1967–73, before slowing markedly after 1973.

term growth appears to have been surprisingly robust, and indeed seems to have survived until several years after 1973.[43]

20.9. Slower Growth Since 1973 and the Productivity Puzzle

The trend of growth established in the 1950s and 1960s broke down sharply in 1974 as the world plunged into the worst recession of the post-war period. The recovery set in from about mid-1976 onwards, but after the initial bounce-back, the rate of expansion seemed to stabilize at about $3-3\frac{1}{2}$ per cent per annum until the second oil crisis of 1979–80 and the further generalized recession of 1981–2. In the intervening period 1976–9 the *level* of output never got back to the previous trend, and unemployment stepped up substantially to about 5 per cent of the labour force on average, compared with about 3 per cent in the previous decade. Unemployment stepped up further with the recession of the early 1980s.

The period is obviously so disturbed that it is very difficult to pick out longer-term trends. If attention is concentrated in the peak years 1973 and 1979, growth in OECD countries slowed down from its previous $4\frac{1}{2}$ per cent per annum to 2·7 per cent (see Table 20.1). In Western Europe the slowdown was greater: growth halved from 4·8 per cent per annum to 2·4 per cent. (In the UK the fall was from 3 per cent to 1·3 per cent per annum.) In Japan, the slowdown was largest of all, from $9\frac{1}{2}$ per cent to about 4 per cent. It is possible, however, to interpret the figures in a slightly different way as due to a once-and-for-all shift downwards in 1974–5. Even if allowance is made for that, however, it appears that the underlying trend of growth became substantially lower.

A better indication of the change in trend is obtained by looking at figures for productivity, measured in GDP per person employed (see Table 20.2). The slowdown in Europe averaged about 2 percentage points; in Japan it was over 5 percentage points. In the United States productivity growth is seen to have slowed down to nearly zero over the period 1973–9. Much of the slowdown occurred, however, in the recession years 1974 and 1975 when productivity growth became near to zero or negative in many countries. It picked up again in the recovery period but not sufficiently to reverse the earlier slowdown, and was generally lower than in the 1960s.[44]

Another feature of the slowdown is that it was not confined to particular sectors such as manufacturing. On the contrary, it occurred more or less across the board, though countries differed in the sectors which were worst hit. Generally, however, the reduction in productivity growth was at least as large in non-manufacturing as in manufacturing. In Japan productivity in the non-

---

[43] This relative optimism about medium-term prospects is still apparent in the 'McCracken Report' [47] published in 1977. See Chap. 19.

[44] In the period 1975–9 productivity grew at 3·4 per cent per annum in France, 3·7 per cent in Germany, 4 per cent in Japan, 2·2 per cent in the UK, and 1·1 per cent in the US. Such figures, however, probably overstate the trend of productivity, since they compare the peak year of 1979 with the recession year of 1975. See Morgan [49].

manufacturing sectors fell particularly sharply from about $9\frac{1}{2}$ per cent per annum in 1962–73 to $1\frac{1}{2}$ per cent in 1973–9.[45]

Such a generalized slowdown in growth and productivity is unprecedented—though perhaps no more puzzling than the earlier acceleration—and there have been many attempts to explain it. The kinds of analysis that have been applied are similar to those outlined earlier in discussing the 1950s and 1960s, but used, so to speak, in reverse. Thus, for example, some have seen the productivity slowdown as occurring on the supply side, others point to demand-side elements, such as the policies followed in most countries.

One of the obvious factors to look at is the 'supply shock' of the rise in oil prices in 1973. It is often argued that oil is a complementary input in the production function, and that a massive rise in its price would affect the productivity of other factors (see Bruno and Sachs [13]. One of the attractive features of this kind of hypothesis is that it would explain the timing of the sudden slowdown, which is hard to account for on other supply-side arguments.

There are, however, some difficulties with this hypothesis. The first is that the oil price rises themselves seem too small to account for such large effects. Important as it is, oil does not have a very large weight in the output of manufacturing or of the total economy. Second, as the OECD noted, the rise in oil prices to the *users* of oil (which is what should matter for this production function approach) did not in fact climb very steeply in most countries until after the second oil crisis in 1979 (see OECD [52] and [53]). Partly for this reason some authors (Bruno [12]) have widened the analysis to take account of the prices of all primary raw material inputs.[46] Other studies have pointed more informally to the possibility that, due to relative price changes and demand shifts, some portion of the capital stock became economically obsolescent following the oil crisis. Estimates of the magnitude of supply effects remain, however, controversial. To the extent that they were important, they explain the slowdown as a shift in productive potential in 1974–5 (and also in 1979–80) and thus have fairly optimistic implications for the future, unless further input price shocks arise.

Conventional growth accounting approaches to the productivity slowdown do not seem to have been very helpful in isolating its causes. As in the case of the preceding rapid-growth period, total factor productivity (or the 'residual') is the major item that varies, and attempts to break it down into the effects of labour force shifts, economies of scale, etc. have tended to produce the rather predictable result that the productivity slowdown is rather broadly based when

[45] See Morgan [49]. The figures refer to 'other goods and measured services', which include financial and related services and community and personal services, including government, where measures of productivity are more or less meaningless. In manufacturing the slowdown was from 10 per cent to about $6\frac{1}{2}$ per cent. As is well known, unemployment was not greatly affected in Japan.
[46] For a discussion of the international commodity price boom see Chap. 19. Bruno estimates that perhaps half the productivity slowdown in manufacturing can be accounted for by such input price shocks, and sees the rest as due to indirect demand effects following from the policy response of governments (see [12]).

imputed to different 'causes', just as it is when looked at across differen countries or different sectors.

The US position is, however, worth singling out. For the US, several studie have suggested that the slowdown was much more gradual, with productivity performance decelerating from the mid-1960s onwards (see, for example Denison [19] and Nordhaus [50]). Moreover, in the 1970s, the US, unlike mos other countries, carried out expansionary policies, and employment ros rapidly. In spite of such relatively favourable elements on the demand side productivity slowed down; and on a growth accounting basis, Denison [20 found that the residual became negative. Thus it can be argued that the US data are more consistent with the idea of some fundamental 'supply-side slowdown, and also that alternative explanations from the demand side are less likely to be appropriate. In Europe and Japan it is hard to explain the sudden break in trend within the growth accounting framework.

Similar difficulties arise with the 'catch-up' thesis—which would, of course explain the slowdown in productivity growth as Continental Europe and Japan came nearer to US levels of productivity. The problem is that this thesis cannot explain the suddenness of the change, nor does it seem to work very well in explaining the pattern of slowdown—why, for example, should the UK be affected, when the productivity differential was still large?[47]

Turning to the 'demand side' of the picture, the obvious explanation o slower growth is the effects of the two oil crises and the generally restrictive policies followed by the OECD governments.[48] The interesting question, then is the extent to which restrictive policies were necessary or appropriate to match a slowdown of productive potential arising from the supply-side changes already discussed,[49] as compared with the alternative hypothesis that slow growth of productivity was *induced* by restrictive policies and slow growth.

It is useful to distinguish between the effects of recession and of slow growth—appealing, as Matthews [45] has suggested, to Okun's Law and the Verdoorn's Law. Okun's Law refers to the adverse effects on productivity as an economy swings into recession (and the favourable effects as it moves out again). The idea is simply that as the economy departs from productive potential, the effect on employment (and unemployment) is less than proportional, and output per head suffers. The usual explanation runs in terms of labour 'hoarding' and similar phenomena which occur when a downswing is expected to be temporary. Verdoorn's Law, as discussed in section 20.6.4, captures the idea that productivity (in manufacturing, or more loosely, in the economy as a whole) depends on the growth achieved. Either or both could account for the slowdown observed in manufacturing, but recession-induced effects would be seen as essentially short term and reversible, and therefore as not affecting the underlying trend of productive potential.

In fact, as noted, the recession was not fully reversed in most OECD countries, focusing attention on the somewhat longer-term induced effects on

[47] For an examination of the 'catch-up' thesis see Marris [42].
[48] See Chap. 19 for a fuller discussion.
[49] See the discussion in Chap. 13 of the IMF's measure of potential output in the UK, which assumes a reduction in 1974–5 due to the oil shock.

productivity. (Labour-hoarding would, for example, tend to cease when a sustained upswing failed to materialize.) These include static and dynamic economies of scale as well as induced effects via a reduction in the rate of capital accumulation. It seems probable that in quite a number of countries job creation schemes and the like further slowed the growth of productivity.

It is possible to go further. We have noted that productivity slowed in other sectors as well as in manufacturing. One reason is probably that shifts into manufacturing from other (lower-productivity) sectors would themselves have been discouraged, lowering the measured rate of productivity advance. Growth accounting procedures, for example, suggest that there was less gain from sectoral redistribution in the post-1973 period. The slower growth of productivity and real wages may in turn have had further effects in these sectors where productivity increases are induced by rising wages. In the extreme case of the dual-economy models applied to some of the fast growers, the whole of the effect of the slowdown could eventually appear as changes in the sectoral distribution of the labour force, with perhaps widening productivity differentials as the economy moved back towards 'underdevelopment'.

It seems likely that induced effects on productivity, both within manufacturing and elsewhere, were important, and explain, in part at least, why the slowdown did not lead to as much overt unemployment as would have been expected on the basis of previous trends in productivity.[50] One of the implications is that the level of unemployment may be a much poorer indicator of the longer-term pressure of demand than is often assumed.

Many of the induced effects discussed here are medium term in nature, and conventional estimates of productive potential would indicate a slowdown. In fact, however, most of them are in principle reversible should growth accelerate again. This is most obvious in the case of scale economies. But with an expansion of output, investment, and with it productivity, would also be expected to respond. Induced sectoral movements could be reversed, and so on. What this means is that a period of slow growth could, just as if it led to overt unemployment, lead to a potential for rapid expansion in the future (although there could be supply-side difficulties in achieving it). Productive potential estimates, which are essentially short term, may be misleading, and the temptation to draw strong conclusions from productivity trends in the recent past should be resisted.

If much of the slowdown in productivity growth was induced (and in many countries the slowdown in manufacturing productivity is remarkably close to what would be predicted by a crude application of the Verdoorn Law[51]) then this suggests that the explanation of slow growth in the 1970s is to be found not on the supply side, but in the economic difficulties of the 1970s and the generally restrictive policies pursued by governments. This is not necessarily an optimistic conclusion, however, since, as described in other chapters, there was

[50] In many countries there are secondary labour markets where wage levels are relatively flexible, and where employment may respond in the way indicated. The development of the 'black economy' in some countries can be seen as a special case of this phenomenon (encouraged by aspects of the tax system), which would, of course, distort the statistics.

[51] i.e. the slowdown in productivity was about half the slowdown in output growth.

a kind of inevitability about the policies followed in the face of major shocks and increasing difficulties with inflationary pressure. Moreover, even if the problem of inflation could be solved, and major shocks did not occur, it does not mean that it would be easy to return to a period of rapid expansion. The successes of the 1950s and 1960s depended to a unknown but probably substantial extent on the general climate of optimism and buoyant expec tations, which justified high investment during the long boom. That climate could prove hard to revive even if the more immediate economic difficultie were to disappear.

Finally, what about the UK? The slowdown in growth and productivity wa (in proportionate terms) as marked in Britain as elsewhere. GDP grew during 1973–9 at a little over 1 per cent per annum, and the output of manufacturing actually fell. Productivity in manufacturing, which in the late 1960s and early 1970s was growing at a relatively high rate of about $4\frac{1}{2}$ per cent per annum grew on average by under 1 per cent per annum during 1973–9. The UK having performed relatively poorly in the 1950s and 1960s, performed relatively poorly in the 1970s as well. After 1979 the UK suffered a further major recession, larger in extent than in most other countries, in spite of self-sufficiency in oil and energy; manufacturing in particular contracted very sharply indeed.[52] Productivity, however, kept up much better than might have been expected. Output per person fell by about 4 per cent in 1980—though by much less if allowance is made for hours worked.[53] It rose, however, by about 13–14 per cent over the next two years—or by about 9 per cent over the whole period from 1979 to the first quarter of 1983, in spite of the reduction in output which was still about 15 per cent below the peak of 1979. For the whole economy the gain in productivity was much smaller: 2·3 per cent over the three years 1979–82 if North Sea oil and gas production is excluded.

These figures indicate the massive shake-out of labour in British manufactur-ing industry in the early 1980s' recession (over 10 per cent of the labour force). The result was that Okun's Law, which would have predicted further reductions in productivity, was, in effect, overridden, and productivity speeded up. There is little doubt that the 'shake-out' was a response to exceptionally adverse economic circumstances and the expectations that they would not be quickly reversed. In the short term this led, of course, to overt unemployment rather than lower productivity. Any longer-term benefits would depend on a revival of output and growth to make use of the labour released. (Chapter 29 looks at this most recent period in more detail.) This UK performance raises the possibility that the growth of productivity is slowly reverting to its pre-1973 rate, and that the puzzle of the slowdown will have proved to be a very temporary one. But as yet it is too soon to say. Such a process may be occurring, but it may be that very severe pressures have brought about a once-and-for-all catch-up of some of the efficiency gains which the UK failed to achieve in earlier periods superimposed on an otherwise slow growth trend.

---

[52] By about 16 per cent from 1979 to the trough in the first quarter of 1981.

[53] The fall in output per person, however, in manufacturing was 1·3 per cent between 1979 and 1980.

Bibliography

SECTION A

Many of the major works on comparative growth experience have been discussed in the body of this chapter. An early survey was undertaken by [61] UNECE, *Some Factors in Economic Growth in Europe During the 1950s* (Geneva, 1964). The OECD considered comparative experience in [51] *The Growth of Output 1960–80* (Paris, 1970). Europe's growth, both in the 1950s and 1960s, and in the 1970s, is surveyed and analysed in [10] A. Boltho (ed.), *The European Economy: Growth and Crisis* (Oxford University Press, 1982), especially in Chaps. 1 and 2.

The most famous book using a 'growth accounting' framework is [17] E. F. Denison, *Why Growth Rates Differ* (Brookings Institution, 1967), which covers the United States and eight European countries. The analysis is extended to Japan in [21] E. F. Denison and W. K. Chung 'Economic Growth and its Sources' in H. Patrick and J. Rosovsky (eds.), *Asia's New Giant* (Brookings Institution, 1976), and applied particularly to the UK by Denison in R. E. Caves and Associates, *Britain's Economic Prospects* (Brookings Institution, 1968). Works representing particular views on the growth process in the 1950s and 1960s include A. Lamfalussy, *The United Kingdom and the Six: An Essay on Growth in Western Europe* (London, 1963); [39] A. Maddison, *Economic Growth in the West: Comparative Experience in Europe and North America* (Twentieth Century Fund, New York, 1964); [35] C. P. Kindleberger, *Europe's Post-War Growth: The Role of Labour Supply* (Oxford University press, London, 1964); [31] N. Kaldor, *Causes of the Slow Rate of Economic Growth of the United Kingdom* (Cambridge University press, 1966). A more recent book which discusses many of the approaches is [15] J. Cornwall, *Modern Capitalism: Its Growth and Transformation* (London, 1977).

The slowdown in growth since 1973 has led to extensive literature. An accessible source which includes a survey as well as a number of different analyses is [45] R. C. O. Matthews (ed.), *Slower Growth in the Western World* (Heinemann, 1982). See also a number of contributions (including one by Denison) in the *Economic Journal* (Mar. 1983).

SECTION B

1] ALDCROFT, D. H. and FEARSON, P. *Economic Growth in 20th Century Britain* (Macmillan, 1969).

2] ALLSOPP, C. J. 'The Management of the World Economy', in Beckerman, W. (ed.), *Slow Growth in Britain* (Clarendon Press, 1979).

3] BAILY, N. M. 'Stabilisation Policy and Private Economic Behaviour', *Brookings Papers on Economic Activity*, 1 (1978).

4] BALASSA, B. 'Some Observations on Mr Beckerman's Export Propelled Growth Model', *Economic Journal*, LXXIII (Dec. 1963).

5] BECKERMAN, W. 'Projecting Europe's Growth', *Economic Journal* (Dec. 1962).

6] —— —— *The British Economy in 1975* (Cambridge University Press, 1965).

7] BERNABÉ, F. 'The Labour Market and Unemployment', in Boltho [10].

8] BLACKABY, F. (ed.), *De-Industrialisation* (NIESR, 1979).

9] BOLTHO, A. *Japan: An Economic Survey 1953–73* (Oxford University Press, 1975).

10] BOLTHO, A. (ed.). *The European Economy: Growth and Crisis* (Oxford University Press, 1982).

11] BOLTHO, A. 'Economic Growth', in [10].

12] BRUNO, M. 'World Shocks, Macro-economic's Response, and the Productivity Puzzle', in Matthews [45].

[13] BRUNO, M. and SACHS, J. 'Input Price Shocks and the Slowdown in Economic Growth: Estimates for UK Manufacturing', *Review of Economic Studies* (1983).

[14] Command 2746, *The National Plan* (HMSO, Sept. 1965).

[15] CORNWALL, J. *Modern Capitalism: Its Growth and Transformation*, (London, 1977).

[16] CRIPPS, T. F. and TARLING, R. J. *Growth in Advanced Capitalist Economies 1950–1970* (Cambridge University Press, 1973).

[17] DENISON, E. F., assisted by POULIER, J-P. *Why Growth Rates Differ* (Brookings Institution, 1967).

[18] —— —— 'Some Major Issues in Productivity Analysis: An Examination of Estimates by Jorgenson and Griliches', *Survey of Current Business* (1969).

[19] —— —— *Accounting for Slower Growth: The US in the 1970s* (Brookings Institution, 1979).

[20] —— —— 'The Interruption of Productivity Growth in the United States', *Economic Journal* (Mar. 1983).

[21] DENISON, E. F. and CHUNG, W. K. 'Economic Growth and its Sources', in Patrick, H. and Rosovsky, H. (eds.), *Asia's New Giant* (Brookings Institution, 1976).

[22] GLYN, A. 'The Productivity Slowdown: A Marxist View', in Matthews [45].

[23] GOMULKA, S. *Inventive Activity, Diffusion and Stages of Economic Growth* (Aahus, 1971).

—— —— 'Britain's Slow Industrial Growth: Increasing Inefficiency Versus Low Rates of Technical Change', in Beckerman, W. (ed.), *Slow Growth in Britain* (Clarendon Press, 1979).

[25] HAHN, F. and MATTHEWS, R. C. O. 'The Theory of Economic Growth: A Survey', *Economic Journal*, LXXIV (Dec. 1964).

[26] HARROD, R. F. 'An Essay in Dynamic Theory', *Economic Journal*, XLIV (Mar. 1939).

[27] —— —— *Economic Dynamics* (Macmillan, 1973).

[28] JONES, H. *An Introduction to Modern Theories of Economic Growth* (Nelson, 1975).

[29] JORGENSON, D. W. 'Issues in Growth Accounting: A Reply to Edward Denison', *Survey of Current Business* (1972).

[30] JORGENSON D. W. and GRILICHES, Z. 'The Explanation of Productivity Change', *Review of Economic Studies* (July 1967).

[31] KALDOR, N. *Causes of the Slow Rate of Economic Growth of the United Kingdom* (Cambridge University Press, 1966).

[32] —— —— *Strategic Factors in Economic Development* (New York, 1967).

[33] —— —— 'Productivity and Growth in Manufacturing Industry: A Reply', *Economica*, XXXV (Nov. 1968).

[34] —— —— 'Economic Growth and the Verdoorn law', *Economic Journal*, LXXXV (Dec. 1975).

[35] KINDLEBERGER, C. P. *Europe's Post-War Growth: The Role of Labour Supply* (Harvard University Press and Oxford University Press, 1967).

[36] KREGEL, J. A. *The Theory of Economic Growth*, Macmillan Studies in Economics (Macmillan, 1972).

[37] LAMFALUSSY, A. *The United Kingdom and the Six: Comparative Experience in Europe and North America* (London, 1964).

[38] LEWIS, W. A. 'Economic Growth With Unlimited Supplies of Labour', *Manchester School* (Jan. 1958).

[39] MADDISON, A. *Economic Growth in the West: Comparative Experience in Europe and North America* (Twentieth Century Fund, New York, 1964).

[40] —— —— 'Explaining Economic Growth', in Banca Nazionale del Lavoro *Quarterly Review* (Sept. 1972).

[41] —— —— 'Long Run Dynamics of Productivity Growth', in Banca Nazionale de Lavoro, *Quarterly Review* (Mar. 1979).

42] MARRIS, R. 'How Much of the Slowdown Was Catch-up?, in Matthews [45].

43] MATTHEWS, R. C. O. 'Why Has Britain Had Full Employment Since the War?' *Economic Journal*, LXXVIII (Sept. 1968).

44] —— —— 'Why Growth Rates Differ', *Economic Journal*, LXXIX (1969).

45] MATTHEWS, R. C. O. (ed.). *Slower Growth in the Western World* (Heinemann, 1982).

46] MAZIER, J. 'Growth and Crisis: A Marxist Interpretation', in Boltho [10].

47] McCRACKEN, P. *et al. Towards Full Employment and Price Stability* (OECD, Paris, 1977).

48] MOORE, B. and RHODES, J. 'The Relative Decline of the UK Manufacturing ector', *Cambridge Economic Policy Review* (Mar. 1976).

49] MORGAN, A. D. 'Productivity in the 1960s and 1970s', in Matthews [45].

50] NORDHAUS, W. D. 'Economic Policy in the Face of Declining Productivity Growth', *European Economic Review*, XVIII (May/June 1982).

51] OECD. *The Growth of Ouput 1960–1980* (Paris, 1970).

52] —— *Economic Outlook* (July 1980).

53] —— *Economic Outlook* (July 1981).

54] PEAKER, A. *Economic Growth in Modern Britain* (Macmillan, 1974).

55] ROWTHORN, R. E. 'What Remains of Kaldor's Law?' *Economic Journal*, LXXXV Mar. 1975).

56] —— —— 'Reply to Lord Kaldor's Comment', *Economic Journal*, LXXXV Dec. 1975).

57] SARGENT, J. R. 'Capital Accumulation and Productivity Growth', in Matthews [45].

58] SEN, A. K. (ed.). *Growth Economics* (Penguin, 1970).

59] SOLOW, R. M. *Growth Theory: An Exposition* (Clarendon Press, 1970).

60] TURNER, W. A. *Is Britain Really Strike Prone?* (Cambridge University Press, 1969).

61] United Nations Economic Commission for Europe (UNECE). *Some Factors in Economic Growth in Europe During the 1950s* (Geneva, 1964).

62] VERDOORN, P. J. 'Fattori Che Regolano lo Sviluppo della Prodittivita del Lavoro', *L'Industria* (1949).

21

Long-Term Industrial Performance in the UK: The Role of Education and Research, 1850–1939

C. BARNETT

21.1. Introduction

The previous chapter examined a number of theories of the process of economic growth and the extent to which they can explain both the pattern of growth rates across industrial countries since the war and the changes in them through time. But there are some grounds for believing that, over a much longer period of history, the UK uniquely has experienced a poorer growth record than elsewhere. That there is some such phenomenon to explain is illustrated in Table 21.1 and Figure 21.1.[1] These suggest that the UK's growth of productivity, measured as GDP per man-year, has generally been amongst the lowest of a number of major economies, irrespective of whether the UK's *level* of productivity was relatively high compared to abroad, as in the earlier part of this century, or relatively low, as more recently. Figure 21.1 strongly suggests that the UK has been the one exception to the otherwise fairly steady catch-up of the US level by other countries, and this might well be reinforced if account is taken of the likely impact of the two world wars on Germany and Japan. On these figures, 1873–99 was the last period when the UK's growth of productivity was near the average of other countries. During this period, if not earlier, it seems likely that factors were developing in the UK economy that were to leave it unable to achieve comparable productivity growth for the ensuing eighty years at least.

This chapter does not attempt a complete explanation of this poor comparative performance. Such a task is beyond our knowledge at present. Rather, it focuses on a particular element of the problem—the impact of the system of education and research in the UK. The rationale for this is threefold. First, much of the work on economic growth has emphasized the very great, if not overriding, importance of technological progress, itself a function of the research and innovative capability of a country, and of the quality, as opposed

---

[1] Both the table and figure are taken from R. C. O. Matthews, C. H. Feinstein, and J. C. Odling-Smee's major work *British Economic Growth 1856–1973* (Stanford, California, 1982).

TABLE 21.1. *Growth of Gross Domestic Product per Man-Year in the United Kingdom Compared With Six Other Industrial Countries, 1873–1973*

Period	UK	US	Sweden	France	Germany	Italy	Japan
Annual percentage growth rates							
1873–1899	1·2	1·9	1·5	1·3	1·5	0·3	1·1
1899–1913	0·5	1·3	2·1	1·6	1·5	2·5	1·8
1913–1924	0·3	1·7	0·3	0·8	−0·9	−0·1	3·2
1924–1937	1·0	1·4	1·7	1·4	3·0	1·8	2·7
1937–1951	1·0	2·3	2·6	1·7	1·0	1·4	−1·3
1951–1964	2·3	2·5	3·3	4·3	5·1	5·6	7·6
1964–1973	2·6	1·6	2·7	4·6	4·4	5·0	8·4
1873–1951	0·9	1·7	1·7	1·4	1·3	1·3	1·4
1951–1973	2·4	2·3	3·0	4·4	4·8	5·5	7·9
1873–1973	1·2	1·8	1·9	2·0	2·0	2·4	2·6
Excess over UK growth rate (per cent)							
1873–1899	—	0·7	0·3	0·1	0·3	−0·9	−0·1
1899–1913	—	0·8	1·6	1·1	1·0	2·0	1·3
1913–1924	—	1·4	0·0	0·5	−1·2	−0·4	2·9
1924–1937	—	0·4	0·7	0·4	2·0	0·8	1·7
1937–1951	—	1·3	1·0	0·7	0·0	0·4	−2·3
1951–1964	—	0·2	1·0	2·0	2·8	3·3	5·3
1964–1973	—	−1·0	0·1	2·0	1·8	2·4	5·8
1873–1951	—	0·8	0·8	0·5	0·4	0·4	0·5
1951–1973	—	−0·1	0·6	2·0	2·4	3·1	5·5
1873–1973	—	0·6	0·7	0·8	0·8	1·2	1·4

Source: Matthews et al., *British Economic Growth 1856–1973*, Table 25, p. 31.

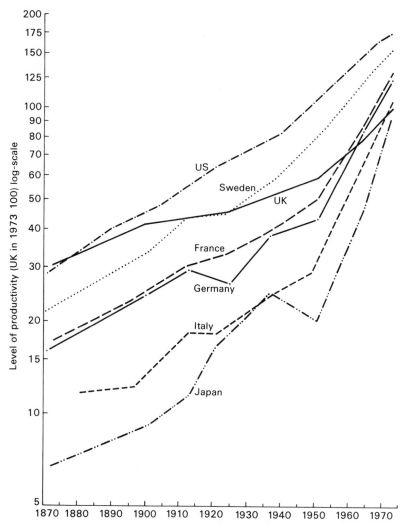

F IG. 21.1. Gross Domestic Product per Man-Year in the UK Compared With Six Other Countries, 1873–1973.

Source: Matthews *et al.*, *British Economic Growth 1856–1973*, Figure 2.2, p. 32. Based on the data used to calculate the growth rates of productivity reproduced in Table 21.1.

to the mere quantity, of the labour force in terms of education, skills, and abilities appropriate to an industrial country. Second, the role of education and research in relation to industrial performance, as will be seen, has been a continuing subject of concern in the UK for at least 100 years. Third, it is an area where there are strong grounds for thinking that the UK has been unique.

Explanations for slow growth which appear plausible in the UK, but which could equally well be applied in other countries, are unlikely to be able to explain the apparently unique record of the UK. However the matter is finally judged, if the UK is experiencing a very long-term slow growth of productivity, it represents an important perspective within which to assess the future economic prospects of the UK.

21.2. British and European Education Before 1870

21.2.1. The Cult of the 'Practical Man'

The development of the British education system between 1870 and 1939 in its relationship to industrial and commercial capability was profoundly shaped by the special British experience in the first Industrial Revolution between c.1780 and c.1850, and by the attitudes and myths that grew out of it. For the British experience of industrialization, and the British view thereafter of the relevance of educational and research institutions to national success, differed markedly from those of the Europeans, Americans, and, later, the Japanese, in that Britain's pioneering lead in the first Industrial Revolution (textile mills, engine-building, steam-power, the first railways) was achieved without benefit of widespread formal education or training at any level, and without benefit of systematic scientific research. Only a minority of the early manufacturers were even *amateurs* of the primitive science of that day. Rather, this first phase of industrialization was the work of the 'practical man' who learned on the job in counting-house or workshop by the traditional means of apprenticeship to his elders. The 'practical man' built up his business, exploited new markets, or devised new machines by applying his native intelligence to the immediate problem, and proceeding by trial and error. The 'practical man' would not have thought that school or university education, as it was in Britain at the time, had anything to do with success in trade and industry. Nor had it.

Around 1800 about half the emerging urban working class in England received no education whatsoever; secondary education for the middle classes (apart from the excellent broad curriculum provided to a minority by the dissenting academies) consisted of decayed local grammar schools and public schools using the same classical teaching as in the seventeenth century, and some private establishments. The English universities of Oxford and Cambridge were sunk in introspective torpor and pedantic cultivation of the classics and mathematics. Their spokesmen recoiled in horror from any suggestion that they should concern themselves with preparing sutdents for careers; they had no conception of research in the modern sense, and as already understood in German universities. Scotland, however, presented a much better picture, with a network of parish schools preparing the talented for the universities, and the universities themselves were concerned early on with science and technology. Glasgow, for example, founded a chemical laboratory in 1763 and a chair of engineering in 1840. Vocational or further education in Britain in the era of the first Industrial Revolution went no further than local mechanics' institutes or corresponding societies.

By 1850 the myth of the 'practical man' had become deeply ingrained in

Britain, with those in industry and commerce disdainful of scientific research and technical education. The 'practical man's' outlook was well expressed by *The Economist* in 1850, when it wrote that 'the education which fits men to perform their duties in life is not to be got in school, but in the counting-house and the lawyer's office, in the shop or the factory.'[2] This may be contrasted with the pronouncement by Dr Arnold, headmaster of Rugby from 1827 to 1841 and a major influence on the development of the Victorian public school ethos, that Christianity took priority over science in education: '. . . rather than have it [science] the principal thing in my son's mind, I would gladly have him think that the sun went round the earth, and that the stars were so many spangles set in the bright blue firmament. Surely the one thing needed for a Christian and an Englishman to study is a Christian and moral and political philosophy.'[3]

And the new or revamped mid-Victorian public schools, for their part, concentrated on the classics and religion; their purpose was to turn out gentlemen to enter the traditional professions or the public service. Oxbridge followed suit: it was only in 1848 that Cambridge set up a natural science tripos, which was taken by a total of 43 students in its first nine years, while in 1850 Oxford created schools of natural science and of maths and physics, though likewise of marginal importance compared with the traditional Oxford prestige subject of classics. Indeed the principal role of mid-Victorian Oxbridge was to produce clergymen, as was also that of the new University of Durham, created in 1837. Only University College, London, with chairs in chemistry, experimental philosophy, botany and, after 1841, engineering, redeemed this other-worldly English university education. Scottish universities, however, continued to give prominence to the sciences. In the industrial regions the sole new university-level foundation before 1870 was Owen's College, Manchester, founded in 1851, imitative of Oxbridge's 'liberal' education, regarded unsympathetically by local businessmen, and by 1861 having only 88 day-students.

A profound gulf of mutual irrelevance had therefore opened by the mid-nineteenth century between Britain's existence as a great commercial and industrial power and even the best of its education—such as it was.

21.2.2. The British Attitude to the State's Role

There was another aspect of the role of the 'practical man' that also contributed to the anarchy and dearth of British education at all levels by 1870, and exercised a dominant influence on developments right up to 1939. Industrialization in Britain had been a 'bottom-upwards' grass-roots transformation brought about by the initiative of the individual 'practical man', and without benefit of state guidance or intervention. This was in accordance with British political and commercial attitudes already deeply ingrained by the time that the Industrial Revolution got under way. For the British had come to prize individualism and localism, as against a strong and effective state, which they saw as the essential feature of the European despotisms they feared and

[2] Quoted in Barnett [16], p. 94.
[3] Quoted in Bamford [15], p. 120.

hated. By the late eighteenth century they had reduced their own central government to the functions of tax-gathering, defence, and foreign policy, and even here its effectiveness was limited by corruption, disorganization, and inefficiency. Otherwise the social and administrative roles of government had been devolved to the counties and the Justices of the Peace, even to the parishes.

This traditional British dislike of the state was sharpened and given fresh doctrinal justification during the Industrial Revolution by the *laissez-faire* political economists, *laissez-faire* becoming, by 1850, a universal article of political faith. Even with regard to education, all must be left to private enterprise or private charity. In any case, it was thought, state intervention in education could lead towards tyranny. A national education system devised and directed by the state was therefore unthinkable. In any case, Britain then lacked the modern state machinery to administer such a system. Therefore modest grants-in-aid to suitable private bodies from government funds marked the practical political limit of the British state's involvement in education before 1870. In 1833 such grants were offered to Church of England and non-conformist 'primary' schools, but even by 1868, while some 1,300,000 children were at grant-aided primary schools of efficient standard, and 1,000,000 at non-grant-aided, non-inspected, and not very efficient schools, no fewer than 2,000,000, mostly in the industrial conurbations, were not at school at all. In terms of secondary education there was not a single school in 1868 over which the state had any control. Apart from the public schools, secondary education still consisted of a random patchwork of ancient and unreformed grammar schools and private establishments. Altogether, there were only 11,000 children in secondary education in England and Wales in 1863.

After 1854 the new but exiguous Department of Science and Art provided grants to selected mechanics' institutes, marking the sum total of British technical education apart from the School of Mines and Science (1851) and the Royal College of Chemistry (1845) in London.

The combined results of the cult of the 'practical man', of *laissez-faire* individualism, and of the other-worldliness of the public school and Oxbridge were that by 1870 Britain still suffered at every level from an almost total lack of education and training geared to its survival as a great industrial nation. As the 1868 Schools Enquiry Royal Commission summed it up:

We are bound to point out that our evidence appears to show that our industrial classes have not even the basis of sound general education on which alone technical education can rest . . . In fact our deficiency is not merely a deficiency in technical education but . . . in general intelligence, and unless we remedy this want we shall gradually but surely find that our undeniable superiority in wealth and perhaps in energy will not save us from decline [3].

21.2.3. The European Attitude to Industry and Education

The approach of European countries to industrialization and the role of education was different from Britain's from the start, and it sprang from a fundamentally different concept of the role of the state itself. Even in the pre- or proto-industrial area of the seventeenth and early eighteenth centuries, European monarchies had regarded it as their function to promote commercial and industrial progress by interventionist measures, including the setting up of training schools for particular crafts and professions. With the advent of the Industrial Revolution, it became entirely natural for European governments to follow their older traditions and seek to guide and foster their countries' industrialization. In particular they saw that the state alone could bring about a structure of national education at all levels which would feed industry with well-educated and trained personnel. More generally, European governments regarded education and research as the great engine of national, social, and cultural progress. Hence in France the *École Polytechnique*, first of the *Grandes Écoles*, and devoted to the production of engineers, was opened in 1794, and a structure of primary and secondary education followed under the First Republic and the Napoleonic Empire. In Prussia universal state primary education was set up in 1806 and became compulsory between 7 and 14 in 1826. As well as the *Gymnasium* in every Prussian town specializing in the humanities, *Realschule* were created to provide a secondary education in science and 'modern' studies. By 1863 Prussia had 63,000 pupils in secondary schools to the total for England and Wales of 11,000, although their populations were comparable (Prussia 18 million, England and Wales 22,700,000).

On the foundation of this provision of general education, Prussia and other German states also created systems of technical education that became the model for the rest of Europe, the United States, and Japan. Higher technical schools were founded at Karlsruhe in 1825, Dresden in 1828, and Stuttgart in 1829, and such institutions were to advance steadily towards university rank. By 1868–72 there were already some 3,500 students in these schools. Moreover, 26 trade schools had been set up in Prussia by 1851. As an example, the metallurgical school at Bochum in the Ruhr was jointly paid for by the government, local industry, and the town. It offered a three-year course with 36 hours' formal instruction a week, covering pure and applied mathematics, physics, chemistry, drawing, metallurgy, machine construction, accountancy, and German language.

In 1855 the *Zurich Polytechnikum* was founded in Switzerland, and was rapidly copied throughout Europe, especially in Germany. Moreover Switzerland had already introduced compulsory day-attendance at trade schools for children who had left school for work.

At the apex of the educational pyramid, the rapidly expanding German universities, though not specifically geared to serving industry, developed during the first half of the nineteenth century into brilliant centres of scientific research, whose discoveries, especially in chemistry, were soon exploited industrially. By 1830 there were 16,000 students in German universities, a figure that bears comparison with the 19,000 total for England and Wales only reached eighty years later. The German model of university was widely followed in America's rapid mid-nineteenth-century educational expansion. The Massachusetts Institute of Technology (MIT) was founded as early as 1865.

The consequences of the immense education and research efforts made by German and other European states became rudely apparent to British observers at the Paris International Exhibition of 1867, and even more rudely in the Paris Exhibition of 1878, which led the Royal Commission on Technical Instruction of 1884 to report that Britain had now been overtaken in terms of industrial science and the quality of industrial management and workpeople: 'The one point in which Germany is overwhelmingly superior to England is in the education of all classes of the people. The dense ignorance so common among workmen in England is unknown' [5]. The commissioners had particular praise for the European technical high schools and polytechnics:

Technical High SChools now exist in nearly every Continental State, and are the recognised channel for the instruction of those who are intended to become the technical directors of industrial establishments. Many of the technical chemists have, however, been, and are being, trained in the German Universities. Your Commissioners believe that the success which has attended the foundation of the extensive manufacturing establishments, engineering shops, and other works, on the Continent, could not have been achieved to its full extent . . . had it not been for the system of high technical education in these schools, for the facilities for carrying on original scientific investigation, and for the general value of that instruction, and of original research, which is felt in those countries [5].

The European states, and above all Germany (newly united in 1871), therefore entered the second Industrial Revolution, that of science-based industries like chemicals and electrical goods, very well equipped by education, training, and research systems to take the lead. Britain, on the other hand, could only deploy a sorry militia of the ignorant led by the 'practical man'. Not merely did Britain lack a modern educational and research structure, it lacked the necessary national understanding and will to create one. Here then is the leitmotiv in British education for the next sixty years: the painful effort against the very grain of national prejudices to remedy what was already by 1870 a half-century of backlog.

21.3. Piecemeal Reform, 1870–1902

The pattern of this epoch was that of monumental investigations of general and technical education by Royal Commissions, which drew up splendid blueprints for emulating European systems, and which thereafter came to nothing, or very little, in the face of a reluctance to raise rates or taxes to pay for them, of denominational pressure groups, and, it may be contended, of a British distaste for coherent, centrally organized structures, and, *per contra*, an instinct for diffused and overlapping responsibilities. As the Royal Commission on Secondary Education of 1895 summed up organizational developments to that date, the growth of the state's interest in education 'has not been either continuous or coherent; i.e. it does not represent a series of logical or even connected sequences. Each one of the agencies [responsible for some aspect of education] was called into being, not merely independently of the others, but with little or no regard to their existence. Each has remained in its working isolated and unconnected with the rest' [6].

21.3.1. Primary or 'Elementary' Education

Having from 1833 onwards locked itself into grant-aiding church and sect schools rather than setting up a non-sectarian state system, Britain found itself gravelled on the denominational issue whenever radical reforms in primary education were mooted—indeed, right up to 1944. In 1861, the Royal Commission investigating the 'State of Popular Education in England' (the Newcastle Commission [1]), though recognizing the appalling deficiencies that existed, had pronounced against central control over school management or interference with church and sect responsibility. The Schools Enquiry Commission (Taunton Commission [3]), set up in 1864, but reporting in 1868, after the Prussian victory over the Austrians in 1866 had demonstrated the power of a well-educated industrial people, had proposed, as part of its general scheme for national education, that elementary education should form a third grade of school as the bottom tier under two kinds of secondary school in a national system under central direction (see below). However, the Forster Act of 1870 (itself a product of the British recognition of the part played by education in Prussia's success in 1866) merely supplemented existing grant-aided denominational schools by providing extra schools where needed, to be administered by elected local school-boards levying a rate. The leaving age was to be 13, as against Prussia's 14, and elementary education was still to be neither free (except to the poor) nor compulsory. Only by 1880 had enough schools been built to enable primary education to be at last made compulsory, fifty-four years later than Prussia. By 1900 the 'board-schools' were educating almost as many children as the denominational schools: nearly 6,000 schools and 2 million children. In 1891, sixty-five years later than Prussia, elementary education became free. The new elementary education under the Forster Act made immense advances in conquering basic illiteracy and drilling children through the three 'Rs', but it was education on the cheap, with basic equipment and buildings, and classes of 60. It did not aim to supply the basis of secondary education, but to be virtually an end in itself appropriate to the lower classes' place in life. In 1894 the odds against an English elementary schoolchild getting a scholarship to a secondary school were 270 to 1.

21.3.2. Secondary Education, 1870–1902

The Schools Enquiry Commission (Taunton Commission [3]) investigated the whole field of school education bar the nine premier public schools, and paupers' schools. Appointed in 1864, it reported in 1868, after the Prussian victory over the Austrians and the year after the fateful revelations about foreign technological achievement at the Paris Exhibition. Its evidence included a comprehensive account of European education by Matthew Arnold HMI. Its diagnosis of British shortcomings was devastating (see p. 673). Its answer was to recommend an adaptation of the Prussian national system of three educational tiers: first grade to age 18–19, supplementing the few and expensive public schools in providing a 'liberal' education for an élite, which the commission saw as classics, mathematics, science, and modern languages; second grade, to age 16, with less classics and more science and languages for the 'commercial' middle class; third grade (as already discussed), for elementary education to 14. These grades the commissioners believed to correspond to the English class structure and the aspirations of the classes. They ruled out free education throughout on the American pattern; they were 'convinced that it is vain to expect thoroughly to educate the people of this country except by gradually inducing them to educate themselves' [3], so also ruling out the Prussian precedent of education from the top as a matter of state policy. But they did say that the existing patchwork of endowed and non-endowed grammar schools and private schools could not fulfil the roles of the first and second tiers in their proposed system. Many towns had no schools of adequate standard. The Schools Enquiry Commission therefore recommended the reform of existing schools and the creation of new secondary schools, the whole to be administered by provincial boards under a new central authority headed by a Minister of Education.

The only result of this massive report was the Endowed Schools Act of 1869, which led to the individual reform of existing endowed schools piecemeal, and the Forster Education Act of 1870, which entirely ignored secondary education and also the commission's administrative recommendations. Otherwise the state's interest in secondary education remained limited to grants-in-aid. By 1895 there were some 218 grant-aided secondary schools in England and Wales, with possibly some 30,000 pupils receiving an approved standard of education. This compares with Prussia's total of 63,000 some thirty years earlier, for a population less than two-thirds as large. Since the Schools Enquiry Commission in 1868 had reckoned the number of middle- and upper-class children between 5 and 20 at nearly a million, it can be seen that the total of 30,000 was grossly insufficient.

The Royal Commission on Secondary Education of 1895 (the Bryce Commission [6]) therefore anatomized all that was still lacking in the provision and organization of British secondary education, and indeed in education in general. The Bryce Commission Report was produced in the midst of renewed national anxiety about foreign technological competition and the superior quality of foreign management and staff. In 1894 a best-selling book appeared entitled *British Industries and Foreign Competition*, and in 1896, a year after the Bryce Commission reported, there was a 'Made in Germany' press panic on publication of a book of that title. No wonder the commission itself noted: 'Not a few censors have dilated upon the disadvantages from which young Englishmen suffer in industry and commerce owing to the superior preparation of their competitors in several countries of Continental Europe. These disadvantages are real' [6].

Repeating the stillborn proposals of the Schools Enquiry Commission of 1868, the Bryce Commission distinguished secondary education into two grades: first, schools whose special function was to form a 'learned or a literary, and a professional or cultured class', and second, those with the function of educating men 'with a view to some form of commercial or industrial life' [6]. The priority is fascinating but only reflects the triumph of the 'liberal education' lobby, represented by such Victorian educational sages as Newman and Edward Thring, and through the media of the public schools and Oxbridge, in forming the mind of the late Victorian governing élite. The commission recommended the creation of local education authorities to set up and run secondary schools, and a central authority for secondary education under a Minister of Education who would unite the powers of existing agencies. But the sole immediate result was an Act of 1899 setting up the Board of Education. Major reform and extension of secondary schooling had to wait until the Education Act of 1902.

21.3.3. Further and Technical Education

The European achievements on display at the 1867 Paris Exhibition inspired the appointment of a Commons Select Committee 'to inquire into the Provisions for giving Instruction in Theoretical and Applied Science to the Industrial Classes' [2]; it reported in July 1868. Its analysis of the weakness of British general education and the virtual absence of technical education was contrasted with an admiring description of European provision in these fields. The committee wrote of British industrial rank and file:

Their [the foremen's] education, and that of the workmen, during the school age, has been received in elementary schools; and owing both to the defective character of the instruction in some of those schools, and to the early age at which children go to work, it is rarely sufficient to enable them to take advantage of scientific instruction at a later period [2].

Of the technical education of smaller manufacturers and managers, the committee reported [2]: 'Unfortunately, this division may be disposed of in a very few words. Its members have either risen from the rank of foremen or workmen . . . or they are an offshoot from the class of smaller tradesmen, clerks etc.' Even the proprietors and managers of 'great industrial undertakings' were uneducated and untrained for their roles. If they had risen from the bottom, 'Any knowledge of scientific principles which they may have acquired is generally the result of solitary reading, and of observation of the facts with which their pursuits have made them familiar.' More generally, however, 'the training of the capitalists and of the managers of this class, has been that of the higher secondary schools' (i.e. classics).

The committee's recommendations were comprehensive and extended to general education as well. It wanted compulsory schooling for every child (finally achieved in 1880); scientific instruction in all elementary schools (achieved only partially and temporarily by the turn of the century—see p. 682); the reconstruction of some endowed schools as regional science centres with entry by open exhibition; state support of higher education in science and technology; courses in technology and applied science in teachers' training colleges; and co-ordination of those government institutions existing in London for scientific instruction. It could be said that these recommendations were only completely fulfilled (if in different form) after 1945. The committee's report was without immediate result at all.

In the same year the British Association for the Advancement of Science made its own report on technical education, and sent a deputation to the government. The consequence was another Royal Commission, on 'Scientific Instruction and the Advancement of Science' (the Devonshire Commission [4]), which reported between 1872 and 1875. Its views corresponded with those of the Commons Select Committee; in particular it noted the 'totally inadequate' number of science teachers even in larger schools, and demanded a vast increase in the proportion of the timetable occupied by science as against classics. The report came to nothing.

The fresh alarm created by the Paris Exhibition of 1878 about the relative backwardness of British technology and business methods led to the creation of yet another Royal Commission, this time on technical instruction *per se* (the Samuelson Commission [5]). This, like its predecessors, did not exclude recommending that greatly improved elementary and secondary education could alone provide the platform for technical training. It noted the excellence of the evening continuation schools and the technical higher elementary schools on the Continent; schools of this latter kind were, it said, 'singularly wanting in our own country'.[4] It admired the European polytechnic system for educating management: to this 'may be ascribed the general diffusion of a high scientific knowledge in Germany, its appreciation by all classes of persons, and the adequate supply of men competent, so far as theory is concerned, to take the place of managers and superintendants of industrial works. . . . In England, there is still a great want of this last class of persons.'[5]

The burden of the commission's recommendations was that Britain should adopt as far as possible the institutions it had admired in Europe; in particular, it recommended that local authorities be empowered to set up technical colleges. The Local Government Act of 1888 having at last supplied Britain with the modern administrative machinery which was the essential prerequisite for a major public involvement in education, in 1889 the Technical Instruction Act empowered local authorities at their own discretion to set up technical and further education out of a penny rate. After 1890 revenue from the whisky duty was diverted to local authorities for this purpose.

Instead therefore of the comprehensive emulation of European systems recommended by various reports since 1868, there was a patchy and highly localized improvement, which only really began in the 1890s. As a result, in the words of one authority, in 1902 British technical education amounted, 'with a few brilliant exceptions such as Owen's College, Manchester, to little more than congeries of technical and literary classes; a small number of polytechnics mainly in London; [and] a rather larger number of organised science schools and evening science and art classes' (Lowndes [17], p. 89).[16]

The failure to implement the recommendations of such bodies as the Royal Commission of 1884 may be ascribed, firstly, to the prevailing political philosophy about the role of the state and central government, coupled with a dislike of public spending and higher taxes; secondly, to the complacency still widely felt by the 'practical man' in industry and the country at large because of Britain's continuing, if inherited, high position as a manufacturing country; and thirdly, to the strong anti-technology bias of British culture, especially within the governing élite as formed by the Victorian public school and Victorian Oxbridge.

Moreover, technical education at a lower level was actually destroyed in

---

[4] [5], Second Report, Vol. I.
[5] Ibid.

1901, when, on the initiative of Sir Robert Morant, Permanent Secretary to the new Board of Education, the higher technical elementary education and evening tuition developed in some 70 schools to age 16 by some school-boards were pronounced *ultra vires* by the Courts.

21.3.4. University Education, 1870-1900

It cannot be said that the ancient English universities of Oxford and Cambridge made much contribution to the success of the British economy in this period. Despite the founding of the Clarendon and Cavendish laboratories in the 1870s, Oxford and Cambridge remained strongly classicist and mathematical respectively, their philosophy of education resolutely non-vocational and high minded. Oxbridge science, as it belatedly developed, became just another form of intellectual mandarinism, with very little spin-off into the world of technological development. This was especially true of chemistry. Even electrical research at the Cavendish in Cambridge, though of incalculable importance for the long-term future, was little related to current industrial development in electrical equipment and applications, in which Germany vastly outstripped Britain in this period. Given the prestige and ambience of a 'liberal' education at Oxbridge, with its anti-industrial values, it is not surprising that even by 1900 fewer than 10 per cent of its graduates went into 'business'.[6]

Rather, late-Victorian Oxbridge positively harmed the prospects of the British economy by completing the work of the public schools in turning out a governing élite imbued with Newmanian ideals of a liberal education in humanistic culture; an élite which both generally and in particular cases (cf. Morant) neglected or even hamstrung developments in technical education.

Scottish universities continued to provide a disproportionate amount of the total national effort in higher education in technology and in industry-related scientific research. Kelvin, of Glasgow, with his outstanding contribution to the development of telegraphy and electrical supply, is the most remarkable example of many fruitful links between Scottish universities and industry (see [20], Chapter 6).

In the industrial Midlands and North of England, new university colleges came into being from the 1870s onwards, in a characteristic unplanned, grass-roots British response to the growing awareness that Britain was backward in number of universities and students. Apart from the existing Owen's College, Manchester, these new foundations comprised Newcastle (1871), Leeds (1874), Bristol (1876), Sheffield (1879), Birmingham (1880), and Liverpool and Nottingham (1881). In Wales there was Aberystwyth (1872), Cardiff (1883), and Bangor (1893). Yet in this founding era the new 'redbrick' universities were not so much universities in the German or American sense, but small-scale amalgams of the functions of the German technical high school, polytechnic, trade school, and part-time further education and evening classes. Their minority of full-time students took the London University degree; and the new university colleges' total graduate output in the 1890s was only about 200 a

---

[6] See Sanderson [20], Chap. 2, for a penetrating account of Oxbridge in this era.

year ([20], p. 95). Moreover the relationship of each university college with local industry, its relative recruitment of students from sons of businessmen, and the relative number of graduates going into business, varied greatly. Leeds, Mason's College, Birmingham, and Newcastle began with a strong technological bias, whereas Manchester and Liverpool aimed at a balance with the humanities. For various reasons, including London University's degree requirements, the civic university colleges did not develop into German-style technical universities, so avoiding, according to some critics, a narrow specialization in favour of a balance between arts and sciences. None the less, it meant that technology had to take merely a share in the available funding and in the number of the new student places being created. As late as 1914, for example, only 198 students out of the 663 at Leeds University College were studying engineering, technology, and agriculture. Nevertheless the university colleges' scientific and engineering departments made significant research and development contributions to local industries. The great English work in this field, however, came from King's College and University College, London, especially with regard to electrical engineering and chemistry.

Clearly the advent of the new university colleges in the provinces, together with the contributions of the Scottish universities and the London colleges, marked a major transformation compared with the bleak period before 1870. But did these grass-roots initiatives amount to a sufficient national effort to make up Britain's backlog and match the current competition? In 1890 there were still twice as many academic chemists in Germany as in Britain, though the British population was three-quarters of the German figure. In 1892 Britain had 287 academic staff in mathematics, science, and engineering compared with 452 in Germany. In engineering in particular the major German technical high schools had 7,130 students in 1901 against a total of 1,443 in British universities.[7] In terms of overall university provision, Britain spent £26,000 in governments grants in 1897, while Germany spent £476,000; in 1902 Germany had 22 universities for a population of 50 million, England and Wales 7 for 31 million.

And, despite notable exceptions adduced by some economic historians, British industry still lagged badly in advanced industries like chemicals, electricals, and machine tools, and even in basics like steel—partly because of a continuing lack of trained personnel at all levels (the 'practical man' still failing to recruit enough of them). Britain's annual rate of growth in the years 1880–1900 averaged 1·7 per cent against Germany's 5·3 per cent and America's 4·5 per cent. Britain's own rate of growth in industrial production was also declining—from 33 per cent in the decade of the 1860s to 24 per cent in the 1890s and 9 per cent in the 1900s ([20], p. 9).

21.4. The 1902 Education Act and After, 1902–1918

The 1902 Education Act, for all its limitations, marked the first British attempt to tackle the whole field of non-university education rather than patch existing

---

[7] These figures are from Sanderson [20], pp. 23–4.

institutions or add on to them piecemeal. In particular, it at last inaugurated a provision of publicly funded and publicly run secondary schools which could bear comparison with that enjoyed by Britain's competitors for half a century. Indeed, the Act was inspired by renewed awareness of foreign commercial inroads into British markets, and by the then fashionable movement for 'national efficiency'. It also marked an attempt to reduce the anarchy of British educational institutions in favour of a system relating the various bodies and roles in some functional coherence. It opened the way for effective measures under the strong-willed guidance of Sir Robert Morant, himself a principal author of the measures in the Act. Nevertheless, the ad hoc policy since the 1830s of grants-in-aid and of creating various responsible organs for particular purposes had created entrenched interests which it was not politically impossible to clear away in favour of a logical, nationally administered system. As a result, even after the 1902 Act bore fruit, British education still fell short of its European rivals in clarity of purpose and articulation.

Organizationally, the Act abolished the school-boards and placed primary, secondary, and technical education under the county and county borough councils. At the same time, in obedience to political pressure, it weakened the existing central superintending powers of the Board of Education, laying the major responsibility for educational policy and initiative on the local authorities; British localism and diversity was again triumphant. The church and sect schools survived (being too strong a political lobby), although they were brought within local government's overall responsibility and financing. New secondary schools were to be set up by local authorities wherever necessary to supplement denominational ones. Further and technical education (such as polytechnics) was to continue to fall under these authorities, the expanding of such provision being a matter of local option.

The second theme of the era of reform ushered in by the 1902 Act is supplied by the prevailing educational ethos, for the ideal of a 'liberal' and academic education took precedence in the new secondary system over practical preparation for a life of work. Here too Morant was influential, being a Winchester and Oxford classicist, and a theologian of evangelical persuasion.

21.4.1. Primary Education, 1902–1918

Except for the fact that the elementary school was no longer regarded solely as a dead end of its own suitable for the lower classes, but a possible springboard, via scholarships, to secondary education, it cannot be said that this basic schooling of the nation made much progress between 1902 and 1918. In particular, the technical higher elementary schools and evening classes destroyed by Morant and the Courts in 1901 were not replaced. The Report of the Consultative Committee on Attendance, Compulsory or Otherwise, at Continuation Schools [8] in 1909 noted that three-quarters of the 2 million children between 14 and 17 in England and Wales were receiving no education at all: 'a tragic waste of early promise', according to the committee. Thus Britain was far from repairing that competitive weakness in the education of its industrial rank and file noted by the Schools Enquiry Commission and the Commons Select Committee on Scientific Instruction forty years earlier.

As late as 1921 only 12·3 per cent of elementary schoolchildren went on to secondary, technical, or other higher education.

21.4.2. Secondary Education, 1902–1918

The 1902 Act led to a major expansion in secondary education, so that by 1914 there were 1,123 such schools, of which 500 were directly run by the local authorities while the remainder was denominational. Unfortunately, the prestige of a 'grammar school' education, itself derived from the Arnoldian public school, with its emphasis on the academic approach to both the arts and science, impressed itself on parents, local authorities, and the Board of Education alike, so excluding a system of alternative secondary education of equal standing, like the German *Realschule*, more related to Britain's existence as a commercial and technical power. Just how far the 1902 reforms failed to remedy the fundamental weaknesses of British secondary education with regard to the needs of the economy was analysed at length by the Spens Report [12] of 1938, which at the same time laid the main responsibility for the academicism of the new British secondary schools on Morant's Regulations for Secondary Schools issued in 1904–5:

Perhaps the most striking feature of the new secondary schools provided by local education authorities, which have so greatly increased in numbers since 1902, is their marked disinclination to deviate to any considerable extent from the main lines of the traditional grammar school curriculum. That conservative and imitative tendency which is so salient a characteristic in the evolution of English political and social institutions, is particularly noticeable in this instance. The natural tendency, however, was greatly reinforced, and in a sense fostered, by the Regulations for Secondary Schools issued by the Board of Education in 1904–5 and succeeding years, and later by the First School (Certificate) Examination as organised in 1917 [12].

The Spens Report noted how Morant had discouraged the science and technical schools that had sprung up in the 1890s so that

... the new Secondary Schools were in effect compelled to take as their model the curriculum of the existing Public Schools and Grammar Schools. . . . We cannot but deplore the fact that the Board did little or nothing . . . to foster the development of secondary schools of quasi-vocational type designed to meet the needs of boys and girls who desired to enter industry and commerce at the age of 16 [12].

21.4.3. Technical Education, 1902–1918

Technical education at the lower level, as given in some elementary schools before being ruled *ultra vires* in 1901, languished (see earlier). Instead, available resources were fed into the secondary schools and their academic objectives. Only about a quarter of elementary schoolchildren could hope for some further education and training to fit them for employment.

Technical schools at a higher level likewise made slow progress, for no government grants were made towards the cost of their construction until 1918. Only 20 new technical schools were built between 1902 and 1918. As a result, in 1908, when Germany possessed 20 technical high schools of university rank (as well as all its polytechnics), with some 14,000 students, Britain still possessed no such university-level technical institutions, but 31 local technical schools with a total of 2,768 students. Yet it was not only the prevailing bias in favour of a 'liberal' education, or lack of funds, that was responsible for this continued weakness. The other factor lay in the 'practical man' of British industry who still did not value proper career training in his employees. As the Annual Report of the Board of Education [7] put it in 1908: 'The slow growth of these technical institutions is, however, in the main to be ascribed to the small demand in this country for the services of young men well-trained in the theoretical side of industrial operations and in the service underlying them.'

21.4.4. University Education, 1902–1918

'Pure' science, especially in the sense of original research, had been expanding in Oxford and Cambridge since the foundation of the Clarendon and Cavendish laboratories in the 1870s. None the less Oxbridge science had few contacts with, or spin-offs to, industry. In 1903 Oxford earned a blistering attack from Professor Perry, later of Imperial College, for 'ostentatiously holding aloof from manufacturers and commerce', and for educationally ruining the sons of industrialists who ought to be replacing their fathers in the business; fathers who, wrote Perry in a blast with his second barrel at the 'practical man', were 'what I call unskilled workmen, that is, unskilled owners of works'.[8] Of 4,025 students at Oxford in 1914, just 21 were reading engineering (Sanderson [21], pp. 243–4). Cambridge certainly set up a chair of mechanics and engineering in 1875, but there was no mechanical sciences tripos until 1894. In 1903 a conference was held in Cambridge to discuss the continuing gulf between the university and industry, and the Professor of Chemistry told the meeting that 'he agreed with all the Vice-Chancellor had said as to the complaint of men engaged in business of various kinds that the University does not provide an education for their sons suited to their needs.' In 1906–14 some 7–14 per cent of Oxford graduates went into business (not necessarily manufacturing industry), although Cambridge did rather better (Sanderson [20], pp. 53–4).

In 1900 London University, hitherto an examining body, became a teaching university incorporating such existing institutions as King's College and University College and the London School of Economics. After 1902 a further wave of 'redbrick' universities or university colleges was founded: Belfast, Exeter, Reading, and Southampton. In 1903 Imperial College, London, Britain's answer to the MIT and Germany's *Physikalish-Teknische Reichanstalt* at Charlottenburg, was founded. Such expansion raised the total student numbers in the united Kingdom to 26,711 by 1913–14. But out of the total for England and Wales alone of 19,458, only 1,901 are known to have taken engineering, technology, or agriculture, plus 2,336 in 'pure' science. This compares with the German figure for science/technology of 24,000 university students (Sanderson [21], pp. 243–4). Britain had therefore by no means remedied its long quantitative backlog in university science and engineering by 1914, although one authority ([20], p. 23) reckons that in quality, British

---

[8] Quoted in Sanderson [20]. p. 37.

university research, both 'pure' and on behalf of industry, was now as good if not better than German.

The Great War of 1914–18, bringing German armies to the Belgian coast and near to Paris, German U-boats to the Atlantic, and German bombers over London, forced Britain at long last to get its education, technology, and industry together in the fashion vainly urged by Royal Commissions and other bodies since the 1860s. The munitions crisis of 1914–15 acutely demonstrated Britain's dependence on foreign advanced technology—drugs and dyes, advanced machine tools, aero-engines, magnetoes, spark-plugs, laboratory equipment, optical glass, and other items. The universities played a key role in the crash national programme to manufacture such products in Britain, and to develop new ones, such as radio equipment and anti-submarine sonar, in order to win the war. Apart from this vital research and development function, they also mounted training programmes for important cadres in war industries. Remarkable successes were achieved, serving to demonstrate what could be done once university resources were mobilized in the service of national survival. Yet the contrast between this wartime university mobilization and the pre-war picture illustrates a new British problem—that British science, though first-class, was normally still too distant from industry, too concerned with 'pure' research. This peacetime problem of insufficient linkage between original research and subsequent technological development to the point of commercial exploitation was to be endemic in Britain in the next half-century during times of peace.

21.5. Too Little and Too Late, 1918–1939

Except for the largely abortive Education Act of 1918, there were no major structural reforms between the two world wars in British education and training, only evolutionary growth and change. Certain basic weaknesses, now built into the system, went unchanged: the highly academic ladder of achievement that led through the grammar school to university and 'pure' science, and the consequent second-class status of young people with a practical rather than an academic talent, with second-class educational institutions to match. A grim paradox persisted whereby the British output of technologists and skilled industrial personnel remained much smaller than America's and Germany's in proportion to population, and yet still exceeded the effective demand from industry for such people, a paradox explained by the survival of the 'practical man' over vast backwoods tracts of British industry. As the biggest-ever investigation of Britain's competitive shortcomings, the Balfour Committee on Trade and Industry, reported in 1929: 'The available information makes it clear that the present response of the leaders of industrial and commercial enterprises to the educational efforts made to train candidates for entry into the higher grades of these organizations is much less certain and widespread than in certain foreign countries, e.g., Germany or the United States' ([11], p. 213).

There also persisted an absence of linkage between Britain's world-class original research in universities and industrial application, even though this was not true of certain outstanding 'modern' firms like ICI. As the Balfour Committee put it:

> Before British industries, taken as a whole, can hope to reap from scientific research the full advantage which it appears to yield to some of their most formidable trade rivals, nothing less than a revolution is needed in their general outlook on science; and in the case of some industries at least, this change of attitude is bound to be slow and difficult, in view of our old and deeply rooted industrial traditions ([11], p. 218).

When British rearmament got under way in 1936, the programme was immediately bottlenecked by lack of skilled personnel, from production managers to tool-setters. It was also held back by Britain's weak base in advanced technology, such as aircraft manufacture, precision engineering, instrumentation, and machine tools. Once again Britain had to carry out a major extension and re-equipment of its industrial resources under pressure of an external military threat, including *ad hoc* extensions of the country's further education and training effort.

21.5.1. Primary Education, 1918-1939

A central feature in the 1918 Education Act was provision of compulsory part-time education from the school-leaving age of 14 up to 18, such as Switzerland had enjoyed since before 1850, but the provision fell victim to the 'Geddes Axe' economy cuts in 1921. Germany introduced such a measure in 1924. Although elementary or primary education was now supposed to be the foot of a ladder leading up through secondary to tertiary education, only 0·4 per cent of elementary schoolchildren got to university in the years 1931-4; in the 1920s only a fifth went on from elementary school to any kind of further education and training (Mowatt [19], pp. 208-9). Britain was still turning out too many people suitable only for unskilled manual jobs, in an era when the old labour-intensive industries lay in terminal decline. Nevertheless there was gradual improvement in primary education: whereas in 1922 there were 28,000 classes in England and Wales with over 50 children, the number had dropped to 6,000 in 1934.

21.5.2. Secondary Education, 1918-1939

Here too the picture was of gradual improvement within the system bequeathed by the 1902 Act. The number of grammar school-type secondary schools in England and Wales rose from 1,205 in 1920 to 1,307 in 1931; the percentage of school-leavers going from such schools to university rose from 4·6 in 1921-4 to 6·4 in 1931-4 ([19], P. 207). The number of junior technical schools rose from 84 to 177, hardly comparable with the number of grammar schools. The dominance of the academic ethos in British secondary education, and the want of provision for the non-academic child, came under criticism by two major reports in the period, the Hadow Report [9] of 1927 and the Spens Report [12] of 1938. The Hadow Report recommended raising the school-leaving age to 15 (finally achieved in 1944), and giving all children a form of secondary education from age 11 + . There should therefore be two broad types of secondary education:

(i) Schools . . . of the 'Secondary' type most commonly existing today, which at present pursue in the main a predominantly literary or scientific curriculum, to be known as Grammar Schools.

(ii) Schools . . . which give at least a four years' course from the age of 11 +, with a 'realistic' or practical trend in the last two years, to be known as Modern Schools.[9]

In recommending this belated adoption of the German *Realschule* the Hadow Report was careful to say it was 'not an inferior species, and it ought not be be hampered by conditions of accommodation and equipment inferior to those of Grammar Schools'.[10]

There followed in the 1930s piecemeal development of the Hadow concept of two kinds of secondary school.

The Spens Report of 1938 followed a track well trodden since 1868 of noting the glaring British deficiency in good technical education at the secondary level. It reported [12]: 'We are convinced that it is of great importance to establish a new type of higher school of technical character, wholly distinct from the traditional academic Grammar.' The training in these schools was 'to provide a good intellectual discipline, altogether apart from its technical value', and the 'schools should be accorded in every respect equality of status with schools of the grammar school type.' Indeed the Spens Report specifically stated that the establishment of parity between all types of secondary school (modern, grammar and technical high) was 'a fundamental requirement'. All this demonstrated an admirable even-handedness which was somewhat belied by the committee's reference to the need for an 11 + selection process to distinguish between 'those pupils who quite certainly have so much intelligence, and intelligence of such a character, that without doubt they ought to receive secondary education of grammar school type; and . . . those pupils who quite certainly would not benefit from such an education'.[11]

In other words, the high-flyers in Britain would continue to be the academics, and the élite path would continue to lie through the grammar school. The Spens Report therefore adumbrated the tripartite system recommended later by the Norwood Committee in 1943 and in the government White Paper on Education [13] of 1943, which itself provided the basis for the 1944 Butler Education Act.

In the mean time, British secondary education remained overwhelmingly academic, both in terms of prestige and quantitative provision.

21.5.3. Technical Education, 1918–1939

In this field too no major reforms took place between the world wars, partly because of stringent government economies, and partly because of the weak demand from industry for the products of technical education. The unofficial Emmott Committee Report [10] of 1927 showed how far Britain still lacked a technical education which in quality and quantity equalled that available to its competitors. The report noted the chaos of the 'system', of which one example

[9] Quoted in Maclure [18], p. 195.
[10] Ibid., p. 187.
[11] Ibid., p. 199.

lay in mining engineering, where 14 institutions offered courses to a total of just 200 students, compared with just 4 mining colleges in Germany handling twice as many students. The Emmott Committee's diagnosis was borne out by the 1945 *Report of the Special Committee on Higher Technological Education* (the Percy Report [14]), which noted that in pre-war Britain responsibility for technical education had been divided between no fewer than 146 local authorities, leading to wasteful competition and yet to an overall shortage of technologists both in quality and quantity.

The Emmott Committee also drew attention to the poverty of equipment in British technical institutions. In one college, for example, 'The equipment for the practical study of electrical engineering is meagre, and the room in which electrical machines are housed is a very small and dingy store in the basement ... The lecture room is so badly lighted that it is impossible to see anything on the blackboard, and in the laboratory the lighting is so poor that volumetric or colorimetric work is impossible' [10]. The recommendations of the 1945 Percy Committee that technical colleges with university status should be created illustrate the broad failure between 1870 and 1939 to emulate the German technical high schools first set up in the 1820s.

Perhaps the major advance in Britain in technical education between the wars lay in the introduction of the Higher National Certificate (HNC) awarded to part-time (evening) students after five year's study. Holders of the HNC in various technologies filled much the same role in British industry as degree holders in German or American industry: a second-class ticket and a second-class status. Between 1922 and 1934 a total of 25,000 HNCs or diplomas were awarded.

21.5.4. Universities, 1918–1939

As has already been noted, in this epoch Britain still failed to set up technical universities. The number of undergraduates reading science and technology rose from 9,000 in 1922 to 10,000 in 1939, which compares to the German figure of 24,000 before 1914. The proportion of students taking pure science or technology actually fell between the quinquennium 1920–1/1924–5 and 1935–6/1938–9 from 30·5 to 26 per cent; more significant still was the fall in those taking technologies from a mere 13·5 to 9·7 per cent (Sanderson [20], p. 263). By comparison the percentage of those reading arts subjects rose from 39·8 to 46·5 per cent ([20], p. 263).

As the Percy Report [14] stated in 1945, 'the annual intake into industries of the country of men trained by universities and technical colleges has been, and still is, insufficient both in quantity and quality.' In particular, the Percy Committee thought that the pre-1939 annual output of engineers, at 700 graduates, had been too small.

Although there were notable exceptions, there was still a tendency for British university science (and scientists) to prize 'pure' original research above industrial involvement, so continuing the gap between discovery and actual manufacturing development. The unquestioned brilliance of university research (cf. Rutherford at the Cavendish) and the many close research links established between provincial universities and their regional industries have

ɔ be balanced against the continued small numbers of science and technology
tudents, both absolutely and relative to the arts, and industry's continuing
ıck of prestige and attractiveness in the eyes of the educational élite.

1.6. Conclusion

'he British education system in 1939 clearly represented an immense advance
n the situation in 1870, when Britain literally did not possess an education
ystem, either in parts or as a whole, in the modern sense, and as already then
reated by its commercial rivals. Yet the size and nature of the backlog still to
e made up in 1939 were to be demonstrated by the spate of major reports and
eforms that followed during the war years and the post-war era. This theme is
ıken up in the next chapter.

Bibliography

SECTION A

1] *Report of the Royal Commission on the State of Popular Education in England* (2794, 1861).
2] *Report of the Select Committee of the House of Commons on Scientific Instruction* (H.C., Session
867–8, XV).
3] *Report of the Royal Commission of Enquiry into Schools* (Command Paper 3966, 1868).
4] *Report of the Royal Commission on Scientific Instruction and the Advancement of Science*
C. 3981, 1872–5).
5] *Report of the Royal Commission on Technical Instruction* (C. 3981, 1884).
6] *Report of the Royal Commission on Secondary Education* (C. 7862, 1895).
7] Board of Education, *Annual Report, 1908* (Cd. 5130).
8] *Report of the Consultative Committee on Attendance, Compulsory or Otherwise, at Continuation
chools* (Cd. 4757, 1909).
9] *Report of the Consultative Committee of the Board of Education of the Adolescent* (HMSO, 1927).
10] *Report of the Committee of Inquiry into the Relationship of Technical Education to Other Forms
f Education and to Industry and Commerce* (1927).
11] *Final Report of the Committee on Trade and Industry* (Cmd. 3282, 1929).
12] *Report of the Consultative Committee of the Board of Education on Secondary Education With
ecial Reference to Grammar Schools and Technical High Schools* (HMSO, 1938).
13] *White Paper on Education* (Cmd. 6458, 1943).
14] *Report of the Special Committee on Higher Technological Education* (HMSO, 1945).

SECTION B

15] BAMFORD, T. W. *Thomas Arnold* (London, 1960).
16] BARNETT, C. *The Collapse of British Power* (London, 1972).
17] LOWNDES, G. A. N. *The Silent Social Revolution* (Oxford University Press, 1937).
18] MACLURE, J. S. *Educational Documents: England and Wales 1816 to the Present Day*
London, 1979).
19] MOWATT, C. L. *Britain Between the Wars* (London, 1968).
20] SANDERSON, M. *The Universities and British Industry 1850–1970* (London, 1972).
21] SANDERSON, M. (ed.). *The Universities in the Nineteenth Century* (London, 1975).

22

Education and Industry Since the War

P. J. A. LANDYMORE

22.1. Introduction

An education system has many roles: to develop the capabilities of the population to live and work in an advanced industrialized society; to provide an understanding of its history, culture, and workings; and to enable individuals to exploit their potential skills and talents. This chapter focuses on only one facet, but the one of most concern from the point of view of this book, namely the part played by the national public education system[1] in the economic system of the UK, and especially its relationship with 'industry', broadly interpreted to include both production and service industries. It will start by considering education as a major (nationalized) industry in its own right: as an employer and user of resources, and as a producer of output. Next, the evolution of the education system, and developments in its various component parts, will be looked at with particular regard to the highly problematic connection with industry.

The underlying theme will be that one of the most important objectives of education is to equip young people adequately to develop a successful working life, and for this objective to be fulfilled a mutually beneficial relationship with industry is needed. Following on from Chapter 21, in which the failure to develop such links over a very long period of the UK's history was described, this chapter suggests that such a mutually beneficial relationship is still largely absent, and that this want constrains economic growth in the UK. This argument, and the reasons for the conclusion just stated, are developed more fully in the following pages. Finally a number of issues raised along the way will be examined, such as: What are the economic benefits to the country of public education? Can they be increased? How much should the nation spend on education? Who should pay? and especially, What currently prevents a better interaction (so long and so widely called for) between education and industry? In examining these issues it is worth stressing at the start that many inside education are equally concerned with the problem of the appropriateness of the system for an industrial society. Indeed many of the constraints on change are

---

[1] Training—meaning in-company, job-specific training such as apprenticeships—is excluded from consideration here.

robably most clearly perceived by those directly responsible for providing
ducation.

There is probably no other industry in the UK that pursues so constant, so
earching, so public, and so absorbing a self-examination as education. Such a
rocess can, however, become introspective: it can militate against an
wareness of the relationship between education and the outside world, and
specially its economic aspect. This relationship is symbiotic. To put it simply,
he provision of resources—almost entirely via taxation—for education
epends on the growth of the economy, which is itself promoted—it has been
apposed—by economic investment in education. Education's 'products'
ecome, in employment, the providers of enhanced resources for improved
ducation, whether for young people or adults. This is not its only, nor its most
mportant function; but education, strictly interpreted as the development of a
erson's abilities, must include the ability to work creatively and productively.
he economist's interest in education, and the place of this chapter in the book,
aight therefore appear self-evidently justified. But the existence among some,
aust be recognized of a view that education is an end in itself, not simply
eparate from, but not to be sullied by materialistic considerations of gain and
oss. As against this latter view, and against simple unawareness of education's
conomic aspect, this chapter examines the education system predominantly
om the perspective of its interaction with industry.

2.2. Education as an Industry

2.2.1. Expenditure, Employment, and Control

aken as a whole, public education is now one of the largest industries in the
JK, absorbing in 1982–3 over £15 billion of taxpayers' money at current
rices, amounting to some 13 per cent of total public expenditure (see Tables
2.1 and 22.2). The largest public spending programme at the end of the last
ecade, education is now second only to health and social services. We spend
nore public money on it than on defence, or on industry, energy, trade,
mployment, agriculture, fisheries, and transport put together, and three times
nore than on law and order. More than a fifth of the total population is
urrently occupied as pupils or students in full-time public sector education,
nd the industry accounts for over 5 per cent of Gross Domestic Product, not
ounting private sector schools (about 6 per cent of all pupils). Some 700,000[2]
ull-time teaching staff are employed in universities, schools, and colleges, and
large number of support, administrative, or part-time staff are also employed,
ither there or in local education authority offices. In all forms of educational
ervices, 1·8 million people were employed in 1981, equal to 7·5 per cent of the
mployed labour force.

Although the term has, somewhat illogically, been reserved for production
adustries like coal, steel, and electricity, education may be classed with law
nd order, defence, and health as one of the nationalized service industries.
ike them, it has no marketed output and its economic weight, in the absence of

[2] DES *Statistical Bulletin*, 1/83.

TABLE 22.1. *Education and Public Expenditure*
(£ million, cash, market prices)

	1978–9	1981–2	1982–3
Education and science*	9·39	14·35	15·30
Health and social services	9·22	15·85	17·27
Defence	7·50	12·61	14·41
Industry, energy, trade, and employment (combined)	3·47	5·92	6·52
Agriculture, fisheries, etc.	1·01	1·63	2·09
Transport	2·24	4·76	5·29
Total planned public expenditure	65·73	104·68	113·01†

* Excluding arts and libraries.   † Estimated.
Source: *The Government's Expenditure Plans* (Cmnd. 8780–II, HMSO, Feb. 1983);
Financial Statement and Budget Report (Mar. 1983).

TABLE 22.2. *Education and GDP*

	1978–9	1981–2	1982–3
Public expenditure on education as a percentage of:			
(a) all public expenditure	14·3	13·7	13·5
(b) GDP	5·5	5·7	5·6

Source: *The Government's Expenditure Plans* (Cmnd. 8789–II); *Economic Trends* (May 1983).

any better approach, is measured by its cost. Throughout the post-war period this cost has increased at a rate well in excess of the rate of economic growth, so that education has absorbed a greatly increased share of national resources. Between 1965 and 1975 alone, current spending increased by over 80 per cent in real terms, rising from 3 to 5·5 per cent of GDP [2]. In addition to the direct public expenditure cost, the occupation of a rising proportion of the 16-to-24 age group in study rather than paid work implies a loss of current output although this may be more than offset by future output gains if education results in enhanced labour productivity. The expansion of education can thus be measured by pupil and student numbers, as well as by expenditure. If success could be equated with growth, we would be looking at a remarkably successful nationalized industry.

Of the nationalized industries, education must be the least monolithic and the most decentralized. By the 1944 Education Act, the Secretary of State for Education and Science has a general responsibility for education in the UK but by custom and practice his powers, especially to initiate change, are tightly constrained. The present 144 local education authorities are the nominal controlling bodies for schools and colleges, but they in turn must act through school and college governors, and in practice it is to the teachers that the larger measures of independence and responsibility are given. Although a long list of national bodies can be compiled, their functions are predominantly advisory. Education in the UK takes pride in independence and diversity, and in consequence the economies of standardization, so often beneficial to manufacturing productivity, and the managerial efficiency of short, clear lines of command, are not to be looked for here. This is obviously not to say that education should or could become more like a production line, but only that it is not so organized as to allow for either central management or rapid change.

In terms of its operational control, therefore, education approximates more closely than most industries to the model of workers' self-management, subject to guidance as to objectives by appointed governing bodies, and to resource constraints determined by local authorities. The flow of those resources is affected by the well-known 'relative price effect': the tendency of the cost per unit of public services to rise more quickly than the general level of prices (see Chapter 9). This is the result of measured productivity gains being disproportionately concentrated in private sector and manufacturing industries. The logical implication is that a given *static* volume of public service provision will require a steadily *increasing* share of private sector income to be exacted in taxation.[3]

Of course, rapid productivity growth (such as occurred in manufacturing especially in the 1945–70 period) will, unless it generates still faster output growth, pose an employment problem. It has long been argued that the spectacular expansion since the war of the public sector, and especially of public services, has helped to solve that problem by expanding employment, as against other areas of the economy where new technology has meant few if any extra jobs in total. In this perspective, education has played an important part in the process, and not only in numbers. To the extent that education both accelerates technological progress and improves the skills and adaptability of the labour force, thus speeding up the adoption of new methods, so will productivity gains be reinforced.

No problem is likely to arise so long as the increased supply of public services satisfies the preference of income earners for increments of public as against private goods. This is another way of saying that the income elasticity of demand for public goods is higher than for private goods. But a static supply at a higher cost creates a different situation. Then the demands of taxation are added to the conflict between labour and capital for shares in the gains from growth. This problem will intensify if, either in quality or in quantity, public services are perceived as poor compensation for the private goods sacrificed by taxation. The likely effects are demands from wage bargainers for *after-tax* real wage increases, and inflationary pressure in consequence.

Viewed in this light, the quality of such services as education, as seen by tax-paying 'customers'—parents and employers (themselves the non-tax-paying

---

[3] For the more general implications of this for economic growth, see R. Bacon and W. Eltis, *Britain's Economic Problem: Too Few Producers*, (Macmillan Press, 1976).

pupils of an earlier generation)—becomes critical. If there are poor communications between them and education's worker–managers, the consequences may be far-reaching. The resulting structural imbalance between private and public demand leads, by this theory, either to continuous inflationary pressure or to demands for cuts in education or other public services in order to release resources for private consumption.

22.2.2. *Defining Performance*

As with all non-marketed services, assessment of education's economic value is complicated by the absence of the usual measures of price and output. Consumers in ordinary markets set limits to output by their choices at the margin. Food is good, but at some point consumption of food becomes progressively less attractive than alternative expenditures. In principle the same is true of education, but it is difficult to reflect this in practice. Since most education is free to the direct beneficiary, without even an opportunity cost until the minimum school-leaving age, there is no easy way to value the direct benefit. Even measures of output are not simple. Using annual numbers of pupils and students 'processed' incurs the criticism of equating mere presence with learning. Examinations passed would be acceptable if they represented known standards of knowledge and intellect. As it is, school examinations have been norm-based; that is, they have used not an absolute, but a relative standard. A GCE A level in French means, in principle, 'better at French than 80 per cent of all pupils'. There has been some recognition of the problems this creates in recent proposals to adopt absolute standards as from 1986. In higher education, examination standards are highly subjective. So while direct costs in education can be measured, direct output cannot.

Thus an enthusiast for education may claim a greater value for extra spending on education as against other uses of funds, but there is no obvious way to establish this claim. If the value of the purpose to which the extra spending would be put is greater than that of existing educational services then this indicates that the present *mix* of expenditure is not correct and requires instead a reallocation of existing expenditure). Those who believe that funds are being wasted in education face the same difficulty.

Moreover there are indirect factors on both sides of the equation. After the legal school-leaving age, the participation of students in full-time education implies a loss of potential output from work. (Grants and like inducements to study, being transfer payments between persons, should be excluded from this figure.) But there are also social benefits external to the direct recipient. Education can clearly contribute to the well-being of the economy in ways that benefit many beyond the initial recipient; and many social, cultural, and aesthetic gains may be transmitted from individual to individual. In addition some argue that education does more than fill voids in empty minds: it counteracts other influences which may be harmful.[4] Schools also provide a child-minding service, releasing parents for work during school hours. Since they also occupy adolescents physically, spending on education may in part be

---

[4] Television is frequently cited.

expenditure on crime prevention, not to mention reduced vandalism, nuisance, and accidents. In the past, some aspects (medical examinations, milk, meals) have been seen as contributing directly to public health. Finally—and a little metaphysically—schools help to inculcate the invisible standards of behaviour that decide the quality of a society. Since decadence (in the sense of a deterioration in social cohesion) is as real a possibility in social relations as progress, this last service has real economic implications, from the resources wasted on refuse collection to those we lock up in prisons.

The upshot of the preceding three paragraphs is that in education the problem—encountered with all nationalized industries (see Chapter 26)—of defining performance targets and performance indicators is especially acute. This hinders every sort of management and economic decision, from hiring and firing to deciding wages and salaries and appraising investments. In addition, there are the difficulties of defining the objectives of education (e.g. is it to impart knowledge or to develop skills?), and finally the inherent constraints on the expansion of people's mental and physical capabilities. These consider- ations complicate the task of assessing the value of public education against its cost. Some of these economic issues in education will reappear in the concluding paragraphs of this chapter. The present intention, in keeping with the economic focus of the book, is to examine the development of education since 1945 in the light of one objective: that of adapting our human resources to the needs of industry and employment. This is not to devalue many other objectives of education—but simply to focus on the link with the economy and the ability of the UK, therefore, to provide adequate education on a national scale.

22.2.3. Education as an Input to Industry

Recently a comparison was made (see Prais [17]) of the vocational qualifications of the labour force in Britain and West Germany (see Table 22.3). We should bear in mind that they refer only to manufacturing and industrial employment; consequently they may reflect a 'hogging' of the skilled work-force by non-industrial employers. Where the comparison is really

TABLE 22.3. *Vocational Qualifications of the Labour Force, Britain (1974–1978) and West Germany (1978)*

Persons with stated qualification levels as percentage of labour force:		
University	Intermediate	None

	University	Intermediate	None
All manufacturing			
Britain	3·3	28·7	68·0
West Germany	3·5	60·8	35·7
All industry			
Britain	5·5	30·0	64·4
West Germany	7·1	59·9	33·0

Source: Prais [17].

striking is in respect of qualifications below university level. Two-thirds of our industrial work-force have no vocational qualifications at all, against one-third in Germany. Less than one-third have some sort of qualification between school-based examinations and university level, against 60 per cent in Germany. The part of the working population qualified in engineering and technology is about 40 per cent lower in Britain; nor are we catching up. Prais estimates that the number of British craftsmen and technicians qualifying in 1977 was some 40 per cent below Germany's. We may also note as relevant in this context a recent estimate[5] that in 1976 German output per employee in manufacturing was about 50 per cent higher than in Britain.

The implication is, of course, that British industry suffers not so much from a shortage of graduates as from poverty in middling skills and qualifications. (We say nothing here of the suspect quality of British time-served apprenticeships compared with Germany's standard-based, examined apprenticeships.) This may become a far more serious hindrance than in the past, when industrialization was based on mass-production with relatively low-level technology and created millions of quite high productivity jobs for unskilled or semi-skilled workers. The new wave of micro-electronic technology is fast inventing robots to do just those jobs. Yet in Britain, until recently,[6] over 70 per cent of pupils left school aged 16, and of these, 80 per cent left full-time education altogether. While higher education has perhaps received more than its fair share of attention, it is the question of how best to provide for the 90 per cent of school levers who do *not* go on to degree courses that is most relevant.

What, then, has education—as a publicly provided good—to contribute to industry? There is a long-standing view that the answer is: 'Very little'. This has at least two radically differing variants. The first is that very little public education of any kind is needed because individuals should assess the private returns of education to themselves, whether in terms of pleasure or of increased earning power, and compare them with the costs. The provision of all forms of education is then properly determined by demand and cost. For job-specific training, as opposed to more general education, individuals may contract with their employers to receive training in return for lower wages, as with traditional apprenticeships. The other variant holds that education must be kept free of the materialistic values of the economic system, and especially of a 'capitalist' economic system. For some who hold this view, education directed to an industrially oriented purpose may help to prop up the existing, but, it would be argued, unjustified, system of organizing production and distribution in the economy.

In between exist a long catalogue of criticisms commonly made concerning education in relation to the UK as an industrial society: for example, school-leavers have little or no understanding of industry and its role in the economy, or of the world of work in general; careers advice at school is inadequate as to employment opportunities and qualification routes; many school-leavers and

[5] See A. D. Smith and D. Hitchens, 'International Industrial Productivity: A Comparison of Britain, America and Germany', *National Institute Economic Review*, **101** (Aug. 1982).

[6] With the onset of recession in 1980 the proportion of 16-year-olds leaving school fell slightly below 70 per cent.

tudents have negative attitudes to industry and commerce; the best students
eek employment elsewhere, especially in the professions or government; school
examinations test mainly academic skills and aptitudes, only relevant for
preparation for higher education; the general level of scientific and technical
knowledge is very low, and even basic standards of literacy and numeracy are
sometimes inadequate; and, especially in sixth forms and above, studies are too
narrow and too highly specialized. There are no satisfactory school examinations for non-academic pupils. In general, resources given to vocational
education are insufficient. The list is not exhaustive.

It is not possible in one short chapter fully to evaluate these views. At best,
they reflect a widespread misunderstanding of what the education system in the
UK provides; at worst, a failure on a very considerable scale to equip people
adequately to cope with the industrial world in which many will spend their
lives. But it has been seen in the last chapter that, historically, education in the
UK had developed up to the Second World War in a manner generally
inconducive to industrial needs. Here we follow that development forward to
see to what extent the position improved after 1945.

22.3. Education in Schools

22.3.1. Achievements, Examinations, and Curricula

In 1983 the Secretary of State for Education, Sir Keith Joseph, attended the
annual conference of the National Association of Head Teachers. In the full
flow of his discourse, Sir Keith—provoked by an interruption—asked his
audience of top teachers, certainly rhetorically, how many of them would really
like to see 16 + examinations swept away completely. He was astonished by the
result: though revealed only by a show of hands, no one could deny the
overwhelming majority in favour. Yet nothing illustrates better the divergence
of views between educational practitioners and their customers. Teachers know
intimately the faults and defects of examinations. These dominate the
curriculum: very little time is allocated to non-examination subjects. Teachers
themselves, by and large, are very well educated, or at least have passed many
examinations. They prefer to teach the brightest pupils in the A-level classes.
But over 80 per cent of pupils do not take A levels. Instead, the greatest
pressures on teachers are in trying to obtain examination passes for the lesser
half of pupils, or dealing somehow with those who will pass in few or none. In
these circumstances, cramming knowledge into heads for examinations is not,
they say, to be confused with education. Yet for outsiders examination passes
are the one visible sign of the benefits of education. For parents they are valued
as access permits to better prospects for their children; for administrators or
providers of taxes they indicate (if imperfectly) the efficiency of a school. It is
probably the superior examination record of private schools that commands
the fees paid from after-tax income—more than equal, for boarding schools, to
an adult's supplementary benefit for a year.

There are numerous and well-known obstacles to assessing the performance
of schools by examination results. Two are as follows. First, anecdotal evidence
from teachers—unconfirmed, but not denied, officially—suggests that the

standards of passes and grades in many examinations have declined. There ha
been some (perhaps not much) depreciation of this currency as a result of th
desire to satisfy demand, and to enhance teachers' own indicators of success
Second, if many more pupils pass examinations that are not useful for them
that does not indicate a better performance by schools.

There have been considerable changes in the system of public examination
over time. In the nineteenth century, public secondary examinations were th
preserve of the eight university examining boards. It was in 1917 that a
national system came into existence, comprising the School Certificate and th
Higher School Certificate. Since the examinations were administered by th
same university examining boards, the certificates exclusively reflected th
requirements and priorities of higher education. It should be stressed that th
national system need not have driven out other more business-oriented
examinations, had they existed in any comparable form. But in their absence
the more visible economic returns to education in the professions, in terms o
income, security of employment, and prestige—all depending o
qualifications—transmitted strong market signals favouring university
oriented objectives. Moreover the system rapidly reproduced and perpetuated
itself in the teaching force.

School Certificate required pupils to pass with a minimum of 33 per cent in a
minimum of 5 subjects, spread between the humanities, foreign (including
classical) languages, and mathematics/sciences. Those offered usually reflected
the 1904 School Regulations, which specified for 12- to 16-year-olds a
minimum curriculum dominated by English, history and geography
mathematics and science, and foreign languages. All these were—with physical
education and 'manual work or housewifery'—compulsory.

When the 1944 Education Act was passed, it was with the chief purpose o
rationalizing a 'system' of secondary education that had evolved in a somewha
haphazard manner. The very distinction between primary and secondar
education was itself only as old as the 1926 Hadow Report. Since the 1902 Act
education had been divided between the elementary and the grammar schools
with no transition at 11.

The 'Hadow reorganization', begun in 1928, sought to establish a secondary
system based on two types of schools, 'grammar' and 'modern', the latte
offering to the age of 13 an essentially watered-down version of the gramma
school curriculum, and thereafter a mainly practical (rather than vocational
instruction. This proceeded slowly, and by 1939 one-third of children remained
in traditional elementary schools.

The 1944 Act was more strongly influenced by the 1938 Spens Report o
secondary education, and especially by its recommendation of technical
schools, with a curriculum based on the sciences, feeding (and closely
integrated with) local technical colleges. While the Act did not lay down any
specific compulsory form of secondary organization, the outcome envisaged by
its authors was a triple system: grammar, technical, and modern school
catering respectively for about 50, 25 and 25 per cent of children. This implied
the creation, almost from scratch, of two entire new systems of curricula and
examinations, tailored to the requirements of the new types of schools.

But if the Act was revolutionary in its implications, it was tentative in its measures. Overwhelmingly respectful of the tradition of local autonomy in education, it left the revolution to generate itself spontaneously in all 155 local education authorities (LEAs). In the event, the creation of a technical education system proved beyond their resources. Only half provided any technical schools at all, and their total coverage was minute. More specifically, neither for technical nor for secondary modern schools were national systems of appropriate examinations devised.

The replacement of the School Certificate in 1947 by the General Certificate of Education (GCE) retained in existence a solitary national examination, still administered by universities, and still solely designed for the purpose of selection and preparation for higher education. There was an element of realism, therefore, in the raising of the minimum mark from 33 to 45 per cent (since GCEs are single-subject examinations, it is unnecessary to keep the pass mark low to avoid mass failures in 'difficult' subjects such as mathematics or foreign languages). By the replacement of the 'block' examination, the grammar school curriculum did become more flexible, but a void in the examination system was left for the 80 per cent of 'non-academic' pupils, until the advent of the CSE (Certificate of Secondary Education) examination in 1965.

Designed for pupils in the 40 to 80 percent range of ability this latter system went almost to extremes in satisfying earlier criticisms of rigidity and academic direction. Single-subject examinations gave a maximum of flexibility to the curriculum, and, moreover, each examination could be taken in one of three different 'modes'. A further fourteen examining boards were created, giving representation to LEAs, further education colleges, and even employers, but a maximum of influence and control over syllabuses devolved on teachers themselves. A further examination, the Certificate of Extended Education (CEE), was subsequently devised to offer CSE holders an alternative to A level for sixth-form study, so as not effectively to oblige them to leave school at 16. There is no pass/failure standard in CSE, whose grades (1 to 5) notionally indicate bands in the ability range from O-level standard (in the top 20 per cent) to above the bottom 40 per cent. Increasingly the drawbacks of this dual system have become apparent, particularly with the advent of a unified comprehensive school system in place of grammar schools and secondary modern schools, and it has now been announced that the systems will be merged in 1986.

The advent of CSE, and the raising of the school-leaving age, have made a considerable difference to the figures for pupils leaving school with no qualifications whatsoever. They have declined sharply in the 1970s from 45 to 12 per cent. The ability ranges notionally tested by GCE and CSE should be seen in their context: today over 80 per cent of fifth-form leavers attempt CSE and 44 per cent attempt O-level examinations.[7]

Table 22.4 shows the most recent figures, at the time of writing, for qualifications of school-leavers. One striking feature is the fall in the proportion of unqualified leavers, but another is that increases at other levels are much

[7] *DES Statistical Bulletin*, 10/82.

TABLE 22.4. *Percentage of School-Leavers with Different Levels of Qualification,*
1973–1974 and 1980–1981

	1973–4	1980–1
1 or more A levels	15·5	16·5
No A-level passes:		
5 or more higher* grades in O levels/CSEs	8·8	9·6
1–4 higher* grades	24·5	26·6
1 or more other† grades	30·8	35·9
no graded result	20·4	11·4

* O-level grades A to C, CSE grade 1: all equivalent to the former O-level pass grades.
† O-level grades D, E; CSE grades 2 to 5.

Source: *DES Statistical Bulletin*, 10/82.

smaller. In recent years the proportion obtaining at least one A level has fluctuated around 16 per cent. The total obtaining the notional equivalent of the old School Certificate—five O levels or better—is still only around a quarter. Forty-seven per cent, or nearly one in two, still leave without a single O level or its equivalent.

In a sense this is as it should be. For GCE examinations are in essence a method of selection. They are not supposed to measure ability, but difference. The same can be said of CSE examinations, for they too are currently norm-based in principle. The main criticism of the examination system as a whole remains the dominance of the GCE syllabuses over the whole of the secondary curriculum. So long as the universities predominate in dictating the requirements of secondary examinations, this must be so, and the requirements of employment, and of vocational education and training, will perforce be obscured. However, employers, parents, and government continue to require schools to direct their activities mainly to the purposes of the national examinations; in consequence only if employers effectively insist, more strongly than the universities, on the development of examinations and curricula better suited to their own needs will schools be given a sufficiently strong incentive to alter their priorities. The proposed amalgamation of GCE and CSE highlights the risk that, in seeking a more 'credible' qualification, the benefits of a more practical form of secondary education may be lost and the predominance of the academic curriculum prolonged.

Exacerbating the problem is the fact that CSE examinations have not won more respect from the public. In part this may be due simply to ignorance of the syllabus and methods of examination, often better suited to employers' needs than the GCE. A major contributory factor to this is the proliferation of qualifications: the 16+ examination is set at two levels by twenty-one examination boards, often in multiple versions (there are, for instance, over 100 mathematics syllabuses). There have been pressures for over a decade for a simplifying amalgamation of O-level and CSE examinations, but the problem of reconciling the academic requirements for future university entrants with the more utilitarian objectives of the other 85 per cent has only now been overcome. The new merged system will, it is proposed, be controlled by only five boards.

Despite the higher apparent success rate, dissatisfaction with the present examination system is general, although agreement on the most appropriate changes is far from that. Recently the Department of Education and Science (DES) has launched several initiatives. One, the technical and vocational education initiative (TVEI), aims through a number of pilot projects to establish new courses for 14-year-olds, initially to 16 but then on to 18, with a strong technical and vocational orientation. A new Certificate of Pre-Vocational Education (CPVE) at 17 + is one the qualifications towards which TVEI may head. If the CPVE were to develop into a qualification taken by a large number of school pupils then it could have a major impact in changing current curricula, teaching methods, etc., and has earned an initial welcome from both the TUC and the CBI. A second is the drive now launched by Sir Keith Joseph to convert both GCE O level and CSE from norm-based, competitive tests to standard-based, objective tests. The stated aim is to enable 80 per cent of pupils to reach the achievement levels currently obtained by only half. The third is the creation of 'half A levels' to allow a broadening of the education of the university-bound academic minority in the 16-to-19 age group.

In a discussion of the links between education and the world of work, these problematic aspects of the examination system deserve to be picked out for scrutiny because there is no better single indicator of the 'production' of schools. For much of the post-war period, some 45 per cent of pupils left school with no examination passes, and recent progress here is to be welcomed. But the continued emphasis on academic values in examinations undoubtedly steers the curriculum away from the interests, aptitudes, and requirements of the largest number of pupils, and hampers, rather than helps, their transition from school to work.

22.3.2. The Extension of Compulsory Schooling

Among OECD countries, the UK alone insists on a national legal minimum of eleven years of compulsory school attendance. In other countries the starting age may be as young, or the leaving age as old, but in most countries one or two years less constitute the minimum full-time school attendance. This situation dates from the raising of the school-leaving age (ROSLA) to 16 in 1973. Actually, the Education Act of 1944, which raised the leaving age from 14 to 15, had simultaneously enacted ROSLA to 16, to be deferred until sufficient resources became available. Consequently ROSLA came into force through an Order in Council rather than through a new Act, and with a minimum of parliamentary debate. This was regrettable. Of course previous ROSLAs (the 1918 Education Act's from 12 to 14, the 1944 Act's) had generally been deemed progressive reactions to the abuse of child labour. None the less, as with all economic decisions, this one involved a choice between alternative uses of resources. In particular, another provision of the 1944 Act called for compulsory part-time continuation courses for school-leavers in the two years to age 18. This also had been deferred through lack of resources, as had the same provision when previously enacted in 1918. So ROSLA's opportunity cost was not only lost production from lower youth employment, but also the non-enactment of compulsory post-school part-time education.

In Germany, by contrast, full-time compulsory education both starts later, at 6, and finishes earlier, at 15. But virtually compulsory vocational education on a part-time basis continues for a further three years, linked to a wide range of professional courses. Youth employment outside the scope of these courses is, in fact, illegal. All courses end in a practical and theoretical examination, administered by the local Chambers of Commerce—in which, incidentally, trade unions participate—usually via the personal medium of a qualified practitioner of the appropriate craft. The pass rate in these examinations is very high (generally over 90 per cent). In short, vocational education combined with employment and training is compulsory in West Germany to the age of 18 and is the means by which the intermediate qualifications noted in section 22.2.3 are becoming even more widely held.

What, then, were the gains expected from the extension to 16+ of compulsory schooling, to be set against its costs? In the UK, as we have seen, the principal school examinations to be taken at 16 are the GCE O levels. Because these are norm-based examinations purporting to cater specifically for the top 20 per cent in the ability range, they have been inappropriate for the vast majority of pupils. The absence of appropriate examinations for the majority had been criticized in the Spens Report of 1938 on secondary education, the Norwood Report of 1943 on secondary examinations, the Crowther Report of 1959 on the 15–18 age group, and the Newsom Report of 1963 on the less and least able. The Schools Council owed its establishment in 1964 chiefly to the decision eventually reached to develop a Certificate of Secondary Education to cater for the 'average' pupil between the 20 per cent targeted by O level and the 40 per cent for whom no examination was deemed suitable. The fact that, in principle, no school examination at all yet exists which is designed for the 'lowest 40 per cent', bears emphasizing.

However, the CSE has attracted continued criticism for being, on the one hand, a still inappropriate imitation of the GCE, and on the other, an insufficient qualification for training and employment. It is thirteen years since its merger with the GCE in some form of unified 16+ examination was first discussed. During this period the presence of a large proportion of former 'non-examination' pupils in school fifth forms has led to considerable problems of co-ordination and supervision, and the belief, prevalent in 1944, that a simple exposure of young minds to a further year's schooling would be beneficial now appears more open to question.

The nub of the question is whether the resources absorbed by ROSLA could be more usefully deployed in strengthening the preparation of young people for employment, rather than prolonging their general education. By itself, ROSLA could make no difference to the extent of access to higher and further education, although it was advocated as improving the 'chances' of the majority. As to vocational education, the legal distinction that exists between School Regulations and Further Education Regulations actually prevents schools from offering a wide range of vocational courses.[8] Also, unlike further education teachers, all schoolteachers must have qualified teacher status: but there is a dearth among teachers of those with the appropriate knowledge and experience to teach industry-oriented subjects such as design, technology, office practice, business studies, etc. Those without a teacher's certificate, if admitted to schools at all, can only be admitted as auxiliaries, whose salaries and terms of employment are significantly worse than those of teachers. The requirement of a teaching certificate otherwise imposes on potential entrants the considerable costs of a three-year training (or, for graduates, one year). Provisions for in-service training to overcome this problem exist in further education, but not in schools.

Consequently the ability of schools to provide the most relevant and useful education—in the sense of entry into employment—for a majority of pupils in the last two years of compulsory education is much restricted, compared with further education. Some efforts have been made to alleviate this, notably in devising more practical and occupationally directed CSE courses, and in the very recent work aimed at the introduction of a Certificate of Pre-Vocational Education. The experiments in unified vocational preparation, trying to integrate employment, training, and further education with the final year in school, and now in the hands of the Manpower Services Commission, are another example. There are a few cases—in our extraordinarily diversified education system there are always a few cases—of tentative steps, through integrated tertiary colleges with both full-time and part-time attendance, towards something like the German system. All that can be said is that it will be a long time before these touch the majority of pupils.

In short, it appears in retrospect that the 1973 ROSLA, whose current cost is around £700 million a year, was, to say the least, a very questionable employment of resources.

22.3.3. *Provision of Teacher Training*

A third barrier with adverse effects is the composition of the teaching force itself. The great majority, in secondary schools, have traditionally entered teaching at an early age, mostly straight from university or teacher-training college. Lack of direct experience or knowledge of the world of work outside education may well impair their ability to educate pupils for it.[9] Careers education in schools has attracted particularly frequent criticism, but careers teachers hardly ever receive an appropriate training on appointment to their new responsibilities. Again, a number of surveys have shown that mathematics, sciences, and even English are very often taught by teachers with insufficient or else no qualifications in those subjects. Yet one obvious remedy for this shortage of supply, supplementary payments for teachers of shortage subjects, continues to date to be successfully resisted, primarily by the teachers' trade unions. Moreover the current DES initiative to alter the training of teachers to meet these points will affect only the 30,000 teachers at present newly qualifying

[8] Except some general courses sponsored by the Royal Society of Arts, Manufactures and Commerce, and by the City and Guilds Literary Institute.

[9] See, for example, [8] and [9].

each year. Even if all subsequently enter education, it would take many years for the effect to be widespread.

22.3.4. Conclusion

The three problems dealt with in the preceding sections—the appropriateness of examinations and curricula, the extension of compulsory schooling, and the lack of flexibility in the teaching force—all concern the central problem of the usefulness of the resources spent on education. There is no doubt that school education serve best those who continue to higher education. For the four-fifths who have typically left school at the first opportunity, mostly for employment, and for the economic system which must employ them, its success is more open to question.

22.4. Further Education

22.4.1. Provision of Non-Advanced Further Education (NAFE)

The Department of Education and Science distinguishes between advanced and non-advanced further education, allowing advanced status to courses that require at least two years of full-time study, or its equivalent, before qualification. A more conventional distinction is between degree and sub-degree courses: the universities are the only institutions of post-school education to offer exclusively courses of degree level or above. The qualifications to be obtained in 'further education' thus range from GCE O level or CSE to the masters' qualifications and doctorates obtainable in universities and polytechnics. What follows will, where possible, defer consideration of degree-level courses and above to the following section on higher education.

Almost 5 million students were registered in colleges of all kinds in 1979–80, nearly 4 million on non-advanced courses. Three-quarters of students take evening courses. Over half of all college students (part-time and full-time) are over the age of 25. Full-time and sandwich students in higher education are in an overall minority: less than half a million, of which 57 per cent attend the 45 universities.[10] It is thus the function of the further education sector to supply the major part of post-compulsory education, both for the 16-to-20 age group, and for those returning to education at all age levels. Further education colleges therefore serve two distinct client groups: school-leavers aged 16 to 20 preparing for employment, and older students mainly on evening courses. Further education as traditionally conceived is combined with adult and continuing education.

The impact of the recent recession has lately increased the take-up of both further and higher education courses. However, in the more typical year 1979–80, 7·5 per cent of school-leavers proceeded to higher education, and 8 per cent to professional and vocational courses other than secretarial. Four per cent went on to college-based O- and A-level courses. Seventy per cent were

[10] *DES Statistical Bulletin*, 1/83.

available for employment.[11] The parity of numbers embarking on full degree courses with those entering the shorter vocational courses is interesting, because there are indications that degree courses give a lower social return than the shorter vocational types. For example, a recent study carried out for the DES of data on education and earnings differentials for the period 1971–8, based on the General Household Surveys, shows the social rate of return on first degrees to average only 4 per cent, whereas the social return on the part-time Higher National Certificate averaged 7 per cent. And yet the inducements offered to students are biased in favour of full-time education: for the *private* rate of return on first degrees averaged 17 per cent, and that for the HNC only 11 per cent. Consequently the type of qualification offering the lowest social rate of return (below the Treasury's then-current test discount rate for public investment of 5 per cent) was subsidized more heavily than that offering the highest.

Riddled as international comparisons in education are with statistical difficulties, it is still interesting to note the distribution of public expenditure on education and training in the European Community, shown in Table 22.5. On

TABLE 22.5. *Allocation of General Government Expenditure on Education and Training, 1978* (per cent)

	General	Vocational
France	71·8	28·2
Ireland	73·7	26·3
Netherlands	75·1	24·9
West Germany	84·9	15·1
Denmark	87·6	12·4
United Kingdom	91·9	8·1
Belgium	93·9	6·1
Italy	96·7	3·3

Source: European Commission.

average, 16 per cent of educational spending in the EEC goes to vocational courses, but in the UK only half of that figure. In contrast, there is no significant difference between the UK's overall education spending per head and the EEC average. Taken together, these indications raise a question as to whether post-school education is too heavily concentrated on the more general, and more expensive, degree-level courses when the advantage to society is greater for shorter, vocational intermediate qualifications. Research on this subject has to date been inadequate.

[11] *DES Statistical Bulletin*, 10/82. The same figures for the latest year, 1980–1, are, respectively, 8, 11, 6, and 63 per cent.

22.4.2. Purpose and Qualifications in NAFE

Unfortunately, evaluating the provision of further education (FE) is complicated by the multiplicity of its tasks. Four can be identified:

(i) building on school education to give post-school qualifications that are vocational/professional without being job-specific, either during or instead of employment;

(ii) making up the deficiencies in the education of school-leavers that have left them less capable of employment in existing market conditions;

(iii) offering post-experience courses to enable workers to enhance their existing skills or retrain in new ones;

(iv) providing part-time education as a form of leisure consumption.

The first two of these apply to post-school education, the last two to adult and continuing education. If we are interested in improvement of the quality of the labour force, we would wish to know how FE resources are deployed between the four aims, but are frustrated by the lack of published information on this point. To what extent does FE patch up the deficiencies of school education and provide evening pastimes, literature, history, and other appreciation classes, other leisure pursuits, etc., or provide the intermediate professional and vocational qualifications which are so much scarcer in the UK than in Germany?

Some indications can be found by looking at the figures for particular courses. The secondary school examinations, intended primarily as preparation for academic higher education, now occupy an increasing proportion of students in FE establishments: in 1978, 17 per cent of full-time students and 14 per cent of all students were enrolled on GCE or CSE/CEE courses, up from 15 per cent and 11 per cent ten years previously. As a proportion of non-advanced courses only, the figures are 28 and 16 per cent respectively; and nearly three-quarters of students on non-advanced courses are of school age (16 to 18). Thus a significant part of FE resources is devoted to the provision of school-type courses to school-age students outside schools, potentially an expensive duplication of resources. As much as one-quarter of all GCE entries are from further education colleges. This may in part reflect local policies of closing school sixth forms in favour of integrated tertiary colleges, but this is not very widespread. Furthermore in LEA committee structures, FE is commonly separated from schools, so increasing the difficulty of integrating provision for the 16-to-19 age group.

A related point is that FE resources are now being directed to provide an element in the Youth Training Scheme for sixteen-year-olds which began in September 1983. Since neither the GCE nor the conventional business and technician courses are suitable for them, a new sort of further education will have to be devised. It remains to be seen how the balance will be struck between useful training and short-term absorption of unemployment for the young people.

If we turn to the conventional vocational qualifications, another disturbing trend appeared in the last decade in the areas of most relevance to the qualifications of the industrial labour force. Table 22.6 shows the number of students acquiring higher national diplomas and certificates in a range of subjects in the last two available years, as a proportion of those passing at the beginning of the decade. We should bear in mind that the relevant age group increased markedly in this decade, and also that a rising proportion of certificate and diploma students in this period came from overseas. Placing them in this context makes some of the declines look still more alarming: for example falls of one-third in those taking the general engineering HNC and OND, and of a half in those taking the electrical, mechanical, and production engineering HNDs.

TABLE 22.6. *Passes in Technical Qualifications (Selected Subjects) in 1977 and 1978, as a Proportion of Passes in 1970 and 1971* (per cent)

	HND*	HNC†	OND‡	ONC§
Engineering	—	67	65	71
Electrical engineering	51	68		
Mechanical engineering	49	—		
Production engineering	49	—		
Foundry technology	97	27		
Metallurgy	33	57		
Chemistry	48	79		
Applied physics	78	59		

* Higher National Diploma.   † Higher National Certificate.
‡ Ordinary National Diploma.   § Ordinary National Certificate.

Source: DES, *Statistics of Education 1978*, Vol. 3.

Recently the HND and OND (full-time) and HNC/ONC (part-time) qualifications have been progressively superceded by new qualifications administered by the Business and Technicians Education Council, making it difficult to bring the picture up to date. These figures must strongly reflect the general contraction of employment in manufacturing industry that has been caused in part by the development of North Sea oil exports and the 1980–1 recession. Nor is there conclusive evidence to support the view that de-industrialization will be reinforced by a deterioration in the quality of the industrial labour force, since the fall in intermediate qualifications could be offset by increased numbers of graduates. Here the evidence is not clear; although numbers of graduates have increased, the proportion in engineering and technology has fallen between 1973 and 1982 from 15 to 14 per cent in universities and from 27 to 17 per cent for Council for National Academic Awards (CNAA) degrees.

To what extent do such changes simply reflect a rational choice by students in response to market signals? In the absence of any attempt at manpower planning in education, supply is chiefly influenced by student choice. Students' preferences will theoretically be formed by their own abilities, previous knowledge and qualifications, estimation of alternative costs and rewards, and ability to predict labour market conditions in the future. It is in any case questionable whether students are capable in the circumstances of making economically rational choices based on these criteria. Moreover wider questions are raised as to the overall structure of the economy, and the presence of distortions in the choices facing students. As an example of the latter, apprentices in industry are paid about 60 per cent of adult wages,[12] and other youth wages have been brought closer to adult levels by trade union bargaining. On the other hand, grants for degree courses are mandatory, but for non-degree courses only discretionary. The direct inducements therefore favour either employment or degree-level study in preference to full-time intermediate vocational studies. Nor is this the full measure of the distortions students face. The sacrifice involved, in terms of lower income, in apprenticeships is very much less than in some other European countries, and there has often been a high level of applications for apprenticeships. But the number taken on has remained heavily constrained, with little sign of the excess supply reducing the income of apprentices relative to other possible activities for the age group concerned.

In 1979–80, expenditure on further education and adult education formed 16 per cent of total education expenditure (excluding administration costs and education-related expenditures), or 15 per cent of all education and related spending. The allocations were as shown in Table 22.7. Unfortunately the published statistics do not distinguish in further education between degree-level education and sub-degree work. It is in fact impossible to know, under present arrangements, how further education is precisely distributed between GCE qualifications, lower-level and higher-level technical/vocational courses, and degree-level work. Some indication may be gleaned from the fact that over

TABLE 22.7. *Allocation of Education Expenditure, 1979–1980*

	% of education spending	% of all education and related spending
Nursery schools	0·6	0·4
Primary schools	28·6	23·9
Secondary schools	37·9	31·6
Special schools	4·3	3·6
Further and adult education	16·3	15·5
Training of teachers	0·7	1·0
Universities	11·7	11·8
Other		12·0

Source: DES, *Education Statistics for the UK* (1982).

[12] See I. Jones and H. Hollenstein, *Trainee Wages and Training Deficiencies*, NIESR Discussion Paper, No. 58.

half the FE sector's full-time students are on degree-level courses, which suggests that higher education may absorb the major part of FE resources.

It is worth recalling in conclusion that not only the 1944 Education Act, but also its 1918 predecessor both legislated for compulsory continuation in technical/vocational education after leaving school—the provision that now operates in West Germany. Yet in both cases insufficient resources were found to give effect to it. In the period of post-war planning, a network of technical schools was envisaged alongside the grammar and secondary modern schools, feeding the technical colleges. These, too, never materialized for any more than 2 per cent of pupils. So far are we from the integrated system of technical and professional education, from school to university level, then envisaged that we have no effective planning or management system for technical education. The nearest substitute is the Business and Technicians Education Council, formed in 1983 from the two separate Councils, BEC and TEC, formed in 1974 and 1973 respectively. The fact that membership of their programme committees is distributed 50–50 between members from education and industry should not be remarkable, but for the sharp and favourable contrast presented with virtually every other examining or advisory board. This is in itself a positive development—for in the end, further education must prove itself by the value to students, and the credibility to employers, of the final qualifications awarded.

22.4.3. Higher Education[13]

Four questions are often raised concerning higher—in the sense of degree level and above—education. They are:

(i) Has the overall expansion of higher education been justified?
(ii) Is the 'binary' principle, which divides university from local authority-controlled higher education, valid and useful?
(iii) Are industry's and commerce's manpower requirements well served by higher education's graduate output?
(iv) Does the economy suffer from a divorce between publicly funded academic research and privately funded industrial research?

The expansion of higher education over, approximately, the fifteen years from 1966 to 1981 owed much to the economic arguments put forward at the time of the Robbins Report of 1963. Among these was the idea that a lack of university-trained manpower, especially in the industry-related courses, contributed to the relative slowness of the UK's post-war growth, both by restraining technological development and by perpetuating poor management. Another point drew on adverse comparisons between the participation rates in higher education in the US and the UK (in 1959 these were 20 and 4·5 per cent respectively), drawing on Denison's work to infer an explanation for lower productivity based on a lower human capital stock (see Chapter 20). As Table 22.8 shows, at the end of the decade higher education's annual output had risen to almost 90,000 graduates a year, plus another 19,000 obtaining postgraduate

[13] This section draws substantially on research carried out by my colleague at the National Economic Development Office, Andrew Kilpatrick.

TABLE 22.8. *First Degree and Other Qualifications Awarded, Year Ended December 1979*

	(1)	(2)	(3)	(4)	(5)
TOTAL	89,384	13,173	19,425	26,540	33,786
Percentages:					
1. Administrative, business, and social studies	26·3	28·4	22·5	28·5	35·4
2. Engineering and technology	14·5	3·6	17·5	45·7	39·7
3. Medicine, dentistry, and health	7·5	4·2	6·6	5·5	0·2
4. Agriculture, forestry, and veterinary science	1·4	0·4	2·6	1·4	1·2
5. Architecture and other professional vocational studies	2·3	5·9	3·5	4·9	11·9
6. Science	19·5	2·6	24·4	11·9	11·3
7. Languages, literature, and area studies	10·1	1·8	6·9	0·1	0
8. Arts other than languages	8·0	1·0	3·6	0·2	0
9. Music, drama, art and design	5·5	0·8	1·7	0·4	0·2
10. Education	4·9	51·1	10·6	1·4	0
Lines 1 to 6	71·5	45·1	77·1	97·9	99·7

(1) 1st degrees.
(2) Postgraduate diplomas/certificates.
(3) Higher degrees.
(4) Higher certificates/diplomas.
(5) Ordinary certificates/diplomas.

Source: DES, *Education Statistics for the United Kingdom* (1982).

degrees and another 13,000 obtaining postgraduate diplomas or certificates. This can be contrasted with further education's 24,000[14] higher and 34,000 lower diplomas and certificates. By this measure higher education has expanded to claim the lion's share of the resources allocated to post-compulsory education.

Despite this expansion, the age participation rate remained, by international standards, much lower than in most comparable countries (see [2]). None the less there are indications of some over-expansion. One is the rate of graduate unemployment, which stood in 1980 at 17 per cent, when of the whole labour force only 6 per cent were unemployed. A second is the marked contraction in the 1970s of income differentials which were previously more in favour of degree holders. Owing to the still considerable subsidy to degree students, however, the personal return on their investment of time was still on average 17 per cent, and as high as 37 per cent for some social science degrees (see Daly [5]), indicating that returns have much further to fall before they have much effect on the demand for higher education. The age participation rate in degree-level courses has remained at just less than 10 per cent in the last three

[14] Excluding 2,307 pre-degree diplomas and certificates awarded by universities.

years, in spite of the growth of the relevant age group, and the recent restraints on student numbers imposed by the Conservative Government.

The forty-five universities in the UK produce 74 per cent of first-degree and 95 per cent of postgraduate-degree holders, the thirty polytechnics and some colleges of higher education accounting for the rest. The binary principle that governed the creation of the polytechnics envisages that resources would be shared equally between the two sectors, the universities maintaining their traditions of academic excellence based on a heavy commitment of resources to 'pure' research, while the polytechnics concentrated on courses and research more directly relevant to industry and commerce. Were this effectively the case, there would be grounds for disquiet over the low share of the polytechnics in the sector's output. This is still more disturbing if we admit the criticism that, far from specializing in the direct requirements of industry, polytechnics have tended to become more like universities.

The 1966 White Paper envisaged three tasks for the polytechnics. They were (i) to provide vocationally oriented degree courses for full-time and sandwich students, (ii) to provide sub-degree courses, and (iii) to provide a part-time route to higher qualifications. In fact between 1970 and 1981 part-time students declined from 43 to 32 per cent of enrolments. By 1978 the number of non-advanced students had already halved, going from 28 to 9 per cent of enrolments, while of advanced enrolments, the proportion on sub-degree courses fell from 64 to 46 per cent. In terms of the courses offered, enrolments in engineering and technology declined from 32 to 20 per cent of the total, while arts enrolments rose as a percentage of advanced enrolments (and there are virtually no non-advanced qualifications in the arts) from 7 to 13 per cent between 1970 and 1981. An analysis of university and CNAA degrees by subject area is given in Table 22.9. The figures in this table require a little interpretation: it should be noted that such subjects as law, sociology, psychology, and philosophy are buried in the same category as 'administrative, business and social studies'. Also the art and design figures are chiefly responsible for the striking figures in the seventh line.

TABLE 22.9. *First Degrees by Subject Area, as a Percentage of Degrees Awarded, 1979 (Excluding Education)*

	Universities	CNAA
1. Agriculture, forestry, and veterinary science	1·9	0
2. Architecture and other professional/vocational studies	1·7	4·5
3. Administrative, business, and social studies	26·6	31·1
4. Engineering and technology	14·1	18·8
5. Medicine, dentistry, and health	9·6	2·5
6. Science	22·9	12·9
7. Music, drama, art, and design	1·8	18·6
8. Arts other than languages	8·4	8·5
9. Language, literature, and area studies	13·0	3·0

Source: DES, *Education Statistics for the United Kingdom* (1982).

These figures are therefore not sufficiently detailed to show whether polytechnics have in reality become carbon copies of universities, as some critics say. What is true is that the subject spread has become much more like that of the universities, with the shares of arts and science rising while the share of engineering and technology falls. Perhaps the most telling point in Table 22.9 is the near-identity in both sectors of the share of arts other than languages, the case for the provision of such studies in polytechnics being rather less evident than that for languages.

Despite the criticism, the binary line is now more entrenched since the recent establishment of the National Advisory Board for Local Authority Higher Education. Here it is worth quoting the evidence of the chairman of the University Grants Committee (UGC), Dr Parkes, to the Education, Science and Arts Committee of the House of Commons in 1980. He said: '. . . the UGC advises the government about universities, but it does so in almost total ignorance of what is happening to the rest of higher education. . . . It no longer seems to me to be efficient to regard higher education as consisting of two distinct parts, each developing separately, and with very little attention paid to the interactions between them.' It is also worth recalling the peregrinations of the nine colleges of advanced technology. These were originally selected from the technical colleges as centres of excellence in the 'maintained sector'. They were then transferred in 1966–7 to the university sector, a decision that required them to shed their non-degree courses and most of their part-time students. But their development into full-scale universities has been sharply cut back by the UGC's recent decisions. They are now to become small-scale 'universities', highly specialized in engineering, technology, and related subjects. These will resemble the idealized notion of a polytechnic so closely, as to cast doubt on the meaning of the binary division.

The last two of the questions raised at the beginning of this section, concerning industry's manpower requirements and the divisions in the UK's research effort, are somewhat intertwined. As to the first of them, we should distinguish between the question of appropriate degree-subject choices, and that of appropriate courses. Concerning choices, it must be emphasized that these are influenced strongly by choices made at A level and even before. The weakness of careers advice in schools has already been mentioned. Given the narrowness of sixth-form studies—a narrowness which universities have acted in recent years to preserve—the decisions made at their inception, at the age of 16, in most cases determined the graduate's specialization at 21 or 22. This long lead-time presents quite a challenge to the predictive powers of a sixteen-year-old. But since the Robbins Report, higher education has declined to attempt to tailor its provision to anything but student choice, dominated as this is by the constraints on choice in school sixth forms. Despite the widely held view that the paucity of scientific manpower is a weakness for the economy, the growth of university places has been led by demand for arts and social studies places. Even now, the reduction of university resources has led to an actual decline in entrants to university courses in computer science, when labour market indicators point strongly to a rising demand.

Additionally, there have been complaints that university courses—especially those most relevant to industry and commerce—have lacked realism. For example, the Engineering Council has recently called for a fourth year of practical applications to be added to a proportion of engineering degrees. Such criticism can only be met on a case-by-case basis, and some difficulty has regularly been experienced in actually determining what the requirements of industry might be. Essentially the difficulty is one of communication, and this is especially aggravated by the lack of interchange of personnel between business and universities, whose career structures diverge virtually from their start.

This last problem also impinges on the question of research. It has long been a cliché that Britain excels in basic research, lags in its development, and fails in its commercial application: 'Invented in Britain, developed in the USA, and made in Japan' runs the wry epigram. Britain's research and development spending is not especially low in relation to GDP, but is so in absolute terms; moreover a large share (55 per cent) is accounted for by publicly financed (especially military) research. This has led to a demand that the research of universities should be more closely integrated with that of businesses. The advantages expected include:

(i) a quicker and better diffusion of advances in knowledge and technique;
(ii) better access to research facilities for small and medium-sized companies, and for new enterprises with less room for large overheads;
(iii) easier and more frequent interchanges of staff between the higher-education and industry sides of their professions;
(iv) increased awareness of industry's needs, with beneficial effects on universities' teaching;
(v) increased awareness in industry of the research capability available in universities, and of their various specialisms.

This question has recently been the subject of a joint inquiry by the two most relevant advisory bodies, the Advisory Council for Applied Research and Development and the Advisory Board for the Research Councils. Their report[15] concludes that 'there is the potential for a substantial strengthening of links between higher education institutions and industry in this country and that action should be considered as a matter of urgency.' Of their twelve recommendations and nine suggestions, the principal one is that the Department of Trade and Industry (not the Department of Education and Science) should establish a £10 million per annum 'industrial seedcorn fund' to be allocated to support industrially-financed university applied research, with an additional £5 million over five years to add to the infrastructure for academic–industrial co-operation. They recommend also that the Science and Engineering Research Council (and other research councils) and the Royal Society for the Encouragement of Arts, Manufactures and Commerce (RSA) should be given co-ordinating roles with respect to projects and the fostering of academic–industrial contacts.

[15] *Improving Research Links Between Higher Education and Industry* (the Muir-Wood Report) (HMSO, June 1983).

22.5. Education and the Economy

We return in conclusion to the questions raised in the introduction. What are the benefits of public education? Can they be increased? How much should the nation spend on education, and who should pay? And what prevents a better interaction between education and industry?

A far from exhaustive list would include as principal benefits, for the population in general and for individuals, intellectual development, social cohesion, the acquisition of useful abilities, and the enjoyment of education as entertainment, as a form of consumption. We might add, as being currently especially apt, the possibility of retraining. To which of these to accord priority is a matter of judgement. For a long time, the moral or cultural objectives were generally considered paramount: for example by Ignatius Loyola ('give me a child at seven, and I will make him mine for life') or Dr Arnold ('a university that did not teach religion would be an abomination'). The more recent growth of education spending was justified on more secular grounds, especially through the human capital approach, as described in Chapter 4. In this, education is seen primarily as producing intellectual development, a capital asset embodied in individuals that yields an enhanced quality of labour over the whole productive life of the person.

The large claims made for the value of investment in education arose from its identification with the very large residual element in post-war economic growth that could not readily be explained by increases in physical capital or flow of labour-time (see Chapter 20). Although the rate of technological progress was taken as given, the speed of its effective application to production was said to depend on education. This identification may now be thought a little more dubious in the light of the slowdown in productivity growth while education spending reached new heights, though it must be remembered that very long lags are probably involved in any feed-through from education spending to economic performance.

Two problems arise in the human capital approach. One is the 'brain drain': the embodiment of a public asset—paid for by taxation—in a person allows him to expropriate it by the simple expedient of leaving the country. This implies that education is a private, not a public, asset, and should be paid for privately. A second is the question of the capital–output ratio. Inability to calculate the output derived from education means that ordinary methods of investment appraisal cannot readily be applied, and there may be a tendency to under- or over-invest in education. Attempts to calculate the output yield have generally been based on the earnings differential commanded by the educated person. This method is rather hard to apply to the two-thirds of education expenditure allocated to the universal, compulsory levels of education. Its results may also be exaggerated by a number of factors, such as failing to separate education from ability, or to take into account artificial entry barriers maintaining high wages in certain occupations in which the better educated are numerous. Thus human capital, although a useful concept, has disappointed so far in its practical application.

An increased return on education could theoretically be gained by various means. In common with any other industry, there could be gains from greater efficiency in the teaching process, to reverse the relative price effect, mentioned earlier, caused by slow productivity growth. Otherwise resources can be reallocated between the various sectors of education by a principle of concentrating on the better return, provided this could be measured. It has been suggested earlier that a redistribution away from secondary schooling—at least as practised at present—and away from degree-level education, to further education and the lower-to-intermediate vocational qualifications would be advantageous. Alternatively (or additionally), curricula and examinations in each sector (but most importantly in secondary schools) could be altered in the direction of a better integration with working life. Lastly, it would be desirable for education—especially post-compulsory education—to be capable of very quick adaptation to new requirements as the structure of production changes, placing new demands both on existing workers and on new entrants to the labour force. Unfortunately, given the very long lead-times inherent in education, hope is very likely always to move ahead of reality, as a reading of the 1928 Malcolm Report (*Industry and Education*) will confirm.

How much education can the country afford, and who will pay? The political stance of the present government, the priority in macroeconomic policy accorded to reducing the public sector deficit, and the growing pressure on the finance of Welfare State commitments have conspired lately to encourage interest in schemes to privatize elements of education, or to reduce its total cost. For instance the education voucher would both promote competition between schools and restrict excess consumption of education by students. That education has, at least in parts, a consumption aspect is well recognized; and the subsidy element in cultural evening classes has been much at risk, even if, unsubsidized, they could claim to be a rational use of rising incomes. Partial replacement of student grants by loans has been much canvassed, even though in theory the graduate repays the social cost of his education already through the instrument of progressive income taxation on his subsequently enhanced earnings.

We may ask not only whether education is properly a public or a private good, but also whether it is an essential or a luxury good. In the private sector of education, the combination of social, cultural, and/or academic advantages offered commands a high price, bearing in mind that this cannot be deducted from the rates and tax payments allocated to state education. This suggests that it is a private good with a high income elasticity. The existence of a private market for a publicly provided good suggests that it is not a pure public good, at least in the strict sense that its provision to one user does not reduce the supply available to another. But the demand may be for a Hirsch good,[16] that is to say for the privilege afforded, and not—or not solely—for the good itself. There is also an argument that education is a right, although to what level is generally left unspecified. As with housing, the right is called a right in the sense that its lack imposes an undeserved disadvantage—meaning a denial of opportunity—on juveniles who suffer as a result of their parents failing to provide, as it were, a

[16] See F. Hirsch, *Social Limits to Growth*, (Routledge, 1978).

sufficient family capital infrastructure. It is also theoretically possible for education spending to have a redistributive effect, large and poor families gaining at the expense of small and rich ones; but the recent evidence is that it is actually the higher-income-earning households that have benefited most from the use of the expanded public resources devoted to education, to the point of nullifying and even reversing the redistribution effect.

TABLE 22.10. *General Government Expenditure on Education and Training Per Head of Population Aged 5 to 24, 1978* (in units of standard purchasing power)

Netherlands	584	Luxembourg	405
Belgium	557	United Kingdom	398
Denmark	499	Ireland	301
France	442	Italy	269
West Germany	424	European 9	402

Source: Commission of the European Communities.

By the best measure, excluding variations in currencies and differences in youth populations, UK expenditure on education is neither particularly high nor low compared with the EEC average (see Table 22.10). Although the last year available for this international comparison is not recent, the DES currently calculates that expenditure per pupil/student has never been higher. None the less, we spent about 8 per cent less than France and Germany, and less than four-fifths of levels in the small north-European states. By themselves these comparisons do not show whether or not this lag is disadvantageous. We should wish to know whether the relative price of education in those countries was simply higher, or whether they enjoy benefits in the form of a more productive and better-adapted work-force, and whether such benefits can be reliably ascribed to education spending. For instance, not many think we should try to match the much higher drop-out rates in university education that accompany the much higher participation rates in Italy, France, and Germany.

At present the total resources available for education are unlikely to grow except slowly. The release of the growth constraint depends, to some degree at least, on re-examining and strengthening the relationship between the education we provide, and the requirements of the economic system. This—to make perhaps an obvious statement—as much requires industrialists to concern themselves with education as it needs educationists to concentrate on the requirements for economic success.

Bibliography

For the basic factual information, see:
[1] Department of Education and Science (DES). *Education Statistics for the UK* (1982)
[2] OECD. *Educational Statistics in OECD Countries* (Paris, 1981).

For the economics of education, see:

[3] BLAUG, M. (ed.). *Economics of Education*, 2 vols. (Penguin, 1968 and 1969).

[4] OECD. *Public Expenditure on Education*, OECD Studies in Resource Allocation (1976).

[5] DALY, A. *The Contribution of Education to Economic Growth in Britain: A Note on the Evidence*, National Institute for Economic and Social Research Discussion Paper (1981).

[6] PRAIS, S. J. *Schooling or Experience: Which is More Valuable?*, NIESR Discussion Paper (1982).

For a discussion of the education–industry divide, see:

[7] RODERICK, G. and STEPHENS, M. (eds.). *The British Malaise* (Falmer Press, 1982).

For some recent official and semi-official discussions, see:

[8] DES. *Teacher Training and Preparation for Working Life* (1982).

[9] —— *Schools and Working Life* (1981).

[10] —— *The School Curriculum* (1981).

[11] —— *17+ : A New Qualification* (1982).

[12] —— *Examinations 16 to 18* (1980).

[13] —— *Education for 16 to 19-year-olds* (1981).

[14] *The Secondary School's Curriculum and Examinations*, Report of the House of Commons Education, Science and Arts Committee (1981).

[15] Central Policy Review Staff. *Education, Training and Industrial Performance* (1980).

On the key area of post-compulsory education, see:

[16] CANTOR, L. and ROBERTS, I. F. *Further Education To-day* (Routledge and Kegan Paul, 1979).

[17] PRAIS, S. J. 'Vocational Qualifications of the Labour Force in Britain and Germany', *National Institute Economic Review* (1982).

23

Long Waves of Economic Activity

G. D. HOBBS[1]

23.1. Introduction

The chapters in Part V have so far been concerned with long-term economic growth and some of the factors underlying it. They have left aside the question of whether there are systematic patterns of faster and slower growth over time. But there has been a growing view in recent years that lack of success in economic policy-making has arisen because there are such major forces at work, operating over very long periods of time, which policy makers have failed to recognize and may well be powerless to prevent. This chapter describes a theory, or more precisely a set of theories, which has led many to believe this to be an important factor in explaining economic performance.

The economies of the Western industrialized world began to behave in an unexpected and unplanned manner in the late 1960s and early 1970s. That it was happening did not really become apparent until the energy crisis of 1973 shook the world into a new state of awareness. Even then, and for some years after, many believed that the world's economic ills had their origin in the abrupt increase in the price of oil brought about by the OPEC cartel and that we would return to the trends of the 1950s and 1960s when that increase had been absorbed. However, the problems of declining growth, rising unemployment, high inflation, and exchange rate instability persisted. As historical trends began to become clearer (Figure 23.1), it could be seen that many of the symptoms had been present even in the 1960s. Realization grew that perhaps the change had more fundamental origins: that perhaps the oil price rise had itself been an effect not a cause.

One facet of this realization was a reawakening to the hypothesis, dormant for many years, that there existed a periodic variation in world economic activity which repeated itself approximately every 50 years. Parallels began to be drawn between the 1970s and the 1920s, and even with the 'Great Depression' of the 1880s.

The history of the 50-year-wave hypothesis is itself long. A useful summary

[1] The author wishes to acknowledge the very considerable contribution made by Dr Martha Cleary in exploring the empirical evidence, and to acknowledge also Michael Jackson, Peter Staardecker, and Paul Floyd for the modelling work. The views expressed are those of the author and do not necessarily reflect those of ICI.

(a) UK industrial production (annual percentage growth)

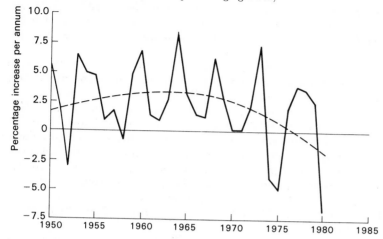

(b) UK unemployment (millions)

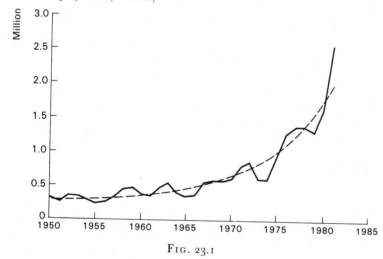

FIG. 23.1

:an be found in Van Duijn [38]. The earliest reference quoted is Clarke [11], who in 1847 suggested the existence of a 54-year cycle in economic activity spanning five regular business cycles. The business cycle of the time was approximately 10 years long, rather than the 4 to 5 years of the modern day. Other authors followed in the early 1900s. In 1913 Van Gelderen [40] published a study of price indices for the US, Great Britain, Germany, and Belgium from which he concluded that there was a long wave in prices covering several decades. The periods of price increases, which he also associated with accelerated economic activity, he called spring-tide periods; the periods o falling prices and retarded economic activity he called ebb-tide periods Further studies followed in the 1920s, the best know of which was carried out b' Nikolai Kondratieff [25], [26]. The 50-year wave is often referred to as 'th Kondratieff cycle'.

Since this early pioneering work, interest in long waves has itself gon through spring-tide and ebb-tide periods, with a notable correlation betwee spring-tide periods of interest and ebb-tide periods in the economy. Studie continued to be reported in the 1930s (readers are referred to Van Duijn [3 for a more comprehensive bibliography), the last, and perhaps most important being that of Schumpeter [37] in which he advanced a technological theory fo the waves' origins. Interest in 50-year waves declined with the advent of wa and the post-war economic boom and did not reappear until the 1970s. Recen authors in the field include Rostow and Kennedy [36], Mensch [32], Forreste [18], Van Duijn [38], Freeman [19], Kucztnski [27, 28], Kleinknecht [24] Delbeke [13], Marchetti [29], Graham and Senge [23], and Freeman, Clark and Soete [2].

The existence of the Kondratieff cycle has been a matter for dispute for th whole of this period. As indicated, numerous empirical studies have bee carried out but, since quantitative economic data are even now only availabl for about four cycles, it is not surprising that conclusive statistical proof (on way or the other) has not yet been forthcoming. There is, nevertheless sufficient evidence, when viewed in its totality, to support the view that th long-wave hypothesis is at least plausible. Equally important, there are nov several theories, of varying degrees of sophistication, which predict th phenomenon. It is on these theories that this chapter will concentrate.

First, however, we should examine a sample of the empirical evidence. Thi is not done in any great depth. A more detailed examination can be found i Cleary and Hobbs [12] and Glisman, Rodemer, and Wolter [22].

23.2. The Evidence

23.2.1. Prices

It was in price-series that the 50-year wave was first observed and in whic some of the strongest evidence is found. Figure 23.2 shows the Wholesale Pric Index for the UK starting in 1790 (see [4]). The series has been truncated a 1970 to prevent the inflation of the last decade overshadowing the pric movements in earlier years (the index had passed a value of 2,000 by 1979). Th eye has no great difficulty in picking out in this, and the comparable chart fo the US (Figure 23.3), a 50-to 60-year periodic movement in prices with peak in the 1810s, the 1860s, and the 1920s. Although of a different order o magnitude, the price rises of the 1970s are consistent in timing with a fourt peak in the 1980s. The peak in the US data in the 1780s is inconsistent with 50-year periodicity. It has its origins in the American War of Independenc (1776–83). There is little doubt that, in general, war has been a contributor factor to some of the sharper price rises, an aspect which is discussed more full later in the chapter.

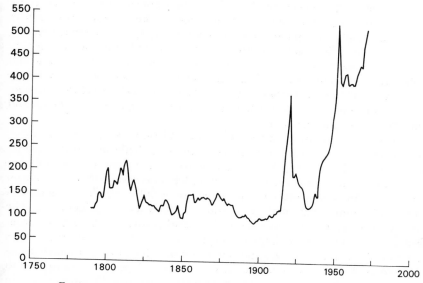

FIG. 23.2. UK Wholesale Price Index, 1790–1970 (1900 = 100).

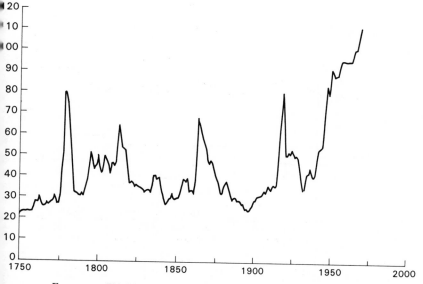

FIG. 23.3. US Wholesale Price Index, 1750–1970 (1967 = 100).

Corroborating evidence for the UK can be found in the wage index, the index of building costs, and the yield on Consols. The wholesale price indices for France, Italy, and Spain also show similar behaviour, albeit over a slightly shorter period. The peaks and troughs are all broadly coincident, the only 'peaks' missing from the set being those for Italy in the 1810s (no data) and 1860s. It is relevant to recall the massive changes that these countries will have seen over the 200-year period, particularly with regard to industrialization and the differences that would have existed between, for example, Spain and the UK at any particular time.

Additional data are available for individual commodities. Some can be found in Kondratieff's [25] original paper and others in the more recent studies by Rostow [33], [34], [35]. Rostow has analysed price-series for foodstuffs and raw materials into 'trend periods'. These he defines as periods during which, on trend, the prices of primary goods either rise or fall in relation to industrial goods. The results of his analysis are shown schematically in Figure 23.4. The timing bears a close resemblance to the broad pattern of changes shown in Figures 23.2 and 23.3—perhaps not surprisingly, as the wholesale price indices are heavily weighted by food and raw materials. The third and fourth cycles differ from the first two in that (a) they are shorter (38 years compared with an average of 53 years), and (b) the fourth which, according to Rostow, 'peaks' in the early 1950s, appears to be an oscillation about an even longer-term inflationary trend. The 'downswing' (1951–72) was a period of stagnant rather than falling prices. An alternative interpretation is that the fourth and fifth cycles should be taken together as a single period of rising prices starting in the mid-1930s and with a peak still to come. Neither interpretation fits very

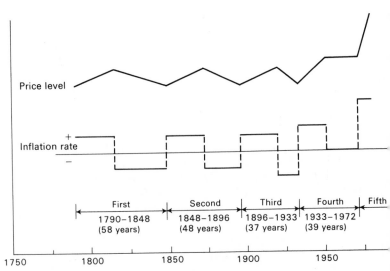

FIG. 23.4. Phases of the Long Wave in Prices (Rostow).

comfortably into a 50-year wave or with the evidence for such waves found in other measures of economic activity.

It can be argued (Warren [41]) that since the world abandoned the Gold Standard in the 1930s paper currencies have become a poor metric for the measurement of value. Although gold may itself not provide a perfect measure it could, nevertheless, be a better one than paper. Kondratieff himself based his own price-series on gold coin or gold-exchangeable currencies. Figure 23.5. illustrates the effect of re-expressing wholesale prices in terms of gold. The last price trough could now be as late as 1939 (making the third cycle 43 years long) and the subsequent peak would be dated at 1967 (47 years after the previous peak). For the believer in long waves this is a much more satisfactory interpretation.

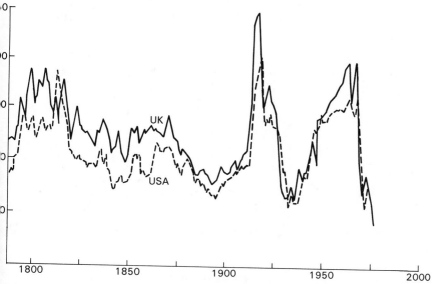

FIG. 23.5. Indices of Wholesale Prices in Gold Terms.
Source: Reproduced from Warren [41].

23.2.2. Output

It is more difficult to find unambiguous evidence for long waves in measures of physical output. One of the problems is that all output-series have strong underlying 'exponential' growth, a trend that makes any cyclical movement that may also exist very difficult to study. If attempts are made to remove the trend directly from the index, the cyclical residual is found to depend critically on the exact nature of the trend line chosen.

A more satisfactory approach is to express the index in growth rate terms. The resulting series is unfortunately so 'noisy' that it defeats the eye in any attempt to find a long wave by examination. Simple smoothing can help to

uncover the underlying movement, although there are statistical hazards
associated with smoothing which the researcher must constantly bear in mind.

Several authors have attempted detailed analyses of output data to test the
long-wave hypothesis, notably Van Duijn [38], [39] and Kucztnski [27], [28].
Van Duijn's chronology for the long wave, based on an analysis of 'crisis,
recession and depression years' and supported by the published historical
perceptions of the times is shown in Figure 23.6. Also shown are the phases of
the long wave suggested by Rostow and by the gold measure of wholesale
prices. Thus a period of prosperity is characterized by a high output growth

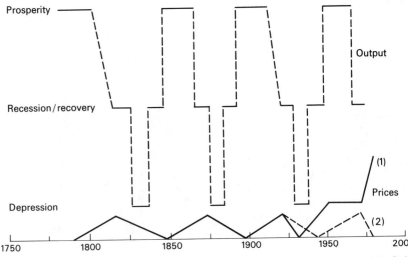

FIG. 23.6. Phases of the Long Wave. (Output—van Duijn; Prices—Rostow (1), Gold
deflated (2)).

rate (and rising prices), recession by declining growth (stagnant or falling
prices); depression is characterized by low growth (falling prices), recovery by
rising growth (stagnant or rising prices). The prosperity phase is typically 15 to
20 years in length, recession 8 to 10 years, depression and recovery each lasting
10 years. Two of the recession phases were delayed by wars (Napoleonic, World
War I). Van Duijn suggests that the current recession phase commenced in the
late 1960s. On the basis of the above chronology a price peak would have been
expected during the same period. Rostow's claim that it occurred in 195
places it too early. If, on the other hand, the price peak is still to come, it is either
late or the recession is unusually prolonged. The gold-adjusted peak, however
fits very well indeed.

Van Duijn has analysed data on industrial production for a number of
countries into *Juglars* (cycles of approximately 10-year periodicity) and has
examined the variation in average growth rate from cycle to cycle. In
aggregate the data are very broadly consistent with the chronology of Figure

23.6. At the individual-country level, however, there are significant deviations from the 'global' pattern. In the UK for example, industrial growth rose sharply into the late 1820s (a period of 'depression') and then declined on trend for the next 100 years. Growth was again high during the 'depression' phase of the 1930s. The picture is only slightly less inconsistent for the US.

Kucztnski has analysed aggregate industrial production data for the capitalist world. The smoothed data are shown in Figure 23.7 and demonstrate

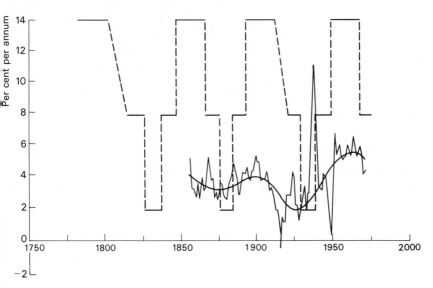

FIG. 23.7. Capitalist-World Industrial Production. (Growth rate in per cent per annum; 11-year moving average.)

how the variation in the growth of aggregate industrial production can be seen as broadly consistent with the long-wave hypothesis. Such a view is strengthened if data on the growth of world energy production (Cipolla [8]) are included (Figure 23.8); they correlate well with the growth of capitalist-world industrial production.

Three other measures of physical output will be given a brief mention because of their relevance to the theories discussed later in the chapter. The smoothed growth of agricultural production in the capitalist world (Kucztnski [28]) is shown in Figure 23.9. Wars so disrupt this series that little can be deduced from it, one way or the other. In contrast the data available on US mineral production (Figure 23.10) do show some sign of long-wave behaviour which is broadly consistent with Van Duijn's analysis.

Several of the theories suggest that investment should show cyclical behaviour more strongly than output as a whole. A graph of UK gross domestic fixed capital formation (less dwellings) expressed as a percentage of total national output (Figure 23.11) shows only the weakest evidence for the peak that would be expected around 1900. The figures for Denmark look very

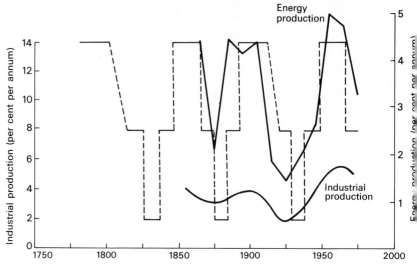

FIG. 23.8. Correlation between World Energy Production (10-year average growth rate, per cent per annum), Capitalist-World Industrial Production, and Van Duijn Long-Wave Chronology.

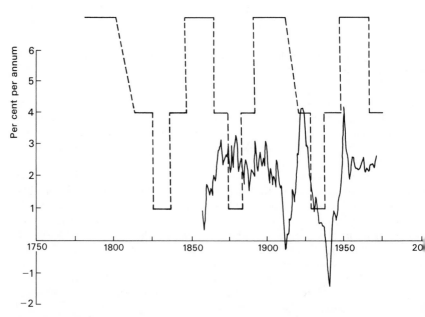

FIG. 23.9. Capitalist-World Agricultural Production. (Growth rate in per cent per annum; 11-year moving average.)

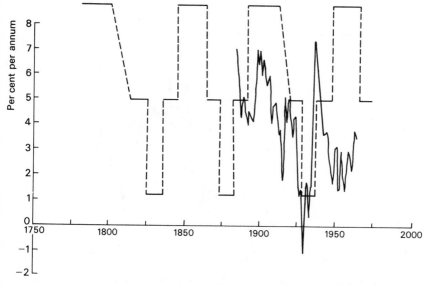

FIG. 23.10. US Mineral Production. (Growth rate in per cent per annum; 11-year moving average.)

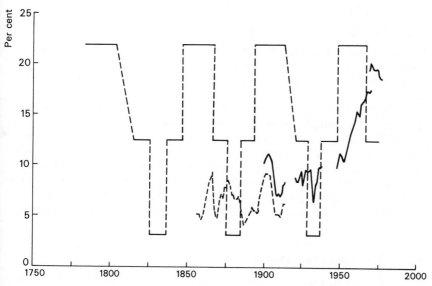

FIG. 23.11. UK Gross Domestic Fixed Capital Formation (Excluding Dwellings) as a Percentage of Total Output.

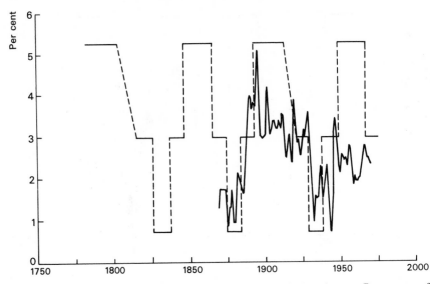

FIG. 23.12. Purchase of Capital by US Manufacturing Industries as a Percentage of GNP.

similar and there is no evidence whatsoever in the data for Italy. The converse is true for the US. Figure 23.12 demonstrates that the variation in the purchases of capital goods by US manufacturing industries expressed as a percentage of GNP conforms rather well with the long-wave hypothesis and Van Duijn's chronology. Similar results can be obtained for Germany (Glisman *et al.* [21]).

23.2.3. *Unemployment*

Unemployment data for the nineteenth century, where available, are fragmentary and not necessarily representative of the total labour force. The data on civilian unemployment for the UK and US are shown in Figures 23.13 and 23.14 respectively. Also included for the UK is a series for unemployment in British trade unions (1851–1926). Both pictures illustrate the very high (up to 25 per cent) unemployment rates associated with the Great Depression of the 1930s. The only other clear peak in unemployment is for the US in the 1890s. This falls too late to be associated with the depression of the 1880s and may have had more to do with the strong protectionist policies (McKinley tariffs) in the US at the time. The cyclical peaks in UK unemployment were higher in the 1880s than during the 'prosperity' phase of the early 1900s. However, they were not significantly higher than those in the preceding 'prosperity' phase of the 1850s.

23.3. Theoretical Explanations

A number of theories have been proposed in support of the long-wave hypothesis. They fall under five broad headings: (i) climatic; (ii) monetary; (iii) wars; (iv) demand/supply imbalance in specific sectors; (v) technological.

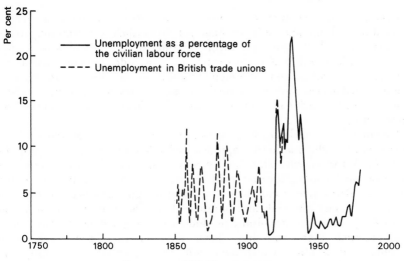

FIG. 23.13. UK Unemployment.

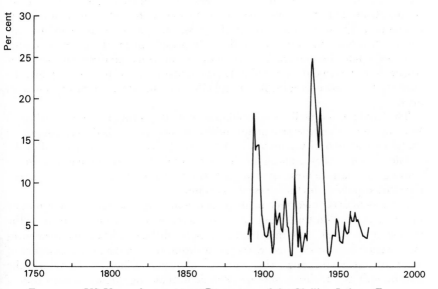

FIG. 23.14. US Unemployment as a Percentage of the Civilian Labour Force.

23.3.1. Climate-Induced Cycles

If climatic cycles exist, then, it is argued, they will induce sympathetic cycles i
agricultural output and prices which will work their way through to th
economy as a whole. An early theory postulated 50-year cycles in sunspc
activity as the origin of climatic variations. A well-documented eleven-yea
sun-spot cycle exists, and, although it would not be expected on physica
grounds, evidence is claimed (Dewey [14]) for a 54-year sun-spot cycle. Ther
is some direct evidence for regular variations in climate—rainfall in the UK
for example.

The only direct agricultural data examined by the author are the series fo
agricultural production in the capitalist world (Figure 23.9), and a series fo
Irish and British wheat yields. Neither of these has provided any evidence fo
long-wave behaviour. However, evidence is claimed for 50-year cycles in tre
rings [14]. Price cycles of course do exist for agricultural products—in commo
with many other materials and products. It has been argued (Rostow an
Kennedy [36]) that if agricultural products are aggregated together with othe
raw materials then there have been cycles in their prices relative t
manufactured products which have induced 50-year waves in supply an
investment. This theory will be described at greater length in section 23.3.5

23.3.2. Monetary Explanations

Some authors studying the long wave in the 1930s suggested that the major gol
discoveries of the 1850s in California and Australia and those of the 1880s an
1890s in Australia, Alaska, and the Transvaal caused the upswing in prices c
the 1850s and 1900s. As most industrialized countries were on the Gol
Standard at that time these dicoveries increased the amount of money i
circulation. This fact, coupled with the theory that when in the long term th
supply of money increases faster than the supply of goods, prices will rise
provides a plausible explanation of at least one influence on nineteenth-centur
prices. However, gold discoveries by themselves do not help to explain th
earlier price peaks around 1780 (in the US) and 1815 or the inflation of recen
years.

The Gold Standard effectively collapsed with the outbreak of the First Worl
War and since then the proponents of this theory have looked increasingly t
the general availability of money as the cause of price waves—in particular th
restrictive monetarist policies of the 1920s and 1930s have been accused o
causing the last depression just as some economists now blame curren
monetarist policies for the present recession.

If monetarists are correct in their assertion that expansion of the mone
supply per unit of output causes prices to increase then the management of th
money supply could explain at least some of the difference between nineteenth
and twentieth-century price levels. In addition there have been a number o
major institutional changes this century—abolition of the Gold Standard, th
advent, with Keynesian economics, of deficit financing, the nationalization o
major industries, the establishment of the Welfare State, and the concentratio

of power in trade unions—all of which have exerted expansionary pressure on the financial sector.

23.3.3. Wars

Another cause of rapid monetary expansion is war. There is a striking correlation between major wars and the sharpest peaks in wholesale prices, as illustrated in Figure 23.15. The War of Independence, the Napoleonic Wars, the American Civil War, and the First World War were funded, according to Galbraith [20], by an expansion of the money supply, either directly by the printing of money (the pound first came into circulation in the Napoleonic Wars, and the 'greenback' in the American Civil War), or indirectly by the suspension of specie (cash) payments and the subsequent issuing of notes.

It is therefore not implausible to theorize that all the observed variations in prices since 1750 have been caused by variations in the supply of money—wartime monetary expansion being responsible for the sharpest peaks and gold discoveries, or the peacetime (mis)management of the money supply being responsible for the slower movements.

Even if this is accepted, however, we are still left with a residual question: has this all been a random process which just by chance appears to be periodic, or have monetary conditions themselves, even war, been dictated by cyclical behaviour having its origin in the management of the 'real' economy?

23.3.4. Demand/Supply Imbalance in the Capital Goods Sector

A system dynamics model of a hypothetical economy (but broadly characteristic of the US) is being developed at the Massachusetts Institute of Technology (MIT)—see, for example, Forrester [16, 18] and Graham and Senge [23]. It is being constructed by the successive linking together of a number of economic sectors (consumer goods, capital goods, financial, etc.). In its early, single (consumer) sector phase the model exhibited a 4- to 5-year business cycle having its origin in inventory and order-book control, and a 20-year Kuznets cycle associated with the accumulation of fixed capital—plant, machinery, buildings, etc. (Mass [30]).

When a sector producing capital goods was added (Figure 23.16) the model exhibited long-wave behaviour. The waves were strongest in variables such as the output and capital stock of the capital goods sector, but also propagated in an attenuated form to the non-capital parts of the economy. They had a periodicity of 40 to 60 years, an amplitude which varied from wave to wave, and were irregular in shape. These oscillations are endogenous to the model, i.e. it has a natural 'ringing' mode of 50-year periodicity which is excited by any external stimulus, even a random one.

The primary cause of the wave was traced to the requirement that the capital goods sector must provide its own capital goods. A steadily rising demand for capital goods arising from the consumer sector causes the capital sector to perceive, through the lengthening of its order-book, the need for more capacity, and it places orders on itself accordingly. This positive feedback loop, strengthened by several others associated with the managerial response to the consequential delivery delays, escalating prices, and profitable investment

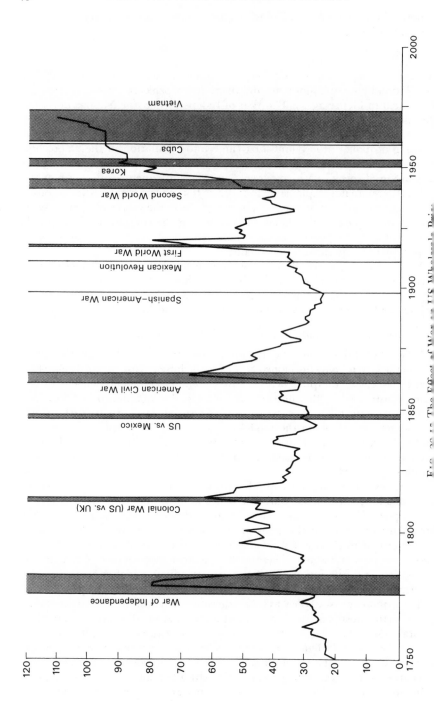

FIG. 20.1. The Effect of War on US Wholesale Price

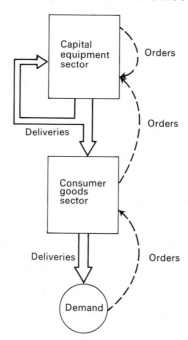

FIG. 23.16. Two-Sector Model of an Economy.

opportunities, leads to an over-expansion of the capital sector. In due course, as order-books are reduced, the over-capacity becomes manifest, ordering declines, and the feedback loops operate in reverse. Ultimately, in a growing economy, demand from the consumer sector overtakes the capacity of the capital sector to supply but, because of the long lead-times associated with the installation of new capital, a period of under-capacity persists until the new (over-compensating) upswing gets under way.

The MIT model is very complex but the behaviour of such a system can be illustrated with a highly simplified and idealized model (Figure 23.17). The capital goods sector possesses a capital stock K having a productivity k (i.e. k is the ratio of output to capital at full-capacity working). The sector's output P is divided between deliveries D_C to the consumer sector and deliveries D_K of new capital to the capital goods sector. For simplicity it will be assumed that D_K takes total precedence over D_C and that there is no delay between ordering and delivery. If it is assumed that a fraction $1/T_K$ of the capital stock is retired each year (T_K is a measure of the asset life), then K is determined by the equation

$$dK/dt = D_K - K/T_K.$$

Consider now the order-book size B, determined by the equation

$$dB/dt = D - D_C$$

where D is the demand (flow of orders) for capital goods arising from the

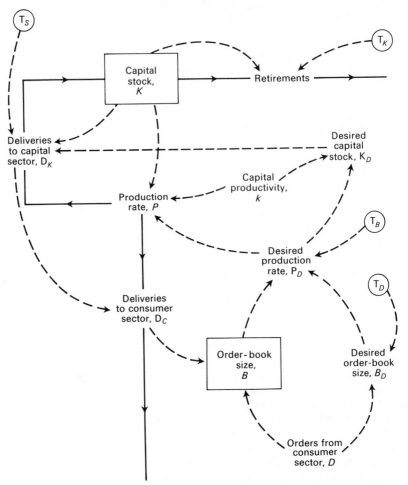

FIG. 23.17. A Simplified System Dynamics Model of the Capital Goods Sector.

consumer goods sector. D_K does not appear in this equation because of the assumption of instantaneous delivery of the capital sector's orders.

It is now helpful to introduce the concepts of a 'desired' capital stock K_D and a 'desired' order-book size B_D. These will, in general, be different from the actual values K and B. These are the levels of K and B that 'management' would like to have in order to meet current levels of demand. Thus D_D, for example, would probably be related to D by a relationship of the form $B_D = D \cdot T_D$, where T_D is related to the number of 'years of cover' desired.

It will be assumed that management attempts to schedule production in order to restore the order-book to the level B_D within a time-scale characterized by T_B, i.e. the desired production rate is

$$P_D = (B - B_D)/T_B, \text{ if } B > B_D$$
$$= 0, \text{ if } B < B_D.$$

The actual production rate P will be given by

$$P = P_D, \text{ if } P_D < kK$$
$$= kK, \text{ if } P_D > kK,$$

i.e. the production must lie within the sector's capacity constraint.

All that remains now is to determine D_K, the rate of delivery of capital goods to the capital sector. The desired capital stock K_D will be dictated by the desired production, thus

$$K_D = P_D/k.$$

Management is assumed to place orders such that any shortfall in capital stock $(K_D - K)$ will be eliminated within a time-scale T_S, thus

$$D_K = (K_D - K)/T_S, \text{ if } K_D > K$$
$$= 0, \text{ if } K_D < K.$$

In this simplified model the consumer sector then has to 'make do' with deliveries met from the residual production, i.e.

$$D_C = P - D_K.$$

The model is now fully specified at the structural level. In general the solution of the equations will fall into alternating phases:

(a) a growth phase in which $K_D > K$ (deficient capacity) and during which K and B are determined by the coupled equations

$$dK/dt + (1/T_S + 1/T_K)K = B/(kT_ST_D) - DT_D/(kT_ST_B)$$
$$dB/dt - B/kT_ST_B = D(1 - T_D/(kT_ST_B)) - (k + 1/T_S)K;$$

(b) a depression phase in which $K_D < K$ (excess capacity), during which capital stock just decays away according to

$$dK/dt = -K/T_K$$

and B tends towards an equilibrium level $D(T_B + T_D)$.

A set of results for $k = 0.16$, $T_D = 0$, $T_B = 2.5$ years, $T_S = 6.0$ years, and $T_K = 40$ years is shown in Figure 23.18. This set of parameters yields a long wave of approximately 50-years periodicity.

While there is no doubt that the model described is a gross over-simplification of reality its behaviour is surprisingly robust, both to parameter changes and to structural improvements (e.g. allocating deliveries on a pro-rata basis rather than giving absolute precedence to the capital goods sector). The key structural feature is the feedback loop associated with the need for the capital sector to supply its own capital goods.

More recently, the MIT model has been extended to include both household and financial sectors. Two mechanisms associated with these sectors, although believed not to induce long-wave behaviour on their own, are found to resonate and strengthen the oscillations originating in the capital sector. They are a

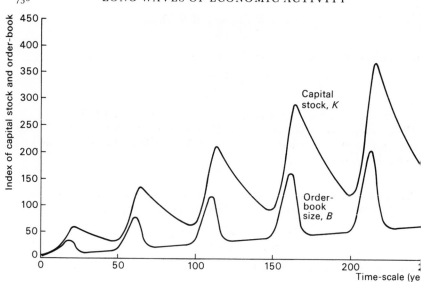

FIG. 23.18 Long Waves Generated by the Simplified Model.

trade-off in the household sector's utility between durable goods and leisure time and, secondly, the balancing of debt in relation to asset values. Over borrowing in the expansion phase, when profitability and asset values are high, leads to a financial restructuring (including some default on debt) when asset values fall and profitability is poor. This more recent version also demonstrates how pressures from the real economy cause a monetary expansion in the upswing, which in its turn fuels inflation. The sequence reverses during the recession/depression phase.

The model has not, at least to the author's knowledge, been validated against US data but is advocated more for the qualitative insights it gives into economic behaviour. However, the evidence that exists for long waves in price, unemployment, and the purchasing of capital equipment by US manufacturing industry lends some support to Forrester's theory. The more crucial data that might display fluctuations in the output or capital stock of the capital sector appear not to be available.

23.3.5. Demand/Supply Imbalance in the Primary Goods Sector

In the preceding theory it was the sector producing capital goods which provided the driving force for long waves; in the theory discussed in this section it is the sector producing primary goods—food, raw materials, and energy. Details of the theory and an analysis of economic history based on it can be found in Rostow and Kennedy [36].

In brief, the theory's proponents argue that alternative periods of over- and under-capacity occur in the primary sector. This failure to follow smoothly the steadily rising demand for these products stems from four causes: the long delays that follow the emergence of a profit possibility and the investment decisions designed to exploit it; the long gestation periods associated with the opening up of new capacity (agricultural areas, mines, oil fields, etc.); the delays between the completion of an investment and its maximum efficient exploitation; and finally, the lumpiness or non-incremental nature of capacity additions to the sector.

The following sequence of events is believed to occur. The demand from manufacturing industry for primary products increases smoothly and reaches a point where it overtakes the existing supply. There are substantial delays before the industry believes it worth-while to develop a new 'lump' of capacity, takes the decisions to invest, and installs and makes the new capacity productive. In the mean-time, supply and demand are out of balance, the price of primary products rises relative to manufactured goods, profitability improves, and investment is attracted preferentially into the sector. Ultimately the new facilities come on stream and overshoot the capacity required to meet the demand. Stocks accumulate, relative prices fall, and further expansion plans are shelved. Investment now swings back to manufacturing until the rising demand once more catches up with the stagnating or declining capacity.

The long-wave behaviour of the model described by Rostow and Kennedy appears not to be fully endogenous in the sense that Forrester's is. It is assumed that the resources available to the primary sector will fall below their long-run balanced growth path—because of the investment delays characteristic of the sector—and that the shortfall will disappear over a period of 40 years. The cycle then repeats. It is the imposition of this assumption on the model that induces a resonant response, albeit of a form consistent with the theory, in the economy as a whole.

23.3.6. Technology and Innovation

This is one of the oldest of the long-wave theories and dates back at least to Schumpeter [37]. It has recently been given a new momentum by the work of Mensch [31, 32] and Freeman et al. [2]. Schumpeter's original theory (cf. Fels [15] for an abridged version) started from the view that innovation (the creation of new products and businesses out of previous inventions) was the driving force behind growth in a capitalist economy and that the level of innovative activity varied substantially from one period to another. Exceptional entrepreneurs saw opportunities in new technology for high (monopoly) profits. Successful exploitation attracted a 'swarm' of imitators and improvers. Provided the technological breakthrough was sufficiently basic (for example, the steam-engine) this swarming created a major wave of new investment and a period of growth and prosperity. Fierce competitive pressures then eroded profit margins and led ultimately to stagnation and depression. The economy then had to await the next swarm of innovative activity. Subsequent workers claimed that the profit erosion would be accelerated by wage pressures during the high-employment prosperity phase and that cost push inflation would be stimulated. As a consequence there would be a progressive shift over time from expansionary investment to cost-saving

innovation and rationalizing investment which would lead to unemployme
during the recession.

Schumpeter's theory embraced concepts such as 'disequilibrium' ar
'imperfect competition', and placed the emphasis firmly on the supply side
the economy with technologically driven, rather than demand-drive
investment. The Schumpeterian economy is not homogeneous but is made u
of industries, of different ages, growing at different rates and subject to differe
rates of technological change. It passes through periods of concentrate
structural change during which older industries mature or decline while ne
industries are born and grow. Schumpeter did not give a satisfacto
explanation for why these periods of restructuring might occur at approx
mately 50-year intervals.

Marchetti [29] has pointed out that these new industrial sectors have, c
each occasion, been based on a new energy form. The upswing of the 1950s an
1960s was based on oil-fuelled technologies, oil achieving its maximu
penetration of the energy market in the recession of the 1970s. The previo
upswing, in the early 1900s, was fuelled by coal, which achieved its maximu
market share in the recession of the 1920s. Before that there was hay (anim.
power) and wood.

Mensch argues, on the basis of his analysis of UK, US, and German dat
that innovation has indeed proceeded at an uneven pace. 'Basic' innovatio
are observed to cluster at 50-year intervals (Figure 23.19), the last clust
occurring in the 1930s. The innovation surges appear to be coincident with th
depression phases of Van Duijn's chronology. The clustering is brought abo
by a shortening, during the depression, of the lead-times between inventio

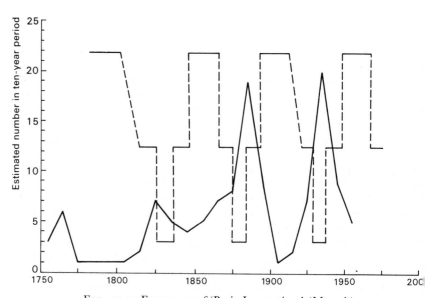

FIG. 23.19 Frequency of 'Basic Innovations' (Mensch).

and innovation. Thus depression triggers the burst of innovative activity which in its turn stimulates the subsequent period of enhanced economic growth. As the wave runs its course improvement innovations become the preoccupation rather than product innovations, a period that Mensch calls 'the technological stalemate'.

Mensch's work is currently the subject of much debate. There is dispute concerning the definition, selection, and dating of the innovations studied. Although the conclusion that clustering did occur in the 1930s is not challenged, the more general conclusion that clustering is strongly correlated with depression is disputed. Freeman *et al.* cite counter-evidence of substantial innovative activity during the post-Second World War boom. They also produce evidence to suggest that 'significant' inventions show a tendency to cluster, but again the clusters occur at times of both depression and prosperity. The claim that the conditions of depression stimulate innovation is rejected on the grounds that the analysis of lead-times does not stand up to scrutiny, that evidence exists showing that research and development expenditures and general patenting activity are reduced during the most severe depressions, and that many case histories quote depression as an inhibiting influence. It has also been suggested by Forrester that the clustering of innovation is a consequence of the long wave, albeit one that leads to amplification, not a direct cause. His theory does not require innovation to cluster but does suggest that there will be a time, near the bottom of the wave, when investment becomes attractive once more, and the climate for product innovation will be much improved. This suggests, however, that the peaks in innovation should be more closely associated with recovery rather than depression.

Freeman *et al.* have put forward their own variant of the technological theory of long waves. It is very similar to Schumpeter's original but puts great emphasis on the concept of 'new technological systems'—clusters of technically and economically interrelated basic innovations, of wide adaptability, which lead to the creation of entirely new industries and stimulate growth and change in some existing ones. They argue that it is the swarming (or diffusion) process around these new technological systems that is important rather than, as Mensch suggests, the clustering at a particular time of a number of unrelated basic innovations. The expansionary phase to which this swarming gives rise is followed by a further wave of secondary and induced inventions and innovations with the emphasis shifting towards process improvement.

Their studies lead them to conclude that the timing of a number of important scientific discoveries played a crucial role in initiating the cluster of innovations of the 1930s. However, they do not believe this was depression-induced. Thus, like Schumpeter, no clear mechanism is put forward to account for the observed 50-year periodicity. They do accept, however, that depression may induce the social and political changes that are needed to enable the new technological systems to evolve. They also accept that Forrester-type mechanisms associated with the capital goods sector may add to the multiplier effects.

Finally they draw attention to the international dimension of the long wave. It appears to be a global phenomenon and individual countries have deviated significantly from the world-wide pattern. Just as each country needs to be considered as a heterogeneous collection of industries, so the world also must be viewed as a collection of nations at different stages of technological and economic development. One particular feature to which attention is drawn is the way in which the focus of technological leadership and economic activity has moved from the UK, to Europe, to the US, and now, possibly, to Japan during the successive long waves.

23.4. Summary and Conclusions

There is sufficient empirical evidence, taken as a whole, to make the long-wave hypothesis at least plausible. The strongest evidence comes from price data and is supported by the behaviour of long-term interest rates, world industrial and energy production, and unemployment. Output data provide less support at the national level. This may, however, not be too significant if the wave really is one of periodic industrial restructuring with technological leadership and the focus of economic activity moving from one geographical area to another.

The main features of the wave are summarized in Figure 23.20. The times at which prices and output growth pass their high and low points are taken from

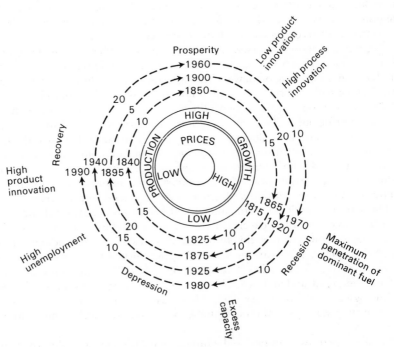

FIG. 23.20. A Long-Wave 'Clock'.

the gold-deflated wholesale price and capitalist-world industrial production indices. The clock revolves every 50 to 55 years. The periods of rising prices, falling output growth, falling prices, and rising output growth come around in the same sequence in each of the three cycles shown. The intervals between peaks and troughs are irregular. Also marked on the 'dial' are Van Duijn's estimates of the prosperity, recession, depression, and recovery phases and the appropriate timing of other economic phenomena referred to in the text.

There are several theoretical explanations; they are not necessarily mutually exclusive. It appears that the variations in absolute prices may be associated with variations in the money supply, whether brought about by war, gold discoveries, or printing. However, it is still possible that these monetary variations themselves are a consequence of what is happening in the real economy. This view is certainly supported by Forrester's model, in which the periodic variations in the real economy have their origins in the over- and under-expansion of the capital goods industries. Rostow on the other hand argues that it is the variations in relative prices, between primary and manufactured products, that is important. In this case waves in the real economy are driven by the over- and under-expansion of the primary sector.

The Schumpeterian theories suggest that technology plays a key role. In one modern version the clustering in time of 'basic' innovations is the prime cause of the recovery and prosperity phases. In another it is the swarming of technically and economically interrelated innovations around one or more of these 'basic' innovations (irrespective of their birth date) that stimulates high growth. In both, competition erodes profits, and the subsequent technological developments shift in emphasis away from product to process innovation, with rising unemployment, stagnation, and then depression. The theories diverge again in explaining why the new burst of innovative activity arises. Mensch argues that the depression itself is the stimulus. Freeman *et al.* argue that it is not, but do not substitute any really clear alternative—except to draw attention to the role of scientific discovery in the 1930s and the possibility of depression-induced social and political change clearing the way for the emergence of a new technological system. The clustering of innovation would be an effect, albeit an amplifying one, rather than a cause, in Forrester's model.

If such a cycle does exist then it is of considerable importance at the present time. A peak around the late 1960s or early 1970s would not only explain the much slower growth experienced since then relative to the rest of the post-war period but would indicate that the oil price shocks of the 1970s might at most be responsible for a speeding up or exacerbation of the shift to slow growth rather than acting as a prime cause (either directly or via the policy responses to them). It would also suggest that a period of relatively slow growth, and probably therefore of high unemployment, is likely to continue for the next decade or so. Whether this will be the case it is impossible to tell. All that can be said is that current developments, in particular the development of a generic new technology—electronic data processing, telecommunications, and associated technology—have some of the features of a Kondratieff downswing, and few more-conventional forecasting approaches see any early end to the current slow-growth era.

Bibliography

SECTION A

The following references (all published since this chapter was written) provide the reader with a comprehensive overview of long-wave theory:
[1] FREEMAN, C. (ed.). *Long Waves in the World Economy.* (Butterworths, 1983) contains a collection of papers from many of the workers currently active in the field.
[2] FREEMAN, C., CLARK, J., and SOETE, L. *Unemployment and Technical Innovation* (Frances Pinter, 1982) provides an analysis of the technologically based theories, including the work of Schumpeter and Mensch.
[3] VAN DUIJN, J. J. *The Long Wave in Economic Life* (George Allen and Unwin, 1983) contains a historical review, an analysis of the empirical evidence, and describes most of the current theories.

Most of the time-series used to illustrate the empirical basis for long waves are taken from:
[4] MITCHELL, B. R. *Abstract of British Historical Statistics* (Cambridge University Press, 1962 and 1971).
[5] —— —— *European Historical Statistics 1750–1970* (Macmillan, 1975).
[6] London and Cambridge Economic Services. *The British Economy: Key Statistics, 1900–1970* (Times Newspapers, 1971).
[7] US Department of Commerce, *Historical Statistics of the United States* (1975).

SECTION B

Other references cited in the text are:
[8] CIPOLLA, C. M. *The Economic History of World Population* (Penguin, 1979).
[9] CLARK, J., FREEMAN, C., and SOETE, L. 'Long Waves and Technological Developments in the 20th Century', Bochum Conference on *Wirtschaftliche Wechsellagen und sozialer Wandel*, 1980.
[10] —— ——, —— ——, —— —— 'Long Waves, Inventions and Innovations', *Futures*, **13**/4 (1981), 308–22.
[11] CLARKE, H. 'Physical Economy', *Railway Register* (1847).
[12] CLEARY, M. N. and HOBBS, G. D. 'The Fifty Year Cycle: A Look at the Empirical Evidence', in Freeman [1].
[13] DELBEKE, J. 'Criticism and Classification of Real Long Wave Theories', Discussion Paper, No. 8001, Workshop on Quantitative Economic History, Katholieke Universiteit Leuven, Centrum voor Economische Studien, 1980.
[14] DEWEY, E. R. Foundation for the Study of Cycles, *Cycles Journal* (June 1970).
[15] FELS, R. (ed.). Abridged edn. of Schumpeter, J. A., *Business Cycles: A Theoretical, Historical and Statistical Analysis of the Capitalist Process* (McGraw Hill, 1964).
[16] FORRESTER, J. W. 'Business Structure, Economic Cycles and National Policy', MIT System Dynamics Group, D-2245-2 (1975); also in *Futures* (June 1976).
[17] —— —— 'New Perspectives for Growth over the Next Thirty Years', MIT System Dynamics Group, D-2251-1 (1975).
[18] —— —— 'Economic Perspective', MIT System Dynamics Group, D-2667-1 (1977).
[19] FREEMAN, C. 'The Kondratieff Long Waves, Technical Change and Unemployment', in OECD, *Structural Determinants of Employment and Unemployment* (Paris, 1979), pp. 181–96.
[20] GALBRAITH, J. K. *Money: Whence it Came, Where it Went* (Andre Deutsch, 1975).
[21] GLISMAN, H. H., RODEMER, H., and WOLTER, F. 'Zur Natur der

Wachtstumsschwaeche in der Bundesrepublik Deutschland', Discussion Paper, No. 55, University of Keil (1978).

[22] —— ——, —— ——, —— —— 'Lang Wellen Wirtschaftlichen Wachstum', Discussion Paper, No. 74, University of Keil (1980).

[23] GRAHAM, A. K. and SENGE, P. M. 'A Long Wave Hypothesis of Innovation', MIT System Dynamics Group, D-3164-1 (1980).

[24] KLEINKNECHT, A. 'Innovation, Akkumulation und Krise. Uberlegungen zu den langen Wellen der Konjunktur vor dem hintergrund neuer Ergebnisse der historischen Innovationsforschung', *Prokla*, **35** (1979).

[25] KONDRATIEFF, N. D. 'Die langen Wellen der Konjunktur', *Archiv für Sozialwissenschaft und Sozialpolitik*, LXVI (1926), 573–609.

[26] —— —— 'The Long Waves in Economic Life', *Review of Economic Statistics*, XVII (1935), 105–15.

[27] KUCZTNSKI, T. 'Spectral Analysis and Cluster Analysis as Mathematical Methods for the Periodization of Historical Processes—A Comparison of Results Based on Data About the Development of Production and Innovation in the History of Capitalism', in *Kondratieff Cycles—Appearance or Reality?*, Proc. of the 7th International Economic History Congress, Edinburgh (1978), Vol. 2, pp. 79–86.

[28] —— —— 'Have there Been Differences Between the Growth Rates in Different Periods of the Development of the Capitalist World Economy Since 1850?—An Application of Cluster Analysis in Time Series Analysis', *Historisch-Sozialwissenschaftliche Forschungen*, Stuttgart, **6** (1980).

[29] MARCHETTI, C. 'Society as a Learning System: Discovery, Invention and Innovation Cycles Revisited', Meeting of the Italian Association for Marketing Studies, Turin, 1980.

[30] MASS, N. J. *Economic Cycles: An Analysis of Underlying Causes* (Wright-Allan Press, 1975).

[31] MENSCH, G. 'Das technologische Patt', *Umschau Verlag* (1975).

[32] —— —— *Stalemate in Technology* (Ballinger, 1979).

[33] ROSTOW, W. W. *The Process of Economic Growth* (Clarendon Press, 1960).

[34] —— —— 'Kondratieff, Schumpeter and Kuznets: Trend Periods Revisited', *Journal of Economic History*, XXXV (1975), pp. 719, 753.

[35] —— —— *The World Economy: History and Prospect* (Macmillan, 1978).

[36] ROSTOW, W. W. and KENNEDY, M. 'A Simple Model of the Kondratieff Cycle', in Uselding, P. (ed.), *Research in Economic History*, Vol. 4 (JAI Press, 1979).

[37] SCHUMPETER, J. A. *Business Cycles* (New York, 1939).

[38] VAN DUIJN, J. J. 'The Long Wave in Economic Life', *De Economist*, **125**/4 (1977), 544–76.

[39] —— —— 'Comment on Van der Zwan's Paper', in Kuiper, S. K. and Lanjouw, G. J. (eds.), *Prospects for Economic Growth* (North-Holland Publishing Co., 1979), pp. 223–33.

[40] VAN GELDEREN, J. 'Springvloed: beschouwingen over Industrieele ontwikkeling en prijsbeweging', *De Nieuwe Tijd*, XVIII (1913), pp. 253–77, 369–84, and 445–64.

[41] WARREN, J. P. *The 50-Year Boom-Bust Cycle* (Warren, Cameron, 1982).

PART VI

INDUSTRIAL POLICY ISSUES

24

Principles of Resource Allocation

H. G. JONES

24.1. Introduction

Most of the chapters in this book have so far been concerned mainly with the determinants of *aggregate* economic activity and numerous factors—domestic, international, historical, and policy—which influence it in the UK. Apart from some aspects of Chapter 9 on public finance, very little has been said about the issue of resource use *within* that macroeconomic aggregate; the distribution of resources between different industries and sectors of the economy; the efficiency with which resources are used in various parts of the economy; and the economic system or systems—competition, planning, or some mix of the two—which constitute the method by which resources are allocated.

These issues are not of course independent of the behaviour of the economy in aggregate. The reasons for studying them separately are first that *microeconomic* resource allocation matters generally have their effect only slowly; second, the method of analysis has traditionally been rather different as elaborated upon in Chapter 1; and third, and by no means unimportant, the *linkages* between underlying principles and application, on which this book tries to focus, are generally far less well established in the microeconomic area than in the macroeconomic sphere, notwithstanding continuing controversy in the latter.

In addition, the types of question raised above are themselves interdependent. Choices between competition, planning, and public ownership (and between various combinations of them) will all in principle influence both the distribution of resources and changes in it over time, *and* the efficiency with which those resources are used. More general issues of fairness, equity, and other possible objectives of society are also affected. Much economic analysis has been devoted to these matters over many years, and no overview of the economic system in the UK would be complete without some description of the various strands of thought involved.

The approach adopted in this section is as follows: in this chapter the question is addressed of whether economic analysis can give any *general* guidance on how best to determine the allocation of resources in an economy, and of what problems emerge in such an approach. This means that this chapter is overtly more theoretical in nature than preceding chapters or those that follow. The next two chapters look at two major aspects of the way in which resources in practice are allocated in the UK, namely performance of nationalized industries in the public sector and competition policy governing behaviour in the private sector. These chapters bring out the extent to which decisions in these two areas have or have not been related to or rooted in the theoretical basis described in this chapter. Chapter 27 examines one industry of sufficient importance to be looked at in its own right, namely North Sea oil. The final chapter of this section then looks more generally at industrial policy and its application over the medium term in the UK.

Although economists' attempts to analyse the general issues associated with resource allocation are often couched in terms of relatively abstract theories and models, it is worth stressing at the start that the central questions of resource allocation—of how the scarce resources of any society *are, could be*, or *should be* allocated amongst the immense variety of competing activities—are at the centre of many areas of political discussion, polemical punditry, and public concern. When, for example, it appears that too few resources are being allocated to the provision of inexpensive and adequate accommodation in Britain, parliamentary questions are asked, leading articles written, documentary television programmes prepared, and new charities formed. Government ministers and economic commentators lament the relatively low proportion of total resources that is invested in modern equipment for British industry. Newspaper headlines insist that 'too large' a proportion of the nation's resources is allocated to a particular industry, 'too little' of a certain service is available, or demand that governments, international organizations, firms, trade unions, or individuals act immediately to alleviate or eliminate a shortage or surplus of energy, paper, beef, butter, or whatever other commodity is currently a cause of sub-editorial concern. To attempt therefore to derive some general principles for answering such questions is of very direct relevance to people's lives and well-being.

An allocation of society's resources can, at any point in time, be viewed as a complete and comprehensive description of the quantities of each and every good and service supplied or used by the government, every productive unit, every household, and every distributive unit in the economy. Although the above description is imprecise, it does convey the vast scale of the problem involved in discussing the allocation of resources. We can however illuminate most of the central problems associated with resource allocation with only modest recourse to formal theorizing.

What, however, are these central problems? At the very least, it is necessary that we discuss:

(a) In what sense, if any, can a particular allocation be described as superior, inferior, or equivalent to some other allocation?—which leads naturally to a discussion of the possibility of a 'best' or 'optimal' allocation of society's resources.

(b) How is the actual allocation of resources in an economy determined, and can any particular method of determination be said to lead to an 'optimal' allocation?

Problem (a) is inevitably associated with the distinction between 'positive' and 'normative' economics which has become widely appreciated since the publication of a celebrated book of essays by Friedman [9] and a well-known textbook by Lipsey [13]. As was seen in Chapter 1, a 'positive' theory is concerned with what *is*—with *prediction* and *explanation* of economic phenomena—whereas a 'normative' theory is concerned with what *should be*— i.e. with *prescription*. Now, it is clear that problem (a) must lead us into the territory of the normative—with all the associated difficulties of making 'value-judgements'. Some writers would assert that if economics is to be considered a science then it has no business with the comparison of alternative allocations— with questions of '*too* much' and '*too* little' and '*better*' or '*worse*'. We return to these questions in section 24.2 where a relatively non-controversial method of limited comparison is discussed.

Problem (b) has been central to economics for most of the three centuries or so in which men have attempted to systematically analyse and study the economic framework of the communities in which they live. There exists, of course, a vast variety of methods whereby the actual allocation of resources in any economy can be determined. Anthropologists have discovered in primitive societies elaborate systems of custom and taboo whereby individuals are assigned to tasks, and the products of labour assigned to individuals. In the Soviet Union and other Communist countries a very large part of the precise allocation of resources is determined within the context of an elaborate plan prepared by the State Planning Commission, Gosplan, and approved at various levels of the political system.[1] In the developed economies of the Western world very large corporations control a significant proportion of total economic activity, and within these corporations varying degrees of hierarchical authority can determine the allocation of resources. Nevertheless, in almost all societies at almost all periods of history at least some part of the actual allocation of resources has been determined by the more or less unfettered free trade of individuals in markets in which the relative prices of commodities, which determine the rates at which different commodities are exchanged for each other, play a central role as indicators of the relative scarcity of commodities and as incentives to individual action. That the price system can co-ordinate a myriad of individual decision-makers in the economy in an ordered manner and produce an 'optimal' allocation of resources is a proposition that has been central to economic and political thought for at least 200 years. In section 24.3 of this chapter we attempt to illustrate the ways in which free-market competition and the associated free-market prices *could* satisfy the claims to order and efficiency and, in so doing, we lay the foundations of a discussion of the strengths and weaknesses of free competition as an allocative mechanism.

24.2. The Efficient Allocation of Resources

24.2.1. *Preferences and Utility*

Most people have some views on the current allocation of resources in the

[1] For an interesting description and discussion of this system see Nove [17], Chap. 2.

United Kingdom—and their views often depend on their own position give1 the current allocation. Some maintain that too much or too little is spent on th aircraft industry, 'luxuries', education, defence, or property 'speculation' Others argue that there are too few doctors, too many students, too many road: or too few houses. Even when a consensus appears to exist, it often breaks dow: when the full implications of a choice are realized. Any allocation of resource that is considered ideal by one individual or group is likely to be anathema t another. The conflicts of interest and diversity of opinion and preference tha are characteristic of most societies constitute formidable difficulties in an attempt to devise criteria whereby one particular allocation of resources can b said to be superior to another. Moreover, it is not generally thougl appropriate to try and overcome such difficulties by assuming a set of 'socia preferences that are defined independently of the individuals of which society composed—for most philosophical and political traditions have been base upon the rejection of an anthropomorphic conception of the state. Sinc economists traditionally assume that, in all but a very limited class of cases, th individual is the best judge of his own welfare, it should be clear that attemp to indulge in the normative comparison of different available allocations, base upon the diversity of individual preferences as to the alternatives, will at be provoke criticism and at worst be impossible.

It is useful if we state the problem formally. In general, a very large numb of feasible allocations of resources will be available in any economy. A allocation can, in principle, be described by a very long list (or, mathematicians would say, vector), $\bar{X}$, of numbers $X_1, X_2 \ldots X_n$ where t particular values of X_1, X_2, etc. are the quantities supplied or used of each inp or output by the government, or by each firm, household, or distributor. Tht for example, X_1 might represent the output of rolled steel and X_2 the output candy floss in the particular allocation represented by $\bar{X}$. If we denote alternative allocation as $\bar{X}'$ then it is necessary to discuss whether there is a way, based upon the preferences of individuals between $\bar{X}$ and $\bar{X}'$, in which o: allocation can be said to be superior to the other.

The problem outlined above has been central to what is called 'welfa economics' for at least 150 years. Welfare economics is not, as might expected, the economics of the social services, but that body of econom analysis which, on the basis of explicit value-judgements, attempts to assess a1 compare different allocations of resources. For many years welfare econom was based upon the assumption that each individual could measure the 'utili' that he or she attached to alternative allocations, that the utilities of differe individuals could be compared with one another, and that, as a consequenc an allocation $\bar{X}$ could be said to be superior to an alternative allocation $\bar{X}'$ i generated a greater sum of total utility. The conceptual problems measurable utility combined with the profound difficulties of interperso1 comparisons of such utility led to the adoption of the so-called Pareto criteric upon which much of this chapter is based.

[2] V. Pareto, an Italian economist and sociologist, devised many of the central concept consumer theory and welfare economics.

4.2.2. The Pareto Criterion

'he Pareto criterion is very simple and apparently reasonable.

An allocation $\bar{X}$ is said to be *Pareto-superior* to an alternative allocation $\bar{X}'$ if, nd only if, (a) *some* individuals or firms are, given their own objectives, *better off* 1 $\bar{X}$ than in $\bar{X}'$, and (b) no individuals or firms are, given their objectives, worse ff in $\bar{X}$ than in $\bar{X}'$. Conversely, in this situation, $\bar{X}'$ is said to be *Pareto-inferior* to $\bar{X}$.

It is important to note that if some individuals or firms are better off and thers worse off in allocation $\bar{X}$ as compared with allocation $\bar{X}'$, then, given the 'areto criterion, we cannot say *anything* about the relative merits of $\bar{X}$ and $\bar{X}'$ nd the two allocations are said to be *Pareto-non-comparable*. Thus it is clear that he Pareto criterion is *very limited* in its applicability, for many of the most nportant and interesting problems in the comparison of allocations *do* involve ome individuals being better off, and others worse off. If only *one* individual is vorse off in allocation $\bar{X}$ compared with allocation $\bar{X}'$ then the allocations are 'areto-non-comparable *even if everybody else* is better off in $\bar{X}$. It is, nevertheless, useful starting-point, and has, as will be seen, been the basis of a number of ar-reaching policies and decisions in the real world. It provides a relatively nobjectionable method of comparing at least some alternative allocations, nd much of the remainder of the section is concerned with a discussion of the nplications of the criterion. We will return to an assessment of the strengths nd weaknesses of the Pareto criterion later in this chapter.

Given the Pareto criterion, it is possible to define a 'best' allocation of esources as follows:

An allocation of resources, $\bar{X}$, is said to be Pareto-efficient or *Pareto-optimal* if, n only if, there is no feasible alternative allocation that is Pareto-superior to $\bar{X}$—i.e. there is no possible way in which the resources can be reallocated so as o make some firms and individuals better off without making some others vorse off.

This definition clearly requires some comment. First, it is necessary to notice he inherent dangers in the word 'optimal'.[3] It is easy to become bewitched by anguage. Casual use of the word 'optimal' can easily lead one to believe that ne is referring to a 'best' allocation of resources in some absolute sense whereas 'areto optimality merely means that an allocation, $\bar{X}$, is better than any lternative allocation *which can be compared to $\bar{X}$ using the very limited Pareto criterion.* hus, for example, a situation in which one man lived in incredible luxury and verybody else in the population was starving could be Pareto-optimal if mproving the lot of the mass of the population involved the wealthy man ecoming worse off. Such is the price of attempting to systematically eschew nterpersonal comparisons of welfare. Second, as will become clear later in this ection, there will typically exist a very large number of possible Pareto-optima nd, unless we are prepared to make further assumptions, there will not be *any* vay in which we can compare one Pareto-optimal allocation with another.

The preceding description of a Pareto-efficient allocation of resources can be nade more precise by considering its implications for (a) the allocation of the

---

[3] This is the reason many writers prefer the description 'Pareto-efficient'.

various productive inputs between the different available production
tivities, (b) the allocation of the outputs of production between the vari
consumers in the economy, and (c) the precise composition of natio
output—i.e. exactly which commodities are produced and in what quantit
We refer to (a) as the problem of *technical efficiency*, to (b) as the problem
exchange efficiency, and to (c) as the problem of *the composition of output*. We n
consider each in turn.

24.2.3. Technical Efficiency

If an allocation of society's resources is to be Pareto-efficient then it is clear t
it must be impossible to reallocate the scarce production inputs so as to prod
more of *all* outputs or *more* of *some* and *no less* of *others*. We can clarify
meaning of this condition of technical efficiency by considering just two typi
production activities—say, the production of wheat and potatoes—wh
require the same two inputs—say, land and labour. Consider, to begin w
the production of wheat. We assume that both land and labour are required
production and that they are substitutable for one another in the sense tha
very large number of different *combinations* of land and labour can be used
produce the same total output of wheat. This ideas is illustrated in Figure 24
The curve *xx* in the diagram represents all the different combinations of la
and labour that, given the state of the technology, can be used to produc
given output of wheat—say, 100 tons. Thus, for example, the point Y in
figure represents a combination of OL^* of labour and ON^* of land which
produce 100 tons of wheat. Moves along the curve from left to right imj
reductions in the input of land and increases in the input of labour. The curv
given a convex shape (when viewed from the point marked O), capturing
idea that it becomes increasingly difficult to substitute labour for land and ke
the output of wheat constant. We define the *marginal rate of technical substitu*
(MRTS) of labour for land in the production of wheat as the amount of ex
labour that is required to keep the level of wheat output constant followin,
small, or marginal, reduction in the amount of land used.[4] It should be cl
that the *MRTS* depends upon the initial allocation—thus it is clearly m
easier to substitute labour for land and keep wheat output constant at poin
in the figure than at point Z.

Given the idea of the *MRTS* of land for labour, it is easy to see that a
allocation of land and labour to wheat and potato production *cannot*
technically efficient if the *MRTS* in wheat production differs from the *MR*
in potato production. Assume, for example, that the allocation of inputs is s
that the *MRTS* in wheat production is 3 units of labour for 1 of land wher
the *MRTS* in potato production is 1 unit of labour for 1 unit of land. T
allocation is inefficient: if 1 unit of land is transferred from potato to wh
production then 3 units of labour can be transferred in the opposite direct

---

[4] The reader will notice that the definition of the marginal rate of technical substitutio
completely analogous to the definition of the marginal rate of substitution for a consumer discus
in Chapter 2. Following the argument of page oo it is not difficult to see that the marginal rat
technical substitution at point Y in Figure 24.1 is measure by the slope of the curve XX at
point.

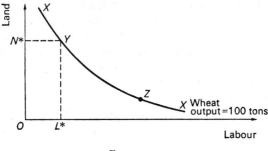

FIG. 24.1

ithout any reduction in the output of wheat. But only 1 unit of labour is
quired to keep the output of potatoes constant following the loss of the unit of
nd, so 2 units of labour are available to *increase the output of wheat, potatoes, or
th*. The initial allocation was therefore Pareto-inefficient. Despite the very
mple nature of the preceding argument it is clear that it will apply to any pair
inputs producing any pair of outputs. We have therefore deduced a very
mple condition of technical efficiency which we summarize as Proposition 1:

oposition 1 (Technical Efficiency)

an allocation of any pair of inputs between any pair of outputs is to be Pareto-
ficient then the marginal rate of technical substitution of one input for the
her must be the same in the production of both goods.

.2.4. Exchange Efficiency

an overall allocation of resources is to be Pareto-efficient then it is clear that it
ust be impossible to allocate the outputs actually produced between the
rious consumers so as to make some better off without making others worse
f. Our discussion of the precise implications of this condition is very similar to
e argument of the preceding section on technical efficiency. We make the
me assumptions concerning the preferences of consumers as in Chapter 2.
onsider the allocation of any pair of outputs—say, wheat and potatoes—
tween any pair of consumers—call them A and B. We have already (see
hapter 2) defined the marginal rate of substitution (*MRS*) of wheat for
tatoes for any consumer as the quantity of wheat that would, given the
rsonal preferences of that consumer, just compensate him or her for a small or
arginal' reduction in the consumption of potatoes—and we have noted that
is rate will depend upon the initial allocation in the sense that it is different at
fferent points on the indifference curve. (See, for example, Figure 2.3.)
Consider, then, a particular allocation of what and potatoes between A and
It is easy to see that the allocation cannot be Pareto-efficient if A's *MRS* of
heat for potatoes differs from B's. Assume, for example, that the allocation is
ch that A's *MRS* is 4 units of wheat for 1 of potatoes, whereas B's *MRS* is 1 unit
wheat for 1 of potatoes. Then the allocation is, given their preferences,
early inefficient. If 1 unit of potatoes is transferred from B to A then 4 units of
heat can be transferred in the opposite direction—and A is, given his

preferences, perfectly satisfied with the deal. But B only requires 1 unit of wheat to compensate him for the loss of the 1 unit of potatoes and, consequently, *3 units of wheat are available to make B, A, or both better off.* It is, once again, clear that the preceding simple argument will apply to any pair of outputs being allocated between any pair of consumers. We summarize the basic condition for exchange efficiency as Proposition 2:

Proposition 2 (Exchange Efficiency)

If an allocation of goods between individuals is Pareto-efficient then their personal marginal rates of substitution between any pair of goods must be equal.

24.2.5. *The Optimal Composition of Output*

Thus far we have used simple intuitive arguments to derive two very basic conditions of Pareto efficiency—the condition of technical efficiency, implying the equality of marginal rates of technical substitution, and the condition of exchange efficiency, implying the equality of personal marginal rates of substitution. We now discuss the final condition of Pareto efficiency relating to the precise quantities of goods produced. In terms of our previous discussions, we are interested in how much wheat and how many potatoes *should* be produced. Intuitively, it is clear that this question relates both to the *preferences* of the individuals in the economy and to the *technical possibilities* of producing the different goods. It should be clear that an economy could not be Pareto-efficient if its resources were being used to produce a bundle of outputs that were considered by the populace to be inferior to another bundle of outputs that *could* have been produced using the same resources.

The necessary condition for a Pareto-efficient composition of output can be most easily appreciated if we assume that only two goods—call them, once again, wheat and potatoes—are produced. The technical possibilities of the economy can be represented in a very simple diagram. Consider Figure 24.2 The curve *AB*, which is usually called the 'transformation frontier' or the 'production possibility frontier', represents all the combinations of wheat and

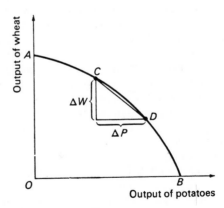

F IG. 24.2

potatoes that could be produced if the scarce resources of land and labour are allocated efficiently—i.e. if the condition of technical efficiency is satisfied. Thus, for example, if all of the economy's resources are used in producing wheat then OA of wheat can be produced. Intermediate points on the curve such as C and D represent other possible efficient combinations of wheat and potatoes— i.e. they show the absolute maximum available production of potatoes for the given levels of wheat production.

Consider the move from the efficient combination represented by the point C to the efficient combination represented by the point D. Such a move involves the production of ΔW less wheat (the symbol Δ means, once again, a 'small change') and ΔP more potatoes. Wheat is being 'transformed' into potatoes—not by any magical method but by the simple expedient of transferring some of society's scarce resources from wheat to potato production. The ratio $\Delta W/\Delta P$ is called the *marginal rate of transformation* (MRT) between potatoes and wheat.[5] It represents the quantity of wheat that must be forgone for a small increment in potato production. The *shape* of the transformation frontier represents the idea that as more and more of society's resources are transferred from wheat to potato production the quantities of additional potatoes produced per unit reduction in wheat production become smaller and smaller.

We have already noted that if the allocation of wheat and potatoes between individuals is to be Pareto-efficient then the personal marginal rate of substitution of wheat for potatoes of any one person must equal that of all others. If, therefore, the condition of 'exchange efficiency' is satisfied, we are justified in speaking of *the* marginal rate of substitution of wheat for potatoes.

It is not difficult to see that if the precise composition of output is to be Pareto-efficient then the technically determined marginal rate of transformation between potatoes and wheat must equal the preference-determined marginal rate of substitution between potatoes and wheat. Consider, for example, an allocation in which the marginal rate of transformation is 3 units of what for 1 unit of potatoes whereas 'the' marginal rate of substitution (given exchange efficiency) is 1 unit of wheat for 1 of potatoes. Then the composition of output is Pareto-inefficient. If resources are reallocated such that 1 less unit of potatoes is produced, then 3 extra units of wheat will become available. Only 1 unit of wheat is, however, required, given the populace's preferences, to compensate for the loss of the unit of potatoes, so 2 units of wheat are now available to make all or any of the consumers better off—depending upon the manner in which the extra wheat is distributed between the consumers. This simple argument clearly applies to the marginal rate of transformation between any pair of outputs and we can summarize our deductions as Proposition 3:

Proposition 3 (Composition of Output)

If the composition of output is to be Pareto-efficient then the marginal rate of transformation of any output into another output must equal society's

---

[5] If the amounts ΔW and ΔP are made very small then the marginal rate of transformation is measured by the slope of the transformation frontier at any point.

marginal rate of substitution (given exchange efficiency) of one output for the other.

24.2.6. Marginal Product and Marginal Cost

It is useful to note a simple relationship between the marginal rate of transformation of one output for another and (i) the productivities of the inputs in producing the outputs, and (ii) the costs of production of the outputs. Let us define the *marginal product* (MP) of an input as the ratio of extra output to small increase in the input, with all other inputs remaining constant. Thus, if ΔN extra acres of land will produce ΔP extra potatoes, then the marginal product of land is approximately[6] $\Delta P / \Delta N$. Secondly, we recall from Chapter 3 the definition of the *marginal cost* (MC) of an output as the ratio of extra costs of production incurred for a small increase in output to the increase in output, i.e the addition to total cost per additional unit of output. Thus, if an increase ΔP in potato production generated ΔC extra cost then the marginal cost of potatoes is approximately $\Delta C / \Delta P$. We now demonstrate that the marginal rate of transformation, $\Delta W / \Delta P$, of wheat for potatoes is directly related to the marginal productivities of inputs in producing wheat and potatoes and to the marginal cost of producing wheat and potatoes.

Let us, for simplicity, assume that the only input to wheat and potato production is land, measured in acres, which is available at a rent of £r per acre Now, consider a small reduction, ΔN, in the acreage made available for wheat production. The fall, ΔW, in wheat output will clearly equal the reduction, ΔN in available land multiplied by the marginal product of land in producing wheat—which, in this context, we denote as MPN^W. Thus we can write:

$$\Delta W = \Delta N . MPN^W \ldots \tag{1}$$

where ΔW is interpreted as a fall in wheat output.

If the acreage, ΔN, removed from what production is used for potat production then the increase, ΔP, in potato production will clearly equal th extra acreage multiplied by the marginal product of land in producing potatoes, MPN^P. Thus we can write:

$$\Delta P = \Delta N . MPN^W \ldots \tag{2}$$

We know, however, that the marginal rate of transformation is defined ε $\Delta W / \Delta P$, *so, dividing equation (1) by equation (2), we obtain*

$$\frac{\Delta W}{\Delta P} = \frac{\Delta N}{\Delta N} . \frac{MPN^W}{MPN^P} = \frac{MPN^W}{MPN^P} \ldots \tag{3}$$

i.e. the marginal rate of transformation of wheat into potatoes equals the rat of the marginal product of land in producing wheat to the marginal product land in producing potatoes. It can be shown[7] that a similar result will hold f any inputs.

---

[6] Strictly, marginal quantities should be defined in terms of infinitesimally small change Nevertheless, it does no great violence to our argument if we follow the present definition.

[7] See, for example, Lancaster [3], pp. 267, 268.

Now, consider the extra costs, ΔC, of producing ΔP extra potatoes. Since we are assuming that land is the only input, total costs, C, will simply equal the amount, N, of land used multiplied by the rent, $\pounds r$ (which we assume unchanged). If the amount of land used increases by ΔN, the addition, ΔC, to costs will be $\pounds r \Delta N$ and we can write:

$$\Delta C = r \, \Delta N \ldots \tag{4}$$

If we divide both sides of equation (4) by the extra potato output, ΔP, we obtain

$$\frac{\Delta C}{\Delta P} = r \cdot \frac{\Delta N}{\Delta P} \ldots \tag{5}$$

Now, from the definitions, $\Delta C / \Delta P$ is the marginal cost of potatoes, MC^P, and $\Delta N / \Delta P$ is the inverse of the marginal product of land in producing potatoes, MPN^P. Equation (5) can therefore be written as

$$MC^P = \frac{r}{MPN^P} \ldots \tag{6}$$

Using an identical argument it is easy to show that the marginal cost of producing wheat is given by

$$MC^W = \frac{r}{MPN^W} \ldots \tag{7}$$

Dividing equation (6) by (7) it can be seen that

$$\frac{MC^P}{MC^W} = \frac{MPN^W}{MPN^P} .$$

But we have already shown (equation (3)) that the ratio of the marginal product of land in producing wheat to the marginal product of land in producing potatoes equals the marginal rate of transformation. It can now be seen that the marginal rate of transformation between potatoes and wheat equals the ratio of the marginal cost of potatoes to the marginal cost of wheat. In the subsequent analysis we will demonstrate the importance of this simple result.

The three conditions of Pareto efficiency discussed above constitute a framework, albeit very limited, in which some questions relating to the relative merits of alternative allocations of resources can be considered. Two important points must be stressed. Firstly, as was mentioned earlier in the section, the Pareto criterion and the efficiency conditions do *not* isolate a uniquely 'best' allocation of resources. Although the conditions of Pareto efficiency *do* rule out many allocations as being unambiguously undesirable, there still remains a very large number of *different* possible Pareto-efficient allocations. Since the Pareto criterion simply makes *no* attempt to compare situations in which some are better off and others worse off, it cannot distinguish between alternative Pareto-efficient allocations that correspond to *different distributions of income and wealth*. Thus one Pareto-efficient allocation might involve substantial inequality of wealth while another might involve perfect equality. If, however, society could by some means or other decide upon and achieve what it considered to be a 'fair' distribution of income and wealth, then there would be every incentive to ensure that the precise allocation of resource corresponding to this distribution was, in fact, Pareto-efficient. Since *everybody* can be made better off in a move from a Pareto-inefficient to a Pareto-efficient allocation, there does not seem to be any obvious reason, whatever one's views on the 'fairness' of the distribution of wealth, why inefficiency should be tolerated if efficiency is available.

Secondly, although the idea of Pareto efficiency is used explicitly in the context of 'cost-benefit' analysis (see, for example, Mishan [4] and Layard [12]), it should be clear that the ideas discussed above are intended to provide an analytical rather than a practical framework for assessment. As is discussed in Chapter 8, real governments have a variety of different objectives—some of which conflict with one another. Now, Pareto efficiency is not an *explicitly* stated government objective and, indeed, it is difficult to conceive of how a real-world Pareto optimum could be identified—even if it was possible to achieve it. Nevertheless, the ideas of efficiency discussed here are not only useful for interpreting the claims to virtue of the proponents of free-market competition but do, in fact, underlie practical discussions of microeconomic policy and practical proposals. (See Chapters 25 and 26.)

24.3. The Price System

In the previous section we identified three basic conditions necessary for an allocation of society's scarce resources to be Pareto-efficient. In the present section we examine how the outcome of a system of unfettered and apparently uncoordinated free competition between self-seeking individuals and firms *could* be Pareto-efficient, and we reserve for the next section a discussion of the problems associated with real-world market behaviour. We concentrate our discussion on a world of free markets and prices partly because such a system is probably[8] the most common allocative mechanism in the West and partly because many of the issues associated with Communist-style command planning do, in fact, arise in the same context. We proceed in three stages. We firstly analyse an 'ideal' form of competition in the context of the market for a single commodity. Secondly, the simultaneous working of the price system for all goods and services (including labour services) is discussed. Finally, the relationship between competition and efficiency is isolated and analysed.

24.3.1. The Single Market

The simplest method of obtaining an insight into the workings of the competitive allocative mechanism is to examine the market for a single good. Our conception of the 'market' for the good (say beer) does not imply a single

[8] It could be argued that, even in an as ostensibly competition-oriented economy as the United States, various forms of corporate and government planning have, in many cases, replaced the market mechanism. For a famous exposition of this kind of view, see K. Galbraith, *The New Industrial State* (Penguin, 1968).

geographical location but is defined simply by the communication between potential buyers and sellers. In a world of 'free competition'[9] the quantities of beer produced and sold will depend upon the preference of consumers, as expressed by their willingness to buy in the market, and the technical conditions of production for the potential sellers, as expressed by their willingness to sell in the market. We define a situation of *perfect competition* as one in which no trader (i.e. buyer or seller) supplies or demands more than a very small part of the total output of the good in question, any new supplier can freely enter if he wishes, all firms produce an identical infinitely divisible product, all have perfect knowledge of all aspects of any exchanges that take place, and transport costs are insignificant. In this case, the demand curve facing any one supplier will be horizontal. Any attempt to raise price above the market level would result in the loss of all demand, while any lowering of price would result in the firm obtaining all the market demand. We can now draw a cost/revenue diagram such as the one shown in Chapter 3 (p. 65), corresponding to a perfectly competitive situation. This is shown in Figure 24.3.

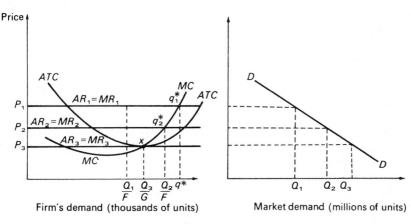

Firm's demand (thousands of units)   Market demand (millions of units)

Fig. 24.3

The average total cost (ATC) and marginal cost curves are as shown in Figure 3.2. If the price were to be at P_1, the demand curve would be horizontal at this level, and is by definition the average revenue curve (see p. 64). The marginal revenue curve will be identical with it because each extra unit of output will add to total revenue an amount exactly equal to the price (equals average revenue (AR)) of the product.[10] The price P_1 will determine total

[9] It is important to note that dangers are inherent in the use of the adjective 'free'. We use it to describe a situation in which buyers and sellers are free to conclude a bargain without outside interference. Some, perhaps many, would claim, however, that 'free' competition is inextricably linked with more general concepts of freedom. Others would disagree.

[10] Any marginal amount always equals the corresponding average if the average is unchanging. An average batting score only rises if the new or marginal innings results in a score above the average. Conversely, it only falls if the marginal innings is below the average. A marginal batting score equal to the average will leave the average unchanged.

market demand Q_1, and with F firms, each individual firm will have Q_1/F units of demand. The profit-maximizing output will, however, be q_1^* where marginal revenue (MR equals marginal cost (MC). Thus the situation depicted would not last. Firms would reduce price in an effort to increase output and profits.

The reduction in price increases market demand, and hence the individual firm's demand, until price P_2 is reached. The firm's demand is Q_2/F which equals the new profit-maximizing output. (The profit-maximizing output has moved from q_1^* because of the change in market price.) No firm in the industry would have any further incentive to change its price or output.

There are three important things to notice about this situation:

(1) The price of the product equals its marginal cost. This will occur as soon as output reaches the profit-maximizing level. At this level $MC = MR$, but under perfect competition $MR = AR$ which is the same as price. Hence price equals marginal cost, which is another result to be utilized in the next section.

(2) Given our assumption, the cost conditions of the producer show how much beer he will be *prepared to supply* to the market at different prices. At price P_2, profit considerations imply that he will be prepared to sell an amount q_2^*, but if the price is P_1 he will be prepared to sell the higher output q_1^*. The points q_1^* and q_2^* represent points on the firm's *supply curve* which relates price to the amount it is willing to supply at that price. Clearly, therefore, under perfect competition the firm's supply curve is its marginal cost curve.

If *every* producer of beer is confronted by a marginal cost curve similar to the one in Figure 24.3 then it is clear that the *total* amount of beer that producers as a whole are prepared to supply will increase as the price increases. This enables us to analyse the individual market in a situation of perfect competition. Consider Figure 24.4. The curve marked DD is the market demand curve for beer showing the quantities of beer that households *plan* to buy at different prices (see Chapter 2).

The curve marked SS represents the quantities of beer that all the profit-maximizing producers are prepared to sell at each price—the quantities being determined by the marginal cost curves of the producers as discussed above.[11]

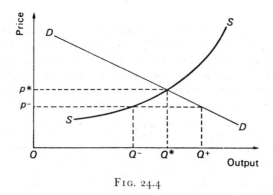

FIG. 24.4

[11] It is, in fact, simply a horizontal summation of the individual marginal cost curves.

Consider the price p^*. At this price, the quantity of beer that producers are prepared to sell just equals the quantity that consumers are prepared to buy. If this price emerged in the market, consumers would find that they were actually able to buy the quantity they planned to buy—there would not be a 'shortage' of any kind. Similarly, at the price p^*, producers would find that there were, in fact, just enough buyers to actually buy all that the producers planned to sell. The price p^* is called the *equilibrium* price for the market—for, it if rules, no trader has any obvious incentive to try and change the situation.

In Chapter 2 we demonstrated how the market demand curve stemmed from households' preferences, incomes, and the price they face. In the present chapter we have shown that market supply depends upon the marginal costs of production. Thus the equilibrium price, p^*, acts as a *signal of the true relative scarcity* of beer stemming from its desirability to consumers and the resources that need to be used in its production. This is what lies behind the intuitive notion of prices equating supply and demand.

Consider the price p^-—which is below the equilibrium price. At this price, the quantity that producers are prepared to supply is OQ^-—which is less than the quantity that consumers plan to buy, OQ^+. In this situation of 'excess demand' some customers will not be able to buy as much beer as they planned, and there are incentives for producers to start increasing the price.[12] Once the price has reached the equilibrium price then plans to buy will once again equal plans to sell—and there will be no more dissatisfied customers. Price acts as an *incentive to individual action* on the part of buyers and sellers and it *co-ordinates their plans* such that the quantity available exactly matches the quantity desired.

(3) Going back to Figure 24.3, at the price P_2, although $MR = MC$, average revenue is above average cost. Super-normal profits are being made and new firms will be attracted in. As F, the number of firms, rises so each firm's demand falls, and further price reductions are necessary to increase overall market demand sufficiently to allow each individual firm to reach its profit-maximizing output. Finally P_3 is reached, with G firms in the industry. Not only does $MC = MR$ (profit maximizing) but $AC = AR$ as well, implying no super-normal profits and no tendency for any firm outside the industry to enter (or any inside to leave). This must be at the minimum point of the average cost curve (point X at output Q_3/G). If $MC = MR$ $MR = AR$, and $AR = AC$, then $MC = AC$. But marginal cost can only equal average cost when the latter is unchanging, meaning a horizontal part of the average cost curve. Given the U-shaped curve, this only occurs at minimum average cost.

Thus, over the longer term, production at minimum average cost is ensured. Higher-cost producers will be unable to compete and will fail to continue profitable production. If there are constant returns to scale and given factor prices, the long-run price level of the product will be independent of the level of demand or output.

Perfect competition in the market for factors of production gives a rather different picture. If firms are profit maximizers they will only employ a factor of

---

[12] There are, in fact, rather tricky logical problems associated with the argument that prices tend to the equilibrium price. If *everyone* acts as a 'price taker' who raises the price?

production, e.g. labour, if the gain to the firm from his production exceeds the cost of his wage. Assuming perfect competition in the product market as well, and therefore an unchanging product price, the gain from employing one more man (all other factors held constant) will be his extra output—the marginal product of labour—times the product price. The cost will be his money wage, which through perfect competition in the labour market will also be given. If the former exceeds the latter the firm will employ the man, and the next, and so on until the marginal product of labour (which is assumed to fall as more men are taken on) falls to the level of the money wage. Any further employment would depress the gain below the cost of the next man, and the firm ceases to employ more men. Its profits are now maximized. The condition is

$$P \times MPL = W$$

where P is the product price, MPL the marginal product of labour, and W the wage rate. This gives

$$MPL = \frac{W}{P}$$

indicating that under the very restrictive assumptions stated the 'price' of a factor of production (the real wage in this case) will equal the marginal product of the factor. While many things will interfere with this, it is not unreasonable to think of marginal product as one element in the determination of real wages under competitive conditions.

24.3.2. General Equilibrium

Equilibrium of an individual market is relatively easy to understand. What, however, is meant by the *general* equilibrium of a perfect market economy? Let us assume that the economy consists of a very large number of households, a very large number of firms, and a very large number, n, of different inputs and outputs. A general competitive equilibrium is then defined as a set of prices, one for each commodity, such that:

(a) *Every* household is in equilibrium in the sense that, given their incomes and the prices of all commodities, they are choosing a preferred bundle of commodities.

(b) *Every* firm is in equilibrium in the sense that, given its technology and the prices of inputs and outputs, it has a production plan that maximizes profits.

(c) *Every* market for each of the n different inputs and outputs is in equilibrium in the sense that planned supplies equal planned demands.

The concept of a general equilibrium is truly staggering. In such a situation, given the prices of all inputs and outputs, there would be no shortages or surpluses of any commodity, and no economic agent, i.e. firm or individual, would have any incentive to alter its pattern of production or consumption. In this situation, the *system of prices* as a whole would be acting as the co-ordinator of a myriad individual decisions by acting as an indicator of relative scarcity and as an incentive to action.

Now it should be clear that the general equilibrium of perfect competition is an abstract concept—no real economy has been, or ever will be, in a situation of general equilibrium. But the concept of general equilibrium represents what might happen in a situation of 'ideal' competition—it shows how the competitive mechanism might co-ordinate an economy in an ordered and, as we will see, efficient manner. A clear understanding of the implications of general equilibrium enables us to understand the effects of anything less than the full equilibrium of perfect competition. We now turn to investigate the kind of allocation of resources that would be associated with general equilibrium.[13]

24.3.3. General Equilibrium and Pareto Efficiency

Given our definition of general competitive equilibrium and our earlier discussion of Pareto efficiency, it is a relatively easy matter to demonstrate that any general equilibrium will, in fact, be Pareto-efficient. Firstly, notice that perfect competition as we have defined it implies that only *one* price can rule for each commodity throughout the economy. All producers face exactly the same price for any input and all consumer face exactly the same price for any output. If any producer tried to charge a higher price than the ruling equilibrium price, our assumption of perfect knowledge on the part of all traders of all aspects of exchange would mean that he would immediately lose all his business. A lower price would result in normal profit not being achieved. Hence, everyone is a price taker, unable to influence the ruling equilibrium prices. Now consider the conditions for Pareto efficiency discussed in section 24.2.

(a) *Technical efficiency.* In section 24.2 it was demonstrated that technical efficiency was implied if the *MRTS* of one output for another in the production of any good was equal to the *MRTS* between the same pair of inputs in producing any other good. Consider an individual producer considering what combination to buy of some pair of inputs given their general equilibrium prices. It is easy to show that he will minimize the costs of producing a given output (or, equivalently, maximize output for a given cost) if he chooses a combination such that the marginal rate of technical substitution of one input for the other is equal to their price ratio. Assume, for example, that £10 will buy 2 hours of capital services or 1 hour of labour services (i.e. the price of capital is £5 per hour and the price of labour is £10 per hour) while the *MRTS* is 1 hour of capital services for 1 hour of labour services. Now, if the entrepreneur purchases 1 hour less of labour services he would save £10. If he spent £5 on purchasing 1 hour of capital services then his output would remain the same (given the *MRTS* of 1 for 1) and he would have made a net saving of £5. Consequently, such a production plan would not have been minimizing cost nor maximizing profit. This simple argument demonstrates that the *MRTS* between *any* pair of inputs must equal their price ratio if costs are to be minimized. Now, if all producers are in equilibrium (see the definition of general equilibrium) then they must *all* be equating the *MRTS*s between any

---

[13] A thorough treatment of these issues would require a discussion of (i) whether general equilibrium is logically possible, and (ii) whether forces exist that move an economy to general equilibrium.

pair of inputs to the ratio of the prices of the inputs. But we have already noted that in general equilibrium they will *all* face precisely the same prices for inputs. Consequently, in general equilibrium the *MRTS* between any pair of inputs in producing any output will equal the *MRTS* between the same pair of inputs in producing any other output—which is precisely our condition for technical efficiency. The price system interacts with the *desire for profit* to ensure the equality of marginal rates of technical substitution.

(b) *Exchange efficiency.* In section 24.2 it was demonstrated that exchange efficiency necessitated that all personal marginal rates of substitution between any two goods must be equal. Now, in Chapter 2 we showed that a consumer freely choosing a bundle of commodities in the market will, given the prices and his income, choose a bundle such that his personal marginal rate of substitution between any pair of goods is equal to the ratio of their prices. If all consumers face uniform prices (and, therefore, uniform price ratios of different goods) then it is clear that all their personal rates of substitution between any pair of goods will be equated. Thus the general equilibrium of perfect competition, by ensuring that all consumers face the same prices, implies that the *self-interest of consumers* will ensure the satisfaction of this basic condition for Pareto efficiency.

(c) *The optimal composition of output.* In section 24.2 of this chapter we demonstrated that the optimal composition of output necessitated that the marginal rate of transformation between any pair of commodities must equal the marginal rate of substitution. In general equilibrium, profit maximization and perfect competition generate exactly this result. This can be seen as follows.

(i) In section 24.2 we saw that the marginal rate of transformation between products 1 and 2 equalled the ratio of the marginal costs of production of the goods in question, i.e. $MRT_1^2 = MC_1/(MC_2)$.

(ii) From Chapter 2 we know that household equilibrium implies that the personal marginal rates of substitution between any pair of goods will equal the ratio of their prices, i.e.

$$\frac{P_1}{P_2} = MRS_1^2 = \frac{MU_1}{MU_2}$$

but we have also seen (pp. 755–6) that Pareto optimality requires $MRT_1^2 = MRS_1^2$. Putting these three together we have that

$$\frac{MC_1}{MC_2} = \frac{P_1}{P_2}$$

which is the necessary condition for the optional composition of output.

(iii) In the present section we have shown that profit maximization in a situation of perfect competition implies that the prices of all goods will equal their marginal costs of production. Therefore the ratio of their marginal costs equals the ratio of their prices which, as we have just seen, is the necessary condition for the optimal composition of output. The conditions that

$$\frac{MC_1}{MC_2} = \frac{P_1}{P_2}$$

can be rewritten:

$$\frac{P_1}{MC_1} = \frac{P_2}{MC_2}$$

saying that the ratio of price to marginal cost for each good (indeed for all goods) must be the same. In fact, further consideration require that the ratio is 1. To take but one reason, some firms cover more than one stage of production. The effect of this can be shown by an example, where $P/MC = 2$:

		Stage 1 MC	Stage 2 MC	Price
(i) Production by 1	firm			
	Wages	£1	£1	
		—	—	£8
	Materials	£2	—	
(ii) Production by 2	firms	MC P	MC	
	Wages	£1	£1	
		£6		£14
	Materials	£2	—	
	Semi-manufacture		£6	

In the second case marginal cost to the first firm carrying out stage 1 of the production process is £2 + £1 = £3. Its price for the semi-manufactured good is £6. So marginal cost for the second firm carrying out stage 2 is £1 + £6 = £7 and the price is £14. For the firm in case (i) with the same inputs, same production processes, and the same output, its marginal cost is £4 in total and the price is therefore £8. Only if the ratio of P/MC is 1 will both cases give the same final price. Perfect competition still gives a Pareto optimum because it does generate $P = MC$.

We have now demonstrated that the equilibrium of an 'ideal' form of competition would, given the associated price system, imply Pareto efficiency. This result provides a precise statement of the sense in which 'free competition' is optimal, given the definition used, the limitations that have been discussed, and the limited applicability of the Pareto criterion. In the next two sections we first examine the principal factors that imply that real-world competition will not generate such attractive efficiency results, and, second, go a little further into the problem of applying the Pareto criterion.

24.4. Market Failure

In the real world, free markets often fail to perform in the idealized fashion required for allocative efficiency—hence the generic title for this section. Below we examine briefly the principal factors that prevent markets from working in the manner described above.

24.4.1. Monopoly and Other Market Imperfections

Perhaps the principal reason for scepticism that the price system will perform effectively as a decentralized signalling system and incentive to action is the

widespread existence in the real world of monopoly and other market
structures which allow individual firms considerable power in the market.
Real-world markets rarely, if ever, conform to the stylized version of perfect
competition described in the previous section. Traders are, as is implied by the
discussion of firms' behaviour in Chapter 3, very often sufficiently dominant in
the market that they can, in fact, choose the price at which they sell their
product. As was demonstrated in Chapter 3, profit maximization in the general
situation implies that firms will choose output such that marginal cost equal
marginal revenue. Since marginal revenue for this kind of dominant firm is *less*
than price, prices must be greater than marginal cost. We have already seen in
the previous section that the composition of output will be optimal only if *all*
prices equal marginal costs of production. No general statement about the
desirability of setting price equal to marginal cost can be made if some other
prices do not equal the marginal cost of their product. We are in what is
known as a 'second-best' world where a more *ad hoc* approach has to be adopted.
Thus any element of market power or monopoly will militate severely against
the claims to efficiency of free competition. This simple, but powerful, resource
allocation argument against monopolistic market structures is not, of course,
the whole story. These matters are discussed in Chapter 26.

24.4.2. External Effects

Many real-world production activities involve side-effects or 'externalities'
which are a pervasive problem if competition and the price system are to live up
to the claims to efficiency summarized in the previous section. Externalities
arise when the activities of one economic agent directly affect the outcome of
the activities of another economic agent in a way not covered by the price
mechanism. Thus, for example, a factory may pollute a river which is the
source of water to another factory, or the air that the local community breathes,
etc. In the absence of a system of licensing or a system of compensation, the
price system *alone* will not provide incentives to minimize this pollution, and
legal prohibition may be essential.

The effects of externalities may be unfavourable—as in the case of the
polluting factory—or favourable—as in the case of the bee-keeper who benefits
from living next door to an orchard. At the heart of the problem of externalities
is the fact that, in the case of many activities, it is difficult to *exclude* others from
the costs and benefits of the activity. If exclusion is impossible (or very difficult)
markets may not exist for the commodity in question—in which case the price
system will not provide incentives to reduce harmful externalities and increase
beneficial externalities.[14]

The factory has no incentive to reduce its pollution because it does not bear
the cost of the pollution, nor would it reap any gain from reducing it (indeed it
would incur the cost of prevention). The orchard-owner receives no payment
from the bee-keeper despite the benefit of the orchard to the bee-keeper, and
hence has no incentive from this source to maintain it, unlike a hive-maker for
example.

---

[14] This is a very terse statement of a profound problem. For an excellent discussion see Bator [7].

Such considerations lead us to distinguish between *private* cost or benefit—the actual cost or benefit incurred by a private transactor such that he will pay for the benefit or need payment to incur the cost—and *social* cost or benefit, which is the cost or benefit which accrue to *anyone* in society irrespective of whether they were involved in the transaction or made or received any payment. There has in recent years been increasing effort in some parts of the public sector to identify such social costs and benefits before taking major resource-allocating decisions.

A problem closely related to that of externalities involves the problem of *public* goods, such as street lighting, the provision of 'defence', or a clean-air programme, where the 'consumption' of these goods by one individual in no way excludes someone else also 'consuming' or enjoying their benefits. Such goods form a significant proportion of the collective purchases made by government on behalf of the community (see Chapter 9).

24.4.3. Intertemporal Efficiency

The ideas of Pareto-efficient general equilibrium developed in the previous section referred to the allocation of resources at a single point in time. A central characteristic of the real-world economy is that resources have to be allowed *now* for the provision of outputs in the future. Thus, for example, a decision to allocate resources for the construction of a new factory must depend upon the demand for the factory's products when it is eventually completed. Now, in principle, all the arguments concerning efficiency in the previous section could be duplicated *if* there existed 'future markets' for all commodities—i.e. markets that quote prices *today* for delivery of goods at future dates. In the real world, however, futures markets are rather rare. Thus the real-world price system does *not* provide signals of scarcity in the future and cannot properly co-ordinate current activities whose outcome lies in the future. Today's beer price reflects today's costs and today's preferences—it will not, in general, provide any information of future costs and future preferences. The price of a raw material might remain very low because of an abundance of it today, irrespective of the fact that it will soon run out altogether. A long-term futures market would allow the future scarcity to be reflected in a high futures price, giving suppliers the incentive to reduce supplies now in favour of supply in the future. This would drive up the current price and lead to an economizing in the use of the ultimately very scarce resource. Many of the ideas of indicative planning stem from this weakness of real-world price systems.

24.4.4. Risk and Uncertainty

All our discussions thus far have involved an implicit assumption of certainty. In the real world, however, the outcomes of activities are frequently uncertain. Now, if insurance companies provided markets for *all* risks it is conceivable that the price system could generate an efficient allocation of resources between activities involving different degrees of risk. But insurance markets are far from perfect and it may be that the price system produces a bias against risky activities, which is inefficient from the point of view of society.

24.4.5. Information and Disequilibrium

The central strand in our argument that the equilibrium of perfect competition would be Pareto-efficient was the idea that all buyers of inputs and outputs would face exactly the same prices—and this proposition stemmed from our assumption of perfect knowledge. In the real world, however, information is far from perfect and is *costly* to obtain. Thus it is not difficult to find two adjacent supermarkets charging different prices for identical products. Consumer organizations frequently reveal astonishing variations in prices for identical commodities. Whatever else may be said about competition in the real world it certainly does not involve uniformity of prices at any point of time—although there are, of course, tendencies to equalization. The costs of acquiring information are a strong reason for believing that equilibrium may never come about—the microeconomy might be in persistent disequilibrium. All the results of section 24.3 are jeopardized by this fact.

24.5. Limitations of Pareto Efficiency

Finally, we return to consider the Pareto criterion itself. Many limitations on its use have been demonstrated; we mention three of these.

24.5.1 Compensation

How do we deal with situations (which are the typical sort) in which some gain by a move from situation A to B, but some lose? Are we unable to say anything at all about the desirability of the change?

It has been suggested that the move could be judged beneficial as long as the gainers gain more than the losers lose, implying that the gainers could compensate the losers for the change. This is only acceptable, however, if the gainers *actually* do compensate the losers. If they compensate the losers sufficiently for them to agree voluntarily to the change then we may presume that they are not worse off at the end. The gainers are still net gainers, however, and thus the Pareto criterion again becomes operative and allows us to judge the move *plus* compensation as Pareto-efficient.[15] The compensation that can be paid, however, and the amount required are both generally dependent on *the distribution* of income, and this may make the compensation procedure unacceptable.

24.5.2. Income Distribution

We have already referred to the problem of income distribution, views on which are explicitly value-based judgements. If decisions determining the distribution of income were independent of those determining resource allocation then, in principle, society could decide through its political system on the distribution of income it desired, independent of its allocation of resources, which could then be made Pareto-efficient separately. In fact, of course, this is largely not possible. A non-Pareto-efficient allocation may be

[15] Many difficulties arise in practice, and even some theoretical inconsistencies may arise, but in principle this compensation principle can sometimes offer a way forward.

preferred to a Pareto-efficient one because the income distribution associated with the former is preferred, but is not in practice obtainable in conjunction with a Pareto-efficient allocation of resources. At best it is only possible to indicate the loss of potential satisfaction that one or more people are suffering in order that a measurable improvement in income distribution is achieved so that society can take an informed value-judgment between the two situations. This in turn will clearly depend on people's views of the importance of equity, incentives, property rights, etc.

24.5.3. Preferences and the Means of Payment

Perhaps the biggest problem of all is the fact that within the Pareto system preferences are only recognized if they are backed up by the necessary money for payment. The strength of a preference for chocolate is assumed to be indicated by willingness to pay for it. For many products this may be acceptable but for a whole range of other products it is not. Inability to pay for a life-saving operation clearly does not indicate the lack of any desire for it, and there is probably general agreement that it is desirable to make such things available irrespective of payment, and hence outside the market system. More controversial, however, are products such as housing, education, minimum standard of consumption, etc. It is generally thought desirable that everyone should have adequate amounts of these irrespective of prices or costs. Clearly, the Pareto-efficient criterion is inadequate to reflect this type of view.

In conclusion, therefore, one can only go a little way with the Pareto criterion. Later, various situations will be examined in which it has been applied, albeit in conjunction with other criteria. There appear to be relatively few examples in the modern market economy where there is both a general agreement that a Pareto-based criterion is paramount and also a sufficient degree of competition to *guarantee* the achievement of the Pareto optimum. The existence of other value-judgements, of externalities, public goods, monopolistic elements, and excessive risk all contribute towards a system in which resource allocation decisions may be extremely complex, political, and subjective.

Bibliography

Section A consists of various expositions of the economic theory of resource allocation. Section B is a selective list of books on welfare economics. Several of the books and articles cited (e.g. Mishan [4]) contain detailed bibliographies.

SECTION A

[1] BATOR, F. M. 'The Simple Analytics of Welfare Maximization', *American Economic Review* (Mar. 1957).
A very well-known goemetrical exposition of most of the central ideas of welfare economics.
[2] DORFMAN, R. *The Price System* (Prentice-Hall, 1964).
A good relatively short account of the theoretical working of the price system.

[3] LANCASTER, K. *Introduction to Modern Microeconomics* (Rand McNally and Co., 1969). Chaps. 9 and 10 constitute a good textbook exposition of most of the issues discussed in this chapter.

[4] MISHAN, E. J. 'A Survey of Welfare Economics 1939–1959), *Economic Journal* (1960). A well-known survey of welfare economics.

[5] SCITOVSKY, T. *Welfare and Competition* (George Allen and Unwin, 1971). Contains a very clear account of the resource allocation implications of free competition.

[6] WINCH, D. M. *Analytical Welfare Economics* (Penguin, 1971). A succinct textbook treatment of welfare economics.

SECTION B

[7] BATOR, F. M. 'The Anatomy of Market Failure', *Quarterly Journal of Economics* (Aug. 1958).

[8] DOBB, M. *Welfare Economics and the Economics of Socialism* (Cambridge University Press, 1969).

[9] FRIEDMAN, M. *Essays in Positive Economics* (University of Chicago, 1953).

[10] GRAAF, J. DE V. *Theoretical Welfare Economics* (Cambridge University Press, 1967).

[11] KOOPMANS, T. *Three Essays on the State of Economic Science* (McGraw-Hill, 1957), Essay 1.

[12] LAYARD, R. (ed.). *Cost-Benefit Analysis* (Penguin, 1972).

[13] LIPSEY, R. G. *An Introduction to Positive Economics*, 4th edn. (Weidenfeld and Nicolson, 1975).

[14] LITTLE, I. M. D. *A Critique of Welfare Economics*, 2nd edn. (Oxford University Press, 1957).

[15] MISHAN, E. J. *Elements of Cost-Benefit Analysis* (George Allen and Unwin, 1972).

[16] NATH, S. K. *A Reappraisal of Welfare Economics* (Routledge and Kegan Paul, 1969).

[17] NOVE, A. *The Soviet Economy*, 3rd edn. (George Allen and Unwin, 1968).

[18] PIGOU, A. C. *The Economics of Welfare*, 4th edn. (Macmillan and Co., 1932).

[19] ROWLEY, C. K. and PEACOCK, A. T. *Welfare Economics: A Liberal Restatement* (Martin Robertson, 1975).

[20] SEN, A. K. *On Economic Inequality* (Oxford University Press, 1973).

25

Nationalized Industries

M. J. BRECH

25.1. Introduction

The origins of the mixed economy stretch back at least to the mid-seventeenth century when the Post Office was constituted as a department of central government. In the nineteenth century the public sector expanded rapidly through the creation of municipally owned utilities to supply gas, electricity, and water. Although there were limited extensions of public control in the interwar period, such as the formation of the BBC in 1927, the foundations of the modern public enterprise sector based on nationalized industries date from the 1946–51 Labour Administration. Control of public utilities was centralized under National Boards and the frontiers of the public enterprise sector extended into new areas such as coal and steel.

Over the ensuing three decades, the public enterprise sector centred on the major nationalized industries and remained broadly constant in size, although one or two industries, notably steel, fluctuated between private and public ownership as ideological symbols of the government of the day. Nevertheless, there were changes at the periphery, such as the growth of 'creeping nationalization' in the early 1970s, involving the creation or take-over by the state of limited liability companies within competitive industries. Since 1979, however, a systematic programme of privatization has been embarked upon which threatens to reduce considerably the nationalized industries in number and in size.

Three types of 'creeping nationalization' can be distinguished:

(i) The 'lame duck' rescue of private firms that are of strategic importance to the UK economy but have experienced temporary financial difficulties, for example Rolls Royce, British Leyland, Alfred Herbert Ltd.

(ii) Intervention to rationalize an uncompetitive industry through enforced take-over, for example the role that the BSC attempted to play in rationalizing the special-steels sector through the take-over of Round Oak and other companies.

(iii) The creation of seed-corn companies to develop and exploit new technologies at an earlier stage in their development than would usually be achieved by the market, for example Celltech under the aegis of the BTG.

In all these cases, the motive for intervention has been pragmatic rather than ideological, to assist in creating an industrial structure that will provide the basis for future economic growth. Public ownership has therefore become an increasingly important instrument of industrial policy.

Despite its long history, the mixed economy has never settled into a generally accepted *modus vivendi*, although few people would deny the state some role in the production of goods and services. Throughout the post-war era there have been disagreements about the objectives to be pursued by the nationalized industries, about the appropriate extent of the public enterprise sector, about the manner in which pricing and investment decisions should be taken in the public enterprise sector, how public enterprise should be financed and how it should be made accountable to the government and to Parliament. This lack of consensus has been most clearly evident with respect to the principal nationalized industries and is demonstrated by a succession of White Papers directed at the problem of their control and financing, and by numerous official inquiries and reports. In the new forms of public enterprise, these problems have been less evident. In part this may be because their objectives are more clear cut, or because they play a less strategic role in the economy than the traditional nationalized industries. However, it may also in part be due to the different control and financing arrangements that they are accorded on the grounds either that they are temporary members of the public sector or that they are more exposed to competitive pressures.

This chapter seeks to outline the main arguments underlying each of these areas of controversy, to show how successive attempts to deal with the problem do not seem to have been successful as judged by the performance of the nationalized industries, and to discuss ideas for reform which as yet remain unattempted. It will argue that the fundamental problem is the failure of successive governments to define a set of consistent objectives for the nationalized industries in the light of which to adapt the control and financing regime.

25.2. The Role of the Nationalized Industries

25.2.1. Motives for Nationalization

The key feature of a public enterprise is that it trades in a commercial environment but its entrepreneurial function is performed by the state. It therefore differs from public services such as health and education in that its outputs are distributed via the market rather than according to administrative rules. On the other hand, it differs from private enterprise in that its profits and losses accrue to the whole population of taxpayers and its shares are not traded on a stock exchange. Consequently, the incentives to respond to market signals that are provided in the private sector by shareholders and the capital market, are absent. A public enterprise is therefore a genuine 'mixed economy' organization in that its operations are subject to a combination of market forces and central direction. In similar vein, the arguments used to justify the main areas of nationalized industry span political ideology, commercial pragmatism, and economic theory.

It was largely ideological sentiments that supported the main wave of nationalization in the late 1940s. In part this may have been prompted by a desire to allow those that had participated in the sufferings of war to have a greater share in the nation's wealth. But the war also served to demonstrate the effectiveness of this form of organization. The logic of the socialist ideal dictated that the appropriate areas for nationalization were the industries that were highly capital-intensive and most open to abuse of monopoly power to the detriment of consumers or employees.

The pragmatic arguments for nationalization centre on the potential role of the major infrastructure industries as instruments of government macro-economic, industrial, and regional policy. Government gains an additional means of influencing aggregate demand through its control over the capital expenditure programmes of nationalized industries, of creating employment on a national or regional basis, and of implementing anti-inflation policies through direct regulation of incomes or prices. In addition, control over the key infrastructure industries in principle allows the planning of facilities in support of rapid industrial growth to be co-ordinated across several areas, for example a co-ordinated transport network involving road, rail, and air.

Although the original motives for nationalization were a combination of ideology and pragmatism, its role has since been rationalized by arguments drawn from welfare economics. These arguments are of two types. One is narrowly related to productive activities and concerns cases where market imperfections lead to a misallocation of resources; the other concerns the wider social welfare-maximizing functions of government. Of the former, there are three kinds of imperfection that are relevant:

(i) The existence of 'natural monopolies' where unit costs decline continuously with increasing scale, as is the case with electricity or gas distribution, or railway services. Competition would entail wasteful duplication of fixed assets, but it is necessary to introduce some regulation to avoid monopoly power being exploited to the detriment of consumers.

(ii) Where there are significant side-effects or 'externalities' attached to the consumption or production of products which are not accounted for by the market. A classic example is pollution from heavy industry or road vehicles which imposes social costs on certain sections of the community which are uncompensated other than through political or judicial intervention.

(iii) The problem of large-scale 'indivisible' or high-risk projects which, in the face of risk aversion in private capital markets, cannot readily be financed through commercial channels, for example nuclear power stations. The social cost of these risks can be minimized via the risk-pooling and the risk-spreading effects of public financing. Because the public sector undertakes a large number of projects simultaneously, it faces a lower variability of returns on the whole portfolio than the entrepreneur who undertakes only a single project. In addition, as the risks are spread amongst the very large population of taxpayers rather than concentrated on a relatively smaller set of private investors, the social impact of these risks is minimized since, for risk-averse people, the negative effect of risk increases more than in proportion to the size of the risk.

Not all of these arguments apply with equal force to all the nationalized industries, nor does the need for regulation or government funding necessarily imply state ownership or control. Moreover, whilst the existence in principle of these market imperfections is clear enough, it is more difficult to define the appropriate response in each case. For example, how should prices be set to simulate competitive market conditions? How much compensation should be paid to health victims in dangerous occupations? What is the maximum level of financial risk that should be accepted by the authorities on new public ventures? In general, economic theory has been more successful in defining the need for state intervention than in defining the rules governing how these interventions should be made.

In addition to the welfare implicatons of the activities of nationalized industries, governments attempt to meet social objectives in wider spheres such as equitable distributions of income or of employment opportunities. Just as governments have found it expedient to use nationalized industries as instruments of macroeconomic or industrial policy, they have also used them as a means of reaching these wider social objectives. However, this role has been promoted rather more systematically than has been the case with macroeconomic or industrial objectives, so that in many cases these objectives have come to be accepted as the social obligations of the corporations themselves. One clear example of this is the maintenance of unprofitable postal services in rural areas, which is seen as a means of redistributing income to less-affluent country dwellers. A further example of using nationalized industries to implement policy can be seen in the field of industrial relations where the industries have been used to spearhead new practices such as the introduction of industrial democracy. In this, as in other cases, the nationalized industries are used to give a lead which it is hoped will be followed by the private sector.

The existence of these wider roles, however, can divert attention from the fact that the mainstream activities of nationalized industries often play a crucial role in influencing the competitiveness of the large sections of private industry which depend on them for vital inputs. This raises the question of how the wider social roles of the nationalized industries should be reconciled with their commercial functions. This conflict is at the root of the problem of controlling the nationalized industries.

25.2.2. The Extent of the Public Enterprise Sector

The size of the public enterprise sector can be measured in several ways. In terms of its contribution to GDP, it has fluctuated throughout the 1970s, reaching a high point of 13 per cent in 1977 since when it has declined to around 11 per cent in 1982. However, as nationalized industries are more capital-intensive than industry as a whole, their share of total employment is lower at around 8 to 9 per cent, and their contribution to fixed capital formation is very much higher at around 20 per cent of the total. This is roughly equivalent to the relative size of public enterprise in France and West Germany. However, a major feature of the UK is the concentration of public ownership in a few nationalized industries in the UK, rather than the more diffuse spread of interests in the other two countries.

Aside from the heavy involvement in primary production, transport, communications, and public utilities, public participation in manufacturing is biased towards mature industries with strong regional concentration, such as steel and shipbuilding, and in traditional engineering sectors which have come under strong competitive pressures from abroad, such as motor vehicles and machine tools. There is also some small-scale involvement in high-technology industries, such as semiconductors, computers, and biotechnology. An important difference from other countries is the absence in the UK of state control in the financial sector, other than the Bank of England.

The importance of the public enterprise sector, and of the nationalized industries in particular, is greater than is implied by their contribution to GDP, due to their strategic role as suppliers of basic inputs to private industry, such as water, gas, electricity, rail and air transport, telecommunications, coal, and steel. Of all intermediate goods and services purchased by private firms from domestic sources, it is estimated that over 20 per cent derive from nationalized industries, and for many of these there is no alternative source of supply. On the other hand, nationalized industries are important customers of private sector firms, both for intermediate purchases and particularly for capital equipment. In both cases a greater proportion of nationalized industries' purchases is supplied by domestic industry than is the case for the economy as a whole. The significance of these purchases is particularly great in those sectors, such as mining equipment, civil engineering, electronics, and pharmaceuticals, where public purchasing accounts for over 50 per cent—rising in some cases to 90 per cent—of total demands. The manner in which public purchasing is conducted, in terms of price, ordering patterns, and performance and technical specifications, plays a role in determining the overall competitiveness of these sectors.

Although relations between public and private enterprise are primarily complementary, there are some industries where the two sectors are in competition, for example steel, which was only partially nationalized, domestic airline services, and surface transport, where rail competes with private road transport. In these cases also, the terms on which the public sector trades are of great concern to the private sector. The danger here is that the public enterprise may receive favourable treatment from government (for example the writing down of its debt in a capital reconstruction) that gives it an unwarranted competitive edge over its private sector competitors.

25.3. Principles and Problems of Control and Financing

In a free-enterprise economy with reasonably competitive markets, the allocation and utilization of resources achieved through the market mechanism is deemed to be more efficient than other practical alternatives. But this is not the case with nationalized industries, which are sheltered from the disciplines of the market both by virtue of their monopoly power—in some cases reinforced by statute, for example the Post Office—and because the continuity of the business in the face of operating losses is implicitly guaranteed by the government. In addition the nationalized industries are given objectives that fall outside the commercial sphere. For these reasons, it is necessary for rules to be devised to govern resource allocation decisions of nationalized industries (the price and quantity of their output, and the extent and direction of their capital expenditure), rules to promote efficiency in the use of existing resources to meet assigned objectives, and rules to define the basis for monitoring performance by government and Parliament. In practice, whilst certain general principles have been developed, no comprehensive control system has yet been achieved that commands wide acceptance and approval.

25.3.1. Arm's-Length Ministerial Control

After the war, the Deputy Prime Minister, H. Morrison, proposed a system of arm's-length control of public enterprise by government. The intention was that the relationship between the Board of a nationalized industry and its sponsoring government Department should be similar to that between the board and shareholders of a private company, and similar accounting and reporting conventions were to be used. However, the major difference in the case of the nationalized industries was that *all* external finance was provided by the government, which became in effect both shareholder and banker. Consequently Ministers wield considerably more *de facto* power through their control over both appointments and external finance than do shareholders of private companies. This has tended to undermine the principle of arm's-length control.

Nevertheless, the principle of arm's-length control, plus the demands of parliamentary scrutiny which have grown over the years, have implied the need for clearly defined targets to be set against which performance may be measured. These targets, together with the rules governing pricing and investment, constitute the regulatory framework within which nationalized industries today have to perate.

25.3.2. Marginal Cost Pricing

The principle of marginal cost pricing (see Chapter 24) was recommended for nationalized industries by the 1967 White Paper [7] in an attempt to put pricing decisions on a sound economic footing. Hitherto nationalized industries had priced their outputs on the basis of overall average cost, charging a uniform price to all consumers, for example a uniform price per therm of electricity independent of the time of day or the location of the consumer. The White Paper recommended that prices should reflect long-run marginal cost—i.e. including the fixed cost of new capacity—on the grounds that this reflected the optimal price-setting which would result under competitive conditions. Provided such conditions were promoted in the private sector, relative prices of public and private sector outputs would reflect relative scarcities and hence lead to an optimal allocation of resources across the economy as a whole. One advantage of this system was that the arbitrary cross-subsidization implicit in the uniform-pricing approach would be eliminated.

Whilst the need for a pricing rule is clear in monopolistic industries, the marginal cost pricing principle faces a number of difficulties. The first of these is that an optimal allocation of resources resulting from marginal cost pricing depends on the absence of imperfections elsewhere in the system. Clearly private enterprise does not match the textbook model of perfect competition, although the distortions may not be too serious when account is taken of the competition that arises from foreign suppliers and potential market entrants. However, there is also evidence that private firms do not always pursue simple profit-maximizing goals as assumed by the competitive model. Under these conditions pursuit of a marginal cost pricing rule in the public sector may be no better than using simpler procedures.

A further complication is the treatment of externalities. Where social costs or benefits are excluded from the marginal cost calculations of nationalized industry outputs, then the resulting prices will produce systematic biases away from the social welfare optimum. If they were to be included, a problem would still remain in that prices in the private sector would still exclude such elements. There would seem to be no way in which relative prices of public and private sector outputs can be made to reflect all the relevant costs and benefits without legislation to 'internalize' the external effects of private sector activities, i.e. to make private sector firms actually pay for the costs they impose on others (or receive payments for benefits received by others).

One important area where imperfections may arise is in the labour market, particularly in the light of the monopolistic market structure and politicized role of the nationalized industries. A long-run marginal cost pricing principle makes no allowance for production inefficiencies or for monopolistic pricing of inputs. Distortions in factor markets are fully reflected in nationalized industry prices as if they were structural contraints embedded in the technical conditions of supply.

However, it is not clear how prices should be set were the presence of these imperfections to be recognized. Theory might suggest that the government should intervene to create the same relative prices as would exist under perfect competition. For example if a nationalized industry was in the position of having to pay particularly high wage rates extracted by a powerful trade union, prices might be set below actual marginal costs and closer to the costs that would occur if wage levels were set in a more competitive framework. This would tend to shift the burden from the consumer to the taxpayer. Or if a nationalized industry faced a private monopolistic competitor who set prices in excess of marginal cost, nationalized industries' prices would also be set above long-run marginal costs in order to create the structure of *relative* prices (though not absolute prices) that would occur under competitive conditions. However, these relative prices may still not create the pattern of output that would exist under perfect competition, since the distortions affect quantities as well as prices; i.e. whilst they may stimulate the same pattern of demand as would exist under perfect competition, supply may not respond because monopolistic interests manage to inhibit this at levels of output below the level of demand.

An alternative approach is to view resource allocation problems as a problem of trying to optimize under constraints, and accept the market imperfections as explicit constraints. (It then turns out that the prices appropriate to an optimal allocation of resources are once more the actual long-run marginal cost prices, despite the presence of imperfections (see Redwood and Hatch [3]).

A second type of problem concerns the setting of prices when costs are continuously declining so that marginal costs are below average costs. Strict marginal cost pricing would imply losses that would have to be made up from general taxation. However, this solution does not necessarily lead to a better overall allocation of resources. Since no tax has a uniform incidence across the whole population, the distortions created through the tax changes could in practice be at least as great as those avoided by adopting a marginal cost pricing rule. In fact this result has been avoided by subordinating the strict marginal cost pricing rule to a requirement to break even, as suggested by the 1978 White Paper [8]. In some such cases, such as electricity or gas distribution, an element of marginal cost pricing can still be preserved. For example, to discriminate between different classes of customer on the basis of the marginal costs they impose on the system, a two-part tariff is used, made up of a fixed charge to cover the fixed costs of the basic service, plus an additional amount that varies in proportion to marginal costs.

In addition to these difficulties with the principle of marginal cost pricing, a problem that arises in practice is that nationalized industry prices have a major impact both on the Retail Price Index (RPI) and on government revenue and the Public Sector Borrowing Requirement (PSBR). Consequently, governments take a close interest in the proposed price changes of individual industries. There have been many occasions, some quite recently, when price increases that could be justified on cost terms have been cut back or delayed. There have been others, such as gas, where prices have been deliberately marked up above marginal costs in order to enforce a particular depletion policy, raise revenue, and preserve relative pricing with other fuels. It is reasonable to speculate that, even if all industries were able in principle to assess marginal costs, they would still face political resistance to the shake-up of existing price structures that a shift to universal marginal cost pricing would imply.

25.3.3. Investment Appraisal

In addition to a pricing rule, a further mechanism is required to allocate capital resources efficiently, both between the public and the private sectors, and between projects within the public sector. The government attempts to do this by imposing criteria for public investment appraisal that reflect the opportunity cost of capital (see Chapter 3, p. 70). The underlying aim is that resources invested in nationalized industries should earn a return at least equivalent to that which would have been achieved in the private sector. The precise mechanisms by which this is to be achieved have varied. The 1967 White Paper [7] recommended that appraisal should be conducted by comparing the net present value of each project, to be calculated using a test discount rate (TDR), or interest rate, that was set at a uniform rate for the whole of the public sector. (See Chapter 3, pp. 76–7 for details of such calculations.) The level of the TDR—initially 8 per cent in real terms, but soon put up to 10 per cent—was based on an assessment of expected returns on large, low-risk projects in the private sector. However, the TDR was difficult to implement in practice because interdependence between new projects and the rest of the business frequently meant that returns to individual projects could not be isolated. Consequently, the 1978 White Paper [8] recommended that the TDR be replaced by a required rate of return (RRR), to be applied to the investment programme *as a whole*, leaving the industries to determine their own methods of assessing individual projects within the overall total. The rate set was 5 per cent per annum in real terms, on the basis of the lower average rates of return achieved in the private sector in the later 1970s.

The first issues that this procedure raises concern the manner in which the opportunity cost should be estimated and whether a uniform rate should be applied to all industries. In a risk-free world of perfect information flows, a uniform criterion based on private sector returns might appear desirable, although even here it could be argued that the *social* rate of time preference (for consumption tomorrow rather than today) may be lower than the private rate, justifying a lower required rate of return in the public sector. In the real world, however, investment decisions are taken in conditions of imperfect information and considerable uncertainty about future economic and technical developments. In the private sector, these factors are reflected in required rates of return which include a risk premium that varies for industry to industry. Therefore, not only is it reasonable that the RRR should vary between nationalized industries according to the individual market and technical risks that they face, but also that the public sector as a whole might be expected to face a lower degree of risk than the private sector, *ceteris paribus*, due to its superior access to information and its greater degree of control over future economic events. On the other hand, the government has argued for a higher RRR in the public sector on the grounds that the absence of the ultimate sanction of bankruptcy encourages 'appraisal optimism' on the part of nationalized industry planners, which needs to be offset.

A further point arising out of this is that attempts to reflect the opportunity cost of capital in public investment appraisals have in practice been crude and insensitive to market conditions. The discount rate has remained constant for periods of years at a stretch, during which the private sector has had to face sharp fluctuations in the cost of capital. Had nationalized industries' investment not been subject to additional controls, such as direct controls on access to external finance, far from creating a balanced distribution of scarce capital resources, this would have loaded the effects of a credit squeeze entirely onto the private sector.

Moreover the changes in the discount rate that have been made have tended to be large and therefore potentially disruptive. For example, the rate was halved from 10 to 5 per cent in real terms with the introduction of the 1978 White Paper, but the effect was even greater since the TDR of 10 per cent was a minimum requirement for all projects whereas the RRR of 5 per cent was an average measure across all projects in a programme. It is possible that this one change was sufficient to tip the balance from investment in diesel- to electric-traction for the railways.

A further issue concerns the appropriateness of these criteria in monopolistic industries where there is little or no market constraint on pricing. If pricing is based on costs, and if the cost of capital based on the RRR is included as a cost, then under monopolistic conditions the RRR will automatically be achieved and the criteria play no allocative role. There are two possible solutions in principle, although neither is widely applied. On the one hand, prices may be regulated at 'competitive' levels and the RRR validly applied; on the other, investment appraisal may be conducted using a social cost-benefit approach and prices subsequently fixed to maximize the net benefit. Both cases serve to demonstrate that investment criteria cannot be divorced from pricng rules in determining the overall allocation of resources.

Finally, there is the question of the choice between an approach based on a discount rate applied to individual projects, and that of a rate of return applied to the whole investment programme of an industry. The adoption of the RRR approach was designed to avoid the interdependence problem and to give the industries the flexibility to appraise projects in a way appropriate to their circumstances, whilst at the same time meeting the target for the programme as a whole. However, it is not clear that the interdependence problem is completely resolved. An investment programme is unlikely to be completely divorced from existing operations and its rate of return will still reflect the particular allocation of joint costs. In addition, whilst the RRR approach might achieve an appropriate allocation of capital between public and private sectors, the same does not hold true for allocation between projects within an industry, for a required average return on the whole programme could allow individual projects with very low returns to go ahead if the programme also included some projects with exceptionally high returns.

25.4. Investment and Financing in Practice

In practice, central control over pricing and investment decisions is not conducted entirely at arm's length through the medium of these guidelines. With regard to investment proposals, sponsor Departments regularly review a sample of projects of each industry to ensure that appraisal techniques are being correctly applied, and monitor all proposals that exceed a threshold amount. In addition, the investment programmes are discussed between the Treasury, sponsor Departments, and the industries themselves, before being presented to Ministers in the annual Capital Investment Financing Review. As a result of ministerial consideration in the context of all other claims on public expenditure, investment levels for the following year are fixed, together with approval for declining proportions of programmes for the ensuing two years to allow some continuity in long-term projects.

In addition to these administrative checks, there are two further constraints which may influence resource allocation, although this is not their primary purpose. First, pricing decisions may be influenced by the need to meet financial targets; second, both pricing and investment decisions will be influenced by the availability of external finance, over which the industries themselves have no direct control. There has been considerable concern in recent years that increasing emphasis on financial performance and independence may in fact have severely impaired the rational allocation of resources in the nationalized industries.

25.4.1. Medium-Term Financial Targets

The primary purpose of setting financial objectives is to encourage efficiency in the nationalized industries and to provide a measure of their achievements. Experience, however, suggests that financial targets do not fulfil this role very effectively. The main problem is that they encourage excessive emphasis to be put on financial performance without recognizing the wider roles of nationalized industries that cannot be monitored in these terms. There is therefore a danger inherent in the system that it will show in a pessimistic light the performance of industries with extensive social obligations. It will also condone the performance of industries that are inefficient in economic terms but nevertheless are able to exploit a monopolistic position so as to produce respectable financial results. In principle, the financial targets are meant to be adapted to the circumstances of the individual industries so that lower targets are set where social obligations are extensive. This is not wholly satisfactory, however, because it does not encourage a sufficient distinction in the public mind between justified losses due to social obligations and unjustified losses due to inefficiency. It would be better for recurrent social obligations to be explicitly assessed and financed by grants from the Exchequer, as recommended in the 1967 White Paper [7], so that they do not distort reported financial performance. Only in the case of British rail has this route been followed.

More serious perhaps are the effects on financial performance of *ad hoc* ministerial directives concerning prices, investment, or employment. On occasion, forms of compensation have been made in order to protect the industry's investment programme, such as the additional external finance that was extended to the nationalized industries in the 1974–5 era of price restraint. However, this type of compensation does not affect reported operating surpluses or rates of return. As a consequence, financial targets are undermined as measures of performance and senior management of the industries becomes demoralized by the lack of an accurate, objective yardstick of its achievements.

Another objection that has been raised to medium-term financial targets is that they are redundant when rules exist to control investment and prices. The investment rules determine the production function, and therefore the scale of operations and the cost structure for a given set of input prices; pricing policy determines the price and quantity of output for a given level of costs. It follows that as revenue and operating costs are determined by these two rules then so are profits. Attempts to apply a direct control on profits, it is held, serve only to over-determine the system.

However, a further degree of freedom may exist in management's ability to influence costs within certain limits for a given stock of capital, i.e.

management is able to influence short-run costs in relation to output independently of prices, which are fixed by reference to long-run costs. In this case, the financial target would exert control over the level of x-inefficiency, the difference between actual costs and the absolute minimum achievable for a given level of output. Moreover, the RRR criterion applies to a longer time-horizon than the financial target, and only to new investment. Its role differs from that of the medium-term financial target, which can be seen as a means of applying a target rate of return to the existing capital stock to be achieved either by reducing current costs or by divestment of relatively unprofitable activities. Nevertheless, it is quite possible for the financial target to conflict with the pricing and investment rules if it is not set with sufficient sensitivity to current economic conditions and the potential for efficiency gains.

Indeed, one of the difficulties met in practice has been that of setting realistic targets in conditions of macroeconomic uncertainty, particularly over the last decade when the trading environment of the nationalized industries has been disrupted by energy price fluctuations and by the decline of manufacturing industry which is their major customer. Other difficulties have arisen due to the distorting effect of inflation on financial targets in the absence of established procedures for inflation accounting. A further problem lies in the medium-term nature of financial targets which reduces their effectiveness as a monitor of current performance and as a test of current management; the average term of office of nationalized industry Chairmen is only four to five years. All that performance against targets can do is indicate to incoming management whether a change of course is desirable or not.

25.4.2. Performance Indicators

In response to some of the objections outlined in the preceding section, a further monitoring device was introduced in the 1978 White Paper [8], with the intention of providing direct measures of operating efficiency and quality of service. Performance indicators were to be a means of avoiding excessive emphasis on financial targets and of preventing financial targets being met purely by increasing prices or lowering standards of service in monopolistic industries. The particular indicators were to be agreed on a case-by-case basis between Boards and sponsoring Departments and were to be reported prominently in the annual report of each corporation.

Whilst the introduction of performance indicators has been generally welcomed as an improvement in the way performance is reported, a number of imperfections exist in the present system. First, no formal targets are set against which performance is compared. Consequently the indicators simply measure the degree of improvement or deterioration relative to the status quo. Perhaps of greater importance is the manner in which the particular indicators are selected. Those who have the greatest interest in the performance of the industries—their customers as represented by user groups—have little or no say in their selection. Moreover the assessment of performance is carried out by the industries themselves and is not subject to independent audit in the way that financial reporting is. It is perhaps therefore not surprising that performance indicators do not carry the same weight with the general public as do financial results.

A further difficulty is that selection of a narrow range of performance indicators may lead to window-dressing—i.e. running the business so as to achieve good scores on the published indicators at the expense of wider aspects of performance that are not monitored. In any case performance indicators appear to be accorded low priority by sponsoring Departments and to be subordinated to financial targets when the two conflict.

25.4.3. External Financing Limits

A further measure of financial control that has come to assume a central role in recent years is the external financing limit (EFL). EFLs are a system of ceilings on the total finance that can be raised by each nationalized industry, and were introduced in the mid-1970s as part of the government's switch to controlling public expenditure in cash rather than volume terms. They constitute a single limit on external funds from all sources, including grants, borrowings from the National Loans Fund (NLF), market borrowing, bank overdrafts, and leasing. EFLs are set annually for the year ahead on the basis of projections of revenue and costs and of the industries' approved investment programme.

EFLs have come to assume a predominate role as instruments of control because they apply an effective sanction on poor financial performance through their impact on an industry's ability to finance capital expenditure or add to reserves. They also have a short time-scale and thereby apply a more immediate discipline than medium-term financial targets. This effectiveness, however, is achieved at the cost of a lack of selectivity in their impact, in that (i) they may impinge on aspects of performance other than those intended or desired, and (ii) they can constrain management from taking certain actions that are in the long-term interests of the industries and their customers.

The cash limit system, of which EFLs are a part, may be used to achieve a number of objectives, including limiting the absorption of real resources by the public sector relative to the private sector, holding down public sector costs, and controlling economic aggregates, such as the PSBR or total public expenditure, as part of macroeconomic policy. However, with respect to the first two objectives, cash limits are blunt instruments in that they cannot discriminate between the impact on costs and that on volumes. Cash limits set with the intention of holding down costs can be evaded by cutting down the scale of operations instead; the same result can also occur unintentionally, if the underlying rate of inflation is underestimated so that the limits are set at an unrealistically tight level. Where a government has the twin aims of defeating inflation and of reducing the relative size of the public sector in 'non-marketed' areas it may find cash limits a simple single instrument to achieve both aims. But in the case of the nationalized industries where market forces play a role in determining the allocation of resources, such a use of the EFL system is inappropriate. It risks imposing arbitrary and unintended constraints on profitable activities and investment.

In recent years, cash limits have come to assume greater significance as instruments of a macroeconomic policy which has centred on reducing the

PSBR as a share of GNP and controlling the growth of nominal income in the economy as a whole. The arbitrary definition of the PSBR—for example, external finance for BL, Rolls Royce, and other publicly owned companies is excluded—has prompted a debate as to whether nationalized industry borrowing should always be accounted against the PSBR. (Under the present rules, nationalized industry borrowing is accounted against the PSBR whatever its source.) It has been argued, for example by the Nationalised Industries' Chairmen's Group, that as nationalized industries are businesses whose activities are primarily commercial, they should be permitted the same flexibility as private enterprises to raise capital from any source: the identity of the ultimate owners should not be allowed to distort their operations. Although this argument is couched in terms of flexibility to raise finance for approved projects, it has been linked with a demand for greater independence for the industries over their actual levels of investment. There are therefore two issues; one of control, that EFLs prevent the industries from implementing minor projects which they could otherwise carry out, and another concerning the method of financing, that there may exist a method that has less undesirable effects on the government's macroeconomic policy.

The response of the Treasury to this demand for greater financial independence is that ownership does make a difference in one important respect, namely that all borrowing by public corporations is implicitly guaranteed by the government. From the point of view of the private investor, securities issued by public corporations would carry no risk of default, and hence would play an equivalent role in portfolios to gilt-edged stock issued by the Treasury. They would therefore have a similar macroeconomic impact. From the point of view of the industries, the implicit guarantee removes the necessity to maintain prudent accounting ratios and a healthy track record in order to attract investors. Hence, it is argued, there is no advantage in granting the industries access to private capital markets.

Whilst the government sees nothing to be gained from greater financial independence for nationalized industries, it does see that it may lose an instrument of an anti-inflation policy that is based on controlling total nominal expenditure in the economy. Where this is the object, the government has on occasions been willing to sacrifice some profitable public investment in order to meet its expenditure targets. Once again, this brings the responsibilities of the industries themselves and the macroeconomic objectives of the government into direct conflict. However, even here, the appropriate target is the capital programme of the nationalized industries themselves rather than the amount of external finance that they are permitted to raise. EFLs are an imperfect substitute since to some extent they can be evaded by raising prices to increase the availability of internal funds to finance investment.

In the final analysis, the effectiveness of EFLs in their various potential roles depends on how the industries in practice respond to them. Whilst the EFLs are not intended in normal circumstances to constrain the investment programmes authorized for the industries, they may turn out to be too tight if the assumptions for inflation and output on which they are based prove too optimistic. When this occurs—as it may frequently do if central government has a bias towards macroeconomic optimism—the industries may respond to this cash flow constraint in one of three ways:

(i) they may cut costs, either by improving efficiency, by holding down pay settlements, or by reducing standards of service;
(ii) they may increase internal funds by raising prices; or
(iii) they may cut back their investment expenditures.

Where EFLs are used as an explicit instrument of anti-inflation policy—i.e. to bring inflation down rather than just to prevent it accelerating—they are intended to act as an influence on unions to accept low pay settlements by imposing an ultimate constraint on the industries' ability to pay higher wages, i.e. they are intended to be a weak substitute for the ultimate sanction of bankruptcy in the private sector. However, there seems to be little evidence that EFLs have had this effect in practice. In the first place there is no reason why EFLs should command any more credibility than medium-term financial targets, since the continuity of the business, and hence of employment, is effectively guaranteed. The only real sanction that EFLs impose is the curtailment of capital expenditure, and this is probably not perceived as a serious threat to employment prospects. On the one hand, new fixed investment could well be labour-saving and hence may actually imply less rather than more jobs than with existing technology; on the other, the effect of the capital programme would not be felt for several years, by which time it may be expected that a change of government or improvement in general economic conditions would have led to a reinstatement of the cancelled investment programme.

If the industries themselves also tend to take the view that the constraints are temporary, they are more likely to evade the effects of EFLs by raising prices rather than by cutting costs. However, their ability to do this will depend on the position of each industry on its demand curve. If, despite the restraint on prices imposed by Ministers, the relative price of a nationalized industry's output is already high, it may be in an elastic segment of its demand curve. Under these conditions, a price rise above the rate of inflation, even if only temporary, may cause significant loss of market share that could endure for several years, and the likelihood of nationalized industries evading the EFL constraint in this manner is therefore lower.

It must be concluded that there is a danger that, whatever the aim of EFLs, their impact may in practice fall on the investment programme. This is clearly a concern felt by the Chairmen of the nationalized industries, who have pointed out the serious commercial costs of a disrupted programme, particularly where performance depends on an interdependent set of annual projects. However, when challenged to do so, they have not found it easy to identify a significant amount of investment that has actually been frustrated by EFLs. In part this may be because in a climate of financial constraint some potentially profitable projects never reach the approval stage. Alternatively the cuts may fall on less readily identifiable types of expenditure, such as on safety and maintenance equipment, which nevertheless have an important impact on the performance of the industry and on the welfare of its work-force.

25.5. Performance of the Nationalized Industries

25.5.1. Problems of Measurement

A major problem with appraising the performance of the nationalized industries is the lack of a comprehensive, stable, and consistent set of objectives for each industry against which performance can be matched. In practice, the greatest attention is given by government and public alike to financial measures because they are the most accessible and the most familiar. However, they can be highly misleading for industries that have extensive social obligations or that are undergoing restructuring in response to major shifts in demand or technology. Some further light may be thrown on underlying performance by examining measures of real performance linked to operating efficiency or to quality of service, or by breaking down results on a divisional or regional basis. Ultimately, however, the performance of a nationalized industry can only be judged by a process of impartial examination of all aspects of its activities over a run of years in the context of its commercial environment and of the complex objectives and directives imposed on it. This section reviews briefly the evidence on financial performance and on some of the measures of real performance that are readily available.

25.5.2. Financial Performance

The financial results of the major nationalized industries for 1982–3 are presented in Table 25.1. The main impression from the table is the diversity in the financial targets set for the individual industries, and the even wider diversity of performance against these targets. This highlights the dangers of making generalizations about the performance of the nationalized industries as a group. Of the eight industries represented, three, the British Gas Corporation, British Telecom, and the Electricity Council, consistently hit or exceed their targets. In 1982–3 they were joined by a fourth, British Airways. On the other hand, the three chronic loss makers, British Rail, the British Steel Corporation, and the National Coal Board, have consistently failed to meet their modest financial targets—despite the receipt of substantial grants by two of them. The difference in performance is particularly stark when portrayed in terms of their impact on public expenditure. The three loss makers required external funds of over £2·5 billion in 1982–3, whereas the three industries in surplus together contributed over £400 million in repayments to government, after taxation and financing their investment programmes.

It is tempting to conclude that the surplus industries are paragons of efficiency whereas the loss makers are grossly mismanaged, but this would be premature before considering the wider circumstances. Of the three consistently good performers, two are energy suppliers. They have been encouraged to match the prices they charge to those of competing fuels, whilst at the same time enjoying access to cheap inputs on the basis of long-term contracts that pre-date the energy price explosion. The third surplus industry, British Telecom, has enjoyed a considerable degree of monopoly as well as a rapidly expanding market. It too has not been slow to raise prices despite the

TABLE 25.1. *Financial Performance of the Nationalized Industries, 1982–1983*

	Target	Out-turn	Profit after interest* (£m)	EFL† (£m)	Actual financing requirement (£m)	Grants and subsidies
British Airways	5·75% return (1982–3/1983–4)	9% (1982–3)	62	−9	−35	
British Gas Corporation	3·5% return (1980–1/1982–3)	4·2% average	634·4	−87	−230	
British Rail Intercity	Break-even by 1985	?	−176	923	?	Revenue subsidy of £887m
Freight	Positive return	Operating loss of £4·4m				
British Steel Corporation	Break-even before interest	Loss of £318m	−386	575	569	
British Telecom	5·5% return	5·8%				
Electricity Council	1·8% return (1980–1/1982–3)	2·3% average	332	−148	−153	
National Coal Board	Positive return after grants (unquantified)	Loss of £111m	−485	962	951	Deficit grant of £374m

* But before taxation and extraordinary items; historic cost basis.
† Including revisions during the course of the year.

capital-intensive nature of its operations and the steady growth of system utilization.

On the other hand, two of the chronic loss makers, the NCB and the BSC, operate in competitive markets in which they compete with foreign producers, some of which receive hefty subsidies from their own national governments. The third, BR, faces strong competition from other modes of transport. One factor which these loss-making industries have in common is that they are all mature industries. Their present capacity was laid down to meet the requirements of an earlier era of rapid industrialization, and the demand for their outputs has been particularly hard hit by the energy price shocks of the 1970s and the rapid rate of de-industrialization experienced in the UK. They are therefore faced with a double adjustment task of contraction and of modernization in order to meet present-day demands. Their performance should ideally be judged against a long-term plan that spells out the financial implications of these adjustments on a year-by-year basis. Such plans do exist as a basis for decisions and evaluation of performance, though unforeseen changes in the economic environment may require modifications which complicate any such evaluation procedure.

25.5.3. Real Performance

A selection of efficiency measures for recent years is presented in Table 25.2 for the major industries. The principal measure of performance shown here is the trend in all-factor productivity—a calculation which includes the contribution of capital as well as labour to overall efficiency and which is particularly suitable for capital-intensive industries. More recent trends in performance are depicted by some of the performance indicators which the industries are now required to publish.

The National Economic Development Office (NEDO) report[1] on the nationalized industries published in 1976 showed that productivity growth in most of the nationalized industries throughout the 1960s compared favourably with the rest of the economy. The figures for the 1970s in Table 25.2 suggest a wider spread of results: only those industries facing relatively strong demand growth, such as BA, the BGC, and BT, achieved average rates of all-factor productivity growth over 1968–78 that exceeded the average of 1·75 per cent per annum for manufacturing industry as a whole. Whilst inevitably there is a correlation between these productivity figures and financial performance, there are also some interesting exceptions that emphasize the dangers of relying on financial performance. For example BR, which has made losses for more than two decades, achieved productivity gains only a little short of the manufacturing average. On the other hand the Electricity Council, which has usually been profitable, achieved annual productivity gains of less than 1 per cent in 1968–78.

An even starker divergence between financial and real performance has occurred since 1978. The industry which appears to have made the most spectacular gains in labour productivity is the loss-making British Steel

[1] 'A study of UK Nationalised Industries: Their Role in the Economy and Control in the Future', NEDO, 1976.

	1968–78* (% p.a.)	1978–9	1979–80	1980–1	1981–2	1982–3	1978–82 (% p.a.)
British Airways							
All-factor productivity	+5·5						+7·7
Available tonne km per employee (000)		135·0	145·2	153·7	157·5	181·6	
British Gas Corporation							
All-factor productivity	+6·5						−0·8
Real operating costs per therm (1973–4 = 100)		90	89	91	87	87	
Electricity Council							
All-factor productivity	+0·7						+2·1
Real total cost per kWh sold (1973–4 = 100)		115	115	119	125	125	
Average supply interruption (mins per customer)		84·3	79·1	76·5	198·5	90·4	+1·8
British Rail							
All-factor productivity	+1·6						+2·2
Passenger/net tonne miles per staff member		144·7	147·8	142·9	146·2	157·8†	
British Steel Corporation							
All-factor productivity	−2·4						
Man-hours per tonne of liquid steel		14·3	13·2	14·5	9·4	9·3	−10·2
Utilization of manned steelmaking capacity		n.a.	n.a.	87%	92%	83%	
British Telecom							
All-factor productivity	+5·2						
National Coal Board							
All-factor productivity	−1·3						
Output per man-year		448	470	479	497	504	+2·4 (1979–82)

* Source: Pryke [5].

† Corrected for distortions due to strikes.

Note: Vertical line implies change in definition.

Corporation in which man-hours required per tonne of liquid steel produced fell by an average of 10 per cent per annum between 1978 and 1982. The two other chronic loss makers, BR and the NCB, have also improved efficiency by over 2 per cent per annum on the measures reproduced here. On the other hand, the profitable energy-producing industries have either become less efficient, such as the Electricity Council where unit costs have risen in real terms and security of supplies deteriorated, or have made only minor gains as in the case of the BGC, where unit costs have fallen by only 0·8 per cent per annum in real terms over 1978–82. This again reinforces the impression that profits in the energy industry owe more to pricing policy than to efficiency, and that the losses in steel, coal, and rail disguise attempts to make constructive responses, possibly belated, to structural problems.

25.6. Proposals for Reform

Finally, this chapter briefly discusses the merits of several proposals for reforming the structure of nationalized industries, proposals that remain largely untried. These proposals vary according to the extent to which they tackle the separate issues of control or of regulation of finance. Proposals aimed mainly at the control problem include the recommendation of the 1976 NEDO Report, subsequently endorsed by others, that an intermediate tier of management be introduced between Ministers and Boards in order to permit greater independence of management from day-to-day governmental control. Another proposal, aimed primarily at easing the financing constraint, is that some areas of nationalized industries' activities be opened up to private finance on certain conditions. Whilst this proposal implies that the government loses some control in that it has to renounce the prerogative to intervene unless it pays compensation, it also involves a shift of the regulatory function from government to the market. A further proposal, which introduces private finance by transferring on a temporary basis certain classes of assets into the private sector, is that of franchising. This differs from the previous proposal in that a considerable degree of control is retained by the state, but a market incentive to minimize costs, subject to an acceptable level of service, is introduced. Finally, there is the possibility of privatization, whereby both control and finance are put into the hands of private investors—although the state could still retain a regulatory function as happens with utilities in the US. It is this last route which the government since 1979 has chosen to follow.

25.6.1. Policy Councils

The aim of this proposal was to reinforce the arm's-length principle of control by interposing a further management tier, termed a 'Policy Council', between the sponsoring Department and the Corporation's Board. The Policy Council was to include the relevant Ministers and Chairman together with representatives of other interests in the industry, of their principal customers or suppliers, and of the City. It was intended that the Policy Council would set objectives and agree the corporate plan and that Ministers would forgo the power to issue directives directly to the industry. Nevertheless the government would retain ultimate control through its powers of appointment to the Policy Council. This proposal would have had the advantage that a wider range of expertise and interests would have been brought to bear on constructing the industry's plan, leading to more stability and better integration with the plans of related industries. Moreover, it would be less easy for Ministers to apply informal pressure on management. Where a Minister did succeed in imposing an obligation, this would be made overt through a submission to the Policy Council so that explicit financial compensation could be agreed.

In practice, this proposal found favour neither with the government nor with nationalized industry managers. The main objection was that a further tier of bureaucracy would be costly and would slow down decision-making. Some commentators speculated that nationalized industry Chairmen did not wish to lose the informal direct relationship with Ministers from which they stood to gain as much as to lose. In the event, the problems of *ad hoc* intervention and the principle of compensation were tackled by other means in the 1978 White Paper [8].

25.6.2. Access to Private Finance

Nationalized industries raise almost all their external finance from the National Loans Fund. But as such borrowing is included in the public expenditure totals, it is subject to the exigencies of the government's targets for overall public spending. If the corporations were permitted to issue securities in their own names, the fact that such stock would be implicitly guaranteed by the Treasury means that in economic terms it would be indistinguishable from gilts—and hence would not constitute grounds of itself for excluding such borrowing from the public expenditure definition.

However, this argument loses force if it is possible to create conditions where no guarantee attaches to an industry's market borrowing—i.e. if some of the risks of the business can be 'privatized' by being transferred to private investors. Where there is a genuine transfer of risk, then, in addition to the freeing of a financing constraint, there can be gains from improved allocation and utilization of resources as a result of exposing the operations of the nationalized industries to the discipline of the market.

However, certain conditions need to hold for there to be a genuine and efficient transfer of risk to private investors. In general terms, investors need to be clear about what risks they are facing, and there must be no way in which one party can subsequently offload its risk onto the other. This gives rise to the following necessary conditions:

(i) That the activity to be financed can be separated from the main business in an accounting and operational sense. Otherwise, returns to the project cannot be isolated from the effects of other parts of the business.

(ii) That government renounces *ad hoc* intervention in these activities unless compensation is paid on previously agreed terms. This limits the extent to which returns can be arbitrarily distorted by political interference.

(iii) That the activity does not involve an unregulated monopolistic position in a market, which might allow returns to private investors to be boosted by exploitation of that position.

(iv) That the activities nominated for private finance cannot subsequently revert to being publicly funded. To allow this would undermine the pressures on the industry to be efficient in order to maintain its credit rating.

A variety of forms of introducing private finance along these lines has been suggested which differ according to the class of risks and the degree of control that are borne by private investors. They include:

(i) *Performance bonds*—a financial instrument for raising general-purpose finance, half-way between a conventional bond and an equity share, whose return would be related to certain aspects of the performance of the nationalized industry, such as the price of the product, revenue, productivity, or a profit measure, adjusted if necessary to offset the effects of monopoly. Investors would have a prior claim in the assets of the business and accordingly there would be no transfer of control.

(ii) *Project finance*—where private finance is provided for a discrete project proposed by a nationalized industry, either via a debt instrument as in (i) but related to the performance and assets of the project alone, or through private ownership of the assets, which are leased to the public corporation for a variable payment related to usage. Investors would therefore bear the risks attached to constructing and maintaining the assets, together with some of the market-related risks.

(iii) *Joint-venture companies*—whereby private equity capital is raised for activities that can be separated from the main business and set up as joint-venture companies, in partnership with a nationalized industry. Control would be shared by public and private interests, and private investors would bear all the risks of the business, since its separate legal identity would ensure that no public guarantee of the private stake would have to exist. However, in some cases there would need to be safeguards on the setting of transfer prices and on the scope for making political directives.

Serious consideration has been given to these proposals, and significant progress was made by British Telecom in 1982 towards issuing a performance bond before it was decided to proceed with full-scale privatization. Some commentators have seen considerable scope for forming joint ventures in many of the peripheral but rapidly expanding areas of nationalized industries, where social obligations do not arise, such as Datapost, Intercity, Sealink, and even electricity-generation. (For further details on some of these, see [9].) However, one stumbling-block has been the suggestion that private financing would be more expensive than traditional borrowing via the NLF. Although the dividend cost of private funds might well be higher than the interest cost of NLF loans, this extra cost is in economic terms illusory. For the true cost of financing nationalized industries via the NLF is masked since it does not incorporate a premium for risk. The hidden cost—which is realized intermittently whenever nationalized industries' debt is written off—is borne by the taxpayer. The apparent higher cost of private finance is due to shifting this burden from the taxpayers to the private investor. Another obstacle has been the apparent unwillingness of the authorities to exempt private funds from the EFL constraint, and this has reduced the attraction of these schemes to the nationalized industries. At the time of writing, the greatest interest in such schemes is being shown by local authorities for the construction of sewage works and trunk roads.

25.6.3. Franchising

Franchising is an alternative to private finance schemes that attempts to meet the same objectives of improving the allocation and utilization of resources within the public sector without complete loss of public control. Under this system, private firms tender for the sole rights to supply certain goods or services for a fixed period using the fixed assets owned by a public authority such as a nationalized industry. At the end of the period, these rights are contested in a new competitive tender. The particular feature that makes this system suitable for publicly supplied goods is that the authority is able to implement its social obligations through the conditions that it sets on the franchise. On the other hand, it can relinquish control of day-to-day operations and financial risks, which pass to the franchisee.

Franchising has the advantage that underlying social objectives have to be spelt out in advance in contractual terms, and therefore cannot be used as an excuse for political interference in day-to-day management. Moreover, an implicit market valuation is placed on the cost of these social obligations as reflected in the tender prices. An additional advantage is the favourable impact on efficiency. Since the private franchisee retains in full the surplus of his operating profit over the fixed royalty payment, he has an incentive to maximize the cost efficiency of the business. Providing that a reasonable number of operators compete for tenders (i.e. that tendering is open to all-comers, and that entry conditions are not too demanding), this contested market will in principle show many of the benefits of competition based on continuous free entry.[2] Franchising can therefore be a useful way of introducing competition in conditions where it is normally either impossible because of natural monopoloy, or undesirable because of wasteful competition.

However, there may be problems in practice. In the first place, this system does not avoid the need for monitoring and regulation. There need to be procedures to ensure that the terms of the contract are fulfilled by the franchisee with respect particularly to social obligations and the quality of the service. Where contract periods are quite lengthy—because the franchisee himself has to invest in specific equipment or in training personnel—retendering may apply an insufficiently strong incentive to maintain high standards of service throughout the contract period. Also, the franchisee might be able to exploit his monopolistic position in the market by charging excessively high prices, unless

---

[2] Cf. Baumol's theory of contestable market in W. J. Baumol, J. C. Panzar, R. D. Willig: *Contestable Markets and the Theory of Industrial Structure* (Harcourt Jovanovich, 1982).

regulated by the terms of the contract. However, even where pricing is uncontrolled, competitive tendering should ensure that at least the extra returns are largely passed on to the franchisor. The franchisor may then attempt to redistribute them directly to consumers or to let them accrue to the benefit of taxpayers via central government finances.

Franchising has some advantages in common with private financing schemes: they both improve the utilization of resources allocated to public uses and bring private risk capital into the public sector. Franchising offers perhaps a simpler way of dealing with social obligations than do many of the private financing schemes, both in terms of determining how they should be compensated and how their control should be separated from day-to-day interference. On the other hand, the benefit of improvements in the allocation of resources between alternative uses appears to be less than in the case of private financing schemes. Whilst cross-subsidization between elements of a franchised service are likely to be eliminated, the overall franchising operation does not face a market test, for the expected return at the margin will be governed by the lowest tender, possibly negative, that the franchisor is prepared to accept. Whether an activity proposed for franchising goes ahead therefore depends ultimately on the existing administrative review procedures governing all nationalized industries' investment and leasing plans.

25.6.4. Privatization

Since 1979 the government's strategy towards the nationalized industries has consisted of two elements, liberalization and privatization. Liberalization seeks to encourage the growth of competition within the sectors served by nationalized industries as a spur to increasing their efficiency. Privatization on the other hand seeks to eliminate at source the problems of controlling and financing nationalized industries by transferring the industries to private ownership. How these two approaches are to be integrated is not entirely clear. Liberalization does not need to be accompanied by privatization to be effective and hence may be used in cases where privatization is not advisable, for example because of extensive externalities or social obligations. On the other hand privatization frequently needs to be backed up by liberalization to avoid the exploitation of monopoly power by private interests. The balance between these policies in each industry should reflect a careful assessment of its market structure and its indirect welfare effects.

Liberalization centres on dismantling the legislation which protects a nationalized industry's monopoly position. Most of the achievements in this field to date (1984) have been restricted to peripheral areas such as allowing competition on long-distance bus routes, opening up the market for telephone handsets to private suppliers, and permitting some competition with the Post Office in the handling of express mail. More significant, however, is the action that may be taken in the case of natural monopoly to force a public utility to share the usage of its network with private competitors, as in the case of the access to the British Telecom system provided to Mercury Ltd.

Privatization, it appears, is being pursued more energetically than liberalization. It has a number of powerful attractions to the present government, including:

(i) the enhancement of economic freedom through the resort to a market-determined allocation of resources in these sectors;

(ii) the improvement in the efficient use of resources through the imposition of market disciplines;

(iii) the weakening of the power of public sector unions over pay bargaining by creating an effective budget constraint;

(iv) the reduction in public sector borrowing due to eliminating the need to provide external finance to these industries, plus the one-off benefit from the revenues generated by asset sales;

(v) the widening of share ownership among the population and to provide better profit opportunities for the private sector.

As has been seen, many of these objectives can be met by other routes. The appeal of privatization is based on the simultaneous achievement of all these objectives, the significant contribution to revenue from asset sales, and an inherent prejudice held by many against public ownership.

Although progress since 1974 towards privatization has been rapid, priorities appear to have been determined less by the need to improve efficiency than by the practical question of the attractiveness of the business to the capital market. Many of the companies offered to the market have been small and operate outside the traditional areas of the nationalized industries, for example Amersham International, Cable and Wireless, and the National Freight Corporation; others have been subsidiaries of public corporations, such as BR Hotels and subsidiaries of the NEB. The two largest sales to date have involved North Sea oil production assets, sold under the name of Britoil, and the country's major airframe and missile manufacturer, British Aerospace. In all of these cases, the businesses involved straightforward commercial activities, unfettered by regulation or obvious social obligations, in sectors where private firms already operated, thereby providing an existing market for the relevant type of share.

Considerably greater problems attach to the proposed privatization of British Telecom and British Gas, and have been responsible for the delays in bringing them to the market. In part this is due to their size and novelty. But to a considerable degree it also reflects the difficulties of producing a regulatory regime that is satisfactory to both consumers and investors. In the case of British Telecom, considerable doubts have been expressed by consumer groups about the possible loss of unprofitable telephone services in rural areas and the reduction in the number of public call boxes. Fears about exploitation of its monopoly position have led to a proposal to restrict increases in tariffs for several years following privatization to a maximum percentage related to the Cost of Living Index. However, this proposal has been criticized on a number of grounds, such as that the ceiling on tariff increases is arbitrary and does not reflect the potential for cost reductions offered by overmanning and new technology; that no adequate mechanism is proposed to regulate prices after the proposed ceiling expires; and that a ceiling on the average tariff allows considerable freedom to change the structure of tariffs to exploit a monopoly position in certain market segments, such as domestic calls, in order to subsidize charges in areas, such as the business market, where greater competition is likely to arise.

In short, the privatization programme of the Thatcher Administration risks being implemented with *ad hoc* solutions rather than with systematic answers to the key problems that underlie public enterprise. In pursuing the short-term gains to public finances from asset sales, there is a danger that the costs of writing-off debt and of funding rationalization prior to privatization may be ignored, together with the long-term revenues that these industries could generate for the public purse in the way of positive returns on their investments. In terms of regulation of prices in the case of natural monopolies that are privatized, and the preservation of social services deemed to be worthwhile in the wider national interest, no widely accepted mechanisms have yet been proposed. It is even unclear in those cases such as British Aerospace and British Airways, in which government will retain around 50 per cent of the shareholding, whether the government will in fact stick to its announced intention of renouncing interference in day-to-day control. It would appear that in overall economic terms, the current privatization programme may only be justifiable if it results in significant improvements in operating and cost efficiency in the industries concerned. Even then it is likely that this gain will be bought at the expense of severe unplanned distributional effects experienced by certain sections of the community.

Bibliography

SECTION A

A comprehensive discussion of the theoretical issues underlying public enterprise is given in [1] M. G. Webb, *The Economics of Nationalised Industries* (Nelson, 1973). Problems of institutional control are discussed in [2] C. D. Foster, *Politics, Finance and the Role of Economics: An Essay in the Control of Public Enterprise* (George Allen and Unwin, 1971), and more recently by [3] J. Redwood and J. Hatch, *Controlling Public Industries* (Blackwell, 1982), which includes some proposals for reform. Attempts to assess the productive efficiency of the major nationalized industries have been made by R. Pryke in [4] *Public Enterprise in Practice* (MacGibbon and Kee, 1971), and more recently in [5] *The Nationalised Industries: Policies and Performance Since 1968* (Martin Robertson, 1981). The landmarks that indicate the changing official attitude to economic and financial objectives are the following White Papers: [6] *The Financial and Economic Obligations of the Nationalized Industries* (Cmnd. 1337, 1961), [7] *Nationalized Industries: A Review of Economic and Financial Objectives* (Cmnd. 3437, 1967), and [8] *The Nationalized Industries* (Cmnd. 7131, 1978). Ideas about reforming the financing of nationalized industries are contained in articles by [9] M. J. Brech and J. C. Whiteman, 'Financing Nationalised Industries: A Third Way', *Public Money*, **2**/3 (Dec. 1982), and [10] S. Lumby, 'New Ways of Financing Nationalised Industries', *Lloyds Bank Review* (July 1981). An informative discussion of the current programme of privatization is to be found in [11] D. Heald and D. Steel, 'The Privatisation of UK Public Enterprises', in *The Annals of Public and Cooperative Economy*, Vol. 52 (1981). Additional material on various aspects of nationalized industries is to be found in various reports of the Select Committee on Nationalized Industries and of the Monopolies and Mergers Commission.

SECTION B

A wider range of readings on particular aspects of public enterprise is the following:

[12] BATES, R. and FRASER, N. *Investment Decisions in the Nationalised Fuel Industries* (Cambridge University Press, 1974).

[13] FOSTER, C. D. *The Transport Problem* (Croom Helm, revised 1975).

[14] HEALD, D. *Public Expenditure* (Martin Robertson, 1983).

[15] —— —— 'The Economic and Financial Control of UK Nationalised Industries', *Economic Journal*, **90** (June 1980).

[16] LAYARD, R. (ed.). *Cost Benefit Analysis* (Penguin, 1972).

[17] MILLWARD, R. *Public Expenditure Economics* (McGraw-Hill, 1971).

[18] MISHAN, E. J. 'The Post-War Literature on Externalities: An Interpretative Essay', *Journal of Economic Literature* (Mar. 1971).

[19] NELSON, J. R. (ed.). *Marginal Cost Pricing in Practice* (Prentice-Hall, 1964).

[20] POLANNYI, G. and POLANNYI, P. *Failing the Nation: The Record of the Nationalised Industries* (Fraser Ansbacher Ltd, 1974).

[21] POSNER, M. V. *Fuel Policy: A Study in Applied Economics* (Macmillan, 1973).

[22] —— —— 'Energy Policy at the Centre of the Stage', *National Westminster Bank Review* (1974).

[23] PRYKE, R. and DODGSON, J. *The Rail Problem* (Martin Robertson, 1975).

[24] REID, G. L. and ALLEN, K. *Nationalised Industries* (Penguin, corrected 1973).

[25] —— —— and —— —— *Economic Analysis and Public Enterprise* (George Allen and Unwin, 1971).

26

Competition Policy[1]

C. J. M. HARDIE

26.1. The Case for a Competition Policy

26.1.1. Monopoly, Competition, and Concentration

The central purpose of competition policy is to promote industrial efficiency through the identification and control of monopolies, cartels, and other potential abuses of market power. Competition policy is therefore very closely related to industrial policy, prices policy, nationalization, and the wide variety of other measures which governments use to influence and improve the performance of the company sector.

The political rationale for policy to promote competition is straightforward. There is a deep-rooted popular belief that businessmen will, if they can, create monopolies to increase their profits, and that monopolies will naturally abuse their power. So too with cartels; price fixing is only to be expected, and damages the interests of the public. The abuses and the damage will be of various kinds. Profits will be too high; that is unfair to customers, and greedy of the businessman. Prices too will be high, and so monopolies are held responsible for inflation. Efficiency—and hence exports, research and development, investment, industrial relations, service to the customer, and everything else which goes to make up a well-run firm—will suffer, because the dominant firm will have no rivals to take business away if it does not keep up to the mark.

If this is the conventional wisdom about the effects of monopolies and cartels, it is not surprising that governments take action. For once, popular belief and economic theory have a good deal in common. Not all the plain man's fears about monopoly are right, and most of them are over-simplified. But the theoretical arguments outlined in Chapter 3 on the behaviour of firms, and developed in Chapter 24 in terms of resource allocation, have had a real impact on the way competition policy legislation has developed and operated. So it is worth looking at the more important points of the theory again.

The central argument for a free-enterprise industrial system is that it will develop and produce the goods and services the community requires, at the lowest attainable cost to society. For this, three basic conditions must be met:

---

[1] Any opinions expressed in this chapter are personal to the author, and do not represent the views of the Monopolies and Mergers Commission, of which he was a member until January 1983.

(i) There must be identity between the private costs which producers take into account in their commercial decisions and the social cost to society as a whole which those decisions entail. In other words, any costs—pecuniary or otherwise—incurred by anyone as a result of the decision must be reflected in the actual cost the producer pays.

(ii) Similarly, there must be identity between the private revenues accruing to producers and the social benefits of their decisions. This, taken with condition (i), means that the pursuit of maximum private profit—the difference between private costs and revenues—will be identical with the pursuit of maximum net benefit to society.

(iii) Producers must single-mindedly pursue maximum profit. If other objectives intrude, then maximum social net benefit will not be achieved even though private and social costs and benefits be equal.

The case for a free-enterprise system can be illustrated by contrasting a monopolist with the firm in a perfectly competitive market (see Figure 26.1).

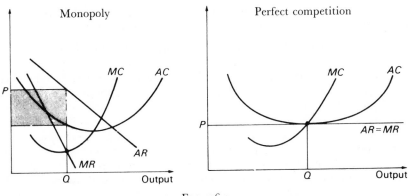

FIG. 26.1

The average and marginal cost curves are the same in each case. Because the demand curve in perfect competition is horizontal, the profit-maximizing firm produces at the minimum point on the average cost curve, and charges the minimum prices consistent with continued production in the long run and no super-normal profits. As compared with monopoly, the advantages of perfect competition are therefore:

(a) Price equals marginal cost. Profit maximization requires that marginal revenue equal marginal cost, but only under perfect competition does price equal marginal revenue and so equal marginal cost—which (as we saw in Chapter 24) is a necessary condition for optimal resource allocation. Under monopoly, price is above marginal cost, meaning that too little of the product will be bought because its price is too high.

(b) Monopoly allows excess or super-normal profits to be made. But they do not act as a signal for new firms to come into the industry to increase production, because of the barriers, natural or man-made, which enable the monopoly to preserve its position. So the monopolist can continue to earn excessive profits and the distribution of income between him and his customers is tilted permanently in his favour. Profit is an important element in the functioning of the perfectly competitive system. It creates the incentive on the sales side to develop and produce successfully the goods and services which customers want, and on the cost side to minimize the use of inputs for the level of output chosen so as to minimize cost for that output. It acts as the incentive and signal for firms to expand production of goods in high demand and for new firms to add to production, or for firms to leave the industry if profits are inadequate.

(c) The combination of a horizontal demand curve (so price equals marginal revenue), profit maximization (so marginal revenue equals marginal cost), and free entry (hence only normal profits, with price equal to average cost) ensures that perfectly competitive firms will end up producing at minimum average cost. Under monopoly, the firm will produce at above minimum cost, and hence inefficiently.

These are the main points of difference between monopoly and perfect competition. But perfect competition has other advantages:

(d) The monopolist has less incentive to improve his product or otherwise increase his efficiency, because unlike the perfectly competitive firm he can survive perfectly well on less than the maximum profits he might get. He can therefore choose a quiet life and still make a more than adequate profit. In terms of Figure 26.1, the average costs of the monopolist may be above the average cost curve, which shows the minimum attainable cost of each output, not what an inefficient company achieves.

(e) Similarly, easy high profits may reduce the incentive to carry out research, development, and innovation, to reduce costs, and to establish new products. These might well increase profits still further, but the urgency to exploit every opportunity will be less than under competition.

(f) Because market dominance has such obvious advantages to a firm, it may become a major company objective, so monopoly no longer just happens to occur sometimes, but is actively promoted and pursued. It thus becomes more widespread and more difficult to control.

(g) These problems arise even if the large firm is not a monopolist in the full sense, but just has a substantial market share. The large firm can often enforce its price leadership by threatening a price war if its smaller competitors do not comply. So prices are raised to much the same level as under monopoly, with all the same harmful effects on output, efficiency, and the rest.

Thus the model of perfect competition plays an important part in justifying competition policy, and more generally in making the case for free enterprise and the profit motive. But the theory is open to objections on both theoretical and practical grounds. For example, many dominant firms will be able to obtain economies of scale—that is, lower long-run unit costs of production—

because of their size. So Figure 26.1 would be inaccurate because it assumes the same cost structure in each case. Economies of scale may mean that prices are lower under monopoly than perfect competition, even though profits are higher.

Economies of scale are the most obvious advantage that large size and dominance may bring, but by no means the only one. The fewer the competitors, the less the uncertainty about their behaviour, and so investment looks more secure. Large firms may therefore be able to attract funds more easily, carry out more investment, and compete more effectively abroad. There may be more innovation than under competition, because only large firms can achieve the scale necessary for effective research and development, and only market power can protect future profits from encroachment and so provide the incentive to innovate.

The evidence of the facts reinforces the argument that competitive conditions may need to be defended, and the popular instinct that something ought to be done about market power. There is a good deal of statistical material to show that large firms have become increasingly important in the United Kingdom and elsewhere since the war.[2] One indicator is the level of aggregate concentration, defined as the share of the hundred largest firms in the net output of the UK manufacturing sector. This has gone up from 16 per cent in 1909 to 27 per cent in the early 1950s, and perhaps around 40 per cent in the 1970s. There have been similar increases in the United States and Germany, but the level of concentration in those economies remains below that in the UK. A similar picture is shown by the evidence on market concentration, usually represented by the five-firm concentration ratio, defined as the proportion of the net output of an industry accounted for by the top five firms. This has grown in almost every industry since the war, and by the end of the 1960s the five largest firms accounted for 90 per cent or more of net output in nearly a quarter of markets.

It does not follow from this that concentration is a bad thing; concentration of net output in the United Kingdom may not matter if imports are significant, and the companies have to be efficient to compete in export markets. But these facts confirm the fears of those who are suspicious of market power, and make them particularly uneasy about mergers and amalgamations which increase concentration.

The case for the free market is not conclusive. It indicates some of the gains which may result from free enterprise and the promotion of competition, but in practice there will be a lot of snags. The arguments for competition make an a priori case for government interference with industrial structures and business behaviour which reveal market power. But they do not prove that the free-market system is the best, nor show what measures would be necessary to make it work competitively. If in a particular case investigation reveals a clear discrepancy between private profit and the public interest, this does not in itself justify government interference, because interference might lead to even worse results than the operations of the admittedly imperfect free market. Even if

---

[2] On concentration ratios generally, see the Green Paper [10], pp. 8 ff. and Annex A.

intervention is justified, it is still necessary to decide the appropriate form. Some very obvious types of discrepancy are dealt with by direct legislation, backed up by inspection and fines—unhealthy working conditions; environmental pollution; safety. In other cases, taxation can be the best instrument. If companies are discouraged from investing by risk and uncertainty, or just ignorant short-sightedness, the aggregate of their decisions may well produce total investment well below what the community thinks desirable at the macro level (where, among other things, individual risks matter less because they are pooled). Hence the taxation system is used to bring private and public benefits closer together—by subsidizing investment in general, or in particular geographical areas. In some cases, like motorways, the Fleet Line, and the Third London Airport, the decision is taken away from the market. Every aspect of social cost and benefit is examined, and the decision rests with the government.

The special role of competition policy (or anti-trust policy as it is sometimes called) is to deal with cases of market power, and with those discrepancies between private and social benefit that occur because of the malfunctioning of the competitive mechanism, where single firms (monopolies) or groups of companies (cartels) escape the discipline of competition because they control a high proportion of a market and there are few potential rivals. It is therefore concerned with what happens when the free market fails to operate properly—excessive prices and profits, sub-optimal output, and lack of incentive to increase efficiency and improve products.

26.1.2. Policy Alternatives

How should the authorities proceed to turn these general propositions about the virtues of competition into statutes which will reduce and control market power? The details of the legislation, and how it operates, are considered in later sections. But the first step is to look at two major issues which the legislators have to face, and which have been settled quite differently here and in the United States.

There is first the problem of whether monopoly, or dominance, can in any circumstances be justified. The extreme view—called the *per se* rule—is that the Court (or other enforcement institutions) need do no more than investigate whether a monopoly or cartel exists. If that fact is established, the case against the company is proved: it only remains to decide on a sentence, or on remedies. The alternative (called here the cost-benefit approach) is to say that the existence of a monopoly or a cartel establishes only a prima facie case against the industry or company, which may be overthrown by further evidence. If, for example, the industry needs a price-fixing agreement to achieve the certainty needed for investment, then the advantage of higher investment can be put in the scales against the harmful effects of higher prices. Sometimes, therefore, a monopolist or cartel will go scot-free. It is all a matter of the particular effects of market power at a particular time.

In either case, if the market power is found to be harmful, the question of remedy must be faced.

One alternative is to restore competition in some way or another, so that the market power is destroyed, and with it the damaging behaviour. In some cases this is quite easy. For example, where the companies have drawn up a formal agreement to fix prices, without which they would find it difficult to co-operate, then all that has to be done is to forbid them to operate such agreements. There are many industries where the number of competing companies is large enough, or their suspicion of each other great enough, that they cannot work together to raise prices without quite elaborate and often legally enforceable provisions. In those cases the elimination of the agreement goes much of the way to restoring competition—not of course perfect competition, but competition sufficiently vigorous that the problems of market imperfection, if they remain, will be relative minor.

In other industries, however, elimination of competitive pressure will not need any agreement. There may be price leadership, a half-conscious understanding not to rock the boat with price cuts which will harm everyone, or a long history of mutual accommodation and respect which amounts to an industry solidarity very like a cartel, but without any formal co-operation. In that case the remedy is not so clear, because there is no agreement to be prohibited. It is impossible to order the companies to 'behave competitively' since that would be irrational and inefficient for them, and very difficult to enforce or even observe. For example, uniformity of prices may show either intense competition or a collusive agreement; heavy advertising may be part of an aggressive competitive strategy, or just the result of an understanding that price competition would be mutually disadvantageous.

The existence of a single dominant firm is the extreme case where no agreements are necessary to avoid competition and no easy solution exists for creating it. In theory (though frequently not in practice) it may be possible to break up such a firm, encourage entry into the industry, or remove tariff barriers to stimulate import competition. But very often it is not possible to promote competition in industries where market power dominates, and so it will be necessary to resort to another kind of remedy—regulation. The authorities can control by agreement or statute the company's prices and profits, or any other aspect of its behaviour, in an attempt to create the result that competition would if it existed.

In most anti-trust policies—certainly in the United Kingdom—there are therefore two strands. First, there is an attempt to promote competition, so that the industry can be left to set prices, plan production, and trade freely in a free market. In this case, competition automatically regulates behaviour in the desired way and prevents any major abuse. Second, there is a more or less explicit regulatory function. The behaviour or performance of the monopolist is examined with a view to modifying it directly, rather than seeking a remedy through the promotion of competition. If the problem is excess profits, it may well be that renewed competition would have eliminated them. But if that is impossible, the alternative is simply to force the company, by administrative decree, to lower prices. Of if market power is associated with wasteful or misleading advertising, the obvious remedy is to tell the company to stop the practice.

The existing legislation and control procedures are in all countries a mixture of the cost-benefit and the *per se* approaches to diagnosis, and of the competition and regulatory approaches to remedy. Much of what follows is to do with the United Kingdom; but our practice is only one example of the mix which may be chosen, and other countries operate quite differently, in particular the United States.

26.2. The UK and EEC Legislation

26.2.1. Anti-Trust Regulations in the UK

Until after the Second World War there was no anti-trust policy in this country. Indeed, the Depression of the 1930s had the opposite effect. It induced governments to persuade industries to concentrate and rationalize, thereby ensuring their survival in times of low demand and inadequate profits. Since 1948, however, with the general improvement in the level of aggregate demand, there have been a series of Acts designed to deal with dominant firms (or monopolies), mergers, restrictive trading agreements (of which price fixing is the most obvious, but by no means the only example), and resale price maintenance, whereby a retailer or other dealer must sell a product at the price laid down by the manufacturer.

Since the Restrictive Trade Practices Act of 1956,[3] the Restrictive Trade Practices Court deals with agreements between companies which relate to the supply of goods or services in the United Kingdom, and with the enforcement of Resale Price Maintenance (RPM) by individual companies. All agreements must be notified to the Director General of Fair Trading, who has to take them to Court, unless they are previously abandoned or are not of such significance as to require investigation. The Court has to decide whether the agreement can be justified in terms of Sections 10 or 19 of the 1976 Act—which allow eight 'gateways', or grounds for justification, of which the most general is (b) 'that the removal of the restriction would deny to the public ... specific and substantial benefits ...'[4]—and whether the advantages of the restriction outweigh the detriments. Similar procedures and provisions apply to RPM.[5]

The Monopolies and Mergers Commission (MMC, or Monopolies Commission for short) was established in 1948, and its powers extended to mergers in 1965. It deals primarily with situations where one company supplies 25 per cent or more of a particular good or service. It deals also with the case where two interconnected companies (e.g. a parent and a subsidiary) control a quarter of the market; and where two quite distinct companies operate in such a way as to restrict competition without any formal agreement. In relation to mergers, the criterion is now that a merger must involve assets over £30 million or a market share of 25 per cent or more, if it is to be examined.

The Monopolies Commission machinery differs in important respects from

---

[3] Here and in what follows the account of the legislation is necessarily summary. Much legal detail which may be of great importance in specific cases must therefore be ignored, and anyone who wishes to know the provisions of the legislation in full must refer to the relevant Act—see Bibliography.

[4] See Appendix 1 for the 'gateways' in full.

[5] See Appendix 2 for the RPM 'gateways'.

that of the Restrictive Trade Practices Court. Firstly, companies do not have to notify a dominant position or the intention to merge—it is for the authorities to identify the situation for themselves. Secondly, the authorities have no obligation to refer a monopoly position or a merger. The vast majority of cases which fall within the criteria for reference have not been, and are unlikely to be, referred to the Commission. This means that though all cartel and RPM agreements have to be examined, few monopoly or merger situations are. Thirdly, the criteria to be used by the Commission under the 1973 Fair Trading Act[6] are much more general than the 'gateways' prescribed under the 1976 Restrictive Trade Practices Act. It is true that there are certain specific matters which the Monopolies Commission must take into account, but it must also consider anything else which seems to it relevant, and it is for the Commission to decide what weight to attach to each factor. Generally, the Commission has to concern itself with 'the public interest'—but this term is nowhere defined. Thus the United Kingdom Monopolies and Mergers Commission procedure is firmly on the 'cost-benefit' side of the fence, with no strong presumption in favour of competition.

The Office of Fair Trading (OFT), and its Director, are responsible under the Fair Trading Act 1973 for a variety of anti-trust functions. The Director seeks out, registers, and refers to the Court restrictive trade practices and cases of resale price maintenance. Although the Secretary of State has similar powers, in practice it is the Director General who identifies cases of dominance, or complex monopoly, and refers them to the Monopolies Commission. For mergers, it is the Secretary of State only who can make the reference; but the OFT, through a committee, is responsible for examining each case and recommending whether it should be investigated. Although, therefore, it has no powers of adjudication or enforcement, the OFT has prime responsibility for the policing of competition and the initiation of proceedings.

The Secretary of State, in addition to his responsibility for merger references, has wide powers to make orders as a result of a Commission report—to regulate prices; end price discrimination; break up a company; ban the merger; and so on. He has, however, no duty to do any of these things, even if the Commission recommends that he should.

Under the 1980 Competition Act (see [5]) the Monopolies Commission was given wide new powers to carry out investigations into the nationalized industries. This was a very important change in its duties; but since such inquiries are almost entirely to do with efficiency, rather than the promotion and encouragement of competition, they are not relevant to anti-trust. The same Act provided what was meant to be a quicker procedure for investigating anti-competitive practices, to be used instead of a full and hence often rather cumbersome investigation by the Commission. The Director General of the OFT can first investigate himself such matters as, for example, refusal to supply bicycles to certain retailers,[7] and may find no fault, or negotiate a change in attitude by the company concerned. If he finds fault, but cannot negotiate a

---

[6] See Appendix 3.
[7] See, Bicycles: A Report on the Application by TI/Raleigh Industries of Certain Criteria for Determining Whether to Supply Bicycles to Retail Outlets (H.C. 67, 1981).

change, the matter may (if he thinks it worth while) go to the MMC, which then carries out a further inquiry. The Commission's recommendations can give the Secretary of State legal power to stop the practice. Only three such references have been made to the MMC since 1980, which may suggest that anti-competitive practices are not that easy to find. Moreover, the new procedure in the event has not proved to be much less cumbersome than the old.

26.2.2. EEC Regulations

The EEC legislation—of which the most important provisions are Articles 85 and 86 of the Treaty of Rome—differs most obviously from the United Kingdom legislation in having no straightforward provision (outside the Coal and Steel Community) for dealing with mergers. Otherwise, there is an obvious parallel between Article 85 and the Restrictive Trade Practices legislation, and between Article 86 and the Monopolies legislation. The EEC provisions deal only with situations where trade between member states is affected. But the coverage is in other ways similar to that in the UK. Under Article 85, agreements have to be notified, and their chances of survival are quite small, as in the UK. Article 86 prohibits abuse of a dominant position within the Common Market or a substantial part of it. A dominant position is not defined in the Article; there is no analogy to the '25 per cent' of the UK legislation. It relates to a position of economic strength enjoyed by an undertaking which enables it to prevent effective competition being maintained. An abuse of that position may be through conduct restrictive of competition, for example by refusing to supply raw material to a purchaser/competitor, or through predatory pricing, or through conduct that exploits that position—excessive or discriminatory prices. As with Article 85, the Commission and the European Court of Justice are building extensive case law on its interpretation.

26.3. How the UK Legislation Works

On the face of it, the Restrictive Trade Practices and Resale Price Maintenance legislation has been very effective. The definition of agreement in the RTP Act is very wide. It covers not only written legally enforceable contracts, but also informal arrangements and understandings. Most agreements are to do primarily with prices, but the Act covers market sharing, discounts, conditions of sale, exchanges of information, and almost everything else to do with the sale or production of goods or services. Of the 3,320 agreements registered since 1956, 2,892 have been abandoned, and only 30 were subjected to a full Court hearing. Of these, only 11 agreements have been approved. In addition, two cases of Resale Price Maintenance were won.

One of the agreements approved by the Court was The Cement Makers' Federation Agreement (Cement)[8] whereby almost all the UK manufacturers set common prices for cement. The Court held that this arrangement reduced the risk facing the industry, and therefore the rate of return which they required. The effect therefore was to reduce prices below what they would have been in full competition, without the agreement; and hence to benefit the

[8] 1961 L.R. 2 R.P. 241.

public under Section 21(1)(b).[9] Although it is not spelled out by the Court in detail, the argument is as follows. Cement production suffers from wide variations in demand. Because capital costs are a large part of total cost, marginal or variable cost is low, and in times of depression producers will be tempted to cut prices far below full cost in order to maintain some cash flow. But such prices will not cover depreciation, so losses will be made. To invest in such an industry, a company will need the prospect of high average prices to make up for these losses. But if, as the agreement provides, price-cutting is outlawed, there will be fewer losses and investors will accept a lower average level of price. The Cement case therefore is an example of the general, if rarely accepted, argument that price competition can be so disruptive that investment is undesirably reduced.

In Medicaments,[10] one of only two RPM cases won by the industry, the main issue was to do with the wholesaling of ethical pharmaceuticals—that is, medical drugs advertised only to doctors, and supplied only on prescription. Each manufacturer fixed the price at which his product was to be sold by wholesalers to chemists, who in turn supplied patients, who typically paid (under the NHS) only the fixed nominal charge for the prescription. Thus the pattern and volume of demand were set not by price or consumer choice, but by the nature of the ailment and the decision of the doctor. A high proportion of the sales of a chemist is accounted for by a few drugs. So his stocks are quite small, and do not include most of the ethical pharmaceuticals that may be asked for. He relies on the wholesaler for frequent (three or four times a day) deliveries of these slower-moving products. The Court found that if wholesalers were free to cut prices, it would be commercially attractive to offer discounts to chemists on the fast-moving products, and either surcharge the others or not stock them at all. Price-cutting would reduce profits; and to compensate for this wholesalers would reduce the range they held, or cut down on deliveries, or both. Either way, service to the public would deteriorate, and the variety of goods available to them be reduced. In these special circumstances, therefore, free competition would have deleterious effects.

The Cement and Medicaments cases are, however, very exceptional. In general, any cartel or trade association whose members form agreements, however informal, on any aspect of the goods or services they supply, or any individual company which practises RPM, has very little chance of receiving official approval. However, it does not follow that restrictive practices are a thing of the past. No doubt many companies still fix prices, but do not register their agreements. From time to time they are caught, often as the result of a Monopolies Commission investigation; but these cases may be just the tip of the iceberg. Very few cases now come to the Court. It was expected that when the legislation was extended in 1976 to cover services, there would be a new crop of investigations. But there have been no further cases; and the Court is therefore inactive.

The evidence of Swann et al. (see [19]) shows that the legislation has

[9] As it then was. See now Appendix 1 for Section 10(1) (b) of the 1976 Act, which is the same.
[10] 1970 L.R. 7 R.P. 267.

encouraged competition and reduced collusion, even if we are still a long way from the free-market ideal. Over 13 per cent of a random sample of agreements which existed in 1956 were found to have been formally abandoned rather than registered; more terminations occurred as the attitude of the Court became clearer; many others were modified in the light of the legislation, and of the cases where an agreement was struck down by the Court, over 50 per cent show an increase in competitive behaviour, predominantly via prices and discounts. On the other hand, perhaps half of the agreements condemned were replaced by some alternative means of restraining competitive pressures, in particular by agreements which involve only the publication of information, but can easily form the basis for understandings on prices. To a lesser extent price leadership took over the role of banned agreements. A further effect of the legislation is to encourage mergers. If prices cannot be maintained by agreement with a competitor, an obvious alternative is to take him over and fix his prices directly, and at the same time make price leadership easier.

Since 1965, when mergers were first caught by the legislation, about 3 per cent of those which met the criteria have been referred to the Commission. Of these the majority have been turned down, or were abandoned when referred. But the deterrent effect of the legislation is certainly much greater than this arithmetic suggests. The City Code on Take-Overs and Mergers[11] requires that the terms of an offer include a provision that the offer lapse if reference be made to the MMC. It may of course be revived when the inquiry is over. But since inquiries take up to six months, and during that time share prices can move to make the agreed terms obsolete, reference often leads to abandonment. And not many large companies will go to the expense and trouble of arranging a deal if there is any real chance of a reference which will at best cause up to six months' delay, and at worst kill it. So there is little doubt that the 1965 legislation has had a severely inhibiting effect on mergers which fall within the statutory criteria.

Rockware[12] is a straightforward case of a merger which was disallowed. Rockware and United Glass each supplied 25 to 30 per cent of the UK market for bottles, jars, and other glass containers; Redfearn had about 16 per cent. The issue was whether either of the bigger companies should be allowed to take over Redfearn. The Commission concluded that the reduction of main producers from three to two 'would constitute a significant loss of competition between suppliers of glass containers . . . and that there would be a serious risk of adverse effects on the reliability of supply and on other kinds of service to customers on the range of containers provided, and on prices'. A merger would increase imports, because customers would place orders on the Continent to guard against shortages; and shortages would be more likely because the two large companies would be more cautious in adding to capacity than the existing three. In this case, therefore, the Commission believed that the merger would lead to many of the classic detriments of decreased competition and market power.

[11] Rule 9.

[12] A Report on the Proposed Mergers of Rockware Group Limited, United Glass Limited, and Redfearn National Glass Limited (H.C. 431, 1978).

In the case of Cross-Channel Ferries[13] the concern was whether the acquisition by European Ferries (a private sector company) of the ferry and port interests of Sealink UK (a company owned by the nationalized British Rail Board) would have anti-competitive effects on ferry operation and on access to ports. The Commission concluded that competition would be reduced, particularly on the Anglo–French short routes. The resulting concentration of ownership of ports would make it more difficult for rivals to get into the business, and they in any case would be deterred by the strength of the newly merged company. The problems of excess capacity could be solved otherwise than by the merger; and regulation of prices did not offer a satisfactory alternative. Since there were no measures available to remedy the adverse effects of the merger on the public interest, it was turned down.

The case of Glaxo[14] involved three companies. Both the suitors for Glaxo's hand claimed that research and development would be more effective if carried on by a larger company; and that the geographical marketing strengths of the two would complement each other to increase world sales of both in countries where one or other was previously unrepresented. But in each case the Commission rejected the idea that the small size of British firms compared with their US and Continental competitors was now an obstacle to effective R & D. Rather, amalgamation would reduce incentives to broaden research. Any of the companies separately might well embark on particular lines of research which would be suppressed in the large company if the partner were already carrying out research in that area. More generally, either merger would eliminate an independent British centre of R & D and thus jeopardize new British products. In the particular case of Beecham/Glaxo, the incompatible philosophies of the two would damage the morale of the Glaxo R & D team. So in this case the Commission ruled against the conventional wisdom that size is necessary for R & D in the international pharmaceutical industry. The traditional argument is that any single line of research is expensive, and unlikely to succeed. Only by having a portfolio of different lines can a company hedge its bets and have a decent chance of the rich winner that will make up for the many losses. But that means a great deal of investment money—which the comparatively small British companies do not have. Against this, the Commission preferred the general virtues of variety and competition, and turned the merger down.

A large minority of mergers do, however, survive reference and the report of the Commission. An example is Unilever/Allied Breweries.[15] In this case there was no question of any reduction in competition, since Unilever was not in the drinks business. The Commission was sceptical of the arguments that Unilever's experience and skill in R & D would improve the performance of Allied, or that the complementarity of their marketing skills would amount to much. More important, it did not in this case see any danger to the public interest simply from the huge size of the new company which was to be created;

---

[13] A Report on the Proposed Merger of European Ferries Ltd. and Sealink Ltd. (H.C. 65, 1981).

[14] Proposed Mergers of Beecham Group Ltd. and Glaxo Group Ltd., and the Boots Co. Ltd. and Glaxo Group Ltd. (H.C. 341, 1972).

[15] Proposed Merger of Unilever Ltd. and Allied Breweries Ltd. (H.C. 297, 1969).

so the view that large conglomerates were *ipso facto* harmful was rejected. The merger was therefore allowed—although subsequently abandoned by the parties—not because it offered any real benefits, but because it would do no identifiable harm. This illustrates well an important general principle—the burden of proof has not been on the companies to show the advantages of the merger, but on the Commission to find dangers to the public interest.

Since 1980, there has been increasing concern about the Commission's treatment of mergers, and the Secretary of State's decisions on whether or not to refer particular mergers. The central criticism is that neither the Commission nor the Secretary of State show enough consistency in their decisions, and do not therefore give the commercial world the certainty necessary to run their affairs. Companies and their advisors are entitled to be able to forecast with at least some accuracy whether a particular merger will be referred; and if referred, whether it will survive. They cannot operate efficiently if merger policy is whimsical. Second, the Commission should concern itself with competition issues only, not with the wide variety of extraneous matters which can be dragged in under the heading of the public interest (which is what the 1973 Act requires to be assessed). Employment, exports, and regional policy may be important issues; but they are nothing to do with anti-trust.

Three particular cases exemplify the difficulties. First, the Royal Bank of Scotland mergers[16]—at that time, the largest in terms of market value ever proposed in the United Kingdom. Competition, in particular the need of the Royal Bank to have a larger partner in order to compete overseas, was one issue, but by no means the only or most important. The Royal Bank was the largest surviving Scottish bank, which raised important issues for the independence and prosperity of that regional economy. The Hong Kong Bank was based, and largely operated, outside the United Kingdom, which raised the question of whether Bank of England control over a UK clearing bank would be as reliable if its parent was not located in this country. A majority of the Commission decided that both mergers were to be refused because of their likely effects on the Scottish regional economy; and the Hong Kong Bank proposal in addition for its effects on Bank of England control. But two members of the Commission dissented from one or both of these conclusions.

The Commission was similarly split in the case of Anderson Strathclyde,[17] where the majority concluded that the effectiveness of Anderson Strathclyde would be adversely affected by the merger; and that employment in a relatively depressed part of the United Kingdom would be damaged, because the merger would detract from the dynamism of business in the region. Two members, including the Chairman, dissented. In this case, the Secretary of State, for the first time ever, refused to accept the Commission's recommendations to stop a merger. As a consequence one member of the majority resigned.

---

[16] A Report on the Proposed Mergers Between Standard Chartered Bank Ltd. and Royal Bank of Scotland Group Ltd., and Hong Kong and Shanghai Banking Corporation and Royal Bank of Scotland Groups Ltd. (Cmnd. 8472, 1982).

[17] A Report on the Proposed Merger between Chartered Consolidated PLC and Anderson Strathclyde PLC (Cmnd. 8771, 1982).

In the House of Fraser case[18] there was much subsequent criticism of the Commission's majority conclusion (again, with a dissentient). One factor, and one only, was the effect on competition between manufacturers of textiles of ownership by Lonrho (a manufacturer) of Fraser (a buyer). More important, the efficiency of the House of Fraser would deteriorate seriously as a result of the merger, because of the effect it would have on the management of the businesses. Consequently, it was disallowed.

It is impossible to identify at all precisely the effects, good or bad, of the increased competition which the Restrictive Trade Practices Court and the Monopolies Commission have encouraged by their restrictions on price fixing, mergers, and market power. Over the last twenty years the dominant influences on efficiency, resource allocation, competition, and the other objectives which anti-trust is meant to serve have been industrial relations, the value of the currency, foreign competition, and a variety of factors which have nothing to do with cartels, oligopoly, or single-firm dominance. For an open economy such as the United Kingdom, anti-trust will at best be a minor instrument of policy. By that modest standard, there is some good evidence that it has done its job well on the restrictive practices, RPM, and mergers front, and made a decent contribution to the country's economic performance.

Since 1948 the Monopolies Commission has produced 109 reports (other than reports on mergers), most of them since the mid-1960s. Of these, six were general references—on such matters as parallel pricing, or refusal to supply—without particular reference to any industry or dominant firm. The remainder cover a wide variety of products, industries, and companies, from bread to accountancy, from Unilever to British United Shoe Machinery to Queen's Counsel. It is impossible to summarize these reports at all helpfully, or to draw any general conclusions on the overall effect of the Commission's recommendations, although a number of individual cases is described by way of example in what follows. First, however, some procedural points. A necessary criterion for reference is, for a single firm, that it have at least 25 per cent of the United Kingdom market (however defined); and for oligopolists, that between them they supply at least 25 per cent, and so conduct their affairs as to restrict competition. So a firm does not have to be anywhere near a 100 per cent monopolist to be caught. But many firms which alone or with others meet the 25 per cent criterion are never seriously considered for reference; and of the rest, by no means all are referred. More than a hundred industries have been investigated since the war by the MMC. Nevertheless, most companies most of the time are in no danger of reference, even if they could be caught by the Act. Of those who are referred, most are criticized in one way or another—not surprisingly, since few companies are likely to come clean out of an investigation into every aspect of their business. The Commission has wide powers of recommendation; and the Secretary of State wide powers to enforce its recommendations. But, with a few celebrated exceptions—British Oxygen; Hoffman La Roche; London Rubber Company; Courtaulds; Roadside Advertising Services—few companies have been seriously disciplined.

[18] A Report on the Proposed Merger between Lonrho Ltd. and House of Fraser Ltd. (H.C. 73, 1981).

Nevertheless, the investigations and conclusions of the Monopolies Commission are important because they show clearly the wide variety of public interest issues which market dominance raises; and warn companies what kind of behaviour they must avoid if they are not to fall foul of the Office of Fair Trading and the Commission. As in the case of mergers, the deterrent effect of Commission reports is quite substantial. Any well-advised large company will, if it is prudent, watch its behaviour carefully to avoid reference; and many do.

26.4. The Attitude of the Monopolies Commission to Business

26.4.1. Introduction

To see more clearly how the Monopolies Commission works, it is useful to start by looking at two important references—Indirect Electrostatic Reprographic Equipment, and Manmade Cellulosic Fibres.[19] The incomprehensible titles are forced on the Commission by the facts that it is the supply of a product, not a company, that is the subject of the reference; and that the product has to be very closely defined to ensure that the market of which the monopolist has 25 per cent is correctly identified to meet the requirements of the Act. In fact, the references were to do with Rank Xerox in the first case, and plain paper copiers; and Courtaulds in the second, and rayon. The conclusions are interesting because very different; one company got an almost clean bill of health, the other was severely condemned.

In the Rank Xerox case, the company had about 90 per cent of the market in 1975, though that share was declining as other powerful rivals such as IBM, Kodak, and the Japanese companies entered the field. Profits on capital employed between 1965 and 1975 ranged from 20·4 to 47·8 per cent—much above the average for British manufacturing industry. This and other evidence led the Commission to conclude that 'Rank Xerox has undoubtedly possessed and exercised substantial market power'. But 'This does not necessarily mean . . . that its monopoly position is itself against the public interest . . .'. Because the company was to be congratulated for having taken the substantial commercial risk of developing a new product, it could not at the same time be criticized for the monopoly position which its success created. Thus the Monopolies Commission was willing to accept the Schumpeterian view (see [15]) that the free enterprise system works by allowing companies to create a monopoly position, and take the profits that go with it; and that is in the public interest provided that they show inventiveness, take risks, and are quite soon subject to new entry or attack by new technologies.

In the Courtaulds case, the Commission took a more hostile position. Courtaulds in 1966 had about 89 per cent of the market in unprocessed rayon. Profits were not strikingly high—between 15 and 20 per cent on capital employed between 1964 and 1967. But the effects of the company's market power were similar to the classic case of monopoly. Production was restricted, and customers had no alternatives if they were dissatisfied or discriminated against. The home market was protected by tariffs, and by deals with foreign

[19] Supply of Man-Made Cellulosic Fibres (H.C. 130, 1968). A Report on the Supply of Indirect Electrostatic Reprographic Equipment (H.C. 47, 1976).

producers to exclude supplies. The effect of Courtaulds verticalization policy had been to foreclose competition and encourage discrimination. The Commission recommended that tariffs be reduced (in 1968, before the Kennedy Round and UK membership of the EEC, they were substantial); all sales should be at list prices to eliminate discrimination; market-sharing deals with EFTA producers should stop; and that Courtaulds should not, without Board of Trade approval, make any more acquisitions in any sector of the textile and clothing industries. This report shows that the Monopolies Commission can be severe when it believes market power to have been abused. Such cases are rare; but act as an example against lesser abuse.

The rest of this section deals with some of the main issues which the Monopolies Commission has to look at when it considers the public interest. Most of these issues have something in common—they concern commercial behaviour which for the authorities suggests danger to the public interest, but to the businessman seems normal or even creditable. Much of what follows is designed to show businessmen why it is that routine commercial behaviour may be suspect to the Monopolies Commission; and also to suggest to professional economists that theory may not always be easy to apply when it is brought face to face with the complexity of commercial behaviour.

26.4.2. Competition and Collusion

For businessmen, competition is above all to do with rivalry, by whatever means are legal and commercially prudent. So an uncompetitive market is where either there are no serious rivals, or the other companies in the industry are sleepy and unaggressive. But for economists rivalry is not enough; whether it is to count as competition depends on what form the rivalry takes, which is partly determined by the structure of the particular industry. Take the case of oligopoly, where there are by definition comparatively few companies—few enough for each to be conscious of his rivals and anxious to anticipate their reaction. This anticipation is thoroughly intelligent commercial behaviour; but it has some unfortunate consequences. Consider price competition. An oligopolist will hesitate to lower his price if he believes that his rivals may follow and he will get no marketing advantage. Thus the industrial structure has the effect that, without any stupidity or malevolence on the part of the oligopolists, competition is muted or diverted into other channels where imitation is not so easy or so quick, such as advertising. When therefore an economist, or the Office of Fair Trading, or the Monopolies Commission, suggests that an industry is behaving uncompetitively, it does not mean that the companies are timid or having a quiet life, but rather that in their circumstances the intelligent and determined pursuit of profit discourages certain desirable kinds of rivalry (e.g. price competition) which would be attractive if the industrial structure were different—in particular, if it were competitive in the technical sense of including a larger number of companies, none of whom was big enough to expect any reaction from the rest, all of whom would therefore act independently in setting price.

The notion of collusion, and in particular of tacit collusion, raises similar problems. There is no dispute that when companies formally agree to fix prices, they are colluding. But what if there is no agreement, and indeed no communication at all, but nevertheless all the companies in the industry set the same prices and change them together? The clearest case is where one company is much bigger than the rest, and acts as the price leader. Economists often call this kind of behaviour (or its close relation, price parallelism) quasi- or tacit collusion: because its effect, that everyone changes price pretty much together, is the same as full collusion, and the uniformity of behaviour arises from the same conscious pursuit of the price that will be best for the industry as a whole, not the price which will cause most trouble to the competition.

For the theorist it is an embarrassing fact that uniformity of price tells him nothing about whether an industry is competitive. Uniform prices may mean that demand conditions are so competitive that no company can afford to diverge from the going price without losing a great deal of business. Or it may be that the companies have succeeded by price leadership or collusion in raising prices to a level where profits will be nearer the maximum available to the industry.

The particular case of Ceramic Sanitaryware[20] shows how difficult it is in practice to define and identify collusion. To quote: 'One of the distinctive features of the ceramic sanitaryware industry is that there is a marked degree of similarity between the major manufacturers' list price . . . and that this similarity has persisted . . . as a result of price changes of the same . . . amounts taking place simultaneously . . .'. The majority concluded that 'it is primarily competitive considerations and input costs similar for all manufacturers which influence each of them in determining such prices and which result in their being largely uniform'. One member of the Commission, however, on the same evidence believed that the companies had pursued a policy of 'live-and-let-live'; not surprisingly, given that the industry has four roughly equal competitors, nothing to fear from imports, and alternative competitive weapons available. In these circumstances 'price competition must seem of doubtful advantage to the industry as a whole and of great potential danger to individual companies'.

26.4.3. Profitability

For most companies profit is a major commercial objective, and an important indicator of business success. For the public interest, however, high profits can indicate an abuse of market power. The company may have deliberately set out (by market segmentation, advertising, the elimination of competitors) to establish a secure niche in the market and premium profits. Such behaviour is admirable by the criterion of profitability and the shareholders' interests. But it also represents a deliberate attempt to create a quasi-monopoly and to enjoy the extra profits which such dominance allows. There is thus a conflict between the valuation of such behaviour and profits by businessmen and the attitude of the community. What is more, governments now encourage companies to set clear objectives, pursue the interests of the shareholders rather than of the management, and in general run their businesses in a purposeful and rational

[20] A Report on the Supply in the United Kingdom and the Export from the United Kingdom of Ceramic Sanitaryware (Cmnd. 7327, 1978).

way instead of in accordance with the sleepy and old-fashioned routines inherited from the inefficient past. It is odd and even offensive therefore for managers who have tried to adjust to those new standards, and have laboured through courses at government-subsidized management schools, to be told that their hard-won profits are a sign of vice.

Of course, profits may be, and often are, associated with wholly admirable qualities. Where a company operates in a competitive market, high profits must mean that the company has reduced costs and developed new products to satisfy that market. But there is no way of discovering from the figures alone whether a rate of return on capital employed of, say, 30 per cent is the reward of virtuous efficiency and risk-taking, or of monopolistic exploitation, or both. What matters is not what profits have been earned, but how they have been earned: and that is a matter of detailed investigation.

It follows that notions of 'reasonable', 'fair', or 'normal' profits are not very helpful. To compare a dominant firm's profit with the average for British industry as a whole, or of that particular industry, of or foreign competitors, only reveals the trivial arithmetic fact that they are higher or lower. If they are higher, no conclusions can be drawn about whether they are deservedly so. If they are lower, this may reflect greater competition or greater inefficiency. If by normal is meant not average or typical, but rather the economist's technical notion of the level of profit required to retain capital in or attract it to that industry, then the question is at least being considered from a useful point of view—that is, what is the minimum profit which has to be offered to this company to induce it to do what the community wants? But very little help can be gained in answering this question from simple arithmetic comparisons. The answer depends on the amount of risk involved, the opportunity cost of the particular resources to the company and to the community, and other factors which required detailed individual examination.   Finally, the accountancy problems associated with the use of rates of return on capital employed are formidable, and of more than merely technical importance. True profitability is calculated by taking into account the duration and time profile of the profits or cash flows associated with a product, which is why the use of discounted cash-flow techniques is encouraged (see p. 75). Rates of return as conventionally calculated are, however, defined simply as the ratio of net profits to net assets employed. Both the computation of profit and the valuation of net assets are notoriously difficult. The most striking example of this is the problem of taking into account inflation in the computation of profits. Moreover, accountants and managers can differ quite legitimately on the treatment of R & D, or depreciation, or stocks, and so on. These variations in treatment will produce quite different calculations for return on capital employed even where the actual experience and profitability of companies are identical. More important, the rate of return on capital employed is a snapshot concept. Where, for example, a product has a pronounced life cycle, to be told that in a particular year it has been highly profitable says nothing about its profitability over its whole life.

Despite these difficulties, the Monopolies Commission almost always looks at accountancy rates of return on capital employed, and some generalizations can be made from its past reports. As the case of Rank Xerox and Courtaulds have already shown, a high rate of return is no sure sign of vice, nor a low rate, of virtue. On the whole, a rate of return on assets at historical cost above 20 per cent will attract attention—though the company will often be exonerated when the circumstances are examined. The most recent and authoritative discussion of this problem appears in the Contraceptive Sheaths case.[21]

26.4.4. Advertising

For the businessman, advertising is an important and often inseparable part of the marketing mix—particularly for consumer goods, but also in a less flamboyant way for producers' goods. To achieve sales by successful advertising is a common and generally admired characteristic of well-run businesses. The peculiar contribution of advertising is not simply that it communicates the existence and characteristics of the product to potential customers. More important, it can be used to distinguish the advertiser's product from the competition, establish its identity and brand name as separate and distinct, and thereby turn it into a branded product where higher profits can be earned than on an anonymous commodity. To establish a clientele which is loyal and captive gives a company an opportunity to raise prices and profits. This, or something like it, is plainly the purpose and effect of much advertising; which is not, of course, to say that any advertising is wholly effective in capturing and tying up any customer, nor that advertising can sell inherently unsatisfactory goods.

All this can look a great deal less admirable from the public policy point of view. In the first place, there is the problem of whether advertising is misleading. To some extent this is an easy matter to deal with—and nothing particularly to do with large or dominant firms. If an advertisement makes factual claims about the slimming properties of bread, or the performance of a stereo set, and those claims are false, plainly harm has been done and the advertiser is culpable.

But very little advertising is straightforwardly of this kind. The real difficulty is that advertising may be used to persuade people to attach ill-defined but psychologically important characteristics to different versions of a product which are essentially the same, or at any rate differ much less than the advertising leads people to believe. Detergents are a classic case. The objection is that although it may be quite harmless if a customer is induced to buy brand A rather than brand B (they are, after all, essentially the same), resources, in particular management time, will have been wasted in inducing the switch, to no purpose save that one company's sales increase at the cost of the other.

Other objections to advertising arise simply from its effectiveness, whether that involves misleading the customer or not. When the advertising achieves its commercial purpose, it succeeds in appropriating a part of the market and attaching it more or less securely to the advertised product. This means that higher profits can be earned, even after charging the costs of advertising. This

---

[21] A Report on the Supply in the United Kingdom of Contraceptive Sheaths (Cmnd. 8689, 1982).

extra profit arises directly from the exercise of market power in the sub-market so created, and need not be the result of any socially useful behaviour by the advertiser—whose only skill may have been to devise a successful advertising campaign. What is more, advertising is often expensive. When it works, it creates barriers to competition. Its effect, therefore, is to limit the threat to the position of the advertised product to rivals who have the time and money to break down the barriers.

Of course, the harm done by advertising will vary a great deal from case to case. Where there are a good number of competing firms, who incur small advertising expenditure, all at about the same level, very little harm will be done; although, to the extent that advertising by competing firms does not affect their competitive position and market shares then resources have been wasted in self-cancelling rivalrous effort.

Advertising can often be justified on more positive grounds. It is in the interests of both the company and the community that new products should be diffused rapidly. It is difficult to know what the optimum rate should be; but it will be faster than that achieved by word of mouth. Advertising not only informs people that the product exists, but persuades them to try it out. It is socially desirable that information on the range and quality of available products should be good; indeed, the simplest models of competition require that it be perfect. Moreover, the company will get its return more quickly if diffusion is fast. This is desirable for the company; from the social point of view, the faster the return if the product is successful, the more willing will companies be to risk money and effort in research and product development. R & D is risky enough anyway; it would be doubly so if advertising were not available to market quickly any saleable products which are created.

In their report on Household Detergents,[22] the Commission concluded that the advertising and price policies of Unilever and Proctor & Gamble were against the public interest. It proposed that substantial reductions (about 20 per cent) should be made in the wholesale price of detergents, and that the companies should cut selling expenses by at least 40 per cent. The Commission's investigation suggests therefore that advertising may be condemned when it replaces price competition, raises prices, and goes further than the socially useful purposes of informing the customer and persuading him to try the product.

26.4.5. Pricing

Whether prices are reasonable is to a considerable extent the same question as whether profits are acceptable. A price which results in an acceptable level of profits will itself be acceptable and vice versa. All the same, difficulties then arise in the evaluation of prices as with profits.

But an additional set of problems arises over price-cost relationships. In any business there will be substantial differences in the gross and net margins[23]

---

[22] A Report on the Supply of Household Detergents (H.C. 105, 1966).

[23] 'Gross margin' means the price less direct costs (that is, the gross profit per unit) expressed as a percentage of the price. 'Net margin' means the price less both direct and indirect costs (the net profit per unit) expressed as a percentage of the price.

earned from product to product at any time. Some of these differences come about because products are at different stages in their life cycle. But in any case it would be a miracle if every product were equally successful in every market. Hence it is an inevitable feature of business life that margins (or price–cost ratios) vary. Even where the company makes only a single product, that product will be sold in a variety of markets, and the margins will differ.

This fact of life is for various reasons suspect. Elementary welfare theory suggests that price should be equal to marginal cost in all parts of the economy if welfare is to be maximized and resources correctly allocated (see Chapter 24). Leaving aside the problems that particular inquiries deal not with all prices but with a particular price (which should not necessarily be equal to marginal cost unless all others are), and that average cost may well be different from marginal cost, this welfare proposition can be translated into the rough-and-ready criterion that prices should all bear the same relation to average cost; which is to say that price–cost ratios, or margins, should be uniform.

That criticism is concerned with resource allocation. The second main concern is to do with fairness, or distribution of income. If two products bear different margins, then the purchasers of one are paying more than the other for the same amount of resources. A very common situation is where the margins earned on export business are a good deal lower than those on home business. In this case, it is said, the home buyer is unfairly treated; the export buyer is being subsidized by the home buyer.

Criticism of this kind is odd to the businessman not only because it is based on unfamiliar propositions of welfare economics, but also because it purports to criticize business practices which are both universal and unavoidable. The consequence of advocating uniform price–cost ratios seems to be that products should all be priced on a cost-plus basis. But this is an odd recommendation when at other times businessmen are asked to pursue rational pricing policies, and abandon ritualistic and mechanical procedures such as cost-plus.

However, the naïve application of uniform price–cost ratios is wrong for another reason. If it is accepted that there is no such thing as a standard 'reasonable profit' to be applied to all situations (because the reward to risk and enterprise must differ from case to case) then different margins on different products become quite acceptable. As for different margins on the same product in different markets, what needs to be considered is not whether price–cost ratios differ (which they do), but whether the overall price earned on the product is reasonable or not. In many cases price discrimination (which is a term synonymous with variations in price–cost ratios) is necessary if adequate profits are to be earned at all. How could airlines cover their costs unless they charged first-class passengers more than the difference in the cost of providing first-class seats can justify? Imposing standard margins may mean that the producer standardizes on the high-margin market and abandons the low-margin market completely—because that is the most profitable way of adjusting. But in that case resource allocation is made worse, because the low-margin market where price was close to cost is abandoned; and the output of the product is even further away from the optimum than previously.

26.4.6. Efficiency

It would be nice to be able to solve the problem of whether high profits were justified by assessing whether the company that earned them was efficient. High profits cannot themselves be taken as an index of efficiency, because their source may just as well be market power.

But estimates of efficiency are extremely difficult to make, and very difficult to know what to do with when you have got them. One measure of efficiency is units of output per unit of input—or productivity. Labour productivity is quite easy to calculate when you can count the output in physical units (apples) and the input in terms of physical units (men). But there are severe difficulties when there are a number of different kinds of products (apples and pears) and of labour input (skilled and unskilled labour). You cannot use market prices to weigh the different products because those market prices themselves reflect market power; and all you end up with is profitability per unit of input. The situation is worse when the value of the capital input has to be calculated; machines are even more difficult to count than men. And all these problems are multiplied when comparisons are made over time to estimate improvements in efficiency, because the nature of the product and the inputs will change, and the valuation measure be further distorted by differential inflation.

Suppose heroically that these problems have been solved, and that productivity is estimated to be currently at such and such a level, and to have improved at such and such a rate over the last ten years. It is very difficult to know whether this performance is creditable or not. If the company were just one among many, it might be possible to compare the company with the average, or the best, of the industry. But the characteristic of dominant firms is that they are often the only, or only significant, member of the industry and that there is nobody else to compare them with. In that case it may be possible to make comparisons with other similar companies in other countries. But international comparisons are very difficult to make fairly. Exchange rate problems add a new set of difficulties to the valuation of inputs and outputs. Different countries have more or less skilled work-forces—and hence differences in production efficiency cannot fairly be imputed to the company alone. And so on.

These problems arise not only with those aspects of efficiency which are in principle quantifiable, but also with the whole range of more general performance indicators which the consideration of efficiency should cover. A company has a record of high and increasing exports, or has steadily improved its production process by research and innovation. But should it not have done even better? How can we tell what it would have achieved in more competitive circumstances?

Even if we were able to attribute high profits to superior efficiency, problems remain. Should not the company have passed on more of its cost savings in lower prices? The consumer would have been benefited directly, demand for the product would have been increased, and resources diverted to the efficient manufacturer of the product. Alternatively, it may be that a high price/profit will attract resources to that activity more effectively, because capital is drawn to the most profitable opportunities.

26.4.7. Equity

One attractive anti-trust policy is to make sure that companies cannot earn profits illegitimately—for example, by vertical foreclosure, predatory price-cutting, or purchase of patents—and then let them set whatever prices the market will bear, and enjoy the resulting profits.

But even if competitive conditions could be created in this way, the policy may result in unacceptably high profits. In the case of personal incomes it is almost universally recognized that the taxation system should limit the take-home salary of the most successful to below what they would earn in a free market. So too certain levels of profit are simply unacceptable, even if properly and openly earned within the rules. For example, the producers of a life-saving drug should not be allowed to charge what the market will bear when that means charging a user his whole earnings to save his life. Even where morality restrains companies from such extremes, very high rates of return by comparison with those earned elsewhere may be unacceptable, both because they represent too high a reward to the producer, and because they involve too high a price to the customer.

It must be recognized, therefore, that a regulatory body will from time to time criticize and reduce profits simply on the grounds that they are inequitably high. This was the case with Hoffman La Roche[24] where although the company was 'a highly competent organization with a product range of high quality', profit levels which resulted in a return on capital employed of 60–70 per cent in the latter part of the patent life were quite unjustified. The remedy proposed was that prices of both Librium and Valium should be more than halved.

26.4.8. Monopolistic Practices

There are a wide variety of other business practices which have been found against the public interest by the Monopolies Commission in some or other of its reports. These findings are summarized in Table 26.1. The practices in the first group are primarily to do with preventing competition via new entry, and generally require some market power if they are to work; you cannot successfully full-line force or refuse to supply if the customer can easily go elsewhere. The practices in the second group do not require market power. What is more, they can in many cases be beneficial—either because they increase efficiency (e.g. vertical integration) or because they enable a small competitor to enter a market against larger rivals (discriminatory pricing). In these cases, the Commission found against the practices; but it does not follow that they are generally to be condemned. It depends on how they are used by whom in what circumstances.

[24] A Report on the Supply of Chlordiazepoxide and Diazepam (H.C. 197, 1973).

TABLE 26.1. *Practices Found Against the Public Interest by the MMC in its Published Reports Since 1959 on the Supply of Goods*

Practice	Number of cases in which practice occurred
Group 1	
Restriction of supply to certain outlets	2
Restrictions on sale of competitors' goods	12
Restrictions on the supply of inputs to competitors	1
Full-line forcing*	2
Rental only contracts	1
Tie-in sales†	3
Group 2	
Discriminatory pricing	7
Vertical integration	3
Acquisition of competitors	2
Patent licensing policy	1
Delivered pricing system	2
Financial interest in competitors	1
Failure to disclose ownership of subsidiary	1

* Full-line forcing is where dealers are required to carry a whole line of the products of one manufacturer in order to keep his business.

† Tie-in sales is where one product is tied to the sale of another; for example, paper may be tied to the rental of a copying machine.

Source: Green Paper [10], p. 73.

In the case of Wholesaling of Newspapers[25] the central issue was whether wholesalers were entitled to refuse supplies of newspapers to retailers who were on the face of it reputable, credit-worthy, and otherwise competent to carry on the trade. The wholesalers argued that they had to restrict the number of retailers to prevent the market being flooded, profits being reduced, and services such as delivery eliminated to save costs. The Commission broadly accepted that in these circumstances refusal to supply was not against the public interest, and made no recommendations against the practice.

26.5. Conclusions

26.5.1. Competition Promotion Revisited

The purpose of those who advocate the 'competition promotion' remedy in anti-trust matters is to identify and eliminate those factors which obstruct new entry, rivalry, and other challenges to market power. Such obstacles may be 'natural', that is not deliberately created by the dominant company (or for that

---

[25] A Report on the Wholesale Supply of National Newspapers and Periodicals in England and Wales, and in Scotland, in Relation to Refusal to Supply and Participating in Retailing (Cmnd. 7214, 1978).

matter by anyone else). The clearest example is where geography, transport costs, economies of scale, and the size of the market combine to create a local monopoly (which may be as large as a state, or a region, or a country). In that market there can only be one major supplier, and he is necessarily protected from competition because there is no room for any producer of similar size in the same place, nor cheap access to the market from the outside. Another problem arises when there are obvious economies in providing a single network of services. Duplicate gas pipes up the same street are evidently wasteful, so too are duplicate railway systems. The least-cost solution is then to have one company establish and operate the network. But that immediately creates a monopoly.

The main difficulty with natural monopoly if not to identify it, but to find a remedy. It is possible, of course, to accept the costs of breaking up the dominant position by subsidizing transport into the local market, or setting up a state competitor, or allowing duplication. But this amounts to the promotion of competition for its own sake, even though it is a less cost-efficient solution. Price control is an obvious alternative—either via regulation or nationalization. But this is only a partial answer. It deals with prices and price–cost ratios, but can do nothing to substitute for competition as a stimulus to efficiency in product development and production. The regulated prices will necessarily be on some kind of cost-plus basis, with all the dangers that involves to incentives and effort.

Some man-made obstacles are in principle easier to deal with. If a company controls all distribution outlets or supplies, then potential rivals are foreclosed from competing, and the dominant firm can relax. In that case the company can be made to give up control. Other obstacles are more difficult, for example patents. It is plain that the possession of a key patent can (if not as often as is popularly supposed) be a crucial protection from challenge. Is this barrier to be condemned? Surely not, since the patent system itself was set up by government to protect an inventor and allow him to reap the fruits of his successful ingenuity. The most general difficulty is that the major obstacle to new competition will often be the existing skill and experience of the historically successful large company. Is that a natural or a man-made barrier? Is it desirable or undesirable? In principle the rules of free enterprise allow companies to compete against each other rather like runners in a race—save for the advantage of effort, energy, and natural ability, all start equal. Then the winner deserves the credit for having developed and displayed the virtues which the system is designed to reward. If he gains experience by persistent competition and success, and thereby becomes even more difficult to defeat, it is further to his credit. Rivals are not entitled to complain that his skill constitutes an undesirable obstacle to their success.

26.5.2. Cost-Benefit Revisited

The competition-promotion approach is comparatively simple. It is based on the proposition that if only competition can be enforced, then efficiency will be achieved—at least so far as it is within the power of anti-trust policy. The approach is admittedly limited—both because competition cannot achieve everything, and because in some circumstances (natural monopoly) competition cannot practicably be achieved.

The alternative approach (which is more like that adopted in the United Kingdom by the Monopolies Commission) can be explained as follows. Competition is not desirable *per se*, but only as a means to socially desirable ends such as efficient production, technical progress, low prices, high exports, and so on. Competition certainly has an important contribution to make to the achievement of these ends—and perhaps for most industries most of the time it is the most appropriate mechanism. But in many cases—not only those of natural monopolies—it will be not simply unattainable, but undesirable. Large scale may be necessary to achieve optimum efficiency in plant, organization, management, distribution, and research. Co-ordination, via cartel or single ownership, is essential when plant has a long and unpredictable gestation period, is large scale, and has to rely for its operation on complementary outputs from other companies. The petrochemical industry, for example, cannot operate at arm's length. The advantages of planning are not simply an ideological matter: they arise from unavoidable technical features of the world, which cannot be reconciled with competition. Efficient economies are full of desirable market imperfections (of which the patent system is one); and it is dangerously simple to pretend that anti-trust policy should aim at the reimposition of competition regardless of its disadvantages.

Considerations of natural justice may also be against a whole-hearted competition-promotion policy. the victors will be dominant. But all they have done is to take the prizes which the system offers. It is not right to change the rules after the game has started—particularly not when it has been won. Unless, therefore, the victory has been achieved by foul means, the verdict should stand, even if it involves accepting the temporary dominance of a single company. There is, of course, a practical reason for this attitude as well as a feeling for natural justice. The incentive system which makes companies strive to be efficient will not operate successfully for long if rewards once achieved are promptly removed.

The theory of competition in its simplest form assumes crudely that it is only by fear of failure or desire for financial success that managers can be successfully motivated. This is plainly a narrow view of human behaviour. Many people, not only inventors, work hard and ingeniously simply from a desire for craftsmanship and to do a good job for its own sake. Internal competition between individuals in a company can be a very good substitute for outside pressure. Management systems such as 'management-by-objectives' or more mundanely efficient budget setting and monitoring can have a substantial effect on efficiency. Of course, the vigour with which the management at the top of the company strives to introduce and operate systems of this kind will depend on what forces are operating to motivate it. But it is evident that the vast majority of people working in industry are not influenced by the direct impact of competition or even of financial gain/loss; and that therefore the effectiveness of these other sources of discipline and efficiency must be assessed before it can be assumed that the absence of competition is associated with incompetence.

The main problem with a broad approach to anti-trust is that it provides no calculus for making the trade-off. Suppose a company to be dominant, and that consequently prices are somewhat higher than they would be in the absence of dominance. But the dominance means that the company is a good deal more successful in exports than it would otherwise have been. What are we to conclude? Does the export disadvantage outweigh the price disadvantage or not? How can we decide these things? There is at present no good answer to this question. However, it is plainly no answer to concentrate solely on the fact of dominance; condemn it as anti-competitive; and therefore seek its elimination.

26.5.3. The Scope of Anti-Trust

The effectiveness of anti-trust policy is necessarily limited. Even if it is possible to identify successfully what is wrong with an industry, there may be very little to do about it. It is often very difficult and damaging to promote competition by breaking up large firms—economies of scale are lost, management morale shattered, and the new smaller firms may still collude and fix prices as effectively as did their parent. Regulating prices and profits is possible, but it is very difficult to increase exports, or investment, or R & D if those are the areas in which you believe that the monopolist has been inefficient.

If anti-trust cannot do the job, then other instruments of economic policy will have to be used. Some of these may be general—price codes; export subsidies; investment grants and tax allowances—and designed to change the behaviour of all companies, large or small, dominant or not. A catch-all remedy for situations where private enterprise does not serve the public interest is nationalization. Whether the problem is to do with employment, or investment, or industrial relations, the government can put it right—or at least believe that it can—by taking direct control of the industry, and removing certain of its decisions from the influence of market forces.

Anti-trust policy must therefore be seen as part and part only of industrial policy. It is one option from a range which extends from whole-hearted *laissez-faire* to centralized state planning. Different diseases will require different remedies.

Appendix 1: The Restrictive Trade Practices Court 'Gateways' and 'Tailpiece'

Section 10 of the Restrictive Trade Practices Act 1976 provides that an agreement relating to goods shall be deemed to be contrary to the public interest unless the Court is satisfied of any one or more of:

(a) That the restriction is reasonably necessary, having regard to the character of the goods to which it applies, to protect the public against injury (whether to persons or to premises) in connection with the consumption, installation or use of those goods;
(b) That the removal of the restriction would deny to the public as purchasers, consumers or users of any goods other specific and substantial benefits or advantages enjoyed or likely to be enjoyed by them as such, whether by virtue of the restriction itself or of any arrangements or operations resulting therefrom;
(c) That the restriction is reasonably necessary to counteract measures taken by any

one person not party to the agreement with a view to preventing or restricting competition in or in relation to the trade or business in which the persons party thereto are engaged;

(d) That the restriction is reasonably necessary to enable the persons party to the agreement to negotiate fair terms for the supply of goods to, or the acquisition of goods from, any one person not party thereto who controls a preponderant part of the trade or business of acquiring or supplying such goods, or for the supply of goods to any person not party to the agreement and not carrying on such a trade or business who, either alone or in combination with any such other person, controls a preponderant part of the market for such goods;

(e) That, having regard to the conditions actually obtaining or reasonably foreseen at the time of the application, the removal of the restriction would be likely to have a serious and persistent adverse effect on the general level of unemployment in an area, or in areas taken together, in which a substantial proportion of the trade or industry to which the agreement relates is situated;

(f) That having regard to the conditions actually obtaining or reasonably foreseen at the time of the application, the removal of the restriction would be likely to cause a reduction in the volume or earnings of the export business of the United Kingdom or in relation to the whole export business of the United Kingdom or in relation to the whole business (including export business) of the said trade or industry; or

(g) That the restriction is reasonably required for purposes connected with the maintenance of any other restriction accepted by the parties, whether under the same agreement or under any other agreement between them, being a restriction which is found by the Court not to be contrary to the public interest upon grounds other than those specified in this paragraph, or has been so found in previous proceedings before the Court;

(h) That the restriction does not directly or indirectly restrict or discourage competition to any material degree in any relevant trade or industry and is not likely to do so.

The 'tailpiece' states that the Court must be 'further satisfied that the restriction is not unreasonable having regard to the balance between these circumstances and any detriment to the public or to persons not party to the agreement . . . resulting or likely to result from the operation of the restrictors'.

Identical provisions apply to services.

Appendix 2: The Resale Price Maintenance 'Gateways' and 'Tailpiece'

Section 14 of the Resale Price Maintenance Act 1976 provides that Resale Price Maintenance may only be operated where the Court concludes that without RPM:

(a) the quality of the goods available for sale, or the varieties of the goods so available, would be substantially reduced to the detriment of the public as consumers or users of those goods; or

(b) the number of establishments in which the goods are sold by retail would be substantially reduced to the detriment of the public as such consumers or users; or

(c) the prices at which the goods are sold by retail would in general and in the long run be increased to the detriment of the public as such consumers or users; or

(d) the goods would be sold by retail under conditions likely to cause danger to health in consequence of their misuse by the public as such consumers or users; or

(e) any necessary services actually provided in connection with or after the sale of the goods by retail would cease to be so provided or would be substantially reduced to the detriment of the public as such consumers or users;

and in any such case that the resulting detriment to the public as consumers or users of the goods in question would outweigh any detriment to them as such consumers or users (whether by the restriction of competition or otherwise) resulting from the maintenance of minimum resale prices in respect of the goods.

Appendix 3: The Monopolies Commission and the Public Interest

Section 84(1) of the Fair Trading Act 1973 provides as follows:

In determining for the purposes of this Act whether any particular matter operates, or may be expected to operate, against the public interest, the Commission shall take into account all matters which appear to them in the particular circumstances to be relevant, and among other things, shall have regard to the desirability—

(a) of maintaining and promoting effective competition between persons supplying goods and services in the United Kingdom;
(b) of promoting the interests of consumers, purchasers and other users of goods and services in the United Kingdom in respect of the prices charged for them and in respect of their quality and the variety of goods and services supplied;
(c) of promoting, through competition, the reduction of costs and the development and use of new techniques and new products, and of facilitating the entry of new competitors, into existing markets;
(d) of maintaining and promoting the balanced distribution of industry and employment in the United Kingdom; and
(e) of maintaining and promoting competitive activity in markets outside the United Kingdom on the part of producers of goods, and of supplies of goods and services, in the United Kingdom.

Appendix 4: European Economic Community: Articles 85 and 86

ARTICLE 85

1. The following shall be deemed to be incompatible with the Common Market and shall hereby be prohibited: any agreement between enterprises, any decisions by associations of enterprises and any concerted practices which are likely to affect trade between the Member States and which have as their object or result the prevention, restriction or distortion of competition within the Common Market, in particular those consisting in:

(a) The direct or indirect fixing of purchase or selling prices or of any other trading conditions;
(b) the limitation or control of production, markets, technical development or investment;
(c) market-sharing or the sharing of sources of supply;
(d) the application to parties to transactions of unequal terms in respect of equivalent supplies, thereby placing them at a competitive disadvantage; or
(e) the subjecting of the conclusion of a contract to the acceptance by a party of additional supplies which, either by their nature or according to commercial usage, have no connection with the subject of such contract.

2. Any agreements or decisions prohibited pursuant to this Article shall be null and void.

3. Nevertheless, the provisions of paragraph 1 may be declared inapplicable in the case of:

—any agreements or classes of agreements between enterprises,
—any decisions or classes of decisions by associations of enterprises, and
—any concerted practices or classes of concerted practices

which contribute to the improvement of the production or distribution of goods or to the promotion of technical or economic progress while reserving to users an equitable share in the profit resulting therefrom, and which:

(a) neither impose on the enterprises concerned any restrictions not indispensable to the attainment of the above objectives;

(b) nor enable such enterprises to eliminate competition of a substantial proportion of the goods concerned.

ARTICLE 86

To the extent to which trade between any Member States may be affected thereby, action by one or more enterprises to take improper advantage of a dominant position within the Common Market or within a substantial part of it shall be deemed to be incompatible with the Common Market and shall hereby be prohibited.

Such improper practices may, in particular, consist in:

(a) the direct or indirect imposition of any inequitable purchase or selling prices or of any other inequitable trading conditions;

(b) the limitation of production, markets or technical development to the prejudice of consumers;

(c) the application to parties to transactions of unequal terms in respect of equivalent supplies, thereby placing them at a competitive disadvantage; or

(d) the subjecting of the conclusion of a contract to the acceptance, by a party, of additional supplies which, either by their nature or according to commercial usage, have no connection with the subject of such contract.

Bibliography

A. THE LAW

The relevant United Kingdom legislation is as follows:
[1] Fair Trading Act 1973.
[2] Resale Price Maintenance Act 1976.
[3] Restrictive Trade Practices Act 1976.

Details of decisions of the restrictive Trade Practices Court can be found in [4] The Law Reports of Restrictive Trade Practices Cases.
[5] Competition Act 1980.
[6] The Reports of the Monopolies and Mergers Commission give a full account of the arguments and conclusions on Monopolies Commission cases.
[7] The Annual Reports of the Registrar of Restrictive Trade Practices, now succeeded by the Director General of Fair Trading, give a good general account of anti-trust policy for the preceding year.

The position in the United States can be seen most easily from:
[8] NEALE, A. D. and GOYDER, D. G. *The Anti-Trust Law of the United States* (Cambridge University Press, 1982).

For the EEC, see
[9] BELLAMY and CHILD *Common Market Law of Competition* (Sweet & Maxwell, 1978).

B. THE ECONOMICS

Much the best general introduction to the issues are the Green Papers
[10] *A Review of Monopolies and Mergers Policy* (Cmnd. 7198, HMSO, 1978).
[11] *A Review of Restrictive Trade Practices Policy* (Cmnd. 7512, HMSO, 1979).
The Annexes to the 1978 Green Paper provide extensive bibliographies on concentration; monopolistic behaviour and performance; economies of scale; mergers; and innovation. These should be used as a detailed supplement to what follows here.

Other general introductions are:
[12] HUNTER, A. *Competition and the Law* (George Allen and Unwin, 1966).
[13] ROWLEY, C. K. *Anti-Trust and Economic Efficiency* (Macmillan, 1973).
[14] HUNTER, A. *Monopoly and Competition* (Penguin, 1969).

The best defence of monopoly is in:
[15] SCHUMPETER, J. A. *Capitalism, Socialism and Democracy* (Allen and Unwin, 1950), Chaps. 8 and 9.

A good deal of the theory behind anti-trust policy is to do with perfect competition, the allocation of resources, and the theory of the firm. For these, see the bibliographies to Chapters 3 and 24 of this book.

For more detailed reading on how the policy is operated see:
[16] Office of Fair Trading. *Mergers: A Guide to the Procedure under the Fair Trading Act 1973* (OFT, 1978).
[17] ROWLEY, C. K. *The British Monopolies Commission* (George Allen and Unwin, 1966).
[18] SUTHERLAND, A. *The Monopolies Commission in Action* (Cambridge University Press, 1969).
[19] SWANN, D. *et al. Competition in British Industry* (George Allen and Unwin, 1974).
[20] KORAH, V. *Competition Law of Britain and the EEC* (Penguin, 1974).
[21] HEATH, J. (ed.). *International Conference on Monopolies, Mergers and Restrictive Practices* (Dept. of Trade and Industry, HMSO, 1971).
[22] GEORGE, K. and JOLL, C. (eds.). *Competition policy in the U.K. and the E.E.C.* (Cambridge University Press, 1975).

For an attack on the effectiveness of mergers, see:
[23] MEEKS, G. *Disappointing Marriage: A Study of the Gains from Merger* (Cambridge University Press, 1973).

27

North Sea Oil

J. C. WHITEMAN

27.1. The Oil Discoveries

The exploitation of oil in the UK continental shelf has been seen as one of the principal developments affecting this country's recent history, to the extent that it has been described as the North Sea 'bonanza'. Its impact on the economy has been so substantial that the industry requires a chapter of its own. The first discovery of oil in significant quantities was made by British Petroleum in November 1970, in the Forties field 125 miles north-west of Aberdeen. That was followed, in July 1971, by a second major discovery in the Brent field, some 200 miles further north, off the Shetland Isles. It had been apparent for decades that large areas of the UK continental shelf could contain oil-bearing rock formations, and production from small onshore wells in Lincolnshire started as far back as the 1930s. However, the main surge of offshore exploration followed the Forties and Brent discoveries, and the bulk of existing proven reserves was established by 1976.

Estimates of how much oil might be recovered from under the North Sea and elsewhere in the UK's continental shelf are necessarily imprecise. First, there is a geological aspect—assessing how much oil is present. Second, there is a technical aspect—assessing how difficult it might be to recover the oil. It is worth bearing in mind that the proportion of oil on average recovered from a field is little more than a third of the total present. This is because of the third aspect—assessing the cost of extraction and the revenue which the oil company will receive for it. At a high price, net of taxes and royalties, it might be worth overcoming technical hurdles—such as undertaking secondary recovery operations—which do not pay at a lower price. Hence any estimate of recoverable oil reserves is contingent upon technical and economic factors at least as much as upon geological ones.

To allow for the uncertainties of assessing reserves, the official (Department of Energy) estimates distinguish 'proven' reserves—those virtually certain to be economically and technically feasible—from other categories with a lesser probability. Table 27.1 shows the official estimates given in mid-1983. It is quoted as a range, further to reflect the uncertainty of any precise estimate. The range given is equivalent to about 20 to 50 years' consumption at the 1980 rate. Unofficial estimates of UK oil reserves encompass a much larger range: the

TABLE 27.1. *Official Estimates of Remaining Oil Reserves in UK Continental Shelf (as of 31 December 1982)*
(in million tonnes)

Remaining reserves in present discoveries (of which, proven* reserves 1,000)	1,325–1,625
Potential undiscovered reserves	225–2,125
Total recoverable reserves	1,550–3,750

* Proven means those reserves which on the available evidence are virtually certain to be technically and economically producible.

Source: Department of Energy.

highest estimate quoted (by Professor P. R. Odell) is equivalent to nearly 150 years' consumption. The actual length of life of the reserves naturally depends upon the rate of extraction, itself influenced by technical and economic factors.

The UK attained self-sufficiency in oil during 1980, when consumption and production were both 80 million tonnes annually, or 1·6 million barrels per day. Self-sufficiency refers to the net position. Much North Sea oil output is exported, in exchange for lower-grade (and cheaper) oil suited to UK refineries. Figure 27.1 shows the profile of output and consumption, with a forecast range—derived from official sources—up to 1985. Assuming there are no dramatic changes in prices or taxes, oil production is expected to peak in the mid-1980s and decline steadily thereafter, probably falling below UK

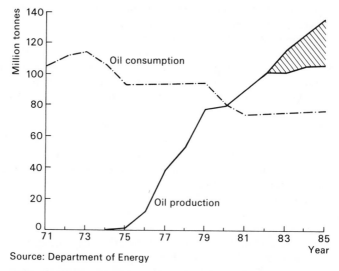

Source: Department of Energy

FIG. 27.1. UK Oil Production and Consumption (in Millions of Tonnes), 1971–1985.
Source: Department of Energy.

consumption sometime during the 1990s. At the peak level the UK will produce about $2\frac{1}{2}$ million barrels per day, making it the sixth-largest world producer (after the USSR, US, Saudi Arabia, Iraq, and Iran—on the basis of their 1979 levels of output). It will account for roughly 5 per cent of total world production.

Over the next decade the UK will be a substantial net exporter of oil, but thereafter it is likely to be a permanent importer. In principle it is possible to assess whether the UK should be regarded as self-sufficient, in a permanent sense: this involves discounting future production and consumption to arrive at a present value of both. The results of such a calculation naturally depend heavily upon the discount rate chosen as well as assumptions about future trends in demand; it tends to suggest that the UK is only a small net exporter.

27.2. The Economics of Oil Extraction

As might be suggested by a moment's reflection on the difficulties of operating oil rigs in deep and frequently stormy waters, the cost of finding and exploiting oil under the North Sea has been very high compared with the costs of extraction in the Middle East. During the 1970s some £25 billion at 1980 prices was spent on equipment alone for oil (and gas) extraction. In 1981 North Sea oil capital spending amounted to 20 per cent of the UK's total industrial capital formation. Allowing for the capital and other inputs, the Department of Energy has calculated that oil from fields discovered prior to 1982 costs US$12 per barrel to extract (in 1982 prices). The expenditure is not just financial: up to the end of 1982, 125 people were killed while working in North Sea oil installations.

Despite the significant human and financial costs, at present prices the North Sea is a very profitable source of crude oil. Hence, in 1981 oil (and gas) extraction generated profits of £11 billion, accounting for more than a third of total corporate gross profits in this country. A significant proportion of the gross profit is siphoned off by the UK Government in the form of royalties and taxes of various kinds. In 1981 the proportion was 50 per cent, but it will rise once the heavy investment of the 1970s has been written off by the oil companies. The complexity of the UK's system of taxation for oil has stemmed from the government's attempt to prevent the oil companies earning excessive profits while also not impeding unduly the exploitation of oil. The accelerated write-off allowed for North Sea investment has caused government revenue to grow more slowly than the value of oil production. Figure 27.2 shows total revenue from oil, with the official forecast up to 1984–5. Unofficial revenue forecasts vary more widely than those of output, since changes in the price of crude oil and in the pound–US dollar exchange rate have a disproportionate effect on profits. The official revenue forecast is at the lower end of the range, with other commentators forecasting up to twice as much in 1985. In that year, even on the government's view, oil revenue will account for 6 per cent of total revenue (and be equivalent to half the revenue from VAT).

North Sea oil's impact on government revenue may be significant, but its effect on the balance of payments statistics is more dramatic. The nature of the

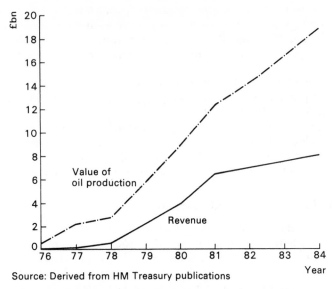

Source: Derived from HM Treasury publications

FIG. 27.2. Government Revenue From North Sea Oil (£ Billion), 1976–7 to 1984–5. Source: Derived from HM Treasury Publications.

balance of payments is such that payments of all sorts by UK residents must balance receipts, so that the actual statistics cannot show what the position would be in the absence of indigenous oil; at best they can show how far other items would have to adjust to compensate for the absence of oil.

There is a further proviso: the effect of North Sea oil on the balance of payments does not equal the savings in net imports it permits. Prior to the full-scale production of oil, and to a lesser extent continuing up to the present, there have been substantial imports of equipment and services; however, these have not generally involved any immediate foreign exchange cost as they have often been paid for by inflows of foreign capital. Consequently, as the production of oil has built up so has the outflow of dividend and interest payments on this foreign investment, partly offsetting the direct savings of foreign exchange allowed by the oil itself. Table 27.2 depicts how the foreign exchange flows related to oil have developed since 1975. The total identifiable impact of oil on the current account in 1983, estimated at £12 billion, was equivalent to 20 per cent of total imports.

Compared with its importance to the balance of payments, North Sea oil's contribution to total net output in the UK economy is rather more modest. In 1981 oil and gas together accounted for 6 per cent of GDP; after allowing for net oil-related dividend payments abroad they accounted for 5 per cent of the UK's GNP. On official estimates the share of GNP is expected to increase relatively little. In international terms, the share of oil and gas in this country's GDP is comparable to that of gas in the Netherlands. The UK is in no sense an

TABLE 27·2. *North Sea Oil—Balance of Payments Impact*
(£ millions)

	1975	1976	1977	1978	1979	1980	1981	1982
Value of oil sales	58	645	2,226	2,805	5,681	8,351	12,341	14,431
Import of goods for oil sector	-341	-536	-531	-185	-171	-144	-377	-451
Net import of services for oil sector	-481	-640	-701	-545	-447	-469	-553	-676
Interest, profit, and dividend payments of oil sector	-23	-24	-550	-666	-1,368	-2,215	-2,355	-2,561
Total impact of North Sea oil sector on *current account*	-787	-555	+444	+1,409	+3,695	+6,023	+9,212	+10,743
Overseas investment in oil sector	946	1,142	1,508	791	696	841	1,638	1,040
Net balance of payments impact of North Sea oil sector	159	587	1,952	2,200	4,391	6,864	10,873	11,783

Source: CSO, *Balance of Payments 1983*.

oil-based economy in the same way as, say, Venezuela—a country with a comparable oil output; oil accounts for a quarter of its GDP, and virtually all of its export receipts.

27.3. Problems in Analysing North Sea Oil

27.3.1. The Key Questions

The build-up of production of oil from the UK's continental shelf, and its evident impact on the statistics of the balance of payments and of government revenue, stimulated an intense debate over its implications for the standard of living in the UK and the structure of the economy. The issues raised can be expressed in four questions which are identified here and then examined in the remainder of this chapter.

(i) *What is the effect of North Sea oil on the UK's exchange rate and, as a result, on the structure of the economy?* In the daily newspapers the pound is frequently referred to as a 'petro-currency', implying that its value is heavily dependent upon the existence of indigenous oil. Supporting this viewpoint, Forsyth and Kay [12] have suggested that a high exchange rate is a necessary consequence of North Sea oil and the extra income which it generates for the UK. On their analysis, oil self-sufficiency implies a decline, at least in relative terms, in the size of the manufacturing sector, and a rise in the exchange rate is the mechanism by which this occurs. The plausibility of their analysis was enhanced as it was published in 1980, when sterling had risen to a record level in real terms and manufacturing output was declining rapidly.

(ii) *Has North Sea oil lifted any previous constraints on the UK's growth rate?* By contrast with Forsyth and Kay, Cripps and Godley [9] have suggested that North Sea oil need not result in a higher exchange rate, and that it permits an expansion of manufacturing. On their analysis, the UK's growth rate was previously artificially limited, because any expansion of demand was accompanied by a rapid deterioration in the current account of the balance of payments. In other words, attempts to expand the economy confronted a balance of payments constraint. According to Cripps and Godley, oil provided a significant saving of foreign exchange, thus easing the constraint on growth; demand could be expanded until the constraint was met again.

(iii) *Has North Sea oil lowered the UK's growth rate, by resulting in deflation of the economy?* We have seen that a substantial proportion of the profit from North Sea oil accrues to the government. It is clear that the way the revenue is used can have an effect on the level and pattern of activity and incomes in the UK. Worswick [15] and others at the National Institute have suggested that, if not allowed for properly, North Sea oil can cause the whole economy—not just manufacturing—to be deflated. This analysis also gains plausibility from the fact that in 1979–82 the UK economy has suffered a more severe decline in output and employment than any other industrial country.

(iv) *Is the UK wealthier as a result of North Sea oil?* This is the fundamental question in relation to the UK's oil, for a number of the other effects can be seen to depend upon it. It would seem only common sense to suppose that the UK is better off by virtue of possessing oil, because of its significant contribution to GDP, or to government revenue. Indeed various suggestions have been put forward for using the resources to improve the standard of living of the UK, either in the short term, for example by expanding public services, or in the longer term, for example by investing in additional productive capacity. However, the Bank of England [1, 2] has suggested that while we are clearly better off than we *would* have been without oil, we are not on that account much better off than we actually *were* before the steep increases in oil prices from 1973–4 onwards.

27.3.2. *Sources of Confusion in the Analysis*

It is difficult, on a first impression, to assess which of these views is correct, or even the extent to which they are inconsistent with one another. This confusion is not surprising. Analysis of the impact of North Sea oil is particularly complicated because the process of oil exploitation during the 1970s was punctuated by sharp changes in the world price of oil, as well as by a significant shift in the focus of domestic economic policy.

In 1973–4, after the initial major oil discoveries, but well before production started, the first OPEC 'shock' doubled the oil price. For several years the UK had to import oil at the higher price. Then in 1978–80, as the UK was approaching self-sufficiency, the oil price doubled again. Also during the late 1970s, but particularly from 1979, the first priority of domestic macroeconomic policy in the UK shifted from the preservation of full employment to the attainment of greater price stability.

From this it can be seen that there are two oil-related influences on economic developments in the UK:

(i) The effect of the growth of North Sea oil production, abstracting from the effect of a changing oil price (i.e. assuming the oil price is constant).
(ii) The effect of changes in the price of oil, abstracting from the effect of the growth of oil production (i.e. assuming oil production is constant at, say, self-sufficiency).

In either case it is appropriate to identify the impact on the UK's standard of living, its level and structure of production, and to ask also how the impact might have been modified by a different government macroeconomic policy stance. The reason for wishing to disentangle the two influences—price and volume—is that in the future one may change without the other. Indeed the particular combination of world price and UK output levels which character-ized the 1970s is certain not to recur. To assess the impact of future changes in output or price it is necessary to identify their separate effects.

27.4. The Impact of North Sea Oil

Discussion of the impact of oil on the rest of the UK economy was first stimulated in 1980 by Forsyth and Kay [12]. Their approach was similar to one used earlier by Gregory[1] in analysing the impact on Australia of a boom in mineral development in the 1960s. Forsyth and Kay's paper prompted a number of responses, mainly from academic economists, while the Chancellor of the Exchequer, Sir Geoffrey Howe, at the time broadly endorsed the views they expressed. In this section their paper, and subsequent critiques of it, are reviewed.

27.4.1. The Forsyth and Kay Analysis

Their paper used what is termed a 'comparative-static' approach, comparing the structure of the UK economy first without, and second with, North Sea oil production but not specifying (as would a 'dynamic' approach) the path of adjustment between the two states. They drew up a table—reproduced here as Table 27.3—summarizing the flows of goods and services within the economy, using 1976 as the pre-oil base. Five broad categories of production were identified; of them, 'primary' includes both agriculture and mining, and 'distribution and services' includes health and education as well as banking. In Tables 27.3 and 27.4, 'production' less 'exports' plus 'imports' equals 'absorption'.

TABLE 27.3. *The Structure of the UK Economy, 1976**
(£bn, 1980 absolute prices)

	Production	Export	Imports	Absorption
Primary production	9·0	− 1·2	+ 8·0	15·8
Manufacturing	48·9	− 24·9	+ 22·0	46·0
Construction and housing	22·5	− 0·2	+ 0·3	22·6
Distribution and services	88·1	− 18·8	+ 16·9	86·2
Public administration	13·5	—	—	13·5
Total	181·9	− 45·1	+ 47·3	184·1

* The 'pre-oil' equilibrium in Forsyth and Kay's analysis.

Source: Forsyth and Kay [12], Table 4.

The figures in Table 27.3 were all converted to approximate 1980 values (by multiplying each element by 1·65). As well as production the table shows exports, imports, and 'absorption'—i.e. final use in consumption or investment. Thus for example in 1976 the UK produced £48·9 billion of manufactured goods, of which it exported £24·9 billion (shown as a minus because it reduces the amount of goods available in the UK). It imported £22 billion of manufactures (counted as a plus for the opposite reason) and so 'absorbed' £46 billion (equals £48·9 billion minus £24·9 billion plus £22

[1] GREGORY, R. G. 'Some Implications of the Growth of the Mineral Sector, *Australian Journal of Agricultural Economics* (1976).

billion). The total line shows overall output, then the net balance of trade (which was then in deficit to the tune of £2·2 billion), and finally overall absorption of goods and services.

It will be noticed that for certain categories—public administration and construction—there is little or no foreign trade. Though the table does not show it, the same is true of many services. These are all termed 'non-tradable' activities, to distinguish them from manufactures, primary commodities, and certain services such as banking and insurance, which are extensively exported or imported and so are known as 'tradable' products.

The 'initial' impact of North Sea oil—in inverted commas because no time path is implied for the chain of events—on the UK economy was illustrated by Forsyth and Kay as an addition to production in the primary sector. They used a figure of £10 billion at 1980 prices, bringing primary production to £19 billion and raising total output by roughly 5 per cent. Several key assumptions were made to determine the effect of the extra output:

(i) Absorption of goods and services is assumed to rise by exactly the same amount in value terms as oil adds to production—i.e. the output of all the non-oil sectors together does not change, and neither does the balance of trade.

(ii) The extra absorption is spread uniformly across the five categories of production in proportion to their pre-oil levels—i.e. absorption in each category rises by 5 per cent.

Since absorption increases uniformly the initial extra output of primary products—oil—must be transformed in some way into the products to be consumed or invested. For tradable goods and services there is no difficulty since extra quantities of these can be imported in exchange for oil (or instead of previous oil imports). However, for non-tradable products there is no alternative but to raise domestic production. So some productive resources— employees, equipment, etc.—must transfer from producing tradables to producing non-tradables. The output of the former falls, being made up by imports, the output of the latter rises to satisfy the extra demand. Table 27.4 shows the 'post-oil' economy: total output and absorption are higher by 5 per cent but manufacturing output is 6 per cent lower.

The process can be summarized in Forsyth and Kay's own words:

The essentials of what is happening are very simple. North Sea oil adds considerably to the growth of the UK economy. However, this growth takes a highly unbalanced form; all of it occurs in a single sector whose size is, even then, small in relation to the overall economy. To use the additional resources which it makes available to us, it is necessary to convert them to a form in which they can be exploited domestically. But there is simply no way in which oil can be converted into houses, or restaurant meals, or retail and distributive services, either directly or through trade; and it is largely on items of these kinds that we shall want to spend our increased income. All we can do is to exchange oil for traded goods—predominantly manufactures—and redeploy the resources released from these sectors into the other, non-tradeable, sectors of the economy. There is no mechanism for deriving benefit from North Sea oil which does not, sooner or later, require this structural change [12].

TABLE 27.4. *The Post-Oil Economy*
(£bn, 1980 prices)

	Production	Exports	Imports	Absorption
Primary production	19·0	(− 2·3)		16·7
Manufacturing	46·1	− 22·2	+ 24·6	48·5
Construction and housing	23·7	− 0·2	+ 0·3	23·8
Distribution and services	88·9	− 16·9	+ 18·9	90·9
Public administration	14·2	—	—	14·2
Total	191·9	(+ 2·2)		194·1

Source: Forsyth and Kay [12], Table 5.

The way this structural change occurs, according to them, is via the exchange rate. They pointed to the rise, of more than 20 per cent, in the value of sterling between 1976 and 1980. The higher exchange rate itself improves the UK's standard of living (since typically export prices expressed in sterling do not fall by as much as import prices do, and the terms of trade therefore improve). The initial gain in income is thus enhanced, with further repercussions for manufacturing and other tradables as spending on non-tradables rises further. Forsyth and Kay calculate the total effect as a gain in absorption of £15·5 billion or 8½ per cent, but associated with a fall in manufacturing output of 9 per cent.

27.4.2. *Critiques of Forsyth and Kay's Assumptions*

Various authors initially responded to Forsyth and Kay, focusing their criticism on the two key assumptions identified in the preceding section. Implicitly, Cripps and Godley [9] criticized the first assumption, that non-oil output in total could not rise (any changes occurring only in its composition). Forsyth and Kay pointed out that their intention was to identify only the effect of North Sea oil itself on the UK economy. Higher non-oil output could only be a result (in the short run, at least) if there was previously a balance of payments constraint on output, which oil revenues eased. Cripps and Godley asserted that there *was* a balance of payments constraint on output. Instead of allowing the exchange rate to appreciate the government should have expanded the economy to absorb the extra imports permitted by oil revenue. They calculated that output could expand by 23 per cent (instead of 5 per cent) and manufacturing by 6 per cent (instead of falling by 9 per cent).

For this increase to be possible there must have been spare productive resources in existence, prior to the exploitation of North Sea oil, which that exploitation allowed to be used. The output of the economy is assumed to have been constrained by an inadequate supply of tradable goods—which is what a balance of payments constraint implies—even though there are some spare resources. North Sea oil, by adding to the supply of tradables, allows (non-tradable) output to expand until the point at which the constraint binds again.

Over a longer-term perspective, when equipment can be replaced and personnel redeployed, resources can clearly shift between the tradable and non-tradable sectors (a shift which the Forsyth and Kay analysis invokes). The notion of a balance of payments constraint is then implausible. At any stage the ultimate constraint is the capacity of the economy to supply the goods and services which final users are prepared to buy: a weak balance of payments may merely be a symptom of meeting that ultimate constraint. Alternatively it may be that the incentive for resources to move between the tradable and non-tradable sectors—the 'real' exchange rate—is inadequate.

In 1976, the base year for Forsyth and Kay, there was some evidence that the UK was temporarily constrained by its balance of payments, because of the rise in oil prices in 1973–4. However, fear of inflation was also a constraint on policy at that time (having reached 25 per cent the previous year).

Cripps and Godley's critique was in fact one particular case of a general analysis, developed by Brooks [4], which identified the theoretical supply conditions required for total non-oil output to increase following the discovery of a new natural resource. A rise in price of non-traded goods (in relation to wage costs in their production) associated with an appreciating real exchange rate could generate an expansion of their output that was not fully offset by a fall in tradable output. In an extreme case, where output is purely demand constrained—in a 'Keynesian' world with spare resources where output can increase at a constant cost of production—no change in prices would be necessary to promote additional output of non-traded goods. If such conditions had prevailed in 1976 the government could have expanded demand even without the existence of North Sea oil. None the less Brooks's basic point is valid, that supply as well as demand factors will determine the response of the economy to North Sea oil.

Like the others, Barker's [3] critique of Forsyth and Kay focused on the assumption of fixed non-oil output, but in his case from a different angle. He reiterated that a substantial proportion of the revenue from oil accrued to the government. If this revenue were used to reduce government borrowing (the PSBR) then the whole economy could be deflated, particularly if the remaining profits of oil companies were not spent by them. Hence the government revenue should be spent—and Barker advocated using it to stimulate specific types of expenditure on equipment which would allow manufacturing to expand rather than contract. So the main focus of his criticism was on the possible dynamic effect on supply capacity from investing North Sea oil proceeds. Forsyth and Kay's framework did not explicitly allow for such effects; however, they suggested that the return on capital invested in manufacturing was too poor for additional investment to be worthwhile.

A critique from Worswick [15] echoed that of Barker in focusing on the way North Sea oil is distributed and its resultant effect on the level of demand in the economy. He also criticized the assumption that non-oil output should remain at its 1976 level—both because of the normal 'trend' growth of output and because of the degree of excess capacity in that year. While growth is continuing, a relative decline in non-oil tradable production is possible without any absolute decline in its level. Strictly speaking, these critiques were invalid or at least not relevant: Forsyth and Kay were not attempting to allow for the passage of time, but only for the impact of oil in a timeless 'comparative-static' sense. Also, the existence of spare resources in 1976 could only be relevant if, as Cripps and Godley argued, it was North Sea oil which would permit their use.

27.4.3. Critiques of Forsyth and Kay's Basis of Analysis

While the contributors reviewed in the preceding section focused on relatively minor defects in, or possible amplifications of, the Forsyth and Kay analysis, the Bank of England [1, 2] suggested—albeit in a restrained tone—that the basic comparison was fundamentally wrong. Forsyth and Kay, it was suggested, were trying to compare a picture of the UK economy self-sufficient in oil with one of the UK without oil but adjusted to having to import at high OPEC prices. However, the UK never underwent an adjustment to importing at higher prices. By 1976 it had certainly not adjusted to the increase in prices in 1973–4. In that year the UK was suffering from a weak exchange rate and a large balance of payments deficit despite having borrowed abroad substantially in anticipation of its future oil revenues. Since it was going to become self-sufficient, there was less requirement to adjust to higher-priced imports.

The Bank of England suggested 1970 as a more appropriate base for analysing the impact of North Sea oil on the UK's standard of living, exchange rate, and structure of production. In that year the UK devoted roughly 2 per cent of its GDP to obtaining oil: the process involved exporting goods and services in return for imported petroleum. Ten years later, in 1980, the UK devoted roughly 3 per cent of a larger GDP to obtain a smaller quantity of oil. It was incidental that this occurred by the rather different route of sinking resources into the North Sea. Expressed another way, the cost of oil from the North Sea in 1980 was £35 per tonne (at 1980 prices) whereas before 1973–4 imported oil cost £23 per tonne (again at 1980 prices).

Compared with the position in 1970, self-sufficiency in oil did not make the UK better off. The evident large profits and revenues should not be confused with an improvement in welfare or standard of living. They arise from a redistribution of real income, within the UK, away from users of oil to producers of it and to the government. Since the resource cost of the oil in 1980 was higher than in 1970 there remained a smaller quantity of other goods and services to be divided between consumers, producers, and the government than previously. Since North Sea oil in 1980 cost more to extract than OPEC oil cost to import in 1970, there was a net *loss* of welfare in the switch to self-sufficiency. This is not to deny that there would have been an even bigger loss of welfare involved in having to continue to import, but at the 1980 OPEC price, which was considerably higher than the cost of North Sea oil. To avoid a loss of income is helpful, but it is not the same as gaining extra income.

There being no 'free' resource endowment from North Sea oil—in the sense of its costing less than the previous (pre-1973) alternative—there is no scope for the lifting of a balance of payment constraint or for affecting the level of the exchange rate, in each case compared with the position in the early 1970s. It might be suggested that some structural change is needed because the form of resources used to extract oil—oil rigs, support services—is rather different from that previously exported in return for oil. However, a large part of the North Sea oil exploitation has been undertaken by imported equipment financed by foreign capital. The subsequent exports to pay profits on this capital could take the same form—principally manufactures—as previous exports made in direct exchange for oil.

Compared with the structure of production that the UK would have had to acquire—and other countries did have to acquire—in the absence of indigenous oil but following the increase in its price, the 1980 position *is* different. In order to export more (on a net basis) it is likely that the tradable sector—particularly manufacturing—would have expanded relative to the rest of the economy. Forsyth and Kay would have been correct in comparing the actual structure with this essentially hypothetical position, but 1976 was not such a situation.

Hence, to summarize, possession of North Sea oil allowed the UK an easier adjustment to the effect of higher world oil prices, easier that is than other countries had to make. It meant that the difficulties apparent in the mid-1970s in attaining a current balance were temporary, and that the associated pressure on the exchange rate could be eased. It did not mean that the UK could enjoy, without extra effort, additional public services or private consumption. Nor did self-sufficiency involve a revaluation of the exchange rate compared with the level that was correct for the early 1970s.

27.5. The Direct Impact of Changes in the Price of Oil

27.5.1. Self-Sufficiency in Oil

The confusion, and consequent dispute, over the impact of North Sea oil was fostered by the combination of first, the growth of production, and second, sharp increases in the price of oil. Disentangling the effect of the growth of oil production, the previous section has shown that the attainment of self-sufficiency *per se* would have had no dramatic effects on the UK economy. The crucial criterion in this was a comparison of the (resource) cost of North Sea oil with the previous cost of importing. However, it is evident that the UK has suffered from abrupt changes in its exchange rate and a sharp decline in manufacturing; the question that remains is whether this can be attributed to changes in the price of oil, or to factors unrelated to oil. In this section the possible impact of changes in the world price of oil is investigated. In order to separate its effect from that of oil production, the discussion will proceed on the basis that the economy was self-sufficient before any price changes occurred. The main emphasis is on increases in price, since these were the dramatic influences in the 1970s; there has been a downward trend in prices from 1981—at least relative to that of other products—but it has been less abrupt.

A common-sense reaction to the direct impact of oil price changes on a self-sufficient UK economy is to think that it should be negligible; if this view is correct then any impact which results must be attributable to mismanagement of policy. However, changes in oil prices do necessitate adjustment in the pattern of consumption and production in the rest of the world. Since the UK is an important trading country, as well as a key financial centre, adjustment elsewhere in the world might be expected to impinge upon the UK. The effects of oil price changes, both direct and indirect (i.e. via the rest of the world), are examined in turn.

27.5.2. The Direct Effects on the UK

The general policy in the UK has been for the price of oil to be set freely on a market-determined basis. This is in contrast to the policy for gas prices which have been persistently below a free-market level. It follows from the oil-pricing policy that, in the absence of a simultaneous change in the pound's exchange rate, movements in the US dollar price of crude oil are reflected quite rapidly in the sterling price of petroleum products. A 50 per cent rise in the price of crude does not result in a similar percentage increase in the price of petrol at the filling station because of downstream refining costs, profit margins, and the substantial tax imposed on petroleum products (in 1982–3 excise duty was 71p per gallon, plus VAT of about 22p, both in relation to a retail price of 170p). None the less the retail price will rise in response to a change in crude oil prices. During 1979–80 the pump price of premium petrol rose from 80p to 132p per gallon, while the crude price in US dollars increased nearly 150 per cent (in sterling the increase was less because the pound appreciated some 20 per cent over the same period).

The increased price of oil encourages users to switch to other sources of energy, which have become relatively cheaper; the price of alternative energy sources is likely to rise somewhat to reflect the extra demand. The combined effect of higher prices for oil and for other energy sources is to encourage conservation and a shift in consumption away from energy-intensive products. Although this tends to occur over a longer period, and is then often irreversible in the short term (for example a switch from oil- to coal-powered generating equipment), the eventual scope for economizing in energy is considerable. Over the second half of the 1970s the energy coefficient of output growth (i.e. the growth rate of energy divided by the growth of output) was virtually half its level in the first part of the decade.

Despite the powerful incentive to shift consumption away from oil, in the short term total expenditure on oil is certain to increase following a price rise. In the first instance the extra revenue accrues as profit to the oil companies. However, the UK tax system for North Sea oil is designed to extract all oil companies' profits (above the level required to keep them exploiting the North Sea resources). The bulk of the additional revenue therefore accrues to the government.[2] If the government succeeds in extracting all the extra profit resulting from the higher price there will be no additional incentive to explore for new oil in the North Sea. Apart from any possible incentive to increase production, the effect of an oil price increase in a self-sufficient UK is the same

[2] The system is slightly more complicated because a large proportion of North Sea oil is exported, but this does not prevent the eventual flow of revenue being from consumers to the UK government.

as that of an increase in excise duty on petroleum products. Its repercussions on the level and pattern of activity depend, as do those of any other tax increase, on the use made of the revenue by the government. As Barker [3] and Worswick [15] suggested, if the revenue is devoted to reducing borrowing it will tend to depress the level of activity and employment in the economy, and since that recession will itself lead to higher public borrowing, the government's aim may be at least partly frustrated.

There is virtually no reason for the increase in oil prices to affect the exchange rate directly: the only small proviso is that a reduction in oil consumption within the UK would permit an export surplus in oil to emerge, increasing the country's foreign exchange receipts. In addition, any general deflation of demand which does result from the revenue being saved by the government may itself contribute to a higher exchange rate.

One likely consequence of a significant increase in oil prices is a temporarily higher level of inflation in the UK. As well as the direct effect of higher prices for oil products sold to final consumers, there is a pervasive influence from the higher cost of energy incorporated—via transport, processing, etc.—in other products. This has the potential of raising the rate of inflation. Whether in fact it does depends upon the use of the extra government revenue from higher oil prices. A reduction in VAT could largely offset the impact of higher oil prices on the general price level. However, if the revenue is used in ways which allow significant changes in real incomes of different groups there may be pressure for higher wages and a more persistent inflation process may emerge. It is more efficient to prevent this process by reducing VAT than to attempt to end it by reducing government borrowing and the level of economic activity. It is worth emphasizing that the government has this option only because the country as a whole does not face a loss of real income.

In summary, a change in the price of oil need not have a dramatic effect on the UK. The higher relative price of energy will imply adjustments in consumption patterns, and some change in the distribution of income is likely. A change in the level of production will occur only if the government does not adjust to its higher revenues.

27.6. The Indirect Effects on the UK

The previous section has shown how the UK can, in effect, choose how far it adjusts in response to a changed oil price. For countries that are not self-sufficient adjustment is obligatory: in the case of oil importers it is adjustment to a loss of real income, in the case of exporters, to a corresponding gain. In the world as a whole, as in the UK, the higher oil price is effectively a tax on consumers for the benefit of producers' governments; the difference for the rest of the world is that the two parties are located in different countries. The analysis of this aspect originated in the Bank of England. It pointed out that the process of adjustment to a sharp change in oil prices—such as occurred in 1978–80—may take several years; during this period there may be temporary effects which differ from the lasting consequences of higher oil prices.

27.6.1. Temporary Effects on the World Economy

In the short term, OPEC and other oil-exporting countries may be unable to increase their spending to match their enhanced income from oil. This is particularly true for the 'low absorbers'—such as Kuwait, and Saudi Arabia—which already have a very high income per capita. By contrast, oil-importing countries perceive a more pressing need to realign spending to their lower income; at a national level, this is because of a current balance of payments deficit, and at an individual level, because the scope to maintain the previous standard of living by reducing savings may be limited. Hence oil exporters are likely to increase their spending less rapidly than oil importers cut theirs. In other words, there is an increase in the world's savings ratio matched by a reduction in demand—a world recession. It may be recalled that during the first oil crisis in 1974–5 Dennis Healey, then the UK's Chancellor of Exchequer, recognized this danger and encouraged Western governments to incur budget and balance of payments deficits during the adjustment period. Unfortunately few countries, apart from the UK, practised what Healey preached. The 1976 sterling crisis was largely attributable to this disparity of practice.

As in 1974 and to a greater extent in 1980, oil-importing governments, far from compensating for the loss of real income by reducing taxes, may wish to further tighten their policy stance and avoid the persistent inflationary process which could result from individuals attempting to preserve their real income level. Unlike the UK, oil-importing countries have to cope with a loss of real income. Any autonomous tightening of policy to combat inflation will exacerbate the world recession. The recession itself will be accompanied by a lower level of international trade, lower demand for UK exports, and so a loss of income and employment in this country. The process is temporary, lasting until the increase in OPEC's spending matches the fall in oil-importing countries'.

This process of extra saving accounts for a demand effect on the UK, but there is also a financial or portfolio effect. While OPEC continues to under-spend its income, it will accumulate financial assets—bank deposits, and government and private bills and bonds. The US is the obvious destination for the bulk of the funds because of its inherent stability and its extensive financial markets. However, it is logical for part of the funds to be placed in the UK to diversify portfolio risks, reflecting this country's 'safe' status as an oil producer and its active financial markets. At those times when OPEC is experiencing a current account surplus in the region of US$100 billion, placing even 5 per cent in the UK would imply a substantial inflow of foreign exchange. In the absence of official intervention, the inflow would lead to a significant appreciation of sterling. This accumulation of financial balances will continue, at a declining rate, until OPEC's collective current account surplus is eliminated. In principle it could be matched by a reduction in sterling holdings by oil importers: however, relatively few countries now hold liquid assets in sterling, and they too would be encouraged to retain them because of the UK's possession of oil. As the OPEC surplus is eliminated the exchange rate will return to its previous level (or trend). The temporarily overvalued rate might, however, have had permanent effects on the 'real' economy, if exporting or import-competing businesses were forced to scrap capacity, or shut down entirely.

27.6.2. Permanent Effects on the World Economy

When the adjustment process is complete, OPEC will be receiving a greater quantity of non-oil goods and services in exchange for a given quantity of oil. The actual volume of oil exported may fall off because of greater conservation and an additional stimulus to domestic energy sources on the part of oil importers. None the less there is likely to be a larger flow (in volume terms) of non-oil products, exported by importers and imported by OPEC. For the UK itself, assuming it retains a position of exact self-sufficiency, there is no change in the net import/export balance of oil or of other products. So world trade in non-oil products will increae but the UK will not participate in the additional trade.

Relative prices—i.e. real exchange rates—will adjust to bring about this situation to the extent that it does not occur automatically. A degree of automatic adjustment is possible as oil importers curb consumption and exporters increase it. Within oil-importing countries there is a cut in consumption; this cut is induced by the increased price level for a given level of income, i.e. by a fall in real disposable income. Some of the fall in consumption will be of tradable goods (i.e. which are imports, import substitutes, or exportables) and so will contribute directly to a correction of the balance of payments. In so far as the reduced consumption is of non-traded products it will not contribute to correcting the balance of payments. So some change in relative prices is necessary, to induce the productive resources involved to switch to production of tradables. (This process is exactly that described by Forsyth and Kay, but operating in reverse.) Viewed in macroeconomic terms, it will appear that the cut in real income caused by higher oil prices is inadequate to correct the current balance of payments deficit without an adjustment of the exchange rate. Within oil-exporting countries any increase in demand for tradables can be met by importing: an increased demand for non-tradables causes their price to rise. In some cases the effect may be strong enough to make trade worthwhile as, for example, construction workers migrate to the Middle East to build airports, hotels, etc.

Depending upon the actual pattern of change in demand in different countries, the UK's exchange rate will rise against some currencies and fall against others. It will only change on average if the pattern of adjustments elsewhere results in a changed demand for UK products—for example, if OPEC increases its consumption of UK products (cars, missiles, power stations) by more than oil importers reduce theirs. (In fact it is the net flow which matters since trade does not have to balance bilaterally between countries. Increased UK exports to OPEC could be matched by increased imports from non-OPEC countries.) As the Bank of England has emphasized, the exchange rate only rises to the degree necessary to divert the net flow of extra trade in non-oil products away from the UK. Unless the shift in real income in the world causes a pronounced shift in preference for UK products, the change in exchange rate is likely to be small.

27.6.3. Summary of Indirect Effects

The UK cannot avoid all the consequences of higher oil prices. In the short term, the higher level of saving in the world depresses demand for the UK's exports. The associated build-up of OPEC liquid assets will cause sterling to rise. Over the longer term these powerful effects will unwind, and there remains only the small revaluation needed to divert the extra trade in non-oil products.

27.7. The Effect of a Reduction in Oil Prices

The 1970s were a period of sharply rising real oil prices; the early 1980s, by contrast, have been characterized by weakening prices. The future trend of prices depends upon political as well as economic factors and so is doubly difficult to predict. Most of the effects of higher oil prices are reversed, with varying lags, when prices decline: in the UK, oil company profits and government revenue fall, but consumers gain directly from the lower prices. In the rest of the world the shift in real income described in the previous section is reversed. Again in the short term this process might depress activity and trade (especially if 'high-absorber' oil exporters have difficulty servicing their heavy debts when their oil income has fallen). A large and sustained reduction in oil prices would eliminate the profitability of the North Sea operations. While variable costs continued to be covered it would pay to continue production (and any loss sustained by the government would be matched by a gain for consumers). However, a permanent return to such a low oil price level appears unlikely.

27.8 The Effect of the UK Being a Net Oil Exporter

So far the discussion in this chapter has proceeded on the assumption that the UK is just self-sufficient in oil: most of the contributions reviewed here have used the same supposition. As an earlier section suggested, on a present-value basis, that assumption appears to be roughly correct. The UK's present exports are almost matched by future imports of oil. However, these exports are substantial and are expected to continue, albeit at a declining rate after 1985, for at least another decade. A recent forecast by Esso has suggested that oil exports *may* continue to the end of the century. Given this uncertainty about the future—and particularly when allowance is made for the cautious nature of oil company and official forecasts—it is useful to consider what modifications are necessary to the analysis of North Sea oil if the UK is (or is perceived to be) a net exporter of oil for the foreseeable future.

It is worth re-emphasizing the point that, if pre-1973 oil prices were still prevailing, the UK would gain nothing from being a net exporter. Indeed it would only become one by subsidizing North Sea oil operations. However, the substantial increases in oil prices since then have yielded a commensurate profit to the UK as a whole (just as they have to OPEC) on that portion of oil which is actually exported (net of any import of oil). In 1982 net proceeds from oil exports (allowing too for imported equipment and profit remittances as well as oil imports) were £1 billion. If the oil price is maintained in real terms this figure will rise to £5 billion in 1985. Most of this inflow represents extra government revenue. The effect on the exchange rate and pattern of production depends on whether that revenue is spent, and if so, how it is spent. It is likely that some of the income will be spent on non-tradables, so that a small-scale Forsyth and Kay effect emerges. In the extreme case where none of the extra consumption were of tradables, the £5 billion revenue in 1985 might induce an increase in the real exchange rate of about 5–7 per cent. At present the assumption that oil prices will even be maintained in real terms up to 1985 appears optimistic. Allowing for that, the medium-term effect of the UK possibly being a net oil exporter is relatively modest.

Ironically the reason for the UK becoming a significant oil exporter is not just the rise in production of oil since 1975 but also the substantial decline in its consumption since the peak year of 1973. If consumption had remained at the 1973 level of 105 million tonnes the UK would barely have achieved self-sufficiency in 1981, and even at peak production levels could have exported only 25 million tonnes per year. While energy conservation may account for part of the reduction in the use of oil (which by 1982 was down to 75 million tonnes), a major contributory factor is the 20 per cent fall in manufacturing output between 1973 and 1982. The major part of this fall occurred after 1979 and may itself be attributed to the high exchange rate and the severe recession which the UK suffered.

27.9. North Sea Oil and Government Policy

While the 1979–82 depression in manufacturing was partly a result of the world recession (following the 1978–80 oil price increase), government policy in the UK may have exacerbated the position. A number of points already made can be drawn together to examine how far the government could mitigate any effect either from the growth of oil production or from increased prices.

The conclusion has already been reached, in section 27.4, that attainment of self-sufficiency should not in itself imply significant changes in the UK's level and structure of non-oil production: hence there is little need for policy action. However, an oil price rise has important direct and indirect effects on the UK, given that it is self-sufficient in oil. The *permanent* effects of adjustments elsewhere in the world economy are intrinsically unavoidable. The UK is bound to experience a smaller share of world trade in non-oil products than if it were an oil importer. The temporary effects from the world recession are also largely unavoidable. However, temporary portfolio effects—an inflow of OPEC funds—could in principle be offset: the Bank of England could neutralize the impact of the inflow on the exchange rate. The difficulty is that, as with any exchange market intervention, it is not possible at the time to separate temporary and permanent influences on the exchange rate, i.e. to know to what extent intervention is appropriate. Also, if monetary policy were aimed at attaining a certain growth of the domestic money supply (such as

£M3) it would be necessary to complement the exchange intervention by action to offset the domestic credit growth which the inflow of funds would permit. In practice, in 1979–80 the government explicitly chose not to intervene to offset the exchange rate; its main action was to remove exchange controls, which did permit an outflow of UK-owned funds. After the event it is possible to conclude that a less agnostic approach to the exchange rate might have been better from the point of view of preserving the level of non-oil activity.

The government also has a choice in its reaction to the direct effects on the domestic economy of higher oil prices: as has been noted, the major potential consequence is a reduction in the (*ex ante*) PSBR, a tightening of government policy. In general the government could offset this, spending the extra proceeds, or reducing non-oil taxes. In 1979–80 the complication was that the extra revenue from higher oil prices did not accrue immediately to the government. This was partly because of intrinsic lags in the tax system, but it was mainly because oil companies had a considerable backlog of depreciation allowances—on North Sea investments—which they could set against any additional tax liability. Hence the higher oil prices merely accelerated the write-off of North Sea investment, and the immediate proceeds accrued to the oil companies. Since the companies are likely to have saved a higher proportion of their income than the consumer of oil would, the net effect was still deflationary. In order to offset this deflation, however, the government would have had to spend money that it had not received. Its fear at the time of the 'crowding-out' effects of the financing of such action, while ill-founded, prevented any offsetting move: indeed, allowing for cyclical movements, the fiscal stance was tightened sharply. In any future price adjustment the government could have greater scope for offsetting, even with the same perception of 'crowding-out'.

Finally, we return to the paradoxical result of the government's tight policy stance in 1979–81 which was to make the UK a more substantial oil exporter, as a result of the decline in heavy manufacturing. Thus the government, by its own inaction, brought about (on a smaller scale) the effect—higher exchange rate, smaller manufacturing sector—which Forsyth and Kay incorrectly regarded as the inevitable consequences of oil production.

27.10. Conclusions—An Emerging Consensus on North Sea Oil?

The intense debate which development of North Sea oil stimulated is beginning to arrive at a consensus. Identification of the separate issues has assisted this process—by specifying the impact of oil production, the effect of oil price changes, and the role of government policy. After reviewing these issues in sections 27.4 to 27.9 it is now possible to answer the questions posed in section 27.3:

(*i*) *Is the UK wealthier as a result of North Sea oil?* The simple answer to this is 'No'. The real (resource) cost of North Sea oil is now greater than that of imported oil was in 1970. It is true that, without indigenous oil, the UK would have been worse off as a whole—though certain groups, particularly manufacturers, would have received a stimulus. As regards oil produced for its own use (or exchanged for foreign oil for UK use), there is a smaller loss of real income than would have occurred in the absence of North Sea oil. As a partial offset, at present the UK makes profits on its net exports of oil. Overall there is no doubt that the oil-related events of the 1970s impoverished the UK. There are no extra resources for new factories, hospitals, or tax cuts.

(ii) *What is the effect of North Sea oil on the UK's exchange rate and, as a result, on the structure of the economy?* The *long*-term effect is minor. During the 1970s the move to self-sufficiency, combined with the effects on other countries of adjusting to a higher oil price, may have caused a small permanent rise in the exchange rate associated with a fall in its share of world trade. An outside estimate of the impact would be a 5 per cent revaluation. Over the *medium* term, while the UK is perceived as a net exporter of oil there is a further impact on the exchange rate—a 'mini' Forsyth and Kay effect—of 5 per cent or so. So the combined effect would not be more than a 10 per cent loss of competitiveness. The relative contraction of manufacturing which this would imply is relatively small.

However, for short periods, following an oil price increase, the disposition of OPEC funds can cause a substantial rise in the exchange rate. This is purely a temporary phenomenon (though one with a duration of years rather than months, on the basis of past experience) and, as far as possible, damaging effects from it on the UK's productive capacity should be offset.

(iii) *Has North Sea oil lowered the UK's growth rate, by resulting in deflation of the economy?* The attainment of self-sufficiency *per se* should have had no effect on the level of activity. Oil price increases are effectively tax increases for the UK, and like other taxes can deflate demand (and raise the exchange rate) if no offsetting reductions are made. Whether by error or design, the oil 'tax' was not offset in 1979–80: in this rather special sense the possession of oil has lowered the UK's growth rate.

(iv) *Has North Sea oil lifted any previous constraints on the UK's growth rate?* It follows from the answers to earlier points that it has not. The UK avoided a tighter constraint on growth (of which the 1974–7 experience gave but a mild hint) but has not acquired an extra source of foreign exchange.

As the discussion of section 27.9 has shown, it does not follow that oil has no implications for policy. At a minimum, policy should be set to mitigate the impact of price changes. There is also scope to encourage investment against the day when the UK has to import oil at a higher cost. Though serious errors have been made in relation to the use of oil revenues, one policy decision so far appears to have been correct. That was the decision to exploit the oil as fast as possible: indeed if a downward trend in the real price of oil continues, the UK may turn out to have achieved its peak surplus of oil production at a time of relatively high price.

Bibliography

[1] Bank of England. 'The North Sea and United Kingdom Economy: Some Longer Term Perspectives and Implications', *Bank of England Quarterly Bulletin*, **20** (1980), 449–454.

[2] —— 'North Sea Oil and Gas: A Challenge for the Future', *Bank of England Quarterly Bulletin*, **22** (1982).

[3] BARKER, T. S. 'De-Industrialisation, North Sea Oil and an Investment Strategy for the United Kingdom', in Barker, T. S. and Brailovstiy, V. (eds.), *Energy, Industrialisation and Economic Policy* (Academic Press 1981).

[4] BROOKS, S. *The Economic Implications of North Sea Oil*, NIESR Discussion Paper, No. 38 (1981).

[5] BUITER, W. H. and MILLER, M. H. 'Monetary Policy and International Competitiveness', *Oxford Economic Papers*, **33** (1980), 143–517.

[6] BUITER, W. H. and PURVIS, D. D. '*Oil Disinflation and Export Competitiveness*', Warwick Economic Research Papers, No. 85 (1980).

[7] BYATT, I. *et al.* 'North Sea Oil and Structural Adjustment', HM Treasury Working Paper, No. 22 (1982).

[8] CORDEN, W. M. 'The Exchange Rate, Monetary Policy and North Sea Oil: The Economic Theory of the Squeeze on Tradables', *Oxford Economic Papers*, **3** (1981), 23–46.

[9] CRIPPS, F. and GODLEY, W. 'The Economic Implications of North Sea Oil', mimeo (1980).

[10] Department of Energy. *Development of the Oil and Gas Resources of the United Kingdom* (HMSO, 1983).

[11] EASTWOOD, R. K. and VENABLES, A. J. 'Macroeconomic Implications of a Resource Discovery in an Open Economy', *Economic Journal* (1983).

[12] FORSYTH, P. J. and KAY, J. A. 'The Economic Implications of North Sea Oil Revenues', *Fiscal Studies*, **1**/3 (1980), 1–28.

[13] HOUTHAKKER, H. S. 'The Use and Management of North Sea Oil', in Caves, R. E. and Krause, L. B. (eds.), *Britain's Economic Performance* (George Allen and Unwin, 1980), pp. 331–70.

[14] WHITEMAN, J. 'North Sea Oil and the UK Economy', NEDO Economic Working Paper, No. 5 (1981).

[15] WORSWICK, G. D. N. 'North Sea Oil and the Decline of Manufacturing', *National Institute Economic Review*, 94 (1980), 22–6.

28

Industrial Policy

D. J. MORRIS and D. K. STOUT

28.1. The Need for an Industrial Policy

28.1.1. Economic Performance in the UK

Part V of this book established that the UK has experienced poor growth of productivity relative to abroad, not only since the war but probably since the nineteenth century. It is therefore a central policy question as to whether this poor record can be rectified through improved industrial performance.

Slow growth of labour productivity is a serious problem for at least two major reasons. First, unless the proportion of the population working rises sufficiently to offset it, a slow rate of increase in labour productivity implies a low rate of increase of material living standards for the population as a whole, i.e. slow economic per capita growth. Second, it is very likely that most, if not all of the economic difficulties that have beset the UK in recent years can be attributed to this factor. In view of the significance of these statements it is appropriate to be slightly more specific about the economic relationships involved.

Low productivity must in nearly all circumstances result either in correspondingly low wages, or high prices, or low gross profits, or, more usually, in some combination of these. This can be seen as follows (taxation is ignored in order to simplify the exposition): total revenue (TR) for a firm by definition equals total cost (TC) plus profit (Π). Total revenue is also equal to the average price level of the firm's products (P) times its output (Q). Therefore

$$TR = P \times Q = TC + \Pi$$

and

$$P = \frac{TC + \Pi}{Q}.$$

The simplest way to see the implications of this is to multiply the right-hand side by W/W which does not change the equation, where W is the total wage bill of the firm, and then by L/L which again leaves the equation unchanged, where L is the total labour force in the firm. This gives

$$P = \frac{TC + \Pi}{Q} \times \frac{W}{W} \times \frac{L}{L}.$$

This can be rewritten as

$$P = \frac{TC + \Pi}{W} \times \frac{W}{L} \times \frac{L}{Q}.$$

However, W/L is the average wage rate per man (w) and L/Q is the same as $1/k$ where k is Q/L, that is, output per man or labour productivity. It is therefore *definitionally* true that

$$P = \frac{TC + \Pi}{W} \times \frac{w}{k}.$$

Thus if productivity (k) is low it follows that either wage rates (w) must be low, or the price level (P) must be high, or the term $(TC + \Pi)/W$ must be low. This in turn entails either that non-wage costs must be low, i.e. raw material costs, semi-manufactured input costs, fuel or rental costs, or gross profit must be low. But all these costs will generally be given for the firm, dependent on the prices charged and the firm's scale of operations and output levels. So in the absence of low wages or higher prices to compensate, low productivity will result in low gross profits.[1]

In practice, all three have occurred. Low wages are, of course, part of the means by which low productivity gets transmitted into low living standards, and many firms in the UK have only been able to remain internationally competitive despite significantly lower levels of productivity because they have paid much lower wages than abroad. Equally serious, low wages and low rates of increase in wages are thought by many to be one major cause of inflation through the resulting attempts of the UK work-force to obtain higher wage increases than can be absorbed through higher productivity. Thus the pressure of low productivity has been partly switched to prices. This has meant an inability to compete adequately in international markets, with a consequent slow growth of export demand, a falling share of world trade, and a tendency to balance of payments deficit. Finally, to the extent that higher prices have not been able to take up all the pressure of wage increases in excess of productivity, gross profits (profits and interest payments) have fallen. This has tended to mean inadequate investment because it curtails either the supply of funds for investment or the incentive to invest, or both.

All this is not to say that other factors have not been important, but that low productivity has been a major and continuing factor in the generation of inflation, low investment, and balance of payments problems in the UK. The problem did not stop there, however. Repeatedly in the 1960s and 1970s, a decline in export competitiveness meant that sterling became overvalued. To defend the exchange rate successive rounds of deflation of aggregate demand were required, and this further reduced investment by reducing the level of demand and increasing its instability. Low profitability led to an ever-growing incentive to invest abroad for both UK and foreign firms, thereby increasing the long-term outflow of capital from the UK. The loss of foreign market share

[1] If industrial costs rise as a result of higher import prices, then to that extent wages have to rise less fast than productivity to avoid inflationary consequences. Or again, if profits are required to rise rapidly, for example from an inadequate level, the same conclusion holds.

also directly operated to reduce investment in the UK. The low rate of investment implies that the average age of the capital stock in the UK may tend to be higher than in most other industrialized countries *and its productivity lower*, further undermining export performance. In short, low productivity has caused or exacerbated almost all the economic problems faced in the UK, and in addition tends to magnify itself. A very large improvement in productivity is therefore an essential prerequisite if the UK economy and living standards are to improve, and the central role of industrial policy is to bring this about. Table 28.1 charts the performance described. This is consistent with the description above, except that over the whole period 1966–82, earnings went up as fast in the UK as in the rest of the EEC despite the slower growth of productivity, pushing more of the adjustment onto profitability. Real earnings none the less grew much more slowly, as a result of inflation, reflecting the constraint on living standards that lower productivity represents.

TABLE 28.1. *Productivity Growth and its Consequences*

	EEC	UK
Growth of industrial output per man-hour 1966–82 (% p.a.)	4·3	3·4
Growth rate of average hourly gross earnings 1966–82 (% p.a.)	13·4	13·4
Rise in wage cost per unit of output 1966–82 (% p.a.)	8·5	9·7
Rise in Consumer Price Index 1966–82 (% p.a.)	8·2	11·0
Growth of export volume 1966–82 (% p.a.)	8·4	5·2
Net operating surplus (% GDP) 1972	25·2	17·3
Net operating surplus (% GDP) 1982	20·0	13·3
Investment (% GDP) 1972	23·6	19·8
Investment (% GDP) 1982	19·9	15·9

28.1.2. The Basic Rationale for Industrial Policy

All the economic policies described in earlier chapters have direct and significant effects on industry. Fiscal, monetary, and exchange rate policies are all main determinants of the level of demand that industry faces, of its ability to earn profits, and of its investment plans and its ability to finance them. The stability of demand, with its implications for long-range financial and investment planning, is also partly a function of the degree to which these policies are successfully pursued. When in operation, prices and incomes policy can have a major effect on industrial labour costs, on the availability of labour to particular firms, on gross profit margins obtainable, and on the continuity of production. Competition policy, planning, nationalization, and privatization all represent policies which are directly concerned with the structure, behaviour, and performance of different sectors of industry. Finally it has been seen how important education and training policy can be in determining the type and quality of the labour force available to the industrial sector of the economy.

With so many possible ways of influencing industry, both short- and long-term, at their disposal, it may be asked why governments should have felt it necessary to develop industrial policies over and above those already mentioned. There are two main answers to this. First, none of the many policies already examined has had sufficient, if any, impact on the key issue of productivity performance. As we have seen, monetary, fiscal, and exchange rate policy have been primarily directed towards managing the level of demand and improving the balance of payments with a *given* productivity level. Except for a relatively brief period when emphasis was placed on productivity bargaining, prices and incomes policy has been mainly concerned with direct control of inflation rather than with productivity improvements. The impact of these policies on productivity has therefore generally been a secondary concern or been ignored altogether because of the shorter-term problems to be dealt with. Longer-term growth and investment strategies of firms may have suffered as a result.

The same point cannot, however, be made with regard to the longer-term anti-trust, planning, and nationalization policies discussed. Each of these has been partly conceived of as a means by which productivity could be increased—anti-trust legislation by generating increased efficiency in the use of resources through the enhanced pressure of competition, planning through provision of a more stable background for investment and to advance identification of potential obstacles to faster growth of productivity, and nationalization by allowing rationalization of production and distribution facilities and the achievement of all the economies of scale inherent in the industries concerned. In practice, each has failed for different reasons to have the impact on productivity necessary to alter radically the performance of the UK economy. For reasons discussed below, planning has not had either the backing or the success necessary to contribute significantly to this aim as yet. The nationalized industries, despite often having faster growth of productivity than the private sector in recent years, have not on average achieved comparable levels with these industries in other countries, and, equally important, cover very little of the manufacturing sector. Yet the manufacturing sector is vital partly because it may well be a main determinant of overall productivity (see ch. 20) and partly because it provides over 65 per cent of the exports of the UK, where, as we have seen, high productivity is a crucial factor in overall performance.

The impact of the anti-trust legislation has been more complex. The Restrictive Trade Practices Act of 1956, augmented by the 1968 Act, together with the abolition of resale price maintenance, are generally thought to have stimulated more competition in the UK initially—an effect which was reinforced by entry into the European Economic Community with its own anti-trust laws and the progressive removal of protective trade barriers which this has entailed. Yet a concurrent phenomenon, almost certainly caused in part by the increase in competition, has been a wave of mergers. These in turn appear to have been the main cause of the increase in industrial concentration which has occurred in recent years (see Hannah [25]). In practice, this has meant an increase in the number and extent of dominant market positions, thus at least mitigating and perhaps reversing the trend towards greater competitive pressure. The largest 100 firms were responsible for approximately 50 per cent of net manufacturing output in 1975 (as compared to 25 per cent in 1950, only 15 per cent in 1910, and a figure of 66 per cent forecast by the NIESR for 1985), and virtually all more comprehensive measures of industrial concentration in the UK support this trend. It remains to be seen whether increased international competition both from the EEC and from other countries currently industrializing will force higher productivity on UK industry, but it must be noted that there is no necessary reason why it should. The intensification of competition may lead to a further weakening of industry's ability to foresee and earn the profits necessary to increase investment in manpower and machinery in the private sector, and an increasing relative rate of decline rather than a reversal of it. Finally, it is difficult to discern any significant effect of the Monopolies and Mergers Commission on the process of concentration or on the overall level of productivity, and the alterations in company behaviour which it has recommended should be made in specific cases have tended to be concerned with price, profit, and advertising levels rather than productivity (although it is difficult to see what such a body could do in this regard except ensure that anti-competitive strategies are halted).

Thus continuing poor productivity performance, together with the inappropriateness or inadequacy of the more well-established policies examined, have necessitated the development of other measures more directly aimed, if not exclusively so, at improving productivity. But, on the more positive side, consideration of the growth process itself suggests important features in it that call for quite different types of policy. The first of these is the need to reduce the costs and dislocation attaching to the faster movement of productive resources between firms and industries, and to help to organize and encourage these movements.

The conditions of 'equilibrium' growth in a long-term 'steady-state' sense can be described without reference to changes in industrial structure. As was described in Chapter 20, the growth of 'productive potential' can be derived on the supply side from the rate of growth of the labour force and the stock of capital, together with the (generally assumed to be independent) rate of technical progress. But the growth of output per head that this implies may be unsatisfactorily low compared with the 'transitional' rate that can be achieved for many decades on end in an industrial (or rapidly industrializing) economy in which the allocation of resources between industries is rapidly altering, away from lower productivity and less competitive sectors, and away from inherently slower-growing markets, towards areas of faster growth and higher productivity. Most models of the growth process often include a residual term in the equations which they comprise, which allows for, but does not analyse or explain, this element of growth that depends on changing industrial structure. One major objective of industrial policy is to accelerate this process.

The second important feature of the growth process which requires special attention is the role of technological advance—inventions and their application to industry to generate new products and processes. Much of the difference between faster- and slower-growing economies appears to lie in the rate at which they develop and exploit new technology as a result of their inputs to research and development, the efficiency which they obtain in the R & D function, and their success in applying the results, marketing them, and therefore realizing their commercial potential. Much of the otherwise unexplained element in countries' growth is often attributed to this.

The third feature of industrial performance which in principle calls for special handling is what may be termed the 'recovery' problem. As was seen in section 28.1.1, poor productivity growth can breed poor productivity growth, and though this was argued at a rather general level it is a very real problem for many companies. A past poor productivity, growth, and profits record makes it very difficult, risky, and often costly to recover to a fast-growth and high-profit record. It may well require innovation, new investment, selling new products to new markets, new management, etc. all at once, when just maintaining current operations may take most or all of management's time, and all on the basis of inadequate internal finance. But heavy external financing may be either costly in the circumstances or unavailable, and even if available may not be attractive to the company concerned. This may be simply because the risks to the managers are too great, or because the impact on the company's overall financial position would make it too weak or even liable to take-over. For all these reasons, switching from a past poor growth and productivity record to a strong one may be very difficult even where it is relatively clear that such changes need to be carried out.

These three factors, restructuring, recovery, and research and development, are the main reasons lying behind industrial policy. It is not just that other policies are directed to other objectives, though this is important. It is also that each is often not susceptible of a market solution in the sense that there are systematic reasons why leaving the matter to competitive markets will not in general give an optimal result. In all three cases the basic reasons for this are uncertainty about the future, and as a result, imperfect capital markets. When companies face problems of restructuring, recovery, or carrying out research, they, and providers of finance to them, face inherently higher uncertainty about the outcome than for more usual investment decisions. In some cases, for example major new technology developments or the recovery of a large, heavy loss-making company, this means that no finance will be made available. More generally it may mean that funds will be available but at higher cost than usual to cover for the additional risk. What is the impact of this on the company concerned? It already faces similar financial risk with regard to internally financed elements of the programme; its managers also face added risk in that their careers and livelihoods may to some considerable extent be at stake. They are then faced, in a market environment, with higher costs of funds. To the extent that they need more external finance because of current inadequacy of internal funds the problem is made still more acute. It may well be the case therefore that companies would only be prepared to proceed if funds were available at *reduced* cost, but this is the opposite of what arises in a market for risk funds. This will then inhibit the provision of such funds. Companies become constrained by their internal funds: the programme of recovery, restructuring, or research and development is constrained or becomes impossible.

It is extremely difficult to gain any direct idea of the extent to which this type of problem exists, primarily because it manifests itself as much in companies not seeking funds to carry out such activities as it does in such funds not being available at low cost. But one thing is more certain, namely, that the problem will be more serious in an economy exhibiting low productivity growth and low profits. This is because the need to take such actions, in particular restructuring and recovery, will be greater *and* the opportunity afforded by current profit levels will be smaller. Reliance on market forces to tackle these three factors is therefore likely, other things being equal, to pose a more serious problem and provide a less adequate solution in the UK than elsewhere in the industrialized countries, given its poor productivity record and very low level of profitability.

The elements of the growth process described here must be kept in perspective. They are not the only nor even probably the most important elements. Such factors as the skill of the labour force, the organizational, marketing, and technical abilities of management, and their combined ability to operate efficiently are all of course central, and to this extent policy aspects can normally only be marginal. But the problems of restructuring, recovery, and research and development are such that they cannot be ignored and require specific policy measures if they are to be overcome. As such they have been the basis for active industrial policies in virtually all industrialized countries.

28.2. A European Perspective

All European countries, including the UK, have been continuously involved in such policies since the Second World War. This section does not attempt to provide a summary of the policy instruments used, not least because all countries have at various times used virtually all of the same wide range of instruments to a lesser or greater extent. Rather, it seeks to identify key phases of post-war industrial policy in Europe and their defining characteristics.

28.2.1. Early Phases

In fact, at least four rather different phases of industrial policy can be seen in Europe since 1945. In the first decade after the war, in a period of unprecedently rapid growth, four main elements dominated industrial policies:

(i) The improvement (and, in some cases, reconstruction) of the basic infrastructure of economies; the development of the coal, steel, and transport industries, and, on the social front, of the housing, health, and education services.

(ii) Incentives to generate a high level of investment and saving.

(iii) The creation of a competitive framework for industry to encourage flexibility and efficiency as both internal and external controls were dismantled.

(iv) The Marshall Plan, which played an important role in providing access to vital materials, encouraging the dismantling of controls and providing investment funds on a large scale to help re-establish industrial growth. It also helped to stimulate an organized approach to identifying industrial priorities.

In the second phase, from the late 1950s until 1973, reconstruction gave way to consumer expenditure as the main impetus to economic growth. The explosion in demand for housing and consumer durables, aided by cheap energy, created fast rates of expansion in engineering and construction and in the complementary materials-processing industries—steel, chemicals, rubber, aluminium, oil-refining, etc. In addition, the development of the Common Market, and the operations of GATT, generated more competition in Europe, in particular from US multinationals. Competition policy remained important in Germany and the UK, but simultaneously size and technology became two of the chief concerns of industrial policy. France and the UK encouraged the creation of large groupings to compete with the US; Belgium's policy of attracting multinational companies brought diversification of the industrial base, together with foreign capital, know-how, and technology. In West Germany, concern about the technology gap led to increasing Federal support for R & D, and the establishment at the end of the decade of the data-processing programme.

Towards the end of the 1960s, divergent growth between the new and older industries, particularly coal, shipbuilding, and textiles, led to renewed concern for regional issues, while increased awareness of environmental damage led to a growing body of regulations in relation to noise, pollution, health, and safety.

28.2.2. The Early 1970s and the First Oil Crisis

The third phase, from the 1973 oil crisis to around 1975–6, was short but of particular importance. In retrospect it can be seen that 1973 marked the end of very rapid post-war growth in the developed countries of the West. But the early 1970s marked more than the end to an era of cheap fossil fuels. In addition, it saw:

(i) a halving of the fast rate of population growth of the 1950s and 1960s with its concomitant demand for new housing, furniture, consumer durables, etc.;

(ii) the beginning of an era when it seemed likely that micro-electronics and its associated technologies (e.g. telecommunications) would dominate developments;

(iii) the emergence of the newly industrializing countries (NICs) as an important element in world trade, exploiting mature and standardized technologies.

At the time, many of these trends were not fully apparent and most European countries treated the 1974–5 recession as they had earlier post-war cyclical downturns, reflating demand and taking steps to support employment in those industries which seemed particularly badly hit. This time, however, these included not only the traditional problem industries, like shipbuilding and textiles, but such industries as steel, tyres, chemicals, and man-made fibres which had previously shown greater resilience.

However, the three major OECD countries—the US, Germany, and Japan, which together account for nearly two-thirds of the output of the developed economies of the West—deflated their economies to deal with the inflationary and balance of payments problems caused by the oil crisis, a stance which they again adopted after the second oil crisis.

The growing pressure for structural change therefore developed against a background of more deflation, high unemployment, and lower real profitability than in the earlier post-war decades. Governments inevitably found themselves deeply involved in 'negative' industrial support policies—that is, policies which attempt to slow down the changes indicated by market signals and to some extent cushion society from their effects—at a time when policy should, viewed from a longer-term perspective, have mainly been encouraging more rapid industrial adaptation and change. But slow growth and uncertainty in themselves created resistance to change.

28.2.3. 1976 to 1983

The most recent phase is characterized by:

(i) Growing awareness of this constellation of forces making for rapid change, in particular of new technologies with ramifications across a wide and diverse spread of products, and of highly concentrated import penetration from Japan and the NICs in certain specific areas.

(ii) The desire by governments to extricate themselves from 'negative' support programmes, initially conceived of as temporary measures to prevent major closures and job losses. In some cases, however, the depths of the recent recession frustrated this for some while, particularly in steel.

(iii) The realization that while adjustment can generally occur relatively easily in an era of fast growth, the process is much more costly both in social and economic terms in conditions of slow or zero growth.

(iv) Acceptance of the fact that such conditions will be major features of the 1980s as a whole. Few countries see any prospect of a return to sustained fast growth before at least the late 1980s. Most explicitly recognize that only rapid reorientation of industry in order to concentrate on certain specific types of product can help to ease this problem.

28.2.4. Current Policy Emphasis in Europe

Although the development of industrial policy measures can often be explained better in terms of various social and political pressures rather than by purely economic factors, current policies in Europe can none the less be understood against this post-war economic background. There is still continuing emphasis placed on competition and free-trade policies, which provide market-oriented ground-rules for commerce; on substantial investment incentives; and on increasingly refined regional support policies. But there are now more attempts (partly at the instigation of the EEC) to modify large-scale sectoral support programmes in order to bring about capacity reductions, restructuring, and de-manning as a condition for further assistance. There is also growing emphasis on measures thought likely to provide flexibility and assist particular types of relocation. Five such policies are particularly important in this respect:

(*a*) *Sectoral support*. All the major European countries have identified certain growth areas for the future, whether or not in a formal planning context, and are providing direct support for them. Most notable are information technology, micro-electronics, biotechnology, robotics, and energy technologies.

(*b*) *Public purchasing*. Increasingly this is being used to foster the same type of industry. The telecommunications and defence industries—important purchasers of new technology—are both exempt from the EEC public purchasing directives, which have in any case so far had little impact.

(*c*) *R & D support*. In many countries this has become a major element in industrial policy, via grants and loans towards specific R & D costs, various tax allowances, support for a range of research institutions, dissemination of technical knowledge, and support for the successful commercial launching of new products.

(*d*) *Small and medium-sized businesses*. This also is a fast-growing area of support, partly to encourage entrepreneurship and innovation but also to assist the application and diffusion of knowledge throughout industries and to maintain the stimulus to competition.

(*e*) *Education, training, and retraining*. These policies reflect not only the preoccupation with new technologies and with increasing the flexibility of the work-force, but also in some countries attempt to make a virtue out of necessity in the current high levels of unemployment. Training and education are increasingly being regarded as an integral part of manpower policies.

How does the UK fit into and compare with this picture? A fuller answer is attempted in section 28.4 after a detailed review of industrial policy in the UK. But two preliminary points may be made. First, there are in general strong similarities in terms of the main objectives and major thrust of industrial policy over time in the UK. Second, this remains true despite considerable change over time in the specific instruments used in the UK to pursue those ends, with or without success. It is to the more detailed application of industrial policy in the UK that we now turn.

28.3. The Development of Industrial Policy in the UK

28.3.1. The Range of Instruments Available

The government can choose to influence industry in a variety of ways ranging from general exhortation ot selective quid pro quo action at the individual-firm level; from simply increasing the intensity of competition (relying upon private decisions to allocate resources) through participation by way of, for example, the (now defunct) National Enterprise Board (NEB), all the way to public ownership and control; from privatization to nationalization (see Chapter 25).

In a mixed economy, there will be some fields of decision where social welfare is likely to be higher if free consumer choice is allowed to decide what goods and services are produced, and how, subject to qualifications about fair distribution. And there will be other fields of decision where the social benefits and costs differ widely from the private, so that state intervention by production, distribution, or rule-making will improve allocation.

Within paraliamentary approval, the government of the day is the ultimate custodian of the public interest. It can and does influence allocation in a number of ways:

(a) as a customer of the private sector, e.g. buying drugs for the National Health Service;

(b) as an employer, e.g. absorbing skilled workers in the electricity industry in competition with private employers;

(c) as the maker of tax and subsidy laws, setting the framework within which private decisions are taken, e.g. determining the relative tax burden on food, construction, and high-technology products, or the relative labour costs inside and outside regions of high unemployment;

(d) as the authority prohibiting some actions, e.g. the pollution of waterways by industrial effluents, and enforcing others, e.g. health and safety measures at work;

(e) as the agent ultimately responsible (within the limits set by world economic conditions) for the level of demand and employment through consistent influence over such variables as the money supply, interest rates, the exchange rate, and the level of public spending and taxation;

(f) as collector and disseminator of statistical indicators and forecasts which influence industrial expectations and decisions, e.g. the Public Expenditure White Paper or the figures of monthly car registrations or housing starts.

The government can also:

(g) make commitments (in return for reciprocal commitments) intended to generate the confidence necessary to invest, or to retrain, or in pursuit of a voluntary pay and prices policy (see Chapter 11);

(h) channel savings to particular industrial activities or classes of firm, through the tax system or by augmenting the lending functions of the private capital market, e.g. by guaranteeing loans to small firms;

(i) intervene directly to change the structure of an industry (its concentration, conditions of entry, capital-intensity, rate of diffusion of new techniques, economies of scale), e.g. by encouraging or preventing mergers through specific industrial support schemes, or by taking over a particular firm, or by returning all or part of a nationalized industry to the private sector.

In some of the above respects, the government directly determines economic choices. In others it sets broad conditions within which market forces allocate resources. Decisions about which to rely upon and how far to try to co-ordinate actions under the several headings into an articulated industrial policy are often primarily political.

28.3.2. The Recent History of Industrial Policy: An Overview

The industrial policy landscape is like a hillside on which overlaying strata from earlier policy periods outcrop side by side, some eroded, some glaciated, others active. The overlapping of the dominant theories and the practical concerns of different policy phases strains the metaphor; but it is convenient to ignore the blurred edges and to distinguish six main types of industrial policy instrument. Each of these has its own period of prominence, each relied less than it might have on what went before, yet each has left its mark on the present policy mix. Each of the six major stages reflects an over-simplified view of the causes of de-industrialization in the UK, overemphasizing the differences from earlier views. Most of them led to policy actions which expected results far quicker and more dramatic than could be expected, which disappointed the political hopes that had been built on them, and which were thereafter treated not as reusable parts of a co-ordinated long-run policy set but as failed panaceas never to be repeated.

The six overlapping approaches, together with their years of maximum emphasis, are:

(i)   regional policy (1930–70);
(ii) investment-led growth (1945–72);
(iii) national indicative planning (1965–7);
(iv) picking champions (1966–76);
(v)   achieving a consensus (1975–9);
(vi) a new supply-side approach (1979–83).

Table 28.2 gives summary figures for some categories of related expenditure for the period 1974–82.

28.3.3. Regional Policy

Regional policy is the deepest stratum of industrial policy. From 1930 onwards long-term local unemployment has been associated with the decline of clustered basic industries like coal, textiles, shipbuilding and, more recently, steel and cars.

Special Areas were designated for tax relief as early as 1934. And Development Areas were set up in 1945, Grey Areas defined in 1967, and later Special Development Areas have widened and narrowed again.

Conceived of purely in terms of differential rates of unemployment, it might be argued that policy could be designed to relocate the excess supply of labour in areas of excess demand, or relocate jobs through inducing firms to expand in the areas of high unemployment. While some gestures have been made towards the former approach, primarily through wider circulation of job opportunities, assistance for interview travel expenses and removal expenses, and through housing policy, it has never represented the main line of attack. Even in terms

TABLE 28.2. *Government Support for Industry by Function, Excluding Nationalized Industries 1974–5 to 1981–2* (1980 prices, £m)

	1974–5	1975–6	1976–7	1977–8	1978–9	1979–80	1980–1	1981–2
Regional (excluding N. Ireland)	878	1,032	1,011	660	731	566	624	773
R & D (industry and energy)	308	333	360	306	299	313	354	300
Employment	280	449	720	922	943	945	1,280	1,539
Investment Grants	199	94	31	7	3	2	1	—
Selective—Schemes and NEB	47	533	115	117	177	170	168	188
Selective—aerospace, shipbuilding steel and vehicles	450	363	427	565	393	391	513	858
Trade	313	264	330	175	279	399	498	529
Redundancy	257	269	252	246	243	259	445	688
R & D (defence and other)	1,400	1,640	2,093	1,962	1,954	2,026	n/a	n/a
Total	4,132	4,977	5,339	4,960	5,022	5,071	n/a	n/a
Capital allowances and Stock Relief	5,875	6,900	6,025	7,125	8,125	7,300	7,925	7,650

Sources: *Economic Trends, National Income and Expenditure,* Inland Revenue, Public Expenditure White Papers (various years); Corporation Tax Green Paper (1982).

of unemployment alone it faces three disadvantages. Firstly, if the skilled and semi-skilled are generally more in demand and therefore potentially more mobile, schemes designed to increase migration from the depressed regions may well have their main impact on skilled workers, thus further reducing the attractiveness of the area to current and prospective employers, and so worsening unemployment among the unskilled. Secondly, movement of labour into the expanding areas not only increases the supply of labour but also the demand for goods, part of which will tend to be met by local traders, services, and manufacturers. Only part of the labour imbalance is therefore removed, and so the total migration required to remove the imbalance may be much larger than initially thought necessary. Thirdly, there is no guarantee that migration will be from among the unemployed or from jobs subsequently filled by someone previously unemployed. The rationale is further undermined if other objectives are brought in. Such migration may well increase the imbalance in congestion and in the demands placed upon various social services and resources such as schools, hospitals, etc. Over- and under-utilization of resources may continue to impair productivity, and the demands on local goods and services may exacerbate inflation. The main line of policy has therefore been to encourage firms to move to, or expand in, the depressed regions.

Here there have been two main types of instrument, the first being a system of control based on Industrial Development Certificates (IDCs). Any industrial development over 5,000 square feet required one of these to be obtained before planning permission could be granted, and they were only readily issued for development in Development Areas, as the officially designated depressed regions became known in 1966. IDCs are now no longer required in these areas. The general policy elsewhere was only to issue an IDC if it was likely that refusal would result in the loss of the development, either because it would not be embarked upon at all or because it would be relocated elsewhere in Europe. It is in fact very difficult to know how stringently this control was applied from the figures on applications and refusals because considerable informal discussion would normally occur first, during the course of which the unacceptability of a proposed development could be indicated.

The second instrument was to give incentives to firms to relocate. Initially these mainly took the form of higher investment incentives in the Development Areas. Cash grants were introduced in 1963 on both plant and machinery and buildings, in addition to 100 per cent initial allowances for the former. When Investment Grants were introduced throughout the country, the rate in the Development Areas at 40 per cent was twice that elsewhere. Buildings also received 25 per cent cash grants in both Development Areas and a new classification known as Intermediate Areas (generally 'fringe' areas suffering the symptoms of regional depression but not so acutely), and 35 per cent in the new Special Development Areas where the problems were most acute. Only the cash grants for buildings (at different rates) were retained after the abolition of Investment Grants in 1970, with 100 per cent initial allowances again becoming the main regional incentive. But this was subsequently regarded as a mistake, not only because it reduced the assistance given but also because it is especially in the depressed regions that firms may be potentially and actually efficient in their operations but still inadequately profitable, and therefore unable to take full advantage of allowances as opposed to grants. So in 1972 cash grants were reintroduced for buildings, plant, and machinery at 20 per cent in Development Areas, 22 per cent in Special Development Areas, and at 20 per cent on buildings in Intermediate Areas. Unlike Investment Grants, these Regional Development Grants, as they were known, did not result in a corresponding reduction in the total annual depreciation permitted. The introduction of these grants provoked criticism on the grounds that they were a capital subsidy with the biggest attraction for capital-intensive firms, whereas the high unemployment in the Development Areas suggested that it would be more efficient to attract labour-intensive ones. Partly in response to this type of argument, the Regional Employment Premium had been introduced in 1967. This was a direct subsidy to all firms in Development Areas per employee per week, with different rates for men, women, and minors. Although it was originally to be phased out in 1974, it continued until 1977. It was then phased out, being too expensive and wasteful insofar as it was paid to inefficient and loss-making companies.

One reason it was so expensive was that it was paid in respect of all jobs in depressed regions rather than just *new* jobs. Against this it can be argued that the size of the problem is so large that job-creating policies could easily be undermined by simultaneous contractions of employment elsewhere in the depressed regions unless prevented through a general subsidy, quite apart from the fact that it would be administratively impossible to identify 'new' jobs for any appreciable period of time. On the relative merits of labour and capital subsidies there is a strong argument for continuing with both. Although labour subsidies may deal more directly with the problem of unemployment in the short term, if the overall problem is to a great extent the dependence on declining industries then in the long term it will require the attraction of new, expanding industries which tend to be, though not exclusively, more capital-intensive.

Many other regional instruments have been used, including the provision of infrastructure—roads, drainage, etc.—government-owned land and buildings at preferential rates, selective measures for land reclamation, clearance of derelict sites, removal grants, cheap loans, and grants to cover the cost of commercial loans. Scottish and Welsh development agencies receive grants to help establish and develop new industrial estates and purpose-built factories. In addition, at one stage, there were efforts to polarize growth in particular areas by concentrating assistance, so that expenditure would have reinforcing 'regional multiplier' effects as funds were spent on locally available goods and services rather than on ones 'imported' from outside the area. The size of these amplifying effects depends also on whether subsidies are used to expand employment, increase wages, increase investment, lower prices, or pay out more dividends (in declining order of effect). There are, however, many unknowns in the process of growth geographically. More recently, 'Enterprise Zones' have been set up in some depressed urban areas. In these zones many of the burdensome regulations that slow up development and put off many small businesses have been set aside. But it is too soon to say whether this attempt to improve conditions from the 'supply' side will have a major effect.

Since 1980 some rather substantial changes in the nature of the regional problem have become evident. First, the pattern has to some extent changed (most notably with the West Midlands moving from being an area of below-average to above-average unemployment). This in part is because regional unemployment no longer only reflects an outdated industrial structure and/or inherent disadvantages such as poor communication and transport links to main markets. Increasingly it also reflects the shift of industry away from major conurbations and cities, towards smaller cities, towns, and more rural areas. Regions with a high degree of urbanization have therefore been affected more than others.

Second, and of fundamental importance, average unemployment in the UK has risen from 1·5 per cent in 1965 to nearly 14 per cent in 1982, with over half the rise concentrated in the last two years of the period. Therefore, while it was reasonable to think that a successful regional policy in the 1960s could balance regional demand more in line with supply, by the 1980s relocation of jobs might simply redistribute unemployment. With unemployment over 10 per cent in the lowest-unemployment region (the South-East), attracting jobs to even more heavily depressed regions might have the claim of equity to support it but little chance of switching demand from overheated regions. Partly because of this, most recent changes in regional policy have been to cut overall support. This, however, leaves unanswered both the question of how to reduce unemployment generally and how, in the process, to have a disproportionately larger effect in the more heavily depressed regions, comprising Northern Ireland, Scotland and Wales, the North, North-West, West Midlands, and Yorkshire and Humberside.

28.3.4. Investment-Led Growth

One widely held but grossly over-simplified theory about low UK growth was that because countries with fast growth rates tended to have high ratios of investment in plant and equipment to GNP (hardly surprising if these were both seen as the results of market success) then what the UK needed to do in order to grow was to invest more heavily. There is, of course, more to the argument than this, and it is widely recognized internationally that the marginal social rate of return tends to exceed the private. Fiscal incentives to invest are therefore ubiquitous.

In the UK, one of the major instruments used by successive governments to improve investment in industry has been the use of tax incentives. As seen in Chapter 3 (p. 56), firms are allowed to deduct from profit an amount to cover the depreciation of assets before arriving at taxable profits. The most common method has been to deduct $1/n$th of the initial cost of a machine, factory, etc. where n is the number of years it is estimated that equipment will last. (Other methods exist however, and all are complicated by such factors as scrap value, inflation, and technological obsolescence.) In 1945 the government introduced a system of Initial Allowances. This permits firms to accelerate depreciation for tax purposes. For example, a 40 per cent Initial Allowance allows firms to deduct 40 per cent of the cost of a machine in its first year, independent of its normal annual allowance in that year. However, the annual allowances in subsequent years must be reduced so that, as before, the total depreciation over the life of the machine is equal to its net cost. The effect is to reduce *taxable* profits in the first year but correspondingly increase them over the remaining years of the machine's life. Taxation is therefore to a certain extent deferred.

In comparison with ordinary straight-line or declining-balance depreciations, Initial Allowances represented an automatic interest-free loan without security from the Inland Revenue. This entailed a net reduction in the cost to a firm of financing its operations and made more funds available than otherwise in the early stages of new equipment. This second effect was not immediate, however, because taxation is normally paid a year in arrears.

In 1954 Investment Allowances were introduced. These operated in the same manner except that no corresponding reduction in subsequent annual depreciation allowances was made. Thus if the Investment Allowance was 30 per cent, the total depreciation allowance for tax purposes over the life of the machine was 130 per cent. Taxation was not only deferred, therefore, but reduced in total because the reduction in the first year was not matched by any increase in later years. In that firms were then being credited with expenditures which they had not in fact incurred this system involved an effective subsidy, and increased the overall expected post-tax profitability of investment.

One or other of these systems, and sometimes both together, have operated for much of the period since the war, the rates being, however, different in general on buildings as opposed to plant and machinery, and being varied over time (sometimes set at zero, thus effectively suspending operation). Increasingly, they were regarded as having several drawbacks. One, the delay in obtaining the benefit, has already been noted. In addition, firms had to make sufficient profit to have an initial tax bill larger than the value of the allowances before the full benefit could be obtained. Thirdly, the system or the rates were changed so frequently, on average more than once every three years, that it was both difficult and risky to take them into account in planning investment.

Partly as a result of these objections, and bearing in mind that the Investment Allowance system had involved an effective subsidy for some years, a new approach, the Investment Grant system, was introduced in 1966. (Such grants had, however, already been employed on a regional basis as part of an incentive scheme to relocate firms; see section 28.3.3.) Investment Grants, generally equal to 20 per cent of the cost of plant and machinery (buildings continued to receive Initial Allowances), were paid in cash, thus making the subsidy explicit. The system was planned to be one on which firms could rely, with the cash payment being made within six months of the capital expenditure and being payable irrespective of whether the firm concerned was making profits. It was therefore hoped that, unlike the previous system, this would help firms making low profits or losses who were attempting to climb out of that situation by modernization, re-equipment, and expansion to obtain economies of scale.

The grants were tax-free, but their net effect is none the less only found by deducting the going company tax rate from them. This is because the total of annual allowances permitted is only the actual expenditure incurred by the firm—the remaining 80 per cent. In obtaining the grant, therefore, total depreciation is reduced by 20 per cent and tax is therefore now paid on this amount. With a tax rate of 40 per cent, a 20 per cent grant is then worth 12 per cent (the same as a 30 per cent Investment Allowance).

In practice, the payments were rarely as fast as had been intended, and the system itself only lasted four years (though payments agreed under it were not tapered out completely until 1980). Criticism focused on the payment of subsidies to loss-making firms, the need for confirmation that investment was eligible for a grant, and the large increase in both government taxation and expenditure figures that resulted. So in 1970 the Investment Grant system was scrapped and a return was made to Initial Allowances at 35 per cent, but at 60 per cent for the first year as a short-term measure to accelerate investment, because of the high unemployment then existing. But in 1972 the rate was increased to 100 per cent (and from 15 to 40 per cent on buildings). In effect, capital costs were on a par with current costs, and there was the maximum deferment of tax liability in the first year consistent with no overall subsidy (other than the zero interest charge on the deferment).

It is, of course, very hard to determine the overall impact of these incentive schemes on the level of investment. Their impact on the supply of funds may only have effect if firms' investment is limited by financial constraints. Except for small fast-growing firms, and apart from a couple of relatively short periods, this generally appears not to have been the case in the UK. Their incentive impact on the expected rate of return may be swamped by the changes to the expected return that relatively small adjustments in sales, cost, and price forecasts make; and their effect may be partly or totally negated if non-profitability criteria are used (explicitly or implicitly), if pre-tax calculations are done, or if the frequent changes in the incentives used have led to their exclusion from investment decision-taking. The majority of studies of the interview type at the microeconomic level support the view that they have not been very effective. More aggregative econometric analysis is inconclusive. Many studies indicate relatively little effect, but a few indicate the opposite. What cannot be disputed is that they have been unable to increase investment in the UK to a level comparable with other countries, and have therefore at best only served to mitigate what would otherwise have been an even worse record of investment and productivity.

The system of 100 per cent Initial Allowances was thought to be appropriate because the generally poor and uncertain outlook for investment induces industry to adopt relatively short time horizons, and because the system heavily concentrated its incentive in the first two years of an investment project. The absence of any effective subsidy nevertheless reduced its impact in comparison with other systems, and it was unlikely that a marked improvement would accrue as a result of it. Partly reflecting this, the 100 per cent allowance system was abolished in 1984.

But there was another more important reason for this. the acceleration of inflation in 1973–4 meant that a considerable proportion of company profits as measured in company accounts arose from the production of goods at an earlier lower-cost period and the sale of them at a later higher-price period, taking no account of the fact that to replace the goods sold at the later-period level of costs would be much more expensive. This stock appreciation element in profits was taxable but did not of course generate any cash to pay the tax. This threatened to hit UK companies very hard in the inflationary period of the mid-1970s and so Stock Relief was introduced, an allowance against tax for the stock appreciation element in profits.

Thus by the early 1980s there were 100 per cent Initial Allowances, Stock Relief, and also tax advantages for financing by borrowing because the interest charges payable, unlike dividends payable on equity finance, were regarded as a cost, according them full tax relief. The system had therefore become complicated and cumbersome, and given the allowances, the overall effective tax rate was very much lower (in some cases even negative) than the notional 52 per cent rate of Corporation Tax. Half of all companies paid no tax at all.

With the abolition of the system there is no Stock Relief, no special allowances on investment (apart from in a transitional period), and therefore no explicit investment incentive in the system. But the rate of Corporation Tax will be reduced progressively to 35 per cent by the end of the transitional period and it was announced that the effect of these changes together would be 'broadly revenue-neutral', i.e. lead to much the same overall tax burden but in a much simpler way and without the 'distortion' of a pro-investment bias. However, it has been estimated (see [26]) that the change will only be revenue-neutral if inflation is about zero, a stated government aim, under which condition Stock Relief would have no value. If, as most people expect, inflation continues to run at 5 per cent or above, then the loss of Stock Relief will matter and the overall effect of the changes (unless the new Corporation Tax rate is itself changed) will be to increase the burden of Corporation Tax substantially.

28.3.5. National Indicative Planning

An alternative approach to the slow growth of GDP in the UK is based on the belief that it stems from the continuous disappointment of demand expectations through the combined effects of caution (of investors, principally) in the face of uncertainty. In that case the preparation and contemplation of a detailed plan showing the feasibility of a higher growth rate than before could lead to a set of simultaneous decisions which might make this growth possible. This approach was embodied in the 1965 National Plan.

The main advantage of this kind of indicative plan is the steadier and higher rate of industrial investment that may result from more confident expectations. But investment may languish in spite of the plan. If this is not to happen, the government needs to do two things. First, it should state the measures it is prepared to take to ensure that expansion is not halted by, for example, a worsening balance of payments. In fact it has to convince investors that the only thing that stands in the way of faster growth is their own timidity—not a very plausible proposition. Second, it has to be able to persuade or oblige firms to act upon those changed expectations. There were no *directives* for actions by firms in the 1965 National Plan. And there is a logical difficulty about expecting firms to act voluntarily in accordance with such a plan.

A simplifying selection out of the possible future states of the environment has to be made to reduce the number of paths and the corresponding sets of hypothetical questions to a manageable level [28]. In the case of the National Plan this reduction was down to a single path. Since one does not know what confidence is attached by industrialists to the chosen outcome, one cannot know for sure how they will behave. All that is known for certain is that producers are likely to make more flexible decisions than would be optimal if they believed that the plan was self-fulfilling. This almost certainly implies less investment, postponed investment, less product specialization, and less training and manpower planning.

It is a pity that the idea of consultative industrial planning across the board should have received such a severe set-back because of the mistakes that were made by rushing the National Plan in 1965 and expecting too much from the 'virtuous circle' theory of growth. With hindsight, the main mistakes are apparent. First, the target growth rate was too high. Since the National Economic Development Council (NEDC) had looked at the obstacles to achieving 4 per cent per annum growth in its 1961–6 study [31], the Department of Economic Affairs (DEA) did not want to aim at less.[2] Second, only one growth rate was considered. But a lower one alongside might have defeated one of the objects of the exercise, which was to raise growth by raising expectations of growth. Third, the increase in the volume of exports required to maintain the balance of payments was $5\frac{1}{4}$ per cent per annum. The rate of growth in the five years before 1964 had been about 3 per cent, and an optimistic view of trends in world trade might have raised this figure to 4 per cent for the Plan period. But $5\frac{1}{4}$ per cent was the needed increase, and the document observed baldly that 'this figure has been taken for the purposes of the Plan' [19, Chap. 7, para. 65]. In justification, the planners offered two straws of comfort: many of our competitors have expanded exports considerably faster' (which was irrelevant) and 'the Industrial Inquiry has shown that industries themselves believe an increase of this order to be attainable' (which meant little more than that if the export demand was there it could be supplied).[3] The paragraph concluded 'the task will not be easy and will require a major effort by all concerned'. It did not show why such an effort should be made by individual firms, given the relative unprofitability of exports at the old rate of exchange. As a matter of fact, the required growth of exports would have been even higher, since the ratio of the growth of imports to the growth of

---

[2] The NEDC settled on 4 per cent in order to bring out the problems of faster growth. Since the rate achieved from 1950 to 1960 was 2·6 per cent, this might have been done by the choice of, say, $3\frac{1}{4}$ per cent. However, the figure was to some extent a compromise between the TUC's desire to countenance as high a growth rate as people could bring themselves to swallow and the Federation of British Industry's equally understandable interest in a rate not too far from what was being used by the corporate planners in their own forecasting. Neither of these reasons ought to have been allowed to influence the DEA's choice of a target growth rate.

[3] The export growth forecast was heavily weighted by absurdly optimistic figures for three of the four largest exporting industries: mechanical engineering (7·8 per cent per annum), electrical engineering (7·7 per cent), and vehicles (5·2 per cent). The report qualified these estimates in terms that exposed them: 'the forecasts represent the rates of growth which industries think are feasible in the context of a rate of growth of 25% in the economy as a whole by 1970'.

consumption over the Plan period (despite devaluation in 1967) turned out to be not the 1·2 assumed in the Plan, but 2·7. The balance of payments measures in the Plan's check-list of action included 'the impact of a successful prices and incomes policy', a condition which would have been all the more necessary had devaluation come in 1965 in time to make the Plan's export target more credible.

Fourth, even if the 1966 sterling crisis had been avoided, the Plan would almost certainly have run up against supply constraints. The forecast manpower requirements exceeded the work-force by almost half a million, a gap which it was optimistic to suppose could be filled by movement between regions or by changes in the organization of work. There were few industrial policies built into the Plan to raise the rate of growth of productivity by the amount the Plan required: rationalization by means of the Industrial Reorganisation Corporation (IRC) was foreshadowed; the investment of nationalized industries was to be based upon the Plan assumptions; the switch to Investment Grants and the discrimination in favour of profit retentions under the newly introduced Corporation Tax were expected to boost industrial investment; and lump-sum payments to redundant workers and transferable pension rights to increase worker mobility. Apart from this, beneath the surface of the 1965 National Plan lay the assumption that the growth of productivity was *demand determined* and could be raised simply by the expansion of capacity which was presumed to follow increased demand.

It is instructive to contrast this plan with indicative planning in France in the 1950s and 1960s. In France the Budget was based on the Plan; general economic policy was co-ordinated around it; the Plan allocated the growth increment, concerning itself with distribution as well as growth; prices and incomes policies were fully tied in; and the industrial detail in the Plan encouraged optimism; but the prime condition of the Plan was a healthy balance of payments surplus. Contracts with individual firms were entered into in the spirit of the Plan, and (to a decreasing extent after the Fourth Plan) financial rewards and penalties attached to their performance [41, Chap. 3].

Table 28.3 compares, for three UK growth studies of the 1960s, planned or projected increases over the period in GDP (and its principal components) with what happened. The ratio of the actual to the projected increases (O/P) is also shown.

It is plain that all three projections or requirements were optimistic. In the third exercise, when higher and lower cases were considered, as well as a basic case, the growth of GDP and investment were well below even the lower case. The expected relation between consumption growth and income growth in the first two exercises was not much different from the actual; but in the third, the share of consumption increased markedly. The income elasticity of demand for imports was 2 over the period of the National Plan, about double the target elasticity, in spite of devaluation. In 1967–72 the growth of imports was almost three times as fast as the growth of GDP, and the income elasticity more than twice what was projected. In all three stages, manufacturing investment grew

---

[4] Income elasticity of import demand is approximately the percentage growth of imports, divided by the percentage growth of income.

TABLE 28.3

(all figures are expressed as percentages)	Growth 1961-6			National Plan 1954-70 (basic plan)			Task Ahead 1967-72		
	Plan	Out-come	O/P	Plan	Out-come	O/P	Plan	come	O/P
GDP	22	16	71	25‡	14‡	56	17	13	74
Consumption	19	14	72	21	11	52	12	14	119
Investment	30	27	89	38	24	64	21	12	55
Public current	19	12	65	27	12	44	9	7	82
Visible exports	28	20†	73	36	37	102*	32	35	110
Visible imports	22	19†	86	26	29	112*	22	36	163
Import growth/GDP growth	100	119		104	209		129	284	
Invest. growth/ Consump. growth	158	160		181	224		175	81	
Consump. growth/ GDP growth	86	94		84	78		71	113	

* Affected by devaluation.
† Goods and services; goods alone in other columns.
‡ GNP.

Sources: NEDC, *Growth of the UK Economy to 1966*; DEA, *The National Plan*; DEA, *The Task Ahead*; CSO, *National Income and Expenditure 1974* Blue Book).

less than had been projected or required; and in *The Task Ahead*, investment as a whole rose more slowly than consumption, instead of very much faster.

It is clear that throughout the 1960s Britain failed to develop industrial policies to permit the sustained faster growth of GDP: consumption and imports grew much too rapidly and industrial investment much too slowly. Above all, little was done to encourage the rapid changes in industrial structure upon which mobility of resources and industrial growth depend.

28.3.6. Selection of Champions

The supporters of industrial policy frequently lay stress on the successes of past French industrial planning and point in particular to the fact that in France, the government was in the habit of dealing with large individual firms chosen for their potential strength. These firms were given cheap loans, tax advantages, export credits, licences, and long-term contracts in return for their co-operation in innovative leadership and orientation to growth.

In a phase of industrial policy which overlaps the National Plan phase and the later focusing on the specific problems of individual sectors of manufacturing (see section 28.3.7), UK industrial policy became for a time fairly firm-specific.

The Industrial Reorganisation Corporation was set up in 1966 to exploit scale economies through mergers and to encourage innovative firms. It was abolished by Heath in 1970 and replaced by the much more ambitious National Enterprise Board in 1975, which in its turn was cut back in 1980, combined with the National Research and Development Corporation (NRDC) to become the British Technology Group (BTG), and now focuses upon a handful of mainly high-technology small firms.

Potentially, these institutions—as well as the legislation to enter into so-called Planning Agreements with leading companies, which were strenuously and successfully resisted by the company sector—might have led towards French-style firm-specific planning. In practice it was sometimes said that Ministers did not 'pick winners'. Rather, through these institutions it was losers like Rolls Royce, British Leyland, and Alfred Herbert who picked Ministers.

The BTG (or NEB and NRDC as was) has started companies in VLSI circuitry, electronic office equipment, computer peripherals, and biotechnology (monoclonal antibodies). It has created an important link (supplied in the US by venture-capital companies) between university research and commercial application. A full-blooded 'winner-picking' industrial policy would go very much further than this, of course. Criteria would be established by which to identify in advance the firms that it would be most productive to assist. For example, industries and individual firms might be classified as either:

(a) intrinsically successful;
(b) having the potential for success if action is taken;
(c) vital for other sectors of the economy.

In general, only firms coming under one of these headings would qualify for assistance, especially if its actual or potential success was based on comparative advantage. It would then be necessary to examine the disaggregated implications of this for particular firms, and in addition there would need to be criteria for deciding which firms in a qualifying industry would receive any aid requested. Again, past performance, potential for the future, and special factors would be the main ones. This was, in fact, part of the intention of the sectoral approach to industrial policy (see section 28.3.7).

All that is now left is a vestige of the discredited winner-picking approach. It was never a very convincing idea, given the poor record of successive British governments in backing expensive industrial projects. And even on the tiny present scale it does not sit well with the Conservative Government's belief in the efficacy of the capital market to separate the industrial sheep from the goats. The main damage this phase of policy did was to confuse politicians and the public alike. What was described as 'picking winners' appeared in practice to amount to spending huge sums shoring up ailing companies, and for many politicians and industrialists,, industrial policy as a whole was unreasonably identified with the discredited activity of 'winner-picking'.

28.3.7. Achieving a Consensus

In the company sector, commercial interest, independently advanced, and higher overall growth can conflict in all sorts of ways. There is no point in expensive in-house training schemes if the effect is that rivals can afford to offer higher wages and bid one's trainees away. It may be good policy not to be the first firm to introduce an untried production technique, if others will benefit from your mistakes and avoid some of the teething troubles. There may be a strong case, in a cyclical industry, for operating a small vertically integrated plant to provide one's own raw material, building it on a scale where it will just supply all one's requirements at the lowest point in the cycle—residual supplies being bought outside from the specialist suppliers, over the rest of the cycle. To the firm integrating in this way the gain from getting most of its requirements from a plant used at full capacity throughout the cycle more than offsets the loss of scale economies and the somewhat higher price that must then be paid for its bought-in supplies from specialists whose average plant utilization over the cycle is now somewhat lower. But productivity in the industry as a whole is reduced since there is an overall loss of economies of scale.

Much of our social organization consists of institutional arrangements to bring individual and public interests closer together. Some of these are market oriented (like the subsidization of research and development expenditure); some are government regulations (like industrial training levies); some are direct and selective interventions by government agencies (like the enforcement of mergers by the IRC in the late 1960s or the *contrats fiscaux* between the French Government and particular firms in successive National Plans); and some follow judicial recommendations (like those on proposed mergers by the Monopolies and Mergers Commission). Typically, the government has a role wherever externalities are important: that is, where social returns are different from private returns.

The role of government is probably most effective when what is required by its economic Departments is knowledge of the behaviour and contingent plans of industries, of employees, and of the government itself. In some cases the exchange of information may become explicit or even be part of some form of social contract. In the latter case, it may include but go beyond purely industrial policy issues to interdependent commitments by those involved. Attempts on the basis of such exchanges of information or commitments to construct a consensus approach to industrial policy issues are likely to be very difficult and bound to be complex. What follows is a highly stylized and over-simplified illustration of this interdependence. It can be thought of as the bare bones of a more realistic and intricate model. It differs from most traditional models of the working of the economy by admitting three separate economic agents, each of which individually controls only one of three levers of the economy—the growth of demand, the growth of money income per man, and the growth of prices. The participants may be thought of as having three principal objectives which they hold in common and which can be achieved only by the concerted action of all of them.

The relationship between the decisions of the three principals in the economy are shown in the diagram represented in Figure 28.1. There are three controlled inputs, one from each of the three principals. These inputs are circled. There are three outputs—the three common objectives—and these are boxed. The wages/profits distribution is assumed to be a common goal, which

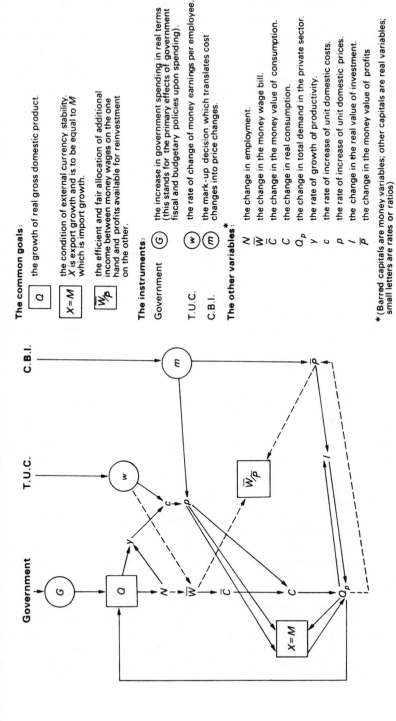

The common goals:

$\boxed{Q}$ the growth of real gross domestic product.

$\boxed{X=M}$ the condition of external currency stability. X is export growth and is to be equal to M which is import growth.

$\boxed{\overline{W}/\overline{p}}$ the efficient and fair allocation of additional income between money wages on the one hand and profits available for reinvestment on the other.

The instruments:

Government $\;(G)\;$ the increase in government spending in real terms (this stands for the primary effects of government fiscal and budgetary policies upon spending).

T.U.C. $\;(w)\;$ the rate of change of money earnings per employee.

C.B.I. $\;(m)\;$ the mark-up decision which translates cost changes into price changes.

The other variables*:

N the change in employment.
$\overline{W}$ the change in the money wage bill.
$\overline{C}$ the change in the money value of consumption.
C the change in real consumption.
Q_p the change in total demand in the private sector.
y the rate of growth of productivity.
c the rate of increase of unit domestic costs.
p the rate of increase of unit domestic prices.
I the change in the real value of investment.
$\overline{P}$ the change in the money value of profits

*(Barred capitals are money variables; other capitals are real variables; small letters are rates or ratios)

Fig. 28.1. Interdependence in the UK Economy.

might be negotiated after exploration of the model and agreement about the dependence of real wage growth upon investment and hence upon profits. (At worst, consideration by all three parties of the model's relationships would make disagreement on the distribution goal explicit. At best, it might make it possible to resolve the disagreement by negotiation against a background of other particular policy objectives.) There are a number of intermediate steps, described below, which connect the inputs and the objectives by way of changes in other key economic quantities like employment, productivity, unit costs, prices, consumption, exports, and imports. The order of cause and effect is shown by arrows. Continuous lines show the links between principal production and expenditure quantities. The dashed lines show the relationship between different components and shares of income.

Starting at the top of the figure, the three levers which the three principals control are these:

(1) (by the government) additional real government expenditure, G, which can be set so that, after the consequent increases in the other sorts of domestic expenditure—consumption and investment—are calculated, and the growth of exports is added, the required growth in real domestic product, Q, is attained. G stands for the much more complicated measures, including changes in taxation and monetary policy, which the government takes in practice;

(2) (by the TUC) the annual rate of growth of earnings per man employed (w in the figure);

(3) (by the CBI) the mark-up (m) which, when applied to the change in unit costs (c), determines the change in price (p).

These three instruments (circled) are the only three 'independent' variables; and together, by way of the principal loops and feedbacks shown in the figure, they determine the behaviour of the economy. In particular, the values they take will determine the degree to which the three collective goals (boxed in the figure) are achieved.

The instruments and the targets (full-employment growth, currency stability, and fair distribution) are connected by a number of pathways through dependent real and money changes.

This may be summarized as follows (see figure): the current rate of growth of real Gross Domestic Product will be reflected partly an changes in employment, and partly in productivity changes. Productivity growth, coupled with the rate of change of money wages per employee, determine the rate of increase in domestic unit costs. This, together with the chosen average mark-up, determine the rate of domestic price increases. In addition, the rate of increase in money wages per employee and the change in the level of employment determine the change in total money wages. This in turn determines the change in consumption expenditure in money terms. Coupling this with the rate of price increases sets the rise in real consumption while the rate of price increases also determines international competitiveness, hence balance of payments performance over time, and the stability or otherwise of the external value of the currency. (This would also, of course, depend on the rise in real incomes which will result from the growth of money wages and prices.)

Thus changes in consumption, exports, and imports will be determined, and these are three of the four components of the change in total demand facing the private sector. The fourth component—investment—depends partly on overall private sector demand itself (i.e. the accelerator relationship) and partly on the profitability of meeting that demand. This will depend on the mark-ups industry wants, or can get, in the light of prevailing demand conditions. The proportion of profits retained will also be important because of its effect on the supply of funds for investment. Finally, adding this total private sector demand increase to that which occurs as a result of government expenditure gives the real rate of growth of domestic product which can therefore be controlled by the government's policy on expenditure and taxation. (In this sketch of the structure, time-lags have been omitted, and so no notice has been taken of the fact that investment may not respond swiftly to increases in private production if there is excess capacity in manufacturing industry.)

Even this very crude sketch illustrates clearly the interdependence of objectives and the dependence of each on all three participating agents. The rate of inflation depends on mark-ups, wage increases, and demand management policy, and in turn directly or indirectly determines the external value of the currency and the growth of real output. The distribution of additional income between wages and profits also depends on the mark-up, money wage, and demand-generating decisions of the three agents respectively.

Much less ambitious and much less collective approaches to industrial policy are of course possible within this general approach. The key characteristic of it is simply the recognition that different groups affect different part of the economy yet the objectives of all are affected by the activities of all the groups concerned. The only institutional attempt to work within this approach was the setting up of the National Economic Development Council in 1962, with representatives of the government, the TUC, and the CBI.[5] Both the role and effectiveness of this body has varied through time, depending not least on the

---

[5] Selwyn Lloyd's statement of the remit of the NEDC, which he made at its inaugural meeting in March 1962, reflects belief in the scope for collaborative action. He said: 'I would define our task as follows:

'To examine the economic performance of the nation with particular concern for the future in both the private and the public sectors of industry.

'To consider what are the obstacles to quicker growth, what can be done to improve efficiency, and whether the best use is being made of our resources.

'To seek agreement upon ways of improving economic performance, competitive power and efficiency, in other words to increase the rate of sound growth.'

On another occasion, the Chancellor observed that he was anxious to secure that both sides of industry, on whose co-operation the fulfilment of 'our' objectives must significantly depend, should participate fully with the government in all stages of the process. It could be argued that on this occasion, as many times later, Ministers allowed themselves to be beguiled by a collective noun into supposing that agreement about the desirability of a set of actions by representatives of 'both sides of industry' would actually result in any voluntary collective action. One notable unilateral counter-example was the CBI's voluntary price restraint in 1971–2.

commitment or enthusiasm of the government of the day to utilize it. In addition to the government, TUC, and CBI, there are on the Council the Governor of the Bank of England, the Chairman of a nationalized industry, the heads of the Consumer Association and the Manpower Services Commission, and the Director-General of the National Economic Development Office (NEDO), and it therefore embraces virtually all the major centres of economic power in the UK. But frequently the divisions of view between the different groups represented have prevented it being as effective as originally envisaged.

None the less, at a meeting of the NEDC held at Chequers in November 1975 the government tabled its proposals for the evolution of an Industrial Strategy, involving the co-operation of the CBI and the TUC. It described a process of setting out annually the main components of the government's medium-term projection, identifying thirty-nine key sectors for individual attention, and involving tripartite working parties for each sector, as well as NEDO which was working in a complementary way on performance and its dependence on structure at the particular-industry level.

By the end of 1978, after three years, this supply-side approach to industrial policy had had some success. About 40 per cent of manufacturing industry was covered. The Sector Working Parties provided the main focus of a policy which influenced many branches of the government. They set themselves five-year objectives to improve upon the trend of their shares of world exports and the UK market. They then began to work out what would have to be done—by government and by management and unions—to reach these objectives. The need to improve both price competitiveness and non-price competitiveness directed attention to the factors of faster growth of productivity and better product design and marketing. And behind these there have been self-referring recommendations about manning practices, specialization and standardization of products, the diffusion of new techniques, and the exchange of information between customers and suppliers. Much of this work has continued in the sector committees in spite of the demise in 1979 of the Industrial Strategy proclaimed in 1975, and recent estimates [21] suggest that the sectors covered by such committees have tended to have a better record of competitiveness than others. The main limitation is that these committees are predominantly in manufacturing, which now represents only 25 per cent of GDP, though it still represents over half of all exports.

28.3.8. A New Supply-Side Approach

The election of the Thatcher Government in 1979 saw the beginning of a new 'supply-side' approach. This was based on three main elements. First, new importance was attached to the setting of a macroeconomic environment favourable to enterprise and the operation of market forces. This was to be achieved by reduction of taxation, particularly of marginal rates of tax, to encourage effort and risk-taking, and by reduction of government expenditure, (particularly on loss-making enterprises) to encourage efficiency, shift more resources to profitable areas, and above all to leave room for the private sector to expand. This latter point was of course heavily influenced by the belief (see Ch. 14, p. 462) that public expenditure 'crowds out' private expenditure via higher interest rates, a higher exchange rate, and/or higher inflation.

The second strand of the new policy was to encourage competition whenever possible, primarily through increased attention to competition policy, privatization whenever possible of publicly owned assets, and through not supporting companies in difficulty. The third element was the heavy reduction and eventual elimination of deficits in some nationalized industries which had constituted a substantial drain on government expenditure.

Three points must be made about this new direction. First, there is little doubt that it will take some time to achieve discernible results, partly because industry will take time to adjust to a new climate and partly because there are long lead-times in the industrial decisions and expenditures that determine industrial performance. None the less, productivity growth has been significantly stronger since 1981, which might be attributable to this new regime. (Recent economic performance is summarized in Chapter 29.) Second, doubts exist about how much difference these changes can make. The notion of public expenditure completely crowding out an equivalent amount of private expenditure has been seen to depend on inherent inconsistency between monetary and fiscal policy (see Chapter 12). It is difficult to see competition policy having a very substantial effect. The limited effect of privatization on competition, whatever its other benefits, has been noted in Chapter 25, although in British Leyland, British Rail, and British Steel, there have been major savings of public money (for a much smaller industry in the case of steel).

Third, it must be asked how the new approach helps to overcome the three problems of restructuring, recovery, and research and development described earlier. On the last of these three there has been an acceleration of support, with a higher proportion of total public funding being shifted into various types of support for innovation, design and application of new technological processes. Whether it will be sufficient to reverse the post-war trend of relative decline in resources to research and development remains to be seen. The UK's civil R & D spending per head of the population, second only to the US in 1964, was by 1978 caught up by France and comfortably surpassed by West Germany and Japan. The UK's military and defence R & D remained strong but this appears to have had little economic spin-off. It is probably unrealistic to believe that a simple realignment of R & D towards civil purposes is possible. This is not just because military R & D is a necessary concomitant of the UK's defence programme, but because the alternative to military R & D in the UK may well be purchase of US defence equipment, rather than more civil R & D. It none the less remains true that the UK's military R & D is estimated to absorb nearly 40 per cent of the UK's R & D personnel, which must have an adverse effect on the civil side. The consequence of heavy defence commitments will have to be a larger overall R & D effort than elsewhere in Europe, rather than less civil R & D; otherwise the UK will increasingly be unable to finance either adequately as its GDP slips further behind that of faster-growing countries.

A further element in the attempts to tackle this problem is on the engineering manpower side. Initiatives started in 1984, and backed by both the Department of Education and Science and the Department of Trade and Industry, are designed to increase substantially the number of people training to be engineers, particularly in the electronic and information technology areas where serious shortages exist. Inevitably such initiatives take time to have an impact, and Chapter 22 indicated how easy it is for attempts at improving the skill and quality of manpower available to industry to fail, either on the supply or on the demand side. But there is probably a stronger recognition of the problem of shortage of industrial training at all levels, and determination to tackle the problem, than for many years.

On cases of restructuring and recovery the position is less clear. At one level there is the view that subsidies are inherently inefficient, either because they remove market discipline or because someone else bears the cost, or both. This, coupled with faith in the efficacy of market mechanisms, has led to a new spirit of 'disengagement' of the public sector from such activities. At this rather general level there is little economic support. As we have seen, certain situations probably do not have efficient market solutions, and there is little reason to believe that intensified competitive pressures will generally strengthen companies currently in a weak position. There is therefore nothing inherently inefficient about subsidies in particular circumstances and certainly no reason to believe that there necessarily will be offsetting costs elsewhere in the economy.

But at another level there are more serious objections. These assert not any underlying incorrectness of public support of various kinds, tailored to particular cases of market failure, but the difficulty or impossibility of identifying those cases, of distinguishing them from those of straight inefficiency or long-term decline, of resisting political lobbying and other pressures to support certain companies or sectors, whether economically justified or not, of ensuring that availability of public funds does not itself constitute a reason for inefficiency, and also of ensuring that the government does not get locked into providing ever larger sums of money in order to prevent earlier expenditure being wasted. These practical obstacles to the implementation of a successful, active, industrial policy can be severe, and although there are examples of companies which would never have come through recovery periods successfully without public support, most notably British Leyland and ICL, there are also others such as Alfred Herbert where the cost has been heavy to no avail. It is not clear that in the past either the information or the expertise existed in government to analyse different companies and sectors, and their prospects, in order to distinguish economically justified calls on public funds to support industry from other often equally pressing but inappropriate calls.

How successful a new spirit of disengagement will be in the 1980s cannot be predicted. In the early 1970s, when a similar approach was adopted, economic and political pressures served to undermine it within two years, leading to major support for Rolls Royce and Upper Clyde Shipbuilders, simultaneously with the passing of the 1972 Industry Act which has been an important instrument of discretionary intervention and support ever since. But this course of events need not necessarily be repeated, provided industrial performance is seen to start to respond to the new style of industrial policy.

28.4. Evaluation of Industrial Policy

28.4.1. Problems of Evaluation

It is virtually impossible to disentangle the impact of industrial policies on growth from the many other economic and social factors which determine it. Nearly all types of instrument have been employed in countries with very different records of growth, and while there are signs that industrial policies have been more coherent and more effective in faster-growing countries, it is not at all clear in which direction the causality runs. Whether current attempts to restructure the industrial base of European countries are successful will not be known for several years.

In addition, macroeconomic policies aimed at inflation and balance of payments deficits have, repeatedly, had more immediate impact on industry and often severely limited the scope of industrial measures. In many countries the problem of trying to reduce inflation and budget deficits has prevented effective implementation of restructuring policies. In Germany, until recently, a policy of counter-cyclical economic management within a framework of moderate monetary growth, coupled with an effective wage determination mechanism, was generally successful, and this meant that support for industry, concentrated on regional, education and training, R & D, and growth sector support, could be maintained as a continuing and viable element of policy. Only in France did a very distinctive industrial policy come to be a continuing, moderately stable, and important element in industrial growth despite often severe and continuing difficulties with inflation, the balance of payments, and unemployment (indeed France deliberately used industrial policy to help solve some of these problems). Even here recent macroeconomic pressures have caused some disruption to the continuity of industrial policy.

It must also be said that there are clearly many different routes by which industrial objectives can be furthered, and no particular policy, institutional framework, nor method of implementation is guaranteed to succeed. Germany throughout the post-war period has chosen a decentralized approach, eschewing any formal or detailed planning and focusing particularly on R & D, and on building up small and medium-sized firms. France, with a comparable level of success, has favoured a highly centralized approach, which, in spite of Barre's attempts to reverse it in 1976–7, probably increased in the late 1970s. Although industrial policy has been largely outside the formal planning mechanism, the approach has been 'planned' in the broad sense and has concentrated on particular key sectors and the building up of major national companies. Among the other European countries there has been a tendency to veer more towards the German decentralized model, although some have attempted more general strategic planning and have identified particular sectors which appear to have good growth prospects. Many have been less able than Germany to reduce sectoral commitments, particularly when political coalitions have been fragile. None appears to have achieved a similar degree of overall success as France or Germany. In addition, while expenditure levels associated with industrial policy have generally risen in all countries, there is little observable relation between expenditure and industrial restructuring and growth. This is not surprising. Many elements of industrial policy involve minimal expenditure, most notably planning exercises and competition policy; many others may have effects considerably out of proportion to actual expenditure, in particular soft loans and guarantees; while tax incentives do not show up as 'expenditures' at all. Differences in the size and financing of the nationalized industry sectors of these countries also cloud comparisons.

A further point which cannot be overemphasized is that, with the exception of a small number of EEC-based initiatives, each country has pursued its industrial policy independent of its European competitors. These policies have in considerable degree therefore been directly competitive with each other— a point which may be obvious when all countries are supporting their micro-electronics industries, but is not necessarily any the less true when they provide regional or employment support which goes predominantly to a small number of hard-hit and regionally concentrated industries. Indeed many of the issues that come up under the heading of non-tariff barriers to competition from foreign trade, such as standard-setting, public procurement policies, etc., are explicitly part of most countries' industrial policy armaments.

28.4.2. Lessons from Europe

These points must make for some agnosticism and put considerable limits on what may usefully be inferred from looking at industrial policy across Europe. Nevertheless some tentative lessons from Europe may be identified. The first conclusion relates to the degree of selectivity involved. In the early 1970s there was a growing tendency towards selection of specific sectors for assistance, and this was exacerbated by the series of industry crises that came in the wake of the 1974–6 recession. Recovery saw attempts to move towards more 'horizontal' measures (i.e. potentially available to all) coupled with restructuring programmes designed to ensure that governments could extricate themselves from heavy support for particular sectors. This shift reflected in part the belief that all sectors have areas of potential growth, and in part the disillusion with previous attempts at selectivity.

To some extent the 1979–81 recession forced governments back to support of specific hard-hit sectors. But there is now an unmistakable move towards selectivity of a new kind. Certain trends, especially concerning import penetration, emerging new technologies, and rapidly expanding product areas, e.g. energy exploration and development, have become much more evident, and there is increased recognition that they are creating inescapable pressures for adaptation. Direction of support in a way that reflects these pressures has therefore been seen to be a necessary element of industrial policy. This new selectivity is reflected in:

(i) Specific priority to major growth sectors, often delineated in terms of generic technologies rather than traditional product areas.

(ii) Promotion of support which in appearance is general (e.g. R & D, subsidized loans, public purchasing) but which in practice can be applied in a highly selective manner.

(iii) More selective impact of some long-standing programmes, in particular employment subsidies and manpower and training policies, but also in some cases investment support and regional assistance.

There are therefore strong indications that despite the apparent shift to more horizontal measures, industrial policy has in practice become more selective recently.

Second, some conclusions about the effectiveness of formal, quantitative planning are possible. It is clearly not a necessary condition for success, and although most countries have attempted centralized forward planning, in general—with the partial exception of France—it seems to have had little impact. In the Netherlands it appears to have helped focus attention on the need for structural change in the post-1973 world, but against this Sweden, with a previously successful planning mechanism, was amongst the slowest countries to recognize the changed environment in which it would have to compete.

There has, however, been a subtle and significant change in attitudes to planning. Some of those countries which continue to adhere to a planning framework (France, Holland, Belgium) have substantially shifted away from the more quantitative indicative planning of the 1960s, instead developing broad sectoral assessments in a more flexible way as a means of identifying and giving priority to medium- or long-term industrial objectives within the broad economic environment envisaged. This approach, though in a more informal way, is also a feature of other economies which do not have planning mechanisms as such, and is linked to the increased selectivity which characterizes industrial policy. As a result, most countries in Europe now have at least some systematic means for considering how the structure of their economy might look in the longer term and the priorities which flow from this.

Third, there are indications that stability and continuity of policy are important. While emphasis of policy inevitably changes over time, many people, observing the very different systems of France and West Germany, believe that these two characteristics have contributed to their success, partly by reducing uncertainties for industry but also (as important if more mundane) by allowing greater familiarity on the part of both government and industry with the instruments used. The West German commitment to the data-processing industry is a particularly clear example of the benefit which may be derived from a policy developed and implemented over a long period. There are also signs that more stability over time provides an environment in which agreement is more readily achieved on movements in prices and incomes.

Fourth, there appear to be substantial gains from linking industrial policy instruments together so that they represent a series of mutually reinforcing measures. One example would be the recent Dutch legislation which introduced a package of measures comprising incentives for investment, R & D, innovation, and training, combined with a reorganization of sectoral aid with the purpose of bringing all sectoral schemes within one framework and aligning them more closely with EC guidelines. The French have long recognized the advantage of putting a package of incentives together into 'growth contracts' with companies, or similar arrangements, in order to secure maximum effect from expenditures. Integration of manpower policies with industrial policies is another factor to which importance is attached.

Fifth, it is noteworthy that despite representing very different approaches, both French and West German industrial policies evince a considerable if varying degree of consensus and commitment amongst politicians, officials, industrialists, bankers, and trade unionists. Although the French system has often been arbitrary and unaccountable, it has generally succeeded because all involved were anxious to see the policies successfully implemented. It is obvious but none the less important that strong opposition to industrial policy measures by any of those involved in implementation is very likely to reduce their impact. General support for policy, therefore, has a considerable value quite separate from the elements actually agreed upon.

Sixth, the long-run success of the German economy is associated by many with its long-run commitment to investment in human resources. This has taken the form not only of more emphasis upon applied science and technology at the university level, but of a long-established tradition of vocational and skill training for all workers. Following this lead, many European countries have been putting increasing emphasis on education and training programmes in the last few years, increasing the number of those participating in apprentice-ship and vocational programmes, sometimes anti-cyclically, as well as trying to increase the proportion of students in higher education, particularly those studying applied sciences. Retraining and skill-upgrading are also seen as vital elements in creating a much more mobile, flexible, and more highly rewarded work-force.

Seventh, the relation between industrial policy and the market mechanism is of fundamental importance. There are three main aspects that merit consideration:

(i) the pressure of market forces;
(ii) the direction of change indicated;
(iii) the responsiveness of companies in following market signals.

With regard to the first, although competition policy remains in place to strengthen market forces, and support for small business has similar effects, recent developments in industrial policy equally clearly recognize the intensity of international competition, particularly from Japan and the US and the need, in appropriate areas, to support larger units. This is almost inevitable in the small European countries, and has always been a feature of the French approach. In Italy it has been an outcome of the larger public sector presence in industry. Only in Germany, a large and successful economy in its own right, has this trend not been so evident. Conflict has therefore developed in some areas between the need to provide support, particularly for large-scale innovative development, and the requirements of enhanced competition.

Second, with regard to the direction of change, policies which have sought to preserve existing positions against the tide of the market have usually taken much longer than initially forseen, have been increasingly costly and have often not, in the end, been very successful; hence the growing emphasis on establishing timetables for contraction of capacity, restructuring of capital base, and reorientation of product mix as conditions of support. In contrast, policies which seek to work with the grain of the market generally prove more successful, though by no means always so. In certain cases there are clear grounds for wishing to override the results of pure profitability criteria, most notably on grounds of greater regional equity, but elsewhere long-term 'negative' support appears unlikely to be justifiable.

On the third issue of responsiveness, there is clear recognition in virtually all European countries that while the market mechanism will generally indicate the required direction of change, market incentives may often fail to generate a sufficiently rapid response. The ratio of return to risk is frequently perceived to be more favourable for established products, familiar processes and technologies, and existing markets than for some of the dramatically new opportunities that have opened up in recent years. Countries have responded to this in different ways. West Germany has sought to encourage risk-taking through its support for R & D and encouragement of medium-sized business, France has sought to provide security for specific companies in key sectors, Belgium has attracted foreign multinationals better placed to generate finance for such activities; Italy has used its public sector. Some countries have been more successful than others, but all, including West Germany, have recognized that the strains currently imposed on the developed countries of the West are unlikely to be met without considerable government involvement.

28.4.3. Continuity of Policy

Of the factors that appear to be associated with successful implementation of industrial policy, the one that seems least well achieved in the UK is that of continuity. Indeed even the briefest summary of the history of industrial policy in the UK reveals major changes of course. In 1970 there was a move to disengagement, with emphasis on increased competition, more efficiency in public and private sector management, withdrawal of subsidies from loss-making companies, and increased rewards for individual enterprise.

Within two years, rising unemployment and the experience of two major rescues had brought home how difficult such a policy would be. The 1972 Industry Act not only developed regional policy and provided new investment incentives, but introduced selective elements in the tradition of the repealed 1968 Industrial Expansion Act.

Continuing lack of success in UK economic performance and dissatisfaction with the 'disengagement' approach led the Labour Party while in opposition in the early 1970s to develop a much more interventionist stance, including a public sector banking institution, planning contracts with individual companies, and much greater information disclosure, all backed by extensive powers, in addition to a major expansion of nationalization. However, when Labour returned to power, the resulting 1975 Industry Act was far more limited in scope than had been envisaged when the party was in opposition. Only one planning agreement was ever made in the private sector and information disclosure rules never took effect. The National Enterprise Board (NEB) did gain some acceptance but its funds were very much more limited than originally envisaged, its activities were dominated by the 'rescues' for which it had to take over responsibility, and the criteria laid down for it were much closer to standard commercial criteria than originally planned, raising doubts about whether it had a role distinct from private sector banks.

Thus by 1976–7 the new measures and institutions which had been the centre of so much attention had become tangential to industrial performance. For that longer term, two other types of development appear to have been more important. First, government expenditure in real terms was increasing significantly, this increase being heavily concentrated on employment measures, regional expenditure, and support for industrial comapnies in difficulty. Stock Relief also made a substantial difference to corporate cash flow under inflationary conditions. In addition a large number of selective support schemes were introduced, though the total expenditure involved on them was relatively small. Second, there was growing recognition in many quarters that the needs of industry had received too low a priority and that by some means this would have to be corrected, not least if other social aims were to be met.

The introduction and design of the Industrial Strategy and the Sector Working Parties created under the NEDC, through which it operated, reflected in part this increased concern with UK industry. It also reflected other strands of thinking—to avoid 'top-down' planning, to achieve some consensus between government, industry, and unions, and to obtain closer co-operation between the Civil Service and industry. In addition it embodied the view that all sectors had scope for improvement. It can be argued that although the Industrial Strategy might have complemented the rather grander designs that initially lay behind the 1975 Industry Act, in the event it filled a vacuum left as a result of the way in which the Act was eventually implemented.

The aims and institutional apparatus of the Industrial Strategy still remain, but as a coherent approach this initiative ended in 1979. A detailed assessment of the Industrial Strategy and indeed of the period of the late 1970s as a whole in the relations of government and industry has still to be written, though this issue is commented upon later. But it may be noted first that it coincided with very much increased external pressures on the UK and also restraint on public expenditure on industry. Second, it coincided with the growing recognition, already commented upon, that pressures for rapid adaptation were increasing and that 'positive' adjustment would be necessary if Europe was to continue to face the competitive pressures of the US, Japan, and the NICs.

As has been noted, the return to power in 1979 of the Conservatives marked the beginning of a new attempt to disengagement, marking the fifth major change of approach in nine years. Naturally some of these discontinuities were directly associated with changes of government. But, equally important, some were not, in particular those of 1972 and 1975–7. These appear to be associated more with the pressure of events, and with changes of Minister and of other individuals involved, the latter changes themselves being in part a reflection of changing perceptions about what was feasible and desirable. Between 1973 and 1983 there have been eight different Secretaries of State for Industry.

Underlying these changes there was, in practice, stability of a sort. Capital investment incentives, a strong regional policy, and a progressively stronger competition policy have all persisted through most of the last thirty years or so. Support for training and R & D and for several major companies in difficulty has been a feature of all governments. The basic stance of trade policy, including commitments to free trade, attitude towards membership of the EEC, export support, limited and selective protection, etc., has not varied significantly. The development of public purchasing and attitudes to standard-setting have been free of major changes of direction. The total expenditure by successive governments on industry in real terms has grown and, naturally, has varied, but has not fluctuated very heavily for many years. Changes in its composition, in particular the growth and decline of regional expenditure and the rise in employment support measures, have generally occurred only gradually over time. It should be added also that most of the major deviations from this pattern have tended to be in the first two years of a government, to have been short lived, and to have had little discernible effect on policy beyond that short period.

But this underlying continuity does not mean that there has been continuity in impact or effectiveness. While most people involved, both inside and outside government Departments, would attest to the underlying stability noted above, many of them, especially those associated with industry, and particularly industry outside the South-East, were also extremely conscious of the instability caused by the apparently major but unsustained changes of direction. Expressed intentions concerning major changes in industrial policy, the rhetoric associated with them, and the attempts to introduce them have been seen to generate considerable instability even where such change has not in the event either occurred or been sustained. This has been damaging to the effectiveness of policy. The very genuine prospect of major changes in the relationship of government to industry has, it appears, frequently created major uncertainties which not only render existing policy suspect but actually make the overall tasks of effective management more difficult.

To take but four examples: first, company decisions about research and development, training, and capital investment are all lengthy processes with consequences running forward many years. Support for all three has been fairly stable for most of the 1960s and 1970s. Yet there has been no point in the last twenty years when companies generally could feel any degree of assurance about industrial policy in any of these fields beyond a five-year time horizon. This partly reflects inevitable uncertainties about the course of economic events; it partly reflects the demands of the democratic process. But in retrospect there appears to be a major difference between the uncertainties that were perceived and the much greater continuity that eventually emerged.

Other, more specific, disadvantages follow. For example, an important part of the increasing association of those concerned in implementing industrial policies with the industries for which they have responsibility is the development of routine and regular contacts with industry. This activity on the part of sponsoring divisions can provide an important element of continuity at a detailed level. Department of Industry officials could take the initiative in seeking the views of industrialists, ensuring that the latter were aware of assistance available and attempting to assess the effectiveness of the measures taken. Some of this was weakened or ceased to happen when policies based more on disengagement were introduced. This was partly a direct result; partly it arose from uncertainty about the future of specific schemes and partly from general uncertainty about the continued acceptability of such contacts.

Another example is the impact on the take-up of various government support schemes when Planning Agreements and new information disclosure rules were first proposed and provision for them introduced in the 1975 Industry Act. The concern of some industrialists that acceptance of support would be linked to involvement in the new arrangements was a factor perceived by some as undermining the framework of industrial support measures at that time. In restrospect, as in many other cases, no change of significance occurred, but this was not relevant to the perception of those involved at the time.

To take another related example, applications for Section 7 assistance under the 1972 Act fell away substantially in 1979 before any change in the regulations and probably to a greater extent than can be explained by the subsequent tightening of the criteria. The onset of recession may well have been a factor (incidentally illustrating the destabilizing effect of the macroeconomy not just directly on industry, but indirectly as well via its effect on the take-up of industrial assistance) but it appears also to have reflected the much lower profile given to such assistance by the Department of Industry and the much lower preparedness of companies to take advantage of support measures once their future was made uncertain.

Discussion of numerous individual issues in the Economic Development Committees can easily experience a hiatus at times of apparent discontinuity. This is not solely or even generally because of the introduction of specific new guidelines or directives at such times. Rather, it simply becomes unclear whether it is worth devoting time and energy to particular avenues of activity. A coherent view, probably built up over a period, becomes uncertain or undermined until a new equilibrium is found perhaps eighteen months or two years later. This period of disruption may at first appear relatively unimportant. But typically a new initiative, for example funds to develop the more rapid application of a new technologically sophisticated product, or aid to assist the orderly run-down and rationalization of a declining sector, may well take up to three years from inception to implementation. In either type of case, therefore, effectiveness can easily be reduced substantially if such uncertainty persists, and this is very inefficient if that uncertainty is largely avoidable.

Such uncertainties can have wider consequences. For example, it is quite likely that in aerospace and shipbuilding continued uncertainty over questions of ownership had debilitating effects on the industry despite the building up of all the vital links between government and the industry in terms of public purchasing, support for research, design, and development, capital allowances, etc.

It is of course true that genuine and perhaps unavoidable discontinuities occur from time to time as events change; and shorter-term macroeconomic problems, such as defence of the exchange rate, the need to control inflation, etc., can vitiate any longer-term framework. It none the less appears that, overall, industrial policy has exhibited more stability than is immediately apparent. The problem has been the considerable uncertainty arising from the much greater fluctuations in what was planned and said rather than what was actually put into practice. This suggests that the explicit goals of industrial policy need to be set sufficiently modestly, sufficiently far from polar extremes, and with sufficient industrial consensus to operate continuously over decades rather than in two- or three-year stints.

28.5. Problems for Industrial Policy in the 1980s

In conclusion it is worth looking at some of the pressures which industry in the UK and the framers of industrial policy face in the 1980s. Perhaps the most significant is the very substantial shift in the structure of UK industry and of its exports and imports. Manufacturing has now shrunk to some 25 per cent of GDP, and in 1983, the UK's imports of manufactures exceeded its exports for the first time in peacetime. Services have expanded, and on the balance of payments side, strength has come from invisible earnings and non-manufactured visible trade, this being partly in food and drink but mainly of course in oil.

Part of the squeeze on manufacturing has resulted from a very high exchange rate which in turn partly reflects the development of North Sea oil. Production of the latter may well peak in 1985 but this is likely to be followed by only a very slow run-down, with the oil surplus disappearing sometime in the early 1990s. It is unlikely therefore that the 1980s will see any great resurgence of manufacturing, if at all, particularly given the recovery problems, described earlier, which many sectors of manufacturing face as a consequence of the period 1979–81, when manufacturing output fell by over 16 per cent.

This situation, in the context of long-term relative decline, and given the difficulty of trying to determine the policy implications of the run-down of North Sea oil, has had a bearing on the stance of industrial policy. Whatever policies are followed, few economists or politicians now expect that British industry will recapture that degree of widely diversified success in world markets which has been slipping away for the past century. By 1983, this belief has infected many policy makers and economists with a kind of weary resignation. A policy of disengagement has after all the merit of saving public money;[6] it cannot make matters much worse, and it may increase initiative by

---

[6] There may be high transitional costs to the taxpayer, however. For example, the privatization of a nationalized industry is an aspect of the shift to disengagement. Yet a heavy burden of irrecoverable debt may be shifted onto the taxpayer, to the benefit of the financial institutions, in the process of persuading them to take up the shares in the denationalized concern.

reducing job and profit security. The albatross of responsibility for industrial decline drops from the neck of the government of the day.

Against this, it has been argued that if a government were to try altogether to disengage, the rate at which manufacturing ran down would accelerate. The unemployment, regional dislocation, and loss of investment confidence that this might cause would force a government towards the *ad hoc* short-term protective measures which slow up both the development of new products and processes and the resource movements which are essential conditions of rising living standards. Britain is not alone in facing the dilemma that piecemeal protectionist lobbying (quotas, so-called 'basement' prices for competing imports, preferential public purchasing, and so on) may be easier for a government to resist when it has a 'hands-on' industrial policy.

At the same time there has been an increased initiative from international bodies like the European Commission and the OECD to formulate industrial policies which are not self-cancelling between countries and which may collectively enable national governments to reflate without running into sectoral supply constraints—like labour bottlenecks or a 'lock-in' to obsolete technology. Such policies can often be the antithesis of protection. They work, so to speak, 'with the grain of the market', intensifying and advancing market signals and quickening the response of labour and capital to these signals. Against this trend, however, there has been an infectious concern throughout the OECD about public sector deficits—swollen, as a ratio of GNP, by high unemployment. This has been a prime reason for the cutting-back of industrial policy spending in Britain, as elsewhere.

Against this background, the UK appears to face at least four major questions with regard to its industrial policy in the future. First, can sectors of industry be identified, on a sufficiently disaggregated basis, where trends in comparative advantage or our ability to *create* a comparative advantage can justify government support, in whatever form is best, to help those sectors succeed? Work by NEDO suggests [34] that such analysis should relate more to the product innovation and associated skills of a sector than to the capital or labour input or process innovation, but it remains to be seen whether this approach can be put into practice.

Second, can the consequences of the run-down in oil be anticipated and prepared for? It may be that as North Sea oil runs down the exchange rate will fall and that this will be sufficient to generate a new resurgence of manufactured goods exports, just as a rise in the exchange rate hit manufacturing very hard. But the impact of large rises and falls in the exchange rate are not necessarily symmetrical. While a large rise can and has very quickly reduced the UK's manufacturing base, a rapid expansion probably cannot be generated purely through a large fall in the exchange rate. Though often ignored in traditional textbook theory, a main determinant of successful industrial expansion is the past record of the companies concerned, as this determines (i) the profits available for innovation and expansion, (ii) the state of the balance sheet, upon which the ability to raise funds is heavily based, (iii) the amount of research and development, upon which future competitiveness heavily depends, and (iv) the extent to which companies have ensured a programme of products, each with a life cycle that is phased to fit with the rest of the programme and which together provide, at any one time, a balanced portfolio of new and established products, high-risk and low-risk ones, cash-generating and cash-absorbing ones. After what may be a decade of relative weakness, a lower exchange rate may be a necessary but far from sufficient condition for rapid expansion of manufacturing. In addition, the UK will be attempting to bring about a structural readjustment already achieved or in the process of being achieved by non-oil-backed industrialized countries.

There is little prospect that the private capital market can overcome this difficulty by providing long-term funds on a large scale to permit continuous development of UK manufacturing throughout the 1980s. Provision of such long-term high-risk funds is a very familiar example of market failure, as is most readily apparent in the high proportion of non-market finance for long-term research and development expenditure. This problem is therefore essentially one of industrial policy and almost uniquely one for the UK.

Third, can the UK cope with the problems of rapid technological advance? In some areas, the US and Japan (and occasionally West Germany) are now technological leaders and unlikely to be matched. The choice for the UK, and indeed for most of the rest of Europe, lies between licensing US or Japanese technology and becoming an assembler of products which embody it, or of uniting within Europe to form a third force in technological competition in the industrial West. The best choice will vary from product to product, but frequently there will not be a feasible option based purely on UK technological know-how. This is at first sight surprising given the UK's enviable performance in scientific research in many fields, but in part reflects concentration on pure and often 'big' science, such as radio astronomy and nuclear accelerators, at the expense of engineering research which is likely to have greater commercial spin-off.

But there are areas where the UK's innovative effort is still both important and excellent. Support for new technology and its application has also been growing fast. Between 1978 and 1982 alone a dozen schemes totalling one-third of a billion pounds were introduced in areas of information technology, micro-electronics applications, biotechnology, computer-aided design, film optics and opto-electronics, computer-controlled machinery, and others. The question still remains whether the UK can afford enough, given what others are also spending, and can concentrate its support enough, to enable the country to match and beat its competitors across a number of advanced, high value-added sectors, thereby increasing the UK's rate of growth.

Finally, as is clear from section 28.4.3, the UK has yet to find a way of generating some continuity of policy, without which the latter is unlikely to be effective. This is partly a question of avoiding naïve choices and fluctuations between unbridled faith in *laissez-faire*, usually presented as letting market forces work unhindered, and *dirigiste* planning and protectionism, often presented as giving industry a breathing space. But also it is a question of trying to find some more general consensus on the broad elements of industrial policy, where governments recognize the possibility that they may not last as long as companies' investment and planning horizons, and of trying to establish the institutional means for providing that continuity. Constitutionally the framework and institutions of industrial policy must remain entirely subservient to the will of Parliament, and the potential for extreme fluctuation in the latter may render all such attempts at stability impossible. But at least one objective of industrial policy in the UK in the rest of the 1980s should be to try to create the climate within which such fluctuations can be minimized.

Bibliography

SECTION A

Industrial policy is inextricably entwined with the general performance of the economy and with the impact, deliberate or otherwise, of other economic policies. Books and papers which none the less focus to some extent on industrial policy issues are:
[1] ADAMS, F. G. and KLEIN, L. R. (eds.). *Industrial Policies for Growth and Competitiveness* (Lexington, 1982).
[2] CARTER, Sir Charles (ed.). *Industrial Policy and Innovation* (Heinemann, 1981).
[3] CARTER, Sir Charles and PINDER, J. *Policies for a Constrained Economy* (PSI, 1982).
[4] GRANT, W. *The Political Economy of Industrial Policy* (Butterworth, 1982).
[5] MIDDLEMAS, K. *Industry, Unions and Governments* (NEDO/Macmillan, 1983).
[6] WOLF, M. *Adjustment Policies and Problems in Developed Countries* (Heinemann, 1981).
[7] DELL, E. *Political Responsibility and Industry* (George Allen and Unwin, 1973).
[8] NEDC, Industrial Policies in Europe', NEDC Council Paper (81) 51 (1981).
[9] NEDC, *Industrial Policy in the UK* (NEDC, 1982).
[10] OECD, *Positive Adjustment Policies* (Paris, 1982).
[11] STOUT, D. K. 'De-industrialisation and Industrial Policy' in Blackaby, F. (ed.) *De-industrialisation* (Heinemann, 1979).

SECTION B

Other works on aspects of the problems discussed in this chapter are as follows:
[12] ACARD. *R & D for Public Purchasing* (HMSO, Feb. 1980).
[13] BLACKABY, F. 'Narrative 1960–74', in Blackaby (ed.), *British Economic Policy 1960–74* (Cambridge University Press, 1978), pp. 11–76.
[14] BROWN, A. J. and BURROW, E. M. *Regional Economic Problems* (George Allen and Unwin, 1977).
[15] CAVES, R. E. and KRAUSE, L. *Britain's Economic Performance* (Brookings Institution, 1980).
[16] Committee on Industry and Trade, *Imports and Exports*, First Report, Session 1980–1, Vol. I (H.C. 109-I, 21 Jan. 1981).
[17] Committee on Industry and Trade, *Imports and Exports*, First Report, Session 1980–1, Vol. II (H.C. 109-II, 31 Jan. 1981).
[18] Committee of Public Accounts, Third Report, Session 1981–2 (H.C. 29, 17 Nov. 1981).
[19] Department of Economic Affairs. *The National Plan* (cmnd. 2764, HMSO, Sept. 1965).
[20] Department of Industry. 'Criteria for Assistance to Industry', App. A, (H.C. 619, 1976).
[21] DRIVER, C. 'Import Penetration and the Work of the Sector Working Parties', *Applied Economics* (Jan. 1983).
[22] FIELD, G. M. and HILLS, P. V. 'The Administration of Industrial Subsidies', in Whiting, A. (ed.), *The Administration of Industrial Subsidies* (HMSO, 1976).

[23] GANZ, G. *Government and Industry: The Provision of Financial Assistance to Industry and its Control* (Professional Books, Abingdon, 1977).

[24] GOLT, S. 'Government Organisation and Support for Private Industry: The United Kingdom Experience', in Warnecke, S. J. (ed.), *International Trade and Industrial Policies* (Macmillan, 1978), pp. 58–87.

[25] HANNAH, L. *The Rise of the Corporate Economy* (Methuen, 1976).

[26] Institute for Fiscal Studies. *Corporation Tax* (IFS, 1984).

[27] MATTHEWS, R. C. O., FEINSTEIN, C. H., and ODLING-SMEE, J. C. *British Economic Growth 1856–1973* (Stanford, 1982).

[28] MEADE, J. *Theory of Indicative Planning* (Manchester University Press, 1971).

[29] MORGAN, A. D. 'Commercial Policy', in Blackaby [13], pp. 515–63.

[30] MOTTERSHEAD, P. 'Industrial Policy', in Blackaby [13], pp. 418–83.

[31] NEDC. *Growth of the UK Economy to 1966* (HMSO, Feb. 1963).

[32] NEDC. *Education and Industry* (NEDC, 1982).

[33] NEDC. *Innovation in the UK* (NEDC, 1982).

[34] NEDC. *Trade Patterns and Industrial Change* (NEDC, 1984).

[35] NEDC. 'Nationalised Industries—Exports of Suppliers: Telecommunications Equipment' (NEDC (76) 81, Oct. 1976).

[36] NEDC. 'Public Purchasing', Memorandum by the Secretary of State for Industry, 26 June 1980 (NEDC (80)/44, Restricted).

[37] NEDC. 'The International Context of the UK', Memorandum by the Director-General (NEDC (83)/7, 1983).

[38] NEDO. *Growth of the Economy* (HMSO, 1984).

[39] Office of Fair Trading. *Anti-Competitive Practices: A Guide to the Provisions of the Competition Act 1980* (HMSO, 1980).

[40] PARR, M. 'The National Enterprise Board', *National Westminster Bank Review* (1979).

[41] Political and Economic Planning. *Economic Planning and Policies in Britain, France and Germany* (George Allen and Unwin, 1971).

[42] TURPIN, C. *Government Contracts* (Penguin Books, 1972).

[43] SHANKS, M. *Planning and Politics* (George Allen and Unwin, 1977).

[44] SMITH, T. 'Industrial Policies in Britain', in Hayward, J. and Watson, M. (eds.), *Planning, Politics and Public Policy* (Cambridge University Press, 1975), pp. 111–27.

[45] —— —— *The Politics of the Corporate Economy* (Martin Robertson, 1979).

[46] STOUT, D. K. 'Capacity Adjustment in a Slow-Growing Economy', in Beckerman, W. (ed.), *Slow Growth in Britain* (Oxford University Press, 1979).

[47] WALKER, G. and ALLEN, K. *Industrial Aids in Britain: 1981, A Businessman's Guide* (Centre for the Study of Public Policy, University of Strathclyde, Glasgow, 1981).

[48] WARNER, F. *Standards and Specifications in the Engineering Industries* (NEDO, 1977).

[49] WATSON, M. 'Conclusion: A Comparative Evaluation of Planning Practice in the Liberal Democratic State', in Hayward, J. and Watson, M. (eds.), *Planning, Politics and Public Policy* (Cambridge University Press, 1975).

[50] YOUNG, S. 'A Comparison of Industrial Experiences', in Hayward, J. and Watson, M. (eds.), *Planning, Politics and Public Policy* (Cambridge University Press, 1975), pp. 141–54.

[51] YOUNG, S. and LOWE, A. V. *Intervention in the Mixed Economy* (Croom Helm, 1974).

[52] *Public Purchasing and Industrial Efficiency* (Cmnd. 3291, HMSO, May 1967).

[53] *The Reorganisation of Central Government* (Cmnd. 4506, HMSO, Oct. 1970).

[54] *Investment Incentives* (Cmnd. 4516, HMSO, Oct. 1970).

[55] *A Framework for Government R & D* (CMND. 4814, HMSO, 1971).

[56] *Industrial and Regional Development* (Cmnd. 4942, HMSO, Mar. 1972).

[57] *A Framework for Government R & D* (Cmnd. 5046, HMSO, July 1972).

[58] *The Reorganisation of British Industry* (Cmnd. 5710, HMSO, Aug. 1974).

[59] *An Approach to Industrial Strategy* (Cmnd. 6315, HMSO, Nov. 1975).

[60] *The Challenge of North Sea Oil* (Cmnd. 7143, HMSO, Mar. 1978).

[61] *A Review of Monopolies and Mergers Policy* (Cmnd. 7198, HMSO, 1978).

[62] *A Review of Restrictive Trade Practices Policy* (Cmnd. 7512, HMSO, 1979).

[63] *Trade policy* (Cmnd. 8247, HMSO, May 1981).

PART VII
CONCLUSIONS

29

The UK in the 1980s: Theory, Policy, and Performance

D. J. MORRIS

29.1. The UK Economy in 1984

29.1.1. The International Setting

It is now conventional wisdom that the 1973 oil crisis marked a turning-point in the economic development of the West, and so it did. It is nonetheless worth recalling two points that have emerged from earlier chapters. First, several of the problems which have beset the Western world in the 1970s and 1980s were well in evidence before 1973 and were only exacerbated by the oil price shock. Most important of these was the rate of growth itself. Figure 29.1 shows a 5-year moving average of the growth of the OECD countries (North America, Japan, Western Europe, Australia, and New Zealand) and for the UK alone. Both follow the same pattern over time but with the UK growing on average some 2 per cent per annum slower, and while it is undoubtedly true that the average rate of growth has been much slower from 1973 to 1983 than in the twenty years preceding, it is also very clear that the average growth rate has been declining since the early 1960s.

This was not the only important change, however, to set in before 1973. Both inflation and unemployment moved to what were then record levels, simultaneously in the early 1970s, again before the 1973 oil crisis occurred. As far as inflation is concerned, greater synchronization of upswings and downswings of the major economies, itself a product of growing trade and financial integration in the 1960s led to greater pressure of demand on commodities in expansionary periods. Inherently, production of commodities is slow to respond to increased demand and certain commodities experienced some supply disruption, all contributing to a substantial inflation of non-oil commodity prices even before 1973. But growing acceleration of earnings inflation was also apparent in many countries, adding to an underlying rise in inflation (see Figure 29.2).

The causes of the rise in unemployment generally throughout the OECD in the early 1970s are less clear. In part the rise in 1971-2 was cyclical, with some recovery afterwards (see Figure 29.3, which shows the average levels of unemployment in successive cycles as well as figures for 1980 and 1982). But the

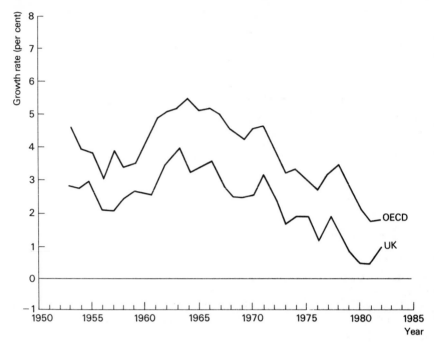

F IG . 29.1. OECD and UK Growth Rates, 5-Year Moving Averages.

Note: Each point gives the average growth for the 5 years for which the year shown is the middle year. Thus the collapse of growth in 1974 first affects the 1972 figures.

Source: OECD.

average level of unemployment never fell back to the levels of the late 1960s. Growing structural unemployment, arising from a growing mismatch, be it in terms of skills or regional location, may have been a factor, especially if the pace of structural change accelerated, but the other usually quoted reason—technological unemployment—has little support. As Figure 29.3 shows, the total level of employment in the OECD rose from 290 million in 1967 to almost 330 million by 1980, a rise of nearly 14 per cent during a period in which technological advance has generally been thought very rapid. Higher unemployment has arisen because even this growth of employment has failed to keep up with the growth of the number wanting to work. The latter has risen by over 50 million in the same period, due to demographic factors and the rising proportion of the population wanting to work, especially women. It must be added that the picture depends heavily on the US and Japan, which together represent over 50 per cent of the OECD. In Europe the labour force has grown much more slowly, employment more slowly still, and unemployment as a percentage has grown faster. If related to technology at all this seems to be a reflection of too slow rather than too fast a rate of technical progress.

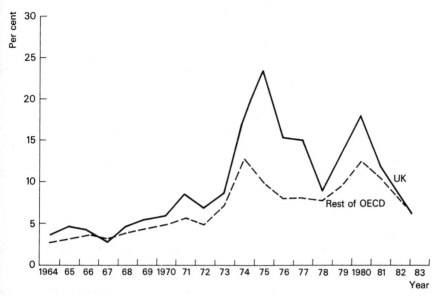

FIG. 29.2. Inflation Rates in the UK and the Rest of the OECD: (Annual average increases in consumer prices.)

Source: OECD.

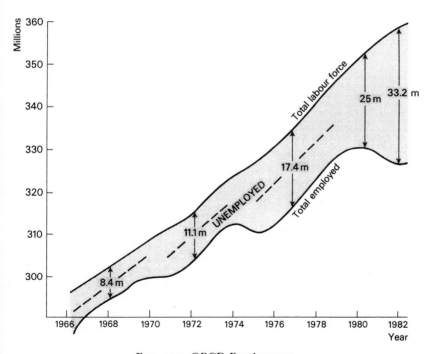

FIG. 29.3. OECD Employment.

The other important change that pre-dates 1973, even if the oil crisis years greatly exacerbated it, was the rise in the personal savings ratio (see Figure 29.4). The trend towards a higher ratio of personal savings out of income started to develop in the 1960s, and has been attributed both to growing unemployment and uncertainty on the one hand and to accelerating inflation on the other, though they are not of course incompatible explanations. While the former seems intuitively obvious—saving is after all to a considerable degree precautionary against an uncertain future and in particular the loss of earnings—the latter is less so. It relies on the type of behaviour described in Chapter 2, in which people save to some extent to be able to buy certain goods and services in the future, and to have financial assets sufficient to give them purchasing power over goods and services in the future. If inflation accelerates then current rates of saving will result in a falling real value of financial assets and a growing inability to attain the future purchase of, for example, a house, leading to an increase in people's personal savings ratios. Recent sharp falls in the savings ratio (see below) at a time of rapidly decelerating inflation have given further confirmation of this relationship, but this does not mean that the link from unemployment is irrelevant, even though the latter has remained high. For if the fear of unemployment triggers higher saving then it is when unemployment is *rising*, rather than its level, that matters. If it stabilizes at a high level then provided people still with jobs start to feel more reassured that their jobs are now safe, their savings ratios may well start to fall. Thus the end to sharp rises in unemployment may have been as important as the fall in inflation in determining the recent path of the savings ratio.

FIG. 29.4. Personal Savings Ratio, OECD, 1963–1982.

The second point to make about the 1973 oil crisis is that a purely mechanical calculation of the likely effect on GDP of a quadrupling of the price of oil, even if allowance is made for the associated rise in the price of competing fuels, does not generate the type of lower GDP figures which ensued. The latter can only be attributed to the oil price rise if allowance is made for three types of reactions: (i) the impact on savings, following the argument above, as still higher levels of inflation and further rises in unemployment drove the personal savings ratio to even higher levels and cut consumption; (ii) exacerbation of inflation as both individuals and companies tried to recoup their lost real income by pushing for higher pay and higher prices respectively; (iii) the reaction of the US, West German, and Japanese governments, all of whom to some extent tried to deflate their economies to fight such inflationary pressures, thereby adding to the recessionary forces arising directly from the oil price rise.

The main point emerging from this brief summary of the 1973 oil price shock is that it provides a list of the factors which went on to dominate the rest of the 1970s and became the setting for the 1980s. Throughout this period the OECD has had to grapple with a continued slowing of economic growth; continued high inflation and high unemployment, the former gradually coming under some control but the latter getting dramatically worse, partly as a result of the determination of a growing number of governments to tackle inflation even if this meant a more deflationary stance and more unemployment than otherwise; and the savings ratio being a key factor in translating higher inflation into stronger recession.

It is true that there was an attempt at some form of internationally co-ordinated but staggered expansion from 1977 onwards, generally referred to as the 'locomotive' approach (see Chapter 19), but only the US succeeded in surpassing even its average growth rate for the decade prior to 1973. In Japan, and particularly in West Germany, resistance grew to the idea of following the US lead, partly because it was at first felt that the West German economy would once again resume strong growth anyway and that little or no government expansion was required. But West Germany's previous success had been founded heavily on its higher export growth, itself a function of rapid world growth and an undervalued Deutschmark. After 1973, with West Germany being looked to as a 'locomotive' to generate fast world growth, and with a very much higher exchange rate, this was now not likely to be possible. Once this became clear there was considerable reticence about expanding government expenditure, or cutting taxes to promote consumer expenditure, because of the problem of financing a higher budget deficit, leading either to higher interest rates or to more inflation as a result of faster monetary growth, or some combination of these. Thus neither the locomotive nor later versions of the plan were in the end very successful, with the US unable to continue to act as a locomotive on its own and fears of inflation acting to inhibit others from following. What success there had been was finally shattered by the onset of the second oil price shock in 1979, which renewed all the pressures described above: still slower growth as a new synchronized recession set in, another resurgence of inflation, unemployment moving to its highest levels for fifty years, another sharp rise in the savings ratio, and renewed macroeconomic policy efforts to contain inflation. Mass unemployment increasingly came to be seen as either inevitable, as less important than defeating inflation, or as only soluble by, or in the context of, low inflation, which therefore had to be the prime objective of government economic policy.

29.1.2. Recession and Recovery in the UK, 1979–1984

The factors described above that have dominated the international economy have also been paramount in the UK, with slower growth than before, higher inflation and unemployment, similar effects to elsewhere on the savings ratio, and increasing pressure to use fiscal and monetary policy to control inflation, despite rising unemployment. Until 1978, a fair measure of success was achieved in tackling these problems: from the end of the 1973–5 recession until 1978, growth averaged 2·8 per cent per annum, exactly equal to the decade prior to 1973. Inflation, after being well above 20 per cent was brought down in three years to a low of 7 per cent, unemployment was held roughly constant. But the particular combination of monetary, fiscal, and incomes (Social Contract) policy that helped, against a background of cyclical upswing, to achieve this could not be held after 1978, with the so-called 'winter of discontent', involving a number of prolonged strikes, bringing both the strategy and the government of the day to an end.

The peaking of the business cycle in 1978 and the second oil price shock in 1979 saw the UK and the rest of the OECD starting to move into recession. Figure 29·5 shows growth in recent years, together with some indication of likely future growth, for both the UK and the rest of the OECD. This reveals, however, that the UK went into a much deeper recession, growth becoming negative in both 1980 and 1981. Also, the low point of the UK's growth rate occurred (in annual figures) two years earlier than that of the OECD.

There were two main reasons for the different profile of recession in the UK. First, inflation in the UK in 1979 and 1980 had surged well ahead of the OECD average, partly as a result of the growing strain on, and then collapse of, the Social Contract, and partly because the incoming Thatcher Government made the defeat of inflation its overriding priority in the management of its fiscal and monetary policy. While there remains disagreement about whether such a strategy helps or hinders growth in the medium to long term, there is virtually no disagreement that, in the circumstances pertaining in the UK in 1979–81, with a history of high inflation, the short-term effect of such a policy would be to depress GDP growth heavily.

Second, from 1978 the effective exchange rate of sterling started to climb heavily, anticipating the build-up of North Sea oil, and by 1980 had appreciated over 15 per cent despite unit labour costs in the UK having *risen* over 25 per cent in the same period relative to abroad, reflecting higher earnings inflation and lower productivity growth than elsewhere. The peak in the effective exchange rate, in 1981–2, occurred some three years before what is likely to be the peak rate of production of North Sea oil. As a result of these events, the balance of payments was in very large surplus in 1981 and 1982, but the competitiveness of non-oil products fell on average by around 40 per cent. This caused a very large decline in manufacturing, which is particularly

FIG. 29.5. Growth of GDP, UK and the Rest of the OECD, 1977–85.

Sources: OECD; Oxford Economic Forecasting.

dependent on exporting, thereby contributing to the severity of the recession. The impact on unemployment was still more severe because the labour content of the lost manufacturing output was very much higher than that of the North Sea oil production coming on-line, even allowing for the UK labour requirements of the inputs to North Sea oil production. By the end of 1982 unemployment had reached 3 million, from which level by 1984 it had changed little. (See Figure 29.6 for a comparison with the OECD.)

But just as Figure 29.5 shows that the UK went into more severe recession earlier, so it also reveals that the UK started to recover earlier. Although it was from a new low base level of GDP, brought about by two years of negative growth, the UK by 1982 was starting to recover at a time when OECD growth was around its lowest point. Even in 1983, with the OECD starting its own recovery, UK growth was still somewhat above the average for the rest of the OECD.

The causes of recovery in the UK are not difficult to identify. Over half of the rise in Total Final Expenditure (TFE) between the first quarter of 1982 and the first quarter of 1983 (ignoring stockbuilding) was due to a rise in private consumption. This resulted from a very substantial fall in the personal savings ratio (see Figure 29.7) as consumer price inflation came down from around 18 per cent to below 5 per cent. This direct contribution to growth arising from falling inflation was helped by the abolition of various restrictions on credit,

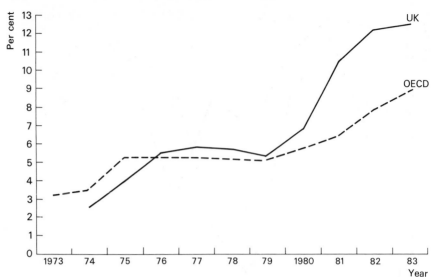

FIG. 29.6. Unemployment as a Percentage of Total Labour Force, UK and the Rest of the OECD (Annual Averages).

Sources: Department of Employment; OECD.

which further encouraged consumer spending. A further 20 per cent of the increase in TFE was due to public sector consumption spending, with almost all the rest due to public and private investment. Exports contributed only 3 per cent of the increase, but given the depressed state of the world economy at the time and the loss of UK competitiveness described above, this was unsurprising.

From the first quarter of 1983 to the first quarter of 1984, the profile of recovery changed. With the effects of the removal of credit restrictions wearing away, with the surge of new consumer-durable spending slowing, and with the savings ratio levelling out at historically very low levels, private consumer spending made a much smaller contribution then in the previous year to the growth of TFE, of just over one-quarter (28 per cent). Government attempts to control public sector current spending resulted in this exhibiting virtually no growth, and the momentum of recovery was taken up first by investment (38 per cent of the rise in TFE) as a result of growing demand, higher capacity utilization, and rising profitability, and second by exports (34 per cent of the rise in TFE).

This in part reflected the beginning of recovery elsewhere in the OECD, in particular in the United States, but also reflected an improvement in UK competitiveness. A sharp improvement in the rate of growth of productivity together with some easing of relative earnings inflation (both discussed below) brought some improvement in relative unit labour costs, which was further

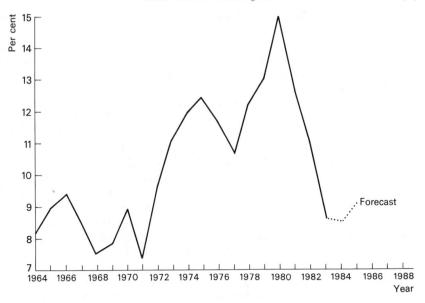

FIG. 29.7. UK Personal Savings Ratio, 1964–1985.
Source: Economic Trends; Oxford Economic Forecasting.

helped by some easing in the effective exchange rate, though most of this was
due to a strong rise in the dollar. The combination of these factors removed at
least half of the 40 per cent loss of competitiveness witnessed up to 1980–1, and
while this still leaves some considerable room for further improvement, it has
helped to generate more export growth than otherwise as world markets have
once again expanded.

None the less, the UK growth rate is likely to peak in 1984. In part, this
merely reflects the relative size of the consumption, investment and export
components in TFE. With public and private consumption accounting
for roughly two-thirds of TFE, investment for 12 per cent and exports for
22 per cent, a slackening of consumption growth would require in compensation extremely large rises in investment and exports if GDP growth were not
to slow. The prolonged miners' strike of 1984, unresolved at the time of writing,
is bound now to have some effect on GDP in 1984, though this may be
compensated for after the strike is over. But underlying all this there is a more
fundamental question, namely, why should it not be possible for economic
growth in the UK to continue at its 1983 rate of 3 per cent, or even higher,
given that there still remain over 3 million unemployed, all the growth of the
1981–4 upswing having been matched by a combination of increases in labour
productivity and in the size of the labour force. To tackle this, it is necessary to
pull together various strands of analysis from earlier chapters.

29.2. Government Economic Policy

29.2.1. Money and Inflation

Economic policy since 1979 has been based on a number of underlying beliefs about how the UK economy works, all of which have been discussed during the preceding chapters. It is none the less worth pulling them together as a summary description of policy in the 1980s. Prime amongst these is the relationship between the money supply and inflation. It has been seen in Chapters 5 and 10 that Friedman and others sought to establish, both theoretically and empirically, that inflation would, with a time-lag, follow the course of monetary growth. In terms of the identify $MV = PY$ (where M is the stock of money, V its velocity of circulation, P the price level, and Y real output) this implies a stable value of V over the medium to long term and a tendency for real output, Y, to move to a level determined by real supply and demand factors independent of the money supply. Part of the rationale for the monetary targets now emphasized by the government (though not the only rationale, see below) is that they can help to control inflation, especially if they are progressively reduced over time.

Clearly, a vital part of this argument is the belief that real output is, in the long run, independent of monetary policy. The main theoretical support for this lies in the expectations-augmented Phillips curve analysis (see p. 226 *et seq.*) which leads to the view that there is a natural rate of unemployment, or at least a 'non-accelerating inflation rate of unemployment' (NAIRU), which generates, and alone generates consistency of actual inflation with expected inflation. The NAIRU, it is argued, may vary slowly over time in the light of structural factors in the labour market, for example skills, sectoral composition, incentives to work or not to work as a result of the tax and benefit system, etc., but at any one broad period of time, no other rate of unemployment can prevail indefinitely. The level of real output that emerges in the long term is then a function of the natural rate or NAIRU, together with the trend level of productivity. An active demand expansion by government can at best make only a short-term change in this level of output and employment, with the longer-term consequences, once employment has returned to its natural level, being entirely one of higher inflation.

29.2.2. Crowding-Out

Such a picture automatically implies that any expansionary effect of government reflation will be fully crowded out, in the sense that there will eventually be an equal and offsetting fall in expenditure elsewhere in the economy. But it is nonetheless worth highlighting the mechanisms by which crowding-out is presumed to occur. If a higher budget deficit is financed by borrowing then this, it is argued, will lead to higher interest rates, which will reduce both private sector investment and some consumer spending financed by credit. Higher interest rates will also push up the exchange rate, hitting exports. Overall, if the money supply is unchanged and the velocity of circulation is in the long term stable, and if inflation will not actually slow under such circumstances, then it follows from the basic identity $MV = PY$ that real output cannot in the long run be higher than it would otherwise have been.

If a higher budget deficit is financed through faster monetary expansion then on the basis of the argument rehearsed in the previous section, inflation will accelerate. This will hit spending via the rise in the savings ratio it generates or via the reduction in the real value of financial assets it causes, the former effect to some extent reflecting the need to restore the real value of such assets. There could none the less be some net expansionary effect were it not for the argument, noted above, that in the long term real output is independent of monetary growth, the full effect of the latter being reflected in inflation. To the extent that an immediate effect of faster expansion of the money supply is to lower the exchange rate, directly or via lower interest rates, the effect on import prices and thence on general inflation comes through all the quicker and more forcibly.

29.2.3. Expectations

On this basis, the central elements of policy have become the establishment of a series of monetary growth targets, which it is hoped can be progressively reduced over time as inflation falls, coupled with a stable Medium-Term Financial Strategy which sets out a series of annual target figures for the Public Sector Borrowing Requirement (PSBR). These are designed to be consistent with monetary growth in that, taking the two together, the part of the PSBR not financed by the target monetary expansion necessary to match real growth can be met through borrowing from the private sector (or abroad) at acceptable levels of interest rates. Without consistency between monetary and fiscal policy, defined in this way, it is doubted whether the policies could remain credible.

In this process of policy formation, expectations play a central role. If it is believed (rightly or wrongly as it happens) that faster monetary growth will shortly lead to more inflation, or that a PSBR exceeding the target will lead to excessive monetary growth and the same inflationary result, then any such failure to meet these targets will quickly lead people to act in certain ways which *will* generate more inflation. Expectations that the exchange rate will fall as a result of excessive monetary growth will lead to sales of Sterling and pressure on the exchange rate. Fears of greater inflation will lead people to price higher or to demand higher wage increases in anticipation. Thus *failure* to meet targets, chosen to inhibit inflation, may very quickly generate inflation, so that meeting and maintaining the strategy is crucial. Similarly, if a government overshoots its PSBR target when committed to monetary targets then this will immediately raise the spectre of higher interest rates as a result of the government needing to sell more gilts. This will lead to sales of gilts, generating a rise in interest rates. Thus crowding-out effects may start to develop very quickly if a government is seen to be exceeding its PSBR target.

Expectations therefore have two main effects. First, they tend to make the consequences of faster monetary growth or a higher PSBR more immediate, and in some cases, primarily in financial markets, almost instantaneous.

Second, they box a government in, making it essential that declared targets be met and exacerbating the costs of failure to meet them.

29.2.4. *The Supply Side*

If monetary and fiscal stance is set in the way described and full employment (or the natural rate of unemployment) does not result it must then be asked what, if anything, adjusts to bring it about. It is here that another main strand of government economic policy comes in, namely the working of the supply side of the economy. Monetary and fiscal policy is geared to achieve a target rate of growth of nominal expenditure $(P \times Y)$. This sets a stable demand framework which is *consistent* with non-inflationary growth (i.e. growth of M sufficient to permit maximum sustainable growth of Y with minimum inflation). The extent to which this is attained, as opposed to higher inflation and slower growth, depends on the strength of the essentially supply-side forces which determine both the feasible rate of growth of real output and the speed with which actual output converges on that rate.

These supply-side factors are of three broad types. First, there is the general efficiency of the management of production and sales and the management of change, including fast structural adjustment and rapid utilization of technological change; second, the structure and pattern of incentives—rewards and penalties—attached to success and failure of effort, ingenuity and risk-taking; third, the flexibility of the labour market, both in terms of readiness to accept changes in work and working procedures within a plant, between companies, and between skills and sectors of the economy, and in terms of remuneration being closely related to the productivity of the employees concerned.

These three are of course heavily intertwined. Moreover all three, but particularly the third, are closely linked to people's expectations again about the economy and economic policy. If competition and flexibility are encouraged, and this is seen to be happening against a background of stable and consistent monetary and fiscal policy, then, it is argued, both the need for labour market flexibility and the benefits in terms of full employment can be seen more clearly and adjustment will occur more quickly. Such change may take a considerable time, especially after many years in which it was *not* necessarily very rational to adjust at some cost in such ways. This was because the emergence of significant unemployment would, it was confidently expected, lead to government action to remove it. In other words it is argued that a commitment by government at the macroeconomic level to maintain full employment led to expectations amongst the labour force which increasingly impeded the microeconomic flexibility necessary to make full employment with low or zero inflation achievable. Supply-side improvement can be fostered by government action through increasing competition in product markets, reducing rigidities in the labour market, and increasing incentives generally, mainly through lower marginal rates of income tax, but productivity depends on employers and employees improving efficiency, seeking out new opportunities for higher earnings or profits, and responding to these market signals.

Within the overall policy the supply side is crucial because it alone can guarantee maximum growth and full employment. This is seen most clearly if it is asked what can be done if the supply side fails to respond. Macroeconomic management cannot be a substitute since, it is argued, the effect of expansionary fiscal policy is crowded out and the ultimate effect of expansionary monetary policy is merely higher inflation. Thus overall it is the role of monetary and fiscal policy to control inflation and provide a macroeconomic environment in which non-inflationary growth and full employment are *possible*. It is the role of an efficiently operating microeconomic supply side to generate these within that framework.

29.2.5. Modelling Economic Policy

Chapter 14 looked at how the economic behaviour of the UK has in recent years been modelled. The approach to economic policy described above has important implications for modelling, whether this is designed to be a basis for forecasting or for simulation work. First, and most straightforward, current policy is based on the view that certain important economic relationships were either represented only weakly or not represented at all in pre-existing macroeconomic models. Increasingly therefore in the Treasury model, but also in other major UK models, linkages such as those between public borrowing and interest rates, between interest rates and the exchange rate, and between supply and demand in the labour market and pay have been re-examined, re-estimated, and improved. In general these changes have tended to increase the amount of crowding-out in the models and confirm that more crowding-out occurs than was previously predicted by some of the models.

Second, current economic policy has focused attention on three weaknesses of most macroeconomic models. The most intractable of these is that until very recently all such models have been essentially demand-based models in the sense that they primarily sought to model and predict components of expenditure, it being presumed that output responded as necessary and that demand therefore determined the degree of capacity utilization in the economy. Supply-side linkages, for example between marginal tax rates and effort, between competitive pressures and productivity, and between the legislative framework of industrial relations and earnings settlements, to name but three, were either impossible to incorporate or at best only able to be fed into the models in a rather crude and arbitrary way, for example by changing the time-trend of productivity growth. It has therefore become increasingly difficult either to criticize or to justify policy by reference to such models, even though they are the only tools of analysis which attempt to incorporate simultaneously the main economic relationships in the economy. This situation should improve as economists attempt to build essentially supply-side-based models, but this is still at a very early stage.

Almost as difficult is the problem of the time-scale of current macroeconomic models. Most are specifically designed to give reasonable forecasts over two to four years, and become increasingly less reliable after that. But much of the economic behaviour on which policy is currently based is explicitly recognized to be longer term than that. While crowding-out and inflationary effects of policy generally operate within such a time-scale, any tendency towards the natural rate of unemployment may, depending amongst other things on people's expectations, take considerably longer. More generally, effective working of the supply side of the economy make take longer, especially if it is believed that for many years it has failed, or has not been encouraged, to operate effectively.

The other big weakness of macroeconomic models generally in this context is their inability to cope fully with expectations. At one level this is a problem of trying to anticipate when market sentiments will change and how soon expectations of certain events will precipitate action, frequently of a self-justifying nature. At another level there is a more difficult problem, namely, that if a model predicts behaviour well then the existence of the model gives people more information about the future, which in turn may alter their behaviour, or at least speed up their reactions, thereby invalidating the model. In some cases this may not be important, or can be allowed for judgementally by the modeller; but in other cases, particularly in relation to the effect in financial markets of the success or failure of government in achieving stated aims, the effects may be of considerable size.

At still another level, models, if accurate, reflect the impact of expectations on behaviour even if they do not model expectations explicitly. If part of the purpose of economic policy is to *change* how people think about the economy, how they form expectations, and, therefore, how they respond to economic events, then policy is specifically trying to change at least some of the factors on which existing behaviour and therefore existing models depend. It may not therefore be very useful to try to assess such policy in the light of the economic performance to which the model predicts it will lead. To take an obvious example, it may be *because* models predict that a tight monetary policy coupled with high earnings inflation will lead to high unemployment that there is reason to expect earnings inflation to abate, in a manner not seen before, if previously it was expected that high unemployment would lead to a relaxing of the monetary policy stance. Whether the reasoning is true or false, assessment based on a conventional macroeconomic model will not provide an answer.

None of this invalidates the use of models for providing some guide to future economic developments, at least for several years ahead, and to the likely consequences of various changes in economic conditions or policy. But it currently does make it very difficult or impossible to examine, in a manner which allows for ramifications throughout the economy, the soundness or otherwise of the basic stance and framework of current policy. To some extent it becomes an inevitable act of faith that the thrust of the policy is correct, depending on observation of broad historical trends in the UK, specific examples of how managers, employees, investors, and consumers have behaved in the past, and personal judgement of how matters may be improved. Clearly this problem eases as more experience is gained of the implementation and impact of current policy, but even here there is considerable room for interpretation. In particular, if a high level of unemployment persists, is this because the natural rate has become very high for structural reasons, is it that the supply side in general and the labour market in particular are failing to respond to disequilibrium fast enough, leaving unemployment well above the natural rate for a long period of time, or is it that this whole way of looking at the economy is incorrect? This and other such problems are reviewed in section 29.3, but it must be noted that effective modelling of the economy depends on finding an answer to such questions rather than the other way round. Progress in understanding the economy may still be made both by analysing individual economic relationships further and by looking at their interaction in the context of macroeconomic models, but if policy is to any significant extent geared to changing behaviour then the policy inferences drawn may remain unaffected.

29.2.6. Progress to 1984

The economic situation which confronted the new economic policy in 1979 was a very difficult one. The period 1979–81 saw a new round of large oil price increases, from below $13 per barrel to over $30, and a world recession developing. The inflationary impact of the oil price rise was exacerbated in the UK by a sharp acceleration of earnings in both the public and the private sector, some of it dependent on the build-up of pressure for larger pay rises which had developed previously during the period of the Social Contract. In addition the objectives of keeping both interest rates and growth of the money supply low, simultaneously with reductions in taxation, could only be reconciled in the short term by very large cuts in public expenditure at a time when recession was pushing up the unemployment-related and social security components of public expenditure. In the event, therefore, in this initial period virtually none of the government's objectives nor even the targets for its instruments of policy were met. Monetary growth targets and the PSBR overshot, interest rates went to record levels, government expenditure and the burden of taxation both rose rather than fell, consumer price inflation rose from around 8 to 18 per cent, and growth of the UK economy went sharply negative. Unemployment doubled to $2\frac{1}{2}$ million. Only the balance of payments was not a cause for concern as recession and the build-up of North Sea oil moved the current account from a small deficit in 1979 into large surplus by 1981. Even here the associated rise in the value of sterling hit non-oil exporting industries very hard, with manufacturing output down by nearly 18 per cent, back to the levels of the mid-1960s.

Between 1981 and 1984 this position in most respects improved substantially. Increasingly the PSBR was brought into line with a revised Medium-Term Financial Strategy, albeit at higher levels of both government expenditure and taxation than originally planned. Monetary growth was brought into line with targets and eventually interest rates were also reduced, though a high level of world interest rates prevented this going as far as was hoped. (In fact there was some success in 1983–4 in 'decoupling' UK interest rates from high US rates, but this was brought to a sudden halt by a sharp rise in UK rates in July 1984.) There was also much more success on most of the main macroeconomic objectives of policy. The annual rate of inflation was brought down to around 5 per cent, having touched a low of 3.7 per cent. This was helped by falling commodity prices and could not have been sustained if Sterling had fallen substantially, but was none the less heavily dependent on a large fall in earnings inflation, down by over a half to around 8 per cent, and, from the second quarter of 1981, on a substantial increase in labour productivity in manufacturing.

Figure 29.8 shows the path of manufacturing output, employment, and productivity since the mid-1960s. As can be seen, each time manufacturing output has fallen, in 1967, 1971, 1975, and 1980–1, the line representing output

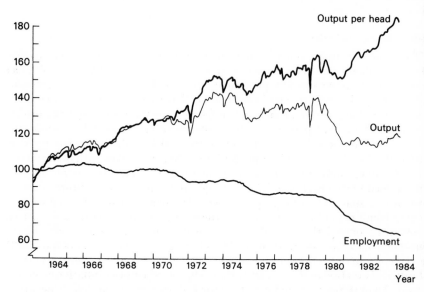

F IG . 29.8. Manufacuring Productivity in the UK (1963 = 100.)

Source: CSO.

per head has risen relative to the line representing output. This implies a 'shake-out' of labour as a result of each recession sufficient to give a 'one-off' rise in productivity, and this effect can be seen in the employment line, which takes a step down in each of these years. At other times productivity tends to follow output rather closely, with employment remaining relatively unchanged.

The path of manufacturing productivity was therefore not unusual during 1981–2. The 'shake-out' effect was stronger but this just reflected that the fall in output, and the associated financial pressures, were stronger. (Also, part of the rise in productivity in this period was no more than a recovery of the sharp fall in productivity in 1980–1.) But since the beginning of 1983 it has become clear that there are differences this time. As manufacturing output has started to recover somewhat, rapid productivity gains have continued, resulting in an average growth per annum in excess of 6 per cent from the second quarter of

1981 to the first quarter of 1984. This figure has only previously been attained on a sustained basis in the strong upswing of 1972–3.

Part of these gains no doubt comes from the large-scale closure of least-efficient plants, the productivity improvement associated with surviving plants being somewhat lower. It may also be that there are limits to how fast productivity improvements can be made in response to falls in output, so that a particularly severe recession will lead to productivity improvements spread over a longer time. But the figures are also consistent with a gradual improvement in supply-side efficiency as employers and employees, no doubt concerned by the possibility of bankruptcy and unemployment, but also recognizing a new determination by government to let markets work to the benefit of the efficient and the detriment of the inefficient, improve their methods of working and the flexibility with which they respond to new pressures and new opportunities. One of the major tests of the new policy, particularly given the importance of the supply side, will be whether this type of faster productivity growth can be sustained.

The rise in productivity growth and fall in inflation were not only objectives in their own right. As we have seen, the fall in inflation, via its effect on savings behaviour, led to a consumer-led expansion which has contributed to GDP growth of over 2 per cent in 1982 and over 3 per cent in 1983. This is not particularly fast given that it represents an upswing phase of the business cycle, and has been insufficient to stop unemployment rising, but it does give some indication of the extent to which the UK economy can recover largely without assistance from fiscal expansion. (Not entirely, however, because there is likely to have been some stimulus in 1983 not apparent in the overall PSBR figure because of some sales of public assets under the privatization programme, which are shown as negative expenditure.)

The major objective which remains unfulfilled is a reduction in unemployment. An overriding commitment to full employment, such as was seen in the 1950s and 1960s, no longer exists, and it is now far from clear what level of measured unemployment would now represent 'full' employment. But with the figure having been around 3 million for two years and still edging up despite growth of GDP at what is likely to be the fastest rate it will record between 1980 and 1986, and with over 1 million now unemployed for over a year, it is more serious than at any time for nearly fifty years. In part this is a European-wide problem but, as Figure 29.6 reveals, it is more acute in the UK. This has been attributed on the one hand to the failure of the labour market in general and of wage bargaining in particular to respond in a flexible enough fashion, and on the other to the failure of government economic policy to promote faster expansion and hence more employment. At a broader level it may be argued that there are inherent weaknesses in the UK economy which can manifest themselves in inflation, balance of payments deficits, low productivity, high unemployment, or some combination of these, depending on circumstances and policy. This raises the question of whether such weaknesses are disappearing, or whether it is just that all of the burden of them is at present falling on unemployment rather than on the other symptoms which have borne the brunt in earlier years.

29.3. Problems of Policy

29.3.1. The Labour Market

There is a clear sense in which the major problem facing policy is that of
unemployment. Unless dramatic changes occur in the UK economy quickly
the 1980s will, like the 1930s, be seen in retrospect as a decade of mass
unemployment in the UK. But the policy stance, as we have seen, is one in
which unemployment cannot be affected much by policy, and will depend on
the working or non-working of the labour market. This issue can be examined
by recalling the expectations-augmented Phillips curve analysis of Chapter 7,
reproduced diagrammatically in Figure 29.9. This shows illustrative curves for
inflation expectations (E) equal to 5, 9, 14, and 20 per cent, and a non-
accelerating inflation rate of unemployment of 8 per cent. The dotted line to
the left of the NAIRU shows in stylized fashion what may happen if a
government, faced with 5 per cent inflation and 8 per cent unemployment,
tries to reduce the latter. Initially a faster rate of price increases, with pay in
relation to productivity still reflecting expected inflation of 5 per cent, creates
higher profit margins and scope for higher employment. But as expectations
catch up with higher inflation, so pay rises accelerate and the rationale from the
employer's point of view for the higher level of employment disappears.
Repeated attempts to reduce unemployment below the NAIRU result purely
in ever-higher inflation.

   The policy implication is often taken to be that the reverse behaviour can
bring inflation down, with unemployment eventually converging once again
on the NAIRU figure. During the process unemployment is higher than this,
but as expectations adjust to lower inflation so the pressure on profit margins

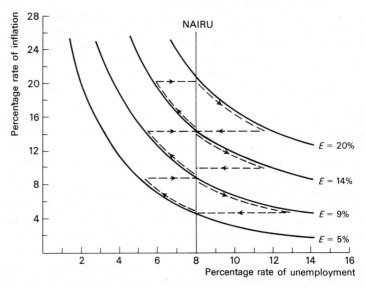

FIG. 29.9. Implications of Expectations-Augmented Phillips Curves.

which generates higher unemployment abates. In the long term the only effect of a macroeconomic policy stance which is tight at 20 per cent inflation is to reduce inflation.

But if Phillips curves are the shape shown, i.e. convex to the origin of the graph (see below for possible reasons for this), then the response is not symmetrical. While attempts to reduce unemployment below the NAIRU run into ever-more sharply rising inflation, an effect which is ever-more severe at high levels of inflation, increases in unemployment have progressively *weaker* effects on inflation and this effect itself becomes progressively weaker the lower is inflation. Thus, as shown, a rise in unemployment to 12 per cent may be sufficient to bring inflation down from 20 to 14 per cent, but insufficient to reduce it from 14 to 9 per cent. Illustrating the same point the other way round, unemployment of 13 per cent may be necessary to reduce inflation from 9 to 5 per cent, even though a fall in unemployment from only 8 to 5 per cent was sufficient to cause the equivalent rise in inflation. At the 13 per cent level of unemployment, the difference between actual and expected inflation is only 4 per cent, suggesting that despite very high unemployment, the forces acting to reduce it are very weak. This is consistent with the situation in the UK in 1984.

Why might Phillips curves be the shape portrayed? (They cannot of course be plotted empirically because *observed* inflation/unemployment points will lie on a series of individually unobservable lines as expectations change.) It might simply be that for any given level of inflation expectations a given reduction of unemployment will generate more inflation the nearer the economy is to full employment. This could generate the sequence of events described above, except that there would be no reason to assume a stronger effect at higher levels of actual inflation. If it is added, however, that the readiness of companies to put up prices as capacity utilization increases, for a given level of inflation expectations, may well be greater the higher is the level of inflation, then this could generate the relationship depicted.

But an alternative explanation is that the whole picture is misrepresented. In an atomistic labour market, where any unemployed person could offer to replace someone currently employed, but at a lower wage, and was taken on to replace the existing employee as a result, then the existence of a large number of unemployed would tend to bring down wage inflation and perhaps even the absolute level of nominal wages. The same result would occur if the existing employee held on to his job but only by accepting a wage cut to a level where the unemployed person could profitably be taken on as well. In practice such situations are rare and confined to a small number of very informal parts of the labour market. Typically, wages are negotiated more collectively than this, reflecting not only trade union organization but the workings of the internal labour market (see Chapter 4) and widespread notions that people doing the same job, at least in a large number of occupations, should get the same pay. As a result wage settlements are generally settled in the light of supply and demand conditions within a company or plant and without direct reference to the existence of unemployed people who would be prepared to work for less. It is of course true that *rising* unemployment will tend to inhibit wage increases because they may lead to redundancies amongst those currently working, and *falling* unemployment will lead to higher increases as it is perceived by both employers and employees that more labour is required.

This is for the most part consistent with the path of inflation as shown by the dotted lines in Figure 29.9, and with recent UK experience. But if unemployment *stabilizes* at a high figure then neither of these effects is likely to continue. Earnings and price inflation may then occur at a significant if unchanging rate because the risk of redundancy to those still employed is very much less. The high level of unemployment will no doubt still have some pervasive effect and this will prevent a strong resurgence of earnings inflation. But there appears no reason to believe that the high *level* of unemployment will necessarily bring earnings inflation down much further—and it may not do so for years if unemployment is not rising significantly—given that companies can pass on these increases in prices, after allowing for productivity growth.

This does not mean that the problem of inconsistency between actual and expected inflation disappears. Rather it means, in terms of Figure 29.9 and the approach that it encapsulates, that the NAIRU *becomes* the new higher level of unemployment (in the figure, 13 per cent), with expectations consistent at this new level. This is shown in Figure 29.10.

There are three strong reasons for believing that this is effectively what has happened. First, the NAIRU is by definition the rate of unemployment at which inflation does not accelerate (or decelerate). UK inflation, having decelerated sharply, now appears to have stabilized. After a low of 3.7 per cent, it has risen to nearly 5 per cent, and there is little expectation that it will fall significantly from that figure. This is occurring at an unemployment rate of nearly 13 per cent, and there is therefore little reason to believe that the

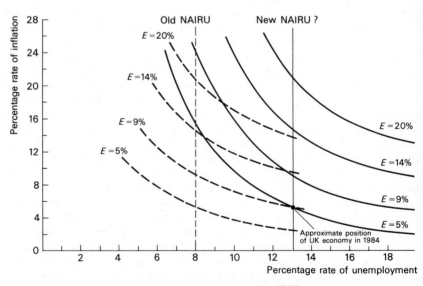

FIG. 29.10. A Shift in the NAIRU.

NAIRU is substantially below this, even though non-accelerating inflation was achieved at a little over one-third of this figure in 1977.

Second, if the basic expectations-augmented Phillips curve analysis is correct, and even if the inherent problem at high unemployment described by Figure 29.9 is correct, then it would be possible to imagine a major expansion of the economy, driving unemployment down towards a NAIRU substantially below present unemployment levels with very little if any effect on inflation. But econometric evidence embodied in various macroeconomic models indicates that the improvement in company financial positions and the *fall* in unemployment that this would generate would set off a new round of inflation. This is consistent with Figure 29.10, but not with Figure 29.9.

This immediately draws attention to the third point, namely, that although earnings inflation fell sharply in 1981–2 as unemployment rose sharply, it has remained virtually constant since then at around $7\frac{3}{4}$ per cent, despite a continuing very high level of unemployment. Again, this is consistent with Figure 29.10, but not with Figure 29.9.

If these arguments are correct then current policy will either result in many years of mass unemployment to achieve its aims, or will fail altogether. While there is an aggregative sense in which the rate of growth of earnings as a whole prices a proportion of the labour force out of work, this is to only a very limited extent true for any given group of employees if unemployment is not rising significantly. Paradoxically, this might be addressed either within a heavily centralized wage-bargaining process covering the whole of the labour force, or within a heavily atomistic labour market as described on p. 915. But neither condition exists in the UK, nor do recent changes in wage-bargaining practices or industrial relations legislation make a significant difference to this even though there are some signs of more decentralized, e.g. plant-based, bargaining.

This does not mean that inflation cannot be brought down further within present policy. If the present cycle peaks, leading to slower growth and to unemployment rising significantly once again, then this will probably reduce inflation. But the underlying problem of reconciling low inflation with low unemployment will be no nearer to being achieved, and a new NAIRU may well thus be established at a still higher level, making such reconciliation still more difficult.

29.3.2. *The Medium-Term Financial Strategy*

A more specific policy problem concerns the Medium-Term Financial Strategy (MTFS). One of the rationales for such a strategy is that by setting out a series of year-by-year targets for government expenditure and taxation, coupled with consistent monetary targets, the impact of shocks to the economic system is reduced. This is certainly true of price shocks. If energy prices were to rise sharply, for example, as a result of a major new conflict in the Persian Gulf, or if earnings inflation rose significantly, then the lack of accommodation of the MTFS to those changes creates a deflationary stance that helps to reduce the inflationary consequences. The more severe the shock the greater the dampening effect.

The same, however, is not necessarily true of an output shock. If GDP were depressed in the UK by a world recession, for example, as the result of an international banking crisis arising out of the current debt problem, then this would tend to increase government expenditure, reduce taxation, and therefore push the PSBR over target. If in order to get back into the MTFS, taxation was raised and/or government expenditure reduced, this would tend to exacerbate the recession. In a world where the supply side responds and unemployment tends back to the NAIRU, this need be no more than a temporary problem. But it the supply-side response is inadequate, and if, as we have seen, there may be no strong tendency for unemployment to revert to a lower level, then the effect of adhering to the MTFS in such circumstances is to worsen the economic position.

As was seen in Chapter 12, this can in principle be handled by targeting the *structural* budget deficit which excludes that part which is caused by fluctuations in demand and employment. The latter part could be allowed to increase in the event of a deflationary output shock, increasing the total deficit but without affecting the structural deficit. But the MTFS makes no such distinction and foresees a relationship of PSBR to GDP over time that is independent of such events. Worse still, the reactions of financial markets to an overshoot may be such that the government could not allow for such events even if it wished to, except at the cost of very much higher interest rates, with the crowding-out which that implies.

This might be thought a problem only in the event of a deflationary output shock, but the same point holds if growth for *any* reason is lower than the $2\frac{1}{4}$ per cent per annum envisaged in the MTFS. If, for example, the economy were to turn down significantly after the next business cycle peak, perhaps giving, as an illustration, growth figures of 2 per cent for 1985 and $1\frac{1}{2}$ per cent for 1986, then it is likely that the budget deficit would start to expand. If the reaction to this is to tighten the stance of policy in order to meet the MTFS then this will accentuate the recession. By the same token, growth at a rate faster than $2\frac{1}{4}$ per cent per annum would reduce the PSBR, allowing room for tax cuts over and above any envisaged in the MTFS, and generate still faster growth. There is therefore a sense in which the MTFS is inherently stabilizing in response to a price shock but inherently *destabilizing* in response to output variations. Within limits this can be handled in practice through varying assets sales and through the use of the contingency element of each year's budget, but beyond this the MTFS would run the risk of losing credibility, with the attendant dangers noted earlier.

29.3.3. *Unemployment*

Given the problems of the workings of the labour market and of the potentially exacerbating effects on unemployment of the MTFS in any downswing, it must be asked whether there is any likelihood of reducing unemployment significantly during the mid-1980s within the policy. The National Economic Development Office has tried to make some estimates of the scale of extra employment that could be generated by various performance changes in the economy, within the macroeconomic strategy. Further improvements in productivity by reducing unit labour costs will improve competitiveness, which in turn can generate increases in exports, thereby generating more employment in export industries and, indeed, more widely as lower inflation makes the impact of the MTFS more expansionary. But the scale of job losses necessary to generate the initial productivity improvement against the background of current output levels would generally be greater than the jobs created, at least for several years, resulting in no net addition to employment in that period. Improvements in non-price competitiveness, for example, in product design, reliability, delivery, and service, could have a much stronger impact in generating jobs because they do not require an initial reduction in employment in order to generate the productivity increase (indeed such improvements may directly increase the requirement for labour with certain skills), but the estimates suggest that the scale of improvement in non-price competitiveness necessary to generate a significant fall in unemployment would be very large. Traditionally the UK has not been very strong on this, which suggests that there is certainly scope for large improvement, but, by the same token, must raise doubts about the feasibility of achieving such change. A lower rate of pay increases would, against the background of the MTFS, also create scope for increases in employment, but the effect is again lagged. More seriously, it appears that basic settlements would almost certainly have to be zero or negative for a number of years if this effect were to be sufficient to reduce unemployment substantially. If, as suggested above, large-scale unemployment will not produce such a result, it is not clear what other means exist for believing that such a change is feasible.

Numerous suggestions exist for reducing unemployment which in one way or another depend on a redistribution of work. These include reductions in overtime working, job-sharing, early retirement, and changes in the system of taxation and social security to encourage more part-time employment. The basic drawback of such schemes is that they only redistribute unemployment rather than reduce it. There may be arguments on the grounds of equity for this, which are not assessed here, but none are likely to reduce the gap between work and income wanted on the one hand and work and income available on the other, whatever the effect on measured unemployment. Reductions in overtime and associated pay might at first sight appear the most promising way forward, partly because those experiencing a reduction in overtime would none the less have full-time employment, and partly because the UK does appear to have a much higher degree of overtime in aggregate than most other countries. Against this, much of it may well represent not occasional overtime as a flexible response to varying demand but permanent overtime worked week after week, the only real purpose of which is to generate a higher weekly wage than would be the case if all the hours regularly worked were paid at basic rates. In this case moves to reduce overtime might well result simply in such hours being incorporated into the normal working week. Any limit on this which resulted in lower take-home pay might well lead only to renewed wage pressure and more inflation or, where possible, the compression of the original amount of work into the shorter period, keeping up the pay of those concerned but then, of course, making available no extra work for those currently unemployed.

All such proposals warrant further examination, but at present it seems unlikely either that they will occur on any great scale or that they would have a large effect on unemployment if they were. Making extended training available to all under the age of 18, thus taking them out of the work-force altogether, is another possibility, but this might well flounder on the cost and on the problem of ensuring that jobs were then available for those coming out of the extended training programme.

Finally it is at least possible to sketch a picture of the UK economy by the end of the 1980s in which it has a high-wage and high-productivity sector of internationally traded goods and services, fully competitive with abroad, and a lower-wage, lower-productivity sector of non-internationally traded goods and services, such that the overall demand coming from abroad and within the UK economy was sufficient to employ the work-force fully apart from frictional unemployment. Thus the productivity level necessary to be competitive would be reconcilable with full employment within the resulting level of demand. This need not involve any great reduction of productivity in the non-traded sector from present levels, and this lower productivity need not adversely affect the traded sector when goods and services are supplied to it from the non-traded sector if wage levels match productivity levels. But there are two great hurdles to achieving this solution to the problem of unemployment, the first being that there is no obvious means of bringing such a state of affairs about. The second is that unless the taxation system were substantially modified, the full burden of adjustment would be felt by those in the non-traded sector as income inequality increased in line with the productivity difference described. Whether the tax system could successfully resolve this by transferring some of the gains in the traded sector to the non-traded sector without impairing efficiency, or indeed at all, is not known, but it seems unlikely that such a change would prove acceptable without some concomitant action on income distribution.

Overall, therefore, the prospects for unemployment under present policy remain very poor. To the extent that the run-down of North Sea oil production leads to a lower exchange rate, encouraging a switch back to manufactured exports, the situation could improve. But as noted in Chapter 27 and 28, the run-down will be very gradual, and manufacturing may find it much more difficult to expand on the basis of a lower exchange rate than on the contraction forced on it from a higher one. In addition it has been estimated by the Department of Employment that as a result of trends in demography and participation rates the work-force seeking jobs will probably rise by over half a million by the end of the decade. With current GDP growth being the fastest for five years but still outstripped by productivity growth, the scope for significantly lower unemployment during the 1980s looks very bleak indeed.

29.4. Alternative Strategies

29.4.1. Reflation

Most alternative approaches to managing the UK economy that have been suggested are generally referred to as one variant or another of Keynesianism.

In as far as most include some element of increased deficit financing in order to generate more employment this is probably correct. But this should not obscure the fact that there are important differences between alternative strategies, and that some may have important elements in common with the current non-Keynesian approach.

The alternative which at a political level is most evident is also the simplest. It entails a substantial expansion of government expenditure and/or reductions in taxation, with particular interest in VAT because of its short-term effect in slowing inflation. The objections to this described earlier are countered by the arguments first, that crowding-out effects as a result of increased public borrowing will be small, as evidenced by the rapid growth and fall in unemployment in the US as a result of large-scale deficit financing, despite high interest rates; second, that the UK's structural budget position is in fact in surplus and much tighter than elsewhere; and third, that to the extent that such effects become serious they can be neutralized by expansion of the money supply. The charge that this would be inflationary are countered on the grounds first, that expansion of the money supply is appropriate to a fiscal expansion because the latter increases the demand for money; second, that there is no inherent tendency to full employment so that such an expansion can, even in the long term, fuel real growth rather than inflation; and third, that with so much spare capacity there are no grounds for thinking that more inflation need result at all. The historical association between monetary growth and inflation is questioned empirically, especially as the velocity of circulation of £M3 has risen substantially over the last ten years, and, where such a correlation does exist, it is seen predominantly as a case of reverse causation, with the supply of money responding to increases in nominal demand. The latter may be the result of inflation, but this is seen as originating from causes other than monetary expansion.

No detailed assessment of this is necessary here because the potential drawbacks are for the most part covered in the arguments that have already been described as the basis of current policy. But is it worth noting two points. First, if the interpretation of the labour market embodied in Figures 29.9 and 29.10 is correct then such a policy would almost certainly lead to a further rapid acceleration of inflation as the demand for labour started to rise again, albeit with a time-lag. The problem is no less serious for this policy than for current policy. Second, economic agents within and outside the UK have adjusted their views of the economy and of policy as a result of the experience of 1979–84. Whatever might have been possible under a different policy at that time, it is now very likely that any major fiscal and monetary expansion would generate severe and immediate pressure on interest rates, on the exchange rate, and on prices generally. The boxing-in that the current government may experience as a result of the expectations it has generated may well apply with equal vigour to another government with quite different aims and policy.

29.4.2. Prices and Incomes Policy

A second alternative in the Keynesian mould also argues for a substantial government reflation, but recognizes that by itself this would generate a new surge of inflation, which in turn would eventually offset some or even most of the original expansionary impetus. This alternative therefore sees a prices and incomes policy as a necessary concomitant of expansionary policy to inhibit the otherwise inflationary consequences.

As was seen in Chapter 11, there are many possible variants of prices and incomes policy, some rather mechanical and narrowly focused on movements in pay and prices. Others are much broader, involving a general understanding between the interested groups on the conduct of economic and social policy, and it is therefore difficult to make any general observation based on economic principles about such proposals. The most frequent criticism of this wider approach is that it has repeatedly failed in the past, leading at best to only a temporary reduction in inflation and culminating in a new surge of inflation when finally each policy has collapsed. Against this it is argued that success in using such policies was improving over time, with later ones having operated successfully over a considerably longer period than earlier ones. Rather like the first attempts at manned flight, all the early attempts crashed, and this was thought by some to be inevitable because they defied the laws of physics. Many regard prices and incomes policies as doomed to failure because they defy the economic laws of supply and demand, but proponents, by analogy with manned flight, believe that this reflects either inadequate understanding of those laws or an inability as yet to design the policy that will operate within those laws to achieve the objective of low inflation.

It is further argued that such policies have always in the past been introduced once inflation was a serious problem. There is no certainty that the same problems and pressures would arise with a policy introduced in a period of low inflation and then maintained as expansion occurred, particularly if the expansion were seen as conditional on the working of the prices and incomes policy.

Irrespective of such debate it remains the case that there is very widespread disenchantment with prices and incomes policy, at least amongst the major political and industrial groupings. Conservative policy regards it as distorting markets and bound to fail; Labour Party policy regards it as resulting, by design or default, in a squeeze on real living standards, and the same is true of TUC policy; the CBI, recalling the interference in company decision-taking and the pressure on profitability that past prices and incomes policies have entailed, is also opposed. Only the Alliance Party offers any support for some form of prices and incomes policy, and here too there are reservations about any form likely to run into the drawbacks of past attempts.

29.4.3. New Cambridge

In the mid- to late 1970s a so-called New Cambridge school of thought emerged. Like the other approaches outlined above it too was essentially Keynesian in its view of the economy, but with some rather specific differences which led to different policy implications.

At the heart of this school was the belief, based on past evidence, that the work-force in effect had a target real wage which rose over time and which in the long run it would always achieve. Therefore, if inflation were to be controlled, productivity growth would have to be fast enough to match the growth of target real wages. This, it was argued, could only be achieved if output grew sufficiently fast, but calculations suggested that this rate would generate a severe balance of payments crisis. A devaluation large enough to offset this would only precipitate further inflation, and it was therefore concluded that import controls would be necessary to make the strategy work.

This school of thought has been less prominent recently, partly because the balance of payments constraint on the UK appears to have been removed by North Sea oil, but also because of doubts about the desirability and effectiveness of import controls. These objections concern the market distortions created by import controls, the threat of retaliation, and the serious possibility, in a world of growing protectionism, that such a move by the UK could lead to a widespread breakdown in free trade. The notion of a target real wage has also been questioned.

None the less, the New Cambridge approach has generated important and interesting insights. Real wages have continued to grow virtually without disruption throughout the biggest UK recession for fifty years and despite unemployment rising to over 3 million. The balance of payments constraint might well re-emerge in the mid-1980s and there remains at present an apparent irreconcilability between high employment and low inflation within conventional policy. These points do not reduce the objections against import controls, in particular the likelihood of retaliation (even though, as the New Cambridge school has argued, the latter would either be irrational or complementary), but the essential question posed by this approach, as to how otherwise to achieve high employment and low inflation, remains unanswered.

29.4.4. New Keynesianism

In 1982, James Meade introduced another approach[1] which he named 'New Keynesianism'. As the name implies, it has certain Keynesian elements, but also some elements in common with current policy. Stripped to its essentials, this sees, first, the government having three macroeconomic targets—growth of *nominal* spending, balance of payments equilibrium over time, and adequate investment in relation to GDP—and three instruments to achieve them: tax policy, interest rates, and the exchange rate. It is argued that the latter three should primarily be assigned to the former three in the order given. This is because although all three policies affect all three targets, tax policy affects nominal spending most directly, the interest rate has very immediate effects on capital flows in the balance of payments, leaving the exchange rate, which ideally should not fluctuate heavily, to move gradually over time to a level such that the interest rate level associated with it is sufficient to permit adequate investment. While this specific assignment of policies to objectives looks novel, it is not clear that it would be so dramatic a change in terms of practical management of the economy, and the view that it is the growth of *nominal* spending rather than of real GDP which the government can target and control

[1] See J. E. Meade, *Stagflation*, Vol. 1, *Wage-Fixing* (George Allen and Unwin, 1982) and D. Vines, J. Maciejowski, and J. E. Meade, *Stagflation*, Vol. 2, *Demand Management* (George Allen and Unwin, 1983).

is an essential ingredient of current policy, even though monetary factors are regarded as more important in achieving this than fiscal ones *per se*.

The quite novel part of the proposal addresses the problem that within the growth of nominal spending there is no policy mechanism for ensuring that the consequence is substantial real growth and low inflation rather than the reverse, and that the working of the labour market does not itself seem able to generate the desired result. The proposal, which amounts to an *employment-generating decentralized* incomes policy, sees all *agreed* wage settlements as going through, but pressure being exerted for non-agreed ones to be referred to an arbitration process. The latter would produce a judgement on the basis of one overriding criterion, namely, given the details of the individual cases, the target growth of nominal expenditure, and the general level of unemployment, the level of pay award necessary to make progress towards (or towards maintaining) full employment. The policy would therefore be employment-generating in approach and would be decentralized in the sense that there would be no national norm and no maximum, and local factors, for example, shortages of particular skills, etc., could be allowed for. None the less the general level of wage settlements would come into line with nominal spending because there would be a general tendency to job losses if it did not.

A number of problems are raised by this approach. First, unless the government could itself refer some settlements, even though agreed between employer and employees, to the arbitration process, it would be quite possible for a large number of inflationary settlements to bypass the constraint completely. Though this would in principle be reflected in a tendency to higher unemployment and therefore to still lower wage increases in disputed cases, the pressure of adjustment would be intense in these cases and the approach might well not survive. Second, there is the problem of employers or employees who refused to go to arbitration, especially as this is not viewed as compulsory. Equally, what would happen if the arbitration award were not accepted? Meade's approach is to suggest that settlements might be binding on employers and that a series of 'levers' be used progressively to weaken the negotiating strength of any employees who refused to go to arbitration, for example, removing certain legal immunities, non-allowance for lost pay in determining income tax and benefits, etc. Whether such pressures would be effective, however, remains open to question.

Other practical problems abound. Allowance would have to be made for productivity improvements, but might well have to be retrospective if this were not to represent a loophole in the system. There is an important question of the level at which groups of employees would be defined for bargaining purposes. National bargaining might well be incompatible with the approach if it involved employees in different sectors and regions and with different skills all coming under one negotiation. Even plant-level bargaining could face similar difficulties. Comparability problems and low pay are just two other factors which would need to be considered, and suggest, as Meade notes, that the possibility of success would depend on substantial accompanying changes in the system of social security and taxation.

Such an approach is of course untried and clearly faces difficulties. The one characteristic that should be emphasized is that it recognizes the labour market problem at the heart of the unemployment/inflation issue and attempts, with what success cannot be known at present, to tackle it.

29.4.5. The Supply Side Revisited

Another alternative would be to try to make the supply side, and in particular the supply side of the labour market, work effectively as a market. This would entail the substantial weakening or abolition of collective bargaining as currently practised, removal of job protection legislation, and modifications to the arrangements for redundancy payment. There could still be legal restraint on unfair dismissal but the latter would not include dismissal in order to recruit someone else to the same job at a lower wage. Supporters of this approach would normally want to couple it with reduction in unemployment benefit in order to increase the incentive to take work.

This proposal more than most moves outside the sphere of economics and into the political arena. It embodies a view of not only economic but also power relationships in society that are very different from those existing at present. It also involves markedly different judgements concerning equity versus efficiency and the role of purely economic incentives in decisions about employment. At this level it is not appropriate in the present context to comment further than this. The main insight gained from such a proposal is that it highlights the difference between the type of labour market that currently exists and the type that might be required if it were by itself to generate high employment and low inflation.

29.4.6. Taxes and Subsidies

Finally, mention should be made of proposal's, emanating primarily from Richard Layard,[2] first, that companies pay a tax on any increase in hourly wage payments over and above a norm for the year established by the government, and second (as a separate proposal), that companies should receive subsidies in relation to the *extra* employment they generate, thereby lowering the cost of employing people but concentrating the effect at the margin. These are the most developed of a number of types of expenditure or tax-based schemes to encourage employment and will not be reviewed here. But, like the Meade approach, these proposals are geared specifically to the problem of the labour market, and will potentially have budget deficit implications, implying that they would need to be integrated into a full macroeconomic strategy that took account of the other macroeconomic goals of government.

29.5. Conclusions

This chapter is to a great extent a conclusion in itself to the whole book. It is perhaps worth ending by emphasizing two points. First, as was emphasized in the first and second editions, and in Chapter 1, the central and unresolved issue is that of how the labour market works and how it might change either under

[2] See R. Layard, *More Jobs, Less Inflation* (Grant McIntyre, 1982).

the pressure of high unemployment or in response to new attempts, legally backed or otherwise, to modify its employment/inflation consequences. This clearly permeates the differences between present policy and the various alternatives listed. It even affects how economic concepts are formed and used. In particular, if it is accepted that output and employment can alter flexibly then it seems appropriate to define increases in demand in terms of nominal expenditure, it being a supply-side question as to whether and to what extent higher demand leads to higher prices or higher output and employment. But this then renders all problems of under-utilization (of capital or labour) as supply side by definition. Thus on this measure any company that believes it is restricted by low demand, i.e. by shortage of orders, is regarded as being restricted only because its price level is too high to achieve the level of orders required. If instead industry costs are viewed as being as low as it is realistic to achieve then real expenditure rather than nominal expenditure is a more appropriate measure of demand.

There is no unambiguously correct answer to this definitional problem, depending as it does on views about the scope for changes in costs, but it underlies the acute differences between those who believe deficient (real) demand is the basic cause of currently high unemployment and those who believe that (nominal) demand has been expanding at a more than adequate rate to generate high employment.

Second, although the position of the UK economy has changed dramatically in a number of respects in the last five years, it still faces, perhaps more acutely than ever, the problem of achieving full employment, low inflation, and external balance. The symptoms of the problem have changed, partly because of the stance of policy and partly because of other events, in particular the rise of North Sea oil, the fall in world inflation after the second oil crisis, and the slow growth of the world economy since then. But inflationary tendencies do not appear to have disappeared from the economic system in the UK, the large balance of payments surpluses of the early 1980s are unlikely to continue, and, above all, there seems little prospect that mass unemployment can be avoided for many years.

Index

accelerating inflation, 158, 159, 400
accelerator, 153
accepting houses, 317
accommodating inflation, 385, 392-3
accounting rate of return, 76
adjustment problem, 485-6, 533-8, 556-9
advertising, 31, 82, 816-17
Advisory Board for the Research Councils, 713
Advisory Council for Applied Research and Development, 713
aggregate concentration, 801
aggregate demand, 9, 10, 12
  consumption function and, 45
  controlling, 253, 262-3
  excess, 195, 218-19
aggregate economic activity, 133-54
agricultural subsidies, 276
Agricultural Wages Board, 333
Akamatsu, K., 538
Alliance Party, 920
American Internal Revenue Service, 359
Amersham International, 795
amortization component, 619
Anderson Strathclyde merger, 810
anti-trust policy, 798-828, 854
  case for, 798-804
  collusion, 67, 69, 182, 803, 813-14
  cost-benefit, 822-4
  EEC law, 804-6
  efficiency, 819-20
  monopolistic practices, 798-802, 820-1
  policy alternatives, 802-4
  pricing, 817-18
  profitability, 814-16
  UK legislation, 804-12
apprenticeships, 696
arbitrage, 181-2, 192
arbitration, 338, 339
arm's length ministerial control, 776, 790-1

automatic stabilizer effect, 604
average cost pricing, 62-3
Average Earnings Index, 144-5, 358
average physical product, 89
aviation subsidies, 277

balance of payments, 168, 175-201, 262
  automatic equilibrium, 193-4
  capital account, 177-8, 187-91
  current account, 177, 178, 195-8
  exchange rate in UK and, 194, 206-7, 213-14
  invisibles, 177, 178, 186-7
  oil and, 179, 182, 206, 207, 213-14, 593, 596-601
  recycling deficit and surplus, 593-6, 597
  short-term capital movements, 179, 190-3, 197
balance sheet, 56-60
Balassa, B., 518
Balfour Committee on Trade and Industry 1929, 685-6
Bank for International Settlements (BIS), 570, 595
Bank of England, 127, 260, 314, 328
  cash ratio, 320-1
  Competition and Credit Control, 169
  debt management, 311-13
  exchange equalization account, 197
  Governor, 878
  intervention, 179, 328
  North Sea oil and, 840, 843
  prudential regulations, 323
bank rate, 169
bankers' balances, 377N, 433N
bankers' deposits, 127, 129, 130
Banking Act 1979, 323
banks, 127-9
  asset structure, 128
  Bank of England and, 317
  financial intermediation, 116
  money creation and, 127
Barber, Anthony (Chancellor), 563